ADMINISTERED POLITICS

ADMINISTERED POLITICS
Elite Political
Culture in Sweden

Thomas J. Anton
The University of Michigan

Martinus Nijhoff Publishing
Boston/The Hague/London

Distributors for North America:
Martinus Nijhoff Publishing
Kluwer Boston, Inc.
160 Old Derby Street
Hingham, Massachusetts 02043

Distributors outside North America:
Kluwer Academic Publishers Group
Distribution Centre
P.O. Box 322
3300 AH Dordrecht, The Netherlands

Library of Congress Cataloging in Publication Data

Anton, Thomas Julius.
  Administered politics.

  1. Sweden—Politics and government—1950–1973.
2. Government executives—Sweden. 3. Legislators—
Sweden. 4. Elite (Social sciences)—Sweden.
I. Title.
JN7791.A57   301.5'92'09485   79–22050
ISBN 0–89838–025–1

Printed in the United States of America.

CONTENTS

PREFACE

Several years ago, freshly returned from a year in Stockholm but deeply enmeshed in the American Malaise of the late 1960's, I sketched out an image of Swedish policy-making that defined a generalized policy-making role and sought to relate that role to both citizen attitudes and the elite political culture in Sweden.[1] Although that sketch seems to have been taken seriously by other foreigners, I think it is fair to say that the principal reaction of my Swedish friends and colleagues was amusement. When I later (1970-71) returned for another year in Stockholm, I found myself being introduced at parties as the man who had written "that marvelously out-of-date sketch of how Swedish politics used to work—hah, hah." Or, I would be referred to as the American who, like Marquis Childs some years earlier, "believed our propaganda." By 1970-71, of course, the Swedish political environment had become more boisterous than it had been in 1967-68. Indeed, during the course of that year my amused colleagues found themselves enmeshed in a strike action against the government that was part of an emotional series of such actions that some observers thought would bring most public services to a halt. If my earlier portrait had been influenced (too much, they thought) by the American Malaise in which I was implicated, so must their later reaction to my portrait have been influenced (too much, I thought) by the Swedish Turmoil of 1970 and 1971.

A SWEDISH MODEL

Policy making in Sweden, I argued in 1969, was dominated by "experts" or expert roles attached to a dual structure of social power: government interacting with an unusually well-developed and quite centralized series of interest group organizations. After describing typical patterns of interaction among these experts, I offered the following summary:

> Swedish policy making is extraordinarily *deliberative,* involving long periods of time during which more or less constant attention is given to some problem by well trained specialists. It is *rationalistic,* in that great efforts are made to develop the fullest possible information about any given issue, including a thorough review of historical experiences as well as the range of alternatives suggested by scholars in and out of Sweden. It is *open,* in the sense that all interested parties are consulted before a decision is finally made. And it is *consensual,* in that decisions are seldom made without the agreement of virtually all parties to them.

Students of American politics will have no difficulty appreciating the significance of these aspects of politics, particularly to a resident of an American city in the late 60's. But these observations were based on a good deal of reading as well as a fair amount of observation and I thought they were quite sound:

> Let me emphasize that systems of "expert" or "specialist" roles, operating in a deliberative, rational, open and consensual fashion, represent the "normal" in Swedish decision-making. Systems operating in this fashion are found at every level, and for every issue . . . This pattern, in short, represents a national style, which is itself a reflection of Swedish political culture. To appreciate how this political culture structures decision-making, we need to look first at citizen attitudes toward government, and then at elite orientations.

Naturally, what most struck me about citizen orientations was the general passivity of the population: people did not seem to be interested in shouting at one another, or at politicians; apart from political parties there seemed to be no citizen groups agitating issues in a publicly visible way; and there were no street demonstrations turning into riots (although bricks were being thrown, regularly, through the windows of the American commercial and cultural centers in protest against our Viet Nam policy). In an effort to explain what seemed to me to be a general state of mass quiescence I began looking at opinion polls and other evidence regarding mass orientations to politics. This, in turn, led me to argue that citizen orientations in Sweden resembled what Almond and Verba had called a "subject" political culture: Swedes seem to have a high level of awareness of things political, they express positive feelings of pride and support for the system, but they also emphasize outputs rather than participation and thus engage in little political activity apart from the act of voting. Above all, Swedes exhibit a well-developed deference to poublic officials, who are accorded high status and generally allowed to go their own way in pursuing their "expert" solutions to public problems.

Within a context defined largely by citizen quiescence and deference to public authority, the small and homogeneous Swedish elite operated with a noticeable sense of independence, according to norms that stressed achievement in problem areas defined by individual competence and training. Referring to this as a "work orientation," I contrasted these norms to the "politics as game" orientation that characterizes much of American politics and suggested that it produced a strong commitment to action (rather than talk) among the Swedish elite. The activist orientation, in turn, produced policy debates that I found "almost totally devoid of ideological or philosophic symbolism, focusing instead on specific proposals to deal with specific problems." Socially, the class and educational homogeneity of the elite, its tradition of widespread consultation and its willingness to be patient in searching for solutions to problems contributed to an atmosphere of calm in policy making, while the work orientation structured a pragmatic approach to problem-solving. That approach was defined intellectually, I suggested, by two habits of mind that encouraged agreement among the elite. One was relativism, or the reluctance to adopt absolutist positions; the other was particularism: "the definition of issues in terms of their specific, rather than generalized significance." Not surprisingly, I summarized all this as "an elite culture in which a highly pragmatic intellectual style, oriented toward the discovery of workable solutions to specific problems, structures a consensual approach to policy making."

Apart from what may now seem to be the "gee whiz!" quality of this portrait, two things about my earlier analysis are worth underlining. The first is that, while never stated very explicitly, I assumed that citizen and elite orientations could provide an explanation either for the range of policies produced by Swedish governments or for the capacity of Swedish government to solve problems, or both. The second point to remember is that this essay on attitudes contained no attitudinal data, as such. I had read a great deal about Swedish politics and decision-making, and I had myself observed and reconstructed some decision-making activities in a Stockholm suburb. These activities encouraged me to draw inferences about the mental processes that produced patterns of observed behavior, but I had conducted no survey, nor had I attempted to conduct systematic, in-depth interviews. There were those in Sweden and the United States who believed the absence of these kinds of data to be a serious weakness in my argument.

Lengthy visits to Sweden in 1971 and 1973 provided opportunities to remedy this weakness through structured interviews with 315 senior civil servants and forty-four members of the Swedish Parliament (*Riksdag*). Moreover, because the interviews conducted in Sweden were similar to interviews conducted at approximately the same time in six other nations (England, France, West Germany, Italy, The Netherlands, USA) by University of Michigan colleagues,[2] it became possible to contemplate an explicit comparison of Swedish thought patterns and ideas expressed by other western elites. This book is the result of those efforts. Whether or not my earlier speculations have any validity, whether Swedish elite officials are different from or similar to other elite groups, and what difference any of this makes in understanding modern political systems are issues that now can be addressed with systematically-collected data.

A MODEL FOR ANALYSIS

The major analytical tool used to illuminate these issues is the concept of role. In simple terms, "role" refers to patterned (i.e., repeated) behavior that takes place in response to the actions of others. Because patterned action is assumed to be a response to other behaviors, rather than a result of some "internal" drive, role is properly regarded as a sociological, rather than psychological, concept. Using the concept obliges the analyst to seek explanations for patterned behavior in the social structures that provide opportunities and incentives to guide individual action. It is important to note, however, that "patterned" behavior is not "determined" by the quality of social interactions. Individuals are assumed to be free to choose their actions; only when similar choices are repeatedly made in similar situations is there evidence of role behavior. Since individual choice defines role, there always is some variability in the actions that can be described as role behavior. This can create problems for the analyst but it also creates opportunities for noticing, then examining, the more dynamic properties of roles and the social structures within which they are played out.[3]

Roles can be observed directly, in actions taken repeatedly by individuals in defined social structures, i.e., organizations. Roles can also be observed indirectly, through interview techniques that ask role incumbents to describe actions they believe to be appropriate to certain relationships or situations. Such responses can be used to summarize an individual's readiness to perform a certain role, in which case they are conventionally referred to as role orientations. Attitudes of warmth or hostility to identified individuals, for example, can be used to estimate the probability that roles such as "friend" or "neighbor" will be entertained. Or, interview responses can be used to define the boundaries of legitimate role behavior, in which case they are conventionally referred to as role expectations. Whether or not an individual believes that a "friend" should be prepared to help pay his or her bills, for example, is an indication of how that individual expects the role of "friend" to be performed. These distinctions between orientations, expectations and behavior help the analyst to choose methods appropriate to the level of analysis desired, and help the reader to understand how analytical results are to be interpreted. In this study, for example, Chapter 3 examines role orientations, Chapters 4 and 5 analyze expectations, and Chapter 8 uses evidence of behavior to develop inferences about the relationship between public roles and private personality.

A major advantage of using the role concept is avoidance of the ambiguity often associated with efforts to study something as nebulous as "political culture." Understanding role as patterned behavior within a specified social structure—in this case, the governmental system—permits a relatively straight-forward and specific identification of expectations to be explored: self, work, colleagues, counterparts (below, Chapters 3-6). Moreover, because roles are chosen rather than predetermined, examination of role expectations can reveal the values around which role choices are organized. Clearly identified values can be linked to specific action expectations, thus avoiding the referential fuzziness often found in less focused studies of "culture." Furthermore, value-based expectations can be related to background characteristics and interaction patterns among elite officials (below, Chapters 2 and 5) to develop analytic statements of considerable general significance.

These important advantages are matched by another: the utility of "role" in clarifying the nature of modern bureaucratic systems. Scholars repeatedly have argued in recent years that public sector expansion into a broad range of welfare-state activities, coupled with rapid technological change, have changed basic perspectives among governmental elites. Older bureaucratic orientations, emphasizing neutral objectivity in the application of clearly-defined rules, have been challenged or replaced by orientations more in accord with the demands of large-scale technology and social reform. While some scholars assert that a shift to newer specialist or political roles *has* occurred, others, noting the tension between older and newer role orientations, have argued that a massive role change should occur, in order to bring bureaucratic roles into closer alignment with new social realities. In point of fact, evidence bearing on the occurrence of a massive role shift is quite ambiguous.[4] Sweden thus provides a perfect opportunity to introduce some clarity to this debate: the pace and scope of social change during the past half century have been extraordinary, in a system dominated by a bureaucratic system that has been entrenched for centuries. If social changes produce tension between older and newer bureaucratic orientations, surely those tensions will be clearly revealed in Sweden. And if some new or different bureaucratic roles have taken hold anywhere, surely they will be apparent in Sweden, one of the most technologically sophisticated welfare states in the western world.

Finally, use of the role concept to probe the thinking of a group that includes politicians as well as bureaucrats will permit analysis of the bases upon which accommodation takes place between these two institutions. Earlier analyses of elite accommodation, focused on societies in which there was considerable fragmentation below the elite level, stressed the significance of common background, continuous interaction, and commitment to system preservation. But, as Presthus has argued, these qualities are likely to be found among any group defined as an "elite."[5] What is more interesting and important is the substantive basis of accommodation, that is, the values and norms that support continuing commitment to the system. As we shall see, the values supporting system commitment among members of the Swedish elite are rather different from elite values in other systems (below, Chapter 7), particularly in the use of complex procedural norms to limit and guide political conflict (below, Chapter 8). Analysis of the values and procedural norms built into Swedish bureaucratic and political roles will permit us to define a uniquely Swedish approach to modern higher administration, to contrast that approach against evidence from other systems (particularly the American system), and to speculate about the significance of that approach in understanding both elite roles and elite accommodation.

ACKNOWLEDGEMENTS

This study builds on the ideas of so many good teachers that it is difficult to separate their ideas from my own. Hans Meijer, now *Rektor* of the University of Linköping, deserves my greatest thanks, both for his ideas and his willingness to help organize and plan the project of which this study is one part. Olof Ruin, formerly Deputy Chancellor of the Swedish University System and now Professor of Political Science at the University of Stockholm, stimulated my thinking in more ways than he probably imagines, including his delightful skepticism about the whole enterprise. Björn Molin, colleague and Member of Parliament, has been a source of continuing support, socially as well as intellectually. For Daniel Tarchys, also a colleague and Member of Parliament, I offer thanks and the hope that he will find some resemblance between Anton III and Anton I. My closest Swedish colleagues on the project, Anders Mellbourn, Claes Linde and Gunnar Lönnqvist, are so much a part of the following pages that no effort to separate their work from my own seems inconceivable. To my Michigan colleagues Samuel J. Eldersveld, Robert D. Putnam (now at Harvard University), Ronald Inglehart and Joel Aberbach I can only offer the hope that their continuing support is repaid to some extent in these pages. Bert Rockman, then at Michigan and now at the University of Pittsburgh, made a very special and very helpful effort to improve the penultimate draft. Kevin Kramer, Thad Brown and Lee Luskin all worked with me at one time or another in Ann Arbor, with good humor and high intelligence.

Among the organizations whose support was essential to this work the most important was the Bank of Sweden Tercentenary Fund, which helped to support me for a year in Sweden and provided funds for the enormously complicated and time-consuming work of interviewing, transcribing, coding, and analyzing. The National Science Foundation, through a grant to The University of Michigan, also supported these efforts, as did the Horace H. Rackham School of Graduate Studies of The University of Michigan and Professor Charles Overberger, Vice President for Research at the University. Neither the Department of Political Science nor the Institute of Public Policy Studies at The University of Michigan expected this study to take so long, and I am exceedingly grateful to both organizations for their patience as well as their support. Finally, special thanks to Kathryn Jones for her unique contribution to this study.

NOTES

1. "Policy-Making and Political Culture in Sweden," in *Scandinavian Political Studies*. Vol. 4 (1969), pp. 90–102.

2. An NSF grant to study "The Political Culture of Bureaucrats and Politicians" funded work led by Professors Samuel J. Eldersveld (Holland), Robert D. Putnam (Britain, West Germany, Italy), Joel Aberbach and Bert Rockman (USA) and Ronald Inglehart (France) as well as portions of this study.

3. The literature on role theory is extensive, but I am most indebted to Talcott Parsons and Edward Shils, *Toward A General Theory of Action*. (New York: Harper Torchbook Edition, 1962), esp. pp. 3–27, 53–109, and 190–233.

4. For a comprehensive recent review of both theory and evidence, see Robert D. Putnam, *The Comparative Study of Political Elites*. (New York: Prentice-Hall, 1975), esp. chapters 5 and 8.

5. Robert Presthus, *Elite Accommodation in Canadian Politics*. (Cambridge: Cambridge University Press, 1973), chapter 1.

ADMINISTERED POLITICS

1 THE FIRST NEW SOCIETY

Sweden is often said to be a dull country, yet it excites powerful emotions among those who observe its people and politics. Since 1935, when Marquis Childs popularized the notion of Sweden as a "middle way" alternative to repressive communism or brutal fascism,[1] two generations of admirers have been fascinated by the transformation of "a clean, well-lighted place"[2] into a model of modern welfare capitalism. Critics, on the other hand, have been equally impressed with the growing intrusion of government into private affairs and vehemently protest against "the new totalitarians."[3] Scholars, meanwhile, are often frustrated because Sweden seldom fits easily into the stereotypical images of social analysis that are tools of the scholarly trade. Sweden has had a "socialist" government for nearly half a century, yet more than 90 percent of industry is privately owned; Sweden has been at peace for nearly two centuries, yet its per capita defense expenditures are fourth highest in the world; Sweden is an intensely secular society, yet more than 90 percent of all Swedes choose to retain their membership in the state Lutheran Church.[4] Especially for foreign observers, Sweden is good, bad or confusing, but never easy to understand.

Part of the scholarly frustration may arise from the feeling that Sweden *should* be easy to understand. It is, after all, a small nation of hardly more than eight million people, the great bulk of whom share the same ethnic heritage,

1

speak the same language (with only moderate regional variations) and participate in the same social and cultural institutions from one end of the country to the other. These characteristics, coupled with geographic isolation and the extraordinary stability of government during the past half-century, might well suggest an absence of social complexity in this distant corner of the world.

Despite a superficial plausibility, this view overlooks both the extent and the pace of social change in recent Swedish history. Indeed, in most important respects, Swedish society has been totally transformed within the memory of most Swedes living today. It is important to remember, to begin with, that industrialization came late to Sweden. In 1870, at a time when industrial development was well advanced in Western Europe, some three-quarters of Sweden's work force was still engaged in agriculture—and faring so badly that roughly a million Swedish peasants uprooted themselves and emigrated to the United States.[5] Not until the 1890's did industrialization gather momentum, but more than 55 percent of Swedish workers were still agricultural workers in 1900, and 44 percent remained in agriculture in 1920.[6] During the formative years of most Swedes now living, therefore, Sweden was a predominantly agricultural and, relative to other European states, a poor society.

Although the foundations of a modern, industrial economy were securely in place by 1920, a worldwide depression inhibited economic development. One important consequence was that population growth almost came to a halt in the 1930's;[7] another consequence was that the traditional Swedish pattern of dispersed industrial production, rather than large and concentrated urban agglomerations, was maintained through the period of the Second World War: Stockholm, Sweden's capitol and largest city, contained scarcely more than 650,000 people as recently as 1945.[8] Industrialization, therefore, not only came late to Sweden, but its advance was limited by an existing Swedish pattern that delayed its full elaboration until the post-war era. Solutions to the problems typically associated with advanced industrialization—rural de-population, growth and overcrowding in urban areas, social disorganization, etc.—did not begin to be implemented on a large scale until after 1945. From a physical point of view certainly, much of what is now visible in Sweden is entirely a product of the last thirty years. Considerably more than half of all Swedish dwelling units, for example, have been built in that time.[9]

Late and muted industrialization thus delayed major social change, but once the process began it proceeded, and continues, at an extraordinarily rapid pace. Continuation of a remarkable rate of social change is due in large measure to the comprehensiveness of the changes initiated within the past three decades. Being slow to experience the problems of industrial growth, the Swedes were in a position to observe how other systems had handled such problems. Observation of successes and failures elsewhere appears to have impressed upon the Swedes the necessity of dealing not simply with problems, but with systems and institutions. The housing pressures felt by Stockholm residents during the war years, for example, were attacked not by efforts to build more apartments, but by efforts to build an entire system of new suburban towns around Stockholm, tied together by a subway system whose construction would be coordinated with new town development. British and American visionaries provided the ideas; Swedish officials put them into effect, and later changed the entire metropolitan government system for Stockholm as a result.[10] In similar fashion, efforts to deal with the welfare and educational problems created by rural depopulation led to a recognition that the local government institution itself required adjustment, for urban as well as rural areas. Beginning in 1952, therefore, a process was begun that led to reduction in the number of Swedish municipalities by a factor of 10—from some 2500 in 1952 to only 274 in 1974.[11]

The process of "solving a problem—changing an institution" obviously can have a "snowball" effect unless restrained by tradition, myth, vested political interest, or some other brake on institutional change. It is a measure of the weakness of such restraints in Swedish society that virtually all major—or minor—Swedish institutions have experienced changes of a fundamental kind within the very recent past. The Swedish *Riksdag* changed from a bicameral to a unicameral legislative body in 1971;[12] all formal political powers were eliminated from the Swedish monarchy with the recent death of King Gustav Adolph VI;[13] educational changes begun in the 1950's have now led to a total transformation of Swedish higher education, from an elitist system limited to an upper-class few to a wide-open "people's university";[14] both the funding and organization of health care have been revolutionized in the past two decades;[15] even the powerful flow of people into Swedish cities that has marked the postwar period has been halted, in part through government policies.[16] Throughout, the Swedish economy has continued to change as it grows: fewer than eight of every 100 Swedish workers are now engaged in agriculture, while close to 60 percent are involved in the "service" occupations that characterize what some observers refer to as "post-industrial" development.[17] And, of course, Sweden is now—barely three decades away from a state of relative impoverishment—one of the richest nations on earth in terms of per capita gross national product.[18] "Stability" may describe the party system or characterize the government well enough, but Swedish society as a whole has been anything but stable. Few societies have ever changed so much, so soon; fewer still have institutionalized processes that encourage the *continuation* of rapid social change.

To understand the genuine complexity of mid-20th century Sweden, therefore, it is essential to recognize that in many respects it is a new society, in which both the physical environment and social relations have been dramatically transformed within the past two generations. Although a similar claim might be made about a number of other Western societies, the interesting characteristic of the Swedish model is the extent to which major social changes have been "planned" rather than "experienced." The economic transformation was stimulated by early application of Keynes-like policies and later accelerated by the well-known "active manpower policy" initiated in the 1950's.[19] Support for expansion of welfare programs was carefully nurtured not only among affected groups but among school children whose educational curricula were gradually changed to reflect reformist values and whose schools were themselves altered to reflect those values.[20] As governmental programs and the number of government officials have grown, more "planning" has been done to inject public authority into more spheres of social relations, gradually diminishing the boundaries of what can be considered "private" and expanding the legitimate scope of public intervention. Swedish willingness to be "logical" and "empirical," with a growing number of programs about which to be "logical," means that few institutions, public or private, are now regarded as beyond the boundaries of public scrutiny and, if necessary, public policy action. In cybernetic terms, Sweden seems well on the way toward becoming a self-correcting society.[21]

Whether or not a change is regarded as a "correction" or an "error," of course, depends on who or what is the focus of governmental activity. With more than 90 percent of Swedish industry in private ownership,[22] reformist governmental action is bound to produce conflict over the control of economic resources. For individuals, reformist governmental action is bound to be experienced by some as a threat to personal integrity, as public policy attacks cultural or social "problems" thought to be outside the purview of state action. And for officials, themselves, reformist action is bound to produce conflict with other officials, as one corrective program "bumps into" another in an already crowded program field. To assert that Sweden has arrived at a new political plateau, in short, is not to say that the politics of institutional self-correction will be either peaceful or static. It is to say that, for the moment at least, Sweden is "out front" among Western systems that combine expanding public sector activity with traditions of corporate and individual freedom. New public-private, citizen-state and official-official relationships will be defined in Sweden earlier than elsewhere, but the content of these new relationships remains unclear, for Sweden is very much in a state of "becoming" rather than "being." That is why she is interesting and, for those interested in the politics of permanent change, important.

THE SWEDISH POLITICAL TRADITION

If the significance of Sweden lies mainly in its ability to institutionalize planned social change, the significance of planners in Sweden can be traced to political traditions that surround public decision-making with values and incentives appropriate to the task of foresighted social choice. Not long after Gustav Vasa had driven the Danes from Sweden and been elected King of Sweden in June of 1523, he began a process of power centralization that very quickly gave Sweden an efficient and centralized administrative apparatus. By the 1530's the power of both the church and the previously independent regional administrators had been eliminated, a national system of taxation and tax collectors responsible directly to the crown had been established, and a central administrative bureaucracy, the *Kansli,* had been created to control state administration. Successive modifications of this system within the next century led to an administrative structure embodying principles that continue to be followed today. Under the leadership of Axel Oxenstierna, Sweden by 1634 had created a system of administrative boards, with regional sub-units, staffed by a professional corps of civil servants. The system has been greatly expanded of course, and we shall see that ministries were added in 1840, but the basic structure was already in place before the middle of the 17th century. Two and a half centuries before the emergence of either industrialization or modern political institutions, in short, Sweden had created a centralized, professional and politically responsible civil service.[23]

The early emergence of a national administrative system, centuries before parliamentary democracy became a reality, permitted administrators to dominate the course of public events in Sweden. As representatives of the crown, often of noble origin, their social status was assured and, over time, came to be reflected in popular respect for the office: to this day, opinion polls show that Swedes place the position of government official close to the top of their occupational prestige rankings.[24] But Swedish administrators had more than respect; they had considerable power. In part this was a function of the absence of other powerful institutions. The *Riksdag,* in which "estates" rather than individuals were represented, met irregularly and could easily be dominated by administrators who were members. Not until the 20th century was the national parliament in a position to exert meaningful political control over the Swedish administrative apparatus.[25] Administrative power was also a function of Swedish insistence that "political" and "administrative" decisions were clearly distinct and that the latter could be made simply by applying law to the facts of a particular case. The administrative boards initiated in the 17th century were designed to provide such legal judgments, and officials were assigned full authority to make those judgments, free from "political" interference. That administrative freedom, based on a judicial view of administrative responsibility, effectively removed the *Riksdag* as a check on administrative behavior and structured a sense of bureaucratic "independence" that also continues to this day.[26]

High status, unimpeachable legal responsibilities and the weakness of other political institutions thus effectively guaranteed civil servant access to policy-making processes from the 17th century onward. Practice became official in the 1809 Constitution, in effect until 1974, which required that "before matters are submitted to the King-in-Council, they shall be prepared by the member submitting them, who shall collect for this purpose the necessary information from the competent administrative officers." With access guaranteed by both custom and official doctrine, Swedish administrators have been able to impose a markedly rationalistic style on policy-making procedures. As Hugh Heclo has noted in his recent study of social policy development in Britain and Sweden, policy deliberation in Sweden typically has ". . . begun from an assumption that the primary requisite for policy decision is more information, clarification, and analysis among the interested parties; British discussion has generally begun from the assumption of divergent interests resolvable only through partisan conflict and certainly not through joint committee work."[27]

Careful research, lengthy deliberation and consultation among all interested parties define a style Swedish historians can trace back to at least the 13th century. Today, Sweden's administrator-politicians have institutionalized that style in the widespread use of Royal Commissions to generate policy innovations, and in the "remiss" process. Royal Commissions are appointed to investigate a problem or problems the government believes may require a legislative solution. Appointed by the Ministry responsible for the problem-area, such commissions typically are dominated by administrators but can include a wide range of members, are provided with paid, full-time staff, and normally produce lengthy reports summarizing the data collected and conclusions reached after what may be years of investigative work. Although the process is often slow, exceedingly few, if any, major reforms are proposed—let alone enacted—without the preparatory work provided by a Royal Commission. Often enough, the work includes outstanding research—indeed, some of the best social research in Sweden is produced for such commissions and published in the prestigious SOU (*Statens offentliga utredningar*) series. The importance of these information-gathering activities to Swedish decision-making is suggested by the fact that some seventy-five new commissions are appointed each year and that, at any given time, some 300 or so commissions are likely to be in existence.[28]

As Christopher Wheeler recently has reminded us,[29] however, the political significance of Royal Commissions extends far beyond their information-gathering and analysis activities. Commissions do their work before any legislation is drafted, so that members can properly feel that their deliberations are likely to have a real impact. Moreover, membership on most commissions includes representatives of affected interests and, especially on politically sensitive topics, members of the opposition parties in Parliament. To the extent that agreement can be reached—and the enhanced probability of influencing legislation through unanimity provides an incentive to agree—later difficulties can be avoided: having assisted in the formulation of policy, party or interest group representatives may well feel bound to support that policy later. Quite apart from the conclusions offered by Royal Commissions, then, the process of reaching those conclusions often provides a mechanism for coopting potential opponents into consensual support for policy recommendations. Here, behind committee doors, in debates over research, can be found much of the genius of modern Swedish politics.

Once completed, commission reports are submitted to the relevant Minister who, if he wishes to proceed to the legislation stage, circulates the report to groups and agencies likely to be affected by commission proposals. This circulation, or *remiss,* to a larger group provides another opportunity for affected parties to influence policy or to go on record supporting a proposal. For the government, particularly the responsible Minister, the *remiss* generates valuable information, as Wheeler notes:

> Comments on the technical aspects of the proposal serve as important checks on the findings of the Royal Commission. Moreover, it is of equal importance at this stage for the government to get a feeling for the intensity of emotions stimulated by a proposal. This *political* information is important for the government as it tries to determine what concessions, if any, should be made to protesting groups, given its long-run desire to be re-elected.[30]

Only after such reports have been prepared, circulated on *remiss,* and *remiss* responses considered, does the government determine whether or not to draft legislation, and what the content of the legislation will be. Bills submitted at the conclusion of this process include generous portions of the research on which proposals are based, a lengthy review of the *remiss* responses from affected organizations, and a consideration of how the proposed legislation has taken account of criticisms, as well as newly-gathered information. Not surprisingly, such bills are extraordinarily bulky documents that, when published, constitute very large volumes by themselves. To read them is to learn exactly what combination of information and argument supported what specific proposals, exactly the positions of interested groups on such proposals, and exactly what changes in proposals were made to satisfy such reactions.

Observers of more volatile systems such as the American or British may regard such policy-making procedures as exhausting no less than exhaustive, and they often are: it is not terribly unusual for Royal Commissions to work for a decade or more, and some have consumed as much as two decades.[31] It is important to bear in mind, however, that the collection and analysis of information by a representative committee is itself a political activity of great significance. By the time a legislative proposal is actually drafted, affected interests have been given a voice, potential opponents coopted if possible, and attention has been paid to implementation issues such as "who will carry out these proposals?" "on whose budget?" "do they want or can they be induced to do this?" Dominated as they are by administrators, Swedish Royal Commissions are classic representations of Mannheim's passing but insightful comment: "The fundamental tendency of all bureaucratic thought is to turn all problems of politics into problems of administration."[32]

This fundamentally cautious and hard-headed policy-making style suggests that Sweden is unlikely to be first to try any new program — and unlikely to try a new program at all without both widespread agreement and convincing evidence that it can work. The practicality of the Swedish approach has obvious advantages, particularly in an era when service delivery has become a major governmental responsibility. But there is a political advantage that may be less obvious, although equally relevant to the pace of social change in modern Sweden. Hugh Heclo's careful comparison of British and Swedish social policy development captures this advantage very nicely and is worth quoting at some length. Summarizing the 20th century experience of the two countries, he writes:

> The 1907 Swedish pension investigation, for example, entailed an analysis qualitatively superior to anything in Britain and produced a plan acceptable to most groups concerned, a plan capable not only of pre-empting a good deal of partisan conflict but of being developed and extended to all citizens in subsequent years. The British pensions of the same period, involving what analysis and consultation could be hurriedly arranged by several civil servants, created from the moment of their passage a persisting and largely sterile party division between contributory and noncontributory antagonists. The point is not that partisan clashes are necessarily unproductive, but that through the British method they remained largely mock battles; they were irresponsible in the sense that the supposed opposition (usually Labor) was unwilling or unable to act on most of its own pension or unemployment proposals when finally in office. In the same way, the 1928 Swedish investigation, which ostensibly was a manifestation of economizing forces, exerted its own independent impact, providing factual and analytic intelligence that seems to have alleviated any strong party clash on the basic lines of a new and more adequate pension policy adopted in the 1930's. Much the same can also be said for the current Swedish investigation of unemployment benefits . . . By no means has the Swedish approach prevented partisan clashes; investigations of a number of important issues have been unable to reach agreement. But the direct consequence of this has been that partisan conflict — for example in superannuation in the 1950's or unemployment in the late 1920's — has been concentrated on precisely those issues of significant disagreement, in contrast to the more vague, often fanciful clashes that have characterized much of British policy.[33]

If Heclo's analysis is sound—and there is much confirming evidence—the Swedish style not only produces reforms that work, it also encourages political learning. Asking the "administrative" questions of impact and feasibility, in other words, produces information that often leads to a clearer conception of the relationship between political preference and program consequence, and it can lead to a change in values as program consequences change through time. Herbert Tingsten long ago argued that precisely this process had eliminated the significance of ideology from Swedish politics.[34] He was right, it seems to me, if "ideology" is defined as an unchanging configuration of values. If values are conceived to change in response to changed social conditions, however, it is clear that they continue to affect Swedish policy-making in a way more precise and more far-reaching than Tingsten had imagined. Indeed, the learning of new values through program implementation and empirical evaluation has become, for Sweden, a more powerful motor of social change than any past ideology.

Apart from a traditional style that emphasizes empiricism, rationality and consultation, the structure of modern Swedish administration stimulates change by providing organizations whose specialized responsibility it is to promote planning and policy innovation. As noted earlier, full responsibility for carrying out programs mandated by law is lodged in administrative boards, which now number about seventy. Each such board is headed by a Director General, appointed by and responsible to the Cabinet. Operationally, Boards are made up of a number of bureaus or, more recently, divisions, and large boards such as the Board of Health and Welfare employ many thousands of people in carrying out their functions. Board responsibilities are spelled out in great detail and civil servants are provided strong encouragement to pay attention to the details of their work by the legal responsibility each of them bears for its proper execution: the lifetime tenure civil servants enjoy can be ended prior to retirement age through action brought in a court of law. Thus, although Directors General are expected to advise the Cabinet from time to time on improvements in Board operations, and although Directors General invest a great deal of time participating in Royal Commission work, the agencies they lead are predominantly engaged in carrying out detailed legislative instructions. They do administration, not politics.[35]

The politics is done by the thirteen ministries (in Swedish, *Departement*). Led by a Cabinet member, each of the ministries is a small (around 100 people) organization with financial and policy-making responsibilities that give it a central position in Swedish politics. The financial responsibilities include coordination of budget preparation for the several administrative boards included within its domain of functional interest; the Ministry of Health and Welfare, for example, is responsible for the budget of the Board of Health and Welfare, the Social Insurance Board, and other welfare agencies. Thus, while

Ministries are excluded from interference in day-to-day administration by both tradition and law, they nevertheless can affect administrative operations through the budget process. How much a ministry affects board operations, of course, depends on the skill and prestige of both Minister and Director General, among other things. But the opportunity for ministerial influence is constantly present, creating a set of overlapping responsibilities among Cabinet, Minister and Director General.

Important as the budget responsibility is—and if anything it has grown in importance in recent years—the most important Ministerial role is the planning of social change through public sector policy innovation. Note that this formulation assumes a governmental responsibility for changes in society as a whole, and that public policies are explicitly formulated in terms of social impact rather than program change alone. Pierre Vinde, himself a long-time official in the Budget Division of the Ministry of Finance, has described and evoked the significance of ministerial activities in his *Hur Sverige Styres*[36] (How Sweden Is Governed). Arguing that planning is the most important job of the Ministries and that current operations must always be placed within a longer time perspective, Vinde suggests that the primary meaning of planning in Sweden is "to determine how the government desires the future society to appear. That means that the government examines existing or potential defects in the society and through activities decided in advance seeks to ameliorate these defects or prevent their existence." Continuing, Vinde offers an interesting example of what he means:

> One area in which the government's desire to change society came to fruition was the supplementary pension program (ATP). In this case the government wanted to provide all groups of citizens a level of old-age security above the minimal level provided by the basic national pension. Earlier only managers and officials had enjoyed such benefits. Behind this reformist desire was the government's political interest in achieving a greater degree of equality among different groups of citizens. Such a reform required long-term planning and comprehensive research. Planning began in the 1940's, the decision came at the end of the 1950's, but the ATP system will not be fully operative until the 1990's. In this case it will have been nearly 50 years between the first initiative and the reform's full operation.[37]

Vinde insists that this long view is neither academic nor exceptional; it is a practical, day-to-day aspect of ministerial operation, if only because daily choices about budgets and programs require awareness of long-term plans: "Since so large a fraction of state activity is controlled through the budget it is natural to require officials who work full-time on state expenditures to be aware of long-range plans and reform objectives. Proposals for new activities are constantly made which must be placed in a long-range context in connection with budget preparation."[38] Often enough, it is precisely this process of considering requests for new programs that leads to special planning studies within ministries—as, for example, an effort to map changing relationships between criminal behavior in society and the personnel needs of the police, state prosecutors' offices, and the courts.

The major instruments of planning, however, are two: Royal Commissions and five-year economic plans. As noted earlier, Commissions are established for all major policy problems, under the control of the relevant Minister who defines the problem to be investigated, recommends members, and provides staff and other resources to support commission undertakings. Ministries, therefore, are the nerve centers controlling major policy innovations for Swedish government, and much ministerial activity is devoted to creation, guidance and support of Royal Commissions. Long-range economic plans are a more recent planning tool, having begun in 1947, but they are no less significant. Such plans, which provide the foundation for national economic policy, attempt to map future development trends in the entire economy, including "not only the public sector but local government activities and the private sector," as well.[39] According to Vinde, the process, no less than the result, is all-embracing: business, labor, and agricultural research organizations work closely with ministries in developing the five-year projections. In both fiscal choice and policy development, accordingly, ministerial politics is very much a politics of the future, and very much a politics of social, rather than merely governmental, change.

"Planning," of course, is an activity that many systems claim to support, but in very few cases is there much evidence to suggest that the activity called "planning" produces much of real consequence. Even in Sweden there are those who are skeptical. Assar Lindbeck, a major figure in Swedish economic thought, convincingly argues that post-war fiscal and monetary policy has been consistently mismanaged and that none of the instruments of "planning" have worked very well. In his view, ". . . there has hardly been any long-term planning in Sweden during the post-war period."[40] Like most economists, Lindbeck draws his conclusions from evidence that government policies have perverse consequences, or unintended consequences, or no significant consequences at all. This "achievement model" of planning, emphasizing the extent to which stated objectives are realized, is not unimportant, but it is outmoded. A "learning model," which emphasizes the extent to which social systems adapt to failure no less than their ability to achieve success, is more comprehensive and thus more relevant.[41] Seen from the perspective of a learning model, Swedish policy planning has been very consequential indeed.

Swedish planning has been consequential partly because a long tradition of empiricism and consultation supports it, partly because specialized structures and processes exist to carry it on, and partly because the political system, while "democratic," is oriented far more toward performance than to participation. It should be recalled that Sweden is one of the most organized democracies in the world, both in terms of the number of special interests, large and small, that have created formal structures to promote their interests, and in terms of the extent to which these various organizations are centralized at the national level.[42] Whether it be a fisherman's league, a labor union, an industrial firm or a political party, the almost universal pattern is a structure composed of many local and regional units that conduct most of their important business through the national headquarters, usually located in Stockholm. Considering the historic centralization of Swedish administration, and the more recent centralization of Swedish local administration, Sweden must be regarded as an extraordinarily centralized organization environment. Recent assignment of some central government agencies to ten cities across Sweden does not alter this conclusion.[43]

Two consequences of organizational centralization are important in appreciating the capacity of Swedish government to plan. One is that citizens tend to participate very little in the activities of organizations in which they are formally enrolled. For most Swedes, joining an organization is a mere formality, required as a condition of employment or desirable because of benefits associated with membership. Only a few are actively interested and for them, the path to the top is so long and time-consuming that only a fraction of the "few" ever make an attempt to follow it. The great majority who are members of organizations seem perfectly content to allow leaders to set policy and look out for their common interests. In politics, most Swedes vote—elections are always held on Sunday to minimize the impact of work on voter turnout—but very few do more than that. Parties are dominated by tiny elites and vehicles for citizen participation outside the party-organizational structure do not exist. The development of neighborhood organizations in the large cities that seemed to become prominent in the early 1970's, stimulated by examples of citizen (student) protest in other countries, has now diminished and citizen passivity once again has come to characterize Swedish political life. As public and organizational citizens, in short, Swedes are among the most practiced followers in the world.[44]

The second consequence, following from the first, is that the number of public and private organizational representatives actively engaged in decision-making is very small and highly concentrated in Stockholm. Once admitted to this circle it is not at all difficult to learn a great deal about other participants in relatively short order. And, since these leaders of organizations are able to speak authoritatively for the members they represent, binding commitments can be arranged by very few people. From a policy-making or planning point of view, the presence of a tiny "apex" elite within a single city certainly must be regarded as helpful. Ease of access to individuals and to organizational intelligence, coupled with familiarity based on repeated personal interaction, produce a climate in which the responsibility of choice is easily assumed and definitively —

if cautiously—achieved. In such a climate it is easy to believe that planned social change can be achieved, for whatever this tiny elite can agree to will be implemented, will be monitored, and will, if necessary, be changed.

THE IMPACT OF SOCIAL DEMOCRACY

The emphasis here on the policy-making aspects of the Swedish political tradition has implicitly rejected more "heroic" versions of national institutional development which focus on individual leaders, or more recently, on dramatic struggles between political parties of the left and right to bring about political modernization. Nevertheless, it is of some importance to assess the significance of the Swedish Social Democratic Party, in power continuously from 1932 to 1976. Originally a Marxist party, the Social Democrats made an early shift away from violent revolution to reform through parliamentary institutions.[45] In keeping with its origins, however, the party has maintained a very close relationship with the Swedish labor union movement and has consistently relied on union proposals to structure its parliamentary program—the drive for income "equality" during the past decade is a good case in point. Surely these labor-reformist inclinations have clashed with the inherent conservatism of the Swedish administrative tradition.

That social democracy has challenged administrative habits can hardly be denied. Party programs have consistently favored more public sector expansion than administrators would have preferred, and the Social Democrats consistently have tailored their economic policies at least as much to the perceived requirements of the next election as to "sound" economic doctrine.[46] The timing of tax increases, or rarely, decreases, for example, has been strongly influenced by the date of the next election, as have decisions such as the hurried creation of a public corporation to assist failing industries. Such decisions are both too "political" (i.e., determined by criteria of electoral success) and too hurried (i.e., not thoroughly studied for administrative feasibility) to sit well with administrators bred to the Swedish tradition. In recent years, moreover, the desirability of maintaining the tradition of "independence" for administrators has come under increasing attack from party members on grounds that the tradition is badly suited to an era when vast social programs are being operated by government.[47] Administrative independence in the welfare state, it is said, undermines political responsibility at precisely the time when it is most needed to restrain government from welfare objectives unsupported by the electorate. All these tensions, rooted in the historical development of party and bureaucracy, remain live issues in a relationship that is bound to be strained.

But the Social Democrats never engaged in a frontal attack on either the administrative system or its personnel. On the contrary, when the party assumed power it took the position that the bureaucracy was a resource that could and should be used in reforming society, relying precisely on the traits of expertise and neutrality that have lately come under attack. Accordingly, the party did nothing to challenge the power base of Swedish administrators. Recruitment remained closely tied to university training, administrators continued to be drawn into the highest policy-making councils, and the Social Democrats continued to honor, by word and deed, the traditions of neutral competence and independence that characterized the development of Swedish central administration.[48] Meanwhile, in order to reform society, the bureaucracy had to be expanded. Officials were also given increasing opportunities to advance themselves, as new programs generated a higher demand for both workers and leaders in the public service. By the 1970's, the bulk of Swedish public administration was engaged in activities that did not exist when the Social Democrats assumed power, many of which were directly traceable to party initiatives.[49] Tension between party and bureaucracy was unavoidable, perhaps, but public sector growth has expanded the common interests of both institutions, and leaders of both institutions know it.

It is important to add that the "conservatism" inherent in any administrative tradition does not, in the Swedish version, automatically imply opposition to social reform. Indeed, Heclo has persuasively shown that Swedish administrators were the most consistent and effective force for social policy reform in Sweden throughout the 19th and 20th centuries—often in opposition to more "democratic" representative institutions such as parliament or local government.[50] In part this seems to have been due to a natural concern for administrative feasibility that, given access to policy-making circles, tended to dampen enthusiasm for ill-considered or overly restrictive proposals. It was due even more, however, to a problem-solving mentality that often led administrators, after typically careful investigations, to propose solutions more far-reaching than anything then being considered: an 1837 Royal Commission report concluded its study of poverty and poor relief by proposing a comprehensive program of public elementary education as the best means of combatting the ignorance it suggested lay at the root of poverty.[51] In this instance, as in many others, Swedish administrators were well ahead of their contemporaries in defining and rationalizing solutions to problems. If the Social Democrats are less "radical" than other parties with a Marxist lineage, the Swedish administrative tradition is similarly less "conservative" than a long tradition of elite status might imply.

Given a pragmatic party of the Left and a tradition of open-minded administration, to say nothing of well-developed habits of widespread consultation, it is more difficult than usual to establish conclusions about who has led and who has followed along the path of reform. Perhaps the major significance of the Social

Democrats is what is most obvious: they maintained power for nearly a half-century, providing an electoral foundation for public sector expansion. Social Democratic continuity has clearly stabilized political expectations as well as political power, including the expectation that public sector activities—what Swedes like to call their "service democracy"[52] —will continue to improve. The partisan effect of creating and stabilizing an expectation that better services will be available at higher standards has been to strengthen the Social Democrats, widely perceived as a major source of service initiatives. The political effect, on the other hand, has been to build a bigger, better and more comprehensive power base for Swedish administrators who, along with their party counterparts, have become active social and cultural engineers. Although form and substance have changed considerably, the tradition of administrative domination lives on.

BUREAUCRATIC ROLE EXPECTATIONS IN CONTEXT: TWO FACES OF THEORY

The continued existence of a politically-dominant civil service, despite a half-century of continuous governmental control by a reformist political party, raises questions that invite further exploration. From a political point of view, it seems essential to ask what factors shaped the accommodation that took place between politicians in the Social Democratic Party and traditionally prestigious senior civil servants. Perhaps the party elite never mounted a frontal attack on the bureaucracy because there was no need to do so: over time, bourgeois party sympathizers could simply be replaced by socialist loyalists more amenable to the party's "reformist" program. Working class people would replace upper class individuals, particularly at the top, and bureaucratic performance would then closely follow political imperatives—assuming, of course, that working class origins and reformist values are closely linked. This "hypothesis of class transformation" is important because it suggests a clear mechanism for translating political power into government action and a clear mechanism for accommodating a bureaucratic system to new political imperatives.[53] Unfortunately, the hypothesis is quite wrong. Although educational backgrounds have changed considerably among senior civil servants, reflecting the growth of new governmental programs,[54] we shall see in Chapter Two that senior bureaucrats continue to be drawn predominantly from the upper and middle classes, in continuing contrast to the predominantly working-class origins of Social Democratic politicians. We obviously need a better explanation.

An alternative hypothesis, more satisfying because it avoids simplistic assumptions about the relationship between childhood origins and adult perspectives, might be thought of as the "shared values" hypothesis. One version of this hypothesis, much discussed by recent students of so-called "consociational" political systems,[55] asserts the existence of a strong commitment to maintain the system among bureaucratic and political elites. Since, among other things, "maintaining the system" implies maintenance of elite status within it, this commitment is hardly surprising; its significance lies primarily in the absence of other strongly shared values among populations that are described as highly fragmented.[56] Given the ethnic and cultural homogeneity of the Swedish population, discovery of a shared commitment to maintain the system would be neither surprising nor, perhaps, very interesting. In Sweden, at least, the significant question is not so much *whether* a shared interest in system maintenance exists, but rather, what are the terms on which that shared interest is founded?

It seems entirely plausible, if the preceding discussion of the Swedish bureaucratic tradition is accepted, that this shared interest is built around widespread bureaucratic acceptance of reformist values. The Swedish civil servant traditionally has been a pragmatist and it is entirely conceivable that senior officials either were or quickly became supportive of socialist reform, despite centuries of entrenched power organized around very different values. Perhaps the ascendance of social democracy created a large number of "bourgeois radicals" in the government, who were able to stave off a frontal attack by choosing to accept the party's program. Or perhaps "traditional" bureaucratic values include some that encourage accommodation to political leadership, whether or not political programs are accepted. Because so much of our attention will be focused on the value-bases of role expectations we can examine these issues in some detail, beginning in Chapter Three, in which we ask whether Swedish bureaucrats are in fact a group of "bourgeois radicals."[57]

The answer to that question leads directly to a formulation that reverses the direction of "accommodation." In view of the traditional power of Swedish civil servants, and the known reluctance of the Social Democrats to confront that power, it is important to consider whether reformist accommodation to the entrenched bureaucracy is not the most important form of political accommodation among the Swedish elite. Most, if not all, of the literature on Swedish politics and policy portrays an extraordinarily quiescent system, guided by highly deliberative, empirical and rationalistic processes.[58] The apparent stability of these processes through time strongly suggests that administrators have not only taken over the high ground of symbol definition but have held that ground against all competition for a considerable period. To the extent that administrative ideologies give meaning to issues and define terms of debate, it is politicians who must do the accommodating rather than administrators. If this is in fact the basis of elite accommodation, we should find supporting evidence both in administrator role definitions (Chapters Three and Four) and in patterns of interaction between civil servants and members of Parliament (Chapter Five).

Clarifying the bases of political accommodation through role analysis will permit us to address a larger theoretical issue, namely, the adequacy of currently-popular conceptions of bureaucratic roles. Max Weber's brilliant imagination remains the source of most current images of bureaucracy as a hierarchy ordered by authority, in which highly-trained officials apply abstract rules in pursuit of objectives defined by law.[59] In the Weberian model officials are appointed to positions on the basis of specialized knowledge, hence they are able to render "expert" judgments. Moreover, because such judgments are presumed to derive from clearly-specified and universally-applicable legal rules, official decisions can be seen to be "neutral" in their derivation. Although constantly monitored for quality of performance by the hierarchical superior, neither partisanship nor personal loyalty can be used to evaluate official performance; objectivity and expert competence are the only legitimate evaluative grounds. The role behavior implied by these characteristics of "bureaucracy" seems clear enough: impersonal, formal, rule-oriented rather than people or problem oriented, distant from both the hurly-burly activities and emotional commitments of politics.

This image of bureaucracy was admittedly something of a caricature, even for Weber, but it nevertheless has motivated a great deal of scholarship. Indeed, it is hardly an exaggeration to suggest that Weber's work is a major foundation of modern organization theory. Focusing, as Weber did, on the inner logic of bureaucratic relations has been helpful in developing expectations about behavior patterns within public organizations. Recent extensions of that theoretical work have been concerned with organizational-environment relationships as well, but the imagery used to conceptualize such relationships seems familiar. In his recent work on politician-bureaucrat relationships, for example, Putnam has made effective use of an image of the "classical bureaucrat," who

> . . . operates with a monistic conception of the public interest – the 'national interest' or the 'interest of the State.' He believes that public issues can be resolved in terms of some objective standard of right, or of justice, or of legality . . . such bureaucrats 'frequently operate on the assumption that problems can be resolved purely objectively . . . without reference to sociopolitical considerations.' This presumption leads naturally to the belief that because the bureaucrat himself is 'non partisan,' his judgment is 'impartial' and 'objective.' Consequently, the classical bureaucrat distrusts or rejects the institutions of politics, such as parliaments, parties, and pressure groups.

While obviously inspired by Weber's conceptualization, these images permit Putnam to develop a model of the "political bureaucrat," who operates with a more pluralistic conception of the public interest, a more relativistic notion of substantive and procedural aspects of decision making, and thus a willing acceptance of political institutions. Understanding the political environment within which he works, the political bureaucrat is prepared to be both an advocate of programs and a compromiser when program goals cannot be wholly achieved. In effect, the political bureaucrat is everything the classical bureaucrat is not— a polar opposite.[60]

Putnam did not intend these images to be accurate descriptions of reality; they do, however, provide a useful interpretive framework within which to place results of empirical work. With some slight embellishment, in fact, we can use this framework to extend our insight into bureaucratic role orientation. If "classical" and "political" bureaucrats stand at opposite poles of some imaginary continuum, the above discussion suggests that two major dimensions structure that continuum: the extent to which officials adopt an active or passive stance toward their responsibilities, and the extent to which officials adopt an open or closed posture toward other political institutions. By placing these qualities in the familiar two-by-two table (Table 1.1), we can more clearly perceive relationships of considerable potential interest.

Table 1.1. Dimensions of Official Role Behavior

	Closed	Open
Passive	Classical Bureaucrat	Judge
Active	Expert	Political Bureaucrat

This array of role types captures several nuances that are hidden in a simple "polar type" formulation. The classical bureaucrat, derived from Weber, may well have been an empirical reality in Germany, and may still be an empirical reality in Italy, but isolation from other political institutions was never part of the Swedish bureaucratic tradition. There was of course a time when Swedish officials believed their responsibilities did not extend beyond exercising judgment on actions initiated by others, but the Swedish tradition always has made clear that senior officials were to be welcome participants in the work of other institutions. This combination of passive responsibility coupled with open access is captured far more accurately by the "judge" concept than by the idea of "classical bureaucrat," although both concepts share expectations of neutrality and objectivity. There is a similarly important nuance that supports a distinction between the classical bureaucrat and the more modern concept of expert. Both roles are assumed to be closed to and perhaps somewhat hostile to less competent institutions. But the scientific underpinning of the "expert" role provides a drive toward activism that is absent from the classical bureaucrat, whose specialized expertise is derived from administrative rather than scientific knowledge. Note, too, that both the judge and the political bureaucrat role are assumed to be open to other institutions, but that the political bureaucrat accepts a responsibility for active intervention and initiation of new programs.

This simple classification scheme suggests a number of conclusions. Given the enormous expansion of public sector activities we know to have taken place in Sweden and other Western systems, a massive shift toward more active bureaucratic role definitions seems self evident. Programs designed to change society — such as welfare, social insurance, health care, and so on — typically aim at income redistribution or broadened access to social services or both. Because such programs are inherently reformist, it is difficult to conceive of competent administration unless the responsible officials are themselves committed to reform, hence activism. Few classical bureaucrats should be found in Europe if this reasoning is correct while, in Sweden, a shift from the judge role to the political bureaucrat role should be quite apparent. Similarly, government operation of complicated technological programs, from nuclear reactors to automated mass transit systems, implies a large and increasing number of "experts," whose authority is based on technical/scientific knowledge and who are also activist in orientation.[61] Finally, a shift from closed to more open orientations to political institutions should be apparent, although accompanied by some tension, particularly between experts and politicians. These expectations may or may not be borne out, or they may be borne out in ways that suggest some new conceptualization not yet apparent. The point is that treating role expectations as a matter of investigation rather than definition permits us to explore reality in a fashion that should enrich our theories of modern governance.

SUMMARY

Sweden is interesting politically because it appears to have come closer to institutionalizing planned social change than any other Western society, without experiencing many of the disruptions typically associated with rapid change. Sweden's good fortune has a number of obvious causes: industrialization came late, permitting resource exploitation without severe problems of urban congestion or rural decay; problems that arose could be dealt with by a competent centralized bureaucracy, in place for centuries; an ethnically homogeneous citizenry traditionally has shown few signs of serious cleavage and great deference to government officials; the small but highly organized population has provided a setting for easy agreement among organizational elites. Good luck aside, it remains true that other nations, less isolated and richer in resource base than Sweden, have not matched the Swedish level of development or rate of change. Surely it is at least possible that elite ideas and attitudes have had something to do with the Swedish record of political and economic success. If so, observing role conceptions among bureaucrats and politicians may help us to perceive the structure of leadership in modern political systems. In the end, Sweden may help us to better understand the political meaning of bureaucracy by showing us the bureaucratic meaning of reform.

2 PUBLIC AUTHORITY AND SOCIAL STRUCTURE

To characterize the parliamentarians and higher civil servants we interviewed as an "elite" is to invoke an ambiguous image. From a structural point of view, the term suggests a small group of individuals located at the top of a socially-defined pyramid, and characterized by possession of more of the attributes that define membership in the social pyramid: if the attribute is wealth, the elite are the most wealthy; if it is notoriety, the elite are the most famous; if it is power, the elite are the most powerful, and so on.[1] Process-oriented studies, however, frequently confound such simple images by challenging the meaning of the quality attributed to an elite. Studies of "leadership" or "influence," for example, often enough show that a "power" elite seldom exercises its reputed power or that other actors, not included in an elite group, in fact determine the course of events in some specific area.[2]

The possibility of some disjunction between structural and behavioral elite attributions imposes an obligation for clarity on all who use the term. Although the Swedish "elite" discussed here is known to make, or participate in making, important decisions, we have not chosen it on those grounds. Nor have we chosen our respondents in terms of wealth or education or prestige or some other quality we might presume to be significant. Instead, the focus here is on individuals who occupy *positions* close to the top of the structure of public authority in Sweden: civil servants just below cabinet level and, later, a sample of parliament members.[3] Are people in such positions "thrown up" somehow, by accident, or is there some pattern to their relationship to the larger social system? If there is a pattern, is it stable or changing and, if changing, how?

In general we know that elite relationships to social structure tend to be quite distinctively patterned. Virtually all studies of public or private sector elites have shown that they are disproportionately drawn from the more privileged strata of society, in large measure because the resources of privilege tend to be cumulative, that is, those who are wealthy also tend to be the best educated, to have the best jobs, the best residences, and so on. Social privilege and elite position, in short, go hand-in-hand.[4] For several reasons, however, one might anticipate that Sweden would be an exception to these widely-observed patterns. Politically, a party professing a strongly egalitarian ideology held government power continuously for nearly a half-century, until defeated in 1976. Despite that defeat, the Social Democratic Party remains powerful, supported by a powerful and well-organized labor movement that has provided both leadership and support for a long string of government programs designed to redistribute income. Finally, and to some extent because of these political conditions, the Swedish economy has grown rapidly, transforming Sweden from a poor to a very rich nation within two generations. Quite apart from ideology, one could plausibly expect these economic changes to have shaken up earlier patterns of resource cumulation. Sweden, in short, might well be a society in which governmental elites come from less privileged backgrounds than they do elsewhere. Let us see whether this speculation can be supported.

ELITE SOCIAL CHARACTERISTICS

Those who make it to the top of the political heap in Sweden are predominantly middle-aged (median age = 51), upper- or middle-class males, raised primarily (80%) in urban areas, and educated to at least the level of the B.A. degree at Swedish universities. These characteristics are very similar to elite characteristics in other advanced nations, but there are obvious gaps between what these data show and the cultural-political aspirations of Swedes themselves. Despite a long history of feminist agitation in Sweden, for example, and despite much recent official support for feminist aspirations,[5] we found that only ten (3.2%) among our civil servants and two (4.7%) of our parliamentary respondents were women. These figures are not significantly different from those reported by Christoffersson and his colleagues, who show that fewer than 6 percent of middle- as well as upper-level bureaucrats are women.[6] It is clear that women remain a rather weak minority in the Swedish civil service as a whole, that the proportion of women declines as the level of responsibility increases, and that women are virtually unrepresented at the highest levels. At the top, Swedish politics is very much a male world.

Perhaps more surprising, in a country where the official ideology has been vaguely "socialist" for the past four decades, is the relatively small proportion of elite civil servants who emerge from the working class. Using the social group classification that has been standard in Sweden for many years, we find that fewer than 15 percent of our respondents are persons of working-class origin (Table 2.1). This, of course, severely under-represents a class that, during the first three decades of this century, constituted the bulk of the Swedish population. By expanding educational opportunities and otherwise removing barriers against working-class assumption of higher-status positions, the Social Democratic government has attempted to promote greater equality in employment, and there is evidence that these efforts have had some success. Studies by Landström (1917-47),[7] Linde and Lönnquist (1957-67),[8] and Christoffersson et al. (1969)[9] show that, over time, there has been a gradual increase in the proportion of civil servants drawn from the working class (Table 2.2). One might argue that these figures represent an impressive accomplishment, yet what they reflect does not remotely approach a position of working-class equity. Indeed, the available evidence makes clear that a social class filter continues to operate at the

Table 2.1. Respondents, by Social Group

	N	%
Social Group I (upper)	129	41.7
Social Group II (middle)	134	43.4
Social Group III (working)	46	14.9

Table 2.2. Government Employees, by Social Origin, 1917-67

	Social Group, %		
	I	II	III
1917	64	33	2
1927	60	37	4
1937	56	39	5
1947	48	43	9
1957	36	47	18
1967	27	51	22

top. Thus, when Christoffersson et al. divide their sample of 1553 individuals into "chief executives" and "other officials," producing a "chief" group that corresponds to our sample, they discover that only 17 percent of their chief officials are of working-class origin—a result very similar to the data in Table 2.1 above.[10] Despite some loosening, then, the administrative elite in Sweden has been, is, and will in all probability continue to be a group in which the upper and middle classes of society are substantially over-represented.

One reason why the above conclusion can be put so strongly emerges from consideration of the educational backgrounds of our respondents. More than eight of every ten upper-level administrators hold a university degree, and another 15 percent have completed the *student-examen,* which is roughly equivalent to two years of college education in the United States.[11] Those who have had no higher education at all amount to only 3.2 percent of our sample. These figures are considerably higher than those reported by Christoffersson et al., who show that only 34 percent of their sample are academics. Separating out the "chief" officials from others in their sample, however, again leads to results closer to these: some 63 percent of the highest group are academics, including 91 percent of executives in ministries and 64 percent in the central administrative boards.[12] Taken together, these studies underline the extent to which university training is required for admission to the highest level of civil service participation in Sweden. This, of course, accounts for the relative lack of working class participants at the top since, until the 1960's, Swedish universities were few in number and attended primarily by students from the more privileged social class. Recent changes in educational policy have enormously expanded opportunities for higher education, but the impact of this expansion on the social origins of elite administrators, if any, will not be felt for some time to come.[13] For the moment, the Swedish higher civil service remains largely a preserve for the well-born and the well-educated.

It is also surprisingly dominated by persons who have been either raised or educated in the Stockholm area. Some 30 percent of all respondents indicated they were raised in Stockholm city or county (recall that 80 percent grew up in urban places) and, of those who hold academic degrees, nearly two-thirds received those degrees from the University of Stockholm, the Stockholm School of Economics or the Royal Institute of Technology, also located in Stockholm (Table 2.3). If those who attended the University of Uppsala—some forty miles from Stockholm—are included, nearly 80 percent of the academic degree-holders in our sample received their degrees from institutions either in or close to the capitol city.[14] Given the historical similarity in the social class backgrounds of students at all Swedish universities, it would be incorrect to conclude that this system is similar to the English system, in which higher civil servants are recruited from the predominantly upper-class "Oxbridge" universities rather than

Table 2.3. Location of Respondent University

	N	%
Lund	37	13
Gothenburg	19	7
Stockholm	180	64
Uppsala	43	15
Umeå	0	0
Foreign, Unknown	4	1

less prestigious "red brick" schools. The Stockholm concentration is more likely a function of the small size and concentration of the higher education sector itself. Whatever the cause, the effect is to give to the administrative elite a regional, no less than urban, quality.

Perhaps the most striking conclusion to emerge from this brief review of background characteristics is that higher civil servants in Sweden are not at all different from civil servants elsewhere. Virtually all men, they were raised primarily in urban areas, 30 percent of them in Stockholm, where most of them were educated and where most of them still reside. If upper- or middle-class origins can be said to bestow privilege, the great bulk of these officials have been privileged. In 1970, the average member of this group had been a civil servant for twenty-four years, and was—by definition—occupying a position in middle age that conferred considerable organizational influence as well as opportunities for interaction with others like himself. In terms of social class, sex, educational attainments or geographic origins this group was, and remains, quite unrepresentative of the Swedish population as a whole, although similar to elites in other advanced countries. Both the homogeneity of the group and its differentiation from the general population make clear that access to elite positions is no accident, but results from patterned social processes—a subject to which we now turn.

FAMILY CONTEXT AND ELITE STATUS

An obvious place to begin a search for social processes that might be related to the achievement of elite status is the family. In Sweden, as in other European systems governed for centuries by large and prestigious bureaucratic organizations, it is entirely plausible to expect public service to become a "tradition" in some families, handed down from one generation to another as the "expected" thing for a son or sons to do. Over time, these inter-generational expectations would create a political class within the middle- and upper-class groups that typically populate leadership positions in society. A political class of this kind may have been powerful at one time in Sweden but if so, little more than remnants remain.[15] Among the individuals we interviewed, only twenty-five reported coming from a "civil service family" and only four indicated membership in a "political" family. A "tradition" of doing political or governmental work, if it ever existed, is not a significant aspect of elite recruitment in modern Sweden.

It is nevertheless clear that the family environments from which these respondents emerged were more hospitable to political matters than the typical family setting. Of the 315 elite administrators in our sample, 120 (31.1%) report that relatives have held government jobs and nearly a third (32.5%) report relatives who have been active in party politics. More significantly, perhaps, some 52 percent indicate that they often talked about politics in their parents' home. Although exactly comparable data for the general population are not available, these figures almost certainly indicate a far higher level of political interest and awareness than would be found among average Swedes. A 1970 Gallup Poll, for example, found that only 11 percent of Swedish men and 4 percent of Swedish women expressed a "very strong interest" in politics (the combined average was 7 percent). Moreover, these figures were identical to a similar poll conducted fifteen years earlier, using a similar sample.[16] Various other surveys, conducted at various times, also report a generally low level of interest in politics among Swedes.[17] Elite administrators, however, are drawn from families in which participation in government was common and discussions about politics occurred with far greater frequency than appears to have been the case for most of their countrymen. From an early age, members of the Swedish elite talked politics and lived politics. If not, strictly speaking, a "political class," these individuals at least grew up in family circumstances that were relatively "politicized."[18]

Because the Swedish elite emerges from families that are relatively politicized, rather than a political class, relationships between family political activity and later elite position are less strong than might have been anticipated. There is a slight tendency for individuals with relatives in public administration to be located within agencies dealing with defense, and commerce, and to identify themselves with technicians or engineers. There is a similarly slight tendency for individuals with relatives in politics to be located in agencies dealing with finance and local government, and to identify themselves with planners. It is also interesting to note that "Director General" is the most frequently-reported title for individuals who have relatives in government, in politics, and for those who report frequent political discussions with parents.[19] Family context thus appears to have some impact on rising to the very top, and some slight impact on the choice of organization within which to pursue a career. But the important point is the relative insignificance of these relationships.[20] In modern Sweden elite

Table 2.4. Family Context and Attitude

	% Relatives in Administration		% Relatives in Politics		% Discussed Politics at Home	
Esteem for	Yes	No	Yes	No	Yes	No
Politicians						
Yes	57	68	67	63	72	58
Middle	17	12	15	13	13	14
No	26	20	18	23	15	28
System Awareness						
Yes	61	68	76	58	75	56
No	39	32	24	42	25	44

status in government is neither inherited nor allocated by family tradition, however much it may be confined to middle- and upper-class individuals.

On the other hand, family context does appear to influence both the extent to which the administrative elite feels esteem for politicians and the extent to which members of this elite exhibit awareness of the larger political context within which they operate. As Table 2.4 suggests, individuals who have relatives in politics and who report frequent political discussions with parents tend to have a more positive view of politicians than those who do not. These politically-sensitive individuals also demonstrate a considerably higher sensitivity to the political system as a whole than is shown by either individuals without politically-connected relatives, or with relatives in administration instead of politics. Having had relatives in politics or government, or having talked frequently about politics at home, therefore seems to have affected basic elite attitudes rather than the nature of elite positions. Administrative leaders in Sweden are disproportionately drawn from politicized middle- and upper-class families, they begin to discuss politics in the home, and what they learn about politics and politicians within the family context structures an appreciation of social life that is carried into adulthood.

ORGANIZATIONAL PROCESSING

The class and educational filters that determine access to the Swedish elite maintain their significance in part because they are able to accommodate other social changes. In the past, middle- and upper-class individuals interested in a government career went to the university, studied law, and moved into civil service positions that required use of their legal training. Expansion of the industrial and welfare state, however, created a demand for more varied educational training among new civil servants. Whereas the proportion of academics with legal training exceeded 60 percent in 1917 and was 52 percent as recently as 1947, by the late 1960's the proportion of lawyers had fallen to little more than 25 percent. Nevertheless, lawyers constitute 32 percent of the persons we interviewed, which suggests the continuing significance of legal experience at the highest governmental levels (Table 2.5). Lawyers are predominant among those working in ministries (55 percent), the Directors General of Administrative Boards (40 percent), and among respondents 41–50 years of age. Social scientists are most strongly represented among ministry under-secretaries (75 percent), other ministry employees (36 percent), and among those of our respondents who are 40 or younger (53 percent). While lawyers remain the most numerous single group in the upper echelons of Swedish administration, the number of social scientists is increasing noticeably in the policy-planning ministries, where they may soon rival lawyers in significance. Law remains the major discipline of the elite, but the new industrial state clearly has opened the way for alternative sources of trained perception.[21]

Attending a university, of course, provides plentiful opportunities for other social interactions in addition to disciplinary indoctrination. Swedish universities traditionally have sponsored very few extra-curricular activities such as athletic teams, but students themselves have created organizations or participated in a variety of non-university organizations during student years. Since nearly two-thirds of our respondents were educated in Stockholm, we may assume they had easy access to an organizational environment at least as rich as the more "campus-type" universities of Uppsala and Lund.[22] Wherever they studied, our respondents were active organization men: more than 57 percent were members of at least one organization and some 40 percent were office-holders in one or more such groups. Table 2.6 indicates the kinds of organizations favored by the elite, both when they were students and now. Apart from the student unions—

Table 2.5. Lawyers as a Percentage of Civil Servants, 1917–67

1917	61
1927	56
1937	54
1947	52
1957	45
1967	28

Source: Landstrom, op. cit., p. 130; Linde and Lönnquist, op. cit., p. 50.

Table 2.6. Organizational Participation, Student and Current

	Union	Service	Cultural	Political	Sport Club	Religious
			Participation Now			
Member	48.1	31.0	31.0	17.4	20.3	0.6
Officer	7.4	10.6	5.5	5.8	2.9	0.6
Total	55.5	41.6	36.5	23.2	23.2	1.2
			Participation Then			
Member		11.9	14.2	5.2	24.5	1.9
Officer	20.6	10.6	6.5	7.4	11.0	1.3
Total		22.5	20.7	12.6	35.5	3.2

called *"kår"*—in which all students are automatically enrolled, sport clubs were most popular and religious organizations least attractive. Rather few of these respondents were active in political organizations as students, but this conclusion should be compared to the much higher proportion who achieved leadership positions in the student *kår*. As the major university-related student organization, the *kår* provided students with their most important opportunities for social and regional identification. *Kår* leadership was therefore based on the ability to articulate general and diffuse sentiment, rather than specific, functional interest. In this sense, *kår* leadership clearly was "political" and may well have presaged abilities that contributed to later assumption of elite status.[23]

Comparison of organizational activities then and now (1970-71) is instructive. It is immediately apparent that the level of current participation is considerably higher; indeed, 72 percent belong to at least one and 59 percent to at least two organizations. It is also clear that the proportion who hold office in other organizations now is smaller (33 percent) than it was when these individuals were being educated. A tendency to belong more but participate with less intensity as responsibility increases is easy enough to understand, particularly if we note the nature of outside interests. The proportion who participate now in service and cultural organization is almost double what it was, as is the proportion involved in political organizations. Participation in sport clubs is much lower, almost entirely because of a cessation of leadership activity. *Kår* participation disappears, but is replaced by heavy participation in union membership. Membership in SACO, the union of academics and professionals, reflects the extraordinary strength of white collar unions even at the highest levels of the government.[24]

How are we to explain the increase in organizational memberships held by these respondents? We know that a relatively strong (gamma = .43) relationship exists between the number of organizations a respondent belonged to years ago and the number he belongs to now, and we know that a similarly positive, though weaker (gamma = .32) relationship between holding office then and now also exists. This suggests a generalized interest in joining and holding office that might well characterize seekers of influence who later gain elite status. Yet, when we examine the relationship between joining-holding office in a *different* organization (*kår* and union organizations excepted), we find no correlations of any significance. Instead of using participation in one organization as a springboard to responsibility in another, these respondents tend to maintain affiliations with the same kinds of organizations through time (Table 2.7). Thus, the "participators" among these elite indicate a participatory interest early and maintain interest in the same organizations later in their careers; some early nonparticipators become active later, but usually in organizations that reflect a specialized existing interest rather than a concern for broadening a base of power. For example, the predominately technical elites in the National Public Authorities, who are *least* likely to have been members of organizations as students, are now *most* likely to be union members and *most* likely to be officers in service organizations. For this elite, in short, organizational participation appears to reflect functional interest rather than a generalized search for influence. To the extent that "old boy" networks exist, therefore, they are more likely to reflect specialization of training and interest than the more diffuse class and/or regional attachments associated with university attendance in some other nations.[25]

Relationships based on function and interest are bound to be reinforced by the overwhelmingly *governmental* quality of elite career patterns. Having risen to the top, members of this elite interact freely with private sector organizations but relatively few have had previous experience in the private sector (Table 2.8). Even if we sum together all first, second and third mentions of experience in business and/or industry, the total barely exceeds a fifth of all mentioned experiences. These respondents typically have entered government service at young

Table 2.7. Organizational Participation Then, Now Compared

	Tau_b	Gamma
Political	.39	.81
Service	.23	.51
Cultural	.39	.77
Sport Club	.31	.63

Table 2.8. Previous Experience, Elite Administrators

Sector	1st Mention		2nd Mention		3rd Mention		Cum.	
	N	%	N	%	N	%	N	%
Education, Research	16	6.0	25	12	11	10	52	9
Private Industry	43	16.0	59	29	18	17	120	21
Interest Organizations	15	6.0	18	9	2	2	35	6
Public Administrations	170	64	94	4.5	65	6.2	329	57
Other	20	7	10	5	7	7	37	6
Mass Media	3	1	1	0	2	2	6	1
Totals	267	100	207	100	105	100	529	100

age, stayed for a long time, moved up, and are now—primarily because of being "up"—moving around; thus 40 percent moved into their present positions from other organizations. Note, however, that the great majority of these "other" organizations are other governmental agencies such as boards, ministries and, to a lesser extent, court positions. It is therefore clear that this is, first and foremost, a *governmental* elite, in which lateral entry to top-level positions seldom occurs. As Christoffersson and his colleagues have noted, "A counterpart to the American system in which many top positions in the administration are filled with people who have previously had a successful career in the private sector does not exist in Sweden.[26]

COLLEAGUES AND FRIENDS

It seems perfectly understandable that individuals with well-defined interests, who spend decades within the same organizational structure, would tend to find their most rewarding personal relationships within the organizations that provide their sustenance. To test this supposition, each person interviewed was asked to describe his or her three closest friends in terms of occupation, origin and type of interaction. Not surprisingly, in view of their own stature, these officials perceive virtually all of their closest friends as members of the upper, not middle class: 89 percent of the first, 89 percent of the second, and 84 percent of the third friends mentioned were placed in this group (Table 2.9). Obviously these men confine their social relationships to the relatively narrow social stratum from which they emerged themselves. They also appear to confine such relationships largely to people whose occupations are very much like their own. Table 2.10 classifies friends of these respondents by type of work. Individuals working

Table 2.9. Elite Friends, by Social Class

	Friend 1		Friend 2		Friend 3		Cumulative	
	N	%	N	%	N	%	N	%
Upper	239	89	233	89	186	84	658	88
Middle	24	9	15	6	25	11	64	8
Working	5	2	13	5	11	5	29	4
Totals	268	100	261	100	222	100	751	100

Table 2.10. Elite Friends, by Type Work

	Friend 1		Friend 2		Friend 3		Cumulative	
	N	%	N	%	N	%	N	%
Works in Same Agency	46	17	27	10	26	11	99	13
Same Type Work, Different Agency	54	20	65	25	43	19	162	21
Professional, Private Practice	24	9	12	5	15	6	51	6
Higher Admin., General	57	21	72	27	45	20	174	23
Other	93	34	87	33	100	44	280	37
Totals	274	101	263	100	229	100	766	100

in the same agency or doing similar work in another agency, along with people who are engaged in higher administration in general, provide most of the friends named by our respondents. When we classify friends by sector, public administration emerges as the dominant source of employment: only 26 percent of the first, 26 percent of the second, and 20 percent of the third friends named, for example, are in private sector occupations.[27] In terms of either social class or occupation, the friends of this elite are people very much like themselves.

Inquiring into the sources of these friendships produces a useful insight into the nature of friendship patterns. Table 2.11 summarizes responses to the question "How did you make these friends?" Since considerably more than half of the respondents could not or did not answer, these data must be regarded with some caution. Nevertheless, the data are consistent with other knowledge we have in suggesting a group whose friendships derive mostly from the work experience or, to a lesser extent, from associations originating in childhood.

Table 2.11. How Did You Make These Friends? (%)

	Friend 1	Friend 2	Friend 3
Childhood friend or classmate	33	21	24
Used to work with him	16	25	9
Work with friend now	36	25	30
Met in organization	4	8	7
Neighbor or relative	9	16	23
Other	3	5	7

Members of organizations to which the respondent may belong do not appear to be important sources of elite friendships. Nor do neighbors or relatives provide many friends, except in the third-friend category. Work is clearly the dominant friendship source, past associations second, and neighbors or relatives a distant third.

We can now be more confident in interpreting the pattern, noted earlier, of increased organizational memberships but decreasing intensity of participation in such organizations. These data suggest that such memberships are largely formal, designed to maintain contact but not as a major source of activity or of friends. While only suggestive, these data again indicate that the Swedish administrative elite becomes increasingly narrow over time; individual careers are pursued largely within the public service, often within the same agency; friendships are made almost entirely within the same class and occupational group—and often the same agency; other organizational affiliations gradually lose their personal significance as the elite increasingly narrows its attention to governmental activities and governmental colleagues, unaffected by the occasional outsider who manages to land a top-level position.

Taken together, these observations about the manner in which members of the elite are processed through organizations suggest a tight, guild-like bureaucracy. The sons of middle- and upper-class Swedes who come to occupy elite governmental positions begin the climb toward those positions by entering a university for training in law, social science or technology. They join non-university organizations during those years, and often become leaders in those organizations. A great many become leaders in the principal student organizations, the *kår*, or student union. Later, these interests continue (except for the *kår*) but the future elite pursues them with less vigor as they climb, relatively slowly, up the ladder of governmental success. The fact that early interests persist, but that organizational pursuit of those interests gradually weakens, suggests that the focus of elite attention is gradually dominated by governmental responsibilities. Closed to outsiders, operated by individuals who lack new outside interests and who reduce their involvement in old interests, the system provides a perfect breeding ground for clearly-defined "governmental" interests articulated by thoroughly-socialized government officers.

PROTECTIVE PENETRATION

The bureaucratic system that processes individuals into elite positions clearly resembles a "guild" model, in that entry is rigidly controlled, leadership is derived from within the system, and outside penetration is minimized.[28] To conclude, however, that the Swedish bureaucracy is therefore cut off from the rest of society would be a serious error. Indeed, one of the most striking characteristics of the Swedish elite is that, having made it to the top, they find themselves deeply involved with a variety of other governmental and private-sector organizations. Thus, nearly 75 percent of these respondents are members of Royal Commissions, members of advisory boards to other national agencies, representatives to international bodies, and holders of other national-level responsibilities; more than 15 percent are active in private sector organizations as board members or consultants; 6 percent even hold office in local government. Having spent decades learning the system and internalizing its norms, members of the administrative elite find themselves circulating freely among the many organizations that guide Swedish society. What are we to make of this quite widespread penetration of Swedish society by the governmental elite?

At a very obvious level, of course, there can be no surprise in discovering that Directors General, Bureau Chiefs and other senior public officials are provided opportunities to participate widely in other activities. They are, after all, well-trained and experienced men, holding high office in a society that has assigned great prestige to such offices for centuries. Little wonder that corporate boards, commissions of inquiry and the like should find use for their services, and for their prestige. At a less obvious, but considerably more important, level there is an additional point that should be made. Extramural participation by senior-level officials who have grown up within the government guarantees that organizational turf will be represented as well as possible. Since these officials, for reasons outlined above, can be expected to be very clear about their own organizational interests, outside activities can be expected to be protective of those interests or, where possible, beneficial to them. If the government's interest can be defined as the interests of the several agencies that make it up, elite circulation guarantees that "the government" will be strongly represented in many segments of society.[29]

The Swedish model, then, is not quite as closed to the external environment as the "guild" notion implies—at the top, the Swedish civil service penetrates other sectors of society comprehensively and competently. Nor is the Swedish model at all like an "entrepreneurial" system, in which lateral entry is common to all middle- and senior-level bureaucratic positions.[30] The Swedish model may be thought of instead as a system of protective penetration, in which external representation primarily by elites guarantees that governmental interests will be protected or advanced, while circulation guarantees that the advancement of government interests will penetrate virtually all sectors of society. In Sweden, the "government" is a very clear and well-established entity, its representatives clearly know what they are about, they are paid great deference, and they shape the external environment as much as they are shaped by it.

SOCIAL STRUCTURE AND ELITE STRUCTURE

It is difficult to resist the conclusion that the public elite in Sweden is virtually indistinguishable in any important respect from what it must have been fifty — or even a hundred—years ago. Now, as then, the elite is overwhelmingly male, middle- or upper-class in origin, and university-trained; indeed, university training is even more pronounced now. Now, as then, elite administrators join the public service early, spend a considerable time in the ranks, and move to top positions from within: neither youth nor outsiders are welcome at the top. Now, as then, the mandarins of welfare enjoy a psychological security and satisfaction founded on their structural independence within the Swedish political system. Now, as then, elite administrators face their more heterogeneous counterparts in the national legislature from a position of superior stature, based on expert knowledge, command of resources, and tradition. Sweden has changed a great deal, and the bureaucracy has grown enormously to monitor these social changes, but at the top, the old system seems quite secure.[31]

Although the stability of the "old system" of privileged recruitment may seem disappointing to those who may have expected Sweden to be different, the conclusion itself raises an interesting paradox: elite stability in the face of massive social change. To some extent, of course, the paradox may be overdrawn. There has been some movement, after all, toward increased working class representation and a great deal of movement toward representation of educationally-based skills that are very different from elite skills a century ago. More generally, however, it is important to understand that elite stability is paradoxical primarily because of the implicit assumption that elite social backgrounds condition elite values. If values are determined or influenced by something other than social background—education, organizational socialization or philosophical commitment are prominent and reasonable alternatives—then the stability of elite recruitment patterns may be of trivial significance. Elite values, in short, may well be quite compatible with rapid social change, regardless of background. Clearly we need to supplement background information with some sense of elite values and perspectives on society.

3 PATHWAYS TO SATISFACTION

It can hardly be surprising to learn that an elite group, however chosen, is satisfied with its general position in society. For members of the Swedish elite, whose origins are overwhelmingly found in the privileged social classes, anything less than similarly overwhelming levels of satisfaction would be particularly surprising. To report that virtually all (97%) of the officials we interviewed accept the present social order in Sweden, therefore, can hardly be regarded as unusual—or even very interesting. As we shall observe in a later chapter, however, this proportion of satisfied officials is higher in Sweden than in any other nation for which we have data.[1] Indeed, only among Swedish officials are there many (12 and 14 percent of administrators and politicians, respectively, or 43 people) who are judged to be "passionate" defenders of the status quo. Privileged origin is surely relevant to any appreciation of Swedish elite satisfaction but, in view of the many programs of social redistribution that have been undertaken during the past two generations,[2] it is also problematic. Why should a privileged elite be so content with the systematic elimination of the very privileges that gained them "elite" status? Should not, in fact, an elite thought to harbor considerable resistance to social reform be quite *unhappy* with the reforms of the past thirty years? Or is this a group of "bourgeois radicals" who willingly accept, and even lead, changes that undermine their own social status?

DIMENSIONS OF SATISFACTION

Let us begin by clarifying the extraordinary levels of satisfaction that exist among higher-level civil servants in Sweden. Midway through each interview, respondents were asked a series of questions about the political system—what institutions are more or less influential, what role citizens do and should play, and so on. In coding these responses, coders were instructed to judge each respondent's degree of acceptance of the political system, with categories ranging from total rejection to total (i.e., passionate) acceptance. Near the close of each interview respondents were asked a similar question about the existing socioeconomic order and coders were instructed to code those responses, too, in terms of similar degrees of affirmation. The results of these exercises, displayed in Table 3.1, suggest that Swedish senior administrators have made a near-total commitment to the system they serve. Minor tinkering, and perhaps a few more significant changes, might find support from these respondents, but the basic message is different: "Hands Off!"

These, of course, are global judgments about very large and necessarily somewhat ambiguous concepts; a more concrete focus may be useful in clarifying these assessments. Early in the interview, respondents were asked to identify the most important problem confronting them in their own work. Later, respondents were asked to discuss the most important problem facing national leaders in the Cabinet and Parliament. In both questions respondents were requested to indicate how they would solve the problems they identified. Discussions of solutions proposed can also be evaluated in terms of the degree of change, in government operations or national politics, implied by respondents' proposals. These evaluations are displayed in Table 3.2, along with evaluations of the degree of change in the distribution of political power desired by respondents. A total lack of revolutionary fervor is again expectedly absent from these data, but there is now

Table 3.1. Elite Attitudes Toward Political and Social Systems

	Political System		Social Order	
	N	*%*	*N*	*%*
Total Acceptance	37	12.1	40	12.7
Accept, Minor Changes	206	66.9	280	66.2
Accept, Major Changes	63	20.5	63	20.1
Reject, Partial	1	0	3	.1
Total Rejection	1	0	0	0
	308	98.5	306	99.1

Table 3.2.   Civil Service, National Policy and Power Changes Desired

	Civil Service Change		National Problem Change		Political Power Change	
	N	%	N	%	N	%
Revolutionary	2	0.7	5	1.8	1	0
Important	74	25.3	92	33.5	44	15.2
Minor	185	63.1	161	58.5	136	46.9
None	32	11.0	17	6.2	109	37.6
Totals	293	100.1	275	100.0	290	99.7

more variation in the proportion who desire "important" changes. Indeed, more than a third believes that important changes would be necessary to solve the most important national problem, and a fourth believes that the solution to the most pressing problem in their own area of responsibility requires important change. Swedish administrators are quite confident that these changes can be brought about without significant alteration of the present power system: only 15 percent believe that important political changes would be desirable, while well over a third reveal a satisfaction so complete that they want no political changes at all. In discussions of solutions to more concrete problems, then, many Swedish administrators are willing to contemplate significant changes, so long as those changes do not impact on the current distribution of political power.

If these data suggest a group aware of its own position and anxious to preserve it, the reasons must be related to the extraordinary contentment with both their jobs and their colleagues expressed by these men and women. During our interviews, each respondent made judgments about the Swedish administrative system on the basis of his (or her) experiences. Each respondent also indicated how attractive he or she found a civil servant position to be. Finally, we asked our coders to evaluate the entire interview as a basis for judging how each respondent felt about his or her colleagues. Table 3.3 reports these summary judgments. Clearly, nearly all of these respondents are pleased with their positions; extraordinarily few indicate any dislike at all. Most would probably agree with one respondent who, when asked what he disliked about his position, replied: "Everything in life has positive and negative aspects, but unfortunately I have nothing I regard as a disadvantage. I have nothing to complain about, so I can offer nothing. It is good, only good." On the other hand, the number of respondents who are unclear in their evaluations of their colleagues seems high. If we assume that some fraction of these unclear responses are in fact individuals who are negative but resist making negative statements about colleagues, an under-

Table 3.3.   Satisfaction With Job and Colleagues

	How Good Is CS?		How Good Are Colleagues		How Attractive Is CS To You?	
	N	%	N	%	N	%
Very Good	24	8.0	33	10.5	70	22.6 Like Very Much
Good	173	57.7	174	55.4	202	65.2 Like
Pro/Con	64	21.3	31	9.9	30	9.7 Pro/Con
Bad	4	1.3	—	—	5	1.6 Dislike
Unclear	35	11.7	76	24.2	3	1.0 Dislike Very Much
	300	100.0	314	100.0	310	100.1

tone of criticism against some officials, if not the civil service as a whole, might be said to exist. We shall explore that possibility, among others, in a moment; for now the important conclusion demonstrated by Table 3.3 is the very great satisfaction with jobs and colleagues experienced by elite administrators in Sweden.

ORDINARY MOTIVATIONS

Why should satisfaction levels among Swedish administrators be so high? Is it because, as persons of upper- and middle-class origin, members of this group are doing what they had always hoped to do or had traditionally expected to do? Is it because they are committed social reformers happy to be in the vanguard of social change, regardless of class origin? In Table 3.4 we list the seven most fre-

Table 3.4.   What Led You To Choose A Public Service Career?

	1st Men	2nd Men	3rd Men	Total	
				N	%
Chance, Happenstance	71	28	11	110	27
Job Because Open in My Area	51	48	4	103	26
Lack of Other Opportunities	29	16	2	47	12
Intellectual Stimulation	15	23	3	41	10
Job Fits My Education	24	7	6	37	9
Family Tradition	20	8	4	32	8
Strong Political Interest	18	14	—	32	8
				402	100

quent answers to the question "What led you to choose public service as a career?" derived by summing the first, second and third responses mentioned by each official. Because the boundaries between these categories are blurred and overlapping, it is best not to take these numbers too seriously. Even with this caveat, however, it seems abundantly clear that family tradition and strong political interests are not very important in explaining why these top administrators chose to enter public service. Indeed Table 3.4 suggests that most of these individuals did not "choose" public service at all. Chance or fortuitous vacancy in an area in which the respondent was working are the two most frequent reasons offered, and there is no close third. More positive attractions such as intellectual stimulation are mentioned infrequently, often as a second or third response. Rather than "choosing" public service, many of these senior officials appear to have drifted in. At the point of entry, at least, their motivations were quite ordinary.

For many of these officials, particularly those above 60, the drift into public service was associated with major world upheavals that increased the attractiveness of public as opposed to private sector employment. One bureau chief (#318),[3] educated in the law but working as an administrator, offered the following response when asked if he had ever thought about private sector employment.

> Not really. Obviously I thought some about becoming a lawyer when I went to the university. But during the thirties – after it had become clear that war was inevitable – everything was so terribly uncertain. Business was down. Salaries were poor and there was risk in private employment. All legal apprentices who finished their court training went without income for years. The same thing happened if you went into the national courts ("hovrätten"), of course, but getting to the point at which you could get a salary was a little quicker and if you then moved into administration you could then get another salary as well. That was a powerful influencing factor at that time.

Another administrator described the attraction of work as a military doctor in the late 1930's in similar terms (#148):

> When I was ready to practice, about six or seven years after my degree, times were relatively poor in Sweden for doctors. I moved into military medicine then not so much because I particularly wanted to do it but because at that time it was a relatively good position. And it had the great advantage that, at that time, one could have a private practice during part of the day and conduct your military practice during the rest of the day . . . That began in 1936 or 1937, I would guess, and then I went over to full-time military work in March 1940, just when the war began. A little uncertainty about future relationships and so on also influenced the choice.

Or as a supervisory engineer in the Telecommunications Administration put it (#120): "In 1936 you were happy to get into public service because it was a job. There were no other jobs then and the public cake seemed best at that time."

Younger officials, less affected either by depression or war, nevertheless frequently offer similar interpretations of their choice of public service careers. Asked why he chose public service, an Assistant Foreign Secretary (#114) said:

> I can say that I did not choose to go over to public service — I chose to go over to foreign service because I am a lawyer and economist, I am very interested in languages and international relations activity interested me . . . It was personal reasons and not idealistic reasons that led me to administrative work in the foreign ministry.

Another official, who completed his university education while employed in the National Postal Service, made it clear that he undertook his education in order to ". . . increase my opportunities, to partly get something else if necessary . . . in other words, to earn money. At that time I saw the possibility that I would either increase my earnings outside the agency or, if the agency offered me something comparable, I would take it. In a sense it was not my decision to make. Then I took my exam, the demand for jurists was low, I was married and everything was tough . . . So I waited around Stockholm . . . an offer came from the postal service and I stayed on."

If as these examples suggest, many senior officials never planned to enter public service, it is nevertheless clear that other choices they made, particularly their choice of academic discipline, exerted considerable influence on the direction in which they drifted. Those who chose to read law at the university — and we have seen that a large number made this choice — took courses that devoted a great deal of attention to public administration. It was therefore "quite typical," as one Bureau Chief (#318) said, "for students entering these schools in Stockholm to be thinking about a public service career." Studying law was also something that many of these middle- and upper-class individuals did when they had no other clear preference (#307):

> I was perhaps among those who at that time had no definite idea of what I wanted to do, only very vague preferences. In those days — I don't know whether it is still true — you arranged to read law because you thought it provided the greatest number of future options. It was a way of putting off a decision until some future time, but preparing yourself to make that decision when you had to.

Those who thought they might be interested in the public service, among other things, but who could not make up their minds could, in later years, read other disciplines as well as law: political economy, statistics, economics, social administration, and so on. Often enough, these choices emerged late, and in occasionally strange ways. One Director General reports that he finally decided on law when a group of churchmen from his hometown attempted to persuade him to read theology in preparation for a church career (#22). An educational official, originally interested in classical languages, turned to economics (at another university) when he learned how poor employment opportunities were likely to be in classical languages (#324). A ministry official had dreamed of becoming a diplomat as a boy and began to read law after graduating from high school. The experience changed his mind and he switched to economics, then back again to law at the end of his studies. Shortly after taking a court position he was offered an administrative position in the Ministry of Social Welfare (#54).

For these kinds of individuals, with a variety of interests and talents, it seems clear that public service of some kind was always a prominent alternative to be considered, even if the specific position could hardly have been foreseen. In this sense their public service is less accidental than they often perceive it to be. What is accidental is their present position, and it is accidental precisely because, as multi-talented generalists, they move around a good deal. A case in point is an official currently in the Ministry of Finance, who describes his move into finance as "pure chance" ("sinkadus" #316). As a youth, he wanted to become a teacher, then he developed an interest in community affairs and, after considering social administration, wound up studying political economy. After a period in county labor market work he considered moving to the Ministry of Social Welfare, the parent organization at that time, but went to Finance instead when they asked him to assume a better position. Here is how this official describes the rest of his career:

> I had a short break for about a year and a quarter when, because of unusually heavy responsibilities, Social Welfare asked me to go over to work on their budget and I did so. Finance then asked me to come back and I have been here most of the time. In short, if we consider my overall background, I have been in both Finance and Social Welfare over the years, I have worked in a Parliamentary Committee, first as a "notarie," as it was called, then as what they now call a division secretary.

In this case, as in many others, one can appreciate the "accidental" character of a current position, but it is also clear that this official was clearly engaged in a public "career."

Perhaps the central theme running through these discussions of public service choices is ambition. As talented people with enough intellectual ability to make it through the university, these individuals typically confronted a variety of opportunities when they finished their education. Some chose private sector positions before entering public service; many others entered public service directly, some because it seemed the best opportunity at the time, others because it provided more fulfillment than was available elsewhere. Few of these people admit to idealistic motivations—many, in fact, go out of their way to deny such motivations. Despite a self-conscious "practicality," however, it seems clear that many chose to study in areas that provided good background training for government service, particularly law. Thus, while government service may not have been seen as a place to "do good," it clearly was perceived as a place to "do well"—to earn a good salary and gain status. In short, public service in Sweden was, and remains, an attractive alternative for young men and women who want to get ahead. A large majority of these individuals saw it that way, and their careers have obviously proved them right.

SATISFACTIONS OF BUREAUCRACY

However "accidental" original entry into the public service may have been, it is clear that, once in a government job, these officials found it enjoyable. Why? In Table 3.5 we tabulate responses to a question each respondent was asked: "What do you find most satisfying about your present position? What would you miss most if you were forced to leave it today?" Again, we show first, second and third responses to reveal some of the complexity of these responses, but this time we have grouped the responses to suggest what we believe to be the dominant sources of satisfaction they reveal: Achievement, Power and Intellectual Stimulation.[4] As before, it should be noted that these categories are blurry at the edges and there is some unavoidable ambiguity in placing a particular response in one or another category. Nevertheless, achievement, power and

Table 3.5. Most Satisfying Aspects of Present Position

	1st	2nd	3rd	Total	
Enjoy my Field	48	42	31	111	*Achievement*
Bldg. Programs, Innovation	19	32	24	75	186 (38%)
Being at Center	48	9	20	77	*Power*
Freedom, Independence	40	11	8	59	173 (35%)
Power to Infl. Decisions	10	19	8	37	
Variety of Experience	39	19	11	69	*Stimulation*
Stimulation	30	24	11	65	134 (27%)

stimulation seem to be the most prominent satisfactions and, we believe, they are listed in roughly accurate order of importance. Let us now examine what they mean.

Many who express achievement values point to the development of new or innovative programs as a main source of satisfaction. One official, who had been lured away from a private-sector bank directorship in order to reorganize a state-controlled bank, had this to say when asked about satisfactions in his position (#117):

> To create a bank. To try to refine and apply ideas from my earlier bank experience as head of this operation. I think that gives a feeling of satisfaction in my work.

Although only a few among these officials had entered public employment in mid-career, the fact that this individual found a public position attractive after a successful private sector career again suggests the competitive strength of government service in Sweden. A more typical "innovator," who had followed legal training and a court career with service in three different ministries and a variety of official commissions, expressed himself as "totally convinced" of the benefits of his public service in general and of his current position in a new consumer affairs agency (#151). Why?

> A great advantage with this work, as I see it, is that it is a new activity, so that you really have a chance to build something different. Nothing is routine, but your work is always new and constantly filled with new aspects of problems. May I also say that I think it is very stimulating that way.

Or, as a Director General said, voicing a recurring theme among innovators, ". . . what is satisfying, from my point of view, is primarily to have an opportunity to influence the development of something new, even if it goes very, very slowly" (#147).

Most achievers, however, give greater emphasis to the enjoyment they feel in doing what they regard as important work. Indeed, our use of "enjoy" is probably misleading to some extent, since these individuals usually say their satisfaction comes from involvement in "urgent" work (welfare) (#143), "the most important supply problem we face" (energy) (#323), or, less dramatically, "something that quite simply has to be done" (foreign aid) (#137). But achievers obviously experience enjoyment, no matter how defined—as is clear in the following response from a senior administrator of education programs:

> A very difficult question—it is almost impossible to answer. It is clear, to begin with a small thread, that when I am out in the schools—which I am quite often—it is a real joy to come into a school and sit in a classroom and watch students work. The opportunity I have to make their education more

effective and better, not just more effective but better as well, is a pleasure that is perhaps my greatest stimulation. You go into a school and students are doing something, even handicapped kids are doing something, linked in groups or sitting by themselves and working, and so on, and that, for me, is the single greatest stimulation. From that I can go to another value, namely that in the position I hold I have very large opportunities, through various means, to influence the educational situation, the educational milieu, for a large number of young people. I believe that this is the most essential thing.

This official obviously believes education to be very important, but it is hard to avoid the conclusion that he derives real pleasure from doing "important" work. For many of these senior civil servants, then, "doing something" is a kick.

Doing something, of course, implies having the power to do something; thus it is to be expected that power is prized by senior officials. The nuances of "power" in the Swedish context, however, are revealing. Conceived as "influence" or "ability to make decisions" in some unspecified subject matter area, power is not mentioned very often—indeed, it is worth emphasizing that discussions of power are typically framed, as the above example suggests, in terms of some specific public responsibility over which the official has influence. Although a generalized "influence" over decisions is conceivable to these officials, their discussions make clear that such power is neither very salient nor very important to them, for reasons that will become more clear as we examine other power-related satisfactions.

What many officials find most satisfying is being at the center of things, being part of a group of active men who are making things happen. In part, this kind of pleasure derives from being on the inside and thus knowing what is going on: the "inside dopester" syndrome.[5] One high-level cabinet official, for example, had indicated great satisfaction with the "overview and insight" he derived from his strategic position. Was it that insight, we then asked, that he would miss most if he left his position?

Well . . . they tell a story about politicians that I think applies to administrators as well, and that is that they talk a lot about power, especially recently. That is not what you miss if you are away for a while, but on the other hand it is psychologically difficult to be away. It's always fun to know what is going on and in this job you know a lot about what is going on. That is fun (#100).

A ministry official put the same idea in a slightly different way: "I would probably miss the contacts with others more than anything else. Contacts are really important in society, especially contacts with people who have both influence and perspective" (#159).

Quite apart from the pleasures of "inside dopersterism," it is evident that being at the center provides opportunities to see the system whole that many officials find deeply appealing. One official in the National Accounting Office (RRV), who had previously been in the Ministry of Finance, provides an expression of this view that is worth quoting at some length, since he has a dual perspective:

> When you have worked at the Ministry level in public administration and particularly in the Ministry of Finance—there is probably no other position in public administration that offers such a total overview—you understand that a Ministry always deals in oversight. Sometimes there is perhaps too much oversight and not enough deep penetration into problems, but particularly in the budget work of the Finance Ministry, you always have contact with other ministries. Either you work as contact man or . . . as we called it, head man, and you always had colleagues who had contacts with other ministries . . . I worked primarily with those parts that had to do with the Finance Ministries' own authorities, including the National Accounting Office, the Central Administrative Bureau, customs, and so on . . . These contacts gave me a really broad overview. It was an incredibly interesting and stimulating job. If you should leave that kind of job and go to something more limited, you would have difficulty . . . I think the National Accounting Office is one of the administrative units that, apart from the Ministries, has the broadest overview of Swedish administration . . . It reminds me very much of my previous work in Finance (#316).

Despite this official's belief that this larger social perspective is available only in ministries and a few other "special" agencies, our data show that a great many officials in more strictly "administrative" units have very similar views. If ministerial officials enjoy the broad perspective that comes from budget review and fiscal planning, line administrators develop an equal appreciation of the system in their efforts to carry out their own program responsibilities. One Labor Market Board official describes—and partly complains about—the various duties assigned to his office, from employment information and education to foreign workers, and emphasizes the many "contacts" generated. A National School Board official makes clear that his work requires contacts with lower-level units as well as across units at the national level:

> This is one of the key positions in the agency. We are responsible for a practical organization plan for the schools, one that works. We also translate what our academic colleagues do into practical educational plans. That is another component. We have what our colleagues produce on the construction side, what administrators give us in the form of regulations and teaching positions—we take all that here and pull it together into a synthetic product, a practical school organization. A great deal comes to focus here, in other words. That means that we are naturally a target of complaints directly, partly with the heads of our regional offices, with local school boards, with county

boards of education, and with school leaders. Then we have our major organizations. We have intensive contacts, of course, with labor and employer organizations, including nearly forty work advisory councils. These councils often make weighty and quite radical proposals on the shape and structure of education. These contacts create a stream of demands, but they are certainly stimulating (#324).

Being at the center, then, is satisfying not only because it offers an insider's view of important events, but more importantly because it enables officials to appreciate the totality of a system in which their activities are only a small fraction of all that is going on. That kind of appreciation comes easily with ministerial employment, heavily oriented to budgeting and planning, but it also emerges from the more common administrative task of designing and implementing programs in a complex governmental system. Whatever its specific source, the widespread appreciation of the many components of the Swedish administrative "system" among senior civil servants is an important fact, to which we shall return below.

At first glance, it may seem paradoxical that "freedom and independence" is nearly as widespread a "power" value as is being at the center. The independence of administrative officials is of course an old Swedish tradition, reflected today in lifetime tenure and legal, rather than administrative, responsibility for performance—that is, senior civil servants are accountable to courts of law rather than to superiors for performance of their duties and can be removed from office only by a court judgment against them. That senior officials enjoy this traditional and legal status is evident from the frequency with which they mention it, often enough in conjunction with their enjoyment of many contacts. Thus a previously quoted ministry official, who had emphasized the significance of contacts with important people, concluded by suggesting that "This (contacts) combined with a great deal of freedom to act on my own is what I would miss most" (#159). Knowing more about what other actors and organizations in the system do, in other words, appears to go hand in hand with appreciation of one's own independence.

Sometimes this system-derived appreciation of independence is expressed in relatively self-centered fashion, as in the case of a Bureau Chief who pointed out that he was the only person in the national administration dealing with a particular problem and thus had ". . . a large scope for my own initiative and freedom to make decisions" (#231). Or, it can take the form of appreciation for the freedom to organize one's work, as expressed by a ministry official:

Independence is perhaps the most notable aspect of my work, particularly if I compare it to the job I used to have in the legal department, where we spent a lot of time writing parliamentary motions, laws, official announcements, and so on. That became quite monotonous. Here there is an incredible excitement in the work, a real rush to do it. But at the same time there aren't so many of these projects that somebody brings in to be done in fourteen days or something. Here I can make my own priorities for my work and set my own pace for getting it done (#74).

More often, however, independence is appreciated in a more political and organizational way—as independent "influence" (#145), independent "decision-making" (#155) or, as one veteran of thirty-five years' service put it, "the relatively great freedom I have had, despite all the rules" (#318).[6] One bureau chief summarized several common themes in explaining his enjoyment:

> It is first of all the colossally interesting work I do that I find attractive . . . where I myself, as it were, can determine a great deal concerning direction and design of the whole thing. That is due to the fact that my situation here is quite unique: there is no one else who has a similar position and a similar education and similar responsibilities and that means, in effect, that I can be quite self-steering . . . My work is very free, and I enjoy it (#308).

Another bureau chief, also fascinated by the work he was doing, added a more colloquial embellishment to the theme of "independence":

> I have had the good fortune to work by myself on my own little thing since coming to the National Board of Education. I have had my own rather large piece of our common cake, in other words a few million crowns, that I have been able to control. I have, in short, never had to experience any lack of influence, if you understand what I mean. Something that, in principle, I think would be extremely stimulating would be to structure a society so that as many as possible had the opportunity to have a little bit of whatever we hold in common—after all it is your money and my money that I sit here and administer, isn't that right? (#311).

Freedom to organize one's own work and the ability to exert independent influence, or control, over some limited but specific portion of a complex environment thus stand out as major social dimensions of "independence." Yet a close reading of these interviews also reveals repeated references—sometimes hidden in other verbiage—to the closely related themes of *personal* integrity and *personal* fulfillment. Consider, for example, the frequent references—some of which have been noted here—to being alone, or being the only person engaged in some activity. The enjoyment of "aloneness," sometimes vividly expressed as "being in my own little corner of the world, in a room, without much outside contact . . . most part sitting in a corner, working pretty much as I please" (#315), contributes to what some officials regard as their "personal integrity" (#256). Others see their independence as a source of opportunities for "self-realization" (#100). The development of self through and by the development of work is

nicely expressed by an official who emphasizes the "very large degree of freedom" he has to do things in his job and who, when asked what is most satisfying,
says:

> Partly that I can influence the shape of this job so very much, and partly that
> I can experience a development of myself as I develop my position. The
> position, you see, is not totally locked in but rather is a job I can shape. I can
> also – theoretically, at least – influence not only my own job but other jobs
> as well, agency objectives and agency policy. I have, if you will, a certain
> possibility to exercise what is normally called power (#238).

Independence, then, has both organizational and personal consequences for many
of these officials, whose attachment to position is clearly perceived as an enrich-
ing personal experience. Freedom from outside controls, influence over decisions
and pleasurable personal growth combine to provide dimensions of satisfaction
for these "independent" public servants.[7]

A third major source of satisfaction, labelled "stimulation," is somewhat less
distinct than achievement or power, largely because it is so often mentioned in
conjunction with either or both of the more prominent values. Both achievement
and power-oriented officials often indicate their "fascination" with the content
of the problems they deal with, or the "stimulation" they derive from dealing
with them. In part, these feelings are a direct outgrowth of university training in
a discipline that forms the core of a current public responsibility, in part they
derive from the intellectual excitement of attempting new things. Most often,
however, they appear to arise from the simple fact of variety – the constant
change in matters to be dealt with. One education official put it well:

> What is most satisfying to me is in fact the variety of my work. You get a
> lot of different problems to deal with. Naturally they are related to some
> extent and some matters such as budget have to be handled, but these things
> are interrupted for various reasons. There may be a trip abroad, there may be
> a committee meeting, or you might be asked to dig into some question quickly
> and give a suggestion to some cabinet official or under-secretary. The prob-
> lems change even if they always start out from a certain common base (#163).

These kinds of comments, made repeatedly, are reminiscent of other comments
suggesting a variety of interests earlier in life and the difficulty many of these
officials had in choosing careers. Whether they suggest impatience and routine,
boredom, or simply an unwillingness to be committed to a single task for a long
period of time is not always clear; what is clear is that these men genuinely
enjoy variety in work and genuinely enjoy the challenge of constantly-shifting
responsibilities.

The other side to this coin, of course, is that constantly-shifting responsibilities often prevent these officials from devoting enough time to any single job.

Indeed, virtually the only complaint that emerges with any force from responses to the question, "What do you find least satisfying about your work?" is that there is not enough time to do everything that is expected. The results, according to these officials, include a high level of stress, occasional frustration, and considerable difficulty in maintaining healthy family relationships. These kinds of responses should not be assigned exaggerated significance: most respondents had little or nothing to say in response to this inquiry. Nevertheless, at the top of Swedish public administration there is enough pressure to perform many tasks quickly and well to cause some officials, at least, to express mild unhappiness.

EXPLAINING SATISFACTION

Given the extraordinarily high levels of satisfaction that exist in all segments of the Swedish administrative elite, it is more than usually difficult to identify relationships that might help us to better understand the attractions of public service. Nevertheless, we have observed some difference in the degree of change desired or the sources of satisfaction among senior officials and it may be profitable to consider those differences in a more systematic way. We have already suggested that agency position may have an important impact on perception, and it is plausible to anticipate that age can have an impact as well. Finally, now that we have some idea of the sources of satisfaction among these officials, we may find something in their general orientation to public service that may be enlightening.

Despite the attractiveness of the hypothesis that age has a major impact on satisfaction, we have few data to support it. In part this is due to the absence of very young people among our sample of senior officials: only 33 of 315 respondents were forty years of age or younger when they were interviewed. Younger officials tend to be slightly more attracted to power values than to achievement values than their older colleagues (Table 3.6), and commitment to achievement

Table 3.6. Percent Who Value "Power" and "Achievement"
           By Age Category

	Power	Achievement	Other
29–45 Years	36.6	37.8	25.6
46–55 Years	32.8	40.8	26.4
Over 55	28.7	44.7	26.6
		N = 301	

appears to grow with age. But these differences are not striking and they are less consistent when age categories are grouped differently. Thus, while it may be true that younger people are more power conscious (in the Swedish sense) than their older counterparts, these data provide no convincing support for that assertion. Nor do we find significant age-related differences in education, outside employment, entry motivation, system support or overall satisfaction. Age, in short, appears to have very little to do with degrees of official satisfaction.

Agency or agency position is more promising, largely because we suspect that agency affects political views and might therefore be expected to affect other views. In Table 3.7 we summarize entry motivations for Director General and other employees of ministries, boards, and public authorities. Although reported motivations vary considerably, we divide them here into two groups in order to emphasize the difference between "drifting" into public service for a variety of accidental or circumstantial reasons, and entering public administration for more positive, less accidental, reasons. Although a substantial majority in each group emphasizes the "chancy" nature of the drift toward responsibility, the majority is somewhat larger among officials in the public authorities. Officials in these largely technological agencies were less likely to mention happenstance and more likely to mention a lack of other opportunities than members of other groups: for them, public service was more likely to be "the only" alternative rather than "a good" alternative. This difference is not very large, but it is a potentially revealing tendency.

Officials in public authorities are also slightly more negative about public service in general: they are more likely to think that government work is not especially attractive, more likely to give a low rating to the civil service, and more likely to want either major or important changes made (Table 3.8). These conclusions emerge from Table 3.8, but we should point out that "negativism" reported there was derived by combining the lowest three positions on a five-point scale (i.e., the neutral position combined with two negative positions). This procedure clearly exaggerates the level of dissatisfaction present among these officials, but the point is not to summarize dissatisfaction so much as it is

Table 3.7. Entry Motivation, By Position (%)

	Circumstantial	Intentional
General Directors (N = 60)	60.0	39.9
Ministry Officials (N = 43)	60.6	39.7
Board Officials (N = 142)	64.6	35.0
Public Authorities (N = 41)	68.3	31.7

Table 3.8. Dissatisfaction, By Group (%)

	Find CS Unattractive	Rate CS As Poor	Want Major or Important Changes
Directors	16.4	31.1	38.2
Ministries	6.8	22.7	17.8
Boards	7.5	20.6	20.9
Public Authorities	19.5	39.4	36.8

to reveal dissatisfaction relationships. Insofar as dissatisfaction exists, Table 3.8 suggests it is more likely to be found among officials in Public Authorities and, interestingly enough, among Directors General. What can this pattern of disparate dissatisfaction mean?

Since second-level administrators in technological agencies (recall that Directors General have been separated from this classification) obviously do rather different things from Directors General, it is probably wise to assume that sources of dissatisfaction are different for these two groups. One source of unhappiness, specific to the conditions prevailing at the time of our interviews, appears to have affected public authority officials more than others in our sample: the lock-out and strike of academically-trained officials that occurred in the Spring of 1971, during the period in which we were talking to respondents.[8] Employees in one of the authorities, SJ (the State Railways), were in the forefront of these activities, and other authorities were quickly drawn in. Shortly after the conclusion of the strike we asked a state railway official if he had ever thought of leaving:

> Yes, during the past few weeks, after the lock-out when all desire to work has totally disappeared. If I had a son I would tell him never to go to SJ.
> Is that because it is a government job, or . . . ?
> Yes . . . it is so damned uncomfortable in every way.
> Is there anything you think to be beneficial?
> Well, I guess I think . . . if you have been with an agency for thirty years and they are locked-out – and by the way, I am not alone in this feeling; there is the same unhappiness in the whole agency – then what you have lost can't be replaced by money . . . it will take a generation before SJ recovers . . . (#133).

Another technician, a supervisory engineer at the Power Authority, had no difficulty in finding sources of unhappiness:

> Today it isn't so pleasant to be with the power authority any longer, especially if you are a universally-trained, high-level civil servant. During the spring strike we heard the governing party call us parasites and saboteurs. At

the same time, when you work in this area, you hear the bourgeois side call you "nature destroyers" and technocrats. They spit at us from all sides and when you have been spit upon enough you begin to prefer stones. We think we are doing as good a job as we can and we certainly believe we are improving our fellow-citizens' welfare in one way or another. But we get criticism from every side and every corner and sooner or later you get tired of it (#132).

The obvious intensity of these feelings surely has roots in the fact that authority employees appeared to be clear and open targets of government action. Nevertheless, there may be more fundamental, less situational roots to such feelings, arising from the nature of work in highly technical, scientific or engineering enterprises.

In order to consider this possibility more systematically we constructed a series of summary indices to measure acceptance of the socio-political system, satisfaction with the civil service and the amount of change desired in society.[9] We also combined these indices into a summary satisfaction score that would permit us to compare levels of satisfaction among different groups and relate satisfaction to other responses. These measures strongly suggest that dissatisfaction among public authority officials is primarily related to their unhappiness with specific events, coupled with a certain lack of perspective on those events which seems structural rather than attitudinal. Authority officials, for example, demonstrate a higher level of acceptance of the status quo than either Board or Ministry employees: the relationship between authority employment and our summary acceptance measure is .40 (gamma). We also know that those who were defined as "technicians" by our coders are likely to exhibit a high level of acceptance of the political-economic order (gamma = .22). Technicians, however, perceive the civil service far *less* favorably than others (gamma = -.31 for relationship between technician role and summary civil service evaluation). Since the bulk of these authority employees see themselves as technicians, it seems clear that these officials are less happy in their work than other groups of officials. But it is the civil service, not the system as a whole, that is the focus of dissatisfaction.

Part of the reason, the lock-out and strike of 1971, has already been noted. Other reasons mentioned in our interviews include red tape, lack of resources or general frustration over inability to implement the "right" technical solutions. Although difficult to demonstrate, we are inclined to believe that most of these "other" reasons also arose out of the lock-out frustration, which provided an occasion for releasing latent attitudes of hostility. At the same time, it is important to note that, structurally, these officials tend to work in ways that give them very little contact with other actors in the bureaucratic-political system. Compared to ministry and board officials, they have far fewer contacts with either parliament (gamma = .68) or political parties (gamma = .51) and thus have far less of the "system" perspective that we have seen to be so important and so pleasurable for many other senior officials.[10] To the extent that system awareness provides a broader frame for reference for interpreting events and thus reduces the significance of single events, such as a lock-out, these officials lack an easily-available mechanism for rationalizing events except in a highly intense and personalistic way. Their unhappiness, then, seems to us to be quite specific, directed at individuals and focused on events. They probably want to change individuals or organizations; they do *not* want to change either the system or their status in it.[11]

The dissatisfaction, such as it is, of Directors General is quite different. To appreciate how different it is we begin with a negative finding: using our combined measure of system acceptance, civil service evaluation and desire for change as a general satisfaction indicator, we find no relationship between agency type or position and general satisfaction (gamma = -.01). Among other things, this is a useful reminder of the artificiality of the scoring mechanism used earlier; although some Directors General may be unhappy, their unhappiness, or others' unhappiness, has little to do with either agency or position. What seems important is not so much position as system awareness, absent from many authority officials, but quite characteristic of Directors General as a group, as well as many other officials in boards and ministries. In contrast to weak agency-position relationships, system awareness relationships seem quite strong: the higher the level of system awareness, the less there is acceptance of the status quo (gamma = .60); the higher the level of system awareness, the more changes are desired (gamma = .34); the higher the level of system awareness, the more dissatisfaction and desire for change is picked up by our summary measure (gamma = .62). Very similar relationships exist for officials who demonstrate a policy-making, rather than technician role: the more oriented to policy-making an official is, the less he is likely to accept the status quo (gamma = .58) and the more he is likely to desire change (gamma = .45).

All this suggests that the dissatisfaction sometimes found among Directors General and other officials is really not so much conditioned by where they sit as by what they do. Those involved in gratifying contacts with people from other parts of the system, and who think of themselves as policy-makers, are occasionally likely to feel a frustration born of both knowledge of the system and the obstacles to achievement built into it. Like their less aware agency colleagues, however, such officials seldom attack the system at its roots. On the contrary they support it, seek to remove its defects, and sometimes feel the kind of frustration expressed by a finance official who, in comparing Swedish and American administrative practices, remarked:

It seems much slower here, there are too many decision points and such. I'd like to see more "go" in the organization—this is clearly the problem you react against most often. You have a real selling job to do every time you want to get something done. You know yourself that you are right . . . a solution to some problem is well-conceived and available, but you have to convince what seems like thousands of offices—people in all possible positions, back and forth, up and down, that your solution is the right way to go. In itself this can be interesting, and even stimulating, but it is a very heavy job (#319).

CONCLUSION

That senior civil servants in Sweden like what they do should now be clearly beyond question—indeed, we have had to strain our analysis to discover dissatisfaction sufficiently strong to be worth investigating. We can also be more definitive about why they are in public service. These are *not* people who entered public employment in order to foment revolution or guide major social change; neither are they people driven by family or class ethic to pursue "traditional" careers. Rather, these are typical middle-class individuals who are bright enough to finish college, who have varied interests and experiences, who find it difficult to decide what to do after college, who more or less "drift" into the civil service and who, over time, float to the top. In large measure, the "drift" into public service is due to the continuing attractiveness of public service employment. Many drift in from a variety of private sector positions but once in, find conditions of work and opportunities for satisfaction to be superior to private sector alternatives. Most who drift in stay for a very long time.

The enduring satisfaction of public service closely resembles the "work orientation" described some years ago by Anton:[12] these officials enjoy achievement and the ability to influence decisions more than anything else, but they are also powerfully attracted to the independence available to them as national civil servants. This sense of independence, derived from legal status, seems closely related to official awareness of the existence of other equally independent entities in a highly complex organizational system. Moreover, "independence" has individual as well as social consequences: "integrity" or "self-realization" are spoken of with some regularity by these officials in describing their satisfactions.[13] These qualities, derived from system characteristics, seem more important in understanding general satisfaction (or dissatisfaction) than characteristics of agency sub-units within the system. At this level, for this issue, there does indeed seem to be a set of understandings shared widely by senior officials, regardless of agency type or position held. We can now begin to speak more seriously about "an elite culture."

4 THE "ORDINARY" CIVIL SERVANT: SOFT ACTIVIST

Rapid social change strains ideas no less than established social relationships. Whether reacting to or anticipating fundamental social changes, such as the shift from agricultural to industrial work, Swedish public servants have organized new programs and expanded public employment to a point at which more than 50 percent of gross national product is now consumed by the public sector. These changes, coming within a relatively brief historical period (i.e., roughly fifty years), have severely challenged prevailing ideas about the proper relationship of government to society as a whole and have undermined civil servant role orientations that had become as comfortable as they were widespread. According to this comfortable view, the appropriate function of government was to enforce rules of fairness and equity in social relationships. The most important requirement for a civil servant, therefore, was training in the law. Knowledge of administrative law together with personal qualities of objectivity and impartiality defined the "classic" Swedish view of administrators as judges, whose chief responsibility was to select and apply legal rules to problems presented to them.[1]

Vastly expanded public programs, self-consciously designed to "reform" society, clearly have challenged the viability of the "judge" model of administrative role. The design of new programs can hardly be assisted very much by knowledge of old law, nor is it likely that meaningful reform can be brought about unless proponents are very partial indeed to the cause of reform. Yet, precisely because these public sector changes have occurred so rapidly, the older, more "comfortable" role definition has maintained some of its earlier popularity, even in agencies far removed from legal responsibilities. Thus, an official in the Ministry of Agriculture (#67), one of the few who admitted that he had always intended to pursue a public service career, indicates that his work affects all Swedes and that, as a consequence, "It is naturally very important that you observe a strict objectivity in your work." A supervisory engineer in the State Railways suggests the importance of loyalty in carrying out his duties and adds, "A revolutionary type, who thinks everything in society is wrong, simply won't do as a leader" (#121). A Bureau Chief, trained in statistics, offered a nice summary of this view when asked if there was something common to the responsibilities of all senior civil servants, regardless of where they worked (#332):

> Loyalty and objectivity are the qualities I think are required. They are certainly pervasive enough. In this office we have relationships with a number of different labor groups, representing different parts of the industrial system, and we deal with them in different contexts. It is easy to see how those who represent a special group in society come driving in here with their own special requests, how often they are unreasonably directed to narrow material interests. It is their obligation to act that way, but I always feel incredibly alienated from that whole posture—to only demand, without regard to obvious realities, more resources only for the interest of their own group. That, of course, is what they are supposed to do, but it is obviously not my style in any way. For those of us in national administration, the problem is to achieve some balance and to produce something as close to the truth as possible. The truth is naturally a complex idea, and we can obviously discuss what it can mean. But our fundamental mission in all events is to achieve it, almost like a judge.

Perhaps unnecessarily, this official added at a later point that "I am among those who continue to believe strongly in the value of the old Swedish administrative traditions, that of course are being picked away a good deal."

That such traditional views continue to exist—and in some strength[2] —cannot and should not be attributed solely to the appeal of some past era. Fairness, objectivity and loyalty, after all, can hardly be regarded as undesirable qualities, particularly in a nation whose citizens have long demonstrated an altogether uncommon respect for the law, both as universal standard and as protection against arbitrary power. Nevertheless, the tension between such views and the requirements of expansionist public policies is evident and, in recent years, openly expressed. As one cabinet official remarked (#54);

> I myself am a lawyer and I certainly think that legal education is good, but on the other hand I have to say that I am quite wary of many of my lawyer

colleagues. I believe that lawyers have been both a help and a hindrance to social development here. Jurisprudence has a certain quality of conservatism in its worst forms and in my view lawyers have been far too influential—in Parliament, in Royal Commissions, in the Cabinet—in persuading politicians that this or that program simply would not work. These people typically base such judgments on the legal system as it is today. On the whole they are unable to imagine any change in it—for that reason I think lawyers often give poor advice. On occasion I have fought against this conservation myself, because I don't like it. We have a more modern view of our responsibilities here, and I think we are much more healthy here than other agencies that have a more static view of the legal system . . . Legislation is nothing more than a means for achieving desired social purposes . . . In my view a good lawyer is one who understands that he is nothing more than a technician, who knows how to structure law to achieve social ends . . . I don't want to do away with legal notions such as applying the law equally to all similar cases. That is an extremely important basis for a just society. But when, as is often the case, the law is experienced as a hindrance to any change in the system, then it is very unfortunate.

This kind of critique is made more openly by politicians than civil servants but, as the above example suggests, civil servants are themselves sensitive to the disparity between their interest in reform and a set of images that tend to deny them a legitimate role in processes of change. A search for alternative role formulations, accordingly, has been under way for some time. Although the search is far from over, it is possible to identify the dimensions of several responses to the problem of justifying bureaucratic status in a rapidly expanding democratic system.

At one extreme, it is possible to imagine a response that represents withdrawal from the processes of social reform yet retains some connection to the Swedish administration "tradition." Among these respondents, there are a few who self-consciously emphasize *expertise* as their basic role qualification and role orientation. Their activities are predicated on the special knowledge they possess and to them it makes little or no difference whether they work for public or private agencies. There are the expert technicians, the "hired guns" who have no conscious interest in the direction—or existence—of political change. Content to follow whatever political wind that blows, these officials nevertheless fit comfortably within that portion of Swedish tradition that emphasizes the significance of technical expertise in the operation of governmental agencies.[3] At another extreme, we find a few respondents who are quite openly political, in a partisan sense. For them, all actions have political significance and are therefore to be judged in terms of who they benefit, rather than what they accomplish. Moreover, since only parties face the electorate on a regular basis, partisanship provides the only mechanism of accountability and responsibility in keeping with democratic norms. These officials, then, treat administrative responsibility as an extension of party membership, seeking to advance party goals through administrative action, often through reformist proposals. For them, as for elected politicians, power and social reform are the appropriate guidelines for officials' action.[4]

Judges, technicians and politicos do not by any means constitute major role orientations among senior civil servants: taken together, adherents of these role orientations constitute no more than 20-25 percent of those we interviewed.[5] We mention them primarily to underline the variety of responses that can be and are made to the problem of devising a workable justification for expanded bureaucratic power in a changing but democratic system. The dominant response among these respondents is clear enough, but as yet it has not been clearly identified and thus has no clear theoretical rationale. Unlike the more extreme responses, the dominant response builds upon the most characteristic quality of the Swedish tradition: administrator "independence." The building blocks, however, are rather different from what might have been expected in this advanced and highly technological society. For want of a better term, we think of this dominant role orientation as the "soft activist."

DEFINING THE SOFT ADMINISTRATOR

We can begin to understand the soft activist posture by recalling who these people are and the kind of work most of them do. By choosing respondents very close to the top of the Swedish administrative hierarchy – Directors General and other officials just below cabinet rank – we guaranteed selection of a group that would share several common characteristics: all would have major administrative or planning responsibilities; all, by virtue of those responsibilities, would have a variety of other public duties to perform; all would therefore be deeply involved in their work, quite busy at a variety of different activities and, as we have seen, occasionally frustrated over their inability to give enough time to many of their problems. To be sure, degrees of responsibility and involvement vary with agency and position but to a considerable extent, individual responsibility for a variety of different activities is as common to each of our respondents as the sense of independence they feel in carrying out those responsibilities. As one bureau chief put it, "I experience my position as a sort of 'man-in-the-middle,' where I have concrete responsibility for a rather large operation, but where I nonetheless have a stimulating freedom to do the job as I see fit" (#324).

What sort of qualities might contribute to successful performance in such positions? To find out, we asked each respondent "How would you generally describe the responsibilities of a higher civil servant?" We then asked a follow-up question: "What personal qualities do you think it necessary for a skillful chief administrator to have?" Responses to these questions were often long and revealing, and we developed an elaborate coding scheme in an effort to capture some of the complexity of these revelations. Each interview was coded twice and, for each coding sequence, traits mentioned by respondents were coded first, a summary coder judgment about the significance of each major trait category was coded second, and an overall summary judgment was coded third. These procedures were time-consuming, but they permit us to be reasonably clear about the yet-to-be-articulated theory that guides most higher civil servants in Sweden.

It is quite clear, for example, that senior officials reject the notion that some particular social background is necessary to perform well at the top. One might of course expect rather few officials in a democratic state to assert a contrary view, or one might anticipate a certain reluctance to deal with the question at all, as a result of democratic norms. For these officials, however, the question is not strange—social class remains a much-discussed topic in Sweden—and is typically dealt with directly, as in the case of a cabinet official (#100):

> Socially . . . I represent an extreme, in that I come from a very poor worker's home, but there are naturally those who come from upper-class environments who function quite well . . . What else is there to say?

Another official, who says he "represents the type of senior civil servant who has more of an expert position than many others," responds in the following way to our question about educational requirements (#95).

> I don't think that, overall, one can say that there is some basic education such as an academic exam or something similar that is required. I don't believe that. Obviously for me, in this particular work, it would be convenient not to be a lawyer.
> But are you saying that, in principle, any education at all will do?
> Yes, I think so.

A third official, this one a bureau chief in the Labor Market Board, offered a useful summary view (#330):

> If you mean formal schooling, a special academic degree or something like that, then I don't believe that is decisive. I myself am trained in a discipline (education) that has little to do with my present work and I have many colleagues here in the agency about whom the same thing can be said. That conceivably can mean that we are not as good as we might be, that for example we do not have sufficient social science schooling, which I occasionally lacked, a basic economics-statistics education which would have been useful for me. But as I said I don't think that one can say that a special education can create

the ideal leader, or chief, for a bureau. I would like to say that I believe that a great deal of what I learned when I was a student I learned outside of my studies. I participated quite a bit in different organizations. I have done that since I was a student as well, in voluntary and professional organizations. That is good schooling. You learn to pay attention, you learn to speak, which is quite important for us. To a considerable extent our work involves providing information and perhaps also being a propagandist . . .

It is easy enough for a group composed almost entirely of persons with academic degrees to deny the significance of such training. Since so few among their daily colleagues lack education, it becomes virtually impossible to use education to explain variation in administrative performance. The same interpretation can be made regarding the perceived significance of class background: with so few working-class colleagues to observe, it becomes impossible to attribute performance variation to class. All this is simply to say that members of this elite, who are aware of structural interpretations of their activities, nevertheless understand and evaluate themselves in terms of individual rather than structural qualities.[6] Thus, while most respondents deny the significance of any particular kind of education, they nevertheless believe strongly that, to be a good administrator, one must have a very high order of intelligence as well as knowledge of the activities for which he is responsible. These two qualities, high intelligence and knowledge of the job, are mentioned repeatedly by these respondents and taken together, represent one of the most powerful themes to appear in these discussions.

Often enough the two qualities are in fact taken together, as in the following comment by a supervisory engineer:

> I think that the higher up you go, the more important it is to have some general perspective on your problems. The chief has to know so much that no subordinate can mislead him, that much knowledge is essential. But he also has to have enough judgment to be able to evaluate the proposals that come to him. You have to remember that in this division, for example, we have a number of technicians — about 390 technicians, civil engineers and down to lower grades. Many are totally wrapped up in their work, which they feel is absolutely essential to give life meaning. They know a great deal and they know how to put their ideas across. Since they work in such a limited sector it is clear that their preferences cannot be very thorough. In that kind of situation it is the chief who has to try to evaluate their ideas from a larger point of view, and naturally do so in a way that will not crush those who have enough initiative to offer proposals (#193).

It follows from this kind of emphasis on general intelligence and work competence that experience is more highly appreciated than education: nearly 60 percent of these officials do in fact mention the importance of some kind of experience, both within and outside of the public sector. As one official (#324) put it, in emphasizing the utility of private sector experience, "There is a world outside of Verona." It follows, too, that expertise—the kind of detailed, sometimes scientific, knowledge of a limited subject area that many have assumed to distinguish Sweden from other advanced bureaucratic systems—is not highly valued, at least at the top. Indeed, there is a distinct undercurrent of hostility to experts in many of these conversations. "I sometimes think," one official said, "that theoretical expertise goes hand-in-hand with a shortage of the common, personal knack of getting along with people that is surprising" (#326). Another said, "We used to say that 'he is poor at working with others, but that is because he is so smart.' That is of course total nonsense" (#22). Still a third official, this one a Director General (#147), described the qualities of a good chief administrator this way:

> I don't think a chief needs to be a clever specialist. He doesn't have to be a specialist at all. You can always hire experts, but what is most important for a chief administrator is first, to define responsibilities, then to have a sense of the problem area as a whole, so that you don't drown in details, and then— and this is colossally important—to try to coordinate the work in a way that gets the best out of each worker. There are plenty of smart people in different areas who want nothing more than to do their best, but they are often specialists in one area who tend to lose sight of the whole. I have profited greatly in my work from having been a union man and having met many people, not only at lunches or other pleasant meetings but also at tough bargaining sessions. I have learned to recognize the other side. Notice that I did not say the *opposite* side, but the *other* side, with whom you have to reach agreement. I have profited enormously from that view.

Among senior Swedish administrators, then, the most celebrated imagery revolves around generalized wisdom, rather than specialized knowledge: "First and last, a good administrator has to have general common sense. He can be as big an expert as there is in some area, but this general, so-called 'farmer's horsesense' [sunt bondförnuft], has to be among the qualities he has" (#211). These references to general intellectual capacity or common sense constitute more than three-quarters of all references to intellectual traits in the interviews. Expertise, i.e., specialized theoretical knowledge, was mentioned only fifty-two times and made up only one-quarter of the 208 references to such traits (first through fifth mentions). Appropriately enough, these images can be—and often are—attached to real individuals who serve as role models:

> It is clearly good to have an academic degree, but there are many, many people who have taught themselves and who have a sure sense of themselves. I mean, take Sträng [Gunnar Sträng, Finance Minister for twenty-one years].

He is the most fantastic chief there is and he has very poor formal education. He is fantastic in the sense that he grasps things immediately, decides what he wants to do quickly, gives clear instructions and then stands behind them, always listens with interest, and is always in good humor. He has to be easier to work for than anyone else. He is tougher to work for too, since he has an incredible memory for detail. He almost always knows more about the details than whoever it is he is talking to, which can be terribly embarrassing. He can also rake up all sorts of things. He has been around longer than anyone else and remembers everything he has heard during all those years, which makes it impossible to think about beating him (#100).

Even if we admit what is surely the case, i.e., that this picture of Gunnar Sträng is more than a little exaggerated, the qualities mentioned do in fact represent what most senior officials believe to be most essential to their work: great native intelligence, mastery of detail, ability to guide and control the work of others. That Sträng is believed to possess these qualities despite a lack of formal education—Sträng left school at twelve, was on his own at sixteen and is sometimes said to have done his university work at the Lövsta garbage dump, where he scrounged scrap magazines to read[7]—gives him a special stature, particularly among those whose education was far more extensive. For many, including the official just quoted, he is the quintessential role model.

The good "soft activist," of course needs more than a high level of native intelligence. In Table 4.1 we summarize the traits mentioned most often as being essential to the work of a higher civil servant. Coders were instructed to record up to six traits mentioned and we show five references here, dividing intellectual traits into "expertise" and "generalist" categories for purposes of argument. Table 4.1 suggests that, important as intellectual traits—particularly generalist traits—are thought to be, their importance is overshadowed by both organiza-

Table 4.1. Trait Characteristics of a Good Administrator

| | Mentions | | | | | TOTAL | |
	1st	2nd	3rd	4th	5th	N	%
Organizational	100	59	68	41	24	282	31
Sociability	19	84	57	51	13	224	24
Intellectual	39	53	43	48	25	208	23
Expertise	13	21	7	11	4	56	6
Generalist	26	32	36	37	21	152	16
						922	100

tional and sociability traits, some of which have been hinted at above. Again, it is important to warn against taking numbers of this kind too seriously, in this case less because of coding ambiguities than because of traits that are so widely "understood" to be important that they are not mentioned at all. We believe, in this case, that intellectual competence is in fact so widely assumed that many failed to mention it, thus understating the extent to which it is regarded as important. If so, the ordering suggested by the totals may be somewhat misleading although not, in our view, seriously so. Quite apart from the totals, however, there are other patterns of interest contained in these figures.

One such pattern that is surely important—and perhaps surprising to those who may view Sweden as a paradise for technologists, engineers and other science-oriented bureaucrats—is the perceived necessity for what we refer to as "sociability" traits, that is, getting along with people, listening to their problems, and other human-centered activities we will shortly explore in much greater detail. Organizational traits such as coordinating work or delegating authority are mentioned more often, perhaps because the question we asked was designed to encourage respondents to think in such "organizational" terms. The number of sociability or, as we shall call them, "soft," responses therefore seems all the more impressive. Moreover, by displaying the order of mention, we can begin to perceive *how* these officials think about such qualities. Asked to identify the qualities of a good senior administrator, Swedish civil servants seldom refer to sociability traits *first:* various forms of organizational competence come to mind first, followed distantly by intellectual qualities. But sociability traits emerge as a strong leader in second mentions and retain considerable strength through third, fourth, and even fifth references. Like intellectual qualities, soft traits appear to be seen as secondary but nonetheless fundamental to the main task, which is organizational. Unlike intellectual qualities, however, these "soft" characteristics are less often simply assumed and more often mentioned explicitly, with some conviction, as though it were important not only to possess such qualities, but to *know* that one possessed such qualities. This emphasis on the soft side of administration is both interesting and somewhat unexpected among Swedes. Accordingly, we begin a closer examination of these several traits by focusing on these soft qualities, before exploring the meaning of more strictly organizational talents.

"SOFT" ADMINISTRATION

Gunar Sträng, in describing the consequences of having left school at an early age, begins by pointing out that *"Man fick lära sig att umgås med folk*—you had to learn how to get along with people."[8] Exactly the same phrase—*"umgås med folk"*—occurs repeatedly in descriptions of the good administrator offered by officials who believe that "you always have personnel problems" (#320) and that a fair amount of psychological insight is necessary to deal with them"; "no matter how clever or capable you are, the whole apparatus can fall apart if you can't deal properly with personnel problems" (#370). For most of these men, dealing properly with people is something you learn through experience, as Sträng did, rather than through books, and it is impossible to fake:

> You have to be really interested in people; otherwise it won't work. You have to be interested in solving problems and not take the attitude that you want to get them out of the way in the easiest possible way—otherwise it won't work. Then of course it is very important that you retain a certain measure of calmness in difficult situations, for you will certainly get into conflict situations where there is no solution and then you have to have enough inner strength to reach at least some resolution. Whether or not the resolution is absolutely right is perhaps not the most important thing in such situations, but you have to have a certain capacity for intuition combined with—what shall we call it—judgment, in order to keep the situation under control. I have friends who have been quite excellent in ministerial positions who then go out to positions as Bureau Chief in an operating agency and are simply not used to the kinds of conflict that come up: people disagreeing, blending their private problems with their work, campaigns between Bureau Chiefs and all these things they are spared in ministries (#318).

However it may appear from the outside, from the inside these officials see the administrative environment as unsettled, characterized by a variety of interpersonal problems, and in constant need of sensitive intervention. The problems differ to some extent, as the above citation suggests. In ministries, with small staffs engaged primarily in planning, budgeting and bill preparation, the leadership problem is primarily to secure sufficient motivation under conditions of constantly changing work loads. One ministry administrator describes his solution in response to our query about the qualities of a good administrator:

> I think he ought to have a good way of dealing with people—he should always have that. He should be determined, but on the other hand he can't be too determined: you can't drive your people too hard. If you drive them hard in some situations you can compensate in other situations by being decent when it comes to vacations or time off at some point if you have asked for overtime work at another. I don't know how well I have succeeded, but my personal philosophy is that you get further with friendliness and fairness and being reasonable than you get through being a dictator. If I disagree with my colleagues on some question I don't say 'no, now we'll do it my way'— naturally there are times when you have to say that too—but we go through the problem together and try to reach an agreement. I would say that in 95

percent of the cases, maybe more, we succeed in reaching agreement on what we both believe to be right (#119).

Problems appear different in the much larger administrative boards that employ many more people and carry out the daily operations of government. Here, as we have seen, larger numbers of people, with more varied educational backgrounds, engaged in more varied talks, lead to more interpersonal and interagency conflict and presumably require more than simple motivational skills. Sensitivity to the emotional needs of subordinates and a persuasive rather than dictatorial decision-making style nevertheless remain at the center of desirable qualities mentioned by agency administrators. One, for example, suggests that a suitable background quality for leaders in such agencies is ". . . to have sat in a low position and learned what it feels like to be shut off from further advancement" (#322). Another (#320) points to the difficulty of moving unsuitable people from one position to another in public agencies. Unlike private sector administrators, ". . . you can't just say 'thanks and good-bye,' but you have a totally different duty to try to help the employee retain his/her position." Superiors and subordinates, in short, are often perceived to be in a different, more sensitive, relationship to government:

> I am convinced that what is essential is to keep the work done in the organization within acceptable bounds and that you adopt the position that your co-workers are not just some subordinates or errand boys that can simply be told to do some job. You have to work together on an equal footing all the time, and your co-workers must feel that they participate in decisions. I'm not talking about some romantic vision of industrial democracy—that simply couldn't be applied here. But there has to be a little bit of that even in this kind of operation. I think it is quite essential that your employees have a feeling of participation, and not that they are ordered around to do things (#74).

Regardless of the kind of agency, then, a large number of senior Swedish administrators typically believe it essential to be genuinely interested in their subordinates' problems, sensitive to their needs, and prepared to listen to them in agency decision-making rather than simply order them around. In dealing with colleagues at their own level of responsibility, too, these administrators repeatedly emphasize sensitivity, willingness to listen and compromise, or, as it is often put, "the capacity to cooperate." One source of this emphasis is identical to the administrative view of subordinate relationships, that is, that more can be accomplished through diplomacy than through rigid insistence on a pre-set position. But there is another, more dynamic, perception shared by many respondents, which asserts that significant changes in administrative practice since 1950 require a greater "capacity to cooperate."

At one level, this view proceeds from a simple recognition of increasing complexity caused by public sector growth through time: "During the past few years we have had much more intimate contacts with ministry-level units. For this unit we have our head ministry, Commerce, but then there is the Ministry of Industrial Affairs, the Interior Ministry where the Labor Market Board is located, with all of whom we have to cooperate. So far as I can tell, we have developed a more multi-faceted relationship, or cooperation, with central administration than we had, for example, in the middle of the 1950's. At that time you wrote and for the most part got a written answer. Now much of this takes place on the personal level, and there is more of it than before, too. That is my experience" (#320). Another official, this one in a technical authority, offered the same ideas: "Today there is a good deal that affects many different agencies . . . so we now routinely work in teams . . . If something special comes up, we get a few people together and go through the problem to divide up responsibilities . . . In principle larger and more significant questions are taken together, in a little collegium, which is a beneficial way to make decisions . . ." (#113).

At another, far deeper level, proponents of this view suggest that changes in administrative style are directly related to continuing changes in the character of the people who are public employees. "The old model," a State Railways administrator suggests, "which existed when I began at the company, the authoritarian leader who made all decisions, and gave orders to do this and that, is disappearing." Now, he continued, an administrator had to be able to "Umgås med folk" (#113). A research director offered an explanation for the same phenomenon:

> It is clear that the art of handling people is becoming more and more useful, because there is no longer the hierarchy in administration we had earlier. You now have to involve yourself with personal problems all the way down to the lowest employee in an agency. In a large agency it can really be a headache. Moreover people will no longer accept merely being informed but also want to be able to influence decisions in a way that is quite different from what it was earlier. This creates demands on higher administrators that were not present before (#118).

Another official, who begins by insisting on the need for technical competence among all higher administrators, goes on to argue:

> . . . that, once you have technical competence as a base, it is quite simply the capacity to cooperate with other people that is demanded more and more today. We are now a society in which people in general are beginning to have pretensions about being treated like human beings, which requires a very different, far more democratic, attitude toward many—but that is true for all administrators, not just state officials. In my case it hasn't been a major problem—I have only been in rather new agencies, the Central Bureau of Sta-

tistics and the National Accounting Office, which have been thrown together quickly with the same kinds of people, but I think the problem exists still in other places. This "command" attitude, which people continue to bring into their agencies — think of the LKAB problem and such [LKAB is a government-owned mine that was subjected to a bitter and well publicized labor conflict in 1969] —it's completely out of date in our country. I think that is essential to bear in mind. But once you have said that, that there is now a need for capacity to cooperate with a new type of person developing here, it means no more than this: that cooperative capacity must be based on a technical competence, that combination (#209).

Although many "soft" administrators might be inclined to reject this juxtaposition of technical and democratic qualities, other components of this view are widely shared and constitute something approaching a "theory of administrative change" in Sweden: social (i.e., educational, economic) changes produce individuals who are more democratic in spirit; more democratic individuals, employed by public agencies reject older administrative styles and force adoption of a more "democratic" leadership style; among senior administrators, this change is experienced as increasing awareness of a need for sensitivity to personal problems of employees and a focus on cooperative capacity. These elements of a theory are plausible enough, but not entirely persuasive. The structural and psychological independence of senior administrators, for example, implies a long-standing need for cooperative skills in dealing among themselves and historical evidence of the existence of such skills is plentiful.[9] During our interviews, moreover, "soft" administrative skills were as likely to be mentioned by older administrators as by younger officials. This is hardly conclusive, but it does suggest that soft skills are traditional skills in Swedish collegial administration. To the extent that change has occurred, it is very likely a change in supervisor-subordinate relations, as well-developed negotiating practices trickle down to color relationships between senior officials and their lower-level subordinates. This kind of change is perceived by many to be widespread throughout operating *and* ministerial agencies:

I would like to say that, apart from standard qualities such as competence and so on, it seems to me that what is most essential in all senior administrative positions is a talent for cooperation, because it plays an incredibly more important role than it did only five years ago or ten years ago. I am talking about operating administration above all, although it is also obviously important in a ministry. But ministries are more involved in preparing decisions for the Cabinet to take . . . while in an administration, an operating agency, there is a colossal mass of operating decisions, low-level practical choices . . . And those choices naturally cannot be recalled. The decisions we make here [the speaker is a ministry official, on leave from an operating agency] only indicate which agency will do what — they do not actually divide up the work. But in an operating agency there are a tremendous number of operational decisions of the type that actually assign work and it is important that such decisions be made in a way that is generally understood and that is acceptable to the organization as a whole. I believe that "cooperative capacity" can stand as a headline, to which I attach great weight (#84).

Or, to borrow an old-fashioned rule-of-thumb from old-fashioned Swedish administration, "Don't push him; pull him."

MANAGEMENT AS LEADERSHIP

Important as "soft" skills are, it will be recalled that these officials give even greater weight to what we have referred to as organizational traits. When asked to indicate the qualities of a good administrator, Swedish officials mention these traits first, and they mention them more often than other kinds of skills. In Table 4.2 we report the first through fifth mentioned organizational traits that were most often suggested by these civil servants. Ability to delegate authority emerges convincingly as the most often mentioned trait particularly if, as we think likely, there is considerable overlap between the kinds of activities coded in the first two categories. Indeed delegation and coordination very often are included together in responses, as in the following report of the administrator's requirements: "To know the contents of the job, to be able to concentrate on it, to be able to divide up your work responsibilities, to be able to have enough trust in your colleagues so that you can coordinate a unit as big as this one is, with five different sections" (#330). Ability to administer, a rather diffuse coding category dominated by practical talents such as knowing rules and regulations, is a distant second, both in total mentions and in the order in which such skills are brought to mind. From the point of view of these officials, then, the

Table 4.2. Organizational Traits of the Good Administrator,
           Number of Mentions

	Mentions						
Ability To:	*1st*	*2nd*	*3rd*	*4th*	*5th*	*Totals*	
						N	*%*
Delegate Authority	51	29	25	12	12	129	54
Coordinate Work	12	9	11	6	3	41	17
Administer	32	16	9	7	3	67	28
						237	99

dominant organizational skill required to succeed in administration is ability to delegate authority.

This, of course, can hardly be surprising, in view of the kinds of multiple responsibilities these officials deal with. As used by the typical Swedish official, however, the concept of delegating authority embraces levels of meaning that are considerably more extensive than the words themselves suggest. One can hardly delegate, after all, unless one has some idea of what to delegate, and the choice of what to delegate implies several others. Consider the following discussion, from an official in the Ministry of Education, noting its "soft" overtones:

> In my division it is clear that the position [of Chief] requires one to be a work leader. Partly it is a question of organizing work, of leading it, of dividing responsibilities, of reaching agreements. In general I work in the following way: I try to think through for myself how something should be. Then I discuss it with the people who will be affected and try to reach some agreement with them on how it will go. On large questions, of course, I may ask people to think about the problem and tell me how they would solve it so that we can reach some agreement after talking it over. That is what I mean when I refer to organizing the work. The second part is leading our personnel. I think the manner in which you handle and get along with people [umgås med människorna] is extremely important . . . It is also difficult (#326).

The overtones of "democratic" leadership in this formulation are interesting, but what seems more significant is this official's determination, on his own, of organizational goals. One need not suggest anything devious at all about the more "democratic" overtones here to realize that achieving agreements with colleagues is likely to be easier if the leader has—as this one tries to have—some idea of where he wants to go. As another official put it:

> Something you must have, which is absolutely necessary if you are to keep the operation working, is some sort of, what they call goal-setting. You really have to know in what direction you want to take something, have some notion of what is right or not right. That is an absolute necessity for guiding yourself and thus also for guiding others. If you don't have that, and a desire to do something, some goal of your own somewhere a desire to reach it—if you don't have that, you might as well pack it in (#136).

To delegate, then, implies direction, but where does that come from? One possible source, education, is not viewed as especially relevant, but even if it were, so many of these officials work in areas distantly related to their educational training that a direct educational influence would be unlikely. A more likely source is political commitment. This seems to be a clear enough influence in ministries, but it seldom appears in responses made by officials in operating agencies. What does appear—and it appears quite often—is a set of inter-related ideas that may well spring from the legal responsibility each of these individuals bears for his office and which together define a distinct posture of activism: understand the purposes your agency was designed to achieve, pay attention to the environment, including the political environment; look for ways to improve your agency's performance—don't wait for changes to be forced on you.

APPRECIATE YOUR PURPOSES

We have already pointed out the significance these officials attach to knowledge of agency operations. They also attach great weight to an appreciation of agency mission as a whole, that is, to how all parts fit together and what it is that these coordinated parts are supposed to accomplish in society at large. "If you have an area of responsibility," one official suggests, "you have an obligation to yourself to define for yourself an overview of the whole area, in part so that you inter-vene when necessary with advice on various matters, in part so that you can sound an alarm with higher authorities when problems crop up that are beyond your power of decision. Developing that kind of overview over the entire area of responsibility is, in my view, a chief administrator's biggest role. If he has it, the system works. If he doesn't, the system will come to a halt and no one will know the effects of stopping at all" (#325). Another Bureau Chief put these ideas into a broader context:

> I think that it ought to be wholly central for a senior official, in the first instance, to look after whatever function in the society it is his responsibility to improve, that is to say, administer. In other words, one should understand oneself more as part of an idea that you want to advance in your area than as a bureaucrat, in the bad sense of that word . . . I sometimes think that a great many really fine intentions are administered away in the agencies because we Swedes are in some ways perfectionists. We sometimes forget what we are supposed to achieve in our efforts to make our "administration" as perfect as possible. It is quite important that one try in some way to have a clear under-standing of the substance of your own area of responsibility that you are supposed to improve—in some sense, that is, to apply means to ends and not the other way around.

PAY ATTENTION TO THE ENVIRONMENT

The outward-looking, social-impact perspective contained in views that stress agency mission implies careful monitoring of the "world outside of Verona" mentioned earlier by one official. Indeed, that official had in fact stressed the need to stay "plugged in" to social developments, experiments and research likely to affect his agency. He also made clear that he makes a strong effort to "keep up with political debates" with a view toward generating clues about the kinds of activities his agency might support (#324). In addition to their efforts to maintain contact with their government colleagues, therefore, these officials repeatedly stress the value of careful monitoring of the non-governmental environment. To the extent possible, they want to know what social or political developments are or will be in a position to affect their work, and much of what Swedish officials refer to as "planning" is in fact composed of efforts to scan a wider environment for clues to future agency activities. One Director General, who admitted to a "fascination" for planning of this kind, but who nevertheless felt he had his feet on the ground enough to know when planning was or was not likely to be useful, described his environmental monitoring program as follows:

> I have the advantage of having a small group of people here, Bureau Chiefs with whom I meet every Monday. One of us may have heard a speech or seen something on T.V. or been irritated by an interview on T.V. or seen a piece in a newspaper or been to a conference where we got an idea. I normally write my ideas down in a little book that I carry and think about them a while. Often I bring them up for a completely open-ended and free discussion in this little group. It is clear that in seven cases out of ten we say "Asch, it won't work, it is hopeless, or that was a crazy idea, we have already tried that." It is true of many fine ideas that, in many, many cases they were in fact tried ten or fifteen years ago and found to be unworkable — much more than young people think. But I have had the good fortune of sitting together with a group of knowledgeable people who can deal with those ideas in the right way. When we have an idea that we think we can try out on a larger group of people we do so, and some of them turn out to be quite firm and significant. I think this is a very, very stimulating responsibility and perhaps the most important of all.

BE ON THE LOOKOUT FOR CHANGE

At the bottom of these mission-defining and environmental-monitoring activities there appears to be a powerful reformist urge, undoubtedly influenced by political awareness, but also traceable in part to the fact that these officials, themselves, are responsible for programs. Whether in ministries, where a search for new programs and changes has become largely routinized in the long-range planning process, or in administrative agencies, still thought by many to be dominated by the *status quo* orientation of judge-like administration, the typical senior official is devoted to reform in programs for which he bears a significant responsibility. "We must always," asserts a ministry official "see before us the possibility of renewal and change if we find something that can be better than it is under current conditions" (#106). But a Director General of wide experience, who enjoys "working with and solving personal problems and dealing with [umgås med] leaders of the personnel organizations" in his very large agency is hardly less reformist:

> What is required of an administrative official who gets up to the top level is that he be constructive. He must have a sense of what is going on in the world and he must constantly try to improve agency activities and try to put forward a variety of reforms, of larger and smaller dimensions. That is what distinguishes a judge from an administrative official: the jurist just sits and makes judgments about facts and what is right or wrong, for what reason, but the administrator must be constantly dynamic, constantly on the alert to see what can be done to bring about improvement. I should think, too that there is nothing that distinguishes an Under-Secretary from a Director General on this point—or, for that matter a Managing Director in industry or a large business. In all cases, what is important is to watch for opportunities to modernize . . . It is also necessary to try to have good relations with people . . . You have to be able to deal properly with people, not just have good arguments. You have to be able to sell them, to sell your ideas (#107).

With this vision of reform through salesmanship we come back again to soft administrators, those who know what they want, change, but who know how to persuade or "sell" others to accept their ideas. Perhaps we can call these soft activists "salesmen of reform." They monitor, plan and push for change, but always with a smile and always with due consideration for the sentiments of others and the need for careful pacing or organizing reform:

> I'd like to say that it is important to be able to take people and get along with people [umgås med folk] in a 'selling' way. People have very different abilities to do this. For some it is natural; for others it can never be learned. But there is a great deal that can be accomplished this way and some experience of it certainly is essential. The word is sell. If you can sell things, sell yourself, convince people in a trustworthy and proper way, a great deal can be accomplished.

SUMMARY: SOFT ACTIVISTS AND BUREAUCRATIC THEORY

In the Swedish public bureaucracy, as in other large and complex organizations, underlying role orientations are likely to vary a good deal, depending on the characteristics of the individual, the nature of the work done, or the qualities of the structure within which public activities take place.[10] Total homogeneity of role orientations is unlikely at any time, but it is particularly unlikely under conditions of rapid social and organizational change, when the invention of new responsibilities outstrips the guidance capacity of older role definitions. It is therefore to be expected that, among the senior-level officials we interviewed, a number of role definitions were found. Some officials felt it appropriate to act as judges, seeking to apply legal principles to causes brought before them, following a role model more popular fifty years ago than it is today. Others described themselves as experts, using their specialized knowledge without regard to political preferences, or as partisan politicos, seeking to advance political causes without regard to the legal or intellectual foundations on which such causes may rest.

Most of these top-level bureaucrats, however, defined the ideal-type civil servant in terms that provide a peculiarly Swedish twist to common conceptions of bureaucracy. On the one hand, the "good" senior-level bureaucrat is seen as an activist, rather than as an uninvolved and unopinionated executor of orders from above: according to our respondents he must have a sense of purpose, awareness of the opportunities available in the environment, and the ability to sell both himself and his program plans. On the other hand, the good bureaucrat is also required to have a variety of "soft" qualities rather than the formalistic insensitivity often attributed to the bureaucratic role: he must be aware of the needs of his subordinates, be willing to participate rather than dictate, and he must be equally sensitive to the problems of his peers, with whom he negotiates. He must, above all, be able to get along with people, to "umgås med folk." The bulk of our respondents believe they should be, and many assert that they are, "soft activists."

Many senior officials assert that these are new qualities among Swedish administrators. The "judge" role said to be dominant until recently was essentially a passive orientation: problems came before such judges through the initiative of others; "judges" could not institute change. Sensitivity to the human aspects of administration is also new, spurred on by changes in the kind of people employed by government. Although our data cannot resolve the issue of "newness," we are inclined to doubt those who make such assertions. For one thing, there is no appreciable difference between younger and older officials in attitudes toward activism or a soft style of human relations. Moreover, there is considerable evidence in other studies to suggest that both sets of qualities have characterized Swedish administration and politics for years.[11] Indeed, there is enough evidence to question the frequently-asserted domination of the "judge" or "neutral executor" orientation in past eras.

Most fundamentally, however, we believe that the combination of attitudes we have labelled "soft activism" is to a considerable extent a function of the structure of the system itself. Once they achieve a permanent civil service position, these officials are individually responsible for something—a piece of the cake, as they might put it. Responsibility, moreover, extends not to a party or to a particular government, but to the law, and failure in exercising responsibility is dealt with by the law.[12] That sense of responsibility is a tradition of centuries, not years, and it encourages two kinds of behavior that show up, attitudinally, as soft activism. First, because responsibility is individually assigned and individually experienced ("independence" discussion of Chapter 3), there is a strong incentive to use that responsibility in a noticeable way, hence "activism." Second, precisely because each responsible official is surrounded by others who are equally responsible, that is, independent, there is a strong incentive to develop techniques of interaction that permit coordination to occur, hence "soft" human skills.[13] Use of those skills with subordinates may well appear "new" to some, but their use with peers is a tradition of some lineage, in a system structured to encourage "soft activism."

5 MANAGING POLITICS AND POLITICIANS

If there is any political relationship that can be regarded as central to the understanding of maturing industrial societies, it is the relationship between senior bureaucrats and party politicians. The rise to power of both groups defines a major political characteristic of modern states, while interactions between bureaucrats and politicians now seem decisive in setting the course for future societal development. In Sweden these interactions have reflected the historic dominance of a public bureaucracy that was a sophisticated and effective organizational system for generations before modern political parties came into existence. Not until this century were party organizations significant in Swedish governance, by which time the social status, legal autonomy and decision-making influence of Swedish administrators had become an important and thoroughly accepted "tradition" of Swedish life.[1]

Perhaps the best evidence of the power of this tradition was the refusal of Social Democratic Party leaders to challenge it. Assumption of governing power by the Social Democrats in 1932 was accompanied by Marxist rhetoric, but in fact little was done to disturb the bureaucracy. On grounds that an effective bureaucracy was essential to social reform, educational criteria for civil service entry were preserved, thus preserving the middle- and upper-class quality of civil service personnel.[2] Administrators could therefore proclaim their willingness to go along with a proletarian party because it cost them nothing: they retained control over entry criteria and, as social programs expanded, they gained even more control over programs increasingly defined as complex and thus in need of "expert" administration. One result, documented recently by Christoffersson and his colleagues, is that after forty years of continuous rule by the Social Democrats, only a third of top- and middle-level bureaucrats expressed a preference for the Social Democratic Party, while 58 percent preferred a non-socialist party.[3] For most of this century, Sweden has had a Social Democratic government, but a bourgeois bureaucracy.

The significance of these labels should not be exaggerated, however. We have seen that Swedish administrators are not as conservative as their backgrounds might imply, nor are Social Democrats as radical as their sometimes inflamed rhetoric suggests. What is more important is the relationship suggested by this continuing tradition of administrator influence. Swedish bureaucrats have been influential for centuries, they have increased the scope of their influence as the scope of government has increased, and politicians from the working-class party have sought out their counsel rather than organizing opposition to them. To a considerable extent, then, Swedish administrators have acted as tutors to the newer political elites, instructing them in the practicalities of government operation from a position of traditional and legal independence. We should therefore expect political discourse to be strongly influenced by administrative conceptions of good and bad, right and wrong, and we should anticipate a general consensus on appropriate procedures for raising and resolving issues. This is not to say that disagreement is impossible—some tension between administrative "independence" and the authority of elected party representatives, after all, must be regarded as unavoidable—but that tension is played out within a context of fundamental normative and conceptual agreement. Both the consensual context and the sources of tension within it are the concerns of this chapter.

THE CONTEXT OF INTERACTION

Members of the Swedish Parliament, from whom we selected our sample of politicians, are far more heterogeneous in social background than their administrator counterparts: a variety of occupations are represented, for example, and only one-fourth of the membership hold university degrees. On the other hand, MP's typically serve for many years and are therefore provided more than adequate exposure to the administrative culture in Stockholm. One result is a remarkable similarity of views regarding major characteristics of Swedish society and politics, including perspectives on power. To investigate power perspectives we began by handing each respondent a sheet of paper on which we had printed three quite different statements about the distribution of power in Sweden. Respondents were asked to read the statements and then place a check mark alongside the statement he or she considered to be the most accurate. Table 5.1, which compares responses of administrators and politicians to this inquiry, reveals that both groups view social power distribution in overwhelmingly pluralist terms. While nearly a fourth of the administrators preferred the elitist alternative, none could bring themselves to support the Marxist view. Scanty support for a Marxist view among politicians is overshadowed by their even more pronounced adherence to a pluralist perspective. Some differences at this level are apparent, but the differences seem of little significance compared to the level of agreement shown.

These are of course rather general questions, subject to a variety of possible interpretations because of their lack of specific content. To generate more specific opinions, we also handed each respondent a paper on which we listed twelve of the most important institutions in Swedish political life, from "banks and insurance companies" to LO, the central labor federation.[4] We then asked respondents to "indicate for each of these groups how much influence you feel they have over policy," with possible responses ranging from "very much" to "very little." Table 5.2 displays the six most influential institutions in Sweden, as seen by the administrators and politicians we interviewed. Rankings are based on the proportion of respondents who rank each institution as "the most" or "very " influential. Precisely the same institutions appear in both lists of the top six and, although not shown in the table, there is considerable distance in raw scores between the sixth and seventh positions on both lists (private industry ranks seventh for administrators and the opposition parties occupy that rank for parliamentarians). Administrators attribute greater influence to LO, the central

Table 5.1. Views of Power Structure

Administrators			Politicians	
%	N		%	N
70	(214)	*Pluralism:* Competition Among Groups	79	(34)
5	(17)	Tend Toward Pluralist View	4.5	(2)
25	(75)	*Elitism:* Rule by Leaders of Government, Business, Politics	12	(5)
–	–	*Marxism:* Rule by Corporate Elite	4.5	(2)
100.0	(306)		100	(43)

Table 5.2. Institutional Influence on Policy: The Big Six

	Administrator Ranking	Politician Ranking
The Government (Cabinet)	1	1
LO	2	4
Social Democratic Party	3	3
Parliament	4	2
Mass Media	5	2
Local Government	6	5

labor organization, and to the mass media, than do politicians. Politicians rank Parliament and local government higher than do administrators, no doubt because of their membership in those institutions—recall that a majority of MP's are active local politicians as well. These differences are not uninteresting, but again, the more striking conclusion is that administrators and politicians have very similar understandings about the influence structure that shapes Swedish public policy.

To this picture of a bureaucratic-political elite that sees the political world in very much the same way we can add several indicators that reveal an overwhelming normative consensus as well. Earlier we reported the high level of satisfaction experienced by administrators; in Tables 5.3 and 5.4 we compare administrator satisfaction with the level of satisfaction experienced by politicians. Quite clearly, most of these respondents believe that the political system as a whole is a good one that ought to be preserved, essentially in its present state. Agreement on the desirability of preserving a good system extends well beyond the social order as a whole, however. After these officials had indicated their views of power structure and institutional influence, we asked them whether they thought the system of power distribution was as it should be, or whether they thought any changes ought to be made in it. Table 5.4, which displays responses to this general question, again reinforces the conclusion that senior-level Swedish officials are extraordinarily comfortable with the present state of affairs. Since the institutions viewed as most powerful by these people are, with the exception of the mass media (Table 5.2), governmental institutions, perhaps we should not be too impressed by these figures. Nor should we be surprised at the almost total absence of interest in adjusting the influence of any of the twelve specific institutions about which we asked questions. This is obviously an elite that sees itself at the center of power, for whom the first rule of the political game is 'don't rock the boat.'

Table 5.3. Satisfaction with the Political System

	Administrators		Politicians	
	%	N	%	N
Passionate, Total Rejection	0.3	(1)	–	–
Rejected, Ameliorative Reforms Proposed	0.3	(1)	4.5	(2)
Accepted, Ameliorative Reforms Proposed	20	(63)	22.7	(10)
Accepted, Little Inclination To Change	67	(206)	65.9	(29)
Passionate Affirmation of System	12	(37)	6.8	(3)
Totals	99.6	(308)	–	(44)

Table 5.4. Satisfaction with Perceived Power Structure

	Administrators		Politicians	
	%	N	%	N
No Change Desired, Generally Satisfied	38	(109)	22.7	(10)
Basically Satisfied, Some Minor Changes	47	(136)	59.1	(26)
Somewhat Dissatisfied, Major Changes	15	(44)	11.4	(5)
Many Significant Changes Proposed	0.3	(1)	4.5	(2)
Totals	100.3	(290)	100.0	(43)

The obvious satisfaction felt by these individuals with both the social order and their place within it might imply considerable anxiety regarding social conflict. Social conflict, after all, might become serious enough to threaten the positions held by members of this elite. No such anxiety emerges from the interviews, however. Most respondents view the various sectors of society to have parallel rather than contradictory interests; they find conflict "healthy"; and they welcome its occurrence. During the course of each interview, administrators and parliamentarians alike were asked whether they thought social conflicts were "healthy and necessary." Table 5.5 displays the responses of both groups. Not surprisingly, politicians appear somewhat more receptive to conflict than admin-

Table 5.5. Evaluation of Conflict

	Administrators		Politicians	
	%	N	%	N
Very Healthy, Normal	9	(27)	7	(3)
Healthy, But No Physical Violence	42	(122)	51	(22)
Pro/Con or Neutral – Can be Either	35	(101)	28	(12)
Sick, Unfortunate, Usually Bad	13	(38)	12	(5)
Very Sick, Dangerous, Deplorable	1	(4)	2.3	(1)
Totals	100	(292)	100.3	(43)

istrators, but few in either group regard conflict as unhealthy. Physical violence, however, is explicitly excluded from the boundaries of "healthy" conflict, as we shall see in chapter six. What is meant by "conflict," accordingly, is disagreement that takes place within the boundaries of a prevailing consensus on values. Non-violent intellectual disagreement, in a society perceived to have no "real" conflicts of interest, is bound to appear "healthy."

Given the assumption of shared rather than divergent interests, conflicting opinions seldom are a real obstacle to elite accommodation. Two of the written questions put to elite administrators (but not politicians) at the conclusion of each interview revealed widespread agreement that the best solution to political controversies was likely to be found "in the middle" instead of among the extreme positions, and that compromise was generally a desirable and appropriate method of resolving disputes. Table 5.6 shows responses to a question put during interviews with both politicians and administrators: "In a case of conflict or disagreement in which one side seems to you to be wholly in the right and the other side wholly wrong, do you think that the side which is in the right should stick to its guns or would you personally be inclined to seek a compromise?" Apart from revealing how little support there is among these officials for taking "hard" (i.e., non-compromising) positions, the table provides additional evidence of similarity among Swedish administrators and politicians. Politicians seem somewhat more inclined to "lean toward" or to be definite about both compromise and sticking to guns, thus reflecting their greater heterogeneity. On the whole, however, both groups reflect the willingness to accommodate that has become the best documented characteristic of the Swedish political tradition.

In order to illuminate the depth of these accommodationist sentiments, we asked our coders to record references to matters of principle that were felt to be

Table **5.6.** Inclination to Compromise Strong Disagreement

	Administrators		Politicians	
	%	N	%	N
Definitely Would Compromise	22	(66)	20	(8)
Leans Toward Compromise	40	(121)	46	(19)
Pro/Con, Depends	26	(79)	20	(8)
Leans to Sticking to Guns	9	(27)	10	(4)
Definitely Would Stick to Guns	2	(6)	5	(2)
Totals	99	(299)	101	(41)

beyond compromise. Slightly more than 11 percent of the administrators mentioned moral or ethical questions, another 7 percent referred to technical or factual matters on which compromise would be senseless, and another 22.5 percent indicated a belief that "certain questions" could not be compromised without specifying the nature of these questions. More than 53 percent, however, made no reference at all to issues that could not be compromised without specifying the nature of these questions. Indeed, their responses made clear that nearly 57 percent thought that it was either "highly" or "somewhat" unrealistic to talk about unresolvable issues of right and wrong in politics. This should not be taken as a sign that these officials lack principle. Rather it suggests that, for the Swedish elite, one man's principle is another man's poison. If so, absolutist positions are unlikely to be politically useful.

The striking degree of factual and normative consensus that prevails at the top of the Swedish governmental system can hardly be regarded as a mystery. Although politicians and administrators come from somewhat different social backgrounds, both groups start their careers early, stay long, and thus accumulate a great deal of knowledge built on increasingly-shared assumptions about how things work. Moreover, both groups have strikingly similar reading habits, as can be seen in Table 5.7. Asked "what newspapers do you read regularly?" administrators and politicians reveal their overwhelming reliance on the Stockholm press, particularly the Independent morning paper *Dagens Nyheter* and the Conservative afternoon *Svenska Dagbladet*. Of these, *Dagens Nyheter*—a combination of the *New York Times* and the *New York Review of Books*—was clearly most significant in 1971. Apart from its news coverage, *Dagens Nyheter* provides a cultural page in each edition in which leading political issues of the day are debated by major public figures, including many of our respondents. A similar

Table 5.7. Newspapers Read Regularly

Administrators % Mentions				Politicians % Mentions		
1st	2nd	3rd		1st	2nd	3rd
56.8	22.9	2.5	Dagens Nyheter	34.1	25.0	13.6
36.8	29.2	5.7	Svenska Dagbladet	11.4	25.0	11.4
0.3	1.9	3.5	Arbetet	11.4	6.8	18.2
1.9	3.2	3.2	Goteborgs Handels & Sjö.	9.1	4.5	–
–	–	–	Sydsvenska Dagbladet	2.3	–	2.3
0.3	9.8	15.6	Expressen	–	6.8	9.1
–	8.9	13.3	Aftonbladet	2.3	4.5	9.1
1.6	7.0	8.9	Other Swedish	27.3	18.2	13.6
1.0	1.0	1.0	N.A.	2.3	9.1	22.7

page is provided in *Svenska Dagbladet,* a paper oriented less to intellectuals than to business executives. Both newspapers thus provide information *and* the arguments necessary to structure information into positions on issues. They also provide a ready means for communicating a sense of the trends in issue development, gossip about career successes and failures and other informational glue for the Stockholm public community. Since *Dagens Nyheter* is so dominant in circulation, it is a fair assumption that this single paper has considerable impact on elite values and attitudes. The information-attitudinal world of the Swedish elite seems relatively constrained.[5]

It is also worth noting, again, that we are talking about a rather small elite group. Swedes never tire of repeating that theirs is a small country. For those who arrive at the top, it is even smaller, since the educational screen through which top-level administrators have been filtered has eliminated everyone who could not make it to and through the university, while an equally effective organizational screen has eliminated all but the most accomplished politicians. These powerful filters, coupled with the historic concentration of government offices in Stockholm, have created effective social, no less than informational, supports for administrator-politician agreement. Because the proportion of any given age-cohort that attends a university is small, and the number who wind up in government or politics even smaller, members of such cohorts tend to be familiar with one another. Settling in Stockholm, they can easily observe the career progress of their colleagues in the press, through service on committees or other joint bodies, or through rumor from mutual friends. Lengthy service plus Stockholm residence three or four days per week provide similar opportunities for legislators. In this system, therefore, there is seldom need for an artificial device to coordinate opinion or spread information; historic familiarity and shared day-to-day experiences—from the morning editorial in *Dagens Nyheter* to the daily commute by subway—provide all the coordination normally required. It is only a slight exaggeration to suggest that, for any given public issue, most members of the elite not only begin by knowing the issue and the participants, but also what their positions are, how they arrived at them and the direction of possible changes in position, if any. In Stockholm, this kind of intelligence is, almost literally, "in the air."

In sum, elite administrators and politicians over time accumulate very similar experiences, they read the same things and see things in very much the same way: they like what they do and are satisfied with their own stature; they generally believe the system to be good and worth preserving; they generally believe that major political institutions are legitimate and worth preserving; and they demonstrate sensitivity to the basic norms that guide their mutual interaction. In this kind of context, it would be surprising indeed if serious disagreements occurred very often or if, having occurred, such disagreements were not resolved with relative ease.

ROLE CONSENSUS

Shared perceptions and norms extend naturally into agreement over more detailed aspects of political and administrative behavior. Each group of respondents, for example, was asked to describe both their own and their opposite's role and to tell us what personal qualities were required to perform such roles. Civil servants were asked, "How do you see the role of a senior civil servant— what are his most important tasks? What personal qualities should a senior civil servant have?" At a later point, the same question was asked, substituting "member of parliament" for "senior civil servant." The parliamentary questionnaire contained the same two questions, in reverse order. All interviews were taped, transcribed, and coded twice, with all coding differences reconciled.

Table 5.8 summarizes legislative and bureaucratic perspectives on the desirable characteristics of senior civil servants. On some issues there is near unanimity on qualities that are *not* important. Neither administrators themselves nor parliamentarians believe that charismatic, representational, ideologue-advocate or mediating traits are very important, and only a few believe that counselor or technician qualities are of first significance. Most of these are qualities associated with political activity and it seems clear that agreement on the non-political character of the senior civil servant role is widespread. Although majorities of both legislators and administrators reject the importance of "character," the substantial fractions (44 and 48 percent) that assign "important" or "very impor-

Table 5.8. Civil Servant Traits, As Seen by Swedish Administrators
            and Politicians

Administrators	Organizational Traits	Politicians
55.6	Very Important	13.6
20.6	Important	9.1
23.2	Not Important	77.3

Administrators	Mediating Traits	Politicians
7.6	Very Important	2.3
9.5	Important	2.3
81.3	Not Important	95.5

Administrators	Sociability Traits	Politicians
51.1	Very Important	18.2
14.6	Important	4.5
33.0	Not Important	77.3

Administrators	Intellectual Traits	Politicians
35.2	Very Important	61.4
26.7	Important	2.3
36.5	Not Important	36.4

Administrators	Ideologue-Advocate Traits	Politicians
1.0	Very Important	–
4.1	Important	2.3
93.3	Not Important	97.7

Administrators	Technician Traits	Politicians
9.5	Very Important	2.3
14.9	Important	2.3
74.3	Not Important	95.5

Administrators	Counselor Traits	Politicians
4.4	Very Important	11.4
5.1	Important	2.3
89.2	Not Important	86.4

Administrators	Neutral Executor Traits	Politicians
22.9	Very Important	77.3
12.4	Important	2.3
63.5	Not Important	20.5

Administrators	Charismatic Traits	Politicians
3.2	Very Important	—
5.7	Important	—
89.8	Not Important	100.0

Administrators	Representational Traits	Politicians
4.8	Very Important	2.3
13.3	Important	—
80.6	Not Important	97.7

Administrators	Character Traits	Politicians
27.3	Very Important	36.4
16.5	Important	11.4
54.9	Not Important	52.3

Administrators	Policy-Making Traits	Politicians
11.4	Very Important	—
17.1	Important	2.3
70.2	Not Important	97.7

tant" ratings to this quality suggest that it is regarded as a significant secondary characteristic. Focusing on the qualities regarded as important by each group, on the other hand, reveals some interesting disagreement. For legislators, it is clear that the single most important quality of a good administrator is that he be a "neutral executor," that is, someone who "loyally represents and serves whatever government is in power." Intellectual qualities, by which legislators mean "expertise, technical, or professional competence," is the second most important trait among members of the *Riksdag.* Smaller proportions believe that organizational or sociability traits are important, but legislators unanimously (98%) reject the significance of policy-making qualities for civil servants. If we recall the general rejection of the more specifically "political" traits noted earlier, we are left with a legislative conception of the good administrator as someone who does what he is told, and is smart.

Although more than a third (35.3%) of the civil servants believe that doing

what they are told is "very important" or "important," administrative conceptions of the desirable are generally quite different. Like members of the *Riksdag*,
administrators accept the importance of intellectual qualities, giving somewhat
more emphasis to the capacity for creativity, imagination and innovativeness.
But unlike their parliamentary colleagues, Swedish administrators stress the
importance of organizational and sociability traits for the good administrator
(Chapter 4). The abilities to delegate authority and to "get things done" are
qualities especially prized by civil servants, as is the ability to establish and maintain good working relationships with colleagues or staff. And note that 28.5
percent of the administrative respondents think that policy-making traits are
either "important" or "very important." The administrator's conception of the
good administrator, then, is someone who can get things done, who can get
along with others, and who is smart.

These differences may be less consequential than they appear to be at first
glance. The proportion of administrators who assert the desirability of policy-
making traits, after all, is not large: most civil servants agree with legislators that
such qualities are really not important. Since administrators do not emphasize
policy-making traits, but do emphasize the ability to get things done, one might
easily argue that the Swedish administrative self-conception is a mirror-image of
the parliamentary view: legislators want administrators to do what they are told
and administrators most prize the ability to do what they are told to do. This
interpretation is somewhat strained, since it avoids the issue of who tells
administrators what to do. But given the level of agreement on the importance
of intellectual qualities and the generally non-political character of administrative work, it seems plausible.

Table 5.9 displays administrator and legislator perceptions of desirable
characteristics of members of Parliament. Perhaps the most striking piece of

Table 5.9. Members of Parliament Traits, as Seen By Swedish
Administrators and Legislators

Administrators	Organizational Traits	Politicians
1.9	Very Important	—
7.6	Important	2.3
89.5	Not Important	97.7

Administrators	Mediating-Bargaining Traits	Politicians
28.3	Very Important	6.8
25.4	Important	4.5
45.1	Not Important	88.6

Administrators	Sociability Traits	Politicians
9.2	Very Important	40.9
8.6	Important	15.9
81.3	Not Important	43.2

Administrators	Intellectual Traits	Politicians
26.3	Very Important	31.8
19.0	Important	27.3
53.3	Not Important	40.9

Administrators	Charismatic Traits	Politicians
28.6	Very Important	29.5
14.9	Important	4.5
55.6	Not Important	65.9

Administrators	Representational Traits	Politicians
34.6	Very Important	79.5
19.7	Important	11.4
44.8	Not Important	9.1

Administrators	Character Traits	Politicians
37.8	Very Important	40.9
11.4	Important	15.9
48.9	Not Important	43.2

Administrators	Policy-Making Traits	Politicians
42.5	Very Important	11.4
16.2	Important	25.0
40.0	Not Important	63.8

Administrators	Ideologue-Advocate Traits	Politicians
25.1	Very Important	20.5
23.5	Important	25.0
50.5	Not Important	54.5

Administrators	Technician Traits	Politicians
0.3	Very Important	—
0.3	Important	2.3
98.4	Not Important	97.7

evidence in Table 5.9 is the relative insignificance legislators themselves attach to policy-making traits: only 11.4 percent regard such traits as "very important" while almost 64 percent believe them to be "not important." Representational qualities—being responsive to constituents or clientele groups, representing constituency interests, interpreting and expressing popular sentiments—are far and away the most important qualities legislators themselves think they should have. A majority of legislative respondents also believe that intellectual, character and sociability traits are important. For Swedish parliamentarians, a good politician is one who can represent constituency interests, is smart, and can get along. He need *not* be especially qualified for policy-making.

Civil servants generally agree that representational skills are essential: some 54.3 percent indicate that such traits are "very important" or "important." A slightly larger fraction (58.7%), however, believes that policy-making skills are important. This appears to reflect a major difference of view, but examination of the detailed responses that were coded under "policy-making" suggests a more cautious interpretation. The quality mentioned most frequently by administrators was vision, or the ability to see the impact of programs. The next most frequently mentioned quality was the ability to formulate and articulate policy. Traits such as decisiveness, decision-making ability, or advice-giving capacity were mentioned only rarely. Policy-making, for these administrators, is clearly an activity associated with foresight and articulation, rather than decision-making. Although only a minority of administrators think that intellectual skills are very important, those who do define such skills in a fashion quite consistent with their views on legislative policy-making qualities: general intelligence and a wide range of experience, rather than highly-trained expertise, are the qualities mentioned most often. Swedish administrators thus prize some skills associated with policy-making, but they do not think that decision-making skills are important for parliamentarians. For them, the good politician is one who represents his constituents, can appreciate the long-term consequences of public programs, and is not narrow-minded.

We can summarize these views in a diagram that is as interesting for what is left out as it is for what is indicated. There is general agreement that the basic role of the legislator is to represent interests; neither administrators nor legislators themselves believe that making policy decisions is important for the role of a *Riksdagsman*. Both sides also agree that the basic role of the civil servant is to administer policy, although the meaning attached to that role is shaded rather differently. Legislators stress "loyalty" in carrying out policy while administrators, as we have seen, emphasize organizational competence in a way that asserts their own freedom to influence policy formulation. This is an important source of strain in administrator-politician relations, and we will shortly explore this tension in greater detail. At this point, however, it is important to note that such

Figure 1 Administrator and Legislator Role Expectations

	Self	Other
Parliament View of	Representative	Neutral Executor
Administrator View of	Administrator	Representative

strain is tempered by a third role, not shown in Figure 1. The role is "policy-making." If, as Figure 1 suggests, legislators "represent" and civil servants "administer," where do policy decisions come from?

The answer is that policy choices are made by the Cabinet or, as it is known in Sweden, *Regering* (Government). Through its control over the normal processes of program development, budget preparation and bill-drafting, and through its control over the activities of the roughly seventy-five new Royal Commissions created each year, the Cabinet dominates the processes of policy formation, using ministries for staff assistance.[6] Administrators in operating agencies often interact with ministry staff over budget and policy problems, of course, and legislators as well as administrators are often appointed to Royal Commissions, whose activities offer opportunities for resolving disagreements over policy matters. An institutionally specialized policy formation process thus enables administrators and legislators to influence policy, through an inter-personal arena that reduces the natural tension between legislative "control" and administrator "freedom." Policy specialization, in short, promotes institutional harmony no less than policy agreement.

ROLE CONSENSUS? A SECOND CUT

The fact of policy specialization underlines the need to look beyond indicators of a general role consensus to evidence that may provide a more sensitive portrait of the differentiated sub-systems that exist within the overall consensus. We have already noted that the ministries, for example, are rather small units, employing between 100 and 200 people, most of whom are younger in average age, and trained in different academic disciplines (i.e., social or administrative sciences, rather than law) than administrators in the large operating units. Christoffersson and his colleagues have shown that, on the policy-relevant dimension of party preference, cabinet ministries are very different from other units. Among their sample of 1553 top-level and middle-level civil servants, some 58 percent indicated a preference for a non-socialist party, while only a third

Table 5.10.   Party Preference Among Swedish Administrators (%)

Level	Party Preference			
	Non-Socialist Party	Socialist Party	No Party Preference	Sum
Chief Administrators	65	29	16	100
Other Administrators	59	34	7	100
Total	58	33	9	100

Source: Adapted from Ulf Christoffersson *et al., Byråkrati och politik,* p. 80.

preferred a socialist, i.e., Social Democratic party (Table 5.10). In the ministries, however, some 47 percent of the chief administrators and 48 percent of the others, indicated a preference for a socialist party. If the Foreign Ministry, traditionally a haven for Swedish blue-bloods, is not included, the proportion of ministry officials who prefer a socialist party rises to 55 percent. Given the policy planning responsibilities of the ministries, it can hardly be a surprise that they are dominated by socialists after forty years of Social Democratic rule; perhaps the only "surprise" is that other units continue to be largely populated by people who prefer the bourgeois parties. The combination of socialist preference and ministerial employment, however, has interesting consequences. Christoffersson and his colleagues developed a "political governance" variable by asking their respondents whether politicians ought to have greater, lesser or the same influence as administrators over future decision-making.[7] They also asked their respondents to indicate their preferences on increasing or decreasing the use of laymen on decision-making boards. On both these questions responses were largely negative. Forty-five percent opposed, and only 35 percent supported the notion of increasing the decision-making influence of politicians, while 63 percent either wished to make no changes in layman influence, or wanted to reduce it.[8] Those who were in favor of increased political influence were also in favor of increasing the influence of laymen, but supporters of these changes were few, compared to opponents.

Socialist preferrers, however, were considerably *less* negative to an increase in politician's influence, and a clear majority of them (57%) were in favor of increasing the influence of layman boards. Socialists preferrers *in ministries* were the most hospitable of all to the idea of increased politician influence: 76 percent of ministerial socialists support an increase in politicians' influence (Table 5.11). Even *non*-socialists employed in ministries turn out to be supporters of more politician influence. It is indeed obvious, as Christoffersson and his col-

Table 5.11. Support For Political Guidance By Party Preference (%)

	Party Preference			
	Non-Socialist Party	Socialist Party	No Party Preference	Total
Ministry Officials	54	76	49	63
Others	31	42	32	34

Source: Christoffersson et al., Byråkrati och politik, p. 127.

leagues conclude, that ". . . ministry officials are a special group. They offer a radically different point of view than all other state officials. They are far more supportive of increased political guidance than all others, and they are also considerably more positive toward politicians than the civil service as a whole."[9] These results, based on a different sample, suggest that Swedish administrators as a whole may be rather more sensitive to political encroachment on their power than was suggested above, but the results are otherwise quite consistent with other portions of our analysis. At the conclusion of each of our interviews, for example, we asked respondents to fill in a closed-item questionnaire containing some thirty-five items. From responses to these questions we later constructed two scales, one measuring what we think of as "populism," or support for popular control over government, the other measuring what we think of as "trust in politicians." (See Appendix to the chapter for the scale items and measures of their significance.) Scoring on these scales is arranged so that a positive score indicates a higher scale value: the greater the positive value the more trust in politicians and the more faith in the wisdom of popular control of governmental decision-making. Summing the differences between the proportion of high and low scorers on these scales by agency, as is done in Table 5.12, enables us to determine both the degree to which there are differences of attitude within agency type, and the direction of these differences. Quite clearly, opinions in the ministries are skewed very much toward a high level of trust in politicians and in the general public, while officials in the public authorities lean very strongly in the opposite direction. Opinions in the boards are split more evenly but there, too, the direction is slightly away from trust in politicians or the general public. The questions used here are not precisely the questions used by Christoffersson and his colleagues, and the samples are very different, but the results are parallel and confirm the very different, very political quality of the ministries.

In place of "consensus," then, it might be more useful to think of majority and minority orientations to administration and politics among top-level Swedish

Table 5.12.   Percentage Differences on Trust in Politicians and
             Populism Scales, By Agency

	Trust in Politicians	Populism
Ministries	+58.6	+48.2
Administration Boards	–7.4	–2.6
Public Authorities	–27.6	–37.5

administrators. For the bourgeois majority, administration involves getting things done, and requires social, organizational and intellectual skills above all. Loyal execution of government policy, regardless of party source, continues to be prized, but there is also some disquiet over "political interference" and a reluctance to increase the influence of politicans. The minority orientation is concentrated within those agencies—ministries—engaged in policy evaluation and program planning, working closely with political leadership in and out of the *Riksdag.* For ministerial civil servants, especially those who are Social Democrats, increased political control over the administration is very much desired, for policy reasons as well as a healthy tonic against the cult of bureaucratic expertise. These are the administrators who regard policy-making and even representational traits (Table 5.8) as important *for themselves,* precisely because they are themselves engaged in the minority, policy-making, system.

THE IMPACT OF PARTY ON LEGISLATIVE ROLE EXPECTATIONS

If administrative orientations are affected by party preference as well as position, it would be surprising if legislative orientations were not also affected by party affiliation. With only 44 legislative respondents, evenly divided between socialist (20 Social Democrats, 2 Communists) and non-socialist parties, it is difficult to provide much more than a speculative evaluation of party impact. Limited as it may be, our evidence is worth some comment.

As far as their own work is concerned, socialists and non-socialists are in general agreement. Both groups agree (socialist = 80 percent, non-socialist = 79.2 percent) that representational traits are "very important" and similar proportions from both groups agree on the importance of intellectual, character and sociability traits. Only 30 percent of the socialists, as opposed to 42 percent of non-socialists, however, believe that policy making traits are important or very important. This might be taken as a reflection of the somewhat greater propor-

Table 5.13. Legislative Perceptions of Important Administrator Traits, by Party Group

Non-Socialists Mentions			Socialists Mentions	
1st	*2nd*		*1st*	*2nd*
4.3	13.0	Advisor Counselor	5.9	6.7
17.4	39.1	Intellectual	–	20.0
4.3	8.7	Organizational	–	13.3
4.3	13.0	Character	–	33.3
69.6	8.7	Neutral Executor	94.1	–
–	4.8	Technician	–	–
–	13.0	Sociability	–	26.7

tion of non-socialist MP's actually appointed to Royal Commissions,[10] or it might be a reflection of a socialist sample that excluded ministers. In a party that refers to itself as "the movement" and emphasizes party discipline as a means of redressing the economic power available to the other side, back-bench MP's might well be expected to think of policy-making as something for the leaders to do, and for them to endorse.

On the other hand, party affiliation does influence legislative views of the administrative role. Table 5.13 summarizes the administrator traits given first and second priority by socialist and non-socialist parliamentarians. While both party groups give heavy emphasis to the expectation that administrators will be neutral executors, socialist MP's appear to view the good administrator as "a good guy who does what he is told," but who need not be an "expert." All this is fully in accord with the opinions of the policy bureaucrats in the ministries, who support increased political influence through increased laymen representation, rather than reliance on experts. Non-socialist MP's, by contrast, expect a more varied set of qualities, even as they emphasize the fundamental importance of "neutral executor" traits. Intellectual qualities of expertise are clearly more important to bourgeois party MP's than they are to socialists. For them, government as an "expert" undertaking remains a powerful concept, perhaps because they are as well-educated as their administrative counterparts and hence are more willing to appreciate the virtues of expertise than are socialist legislators.

ROLE SPECIALIZATION AND COMMUNICATION

Whether or not an administrator falls generally into the large group of administrative generalists or the much smaller group of policy bureaucrats seems very

Table 5.14. Swedish Administrator Partisan and Policy-Making
            Orientation, by Contact with Political Parties

			Contact With Parties			
Partisan Orientation (%)				Policy-Making Orientation (%)		
Very	Some	None		Very	Some	None
33.3	66.7	0	Very Often	33.3	66.7	0
35.3	35.3	29.4	Often	35.3	52.9	11.8
5.0	23.0	72.0	Seldom	15.0	40.0	45.0
1.1	11.0	87.9	Never	3.8	25.3	70.9
gamma = 0.65				gamma = 0.59		

clearly related to the amount of contact he has with other components of the policy-making system—the parties and Parliament. A third or more of those who reported that they were in contact with political parties "very often" or "often" were judged to have very strong partisan and policy-making orientations (Table 5.14). Among those who reported no contact with parties, 88 percent had no partisan orientation and 71 percent had no policy-making orientation. Similarly, among those who reported a great deal of contact with the *Riksdag,* a quarter were judged to be very partisan and a third were coded as having a very strong policy-making orientation. Of those reporting no contact with the Parliament at all, 94 percent had no partisan orientation and 76 percent gave no emphasis to policy-making (Table 5.15). Precisely the same pattern emerges when contacts with LO, the central labor federation, are compared to role orientations: the more contact, the less technician, the more partisan and the more policy-making orientation these administrators exhibit.[11] LO and the Social Democratic Party are of course very closely related in devising social policy innovations—a relationship that underlines the "special" character of the ministry-centered policy-making system under a Social Democratic regime. A better understanding of the significance of communication patterns for role specialization can be obtained from a more comprehensive view of those patterns. Each respondent was asked to fill in a sheet on which we had listed a number of different institutions and a number of boxes reflecting the frequency of his contact with those institutions, as well as the initiator of the contact. In Figure 2 we show that results of an analysis of those responses, based on a scoring convention that assigns a low number (1–3) to frequent contact and a higher number (4–7) to little or no contact. Arrows indicate whether the respondent or the other party typically initiates the contact; where there is no arrow, both parties are reported as equal

Table 5.15. Swedish Administrator Partisan and Policy-Making
Orientation, by Contact With Parliament

Contact With Parliament						
Partisan Orientation (%)				Policy-Making Orientation (%)		
Very	Some	None		Very	Some	None
25.0	41.7	33.3	Very Often	33.3	45.8	20.8
8.6	31.4.	60.0	Often	11.4	50.0	38.6
1.3	4.8	93.7	Never	1.6	22.2	76.2
gamma = 0.65				gamma = 0.48		

in the initiation of contact. Observation of the mean scores for administrator-Parliament and administrator-political party contacts makes clear how infrequent such contacts are. Contacts between administrators and political parties occur at a reported rate of somewhere between "seldom" and "never," while parliamentary contacts appear to take place at a rate approaching "seldom." Although these are gross indicators, they nevertheless suggest how little most civil servants have to do with politicians and how atypical, therefore, the policy bureaucrats of the ministries are. Note, too, that when such contacts occur, they tend to be initiated by the politicians rather than the civil servants.

If the average administrator has little to do with politicians, he has a great deal of contact with ministries and administrative boards; indeed, the only relationships which occur with a frequency equal to a stated "often" or more are contacts with ministries and boards. This suggests a great deal of center-periphery communication but, as the higher mean scores for contacts with other institutions suggest, not much lateral contact between bureaucrats and institutions outside their own spheres of competence. If so, we should expect to find lower mean scores (i.e., more contact) on measures relating individual agencies to their clientele groups. Examination of contact scores by agency indicates that this expectation is in fact true: whereas contacts between all civil servants and local governments average 4.6 (close to "seldom"), contacts between local governments and administrators in agencies under the Ministries of Interior and Civil Affairs—both heavily involved in local government responsibilities—average 3.0 and 2.5, or "often" to "very often." Similarly, while contacts between all administrators and private industry average 3.7 (between "often" and "seldom"), contacts between administrators associated with the Ministries of Industry and Commerce average 2.9 and 2.4, respectively, or "often" to "very often." High levels of contact between all administrators and the central administrative organs (ministries and boards) reflect the institutionally specialized system of policy-making, while high levels of contact between administrators and their respective clientele groups reflect both the specialization of function that is typical of modern bureaucratic systems and the gradual blurring of "public-private" boundaries in increasingly corporatist states. Communication in such systems follows the spokes of a wheel, from center out to the rim and beyond, rather than moving around the rim.

Figure 2 also permits us to contrast administrator and politician contact in interesting ways. Unlike administrators, whose contacts are largely with their own board/ministry or the clientele they service, most politician contacts are with citizens, local governments and the mass media, thus reflecting both their representation interests and the fact that most parliamentarians are active local politicians. Moreover, with two exceptions (white collar unions and private industry), parliamentarians generally are in more frequent contact with all of the institutions listed, which suggests that the political role, too, is subject to a specialization defined by thicker and more varied relationships with the larger society. Perhaps it is this generally more multi-faceted interaction network that leads politicians to report more contact with ministries and boards (means = 3.6 and 3.8) than civil servants in general report having with members of Parliament (mean = 4.6). Since both sides agree that legislators typically initiate such contacts, these differences in frequency estimates are probably not very significant.

On the other hand, the overwhelming directional bias of the arrows seems very significant. As we have repeatedly noted, members of the Swedish governmental elite enjoy extraordinary social status, feel themselves to be powerful and independent, and believe that they have a good deal to do with the direction of Swedish society. It is totally consistent with these attitudes that members of this elite quite literally see themselves in the center of Swedish public life, as recipients of requests for communication or information from other major social institutions. And within this central group, civil servants are most central of all, for it is they who respond to initiatives from politicians rather than the other way around. As the directional arrows make clear, administrators command the informational resources most essential for the conduct of Swedish affairs now, as in the past.

ADMINISTRATION AND THE CONTROL OF CONTEXT

One way to summarize the preceding argument is to suggest that disagreement about the appropriate boundaries for administrative and legislative action among the Swedish elite is organized around two major intellectual paradigms. The first

Figure 2   Mean Scores, Civil Servants & Politicians, by Frequency of Contact

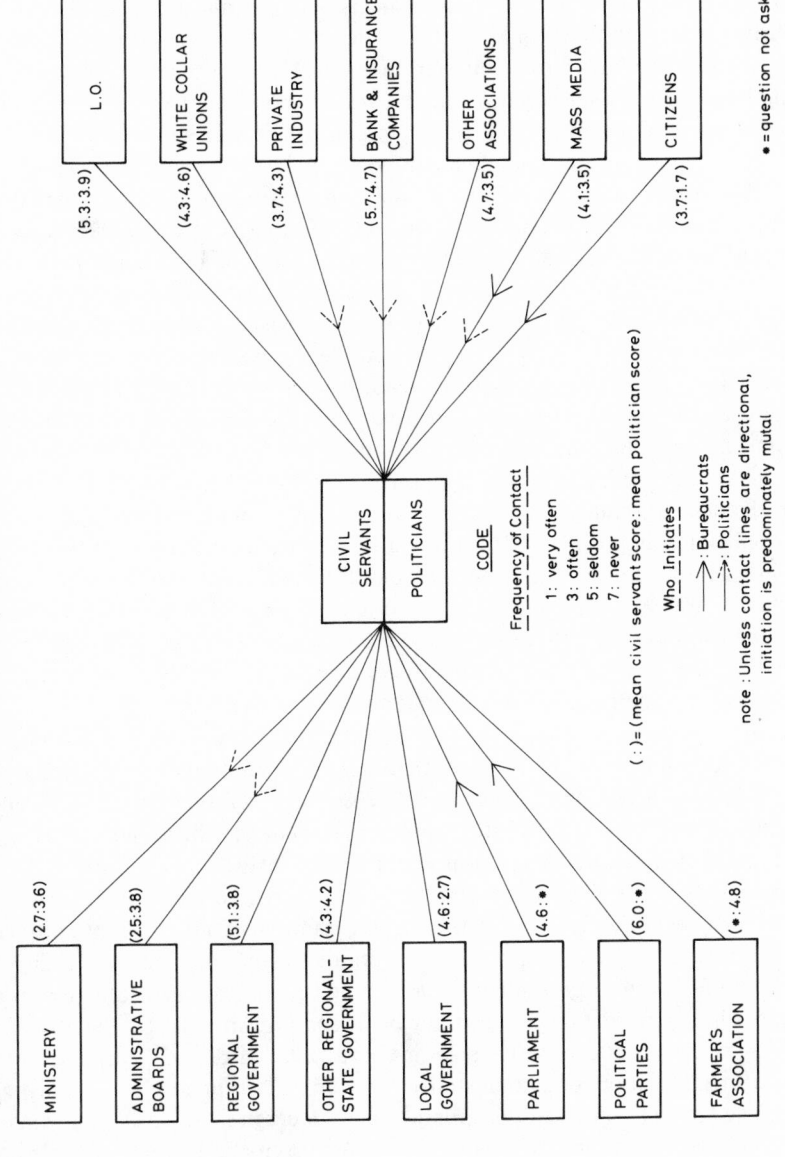

L.O. (5.3:3.9)

WHITE COLLAR UNIONS (4.3:4.6)

PRIVATE INDUSTRY (3.7:4.3)

BANK & INSURANCE COMPANIES (5.7:4.7)

OTHER ASSOCIATIONS (4.7:3.5)

MASS MEDIA (4.1:3.5)

CITIZENS (3.7:1.7)

CIVIL SERVANTS
POLITICIANS

MINISTRY (2.7:3.6)

ADMINISTRATIVE BOARDS (2.5:3.8)

REGIONAL GOVERNMENT (5.1:3.8)

OTHER REGIONAL – STATE GOVERNMENT (4.3:4.2)

LOCAL GOVERNMENT (4.6:2.7)

PARLIAMENT (4.6:●)

POLITICAL PARTIES (6.0:●)

FARMER'S ASSOCIATION (●:4.8)

CODE

Frequency of Contact

1: very often
3: often
5: seldom
7: never

(:)=(mean civil servant score : mean politician score)

Who Initiates

→ : Bureaucrats
⇢ : Politicians

note : Unless contact lines are directional,
initiation is predominately mutal

● = question not asked

may be thought of as the "traditionalist" paradigm, still subscribed to by a majority of administrators and perhaps half of Parliament. Legislators and executives whose orientations are constrained by this paradigm believe that Parliament should represent societal interests and that civil servants should have independent authority to administer programs. Various shades of opinion regarding how much "independence" administrators should have are found within this paradigm, but there is fundamental acceptance of a strict separation between political representation and administration of policy. Indeed, a major component of this viewpoint is the belief that only such a strict separation, coupled with administrator independence, can guarantee citizens against legislative excess.

The second, "activist," paradigm, is subscribed to by a small minority of administrators, but a larger fraction of the Parliament. Politically, the minority is dominated by Social Democrats in both the *Riksdag* and the administration. Organizationally, the minority is concentrated in the ministries. This group believes even more strongly than the majority that administrators in the operating agencies should do what they are told, that the Parliament should represent interests, and that the administrators and politicians who are involved in the work of the ministries should set policy. For the activists, boundaries between setting and carrying out policy are blurred: some administrators should be good at policy-making, while politicians and laymen should have more influence over administration. From this point of view, the problem of policy is not so much who, or how, but what and when. Accordingly, there is less concern over legality or the danger of legislative excess, and more concern about social reform.[12]

Focusing on these kinds of differences is important, if only to make clear that Swedish government is a complex undertaking that necessarily generates differing points of view about matters of fundamental importance. At the same time, it is even more important to recognize that these differences are nuances that do not significantly affect the dominant consensus over substantive and procedural values. Images of social structure, political power and institutional influence are widely shared, as are preferences about change in the socio-political order and procedures for dealing with public issues. If these shared values seem self-serving, it is partly because they emerge from a long tradition of administrative influence, publicly-endorsed, that legitimizes elite status for the small circle of individuals who guide Swedish government. Elected politicians have gained access to that circle, but only in this century and on terms primarily set by the established elite—i.e., administrators. Those terms have included general acceptance of the traditional position of administrators, including acceptance of administrator-defined conceptions of appropriate policy processes. Swedish policy-making is deliberative, rationalistic, consensual and pragmatic because administrators control the context within which policy is made.[13] There are occasional lapses, to be sure, but alternative styles are short-lived among elites who define politics as administration.

APPENDIX: POPULISM AND TRUST IN POLITICIANS SCALE ITEMS

Populism Scale

1. Certain people are better suited to lead Sweden because of their social background (factor loading = .57).
2. Most important questions are too complicated for the public to understand (factor loading = .67).
3. Technical considerations are of greater importance than political factors when it comes to solving social and economic problems (factor loading = .46).
4. The strength and efficiency of a government are more important than its specific programs (factor loading = .57).

Trust in Politicians Scale

1. Many who enter politics often think more about their own welfare or that of their party than about the welfare of citizens (factor loading = .65).
2. The interference of politicians in affairs which are properly the business of administration is a disturbing feature of contemporary public life (factor loading = .54).
3. The general welfare of the country is seriously endangered by the continual clash of interest groups (factor loading = .60).
4. Although parties play an important role in a democracy, they often uselessly exacerbate political conflict (factor loading = .69).
5. Many of the doubts and fears expressed about the growing intervention of the state in economic affairs are fully justified (factor loading = .73).

6 IMAGES OF SOCIETY AND POWER

It is a fair guess that Swedes are more self-conscious about the kind of society they have created than any other people in the world. The rapidity of a social transformation that created enormous national wealth where enormous national poverty had existed barely fifty years earlier provides an easily-accessed supply of comparative images—how different it was when I was young!—that encourages national self-awareness. Swedes also receive large quantities of information about other nations from media institutions that usually have appeared committed to portraying other societies as less advanced, less wealthy and less tranquil than is Sweden itself. In a nation of virtually total literacy, these media biases structure widespread acceptance of clear national self-images: small, different, better. Among the governmental and commercial elites who regularly travel abroad, these general images are supplemented by detailed knowledge of other places, leading to a very sophisticated awareness of how and why Sweden is different. Assessments of Swedish society by senior government officials frequently rest on comparisons with other systems, personally experienced. More than most other national elites, perhaps, these officials know why they are what they are; they also know why Sweden is Swedish.

A CONGENIAL, ORDERLY PLACE

The Swedish governmental elite is very much aware of the privileged position Sweden occupies in the world; although small in size, Sweden is among the richest and most technologically advanced nations in the world, and elite administrators as well as politicians know it. They could hardly *not* know it, given the amount of attention paid to poverty in other countries by the Swedish media and the sustained attention focused on the issue of foreign aid during the past decade by the political party organizations.[1] Nevertheless, wealth and technological sophistication are not regarded as important "Swedish" qualities. Other nations are as rich or as sophisticated, and some even combine these qualities as much as Sweden does. From the elite point of view, what really distinguishes Sweden from other systems is a peculiar combination of social harmony within a dense organizational field—a combination sometimes referred to as "organization Sweden."[2]

We have already pointed out, in Chapter 2 above, that senior Swedish officials typically belong to several organizations. It can hardly be surprising, therefore, that members of this elite imagine society to be composed of a multitude of competing interest groups, or that public policy is seen to be largely a product of interaction between various groups and the government. A perceived absence of a single dominating group—recall the "power" images reviewed in Chapter 5—is also understandable for a group of individuals who are close enough to decision-making to observe interest-group influence. From the elite point of view, Sweden is something of a pluralist paradise, where every interest has an organization, every organization has a say, and every say has a policy impact.[3]

The striking characteristic of this dense network of energetic organizations is that interactions between them are rarely perceived as challenges to fundamental interests. Disagreements occur, of course, but less often than one might expect, and when they do a satisfactory resolution is typically found. This view of a rather benign social environment emerges clearly from an extended series of questions about the nature of causes of conflict. At the outset, respondents were asked whether they perceived conflict or consensus to be more typical of social relations in general. Slightly more than a third of these officials believe conflict to be typical in social relations (Table 6.1), as compared to nearly 43 percent who believe that consensus is more characteristic of intergroup relations. This does not seem a very large majority for a consensus view, but a closer examination of the meanings attached to "conflict" makes clear that the activities referred to assume an underlying consensus. Only a third of those who discussed conflict used the phrase "class conflict" and, when even these responses are analyzed more closely, "class" very quickly turns into "group": more than 55 percent of those using the term "class" referred to disputes between business

Table 6.1. Perception and Evaluation of Conflict

	%
Consensus is Typical	41.6 (127)
Neither	22.3 (110)
Conflict is Typical	36.1 (110)
	100.0 (305)

and labor organizations; fewer than 20 percent thought of "class" in terms of rich versus poor, workers versus capitalists, or other more loaded terms. Indeed, most (62%) of those who discussed conflict specifically were in fact thinking about non-electoral disagreements between interest groups or personal disagreements between ambitious politicians. Overall, elite views of conflict appear to have all but eliminated the concept of class or other "fundamental" opposition and replaced it with far less threatening meanings that emphasize personal disagreement or the simple exchange of different ideas. It is therefore easy enough to accept the conclusion of one respondent (#136) who referred to group differences as "shadows, nothing more," and went on to suggest that, "Apart from the tiny extremist groups, which of course you always have and we had during the thirties when the Nazis and other such were around, basic differences of interest cannot be found . . . At bottom, everyone in Swedish society has common interests."

These perspectives help to explain why so few among the officials we interviewed (14.4%) believed that conflict was bad, unhealthy and dangerous. Defined as disagreement or an exchange of viewpoints among individuals or group representatives, "conflict" is bound to seem useful. The utility of conflict is expressed in a variety of ways, but primarily as a mechanism for generating new ideas and solutions to problems. Most (64.3%) of those who discussed the virtues of conflict suggested improved problem-solving as the chief benefit, including one (#113) who thought it necessary to ". . . have a war now and then in order to clear the air." For him, inter-group conflicts were events to be viewed positively as social cleansing mechanisms. Another (#211) argued that "It is absolutely essential that there be different points of view and that these different views be debated. Otherwise," he asserted, "there would be no change." A third administrator defined the connection between conflict and the typically Swedish mode of problem-solving: "I can't say that all conflicts are necessarily healthy, but if it is the case that there are opposing interests on some question, with different groups in opposition, then I think it is important that these different interests be spelled out. They should not be covered over and treated as though they didn't exist. In this sense conflicts are useful because they can clarify. I mean that you can clarify a point of departure by clarifying different values. Then you can more readily move toward a solution, most often through compromises."

This benign view of conflict and its consequences is accompanied by a widely-shared perception that more fundamental kinds of disagreements have been declining. Toward the close of our discussions of conflict we asked each official whether he or she believed there "were greater cleavages in Swedish society today than there were fifteen or twenty years ago," and whether he or she thought the current situation was positive or negative. By using a word—"motsättningar"—that connotes antagonism as well as opposition, we hoped in this later question to avoid responses based on the benign view of conflict noted above. Table 6.2 displays responses to these two questions. As we can see, the vast majority of those responding believe that the kind of fundamental hostility and opposition that characterized the "old" Sweden have been done away with, to the considerable benefit of the current generation of Swedes.[4] This distribution of responses is especially interesting since a great many of our interviews took place during and after a much-publicized confrontation between the police and various citizens' groups in downtown Stockholm. One might have anticipated, perhaps, that the obvious danger to public order created by a large gathering of sometimes unruly individuals might have caused a larger number of respondents to assert that cleavages had increased. Some obviously were affected in this way, but the more common response, reflected in the figures displayed in Table 6.2, was to offer a more reflective answer, one that considered the difference between that demonstration and other kinds of disputes that characterized the old society. "Personally," one official said, "I find the conflicts in today's society to be tedious, regrettable and a little frightening. But viewed in the broader perspective of our own historical development, you have to recognize that conflicts are often useful in moving society forward" (#308). In the typical perspective, Sweden had passed through the era of fundamental class or group contradictions, into a period of what might be called "progressive conflict."

Table 6.2. Perspectives on Social Cleavage

	%			%	
More Conflict Now	22.5	(65)	Current Situation Good	65.8	(144)
Same as Before	14.2	(41)	No Opinion	13.7	(30)
Less Conflict Now	63.3	(183)	Current Situation Bad	20.5	(45)
	100.0	(289)		100.0	(219)

Disputes can be very difficult, but having them is a very useful way to advance the general interests shared by all Swedes.

PLACID INSTITUTIONS

Congenial perspectives on the structure and inter-relationships between groups in society support equally comfortable images of central political institutions. Major political parties, for example (see Table 6.3), are perceived to have been drifting toward one another for the past two decades. Barely one of every ten among these respondents believes that there are significant differences between the parties now—they are, to repeat an image, nothing more than shades of the same color.[5] To be sure, most administrators recognize continuing differences in ideology that separate the "socialistic" parties from the non-socialists: "The dividing line comes at the socialistic proposition that society as a whole should do things and can do things best, while others maintain that human beings as private persons—and above all as companies—can do certain things best. Whether one side or the other shall be given these responsibilities is the decisive difference [between parties]" (#84). It is precisely these kinds of ideological differences that characterize responses from those who believe that "major" differences exist. Most respondents, however, find it increasingly difficult to tell the parties apart, even at the extremes. The official just quoted, for example, notes that the Left Communist Party (VPK), the smallest and most radical party represented in Parliament, has abandoned its former "commitment to the East" and thus appears more like a national party of reform. On the other extreme, the recent metamorphosis of the "conservative" party into the Moderate Party, symbolizing its acceptance of virtually all major reforms of recent years, places even that party of big business well inside the prevailing centrist consensus. Most respon-

Table 6.3. Party Change and Party Differences

During Past 15-20 Years Party Differences Have			Party Differences Now Are		
%			%		
Increased	7.8	(24)	Major or Important	12.8	(39)
No Change	14.7	(45)	Some Differences	36.7	(112)
Decreased	77.5	(238)	Few or None	50.5	(154)
	100.0	(307)		100.0	(305)

dents (62.2%), in fact, believe that the political parties exaggerate social differences in order to drum up electoral support.

For a few, the lack of significant differences between parties is altogether unfortunate. Consider the following argument which, in retrospect, seems to have been prophetic:

> The only real party we have now in this country, with the developments that have taken place, is the Social Democratic Party, and the one thing you can say about them is that it is not good to have sat in such a dominant position for such a long time, so that you get no opportunity to renew yourself. But prestige and other similar considerations dictate that you stay in power, mislead the people, and so on. It would be good for politics in general if we got a breathing pause every so often so that, without having it hurt so much or taking away too much prestige, you could clean out the leadership, bring in some young people and so on. Those other parties probably have been destroyed from having sat in opposition for so long . . . There is very seldom a useful idea to be found among them. That is unfortunate, because I think it would be helpful to have, say every ten years or so, a change in governments— not too often, but at least once in a while to give everyone a chance to rethink things like political programs. But I can't see any real possibilities for such changes (#132).

This view, we should point out, was the expression of an individual whose union had been "locked out" by the government during the course of the 1971 labor dispute—a circumstance that surely explains his evident hostility toward the Social Democrats as well as his misplaced (as we now know) hopelessness about change. Officials with more sympathy for the Social Democratic cause were more likely to perceive considerable differences between the parties. "Everyone knows there are differences between the parties," said one Division Chief who, like his grandfather and father, was a convinced Social Democrat, "and some of those differences are quite large. We have all experienced the very heated and intensive recent arguments, including some very serious accusations, regarding what we think we can afford and what we think we can't afford. Whether we should spend two billion or four billion in the present situation seems to me to be a really essential difference between the parties" (#327). These perceptions of no differences or major differences may be interesting, but they represent small minorities, at the extremes. For most of our respondents, the political parties were seen, as one respondent put it, to be "more and more alike" (#136).

Political parties are not, of course, the only institutions of significance in Swedish society, nor are they necessarily the most salient institutions for senior civil servants. If, as we have seen, senior administrators perceive Swedish society in terms of competing groups, it is important to know *what* groups are viewed as significant, particularly in areas that affect the work of government. To develop an estimate of institutional or group influence, we handed each official a card on which we listed a number of different institutions and asked him or her to indicate how much influence each group had over policy in the areas that had been discussed in the interview. The results displayed in Table 6.4 provide an interesting context in which to interpret earlier perceptions of pluralism and party dominance. It appears from this inquiry, for example, that the perception of the Social Democrat Party as the only meaningful political party (at least in 1971) was not so far-fetched after all. All of the parties may have come together in the center of the political spectrum, according to senior administrators, but only the Social Democrats are regarded as influential, while fewer than 5 percent see the opposition parties as powerful institutions. But neither the Social Democrats nor their close ally, the Central Labor Organization (LO), both of whom are viewed as very influential by roughly two-thirds of these officials, match the perceived power of the Cabinet, which outdistances other institutions by a clear and considerable margin. Ratings for each of these three dominant institutions are distinguished not solely by the proportion who think they are "very" influential, but also by the virtual absence of anyone who believes that they have "little or no" influence at all. At the top, cabinet-labor-party structures an obviously dominant triumvirate.

Not quite half of these officials view Parliament as very influential. Since most of the work done by the national legislature is initiated, defined and controlled by the Cabinet, which is in turn controlled by the governing party, this proportion seems, if anything, too high. That so many view Parliament as influential

Table 6.4. Administrator Views of Swedish Power Structure

Institution	Degree of Influence, %			
	Very	Fairly	Little	N
Cabinet	87.3	12.7	0	308
LO	67.6	30.7	1.6	306
Social Democrats	65.1	32.9	2.0	304
Parliament	47.7	32.9	2.0	308
Mass Media	45.0	43.0	12.0	298
Local Government	35.1	53.8	11.1	305
Private Enterprise	13.5	54.8	31.7	303
Banks, Insurance Companies	12.9	47.8	39.2	301
Administrative Boards	7.6	63.0	29.4	303
White Collar Unions	5.9	53.6	40.5	304
Opposition Parties	4.6	41.8	53.6	304

despite what appears to be a purely formal role may be due to the important work done by individual members, both in parliamentary committees and in the various investigative commissions that prepare the political and intellectual foundations of major policies.[6] Neither committees nor individual legislators are as important as they might be in, for example, the United States Congress, but committee charmen are significant figures nonetheless, while individual *Riksdagsmen* often are powerful local politicians as well as national legislators and thus speak with the added weight of regional interest.[7] This powerfully *local* orientation of the national Parliament may well be a major reason why so many among our respondents (35.1%) believe local government to be very influential. The limited proportion (7.6%) who believe administrative agencies of the national administration to be very important must, on the other hand, be seen partly as reluctance to over-rate themselves. These agencies command vast personal and financial resources that, as portions of an expanding public sector, have had major impacts on Swedish society, whether or not the administrators who lead them are willing to admit to that fact.

A final conclusion of interest that emerges from the data in Table 6.4 is the limited influence attributed to private-sector organizations. Many respondents believe the mass media to be influential, but exceedingly few regard industry (13.5%) or banks and insurance companies (12.9%) as powerful. In part, of course, these estimates arise from the natural tendency of administrators, when asked to discuss important national problems, to focus on issues for which they have some direct responsibility. When we later ask for influence estimates on the kinds of problems discussed earlier in the interview, it is not surprising that private sector organizations are perceived as without a great deal of influence. On the other hand, the responsibilities discussed were often in areas—taxation, economic regulation, welfare—that are typically the focus of much private-sector concern in other systems, which suggests that there is a base of reality to support these images of public policy arising from a predominantly *governmental* elite, assisted by the nation's major labor organization. So long as we remember that all important policy initiatives in Sweden, including economic policy, arise typically from consultation with all affected parties, the perspectives summarized in Table 6.4 do not seem unreasonable.

How appropriate, we wondered, was this pluralist, increasingly homogeneous and government-dominated power structure to existing social conditions in Sweden? By 1971, when these interviews were conducted, both Europe and the United States had experienced several years of turbulent political unrest, characterized by frequently-violent street demonstrations and well-publicized demands that governments do what the demonstrators desired. Sweden itself had experienced an increasing number of violent street demonstrations, usually aimed at American foreign policy, as well as a surprising number of wildcat strikes in

1969–70, including one that took place in a government-owned and operated mine.[8] Moreover, we began our interviewing just weeks after a bitter disagreement between civil servants and the government had been settled. Finally, many of our interviews were in fact conducted during and just after a fourteen-day confrontation between citizens and the government in downtown Stockholm.[9] We were therefore pleased that we had decided, for other reasons, to ask each official not only about his or her view of social influence, but also his or her opinion about whether the structure of influence was "as it should be, or should it be changed?" Surely the turbulence of the late 1960's and early 1970's would have altered preferences, if not conceptions, about social power.

Among Swedish administrators, however, this expectation turned out to be quite wrong. More than a third of these officials (37.6%) were so satisfied with the power system they had just described that they could think of no changes to recommend. Another 46.9 percent were basically satisfied but willing to suggest a few minor changes. Among the few (15.5%) who thought it desirable to make "significant" changes, only one believed that many such changes were necessary; the remainder felt only that "some" such changes were desirable. A somewhat more specific insight into elite satisfaction with existing influence patterns is provided in Table 6.5 which summarizes the magnitude and direction of the net change desired for each of the eleven institutions referred to in the previous table. By "net" change desired we refer to the difference between those who indicated that a given institution should have "more" power and those who said it should have "less." The direction is given by the sign, but in interpreting these

Table 6.5. Changes in Power Desired by a Satisfied Elite

Institution	should have	Percent	
		More Power	Less Power
Parliament		+14.0	
Opposition Parties		+13.3	
White Collar Unions		+ 3.7	
Cabinet		+ 1.7	
Local Governments		+ .3	
Mass Media			−10.2
LO			− 7.5
Social Democrats			− 6.8
Private Industry			− 4.4
Banks, Insurance Companies			− 4.1
Administrative Boards			− 2.1

numbers it is important to remember that their magnitude is heavily influenced by the overwhelming proportion of respondents who indicated preferences for each institution having the "same" degree of influence it now has, rather than an increase or decrease — indeed, the mean proportion of respondents who chose the "same" alternative for these institutions was 91.6 percent. Thus the generally small percentages accurately reflect the central fact about senior administrators: they overwhelmingly accept the existing power system and reject major changes in it. There is some sentiment for increasing the influence of Parliament and the opposition parties, but these views are not widely-shared. There is noticeable sentiment for decreasing the influence of the media, and some feeling that the power of both the LO and the Social Democrats ought to be decreased, but the latter sentiments appear too weak to be judged very significant. On the whole, senior Swedish administrators can only be regarded, from this evidence, as unusually content with the system of social power, with individual components of that system, and with their own position within the system components.

ELMS AND POLITICAL ATTITUDES

To report such extraordinary levels of institutional satisfaction against a background of environmental turbulence may suggest either a lack of awareness or a lack of concern on the part of senior civil servants. Neither suggestion is accurate. As noted earlier, many of these interviews took place during and just after a much-publicized confrontation between governmental authorities and various groups of Stockholm-area citizens. The confrontation centered ostensibly on the city's decision to cut down the last remaining stand of elm trees in a major and centrally-located downtown park, *Kungsträgården*, in order to build an entrance to a new subway station. The decision to fell the trees had in fact been made months earlier, after the usual round of reviews by three different City Council committees and the City Council itself. Indeed, the issue is interesting precisely because, as I have noted elsewhere, it was ". . . a classic example of how the game was supposed to be played. The process had taken a great deal of time, several different city decision-making bodies had been involved, a variety of organized interests were represented on those bodies, appeals were considered all the way up to the Prime Minister himself, and a great effort was made to 'rationalize' the decision in terms of a larger plan for expanding the metropolitan subway network to accommodate citizens and institutions (such as the University of Stockholm) in need of transit service."[10] Nevertheless, when it was announced that workmen would begin setting up equipment to cut down the trees, large (therefore organized) crowds began to gather under the trees, hammocks were strung in the trees and occupied by young men and women who refused to leave, and several thousand people decided to camp out in the park to prevent the work from getting under way. Observing this gathering, gangs of motorcycle toughs descended on *Kungsträgården* and were driven off by hastily-mustered police only after a series of acts of violence.[11] As a result of this activity, city authorities at first postponed, and later cancelled, their decision to fell the trees. The entrance to the new subway station has since been located elsewhere.

Because this was as much a media event as a real confrontation, it caused a great deal of consternation even among Swedes who did not live in Stockholm or who knew little about either the park or the issue. For the senior civil servants we interviewed, the issue was especially salient, partly because most of them live in or around Stockholm, partly because they could imagine themselves in such a situation, and partly because we encouraged them to think about its significance by asking two questions in connection with our exploration of power perceptions. The first question focused exactly on citizen participation: whether a respondent thought more of it was desirable, what kind of participation was desirable, and why. We then asked whether the respondent felt that "socially dangerous" methods were often used by action groups and if so, what society should do about the use of such methods. Each of these questions, in turn, was surrounded by a series of follow-on or probe questions, so that we were able to develop a well-rounded view of elite perceptions. Responses to these questions enable us to conclude that elite administrators were extremely troubled by the events in *Kungsträgården,* that they are *not* generally in favor of increased citizen participation, and that their hostility to increased citizen participation may well have become more intense because of a breakdown in respect for democratic rules of the game perceived to have taken place under a stand of trees in downtown Stockholm. All of these factors contributed, we think, to their affirmation of the virtues of the established order. Let us turn now to the evidence for these propositions.

On first glance, these officials appear favorable toward the notion of increased citizen involvement: more than half (57.1%) say "yes" when asked whether they believe "increasing citizen participation" would be desirable in Sweden. Analysis of what they mean by participation, however, makes clear that senior administrators prefer citizens to act in channels that already exist rather than attempt to expand their own direct involvement—indeed, only seven individuals among our respondents favor any form of *direct* citizen involvement. A few (52) suggest that it would be helpful if citizens "paid more attention" to governmental affairs, some (58) believe that greater efforts by citizens to make their views known to Parliament and government leaders would be helpful, and a third group (35) proposes increased involvement in political parties or local governments. Apart from their general weakness, these sentiments reflect the difficulty senior administrators had in thinking specifically about the problem: barely half (54%) could offer a specific proposal for increasing participation. More than three-quarters of the respondents (76.2%), on the other hand, could offer specific reasons why an increase in participation might be dangerous. It is precisely these perceptions of potential danger from increased participation that appear to have been heightened by the battle of the elms.

The reason for heightened concern, of course, was the violence associated with the elms dispute. As we have seen, these officials generally believe conflict to be healthy so long as it is expressed in the forms of verbal argumentation, or even opposing public demonstrations. When conflict becomes violent, however, it generates great consternation among elite administrators, both because of harm done to individuals and because of the difficulty of shaping a governmental response in keeping with Swedish traditions. Consider the following response to the question of whether socially dangerous actions were being used and if so, what might be done to deal with them:

That is of course a really complicated problem. We have a good example with those famous elms. There we had a political decision made according to fully legal procedures—I think everyone agrees on that. But it also was something that a certain group—and I say "certain" group because we don't know how many Stockholmers really supported these actions. I thought I saw something in the papers that reported a statement from the labor unions that was very critical of these actions, which suggests that it was not much of a majority that supported the demonstration, in any case not a majority of workers. But that this group should be permitted to agitate, demonstrate and express its dissatisfaction is totally self-evident, that really should not be hindered. Afterwards, I naturally became more doubtful when I saw how the demonstration developed, with efforts to use violence. I think, in any case, it was violence. I wasn't home when it happened but read about it in the papers. But I have the impression that the group tried, with physical opposition, to prevent implementation of this decision, which resulted in the police being called, and then all hell broke loose. And that is terrible, that this had to happen. I don't know how we'll be able to set things right again. What would have happened if the police hadn't been called in? Obviously, workers who were standing there with saws would have been forced to get out. They were forced away anyway, despite the police, which may indicate that the police weren't as effective as they usually are. It is really unfortunate, nevertheless, that society finds itself forced to use violence to cope with this kind of demonstration, and it is something we must be extremely careful about and preferably not use. I don't want to go so far as to say that society should be wholly passive and never act against demonstrations . . . but once you get started with nightsticks and such, things really come unglued. I must say I feel myself really divided about this and can't find any good solution. I know the answer, naturally, is that in this country citizens should participate and decide so that situations such as this don't arise. But then, if the question is 'shall all citizens participate?' it is quite possible, in precisely this concrete case, that there would have been a majority for the proposition that these poor trees should go. And then you have to ask yourself whether the group that started the whole thing would have yielded (#74).

Although this official agonized primarily about the use of force by public authorities, others were more inclined to worry about social conditions that seemed to them to increasingly require the use of force. One official, concerned about the breakdown of family authority in an increasingly urbanized society, recalled that he had in fact favored the purchase of a water cannon to control demonstrators when, years earlier, he had worked in local government. Now, as a national official, he continued to feel a need for stronger governmental response:

> If one reviews the different methods of expressing group opinions that developed during the 1960's—throwing eggs and tomatoes at ambassadors, the fight over the elms, and all that—I think it is quite clear, despite everything, that the authorities have perhaps been a bit too easy on groups that ignore the rules about what we used to call law and order. You can present your views in a convincing way without destroying law and order. There were, as I understood it, two groups of demonstrators down here in *Kungsträgården*. One was Alternative City, which put forth its views in a strong but orderly way, in order to wake up city authorities and get them to understand that there was a broad opinion here in Stockholm that had a different understanding about the elms. Then there was another group, I assume without any invitation from Alternative City, that hung around and engaged in direct destruction, a very different kind of activity. It must have been unusually difficult for the authorities to control these wilder adult thugs who were carrying on down there, who didn't really know why they were there in the first place, and who perhaps threatened order in another, more irritating way for those around them. How do you deal with them? When you see their way of demonstrating . . . I no longer believe in the water cannon, of course, but I used to think there was something to it . . . maybe . . . (#138).

For others, the question of dealing with violence was a less agonizing, more clear-cut problem:

> Let me put it this way—and now I will answer as a reactionary because I think like a reactionary on just this question, even though I would not want to be painted as one. You have to meet violence with a hard response because the society we have now is based on peaceful coexistence, and if anyone wants to take up extra-parliamentary methods for his own purposes, then we no longer have peaceful coexistence. The gangs and those elements that want to fool around with violence ought to take off and build their own society someplace, where they have room for all kinds of fights. Of course they will

come up against groups that have different ideas than they do and who are also interested in fighting. They can all get together well enough in that kind of place, where everyone thinks violence is fine, but I don't think it ought to happen where we have chosen to live together peacefully. These toughs, therefore, ought to be put out of the way, one way or another, as quickly as possible (#170).

These three individuals have different ideas about appropriate governmental response to violence and thus roughly reflect opinion differences among all respondents: slightly more than a third favor more communication and persuasion as the solution to violent actions, slightly less than a third favor stronger measures of control, and the rest can think of no solutions that differ from current procedures. The problem is clearly complicated, and the responses of these officials reflect that fact. Nevertheless, there is a common theme uniting many of these responses that may well have been brought closer to the surface of consciousness by the elms, namely, affirmation of the legitimacy of existing institutions and recognition of the virtues of established procedures. The virtues of the established order are often defined by comparison with other, less fortunate, systems, as in the following response to our question about the desirability of increased citizen participation in Sweden:

As an answer I will offer a comparison between the situation in Sweden and in other countries. It is in fact the case that Sweden for a long time has provided a very much greater public view of administration, that is, public administration, than any other country, so far as I know. In Sweden the publicity principle [guaranteeing public access to all government papers] has been established for a very long time. That principle is totally unknown in many other nations. We have to go no further than Denmark and Norway to see that the principle of publicity is not at all used in the same way that it is used here in Sweden. There are exceptions here of course, through use of the secrecy legislation to declare that some matter is not for public view. But these are exceptions that can only be justified for special reasons. Otherwise everything is public, even patent applications, which can be kept secret only for a short time. After that even they are public. That is one example of how far we have gone. For that reason I think the need to provide greater access to administration is not as real in Sweden as it is in many other countries, where the concept of public information is unrecognized. In principle I think there should be public access to governmental administration. It should be the way it is here in Sweden. That is my understanding. But it ought to be implemented in other countries — we have been the leaders in this area (#310).

Or, the established order is defended simply because it is there and already provides opportunities for influence:

> Don't we have the possibility already now? We have our local elections and
> our Parliament . . . We have employee representatives on our agency board
> and we have a laymen board and we have continuing contacts with our cus-
> tomers in our local offices. There are channels everywhere. What more should
> one do? (#134).

What these kinds of responses suggest, more than anything else, is a feeling for
the "special" quality of the Swedish polity, with its ancient traditions of democratic control, its carefully-crafted institutional structure, and its "advanced"
state when compared to other polities. Thus the "danger" in citizen participation
is not really perceived to be violence which, after all, remains uncommon among
the Swedes, however much violence under the elms was publicized. The more
significant danger, for elite administrators, is that this satisfying institutional
structure would be fundamentally altered by increased citizen activity.

Broadly speaking, Swedish administrators see three major categories of problems arising from additional citizen involvement. The first, and most commonly
mentioned, category may be termed "technocratic," or the danger of making
wrong decisions. Officials who hold this view often are employed in technological
agencies, where "right" decisions are easier to conceive; they often express
concern over a perceived trend toward greater complexity in the issues to be
resolved by public action, and they quite often doubt the capacity of ordinary
citizens to participate intelligently in such complex issues. Sometimes the technocratic response can be blunt. Should citizen participation be increased? "No.
You hear this 'power to the people' and other nonsense in some places, but the
people have power in this country and in many others . . . To drag in the grass
roots on every decision to build a house or cut down some elms just isn't right
. . . I also think it is a bit dangerous, with all due respect for the people . . . To
make a wise decision you have to know what you're doing and not allow yourself to be influenced by affect or temporary opinions; decisions therefore have
to be delegated to people who are trained and have the capacity to really consider all aspects of a problem" (#121).

Sometimes, the technocrat is more gentle. Is increased citizen participation
desirable?

> Well, naturally you can say that it is desirable in principle, but then you have
> to add that if a development in that direction should take place, it would
> demand so much from people that you wonder whether they could develop
> enough knowledge to be able to contribute anything essential to it. You
> know yourself that many questions are quite out of the ordinary — you don't
> have a solution for them right at your fingertips since you know too little
> about a certain area. You have to get to yourself in the pictures, really dig
> into it. Before you do that to get the general picture you really cannot con-
> tribute to a wide choice. Many of the questions dealt with by the country's

leaders are so complicated that a considerable knowledge increase would be required if we were to change in the direction of more citizen contributions (#211).

A second problem perceived by the elite is stagnation, or the danger of making no decision. Particularly in a system characterized by increasingly complex decisions on top of traditionally cumbersome procedures,[12] any increment of citizen action would be little more than an additional hindrance to effective governmental response. One official was persuaded it would be quite unwise to "complicate the apparatus through bringing citizens into all kinds of situations" (#113), while another argued that ". . . it would be more difficult and more burdensome to work in the direction of continued progress in society." He then explained that

> . . . the entire administrative apparatus and the social machinery in general would naturally be much more formless if all decisions had to reflect hundreds of opinions from different places, all of which had to be weighed together. That is one thing, the formlessness. The other is that such a system would also probably be unmanageable from another standpoint, because it would become even more difficult to choose a solution that could satisfy all groups. I believe, therefore, that despite many complaints because power is said to be concentrated in too few hands, most people believe that is the only practical possibility, if we are to move society forward. I think most people accept that. The important thing to them is to make sure that the right people have the power—that is where judgment comes in. It is generally dangerous to spread citizen influence around too much, not because people don't have opinions or that they don't have opportunities to express their opinions, but because it makes the process of collective decision-making even more difficult. It is very difficult to devise such mechanisms that function in a practical way (#138).

The third, and clearly most fundamental, difficulty is the political danger of having the wrong people in a position to make decisions. The problems of collective decision-making in a system so advanced and so changeable persuade many of these administrators that direct citizen involvement is a very poor idea. "I find it very hard," said one official, "to believe in any of the forms of direct democracy in a country such as this. In fact, I think that the only effective governing form that one can reasonably work with is representative democracy— although we can of course make it better" (#106). One of the perceived discomforts of a more direct form of democracy, alluded to in the above citation, is the loss of orderly procedures, the formlessness of it all: one official refers to the unhappiness of having "national debates on small issues" (#117), while another, clearly irritated at the idea, thought that mass participation could only result in making a "mish-mash of everything" (#134). To avoid disorganized chaos, orderly and well-understood procedures are perceived to be quite essential by the bulk of the Swedish administrative elite.

Although it would be easy enough to interpret this emphasis on order and regularity in authoritarian terms, the moral "bite" in this concept arises from the perception that the order developed very slowly and carefully over a period of several centuries to guarantee an equitable system of majority rule. To move toward direct citizen influence would, from the administrator point of view, be to run the risk of creating a non-democratic system of minority, rather than majority, government. One official expressed deep concern over what "a demagogue" might do in a system based only on citizen opinion (#74), while another could see nothing but risks because "I think it would be those who mouth-off the loudest, usually a very small group, who would get influence. In reality you would not get the kind of society most people want, but the kind of society amenable to those small groups who are able to make themselves heard. That is a very large risk" (#319). In this sense, "Order" is a protection against a potentially tyrannical minority as well as a means of ensuring the implementation of majority rule.

From this very Swedish point of view, then, emphasis on order and form springs from deeply-held sentiments that are more democratic than authoritarian, for they reflect an ingrained determination that society's rules should apply equally to all persons. Efforts to influence policy directly are thus efforts by small groups to gain what the majority does not have. If successful, such efforts are doubly unfair: groups achieve benefits for themselves that are not available to other citizens, and they do so by breaking rules that all other citizens follow. A fetish for following the rules, particularly if they are expressed as law, is an old Swedish stereotype, of course, as is Swedish unhappiness with success that appears to be unequally distributed (often covered in the phrase "Royal Swedish Envy"). Yet overtones of these stereotypes are unmistakable in our interviews:

> We really can't have it the way it used to be during the times of village meetings, when everyone participated. Now it is elected representatives who must decide. Whether you then want to increase citizen influence or not is naturally difficult to say. You have a local council here of 100 people, which means that their decisions don't always agree with your preferences. But in general the division we have seems to me to be right. The people who are governing are selected through democratic procedures and if they have made a decision, you can't just rip it up. On the other hand, expressions of opinion can be very useful in generating an issue, bring it to discussion, and perhaps influencing its resolution in the right way. But I don't think we should allow any "governing," so to say, outside of the forms we have. If they are not good enough, then the forms can be changed. We have heard some political talk about not making decisions here in Stockholm without consulting with

these neighborhood associations. That's fine—you should always consult as widely as possible. But you cannot, in my opinion, take decision-making authority away from the agencies we have that generally operate according to the rules . . .

If an authorized public agency in a democratic system, has made a decision, then the decision has to be carried out. There have to be exceptional reasons to give way before an opinion whose strength and breadth you don't know. Just because a group of who-knows-how-many people creates an action group and says "We don't want this and will you kindly change that" is no reason to change. If you have a properly-made decision you have to stand fast with it— next time you can elect somebody else to fill those positions if you don't like the decision. I personally don't like the way Stockholm is being developed at all, for example, razing buildings everywhere and building new highways and such. But it would never occur to me to try to prevent the implementation of one of those decisions. If I want to change I can do that by voting for people who I hope would have the same opinions I do (#119).

Nothing is dangerous to society if it is kept within the rules of the game that, so to speak, are provided by legislation. Anybody can go to it to try to build support for some opinion, which is fully correct and always has been fully correct. When people go outside of society's rules of the game, however, then I think you cannot permit it. I think this business about the elms is a dangerous road. I believe it is really dangerous to allow certain action groups to have their way because you don't really know how many people they have behind them. One can easily imagine that these loud shouters are not at all reflective of any broad-based opinion and I am definitely opposed to forcing people to do things or not do things in the way that has been followed over there. If we have rules for the way society is to be governed, we should follow them. Otherwise we should change them (#107).

Senior civil servants in Sweden are thus in favor of increased citizen involvement "in principle," so long as involvement occurs within the framework of the existing system of representative democracy. They are clearly opposed to direct democracy, an impractical and dangerous scheme in their view, and tend to be suspicious of citizen or neighborhood action groups that appear to support "direct" participation by citizens in the affairs of governmental institutions.[13] They are especially suspicious if such groups act in ways that contribute to any breakdown in the social prohibition against acts of violence. Hostility to violence in any form is to a considerable extent grounded in a strong commitment to "play by the rules" as they exist at any given time, rather than attempting to place oneself above others by breaking the rules. The rule-following commitment is in turn related to deeply-ingrained preferences for orderly procedures, for routine, for structured—and therefore predictable—ways of doing things. Only through strict adherence to established forms and rules, according to these administrators, can society be protected against minorities seeking to impose their preferences on the majority; order is therefore seen as a necessary precondition for the preservation of Swedish democracy, whatever it may signify in other systems.

FUNCTION AND CONSCIOUSNESS

These various preferences, opinions and beliefs are obviously self-serving, in the sense that their social consequence is to preserve elite status. At the conscious level, however, they are rationalized in terms of high principle: democracy, equity and Swedish "tradition." There can be no surprise in this, of course, since members of elite groups typically justify their claim to high office with acceptable symbolic rationalizations. Nevertheless, the stress on "democratic order" by an elite that we have shown to be tiny, homogeneous and generally unfriendly to most forms of direct citizen participation seems sufficiently striking to invite further exploration. Although the kinds of data we have will not permit definitive statements about causes, we can combine the data in a number of ways in order to show relationships that may be interesting.

Let us recall, for purposes of this analysis, the central ideas that structure elite thinking about socio-political institutions. One set of ideas has to do with evaluations of conflict—whether officials think conflict is good or bad; another group of ideas clearly revolves around hostility toward, or acceptance of, greater citizen participation; still a third important set of notions focuses on the extent to which these respondents desire, and feel themselves obligated to work for, major changes in Swedish society. Because we have several indicators that can be used to measure these ideas, we can construct multiple-item indices for each set of core ideas and use these indices to describe their distribution among our respondents. In Table 6.6 we list the questions, scoring conventions and inter-item correlations for each of three indices, labelled Fear of Conflict, Establishment Satisfaction, and Mobilizing Change (FCI, ESE and MCI). Several items are used in constructing each index, in order to avoid the potentially misleading effects of unusually powerful or weak single items. Reasonably strong inter-item correlation among items used in each index suggests that each of the core idea groups is coherent. By calculating a mean score on each index for each respondent and then grouping individuals in different ways, we may be able to observe useful relationships. Note, however, that our interest at this point is only in the relationships that may emerge. That is, we already know that the great bulk of our respondents have very little fear of conflict, are satisfied with the present "establishment," and have very little interest in promoting change. What we now seek to examine is whether there are degrees of difference in these perspectives among different sub-groups within this elite.[14]

Table 6.6. Core Idea Indices

I Fear of Conflict Index	II Establishment Satisfaction Index	III Mobilizing Change Index
Is conflict healthy or sick?	To what degree does R favor increased citizen participation, yes–no.	How much future change is desired? (Revolutionary to None)
Does R distinguish between actual and meritable conflict?	Is R enthusiastic or not enthusiastic about citizen participation?	To what extent does R view his role as fighting for a cause?
Is conflict good or bad?	What is citizen's proper role, from voting to direct influence?	Does R use a unified conceptual scheme in discussing politics?
Is conflict necessary or unnecessary?	Does R accept or reject existing social order?	
min score = 4 max = 20	min score = 4 max = 25	min score = 3 max = 17
Mean Inter-Hem Correlation = .520	Mean Inter-Hem Correlation = .539	Mean Inter-Hem Correlation = .306

Among the principles that might be used to classify individuals for more detailed examination, agency and position seem likely to generate useful insights. We know that agency activities differ, and it seems reasonable to expect these differences to be related to perceptions of conflict and change. On the whole, this expectation is supported by our data—but only slightly. Whether or not an official is employed in a ministry, an administrative board or a public authority makes some difference in his evaluation of conflict: ministry people are more likely to believe that conflict is good and healthy than are other employees, but this relationship is not very powerful (eta = .148). Ministry officials are more likely than others to favor increased citizen participation, but again, this relationship is not very powerful (eta = .217). The strongest agency impact is on scores for the Mobilizing Change Index. Although we know that very few among these officials favor major change, those who do are more likely to be found in ministries or administrative boards than in public authorities (eta = .235). Despite the general weakness of these relationships, they seem consistent with expectations derived from knowledge of what these agencies do.

A more detailed view of what these general relationships mean can be obtained by examining index scores by position, as well as agency. In Table 6.7

Table 6.7. Index Scores, By Position

	FCI		ESI		MCI	
Under-Secretaries	7.77	(9)	11.77	(13)	11.58	(12)
Directors General	8.64	(44)	13.71	(44)	10.93	(44)
Prime Minister's Staff	8.64	(22)	13.55	(20)	10.96	(24)
Division Chief	9.32	(22)	15.94	(18)	11.82	(22)
Supervising Engineer	10.03	(32)	13.75	(32)	11.43	(35)
Bureau Chief	10.10	(42)	13.07	(42)	11.28	(46)
Grand Means	9.48		13.49		11.36	

we show mean index scores for six important groups of officials, compared to the grand mean for each index. Scores on the Fear of Conflict Index are generally low (recall that the maximum possible score is 20, compared to a grand mean of 9.48), reflecting the generally favorable view of conflict discussed above. Within this generally favorable group, however, those who are *least* fearful of conflict are the Under-Secretaries, followed by Directors General and officials from the Prime Minister's Office (*Kansli*). Officials in less central, more purely "administrative" positions—Division and Bureau Chief, Supervising Engineer—tend to be more fearful of conflict. Under-Secretaries also tend to be considerably less committed to establishment procedures and favorable toward more citizen participation than other groups, including Directors General and officials from the Prime Minister's staff, both of which groups are above the grand mean score for establishment satisfaction. Note, however, that it is precisely the latter two groups, which tend toward hostility toward greater citizen participation, which also show the most change-oriented (i.e., lowest) scores on the Mobilizing Change Index. Directors General, who circulate freely at the central level, and the central government's executive staff, who are primarily engaged in planning, evaluation and budgeting, are thus more inclined than other officials to find conflict useful, more inclined to favor change, but not more inclined to favor the procedural-institutional changes implied by greater citizen participation.

Put another way, most of these officials, regardless of how much change they want or how they evaluate conflict, seem deeply committed to the desirability of following established rules of political procedure. For these very Swedish public servants, democracy implies order and careful attention to existing rules of procedure, but order does *not* imply resistance to change. On the contrary, the implication of these sentiments is that change of the kind that might be acceptable in the Swedish context can only be achieved through orderly procedures, widely accepted and observed. In Swedish elite eyes, democracy, order and social change are fully compatible. The country is Sweden, after all, and they are Swedes.

EQUALITY YES, MORE EQUALITY NO!

These wary opinions regarding increased citizen participation, taken together with earlier evidence of overwhelming satisfaction with other political institutions, make clear that the higher reaches of the Swedish civil service are no breeding ground for radical changes in institutional relations. Senior administrators by and large believe the system to be well-enough organized and, as the discussion of citizen participation demonstrates, they believe that most citizens agree with them. This reluctance to support institutional change can be explored from another, deeper, perspective that also implies something about elite views of popular Swedish attitudes. The vehicle for such an exploration is a series of questions put to administrators regarding several policy issues under debate in Sweden in early 1971, of which the most interesting for our purpose was the question of income equality. By 1971, the so-called "incomes" policy of the Social Democratic government, aimed at reducing the differences between white-collar and blue-collar incomes, had been in effect for several years and *"ökad jämlikhet"* — increased equality — had become a Social Democratic slogan.[15] Implementation of the policy by permitting higher percentage increases for blue-collar workers had created considerable resentment among many white-collar professionals including, as we have seen, a number of government executives. Increased equality nevertheless was official government policy, to be enforced by public officials whether or not they agreed with it. The evident tension between duty and perceived self-interest among many officials provided an excellent opportunity to probe elite views of citizen motivations.

At the outset we wanted to be clear about the context in which officials thought about this issue and therefore asked an obvious question: "One of the most common phrases in today's political debate is 'equality.' Do you think that any social equalization has taken place in this country during the past fifteen to twenty years?" As expected, only one among the 305 officials who answered this question said "no," although eight more argued that a trend toward greater equality in social life was more apparent than real. All of the remaining respondents — really, the entire sample — believed that equalization had taken place, a perception that seems quite unchallengeable with any known evidence, although the extent of *income* equalization in recent years has been questioned in a much-publicized study by the Commission on Low Income Earners. The significance of this view is less its unanimous acceptance, however, than its "fit" with other views, noted earlier. By very large proportions, these officials believe that fundamental social cleavages have been reduced in Sweden, that political parties have drifted toward one another in the middle of the political spectrum, and that social equalization has become a powerful trend in Swedish life. From the perspective of nineteenth or early-twentieth-century political ideologies, certainly, it appears that Sweden had achieved most of what reformers had always desired—at least from the point of view of senior administrators. Surely one might expect that a group holding such views would have difficulty accepting the proposition that more reform was needed.

Remarkably enough, however, nearly 60 percent of these officials appear to favor even more levelling of incomes. When we asked "What is your position on increased income-levelling here in this country? Are you for the most part positive or negative?" some 59.5 percent gave answers that supported greater equalization, including four who suggested complete income equality and fifty-five others who supported "considerably more" equalization than had already occurred. At the other extreme, only ten thought that equalization had gone "too far," and another twenty-nine felt that it had come far enough. But even if centrist, pro-con opinions are included with these more explicitly negative positions, the proportion who indicate generally negative sentiments toward stepping up the pace of income equalization fails to reach 40 percent. The results seem paradoxical: a group whose members generally feel that cleavages have been reduced and equality increased nevertheless appears to want to "rev up" the pace of change even more. How should we interpret this apparent paradox?

One interpretation is that the data have been misinterpreted. Most (122) of the responses judged to be favorable to greater equality fall into a category coded "yes, some," and it is easy enough to imagine that such responses reflect no great commitment to equality, but rather a convenient and acceptable response that moves the interview from one subject to another. Another interpretation might well be that there is no paradox at all. These officials really do want to see a more equitable distribution of social rewards and simply feel that the obvious progress that has been made is not enough. Other interpretations are possible but these two, which focus on the validity of the data, are enough to motivate a closer examination of the meanings attached to these responses.

All respondents were asked to indicate the grounds on which income differences could be justified, in their view, regardless of the position taken on the desirability of more equalization. The results are summarized in Table 6.8 which reports the four most-mentioned categories of justification, using first, second and third responses. The total impression created by these figures is that senior civil servants continue to believe in the motivational power of income differences within a market environment. Although equality may be a generous and popular ideal, senior administrators do not believe that all persons contribute equally to work. Some do more, some do it longer and some do it better—and if they do

Table 6.8. Why Incomes Should be Different

	Mentions				%
	1st	2nd	3rd		
Contribution to Work	52	74	25	151	33
Provides Incentive	89	28	11	128	28
Heavier Responsibility	43	45	11	99	21
Reflect Market Mechanism	54	19	10	83	18
				461	100

their income should reflect that "unequal" contribution. In fact, these officials also believe that one way of generating effort is precisely to pay more in order to encourage greater effort, or assumption of greater responsibility. Those with more talent, who can command higher salaries on the market, should also receive more in recognition of their greater market power, whether they work in private or public sector organizations. Note that these responses are made to a question about reasons for different incomes *in general,* not solely in governmental employment, and thus may be said to reflect attitudes about the labor market as a whole. Those attitudes provide a strong indication that our second interpretation, above, was inadequate. When asked, senior administrators are willing to say things about more income equality that sound favorable, but when pressed, they make clear that capacity, responsibility and old-fashioned hard work continue to justify higher incomes. We can appreciate the power of these "old fashioned" sentiments by observing their expression:

> [An Administrative Director] I think that what must continue to be decisive in wage-setting policy is performance — we must never get away from that. I believe that we will have done society an injustice if we use the notion of equality to mean that everyone should have the same income regardless of what they produce. In my view, this equality is very difficult to deal with. I think what you can do is put in some kind of equity requirement so that those who can do something will be rewarded, economically, for it (#135).

> [A Supervisory Engineer] If I look at this from the background of my own work I would have to say that to try to achieve a powerful equalization is a questionable idea. Despite everything there are — whether one thinks there should be or not — there are people who want to put a great deal of effort into their work often spurred by the thought that there is some payoff, that they will get something for it. You work for your extras in a sense. Now we have to be very concerned about these incentives. If we were to say that some were less essential than others, or that those who have such incentives should be treated the same as those who don't, then we would without any discussion

at all arrive at a position of inferiority with regard to other nations, and that we cannot accept. I do not accept this line in principle (#210).

[A Director General] No, there is no possibility of establishing the equal income idea, because it would not stimulate ambition and future progress. So it must come to a certain boundary: it must pay for good people to really work and make their inputs.

But if you would differentiate incomes, what would be the criteria?

Here you have to talk in rather loose terms. I would say quality of work and responsibility . . . quality and responsibility; that must be decisive. It might be that you'd have to change present methods and measure, for example, the division of responsibility. What is or isn't responsibility? Or more or less responsibility? But these are the two primary things (#107).

Among these officials, income differences are often justified with reference to the international market no less than the national economy. Sweden's heavy (50%) reliance on exports in generating national product means that Swedish goods must be competitive, which in turn means that incomes should respond to those activities and jobs that help Sweden compete in foreign markets. But it is the national system and individuals within it that elite administrators refer to most of all, and they clearly believe they are expressing views shared by most Swedes when they justify income differences.

"There are economic reasons for increased equality, nothing more, and I doubt anyone can change that," said a Division Chief. "All people strive for an improved economic situation, a better relative standard of living. This demand for a better standard would have to be replaced by some other vision in order for people to accept economic quality. But I can't for the life of me imagine what we in Sweden would find as a surrogate for this striving. It would have to be something of a religious or idealistic interest, which might come some time, but I don't see it for the present time . . . I can't dream of how you could continue to have future progress with total income equality" (#315).

Most of the officials we interviewed, therefore, reject extreme visions of income equality, continue to believe that hard and good work should be rewarded and, judging as much from the tone of their comments as from what they say, are not much inclined to pursue major additional changes. The few who do think it desirable to make additional major changes tend to be the younger and more politically active people in the ministries. A good example is the following exchange between our interviewer and a ministerial Under-Secretary who is young, a Social Democrat, and something of a political strategist:

I sense that you are in some degree positive toward greater income equality, but how far would you go? Would you think of yourself as a supporter of the equal pay principle in some form?

No, I don't believe anything will be solved that way, because Sweden is not isolated. We have a nordic labor market, at least for the time being—we'll see how it goes with EEC. But you also have, of course, with a progressive tax system and through reducing side benefits, we can see to it that these major income differences are reduced. What you have to do is increase from the bottom, with large amounts, rather than decreasing at the top. If we don't solve the problem through an incomes policy we will have to take the legislative road, through tax policy and in that case, major needs-tested reforms, not least in the schools, children's allowances, pensions and the like (#139).

SUMMARY: THE RAZOR'S EDGE OF PROGRESS

In judging the significance of elite social perspectives, it is useful to ask what might have been different about these responses if the questions had been asked one or two years earlier or later. Images of power, conflict and institutional adequacy are bound to be influenced by current context to some extent; the trick is to know how to separate out the more fundamental from the less stable images. Without information gathered at different points in time, the trick is not easy to perform well, but with sufficient attention to other available evidence, it can be attempted. It is extremely difficult, for example, to dispute the validity of images characterizing Sweden as wealthy, privileged and generally harmonious, just as it is difficult to dispute the widely-shared belief that cleavage and conflict have declined as wealth has both increased and been spread around more evenly. Images of power are perhaps more questionable, since they are based, of necessity, on unevenly distributed information and even more varied criteria of significance. It is nevertheless clear that senior civil servants overwhelmingly agree with one another regarding institutional influence over public policy. It is also clear that their perceptions are very similar to the perceptions held by members of the Swedish Parliament. These shared perceptions may be inaccurate—although we doubt they are—but they are extraordinarily alike.

Had the question of income equalization been raised earlier, we suspect that the result would have been far more favorable to the concept. In 1971 income equalization was a live issue, an issue that had partly shaped the context of a lockout-strike in which many of our respondents had participated, and thus an issue on which experience had created more intense opinions. The issue, in short, was no longer one on which responses could be shaped by theoretical preferences: more equality, for many of our respondents, meant less money in the pay-check. Under these conditions, we think it quite understandable that support "in principle" would be qualified in a variety of ways. We also think it understandable that the pressure of actual, rather than theoretical, income loss might lead to a careful and more focused assessment of the grounds on which *any* income differential might be justified. Finally, the emergence of merit, responsibility, and willingness to work a little harder as criteria for wage differences seems to us totally consistent with Swedish work habits and opinions. So far as the available evidence can show, Swedes in general are competitive, they do generally strive to improve their year-to-year living standard, and they do expect to be compensated for the contributions they make.[16] Elite administrators know their fellow citizens.

The issue of citizen participation was probably more influenced by current controversy than any of the other issues we raised and the result again, in our view, was a more intense reconsideration of appropriate and inappropriate citizen actions, leading to a stronger affirmation of the virtues of the established system than might have occurred five years earlier, or later. The virtues affirmed, however, are not so much the advantages of an existing government or other institutions. What is most strongly affirmed is the desirability—indeed, the necessity—of orderly public procedures and rules that channel political participation into structured, thus predictable, patterns. Although elite emphasis on order as a prerequisite for democracy will doubtless seem hypocritically self-serving to some, in our judgment it represents a view honestly held, among individuals in a group that clearly reflects a peculiar national culture. Willingness to accept conflict, it will be recalled, rests on the assumption (universally made) that conflict will not result in violence, but rather will be conducted according to rules of decorum that define conflict as little more than debate. Beneath the surface of these positive evaluations of conflict are undertones of concern over the consequences of uncontained conflict—the "chaos" or "mish-mash" or even mob violence that might occur if the accepted rules were to break down. The suggestion that total breakdown is only a rule away seems strange in a society at peace for the best part of two centuries, but fear of violence is clearly evident in these interviews.[17] Affirmation of rules emerges with such strength here precisely because violence did in fact occur. To avoid that ultimate horror, even citizen political participation may be justifiably curbed.

7 SWEDEN COMPARED

Are Swedish elite officials different from public elites in other western political systems? In this chapter we propose to answer that question, using administrator and politician data drawn from the Michigan seven-nation study.[1] Those data make clear that, in some respects, Swedish officials are not at all different from their colleagues in other systems: they are predominantly men, drawn from middle- and upper-class backgrounds, and educated to at least the first university degree. But they are also Swedes and therefore subject to a variety of historical and political experiences markedly different from elite experiences in other nations. It is thus reasonable to assume that responses to a variety of subjective questions will exhibit a characteristically "Swedish" pattern derived from characteristically different experiences, in a different cultural setting. Because a large number of similar questions were asked in each nation, we can illuminate Swedish differences, as well as cross-cultural similarities, in some detail.

INSTITUTIONAL LINKAGES

The work of the Swedish public elite takes place in a world that is small, comfortable, well-understood and highly specialized. As we have seen in previous chapters, there is widespread agreement on what the various actors in the system should do and a great deal of information is available on actual performance. Senior administrators are understood to be running their programs, with more or less autonomy; Parliament is understood to be representing various social interests, more or less well; the Cabinet is understood to be reviewing old, and establishing new policies, with more or less dispatch and with greater or lesser skill in coopting social interests into the policy-making activities of Royal Commissions. Shared expectations, built upon centuries of tradition, permit the system to run smoothly, adjusting to unexpected developments through procedures that are also based on centuries of experience in crisis-management. At the top, the conduct of public business in Sweden resembles the operations of a well-oiled machine. As a result, actor linkages take on a highly specialized quality.

In a previous chapter, for example, we observed the multiple contacts administrators have within their own agencies and with the supervising ministries, yet their relative absence of contact with other agencies, or with politicians. This pattern of internal and hierarchial communication suggests a functional (or programmatic) specialization that is noticeable in Sweden, but also quite typical of the other nations included in the Michigan study. Thus Rockman's analysis of the Michigan data leads him to conclude that bureaucrats in all nations are oriented (measured by contacts) chiefly to their respective departments.[2] Within national administrative systems, differences exist in the extent to which there is cross-departmental contact. Senior civil servants in The Netherlands and in West Germany report somewhat higher levels of contact with officials in agencies other than their own than are reported by other national elites. These differences are not large, however, and they seem entirely due to the peculiar qualities of German and Dutch politics rather than to a less developed level of functional specialization. Although the Swedish data are not precisely comparable on this point, cross-agency contact probably occurs less frequently among Swedish administrators than it does in other systems except at the ministry level—a point to which we will return shortly. At the sub-ministry level, Sweden seems somewhat more specialized than other systems, with little cross-agency contact but a great deal of hierarchical and within-agency contact.

Senior Swedish administrators share another communication characteristic with other national elites, namely, a considerable amount of interaction with clientele groups. Images of bureaucracy that emphasize its isolation from society at large are clearly contradicted by the rather high levels of contact with clientele groups reported by bureaucrats in six nations: the proportion of each national sample reporting at least "regular" contacts (Table 7.1) ranges from a low of 49 percent (Italy) to a high of 94 percent (USA). Data for Sweden are again not precisely comparable, but we have already observed (Chapter 6) the high level of interaction between Swedish administrators and the clientele groups their respec-

Table 7.1. Administrator Contact With Clientele Groups, Citizens, Parliaments

Percentage Reporting "Regular Contacts"	Britain	Germany	Italy	Netherlands	USA	Sweden	
						Ministries	Other
Clientele Representatives Mean = 74.8	67	74	59	64	93	ND	
Citizens Mean = 48.7	9	29	66	29	68	69	52
Members of Parliament	5	74	50	16	64	86	17

Source: Bert a Rockman, "Linkages at the Top: The Sociometric Nets of Bureaucrats and Politicians" (unpublished paper).

tive agencies were created to serve. Social groups of various kinds thus appear clearly integrated into the activities of public agencies, particularly in the United States and Sweden, where close contact between administrators and group representatives is taken for granted. Contact with ordinary citizens is far less frequent, again with the exception of the United States and Sweden, where senior civil servants obviously find citizen contacts to be part of the normal routine.[3] American and Swedish social structures are certainly very different, but public bureaucrats in each of these systems stand out for their willingness to interact with the larger society, rather than isolating themselves from it. Indeed, civil servants in all systems included in the Michigan study share this integrative quality to a larger extent than earlier theories of bureaucracy have suggested.

Earlier theories, of course, were built around the differences between political and administrative action, which were presumed to be substantial and presumed to structure bureaucratic unwillingness to interact with these representatives of the larger society. Such theories, interesting enough at a general level, overlook the impact of institutional relationships. Although it is true that few civil servants report regular contacts with political party leaders, it is also true that considerable interaction takes place between civil servants and members of national parliaments (Table 7.1). That interaction seems negligible in Britain and The Netherlands, where contacts are mediated through ministries, but it is frequent in Germany, where civil servants often serve as staff aides for *Bundestag* committees. Civil servant-legislator contacts are also frequent in the United States, where the power of individual Congressmen, the absence of party discipline and congressional control over agency budgets combine to structure powerful incentives for close cooperation. Most bureaucrats have little to do with members of the *Riksdag* in Sweden, but the proportion of civil servants in the ministries who report regular parliamentary contacts is higher in Sweden than in any other nation, including the United States. These contacts reflect the highly specialized policy-making activities of the Royal Commissions, which typically include MP's and senior administrators as members, and which are coordinated by ministry officials. Compared to the United States, administrator-politician interaction in Sweden is less extensive, but it is equally or more intensive among those who are called upon to participate in policy-making. In each case the institutional framework is different, but the result is considerable interaction and, in Sweden, a policy-making routine clearly distinguished from "normal" politics or "normal" administration.

Comparison of contact patterns reported by various national elites thus enables us to gain a better appreciation of institutional impacts on elite behavior. Like high-level officials in other systems, Swedish administrators tend to focus their activities on their own departments, they tend to have little to do with politicians, but they are in frequent contact with clientele groups, particularly those whose interests are directly served by their respective agencies. Politicians have frequent contacts with citizens and interest groups in all systems, but less contact with administrators at the operating level and more contact with ministry-level civil servants. These similarities aside, the Swedish system seems clearly more specialized than other systems, in two important respects. First, second and third rank administrators have fewer cross-agency and political contacts, but as much or more clientele contact, than other elite administrators. At these levels, administrators seem to stick to their own knitting, but the knitting is done in close cooperation with non-governmental groups that are integrated into public processes. This pattern, as Ruin has suggested,[4] may well reflect a more advanced state of corporatism in Sweden than in other systems. Second, the specialized policy-making role of the ministries is reflected in interaction between politicians and top-level administrators that are more frequent in Sweden than in any other nation investigated. The frequency of these contacts, coupled with a high level of reported contact with citizens, suggests that on these dimensions the Swedish elite is most like the American elite, whose contact patterns also reflect a great deal of politician-administrator interaction as well as citizen contact.

VIEWS OF POWER AND POLITICAL INFLUENCE

We have already seen (Chapter 6) that the Swedish elite has a very clear understanding of institutional power in Sweden. Administrators and politicians alike agree that the Cabinet and its ministers are most influential, and that the Social Democratic Party, the central labor federation and the Parliament are among the other institutions of influence. Although institutional and cultural variety renders comparison hazardous, it is interesting to compare these Swedish responses to responses offered by other national elites. It will be recalled that each respondent was asked to estimate the influence of a variety of institutions "on the formulation of public policy." The institutions were listed on a card handed to the respondent and estimates were made by checking one of five available boxes, ranging from "the most powerful" to "no power at all," for each institution listed. Despite some ambiguity in institutional identification (i.e., "the press" rather than individual newspapers), more than 60 percent of those who filled in the form did so without any indication of hesitation or confusion. To the extent that "formulation of public policy" is a useful conceptualization of institutional power, these responses should be provocative.

The results for all nations, trichotomized for ease of interpretation, are summarized in Table 7.2. Public policy in advanced Western nations is perceived by the elite to be largely controlled by government ministers, leading political party members (who are often enough ministers), and trade unions. The modest

Table 7.2. Perceptions of Institutional Influence

	%		
	A Lot	Some	Not Much
Members of Parliament (1413)	29.7	24.2	46.1
Leading Party Members (806)	55.5	25.4	19.1
Trade Unions (1080)	47.4	26.9	25.3
Business-Finance (944)	22.2	28.8	48.2
Religious Organizations (723)	8.2	15.4	80.1
The Press (1076)	35.9	25.5	38.1
Senior Administrators (1235)	26.6	25.0	47.9
Ministers (963)	67.7	21.9	9.8

influence of parliamentary bodies, so often asserted in recent years, is reflected here in the rather small fraction that perceives members of parliaments to be "very" influential. Nor do these respondents, most of whom are senior civil servants, see themselves as having much influence. Private industry and finance, so often the foil against which social reformers aim their attacks, are not perceived to have much policy influence at all, and barely more than a third of those interviewed felt that the press had a large influence over policy. Overall, public policy is seen to be securely in the hands of senior ministers and party officials, consulting with trade union leaders.

But of course there is no policy that is developed "overall"; policies are shaped within nations, by national elites. It is therefore more instructive to compare influence rankings by nation, as shown in Table 7.3. The modest number of respondents who thought parliamentary bodies were very powerful in Table 7.2 can be seen, in Table 7.3, to include some national elites who hold far more exalted views of legislative power. In both the United States and Sweden, but especially in the United States, very large fractions of those interviewed believe members of the respective national legislative bodies to have considerable policy influence. In The Netherlands, too, nearly half of the civil servants interviewed believe MP's to be very influential. Because of wording differences it is quite likely that these ratings reflect somewhat different criteria. In the United States, where respondents were asked to rate the influence of "members of Congress," estimates are almost surely based on the perceived ability of *individual* Congressmen to influence appropriations and policy. In Sweden, where respondents were asked to rate the influence of "the Parliament," the institution itself, rather than individual members, was the focus; had "members" been the focus, ratings might have been considerably higher, primarily because many

Table 7.3. Percentage Indicating Listed Organizations Are Very Influential

	Administrator Perceptions					
	Britain	Germany	Italy	Netherlands	Sweden	USA
MP's	1.6	13.0	9.5	48.7	45.5	56.4
Leading Party Members	41.3	80.4	69.6	48.7	—	13.5
Trade Unions	6.4	38.4	64.4	69.7	64.6	—
Private Industry	11.1	29.0	27.8	—	12.0	—
Religious Organizations	0.0	2.1	15.6	17.1	—	—
The Press	5.6	44.2	24.3	53.9	42.3	—
Senior Civil Servants	42.0	4.3	10.5	34.2	5.7	26.2
Ministers	84.9	58.0	52.2	68.4	84.8	49.2
Other Groups	2.4	12.3	19.1	—	2.8	—
	Politicians' Perceptions					
MP's	11.1	17.2	3.0	—	50.0	84.4
Leading Party Members	38.9	47.6	30.0	25.0	—	—
Trade Unions	15.7	18.0	34.0	43.2	29.5	—
Private Industry	21.3	21.1	33.0	—	6.8	—
Religious Organizations	0.0	3.9	16.0	9.1	—	—
The Press	12.1	42.2	15.0	38.6	22.8	—
Senior Civil Servants	51.0	13.3	23.0	56.8	9.1	70.1
Ministers	74.1	48.5	22.0	86.4	72.7	61.0
Other Groups	1.9	4.6	9.0	—	0.0	—

members are simultaneously ministers. Despite these interpretive difficulties, national rankings of legislative influence seem plausible: in no case except the United States is the parliamentary body or its members ranked first in influence, but in nations such as Sweden or The Netherlands, the parliamentary body is clearly included among the more significant institutional actors.

More systematic comparison of the top three institutions in each nation suggests both that ministerial government is alive and healthy in the West and that there is considerable agreement between administrators and politicians regarding the specific national characteristics of influence structure. In Britain, the highest number of "very influential" ratings from both administrators and politicians are assigned to Ministers, Senior Civil Servants and leading party members; in Germany both groups of respondents agree that the top three power ranks belong to leading party members, ministers, and the press, although ranks one and two are reversed; in Sweden, we note again that ministers (the Cabinet), trade unions (LO) and Parliament are agreed to be in the top three. There is less politician-administrator agreement in The Netherlands regarding the top three, but note that the top five include the same institutions for both groups. Ministers and party leaders are perceived to be at the helm of Western European governments, with parliaments and trade unions in more or less close association, depending on which nation is considered. Swedish images, drawn from a system in which leading party members are simultaneously members of Parliament and where cabinet ministers are often selected from members of Parliament, seem quite similar. Our measures are admittedly crude, but the general coherence of within-nation rankings and the interesting between-nation differences both suggest that these results may reflect reality.

Finally, two comparisons between all administrators and all politicians seem suggestive enough to be worth comment. Politicians in all nations tend to see senior civil servants as more influential than civil servants perceive themselves to be, while administrators tend to attribute more influence to trade unions than is assigned by politicians. Perhaps this difference reflects the difference between being on top and wanting to be on top. Interestingly enough, administrators tend to be more conscious of press influence than are politicians. This may be yet another indication of greater political/environmental sensitivity among civil servants than is commonly supposed.

ON SATISFACTION AND SOCIAL CHANGE

We have observed, using a variety of measures, that the Swedish elite seems quite content with the existing state of society and politics: they like one another, they like what they do, they believe the system they serve to be a good one, and they are not much inclined to press for either social or political change. From one point of view, none of this is very surprising. Almost by definition, "elites" are bound to feel satisfied with what they do and what they are, except in highly unstable conditions. Nevertheless, there are bound to be differences in the degree of satisfaction experienced by different national elites, or by sub-groups within an elite structure. Given what we know about the contrasting contact patterns of bureaucrats and politicians, for example, we should expect politicians to be less satisfied than administrators and more interested in changing society. We might also anticipate that overall levels of satisfaction would differ from one national elite to another.

Tables 7.4 and 7.5 provide some evidence to evaluate these speculations. Table 7.4 compares responses of administrators and politicians from five countries to one of several questions designed to estimate satisfaction with the existing political system. The proportion of each national elite group that falls within each response category is displayed along with mean scores (scale = 1–5). A glance at the first and last response categories makes clear that the satisfaction experienced by members of the Swedish elite is quite common among other national elite groups. Very substantial fractions of all national elite groups indicate that they have "little inclination" for change in the political system. If the "affirmation" and "little indication" categories are combined, the proportion of national administrators who seem basically satisfied exceeds 50 percent in all but one case. Only among Italian officials does there appear to be substantial disaffection from current political institutions and a desire for another order. At the other extreme, the Swedes stand out in terms of both the level of satisfaction they express—79 percent of Swedish administrators and 64 percent of Swedish politicians want little or no change—and the unanimity with which they express that sentiment. For them, Sweden appears to be a political utopia.

What is perhaps most remarkable about the satisfaction experienced by the Swedish elite is not so much its magnitude, which is remarkable enough, but the fact that politicians are nearly as satisfied as administrators. Other columns in Table 7.4 reveal that politicians typically are less content and more interested in change than are administrators: French, German and British politicians are all substantively more change-oriented than their administrative counterparts. Swedish politicians are also more reform-minded than their administrator colleagues, but almost two-thirds indicate little or no interest in change. This level of disinterest in political reform is perfectly understandable for the Social Democrats among the Swedish respondents, in power for four decades at the time of these interviews. It seems less understandable for members of the (then) opposition parties, who presumably should have had a vital interest in at least a change in government. That such an interest was so poorly reflected in these conversations suggests, again, how fundamentally content and remarkably unified in outlook all members of the Swedish elite seem to be. It also reflects

Table 7.4.   Satisfaction With Existing Political Order, Bureaucrats and Politicians

| | Percent | | | | | | | | | | | | |
| | Britain | | France | | Germany | | Italy | | Holland | | Sweden | | USA | |
	B	P	B	P	B	P	B	P	B	P	B	P	B	P
(1) Passionate, Total Rejection	–	–	–	2	–	–	–	5	–	–	–	–	–	–
(2) Rejected, Ameliorative Reform Proposed	–	3	1	13	1	1	14	22	–	–	–	2	–	–
(3) Accepted, Ameliorative Reform Proposed	27	48	46	62	45	58	54	67	–	–	20	33	–	–
(4) Accepted, Little Inclination to Change	73	44	53	22	54	38	31	5	–	–	67	50	–	–
(5) Passionate Affirmation of System	–	5	–	–	1	3	1	–	–	–	12	14	–	–
TOTAL PERCENT*	100	100	100	99	101	100	100	99	–	–	99	99	–	–
Mean Scores	3.7	3.5	3.5	3.0	3.5	3.4	3.2	2.7	–	–	3.9	3.8	–	–

*Percents do not always equal 100% due to rounding.

Table 7.5. Attitude to Existing Socio-Economic Order, Bureaucrats and Politicians

	Britain		France		Germany		Italy		Holland		Sweden		USA	
Percent	B	P	B	P	B	P	B	P	B	P	B	P	B	P
(1) Passionate, Total Rejection	–	1	–	2	–	–	–	5	–	7	–	–	–	–
(2) Rejected, Ameliorative Reform Proposed	2	21	3	12	–	6	9	21	7	29	1	4	–	–
(3) Accepted, Ameliorative Reform Proposed	44	42	77	80	46	53	56	55	35	41	20	23	–	–
(4) Accepted Little Inclination to Change	50	21	19	6	51	38	33	16	57	22	66	66	–	–
(5) Passionate Affirmation	3	15	1	–	3	3	2	2	1	–	13	7	–	–
TOTAL PERCENT*	99	100	100	100	100	100	100	99	100	99	100	100	–	–
Mean Scores	3.5	3.3	3.2	2.9	3.6	3.4	3.3	2.9	3.5	2.8	3.9	3.7	–	–

*Percents do not always equal 100% due to rounding.

the fact that, for opposition party members, being out of office does not necessarily imply being out of power. Opposition partisans serve on parliamentary committees, are appointed to Royal Commissions, and otherwise enjoy the perquisites of national policy office. In this context, a change in partisan control of government might well seem one among a number of "minor" changes.

Another interesting clue to the extraordinary political contentment of the Swedish elite emerges from Table 7.5, which compares elite satisfaction with the existing *social* order in six nations. Again there is considerable variation among national elites, with the French joining the Italians and the Dutch politicians on the low end of the societal acceptance scale, the Germans, British and Dutch bureaucrats hovering near the middle, and the Swedes all by themselves close to the very end of the acceptance continuum. If the two most positive acceptance codes (4 and 5) are combined no other group of administrators comes closer than 25 percentage points away from the Swedish level of societal affirmation, and no other group of politicians comes closer than 32 percentage points of the Swedish level of politician satisfaction—in both cases the closest "satisfaction" competitor is Germany. The Swedish elite, in short, is not only manifestly contented with its political position and influence, but also wholly persuaded that the society within which that influence is exercised is a good society. Swedish politicians, in fact, are rather more contented with the existing social system than the political structure. This contrasts sharply with the British or the French elites, but resembles the Italian pattern of strong commitment to social rather than political relations. Unlike the Italians, however, the level of support for society and its political institutions is extraordinarily high among the Swedes. Indeed, Swedish elite satisfaction is so high compared to other national elites that we can almost think of Sweden as a deviant, Panglossian, state.

IS CONFLICT NECESSARY?

Other indicators of deviant satisfaction are readily found in administrators' responses to a series of questions we asked about social conflict. On the assumption that perceptions of conflict were an important key to understanding ideologies, all respondents were asked the following question:

> Some people say that in politics and society generally there is always conflict among various groups, while others say that most groups have a great deal in common and share basically the same interests. How do you feel about this?

In Table 7.6 we compare national responses to this question and discover that Swedish administrators are far more likely than civil servants in other countries to view society in terms of parallel rather than competing or conflicting interests.

Table 7.6. Administrator Perceptions of Conflict (%)

	Britain	France	Germany	Italy	Holland	Sweden	USA
Consensus is Typical	30.1	16.4	14.6	24.8	19.1	41.6	21.7
Neither, Both	25.7	57.0	25.4	18.3	20.6	22.3	19.4
Conflict is Typical	44.2	26.6	60.0	57.0	60.2	36.1	58.9
	(N=113)	(N=79)	(N=130)	(N=93)	(N=68)	(N=305)	(N=124)

We know, of course, that differing definitions of "conflict" can confuse interpretation of such responses. Among Italian administrators, for example, "conflict" was primarily (62%) defined as class conflict, as it was by the British (52%). Among the German administrators, interest group (44%) and class (34%) were the dominant interpretative criteria. And we have already seen (Chapter 6) that the Swedes see conflict primarily in terms of competition between interest groups (47%) or as an exchange of ideas (41%) in which there is not even a hint of violence. Bearing in mind these differences, it remains clear that Swedish administrators, far more than their counterparts in other systems, perceive their society to be structured by common rather than competing interests.

None of this should be taken to mean that Swedish administrators do not perceive these group-intellectual conflicts to be real, or serious. On the contrary, a smaller proportion (42%) of Swedes believe that conflicts are "usually reconcilable" than any other national group. Nor does the Swedish view imply an unusually negative evaluation of conflict as something "sick" or "unhealthy," to be avoided at all costs: Swedish scores on these kinds of questions are close to the mean scores for all respondents. Swedish administrators simply perceive less conflict in the world than their colleagues in other countries do, and they therefore conclude that common interests are more likely to characterize social relations. Thus, when asked to discuss the "most important problem" facing the country, Swedish administrators were the *least* likely to mention conflicting interests in discussing either the problem or possible solutions to it (Table 7.7). Interpretation of this table is complicated somewhat by slight differences in wording: in some countries administrators were asked to indicate the most important problem *in their area of interest,* while in others the question referred to the most important problem facing the nation as a whole. It seems reasonable to assume that directing the question to an administrator's particular responsibility

Table 7.7.   Perceived Conflict in Problem Resolution (%)

In Discussing Problem, Conflict Is Seen To Be:	Britain	France	Germany	Italy	Holland	Sweden	USA
Very Prominent	6.8	4.5	3.8	4.0	13.3	1.7	23.4
Important	13.6	3.6	7.5	7.0	21.3	9.0	15.3
Present	23.7	25.5	27.1	14.0	16.0	13.7	19.8
Minimal	37.3	36.4	28.6	36.0	32.0	28.4	20.7
Absent	18.6	30.0	33.1	39.0	17.3	47.2	20.7
	N = (118)	(110)	(133)	(100)	(75)	(299)	(111)

would be more likely to produce a response that focused on the technical, less conflictual, aspects of a named problem. This, in fact, seems to account for the generally low levels of conflict perception revealed in Table 7.7, except in Holland and the United States, where a third or more of senior civil servants give conflict a prominent position in problem definition. From this point of view, however, Sweden represents the hard case, for in Sweden the question was put in very general, hence very political, terms: "What do you think is the most important problem for the Swedish Cabinet and Parliament to try to solve today?" That nearly half of a large administrator sample could answer such a question without referring to conflict at all is powerful testimony to the benign environment inhabited by the Swedish elite. Conflicts exist, and they are real enough and healthy enough, but they amount to debates between members of the same social family over the best means of furthering a common good that all are presumed to share. In no other country are such views as pronounced or as characteristic of a governing elite.

THINKING IDEOLOGICALLY

Ever since the Swedish political scientist-editorialist Herbert Tingsten asserted an "end" to ideology in the late 1930's,[5] there has been considerable speculation over the extent to which old left-right ideologies and their associated "grand theories" of social change organize the activities of governments. The sources of this speculation seem clear enough. Higher levels of national wealth generated by industrial development, coupled with numerous welfare-state programs—from unemployment compensation to health insurance—have simultaneously increased national affluence and spread that affluence around more evenly than would have been thought possible a century ago. Reduction of income and class disparities, in turn, is often said to have weakened or even eliminated the bases of political conflict. No longer are individual or group interests fought out in the streets, using slogans urging revolution. White-collar bureaucrats now define and protect social interests, using managerial formulae rather than large conceptions derived from theories of social revolution. Scholars recently have assured us that these trends have pushed Western societies into a "post-industrial" era, characterized by a focus on more individualized human values rather than the epic group and economic struggles of the past. Ideology has become technology, politics become administration, and comfortable self-realization has replaced social change as the driving force of modern politics.[6]

Data drawn from our interviews in seven nations certainly suggest that these perspectives are reflected in some of the ways Western elites think about the world. Western administrators and politicians, as we have seen, are generally quite satisfied with who they are and what they do, and they are similarly contented with the "mixed" economies they guide: more than 83 percent of senior civil servants and 77 percent of politicians support the present balance between public and private sector activities. Moreover, while senior administrators perceive a good deal of conflict in society, except in Sweden, those social conflict perceptions do not seem to affect the problems with which they deal every day—the activities they manage are in this sense less conflict-ridden than society at large. In thinking about social problems and appropriate solutions to them, therefore, European elites display precisely the values one might anticipate from managers, rather than politicians. Responses to questions about problems and solutions were coded to reveal how much each respondent "framed" his response: what words were used, whether the discussion referred to past or future states of society, whether tradition, law, morality and a number of other criteria were used. The most prominent criteria used to evaluate solutions were political acceptability, mentioned by more than 55 percent of those interviewed, followed by practicality (54.1%) and cost (47.1%). These "managerial" perspectives, coupled with the high levels of satisfaction with existing mixed economies, appear to mark Western elites as clear-cut products of a new order, defined by social stability and political consensus.

But these data do not permit such easy conclusions. Although managerial perspectives exert a powerful influence on conceptions of social problem-solving, it is also true that some 45.1 percent of the responding civil servants and politicians refer to "group benefits" as a relevant criterion for evaluating proposed solutions. Judging a plan according to which group or collectivity will benefit is of course an inherently political standard, which furthermore assumes that society is structured into a variety of groups with *different* rather than common interests. Elite Swedes, who perceive little conflict in either society or the programs they manage, express thought patterns that resemble what might be expected in the new industrial-welfare state, but other national elites continue to perceive considerable social conflict, however orderly their own programs appear to be. If so, other national elites should exhibit more "ideological" patterns of thought than the Swedes, and Swedish patterns should be clearly located at one end of a thought-pattern dimension.

In coding the interviews, several efforts were made to generate data that might permit an evaluation of more and less ideological styles of thinking. On the assumption that use of general theories was a good indicator of ideological styles, we asked coders to judge respondent use of such theories in several places: once at the conclusion of the "most important problem" discussion, again after the respondent had been asked a series of questions about political parties, and still a third time after the coder had read the entire transcript. On each occasion, coders were asked to make a judgment based on the assumption that use of theories could be more or less obvious, more or less pervasive in a respondent's thinking, and we tried to formulate clear instruction for coding. Thus, the end-of-interview judgment flowed from the following instructional question: "Does this respondent have a single, simplified conceptual explanatory scheme which he applied to all discussion of public policy issues? Do all his discussions of politics revert to a single, fairly coherent set of concepts? Use as a continuum." Responses were coded in each case on a low (1) to high (5) continuum to facilitate comparison with other questions.

Comparing responses to these questions makes clear that ideological thinking is indeed very much alive among Western elites, in patterns that seem quite expected. Thus, conceptual thinking is associated with the use of general theories to analyze political parties ($r=.255$), with the desire for major social change ($r=.412$), with rejection of the socio-political system ($r=.426$), with the perception of much social conflict ($r=.195$), with an inclination to avoid compromise ($r=.116$), although the latter relationship is not uniformly powerful. All of these relationships, in turn, seem powerfully conditioned by partisan (i.e., left-right) party affiliations within each country. Individuals who think about politics ideologically remain important throughout Europe, despite premature predictions about ideological demise.

These relationships permit us to infer that the desire for social change filtered through a traditional left-right conceptual lens remains a significant feature of elite thought patterns, but national differences are not clearly shown. To reveal national patterns we can compare marginal responses to three of the conceptual-theoretical questions and the "compromise" question, as shown in Table 7.8. Evidently the willingness to compromise, for which the Swedish elite is so well known, has become a widely-accepted style in the West, particularly among administrators, few of whom indicate an inclination to maintain hard and fast positions even when they think they are right. British and Dutch politicians, and British administrators, stand out as hard-liners, but the proportion of hard-liners among these groups is relatively small. To be sure, these data reflect nothing more than inclinations, although in some cases (i.e., Sweden) there is considerable behavioral evidence to support the reported inclination toward compromising disputes. To the extent that these data reflect real process in these national settings, they suggest a fairly widespread willingness to engage in negotiation rather than confrontation in the resolution of disputes.

What, then, are we to make of the data in the remainder of Table 7.8, which clearly reveal the considerable extent to which conceptual and theoretical frameworks are used by Western elites, and in particular by politicians? Whether explicating solutions to a "most important" problem, or discussing political parties, or discussing politics in general, very substantial factions among these respondents resort to general theories. Indeed, an average of more than 59 percent of each nation's politicians has been judged to use a "single, simplified conceptual explanatory schema" in discussing politics. Yet most of them are

Table 7.8.   Use of Theory/Conceptual Framework, Bureaucrats and Politicians

Question	Britain		France		Germany		Italy		Holland		Sweden		USA		Overall	
	B	P	B	P	B	P	B	P	B	P	B	P	B	P	B	P
General Theory	43	71	50	65	44	66	45	80	–	–	21	–	41	45	37	65
Framework Politics	37	66	58	52	48	68	73	77	–	–	23	46	–	–	42	64
Ideology	41	65	–	–	44	63	71	93	57	68	57	75	36	79	52	75
Scope	75	85	–	–	16	28	10	11	25	37	32	67	57	56	36	49
Concept	20	76	46	72	35	67	47	75	65	84	29	51	53	56	38	69
Inclination Compromise	25	42	–	12	15	29	20	16	17	34	11	15	9	–	13	26

compromisers, and we have seen that there is a negative, if weak, relationship between inclination to compromise and use of conceptual schemes.

Perhaps the most reasonable response to this dilemma is to recognize that the apparent compromise-theory relationship is too weak to be significant. Inspection of national correlations reveals that the relationship does not exist in France (r=.01) or Italy (r=.006), is extremely weak in Sweden (r=.115) and Germany (r=.151), and moderately strong only in The Netherlands (r=.298), where it is largely a product of responses made by politicians. Furthermore, inspection of correlations between the compromise measure and other "theory" measures reveals a complete absence of meaningful relationships, positive or negative. Western elites *do* use coherent intellectual schemes to interpret the world and they *do* apply general theories to their analyses, but their use of such theories has little or no impact on their willingness to compromise disputes arising from the increasingly complex interactions among well-organized social groups. These elites are ideological, but they are not ideologues.[7]

We are now in a better position to appreciate the unique qualities of the Swedish elite, which is far less likely than other elite groups to derive solutions to problems from general theories, to interpret political parties in theoretical terms, or to apply a single conceptual scheme in discussions of political life. In all these respects Swedish officials demonstrate attributes of the concrete and pragmatic problem-solvers so often portrayed in studies of Swedish politics. At the same time, they very clearly see party differences in terms of ideologies, and they resemble both the British and the Americans in perceiving the scope of government intervention to be a major difference between parties. These views are perfectly understandable, since Swedish political parties do attempt to state coherent ideological positions based on public intervention into private-sector affairs, among a people for whom the issue is far from settled. Private capitalism remains healthy in Sweden, continuing to generate debate over how much government should do, at whose expense.[8] The Swedish elite is far less theoretical than other national elites in its approach to social problem-solving, but accurately perceives the theoretical structures that serve to mobilize popular opinion and motivate various public programs. If they seem somewhat more distant from grand theories than other elites, perhaps it is because they work in a social structure that provides a more explicit and better articulated division between ideology and public responsibilities.

VALUE HIERARCHIES

Speculation regarding the significance of ideological or other modes of political thought lends itself naturally to speculation over long-term changes in values. The phenomena that are said to cause an "end" to ideology—increased national affluence, reduction of class differences and thus class conflicts, the shift from industrial production to social service—are also alleged to cause changes in fundamental values among both elites and mass publics. Phrases such as "post-industrial" or "post-materialist" are used to summarize a shift in basic value orientations away from material enjoyment or security and toward more humane interests such as community, or belongingness.[9] As elites move closer to management rather than ideological values, mass publics are said to be moving closer to individually-defined and experienced satisfactions. Elites manage, mass publics enjoy, and conflict-dominated politics is swept away by a growing wave of affluence.

No citizens were interviewed in the Michigan study, but we were interested in gathering evidence that might shed light on value hierarchies among Western elites. After having read the respondent's discussion of political roles, problems and solutions, coders were instructed to judge the "implicit top priority of the respondent throughout the entire interview. Code only one priority, the one which dominates the respondent's total discussion of the questions." Given the nature of the questions, it was anticipated that values coded at this point would largely reflect current, shorter-run, considerations, and that these might well differ from more basic, longer-term values. To get at these longer-term goals, the following question was asked close to the end of each interview: "How would the society you would like to see for your children differ from today's society?" Coders were instructed to code up two indications of a top priority on this question, using categories identical to those used for the prior question. In a recent analysis, Inglehart has shown considerably less variability in responses to the "futures" question than was apparent in codes recorded for the discussion of current activities. These projected value preferences, he argues, are therefore entitled to be regarded as more "basic" than current formulations.[10] Whether or not these responses are more "basic," they are clearly more stable; hence the following discussion will make use of them.

Table 7.9 displays response percentages and rank orders for the value hierarchy codes, arranged by position and system awareness, a variable of some potential interest. It is immediately apparent, despite a small political sample, that bureaucrats and politicians express rather different long-run values. Material welfare, ranked first by senior administrators, ranks no better than fourth or fifth (depending on scoring convention) among politicians. Security, another more or less traditional value, comes in second among administrators but last among politicians—the obverse case is Political-Institutional Reform, ranked last by administrators but second by politicians. Social Justice and Equality is ranked first by politicians, but only third by administrators. Overall, senior civil servants appear to reflect value preferences quite consonant with their class

Table 7.9.　Justice Position and System Awareness

Value Hierarchy	System Awareness				Position			
	YES		NO		Bureaucrats		Politicians	
	%	RANK	%	RANK	%	RANK	%	RANK
(1) Political/Ins. Reform	6	7	4	8	5	8	19	2
(2) Social Justice and Equality	18	2	5	7	14	4	21	1
(3) Knowledge-Education-Culture	4	8	10	5	6	7	10	6
(4) Material Welfare	21	1	26	1	23	1	14	3
(5) Liberty	8	6	15	3	11	5	10	6
(6) Morality	11	5	9	6	10	6	10	6
(7) Security-Stability	16	3.5	19	2	17	2	12	4
(8) Belongingness	16	3.5	12	4	15	3	5	8

backgrounds, but there is little evidence of a "new" value syndrome. Politicians, who reflect a continuing interest in justice and reform, clearly want to provide the motor for change but again, it is difficult to interpret these interests as anything "new." From this point of view, elite values in Sweden seem, if anything, quite conventional, in keeping with a society anxious to promote continued industrial and economic growth. The exception, if it is one, seems to lie in the 12.6 percent of Swedish bureaucrats who stress "belongingness" as a major value.

Grouping respondents according to high or low scores on our measure of "system awareness" seems more interesting. Recall that this measure taps the extent to which an official feels himself to be part of a larger set of interactions that collectively define "the system," and that our earlier analyses have shown high levels of awareness to be associated with planning and policy-making positions. It now appears (Table 7.9) that high or low levels of system awareness have little effect on value rankings, which are identical, or close to it, in five of eight possible cases. Note too that material welfare is not affected by system awareness, again suggesting that Swedes of all shades of opinion and position are committed to maintenance of a strong economic foundation for their public programs. Those with high sensitivity to the larger system seem inclined to give equal or greater priority to social justice, a value that is ranked last by the less aware respondents. Top priority for low scorers is assigned to liberty, a value that comes no higher than fifth for high scorers. System awareness thus seems to distinguish two clearly-defined groupings. Members of each group appear to assume that material welfare is essential; the question is the direction toward which further development should be aimed. Officials in the ministries or near the top of the traditional civil and service agencies, whom we know from Chapter 3 to have high levels of system awareness, want to shade future development toward greater equality. The engineers, and other specialists in the industrial, commercial, agricultural and transportation bureaucracies score low on system awareness and want to shade development toward greater liberty. For them, perhaps, close clientele relationships and memories of unhappy wage negotiations with governmental leaders may have nourished a concern over continued public sector expansion that is expressed as a desire for more liberty.[11]

Comparing these priorities to those expressed in other nations for which we have data (Table 7.10) suggests that the Swedish elite is not much different from other European elites. Politicians of all these countries, not just Sweden, rank social-justice-equality first among their long-term priorities. Other European administrators, not just Swedish administrators, typically rank material welfare first among their long-term priorities. There are striking exceptions among administrators, however. Among bureaucrats in West Germany, where a massive wall is a continuous reminder of East-West tension, Security-Safety is the top

Table 7.10. Value Hierarchy Rankings, By Country Bureaucrats and Politicians

"Basic"	Britain B Rank	Britain P Rank	France B Rank	France P Rank	Germany B Rank	Germany P Rank	Italy B Rank	Italy P Rank	Sweden B Rank	Sweden P Rank	USA B Rank	USA P Rank	Overall B Rank	Overall P Rank
(1) Pol./Inst. Reform	7	8	4	2	5.5	5	1	4	8	2	—	—	5.5	4.5
(2) Social Justice and Equality	2	1	2	1	2	1	2.5	1	4	1	—	—	2	1
(3) Knowledge/ Educ. Cult.	6	7	3	7	5.5	8	7	8	7	6	—	—	8	8
(4) Mat./Phys. Welfare	1	2	1	3.5	7	6	2.5	6.5	1	3	—	—	1	4.5
(5) Liberty	8	3	8	8	3.5	2	5.5	2.5	5	6	—	—	7	2.5
(6) Morality	4	4	5	3.5	3.5	4	4	2.5	6	6	—	—	4	2.5
(7) Sec./Safety Stability	5	5	6.5	6	1	3	5.5	6.5	2	4	—	—	3	6
(8) Belongingness	3	6	6.5	5	8	7	8	5	3	8	—	—	5.5	7
*Rounding in effect N	112	72	90	72	121	95	100	50	273	42	—	—	696	333

long-term priority, with material welfare no better than seventh. In Italy, whose political institutions are widely regarded as among the least effective in Western Europe, senior bureaucrats place institutional reform at the top of their long-term priority list, with material welfare tied for second. These are perfectly understandable exceptions to a general pattern that is itself an obvious reflection of administrative concern for economy and political concern for mobilization.

Further interpretation, while hazardous, is also suggestive. To the extent that knowledge or belongingness can be regarded as "new" values, these data make clear that such values have yet to capture the imagination of Western European elites. The material welfare-equality-security-morality values that dominate the priority lists in fact seem quite old-fashioned, compared to "post-industrial" or "post-materialist" expectations. The persistence of such values suggests that conflicts from which they emerge—over income, status, and the distribution of both—remain live issues, even in Sweden, which in many respects seems to be more advanced than any other welfare state. Indeed, when value hierarchies are grouped by political party preference, major differences between the traditional parties of the right and left emerge, particularly over social justice and equality. Left parties in all nations continue to drive for greater public action to promote equality, while center and right parties continue to value material welfare and liberty. The considerable support for liberty among these elite cadres thus appears to be a direct reaction against further state intervention, with its promise of greater restriction on income, thus choice, among individuals who hold established positions.[12] If these value hierarchies are any guide, the future shape of Western societies will be structured by preferences that have a lengthy past as well as a very lively present existence.

BUREAUCRATIC AND POLITICAL ROLES

In Sweden, we have suggested, public roles are specialized and clearly understood by political elites: parliamentarians represent constituency and/or clientele interests, administrators run their programs (with more or less autonomy), and the Cabinet makes policy. These role expectations are clearly understood in part because they have a lengthy historical existence, in part because institutional specialization reinforces behavior patterns that meet specialized institutional needs. If official roles reflect unique national histories as well as imperatives common to technology and position, national role expectations should differ in revealing ways. To test this appealing idea we can turn to the considerable information generated in response to questions about the kinds of activities engaged in by bureaucrats and politicians in the several nations included in our study. It will be recalled that early in each interview, respondents were asked to describe their role in terms of tasks required and desirable personal qualities. Answers were then coded twice: once as direct responses, and again in summary categories of a series of analytical "traits." By assigning a numerical value to the significance attached to these traits we can generate data that will permit us to compare Swedish role definitions to similar definitions in other nations.

Since we are interested primarily in showing Sweden-other comparisons, Table 7.11 presents mean values in Swedish bureaucrats and politicians on several important dimensions of political "role," as compared to mean scores for bureaucrats and politicians in the six other nations in which interviews were conducted. Swedish administrators resemble administrators in other countries in how they rank the significance of these traits: in all nations, including Sweden, civil servants believe policy-making traits to be rather important for politicians, with representation qualities seen as somewhat less significant, and sociability traits hardly important at all. Far more than administrators in other nations, however, Swedish administrators believe qualities of character to be important for politicians, as do both Swedish and other politicians. On other dimensions, Swedish politicians seem to have markedly different views of desirable politician traits. The most striking contrasts center on policy-making and representation traits. Regarded as quite important by politicians in other systems, policy-making traits are seen by Swedish politicians to be rather unimportant. What Swedes see to be very important indeed are representation traits, which other politicans see to be less significant. Swedish politicians also view sociability traits to be important, unlike their political colleagues in other nations. These data again reflect the institutional specialization that is characteristic of Sweden, with its separation between parliamentary representation and cabinet policy-making, but they also reflect the interesting Swedish emphasis on "character" and "sociability" qualities. Swedish politics, with its endless round of committee meetings and intense inter-personal communications, could hardly be carried on without such qualities.

Emphasis on these qualities shows up again in comparing Swedish notions of desirable administration traits with views generated in other systems. Administrators everywhere think that intellectual and organizational traits are important in their own work, although Swedes give somewhat less emphasis to intellectual and somewhat more to organizational traits (Chapter 4) than other administrators do. The really noticeable difference between Swedish administrators and others, however, is the contrasting level of significance attached to sociability traits. In other systems such traits are seen to be of little consequence; in Sweden, they emerge as quite important in the minds of administrators themselves. The significance Swedes attach to sociability/organizational qualities, coupled with their rejection of "technician" or "neutral executor" qualities— both of which are more highly prized in other systems—set them apart from administrative elites elsewhere (Table 7.12). Swedes think they need smarts and social skills to run their organizations, but they do not see themselves as "mere" technicians, following orders from others with no input of their own.

Table 7.11. Important Traits of Politicians, Sweden and Other Nations
(Scale: 1 = Very Important; 5 = Not Important)

	Administrators			Politicians		
	6-Nation Mean	Sweden	Difference	6-Nation Mean	Sweden	Difference
Representation	3.5	3.2	-.3*	3.0	1.6	-1.4*
Policy-Making	2.5	2.9	.4*	2.5	4.0	1.5*
Character	4.3	3.2	-1.1*	3.1	3.0	-.1*
Sociability	4.4	4.5	.1	3.9	3.0	-.9*

*Significant at .01 level, two-sample T-test.

Table 7.12. Important Traits of Administrators, Sweden and Other Nations
(Scale: 1 = Very Important; 5 = Not Important)

	Administrators			Politicians		
	6-Nation Mean	Sweden	Difference	6-Nation Mean	Sweden	Difference
Sociability	3.8	2.6	-1.2*	4.0	4.2	.2
Organizational	2.6	2.3	-.3	3.1	4.3	1.2*
Intellectual	2.6	3.0	.4*	2.5	2.5	—
Character	3.5	3.6	.1	2.7	3.3	.6
Technician	3.2	4.3	1.1*	2.9	4.9	2.0*
Neutral Executor	3.4	3.8	.4	2.8	1.9	-.9*

*Significant at .01, two-sample T-test.

If Swedish administrators do not see themselves as "mere" spear-carriers, it is nevertheless clear that Swedish politicians come very close to adopting precisely that view. Politicians elsewhere believe that intellectual, character, and technician-executor traits are important, but Swedish politicians have a more narrow view; administrators should be smart and willing to carry out the directive handed out by Parliament. But note the ambiguity in the Swedish response. It is very important that administrators be neutral executors, but at the same time it is not regarded as at all important that they be "technicians." Swedish politicians evidently want their administrators to do what they are told while recognizing that what they are to do may require wisdom as well as expertise, and that some of that wisdom may have to come from administrators themselves. Swedish administrator willingness to accord policy-making functions to politicians thus has its counterpart in politician willingness to view administration as something quite different from "mere" technique, particularly since both sides help to shape the directives that politicians expect to be "neutrally" executed. These subtle nuances, shaped by historical experience no less than function, help to define a uniquely Swedish pattern of accommodation.

SUMMARY

Are Swedish elite officials different from public elites in other Western political systems? The answer, we can now assert with some confidence, is clearly "yes," and the differences seem both interesting and theoretically significant. To appreciate the significance of the Swedish difference one need do no more than recall what is *not* different about the Swedes. Like other Western elites, Swedes are middle-class, middle-aged university graduates who have spent most of their adult lives working themselves up a variety of bureaucratic and political success ladders. Like those other elites, Swedes perceive their system to be dominated by senior government ministers and labor union leaders, and are not inclined very much to challenge existing systems of power. Like other elites, too, Swedes seem to hold fairly conventional values: material welfare remains the primary long-run concern among Swedish administrators; social justice-equality remains the primary long-run concern among the more reformist cadre of Swedish politicians. None of these characteristics suggests anything more than a privileged, well-paid, rather smug, and wholly conventional official establishment. Apart from language differences, it would be difficult indeed to distinguish between conversations held in London, Bonn, Washington or Stockholm if these were the only grounds for differentiation.

The Swedish difference is real, however, and it is most evident in general viewpoints about both society and administration. Among groups for which a generally high level of satisfaction is to be expected, the Swedes stand out as the most thoroughly satisfied elite of all. Swedish politicians are as satisfied as

Swedish administrators—in sharp contrast to administrator-politician satisfaction levels in other systems—and elite satisfaction extends beyond politics to the social system as a whole. In the elite view, Sweden may not yet have become a utopia, but it seems close. Given these levels of satisfaction, it is not surprising that Swedes perceive less conflict in society than any other elite group, despite their general view that social conflicts are healthy and good for society. Nor is it surprising that Swedes are less likely than elites from any other nation to use ideological or theoretical categories to interpret social and political life. As many other studies have reported, and this one confirms, Swedes tend to think pragmatically about specific solutions to concrete problems. This is not to say that no coherent conceptual schema are used to organize thought, but that no single set of conceptual lenses dominates. The Swedish elite clearly appreciates the ideological battles that continue to mobilize political participation in Sweden (as in the rest of Europe), but its intellectual foci are problem-focused rather than theory-focused. Along each of these dimensions—satisfaction, social harmony, pragmatism—Swedish perceptions reflect a distinctively different point of view.

There is another distinct difference that seems even more interesting. Swedish administrators, more than administrators in any other nation, stress the significance of social skills in the conduct of public administration. In contrast to the power-oriented theories of administration that have recently become popular, particularly in the United States, Swedish administrators appear to follow a more people-oriented approach, in which (as we have seen in Chapter 4) motivational and reconciliation skills are prominent. Swedish politicians, too, give greater emphasis to sociability traits than do their colleagues in other systems. It seems plausible to believe that some of this emphasis on what we have called the "soft" side of administration and politics may be due to the specialization of Swedish public interactions, which simultaneously generates a "need" for numerous personal interactions and encourages appreciation of the skills that "work" in such encounters.

But it is also plausible to view the Swedish stress on sociability, more subjectively, as a function of a deep aversion to conflict that characterizes much of Swedish society. Specialization of activity can itself be regarded as a mechanism of conflict avoidance, particularly in a system in which open conflict is so sensitive a problem (Chapter 6), and so ambiguously perceived: society is composed of many different groups (pluralism), each pursuing its interest, yet relatively little "real" conflict occurs; conflict is "good" and "healthy" for society, yet there is less of it today than two decades ago, and that is also "good." Social conflict is so central to interpretations of modern political development, and Swedish perspectives on conflict so ambiguous, that a more extended treatment of the issue of conflict seems useful. That issue will be our concern in the following chapter.

8 NO PLACE TO HIDE: POLITICAL SKILL AND THE SOCIAL PSYCHOLOGY OF CONSENSUS

No image of modern Swedish politics is more widely celebrated than that of the rational, pragmatic Swede, studying problems carefully, consulting widely, and devising solutions that reflect centuries of practice at the art of compromise. For some observers of Swedish political behavior, schooled in different traditions, Swedish practices seem impossibly civil and altogether impenetrable. Andrew Schonfield, in his interesting examination of *Modern Capitalism*, captures the essence of the frustration outsiders often experience in their efforts to understand Swedish practices: "I recall," he writes, "a British trade union leader after an organized visit to Sweden — there were several such visits undertaken by the British trade union movement in the early 1960's in an attempt to discover the secret of Swedish labor's success — expressing his frustration over the whole business. The secret was either too banal or too opaque to yield intelligent investigation. 'All they can tell you when you ask them how they do it,' he said, describing some particularly difficult decision which involved the concerted action of competing interest groups, 'is, "We has a meeting." *We has a meeting!* I'd like to see how they'd make out with our blokes over here.'"[1]

These observers were of course much too pessimistic. By now a good deal more "intelligent investigation" of Swedish practices has been carried out, with the result that the "secret," if that is an appropriate word, is no longer much of a secret. Studies of policy-making behavior at all levels of Swedish government, and in private as well as public-sector organizations, have documented the extraordinary extent to which those activities follow a problem-solving mode: decisions are made very deliberately, sometimes requiring years before a choice is made; few decisions are ever made without a great deal of preparatory research followed by pre-planning for administrative implementation; administrators and politicians involved in these deliberations show remarkable willingness to agree with one another and, once agreement has been reached, an even more remarkable *un*willingness to display lasting opposition to decisions they regard as unfavorable to them. Decisions are themselves structured to avoid lasting opposition. Seldom are there overwhelming "winners" or clear-cut "losers." The typical political/administrative choice distributes a little bit of some benefit to all involved participants, excluding none from some share of the "action." These processes can be regarded as sluggish and unexciting, but there is nothing mysterious about them. Swedes play cautious, rational, and positive-sum games.[2]

Our own research, furthermore, reveals patterns of perception and evaluation that seem quite consistent with these observed behavioral processes. High levels of satisfaction and trust, political sensitivity, awareness of procedural rules and willingness to compromise are all qualities that seem to support the pragmatic bargaining so often portrayed in descriptions of behavioral processes. It certainly should be easy to negotiate compromises, for example, when all participants tend to perceive their interests to be similar, rather than divergent. We know, too, that in many respects, these attitudes are uniquely Swedish. Elites in most Western systems express a willingness to compromise not unlike the Swedish attitude, but in Sweden that attitude is embedded in a very different context. Compared to elites in other nations (Chapter 7), Swedes are far more "satisfied" with both their status and their society, far less likely to perceive "real" conflicts of interest in society, far less likely to view social institutions in stereotyped ideological terms or simple conceptual schemes, and far more likely to stress the importance of social skills—what we referred to earlier (Chapter 4) as "soft" administration—in the conduct of public affairs than anyone else. These peculiarly "Swedish" qualities also seem quite consistent with rationalistic behavior patterns: indeed, it is the obvious consistency between such attitudes and described behavior that often strikes observers as "banal": the apparent congruence between attitude and behavior leaves nothing to be explained.

The ambiguities that surround the Swedish elite view of conflict, however, suggest that the attitude-behavior nexus is neither obvious nor banal. Conflict is good, but the Swedish elite is very happy with a society in which they admit there is far less conflict than before. Disagreements over policy, including public demonstrations in opposition to an announced course of action, are perfectly legitimate, but only so long as they stay within the narrow confines of existing procedural rules. The surprising vehemence with which many members of the elite discuss what should be done if and when "legitimate" demonstrations spill over into violence, furthermore, suggests a level of anxiety about disorder that may have important implications. Assumptions about society and politics that support a desire *to reach agreement* may in fact be very different from assumptions that support a desire *to avoid conflict.* Before we accept the "banality" of Swedish political processes, therefore, we would do well to attempt a deeper exploration of the less obvious sources of Swedish civility.

THE INSTITUTIONALIZATION OF CONFLICT

We begin, as we should, with the institutions that set parameters for individual behavior. To the outsider, Swedish public institutions represent nothing so much as an elaborate structural labyrinth designed to prevent the occurrence of open conflict, channel it into acceptable forms if it does occur, and ritualize its consequences. Consider the more important characteristics of those institutions:

Functional Specialization

Earlier we noted the conflict-suppressing consequences of a highly specialized policy-making role at the national level (Chapter 5). The natural tension between administrators, who seek discretion, and legislators, who seek control, is ameliorated by generally-accepted and clearly-defined divisions of responsibility. All assume that the Parliament will concentrate its institutional attention on general policy debates in which various constituency views can be articulated, and on formal ratification or defeat of proposals initiated elsewhere. Since Parliament has no legal authority to intervene in the daily conduct of administration, legislative oversight—apart from committee requests for information—is confined to an annual efficiency report issued by a committee of senior members, an occasional report by the Constitution Committee, and the work of the three *ombudsmän,* who are responsible to the Parliament, but quite independent from legislative control. Indeed, the ombudsmen themselves reflect another specialized function—the investigation of complaints against governmental actions—that is set apart from the essential work of the national legislature. Sweden is a representative democracy and, within the framework, the business of Parliament is to engage in representation, nothing else.

Similarly, Swedish administration continues to be operated on the premise that a clear distinction can be made between political and administrative action. Legislation creating programs and assigning responsibility for their conduct is immensely detailed, while General Regulations, Royal Instructions and agency-defined Rules of Procedure provide further instructional detail that can run on for hundreds of pages—there is even a rule to instruct administrators on what to do when there is no rule on which to base a decision![3] Administrators are instructed to apply rules defining their responsibilities with "objectivity," applying the relevant laws without personal or political prejudice, and they can be held legally responsible in the event that a law is violated or some individual or social harm is produced by their actions. When official decisions are made, the names of all those participating must be recorded, along with their preferences; individuals who do not publicly state their disagreement are presumed to approve of the decision and are thus legally liable for the consequences produced. And, according to Sweden's "sunshine law," all official documents and records of action must in principle be made immediately available to the public, including letters received and sent. Thus there is always a publicly available indication of who did what on what grounds—there is no place to hide. This view of administration as the objective application of detailed rules seems quaint in the welfare state era, but it reflects the traditional Swedish interpretation of administration as a legal process, wholly different from the exercise of discretion or judgment, which is what politics is supposed to be about. Whether or not administrators behave in this way is less important than the continuing expectation that they can: as administrators, Swedish officials can act only in carefully defined areas of responsibility, according to precise rules of behavior, but with complete freedom from legislative or political intervention. More clearly than the parliamentary role, perhaps this one is highly specialized.

By keeping administration conceptually and legally free from parliamentary interference, and by confining the parliamentary responsibility to representation, the Swedish system effectively insulates each specialized role from the conflict-generating excesses of the other. Both parliamentarians and administrators, however, are regularly brought into the third, equally specialized, policy-making role through participation in the numerous Royal Commissions established each year. If this role did not exist, it would surely have to be invented, for the Royal Commission has been the traditional mechanism through which problems in current operations are investigated, solutions proposed, and new policies developed. Widespread use of the Royal Commission device allows Parliament and administrative officials to maintain narrow conceptions of their own appropriate spheres of action without sacrificing adjustment capacity. Indeed, that capacity is enhanced because the Cabinet, rather than individual members of commissions, bears legal responsibility for new proposals, freeing participants from the caution encouraged by the legal requirements of "normal" administration. Less constrained use of administrative and parliamentary expertise, in settings that encourage frequent interaction, with easy access to ministry personnel and financial resources, structure a policy-making tool that is not only specialized, but effective. Policy changes are developed, a sense of participation is spread among many members of the elite, institutional purity is maintained and conflict—either between roles or over policy—is resolved, privately.

Political role specialization is of course characteristic of far more than the normal representation-administration-policy-making functions of the elite. We have already noted that the function of investigating charges of governmental excess is accomplished by another clearly-defined and independent role: that of the *ombudsman*. The role of citizens is another well-understood pattern of behavior. Swedes have a number of clear legal rights (free expression, access to public documents, etc.), but the fundamental political expectation is that a citizen should vote. Swedes do vote, usually with higher rates of participation than other democratic systems, but there is a striking absence of other political activity among citizens. Citizen or voter "leagues," neighborhood or community organizations, or "coalitions" for this or that cause have seldom been found in Sweden, and participation in the affairs of political parties or interest groups is typically confined to the few activists who have enough interest to pursue leadership positions. Government, party and group leaders expect citizens to provide support, and citizens do so at the polls and at annual organizational meetings, but neither leaders nor citizen followers expect that the average Swede will participate in the day-to-day activities of the various organizations to which he/she belongs. Like other political roles in Sweden, this one is specialized to the function of providing support.[4]

The pattern of seeking a clear definition for a limited, highly-specialized activity, creating a position to carry on that activity, and then permitting that activity to go on without further interference is a major characteristic of Swedish politics. One result is a proliferation of positions and titles with clear, but very subtle, distinctions. A person elected to a local or national legislative body is a *"förtroendeman,"* a man in whom one invests "trust" to act in behalf of others. The much-used title of *"ombudsman"* refers to a person who is a "representative" of either individual or group interests; that kind of person is neither expected nor required to be concerned about the interests of any collectivity apart from the one he "represents." When the interests of two or more organizations are in real or potential conflict, Swedes often appoint a *"förlik-ningsman,"* a "negotiator," to achieve a resolution that is assumed to be impossible to achieve at all or as well through the actions of conflicting parties. Each of these titles implies a somewhat different notion of "interest"—public, partial or joint—and each of them is surrounded by clear but quite delicate expectations about behavior that is or is not appropriate to the role. What often appears to outsiders as a "fetish" about legal and other rules in Sweden is thus nothing more than an attempt to be clear about the permitted boundaries of one's own action, or about the appropriate title or concept to be attached to some position or status that is under consideration. Precisely because there are so many specialized political functions defined in Sweden, choosing a title or status designation is in fact to choose what an occupant of that position can or cannot do, with or to whom, when, and how.

Being as clear as Swedes try to be about political roles represents a traditional, and by now well-developed, effort to reduce conflict or avoid it altogether. If everyone is clear about their authority and responsibilities, then there will be no cause for dispute and no reason for conflict to occur. Thus even public demonstrations in Sweden take place according to carefully defined rules about what a "demonstrator" or "protestor" can and cannot do, as well as what other roles can or cannot do in response. The results may seem incongruous to observers from other political systems, with less respect for specialized action—squadrons of police motorcycles guiding (and protecting) street demonstrators whose flags and banners call for violent revolution seems curious to some foreigners—but when it works, role specialization does in fact suppress open and visible conflict. Potentially unstable environments become orderly, calm, and quite predictable.

Remiss: Hostages to Policy

If political role specialization prevents the occurrence of many conflicts, another Swedish institution serves to channel conflicts that do occur within safe and manageable bounds. The institution is called "*remiss,*" and refers to the widespread practice of submitting proposals for major policy change to all parties or organizations likely to be affected by the proposals, or likely to have an interest in responding to them. Actual referral of proposals to affected parties takes place at somewhat different stages of the process, depending on level of government and source of proposal, but it is always done before a *final* proposal or plan is drafted. Royal Commissions, for example, submit their reports (which may have taken years to prepare) to the relevant Minister who, after his own review, decides whether or not the matter should go further.[5] A decision to go further implies submitting the proposal to national and local government agencies, interest groups, private firms, party organizations, and any other group or interest thought to be affected: on major proposals the "affected" organizations can quite literally number in the hundreds. Each organization is sent a copy of the proposal and asked to comment on it. Comments received by the ministry are themselves reviewed and, where necessary or appropriate, changes are made before submitting the final proposal and explanatory text to the Parliament, in the form of a government bill ("proposition"). Although it is difficult to capture the thoroughness, comprehensiveness and sheer bulk of bills on major problems, a simple listing of *some* of the organizations invited to submit *remiss* comments on the 1967 housing bill, chosen more or less randomly from various sections of the bill, would include: The National Housing Board, the Swedish League of Cities, the Board of Agriculture, City of Gothenburg, City of Stockholm, City of Linköping, Swedish Association of Counties, Uppsala University, Post Office Board, the National Building Board, City of Västerås, the National Water Authority, National Association of Renters, Malmö Budget Office, Swedish Association of Industries, TCO (white collar union), LO (the confederation of labor unions), SABO (the national organization of public building authorities). Gothenburg League of Suburbs, Five Members of the Greater Stockholm Planning Board, Five *Other* Members of the Greater Stockholm Planning Board, and so on, and so on.[6] Before presenting legislation for a new cultural policy to the Parliament in 1974, the Ministry of Education and Culture worked its way through some 562 *remiss* statements—surely a record of sorts, in a year when more than 5,000 *remiss* comments were generated for the 188 government bills submitted.[7] If nothing else, writing *remiss* responses must be regarded as a major industry in Sweden.

To notice the comprehensiveness of this consultative process, and its obvious impact on policy, is to notice only part of what is important. It is equally important to remember that these consultative processes are largely sheltered from public view: proposals are generated by commissions whose activities are seldom open to the public, they are circulated by ministry officials following routine operating procedures, and responses to them are prepared by specialized governmental or interest group staff personnel, working in the privacy of their headquarters offices. Individuals involved in these activities know who is saying what, and why, but widespread public awareness is largely absent until the point at which the final proposal is released. Royal Commission reports and government bills indicate considerable disagreement on major proposals, but the *remiss* process usually keeps such disagreement confined behind closed doors or along the metallic strands of telephone wire that link various members of the involved elite. If disagreement surfaces in the written reports, it is primarily to show how the problems mentioned have been dealt with or why, having been noted, they cannot be dealt with. *Remiss* procedures do not eliminate conflict, but they surely domesticate it by reducing the possibility of public controversy. Disagreements are confined to disputes among officials; they are expressed through appropriate written channels using the appropriate argumentative means; and they are typically resolved *before* proposals are made public.[8]

The processes of avoiding citizen participation while encouraging the broadest possible range of official and interest group involvement obviously reflect the traditional preference for "informed" policy-making: those who participate have experiential knowledge and thus a more profound basis for formulating judgments than do "uninformed" citizens. But consider the political consequences of such processes. Having been invited to participate, having participated, and having had its ideas either implemented or dismissed for explicitly stated reasons, what does an organization then do if it wishes to oppose part or all of some major proposal? Claims based on lack of information or participation will obviously lack credibility, and even a simple disagreement will lack credibility unless that disagreement was expressed openly in *remiss* responses. Expressing disagreement at that stage, however, permits a ministerial response to be made that will undercut the significance of that disagreement in the final proposal. Agreeing to participate in the processes leading to a final proposal thus imposes severe constraints on later, more public, disagreement. Since the number of participants is typically large, particularly on major proposals, *remiss* procedures have the effect of creating a large number of agency and interest group organizations who, because they have participated in shaping a proposal, are effectively prevented from opposing it. We have elsewhere referred to these processes of implicating as many leaders as possible into major proposals as the "hostage principle."[9] The principle is more elaborately pursued at the Royal Commission level than at other levels, but it is in fact widely followed at all levels of Swedish politics. Hostages are the essential ingredient of Swedish political consensus.

Institutional Ritualization

"Hostage" is a useful concept because it implies what is often true, namely, that a consensus on any given proposal may be made up in part of individuals who agree with the proposals, and in part of individuals who in fact disagree but who have no effective way to express that disagreement. This is almost certain to be true of many important national proposals because ministerial control over policy-making processes is often very strict, beginning with careful specification of the charge given to a Royal Commission, extending to the selection of personnel for the Commission (whose positions, remember, are well-known), and continuing to the choice of substantive recommendations to be made and organizations to be invited to submit *remiss* responses. Increasing sophistication in the use of these controls in recent years has led to increased ministerial-cabinet domination of the policy process: in one year, for example, the Parliament accepted 226 of the 258 bills introduced by the cabinet—220 of them without change![10] Under these conditions the ratio of hostages to supporters might be expected to grow, and along with it, the sense of frustration associated with lack of political impact.

In Sweden, however, there is a perfectly acceptable method of giving expression to disagreement, thus relieving some of the frustration, if nothing else. If, despite all the consultations and all the accommodations and all the adjustments, something objectionable remains, it is always possible to attach a "reservation," indicating both the nature of the objection and the grounds for it. In some ways the "reservation" resembles a negative vote on some proposal, but there is a crucial difference: a "reservation" can be attached to some portion of a proposal without affecting support for or opposition to the proposal as a whole. It is thus the perfect way to express individual preferences without destroying the general consensus—the perfectly Swedish device. The Swedish system assumes that decisions are a collective responsibility and that all participants support the collective choice *unless they explicitly record a different view.*[11] Since decisions are made in private settings, by people who know each other well and have worked together for long periods of time, it is easy to imagine that the pressure to go along is the foundation of the richly suggestive aphorism, 'Don't push him, pull him.' What better way to deal with the pressure than to accept the whole, but attach statements of opposition to various parts? The gesture can only have symbolic value, since the basic decision remains unaffected, but it permits officials to be in disagreement without being in conflict. Symbolic affirmation of that possibility, of the legitimacy of strongly-held opinions, and of the rational discrimination involved in selecting portions of a proposal to oppose lends credibility to important Swedish political values without the slightest hint of obstructionism. Ritualized opposition, in short, has significant longer-term consequences even when it lacks immediate impact. In the long-run, the chief product of these rituals must be affirmation of the Swedish consensus.

USEFUL SKILLS AND SKILLFUL USES

Institutions that suppress conflict, direct it into privatized settings, and ritualize its expression when it does break out obviously require highly-developed but very subtle political skills. Because open conflict occurs so infrequently, a whole range of political techniques useful in more boisterous political systems (such as the American) are either unnecessary or unproductive, or both. "Going public" to dramatize a policy disagreement is regarded as very bad form and is almost never done by officials. Public displays of anger, real or simulated, are similarly rare, as are spontaneous demonstrations, confrontations, or other less orderly political actions. Public debate is thus devoid of the language excesses used in other systems to mobilize or maintain support for a cause. Even a relatively mild suggestion, made by a party leader in the midst of a recent election campaign, that an opposition party proposal should be treated as waste paper and thrown away, was regarded by many Swedes as rather too strong a statement to be made in a Swedish campaign.[12] The mass public is simply not a relevant part of the system except for elections, at which time official debates are expected to "inform" (not mobilize) in order to justify (not cause) their highly organized and quite predictable support.[13] Displays of verbal or behavioral aggressiveness seem quite out of place in this environment.

Skills that matter are those that permit officials to maneuver their way to success in the conference room, behind closed doors, that provide settings within which "successes" are defined and achieved. Swedish institutions, which assume collective responsibility for policy but assign individual guilt for failure, virtually guarantee that no change from established procedures will be attempted by an individual official: the most fundamental rule of Swedish politics must be 'always take hostages.' And since officials and their preferences are so well-known, building a successful consensus around some proposal will typically require the ability to secure participation prior to any effort to modify positions. Securing participation obviously requires highly-developed verbal skills – to identify the grounds on which participation can be based, to state those grounds without compromising goals, and to communicate those grounds persuasively yet with enough flexibility to avoid unretrievable commitments prior to final agreement. The skills required are extremely subtle because they are extremely personal. Such negotiations must be conducted in person or by telephone before anything can be written down: as we have seen, an agreement to do no more than participate in the *remiss* process carries important political implications and must therefore be approached with caution. Securing participation thus requires well-developed inter-personal skills, the "sociability" skills about which Swedish officials talk so much.

Elite sensitivity to the personal aspects of official interaction shows up clearly in responses to our hypothetical question about the action consequences of being right. "Suppose," we said, "there were a disagreement in which one side was thought to be wholly right and the other side wholly wrong; do you think that the side that is right should maintain its position or do you think it should seek a compromise?" Most respondents, as we have seen (Chapter 6), believe that compromise is desirable, in part because it makes little sense to them to speak of being "wholly" right or wrong. While few would go as far as equating what is right with what is possible (#218), most nevertheless doubt that their world can be so simply understood:

> In the first place, I don't believe there is any conflict situation in which one side is totally right and the other totally wrong; from this point of view the question is stated incorrectly. But even if there were such a situation it would be impossible to give a very simple answer because, in thinking about resolving conflicts and all that goes with it you have to see things over the long run as well as for the short term. When you do that it becomes clear that it can

often go just as bad for someone who tries to absolutely maintain his position as for the other. It can go just as poorly for him as for the dog in the fable who dropped the piece of meat he had in his mouth when he tried to get the piece of meat he saw in the mirror. If you maintain a longer-range perspective it is often possible to give up something in the short run in order to gain a compromise that is a long-run benefit. That kind of gain can in fact be much better over the long run than to obstinately stick with a position you think to be the right one (#106).

Note that this is basically a self-interested view of the virtues of compromise: your own long-run interests remain central but you hold onto them best by not trying to achieve all of them at once.

The reason for not trying to achieve everything you might want is that the effort is almost certain to produce what one official calls "secondary psychological consequences":

> If I think I'm absolutely right I will probably want to push my position hard. But I will often say that perhaps it wouldn't be right to push 100 percent because that can lead to secondary psychological consequences, and thus it would not be 100 percent right to push so hard . . . There are psychological factors that are important realities to take into account. People who talk only about what is right and wrong are really dangerous (#54).

Another official clarified the nature of those psychological consequences when he suggested that the "right" side in such a situation would certainly want "to show a little bit of generosity to the losing party in the debate, to round off the disagreement as much as possible, *in order to avoid establishment of a permanent opposition.* You can try to show a little generosity rather than taking everything you have coming, in that way avoiding a situation in which someone permanently stands as a loser" (#134). The desire to avoid creation of a permanent opposition must of course be quite widespread and wholly realistic in a system that provides both permanent tenure and independent authority for senior civil servants. To antagonize someone whose cooperation is essential and who will hold his position for years to come would seem imprudent, at the very least. Swedish officials are bound to be sensitive to this problem because each one of them measures his own anticipated tenure in decades rather than years. Thus, as one official sums it up,

> In order to create a better climate of cooperation it can often be useful to follow what an old-timer in this agency used to say: 'Yes, I'm right, so I can give in a little bit.' There is something to that. If a person is completely right, he can still generously give something to the other party in order to shape a better future relationship between them. I think one has to do that, considering all the circumstances (#213).

Giving in a bit when you are ahead, being "generous" with other parties to a negotiation who may gain less than you do, and doing what you can to prevent anyone from feeling himself a "loser" (and thus a potential opponent in future negotiations) all are sentiments that reflect what we now know to be the characteristically Swedish concern for the social aspects of administration and politics. Within an institutional setting that operates to suppress and moderate conflict, such sentiments encourage the elaborately stylized courtesies that characterize personal interaction among officials: the ritual use of titles among the less familiar, the carefully-calibrated calculations leading to the "dropping of titles" in favor of the more familiar "*du*,"[14] the similarly-calculated cultivation of relationships through small favors that, over time, build up to large obligations. Swedish officials, with anticipations of many years in office, can use time to develop relationships through such courtesies; having developed networks of personal obligations, officials can use them to develop support for changes that can be made without overt conflict, by individuals who are institutionally motivated to be at least as concerned about maintaining relationships as they are about organizational performance. The most essential, and most characteristic, skill among members of the Swedish elite, accordingly, is not the intellectual capacity for analysis or the organizational capacity to make decisions; it is a social capacity for agenda management.

Both our own data (Chapter 4) and other studies document the extent to which Swedes attempt to monitor the environment in which they work and act. Swedish public statistics, of course, are among the best in the world, which means that opportunities for some public response are constantly being generated by "official" information demonstrating unanticipated consequences, or revealing gaps between expectations and performance. Officials are not only sensitive to such information, they actively seek to generate it where it does not exist. Wheeler, for example, has shown that major interest group organizations in Sweden go to elaborate lengths to identify the concerns of their members. In addition to the common mechanism of periodic or annual meetings, interest group leaders have created various kinds of advisory groups, they routinely do surveys of membership opinions on various organizational and political issues, and they maintain a variety of publications to report this kind of information as well as to generate feedback from it.[15] More or less constant monitoring of relevant environments ensures a constant supply of program ideas to be funneled into processes of agenda building.

Since there is no lack of ideas for agenda building, the crucial component of agenda management is the coordination of people rather than programs. Intimate knowledge, generated over a period of years of interaction, is not only helpful, it is absolutely essential to the variety of extraordinarily subtle judgments that have to be made in deciding whether to raise an issue, with whom, and when. Consider a sequence of events, stretching over a period of three decades, we have described elsewhere. A city politician, hoping to implement a twenty-year-old plan to reform urban government, refuses for years to press for reform, knowing that three party colleagues who are leaders in the county government that would in part be "reformed," are strongly opposed. Instead, he coopts these and other regional political leaders into an organization to promote increased housing production, and persuades the national government to provide the necessary resources. He then persuades the national government to press the city and its surrounding suburbs into an agreement to create a metropolitan transportation system; he agrees to give up city control of rolling stock but in return achieves national subsidy and suburban participation in financing the new system. Two of the three suburban opponents suddenly pass away and within a month, the city politician has organized a coalition to support a reform plan that is publicly presented before opposition can be generated. The coalition includes the third suburban colleague, who has been persuaded to change his mind. A phased plan is prepared, more national assistance is secured and, although the city leader is later displaced, a "reformed" metropolitan government is created within six years.[16]

Although it is clear that the city leader had to have detailed familiarity with national as well as local government structures in order to promote his reform successfully, what seems particularly significant to these activities are the judgments he had to make about people. He judged that the three suburban opponents to reform (one of whom, incidentally, served simultaneously in the national parliament) were so strongly opposed that it would not be useful to challenge them, despite party allegiance. He later judged, accurately, that one of the three could be persuaded to change his mind when the support of the other two was suddenly taken away. Finally, he judged it to be possible to gain quick support from a number of other crucial county and national leaders in order to promote a plan for major institutional change that had never before been presented in operational form. By presenting the operational design and giving it a name, the official succeeded in defining new terms in which an old issue would thereafter be debated. And by quickly arranging a series of meetings in which successively more detailed versions of the plan were worked out, he effectively monopolized the arena within which the reform would be negotiated. Timing— the art of knowing when to take what actions—no less than judgments about individual actors and their motivations is an essential component of political success in Sweden as elsewhere.

To interpret judgment and timing skills solely in individual terms would miss much of their significance, for the context within which they are exercised has a great deal to do with the quality of their use. Long tenure and an extraordinary degree of positional overlapping remove much of the "guesswork" from judgments about individual motivations. In a discussion with Christopher Wheeler, a Swedish Board of Education official describes the governmental perspective on proposals put on the agency's Executive Board, on which numerous interest groups are represented: "We have pretty good intuition. We don't propose crazy ideas to the Executive Board which will only be voted down. We're able to say in the discussion within the agency that precedes a meeting of the Executive Board whether groups will or won't accept a proposal." The view from the interest group side is equally plain: "We from our organization must make a judgment as to where the other groups in the Executive Board and the agency officials stand when we draw up our proposals. The agency must do the same. They know if they write a proposal this way or that, they are very likely to have this or that group in opposition. They may accept that; but they never go so far as to risk a situation where the agency's proposal will be voted down." Wheeler goes on to make clear that this high level of government-group knowledge of one another's interests and motivations is a direct product of overlapping positions held by members of the Executive Board:

> . . . during the time field research was carried out for this study, TCO (the major white collar union) SACO (the union of university graduates), and LO's (the central labor federation) educational representatives and the general director and deputy director of the agency sat together on the Ministry of Education's Planning Council. TCO, LO, and SAF's (the Swedish Employers Federation) representatives in the planning council sat together on the Royal Commission dealing with major education reforms. Often a high-ranking member from the SO (Board of Education) sat on these commissions as cairman or secretary. LO and SAF's education representatives sat together on the labor market board. As one participant put it: "As you surely have been able to see since you have been in Sweden, it is really a small circle of people who deal with practically everything."[17]

One obvious consequence of this system of structured familiarity is that the "law of anticipated reactions" is much more accurately used in Sweden than elsewhere, because it can be. To cite another of Wheeler's respondents, "The more organs in which we have common posts, the better we get to know one another and the better this process of mutual attempts to influence one another works."[18] Unacceptable proposals are seldom offered, allowing members of the elite to concentrate their "official" energies on the details of predetermined agreements. If unacceptable proposals are made, ways are found to temporize until conditions change rather than forcing the proposal on those to whom it is unacceptable. Another, perhaps less obvious, consequence, is that the personal coordination so essential to the functioning of the system is easily arranged once a course of action has been chosen. Precisely because of multiple offices, individual members of the elite typically are clear about who should be involved in a given decision and about how such involvement can be arranged. A Stockholm official's ability to achieve agreement among twenty-seven area municipalities plus a dozen different agencies of the national government is no surprise, because he has previously served with all of the individuals, either as participant in some cooperative venture, member of some Royal Commission, colleague in one or another group, or perhaps as member of a political party organization. Wheeler's excellent analysis of a major interest group is filled with reports of similar behavior: coordination achieved through the personal contacts enjoyed by one or another leader in the interest organization. Knowledge, judgment and timing skills are thus structurally induced, and not simply matters of individual talent. Their use by members of the elite often permits quick action in a system otherwise devoted to very slow and very deliberate processes. Both the "normal" processes of visible inaction and the occasional bursts of rapid implementation, however, are products of the same array of structurally-defined sociability skills.

Institutions designed to avoid public conflict, attitudes that reflect sensitivity to inter-personal accommodation, and numerous reports of effective interpersonal coordination all suggest widespread agreement on a series of procedural norms to guide Swedish administrative policies. We can summarize this normative consensus in the following loose rules of thumb:

1. *Always know where you stand* The status and legal authority to act conferred by official position are important political resources in a system so sensitive to precise behavioral boundaries. Since knowing the limits of one's own authority implies knowing the limits imposed on others, such knowledge is an effective tool for avoiding conflict. It is also an essential component for any calculated strategy to change either relationships or programs.

2. *Always take hostages* Although it is sometimes possible to act alone on some matter, particularly if it is a new problem or activity not clearly assigned to one or another office, acting alone would be interpreted either as aggrandizement or stealth, leaving the actor with little or no political support. It is therefore always preferable, and usually necessary, for an actor advancing a proposal to secure advance commitments of support from other influential actors. The more significant the proposal, the more essential it is to secure broad support, from a coalition large enough to be successful, even in the face of opposition. Since premature public awareness of major change proposals can strengthen the opposition, it is important to build the coalition informally, through personal or mediated conversations, and to avoid commiting either the proposal or the identity

of its potential supporters to writing before the coalition is securely in place.

3. *Fight in private*   Strong disagreement over proposals for change is both unavoidable and useful, but expression of such disagreement should be confined to the closed committee rooms or other information settings in which negotiations can proceed in private. Public expression of strong disagreement is not only unseemly, it also suggests that officials have not given sufficient study to the issue to produce a solution that all can agree is the "right" one. Disagreements that remain after lengthy negotiations can always be expressed in writing, the "proper" way, since it offers no obstacle to proceeding. Proposals that are made public should always reflect the consensus agreed to by the majority coalition; care should be taken to create a large coalition if there is a possibility of written objections that reflect significant opposition.[19]

4. *Take time*   Since most officials measure their expected tenure in decades rather than years, there is seldom any strong reason to hurry, and often much to be gained by simply waiting. With the passage of time incumbents in positions may retire, new positions can be created, or new formulations given to old issues – these and other factors often make possible in one year what might have been quite impossible in a previous year. Waiting, therefore, is sometimes both the "only" and the "best" strategy.

5. *When you are winning, compromise*   In Sweden, the late Mayor Daley's rule, 'don't back no losers,'[20] is transformed into the more Swedish 'don't *make* no losers.' Confining conflict to private settings is of course a method of avoiding public embarrassment for the losing side, but Swedes also go to great lengths to avoid having a losing side at all. Giving up a little bit when you are ahead is, as we have seen, the typical formulation of this attitude. The typical result is a settlement in which winners and losers are virtually indistinguishable, because everybody wins something. For Swedes this is less a matter of good will than of good sense: compromising away some of what has been won helps to maintain the good social relationships that are essential to long-term cooperative interactions, even if it sometimes produces less impressive short-term gains.

6. *When you are losing, join the winners*   Maintaining a contrary opinion against a prevailing consensus is difficult enough when the individuals who define the consensus are strangers. When the consensus view is widely shared by individuals who have been, and will continue to be, colleagues for a long time, maintaining a divergent position is not only more difficult, but risky: a reputation for obstructionism is not easily lived down in such an environment. Thus the same factors that encourage winners to compromise – long expected tenure, desire for good relation-

ships during that tenure—also encourages losers to become part of the prevailing consensus. As words are changed to accommodate issues of "principle" that must be given a different public expression, and as negotiated benefits are distributed to all participants, differences between individual positions generally diminish. Over time, elite behavior gives the impression of substantial underlying consensus, with few obvious losers but a great many satisfied (if only partially) winners.

PERSONALITY AND STYLIZED CONSENSUS

Understanding the institutional context of elite interaction takes us some distance toward understanding the sources of conflict-avoidance behavior among Swedish administrators. Institutions induce patterns of role orientation and behavior that can be observed and explained without resorting to individual-level psychological theories. Even negotiating and bargaining skill, usually thought of as an inherently individual attribute, can be shown to have sources in the institutional structures that define opportunities and offer more or less effective strategies of achievement. Multiple centers of independent authority, lifetime tenure, overlapping positions, and comprehensive consultation define a context that both encourages and rewards the sociability skills necessary for administrative success in Sweden. It seems interesting, nevertheless, to speculate about possible relationships between personality characteristics and institutional structure that seem to have no obvious structural source. Having described the elaborate institutional devices used by the Swedes to avoid conflict, for example, it remains unclear why such devices should exist at all. Swedes go to great lengths to avoid conflict, and do so with great success, but why? Why not allow conflicts that exist within society to blossom more publicly, creating more distinct cleavages and generating more sustained public attention? Is there a psychological resistance to public conflict that is somehow rooted in Swedish personality structure?

One reason this line of speculation seems interesting is that elite administrators seem determined to maintain a clear boundary between their official roles and their personal lives. Swedish administrators work hard and are strongly-motivated to succeed, but not to the exclusion of other, more personalized, values. Our interviews suggest that these middle- and upper-class individuals retain their interest in a variety of non-official activities, that they guard their ability to participate in such activities outside of working hours with considerable energy, and that they tend to compartmentalize their work, treating it as something quite apart from more private personal concerns. Unlike the totally-committed organization men portrayed in other literature,[21] these officials typically avoid taking their work home with them, and they report a low level of discussion of work problems with friends. Swedish elite administrators, in short, are not totally consumed by their jobs; only a portion of an individual's personality is identified with position, in what we think of as a *pattern of limited commitment:* there are well-defined behaviors associated with official status; they are not related to individual personality and, provided only that such behaviors are maintained, these officials are free to undertake any action consistent with their responsibilities. Since personality is not heavily invested in position, personality problems are less significant in the conduct of public business. Personal antagonisms or status anxiety, for example, seldom impose barriers to official interaction.

From a structural point of view, limited commitment provides yet another explanation for Swedish ability to generate agreement among large numbers of independent officials. From an individual point of view, however, limited commitment can be viewed as a device for protection of the self from public exposure. Role masks worn during the day prevent other individuals from gaining knowledge of the value and motivational configurations that define the other, non-official, personality. Protection of the private self through stylized public role behavior is of course a ubiquitous feature of social life in complex societies; indeed, it is doubtful that complicated modern societies could function at all without the highly specialized and partial roles that characterize institutional structure in such societies.[22] The intensity with which such public faces are maintained in Sweden – the extraordinary role specialization, the careful specification of permitted and excluded behavior, the emphasis on organized rather than spontaneous settings for personal interaction – all suggest a degree of commitment to maintenance of the privatized self that must be regarded as unusual. That strong a commitment may in fact offer a clue to the elaborate defenses against public conflict that the Swedes have erected, since it is clear that open conflict can create situations in which no established role definitions are appropriate. In such spontaneous situations, some individuals are likely to engage in behavior that reflects private personality rather than public role, thus "exposing" a portion of the self that had previously been protected from observation by others. If such "exposure" were to reveal values markedly different from those associated with an individual's "public" role it might lead to embarrassment, ridicule, or other expression of distaste for deviation from established expectations. Perhaps to prevent such "exposure" and the possibility of unfortunate consequences for the exposed self, Swedes do whatever they can to avoid open conflict.

Although we made no attempt to gather data that might offer direct support for these speculations, there is considerable indirect support available in other work, of various kinds. The existence and power of group and community norms, for example, has been well-documented by social scientists, journalists and other observers. From an early age, Swedish children are taught the virtues of collective action and the desirability of working cooperatively with others rather than going it alone. School curricula coupled with an elaborate network of organized youth groups stress the same values, producing adults who are practiced "members" of various organizations and whose behavior is carefully attuned to the elaborate codes that reflect communal judgments about appropriate conduct.[23] Deviations from accepted standards of behavior, language or even dress are quickly corrected through standard informal techniques (staring, frowning, moving away, etc.) or, when necessary, use of formal authority. Over time, observable behavior becomes quite uniform across individuals, producing a predictability that apparently becomes both habitual and comfortable, since there is seldom any question about expected behavior.[24] Swedish films often portray personal unhappiness produced by observed deviation from common standards, which suggests that anxiety over the possibility of being seen to be deviant is probably experienced by many Swedes. Neither eccentric people nor eccentric behavior are easily tolerated in Sweden.[25]

If socialized "other-directedness," reflecting the power of group norms to control the public behavior of individuals, is clearly documented, so too is the determination of Swedes to protect their privacy. Visitors to Sweden typically notice an absence of public sociability rituals that suggests an absence of interest in other people—variously described as "shyness" or "aloofness" or "stiffness."[26] Although foreigners sometimes attribute these qualities to their own obvious strangeness, two decades of research into community behavior have now established that Swedes self-consciously maintain as much distance from their own countrymen as from the visitors who occasionally wander by. Swedes do not make friends easily and are not, therefore, members of large friendship networks; although enrolled as members in various organizations, Swedes seldom participate in organizational activities; communal life in residential areas is characterized by extraordinarily low levels of personal interaction; leisure-time activities typically involve getting away from other people as much as possible, to isolated cabins or camps where individuals or family units can be alone. Furthermore, these privacy-maintaining behavior patterns seem quite stable through time, despite other major social changes. Thus recent studies by Daun[27] and Popenoe[28] report levels of "neighboring" behavior—saying hello, visiting, shopping together, family care assistance—that are as low in the mid-1970's as they were in the mid-1950's, when Dahlström conducted very similar investigations.[29] The persistence of such patterns in the face of large-scale social and technological changes and organized campaigns to "loosen up" Swedish social relations suggests an unusually powerful desire to protect the inner self against external intrusions.

It is easy enough to imagine the relationship between behavior-controlling community norms that are comprehensively pervasive and individual desires to be free from the power of those norms, if only in the shelter provided by home or the opportunity provided by some isolated vacation cabin. Knowledge that even a minor slip into inappropriate behavior will result in immediate sanction, because everyone knows what is "appropriate," is a heavy burden that Swedes themselves sometimes describe as "suffocating." Home, vacation alone, or even foreign travel each can provide a release from that burden and an opportunity to exercise the "real" self. Within Sweden, however, release is possible only when other Swedes are not around, since the fear that other Swedes would continue to sanction community norms would be enough to prevent release. Swedes therefore do not invest heavily in "friendship," entertain sparingly, vacation alone if they can and even go abroad when possible to avoid being totally consumed by socially-defined rules of behavior.

These observations imply that, explicitly or implicitly, Swedes maintain an "inner self" that is clearly distinct from the public roles they play. They imply, too, that the inner self has very little to support it apart from individual ego strength—in sharp contrast to the strong support available for acceptable public roles. Precisely because of the absence of inter-personal support for the inner self, exposure can have shattering consequences. Once the portion of self that has been carefully cultivated and jealously guarded from outsiders is exposed, there is—almost literally—nothing left of the most important aspect of personality. Without support for the private personality, exposure commonly leads to individual crises that seem impossible to handle. Withdrawal, flight from the area or job or, in very extreme cases, suicide, are among the responses to exposure reported for Swedish professionals.[30] The political analog is the phenomenon of the "spoiled" personality: someone who has behaved so unusually, or has been so controversial, or has so obviously failed to follow accepted norms, that he or she is no longer considered acceptable for significant public responsibilities. "Spoiled" personalities are typically assigned to one or another of the many honorific positions maintained for just such persons, unless the process of "spoiling" has been so public that banishment from further public activities seems advisable.[31]

Detailed regulation of behavior by comprehensive community norms, a consequent search for a privatized self beyond the reach of those norms, and highly individualized but easily shattered definitions of the private self create a social-psychological context in which the individual consequences of engaging in public conflict can be very severe indeed. To enter into a public controversy, in which there are no clear rules governing appropriate behavior, is to risk exposure of the private self; to expose the private self is to reveal attributes that are likely to be defined as "deviant"; to be defined as deviant is to lose the protection of the self offered by the stylized public role and thus to risk spoiling the personality required to play the public role. To engage in conflict, in short, is to risk both loss of self and destruction of career. The risk is taken, but not often and not without extreme caution.

We are now in better position to appreciate the significance of some of the themes that emerge in our conversations with Swedish elite administrators. Swedish officials prefer to pull rather than push, avoid confrontations, are generous when ahead and accommodating when behind less because they are humane individuals—although they may be—than because they perceive the potential consequences *for themselves* that can arise from different styles of action. By their very nature, conflicts are difficult to contain; out of control, they can as easily destroy initiators as targets. It is far better, then, to follow procedures than minimize the occurrence of conflict and keep it under strict control if it should occur. When these officials speak of "integrity," either as a requirement or as something enjoyed (Chapter 4), they clearly refer to their own ability to maintain a coherent and uncorrupted self-definition behind a similarly clear conception of what they can and cannot do as officials. Integrity is in this sense a product of conflict-free environment that offers few challenges to existing conceptions. Integrity, no less than sociability, has its roots in self-interest—or, to put it differently, a highly interested pursuit of self-preservation.

Our search for psychological components of conflict-avoidance behavior among the Swedish elite is not an attempt to "reduce" that behavior to a single explanation. As we have suggested, we can account for a great deal of the behavior we seek to explain without resorting to psychological characteristics. It is also true that psychological qualities such as "fear of exposure," or phenomena similar to "spoiled" personalities, can be found among individuals in many systems, not only in Sweden. What *cannot* be found in many systems, and what we have tried to portray, is the pattern of structural and individual qualities that together form a *context* for action that is peculiarly Swedish. Institutions that suppress open displays of conflict and control conflict when it takes place, structural incentives to develop and use a variety of "sociability" skills, and psychological concern over a potential loss of individuality through conflict are references to very different aspects of Swedish social relations. Each of these contextual components, however, produces a reduction in the level of open conflict. Together they given an amiability to Swedish administrative and/or political behavior that is unique among nations that pretend to be both modern and democratic.

9 POSTSCRIPT: ON THE POLITICS OF ACCOMMODATION

Studies of politics often pose questions to which the only available answers are bound to be misleading. If one were to ask whether bureaucrats or politicians were more powerful in modern Sweden, for example, any response that could be made would be unenlightening. Observing the growing resource base available to senior civil servants, the Swedish traditions of administrative independence and prestige, and the widespread participation of bureaucrats in policy-making roles, one might be tempted to conclude that the bureaucracy is clearly the dominant force. Yet the country has been strongly influenced by a reformist political party that retained power for forty-four years and used that power to initiate a variety of new programs, whether or not the bureaucrats were very much in favor of those programs. However pragmatic or activist Swedish administrators may be, politicians—including many in the so-called bourgeois parties—obviously have been more innovative in devising new programs. Who is more powerful? There can be no good answer because the question itself admits none. If Sweden suggests anything, surely it is that governance in modern democratic states is collective governance, widely shared, about which the interesting questions are not who is or who is not on top, at any given time, for any given issue, but rather, what relationship exists between those who wield power, how are they mediated, and how do they change through time.

The Swedish experience makes this point so well because the tradition of administration participation in politics is so strong and so obvious. An equally strong tradition of widespread consultation between interest groups and the government is institutionalized in a very visible *remiss* process. Modern Sweden thus emphasizes the extent to which administrative institutions must be viewed *in the context of relationships to other institutions* if they are to be properly understood. For students of leadership in modern societies, it is particularly important that bureaucratic-political relationships be clearly seen, since those relationships have become central sources of guided social change.

Consider how misleading it would be, for example, to draw conclusions about either the exercise of power or social policy from a narrow focus on the bureaucratic institution itself. Conclusions derived from such a narrow focus abound in recent writings about "representative bureaucracy," which often imply that public programs only service groups that are "represented" among administrators of those programs.[1] Although evidence to support these implications is seldom offered, the idea that public officials are likely to be more sensitive to various groups if members of those groups hold official positions seems intuitively sound. Yet we have shown that the Swedish civil service is led by officials who have been, are, and in all probability will continue to be distinctly *un*representative of their fellow citizens: they are almost all men, they are virtually all university graduates, they are predominantly products of middle- and upper-class backgrounds, and they are considerably older than the average Swede. Leaving aside for the moment the questions of who has led or followed, what is clear is that these *un*representative officials have participated in programs that have vastly improved the life-chances of those whom they do not represent and, in the process, they have undermined their own status. Thus life expectancy for the average Swede has increased by six years during the past three decades, per capita national income has nearly tripled within the past decade, and various quality of life indicators, from retirement income to size of living space per person, all reveal remarkable progress for the "average" Swede during the past four decades.[2] The Swedish bureaucratic elite is demonstrably unrepresentative, yet it has served the "interests" of a mass population, and served those interests well.

This paradox cannot be explained away by pointing to elite motivations—indeed, our review of thought patterns among the elite only deepens the paradox. At the top, Swedish social reformers are not "bourgeois radicals," nor are they ideologues of social change. For the most part they are very similar to other Western elites: materialistic, wholly conventional in their thinking about the present and the future, pragmatically activist but conservative in analyzing social problems, and judging from their extraordinary satisfaction with the world they inhabit, rather smug about general conditions in that world. If one were to predict the kinds of initiatives these perspectives might produce, one would have to predict a low rate of carefully-tested programs, implemented with great caution. If one were to take into account the unrepresentative character of the elite as well as these non-reformist attitudes, one would be forced to predict elite conservatism, bordering on inaction, in dealing with social problems.

Fortunately not many analysts believe that social and motivational characteristics of bureaucratic elites, taken by themselves, can tell us very much about processes of governmental or social change. The impact of such characteristics depends on the quality of elite interactions with other institutions, or to put it differently, on the context within which institutional elites interact.[3] Four aspects of the Swedish context seem particularly relevant to understanding why an unrepresentative and conservative elite has nevertheless participated so actively in guiding social change:

1. *Tradition* Historical precedent can be a powerful force in shaping behavior as well as attitude. Swedish civil servants hold positions to which great prestige has been attached for centuries. This tradition is reinforced daily in the deference shown them by their fellow citizens, the respect with which they are treated by peers, and the perquisites that attach to their offices. But the tradition is more than just prestige; it is, as we have seen, the considerable independence elite officials enjoy in carrying out their responsibilities. This aspect of the tradition is reinforced by current law and administrative rules, giving elite administrators a psychological security that we have argued is a direct function of political and legal independence. Knowledge that prestige and independence have existed for centuries creates the expectation that these qualities will continue into the indefinite future. Swedish officials are thus politically and psychologically free to participate in experimental programs as they see fit, knowing full well that they will be in authority long enough to correct deficiencies if necessary, and that their careers will be judged on the basis of overall performance through time, rather than the outcome of a single program. In this sense, Swedish tradition encourages innovation.

2. *System Loyalty* Although no specific questions were addressed to this issue during our interviews, the transcripts reveal a high level of pride in being so closely identified with a system that is perceived to be both different from and better than other systems. Some of this comes through in references to the generally high quality of colleagues, some of it comes through in discussions of why certain roles are appropriate or not in Sweden, and some of it is evident in responses that suggest no need to seriously consider major changes in Swedish society. We have pointed out, moreover, that most of the senior officials we interviewed demonstrated a

high level of "system awareness." All of this suggests a continuing high level of commitment to the system as a whole, regardless of the party in power. If, as we suspect, "tradition" also plays a role here, it is to help shape an orientation that *has* been clearly shown (*cf.* Chapter 6), namely a feeling that "we are all Swedes, we are all in the same boat together, so if some political group wants to try something, let them. If things don't work out, we can change things later." Pride, patience, and confidence in the long-run capacity of the system to adjust, structure a built-in loyalty to the system that itself motivates innovation.

3. *Political Style* Both tradition and system loyalty contribute to the rationalistic-consultive style that governs interactions between bureaucrats and politicians in Sweden. System loyalty implies that bureaucrat-politician interactions are to be welcomed and, as we have seen, such interactions are quite frequent (albeit specialized); had we interviewed party leaders rather than back-benchers, in fact, these contacts would have seemed even more numerous. The tradition of administrator domination is largely responsible for the terms in which these interactions take place: empirical, problem-focused, rationalistic, consultative, all leading to a conflict-free final consensus. Given those terms, there is little reason for administrators not to participate, even in discussions of quite radical ideas. Thus the Swedish style, by reducing the intellectual distance between politicians and bureaucrats, encourages communication, on terms that emphasize the interest both sides have in achieving solutions to problems.

4. *System Clarity* Although difficult to measure with precision, a major aspect of the Swedish system of governance is role clarity: governing elites have very clear and carefully specified understandings about what they are obliged to do, what they are encouraged to do, what they are permitted to do, and what they have no right to do. In large measure, of course, these clear understandings are a direct result of centuries of experience with a national civil service. But, as noted earlier, the Swedish elite also works very hard at maintaining role clarity. Bureaucratic, parliamentary and policy-making roles are very carefully delineated, and careful attention is given to role specification in developing rules to implement any new piece of legislation or cabinet directive. Moreover, because the circle of elite participants is both small and quite centralized in Stockholm, actors in governmental dramas have a very sophisticated sense of the "who" as well as the "what" of any contemplated action. Battles over political or organizational "turf" are less frequent and less intense in this environment, because they are less necessary. Individual anxiety over status or power, often the source of inter-personal antagonisms in less

clear systems, seems largely absent from Swedish governance. Clarity of role expectations, in short, structures an environment in which feelings of both organizational and individual security are widespread.

These considerations reinforce a conclusion that should now be obvious: the intellectual framework within which Swedish governance is conducted is derived primarily from the beliefs and norms of a centralized system of administration that has been established for centuries. As tutors to the new political elites of the twentieth century, senior civil servants in Sweden have taught their junior political colleagues a language of practicality, rationality and empiricism that has served both groups well in coping with the strains of modern politics. This conclusion does not at all imply that political elites have been ineffective. On the contrary, the agenda of problems to be addressed and strategies to be developed has been firmly controlled by reformist politicians for the past half century. By accepting the legitimacy of these new claimants to political power, however, senior administrators have succeeded in maintaining the intellectual power of their own values and norms. Thus, while politicians have won many battles, the wars have been fought on a territory staked out and defined by administrators. Politicians, rather than administrators, have done most of the accommodating in modern Sweden. In return, administrators have accepted a great many changes, or accepted them more rapidly, than would have been thought possible in the absence of reformist politics. On the whole, it seems to have been an effective exchange.

ON THEORIES OF CHANGING ORGANIZATIONAL ROLES

The data we have analyzed also make clear that some recent speculations regarding the effects of changes in public leadership cadres are premature. It is true, as we have seen, that larger numbers of working class individuals have arrived at the top of Swedish public organizations, and it is true that larger numbers of technical experts and social planners have been recruited to guide vast new programs of technology or social welfare. Yet, as Anders Mellbourn makes clear in his analysis of these data,[4] remarkably few of these respondents express ideas that suggest either a predominantly political or a predominantly technical orientation. Of 315 senior civil servants interviewed, Mellbourn finds only twenty-eight (8.9%) politicos and thirty-eight (21.1%) "experts," or officials who predominantly reflect a technological perspective. If overlapping codes are eliminated, i.e., if those who are coded as both "soft activists" and either politicos or experts are eliminated, the number of "pure" politicos or experts virtually disappears. Vast new programs are obviously being operated in Sweden, but these numbers plainly indicate that, at the top, politically-committed administrators are *not* required to manage social programs and technical experts are *not* essential to the management of large-scale programs based on advanced technology.

More traditional role conceptions, in fact, seem considerably more widespread among the elite than these newer models. Mellbourn also reports, for example, that ninety-seven (30.9%) officials can be classified in the "neutral executor" category derived from Max Weber's classic analysis (although this number is reduced to fifty when overlapping codes are eliminated). Assuming that this role conception reflects an earlier period, when government programs were small and largely confined to maintaining fair and civil relationships between citizens, the presence of so many "neutral executors" in our sample suggests the continuing utility of such models, even in a period of vast governmental expansion. Loyalty to political leaders and the pursuit of administrative competence in program implementation—whether or not the "program" is congenial—clearly are qualities likely to survive in any public bureaucracy, however complex or technologically advanced it may become.

To say that the newer models we *expected* to find were not found is not to say, however, that nothing new was found. What is most striking about the Swedish elite is what we have referred to as "soft activism": the unusual emphasis placed on social skills in administration. Again and again, Swedish civil servants refer to the need to be able to get along with people (umgås med folk), to be aware of individual sentiments through continuous monitoring, or to be able to devise techniques that encourage individual accommodation. As we have seen, these kinds of sentiments are far more common and far more powerful among the Swedish elite than among elites in other Western nations. We are thus confronted with yet another Swedish paradox: the Western system which is perhaps more technological in orientation than any other, and arguably more reformist in public policies than any other, is led by an elite that is neither very technical nor very political, but overwhelmingly social.

From the point of view of modern, technological societies the "soft" orientation of the Swedish elite has a dual significance. First, it calls into question more individualized models of leadership. Other systems, of which the American may be the best example, encourage confrontational styles of interaction among elites by diffusing power and confusing responsibility. To "get anything done" in such systems, it is said with increasing frequency, a "hero" is required: an individual intelligent enough to perceive the correct issue and ruthless enough to put together an effective (i.e., winning) coalition. Absent heroic leadership of this kind, modern societies become increasingly threatened by political fragmentation and technological complexity. But in Sweden there are seldom any "heroes" to celebrate. Negotiation, debate and compromise are highly-developed arts that lead to collective rather than individual decisions on virtually all issues—

including complex questions of technology. It may well be true, as one of our respondents suggested, that there is not enough "go" in the Swedish system, but it can hardly be maintained that the system is incompatible with rapid social or governmental change. Indeed, collective decision-making structured by "soft" attitudes may be more effective than individualized leadership in coping with complex problems, since it broadens the base of knowledge that can be brought to bear on a problem. Decisions that emerge may not always be the best, but bad decisions are almost certain to be eliminated.[5]

A second, perhaps more exciting, prospect is the apparent transfer of these "soft" techniques downward in the organizational hierarchy, leading to fundamental transformations in the "inner logic" of organizations themselves.[6] Several respondents suggested that greater sensitivity to the social aspects of administration at all levels is a direct consequence of governmental expansion, which increases programs, increases the number of organizations required to serve program needs, and increases the rate and complexity of inter-organizational relationships. Moreover, since public programs now strive to do more, with more technological sophistication, each new program requires a high level of skill and education. Better education increases the number of experts or technicians who, precisely because they are so well-trained, are highly sensitive to how they are treated, no less than what they do. Leading such organizations requires technical ability to be sure, but it is even more essential to be skillful in dealing with people. Administrative leadership in this new setting is increasingly similar to political leadership: building consensus is more relevant than goal-setting; coordination is more central than direction; negotiation is more effective than giving orders. In the new world of administration, social sensitivity rather than technology will prevail.

These views of emergent trends in modern administration have usually been discussed prescriptively, that is, as recommendations for resolving administrative tension,[7] but little evidence of their existence has been offered. The views of the Swedish elite are thus important in suggesting a current reality and future viability to a "soft" or collegial administrative style that has not been previously observed. Diffusion of education-based technical competence throughout an organizational structure does indeed appear to undermine the practical, thus theoretical, basis for hierarchical control. It also undermines the more manipulative aspects of the "power" theories of organizations currently popular in the United States. According to "power" theorists, organizations are best understood as shifting coalitions of influence, held together by "tough" individual leaders, who gain control by offering inducements to organizational members in return for political support.[8] This view implies that leaders and followers within organizations are more interested in gaining and maintaining influence than in programs, and quite willing to manipulate or be manipulated to achieve influence.

In Sweden, however, highly-trained specialists are likely to be *very* interested in goals and extraordinarily sensitive to inter-personal relationships. Such people are unlikely to be as easily manipulated into uncertain coalitions as the "power" interpretations suggest.

Power theories, of course, are popular primarily in the United States, where the governmental setting is very different. Senior officials often are selected entirely on political grounds, they anticipate a short tenure, and they are therefore often quite anxious to "make a record" as quickly as they can. Because programs and responsibilities are often deliberately vague,[9] however, there is no established script to follow in "making a record." The result is a great deal of variable and often frenzied behavior, deliberately manipulative, designed (hopefully) to create a political base capable of supporting "notable" actions.[10] The contrast between American and Swedish environments is striking to observers of both:

> The idea of treating people like human beings is very novel! Americans sound awfully humanistic when they talk about problems of the society, but they sound more paranoid and concerned with their status when they talk about superordinate-subordinate authority relationships in the work setting. They seem to be concerned with who has power. And part of the reason for this is that they are concerned with being activists—in making things happen. In other words, they are *not* hypocrites, but they are in a role setting where they must be quite conscious of their power and the resources held by other actors. The Swedes play a well-defined game; the Americans don't—and that makes for a big difference.[11]

These contextual differences suggest a need for caution in stating general propositions, particularly cross-cultural propositions. One can nevertheless speculate that Swedish public organizations will move further down the road toward "soft" administrative behavior, at a faster pace, than will be true in other advanced but more "power oriented" systems. Swedish public sector employment increased from 700,000 to 1.2 million in the decade 1965–75 alone, largely as a result of growth in local and regional government. Many of these new employees—and virtually all of those who are likely to reach the top levels of administration—were recruited directly from the universities, which doubled the number of graduates produced between 1967 and 1972.[12] Presumably the Swedish public bureaucracy is now even better-educated and thus more sensitive, in addition to being significantly larger. Depending on how rapidly elite bargaining skills filter down into the lower levels of this system, increased employee sensitivity can lead to new and more humanistic styles of interaction accompanied by better public service.

But increased sensitivity can also mean more rapid perception of problems, less patience at failures to remedy obvious wrongs, and even rejection of traditional political styles that "take too long." Which of these scenarios is more likely to occur cannot be predicted, although Sweden, like many other Western nations, faces the 1980's with serious unresolved problems in energy, the economy and inflation that could produce a great deal more social tension than was apparent during the 1970's. It is entirely possible, moreover, that changes in government will occur far more frequently in the next decade than during the past half century of political stability. The new (1974) Swedish Constitution contains electoral rules that enhance the possibility of government change at a time when voter preferences in Sweden, as in other democratic systems, appear to have become unhinged. Olof Petersson concludes his recent analysis of the 1976 election by suggesting that "The image of the stable Swedish voter is today becoming a myth." Long-term processes of change, he writes, dissolve old stabilizing forces and "The electorate becomes more floating . . . More and more voters abandon their old parties. Class voting decreases. A growing number of voters make their decisions shortly before the election. The gap between electors and voters widens."[13]

Should these indicators of potential political instability presage a period in which political leaders are changed every third or sixth years, the world of the senior civil servant will of course seem very different. If such political changes are compounded by unsolvable economic and social problems, perhaps accompanied by a more visible social unrest, senior officials will face a far more turbulent environment at a time when their own resources are bound to seem less certain. In that event, the "soft activists" portrayed here will require all the strengths of a formidable administrative tradition to retain either their capacity or their satisfaction.

APPENDIX A:
SAMPLE SELECTION

Two groups of respondents were selected for interviews among the top strata of the Swedish government. The first group was not a sample but a total population: we attempted to interview all sixteen "State Secretaries" in the ministries, all sixty chief executives of the central administrative boards (usually called "Director General"), and the chief executives of the seven public authorities. These eighty-three individuals constitute the most senior group of administrators in Sweden other than those in the Cabinet itself.

We also chose a sample of individuals from a population consisting of officials at the highest salary levels, as indicated by their listing on salary-list C. Persons on this list were stratified by type agency—i.e., ministry, administrative board, or public authority—and respondent selection was proportional to the number from each type agency in the total population. The total population included the following:

1.	Ministry Officials (excluding State Secretaries)	166
2.	Central Administrative Boards (excluding General Directors)	566
3.	Public Authorities	141
	Total	873

Our goal was 200 respondents, which required a sample of 270 persons, assuming a response frequency of 75 percent. The 270 persons were distributed as follows:

a. $\dfrac{166}{873}$ × 270 = 52 persons selected from ministries

b. $\dfrac{566}{873}$ × 270 = 175 persons selected from boards

c. $\dfrac{141}{873}$ × 270 = 44 persons selected from public authorities.

Respondents were selected randomly and, because our response rate exceeded the 75 percent projected, we achieved 315 interviews.

A sample of fifty Members of Parliament, stratified by party and randomly selected from among MP's not serving as Ministers, produced forty-four usable interviews, evenly divided between socialist and non-socialist parliamentarians.

INTERVIEW QUESTIONNAIRE: SWEDEN

1. What positions have you had earlier in your working career?
2. How long have you had your present position?
   a. Can you tell me briefly how you obtained this position?
   b. Have you ever thought of moving into something other than public administration? In which case, what kind of work?
3. What do you find most satisfying about your present position? What would you most miss if you were forced to leave it someday?
4. On the other side, what do you find least satisfying about the position?
5. What do you think is the most important problem in your own area of responsibility?
   a. What do you think ought to be done to solve this problem?
6. What do you think are the most significant barriers toward solving this problem?
7. More generally, how would you describe the responsibilities of a senior civil servant?
8. What personal qualities do you think are necessary for a good senior administrator?
9. What kind of background should he or she have?

10. Do you think that there are any major differences between work in the ministries and work in the administrative agencies in terms of character of the work?

11. Through our work in other countries we have come to believe that a higher administrator often works in a gray area between administrative and political responsibilities. Do you enjoy the more political aspects of your work?

12. We are interested in comparing the job of a senior civil servant with the job of a senior politician. How would you describe the responsibilities of a politician?

13. What personal qualities do you think are necessary for a senior politician to have?

14. Do you think that politicians are as responsible and well trained as senior administrators?

15. In general, what problem do you believe is most urgent for the Swedish government and Parliament to solve at present? What do you see as the main cause of this problem?

16a. One of the most common slogans in today's political debate is equality. Do you think that any social equalization has taken place in this country during the last 15 or 20 years?

16b. What is your inclination toward an increase in income equalization here in Sweden? Are you in the main positively or negatively inclined toward further equalization? (If positive: would you like to see a total income equalization or do you think that certain income differences can be justified? In the latter case, on what grounds? If negative: according to what principles do you think that income differences can be justified?

17. As you think about the division of power in Sweden, do you think that it is as it should be, or would you like to see some changes? If so, what kind of changes?

18. There has recently been much discussion in a variety of countries concerning increasing citizen influence over public activities as well as increasing citizen participation in the work of government and administration. Do you think that this would be desirable here in Sweden?

19. Do you think that there are any risks or problems associated with increased citizen participation in the work of government and administration?

20. In connection with these discussions about increasing direct citizen influence, it is sometimes said that certain action groups make use of what might be called socially dangerous methods. How do you think that society ought to deal with such activities? (Follow up question:

What kinds of activities would you judge to be socially dangerous? In what way should authorities respond to such activity?)

21. Some maintain that in politics and social life generally there will always be conflicts between various groups, while others maintain that most groups at bottom have the same interests. What is your opinion about that? (Follow up question: For those who answered that conflict always exists, Do you think that such conflicts can at bottom be overcome or not?)

22. Some say that social conflicts have their origin in ignorance or selfishness, while others instead maintain that conflicts are healthy and necessary. What is your opinion on that question?

23. If there were a conflict or difference of opinion in which one side was thought to be wholly right and the other wholly wrong, do you think that the side which was wholly right ought to maintain its position or should it seek a compromise?

24. Political parties play an important role in Sweden, as they do in other countries in which we are conducting our research. When all is said and done, do you think that there are large, certain or very small differences between the Swedish parliamentary parties? (Follow up question: To those who answered large or certain differences—What do you think are the most important differences?)

25. Do you think that these differences have increased or decreased during the last 15 to 20 years?

26. Do you think that the differences that may exist between the political parties primarily reflect existing political differences in the country, or do you think that the parties exaggerate those differences?

27. Do you think that Swedish society today has more conflict than was present 15 to 20 years ago? Do you think this is good or bad?

28. Do you think that today's situation is satisfactory or not?
We would also like to ask you some questions regarding your own personal experiences:

29. If you first think about the time when you were growing up, which person or experiences or perhaps historical events have had significance for your life and your work?

30. Is there anyone among your relatives who has been active in public administration?

31. Are there any who have been active in political parties?

32. Did you often talk about politics in your parents' home?

33. Looking ahead, what do you think you're likely to be doing in five years?

34. If you think for a minute about the kind of society you would like to

see for the generation after your own, how would that society be different from what we have today?

35. How close to that kind of society do you think we can come?

Finally we would like to ask a few questions regarding your contacts and sources of information.

36a. Can you tell us what kind of work your two or three closest friends do?

36b. Do you often talk to them about your work?

37a. Which daily newspapers do you read regularly and which do you find most useful?

37b. Which professional margazines do you regularly read and which do you find most useful?

38. We are interested in the contacts that higher officials have in their working lives. Can you tell me what other institutions and organizations you are in regular contact with, and with what frequency.

NOTES

1. THE FIRST NEW SOCIETY

1. Marquis W. Childs, *Sweden: The Middle Way.* New Haven: Yale University Press, 1937.

2. Kathleen Nott, *A Clean Well-Lighted Place.* London: Heinemann, 1961.

3. Roland Huntford, *The New Totalitarians.* New York: Stein and Day, 1972.

4. For a useful introduction to some of these ambiguities, see Frederic Fleisher, *The New Sweden.* New York: David McKay Company, Inc., 1967.

5. The total Swedish population in 1910 was 5.5 million. Loss of one million inhabitants through emigration between 1870 and 1910, therefore, represented a major cultural as well as economic shock that continues to fascinate Swedish analysts. For a good brief treatment, by a major authority, see Franklin D. Scott, *Sweden: The Nation's History* (Minneapolis: University of Minnesota Press, 1977) pp. 366-378. The theme of emigration is an important concern of Swedish literature, powerfully expressed in Wilhelm Moberg's novels, of which *The Emigrants* (New York, 1951), may be the best-known.

6. M. Donald Hancock, *Sweden: The Politics of Postindustrial Change.* Hinsdale, Illinois: The Dryden Press, Inc., 1972, p. 23.

7. For a brief review of this problem and efforts to deal with it, see Stig Hadenius, Bjorn Molin and Hans Wieslander, *Sverige efter 1900* (Stockholm: Aldus/Boniers, 1972), pp. 136-137.

8. W. Wilhaem-Olsson, *Stockholm: Structure and Development.* Stockholm: Almquist and Wiksell, 1961, pp. 27-33.

9. Derived from Ministry of Labor and Housing, "The Financing of Housing in Sweden," (mimeo, 1971). The current (1978) fraction, of course, is considerably higher.

10. For an analysis of these events, see my *Governing Greater Stockholm: A Study of Policy Development and System Change.* Berkeley: University of California Press, 1975), ch. IV.

11. The significance of these changes is assessed in my "The Pursuit of Efficiency: Values and Structure in the Changing Politics of Swedish Municipalities," Terry N. Clark, ed., *Comparative Community Politics* (New York: John Wiley and Sons, 1974), pp. 87-110.

12. The *Riksdag's* Administrative Board has published a very useful pamphlet describing the origins and functions of the new Riksdag. See *Sweden's Riksdag.* Stockholm: The Riksdag's Administrative Board, May 1971.

13. "Swedish Government in Action," (August 1975), one of the *Fact Sheets on Sweden* series published in the United States by the Swedish Information Service, New York.

14. See Richard F. Tomasson, "Radical Restructuring of Higher Education in Sweden," *Educational Records,* Vol. 56, No. 2 (Spring 1975), pp. 78-88.

15. Arnold S. Heidenheimer, Hugh Heclo, Carolyn Teich Adams, *Comparative Public Policy.* (New York: St. Martin's Press, 1975).

16. For a useful review of Swedish policies, compared to policies in several other nations, see James L. Sundquist, *Dispersing Population* (Washington: The Brookings Institution, 1975).

17. "The Swedish Economy" (August 1972), one of *Fact Sheets on Sweden* series, *loc. cit.*

18. Eric Einhaon analyzes recent economic gains in Sweden, Scandinavia and the United States in his "The Middle Way Forty Years On: Scandinavian Public Policy Issues in a Comparative Perspective." Paper prepared for a Council of European Studies Workshop, Madison, Wisconsin, April 1975.

19. "Active Manpower Policy in Sweden" (April 1972), one of *Fact Sheets on Sweden* series, *loc. cit.*

20. See Christopher Wheeler, *White Collar Power* (Urbana, Chicago and London: University of Illinois Press, 1975), pp. 182-191, for an analysis of these reforms.

21. This idea is developed in Karl Deutsch's pioneering work, *The Nerves of Government* (New York: The Free Press of Glencoe, 1963). But see Donald A. Schon, *Beyond the Stable State* (New York: W.W. Norton and Co., 1971), for a valuable recent elaboration.

22. "The Swedish Economy," *loc. cit.*

23. Franklin D. Scott, *op. cit.,* ch. VI.

24. Richard F. Tomasson, *Sweden: Prototype of Modern Society.* (New York: Random House, 1970), pp. 226-228.

25. Still the best analysis of this political transition is Dankwart Rustow, *The Politics of Compromise.* Princeton: Princeton University Press, 1955.

26. For an analysis of bureaucratic "independence," based on responses to closed questions, see Thomas J. Anton, Claes Linde and Anders Melbourn, "Bureaucrats in Politics: A Profile of the Swedish Administrative Elite," *Canadian Public Administration,* Vol. XVI., No. 4 (Winter 1973), pp. 627-651.

27. Hugh Heclo, *Modern Social Politics in Britain and Sweden.* New Haven: Yale University Press, 1974), pp. 313-314.

28. Royal Commission activity is analyzed in Hans Meijer, "Bureaucracy and Policy Formulation in Sweden," *Scandinavian Political Studies,* Vol. 4, (1969), pp. 103-116.

29. Christopher Wheeler, *op. cit., passim.*

30. *Ibid.,* p. 42.

31. Meijer, *loc. cit.*

32. Karl Manheim, *Ideology and Utopia*. New York: Harcourt, Brace and World, Inc., 1936, p. 118.

33. Heclo, *op. cit.*, pp. 314–315.

34. Herbert Tingsten, *Den Svenska socialdemokratiens ideutveckling* (2 vols). Stockholm: Bonniers, 1967.

35. On the functions and structure of Swedish administrative boards, see Joseph B. Board, Jr., *The Government and Politics of Sweden*. Boston: Houghton Mifflin Company, 1970, pp. 161–167.

36. Stockholm, Bokförlaget Prisma, 1968.

37. *Ibid.*, pp. 48–49.

38. *Ibid.*, p. 51.

39. *Ibid.*, p. 50.

40. Assar Lindbeck, *Swedish Economic Policy*. Berkeley: University of California Press, 1974, p. 182.

41. On "learning" systems generally, see Deutsch, *op. cit.*, Schon, *op. cit.*, D.N. Michael, *On Leaning to Plan and Planning to Learn*. San Francisco: Jossey-Bass Publishers, 1973.

42. Wheeler, *op. cit.*, p. 2 writes: "A staggering 79 percent of the population between the ages of eighteen and eighty, for example, belongs to one or more organizations. This makes Sweden the most organized Western democratic society."

43. Sundquist, *op. cit.*, and "Regional Development Policy in Sweden" (August 1972), one of *Fact Sheets on Sweden, loc. cit.*, discuss this effort.

44. For a review of evidence supporting this point, see Anton, "The Pursuit of Efficiency . . . ," *loc. cit.*

45. Tingsten, *op. cit.*, analyzes this shift.

46. Andrew Martin has effectively documented this point in his paper, "Economic Dilemmas Along the Middle Way: Power, Policy and Planning." (mimeo).

47. For a discussion of this development, and some clarifying data, see Ulf Christoffersson, Björn Molin, Lennart Månnsson and Lars Stromberg, *Byråkrati och politik*. Stockholm: Bonniers, 1972, pp. 132–148.

48. *Ibid.*, pp. 45–57.

49. A useful review of the Swedish transformation can be found in Kurt Samuelsson, *From Great Power to Welfare State*. London: George Allen and Unwin, 1968.

50. Heclo, *op. cit.*, esp. ch. 6.

51. *Ibid.*, p. 60.

52. The phrase is attributed to Professor Jörgen Westerståhl, in *Dagens Nyheter*, August 4, 1956.

53. For a more comprehensive treatment of elite transformation theories see Robert D. Putnam, *The Comparative Study of Political Elites*. (New York: Prentice-Hall, 1975), ch. 8.

54. See Chapter Two, below.

55. In particular Arend Liphart, *The Politics of Accommodation: Pluralism and Democracy in the Netherlands*. Berkeley and Los Angeles: University of California Press, 1968.

56. For a discussion, see Martin O. Heisler, ed., *Politics in Europe*. (New York: David McKay Co., Inc., 1974), chapters 2–5.

57. Gamson, in his *Power and Discontent* (Homewood, Illinois: The Dorsey Press, 1968), discusses the conditions under which an elite group may undermine its own position.

58. For an exception see Sture Källberg, *Off the Middle Way*. New York: Pantheon Books, 1972.

59. Max Weber, *The Theory of Social and Economic Organization* (translators A.M. Henderson and Talcott Parsons, Talcott Parsons, ed.) New York: Oxford University Press, 1947.

60. Robert D. Putnam, "The Political Attitudes of Senior Civil Servants in Western Europe: A Preliminary Report," prepared for the 1972 Annual Meeting of The American Political Science Association, Washington, D.C., September 1972. (mimeo).

61. This, of course, may be seen as a direct extension of the Weberian emphasis on "rationality" in his ideal type model of bureaucracy. For an argument that European elites are now dominated by "technocrats," see Daniel Lerner and Morton Gorden, *Euratlantica: Changing Perspectives of the European Elites.* Cambridge, Mass.: The M.I.T. Press, 1969, esp. ch. 8.

2. PUBLIC AUTHORITY AND SOCIAL STRUCTURE

1. The popularity of the "elite" concept in recent American social science probably is due as much to the late C. Wright Mills as to any other scholar. His *The Power Elite* (New York: Oxford University Press, 1956) portrayed a small group of corporate, political and military leaders who, he argued, were able to dominate American society. Powerfully argued and controversial, the book stimulated a great deal of scholarly activity designed to support or refute the central thesis. Even before Mills had published this work, Floyd Hunter had presented a similar portrait of an urban "elite" in his *Community Power Structure* (Chapel Hill: University of North Carolina Press, 1953). Hunter's work, too, has stimulated much additional research activity.

2. Robert A. Dahl's study of New Haven – *Who Governs?* (New Haven: Yale University Press, 1961) – was designed to refute Hunter's assertions by describing actual processes of decisionmaking in specific policy areas and showing how large and varied the participants in those processes were. The intellectual roots of these two views are traced in my "Power, Pluralism, and Local Politics," *Administrative Science Quarterly,* Vol. 7, No. 4 (March 1963), pp. 425–457. This and other articles tracing the flow of debate over the issue of 'elitist' interpretations of society can be found in Michael Aiken and Paul E. Mott, eds., *The Structure of Community Power.* New York: Random House, 1970.

3. The procedure for choosing respondents is described in Appendix A, pp. 188–189.

4. See Robert D. Putnam, *The Comparative Study of Political Elites.* Englewood Cliffs, N.J.: Prentice-Hall, 1976.

5. Richard F. Tomasson discusses feminism in Sweden in Chapter VI of his *Sweden: Prototype of Modern Society.* New York: Random House, 1970.

6. Christoffersson et al., *op. cit.,* p. 171.

7. Sten-Sture Landström, *Svenska Ämbetsmäns Sociala Ursprung* (Uppsala, 1954), p. 85.

8. Claes Linde and Gunnar Lönnquist, "Personal rekryteringen till vissa offentliga forvaltningar 1957 och 67" (mimeo), p. 33.

9. Christoffersson et al., *op. cit.,* p. 35.

10. *Ibid.*

11. Exactly what the *student-examen* is equivalent to is very unclear. The *gymnasium* or academic secondary school whose graduates are entitled to take the *student-examen* is similar to American high schools, yet the curriculum includes material usually taught in American universities.

12. Christoffersson et al., *op. cit.*, p. 38.

13. Tomasson, "Radical Restructuring . . ." *loc. cit.*

14. This result is consistent with what Christoffersson et al., report (p. 57), and it is similar to reports from other studies that document a consistent "urban" and "center" bias in the origins and/or education of Western elites. Compare John A. Armstrong, *The European Administrative Elite* (Princeton: Princeton University Press, 1973), esp. ch. 14.

15. For years, appointment to state positions had been monopolized by Swedish noblemen and, as Christoffersson and colleagues point out, a third of the Foreign Ministry's officials were of noble birth as recently as 1947. The change reflected in these data thus reflects another twentieth century phenomenon. See Christoffersson et al., *op. cit.*, pp. 45-46 for a discussion.

16. Svenska Gallupinstitutet, *Svenska Folket* (Stockholm: 1971). p. 86.

17. Anton, "The Pursuit of Efficiency . . .," *loc. cit.*, reviews some of these other studies.

18. For an interesting discussion of this phenomenon see Kenneth Prewitt, "Political Socialization and Leadership Selection," *Annals of the American Academy of Political and Social Science*, Vol. 351 (September, 1965), pp. 96-111.

19. Thus 33 percent of those who report relatives in administration are Directors General, as opposed to 18 percent holding this title among those without administrative relatives; 30 percent of those with political relatives are Directors General compared to 22 percent of those without political relatives; 27 percent of those who report they discussed politics with their parents are Directors General compared to 21 percent of those who report no such discussions.

20. Differences between these various groupings are neither powerful nor statistically significant.

21. For an assessment of the significance of this trend see Robert D. Putnam, "Elite Transformation in Advanced Industrial Societies: An Empirical Assessment of the Theory of Technocracy," *Comparative Political Studies,* Vol 10, No. 3 (October 1977), pp. 383-412.

22. As the oldest Swedish universities, Uppsala and Lund are considered by educated Swedes to have somewhat more prestige than newer universities such as Göteborg, Stockholm, or Umeå.

23. Experience in student politics is often characteristic of national leaders. Former Prime Minister Olof Palme, for example, was a well-known student leader when studying at Lund.

24. Arnold J. Heidenheimer has provided a valuable analysis of SACO in his "Professional Unions, Public Sector Growth, and the Swedish Equality Policy," *Comparative Politics* (October 1976), pp. 49-73.

25. Neither the "club" memberships that structure informal interaction among British leaders nor the "ivy league-country club" networks that are common in the United States have obvious counterparts in Sweden.

26. Christoffersson et al., *op. cit.*, p. 59.

27. In contrast, 73.1 percent of the first, 69.9 percent of the second, and 58.8 percent of the third friend named are in non-military public administration.

28. I am indebted to my colleague, Samuel J. Eldersveld, for suggesting the significance of "guild" versus open systems. Further analysis of this distinction will be forthcoming in the work of Eldersveld and my other colleagues in the Michigan project, Joel Aberbach, Robert Putnam, and Bert Rockman.

29. See below, Chapters 6 and 7, for further analysis of interaction between government officials and the larger society.

30. For an interesting examination of mobility in the American federal service and some

of its consequences see Eugene B. McGregor, Jr., "Politics and the Career Mobility of Bureaucrats," *The American Political Science Review,* Vol. LXVIII, No. 1 (March 1974), pp. 18–26.

31. For a useful evocation of the old system see Nils Herlitz, *Sweden: A Modern Democracy on Ancient Foundations.* Minneapolis: The University of Minnesota Press. 1939.

3. PATHWAYS TO SATISFACTION

1. See below, Chapter 7.

2. Albert H. Rosenthal, *The Social Programs of Sweden.* Minneapolis: University of Minnesota Press, 1967.

3. Here, and later, numbers within parentheses refer to interview transcripts. All translations into English are mine.

4. My colleague, Anders Mellbourn, believes that "power" is an inappropriate summary concept; he prefers "independence." My reasons for choosing "power" are made clear below.

5. On "inside dopesterism," see David Riesman, Reuel Denney and Nathan Glazer, *The Lonely Crowd.* New Haven: Yale University Press, 1950.

6. These suggestions that influence is the central quality of "independence" account for my choice of power as the key value in these responses.

7. See below, Chapter 8, for an examination of the personal significance of official "independence."

8. Heidenheimer, "Professional Unions . . . ," *loc. cit.,* analyzes this sequence of activities.

9. The indices merely add individual scores on variables reporting satisfaction with the social system, the political system and the civil service, together with the score on a question investigating the amount of change desired in society. Grouping individuals by different characteristics enables us to portray variation in the summed scores by group.

10. CF., Chapter 2.

11. Given the social origins of higher civil servants in Sweden (Chapter 2) a tendency to favor caution is understandable.

12. "Policy-Making and Political Culture in Sweden," *Scandinavian Political Studies,* Vol. 4, (1969), pp. 88–102.

13. See below, Chapter 8, for an analysis of the theme of "integrity."

4. THE "ORDINARY" CIVIL SERVANT: SOFT ACTIVIST

1. See Herlitz, *op. cit.,* for a discussion of traditional Swedish administration. A more recent view, encouraged by a consideration of various administrative reforms, can be found in *SOU 1968: #47, Forvaltning och folkstyre,* ch. 5.

2. In his forthcoming analysis of these data, Anders Mellbourn places more than 30 percent of these respondents in the traditional category. For a preliminary view see his "The Faces of Bureaucracy – Role Conceptions in the Higher Swedish Civil Service," University of Stockholm, Department of Political Science, 1977 (mimeo).

3. Mellbourn places 12 percent of these respondents in the expert category, *Ibid.*

4. Not quite 9 percent of the respondents fit into this political category, using Mellbourn's classification method. *Ibid.*

5. This percentage estimate is lower than the above numbers suggest because of overlapping coding. When officials coded twice are eliminated, the fractions are reduced as reported here.

6. And thus implicitly reject assertions to "technocratic dominance" or other training based assertions of new power relations. Compare Putnam, "Elite Transformation . . . An Empirical Assessment of the Theory of Technocracy," *loc. cit.*

7. See Sträng's conversation in Nordal Åkerman, *Apparaten Sverige.* Stockholm: Wahlström and Widstrand, 1970, pp. 86–87.

8. *Ibid.,* p. 87.

9. Anton, *Governing Greater Stockholm, op. cit.,* Anton, "Policy Making and Political Culture in Sweden," *loc. cit.,* Heclo, *op. cit.;* Wheeler, *op. cit.;* Andrew Shonfield, *Modern Capitalism* (New York: Oxford University Press, 1965) ch. 9, are among numerous examples that might be cited.

10. Efforts to conceptualize bureaucratic role types are numerous. For one of the more interesting attempts, see Robert Presthus, *The Organizational Society.* New York: Alfred Knopf, 1962.

11. *Cf.* note 9, above.

12. Vinde, *op. cit.,* pp. 199–210, discusses the details of the Swedish system of legal responsibility.

13. Compare Anton, *Governing . . . , op. cit.,* pp. 159–160.

5. MANAGING POLITICS AND POLITICIANS

1. Numerous idealistic organizations, committed to improving the lot of the poor, or increasing Swedish foreign assistance, or otherwise seeking "good works" to do, maintain constant pressure on the political parties. Sweden now devotes one percent of her Gross National Income to foreign assistance each year.

2. For recent analysis of Swedish organizations, see Wheeler, *op. cit., passim,* and Hancock, *op. cit.,* ch. 6. The phrase "organization Sweden" is taken from Frederic Fleisher, *The New Sweden.* New York: David McKay Co., Inc., 1967, p. 41.

3. I emphasize that this is a summary of the *elite* view. Non-elite views of Swedish society are often very different and considerably more hostile to organizational leadership. See, for example, the views reported in Sture Kallberg, *Off the Middle Way: Report from a Swedish Village.* New York: Random House, 1972.

4. Analysis of these responses shows no relationship (Tau = .0065) between estimates of the current situation and estimates of changes in conflict, i.e., those who perceive the present situation to be good do not do so because these see less conflict. Nor do those who perceive less conflict believe the present to be better on that account. The two judgments appear to be made independently.

5. For an academic analysis that makes the same point, see Nils Stjernquist, "Sweden: Stability or Deadlock?" in Robert A. Dahl, ed., *Political Oppositions in Western Democracies.* New Haven and London: Yale University Press, 1966, pp. 116–146.

6. See Meijer, *loc. cit.,* for an analysis of Royal Commission and Board, *op. cit.,* pp. 131–135, for a discussion of the Parliamentary committee system.

7. Hancock, *op. cit.,* p. 95, reports that 71.7 percent of the (then) lower and 78.2 of the upper houses were active in local politics (1965 data).

8. For an analysis of this strike and its significance see Edmund Dahlström et al., *LKAB och demokratin: rapport om en strejk och ett forskningsprojekt.* Stockholm: Wahlstrom and Widstrand, 1971.

9. Reactions to this confrontation are analyzed below.

10. See Anton, *Governing . . . , op. cit.,* pp. 205–206.

11. *Ibid.*

12. Recall our earlier discussion of *remiss* procedures, Chapter 1, *supra.*

13. In this respect Swedish officials resemble American officials who, according to recent surveys, have little enthusiasm for participation. See, for one recent example, F. Thomas Juster, ed., *The Economic and Political Impact of General Revenue Sharing.* Ann Arbor: Survey Research Center, 1976, ch. 9.

14. Readers should bear in mind that the variables we are using can be interpreted in various ways, hence no dramatic significance should be attached to their manipulation in the following argument.

15. The foundations of this policy are now available in English. See *Toward Equality: The Alva Myrdal Report to the Swedish Social Democratic Party.* Stockholm: Prisma, 1971.

16. For evidence, see Svenska Gallupinstitutet, *Svenska Folket* Stockholm: 1971–72, *passim.*

17. See below, Chapter 8, for an analysis.

6. IMAGES OF SOCIETY AND POWER

1. Heclo, *op. cit.,* ch. 2, outlines the development of this tradition.

2. Tingsten, *op. cit.*

3. Christoffersson et al., *op. cit.,* p. 80.

4. See p. 99 below, for the complete list.

5. A recent decline in the number of newspapers published has further constrained information sources in Sweden as a whole. Thus in 1971 nearly 43 percent of total circulation was accounted for by just five newspapers. See "Mass Media in Sweden" (Stockholm: The Swedish Institute, 1972).

6. See Chapter 1, above, for a discussion. See also Vinde, *op. cit.,* pp. 48–75.

7. Christoffersson et al., *op. cit.,* pp. 116–123.

8. It should be noted that the test used in this work was a stiff one: to be regarded as "positive" toward political guidance, respondents had to check a box indicating their agreement that "politicians ought to have greater influence in relation to administrative officials." *Ibid.,* p. 160.

9. *Ibid.,* p. 128.

10. Meijer, *loc. cit.*

11. The gamma statistic for contact with LO and technician orientation is –0.46; for LO contact and partisanship it is 0.45; for LO contact and policy-making orientation it is 0.40.

12. These orientations will have been altered, of course, by the electoral defeat suffered by the Social Democrats in September, 1976.

13. See Anton, "Policy Making and Political Culture in Sweden," *loc. cit.,* for development of these summary terms.

7. SWEDEN COMPARED

1. Similar investigations were conducted in Holland by a team led by my colleague Samuel J. Eldersveld, in France by a team led by Ronald Inglehart, in Britain, Italy and West Germany by teams led by Robert D. Putnam, and in the United States by a team led by Joel D. Aberbach and Bert A. Rockman.

2. Bert A. Rockman, "Linkages at the Top: The Sociometric Nets of Bureaucrats and Politicians" (unpublished paper).

3. The data reported here for Italy are probably misleading, since other data suggest that Italian bureaucrats are too rigid to welcome the rather high level of citizen interaction these figures portray. For further analysis of the Italian data, see Robert Putnam's forthcoming work.

4. Olof Ruin, "Participation, Corporativization and Politicization: Trends in Present-Day Sweden." Paper presented for the 62nd Meeting of the Society for the Advancement of Scandinavian Study, New York, May 5–6, 1972.

5. Tingsten, *op. cit.*

6. For an interesting discussion of these themes by several authors see Leon N. Lindberg, ed., *Politics and the Future of Industrial Society.* New York: David McKay Company, Inc., 1976.

7. The notion that ideological thinking prohibits more pragmatic styles of interaction is clearly an oversimplification, albeit a common one. For a discussion see Robert D. Putnam, "On Studying Elite Political Culture: The Case of Ideology," *American Political Science Review,* Vol. 65, No. 3, September 1971.

8. See, for example, the perspectives reported in the *New York Times,* March 24, 1978, p. 1.

9. The most comprehensive analysis of these themes is Ronald Inglehart, *The Silent Revolution.* Princeton: Princeton University Press, 1977.

10. Ronald Inglehart, "The Values of Bureaucrats and Politicians: Basic and Situational Priorities" (unpublished paper).

11. Given the rather different priorities of the new government that assumed power after the September 1976 elections, it is probable that these observations would be modified if our interviews were conducted now.

12. The new Swedish government's interest in reducing taxes seems to reflect exactly these views.

8. NO PLACE TO HIDE: POLITICAL SKILL AND THE SOCIAL PSYCHOLOGY OF CONSENSUS

1. Andrew Shonfield, *Modern Capitalism* (New York and London: Oxford University Press, 1965), p. 199.

2. Many of the studies that are available in English are reviewed in Chapter 1, above.

3. Vinde, *op. cit.,* pp. 85–109, provides a useful discussion.

4. Anton, "The Pursuit of Efficiency . . . ," *loc. cit.,* reviews evidence for these propositions.

5. Anton, "Policy Making and Political Culture in Sweden," *loc. cit.,* discusses *remiss* procedures.

6. *Kungl, Majlts proposition 1967: 100, passim.*

7. See *Administration TEMA*, Vol. 4 (1975), No. 4 (Stockholm: Statskontoret), for these numbers and a more detailed discussion of the *remiss* process.

8. Perhaps the most detailed report of *remiss* politics in English is Wheeler, *op. cit.,* pp. 38–48 and 118–132.

9. See my *Governing Greater Stockholm* . . . , p. 158.

10. Hancock, *op. cit.,* p. 193.

11. Vinde, pp. 85–109, discusses the rules set forth in government regulations.

12. The suggestion was made by Liberal Party leader Per Ahlmark.

13. On the stability of Swedish electoral patterns, see Bo Särlvik, "Political Stability and Change in the Swedish Electorate," *Scandinavian Political Studies,* Vol. 1 (1966), pp. 188–222. A more recent interpretation, drawing on data from the historic 1976 election, is Olof Petersson, *Väljarna och valet 1976.* Stockholm: Statistiska centralbiyrån. 1977.

14. One humorous and celebrated incident involving the dropping of titles is reported in my *Governing Greater Stockholm* . . . , p. 157.

15. Wheeler, *op. cit.,* pp. 118–163.

16. Anton, *Governing Greater Stockholm* . . . , ch. IV.

17. Wheeler, *op. cit.,* p. 123.

18. *Ibid.,* p. 124.

19. None of this should be taken to mean that public disputes between officials do not occur, only that their occurrence is usually a sign of system breakdown.

20. Milton L. Rakove, *Don't Back No Losers.*

21. William H. Whyte, *The Organization Man.* New York: Simon and Schuster, 1956.

22. See Robert K. Merton, *Social Theory and Social Structure* (The Free Press of Glencoe, 1957, rev. ed.), esp. Part II.

23. Swedish socialization practices are analyzed in Hancock, *op. cit.* Chapter 10 and Wheeler, *op. cit.,* Chapter 10.

24. Titles are still extraordinarily important among Swedes, less because of any innate respect for status than because of the cues to appropriate inter-personal behavior associated with various titles.

25. The theme of deviant ridicule and resultant personal anxiety is of course central to the films of Ingmar Bergman.

26. For a discussion of these and similar images, see Fleisher, *op. cit.,* ch. 16.

27. Åke Daun, *Förortsliv* (Stockholm: Prisma, 1974), esp. ch. 6.

28. David Popenoe, *The Suburban Environment: Sweden and the United States.* Chicago: The University of Chicago Press, 1977.

29. Edmund Dahlström, *Trivsel i söderut* (Stockholm: Stockholm City Administration, 1951).

30. Herbert Hendin, *Suicide and Scandinavia.* Garden City, New York: Doubleday Anchor Books, 1965.

31. Steven Koblik describes one such case in his "Neutrality and Swedish Politics: Dogma, Games, Consequences" (undated, unpublished paper).

9. POSTSCRIPT: ON THE POLITICS OF ACCOMMODATION

1. The extensive literature on representative bureaucracy has been extensively, and critically, reviewed recently in Kenneth John Meier, "Representative Bureaucracy: An Empirical Analysis," *APSR,* Vol. LXIX, No. 2 (June, 1975), pp. 526–542, and Kenneth John

Meier and Lloyd G. Nigro, "Representative Bureaucracy and Policy Preferences: A Study in the Attitudes of Federal Executives," *Public Administration Review,* Vol. 36, No. 4 (July–August, 1976), pp. 458–468.

2. Einhorn, *op. cit.,* reviews these and other statistical measures of progress.

3. On the importance of context, see Charles W. Anderson, "System and Strategy in Comparative Policy Analysis: A Plea for Contextual and Experiential Knowledge," in William B. Gwyn and George C. Edwards, III, eds., *Perspectives in Public Policy Making.* New Orleans: Department of Political Science, Tulane University, 1975.

4. Mellbourn, *op. cit.*

5. I have made this point in the context of land-use decisions in my "Politics and Planning in a Swedish Suburb," *Journal of the American Institute of Planners,* Vol. XXXV, No. 4 (July 1969), pp. 253–263.

6. The necessity of hierarchical organizational forms, postulated in Michaels' famous "iron law" of oligarchy, clearly becomes questionable as inner logic conceptions change. See Robert Michaels, *Political Parties.* (Glencoe, Illinois: The Free Press, 1949), pp. 31–37 for his argument that "Organization implies the tendency to oligarchy."

7. See, for example, Robert T. Golembiewski, *Organizing Men and Power: Patterns of Behavior and Line-Staff Models.* Chicago: Rand McNally and Company, 1967.

8. Richard M. Cyert and James G. March, *A Behavioral Theory of The Firm.* Englewood Cliffs, N.J.: Prentice-Hall, 1963.

9. The causes of deliberate vagueness are discussed in my "Federal Assistance Programs: The Politics of System Transformation," in Douglas Ashford, ed., *Urban Choice and State Power.* Chicago: Maroufa Press, forthcoming 1979. See also Charles L. Schultze, *The Politics and Economics of Public Spending.* (Washington: The Brookings Institution, 1968), p. 47.

10. For a sampling of the vast literature on the games bureaucrats play in the American setting, see Morton H. Halperin, *Bureaucratic Politics and Foreign Policy.* (Washington, D.C.: Brookings Institution, 1974).

11. Personal communication from Professor Bert Rockman.

12. Högskolestatistik I. Stockholm: Statistiskacentralbyrån, 1975: 2.

13. Olof Petersson, "New Trends in the Swedish Electorate: A Focus on the 1976 Election," (Uppsala, Sweden: Department of Government, University of Uppsala, 1978), p. 18. (processed).

CLINICAL
AND
BEHAVIORAL
NEUROPSYCHOLOGY

An Introduction

ARTHUR MacNEILL HORTON, Jr.
DANNY WEDDING

PRAEGER

PRAEGER SPECIAL STUDIES • PRAEGER SCIENTIFIC

New York • Philadelphia • Eastbourne, UK
Toronto • Hong Kong • Tokyo • Sydney

Library of Congress Cataloging in Publication Data

Horton, Arthur MacNeill, 1947–
    Clinical and behavioral neuropsychology.

    Bibliography: p.
    Includes index.
    1. Psychodiagnostics.   2. Neuropsychology.
I. Wedding, Danny.   II. Title.   [DNLM: 1. Neurophysiology.
2. Psychophysiology.   3. Mental disorders.   4. Nervous
system diseases.   WL 102 H823c]
RC469.H67   1983   616.89   83-13766
ISBN 0-03-057607-5 (alk. paper)
        0-03-069351-9 (pbk)

Published in 1984 by Praeger Publishers
CBS Educational and Professional Publishing
a Division of CBS Inc.
521 Fifth Avenue, New York, New York 10175 U.S.A.

456789   052   987654321

Printed in the United States of America
on acid-free paper

*This book is
dedicated to our wives,
Mary and Cynthia*

PREFACE

A great deal of time and more than a little suffering went into the preparation of this book. However, it was not unduly aversive because we are genuinely fascinated with the subject matter and because we believe that a meaningful interface does exist between clinical neuropsychology and behavior therapy. Unfortunately, few training programs currently exist where one can be well trained in both disciplines. We hope this will change and we like to think of ourselves as contributing to the change. A guiding principle behind all our efforts has been the belief that the techniques of behavior therapy are a natural match for the assessment procedures of clinical neuropsychology and that their union can be both joyous and fecund.

A number of people contributed to the present volume, directly or indirectly. We are indebted to our teachers first of all: neuropsychologists such as Howard Gudeman, James Craine, William Tsushima, Richard J. Browne, Thomas J. Boll, Daniel Hallahan, and Ralph M. Reitan; behavior therapists such as Len Ullmann, Roland Tharp, Scott MacDonald, Terence Keane, Carl Johnson, James M. Kaufman, Julian Libet, Dean Kilpatrick, and Marian MacDonald; personal mentors Donald M. Medley, Virgil S. Ward, Paul B. Walter, R. Dean Taylor, Elisabeth B. Decker, Kashmiri Parakh, and Francis R. O'Brien. A number of colleagues reviewed portions of the manuscript or took time over coffee to discuss some of the ideas we present in *Clinical and Behavioral Neuropsychology*. These include Mike Woodruff, Hugh Criswell, Eddythe Carr, Pat Sloan, Larry Hartlage, Charles Golden, Charlie Long, Bruce Becker, Jeff Webster, Paul Malloy, George W. Hynd, Cecil K. Reynolds, Raymond S. Dean, Robert Owens, Peggy Michaelis, and Michelle Timmons. They were willing to share their ideas and were patient with our own and we appreciate their support.

Typing and clerical support were provided by Wanda Davis and Janice Lyons and we appreciate their patience with our constant visions and revisions. Finally, we wish to note the contributions of our wives, both of whom were pregnant during much of the writing of this book. They were long suffering and patient and only occasionally questioned the length of our travail.

CONTENTS

APPENDIX

LIST OF
TABLES AND FIGURES

1

OVERVIEW

A number of years ago, a young psychologist began his internship experience in a Veterans Administration Medical Center.* A primary feature of the clinical experience was weekly attendance at the Neurology Service staff lectures. The young psychologist was somewhat taken aback by the neurological terminology. Five minutes into a lecture by a neurology resident, the psychology intern understood almost nothing of the presentation and began to have doubts about his abilities to interact with neurologists.

About the only thing he could grasp of the lecture was the incomprehensible term "arthropod vector," apparently a central theme of the talk. At the conclusion of the lecture, another psychology student had the courage to ask the meaning of the term "arthropod vector." The neurology resident changed his expression to a somewhat sheepish grin and said a mosquito. The moral of the story is that things are not always as conceptually difficult as they first appear.

BASIC DEFINITIONS

In order to provide some conceptual clarity, the following brief definitions are provided. Remember that the terms to be discussed are often used in an idiosyncratic manner by various authors and different writers are prone to utilize different concepts while retaining a common term as a descriptor. While this sort of behavior tends to

---

*Dr. Horton's contributions to this book were made in his private capacity and without support or endorsement by the Veterans Administration.

diminish the conceptual clarity of scientific/clinical investigation, as yet, no satisfactory means of correcting this situation has been identified.

Brain Lesions

A brain lesion is a rather specific pathological alteration of brain tissue. Usually it can be verified by neurobiomedical diagnostic procedures such as electroencephalography, roentgenography, and cerebrospinal fluid examination, among others.

Brain Damage

Relative to a brain lesion, the term brain damage is used in a somewhat broader sense (Davison, 1974). While brain damage clearly subsumes brain lesions, it also includes alteration of brain physiology without structural change. For instance, a toxic condition could cause brain damage yet fail to show obvious structural changes. On the other hand, a clear example of structural brain damage would be an open head injury in which a foreign object enters one of the cerebral hemispheres. In cases where there is unlikely to be clear structural impairment of the brain, the term "cerebral dysfunction" can serve the purpose of indicating some functional changes while holding the question of structural damage in abeyance. To a certain extent, this usage reflects the difference between "acute" and "chronic" brain damage, which is discussed under the term organic brain syndrome.

Intellectual Impairment

Intellectual impairment implies a certain degree of confidence in a particular definition of intelligence. Unfortunately, there is no universally acceptable definition of intelligence (Sattler, 1974). The following four definitions illustrate the problem. Binet (Binet & Simon, 1905), the first developer of an IQ test, said intelligence was judgment, practical sense, initiative, and the ability to adapt oneself to circumstances. Terman (1921), the American who revised Binet's IQ test, regarded intelligence as ability in abstract thinking. Wechsler (1958), who originated the Wechsler Intelligence Scales for adults and children, suggested that intelligence was "the aggregate or global capacity of the individual to act purposefully, to think rationally and to deal effectively with his environment" (p. 86). Piaget provides an altogether different perspective (Elkind, 1969) by postulating that intelligence is an extension of biological adaption whereby the individual deals with both inner promptings and environmental intrusions. Alternate points of view are provided by Cattell (1963), Guilford (1967), and Jensen (1970), among many others. From the above, it should be clear that these many definitions of intelligence present a conceptual dilemma in that it is difficult to determine if an individual's intellectual ability has been impaired unless one is able to adequately specify just what constitutes intellectual ability.

It was precisely this controversy over intellectual processes that prompted the creation of the first clinical neuropsychological test battery (Russell, Neuringer, & Goldstein, 1970). Ward Halstead, about whom a more detailed discussion follows, was attempting to make a distinction between intelligence measured by standard psychological tests ("psychometric intelligence") and intelligence dependent on the organic integrity of the brain at the level of the cerebral hemispheres ("biological intelligence") (Halstead, 1947). Experience has shown that there are some advantages in this distinction.

While the statement that intelligence is what intelligence tests measure is clearly circular, there is some value in utilizing this operational definition. It provides a measurable criterion for evaluating the effects of brain damage and reflects current practice. Therefore, within the context of this volume, intelligence is operationally defined as what intelligence tests measure. It is realized that this inadequate definition presents additional difficulties in that intelligence tests may differ in the specific abilities they measure. For example, the Stanford–Binet Intelligence Scale is almost entirely verbal at the superior adult level while the Wechsler Adult Intelligence Scale retains performance items regardless of an individual's ability.

The major advantage of this operational definition of intelligence is that it permits some specificity with regard to the effects of intellectual impairment. Intellectual impairment is present whenever one observes a decrease in intellectual ability as measured by an IQ test. This definition, while conceptually inadequate, is exquisitely pragmatic and cuts through the Gordian Knot of defining intelligence.

Sensory–Motor Deficit

Sensory–motor deficits can be interdependent with intellectual impairment (Luria, 1966; Reitan, 1970). However, it is well to make an operational distinction between intellectual impairment and a deficit in sensory or motor functioning. Sensory processes can include visual, auditory, and tactile functions, among others, whereas motor functions may subsume strength, speed, and coordination. For ease of comprehension, the terms agnosia and apraxia are applied to sensory and motor losses. Agnosia generally refers to the failure to recognize familiar objects perceived by the senses while apraxia refers to the inability to carry out complex movements not due to confusion, lack of sensory feedback, or motor paralysis (Chusid, 1976).

Affective Functioning

Affective functioning refers to an individual's constellation of personality traits and mood changes and to the resulting interpersonal style produced by their interplay. Affective functioning is separated from both intellectual ability and sensory–motor adequacy. These concepts by no means imply that the relationships are orthogonal since they interact in a reciprocal manner.

Adaptive Ability

Most of the definitions of intelligence noted earlier include the concept of adaptation (e.g., Binet & Simon, 1905; Elkind, 1969; Wechsler, 1958). Adaptive ability can be defined in terms of intellectual, sensory–motor, and personality functioning (Davison, 1974).

In essence, the earlier distinction made between biological and psychometric intelligence (Halstead, 1947) is utilized as a model for adaptive ability. That is, adaptive ability is defined as the manifestation of the organic integrity of the brain at the level of the cerebral hemispheres. Like Halstead's concept of biological intelligence, this definition separates the concept of psychometric intelligence from earlier definitions of intelligence. Unlike Halstead (1947), we do not believe adaptive ability necessarily resides in the frontal lobes of the cerebral cortex. However, impairment of the frontal lobes would surely produce a decrement in adaptive ability. Thus, adaptive ability, as narrowly defined here, is a measure of neuropsychological adequacy that attempts to explain what is inferred from a neuropsychological evaluation.

THE DISCIPLINE

Definition of the Term Neuropsychology

"Neuropsychology is the scientific study of brain–behavior relationships" (Meier, 1974).

The above definition does not specify that neuropsychology would consist of three major research styles or approaches or that neuropsychology would only include the scientific study of brain–behavior relationships in humans (Davison, 1974). These modifications are a reflection of changes that have been made in neuropsychology in recent years. For example, it is appropriate to allot more than three research approaches to the scientific study of brain–behavior relationships due to the recent emergence of behavioral neuropsychology (Horton, 1978) as a separate subfield of neuropsychology.

The following sections offer a brief survey of the various subfields of neuropsychology: clinical neuropsychology, experimental neuropsychology, behavioral neurology, and behavioral neuropsychology.

While other areas such as speech pathology and physiological psychology (Meier, 1974) could be included, they are excluded here due to the acknowledged preliminary and tentative nature of the following remarks. Special attention, however, is devoted to unique contributions of each subfield.

Clinical Neuropsychology

For the purposes of this volume, the term clinical neuropsychology is used to refer to "that component of the human Neuropsychological enterprise which emphasizes the use of objective psychological methods in the assessment of higher cortical functions" (Meier, 1974, p. 289). This definition focuses on the psychometric aspects of clinical neuropsychology. We recognize that not all contemporary workers who identify themselves as "clinical neuropsychologists" would be willing to accept the above definition as a suitable description of their area of expertise. The rationale for favoring this definition is one of specificity, that is, the psychometric basis of clinical neuropsychology is clearly emphasized and this serves to limit the field.

As observed by Davison (1974):

> Clinical Neuropsychology relies on standardized behavioral observations, emphasizing psychological tests with norms and cutting scores. Behavior, in the context of this approach, is defined in operational terms and, usually, quantified on continuous distributions— the concept of behavioral effects of brain damage, is in this approach, a very differentiated one. In his diagnostic task, the Clinical Neuropsychologist is not merely interested in differentiating brain damage from other diagnostic possibilities, he is also interested in making refined descriptions of clinical conditions including inferences as to location and extent of brain damage, if any, and probable medical and psychological conditions accounting for the abnormal behavior. (p. 3)

From the above quote, two points should be clear. First, clinical neuropsychology is applied in that it focuses upon the clinical problem of assessment of higher cortical functions in humans. Second, clinical neuropsychology is based upon objective psychological tests that meet recognized psychometric standards of validity and reliability. Stated simply, levels of measurement refer to methods of describing observations. In clinical neuropsychology, a good portion of the data are expressed in continuous distributions as opposed to merely categorical descriptions.

The field of clinical neuropsychology was founded through the efforts of two individuals, Ralph M. Reitan and Arthur L. Benton. The major contribution of Reitan has been the revision and careful validation by neurological criteria of an extensive battery of neuropsychological tests initially developed by Halstead (1947). This work has produced separate batteries for the following age groups (Davison, 1974):

Test battery	Age group
Halstead Neuropsychological Test Battery for Adults	15 and above
Halstead Neuropsychological Test Battery for Children	9 to 14
Reitan–Indiana Test Battery for Children	5 to 8

There is a massive body of cross-validated and cross-cultural research establishing the worth of these tests for the assessment of a wide variety of adaptive behaviors dependent on the organic integrity of the cerebral hemispheres (Reitan and Davison, 1974). This work has included investigations of head injuries (Klonoff & Paris, 1974), epileptics (Klove & Matthews, 1974), and the mentally retarded (Matthews, 1974), among others. Later chapters are specifically devoted to Reitan's contribution.

In contrast, the work of Benton has focused on the sequential study of a number of topics drawn from neurology (Meier, 1974). Benton's contribution has been the application of psychological measures to various conceptual issues in neurology. His approach is markedly different from that of Reitan. While Reitan focused on the development of a fairly comprehensive battery of neuropsychological tests, which were admittedly not theoretically based (Reitan, 1968), Benton's work concerned the development of separate tests and relied on a rather careful emphasis on theories other than those identified with clinical neuropsychology (Benton, 1963, 1967, 1968).

Experimental Neuropsychology

The major focus of experimental neuropsychology is "to discover fundamental principles of brain–behavior relationships, regardless of practical application" (Davison, 1974). The assumption is that the study of the basic neuropsychological mechanisms will ultimately provide an elucidation of brain–behavior relationships. Illustrative research areas include learning, memory, and lateralization of cerebral mechanisms.

Karl Pribram and Michael Gazzaniga are neuropsychologists working in the area of experimental neuropsychology. Pribram is well known for his work on the frontal lobes (1974), while Gazzaniga's work (1977) on split-brain patients is internationally famous. As quite a bit of the work in this area is focused on infrahumans and since the generalizability of animal models to modes of human cognitive processing is under challenge (Lockard, 1971), the work of experimental neuropsychology is not always apparent to the clinician. Indeed, the author can recall a clinical neuropsychologist who characterized experimental neuropsychology as "monkey stuff." This viewpoint raises the danger of ignoring a number of possible valuable insights. Investigation of the effects of frontal ablations on the rhesus monkey (Pribram, 1974) has provided a body of data that elucidates the riddle of the frontal granular cortex. Pribram (1974) suggests the frontal lobes are the site of the integration of cerebral perceptions of the world external to the skin with the information arising from the physiological functioning of the human body. Essentially, the frontal cortex may serve to mediate the resolution of possible conflicting demands of the external environment and internal visceral desires. While this interpretation is based upon infrahuman experimentation and the generalizability of this animal model will have to be subjected to scientific test with human beings, a major advantage is readily apparent. A testable hypothesis has been generated from neuropsychological findings and future work can be undertaken to verify or disprove its scientific worth. This brief example demonstrates the heuristic value of basic experimental inquiry in neuroscience. The ultimate problem in modern-day science is not so much the ability to test hypotheses but rather the creative derivation of testable hypotheses.

Behavioral Neurology

One of the most lucid descriptions of behavioral neurology is that provided by Meier (1974). Behavioral neurology is Meier's term for "the traditional medical approach to brain–behavior study." Meier (1974) also effectively describes the etiology of behavioral neurology:

> This approach evolved from 19th century European neurology, based largely upon data obtained by means of strategies applied during clinical neurological examination. Since language disturbances are among the most dramatic changes to occur in focal

cerebral disease and are readily amenable to behavioral analysis at
the bedside, attention understandably was directed to the aphasias,
apraxias, and agnosias. Extremely innovative and imaginative
evaluative strategies were brought to bear on these problems. The
resulting findings added impetus to the entire neuropsychological
effort and yielded considerable knowledge of behavior change in
patients with focal cerebral lesions. (p. 300)

Interestingly, it is possible to pinpoint a pivotal publication that
stimulated American interest in behavioral neurology. In a seminal
paper appearing in the journal *Brain*, Geschwind (1965) integrated
the European literature on behavioral neurology and initiated the
start of real growth in this area.

Language assessment was the central concern of behavioral
neurology as conceptualized by Meier (1974). This quest for assessment devices for the specific quantification of language disturbance
points out a salient aspect of Meier's conceptualization of behavioral
neurology.

Behavioral Neuropsychology

Of the subfields of neuropsychology reviewed in this chapter, the
most recent to emerge has been behavioral neuropsychology. A
tentative definition for behavioral neuropsychology was suggested by
Horton (1978).

Essentially, Behavioral Neuropsychology may be defined as the
application of Behavior Therapy techniques to problems of organically impaired individuals while using a Neuropsychological assessment and intervention perspective. This treatment methodology
suggests that inclusion of data from neuropsychological assessment
strategies would be helpful in the formulation of hypotheses regarding antecedent conditions (external or internal) for observed phenomena of psychopathology. That is, a neuropsychological perspective will significantly enhance the ability of the behavior therapist to
make accurate discriminations as to the etiology of patient behaviors.
Moreover, the formulation of a cogent plan of therapeutic intervention and its skillful implementation could, in certain cases, be
facilitated by an analysis of behavior deficits implicating impairment of higher cortical functioning. (p. 1)

While a focus on organically impaired individuals is fairly
straightforward, less salient features of this definition include:

1. The application of behavior therapy techniques
2. Utilization of a neuropsychological assessment and intervention
   perspective

First, there is less than complete agreement as to exactly what set or group of procedures would qualify as "behavior therapy techniques" (Wilson, 1978; Wolpe, 1976a, 1976b). Indeed, Kazdin (1980) observes that behavior therapy is currently undergoing an identity crisis with rather mixed emotions as to some of the resultant developments (Ledwidge, 1978; Mahoney, 1977; Wolpe, 1976a). Second, given the rapid development of neuropsychological assessment, it is difficult to predict which test, group of tests, or neuropsychological test battery would provide the most appropriate data on which to base a behavioral intervention. For example, CT scanners only recently came into widespread use and have significantly affected the demand for Halstead–Reitan Neuropsychological Test batteries for diagnostic purposes. As technology progresses, it may be that a number of traditional techniques and methods will be superseded by more valid and reliable neurodiagnostic methods. Therefore, it would be unwise to link behavioral neuropsychology to any single set of neuropsychological diagnostic procedures.

NEUROPSYCHOLOGY AND TRADITIONAL MEDICAL SPECIALITIES

The three traditional medical specialities most directly involved with clinical neuropsychology are: neurology, neurosurgery, and psychiatry. This rather arbitrary limitation is not meant to suggest that neuropsychology does not enjoy mutually beneficial relationships with other medical specialties such as rehabilitation medicine, family practice, pediatrics, or cardiology. On the contrary, no rigid boundaries are implied. Rather, because the previous evolution of neuropsychology could have taken place only with the assistance of neurologists, neurosurgeons, and to a lesser extent psychiatrists, it would be inappropriate not to include a brief discussion of these relationships.

It is happenstance that neuropsychology as a discipline in the United States is primarily practiced by individuals trained as psychologists. It should be noted that the famous Russian neuropsychologist, A.R. Luria, was trained as a physician and that many prominent neuropsychologists, particularly from the behavioral neurology (nineteenth century) tradition, are physicians by training and professional identification.

The primary areas of concern of neurologists, neurosurgeons, and psychiatrists are quite well delineated. Grossly oversimplified, neurologists diagnose and treat various central nervous system (CNS) disorders. Neurosurgeons operate when the particular variety of intracranial pathology is amenable to surgical intervention (e.g., space-occupying mass lesions such as meningiomas). In contrast, psychiatrists generally attempt to exclude patients with brain damage from their spheres of practice. In the past, neuropsychology has tended to perform a diagnostic function for all three medical specialties. Clinical neuropsychological test batteries were used as noninvasive methods to provide information regarding the presence or absence of brain damage, lateralization, localization, etiology of the cerebral dysfunction, and prognosis. The first role of the clinical neuropsychologist was to provide neurologists with information useful in the practice of medicine. Indeed, without the aid of neurologists and neurosurgeons, valid and reliable psychological–behavioral measures sensitive to the organic integrity of the brain at the level of the cerebral hemisphere might never have developed. On the other hand, neuropsychology has returned the favor by providing quantitative measures of cerebral function that can be used to elucidate a number of areas of scientific inquiry in neurology and neurosurgery. While in the past, the major flow of information was from the medical specialists to the neuropsychologist (Davison, 1974), there are signs that the trend may be reversed. For example, due to clinical neuropsychological studies of the cognitive and affective sequelae of head trauma and neurosurgical intervention, there is an increased awareness among neurologists as to the need for long-term follow-up and counseling (Boll, 1978).

Quite different relationships have existed between neuropsychology and the traditional medical speciality of psychiatry. The psychological speciality that developed under the aegis of psychiatry was clinical psychology, not any variant of neuropsychology. Actually, the advent of neuropsychology, primarily clinical neuropsychology, applied to the practice of psychiatry, is a fairly recent event. The classic focus of the psychiatrist is, of course, on functional disorders such as schizophrenia, neuroses, and character disorders. The various phenomena of organicity are usually seen as falling under the purview of neurology. More recent thinking, however, has tended to emphasize the interrelationship between cerebral organization and classic dimensions of psychopathology (Pincus & Tucker, 1974). In addition, the emotional concomitants of neurological insult and impairment have received a greater degree of attention from contemporary psychiatrists (Lipowski, 1978). Golden (1978) has recently reviewed the contributions clinical neuropsychology can offer to psychiatry. While some clear trends toward a more liberated view of brain–behavior relationships are readily apparent, the psychiatric conceptual map of cerebral functions continues to be tantamount to a dichotomous model of organicity (Davison, 1974). As this issue is the central determinant of a rather substantial number of differences between the goals, methods, and procedures of traditional clinical psychodiagnostics and the evolving neuropsychological perspective, a separate section is devoted to this issue.

ASSESSMENT IN CLINICAL PSYCHOLOGY AND CLINICAL NEUROPSYCHOLOGY

Clinical neuropsychology and clinical psychology emerged, evolved, and prospered, linked to the respective fields of neurology and psychiatry. Each had a distinct influence on assessment strategies.

Essentially, the primary difference between clinical neuropsychology and clinical psychology relates to conceptualization of neurocognitive processes. The model of brain–behavior relationships most often utilized by the majority of practicing clinical psychologists is markedly dissimilar from the view of psychological/neurological functions endorsed by contemporary human neuropsychologists. These incongruent models are fairly direct reflections of the traditional medical specialities associated with each psychological speciality.

Looking at clinical psychology first, the behavioral syndrome or cluster of behaviors of paramount importance is organic brain syndrome (OBS). As described by Libet and Kilpatrick (1974), OBS usually refers to the following primary behaviors.

OBS Sx.

1. Inability to integrate external stimuli (visual, auditory, or kinesthetic) adequately in space and/or time
2. Disorientation
3. Short-term, recent, or long-term memory losses
4. Impaired judgment
5. Decreased attention span
6. Loss of ability to "track" environmental contingencies (i.e., the consequences of one's behaviors)

Second, behavioral concomitants may include:

OBS behavior

1. Erratic verbal and motor behavior
2. Labile affect
3. Perceptual distortions such as illusions and hallucinations
4. Delusional ideation
5. Confabulation

In the interests of conceptual clarity, it might be remarked that the mnemonic "RIP," which stands for *R*etention (memory), *I*ntegration (cognitive, sensory or motor), and *P*erception (visual, auditory or kinesthetic), is a shorthand but grossly oversimplified way of obtaining a degree of understanding of the OBS concept.

Essentially, organicity or the OBS pattern is a central feature of the clinical psychologist's cognitive map. As observed by Davison (1974):

> The basic concept…is that of organicity, a unitary concept. The concept includes the assumption that any and all kinds of brain damage lead to similar behavioral effects, and that behavioral

differences among the brain-damaged are due primarily to severity
of damage and to premorbid personality characteristics. (p. 14)

The historical support for the OBS conceptualization is often
attributed to Lashley's (1929) work on rats and Goldstein's (1942) work
with brain-injured soldiers. Both of these are discussed in later
chapters. For now, all that is necessary is to realize that to understand
brain damage as existing on a single dimension is as realistic and
useful as the assertion that human beings vary on the dimension of
height. To be sure, the assertion is true in a general sense, and, in
special situations, could be quite useful (e.g., college basketball) but in
many circumstances there will be a need for additional data with
regard to sources of variation. Using the human analogy, the variables
of age, gender, weight, socioeconomic standing, and education, among
others, could be profitably considered in most contexts.

A more highly differentiated matrix of psychological/neurological
functions is generally endorsed by contemporary neuropsychologists.
While it is extremely difficult to obtain widespread agreement on
many scientific topics, the following factors would probably be
vouchsafed as important by a majority of neuropsychologists:

1. Laterality of lesion (right or left hemisphere)
2. Localization of lesion within the hemisphere
3. Etiology of the lesion (vascular, tumor, trauma, etc.)
4. The patient's age
5. Chronicity

Other parameters that might be included are:

6. Premorbid level of adaptive ability (Lansdell, 1971)
7. The patient's condition at the time of assessment apart from the
    effects of brain damage (Stein, 1970)
8. Dominance (Hecaen & Ajuriaguerra, 1964)
9. Size of the lesion (Chapman & Wolff, 1959)
10. Severity of the lesion (Chapman & Wolff, 1959)

Clearly, the contemporary neuropsychological viewpoint of the
parameters along which a given lesion can produce behavioral deficits
is quite complex. It is understandable that the psychological sequel of
injury to the cortex is multifaceted. Just as the human brain is
incredibly complex and so diverse in its functions that it is perhaps
ludicrous to expect to ever fully understand it (Sagan, 1977), so it
would appear that injury to the marvelous collection of tiny neurons
will cause consequences that need careful study if we are to understand
them in even a very rudimentary way. It is interesting to reflect for a

moment that this movement from simple conceptualization to complicated theoretical structure appears to be a general trend in almost any scientific inquiry.

As earlier noted, clinical psychology sprang up within the domain of the traditional medical speciality of psychiatry. This event had profound influences upon the practice of clinical psychology. Basically, psychologists in clinical settings were required to work with those questions of paramount interest to psychiatrists. As observed by Davison (1974) a major area of concern to psychiatrists identified with psychoanalysis was the suitability of patients for analytic therapy. Since the clear majority of psychiatrists trained before World War II were psychoanalytically oriented, a valid prognosis of a patient's ability to profit from psychoanalytically oriented treatment methods was a highly desirable product for the clinical psychologist to produce from an assessment battery. Similarly, as the most common diagnostic classification in many psychiatric settings was and is schizophrenia in its many and varied forms, an ability to assess disordered thought processes in an apparently valid manner was also valuable. Thus, the two factors of suitability for psychoanalytic therapy and the base rates of psychopathology were powerful determinants of the assessment approaches of clinical psychology within psychiatric settings.

In order to address these questions, a fairly standard set of clinical psychological tests has evolved through the years. The following instruments are among those most often used (Lubin, Wallis, and Paine, 1971):

1. Rorschach Method of Personality Assessment
2. Thematic Apperception Test
3. Wechsler Intelligence scales
4. Minnesota Multiphasic Personality Inventory
5. Bender–Gestalt Test

Indeed, this selection of tests to a large degree typifies the psychodiagnostic approach of clinical psychology (Davison, 1974).

Frequency of usage suggests that the above set of tests may be helpful in describing various types of mental disturbances in general and thought disturbances in particular. The psychometric problems associated with the Rorschach Method of Personality Assessment and the Thematic Apperception Test are well known and are not discussed in this context. What is of more interest is the interface of this collection of tests with the brain-damaged patient.

The overriding question of prognosis for psychoanalytically oriented psychotherapy has played a major role with respect to traditional clinical diagnosis of the brain-damaged individual. A diagnosis of brain damage or "organicity" renders a patient inappropriate for verbal, insight-oriented therapy, at least as practiced by most clinicians. This makes the concept of OBS important for clinical psychologists. Unfortunately, however, the emphasis is on a negative inference. Clinical psychologists are looking for a class of patients to exclude as opposed to various classes of patients with common problems that can be treated. The lack of a positive treatment orientation may have been a crucial factor in the relative neglect of the emotion and social adjustment problems of brain-damaged patients treated by clinical psychologists over the years. Clearly, the negative focus on solely identifying the brain damaged for the purpose of excluding them from consideration for treatment in no way fostered a search for better methods to validly describe various categories of organically impaired individuals.

A contributing factor to this situation may have been a tendency to conceptualize certain tests as applicable to all purposes. Clinical psychologists often naively argued that a battery of tests similar to the one described earlier contains sufficient information for all diagnostic purposes, including those related to clinical neuropsychology. However, the classic tests in clinical psychology were selected because of the need to describe functional, as opposed to organic, disorders. There is currently considerable debate over how adequately tests serve this purpose (e.g., Mischel, 1968). An unfortunate myth, but a persistent part of clinical lore, is the belief that some psychologists can use certain instruments to diagnose almost all types of psychopathology. Like most religious delusions, there is little basis in reality for these assertions, and a number of unfortunate consequences. The logic behind the search for the "all-purpose" test is most difficult to comprehend. The authors are aware of clinical psychologists who will glibly assess intellect, personality, and organicity all on the basis of a single test. This is poor practice and worse science.

A very different set of assumptions underlies the clinical neuropsychological approach to assessment. Essentially, clinical neuropsychologists use a highly differential model of brain functioning when they develop and interpret test instruments. The crucial elements in interpretation are awareness of relevant brain–behavior relationships and accurate knowledge of the neurological significance of various psychometric signs, patterns, and cutting scores. The majority of the test instruments used in clinical neuropsychology either were developed with the specific purpose of predicting brain–behavior relationships or were developed for other purposes, yet by happenstance have proved to be particularly sensitive to cerebral dysfunction (e.g., the Digit Symbol Subtest of WAIS). Clearly, instruments that were developed for specific purposes in special settings and subjected to vigorous validation procedures should be quite effective. So it is that neuropsychological assessment techniques, by virtue of emerging within the domains of neurology/neurosurgery, would be more sensitive to the organic integrity of the human brain than those developed in psychiatric settings.

A more difficult problem relates to the actual assessment instruments used in clinical neuropsychology. While the seminal influence of the Halstead–Reitan Neuropsychological Test Battery is fairly well accepted, it would be unwise to suggest that the Halstead–Reitan is the only appropriate approach to neuropsychological assessment. There are those who would advocate a qualitative or "clinical" approach (Goodglass & Kaplan, 1979; Lezak, 1976; Luria, 1966), which is quite at variance from the Halstead–Reitan approach. Moreover, even within the framework of a standardized battery approach, there has arisen a rival to the Halstead–Reitan Battery. The Luria–Nebraska (Golden *et al.* 1978) appears to have a number of methodological strengths, yet this battery was constructed with the express purpose of standardizing Luria's "clinical" approach.

One basic distinction between assessment in clinical psychology and that in clinical neuropsychology is attention to the laterality of hemispheric functioning. To be sure, this is a very gross level of analysis and neuropsychological assessment clearly can provide a more sophisticated analysis of higher cortical functioning and resultant adaptive behavior. In explanation of this point, however, a clinical horror story might be offered. It might be noted that this case is from the senior author's personal experience.

The patient assessed had documented (history and EEG) damage to the left temporal parietal area. He was tested by a third-year clinical psychology student with the Bender–Gestalt and Memory for Design tests. Because the patient performed within normal limits on both of these tests, the student concluded that there was a complete recovery from brain damage. If one recalls that the Bender–Gestalt and Memory for Design tests are visual–spatial assessment instruments and somewhat specific for the right cerebral hemisphere (Golden, 1979), and that the patient's documented lesion was in the left cerebral hemisphere, then the error in neuropsychodiagnosis becomes quite clear. The selection of clinical tests failed to include a measure specific to the left cerebral hemisphere. Thus, a rather gross diagnostic mistake was made.

In summary, the major distinctions between clinical psychological diagnostic approaches and the evolving neuropsychological strategies are apparent. In later chapters, further elucidation of the most popular contemporary neuropsychodiagnostic techniques will be undertaken.

SUGGESTIONS FOR FURTHER READING

Davison, L.A. Introduction. In R.M. Reitan & L.A. Davison (Eds.), *Clinical neuropsychology: Current status and applications.* New York: John Wiley, 1974.

Crockett, O., Clark, D., & Klonoff, H. Introduction: An overview of neuropsychology. In S.B. Filskov & T.J. Boll (Eds.), *Handbook of clinical neuropsychology.* New York: John Wiley, 1980.

Gaddes, W.H. An examination of the validity of neuropsychological knowledge in educational diagnosis and remediation. In G.W. Hynd & J.E. Obrzut (Eds.), *Neuropsychological assessment and the school aged child: Issues and procedures.* New York: Grune & Stratton, 1981.

Horton, A.M., Jr., Wedding, D., & Phay, A. Current perspective on the assessment of and therapy of the brain-damaged patient. In C.J. Golden, S.S. Alcaparras, F. Strider, & B. Graber (Eds.), *Applied techniques in behavioral medicine.* New York: Grune & Stratton, 1981.

2

HISTORY

The materials covered in this chapter fall within two quite different categories. These are: (1) concepts of the functional organization of the brain and (2) development of neuropsychological test batteries.

The first area relates to psychomorphological conceptualizations of the cerebral cortex, whereas the second area relates to the comprehensive quantification and measurement of higher cortical functioning. As with intelligence, the problem of the brain as the seat of complex mental activity is far from solved and areas of theoretical research and practical application are not necessarily synchronized.

In the discussion of the functional organization of the brain, previous points of view on neocognitive structures are reviewed. These include the earliest theories of brain function, later localizationist thinking, and the opposing equipotential positions, as well as more modern integrationist views.

The psychometric representation of cortical structure by psychological behavioral tests comprises the second broad area discussed in this chapter. Much of what we discuss is an outgrowth of the work of Ward Halstead and, in a more applied context, of his student, Ralph M. Reitan, with additional contributions by Reitan's students, Thomas J. Boll and Lawrence C. Hartlage. The more recent trend in neuropsychological assessment might be described as an attempted marriage between modern views regarding mental functioning and their localization as represented by the work of the Russian neurologist A.R. Luria, and standardized methods of quantifying behavior based upon Luria's conceptualizations. In this vein, the pioneering efforts of the American clinical neuropsychologist Charles J. Golden have been of the utmost importance.

CONCEPTS OF THE FUNCTIONAL ORGANIZATION OF THE BRAIN

Preliminary Remarks

It should be stressed that these problems are of an exceedingly difficult type and that an exhaustive discussion is not provided here. More detailed treatments can be contained in any number of textbooks on neurology or neuroscience.

For many years preconceptions of the nature of mental life prevented a true understanding of the functional organization of the human brain. This situation is eloquently described by Luria (1966):

> Many generations of research workers have given their attention to the problem of the brain as the seat of complex mental activity and to the associated problem of the localization of functions in the cerebral cortex. Nevertheless, the solution of these problems has depended not only on the development of technical methods of studying the brain, but also on the theories concerning mental processes predominant at any particular time. For this reason, endeavors to localize cerebral cortical functions were for a long time restricted to futile attempts to "fit" the system of abstract concepts of modern psychology into the material structure of the brain. (Luria, 1966, p. 3)

While these attempts yielded much valuable empirical material, they failed to provide a scientific solution to the problem. It is only in recent years that new principles for its solution have evolved, and new evidence has accumulated to enrich our ideas of the functional organization of the human brain in health and disease.

Earliest Solutions

Initial attempts to elucidate the structural basis for cognitive and affective phenomena are lost in antiquity. Perhaps the earliest recorded scientific investigation of cerebral processes was undertaken by Hippocrates in the fifth century B.C. He was noted as identifying the brain as the organ of the "intellect" (Luria, 1966). Also, he is credited as the first individual to reliably observe that massive injury to a particular cerebral hemisphere resulted in contralateral motor and sensory impairment (Golden, 1978). Further progress is apparent in the work of Galen (second century B.C.), who is credited with devising the notion that the cerebral ventricles (actually, their fluids) were the seat of complex mental functions. He postulated that stimuli received by human beings from the environment enter the ventricles of the brain by means of the eyes in the form of humors. Supposedly these external humors stimulated internal humors and were transformed into various psychic processes (Luria, 1966).

The hypothesis that the cerebral ventricles were the material substrate of mental processes underwent further development prior to its eventual rejection. Additional differentiation of the structure of the ventricles and ascription of particular activities to various portions were undertaken. Nemisius (fourth century A.D.) first suggested that there were three separate and distinct ventricles of the brain and each subserved an independent function. These were as follows: the anterior ventricle was seen as the basis of imagination, the middle ventricle was most involved with intellectual and logical operation, and the final ventricle was credited with the task of subserving memory functions. Curiously, this notion of the three ventricles of the brain as the source of neurocognitive abilities persisted for centuries and savants such as Leonardo da Vinci accepted it as a scientific fact (Luria, 1966).

The emergence of psychology as a recognized field of scientific inquiry aided in a reevaluation of the initial conceptualization of the material substrate of principle mental abilities. This development is described by Luria (1966):

> The subsequent history of concepts of cerebral localization of mental processes was associated with the development of psychology (which for a long time remained a branch of philosophy), on one hand, and with the beginnings of descriptive anatomy of the brain, on the other. The conception of mental functions began to become less rigid while the structure of the brain began to grow clearer. Nevertheless, the basic principle of direct superposition of nonmaterial psychological principles on the material structure of the brain continued unchanged for many years. This explains why the first steps in the development of the science of anatomy in the new era were marked by the search for the particular part of the solid tissue of the "cerebral organ" that could be regarded as the material substrate of mental processes. (pp. 6–7)

As could be expected, there was considerable diversity of opinion as to exactly which specific organ of the human brain served as the material substrate of principal mental abilities. For example, Descartes (1686), famous for his description of the mind and body problem, believed that the pineal gland was the physical seat of mental processes. His conclusion was based, at least partly, on the location of the pineal gland in the center of the brain. Willis (1664) considered the corpus striatum to house mental functions. Vieussens (1685) placed the seat of principal neurocognitive abilities within the mass of white matter of the cerebral hemispheres—the centrum semiorate. Lancisi (1789) theorized that the logical place for mental faculties to reside would be the corpus callosum, the structure that permits communication of information between the two cerebral hemispheres. In sum, the common element of all of these early attempts to better comprehend the relationship between neuroanatomy and mental phenomena was the hope that there was one particular part of the brain that could serve as the direct substrate of the principal mental abilities.

Localizationist Solution

As might be expected, the multiple choices for the material substrate of mental functions led to a new conceptualization. In one sense, it subsumed the ideas of Descartes, Willis, Vieussens, and Lancisi and in another sense, it rejected them all. The next major trend in the study of the functional organization of the human brain was an attempt to identify separate mental functions subsumed by individual portions of the brain.

> Psychology was no longer dominated by the view that consciousness was an indivisible whole. A school of psychology developed that subdivided mental processes into separate, specialized "faculties," and this led to a search for the material substrate for these faculties. The brain was now regarded as an aggregate of many "organs," each of which was supposed to be the material carrier of one particular "Faculty." (Luria, 1966, p. 8)

The first attempt to suggest a differential solution to the perplexing problem of the cerebral localization of mental processes was made by Meyer (cited in Luria, 1966). His highly speculative proposal was to place memory in the cerebral cortex, logic and imagination in the white matter, and apperception and will in the lower brain areas.

A more popular paradigm was advanced by Gall, who proposed that differences in individuals were related to differences in particular brain areas in those individuals (Krech, 1962). Gall was a leading neuroanatomist and is credited with being the first to perceive the value of the white matter of the cerebral hemispheres (Luria, 1966). Despite considerable evidence of Gall's scientific acumen, his framework for relating individual mental abilities to particular sections of neuroanatomy was quite speculative and far beyond limits of his knowledge base. Gall merely took ideas from then current psychological thinking and attempted to place them in a definite group of brain cells. He attempted to shape neuroanatomy into the image of the psychological areas in vogue during his era. A flavor of these phrenological views is apparent from listing some of the mental faculties localized by Gall in the human cerebral cortex. These included "justice," "prudence," "loyalty," "sexual love," and "hope." While these ideas were clearly lacking in scientific support, they were helpful in that they popularized the concept of "localization" and thus provided a basis for later and more realistic thinking along these lines.

Most notable among those providing scientific support for a localizationist point of view was the work of Paul Broca. During April of 1861, before a meeting of the Paris Anthropological Society, Broca exhibited the brain of a patient who had motor speech impairment while alive. Postmortum inspection of this individual's cerebral cortex revealed a lesion of the posterior third of the inferior frontal convolution of the left hemisphere. Broca's continued research soon produced a second subject with an identical clinical syndrome and a similar brain lesion. This finding led him to assert that articulated speech arose from a single specific brain area and that this section of the human cerebral cortex is the "center for motor forms of speech." Supposedly, images of the motor movements constituting speech were stored in the left posterior frontal lobe.

Broca's work, in addition to marking the beginning of scientific support for localizationist theory, encouraged others to explore this line of research. Of those who followed Broca, the major contribution was made by Wernicke (Golden, 1978).

In 1874, Wernicke (cited in Luria, 1966) presented a clinical case in which a deficit in speech comprehension, during the subject's life, was found to correlate with postmortum findings of a lesion of the posterior third of the superior temporal gyrus of the left hemisphere. This impairment of the posterior temporal lobe was independent of any lesion in the left posterior frontal lobe or any motor speech deficits. Wernicke postulated that a center for "sensory images of speech," as distinct from motor images of speech, resided in the posterior third of the superior temporal gyrus of the left hemisphere.

These insightful observations of Broca and Wernicke have stood the test of countless replications and were a major advance in the study of higher cortical functioning. There was an avalanche of "discoveries" that various other mental processes were also localized in relatively small areas of the human cerebral cortex. In what could be seen as a classic example of disregard of the scientific dictum that "correlation doesn't mean causation" many investigations attempted to match clinical syndromes with lesion locations at postmortem examination. Few of these have withstood the test of time. Among these many hypothesized discoveries were centers for "visual memory" (Bastion, 1869, cited in Luria, 1966), "writing" (Exner, 1881, cited in Luria, 1966), and "ideation" (Charcot, 1887, cited in Luria, 1966).

Of more enduring interest were the ideas of Fritsch and Hitzig (1870). These researchers found that stimulation of the sensory–motor area would produce the contraction of specific muscles. This identification of "motor centers" was collaborated through the association of the giant pyramidal cells in the cortex of the anterior central gyrus with motoric functions by the Russian scientist Betz (cited in Luria, 1966). These giant pyramidal cells are, to this day, known as "Betz cells."

Additional support for the localizationist position was gleaned from the investigation of additional clinical syndromes. Musk (1881, cited), working with animals, showed that change to the occipital region could cause visual discrimination difficulties while sparing sight and other cognitive functions. Luria (1966) provided evidence for the role the anterior divisions of the brain play in "attention" and "intellectual activity."

It should be observed that the localizationist position failed to provide a satisfactory answer to the riddle of the functional organization of the human brain.

> The suggestions that different areas of the cerebral cortex are highly differentiated in their structure and that complex mental functions are not uniformly related to the various areas of the brain were basically very progressive. They stimulated the more careful study of the brain and its functions. Nevertheless, the idea that highly complex mental phenomena may be localized in circumscribed areas of the cerebral cortex and that the circumscribed area responsible for a particular function can be directly deduced from a symptom naturally continued to arouse deep misgivings. (Luria, 1966, p. 14)

Equipotential Solutions

As might be expected, there was less than complete acceptance of the localizationist position. Two major reasons for this are related to observations of clinical neurology patients. First, physicians noted that it was possible for a higher-level cortical function to be impaired by multiple separate local brain lesions. Complex skills such as writing or reading could become disturbed by a single local lesion but the single local lesion could be in any number of areas in the brain. As numerous individuals were hoping to make discoveries similar to those of Broca and Wernicke, it would appear almost preordained that when careful correlations of clinical behavioral syndromes with postmortum examination failed to generalize, dissatisfaction with a localizationist paradigm would result. A second consideration is related to the retention of certain skills supposedly dependent on a particular area of the cerebral cortex. Despite the assertion by localizationists that selected small sections of the human brain controlled a specific function, observations were recorded where an individual was injured in the neuroanatomical area supposedly specifically subserving a function and yet were still able to effectively perform the function (Golden, 1978). As a result of these data, incompatible with a patchwork quilt model of functional brain organizations, some scientists favored an alternate view of higher cortical functioning.

Haller (1869, cited in Luria, 1966) suggested that while different sections of the brain might subserve separate functions, the brain is a single organ and is composed of parts of similar importance. Data for this hypothesis could be gleaned from observations that a single brain lesion could impair a number of widely separate neurocognitive skills and, on the other hand, it was also possible to compensate for the disruption caused by such a specific local lesion (Luria, 1966). The uncontrolled nature of Haller's observations was a major factor preventing their unanimous acceptance.

More rigorous proof was offered by Flourens (1824, cited in Luria, 1966). Perhaps the major figure on the early equipotentialist side, Flourens' greatest contribution was to provide experimental evidence that directly contradicted the localizationist position. His scientific paradigm was a physiological experiment in which he arranged the destruction of specific demarkated sections in the cerebral hemispheres of birds. Research of this type became known as ablation studies.

There were essentially three major hypotheses that Flourens claimed had been proven by his experiments. These were summarized by Golden (1978, p. 6):

(1) The process of perception involves the whole brain but sensory input at an elementary level is localized.
(2) Loss of function is dependent on the extent of damage, not on the location.
(3) All cerebral material is equipotential. By equipotential, Flourens meant that if sufficient cortical material is intact, the remaining material will take over the functions of any missing brain tissue.

Although Flourens performed a great service to neuropsychology by injecting scientific evidence into the localizationist versus equipotential debate, his methodology was flawed. The major difficulty was his use of infrahuman subjects and the assumption of considerable similarity between the brains of birds and humans. Flourens overlooked the biological fact that in lower vertebrates the brain is much less differentiated than in human beings and that functioning is inadequately corticalized.

Regardless of these limitations in the research methodology of Flourens, the equipotentialist position continued to garner support. An important factor in this development was a reanalysis of one of the major discoveries in the localizationist tradition. In 1906, Marie inspected one of the preserved brains on which Broca based his internationally famous observation implicating the posterior third of the inferior frontal convolution of the left hemisphere as the specific brain area subserving motor speech. Marie's examination revealed cerebral damage in areas other than the left posterior frontal lobe. On the basis of these findings, Marie argued that the area identified by Broca was not necessarily responsible for the patient's motor speech deficits, but rather a more diffuse sort of impairment that could have disrupted the patient's global intellect and thus produced an expressive language deficit (Golden, 1978).

In a more positive manner, other researchers in the equipotentialist tradition contributed findings in support of the position that the "mass of the cerebral hemisphere is physiologically just as homogeneous and uniform in its importance as the mass of any gland" (Flourens, 1842, cited in Luria, 1966). Of these neurological scientists, perhaps the best known were Goldstein and Lashley. Their experimental findings were crucial contributions to the equipotential position.

It is simplistic to assume that both Goldstein and Lashley professed a slavish adherence to the views of Flourens. Both men quite clearly accepted as proven scientific fact the localization of elementary sensory and motor skills (Golden, 1978). On the other hand, both Goldstein and Lashley strongly asserted an equipotentialist point of view relative to other human cortical functions.

Goldstein is particularly noted for his work with brain-injured veterans of World War I. He (1927, 1939, 1944, 1948) attempted to apply a Gestalt psychological conceptualization to neurocognitive abilities.

> Goldstein believed that every brain lesion gives rise to a disturbance of abstract orientation or categorical behavior. This assertion forced him to adopt a unique position in regard to disturbances of elementary and higher mental functions. In an attempt to elucidate the cerebral mechanisms of these processes, Goldstein distinguished between the "periphery" of the cortex, in regard to which he retained the structured localization viewpoint, and the "central part" of the cortex, which, in contrast to the periphery, he regarded as "equipotential" and functioning in accordance with the principle of the creation of "dynamic structures" against some form of dynamic background....A lesion of the central part of the cortex causes a profound change in both abstract orientation and categorical behavior. (Luria, 1966, p. 20)

Goldstein's assertion that concrete thinking is a general characteristic of the brain-injured individual was a major conceptual achievement and his major contribution. In addition, his use of human subjects and his utilization of psychological tests to study brain–behavior relationships clearly establishes his place as the father of human clinical neuropsychology.

In contrast, Lashley's research concentrated on nonhuman subjects. Unlike Flourens, who ablated bird brains, Lashley's work involved the extirpation of selected portions of rat brains. Lashley's experimental paradigm required the study of the maze running by rats who had suffered cortical surgery with specific brain areas removed. Maze-running deteriorated following brain injury. The results of these experiments suggested that the location of the brain areas extirpated made little difference. Lashley summarized his results in two general laws (Golden, 1978).

1. *The laws of mass action:* The extent of behavioral impairment is directly proportional to the mass of the removed tissue.
2. *The law of multipotentiality:* Each brain part participates in more than a single function.

Lashley's work was almost uncritically accepted. However, Pavlov had made the point that the interpretation of ablation experiments by the undifferentiated concepts of contemporary psychology invited unwarranted inferences (Luria, 1966). In retrospect, it is possible to appreciate the wisdom of Pavlov's view. The extirpation of brain tissue in no way reveals the physiological mechanisms of behavior. Because of this fact, Lashley's conclusions that brain tissue is equipotential were preordained by his choice of experimental methodology.

There are other deficits associated with the equipotentialist position.

Equipotentiality fails to account for the specific deficits often seen in absence of general impairment in intellect, abstract attitude, perception, or other global abilities. The theory also fails to account for the correspondences between sites of injury and higher cognitive deficits that have been repeatedly reported. (Golden, 1978, p. 8)

Neither the localizationist nor the equipotential position adequately described all of the amassed research data and clinical observations. A more moderate position appears justified; that is, the brain is both localized and equipotential. Given the normal course of things, this would be a natural development and indeed might be termed a "political" solution to a psychomorphic problem.

Fortunately, however, a more scientific alternative to these two positions was developed. However, prior to discussing these alternatives, we can sum up the major contributions of both the localizationist and equipotential positions. On the plus side, those who attempted to relegate neurocognitive processes to relatively circumscribed areas of the cortex, with the brain working as an aggregate of separate organs, made a positive advance through their attempts to study mental life and the structure of the brain in an analytic manner. These careful investigations, in the end, provided us with the modern neurosciences that we know today. Also, important clinical benefits were derived from the identification of particular functional zones in apparently homogenous brain tissue. At the same time, substantial contributions toward the development of modern ideas of the functional organization of the brain were also made by those endorsing an equipotentiality stance. Indeed, through a concentrated focus on the unitary functioning and essential plasticity of brain tissue, the advocates of an equipotential theory paved the way for contemporary neuropsychological models of cerebral organization (Luria, 1966).

Still, in spite of these important steps forward, a better paradigm was necessary for further progress in understanding the actual nature of the functional organization of the human brain.

An Integrated Solution

Luria (1966) has eloquently summarized the intellectual precursors of his own theoretical position:

> The entire history of the attempt to localize mental processes in the cerebral cortex, whether these attempts were made from the standpoint of localizationism or antilocalizationism, betrays one false assumption, and this led to the most serious misconceptions. However much the two concepts that have been described may differ from each other, they share a common psychomorphological feature: they both look upon mental functions as phenomena to be directly correlated with the brain structure without intermediate physiological analysis. In other words, they both attempted to "superimpose the nonspatial concepts of (then) contemporary psychology on the spatial construction of the brain" (Pavlov) and they continued to regard mental processes as properties incapable of further analysis, to be understood only, as the direct product of the activity of cerebral structures. In fact, the belief in the material basis of mental activity, which had been openly incorporated in the medieval notions of the "faculties of the mind," persisted unchanged in all these theories, and the true scientific analysis of the mechanisms by which the brain adequately reflects the outside world was replaced by parallelistic views that complex mental functions correspond to circumscribed or extensive areas of the brain. (p. 22)

Essentially, brain functioning, a neurophysiological phenomenon, was placed in the Procrustian bed of contemporary psychology and the limitations of the psychology of the day precluded major advances in neuropsychological theory.

A view more compatible with the actual realities of brain anatomy and physiology was proposed by the English neurologist Thomas Hughlings Jackson. It is difficult to overestimate the influence of Jackson's thinking on modern concepts of psychomorphology. His model of brain functioning essentially underlies all contemporary theoretical attempts to analyze neurodynamic changes associated with local lesions of the brain.

Given this major impact on modern psychology/neurology, it is ironic that Jackson's ideas were initially unnoticed (Golden, 1978). Only after other neurological workers such as Pick, Head, and Forester, during the early part of the twentieth century, quoted Jackson's views did he receive attention. Indeed, his investigations were only published in summary form in England after World War I (1932) and in the United States after World War II (1958) (Luria, 1966).

Jackson, who was a contemporary of Broca, began by studying epileptic fits on a localized basis. By investigating the motor and speech deficits that follow local brain lesions, Jackson was able to develop a consistent theory of the neurological organization of behavioral functioning (Luria, 1966). The impetus for Jackson's theorizing was a single clinical case. One of his patients was unable to say "no" while trying to do so voluntarily but when pressured by Jackson, the patient became exasperated and replied with some anger "No, doctor I never can say no!" The important point is that the patient could produce the word "no" as an automatic response but not as a voluntary skill. This clinical observation suggested that there are multiple avenues for the performance of a behavior. Jackson postulated that each function has a complex vertical organization. Three levels of representation were suggested. First, functions were represented at a "low level" such as the spinal or brain stem. Second, functions were also represented at a "middle level" such as the motor or sensory division of the cerebral cortex. Third, functions were represented at a "higher level" such as the frontal divisions of the brain. It is important to stress that Jackson believed that single functions were represented simultaneously at three different levels of neurological organization. Because of this view of neurocognitive and neurobehavioral processes, Jackson makes a clear distinction between "the localization of a symptom" and the "localization of a function." The localization of a symptom, in Jackson's view, refers to the impairment of a particular function and is quite different from the localization of a function. As a "function" is represented in the central nervous system at three distinct and different levels, it may have an entirely different and more complex cerebral organization (Luria, 1966).

All three levels, in Jackson's view, worked together to perform behavioral tasks in the normal human being. Even an elementary act, such as standing up, requires the simultaneous coordination of all three levels of the nervous system from the spinal cord to the cerebral cortex. At the same time, however, the nature of the behavioral task performed would dictate the degree of involvement of each level. While simple motor activities might not maximally utilize the cerebral hemispheres, complex mathematical computation would require a lesser degree of input from the spinal or brain stem level of neural organization. Jackson believed that higher mental abilities were composed of a number of simple and basic skills which were combined to produce the complex and multivariant cognitive and behavioral abilities manifested by human beings (Golden, 1978).

In applying Jackson's model to neurological realities, a number of implications are readily derived:

1. Localization of an area which impairs a function is not the same as localizing a function.
2. A function is represented in the central nervous system on many different levels.
3. Because of multiple representation of function, a specific behavior is rarely completely lost following a local brain lesion.

Because of the neurodynamic flavor of Jackson's views, they were originally considered to be part of the equipotentialist position. As noted by Luria (1966), "Jackson's contemporaries took an incorrect and biased view of his ideas....His hypothesis pertaining to the complex character and vertical organization of functions was many decades ahead of the development of sciences at that time, and for a long time it remained forgotten, having been confirmed only very recently" (p. 18).

Jackson's views were a major advance over both the equipotential and localizationist positions. In recent years, a great deal of research data on the problem of the brain as the seat of complex mental activity, and the associated problem of the localization of function in the cerebral cortex, have essentially confirmed Jackson's nineteenth century insights. Harlow (1952), working with animals, suggested that a limited lesion did not appear to entirely destroy an ability, despite clear evidence for localization of function. Similarly Krech (1962) and Chapman and Wolff (1961) concluded that learning requires the involvement of multiple cortical areas and that brain areas play differing roles depending on the specific task requirement of particular functions. These data are more compatible with Jackson's views than with either a localizationist or equipotentialist position (Golden, 1978).

During modern times, the integrationist solution first advanced by Jackson has been further developed by Luria. A point of maximal similarity with Jackson's views is found in Luria's model of brain organization. Essentially, Luria considered the human brain to be made up of three distinct blocks. Each of these sections subserves certain basic functions. As theorized by Luria (1973), these three principal functional units of the brain were as follows:

1. The unit for regulating tone or waking
2. The unit for obtaining, processing, and storing information
3. The units for programming, regulating and verifying mental activity

At a glance, it can be seen that these units closely parallel the vertical organization proposed by Jackson.

Each of these units regulates a specific neuropsychological function. The first block regulates the energy level and tone of the cortex and thus insures a stable basis for the organization of mental processes. This unit is located in the upper and lower sections of the brain stem and reticular formation. Injuries to these areas cause a deterioration of mental processes due to disturbance in attention, memory, and wakefulness. The brain's ability to differentially respond to stimuli is markedly attenuated.

The second block, in Luria's theory of higher cortical functioning, has received the greatest amount of scientific scrutiny. This unit is primarily associated with the analysis, coding, and storage of information through sensory modalities. Specific areas are assigned to the translation of optic, acoustic, cutaneous, and kinesthetic stimuli into neurocognitive phenomena. The second block of the brain is located in the posterior sections of the cortex. It includes the temporal lobes, parietal lobes, and occipital lobes. Quite interestingly, injuries to parts of the second block evoke very distinct deficits. The effects of lesions are directly related to the specific lobe (or lobes) involved.

The third unit of the human brain consists of the frontal lobes. These areas are at once the least understood and potentially the most exciting of all neural structures. In Luria's theory, the frontal lobes are responsible for the programming, regulating, and verifying of mental activity and are intimately involved in every complex behavioral process. First, they serve, through connections with the brain stem, to regulate attention and concentration. Second, the frontal lobes set levels of aspiration and determine if the individual's behavior conforms to his/her personal standards.

Luria's concept of hierarchical organization applies especially to the second block. Luria sees this area as further subdivided into zones. Each of the three lobes—temporal, parietal, and occipital—are made up of three additional zones. These sections are called primary, secondary, and tertiary. The primary zone sorts and records sensory information (optic, acoustic, and cutaneous). The secondary zone organizes this information and codes it further. In the tertiary zone, data from the different sources overlap and are combined to provide the foundation for the organization of behavior. The overlapping arrangement provides for a fully crossed analysis of variance factoral structure. This ensures the representation, at the neurocognitive level, of all combinations of optic, acoustic, cutaneous, and kinesthetic stimuli. This matrix of sensation provides a complete representation of external reality.

Injury to the primary zone results in direct sensory deficits, for example, clear-cut inability to perceive optic, acoustic, cutaneous, or kinesthetic stimuli. In contrast, injury to the secondary zone interferes with the *analysis* of sensory stimuli. Perceptions are poorly organized and incorrectly coded. With acoustic stimuli, for example, an injury to the secondary zone does not produce an inability to perceive sound but precludes an effective analysis of phonetic sounds so that speech comprehension may be seriously impaired. The situation for other sensory modalities is tantamount to that described for acoustic stimuli.

Injury to the tertiary zone prevents the synthesis of information into a Gestalt, causing complex disturbance. This sort of deficit precludes the integration of data from two or more different modalities at one time. The appreciation of optic, acoustic, and kinesthetic cues in a unified fashion is necessary for someone wishing to drive an automobile. The inability to blend these sensory modalities into a coherent whole results from an injury to the tertiary zone.

A final consideration is Luria's theory of functional systems. Essentially, Luria thought that every complex form of behavior depends on the joint operation of several faculties located in different zones of the brain. Disturbance of any one of a number of faculties will change behavior in a different way. But in another way, this means that no single behavior is localized in a specific brain area and that each behavior is the result of a specific combination of separate brain areas. Also, the damage to a single brain area causes the behavior to be changed but not necessarily lost. Golden (1979) uses this equation to illustrate this concept:

$$Y_1 = X_1 + X_2 + X_3 \dots X_n$$

where Y_1 = behavior in question;
   X_1 = brain area 1;
   X_2 = brain area 2;
   X_3 = brain area 3;
   X_n = brain area n. Different behaviors imply different weights
for each brain area.

The formula demonstrates that it is not a specific region but rather a pattern of interaction among brain areas that produces a specified behavior. Some examples may be helpful at this point. Consider the act of writing. This includes the use of a number of brain areas such as the sensory–motor area and frontal lobes. It would appear straightforward, however, that the motor area is most important and that the other areas vary in their contribution to this behavior. Nonetheless, the loss of the frontal areas would handicap the act of writing since the writer would be unable to evaluate his performance. Likewise, consider the act of singing a song. This too involves areas for producing sound, hearing sounds, and evaluating the appropriateness of what is heard. Some of these areas are the same as those utilized in the act of writing, yet these areas are less important and are used in a different fashion. The loss of the same area, even though involved in both acts, will have different effects upon each behavior. The effects of a brain injury vary according to the behavior of interest.

A major implication of Luria's theory of brain functioning relates to brain-injured individuals. Basically, Luria sees brain systems as plastic. This can be illustrated by recalling the patient who said "No, doctor, I can't say no." On an automatic level, she retained the response, but on a voluntary level, she had lost the ability to say no. Similarly, brain-damaged patients who lose the ability to perform mathematical calculations "in their heads" can use paper and pencil to solve problems. In both instances, the final result can be achieved through the use of alternate functional systems. The general principle is analogous to deaf individuals utilizing lip reading to compensate for their loss of hearing. The application of this overall idea to the brain-injured is straightforward. Patients who have suffered specific localized brain injuries may be provided with retraining and rehabilitation programs to overcome their behavioral disabilities. Luria's concept of functional systems offers a heuristic theoretical framework for rationally designing such programs.

Having provided an appreciation of the primitive state of contemporary concepts of cerebral localization of mental processes, the stage is set for the discussion of a more difficult problem—the valid and reliable applied psychological measurement of higher cortical functioning.

NEUROPSYCHOLOGICAL TEST BATTERIES

Introduction

This section is devoted to a cursory overview of the development of neuropsychological test batteries. Only a few neuropsychological batteries are described. While there are some data to suggest that the batteries selected for review in this volume are superior instruments for neuropsychological assessment, there are many contemporary neuropsychologists who would vouchsafe different viewpoints. Many neuropsychologists reject the very idea of a standardized battery and prefer to employ a more "clinical" approach to the evaluation of brain–behavior relationships.

Halstead's Contribution

To a large extent, clinical neuropsychology in America began with the work of Ward C. Halstead. In 1935, Halstead received his PhD in physiological psychology from Northwestern University after completing a dissertation documenting postrotational nystagmus in pigeons. During the same year, he established the first neuropsychology laboratory for the study of brain–behavior relationships in human beings at the University of Chicago (Halstead, 1947). As documented by Ralph Reitan, his first doctoral student, Halstead was a most creative psychologist. Halstead made numerous clinical observations of brain-damaged individuals in order to understand how they were different from "normal" individuals. He observed them going to parties, taking walks, and engaging in other essential social interactions. These naturalistic observations provided a basis for the development of test procedures particularly sensitive to the organic integrity of the brain at the level of the cerebral hemispheres.

Halstead's primary goal was the investigation of "biological intelligence" (Halstead, 1947). As described in his major work, *Brain and Intelligence* (1947), Halstead was attempting to discover a better way to understanding cognitive abilities in humans. At about the time Halstead began his work, there were a number of difficulties relative to intellectual assessment. Perhaps the most telling problem was that there was no commonly accepted theory of primary mental abilities. Because of this fact, the many test instruments purporting to assess cognitive abilities were essentially unsupported on conceptual grounds (Russell, Neuringer, & Goldstein, 1970). A second conundrum was the nature and nurture controversy. While Halstead attempted to avoid this problem it is clear that biological intelligence falls squarely within the category of nature. In defining biological intelligence, Halstead (1947) said it was free of cultural considerations and was "general." It was based on the integrity of the brain and was supposedly centered in the frontal lobes of the human cerebral cortex. In a rather dramatic way, biological intelligence constituted the capacity of an individual to adapt to his or her environment during day to day living. Quite definitely, biological intelligence is differentiated from "psychometric intelligence." Halstead saw psychometric intelligence as those abilities that are measured by standard intelligence tests (Halstead, 1947). The contribution of education and experience to psychometric intelligence is straightforward.

In attempting to elucidate biological intelligence, Halstead devised an elaborate research plan. He arranged for physicians at the University of Chicago Medical School to refer subjects to his neuropsychology laboratory on a regular basis. As Halstead (1947) observed: "For perhaps the first time in the history of modern neurosurgery, a group of neurologists and neurosurgeons have fully cooperated in making their cases available for careful study by experimental methods" (p. 31). This availability of neurosurgical data with regard to the actual neuroanatomical site of the brain lesion was of tremendous value. The fortunate relationship between Halstead's neuropsychological laboratory and the neurological physicians and surgeons at the University of Chicago Medical School insured careful specification of the neurological criterion variable that Halstead attempted to study by psychological tests.

Halstead selected 13 tests (from an original group of 27) based on their face validity for measuring biological intelligence. According to Reitan (pers. comm.), Halstead had initially used a large number of procedures drawn from the then current methodologies of experimental and physiological psychology. Depending on their suitability, these instruments were either discarded or retained. Reportedly, a large room filled with discarded instruments was mute testimony to Halstead's rigor, energy, and persistence in this endeavor.

Halstead's plan was to statistically isolate those mental abilities that were essential to brain integrity at the level of the cerebral hemispheres. Having arranged for the assistance of neurologists and neurosurgeons, Halstead was assured of an adequate sample of brain-damaged subjects. Also, his use of multiple psychological tests gave him extensive data to correlate with the effects of brain lesions. The next step was selection of an appropriate statistical methodology to describe these brain–behavior relationships. Halstead's choice was factor analysis. It was a procedure rapidly being advanced and he was fortunate enough to have Louis Thurstone, the famous statistician, available at the University of Chicago at that time. It was expected that the factor analysis of the data from the psychological testing of a large group of brain-damaged subjects would provide some support for Halstead's concept of biological intelligence (Russell, Neuringer, & Goldstein, 1970).

The results of this experiment are detailed in Halstead's 1947 book. Essentially, the factor analysis (which by present day standards was rather crude) produced four factors. These were designated C, A, P, and D (Halstead, 1947). The isolation of the factors was easy, while it was quite difficult to understand what the factors truly represented. At first, Halstead concluded that factor C represented a "central integrative field factor," factor A was an abstraction measure, factor P was a power factor, and factor D was a measure of a person's ability to use different modalities. Later work (Shure & Halstead, 1958), however, produced results which led Halstead to decide that factor C was a measure of verbal intelligence and factor P was actually a measure of attention.

It appears in retrospect that two of the factors Thurstone isolated were related to the functional organization of the human brain. As observed by Russell, Neuringer, and Goldstein (1970), factor C could be considered as primarily a left hemisphere factor, while conversely, factor A could be considered a right hemisphere factor. Thus, Halstead anticipated much of the current interest in lateralization of function in the cerebral hemispheres.

Halstead's concept of biological intelligence could not stand on its own but paved the way for later developments. One major difficulty was that Halstead's basic conclusion that his group of tests was especially sensitive to frontal lobe lesions was in error. Halstead's main subject group consisted of 50 lobectomies. Unfortunately, it appears that the major cause of impairment on Halstead's tests was the amount of brain tissue destroyed—not the specific frontal location of the lesion (Meier, 1974). In fact, it seems that Halstead's tests were actually better for identifying nonfrontal lesions (R. Reitan, pers. comm.).

In spite of the failure of Halstead's concept of biological intelligence to escape falsification, he made a number of important contributions to present day neuropsychology: (1) the development of the impairment index; (2) the concept of a neuropsychological test battery; and (3) the use of nonpsychologists as test administrators. Some feel the development of the Impairment Index may have been Halstead's most important contribution (Russell, Neuringer, & Goldstein, 1970). It was his pursuit of biological intelligence that led to the development of the impairment index. Halstead felt that if a composite measure made up of his tests could differentiate brain-damaged normal subjects, it would offer strong evidence for the concept of biological intelligence.

Essentially, the impairment index was a linear composite of the tests selected by Halstead. Halstead selected ten tests especially sensitive to cerebral dysfunction, set cutting scores for each test, and computed a ratio to show how many of the ten tests had cutting scores suggestive of brain damage (Halstead, 1947). An example might be helpful at this point. If an individual obtained only two test scores in the brain-damaged range out of all ten of Halstead's tests, the individual impairment index would be represented as .2. Similarly, if an individual had obtained seven test scores which fell within the brain-damaged range, that individual's impairment index would be .7. A lack of any scores in the brain-damaged range would be represented as 0 while all scores in the brain-damaged range would yield an impairment index of 1.0. Halstead decided against the traditional method, used with intelligence tests, of averaging subtests. He reasoned that such a procedure sacrifices important individual variations in the test data (Russell, Neuringer, & Goldstein, 1970). While such an objection simply would appear to be common sense today, it was a remarkably astute decision on Halstead's part and one that again demonstrated his own intellectual prowess.

The use of a neuropsychological test battery was also an important contribution. Halstead was the first to utilize a battery of tests to describe brain–behavior relationships. The results he achieved in the differentiation of normal from brain-damaged individuals, however, were quite good. Indeed they were apparently much better than those obtained with any single measure of brain–behavior relationships (Russell, Neuringer, & Goldstein, 1970). Additional advantages included detailed knowledge of a patient's strengths and weaknesses and a more precise understanding of the nature of his/her brain condition (Reitan, 1966). The majority of neuropsychology laboratories in existence today utilize some form of test battery (Craig, 1979).

The use of nonpsychologists as test administrators was another innovation of Halstead's. An important facet of this practice is that it allows for more extensive data collection than if the test battery were to be administered only by professional psychologists (Russell, Neuringer, & Goldstein, 1970). It is difficult to comprehend how it would be practical to administer a battery of tests without nonprofessional assistance.

Reitan's Work

Reitan, who had a rather unusual background, having been both a minister's son and a boxer, was planning to study psychology with Carl Rogers at Ohio State University. In order to earn money for graduate school, Reitan took a job as a psychologist at an Army hospital in Illinois. Reitan became intrigued with some brain-damaged patients and through this interest happened to meet Ward Halstead. Halstead asked Reitan to become his first doctoral student (R. Reitan, pers. comm.).

Reitan extended Halstead's basic work and added a more pragmatic focus. Reitan also provided the scientifically vigorous validation of Halstead's test battery. In a massive research program spanning two decades, Reitan repeatedly cross-validated Halstead's findings and exhaustively documented his own results in over 150 professional publications.

The actual details of this "grand experiment" are quite interesting. Reitan received his PhD degree from the University of Chicago for a dissertation relating the Rorschach Ink Blot Test and the abstraction and power factors in biological intelligence (R. Reitan, pers. comm.).

In the early 1950s, Reitan obtained a position at the Indiana University Medical Center. There, with the help of Dr. Robert F. Heimburger, Director of Neurological Surgery, Reitan founded a neuropsychology laboratory (Russell, Neuringer, & Goldstein, 1970). Heimburger was also a University of Chicago graduate and during his early years of study had spent time in Halstead's neuropsychological laboratory. Reitan and Heimburger had planned during their student days to prove the worth of Halstead's tests for the assessment of higher cortical functions. Reitan (pers. comm.) has observed that when the two of them went to see the dean of the medical school with regard to the establishment of the Neuropsychological Laboratory, the deciding factor was their emotional commitment to the research project. The dean was impressed by their personal involvement and the project was approved.

After the neuropsychology laboratory was founded, research began in earnest. To a large extent because of Heimburger, Reitan was able to develop excellent relationships with the neurology and neurosurgery departments. These physicians and surgeons took particular care to refer the most interesting neurological cases to Reitan. He then had his technicians test these patients while he blindly interpreted the results. This "blind analysis" procedure was crucial to Reitan's validation of Halstead's tests. Reitan never saw the patients and at the time he reviewed the test results, he was ignorant of the neurological findings. Only after the neuropsychological report was completed did Reitan learn the actual neurological diagnosis. This research plan, by which neurological findings served as the criterion variable, and the blind interpretation of Halstead's tests served as the predictor variable, went on for many years and eventually over 8,000 cases were accumulated.

Reitan's major contributions include three specific accomplishments: the validation of Halstead's Neuropsychological Test Battery with respect to neurological criteria; the modification and expansion of Halstead's Neuropsychological Test Battery in accordance with clinical needs; and the development of neuropsychological test batteries for younger and older children.

The validation of Halstead's Neuropsychological Test Battery was, of course, the cardinal goal of Reitan's entire research effort. As observed by Reitan (1966): "One of the principal aims of the Neuropsychological Laboratory has been to effect a meaningful subdivision of the concept 'brain damage' as such subdivisions relate differentially to psychological measurements" (p. 159).

Essentially, five questions were addressed in the course of Reitan's experimental work:

1. Is the subject brain damaged?
2. Is the damage lateralized to one hemisphere?
3. Is the damage localized to a specific area within the hemisphere?
4. Is the lesion acute or chronic?
5. What is the neurological diagnosis?

The first question, with respect to the ability of Halstead's tests to predict brain damage, was addressed in a 1955 study reported in the *Journal of Clinical Psychology*. As observed by Russell, Neuringer, and Goldstein (1970):

> A matched pair design was used in which the 50 brain damaged subjects were matched on the basis of color, sex, age, and education with 50 normals. The brain damaged subjects had diverse diagnoses and 76% of the controls were hospitalized patients whose medical problems did not involve brain functioning. Among the 50 pairs, not one control had a higher (Halstead impairment) index than his matched partner. Eighty-eight percent had a higher index and 12% had an equal index. (p. 8)

This study, along with an independent cross-validation (Vega & Parsons, 1967) established the ability of Halstead's tests to detect brain damage.

The second major contribution of Reitan was the modification and expansion of Halstead's tests in accordance with clinical needs. As noted by Russell, Neuringer, and Goldstein (1970): "Almost from the beginning, the emphasis of Reitan's studies were not directed toward Biological Intelligence. In his concern with the nature of brain functioning, his work has generally been closely related to pragmatic neurological problems" (p. 9).

Reitan added a number of tests to Halstead's Neuropsychological Test Battery and modified still others. These included measures of cognitive functioning, perceptual functioning, language abilities, motor abilities, lateral dominance, and affective functioning. As the Halstead–Reitan Neuropsychological Battery is discussed in a separate chapter (Chapter 7), only the briefest of comments will be offered here.

To assess cognitive functioning, Reitan added the Wechsler–Bellevue scale Form I (W-BI) (Wechsler, 1944). In a study comparing the W-BI with Halstead's tests, Reitan (unpublished, 1959) found that while Halstead's tests were more sensitive to cerebral dysfunction, the W-BI also contributed valuable information. In a like manner, Reitan (1958) found that the Trail Making Test (TMT) was particularly sensitive to brain damage and it was also included.

One basic consideration that influenced Reitan's choice of tests was his goal of providing direct clinical service. He appeared to focus on tests that would most effectively differentiate brain-damaged patients from "normals." This was a reasonable strategy and given the need to demonstrate rudimentary levels of predictive validity, entirely acceptable. However, given a more contemporary perspective, there is a serious limitation inherent in such a test selection strategy, especially when one's eventual purpose is to develop a comprehensive clinical neuropsychological battery. Such a test selection strategy may limit the number of diagnostic questions that can be answered by the clinical application of a neuropsychological test battery. A "yes or no" approach to the question of brain damage is adequate for many purposes, but may seriously limit the clinical utility of the battery. In addition, in many psychiatric settings the referral question is not one of brain damage per se but rather one of determining the relative contributions of organic and psychiatric factors. It is here that many clinicians have felt the Halstead–Reitan Battery is most limited. Relative to clinical decision making, the questions of lateralization, localization, process and etiology, prognosis, retraining potential, and therapeutic management are all legitimate issues of concern. To a large degree, the neuropsychological test battery devised by Halstead ignored these questions. While, on one hand, this is an understandable development in that Halstead's goals were primarily research oriented ("biological intelligence"), on the other hand, it is a significant difficulty should one wish to use Halstead's tests to answer questions other than the classic one of presence or absence of damage in a specific patient.

An example would be helpful in illustrating this issue. Reitan (pers. comm.) relates that while he was pursuing his graduate work as Halstead's student in the neuropsychology laboratory at the University of Chicago, one of his tasks was to administer neuropsychological tests to subjects. One of the many tests Halstead had him administer was the entire Seashore Battery of tests of music appreciation. This test battery includes a number of subtests. Two of these are the rhythm test and tonal memory test. Reitan, after evaluating the performance of many brain-damaged individuals, noted that the rhythm subtest by itself did as good a job of distinguishing between the groups of brain-damaged and normal individuals as the entire Seashore Battery of tests. Thus, Reitan suggested to Halstead that in the interests of economy only the rhythm subtest be administered. Halstead agreed and, as a result, only the rhythm test is part of Halstead's Battery of Neuropsychological tests. More recent work (Thomas J. Boll, pers. comms.), however, has suggested that the Tonal Memory Subtest of the Seashore Battery of tests of music appreciation may be particularly sensitive to impairment of the right temporal lobe. Therefore, it would appear that due to a rather specific criterion, a potentially quite valuable neuropsychological test was excluded from the Halstead Battery.

Tests that were selected for their abilities to answer specific questions usually answered these questions quite well. Tests that are not specifically selected to answer certain questions are much less likely to provide adequate answers. Indeed, it is common to see tests developed for rather specific purposes used to answer questions completely foreign to the original goal of the test constructor.

On the basis of his clinical judgment, Reitan added a number of tests to the Halstead Battery (Russell, Neuringer, & Goldstein, 1970). The specific range of psychological–behavioral measurements included perceptual functioning, language, motor ability, lateral dominance, and personality, among others. In certain instances, many of these test instruments were modified prior to adoption by Reitan.

In order to assess perceptual functioning, a number of techniques from the classical neurological examination were included. These included measures of sensory imperception in the optic, acoustic, and tactile modalities as well as tests of finger agnosia, fingertip number writing, and tactile form recognition (Reitan, 1966). These tests provide information on the comparative functioning of the two sides of the human body. Because of this fact, they may provide important information with regard to the lateralization of brain damage (Wheeler & Reitan, 1962). The major focus in Reitan's procedures for assessing perceptual functioning is on the tactile/kinesthetic modality, while the optic and acoustic modalities receive far less attention.

To assess language, Reitan needed a systematic evaluation of the major aphasic symptoms. He met this need by adding a shortened version of the Halstead–Wepman Aphasia Screening Test (Halstead & Wepman, 1949). This test provided a brief evaluation of major aphasic symptoms. Also, later investigation confirmed that it is sensitive to cerebral dysfunction and, in addition, lateralization of brain damage (Wheeler & Reitan, 1962).

Motor ability was also an important area that clearly needed to be assessed. As tests for simple motor ability (the Finger Oscillation or Tapping Test) and more complex psychomotor problem solving

(Tactual Performance Test) were already part of Halstead's Neuro-psychological Test Battery, Reitan's contribution was to modify the method of administration and scoring. Specifically, Reitan had the Finger Tapping Test performed by both the dominant and the nondominant hand so that the comparative adequacy of performance could be judged. Also, the scores for the dominant and nondominant hands on the Tactual Performance tests were compared in the same manner. In addition, a test for strength of grip of both hands was added. As with the other tests, later research found significant relationships between adequacy of motor performance and actual tissue damage to a single cerebral hemisphere (Reitan, 1958; Dodrill, 1979).

Given the need to properly evaluate individual neurological organization, a measure of cerebral dominance was devised. Reitan's Test for Lateral Dominance assessed eye, hand, and foot dominance (Russell, Neuringer, Goldstein, 1970). This facilitated the interpretation of scores generated from other tests in the neuropsychological test battery.

Similarly, Reitan added the Minnesota Multiphasic Personality Inventory (MMPI) as a measure of personality functioning. The rationale for Reitan's selection was the need to accurately assess the affective sequelae of cerebral dysfunction in both an objective and reasonably comprehensive manner. Given the preeminent position of the MMPI as the most heavily utilized and researched measure of personality functioning (Dahlstrom & Walsh, 1960) his choice was quite wise.

The last specific accomplishment of Reitan was the development of neuropsychological test batteries for younger and older children. Reitan, over a period of many years, administered Halstead's tests to progressively younger groups of children in order to evaluate their clinical utility. Essentially, he found that with minor modifications a battery could be devised for older children between the ages of 9 and 15. Because this battery was basically a direct downward extension of Halstead's work, it was named the Halstead Neuropsychological Test Battery for Children (Davison, 1974). After additional years of work, at the neuropsychological laboratory of the Indiana University Medical Center, Reitan developed a second modification of Halstead's tests for still younger groups of children. This child neuropsychological test battery was developed for children between the ages of 5 and 8. Because of Reitan's greater contribution to this second child neuro-psychological test battery, it was titled the Reitan–Indiana Neuropsy-chological Test Battery for Children (Davison, 1974), and contains a number of tests primarily devised by Reitan for this age group. These include the Matching Test, the Color Form Test, the Matching

Pictures Test, the Target Test, and Matching V's. An additional test, the Progressive Figures Test, is an adaption of the Trail Making Test (Boll, 1978). *In toto*, these tests were the ones Reitan hoped to use to effect a meaningful subdivision of the concept of "brain damage," as such subdivisions relate differentially to psychological measurements (Reitan, 1966, p. 159).

Reitan's findings were replicated and extended at a number of independent centers. Two of these deserve special note—the Topeka, Kansas, Veteran's Administration Neuropsychology Laboratory and the Hawaii State Hospital Neuropsychology Laboratory. Both laboratories were founded by individuals influenced by Halstead's work.

The Topeka Veteran's Administration Hospital Contribution

Phillip M. Rennick worked extensively with both Halstead and Reitan (Russell, Neuringer, & Goldstein, 1970). During these associations, he became entirely familiar with Halstead's tests and Reitan's modifications. In turn, Rennick made his own modifications. Unfortunately, many of these changes were unpublished (Russell, Neuringer, & Goldstein, 1970) so the best source for information about them has been Gerald Goldstein, who worked with Rennick and adopted Rennick's approach for use at the Topeka, Kansas, Veteran's Administration Hospital. Goldstein, a University of Kansas PhD in clinical psychology, was employed at the Topeka, Kansas, Veteran's Administration Hospital as a research psychologist for many years. During this time he conducted an active neuropsychology research program and collected large amounts of data on the veteran population served by his hospital.

The cardinal modifications introduced by Rennick centered on quantification of the clinical data produced by Reitan's modification of Halstead's tests for adults. These included new rating scales for Reitan's modifications of the Halstead–Wepman Aphasia Screening Test, and the perception disorder examination, and also a new method of computing the impairment index (Russell, Neuringer, & Goldstein, 1970).

Rennick also devised a method of quantifying the results from the Halstead–Wepman Aphasia Screening Test in order to make the results more objective. As the test was previously formulated, one merely listed in the presence or absence of various dysphasic or aphasic deficits. Rennick, mindful of the heterogeneous nature of the test, developed two rating scales. One was for verbal items and the other was for visuospatial items (Russell, Neuringer, & Goldstein, 1970). This organization, of course, reflects the specific contribution each portion makes to laterality decisions. The verbal items reflected the organic integrity of the left cerebral hemisphere (assuming right-handedness) and the visuospatial items reflected the organic integrity of the right cerebral hemisphere.

Rennick also devised a rating system for the perceptual disorders examination. This test, which was devised by Reitan and Klove, is largely borrowed for the behavioral neurology traditions. Optic, acoustic, and tactile perception are examined under both single and dual simultaneous stimulation modes of administration. Also, errors in finger agnosia and perception of numbers written on finger tips are recorded. As before, Rennick's rating scale put these data in an objective and quantifiable form (Russell, Neuringer, & Goldstein, 1970).

Rennick introduced his own method of computing the impairment index, which became known as the "Average Impairment Index." Halstead has used ten tests, sensitive to cerebral dysfunction, to form his impairment index and each test which exceeded a cutoff point contributed to the index. Reitan's version used only seven tests but was computed in the same manner. Rennick revised this method by scaling each test on a 6-point scale (0–5). The numbers corresponded to the levels of deficit listed below:

Rating	Level of Deficit
0	Better than normal functioning
1	Normal functioning
2	Mild cerebral impairment
3	Moderate cerebral impairment
4	Severe cerebral impairment
5	Profound cerebral impairment

Rennick did this for all 12 of the tests he used in his index. Generally numerical norms were used to transform raw scores into the rating point system. One standard deviation from the mean usually included the scores rated "1". The normative distributions were garnered from a sample of patients evaluated in Reitan's neuropsychological laboratory (Russell, Neuringer, & Goldstein, 1970).

The average impairment rating scale can be used to evaluate not only presence of brain damage but also severity. An unpublished statistical analysis found Rennick's Average Impairment Rating Scale to be equivalent to the index in determining whether or not the subject has brain damage (Richard J. Browne, pers. comm.). Experience with this scaling method has demonstrated that most of the scores are fairly good indicators of degree of brain damage. A few of the tests, however, overestimate or underestimate the degree of brain damage and so they need to have their scale scores reset (Russell, Neuringer, & Goldstein, 1970, p. 14).

Goldstein had utilized Rennick's methods in setting up a neuropsychology laboratory at the research facilities of the Topeka, Kansas, Veteran's Administration Hospital. The major change introduced by Goldstein was the substitution of the Wechsler Adult Intelligence Scale (WAIS) for the Wechsler–Bellevue Scale (Form 1) (Russell, Neuringer, & Goldstein, 1970). For all practical purposes, the Goldstein Laboratory can be seen as a mirror image of Rennick's.

The neuropsychology laboratory at the Topeka, Kansas, Medical Center produced a steady stream of research under Gerald Goldstein that continued under his successor Dennis Swiercinsky. However, the most noteworthy contribution can be attributed to a student, Elbert W. Russell. In the course of fulfilling the dissertation requirement for his PhD degree, Russell developed new methods for the conceptualization of clinical neuropsychological data (Richard J. Browne, pers. comm.).

Russell's insight was that a "biological key" could be applied to clinical neuropsychological data in an actuarial fashion. As observed by Russell, a key in biology is a "method of locating the name of a species in a taxonomic manual" (Russell, Neuringer, & Goldstein, 1970, p. 14). It is a way of selecting the appropriate classification for a specimen in a preexisting system. As explained by Russell, Neuringer, and Goldstein (1970):

> A key uses the characteristics of a species to locate the class or category to which the species belongs. Logically, it is a form of reasoning by elimination. If a person has a specimen in hand, he can "run" the key until he locates the name of the specimen by using characteristics of the organism. Keys use objective and rather invariant characteristics of organisms in a systematic manner. They consist of a series of statements about the group of organisms to which the species belong which systematically subdivides the total group into smaller and smaller groups until the desired organism is located. (p. 15)

It should be noted that the key method of interpretation of clinical test data did not begin with Russell. Indeed, there has been quite a body of research literature with respect to applying keylike methods in clinical psychology. The majority of the studies have dealt with the Minnesota Multiphasic Personality Inventory (MMPI). It has been averred that the MMPI invites application of such methods (Russell, Neuringer, & Goldstein, 1970). Basically, these methods can be seen as utilizing an ordered set of rules for the categorization of MMPI test data. Paul E. Meehl, who is well known in American clinical psychology for his exemplary research on clinical versus statistical prediction (Meehl, 1954), has performed the best of these studies. In one study, Meehl and Dahlstrom (1960) found that a system of objective rules for classifying psychological test data was superior to the clinical judgment.

Russell's dissertation performed the same function of validating the worth of keylike methods for neuropsychological test data that Meehl performed using similar objective systems for MMPI test data. Like Meehl, Russell developed an objective set of rules for classifying psychological test data. Two major neuropsychological keys were developed by Russell. One determined localization (i.e., whether or not brain damage was diffuse or lateralized to the left or right cerebral hemisphere). The second key dealt with process. It addressed the question of whether or not damage was acute, static, or congenital, if in fact brain damage was present. These keys were combined to provide a neuropsychological classification for particular patients (Russell, Neuringer, & Goldstein, 1970).

The Hawaii State Hospital Neuropsychology Laboratory Group Contribution

In certain respects it is somewhat premature to discuss the contribution of the Hawaii State Hospital group. Their contributions are of quite recent origin and there are relatively few published studies by which to evaluate the work of this group. However, they have produced some seminal findings, especially in the area of cognitive retraining.

The major focus of the Hawaii State Hospital group had been on retraining of the brain injured. They have produced concrete methods for remediating patients who have suffered organic impairment at the level of the cerebral hemispheres. In keeping with the empirical tradition in clinical neuropsychology, the Hawaii State Hospital group has published preliminary results of their work (Gudeman, Golden, & Craine, 1978).

CONCLUSION

In this chapter, two diverse historical trends have been developed: The story of attempts to understand the functional organization of the human brain and the chronology of efforts to develop comprehensive standardized methods for the assessment of human higher cortical processes. It would be entirely misleading to imply that definitive solutions to either of these important problems have been obtained. More correctly, these pages are impressive testimony to the complexity of neurocognitive processes and the profound difficulties inherent in any systematic effort to comprehend the various manifestations of cortical malfunctioning.

Still, a careful and sensitive appreciation of the past efforts to unravel the complex mysteries of the problem of the brain as the seat of mental activity and to understand the associated problem of the localization of functions in the cerebral context is an essential step in the journey toward more sophisticated understanding, measurement, and treatment of disturbances of higher cortical functions.

SUGGESTIONS FOR FURTHER READING

Golden, C.J. *Diagnosis and rehabilitation in clinical neuropsychology.* Springfield, Ill.: Charles C. Thomas, 1978.

Luria, A.R. *Higher cortical functions in man.* New York: Basic, 1966.

Luria, A.R. *The working brain.* New York: Basic, 1973.

Luria, A.R. *The making of a mind.* Cambridge, Mass.: Harvard University Press, 1977.

Meier, M.J. Some challenges for clinical neuropychology. In R.M. Reitan & L.A. Davison (Eds.), *Clinical neuropsychology: Current status and applications.* New York: John Wiley, 1974.

3

BRAIN–BEHAVIOR RELATIONSHIPS

The structure of the human brain is intimately related to behavioral function. The focus of the present chapter is on an elementary description of these brain–behavior relationships.

STRUCTURES AND FUNCTIONS OF THE HUMAN BRAIN: PRELIMINARY REMARKS

In order to facilitate the later understanding of some rather complex material, a number of preliminary remarks are offered in an endeavor to provide a useful cognitive structure. Three issues receive special scrutiny: (1) the neurocortical structures and behavioral correlates; (2) the three-dimensional character of the human brain; and (3) the evolution nature of the human brain.

This chapter is *not* intended as a standard review of neuroanatomy. There are quite a number of neurological textbooks that have already quite adequately addressed this subject (e.g., Chusid, 1976). The present chapter is intended as a brief review of primary neurocortical structure and its behavioral correlates with the sole purpose of aiding the reader in the comprehension of later material. The organization of this chapter follows the earlier material on the history of attempts to solve the problem of the brain as the seat of complex mental activity and to the associated problem of the localization of the functions in the cerebral cortex.

A second limitation of this chapter relates to the neuronal and architectonic structure of the cortex. The cellular substrata of the human nervous system is not discussed. Our selective treatment concentrates on large aggregations of cells in particular regions. This in no way suggests that the cytoarchitectonic layers of the cortex are not suitable subjects for neuropsychological study or that particular cortical neurons may be ignored, but rather reflects the essentially primative state of contemporary neuropsychological knowledge. Despite the facts that the major effort of experimental neuropsychology has been the identification of the structural and functional aspects of the brain and that many significant advances have been made in recent years, neuropsychologists still remain essentially unable to confidently define such basic neurophysiological processes as those that subserve learning and memory (Golden, 1978). This situation adequately mirrors the sad truth that the biochemistry of the brain is only indirectly seen on behavioral tasks. It is not possible to study the action of single cells by psychological–behavioral testing. What can be ascertained, however, is the comparative functioning of large zones of relatively homogeneous cells. These fields of cells with quite similar structure are therefore the focus of this chapter.

It is important to be cognizant of the three-dimensional character of the human brain. It is quite remarkable that the vast majority of neuropsychological research appears to presume a two-dimensional model of brain functioning. Functions can be seen as depicting either laterality, which means the separation of functions to either the left or right hemispheres of the neocortex, or caudality, which relates to how posterior a function can be localized in the cerebral cortex. Of these two, most research has dealt, through mountains of dichotic listening, tachistoscopic, and lateral eye movement studies, with laterality. There has been little self-reflection on this restricted neuropsychological conceptual model of central nervous system functioning.

At this point, some elementary terminology may be of use. For purposes of explanation, a brief discussion of the terms used to describe the three-dimensional character of the brain are presented. Consider a car for a moment. Note the six sides. This will be a model for the exploration. The left and right sides are straightforward. These pertain to lateralization. More problematic are the front and back. When speaking of neuroanatomy, the front becomes "rostral" and the back "caudal." There has been relatively little attention to this dimension in clinical neuropsychology (Meier, 1974). Looking at the top and bottom of a car, the proper terms, if the auto were magically transformed into a human brain, would be "ventral" for the bottom and "dorsal" for the top. These then are the major directional terms used to Neuroanatomy. However, many neuropsychologists prefer the simpler terms superior, inferior, anterior, and posterior when talking about, respectively, the top, bottom, front, and back of the brain. In addition, medial refers to structures near the midline of the brain (or a brain part), whereas lateral refers to structures near the side of the

proximal
distal

brain. Finally, proximal structures are those close to a specified point whereas distal structures are those farther away.

The last preliminary consideration is the evolutionary character of the brain. It is important because it explains the apparent redundancy of behavioral function in the human brain. Human beings evolved over many millions of years from more primitive creatures whose neural structures bore a reasonable resemblance to our own (Sagan, 1977). Over time, these primitive brains changed and added additional neural structures until the contemporary human central nervous system reached its present form. While it would be far beyond the intended scope of this volume to attempt to discuss brain evolution in any reasonable amount of detail, we do discuss cursorily one rather engaging view of the evolution of the brain, the triune brain theory, as a heuristic device.

The triune brain theory suggests that the most recent evolution of the human brain can best be understood as three separately independent cognitive systems (MacLean, 1973). Three successive layers of specialized neural tissue have developed over the initial fishlike brain structures. These layers, quite clearly, all share some common functions, but each successive layer adds some new higher levels of mental specialization. However, at the same time, the older layers still exist and play a role in higher-order behavior. Each layer is a biological computer with multiple interconnections to each other layer, at the same time containing its own special and unique abilities.

MacLean's (1973) three brain layers are the reptilian (or R-complex), the limbic system, and the neocortex. Each of these three layers in the triune brain theory constitutes a separate major evolutionary step.

As earlier stated, the three layers of the triune brain are further elaborations of those neural structures that humans share with fish. The reptilian complex (or R-complex) represents the level of evolution that humans share with reptiles. As conceptualized by MacLean (1973), the R-complex controls aggressive behavior, ritualistic actions, and territoriality.

Parenthetically, it might be recalled that the reason that the older brain layer remains is that evolution advances by addition, not subtraction. Put another way, there is usually no way of eliminating a preexisting system that is consistent with the survival of the species. Therefore, new neural structures must compromise with older layers.

The second brain layer in MacLean's (1973) triune brain theory is the limbic system. This neural structure is shared with the lower mammals but not the fishes or reptiles. Its function is to subserve affective states. Other functions of the limbic system include sex, smell, and in a particular way, memory. As observed by Sagan (1977):

Electrical discharges in the Limbic System sometimes result in symptoms similar to those of psychoses or those produced by psychedelic or hallucinogenic drugs. In fact, the sites of action of many psychotropic drugs are in the limbic system. Perhaps it controls exhilaration and awe and a variety of subtle emotions that are sometimes thought of as uniquely human. (p. 66)

The third brain layer postulated by MacLean's (1973) triune brain theory is the neocortex (or cerebral cortex). This neural structure is unique to humans and the higher mammals such as dolphins and whales. The neocortex can be described as the seat of our characteristically human behaviors such as written language and the cognitive anticipation of events, as well as a host of other complex perceptual, motor, and intellectual abilities.

It is important not to forget the interrelated nature of these three "biological computers." While there is a degree of overlap of each successive new evolutionary layer, it would be folly to ignore the fact that a great deal of human behavior seems to come from the neural structures we share principally with reptiles. A classic example of a complex behavioral system that utilizes inputs from each of the three brains would be sexual functioning.

The overall effect is a multifaceted and at times contradictory picture of base motivation, warm emotion, and logical abstraction. Sagan (1977) captures this difficult conceptual paradigm quite well in the following quote:

A superior agreement is found in the metaphor for the human psyche in the Platonic dialogue, Phadrus. Socrates likens the human soul to a chariot drawn by two horses—one black, one white—pulling in different directions and weakly controlled by a charioteer. The metaphor of the chariot itself is remarkably similar to MacLean's neural chassis: the two horses, to the R-Complex and the limbic cortex; and the charioteer barely in control of the careening chariot and horses, to the neocortex. In yet another metaphor, Freud describes the ego as the rider of an unruly horse. Both the Freudian and Platonic metaphors emphasize the considerable independence of and tension among the constituent parts of the psyche, a point that characterizes the human condition...(p. 83)

MORPHOLOGY OF THE CENTRAL NERVOUS SYSTEM WITH SPECIAL ATTENTION TO THE HUMAN CEREBRAL CORTEX

The gross subdivisions of the central nervous system are the spinal cord and brain. As observed by Lezak (1976):

The brain consists of the complex neural structures that grow out of the front end of the embryonic neural tube. The hind (lower in humans) portion of the neural tube is the spinal cord. The brain stem and spinal cord serve as the through way for communication between the brain and the rest of the body. (p. 33)

SPINAL CORD

The primary function of the spinal cord is the transmission of nerve impulses to the brain and the conduction of motor impulses from the brain to muscles to effect motor acts. The spinal cord segments are referred to as cervical, thoracic, lumbar, or sacral to correspond with attachment groups of nerves. The cervical region includes the neck region while the sacral area relates to the pelvis. A rather sardonic medical student saying is "C-5 then alive"—with reference to the fact that the fifth segment in the cervical region controls respiration.

BRAIN

The brain consists of three major regions. These are the hindbrain, midbrain, and forebrain. The forebrain consists of the two cerebral hemispheres and includes a number of interior structures such as the thalamus and hypothalamus. The hindbrain is composed of an enlargement of brain stem immediately rostral to the foramen magnum, which is the point of demarcation between the spinal cord and the brain. Major areas of the hindbrain include the medulla, pons, and cerebellum. The midbrain is the zone intermediate between the forebrain and the hindbrain (Figure 3.1).

Hindbrain

Medulla Oblongata

The first neural structure above the foramen magnum is the medulla oblongata. It is important as the area responsible for participation in the regulation of a number of activities essential for life. These include the control of respiration, blood pressure, and heartbeat. Injuries at this level can be immediately fatal.

Pons

The pons is an enlargement of the ventral section of the brain stem just above the medulla oblongata. Besides serving as a communication channel to forebrain areas, the pons also includes commissional fiber that connects the two hemispheres of the cerebellum.

roof of the mouth (Gazzaniga, Steen & Volpe, 1979). Chusid (1976) sees this complicated structure as including four parts:

> (1) The mamillary bodies, 2 adjacent pea-sized white masses inferior to the gray matter of the floor of the third ventrical and rostral to the posterior perforated spaces, (2) The tuber cinereum, an eminence rostral to the mammillary bodies, (3) The infudibulum, a hollow process extending downward from the under surface of the tuber cinereum to the posterior lobe of the hypophysis, and (4) The optic chiasm. (p. 20)

The hypothalamus controls a number of supposedly involuntary functions of the body through the anatomic nervous system. While the totally involuntary nature of these functions is a question of controversy at this time, their importance to the maintenance of life-support systems is unquestioned. The particular areas in which hypothalamic participation has been implicated include the regulation of eating, drinking, sexual behavior, sleeping, blood pressure, body temperature, and emotion (Gazzaniga, Steen & Volpe, 1979). It should be stressed that while lesions of the hypothalamic region may produce a variety of symptoms, this is evidence for participation of the hypothalamus in some way as part of the function. It is not data suggesting that the function is entirely localized in the hypothalamus. Hypothalamic lesions induce appetite and temperature changes (Chusid, 1976) as well as mood state alterations (Lezak, 1976) and violent behavior (Lindzey, Hall, & Thompson, 1978).

The Limbic System

Interconnected with the hypothalamus is the limbic system. The limbic system is actually an extensive series of structures rather than a single body. This system includes the amygdala, cingulate cortex, hippocampus, and septal area. Walsh (1978) makes the insightful observation that: "The term limbic system includes so many structures and pathways that the general usefulness of the concept of a united system is open to question. Certainly, it is a region where a large number of circuits relating to different functions come together" (p. 40).

Indeed, there is substantial overlap between the thalamus and hypothalamus and the limbic system. According to Lindzey, Hall, and Thompson (1978):

> All parts of the limbic system are interconnected by nerve pathways that also are connected to many other parts of the nervous system, including the frontal region of the cerebral cortex. The precise role of each component remains unknown but the limbic system as a whole clearly is involved in the expression of emotional and motivational states. (p. 113)

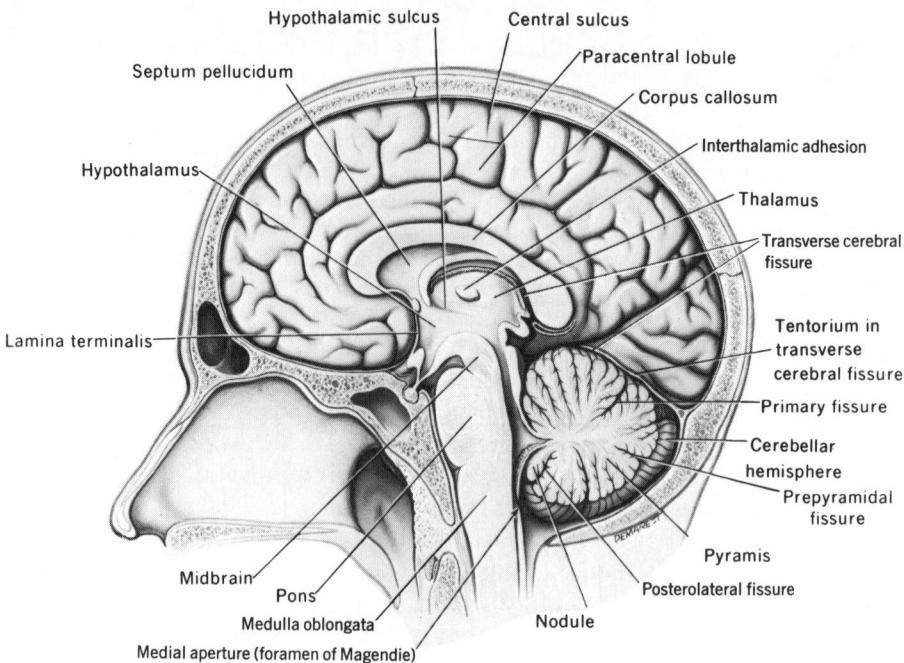

Figure 3.2. Median sagittal section of the brain and part of the head. From Noback, C.R. & Demarest, R.J. *The Human Nervous System.* New York: McGraw-Hill, 1981.

The major function of the thalamus is to serve as the central relay station of the brain. The thalamus performs the work of receiving specific sensory stimuli input from the ascending sensory pathways and then relays this information to the appropriate sensory region of the cerebral cortex. For example, a major nucleus (the lateral geniculate body) in the thalamus takes in sensory data from visual fibers and transmits them to the visual area of the cortex. The same procedure is followed for auditory and somatic sensory data, as well as information from the limbic system and other areas. Chusid (1976) suggests that the thalamus, rather than the cerebral cortex, is the crucial structure for the perception of some sorts of sensation.

A second function of the thalamus is the control of brain electrical activity (Walsh, 1978). Quite clearly, the integrative role of the thalamus is crucial for effective information processing by the brain.

Impairment of the thalamus gives rise to serious disruption of mental activity. Thalamic lesions have been associated with attention and concentration deficits as well as memory problems and in some cases, a behavioral pattern characterized by apathy, disorientation, and confusion (Lezak, 1976).

Hypothalamus

The hypothalamus sits ventral to the cerebrum at the point where the thalamus and midbrain meet. To provide a degree of perspective, one might keep in mind that this places the hypothalamus above the

(Lindsay, Hall, & Thompson, 1978). These functions are vital for adaptive behavior. As observed by Lezak (1976): "The sensory correlations that take place in midbrain nuclei contribute to the integration of reflex and autonomic responses involving the visual and auditory systems. Motor nuclei play a role in the smooth integration of muscle movements and in the patterning of automatic posture" (p. 36).

Reticular Activating System

The reticular activating system includes the central region of the midbrain and the upper section of the hindbrain. The reticular activating system is not a solitary functional unit but more properly contains many clusters of functionally related nerve cells. The major role of the reticular activating system is the control of attentional processes. It regulates cortical tone and directs the organism's attention to incoming stimuli. Damage to this system can cause global disorders of consciousness causing the individual to fall asleep or to go into a coma. The reticular activating system has a special relationship with the frontal lobes of the cerebral cortex, which is discussed later in this chapter.

Forebrain

The forebrain is the most recent evolutionary development of the vertebrate nervous system (Gazzaniga, Steen & Volpe, 1979). Its amazingly specialized nature and unique cellular structures are among the factors that distinguish man from other primates. Its importance in cognitive development is difficult to overstate.

Thalamus

The word thalamus means "bridal chamber." Golden (1978) has suggested that the name connotes its secure and deep location within the two hemispheres. In truth, the thalamus appears to reside quite close to the exact center of the brain (see Figure 3.2). As befits this special location, the thalamus is much older, genetically, than surrounding brain structures such as the cerebellum or cerebrum. In some of the less advanced life forms, the thalamus is the largest structure of the brain. In reference to the last observation, one might recall the dictim that the relative size of a brain structure is a possible clue to its importance.

Physically, the thalamus is a somewhat football-shaped gray mass that resides at the rostral end of the brain stem immediately above the limbic system. The thalamus is composed of two hemispheres, each within the orbit of one of the cerebral hemispheres. It is made up of closely packed nerve cells that have diverse connections.

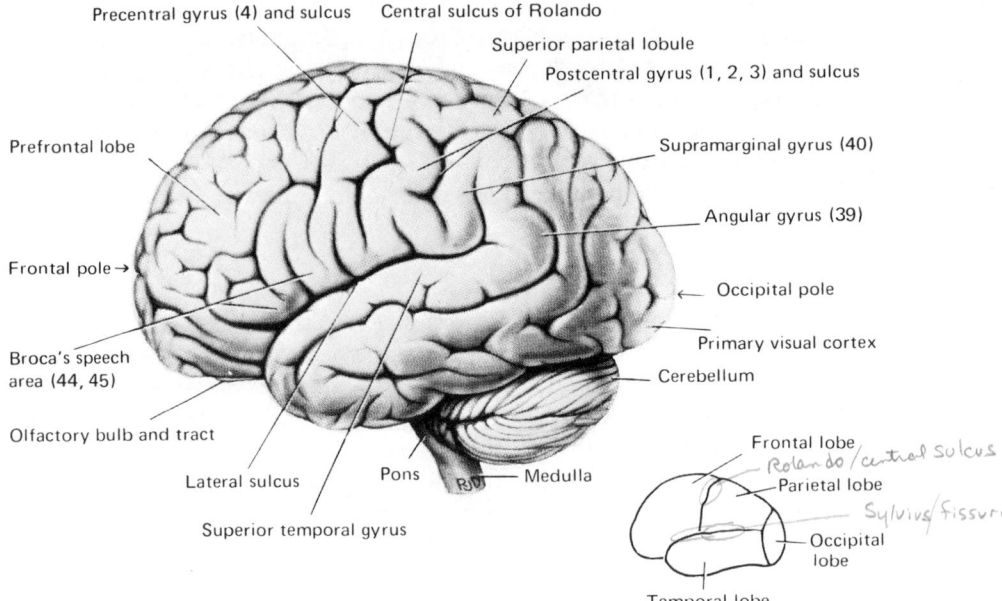

Precentral gyrus (4) and sulcus   Central sulcus of Rolando

Superior parietal lobule

Postcentral gyrus (1, 2, 3) and sulcus

Prefrontal lobe

Supramarginal gyrus (40)

Angular gyrus (39)

Frontal pole →

Occipital pole

Primary visual cortex

Broca's speech area (44, 45)

Cerebellum

Olfactory bulb and tract

Lateral sulcus   Pons   Medulla

Superior temporal gyrus

Frontal lobe / Rolando / central sulcus
Parietal lobe   Sylvius / fissure
Occipital lobe
Temporal lobe

Figure 3.1.   Lateral surface of the brain. Numbers refer to Brodmann's areas. From Noback, C.R. & Demarest, R.J. *The Human Nervous System.* New York: McGraw-Hill, 1981.

Cerebellum

Dorsal to the pons, the cerebellum sits on the brain stem. The major contribution of the cerebellum is regulation of motor control and coordination. Both the pons and the cerebellum work together in the task of regulating motor impulses in response to postural and muscle movement areas. The unique contribution of the cerebellum is that it makes smooth movement possible. For example, removal of the cerebellum causes spastic movements of the limbs and halting speech (Gazzaniga, Steen & Volpe, 1979).

Physically, the cerebellum is made up of two separate hemispheres connected by the vermis. Typically, the cerebellum appears quite convoluted as it has a large number of little lobes separated by several deep fissures that impart a layered appearance.

Midbrain

The midbrain is located at the point where the brain stem merges with the thalamus and hypothalamus. The two portions of the midbrain, the tectum and the tegmentum, are quite important for perceptual processing. More specifically, the tectum is the site of two pairs of relay nuclei for the visual and auditory systems, while the tegmentum holds nuclei for cranial nerves that dictate eye movement

The brain consists of the complex neural structures that grow out of the front end of the embryonic neural tube. The hind (lower in humans) portion of the neural tube is the spinal cord. The brain stem and spinal cord serve as the through way for communication between the brain and the rest of the body. (p. 33)

SPINAL CORD

The primary function of the spinal cord is the transmission of nerve impulses to the brain and the conduction of motor impulses from the brain to muscles to effect motor acts. The spinal cord segments are referred to as cervical, thoracic, lumbar, or sacral to correspond with attachment groups of nerves. The cervical region includes the neck region while the sacral area relates to the pelvis. A rather sardonic medical student saying is "C-5 then alive"—with reference to the fact that the fifth segment in the cervical region controls respiration.

BRAIN

The brain consists of three major regions. These are the hindbrain, midbrain, and forebrain. The forebrain consists of the two cerebral hemispheres and includes a number of interior structures such as the thalamus and hypothalamus. The hindbrain is composed of an enlargement of brain stem immediately rostral to the foramen magnum, which is the point of demarcation between the spinal cord and the brain. Major areas of the hindbrain include the medulla, pons, and cerebellum. The midbrain is the zone intermediate between the forebrain and the hindbrain (Figure 3.1).

Hindbrain

Medulla Oblongata

The first neural structure above the foramen magnum is the medulla oblongata. It is important as the area responsible for participation in the regulation of a number of activities essential for life. These include the control of respiration, blood pressure, and heartbeat. Injuries at this level can be immediately fatal.

Pons

The pons is an enlargement of the ventral section of the brain stem just above the medulla oblongata. Besides serving as a communication channel to forebrain areas, the pons also includes commissional fiber that connects the two hemispheres of the cerebellum.

Electrical discharges in the Limbic System sometimes result in symptoms similar to those of psychoses or those produced by psychedelic or hallucinogenic drugs. In fact, the sites of action of many psychotropic drugs are in the limbic system. Perhaps it controls exhilaration and awe and a variety of subtle emotions that are sometimes thought of as uniquely human. (p. 66)

The third brain layer postulated by MacLean's (1973) triune brain theory is the neocortex (or cerebral cortex). This neural structure is unique to humans and the higher mammals such as dolphins and whales. The neocortex can be described as the seat of our characteristically human behaviors such as written language and the cognitive anticipation of events, as well as a host of other complex perceptual, motor, and intellectual abilities.

It is important not to forget the interrelated nature of these three "biological computers." While there is a degree of overlap of each successive new evolutionary layer, it would be folly to ignore the fact that a great deal of human behavior seems to come from the neural structures we share principally with reptiles. A classic example of a complex behavioral system that utilizes inputs from each of the three brains would be sexual functioning.

The overall effect is a multifaceted and at times contradictory picture of base motivation, warm emotion, and logical abstraction. Sagan (1977) captures this difficult conceptual paradigm quite well in the following quote:

A superior agreement is found in the metaphor for the human psyche in the Platonic dialogue, Phadrus. Socrates likens the human soul to a chariot drawn by two horses—one black, one white—pulling in different directions and weakly controlled by a charioteer. The metaphor of the chariot itself is remarkably similar to MacLean's neural chassis: the two horses, to the R-Complex and the limbic cortex; and the charioteer barely in control of the careening chariot and horses, to the neocortex. In yet another metaphor, Freud describes the ego as the rider of an unruly horse. Both the Freudian and Platonic metaphors emphasize the considerable independence of and tension among the constituent parts of the psyche, a point that characterizes the human condition...(p. 83)

MORPHOLOGY OF THE CENTRAL NERVOUS SYSTEM WITH SPECIAL ATTENTION TO THE HUMAN CEREBRAL CORTEX

The gross subdivisions of the central nervous system are the spinal cord and brain. As observed by Lezak (1976):

Perhaps the two most studied structures of the limbic system are the amygdala and the hippocampal areas. The primary identification of the amygdala has been with the expression of aggressive behavior. This conjecture is based on research that has associated bilateral removal of the amygdala with a taming effect in animals (Lezak, 1976).

Other symptoms of bilateral ablation of the amygdala include inability to recognize objects visually and indiscriminant sexual activity (Golden, 1978). There is some evidence for positive behavior change in humans following bilateral removal of the amygdala (Balasubramanian & Ranamurthi, 1970).

By contrast, the hippocampal region has been most often associated with memory disorders (Penfield & Milner, 1958; Scoville & Milner, 1957). The difficulty is associated with the acquisition of new long-term memories. The primary defect arises after bilateral impairment of the hippocampal structure. The degree of deficit is not as severe if a single hippocampal gyrus is lesioned (McLardy, 1970). With regard to specific effects, the loss of the left hippocampal gyrus decreases verbal memory (Russell & Espir, 1961), while the removal of the right hippocampal gyrus interfers with memory for nonverbal stimuli such as maze learning (Corkin, 1965; Milner, 1970).

A particularly famous case illustrative of the effect of bilateral ablation of the hippocampus was that of "H.M." Surgery was performed to reduce seizures and was somewhat successful. Unfortunately, there were serious side effects. H.M. developed marked memory difficulties, while still retaining normal perceptual functioning and motor skills. Most remarkably his IQ *improved* after his hippocampectomy (Sagan, 1977).

While many dysfunctions such as "sexual difficulties" (Rosenblum, 1974), catatonia (Robert, 1965), and general psychosis (Heath, 1975) have been ascribed to limbic system impairment, there is little rigorous scientific evidence in support of these beliefs (Golden, 1978).

Basal Ganglia

The basal ganglia are masses of gray matter that lie deep within the cerebral hemispheres. The major subdivisions are the putamen, the globus pallidus, the caudate nucleus, and amygdaloid complex (Walsh, 1978). Along with the cerebral cortex and midbrain, the basal ganglia form the extrapyramidal system (Chusid, 1976). The specific parts of the basal ganglia are the putamen, globus pallidus, and caudate nucleus. The putamen is a large convex gray mass that lies just beneath the insular cortex. By contrast, the globus pallidus is smaller and, as its name would suggest, is a lighter shade. The caudate nucleus is a pear-shaped structure situated adjacent to the inferior border of the anterior horn of the lateral ventrical. All the bodies of the basal ganglia are interconnected with various other brain structures.

It is most heuristic to discuss the functions of the basal ganglia within the context of the extrapyramidal motor system. As earlier noted, the basal ganglia are a component of this system. The major functions of the extrapyramidal system are "associated movements, postural adjustments, and autonomic integration" (Chusid, 1976). A clinical syndrome of major importance that has been associated with disorders of the extrapyramidal system is Parkinson's disease.

At present, the exact role of the basal ganglia in the extrapyramidal system is in need of additional study. Golden (1978) records that there are two theories on the role of the basal ganglia that are currently under active consideration by contemporary workers. The first averes that the basal ganglia serve an integrative function. That is to say, the basal ganglia combine information from the visual modality with that of the brain and are centers to regulate the joints and muscles of the body in a coordinated fashion. The second theory postulates a lesser role. Essentially, it suggests the basal ganglia only act as relay points and, in contrast to the first theory, do not serve an integrative function. The most parsimonious conclusion would appear to be that the basal ganglia clearly have a role in the production of motor behavior within the extrapyrmidal system. At present, the precise dimensions of that role are still an object of scientific scrutiny (Williams & Wartick, 1975).

Cerebral Cortex

It should be kept in mind that the term cerebral cortex is sometimes used interchangeably with the terms neocortex, or, simply, cortex. The cerebral cortex is the "structure responsible for most of the things that make up human-language, complex learning, thought and cognition, religion, war, poetry, music, love and hate" (Lindsay, Hall, & Thompson, 1978). As mentioned earlier, the expansion and elaboration of this brain structure in the last 2 million years is the crucial point in the differentiation of man from the higher animals.

The cerebral cortex is divided into two cerebral hemispheres. These are essentially mirror images of each other and impressionistically are not entirely unlike two gray-pointed underinflated footballs laid beside each other. Actually, however, one of the two hemispheres is usually a trifle larger than the other. In humans who are right handed, this is almost invariably the left hemisphere. This minor size differential is an excuse to designate the larger hemispheres, the dominant hemisphere, and the slightly smaller one the nondominant hemisphere. Future references in this volume assume the dominant hemisphere to be the left hemisphere and the nondominant hemisphere the right hemisphere. This convention, of course, does not hold for a number of people.

The geography of the cerebral cortex is quite interesting. The two cerebral hemispheres are separated by the longitudinal cerebral fissure. The actual surface of the brain is made up of many convolutions known as gyri and sulci. The degree of regularity of these features various as a function of the brain location (Chusid, 1976).

The major landmarks on the cerebral cortex are two very deep fissures (see Figure 3.1). Fissures are like sulci but much deeper and wider. The fissure of Rolando (otherwise known as the central sulcus) lies in the middle of each cerebral hemisphere and divides each hemisphere separating the parietal and frontal lobes. The fissure of Sylvius (otherwise known as the lateral cerebral fissure) arises at the base of the brain and separates the frontal and temporal lobes rostrally and the parietal and temporal lobes caudally (Walsh, 1978).

There are four major lobes in the brain: the frontal, temporal, parietal, and occipital lobes. Each hemisphere contains each of these four lobes. The boundaries of each are as follows. The frontal and parietal lobes are separated by the fissure of Rolando. The frontal and temporal lobes are separated by the fissure of Sylvius. The parietal and occipital lobes do not have clear anatomical divisions. However, a much smaller fissure, the parietoccipital fissure marks the beginning of the occipital lobe approximately three quarters of the way back from the frontal pole and provides the starting point for an imaginary line that separates the parietal and occipital lobe.

Another important landmark is the corpus callosum. This structure is a band of white fibers that connects the two hemispheres. The corpus callosum is the primary direct communication between the two hemispheres.

Additional structural differentiation is provided by appreciation of the cellular layers of the cortex. It is customarily taught that there are six cellular strata of the cerebral cortex. Walsh (1978) describes them as (1) plexiform, (2) external granular, (3) outer pyramidal, (4) internal granular, (5) inner pyramidal, and (6) polymorphic. Depending on differing degrees of development of particular layers, the various cortical areas are affected. Perhaps the most popular paradigm for organizing the cerebral cortex is that proposed by Brodman (Figures 3.3 and 3.4). This cytoarchitectonic scheme assigns numbers to various cortical areas. For example, the primary motor projection area is number "4" and is immediately rostral to the fissure of Rolando; primary sensory projection areas (1, 2, and 3) lie immediately caudal to the fissure of Rolando. The primary visual receptive area is No. 17 and is located on the posterior pole of the occipital lobe in the cortex behind the calcerine fissure. The primary auditory receptive area is No. 41 and lies at the floor of the fissure of Sylvius in the transverse temporal gyrus (Heschl's gyrus). There are some drawbacks to the mechanical use of these numbers in that they are of questionable validity with human beings (Golden, 1978).

CRANIAL NERVES

There are 12 pairs of cranial nerves. Cranial nerve I is the olfactory nerve. It is a sensory nerve and subserves the sense of smell. Cranial nerve II is the optic nerve. It also is a sensory nerve and its function is the sense of vision. Cranial nerve III is the oculomotor nerve. This is a motor nerve. Its function is the control of eye movements when following objects. Cranial nerve IV is the trochlear nerve. It is also a motor nerve related to eye movements. Cranial nerve V is the trigeminal nerve. A mixed sensory–motor nerve, it regulates chewing and visceral function. Cranial nerve VI is the abducens nerve. Like cranial nerves III and IV, it is involved in eye movement, particularly lateral eye movements. Cranial nerve VII is the facial nerve. Although mixed, it is primarily a motor nerve. It functions to control the muscles of facial expression. Cranial nerve VIII is the

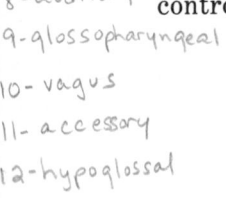

1 - olfactory
2 - optic
3 - oculomotor
4 - trochlear
5 - trigeminal
6 - abducens
7 - facial
8 - auditory
9 - glossopharyngeal
10 - vagus
11 - accessory
12 - hypoglossal

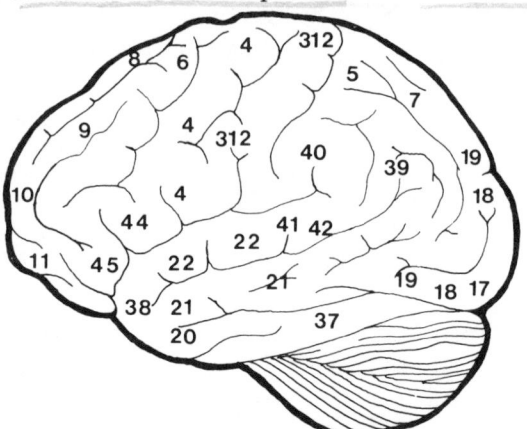

Figure 3.3.   Lateral view of the left hemisphere, indicating Brodmann's cytoarchitectonic fields. Area *4:* precentral region (motor cortex) with Betz cells. Areas *1, 2,* and *3:* postcentral region (sensory cortex). Areas *17, 18,* and *19:* visual cortex. Area *22:* auditory cortex. Area *44:* motor speech cortex (Broca's area). Ill-defined functional centers (see text): Areas *5* and *7:* astereognosis, amorphognosia, ahylognosia. Area *40:* apraxia. Area *39:* agraphia, alexia, acalculia, right-left disorientation, finger agnosia. Areas *41* and *42:* sensory (Wernicke's) aphasia. Area *20:* amusia. These centers, some of which are disputed and poorly defined, apply onto to right-handed individuals. Amnestic aphasia (word blindness) usually is a symptom of a generalized cerebral disorder but occasionally it localizes the lesion to the temporoparietal region. From Suchenwirth, R. *Pocketbook of Clinical Neurology.* Chicago: Year Book Medical Publishers, 1979.

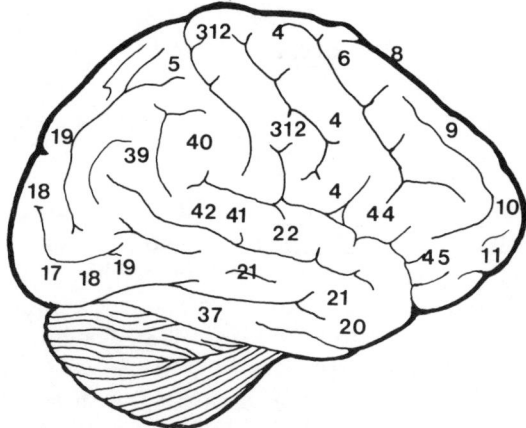

Figure 3.4. Lateral surface of right hemisphere indicating Brodmann's cytoarchitectonic fields. Area *4:* precentral region (motor cortex) with the following topographic localization: Pyramidal cells for the foot in the upper part, for the leg in the middle part, then for the arm, and in the lowest part those for the head musculature. The use of this classification in Areas *1, 2,* and *3* for a corresponding sensory "homunculus" is less clear-cut. The function of the right temporal lobe in right-handed individuals is uncertain. Areas *17, 18,* and *19* represent the visual cortex. Areas *5, 7, 39,* and *40* serve several complex functions, notably orientation (see text). Temporal lobe lesions of either hemisphere may cause homonymous hemianopia. From Suchenwirth, R. *Pocketbook of Clinical Neurology.* Chicago: Year Book Medical Publishers, 1979.

auditory

vestibulocochlear nerve. It is a composite sensory nerve and, as the name suggests, is related to hearing and equilibrium. Cranial nerve IX is the glossopharyngeal nerve. A mixed nerve, its major duties are the gag reflex, taste, sensation in the posterior third of the tongue, and pain in the ear region. Cranial nerve X is the vagus nerve. This nerve is also mixed and controls a multitude of functions. Chief among these are sensation in the abdominal and thoracic regions as well as the pharynx and larynx. Cranial nerve XI is the accessory nerve. This motor nerve controls movement of the shoulders and head. Cranial nerve XII is the hypoglossal nerve, which controls tongue movement.

COVERINGS AND VASCULARIZATION
OF THE CEREBRUM

The Cerebrospinal Fluid System

Cerebrospinal fluid is a clear transparent fluid composed mainly of water. Its primary purpose is to serve as a buffer to protect the brain and spinal cord (Walsh, 1978). Secondary functions include the maintenance of constant pressure with the skull and the disposal of particular waste products in the brain (Golden, 1978).

The system of managing the cerebrospinal fluid is quite complex, and only a very oversimplified explanation is presented here. Within the brain, there are four cerebrospinal fluid-filled cavities. These cavities are termed ventricles (see Figures 3.5 and 3.6). Each is interconnected with each other, the subarachnoid space, and the spinal cord. One of these ventricles lies within each cerebral hemisphere. Together, these are called the lateral ventricles. Each has a somewhat C-shaped contour (Walsh, 1978). The lateral ventricles are connected to the third ventricle, which lies between them at about the level of the thalamus. Directly beneath the third ventricle lies the fourth ventricle, just beneath and in front of the cerebellum (Golden, 1978).

The flow of cerebrospinal fluid proceeds from the lateral ventricle to the third ventricle to the fourth ventricle and then through the subarachnoid space (Figure 3.6). The cerebrospinal fluid is produced by the choroid plexus tissue, which is principally located in the two lateral ventricles (Walsh, 1978). It is absorbed into general circulation by the arachnoid villi within the subarachnoid space (Golden, 1978).

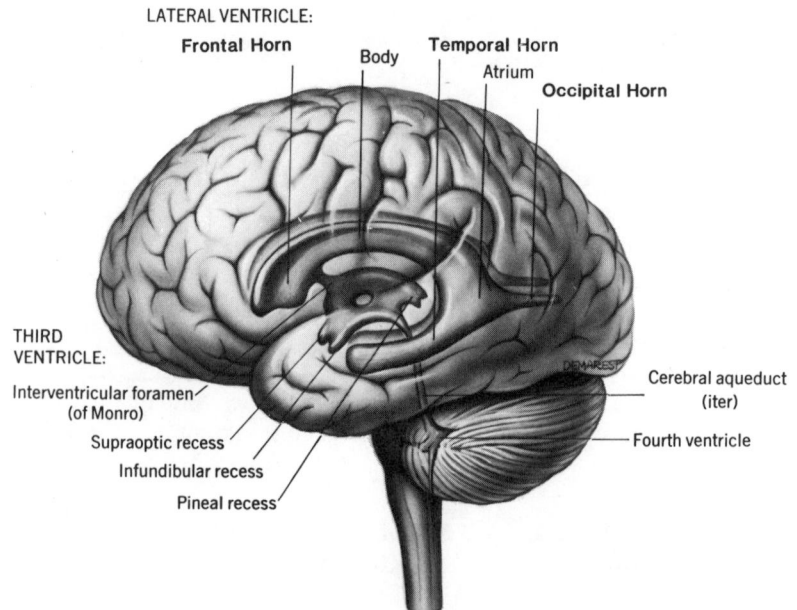

Figure 3.5.   Lateral view of the ventricles of the brain. From C.R. Norback and R.J. Demarest. *The Human Nervous System.* New York: McGraw-Hill, 1981.

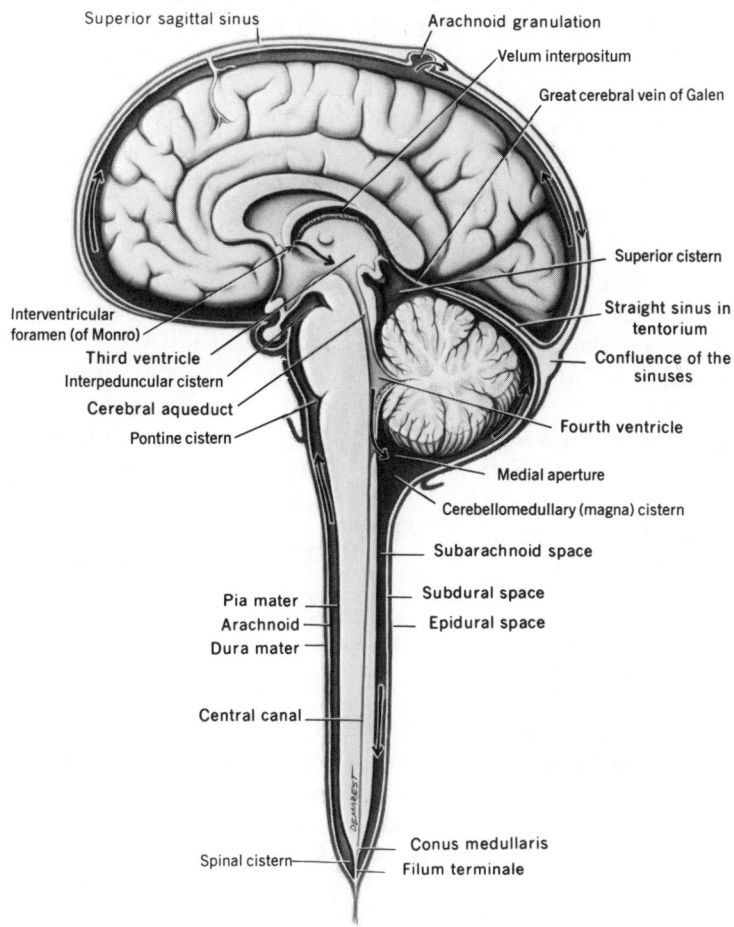

Figure 3.6. Meninges, brain ventricles, and subarachnoid spaces. Arrows indicate the normal direction of flow of the cerebrospinal fluid. From C.R. Norback and R.J. Demarest. *The Human Nervous System.* New York: McGraw-Hill, 1981.

Basically, the brain and spinal cord are completely surrounded by the three meningeal membranes. The outermost meninx is the dura mater. The arachnoid membrane is in the middle while the pia mater is the innermost meningeal layer. The purpose of these membranes is to support and protect the central nervous system. The dura mater is quite tough and resilient and adheres to the inner surface of the skull. The name dura mater means "hard mother" in Latin. The second meningeal membrane, the arachnoid, is very thin and delicate (Walsh,

1978). An idea of its appearance can be gained by realizing that its name derives from the Greek word for spider. The arachnoid membrane is noted for looking like a spider's web of tissue. Beneath this space flows the cerebrospinal fluid. The pia master is also very delicate and highly vascular. It molds itself closely to the brain's surface. Pia mater means "little mother" in Latin. The space between the dura mater and arachnoid membrane is known as the subdural space. The space between the arachnoid membrane and the pia mater where the cerebrospinal fluid flows is known as the subsarachnoid space.

A number of neuropathological conditions can arise that are related to the cerebrospinal fluid system. Two very common ones might be mentioned. First, in cases where there is an obstruction of one of the inner connections of the cerebrospinal fluid system, pressure on the brain can build up to a dangerous level. This condition, termed hydrocephalus, may lead to generalized cerebral impairment if not corrected by some surgical method. The second problem relates to traumatic injuries. A very frequent occurrence is that an individual will receive a blow to the head and as a result of the tearing of some tissue, blood will collect in the subdural space. This condition is known as a subdural hematoma. If not promptly corrected by a neurosurgeon, permanent brain damage can result.

The Cerebrovascular System

In order to properly nourish the brain's 10 billion neurons, a copious supply of oxygen-rich blood is essential at all times. Impairment of the blood supply is the single most common cause of lesions in the central nervous system (Walsh, 1978). Chusid (1976) has contended that an illustration of the vital need of the brain tissue for oxygen by means of the vascular system is the fact that experimental workers have found severe permanent lesions in the cortex of a cat after an interruption of blood flow as brief as 3 minutes.

The blood for the brain comes from the heart by means of two vertebral and two internal carotid arteries. Of these, the vertebral arteries join to create the basilar artery. At the base of the brain, the basilar and internal carotid arteries meet a number of communicating arteries to form the Circle of Willis. This great ring of intertwined blood vessels encircles the optic chasm and the region behind the cerebral peduncles. The Circle of Willis is truly unique in that it appears to be a fail-safe system for the brain's blood supply. The Circle of Willis is an arrangement that permits bypassing any blockage that may occur. These alternate pathways are known as amostomoses.

From the Circle of Willis, three separate arterial systems branch off to supply the two cerebral hemispheres with blood. These are the anterior, middle, and posterior cerebral arteries (Figure 3.7). The

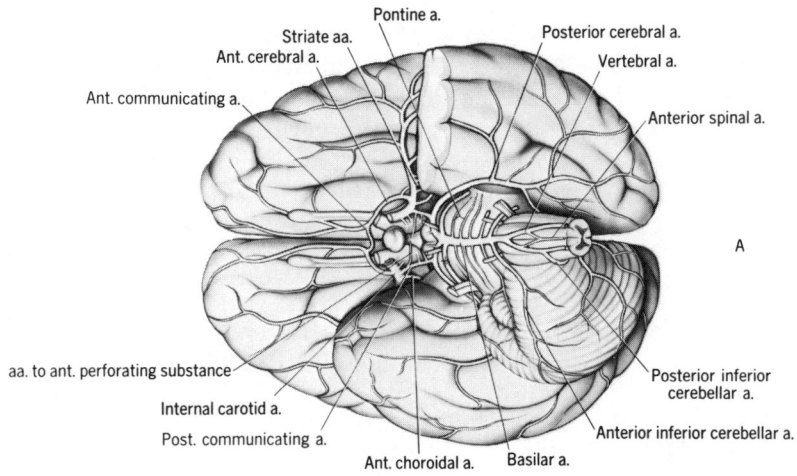

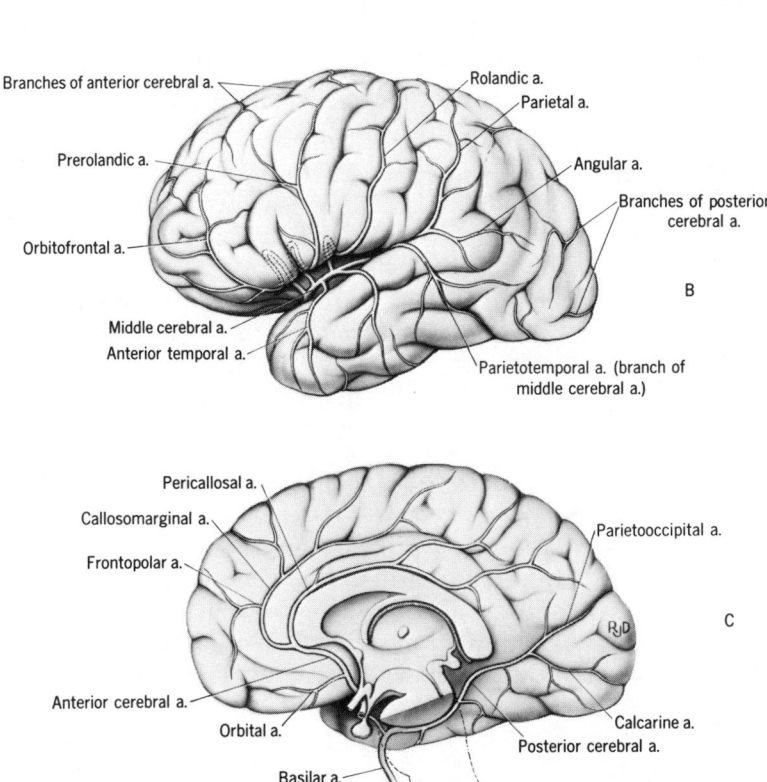

Figure 3.7. Distribution of the arteries on the surface of the brain. *(A)* Basal surface. *(B)* Lateral surface. *(C)* Medial surface. From C.R. Norback and R.J. Demarest. *The Human Nervous System.* New York: McGraw-Hill, 1981.

anterior cerebral artery nourishes the medial aspects of the frontal and parietal lobes. The middle cerebral artery is the major blood source for the surface of the hemispheres. The posterior cerebral artery sends blood to the occipital lobe and the medial portions of the temporal lobe. Drainage is accomplished by three sets of vessels. They are the superficial veins, which drain the lateral and inferior surfaces of the brain, the deep veins, which drain the internal area of the brain, and the venous sinues (Walsh, 1978).

BEHAVIORAL CORRELATES OF THE HUMAN CEREBRAL CORTEX

> Lovers and madmen have such seething brains
> Such shaping fantasies, that apprehend
> More than cool reason ever comprehends.
> The lunatic, the lover, and the poet
> Are of imagination all compact...."
> (William Shakespeare in *A Midsummer Night's Dream*)

In this section we discuss the behavioral capabilities of the neocortex. Comments are offered on a paradigm for conceptualizing the brain's functional organization. Also, a suggested framework for examining the behavioral effects of brain lesions at the level of the cerebral hemispheres is outlined.

There are a vast number of research studies on neurocognitive processes. Using a variety of research methods such as dichotic listening, tachistoscopic recognition, and reaction time tasks, great masses of experimental data have been accumulated.

CONCEPTUAL MODELS OF FUNCTIONAL UNITS

In the ensuing discussion, a fairly straightforward classification of the brain into specific areas is utilized. As can be recalled, there are two hemispheres in the brain and four lobes in each hemisphere. Luria proposed a different conceptual model for the organization of higher mental processes and the behavioral correlates subserved by various functional areas of the brain (Luria, 1966). Luria's theory of brain organization postulated three major blocks: (1) brain stem structures; (2) cerebral cortex posterior to the Rolandic fissure, and (3) cerebral cortex anterior to the Rolandic fissure.

The brain stem structures regulate the energy level and tone of the cerebral cortex. The cerebral cortex posterior to the Rolandic fissure subserves sensory function and is responsible for the reception, organization, and retention of optic, acoustic, cutaneous, and kinesthetic stimuli while the cerebral cortex anterior to the Rolandic fissure subserves motor functions and the formulation of intentions and programs for behavior as well as the evaluation of the behavioral performance. As the brain stem structures have been already discussed, no further attention is devoted to them here. Luria (1966) subdivides the regions of the cerebral cortex further into primary, secondary, and tertiary areas. The primary areas perform very basic functions of either sensory input (cerebral cortex posterior to Rolandic fissure) or motor output (cerebral cortex anterior to Rolandic fissure). The secondary areas provide an enhanced capability to perform more elaborate varieties of sensory–motor functions. For example, a primary area motor function would be simple leg movement; the secondary area motor capability would be necessary in order to dance. Tertiary areas combine the secondary areas. As observed by Golden (1978): "They act to integrate information received from different senses, as in combining of visual and auditory data. These areas are responsible for higher cognitive functions, such as reading" (p. 32).

These areas act in union to produce complex behavioral functions. No single area is solely responsible for a certain observable behavior. Lezak (1976) states:

> The uncertain relation between brain activity and human behavior obligates the clinician to exercise care in his observations and caution in his predictions, and to take nothing for granted when applying the principles of functional localization to diagnostic problems. However, this uncertain relation does not negate the dominant tendencies to regularity in the functional organization of brain tissue. (p. 68)

THE CEREBRAL HEMISPHERE: GENERAL CONSIDERATION

Contralateral control refers to the "cross-wiring" of the human nervous system. The cerebral hemisphere on one side controls motor and sensory functions on the opposite side of the body. The left cerebral hemisphere controls optic, acoustic, cutaneous, and kinesthetic sensory functions as well as gross and fine motor functions on the right side of the body, while the right cerebral hemisphere controls the same functions on the left side of the body. The classic example of this phenomenon is the patient who has a cerebrovascular accident (stroke) in one cerebral hemisphere that results in at least partial loss of sensory and motor functions on the opposite side of his/her body.

Cerebral asymmetry is the term used to denote some morphological differences between the two cerebral hemispheres. Specifically, the two cerebral hemispheres, although physically very similar, are not identical. The left hemisphere (in right-handed persons) is slightly larger than the right hemisphere (Connolly, 1950). The presumed reason for this size differential is that the left cerebral hemisphere subserves language functions and that those areas that deal with the use of spoken and written symbols for communication between human beings have increased in size to handle this fairly unique human ability (Geschwind & Levitsky, 1968). This type of assymmetry is not found in animals below the level of the primates.

Point-to-point representation refers to the primary motor and sensory areas of the brain. The primary motor area is immediately anterior to the Rolandic fissure and the sensory area is immediately posterior to the Rolandic fissure. There are specific areas that correspond to specific body parts. Lezak (1976) explains:

> The amount of cortex identified with each body portion or organ is proportional to the number of sensory or motor nerve endings in that part of the body rather than its size. For example, the area concerned with sensation and movement of the tongue or finger is much more extensive than the area representing the elbow or back. (p. 40)

THE UNIQUE ABILITIES OF THE CEREBRAL HEMISPHERE

It is a well-accepted fact that the two cerebral hemispheres subserve unique functions. Hughlings Jackson first suggested this idea in the 1870s. Jackson based this assertion on his observations of individual patients. Reitan (1966), in his research program on the Halstead–Reitan Neuropsychological Test Battery, encountered clinical areas of lateralized brain damage that demonstrated differential patterns of ability impairment. Reitan likened the strength of his conviction in this principle of different functions of the two hemispheres to the statement of "how many two-headed cows do you need to see before you know they exist." Despite the substantial mass of evidence attesting to this scientific fact, the reality of hemispheric specialization was only widely accepted after a program of research on the behavioral effects of neurosurgical division of the forebrain commissures was reported to the public (Golden, 1978).

The series of highly significant experiments with commissurotomized patients is of the utmost importance in comprehending the behavioral specialization of the cerebral hemispheres. One method of dealing with extreme cases of epilepsy is to cut the corpus callosum, the main set of interhemispheric fibers. This neurosurgical operation is performed in the hope of controlling epileptic seizures. The anterior commissure and hippocampal commissure are also sometimes cut. The operation has proved quite successful. These patients experience a decline in both the rate of seizures and their severity. These commissured or "split-brain" patients experienced few ill effects from the operation. There are, however, subtle cognitive changes. As recorded by Nebes (1974):

> Section of the interhemispheric tracts has been found to eliminate much of the normal integration of sensory information between the two sides of the body, leaving each hemisphere cognizant only of contralateral sensory input. The left hemisphere thus receives detailed information about visual stimuli only if they fall in the right visual half-field.... This division of the subject's peripheral sensory world makes it possible to restrict a stimulus to just one hemisphere. The right and left hemispheres in these individuals can thus be examined independently on exactly the same task, making the commissurotomy patients ideal subjects for the investigation of lateralization of cerebral function. (p. 1)

> In contrast to earlier studies of patients with unilateral brain damage where there are great difficulties in controlling for multiple confounding variables, in the commissurotomy patients the two cerebral hemispheres are relatively intact and available for separate testing, allowing comparison within a single person of the two sides of the brain on a given task. (p. 1).

In order to better understand the methodology of the split-brain experiment, some brief comments on visual information processing are appropriate. Each eye sends information to both cerebral hemispheres. The left half of each eye sends its fibers to the left hemisphere and the right half of each eye sends its fibers to the right hemisphere. This is a very complex system. What should be remembered, however, is that if a subject looks directly ahead at a central fixation point, then information present to his left body side will enter the right cerebral hemisphere and information presented to his right body side will enter the left cerebral hemisphere. In the normal person, the information entering one cerebral hemisphere is quickly transferred to the other hemisphere via the corpus callosum. In the split-brain patient, however, there is no bundle of neural fibers processing information between the two hemispheres. Thus, two separate information-processing centers are available for study (Gazzaniga, 1977).

A number of carefully designed studies explored the unique abilities of the individual hemispheres. The classic paradigm used with the split-brain patients utilized unilateral presentation of information. For example, the name of an object such as a dime or pencil is flashed to the right side of a split-brain subject's body while his eyes are fixed on a central point. The subject is able to immediately name the object because the left cerebral hemisphere (in most individuals) is specialized for language comprehension and expression. If the opposite is done, that is, the same information is flashed in the left visual field, the subject is unable to immediately name the object because the right cerebral hemisphere is specialized for the perception of spatial and part–whole relationships (Nebes, 1974).

Researchers have devised methods to tap the separate cognitive functions of the right hemisphere. This was done in a number of ways. For instance, the left hand, which is, of course, controlled by the right hemisphere, could perform a motor response indicating that information was received in the right hemisphere. Examples included selecting a physical object to match a picture presented on the left side of the body. Interestingly, there also appeared to be some verbal comprehension abilities in the right hemisphere. Split-brain patients can comprehend simple words, such as pen, flashed on the left side, and select an object to match the word (Gazzaniga, Steen, & Volpe, 1978).

Sperry (1961), in the context of this research program, investigated the results of information partly presented to each cerebral hemisphere. The word "heart" was the stimulus and the "he" portion was presented to the right cerebral hemisphere and the "art" portion was presented to the left cerebral hemisphere. The patients would say that they had seen the word "art" as only the left hemisphere is specialized for speech but when asked to point with the left hand to either the word "he" or "art," they pointed to the word "he." This demonstrated an instance where the right hemisphere prevailed over the usually dominant left hemisphere.

Other areas of right hemisphere competence include the perception and manipulation of spatial patterns. Interestingly, drawings made by the left hand of a right handed split-brain patient are usually superior relative to those made by the right hand (Gazzaniga, Steen, & Volpe, 1979)!

Gazzaniga (1967) attempted to synthesize some of the implications of this important and exciting research:

> All of the evidence indicates that separation of the hemispheres creates two independent spheres of consciousness within a single cranium. That is to say, within a single organism. This conclusion is disturbing to some people who view consciousness as an indivisible property of the human brain. It seems premature to others, who insist that the capacities revealed thus far for the right hemisphere are at the level of an automaton. There is, to be sure, hemispheric inequality in the present cases, but it may well be a characteristic of the individuals we have studied. It is entirely possible that if a brain

human were divided in a very young person, both hemispheres could as a result separately and independently develop mental functions of a high order at the level attained only in the left hemisphere of normal individuals. (p. 29)

Gazzaniga maintains that hemispheric specialization occurs due to the development of language. Because the left hemisphere is utilized to perform various types of activities such as reading, writing, speech comprehension, and speech production, among others, there is no space for the development of skills in geometrical visualization and physical manipulation of spatial materials.

The right hemisphere subserves the less culturally valued functions because the left hemisphere is already programmed for language skills.

Despite the impressive and exciting nature of the split-brain research, it would be wise to maintain some degree of scientific caution. Ornstein, Johnson, Herron, and Swencoinis (1980) made the follow-up observation: "One must also be cautious in attempting to infer from split-brain research how the hemispheres function in normals. The disconnection or the epilepsy for which the operation was performed may make brain function in split-brain patients quite different from that in normals" (p. 50).

There are different ways of conceptualizing how the hemispheres work. Sperry (1961) has advanced the view that the left brain is analytic in nature whereas the right brain utilizes Gestalt strategies. Das, Kirb, and Jarmin (1979) postulate that the left hemisphere operates in a successive fashion, while the right hemisphere performs mental operation in a simultaneous manner. This model of information processing is based on the one developed by Luria.

There is a certain amount of data that support a combined theory in which the actual factors that control hemispheric utilization are *not* the demands of the tasks themselves but rather "the cognitive strategies used to solve the tasks" (Ornstein *et al.*, 1980, p. 61). The crucial fact to gleen from this discussion is that what determines the hemisphere utilized is not the input or output modality but rather the way in which the material is to be processed. Nebes (1974) concludes:

It is not just the type of perceptual stimulus or the mode of readout used that determined which hemisphere is dominant, but rather the type of information processing required to solve the given problem. If only visual recognition is called for, even if the material is verbal, the right hemisphere acts. If however, a verbal transformation is demanded, even if the material is nonverbal, it is handled by the left hemisphere. This division of the two hemispheres according to the functions they perform rather than their preferred input or output has led several investigators to propose a model of hemispheric action in which the minor hemisphere is seen to organize and treat data in terms of complex wholes, being in effect a synthesizer with a predisposition for reviewing the total rather than the parts. The left hemisphere in this model sequentially analyzes input, abstracting out the relative details to which it associates verbal symbols in order to manipulate and store data more efficiently. (pp. 131–132)

Thus, it can be postulated that this synthetic–simultaneous versus analytic–sequential model suggests that hemisphere activation is a function of preferred strategy. Evidence for this hypothesis is provided by studies of complex spatial processing. Ornstein and colleagues (1980) found, while using some elegant procedures for comparing ongoing EEG alpha asymmetry in neurologically normal adults, that complex mental rotation, a classic spatial task, evoked more left hemisphere than right hemisphere engagement. They concluded that because of the complex nature of the mental rotation, the brain of their subjects elected to utilize an analytic and sequential strategy to process these spatial data as opposed to the expected synthetic and simultaneous strategy. This finding is consistent with the results of many years of work by De Renzi's group on spatial tasks. De Renzi (1978) summarized his thinking on the matter in the following statement:

> The broader hypothesis can be advanced that whenever the processing of perceptual data goes beyond the level of "pure" detection of spatial orientation and involves intellectual analysis (such as deduction of relationships or discovering a hidden solution intermingled with irrelevant information), the contribution of the left hemisphere to performance increases and tends to attenuate the right hemisphere's superiority. (p. 67)

In the context of above remarks, it is naive to place great reliance on the results of lesion studies of the effects of brain damages in human beings. Yet the vast majority of the voluminous literature on the specific effects of brain damage are of this type. Indeed the state of the art has only in recent years begun to go beyond correlating loss of specific behaviors with lesion sites.

Left Hemisphere Functions

The left hemisphere is specialized for symbolic processing. The use of symbols for communication purposes includes the comprehension and production of spoken speech, reading, and writing, mathematics, spelling, grammar, and remembering verbal material (Golden, 1978).

Another point of interest is the way data are organized in the left hemisphere. Organization occurs on the basis of conceptual similarity (Nebes, 1974). For example, a table and a chair are classified together because they are both furniture. This framework enables the left hemisphere to be the logical–scientific side of the brain.

There is some evidence that tissue damage in either hemisphere can exaggerate the thinking pattern of that hemisphere and precipitate emotional reactions. When the left hemisphere is damaged, the patient is more likely to develop serious affective maladjustment, including anxiety, depression, paranoia, and psychosis (Davison & Reitan, 1974; Gainotti, 1972). One factor in the development of emotional disturbance with left-hemisphere-impaired individuals is postulated to be the loss of the means of communicating with others. The famous "catastrophic reaction" observed by K. Goldstein, in which the brain-damaged individual completely breaks down, is more often associated with left hemisphere lesions, although it would be folly to suggest that the patients with strictly right hemisphere injuries do not also exhibit this syndrome.

Right Hemisphere Functions

The right cerebral hemisphere subserves visuospatial orientation and awareness. The abilities of the right hemisphere include orientation in space, visual neglect, drawing geometric patterns, discrimination and recall of nonlanguage material (e.g., musical sounds and color hues), and facial recognition (Golden, 1978).

The right cerebral hemisphere organizes data on the basis of structural similarities (Lezak, 1976). Patterns, forms, and configurations are the basis for sorting data in the right cerebral hemisphere. For example, while the left hemisphere link between a table and chair is that both are furniture, in the right cerebral hemisphere, the point of structural similarity might be that each have four legs.

Patients who have sustained serious injury to the right hemisphere often ignore or deny their very real deficits (Gainotti, 1972). This general emotional absence of distressful affect stems from the patient's decreased self-awareness of his or her behavior. Lezak (1976), made the following very apt observation:

> Although many patients with right hemisphere damage may at first appear to be free of emotional disturbance, particularly in comparison to those who have sustained left hemisphere damage, their complacency and diminished appreciation for their defective per-

formances may result in irresponsible and childlike behavior. These patients are often unable to profit from experience and are unlikely to improve very much. (p. 48)

It is important to stress that emotional reactions to lateralized brain damage are quite variable and one cannot apply the above characterizations of emotional disturbance and side of lesion to individual cases in a mechanical manner. Lezak (1976) makes the point that factors such as mourning reactions and premorbid personality, among others, can interact to produce the patient's affective state.

Specific Functions of Cerebral Lobes

Behavior is the result of the concerted effort of many diverse brain areas acting in a systematic fashion. As observed by Golden (1978), "Any task which is complex enough or demands sustained and continuing attention is likely to be severely impaired to any part of the cerebral hemispheres" (p. 27).

Frontal Lobes ― *(time Sense "prog'g motor acts chronologically)*

Perhaps the most interesting of all neural structures are the frontal lobes. These brain areas are "responsible for the planning, performance, and evaluation of all motor behavior" (Golden, 1978, p. 41). For many years an enormous controversy surrounding the actual behavioral functions subserved by the frontal lobes. Initially, it was thought that the frontal lobes were the seat of intellectual ability (Morgan, 1943, cited in Luria, 1966). Later work, however, found data that contradicted this preliminary hypothesis. Many studies of head injuries and psychosurgery made it clear that there could be unequivocal destruction of frontal lobe tissue without notable impairment on conventional intelligence tests.

Structurally, the frontal lobes can be divided into three areas. The primary area is Brodmann's area 4 (i.e., the motor strip immediately rostral to the central sulcus). The major Brodmann areas are presented in Figures 3.3 and 3.4. This brain region is intimately involved in the basic motor functioning of the human body. Various body regions are represented on the motor strip. This is one of the few areas of the brain where there is a relatively discrete localization of function.

The motor strip contains some sensory cells. Neff and Goldberg (1960, cited in Luria, 1966) suggest that 20% of the motor strip cells are specialized for sensory input. This permits the sensory–motor integration necessary for the proper coordination of voluntary behavior.

The secondary frontal regions are rostral to the motor strip. This section includes Brodmann's areas 8, 6, and 44. Area 8 controls oculomotor activity while area 6 regulates general motor organization (Golden, 1978). Area 44 is known as Broca's area (in the left hemisphere) and is known to regulate motor speech. In the right hemisphere, this area subserves the ability to sing (Lezak, 1976).

The major importance of the secondary frontal areas appears to be in the production of "motor melodies" (Luria, 1966). These areas control fluid complex motor movement. Golden (1978), in the following passage, summarizes these functions of the secondary frontal areas:

> Tasks (motor) continually demand ever-changing reactions to adjust for the past movements and environmental demands. The secondary areas, using the feedback they receive from the sensory areas of the cerebral hemispheres, provide these adjustments. Consequently, they are extremely important for smooth skilled behavior on the opposite side of the body. (p. 42)

The classic deficit produced by lesions in the secondary frontal lobes is the inability to rapidly perform alternate fine motor movements. An example of this can be seen if a patient with exactly this sort of impairment attempts to rapidly write in cursive script M's and N's. The usual result will be an inability to correctly alternate the two letters. A common result is that one letter will tend to be repeated. This *perseveration* deficit is known as perseveration. The patient cannot successfully inhibit a movement and unintentionally repeats it.

The tertiary frontal lobe areas form the prefontal cortex. This region includes Brodmann's areas 9, 10, 11 and 46 and is most crucial to the successful programming, regulation, and verification of motor activity (Luria, 1973). Disturbance may involve states of activity, mental activity, mnestic actions, and goal-directed behavior. In this discussion, however, two somewhat different categories of deficits will be examined: cognitive deficits and affective deficits. Lezak (1976) makes the valid point that injuries to the prefrontal areas impair the "how" rather than "the what" of cognitive and affective behavior. The character of the deficit is more of an organizational nature rather than a simple absence of a specific ability.

Cognitive deficits in the prefontal areas are associated with lesions of the lateral surface. Patients with a prefrontal lobe injury on the lateral surface often are very distractible and unable to ignore insignificant events (Golden, 1978). Luria (1966), for example, observes whether or not a patient intrudes in conversations. The presence of this behavior alerts the clinician to the possibility of a prefrontal injury. Additional cognitive deficits include an inability to be flexible in one's thinking and subsequent difficulty in adapting to novel situations or performing tasks in an alternate manner (Milner, 1963a). Also, there is an apparent inability or lessened ability to use self-generated verbal cues to regulate action (Luria & Homskaya, 1964). Moreover, destruction of the brain tissue in the tertiary frontal lobe region has been implicated in time sense deterioration. Benton (1968) has found disorientation to time in patients with frontal lobe damage. Additional deficits include problems with time-span judgments and time recency sense.

Affective disturbances associated with the tertiary frontal lobe regions occur most commonly with lesions of the medial and orbital surfaces (Golden, 1978). This fact points out the important role of subcortical structures in human emotional and social adjustment. Luria (1973) clearly recognized this relationship:

> In view of these two important functions of the frontal lobes, it is perfectly logical to regard these structures as tertiary zones for the limbic system, on the one hand, and for the motor cortex on the other hand. These functions also enable us to understand the important role of the frontal lobes in the regulation of vigilance and in the control of the most complex forms of man's goal-linked activity. (p. 188)

Affective changes due to injuries of the medial and orbital surfaces of the frontal lobe are generally motivational. The patient may be either hypo- or hyperactive (Luria, 1973). Also, a lack of social inhibition may result in inappropriate interpersonal behavior such as the use of foul language (Kramer, 1955). Moreover, some emotional flatness, apathy, and carelessness is commonly seen with lesions of this area. It is worth recalling that psychosurgery operations were concentrated in precisely this region of the brain. In patients with particularly violent behavior, ablation of the medial and orbital surfaces of the frontal lobes was done to induce a calming effect. While modern views are generally negative toward this sort of behavior control, the originator of this operation did receive the Nobel prize for medicine in the 1930s!

The frontal lobes are found to be less differentiated than many other brain regions. Still there are some verbal–nonverbal distinctions between the dominant and nondominant hemispheres (Lezak, 1976).

Left Frontal Lobe

The classic left hemisphere–right hemisphere difference is manifested in the left frontal lobe specialization for motor speech. As earlier mentioned, Brodmann area 44, commonly called Broca's area, is intimately connected with motor speech. While the person with a Broca's aphasia may be able to utter individual sounds, he or she is unable to move from one sound to another in the rapid sure way necessary for appropriate speech. Luria (1966) calls the syndrome produced by a lesion in Broca's area "motor aphasia." This area of the brain is most important in Luria's scheme since all higher thought processes are postulated to be dependent on speech.

Lesions of the left frontal lobe tertiary area have real but largely latent effects. A central feature of this sort of brain injury lies in a loss of word fluency. For example, if given the letter "H" and asked to produce as many words as possible that start with this letter, the patient with a lesion in the left frontal tertiary area experiences great difficulty (Benton, 1968). Luria (1966) has labeled this syndrome "dynamic aphasia." Extreme verbal memory difficulties may also be present with this sort of local cerebral impairment, and this problem may play a role in the widely reported difficultly these patients have in regulating their behavior thought internal speech cues. Quite commonly, these patients are incapable of adapting their behavior to anything but the simplest of verbal instruction.

Right Frontal Lobe

There is a right hemisphere deficit that corresponds to the motor aphasia found with impairment to Broca's area in the left hemisphere. In the right hemisphere, an injury to this area produces an inability to sing or "avoculia" (Botex & Wertheim, 1959).

Similarly, lesions in the right frontal lobe tertiary area have nonverbal effects. The most commonly reported deficits include visual–spatial integration (Teuber, 1966), visual–spatial memory (Milner, 1971), and problems in maze learning (Corkin, 1965). The visual–spatial difficulties seen with lesions of the right frontal lobe tertiary area may relate more to the motor than to the visual–perceptual dimensions of the task. The unique character of the assessment measures used in research and clinical practice may have almost as much influence in determining the results obtained as the actual condition of the brain. This conondrum clearly warrants extensive thoughtful consideration and is particularly crucial with an area such as the frontal lobes, where there is less than universal agreement concerning basic functions.

Temporal Lobes

In an effort to provide a thumbnail sketch of brain localization, each pair of lobes of the brain can be characterized by a single unique ability. The frontal lobes would be intimately concerned with time sense and the programming of motor acts in chronological sequence, the parietal lobes are the center for tactile sensation, as the occipital lobes subserve the function of vision. Similarly, the temporal lobes are concerned with hearing and the analysis and retention of acoustic stimuli. Luria (1966) states:

> The temporal region of the cerebral cortex is complex in structure and in functional organization. It includes divisions acting as the cortical nuclear zone of the auditory analyzer (Areas 41, 42, and 22), extra nuclear zones of the auditory portion of the cortex (Area 21), and the formations of the inferior and basal divisions unconnected with the functions of auditory analysis and integration (Area 20). In addition, the temporal region also includes, in its medial surface, those formations belonging to the archipallium and the transitional portion of the cortex constituting part of the limbic system; these formations are associated with apparatuses closely involved in the regulation of afferent processes and form a specialized structure of the cerebral cortex. Finally, the temporal zones bordering the parietal and occipital regions (the posterior portions of Areas 22 and 37), as well as the wholly specialized areas formed by the structures of the interior of the temporal lobe, constitute other divisions (p. 94).

The primary areas of the temporal lobes receive sounds for the cerebral cortex. As in the majority of sensory functions, one finds contralateral control as demonstrated by Kimura's (1963) landmark studies of dichotic listening. In cases where there is destruction of both primary temporal areas, a complete loss of hearing is likely to result (Jerger, Lovering, & Wertz, 1972).

The role of the temporal lobes in memory functions is quite complex, as is the whole area of amnestic processes. Luria (1976), in his book, *Neuropsychology of Memory*, makes the point that amnestic processes themselves are a functional system that require the coordinated and integrated working of many cerebral structures in order to perform in an optimal manner.

The hippocampal structures result in the brain's ability to retain anything new other than motor skills (Corkin, 1968). The ablation of a single hippocampal structure causes lateralized deficits. Lesions on the left side impair verbal memory while lesions on the right side disrupt nonverbal memory (Milner, 1970).

The contribution of the temporal lobes to this process appears to be in the reception and analysis of verbal and nonverbal stimuli. The temporal lobes receive specific stimuli and make fine discriminations among complex stimuli for proper information coding. However, the actual entry of the stimuli into relatively enduring amnestic storage is dependent on the hippocampus. As observed by R.B. Livingston:

"The hippocampus appears to contain a mechanism capable of emitting a signal amounting to a 'Now print!' message without which no recording can take place. This 'Print!' message could be related to 'affective color or emotional tone'" (Quoted in Nauta, 1964, p. 19). Given the previously mentioned role of the limbic system in emotional responding, it is quite likely that memory may have a basis in affective life. The temporal lobes subserve the function of receiving and analyzing acoustic data while the limbic system may or may not send the 'Print' message.

A final point relative to psychiatric disturbances and the temporal lobes is that injuries to the temporal lobes have been known to cause visual or auditory hallucinations (Mullan & Penfield, 1959). Also, disorders of consciousness may arise (William, 1968). Pincus and Tucker (1974) have concluded that some patients with temporal lobe epilepsy display a schizophrenic-like psychosis.

Left Temporal Lobe

The left temporal lobe is specialized for the auditory perception of verbal stimuli such as words and numbers. Impairment of the primary areas results in an inability to comprehend linguistic symbols (Gazzaniga, Glass, Saino, & Posner, 1973). In addition, perception of acoustic intensity may be disturbed (Swisher, 1967).

Impairment of the secondary areas of the left temporal lobe may produce difficulties in the analysis and integration of language sounds (Luria, 1966). There is a diminished ability to comprehend spoken speech through phonic analysis. These deficits may also cause diffi-culties in other language arts such as reading, writing, spelling, and speaking since the decoding of language phonemes plays a role in these processes (Golden, 1978). As already noted, the left temporal secon-dary area is involved in verbal memory (Milner, 1958).

The tertiary temporal–occipital area is involved in the coordina-tion of auditory and visual information (Luria, 1966). Lesions in this area usually result in either the inability to recognize letters (visual letter agnosia) or numbers (visual number agnosia), or difficulty in reading (alexia) despite normal visual acuity.

Right Temporal Lobe

The right temporal lobe is commonly thought to subserve the ability to comprehend nonverbal auditory patterns (Golden, 1978). Like the left temporal lobe, damage to the primary area causes a straightforward loss of hearing in the contralateral area.

The secondary right temporal lobe is involved in the comprehen-sion of visual and auditory nonverbal configuration (Kimura, 1963; Meier & French, 1965). The abilities to comprehend rhythmic pat-terns (Luria, 1973) and pitch (Milney, 1958) are thought to be somewhat localized in the right temporal secondary area. Other functions appear to involve visual closure (Lansdell, 1970) and non-verbal memory (Meier & French, 1965). In addition, patients with lesions in this area may be unable to comprehend music (amusia). Some have suggested that impairment to the anterior portion of the right temporal lobe produces an inability to correctly arrange cartoon pictures as in the Wechsler Adult Intelligence Test picture arrangement subtest (R. Reitan, undated). Others localize this function in the frontal lobes (Luria, 1966). Tonal memory is another ability that has been attributed to the right temporal lobe (T.J. Boll, pers. comm.).

Parietal Lobes   —tactile sensation

The parietal lobes subserve functions of tactile and kinesthetic perception. The primary region of the parietal lobes is Brodmann's area 3. Interestingly, this area is opposite the motor region, Brodmann's area 4. As in area 4, area 3 is one of the few regions of the brain where there is relatively discrete localization of function. Tactile perception of the various parts of the body, face, hands, torso, and so on is situated in such a way that these areas lie in sequential order with the relative importance of the somatosensory region determining the amount of space devoted to each function. For example, the face has a greater portion of area 3 devoted to it than the back of the leg.

When considering the contribution of area 3, it is important to remember the joint coordination of motor and tactile perceptual functions. Luria treats Brodmann's area 3 and 4 as a single region of the brain. The rationale for this organization of cerebral structures rests on the need for somatosensory feedback in controlling motor activity. Luria (1973) has observed that 20% of the cells in the primary parietal region (area 3) are motor cells. Since 20% of the cells in the motorstrip (area 4) are specialized for sensory input, it can be seen that there is a neuroanatomical basis for the reciprocal control of human motor activity. The fact that the central sulcus separates the motor strip (Brodmann's area 4) and the sensory strip (Brodmann's area 3) leads to overemphasis on the differences between these regions and obscures the important role of sensory input in producing appropriate motor output.

Lesions in the primary area of the parietal lobes produce deficits in the ability to accurately appreciate tactile stimuli. Golden (1978) distinguishes between two forms of astereognosis. One refers to an inability to recognize objects by tactile sensitivity. The other involves impairment of the facility to integrate tactile input with kinesthetic information. The first deficit is the sort found with lesions of the sensory strip (Brodmann's area 3). While this sign may be of use in lateralizing brain lesions, one should be cautious, as massive lesions of the primary area of either the left or right parietal lobe can cause bilateral sensory impairment (Corkin, Milner, & Taylor, 1973).

The secondary areas of the parietal lobes are Brodmann's areas 5, 7, and 40. The second type of astereognostic difficulty, the inability to coordinate tactile and kinesthetic stimuli, is thought to be subserved by these areas. Luria (1966) wrote that this deficit could be attributed to an inability to consider more than a single attribute of an object at a time. The patient with a lesion in this region is unable to consolidate all of the dimensions of an object together into a complete entity. For example, if handed a solid Greek Cross, under conditions where no visual feedback is possible, a patient with this sort of lesion would be unable to deduce what he holds until he saw the cross, at which time he could identify it quite quickly.

Another difficulty associated with lesions of the secondary parietal lobe is locating and coordinating one's limbs in space without visual feedback (Golden, 1978). Essentially, the brain is unable to deduce from tactile and kinesthetic cues alone the location and movement of the limbs. Luria (1966) tests this sort of deficit by blindfolding the patient and guiding one of the patient's arms in a number of motor movements. Luria then tests to see if the patient is able to imitate these movements with the other limb. If the patient is unable to adequately model the guided limb, Luria assumes that the brain has received inadequate somatosensory feedback.

An *apraxia* is "a disturbance in the ability to carry out purposive, useful, or skilled acts" (Lewinsohn, 1973). There are many varieties of apraxias; however, each of these can be classified into one of four groups: (1) motor apraxia, (2) ideational apraxia, (3) ideomotor apraxia, and (4) constructional apraxia. Motor apraxia refers to the inability to carry out fine motor acts in the absence of muscle weakness. Ideational apraxia is used to describe a deficit in which the patient is unable to formulate a program of actions. While individual motor actions are preserved, the sequence of actions cannot be coordinated. Ideomotor apraxia refers to a condition in which the patient is unable to voluntarily perform what can be done on an automatic level. For example, the patient may be unable to use his or her hand intentionally but will slap at a bug. Constructional apraxia refers to failure in the assembly of a spatial whole. This can be demonstrated by an inability to draw simple geometric shapes or put together parts of a puzzle (Lewinsohn, 1973). These apraxias are usually thought of as arising from lesions in the parietal lobes. Generally speaking, the more ideational the deficit, the further the lesion lies from the sensory strip (Luria, 1966).

Agnosia refers to an inability to perceive incoming stimuli. One example, arising from damage to the parietal lobes, is finger agnosia (Neimburger & Reitan, 1961). In this disorder, the patient is unable to report which finger is touched by the examiner. Visual feedback, of course, is denied. Astereognosis, a very similar problem, has already been discussed.

Left Parietal Lobe

Speech and writing are frequently impaired by lesions in the left parietal lobe (Luria, 1966). The cardinal reason for these difficulties may reside in the fact that "precise sensory information is not available to the motor areas involved with speaking and writing" (Golden, 1978, p. 37). The patient with a deficit in this area is unable to control words formed by similar speech muscle movements.

Functions subserved by the tertiary areas of the left parietal lobe are of special interest to the neuropsychologist since the afferent systems of vision, audition, and body sensation overlap in this part of the brain (Lezak, 1976). The tertiary portion of the parietal lobe may be divided into two separate sections. First, there is the parietal–occipital–temporal area (Brodmann's area 40), where all three of the lobes caudal to the central sulcus overlap. The second area is the parietal–occipital area (Brodmann's area 39). This second area is responsible for the coordination of visual and somatosensory stimuli (Golden, 1978).

The parietal–temporal–occipital area of the left parietal lobe is of the utmost importance for verbal information processing. Lesions in this region produce dramatic disruptions in language communications since this area is primarily responsible for coordinating information from visual, auditory, and somatosensory modalities. Many aphasic deficits can be traced to impairment of this particular section of the brain. Among other difficulties, lesions in the parietal–occipital–temporal area produce problems in reading (alexia), writing (agraphia), and in naming common objects (anomia) (Butters & Brody, 1969).

It is important to note that there are two types of anomia and that difficulties in naming can be traced to either the parietal or the temporal lobe. Luria (1966) believes that one way to differentiate these two syndromes is to give the patient the first part of a stimulus word. If this clue enables the patient to recall and verbalize the word it suggests that the lesion is in the parietal–occipital–temporal area.

Another difficulty found with parietal–occipital–temporal lesions of the left parietal lobe is type of verbal memory disorder (Luria, 1966). It will be recalled that there are verbal memory difficulties associated with lesions of the left temporal lobe—that is, acoustic-mnestic aphasia. In the left parietal tertiary area, the memory deficit is due to difficulties in correctly organizing verbal material, so that particular information can be successfully retrieved (Luria, 1973). This syndrome has been referred to by Luria (1966) as semantic aphasia. Interestingly, disturbed logical–grammatical operations are also associated with these lesions. For example, these patients are likely to have difficulty with complex verbal comparisons such as "Olga is lighter than Sonia but darker than Kate" or the use of the attributive genitive case such as "father's brother" or "brother's father," "The dog's master" or "The master's dog." As observed by Luria (1966), adequate comprehension requires the logical synthesis of the elements of these expressions into an integral whole.

Failure in color naming is another deficit in normal behavior that often follows injury to the left parietal tertiary area (Neiley, 1974). This refers to loss of the ability to verbally label an object with the correct color. However, it is an error to attribute the inability to separate various objects according to hues to the tertiary region of the left parietal lobe. This function is generally thought to be subsumed by other cerebral structures.

Disorders of the parietal–occipital area share a number of characteristics with lesions of the parietal–temporal–occipital area; common to both are problems with somatosensory stimuli and spatial relations. For example, body agnosia, the inability to correctly identify parts of one's own body in space, can be attributed to lesions in the parietal–occipital area (Butters & Brody, 1969). A related difficulty is finger agnosia, the inability to adequately perceive if one's fingers are touched (Kinsbourne & Warrington, 1964).

Spelling apraxia, the inability to spell fairly simple words that were once known, is often found to accompany lesions in the parietal–occipital area of the left parietal lobe since letters are recalled in an inappropriate sequence due to disturbed spatial processes in verbal memory.

Constructional apraxia refers to impairment in the ability to assemble elements of an object to form a meaningful whole or to draw geometric shapes without distortion of the spatial configuration (Lewinsohn, 1973). In the United States, multiple investigations have established that constructional apraxia can result from lesions of either the left or right cerebral hemisphere. The clear majority, however, arises from lesion of the right cerebral hemisphere. European investigations, on the other hand, have reported that two-thirds of their cases with the identifiable syndrome of constructional apraxia have lesions of the right hemisphere while the remaining one-third have lesions of the left hemisphere. Why is there this discrepancy? One hypothesis relates to cultural differences; however, this possibility is unlikely in view of the massive evidence of relatively excellent cross-validation of neuropsychological tests in different cultures. (For example, Golden's adaptation in America of Luria's (1966) neuropsychological evaluation appears to be a successful instance of just this sort of cross-cultural neuropsychological validation.)

Another hypothesis, which seems more attractive, relates to stimulus materials. Some studies (Ornstein, et al., 1980) suggest hemispheric utilization may depend on the cognitive strategies used to solve tasks. The usual stimulus material employed by European neuropsychologists to assess visuospatial skills is generally quite complex. An example of this sort of visually involved figure would be the Rey–Osterrith design (Lezak, 1976). On the other hand, stimulus materials employed by American neuropsychologists are more likely to be quite simple geometric figures. An example of this type of material would be the Greek Cross in the Reitan–Indiana Aphasia Screening Test, which is part of the Halstead–Reitan Neuropsychological Test Battery (Reitan, 1966). It may be that less complex designs are particularly sensitive to right hemisphere lesions while more complicated and complex figures require more verbal and analytic mental processing and, as a result of the need for a different cognitive strategy, may require a different pattern of hemispheric utilization. Still, it should be clearly understood that this conjecture is purely speculative.

The parietal–occipital area of the left parietal lobe is also an important contributor to other complex tasks that require the integration of visual and kinesthetic abilities. Ideomotor apraxia and ideational apraxia, which were mentioned earlier, are typical of these tasks (Lezak, 1976). Another difficulty that often occurs with lesions in this area is the inability to use numbers and arithmetical processes. This deficit is due to neurological damage and is not simply the failure to have acquired arithmetic skills (Lewinsohn, 1973). A patient with deficits in this area may retain an ability to do practical arithmetic problems. Golden (1978) notes that overlearned math computations may primarily involve memory processes and not arithmetic ability. This is particularly true of patients whose occupations involved extensive mathematical facility such as engineering and accounting.

Still another behavioral ability that involves the parietal–occipital area of the left parietal lobe relates to the relationship of verbal and spatial concepts. Luria (1966) cites the example of the patient who loses the ability to tell time by looking act the face of a traditional clock and noting the positions of the hands. In addition, the understanding of words which imply spatial relations (such as below and above) may be impaired.

Right Parietal Lobe

Defects of the primary and secondary areas of the right parietal lobe are almost identical to those of the left parietal lobe (Golden, 1978). Thus, this section primarily focuses on deficits arising from impairment of the tertiary areas of the right parietal lobe. The tertiary area of the right parietal lobe has been thought to be important in the recognition of faces (prosopagnosia) (Luria, 1973). Also, the difficulties in combining elements to form a conceptually meaningful whole or the spatially faithful drawing of geometric shapes (constructional apraxia) are associated with lesions in the tertiary area of the right parietal lobe. Lezak (1976) observes that constructional apraxia is the most commonly seen apraxia associated with the right parietal lobe. Moreover, the tertiary area of the right parietal area subserves functions of determining shape and directionality of lines (Golden, 1978). In addition, certain types of mathematical operations are vulnerable to disruption in cases of an injury to the tertiary area of the right parietal lobe (Golden, 1978). For instance, multiplication problems may be difficult or impossible to perform. Lezak (1976) observed that this problem relates to the inability to manipulate numbers in space during written calculations. Oral arithmetic problems may be spared.

Two final difficulties often associated with lesions in the tertiary region of the right parietal lobe are dressing apraxia and neglect of the left side of the body. Apraxia for dressing refers to those situations in which the patient encounters difficulty putting on his or her garments. The root cause for this apraxia is thought to be disturbed spatial orientation. The patient is unable to successfully organize the complex body movements necessary to dress.

The phenomenon of inattention arising from lesions of the right parietal lobe is a perplexing conundrum. Golden (1978) has aptly summarized what is presently known concerning the character of this disorder:

> Inattention may involve the neglect of the left side of a person's body and of all objects or parts of objects within the left visual field. Such patients may only copy the right side of a figure or read the right half of a sentence. They may deny the left side of their body, saying it belongs to someone else, or express hatred for an impaired left limb. The patient may have trouble dressing, because the left side of the body is not taken into account. There may be denial of any injury; the patient states that there is no reason to be hospitalized or helped. (p. 29)

It is noteworthy that mild forms of this disorder can consist of such subtle instances as failure to use the left hand spontaneously or awkwardness on the left side of the body (Lezak, 1976). In more extreme cases there is a marked denial of left-sided disabilities (anosognosia); this problem can constitute a major obstacle to any sort of retraining effort.

Occipital Lobes — Vision

The occiptal lobes subserve visual functions. The primary visual projection region of both occipital lobes is Brodmann's area 17 at the most posterior portion of the cerebral hemispheres. Each visual field is controlled by the opposite occipital lobe, following the principle of contralateral control.

The eyes are each divided into two visual fields. To appreciate this organization, imagine an individual staring at the *Mona Lisa*. This person will not move his eyes but will look directly at the painting. The visual image of the left side of the *Mona Lisa* is projected to the individual right side of each of the observer's eyes and the visual image of the right side of the *Mona Lisa* is going into the left side of each eye. This particular organizational feature has straightforward evolutionary advantages. For example, if one eye is blinded, the individual is still able to appreciate both sides of the picture. Later on when information is transferred from the eyes to the visual cortex, there is a cross-over of visual stimuli so that information from the left visual field all goes to the right hemisphere's visual cortex and information from the right visual field all goes to the left hemisphere's visual cortex. As can be seen in Figure 3.8, this cross-over takes place at the optic chiasma. Also, in Figure 3.8, the particular form of visual field disruption particular to a lesion at the optic chiasma is displayed. This is of the utmost importance to the clinical neuropsychologist since it serves as a pathognomonic sign of a tumor or some other serious disorder.

It is important to understand the terminology used to describe visual field deficits. "Hemianopsia" refers to the loss of visual function in one-half of the visual field. A "homomymous hemianopsia" means both eyes have lost one-half of the visual field. Quadrantanopsia refers to the loss of vision in one-fourth of the visual field. Scotomata are blind spots in the visual fields. Some varieties of scotomata are due to lesions.

After leaving the optic chiasma, most visuosensory stimuli enter the lateral geniculate body, while the rest go to the superior colliculi of the midbrain tectum (Gazzaniga, Steen, & Volpe, 1979). The lateral geniculate nucleus of the thalamus is primarily a sensory relay station for neural signals from the retinal ganglionic cells to the cortex (Hubel & Wiesel, 1961). In contrast, the superior colliculi play a more differentiated role. In nonmammals, for instance, the superior collicus is the major visual processing center. In mammals, however, its function appears to be one of directing the eyes (Bizzi, 1971). The retinal–cortical system tells what is being seen, while the collicular system tells where to look (Gazzaniga, Teren, & Volpe, 1979).

After leaving the lateral geniculate body, visuosensory information arrives at the primary area of the visual cortex. This region surrounds the calcarine fissure at the most posterior section of the cerebral cortex. Lesions in this area may produce any of the variety of visual field deficits already discovered.

The secondary areas of both occipital lobes are Brodmann's areas 18 and 19. Some appreciation of the differences between areas 17, 18,

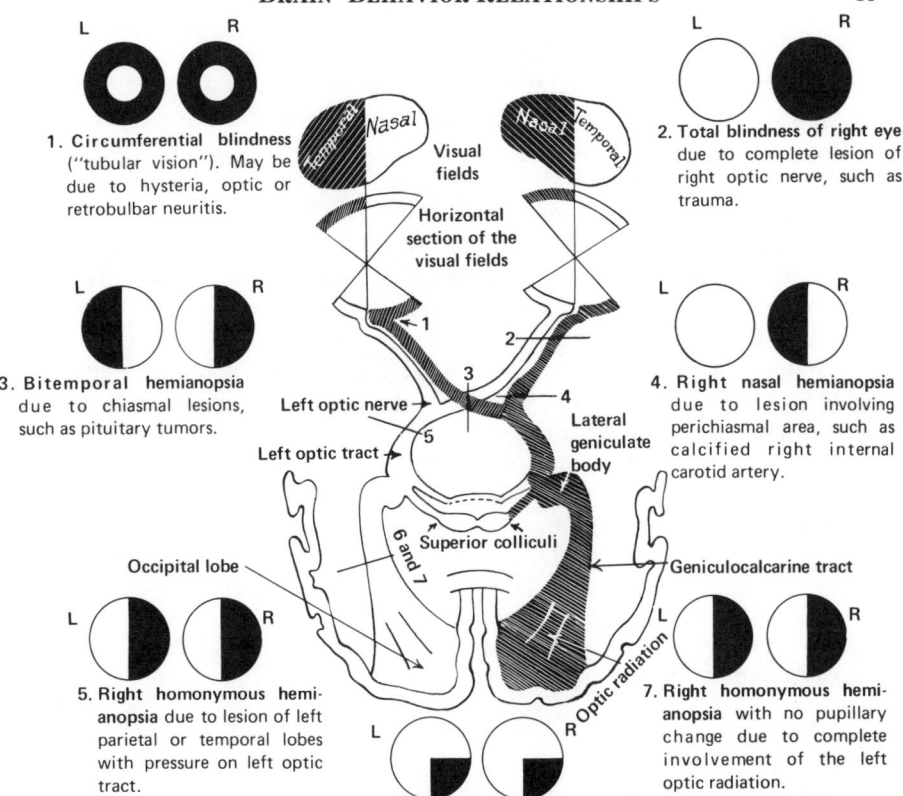

1. **Circumferential blindness** ("tubular vision"). May be due to hysteria, optic or retrobulbar neuritis.

2. **Total blindness of right eye** due to complete lesion of right optic nerve, such as trauma.

3. **Bitemporal hemianopsia** due to chiasmal lesions, such as pituitary tumors.

4. **Right nasal hemianopsia** due to lesion involving perichiasmal area, such as calcified right internal carotid artery.

5. **Right homonymous hemianopsia** due to lesion of left parietal or temporal lobes with pressure on left optic tract.

7. **Right homonymous hemianopsia** with no pupillary change due to complete involvement of the left optic radiation.

6. **Right homonymous inferior quadrantanopsia** due to partial involvement of optic radiations (upper portion of left optic radiation in this case).

Figure 3.8. Visual field defects associated with lesions of the visual system. From Chusid, J.G. *Correlative Neuroanatomy and Functional Neurology.* Los Altos, Calif.: Lange, 1976.

and 19 can be gleaned from realizing that area 17 contains simple cortical cells, area 18 contains complex cortical cells, and area 19 contains hypercomplex cortical cells (Gazzaniga, Steen, & Volpe, 1979). The secondary areas of the occipital lobes integrate and coordinate the visual stimuli sent from the retina to the primary visual areas (Golden, 1978). Lesions that only involve the secondary areas and not the primary area usually do not cause an obvious loss of visual acuity (Luria, 1966).

Left Occipital Lobes

In addition to a general inability to integrate visual sensory stimuli into a meaningful Gestalt (i.e., an associative visual agnosia), another type of agnosia exists in which the patient displays an inability to adequately perceive two objects at the same time. This second type of visual agnosia, referred to as simultaneous agnosia, makes the comprehension of more than a single aspect of an object or form quite difficult. Luria (1966) postulates that difficulties in visual scanning are the cause of this difficulty. An interesting test for optic disturbances suggested by Luria involves drawing unnecessary lines across an outline drawing of an object or a word. These crossed out figures or verbal stimuli will pose difficulties for patients with lesions in the secondary areas of the left occipital lobe.

Lesions in the left secondary area of the occipital lobe impair verbal and numerical stimuli perception. For example, the inability to recognize and identify the symbolic significance of individual letters (visual letter agnosia) or numbers (visual number agnosia) are usually attributed to this region (Golden, 1978). This sort of visual perception problem obviously contributes to difficulty with reading, writing, and arithmetic. Lezak (1976) observed that:

> With lesions confined to the occipital lobe, the reading problem stems from deficits of visual recognition, organization, and scanning rather than from defective comprehension, which usually occurs only with parietal damage. Writing deficits associated with occipital lobe lesions may result from inability to recall the visual image of the required symbol or the sequence of the discrete symbols that make up a number or word, or from faulty scanning. (p. 53)

Right Occipital Lobe

Distortions in the visual perception of nonverbal form appear to be the general characteristic of lesions of the secondary areas of the right occipital lobe. Relative to left occipital lobe impairment, right occipital lobe damage is more likely to involve disturbed abilities in the recognition and differentiation of forms through the visual modality (visual form agnosia) (Lezak, 1976). Other deficits associated with lesions in the secondary areas of the right occipital areas include difficulties in face recognition and failure to comprehend complex unfamiliar visual patterns (Golden, 1978). Also, impairment of the ability to differentiate color hues, as opposed to verbal labeling of colors, has been associated with lesions of the right occipital lobe (Scotti & Spinnler, 1970).

Often visual inattention, such as unilateral spatial neglect, is thought to be a result of a lesion in the secondary area of the right occipital lobe. A more appropriate assessment would suggest that this sort of difficulty most typically occurs in those cases where there is right parietal lobe damage at the same time as right occipital damage (Lezak, 1976). The deficit is more properly associated with tertiary impairment of the area of overlap between the parietal and occipital areas.

CONCLUDING COMMENTS

It is important to realize that in actual practice, the cerebral cortex operates in a dynamic system and cannot be divided up quite as neatly as we have suggested. As observed by Golden (1978): "Although each part of the brain plays a unique role in each behavioral configuration, no part can operate effectively without the other" (p. 44).

Every day tasks such as driving, writing letters, and walking to a corner drug store all require multiple sensory inputs of optic, acoustic, and tactile/kinesthetic nature along with precise fine and gross motor activity and prompt self-evaluation of one's performance. Clearly, cerebral integration of function is more the rule than the exception.

Second, one should be quite circumspect about drawing conclusions with regard to the locus of a focal brain lesion on the basis of a single sign of brain impairment. At one time, precise localization of specific disturbances of cognitive function was a popular academic past time.

> Variation in the size, position, and nature of the lesion and variations in cortical organization make it impossible to infer the location of a lesion from behavior alone with a high degree of certainty.... However, this uncertain relation does not negate the dominant tendencies to regularity in the functional organization of brain tissue. Knowledge of the regularity with which brain–behavior correlations occur enables the clinician to determine whether a patient's behavioral symptoms make anatomical sense. (Lezak, 1976, pp. 67–68)

It is important that one does not overinterpret neuropsychological data. In a clinical sense, brain–behavior relationships, when applied at the level of the individual patient, have a disturbing tendency to vary. The clinical neuropsychologist, either tyro or expert, should never lose sight of the vagaries of individual differences. The ones that exist at a neurological level are every bit as real as those found in the domains of personality or intelligence.

SUGGESTIONS FOR FURTHER READING

Chusid, J.G. *Correlative neuroanatomy of functional neurology.* Los Altos, Ca.: Lange, 1976.

Gazzaniga, M.S., Steen, D., & Volpe, B.T. *Functional neuroscience.* New York: Harper & Row, 1979.

Kolb, B. & Whishaw, I.Q. *Fundamentals of human neuropsychology.* San Francisco: Will Freeman, 1980.

Lezak, M.D. *Neuropsychological assessment.* New York: Oxford, 1976.

Luria, A.R. *Higher cortical functions in man.* New York: Basic, 1977.

Pincus, J.H. & Tucker, G.J. *Behavioral neurology* (2nd Ed.). New York: Oxford, 1978.

Watson, C. *Basic human neuroanatomy* (2nd Ed.). Boston: Little, Brown & Co., 1977.

4

MAJOR NEUROPATHOLOGICAL CONDITIONS

This chapter discusses two general topics. First, principles of neurodiagnosis are elucidated. Second, major central nervous system disorders are described. It should be clearly understood that this treatment of selected portions of clinical neurology is at the most rudimentary level. The sole aim is that of providing a preliminary framework for neophyte neuropsychologists.

INTRODUCTION TO NEURODIAGNOSTIC PROCEDURES

It is important to realize that all neurodiagnostic measures provide some information while not one is totally accurate. Some neuropsychological research has suggested that each neurological test used by itself has serious diagnostic limitations when applied to the full range of possible central nervous system disorders (Filskov & Goldstein, 1974) since each neurological test has a varying degree of diagnostic validity depending on the specific sort of cerebral dysfunction under study. For example, some tests are excellent in identifying tumors but might fail to correctly evaluate the effects of mild trauma to the central nervous system.

The usual problem is one of insufficient diagnostic power and the false-negative diagnosis. Specifically, the neurological test will produce results indicating normalcy when in fact brain damage has occurred. Usually, if a neurological test indicates cerebral dysfunction, one can be very confident of this result.

Neurological tests may be grouped under four headings: (1) the physical neurologic examination; (2) electroencephalography; (3) cerebrospinal fluid examination; and (4) radiologic examination.

This list is quite arbitrary and the inclusion of other procedures such as the examination of cerebrospinal fluid or ophthalmologic tests could be justified. Still, on the basis of frequency of use, the categories listed above include the most often utilized procedures in neurodiagnoses.

PHYSICAL NEUROLOGICAL EXAM

The physical neurological examination includes three major sections: (1) a complete history of the presenting and associated complaints, (2) a general physical examination, and (3) a specialized neurologic examination. As in any other medical specialty, basic data concerning nature, onset, and course of the patient's symptoms are gathered, along with standard medical, personal, family, social, and occupational information. Chusid (1976) points out that detailed information is particularly useful with regard to such complaints as headache, seizures, pain, and visual disturbances.

Next, a physical examination is generally performed. This would typically include study of the circulatory, respiratory, genitourinary, gastrointestinal, and skeletal systems.

After the general physical examination, particular attention is devoted to the central nervous system. However, the neurologic examination is a clinical investigation and not a standardized procedure. Thus, there is considerable variance among neurologists as to the completeness with which each component is assessed. Also, the accuracy of the procedure may to a large degree be a reflection of the skill and acumen of the individual neurologist administering the exam. The neurologic exam is quite adequate for gross disorders but may fail to detect very subtle problems (Golden, 1978). The typical neurological examination would include the cranial nerves, reflexes, sensory–motor functioning, and mental status.

Cranial Nerves

Classically, each of the 12 cranial nerves (listed in Chapter 3) are assessed during the neurologic exam. Methods for the clinical assessment of the cranial nerves are provided in standard textbooks of neurology.

Reflexes

Chusid (1976) observed that "reflexes are inborn stimulus–response mechanisms. The instinctive behavior of lower animals is governed largely by reflexes: in man, behavior is more a matter of conditioning, and reflexes are subordinated as basic defense mechanisms. The reflexes are, however, extremely important in the diagnosis and localization of neurologic lesions" (p. 206). Reflexes that are routinely tested include deep reflexes such as the biceps, triceps; knee, and ankle, as well as superficial reflexes such as the abdominal, cremasteric, planter, and clonus. Extreme brain damage may produce pathologic reflexes. Usually these reflect suppressed cerebral inhibitions. The most well known of these is the Babinski sign, which is produced by stroking the plantar surface of the foot. The behavior sign is the extension of the large toe with fanning of the small toes. In the neurologic examination, the presence or absence of certain reflexes can serve as a reliable guide to the anatomic level of a lesion.

Sensory–Motor Functioning

Various types of sensory modalities are tested in the neurologic examination. These may include pain (pin prick and deep pain), temperature (hot and cold), touch, vibration, position sense, two-point discrimination, double simultaneous stimulation, and the capacity to recognize objects by touch without the aid of vision.

Motor examination includes a number of tests of coordination, gait, equilibrium, and strength. Assessment may include walking, standing with the eyes closed and the feet together (Romberg Test), finger to finger and finger to nose tests, heel to toe walking, and rapid alternating motor movements. Physical strength is assessed by testing resistance to muscle contraction and extension. Involuntary motor movements such as tremors, chorea, and tics are reliable diagnostic clues as are muscle tone alterations that may produce cogwheel rigidity, spasticity, spasms, and hypotonia.

Mental Status

As noted by Chusid (1976):

Mental changes are frequently encountered in clinical neurology, and an understanding of them is helpful for diagnosis and treatment. Mental deterioration, confusion, excitement, mania, lethargy, apathy, anxiety, depression, neurotic behavior, psychotic reactions, personality disturbances, and character disorders may be associated with neurologic disease. The type of mental disturbance is not specific to any given neurologic disorder, although impaired intellectual functioning is very common in cerebral disease. The insidious onset of certain neurologic disorders (e.g., brain tumor, multiple sclerosis, paralysis agitans), with remissions and exacerbations, frequently results in the faulty diagnosis of psychogenic illness. (p. 421)

Given the importance of an accurate assessment of mental abilities for clinical neurology, it is distressing to note that the usual form of mental status exam administered is inadequate for purposes of cognitive evaluation. For example, it is possible to find physicians who would suggest that a mental status examination might be so brief as to include only evaluation of state of consciousness, orientation to time, place, and person, and memory and counting tasks. More typically, mental status exams include observations of general behavior, mood, affect, and thought processes, as well as brief assessments of attention and concentration, sensorium, memory, abstraction, judgment, and insight. In special instances of extremely complete examination, informal assessments of general information, vocabulary, language competence, and arithmetic ability may be conducted. Unfortunately, the unstandardized nature of even this elaborated mental status examination limits its diagnostic power.

It has been suggested that the reason clinical psychology was able to gain recognition as an important part of modern mental health services was because of the poor validity and reliability of judgment based on the psychiatric mental status examination. It should be remembered that the test perhaps most closely associated with traditional clinical psychology, the Wechsler Adult Intelligence Scale (WAIS), was essentially an attempt to develop a standardized mental status examination that provides valid and reliable measures of individual mental abilities.

ELECTROENCEPHALOGRAPHY

Electroencephalography is the measurement of the electrical activity of the brain. Essentially, fluctuations in brain electrical activity are recorded by electrodes attached to the scalp. The potentials of the brain are recorded on paper in a record called an electroencephalogram (EEG). The potentials are amplified and the fluctuations in voltage that appear on the EEG have a fairly rhythmic character. The wavelike patterns that are produced will vary with the brain region being recorded as well as the age and state of alertness of the patient.

As a general rule, it is possible to predict what sort of brain wave pattern an individual will produce in the absence of cerebral dysfunction. Variations from the expected patterns can constitute a basis for postulating impaired brain functioning. As noted with Lewinsohn (1973), the major pathologic changes include waves that are too fast, too slow, or too flat, with all of these conditions being either focal or diffuse.

A major limitation of electroencephalography, however, is that normal-appearing records may be obtained in the presence of clear-cut evidence of severe organic brain disease (Chusid, 1976). Also, 15–20% of a normal population produce abnormal EEGs (Mayo Clinic, 1976). Diagnostically, Filskov and Goldstein (1974), in a landmark study, found the EEG to have about 60% overall accuracy. The area where electroencephalography has proven most useful has been the diagnosis of epilepsy.

More recent work in electroencephalography has focused upon evoked potentials, that is, the recording of the brain electrical activity when standardized stimuli are presented. The EEG data are analyzed by a computer that controls for random and systematic error. This procedure allows for the moment to moment monitoring of a patient's cortical activity and presents a method of looking at the changes that result from brain processing of particular types of stimuli. For example, different patterns of hemispheric activation during the solving of mathematical problems of varying difficulty and type can be elicited with relative ease.

CEREBROSPINAL FLUID EXAMINATION

Since normal cerebrospinal fluid (CSF) is clear and without either odor or color, pathological changes in its composition are easily detectable. Also, various chemical tests may be performed. The cerebrospinal fluid is obtained through the procedure known as the lumbar puncture. This involves the drawing of a small quantity of spinal fluid usually from the spaces between either the third and fourth or the fourth and fifth lumbar vertebrae (Lewinsohn, 1973).

RADIOLOGIC EXAMINATION

Roentgenography of the brain comprises three different categories of investigations: (1) plain view X rays of the skull, (2) contrast studies, and (3) computerized axial tomography.

Plain View X Rays of the Skull

This approach involves simple X rays of the skull. For most purposes only a right and left lateral view, a posteroanterior view, and an oblique anteroposterior view will serve adequately (Chusid, 1976).

Contrast Studies

The introduction of a foreign substance into the brain provides the opportunity for superior visualization when X rays are taken of the skull. There are four types of contrast studies: (1) ventriculography, (2) pneumoencephalography, (3) angiography, and (4) brain scanning.

Ventriculography and pneumoencephalography are quite similar. The basic procedure requires replacing the cerebrospinal fluid with air or oxygen. X rays of the skull are then taken and the contrast between the air-filled ventricular and subarachnoid systems allows the neurologist to better discern if there are abnormalities with regard to the size, shape, or position of the ventricles (Lewinsohn, 1973). Ventriculography differs from pneumoencephalography in that a burr hole is made in the skull and a needle is inserted through the cerebral wall into the ventricles, whereas in pneumoencephalography a lumbar puncture is made. Unlike the cerebrospinal fluid examination, pneumoencephalography involves injecting air into the lumbar subarachnoid space. The air rises up the spinal column and enters the ventricles and subarachnoid spaces of the brain. This procedure results in painful headaches that may last for as long as 2 days. The pneumoencephalogram has been reported to be 80% effective in the diagnosis of space occupying lesions and degenerative diseases (Filskov & Goldstein, 1974).

In contrast, the focus of angiography is on the cerebrovascular system. In this procedure, a radioopaque substance is introduced into an extracranial artery. After the substance has been transported through the cerebrovascular system, X rays are taken of the skull. The location and size of cerebral blood vessels may be visualized on X rays since the radioopaque substance will outline the vascular pattern of the brain (Lewinsohn, 1973). Angiography is of value in the diagnosis of intracranial aneurysms, vascular disorders, hematomas, and tumors. Abnormalities in the location and structure of the cerebrovascular system provide a basis for various diagnostic inferences. An important consideration relative to angiography is that it carries risk of both morbidity and mortality. Still, when used to identify cerebrovascular disorders or tumors, an accuracy rate of 85% was found (Filskov & Goldstein, 1974).

The brain scan utilizes technology developed from nuclear medicine studies. The procedure requires that the patient take a radioactive substance either orally or intravenously. Since lesions that cause brain tissue destruction disturb the blood–brain barrier, the radioactive substance is likely to enter the lesion area from the vascular system. In order to ascertain if there has been damage to brain tissue, the head is scanned by a radiation counter. Positive finding of increased focal uptake of the radioactive substance may be obtained with tumors, subdural hematomas, brain abscesses, and cerebral infarcts (Chusid, 1976).

Computerized Axial Tomography

Computerized axial tomography has prompted a revolution in the field of neuropsychology. Alternately described as "computerized tomography" (CT), this neurodiagnostic method was first introduced in 1972 by the European Musical Instruments (EMI) laboratories in England (Wedding & Gudeman, 1980). The CT scan illustrates the promise of computer technology applied to clinical neurologic diagnosis.

The basic CT technique is rather straightforward. While the patient lies still, a mobile X ray device scans various transverse axial slices of the brain. These neuroradiologic data are fed into a computer and the results are displayed in a pictorial manner. These pictures indicate the relative density of various brain structures. As the density of space occupying mass lesions will differ considerably from that of normal brain tissue, these pictures provide a graphic view of neuropathology. Due to the insensitivity of earlier methods of recording radiographic images, much information about soft tissues was previously lost. The CT scan uses computer technology to save these important neurodiagnostic data.

A major consideration with all neurodiagnostic tests is the degree of discomfort or risk to the individual patient associated with the procedure. Fortunately, the CT scan is a noninvasive diagnostic method that carries virtually no risk of bodily harm to the patient, especially when contrast material is not used. Also, the degree of discomfort is minimal since the only requirement for administration is that the patient be able to remain still (Wedding & Gudeman, 1980). Indeed, the CT scan examination can be conducted on an outpatient basis or with a comatose patient.

A fairly extensive body of research literature has accumulated on the diagnostic ability of the CT scan. Gawler, Bull, DuBoulay, and Marshall (1975) have presented data suggesting that the CT scan has a hit rate of 92% in the correct diagnosis of brain tumors. Similarly, Dublin, French, and Rennick (1977) found similarly encouraging results in the discernment of head trauma cases. Huckman, Fox, and Ramsey (1977) found high accuracy rates for the prediction of head trauma and reported that the CT scan is useful in detecting degenerative disease. Although accuracy rates of 80% or better have been reported in the literature (Tsushima & Wedding, 1979), it would be premature to conclude that the CT scan is a diagnostic panacea and there are some clear limitations with CT scans. Wedding and Gudeman (1980) have observed that problem diagnoses for the CT scan include recent cerebral infarctions, subcortical lesions, early trauma, and multiple sclerosis. Similarly, Jacobs, Kinkel, and Haffner (1976) found that false negatives resulted from all cases of small metastasis and approximately half of all brain stem infarctions. An additional concern is the fairly high cost of the CT scan at present.

Despite these considerations, the promise of CT technology is clearly evident. There is an apparent consensus of opinion among contemporary works in neuropsychology that CT scanning is beginning to replace more traditional neurodiagnostic tests such as pneuroencephalography, cerebral angiography, and radionuclide brain scanning (Tsushima & Wedding, 1979; Walsh, 1978). Moreover, given the rate of technological progress in computer technology, it would be naive to expect that the present-day methods of CT scanning represent the ultimate development of this technique. In fact, positron emission transaxial tomography (PETT scanning) promises to offer even more information about neurological function. This unique procedure requires injection of radioactively tagged glucose and allows observation of the decay of these isotopes over time. Thus, both structural and functional information is available simultaneously. Although expensive and not widely available at the current time, the technique holds great promise.

Many other innovations in computerized tomography appear to be quite promising in terms of increased neurodiagnostic power. While it would be beyond the scope of this book to include an exhaustive list of new developments in this field, a few examples might be mentioned. Clearly, the use of contrast mediums allows increased delineation of neural structures. In addition, the technological creation of three-dimensional scanners is a significant forward step (Wedding & Gudeman, 1980). There is also evidence to suggest that the use of the actual numerical information contained in the computer in computerized tomography may be useful in cases of differential diagnosis (Neeser, Gebhardt, & Levine, 1980). Clearly, it is difficult to predict the ultimate outer boundaries of neurodiagnostic accuracy of computerized tomography.

INTRODUCTION TO NEUROPATHOLOGY

Intimate knowledge of the onset, course, and symptoms of neurological disorders is of the utmost importance for a practicing clinical neuropsychologist. It is possible to infer brain damage as a binary decision (i.e., brain-damaged or normal); however, without an understanding of the major conditions resulting in intracranial pathology, this, in itself, is a very meager contribution.

A more liberal conceptualization of clinical neuropsychology allows that major statements concerning diagnosis, prognosis, and rehabilitation planning can be generated from thoughtful inspection of a body of neuropsychological data. In order to harvest this rich crop, however, it is necessary to be acutely aware of the many complex patterns that various neurological disorders may produce on a battery of neuropsychological tests. As noted by Golden (1978), a proper diagnosis requires a knowledge of neuropathological processes, an awareness of their possible courses, and an understanding of secondary problems that may arise. The advantage of a blend of psychometric acumen and neurological wisdom is straightforward. One is able to exclude various possibilities when viewing a set of neuropsychological data, and thus optimize diagnostic accuracy. Moreover, as the course of various neuropathological processes is known, it becomes possible to insightfully generate meaningful predictions by contrasting the current state of neuropsychological functioning with normal expectations for a particular individual. In addition, information concerning the various cognitive emotional and behavioral correlates of a specific neurological disorder may aid in devising a realistic rehabilitation program. Here, an important clinical concern is the formulation of achievable goals. As an illustration, a clinical neuropsychological case seen by the senior author might be briefly mentioned. Essentially, the question of interest was the determination of the effects of a drug toxicity (lithium) on an older man who was experiencing difficulty walking. After administration of an extensive battery of neuropsychological tests and perusal of the test results, it was clear that the pattern of strengths and weaknesses in cognitive, language, intellectual, sensory–perceptual, psychomotor, and gross motor abilities was more consistent with what would have been expected from a small cerebrovascular accident (CVA) than with what is usually seen with drug toxicity. Based on this inference, careful questioning revealed that the patients had suffered small strokes just before the occasions of drug toxicity. This bit of data enabled the author to postulate an infarction of the left anterior cerebral artery as the reason for the ambulation difficulties and to accurately predict the course of recovery. Without a working knowledge of neurological correlates of the clinical neuropsychological test results, this would have been impossible. Thus, it becomes quite clear that an awareness of the neurological context within which hypotheses must be generated is of the utmost importance for the clinical neuropsychologist.

The various causes of brain impairment may be divided into two categories. The first can be characterized as those that most often produce maximal neuropsychological deficit in a single cerebral hemisphere. The second type is composed of those neurological disorders that most often produce some impairment of both cerebral hemispheres. It should be explicitly stated that this dichotomization is made on the basis of probability only and that there are multiple exceptions.

Neuropathological conditions that typically produce lateralizing signs are intracranial neoplasms, cerebral vascular disorders, and head injuries. These categories may be further differentiated. Intracranial neoplasms include infiltrative tumors (most typically, gliomas) and noninfiltrative tumors (most typically, meningiomas). Neurological disorders that most often cause impairment to both cerebral hemispheres include, among others, degenerative and demyelineating diseases, intoxications, and schizophrenia.

LATERALIZED NEUROPATHOLOGY

Cerebrovascular Accidents

A cerebrovascular accident (CVA) is a disorder that occurs when there is a disruption to the brain's blood supply. Usually, either blood vessels are damaged or the blood supply is interrupted. As the brain cells in the cerebral cortex are highly dependent on a constant supply of oxygen for their survival and the cerebrovascular system is the oxygen transportation method, damage to blood vessels or an interruption of the blood supply will result in the death of brain cells in the cerebral cortex. As in all neurological disorders, the specific effects are dependent on a number of factors including location, type, and extent of the CVA.

Diverse psychological and behavioral effects follow disruption of the blood flow to particular arteries. The middle cerebral and internal carotid arteries are so similar that damage or disruption of one is indistinguishable from the other. The most typical deficits following CVAs are aphasic disorders when the left hemisphere is involved and visuoconstructive dyspraxias when the right hemisphere is involved. Also, there will usually be sensory–motor difficulties contralateral to the hemisphere involved. Golden (1978) mentions that since one branch of the internal carotid artery transports blood to the eyes, sometimes blindness in one eye is a clue to the level of vascular vessel damage or disruption. Middle cerebral artery disorders are not usually associated with unilateral blindness. It might also be mentioned that relative to base rate considerations, CVAs occur most commonly in the middle cerebral artery (Boll, 1978).

By way of contrast, damage to or disruption of the blood supply of the anterior cerebral artery has different psychological and behavioral effects. The typical signs of an anterior cerebral artery stroke include contralateral paralysis of the leg but not the rest of the body, language disorder, and mental symptoms characteristic of prefontal disorders (Golden, 1978). Interestingly, the relationship of the posterior cerebral artery to the basilar artery is quite similar to that of the middle cerebral artery and the internal carotid artery. Simply stated, should the posterior communicating artery be absent, then the psychological and behavioral effects of the posterior cerebral artery are very difficult to separate from those resulting from impairment of the basilar artery. Symptoms may include visual field deficits, visual agnosia, and possible sensory difficulties (Golden, 1978).

There are two types of CVAs: situations in which the blood supply to the brain is inadequate and situations in which blood vessels are damaged. An inadequate blood supply to the brain may be due to a number of causes. One of the most common is arteriosclerosis. Fat deposits accumulate in the blood vessels as an individual gets older. These fat deposits cause the blood vessels to become smaller and consequently less blood is delivered to brain cells. This condition may progress to the point where a number of brain cells die due to lack of oxygen. A thrombus occurs when a blood vessel is closed due to a "plug" that forms at a particular location.

Another way the blood supply to the brain is interrupted is through abrupt blockage of a blood vessel. This condition is called an embolism. A bit of fatty tissue, tumor, clotted blood, or other material is carried by the blood to a smaller portion of the cerebrovascular system where the substance is lodged and the blood supply is disrupted. Both thrombi and emboli are common causes of occlusion of blood vessels (Boll, 1978).

The other sort of cerebrovascular disorders to be described refers to damage to blood vessels. Aneurysms are dilations in the blood vessel wall. Basically, weak areas of an artery allow blood to bulge and create a space-occupying disorder. Usually, this is thought to be due to congenital weakness in the blood vessel. The most common areas of involvement are the basilar surface of the brain such as the Circle of Willis, with the internal carotid and middle cerebral artery as the specific site of impairment in approximately half the cases. Golden (1978) notes that aneurysms may present as highly focal signs on neuropsychological testing. For example, aneurysms prior to bursting typically show impairment indices of .4 to .6 on the Halstead–Reitan Neuropsychological Test Battery for adults. This level of impairment suggests only mild decrements in adaptive ability. When the balloon bursts, however, there is a pattern of severe neuropsychological impairment.

Bursting of an aneurysm or disruption of a blood vessel due to the twin effects of hypertension and arteriosclerosis results in a hemorrhage. Essentially, the blood vessel is damaged and blood is spilled into cerebral tissue. These are extremely serious disorders and produce massive lateralized patterns of deficit. Also, prognosis for the recovery of adaptive function varies invariably with the level of deficit. On neuropsychological testing, the classic pattern is one of severe impairment. For example, on the Halstead–Reitan Neuropsychological Test Battery, impairment indices of 1.0, indicating extreme brain damage, are not uncommon. Most often, ruptures of blood vessels occur in older individuals in whom the effects of arteriosclerosis have contributed to the weakening of arterial walls. In cases where arteriosclerosis has contributed to the hemorrhage, the lateralized deficits are superimposed on a picture of diffuse deterioration throughout the brain.

Brain Tumors

A classic distinction between types of brain tumors separates those that arise from within the brain from those that develop in the meninges, the tissues that cover the brain. The tumors within the brain take over and destroy brain tissue, whereas those that develop in the meninges cause deficits by compressing brain tissue. Golden (1978) terms the first type "infiltrative tumors" and the second type, "non-infiltrative tumors." There are a number of different characteristics of these two types with respect to etiology, course, symptoms, prognosis, and patterns of neuropsychological test results.

Inspection of data with regard to the frequency of major types of brain tumors may serve to clarify these relationships. As reported by Chusid (1976), 50% of all brain tumors are gliomas. These are the most common of the infiltrative tumors (Golden, 1978). Of the gliomas, 50% are glioblastoma multiforms, an extremely malignant growth that characteristically originates from the white matter of the cerebral hemispheres. These are the most common primary tumors of the brain, particularly in the fifth and sixth decade of life. These tumors are most frequently found in the frontal, temporal, and parietal lobes. By contrast, meningiomas, which are noninfiltrative tumors, account for approximately 20% of all brain tumors (Chusid, 1976). They are slow growing, benign neoplasms of adulthood and are most often seen after age 40. Meningiomas usually arise from the archnoid layer of the meninges and produce their deleterious effects by compressing brain tissue. Most commonly, meningiomas arise from the parasagittal region, frontoparietal convexity, sphenoid ridge, and cribriform plate. Gliomas and meningiomas account for approximately 70% of all brain tumors; about 25% of all brain tumors are glioblastoma multiforms.

The metastatic tumor is a growth that is usually secondary to carcinoma. Tumors can be metastasized to the brain from carcinomas in the lung, breast, gastrointestinal tract, and kidneys as well as other areas. It is of particular note that metastatic tumors account for 40% of all tumors in the elderly (Earle, 1955).

Within the category of gliomas there are also astrocytomas, ependymomas, medulloblastomas, and oligodendrogliomas, as well as mixed tumors. In addition to meningiomas and metastatic tumors, in considering brain tumors exclusive of gliomas, Chusid (1976) lists nerve sheath tumors, congenital tumors, and miscellaneous tumors.

Neuropsychologically, gliomas produce severe destruction of brain tissue in a focal area. There are typically very marked disparities between the two sides of the body that go far beyond normal expectations. The disparities are usually consistent over a broad range of motor, sensory–perceptual, and cognitive abilities. In addition, if primary sensory areas are involved, there may be clear suppression of visual, auditory, or tactile modalities. Also, there are general effects caused by increased intracranial pressure. On the Halstead–Reitan Neuropsychological Test Battery (HRNB), for instance, the impairment index is most typically 1.0 (indicating severe impairment) and the tests most sensitive to generalized cerebral dysfunction, such as the Categories Test, are very poorly performed or else cannot be done at all. To a certain degree, the general effects are due to the fast growing nature of gliomas. A clinical point of interest is that while the glioblastoma multiform grows quite rapidly and the history of the patient complaint may be very brief, other tumors often grow at a slower pace. For example, Golden (1978) suggests that astrocytomas, a type of glioma that arises from glia cells known as astrocytes, vary in growth rate from very slow to very rapid. One diagnostic clue suggesting an astrocytoma would be a longer history of patient complaints.

The major diagnostic conundrum with the neuropsychological assessment of a patient with a suspected glioma, however, usually relates to cerebrovascular disorders. It is quite difficult to distinguish a glioma situated along the motor strip from a hemorrhage of the middle cerebral artery (Golden, 1979). Both conditions produce a strongly lateralized and very severe neuropsychological impairment. Clinical lore suggests that the best way to differentiate between these two conditions is to examine measures of motor performance. In vascular disorders, typically motor ability is severely impaired. In contrast, brain tumors produce mild to moderate impairment in motor functions (Russell, Neuringer, & Goldstein, 1970).

Somewhat different effects are seen with meningiomas. Golden (1978) observed that meningiomas characteristically produce less severe deficits in behavior than gliomas. He suggests that Halstead Impairment indices of .4 to .8 are the norm. Here too, clinical lore suggests that the lack of verbal–performance differences on the Wechsler Adult Intelligence Scale in the presence of moderate to severe adaptive ability impairment suggests the presence of a meningioma. In summary, these deficits result more from compression than from intrinsic destructive process.

Metastatic tumors are even more difficult to discern from neuropsychological test results. In fact, the inclusion of metastatic tumors in a section devoted to lateralized brain damage is questionable. While a single metastatic tumor may produce effects quite similar to those of gliomas, it is important to remember that metastatic tumors frequently multiply and, as they are secondary to primary tumors in other parts of the body, may involve multiple areas of the body and brain. When this happens, neuropsychological testing is likely to reveal multiple focal sites of specific impairment. As noted by Golden (1978), a pattern of alternate good and bad areas may result, while the most sensitive tests may be uniformly bad. Usually, metastatic tumors are devilishly difficult to diagnose from neuropsychological testing since, in the later stages of the condition, a pattern of marked diffuse impairment of adaptive ability results.

Another disorder that presents assessment difficulties for the clinical neuropsychologist is the subtentorial tumor. Boll (1978) observed that supratentorial tumors such as gliomas and meningiomas almost invariably produce marked cognitive impairment. By way of contrast, subtentorial tumors usually present primary signs of movement disorder with some secondary indications of fairly mild, later-occurring, cognitive difficulties. Most typically, motor performance problems such as ataxia, dysdiadochokinesia (inability to perform alternating movements in a smooth manner with any speed) and speech difficulties are noted. Interestingly, one research study (Horton & Matthews, 1972) found that patients with subtentorial lesions evidenced marked impairment on simple and complex motor tasks while retaining average intellectual ability and only mildly impaired cognitive skills. In contrast, severe deficits were found on inspection of neuropsychological data for a group of patients with supratentorial lesions. The patients with supratentorial lesions did worse on cognitive measures but better on motor tasks than patients with subtentorial lesions. Charles Matthews has developed a comprehensive battery for the assessment of neuropathological conditions that impair motor performance.

Prognosis for recovery varies widely across the various tumor types. The most optimistic prognosis is for the patient with a meningioma. Neurosurgery usually results in an excellent recovery with minimal after effects. Less positive results occur in cases of gliomas or metastatic tumors. Patients with malignant invasive brain tumors are much more likely to show residual ability deficits assuming the infiltrative tumor fails to redevelop. Still, given modern neurosurgical techniques, radiation therapy, chemotherapy, and aggressive cancer research programs, there is always room for hope. An organization of relatives of individuals with brain tumors has recently been formed to fund research and to provide information about the management of brain tumor patients.

Head Trauma

Head traumas are classified as open or closed head injuries. Closed head injuries are cases where the brain is traumatized but the skull is not penetrated. In open head injuries, there is actual invasion of the cranium and direct destruction of brain tissue. As noted by Golden (1978), the actual neuropsychological effects of head injury are quite variable and, to a degree, depend on the quality and quantity of the force producing the trauma, the premorbid adaptive ability of the person sustaining the head injury, and the actual physical circumstances of the blow. The precise relationship of the victim's head relative to the injuring object or objects is quite important in determining the psychological and behavioral sequelae of brain trauma.

Closed head injuries are generally considered to fall into three broad groups: concussion, contusion, and hematoma.   concussion

A concussion is a relatively mild closed head injury where there is often no major structural damage. However, these patients frequently lose consciousness. Common examples include incidents in football games where one of the participants has his "bell rung" or boxing matches in which a fighter is knocked unconscious for a brief time and will be dazed on awakening. Concussions are typically associated with confusion, disorientation, memory difficulties after regaining consciousness, and short-term loss of consciousness, which may be due to brain stem reticular formation injury (Walsh, 1978).

Fairly closely related to concussion is the second form of closed   contusion head injury, contusion. The basic distinction between the two is that in contusion, the brain undergoes more notable structural damage. In actual clinical practice, this differentiation may be difficult to make with any reliability. Indeed, the behavioral symptoms of the two conditions overlap a great deal (Elliott, 1971). With a contusion, the period of unconsciousness is considerably longer than with a concussion and the difficulties with disorientation, memory, and confusion are more pronounced and enduring. As observed by Boll (1978), contusion is characterized by a tearing of the small blood vessels connecting the brain to the meninges and with some disintegration of nerve cells.

The pattern presented by concussions and contusions on neuropsychological testing is similar in configuration but differs in the degree of impairment seen. Paradoxically, closed head injuries may often show considerable damage to the region of the brain opposite to the side of impact. This phenomenon is described as a *contrecoup* injury. What happens in these cases is that the brain receives the impact of the blow on one side of the skull and then rebounds off the other side of the skull. It should be recalled that the brain is capable of moving in relation to the skull. Normally, there are mechanisms to compensate for typical stresses, but a sharp jerk or strong blow will cause the brain to hit the bony inner table of the skull with considerable force and will produce residual effects. This phenomenon is responsible for many of the head injuries that occur in automobile accidents. The abrupt shock of a car accident frequently results in contusions for the driver or passengers in the car. The impact of the victim's head striking the dashboard commonly affects the basal portions of the frontal lobe and poles of the temporal lobes (Courville, 1942). These trauma patients often exhibit the classical frontal lobe signs of inadequate planning skills and deficient self-control.

Neuropsychologically, closed head injuries produce identifiable patterns. The *contrecoup* injuries are quite distinct. There is usually one focal area of deficit with a less focal area of deficit opposite to the first (Golden, 1978). At the same time, major sensory or tactile perceptual losses and marked verbal–performance differences on the Wechsler scales are uncommon (Boll, 1978). The areas most likely to be seriously impaired are the higher cognitive functions (Golden, 1978). As observed by Boll (1978):

> Higher-level problem solving, concept formation, new learning, and mental flexibility tend to be the most impaired and the slowest to recover. Such deficits may be present in persons whose appearance, conversation, and even IQ scores suggest good abilities, and it is this type of mental ability which seems to recover most slowly. (p. 618)

A common problem for clinical neuropsychologists is the patient who has sustained a closed head injury and evidences subtle cognitive impairment, yet wishes to return to work or school. Physicians may be unable to collaborate the nature and degree of adaptive ability deficit due to limitations in their assessment techniques. This situation requires considerable diplomatic and counseling skill on the part of the clinical neuropsychologist, since the consequences of returning to normal vocational and academic pursuits prior to complete recovery of neuropsychological abilities are often anxiety, frustration, stress, and ultimate failure on the part of the patient. The role of the clinical neuropsychologist in correctly describing the actual state of the patient's higher cognitive functions and using this vital information in a therapeutic fashion to prevent unnecessary emotional distress is an important contribution to patient care.

The third type of closed head injury to be considered is the hematoma. Essentially, this is a disorder in which blood vessels are torn as a result of head injury trauma, and pools of blood accumulate. These pools of blood may lie either within or between the meninges. When bleeding collects between the meninges, an extradural hematoma results. This problem is usually a neurosurgical emergency and is not of great relevance for clinical neuropsychologists (Walsh, 1978).

Of more immediate interest is the condition in which the pool of blood collects beneath the dura mater in the subdural space. This pool of blood is then referred to as a subdural hematoma. The onset of this condition may be either acute or chronic. If acute, then medical treatment is usually obtained promptly and the services of a clinical neuropsychologist are not required. When the disorder is chronic, however, the onset may be so slow that it is difficult to correlate the condition with the head injury. This situation is particularly common with older individuals whose vascular system may be impaired by very mild head trauma, such as bumping one's head on a low ceiling. As the subdural hematoma may develop several weeks after the mild head injury, the condition can be mistaken for senile dementia.

From the viewpoint of neuropsychological testing, a subdural hematoma may imitate another condition. As it is a space-occupying mass that has the effect of compressing the brain, a subdural hematoma may appear similar to a meningioma on neuropsychological tests (Golden, 1978). In cases where two subdural hematomas have formed, however, it is a great deal more likely to be correctly diagnosed, particularly if the aforementioned secondary effects of brain trauma are present. Still, the correct diagnosis of subdural hematoma is to a large degree dependent on the careful examination of a patient's history.

Open head injuries are often referred to as lacerations. Usually *laceration* they involve penetration of the brain by an object. The classic example is a bullet wound inflicted during wartime. Golden (1978) notes that lacerations also can result from severe *contrecoup* injuries.

On neuropsychological testing, lacerations produce a fairly distinct pattern. A precise focal area of deficit, which is quite severe, can usually be identified. The extent and location of the injury will determine the amount of generalized impairment of adaptive ability.

When primary sensory areas are involved, clear suppressions are likely to occur.

Secondary problems produced by head trauma include possible hemorrhage or abscess formation. In addition, with both contusions and lacerations, scars may result and provide a basis for the development of epilepsy (Golden, 1978). The comments averred earlier concerning concussions, contusions, and cognitive deficits also hold for subdural hematomas and lacerations after the acute medical emergency phase has passed.

The neuropsychologist is in the position to make an important contribution because of the particular sensitivity of neuropsychological testing methodology to the presence and type of cognitive and behavioral deficit. This sort of understanding is the first step toward developing plans to insure eventual return to preinjury status with a minimum of distress and disruption.

Klove and Cleeland (1972) found that neuropsychological examination was more effective in predicting recovery from head injury than the traditional measure of duration of unconsciousness. They concluded that, in some cases, the patients with skull fractures may show less neuropsychological impairment than patients with comparable signs on the EEG and physical neurological exam. This may result from the fact that the skull fracture resulted in the reduction of forces that otherwise would have produced additional neuropsychological impairment. Boll (1978), from his extensive clinical experience with head trauma patients, has identified a pattern that relates to the affective status of the patient. Immediately after the head injury, the patient presents a fairly flat emotional picture on an objective personality measure such as the Minnesota Multiphasic Personality Inventory (MMPI). Conversely, a few months later, as the patient's cognitive functions are beginning to recover and there is some realization of the pervasive nature of the adaptive ability deficits he or she will have to face, affective status deteriorates markedly. An MMPI taken at this time will suggest a highly disrupted emotional picture. One explanation for this phenomenon is that as the injured individual regains mentation, there is an increased awareness of his/her neuropsychological status and the emotional reaction is a result of the increased awareness.

NONLATERALIZING NEUROPATHOLOGY

At this point, consideration will be given to those neurological disorders that most often produce some impairment in both cerebral hemispheres. As earlier noted, the dichotomization of neurological disorders into those that most often show maximal impairment in a single cerebral hemisphere and those that are characterized by noticable damage/dysfunction in both cerebral hemispheres is made on the basis of probability only, and there are multiple clinical cases that fail to fit this framework.

Specifically, five neurological conditions are covered: (1) degenerative diseases; (2) infections; (3) toxic disorders; (4) schizophrenia; and (5) Epilepsy.

Degenerative Diseases

Degenerative diseases are neurological disorders of generally unclear etiology in which premature morphological dissolution of nerve tissue takes place with corresponding functional loss. A respected textbook (Chusid, 1976) has identified over 30 separate listings under the heading degenerative diseases of the central nervous system.

The specific degenerative diseases to be discussed here will be: Alzheimer's disease, Pick's disease, Parkinson's disease, and multiple sclerosis.

Alzheimer's Disease

The neurological condition known as Alzheimer's disease entered the scientific literature following its careful description by Alois Alzheimer in the early 1900s. Clinically, the course is well known. Early effects are gradual deterioration of memory, speech, and spatial orientation abilities, followed by disorientation to time and place. In the final stages of this disease, there is complete disruption of intellectual and emotional functioning. Neuropsychological difficulties most often arise between the ages of 50 and 60 but may appear as early as 30 years of age.

Postmortum examinations reveal diffuse atrophy of the brain (Elliott, 1971). Chusid (1976) observes that: "Alzheimer's Disease is characterized by neurofibrillary degenerative changes in the neurons, loss of nerve cells, and argyrophilic plaques in the cerebral cortex and less often, in the basal ganglia" (p. 346).

Unfortunately, there is no known cure for this disease, which generally runs its course in less than 10 years (Kolb, 1977). On neuropsychological testing, the usual profile is one of severe generalized loss. Golden (1978) has observed that the WAIS IQ is frequently less than 60, while the Halstead impairment index is usually 1.0.

Pick's Disease

Pick's disease is sometimes combined with Alzheimer's disease under the heading presenile dementia (Chusid, 1976). Both disorders are characterized by progressive cognitive and speech deterioration.

Pick's disease was first described by Arnold Pick in the late 1800s and may be distinguished from Alzheimer's disease on the basis of the brain lobes involved (Chusid, 1976; Golden, 1978). However, the clinical course of both diseases is quite similar. In Pick's disease, neuropsychological deficits usually occur between the ages of 45 and 60 just as in Alzheimer's. Likewise, Pick's ultimately results in complete intellectual and emotional incapacity. Mutism is somewhat more characteristic of Pick's disease than Alzheimer's and in some very early cases of Pick's disease it may be possible to identify a frontotemporal focus (Golden, 1978). Most commonly, though, it is usually necessary to have a postmortum examination of brain tissue to confidently determine whether a patient had Pick's disease or Alzheimer's disease.

Sadly, as with Alzheimer's disease, there is no known cure for Pick's disease and treatment recommendations are limited to institutional care. Its course, like that of Alzheimer's, usually results in death in less than a decade.

Neuropsychological test profiles are usually indistinguishable from that already outlined for Alzheimer's disease. The only exception to this rule would be the frontotemporal focus, which might be evident in a very early case. Most commonly, however, the picture is one of profound generalized cognitive and affective deterioration.

Parkinson's Disease

James Parkinson's original description was quite accurate. He claimed that this disease was characterized by: "...involuntary tremulous motion, with lessened motor power, in parts not in action and even when supported; with a propensity to bend the trunk forward and to pass from a walking to a running pace, the senses and intellect being unimpaired" (Chusid, 1976).

There is substantial agreement that the symptoms of Parkinson's disease stem from a disturbance of the extrapyramidal system and are related to biochemical metabolism. Extremely low concentrations of dopamine (a neurotransmitter) have been consistently reported when the brains of parkinsonism patients have been submitted to postmortum examination (Chusid, 1976). The exact details of the disordered mechanisms are the subject of current investigations. It is noteworthy that there are seven different forms of Parkinson's disease that have been identified (Golden, 1978).

Parkinson's disease may be precipitated by a number of conditions. Although Parkinson's disease occurs most often after age 50, numerous varieties have been found in younger adults. Chusid (1976) notes: "It [Parkinson's disease] may follow an attack of epidemic encephalitis or may be due to cerebral arteriosclerosis, carbon monoxide, manganese poisoning, trauma to the head, neurosyphillis, or cerebrovascular accidents" (p. 346).

The course of parkinsonism is usually progressive over 20–30 years with significant adaptive ability deficits occurring in 10 years. Golden (1978) suggests that there are five stages of Parkinson's disease. These range from initial symptoms which are mild and unilateral to total disability. Characteristic signs of Parkinson's disease, which become progressively more pronounced, are increasing tremor, muscle rigidity, general movement difficulties, and immobility of facial expression. More specifically, intermittent tremors become worse when the limb is at rest and are frequently of the pill-rolling type. Muscle rigidity can be observed in the "cogwheel" action of limb muscles on passive motion. Also, there is a gait disturbance particular to Parkinson's disease. Essentially, when these patients attempt to walk, they have a tendency to break into a run.

Despite this rather gloomy picture, there are some encouraging developments in the treatment of Parkinson's disease. In stark contrast to the other degenerative disorders, there are established medical treatments for Parkinson's. L-Dopa, among other drugs, has been shown to have a therapeutic effect on the symptoms of tremor, rigidity, and muscle weakness associated with Parkinson's disease.

Neuropsychological test profiles obtained from parkinsonian patients have many elements of similarity with those obtained from patients with other degenerative diseases. In those cases where the disease has run its course, there is evidence of extreme loss of adaptive ability. In the earlier stages of parkinsonism, there are a number of characteristic features. One of these is the characteristic tremor which will show up on drawings of various shapes. Another is micrographia, that is, extremely small writing and drawing. In a landmark study, Reitan and Boll (1971) found that while Parkinson's patients had their greatest difficulties on motor-related tasks, they also demonstrated considerable impairment on abstraction-, learning-, and attention-related tasks. When compared with a control group that had been matched for both age and education, the parkinsonian patients had markedly lowered full scale IQs on the Wechsler Scales (106 versus 122). Golden (1978) has noted that while the IQ may be within normal limits, the score on the category test is invariably impaired to a significant degree.

Multiple Sclerosis

As observed by Chusid (1976): "Multiple sclerosis is usually a diffuse, chronic, slowly progressive disorder that has its onset in early adult life and is characterized by irregular, fluctuating periods of exacerbation and remission" (p. 364).

Essentially, multiple sclerosis results in the degeneration of the myelin sheath covering the nerve axons. The brain stem and spinal cord are usually principally involved. Usually, the disease is diagnosed in persons between 20 and 40 years of age (Chusid, 1976). Multiple sclerosis is common in cold climates, but almost unheard of in tropical areas. Neuropsychological profiles of multiple sclerosis patients have some points of dissimilarity compared with other patients with degenerative diseases such as parkinsonism. While motor deficits (perhaps the most common sign of a degenerative disease) are clear, multiple sclerosis patients characteristically show only mild impairment on tests of complex cognitive functioning and IQ, relative to a normal control group (Reitan, Reed, & Dyken, 1971). This stands in marked contrast to patients with parkinsonism or other degenerative diseases, who usually demonstrate moderate to severe impairment. The clinician should be alert to visual disorders that result from involvement of the optic nerve (Reitan, Reed, & Dyken, 1971). In addition, the characteristic MMPI profile of the patient with multiple sclerosis is worthy of comment. Often, these patients will produce an MMPI profile with elevations on the hypochondroasis (Hy) and hysteria (Hs) scales. This sort of 1–3, or "conversion V" profile is often interpreted as suggesting hysterical neurosis or "conversion reaction" (Lachar, 1974). However, there is evidence (Cleeland, Matthews, & Hooper, 1970) indicating that the 1–3 MMPI profile is a consequence of the multiple sclerosis and not a somatoform disorder.

Infections

Infectious agents such as viruses and bacteria may produce brain dysfunction of a diffuse sort. The three most common groups of infection, for the human neuropsychologist, are encephalitis, meningitis, and neurosyphilis (Lahey & Ciminero, 1980).

Encephalitis

Encephalitis is an infection of the brain resulting from a virus or other disease agent. Symptoms develop rapidly and include drowsiness, fever, stiff neck, and vomiting. Usually, children suffer more severe aftereffects (Golden, 1978). Butters and Cermak (1980) have demonstrated a specific pattern of memory impairment with patients surviving herpes encephalitis. Essentially, postencephalitic patients tend to show adequate short-term memory but retrograde amnesia. Also, postencephalitis patients, depending on the type and extent of infection, may show lateralized dysfunction (Golden, 1978).

Meningitis

Meningitis is a bacterial or viral infection of the meninges, the layers of tissue which protect the brain. Symptoms are similar to encephalitis. Failure to receive prompt treatment results in death. Usually, neuropsychologists are called on to evaluate intellectual and cognitive deficits secondary to meningitis. Typically, children more often show deficits than adults.

Neurosyphilis

Neurosyphilis refers to brain infections caused by syphilitic spirochetes that are corkscrew-shaped bacteria. Cases a neuropsychologist would see are usually individuals in whom the disease was undetected and who have already suffered considerable cerebral impairment.

Toxic Disorders

Many other substances, such as lead, mercury, pesticides, carbon monoxide, or fumes from glue or gasoline, can cause toxic brain disorder. At present, however, neuropsychologists have focused the majority of attention on alcoholism and drug abuse.

Alcoholism

Alcholism is clearly the most abused single toxin. Estimates in the United States are at 9 million problem drinkers and alcoholics (Parsons & Farr, 1981). The classic brain disorder associated with chronic alcoholism is Korsakoff's syndrome (Butters & Cermak, 1980). Essentially, the Korsakoff's syndrome is a chronic condition where the patient, after many years of alcohol abuse, demonstrates severe impairment of the ability to learn new verbal and nonverbal information. Long-term memory is also impaired but to a less striking degree.

The neuropathology of Korsakoff's syndrome has recently been clarified. Butters and Cermak (1980) have concluded that atrophy of the dorsomedial nucleus of the thalamus and mammillary bodies are the two structures most frequently associated with the amnestic symptoms of Korsakoff's syndrome.

Recent work by Butters and Cermak (1980) has found neuropsychological test patterns indicative of Korsakoff's syndrome patients. The pattern is a severely impaired short-term memory in the context of normal measured psychometric intelligence. In terms of commonly used neuropsychological tests, this pattern translates into a 20- to 30-point scatter between the full-scale IQ value of the Wechsler Adult Intelligence Scale (WAIS) and the Wechsler Memory Scale (WMS).

Alcoholic Korsakoff's patients also do quite poorly on the digit symbol subtest of the WAIS, relative to control subjects. Butters and Cermak (1980) note a number of other secondary neuropsychological deficits. These include impairment of visuoperceptive and visuospatial capacities. Personality changes also accompany Korsakoff's syndrome, most commonly apathy and passivity.

While the neuropsychological impairment of Korsakoff's patients has been well known for many years, only in recent years has the riddle of neuropsychological impairment in chronic alcoholics and social drinkers been answered to any appreciable degree. With respect to chronic alcoholic patients and their neuropsychological deficits, Parsons and Farr (1981), in a superb review of the literature focusing on the HRNB, provided some data-based answers. They conclude that chronic alcoholics are neuropsychologically impaired, demonstrating: "... less efficient non-verbal abstracting and problem-solving, visual-spatial and tactual-spatial difficulties, and slowed visuomotor performance" (p. 355). WAIS verbal abilities or general language functions do not appear to be markedly impaired.

Specific tests that Parsons and Farr (1981) suggest indicate impairment of adaptive ability, premature treatment termination, and relapse are the WAIS Digit Symbol and Block Design subtests, the Category Test, the Tactual Performance Test (time and location scores), and the Trail Making Test, Part B.

In another line of research on neuropsychological deficits in chronic alcoholics, Butters and Cermak (1980) have elucidated the dimensions of memory impairment. They demonstrated, on both verbal paired-associate learning and modified Peterson short-term memory tasks, that chronic alcoholics have memory difficulties that fall in a range midway between Korsakoff's patients and nonalcoholic controls. With respect to social drinkers, the line of research of Butters and Cermak (1980) would predict mild memory impairment by social drinkers. Preliminary findings reveal that social drinking may produce marked loss of cognitive and neuropsychological capacities previously believed to be affected only by long-term chronic alcoholism (Parker & Nobel, 1977). There has arisen some interest in the cognitive retraining of alcoholics to aid their recovery of neuropsychological abilities. At present, this area is promising but largely unexplored (Parsons & Farr, 1981).

Psychoactive drugs

Despite multiple reports of brain damage resulting from psychoactive drug abuse, the available research literature is not clear. For example, Parsons and Farr (1981) state: "...when large groups of abusers are assessed under controlled conditions with the HRNB (Halstead–Reitan Neuropsychological Battery), the findings are far from conclusive in demonstrating a picture of consistent impairment that is clearly the result of substance abuse" (p. 346).

Parsons and Farr (1981) have found polydrug abuse to be an exception. Interestingly, Igor Grant and his associates (Grant, Mohns, Miller, & Reitan, 1976; Grant, Adams, Carlin, Rennick, Judd, & Schooff, 1978) showed that persons routinely using several drugs on a daily basis demonstrated behavioral deficits in the areas of abstraction and problem solving.

While Parsons and Farr (1981) decline to conclude that drugs produce a lowered level of neuropsychological ability, they do identify a typical pattern of deficits. Certain subtests of the HRNB are more likely to be impaired. Similar to chronic alcoholics, polydrug abusers perform poorly on Categories and Trails B. Other impaired tests often include rhythm and finger tapping. This is at counter point to chronic alcoholics who usually show deficits on the time and location scores of the Tactual Performance Test as well as Digit Symbol and Block Design Subtests of the WAIS. Drug abusers appear to demonstrate considerably less impairment than alcoholics on the only other widely used standardized neuropsychological battery, the Luria–Nebraska (C.J. Golden, pers. comm.).

Schizophrenia

Lahey and Ciminero (1980) define schizophrenia as: "A group of serious behavior disorders in which cognitive, emotional, and social processes are disrupted and disorganized. Most prominent features include thought disorders, blunted affect, and social withdrawal" (p. 605).

The cognitive dimension is usually emphasized as would seem understandable since the term schizophrenia was derived by the Swiss psychiatrist Eugen Bleuler from the Greek words meaning "split mind." Subtypes of schizophrenic disorders, in DSM-III, are disorganized (hebephrenic), catatonic, paranoid, and undifferentiated. Schizophrenia usually is developed around age 20 and very rarely after age 45. The genetic basis of schizophrenia is well established from twin studies but there is a clear role for stressful life events in the onset of psychotic symptoms (Meehl, 1962).

For many years there was considerable debate with regard to the presence or absence of brain damage in schizophrenics. To a large degree, neuropsychological test batteries were faulted for their failure to make the differential diagnosis of schizophrenic brain damage (Heaton, 1976).

More recent research using new technology (CT scanners), however, has demonstrated the presence of structural brain deficits in schizophrenia (Golden, Graber, Coffman, Berg, Newlin, & Block,

1981). This research has shown that there is a subgroup of schizophrenic patients (60% at one investigator's institution) who appear to have significantly enlarged ventricles and increased sulcal widths. This group of patients appears to have deficits in the anterior area of the left (dominant) hemisphere.

The hypothesis of left hemisphere dysfunction with schizophrenia has obtained considerable collaboration (Flor-Henry, 1976; Gur, 1978). Work by Golden and his associates (Golden, Moses, Zelazowski, Graber, Zatzy, Horvath, & Berger, 1980) has found relationships between cerebral ventricular size and neuropsychological impairment as measured by the Luria–Nebraska Neuropsychological Battery.

In another line of research, investigators have attempted to use the MMPI to distinguish between schizophrenic and neurologic patients. Russell (1975) has suggested using neuropsychological tests to separate brain-damaged and schizophrenic groups from normals and has proposed an MMPI key to make the schizophrenic versus brain-damaged differential diagnosis.

Along the same lines but using a different methodology, Watson and Plemel (1978) devised an MMPI special scale, the Psychiatric–Organic (P–O) Scale, to separate schizophrenic from brain-damaged patients. Cross-validation of the P–O scale by Golden and his associates (1980) and Horton and Wilson (1981) found hit rates of 67 and 78, both better than Watson and Plemel's (1978) original 64.5 figure.

As long as schizophrenia is a poorly described construct, diagnostic problems will remain. Hopefully, new improved technology such as the CT scan will provide a valid and reliable basis for delineating schizophrenia subtypes.

Epilepsy

Epilepsy refers to a variety of seizure disorders involving neurochemical disturbances that result in excessive or abnormal firing of brain cells (Lahey & Ciminero, 1980). Epilepsy is not a specific disease but rather a symptom of a number of different disorders. Indeed, epilepsy is considered by some to represent a spectrum of disorders that are complex and multifaceted in their expression with etiologies that are equally varied (Dodrill, 1981). Both the terminology for describing and the criteria for diagnosing epilepsy are often changed (Boll, 1978). One system in general use is the International Classification of Seizure Disorders (Gastaut, 1970). It dispenses with the old terms of *grand mal*, *petit mal*, and *psychomotor* and introduces a system based on multiple types of information. The basic dichotomy in this system exists between partial and generalized seizures. Partial

seizures have a focal onset, whereas generalized seizures are bilater- *partial:*
ally symmetrical and without focal onset. The category of partial *complex*
seizures is further subdivided into those with impairment of con- *elementary*
sciousness (complex symptomology) and without (elementary symptomology). Psychomotor or temporal lobe seizures are in the first
group. Generalized seizures, on the other hand, involve the total brain *generalized:*
and subsume the old categories of *petit mal* and *grand mal.* Under the *- absence attack*
new system, what was *petit mal* (little bad) is now absence attacks. *(petit mal)*
These seizures often involve only a few seconds of unresponsiveness to
environmental stimuli. Classically, these are not seen after age 20
(Dodrill, 1981). What used to be *grand mal* (awful) seizures are now *- tonic-clonic*
known as tonic–clonic seizures. These are usually associated with a *(grand mal)*
general convulsion. *Grand mal* seizures are the classic seizures
associated with epilepsy and include four stages. First, a sensory aura
is present that can take many forms. Second, there is a tonic phase in
which the person loses consciousness and all muscles contract in a
rigid fashion. Third, in the clonic phase, the muscles repeatedly relax
and contract in a jerky fashion. During this stage, there is the potential
for self-harm. The fourth stage is a postconvulsive coma in which the
person enters a deep sleep and later awakens confused with no
memory of the seizure.

With respect to neuropsychological profiles, there is some agreement that "no specific pattern or type of psychological deficit is
diagnostic of epilepsy" (Boll, 1978, p. 626). Thus it is not possible to
infer epilepsy from neuropsychological results.

In epilepsy, the electroencephalogram (EEG) is often the primary
diagnostic tool, second only to the clinical history. Klove and Matthews
(1974) found some important relationships between neuropsychological impairment as manifested on the HRNB and epilepsy. Epileptics
with known etiology are more cognitively impaired than those with
unknown etiology. Similarly, patients with major motor or mixed
seizures are more damaged than patients with psychomotor seizures.
Finally, increasing frequency of seizures is associated with greater
neuropsychological deficit.

Dodrill (1981) has devised a battery of psychological tests to
evaluate neuropsychological deficits in epilepsy. This battery includes
a number of measures from the HRNB as well as a number of other
tests especially selected for their sensitivity to epilepsy related
impairment. Dodrill reports a summary measure from this battery is
more effective in discriminating epileptics from normals than is the
Halstead impairment index. In addition, it is more stable in estimating functional abilities.

In closing this section, it might be mentioned that while drugs
such as Dilantin are usually prescribed for treatment of seizures, some

behavioral techniques also have shown promise. Mostofsky and Balaschek (1977) demonstrated an intervention as straightforward as providing candy for reducing seizures could be effective. Similarly, using biofeedback, Sterman and Friar (1972) demonstrated that reinforcement of a particular EEG pattern could produce therapeutic benefits.

CONCLUSION

In this chapter, the major neuropathological conditions have been briefly described. Also, basic principles of neurodiagnosis were elucidated. The intent was to provide a preliminary framework for neophyte neuropsychologists. It is clear that a great deal of further study and supervised experience in a clinical setting is necessary before one achieves even minimal understanding of the gamut of neurological disorders and how they relate to neuropsychological test results.

SUGGESTIONS FOR FURTHER READING

Butters, N. & Cermak, L. *Alcoholic Korsakoff's syndrome.* New York: Academic, 1978.

Chusid, J.G. *Correlative neuroanatomy of functional neurology.* Los Altos, Ca.: Lange, 1976.

Dodril, C.B. Neuropsychology of epilepsy. In S. Filskov & T.J. Boll (Eds.), *Handbook of clinical neuropsychology.* New York: John Wiley, 1980.

Golden, C.J. *Diagnosis and rehabilitation in clinical neuropsychology.* Springfield, Ill.: Charles C. Thomas, 1978.

Parsons, O.A. & Farr, S.P. Neuropsychology of alcohol and drug use. In S. Filskov & T.J. Boll (Eds.), *Handbook of clinical neuropsychology.* New York: John Wiley, 1980.

Pincus, J.H. & Tucker, G.J. *Behavioral neurology* (2nd Ed.). New York: Oxford, 1978.

Weiner, H.L. & Levit, L.P. *Neurology for the house officer* (2nd Ed.). Baltimore: Williams and Wilkins, 1978.

5

ISSUES IN CLINICAL NEUROPSYCHOLOGY

As any emerging discipline, clinical neuropsychology is beset with a variety of issues and problems, most of which remain unresolved. This chapter highlights a number of these issues.

Perhaps the major issue confronting the field of clinical neuropsychology is that of the relative merits of a clinical approach to assessment versus a standardized battery approach. The former approach is characterized by the work of Luria who maintained that every patient and every problem was unique and hence a standardized battery was inappropriate for neuropsychological purposes. The standardized battery approach is typified by the work of Reitan, and is currently the preferred approach in American clinical neuropsychology. The chief advantage of the clinical or ipsative approach is that it is extremely flexible and provides the maximum amount of information with the minimal amount of testing time. In the hands of a skilled examiner, such as Luria, it is possible to amass tremendous amounts of information in a relatively short time. However, the disadvantage of the approach is that most psychologists do not possess Luria's insight, understanding, or experience, and their clinical hunches are apt to be wrong and misleading as often as not. With the clinical approach, one runs the risk of failing to adequately survey an important functional domain, missing critical information necessary for the adequate assessment of the patient. Reitan (1974) has criticized Luria's neuropsychological approach, claiming that it is strongly biased toward left hemisphere skills, is too closely tied to the skill level of the examiner, and cannot be cross-validated. Likewise, Luria and Majovski (1977) have suggested that Reitan's standardized approach is cumbersome, overly lengthy, and is not firmly grounded in a theoretical formulation. This debate highlights the essential differences between clinical neuropsychology and behavioral neurology.

117

There are a number of advantages to the nomothetic or standardized battery approach to assessment. First, with continued exposure to the same battery of tests, one quickly becomes quite adept at interpreting the nuances present in the test results. In addition, the batteries frequently include standardized instruments, such as the WAIS, for which a tremendous amount of research data has accumulated. The scientific merit of the battery approach is readily apparent insofar as this method allows comparison of test results across the variety of subjects tested at different times. Statistical analysis become possible when one is collecting the same data on a large subject pool and, given an adequate sample size, the power of multivariate methods can be applied to data analysis. In addition it is possible to plot profiles on patients when a standardized approach is used and information may be present in the profile structure that is not readily discernible when a potpourri of individual tests are administered. Perhaps the major disadvantage of the standardized batteries (e.g., the Halstead–Reitan Battery) is that they require a collection of data that may or may not be relevant to every patient and to every clinical question. In addition, these batteries are typically somewhat cumbersome and almost inevitably longer than the testing that accompanies the clinical approach. Some researchers such as Golden (1976) and Erickson, Calysyn, and Scheupback (1978) have developed abbreviated versions of the Halstead–Reitan Battery in an attempt to circumvent the problem of time. However, whereas these abbreviated batteries are useful as a screening measure, they do not provide the wealth of information present in the longer test battery.

In some ways, we find the clinical versus standardized battery controversy an artificial one. It is obvious to us that the nature of the assessment is closely tied to the purpose for which an examination has been requested. We see patients that are referred for screening for brain damage, for localization of a suspected lesion, for forensic purposes, and for rehabilitation planning. Many times, cost considerations will play a dominant role in the decision-making process. For example, a complete Halstead–Reitan Battery currently costs about $350. We believe it is the most comprehensive neuropsychological battery available today and we use it whenever possible. However, many patients lack the financial resources to pay for the entire battery and many times the wealth of information that it provides is clearly a luxury. In addition many patients will lack the stamina required to complete the entire battery, or their tolerance for frustration will be too low for them to complete each of the individual subtests. In these cases, we go first to those tests that are most likely to answer the referral question. Many times consults can be answered with a mental status exam that is comprehensive and complete. Strub and Black

(1977) have provided an excellent outline of a comprehensive neuro-psychological mental status evaluation. It is especially useful when seeing a nonambulatory patient or testing a patient at bedside. We find that a 1-hour evaluation is adequate for screening for brain lesions and will provide some information about lateralization and even localization. However, if we are assessing a patient for rehabilitation planning or especially if we are examining a patient for forensic purposes, we prefer to have a detailed evaluation conducted in our laboratories. We have learned that attorneys have become familiar with the Halstead–Reitan Battery and are quick to challenge our findings whenever an "incomplete" evaluation is conducted.

We have found it useful to ask six basic questions. These questions can all be addressed by a competent clinical neuropsychologist; however each additional question requires a greater degree of test information to be assessed adequately. The questions are:

1. Is functional impairment present that cannot be accounted for in terms of retardation, education, or age?
2. Is this impairment related to a demonstrable brain lesion?
3. Is the damage diffuse throughout the cerebral cortex or is there any evidence for lateralization?
4. Is the damage diffuse within a single cerebral hemisphere or is there any evidence for localization?
5. Can neuropsychological test findings be used to infer the neuropathological process present?
6. What is this patient's prognosis and what is the potential for rehabilitation?

Questions 1 and 2 are separated because function does not necessarily parallel structure. We have seen patients with massive frontal lesions who displayed minimal behavioral manifestations, while other patients who were clearly neuropsychologically impaired looked neurologically intact on CT scans, EEGs, and a variety of other neurodiagnostic measures. We believe that in general neuropsychologists are too quick to apologize when they have labeled a patient as being brain impaired when in fact medical tests do not suggest that brain damage is present. False negatives are not uncommon in neurology and many patients will have lesions that can be demonstrated only at autopsy.

lateralization

The question of lateralization of lesions is addressed by examining language and spatial deficits (the province of the left and right hemispheres, respectively, in the right-handed individual), and by examining sensory and motor deficits contralateral to the presumed lesion. At times, the evidence for lateralization is incontestable, such as in the patient who presents with a left hemiparesis. At other times, the signs may be subtle and elusive, such as an impaired ability to construct spatial designs in an otherwise functionally infact indi- vidual.

Inferring neuropathological processes from psychological test results requires extensive training and considerable experience with both neurological patients and the tests themselves. In the hands of a skilled examiner, however, amazingly detailed inferences can be made. Sometimes these inferences are fairly obvious. For example, a receptive aphasia suggests left posterior temporal damage and is most likely caused by a cerebrovascular accident. A cerebrovascular accident will usually impair abstraction ability and is contraindicated by a good score on a test of abstraction such as the Halstead–Reitan Categories Test. Cerebrovascular accidents will also affect tapping speed and, in the acute case, will typically produce a difference between verbal and performance IQ. One finds that an occlusion of the middle cerebral artery will produce contralateral paralysis in the lower part of the face and arm as well as sensory deficit. When this occurs in the left hemisphere it is the primary cause of aphasia. Occlusion of the anterior cerebral artery results in paralysis and sensory deficits in the contralateral leg.

When speculating about the likelihood of a vascular accident versus neoplastic disease, it is frequently useful to compare abstrac- tion ability with motor function. If motor function (e.g., finger tapping and grip strength) is considerably more impaired than abstracting ability, it is likely that a vascular disorder is present. If impairment in abstraction and motor skills is about equal, one is more likely to be working with a patient with neoplastic disease. In addition, the cerebrovascular accident will typically result in some signs in the opposite hemisphere, while tumors are more apt to present clearly unilateral signs.

In the case of neoplastic disease, one can sometimes make inferences about the type of tumor that is present. For example, intrinsic tumors typically result in far more serious functional deficits than do extrinsic tumors. An intrinsic tumor is more apt to produce unilateral signs while the extrinsic tumor, because of pressure on the opposite hemisphere, will typically result in bilateral deficits and a smaller VIP–PIQ difference. An intrinsic tumor such as a glio- blastoma multiforme is branching and deadly and will usually depress all scores on the affected side. In a patient with a glioma, it is very unusual to find pockets of strength in the damaged hemisphere. On the other hand, a patient with a metastatic tumor is likely to show a more varigated ability pattern.

Inferences of the type illustrated are complicated by the fact that two or more lesions may exist simultaneously in the same patient. This problem is especially apparent in the case of the alcoholic, for example, who may present with a generally depressed functional pattern due to alcoholic degeneration while showing specific deficits related to trauma secondary to falls while drunk. It is important to remember, however, that whereas inferences about localization of process are fascinating intellectual exercises, they may contribute little to the patient's treatment and are perhaps best left to more specialized neurodiagnostic methods such as CT scanning. What is crucial is that the patient be provided with a total and comprehensive picture of abilities and deficits and a realistic estimate of the potential for recovery from brain damage. This information will be critical to the patient, his family, and to those health care providers working with the patient, and it is a contribution that the clinical neuropsychologist is uniquely qualified to make.

In time, one develops a certain clinical intuition about the localization of lesions. The frontal patient, for example, is character-ized by disinhibition and a lowered level of anxiety. One finds that motor deficits are more pronounced than sensory deficits in these patients. Left frontal lesions produce impaired performance on the Category Test and on the Wisconsin Card Sorting Test. Trails B on the Halstead–Reitan Battery is typically performed poorly while Digit Span and Full Scale IQ from the WAIS remain stable. Right frontal lesions result in impaired picture arrangement on the WAIS as well as impaired Digit Span Performance. Memory for designs and spatial skills are also apt to be impaired. Parietal lesions are most commonly characterized by contralateral sensory deficits. With left parietal lesions, one is apt to find poor performance on the Arithmetic, Digit Span, and Block Design subscales on the WAIS. In addition, Gerst-mann's syndrome may be present (finger agnosia, agraphia, acalculia, and right–left confusion). Right parietal lesions are characterized by poor performance on Block Design and Picture Arrangement, and by impaired performance on the tactual Performance Test and Trails A from the Halstead–Reitan Battery. Temporal lobe lesions are charac-terized by a loss of hearing acuity in the contralateral ear, the presence of auditory suppressions, and sometimes a loss of the upper contra-lateral visual field. With medial lesions, emotional problems may be present because of the proximity to the limbic system, and, if bilateral damage is present, the ability to consolidate memories may be lost. Olfactory hallucinations may also be present in the patient with medial temporal lobe lesions. Left temporal lesions are characterized by problems in speech and impaired performance on the Similarities

Subtest of the WAIS. Right temporal lesions are characterized by adequate speech but problems with rhythm and the perception and understanding of music. Finally, lesions of the occipital lobes are characterized most saliently by homonymous hemianopsias. This is a condition in which one-half of the visual world is lost to the patient. With a right occipital lesion the patient is apt to totally ignore the left visual field. In the left occipital patient, the individual will be more likely to compensate with head and eye movements that make up for the lost visual area.

METHODS OF CLINICAL INFERENCE

We believe that much of the confusion that exists in the older neuropsychological literature is the direct result of the limited methods of clinical inferences used by the researchers conducting the studies. Ralph Reitan has been instrumental in pointing out the need for multiple methods of inference in making diagnostic decisions. Reitan has outlined four basic methods of inference: level of performance, patterns of performance, right–left comparisons, and pathognomonic signs. Level of performance refers to an essentially dichotomous interpretation of data in which cutoff scores are used to classify patients into two basic categories—either brain damaged or normal. For example, patients with an impairment index of .5 or greater may be arbitrarily classified as being brain impaired while those with an index of less than .5 are classified as normal. This approach is analogous to interpreting the MMPI and labeling as schizophrenic all those patients who scored above 70 on the schizophrenia scale. Obviously this approach wastes the vast amount of information present in a comparison of scaled scores. Considerably greater information is present when inner test scatter is analyzed as in the second level of inference, analysis of patterns of performance. An example of the analysis of patterns of performance is found in the comparison of verbal IQ with performance IQ or in the analysis of specific weaknesses on the Wechsler scales. A third level of inference of particular value to the clinical neuropsychologist is the comparison of performance on the right and left sides of the body. For example, motor speed and grip strength on the left and the right can be compared as well as sensory ability and form recognition. Performance can be compared with normative data, and, in addition, the patient can in effect serve as his own control in the comparison of the two sides of the body.

Finally, pathognomonic signs are rare but extremely valuable when present. Pathognomonic signs refer to specific deficits that are almost inevitably indicative of brain impairment. Examples include language disorders, construction dyspraxia, the presence of consistent suppressions, and homonymous hemianopsias. These are disorders that fall outside the range of normal variation and offer *prima facia* evidence of the existence of cerebral impairment.

SUBJECT FACTORS

Age

Interpretation of neuropsychological tests is an art as well as a science. It is an art because of the presence of a number of confounding variables that clearly affect performance of the patient and the interpretation of test results. Age, for example, is clearly related to performance on a variety of neuropsychological measures. Although age is not often mentioned in the research, it affects cognitive function as well as motor and sensory abilities. Reid and Reitan (1963) found that the effects of age were greatest on problem-solving tasks and on those tests which involved learning of new material. Raymond Cattell has provided a useful heuristic in his description of fluid and crystallized intelligence. Essentially, fluid intelligence declines with increasing age while crystallized intelligence holds steady or even increases slightly. Vocabulary skills, for example, illustrate crystallized intelligence and vocabulary has been shown to continue to increase throughout the life span. It is interesting that aging produces the greatest deficits on those tests traditionally associated with right hemisphere function while those tests that hold with age—for example, vocabulary and information—are traditionally associated with the left hemisphere. Some researchers (e.g., Kliez, 1978) maintain that the hemispheres age at a different rate with deterioration of the right hemisphere proceeding more rapidly than that of the left.

It is well documented that dementia is diagnosed far more commonly in the United States than in other countries and in particular it is less prevalent in third world countries. This may be due to the increased prevalence of coronary arteriosclerosis in the United States which in turn is linked to our dietary habits and patterns of living. It is also clear that age interacts with psychiatric status, and loss of a significant other such as a spouse can lead to depression, which in turn will result in poor neuropsychological performance. The data are clear that age interacts in a meaningful way with neuropsychological test performance and must always be considered in the evaluation of any patient's test data. The reader is referred to Albert (1981) for a cogent review of geriatric neuropsychology.

Age at the time of cerebral insult is a major factor in determining the ultimate consequences of a brain injury. Chelune and Edwards (1981, p. 779), after reviewing the extensive literature on early brain lesions, reported two consistent findings: (1) "long-term deficits associated with static cerebral lesions are rarely as severe as the initial deficits," and (2) "the earlier brain damage is sustained in life, the less deleterious its eventual impact on behavior than similar damage incurred by the mature brain."

Although this plasticity model of functional recovery following early brain damage has been challenged (see Satz & Fletcher, 1981), it is accepted by most practicing neuropsychologists. Indeed, the emerging brain is so sufficiently different from the adult brain that many neuropsychologists (including the authors) restrict their practice to either adults or children and do not attempt to master the voluminous literature in both areas.

Sex

Sex is another variable that has generally been disregarded in neuropsychological research. However, differences clearly exist in the morphological structure of the male and female brain and ability differences exist that cannot be accounted for merely on the grounds of environmental influence (Benbow & Stanley, 1980). It behooves the neuropsychologist to consider sex as a moderator variable and to possibly reinterpret particular test performances (e.g., a particularly low score on the arithmetic subtest of the WAIS) in relation to the existing differences in ability of each sex.

Education

Education is an additional factor that will temper the interpretation of every neuropsychological profile. Finlayson, Johnson, and Reitan (1977) have shown that both education and brain damage affect performance on the Halstead–Reitan Battery, whereas Prigatano and Parsons (1976) have shown a high correlation between education and test performance in medical surgical patients but not in psychiatric patients. It is obvious that an IQ of 125 reflects exceptional intellectual ability; however, it may also reflect substantial intellectual impairment in the PhD physicist who was previously performing at a much higher level. Educational information can be especially beneficial as a means of establishing basic intellectual level in those patients for whom premorbid test data are not available.

Medication

Motivation

Another critical subject variable is patient motivation. In our own experience we have realized that keeping the patient's interest and reducing patient fatigue are far more important than maintaining a standardized presentation of test items and we will frequently allow breaks for the individual patient. Motivation is critical if the test results are to be meaningful since so many of the individual tests are based on the assumption that the patient is performing at maximal levels. Occasionally, one will find patients who are motivated to perform poorly. This is most commonly found in those patients who are involved in litigation following a traumatic injury. Heaton, Smith, Lehman, and Voit (1978) compared deliberate malingerers with head trauma patients taking the Halstead–Reitan Test. A discriminate function was able to correctly categorize over 95% of the subjects as malingerers or head trauma victims. In general, few patients have the neuropsychological sophistication necessary to successfully malinger. For example, the second author has tested one patient who presented with a number of right-sided motor deficits following an automobile accident in which he suffered a right hemisphere injury. The test performance was incompatible with the effects of *contrecoup* and the ipsilateral deficits that the patient displayed were clearly an attempt at malingering.

Other Factors

Psychotropic medication can also have a profound effect on neuropsychological performance. Klonoff, Fibiger, and Hutton (1970) demonstrated that increasingly large doses of psychiatric medication resulted in decreasing test performance; however, the study is confounded by the fact that the more significantly impaired patients were those receiving the larger levels of psychotropic medication. Small, Small, Milstein, and Moore (1972) showed that psychotropic medication actually improved performance of many psychiatric patients on the Halstead–Reitan Battery. Clearly, this is a complex research area. It is likely that those patients whose neuropsychological performance is significantly affected by psychiatric symptoms (e.g., delusions, hallucinations, affective disorders, etc.) will demonstrate improved performance as their symptomatology abates. However, drugs that produce sedating effects are apt to impair test performance, especially on those tests in which speed is a critical factor. One finds wide individual differences in response to psychotropic medication, and so dosage levels become as important as the particular class of drug administered. It is simplistic to lump all drugs given to psychiatric patients together and to label them simply as psychotropic medication without investigating their individual response characteristics. In general, caution must be exercised whenever the possibility exists that a patient's poor test performance may be secondary to drugs taken for psychiatric problems or for medical problems such as epilepsy in which the drugs administered have sedative properties. One finds that other somatic treatments (e.g., electroconvulsive therapy) can also profoundly affect test performance and must always be considered in evaluating test results.

Chronicity is yet another variable that must be considered in every neuropsychological evaluation. Almost every neuropsychologist has had the experience of testing a patient who was profoundly impaired but who showed dramatic improvement on subsequent testing. Often times these patients will be assessed periodically as part of a comprehensive rehabilitation program and it is a gratifying experience to see improvement occurring and to be able to graphically display the patient's functional gains. Of course, it is important to control or at least minimize the practice effects involved in multiple administrations of the same test battery. It is unfortunate that so few tests in neuropsychology are available in alternate forms. The Weschler Memory Scale is a notable exception.

There are two factors that are implicated in the very poor test performance of brain trauma patients immediately following their head injury. The first of these is edema or brain swelling. Many times patients who present with profound cognitive disturbance in the emergency room following a head injury will improve dramatically several days later, merely as a result of the brain returning to its normal size. The effects of edema tend to be marked and generalized and are typically found to be bilateral. A second factor affecting chronicity is diaschisis or distance effects. Diaschisis refers to the fact that a lesion in a given area may affect distant portions of the brain totally removed from the affected portion. Typically, diaschisis occurs in the same hemisphere as the lesion; however, its effects can cross the corpus callosum and affect the opposite hemisphere. In general, the effects of diaschisis diminish with increasing distance from the lesion producing the effect, and the effects abate with time.

Type of disorder is another factor that interacts with chronicity. With a traumatic lesion, such as an open head injury, one finds that the more chronic lesions are apt to result in less serious behavioral deficits. However, with a progressive degenerative disease (e.g., Parkinson's, Huntington's chorea, or multiple sclerosis) one finds that the disorder increases in severity as chronicity increases. These facts hold important implications for rehabilitation planning. The patient who suffers from a traumatic closed head injury, for example, is very apt to regain much of whatever function is lost after the injury; the Alzheimer's patient, however, is characterized by progressive deterioration of function, regardless of intervention or rehabilitation efforts.

All of the issues discussed above have related to patient characteristics. However, it is obvious that patients interact with examiners in the testing situation and examiner characteristics in neuropsychology remain virtually unexamined. Although there has been some research on examiner characteristics and intelligence testing (e.g., effects of a white examiner on IQ scores of black children), virtually nothing is known about the effects of various examiner characteristics on testing behavior with other neuropsychological measures. This is a neglected but important research area. In particular, research is needed to assess the interaction between the expertise of the examiner and the test behavior of patients. With an ipsative approach, this is not so much of a problem because typically the psychologist will personally administer all tests. However, when a standardized battery is used, it becomes possible to train technicians in administration of the various tests included in the battery and considerable economy results. The Luria–Nebraska Battery, for example, can be administered at a cost of about $25 per patient using a psychological examiner who has been trained in administration of this battery. However, the effectiveness of examiner administration versus professional administration has yet to be tested.

A handful of studies have compared the accuracy of neuropsychological assessment with traditional neurodiagnostic measures such as angiograms, pneumoencephalograms, electroencephalograms, and computerized axial tomography. Although not widely appreciated in the neurological community, these studies consistently have demonstrated equal if not superior hit rates for the neuropsychological approach. Most of these studies have utilized the Halstead–Reitan Battery. Schreiber, Goldman, Kleinman, Goldfader, and Snow (1976) compared standard neurological methods (e.g., a neurological examination, X rays, electroencephalogram, angiogram, brain scan, lumbar puncture, etc.) with interpretations of the Halstead–Reitan Battery made by experienced clinical psychologists. Of the 78 patients studied, there was diagnostic agreement in all but five cases. Filskov and Goldstein (1974) conducted a very sophisticated study in which they compared the Halstead–Reitan Battery used as a screening instrument with brain scans, flow studies, electroencephalograms, angiograms, pneumoencephalograms, and skull X rays. Furthermore, they examined the accuracy of these methods in predicting presence, lateralization, and the neuropathological process involved in each case. Filskov and Goldstein found that the psychological tests were superior to the neurological tests for virtually every question asked. This is particularly important since many of the neurodiagnostic tests involved considerable risk of both morbidity and mortality for the individual patient. Angiography, for example, involves a morbidity/ mortality risk of somewhere between 4 and 9% (Filskov & Goldstein, 1974).

Tsushima and Wedding (1979) extended this comparison to computerized axial tomography, a safer and noninvasive neurodiagnostic method not generally available at the time of the Filskov and Goldstein study. Tsushima and Wedding found that there was little overall agreement between electroencephalography, computerized axial tomography, and Halstead–Reitan results, with the Halstead–Reitan Battery providing the highest overall agreement (78%) with the neurological/neurosurgical diagnosis. One can speculate that as neurodiagnostic methods become increasingly sophisticated (e.g., nuclear magnetic resonance studies and positron emission tomography) the importance of neuropsychological methods in predicting the presence, localization, or process of neurological disease will decline. However, psychological tests will still be important as screening measures. In addition, the major and unique contribution of neuropsychology lies not in neurodiagnosis but in the assessment of the functional strengths and weaknesses of the individual so that appropriate rehabilitation planning can take place.

The studies reviewed above all involved clinical interpretation of neuropsychological test results. However, few researchers have investigated the accuracy of neuropsychologists as judges. In one early study (Goldberg, 1959) the ability of Ph.D. clinicians to determine the presence of brain damage on the basis of Bender–Gestalt Test data was investigated. The results, unpalatable at best, suggested that hospital secretaries, psychology trainees, and doctoral psychologists were all equally inaccurate in assessing brain damage based on the Bender–Gestalt Test. In addition, the clinicians rated themselves as less confident in their judgment than the secretaries, despite the fact that the clinicians worked with the Bender as a tool for assessing brain damage on a daily basis. Despite these generally negative findings, one of the world's leading authorities on the Bender–Gestalt Test (Max Hutt) was able to diagnose 83% of the patients accurately, outperforming every subject in the initial study. This excellent performance, however, was achieved at the cost of 20 hours of data analysis. It is likely that the poor performance of the psychologists in the Goldberg study in part resulted from the inadequacy of the instrument itself. Goldstein, Deysach, and Kleinknecht (1973), using the Halstead–Reitan Battery, found that inexperienced clinicians were far more

effective than highly experienced clinical judges using more traditional measures such as the WAIS, MMPI, and the Bender–Gestalt
Test.

QUANTITATIVE APPROACHES TO ASSESSMENT OF BRAIN DAMAGE

Actuarial Models

While the early clinical history of neuropsychology was largely
restricted to the use of prevailing tests such as the Rorschach and
Bender–Gestalt, it soon became apparent that brain damage was
multifactorial in nature and no single test *in iso* was adequate for
assessing the presence or absence of brain damage. However, the
Wechsler Intelligence scales were designed to assess several cognitive
dimensions and appeared to hold some promise as a measure of
cerebral integrity as well as intellectual function. Weschler (1944) had
popularized the concept of a deterioration quotient (DQ) based on the
ratio between "hold" and "don't hold" scores. "Don't hold" scores were
those subtests that were most susceptible to the effects of cerebral
impairment. "Hold" scores were those subscales least likely to be
affected by cerebral insult. Matarrazo (1972) has critiqued the
available research on Wechsler's Deterioration Quotient and related
actuarial approaches to the Wechsler tests (e.g., Hewson ratios) and
suggests they are inadequate for the task of assessing brain impairment. Instead, he feels that the discrepancy index (verbal minus
performance IQ) might be a more meaningful index of pathology.
While acknowledging that the Wechsler tests by themselves are
inadequate instruments for assessing brain damage, Matarrazo maintains that a 15-point discrepancy between the two major scales (verbal
and performance) is usually clinically meaningful. A number of
investigators (e.g., Satz, 1966; Simpson & Vega, 1971; Zimmerman,
Whitmyer, & Fields, 1970) have found that depressed verbal scores are
associated with left hemisphere lesions while depressed performance
scores are more commonly found in those patients with right hemisphere lesions. However, Smith (1966) was unable to find the effect
when he investigated a variety of left hemisphere cases and claimed
that brain damage of either hemisphere was more apt to affect
performance scores. In addition, Todd, Coolidge, and Satz (1977), in
the most recent and most important study of the discrepancy index,
were unable to find significant differences between left and right
damaged groups on this scale. Furthermore, the index could not

discriminate between these two groups and a diffuse damage group or between these three and a psychiatric control. These authors report that "the Verbal IQ/Performance IQ discrepancy cannot be used as a diagnostic screening tool in those institutions in which both brain-damaged and psychiatric clients are seen" (p. 453). This finding, based on a sample of 335 clearly defined cases, is especially important because it runs contrary to a vast amount of clinical lore and to the everyday practice of most clinicians. No one to date has replicated the Todd, Coolidge, and Satz (1977) study; it is clear that if the results do hold up to replication they will challenge the adequacy of the inferential process of the majority of practicing neuropsychologists.

Two other actuarial approaches to the WAIS have been developed and appear to offer some utility as a screening measure. DeWolfe (1971) proposed three simple discrimination rules that are a model of parsimony. These were as follows: (1) if digit span is greater than comprehension, classify the patient as schizophrenic, (2) if digit span is less than comprehension, classify as brain damaged, and (3) break ties by classifying all patients as schizophrenic who have a digit span score greater than their vocabulary score. DeWolfe cross-validated his findings at two age levels (29–60 and 60) and was able to achieve substantial predictive power (76% overall accuracy). Whereas these results are not adequate for clinical purposes, in conjunction with other measures they may serve as a useful predictive tool.

Simpson and Vega (1971) developed a set of similar but more elaborate rules for predicting unilateral damage from WAIS subtest variation. They cross-validated their rules by applying them to published data from three other studies. In every case, group means substantiated their findings. Unfortunately, application of the rules to group means tells one little about predictive power in the individual case. This critical test is yet to be done. In addition, while the DeWolfe rules were developed with a sample of diffusely damaged patients, the Simpson and Vega cases were unilateral lesions. No one to date has compared the utility of the two actuarial models across diagnostic subgroups or on the same sample groups.

Actuarial models have also been developed for application to the Halstead–Reitan Battery. The first and still the most important of these is the impairment index, developed by Halstead as a global indicant of cerebral impairment. In developing the index, Halstead chose the ten tests that had the most discriminating power (in terms of separation of brain-damaged patients from normal controls). The impairment index reflects that proportion of scores that fall into the predetermined brain-damaged range. By inspecting the final distribution of index scores Halstead was able to determine that a cutting point of .50 provided optimal discrimination between groups. Halstead felt this technique was less likely to obscure the kind of unique and idiosyncratic (but important) information that might be hidden in an average. Despite the seemingly data-wasteful nature of the dichotomous method, it is a measure that has stood the test of time and one that is still used (with some minor modifications by Reitan) on a daily basis by the practicing clinician. In fact, several studies have found the index to be as efficacious as far more elaborate statistical techniques (e.g., Wheeler, Burke, & Reitan, 1963; Struss & Trites, 1977). However, the index was developed for empirical rather than mathematical reasons—empirically, it works quite well, seemingly ignorant of Lord's (1962) proof that cutting score methods are necessarily less accurate than point estimation methods.

In one of the first studies to offer an alternative to the impairment index, Vega and Parsons (1967) proposed T-score averaging. Use of this method allows more ready visual inspection and comparison of subtests and, with the Vega and Parsons data, increased predictive accuracy from 73 to 79%. In the only other study to address this issue, Kiernan and Matthews (1976) found the T-score averaging method to be slightly superior to the impairment index which, in both studies, had a tendency to label older, nonimpaired subjects as brain damaged (e.g., false-positive errors). Given this empirical support and the seemingly obvious fact that cutoff scores waste prodigious amounts of data, it is surprising that there has been so little clinical interest in generating more viable approaches to classification.

Computerized Models

Not all classification models have been as simple as those described above. Several researchers have addressed the question of computerized interpretation of Halstead–Reitan results. The first successful attempt was a program developed by E.W. Russell as part of his doctoral dissertation research at the University of Kansas. Russell rejected standard statistical approaches and instead developed a taxonomic key, modeled after the keys used in biology to classify plants and animals. The result, described in Russell, Neuringer, and Goldstein (1970), is a set of decision rules loosely approximating the thought process of the neuropsychologist. The successive key approach was used to develop two sets of algorithms, one for localization (left, right, or diffuse) and one for process (acute, static, or congenital). Accuracy rates for the computer model were compared with accuracy rates for the neuropsychologists participating in the study and it was found that the taxonomic keys compared favorably. In terms of localization, the clinician was slightly more accurate (67% compared to 56% for the keys) and both were approximately 75% accurate in terms of process. However, these figures reflect agreement with the diagnostic impressions of the treating neurologist, a criterion measure that in itself is quite imprecise (Filskov & Goldstein, 1974). In addition, Russell's program was validated on a limited sample of cases (N=104) and determination of lateralization was inferred when this information was not available from medical records. Despite these flaws, the Russell study was the first to demonstrate that the cognitive process of the neuropsychologist could be approximated with an actuarial model. In its final form, the model was presented as (1) a set of keys that a file clerk could "run through" to arrive at a neurological diagnosis and (2) a computer program that would output the lateralization and process information in seconds. Unfortunately, the value of the Russell keys is at this point largely heuristic since adequate validation information has not been collected.

Adams (1974) and Gregory (1976) have also developed computer models for analyzing neuropsychological test data. However, the Gregory program was developed on a sample of only ten cases and, while conceptually important, offers little practical utility. The Adams program, also developed as part of a dissertation, attempts to capture the essence of clinical judgment. It only partially accomplishes this goal, achieving 75% accuracy in predicting the presence or absence of brain damage, 66% accuracy in predicting lateralization, and 44% accuracy in predicting both criteria jointly. The Adams program is quite complex (the flow chart describing the logic runs to 61 pages) and neither the program nor the study has been published to date.

The most impressive—and potentially the most important—computer model developed so far was the outgrowth of Finkelstein's doctoral dissertation (1976). Called BRAIN, the program accepts Halstead–Reitan variables as input and attempts to classify (1) presence or absence of brain damage, (2) lateralization of lesion, (3) presence or absence or recent tissue destruction, and (4) most likely neurological diagnosis. The program was written according to a logical decision tree model and was validated on a sample of 144 of Reitan's brain-damaged cases chosen to represent the full spectrum of neurological diagnoses. BRAIN correctly classified 96% of the brain-damaged subjects and 92% of the controls (N=36). It correctly lateralized 75% of the lesions, predicted presence or absence of recent tissue destruction in 83% of the cases, and correctly predicted 1 of 11 specific neurological diagnoses in 64% of the cases. Although not yet published or widely disseminated, the actuarial version of BRAIN (i.e., the Finkelstein–Reitan rules) is being promulgated in a series of workshops conducted by Dr. Reitan and his associates. It is likely that the endorsement of the foremost living neuropsychologist will result in even greater use of both the actuarial rules and the BRAIN program as neuropsychologists become increasingly familiar with each. However, uncritical adoption of either Russell's program or BRAIN is clearly premature, especially if one is using the program to address more than the basic question of brain damaged or not. In the only published study to compare these two programs (Anthony, Heaton, & Lehman, 1980) it was found that both computer models would classify subjects as brain damaged or not brain damaged with acceptable degrees of accuracy. However, neither program was significantly superior to use of the Halstead impairment index in reaching this decision (BRAIN was somewhat more accurate in classifying the true brain-damaged subjects; however, this accuracy was achieved at the cost of a substantial increase in false-positive diagnoses). Russell's lateralization key was found to be minimally useful, while the process key failed to classify subjects at more than a chance level. Likewise, lateralization and prediction of diagnosis were both at chance level with the BRAIN program.

Despite these somewhat dismal results, we expect to see increasing use of computer programs of this type in neurodiagnostics. The advantages of actuarial methods in psychiatry have been well documented (Meehl, 1954; Sawyer, 1966; Spitzer & Endicott, 1974) and we see no reason why the same superiority should not hold in neurology.

Discriminant Functions

The use of discriminant functions with the Halstead–Reitan Battery offers still another approach to classification and prediction. In an early set of studies Wheeler and his colleagues (Wheeler, 1963, 1964; Wheeler, Burke, & Reitan, 1963; Wheeler & Reitan, 1963) demonstrated that discriminant functions could effectively classify patients into left, right, and bilateral (diffuse) groups with a high degree of accuracy, exceeding the performance of every single measure and outperforming the impairment index. In a cross-validation study (Wheeler & Reitan, 1963) 10–20% shrinkage of predictive accuracy occurred but the functions still classified individuals into the appropriate groups with about 80% accuracy (with the exception of discrimination between left hemisphere and diffuse damage, which was essentially at chance level). Following this analysis the authors conclude that the greater accuracy rate found with clinical interpretation of the data must rest in nonlinear combinations of the salient cues. In his last study (1964) Wheeler was able to obtain 80–90% accuracy using the same criterion groups and seven dichotomized measures from each of 224 patients. This study demonstrated the utility of age as a predictor of neurological status and the (slight) superiority of discriminant functions in relation to the impairment index. *Per contra*, Goldstein and Shelly (1972), in one of the few studies to directly assess the utility of the Russell, Neuringer, and Goldstein (1970) Average Impairment Rating, found this simple actuarial measure to be just as accurate (about 70% overall accuracy) as the more complex 22-variable discriminant function. These authors term the discriminant analysis procedure "highly uneconomical" for the purpose of determining the presence or absence of brain damage. However, it is interesting to note that the following year, in a different journal, the same authors (Goldstein & Shelly, 1973) presented the results of another study in which they extoll the virtues of discriminate functions in lateralizing brain damage (relative to factor scores and single variable methods).

Struss and Trites (1977) conducted an interesting study using discriminant functions to separate three groups of 34 subjects each: a control group, a group with positive evidence of brain damage and a positive neurological examination, and, most importantly, a group with definite evidence of brain damage but with no signs of damage present during the physical neurological examination. Discriminant functions were correctly able to discriminate as brain damaged 73.5% of those subjects with negative findings on the neurological exam. This finding supports the results of other researchers (e.g., Filskov & Goldstein, 1974; Klove, 1974; Tsushima & Wedding, 1979) who have suggested that the Halstead–Reitan Battery is a more accurate screening instrument than the more traditional neurological examination. Despite these positive results, Struss and Trites (1977) found that the impairment index alone was as effective as their discriminant function in separating brain damaged from normals. These results are similar to those of Golden (1977b) who found the impairment index as effective as discriminant functions in classifying brain-damaged patients but inferior for purposes of separating psychiatric cases from brain-damaged cases.

Finally, in the only study to directly compare the accuracy of the Russell keys with discriminant functions, Swiercinsky and Warnock (1977) found that the former method (i.e., a key approach) was superior in predicting the presence of brain damage (87% versus 69% for discriminant functions) while discriminant functions provided superior classification into left, right, diffuse, and control categories. However, none of the methods of analysis were good at predicting lateralization with the keys correctly identifying 43% of the cases, the key variables in a discriminant function predicting 52%, and a 21-variable discriminant function predicting with 57% accuracy.

The generally poor performance of discriminant functions in lateralizing, relative to their excellent performance in predicting presence or absence of brain damage, suggests that either (1) the success of the clinician in lateralizing lesions results from his or her ability to analyze nonlinear and configural relationships in the data set that are not amenable to analysis with linear statistical methods or (2) prior researchers have not coded their data in a form which would maximize the predictive utility of discriminant equations. Both possibilities seem likely. As previously discussed, Reitan (1974) uses four levels of inference in making decisions about lateralization and localization of lesions: level of performance, comparisons of the relative efficiency of the right and left sides of the body, pathognomic signs, and patterns of performance. Prior actuarial approaches (e.g., Russell, Neuringer, & Goldstein, 1970; Finkelstein, 1976) have attempted to incorporate these various inferential modes into their program logic; in contrast, statistical approaches (e.g., Swiercinsky & Warnock, 1977) have coded only for level of performance and have neglected the possibilities offered by the other levels of inference. It is possible to speculate that coding variables in a manner more isomorphic to the inferential level of analysis employed by the clinician might greatly enhance the accuracy of the functions generated. Despite the extensive literature on the Halstead–Reitan tests, no one to date has examined this possibility.

In concluding our discussion of discriminant functions, it is important to point out that this technique is frequently abused. This is in part due to the proliferation of canned computer programs that permit elaborate data analyses to be conducted with minimal understanding of the statistical properties of the method employed. For example, we have seen published journal articles in which the number of variables used to generate discriminate functions exceeded the number of subjects in the study. This type of superficial analysis maximally capitalizes on error variance and yields highly unreliable results. At a minimum, every study employing discriminatative functions should include a separate group of subjects used solely for cross-validating the functions obtained from the primary sample.

Factor Analysis

Factor analysis is a multivariate statistical technique closely related to discriminant function analysis. Halstead (1947), working with L.L. Thurstone, one of the pioneers of factor analysis, conducted one of the earliest factor analyses of neuropsychological data. Halstead obtained a 4-factor solution and labeled his factors as C, A, P, and D. C was labeled as a "central integrative memory" factor, A an abstraction factor, P was considered to reflect "power" (alertness), and D was called a directional or modalities factor (Russell, Neuinger, & Goldstein (1970). Other investigations (e.g., Goldstein & Shelly, 1972; Royce, Yeudall, & Bock, 1976; Swiercinsky, 1979) have also examined the factor structure of the Halstead–Reitan Battery with generally similar results. Royce, Yeudall, and Bock (1976) found that about half of their interpretable factors had some localizing value. These included right hemisphere factors termed perceptual–motor speed, temporal resolution, and spatial orientation as well as three left hemisphere factors termed verbal comprehension, memory, and verbal memory. Although none of these studies have been adequate to establish a functional topography of ability, we believe the techniques hold great promise for neuropsychology and that our awareness of ability structure will parallel increases in our knowledge of the basic morphology of the brain.

Methodological Issues

In addition to the physical problems outlined above, a variety of methodological issues are found in the neuropsychological literature. Perhaps one of the most salient is that a number of studies are recorded in the psychological literature using large groups of patients and inferential statistics that report statistical group differences that are of little clinical significance. In contrast, medical journals rarely report findings that are not applicable to the individual patient. The second methodological issue is the failure of many studies to employ the proper control group for comparison purposes. The neuropsychological literature is beset with studies showing that brain-damaged individuals differ from normal controls on any number of measures. Demonstrating this fact is the simple belaboring of the obvious that contributes little to the advancement of our science. Matthews, Shaw, and Klove (1966) discussed the need for using "pseudo-neurologic" patients as appropriate controls; that is, patients who have been referred for a presumed neurological problem provide a more clinically meaningful control than do normal subjects who show absolutely no evidence of cortical impairment. A related problem is that frequently patient groups are comprised solely on the basis of psychiatric or neurological *opinion* rather than on the basis of more substantial neurological findings and tests. Heaton, Baade, and Johnson (1978), committing on this phenomenon, remark "in practice, organic brain syndrome is frequently a presumptive diagnosis based largely upon results of unstandardized clinical exams that are less sensitive to cerebral disorders than are many of the psychological tests under investigation in these studies" (p. 143). It seems clear that haphazard assignment of subjects to groups has often set an upper limit on the accuracy of the neuropsychological tests used to assign patients to those groups. We hope that advances in technology such as computerized tomography will result in more careful screening and more accurate assignment of subjects to categories in the future. One final methodological issue deserves comment. This is the issue of base rates. It is an issue frequently neglected by psychologists and researchers in neuropsychology; however, both the tests selected for assessment and the rigorousness of the criteria set for classification should be affected by the clinician's knowledge of base rates. One may choose to adopt less rigorous criteria in a population that would include a great many nonimpaired patients apt to do poorly on a neuropsychological test (e.g., a geriatric population), while using more rigorous standards for the evaluation of a relatively healthy population (e.g., military inductees).

NEUROPSYCHOLOGICAL EVALUATION OF PSYCHIATRIC PATIENTS

The ability of standardized neuropsychological measures to differentate between brain-damaged patients and normal controls is well documented. However, it has not been conclusively shown that the tests can differentiate patients with known evidence of cerebral pathology from patients whose abberant behavior can best be attributed to "functional" causes. Watson and his colleagues (Watson, Thomas, Anderson, & Felling, 1968) found the Halstead–Reitan Battery totally unsuited to this purpose—both actuarial interpretation and clinical judgment produced hit rates that were just slightly above chance. In response to criticism from Levine and Fierstein (1972), who felt that Watson had failed to adequately control for chronicity, Watson (1974) matched subjects from the initial investigation on the chronicity variable and again failed to achieve either statistical or clinical separation of the two groups. In contrast, the Levine and Fierstein (1972) study demonstrated highly reliable separation, with the brain-damaged subjects scoring worse on every individual measure and doing significantly more poorly on the Impairment Index, Finger Tapping, Rhythm, Digit Span, and Digit Symbol tests. However, this difference may well be accounted for in terms of sampling differences between the two studies. The Levine and Fierstein study used only "diffuse brain disease" cases and excluded those cases where neurological findings were apt to be more equivocal (e.g., psychomotor seizure, multiple sclerosis, etc.). In addition, Watson's patients were considerably older than those used in the Levine and Fierstein study.

Other researchers have also produced equivocal results. Stack and Phillips (1970) compared the Halstead–Reitan performance of 24 acute schizophrenics with that of 18 brain-damaged patients and 18 medical controls. In contrast to Watson, these investigators found that the tests could discriminate between schizophrenics and organics and that clinicians could make this determination with 72% accuracy. Their results are even more impressive insofar as the effect was maintained when age and education effects were partialed out of the data set through analysis of covariance. However, it is likely that these investigators were looking at a group of relatively intact schizophrenic patients since only patients with enough stamina to complete the lengthy MMPI were included. In addition, the Stack and Phillips patients were, on the average, 15 years younger than those in the Watson *et al.* study.

An important consideration in each of the studies reviewed above is that brain-damaged patients were treated as a homogeneous group without regard for lesion type or lateralization of defect. Boll (1974), in a far more sophisticated study, was able to use the results of a single test (Trailmaking, parts A and B), to discriminate between 20 schizophrenic and 120 brain-damaged controls broken down into three subgroups: cerebrovascular, neoplastic, or traumatic disorders. All schizophrenic patients were inpatients in an acute, intensive-care ward. Boll rejected the option of matching individuals or groups by age because he felt age was in itself a potent neuropsychological variable and "any attempts to force age equality upon groups with different types of cerebral disorders might render them nonrepresentative of the total population of persons with the disorders involved" (p. 456). This decision may have been important in light of the results of Barnes and Lucas (1974), who obtained highly significant discrimination between their brain-damaged subjects and the psychogenic subjects on 10 of the 12 Halstead–Reitan measures they employed. Following an analysis of covariance where age and intelligence were statistically controlled, only two variables were found to be discriminating. However, it is naive and inappropriate to covary on IQ scores that were obtained after cerebral insult or injury; insofar as intellectual measures are sensitive to the effects of brain impairment, meaningful variation between brain-damaged and non-brain-damaged groups will be statistically removed and the effect of the independent variable will be diluted. Given this caveat, there is little that the Barnes and Lucas study can tell us. However, it is interesting to note that factor analysis of their data produced quite different factor patterns across groups, again suggesting differences in Halstead–Reitan performance across diagnostic categories. More direct comparison with earlier studies is hampered by the fact that their psychogenic group was largely comprised of neurotics and character disorders.

Fields and Fullerton (1975) compared the performance of three groups (N=25 each): organics, schizophrenics, and medical controls. Subjects were matched for age and education. Their results indicated that six of nine measures clearly differentiated brain-damaged from schizophrenic patients. These authors report data on chronicity of diagnosis (mean chronicity was 4.5 years for the schizophrenic group) but no information on total years of hospitalization, although previous research (e.g., Stack & Phillips, 1970) found this to be the more potent variable.

Not all findings have been as positive as those reported above. Lacks, Colbert, Harrow, and Levine (1970) found the relatively brief Bender–Gestalt Test was more effective in separating organics and schizophrenics than the longer and more complex Halstead–Reitan Battery. However, it is impossible to adequately evaluate this study because of the perfunctory way in which subject selection is described. Their organic group is not described other than as representing "categories such as encephalitis, Pick's disease, Korsakoff's syndrome, etc." (an atypical assortment at best) while the schizophrenic sample is not described at all. In a similar experiment, DeWolfe, Barrell, Becker, and Spaner (1971) failed to find significant differences between the performance of brain-damaged subjects and schizophrenic subjects (chronic) when mean levels of performance of the two groups were compared. However, when pattern of deficit was compared across groups, meaningful differences were apparent. DeWolfe et al. regard the qualitative differences in performance as more meaningful than the insignificant quantitative differences that separated the two groups. However, the one attempt to date to replicate these findings (Watson, 1971) failed and the utility of pattern analysis remains moot.

In one of the best studies to address the problem of differential diagnosis with schizophrenic and brain-damaged patients, Fredericks and Finkel (1978) found that their schizophrenics (N=44) performed better than the brain-damaged group on all Halstead–Reitan tests except categories. However, this otherwise sound study is marred by the fact that the brain-damaged and medical control samples were borrowed from Reitan's files. Testing occurred in a different part of the country, at a different time, with a different examiner. Unfortunately, it is impossible to tease out real differences from differences that might arise due to sampling artifacts.

Each of the above studies lumped all brain-damaged subjects into a single group, perpetuating a uniformity assumption myth (Kiessler, 1966). With one exception (Boll, 1974), no distinction was made between patients suffering from trauma, neoplastic disease, cardiovascular disorders, or degenerative conditions. This consistent failure to subdivide the neurological group into meaningful categorical groups could be in part responsible for the ambiguity that characterized research findings in this area. In the single study to date to adequately treat the issue of lateralization, Golden (1977) used discriminant function analysis of the Halstead–Reitan tests to achieve 90% overall effectiveness in classification. Using all tests to separate the two major groups in the study (brain damaged and psychiatric) Golden was able to achieve 100% classification of the psychiatric group and 94% classification of the brain-damaged group.

In summary, the research dealing with the utility of the Halstead–Reitan Battery in separating schizophrenics from brain-damaged patients is equivocal. Studies have varied on a number of dimensions and it is not yet apparent what dimensions are critical in those studies reporting positive results. At the very least, it appears that total length of hospitalization and chronicity of disorder are potent mediators of performance in schizophrenic samples while failure to control for lateralization and type of lesion may have contributed in part to several of the negative findings reported above. It is possible that additional investigation, with proper controls for lateralization, chronicity, and hospitalization, may clarify this issue considerably. The reader interested in a more comprehensive review of this problem is referred to Heaton and Crowley (1981).

It is possible that a good bit of the problem of separating schizophrenics from brain-damaged individuals lies in the fact that the two populations overlap and do not represent dichotomous entities. Both terms are extraordinarily vague. Just as in neurology and neuropsychology, it has become increasingly apparent that the term organic brain syndrome conveys little information about a particular patient's problem or prognosis, so to in psychiatry has it become clear that schizophrenia refers to a heterogeneous *group* of disorders of varying etiologies. The literature on schizophrenia is clarified somewhat by the application of a process versus reactive distinction. Process schizophrenia is characterized by early onset and a history of progressive deterioration with a poor prognosis. The reactive schizophrenic, on the other hand, is characterized by a relatively later onset, an onset that is usually in response to psychosocial stressors, and a relatively good prognosis. The development of research diagnostic criteria (Spitzer, Endicott, & Robins, 1975) and the third edition of the diagnostic and statistical manual of the American Psychiatric Association (DSM - III), both of which specify the specific operational criteria required for a diagnosis of schizophrenia, offer meaningful conceptual categories for classification of schizophrenic subgroups and should help to clarify future research.

It is becoming increasingly clear that a good many patients traditionally diagnosed as schizophrenics do in fact display neurological abnormalities on closer examination. Differences between the brains of schizophrenics and normal individuals have been demonstrated on gross neurological examinations, pneumoencephalograms, EEGs, and with detailed histological examination. Heaton, Baade, and Johnson (1978) suggest that the base rate for organicity in most populations of psychiatric patients seen for neuropsychological testing is about 30%. The behavioral deficits noted for these patients on neuropsychological examination does not appear to be an artifact secondary to institutionalization, decreased motivation, or psychotropic medication. These findings have considerable significance for the clinician working with schizophrenic patients because of their prognostic implications. It is commonly observed that many schizophrenic patients do not respond to standard psychotropic medications such as the phenothiazines. It is reasonable to speculate that many of these patients may fail to respond because of the fact that their behavioral problems result from structural and morphological anomalies rather than from the biochemical aberrations that are most likely to be responsible for the behavioral deficits noted in the vast majority of schizophrenic patients. If we can identify this subset of schizophrenics who do in fact exhibit morphological anomalies, we may be able to develop more appropriate treatment strategies employing token economies and the methods of behavior therapy in lieu of medication alone.

Unfortunately, the particular brain anomalies present in the neurologically impaired schizophrenic are varied and diffuse. Golden et al. (1980) found that the brains of schizophrenics were less dense bilaterally than were the brains of normal controls. Ingvar and Franzen (1974) conducted a number of regional cerebral blood flow studies that demonstrated frontal lobe deficits in chronic schizophrenics. Gur (1978) has conducted studies that demonstrate left hemisphere dysfunction with compensatory overactivation in schizophrenics. These results are consistent with those of Ingvar and Franzen; however, they have been challenged by Walker et al. (1981), who reinterpret Gur's findings and suggest that these results are best explained as secondary to a deficit in interhemispheric transfer. Other studies have demonstrated enlarged sulci, atrophy of the cerebellar vermis, and backward hemispheric asymmetry in the brains of schizophrenic patients. While these findings are not always consistent, they are highly provocative and tremendously exciting. We anticipate major breakthroughs in the 1980s in our efforts to elucidate the relationships between morphology and function in psychiatric patients and particularly in the chronic schizophrenic.

TRAINING ISSUES IN NEUROPSYCHOLOGY

The vast majority of clinical neuropsychologists find themselves working in a field for which they have had minimal graduate training, if any at all. This results from the fact that neuropsychology is a new and emerging specialty area and most major training programs have been in existence for just a few years. The typical clinical neuropsychologist has had courses in physiological psychology and traditional psychometric testing but has learned the rudiments of neuropsychological assessment through a series of workshops and self-structured learning experiences. Likewise, the average clinical neuropsychologist learned neuroanatomy and neuropathology on his/her own not having had an opportunity to pursue these areas as part of their graduate training. Oftentimes these skills are acquired during the internship year or during a specialized postdoctoral year in neuropsychology. Although we believe that this model is adequate for insuring competency (it was the model under which we were trained), it is clearly unsatisfactory in general and needs to be replaced by more rigorous training standards. Meier (1981) has described four models for graduate training in clinical neuropsychology. In the first, neuropsychology is taught as a subspecialty area in a traditional applied psychology program, usually clinical psychology. The second model involves an interdepartmental supporting program with the combined efforts of neuropsychology and clinical neurosciences. The third model is a variant of the scientist–practitioner model promulgated at the Boulder conference. The goal of this model is to prepare a generalist who can function in neurological and neurosurgical settings. The fourth and final model involves a coordinated graduate curriculum in which the student earns separately both the PhD and PsyD degrees. Whichever model is adopted, it is clear to us that neuropsychologists need to be trained either at the graduate level or during internship or a postdoctoral year, in a medical setting where they can be exposed to a variety of brain-impaired patients as well as to psychiatric patients so the student can appreciate issues of differential diagnosis and the vagaries of behavior found on both neurology and psychiatry wards. In addition, it is important that students be exposed to appropriate role models working in medical settings and that they have the opportunity to interact and learn from professionals in a variety of other specialty areas including neurology, neurosurgery, physical therapy, speech pathology, audiology, and psychiatry. Students should have an opportunity to attend grand rounds in both neurology and psychiatry as well as walking rounds in both disciplines. In addition, attending brain cuttings provides first-hand exposure to neuropathology and allows for a fuller appreciation of some of the neurological causes of abnormal behavior. Finally, the hospital experience will provide exposure to and appreciation of the other neurodiagnostic techniques that are available—angiography, pneumoencephalography, brain scanning, and computerized axial tomography. Both the International Neuropsychological Society (INS) and Division 40 of the American Psychological Association are currently studying training models and are developing plans for credentialing in neuropsychology. We eagerly await developments in both areas and anticipate the development of neuropsychology as a specialty area within its own right.

SUGGESTIONS FOR FURTHER READING

Craig, P.L. Neuropsychological assessments in public psychiatric hospitals: The current status of the practice. *Clinical Neuropsychology*, 1979, *1*, 1–7.

Davison, L.A. Introduction. In R.M. Reitan & L.A. Davison (Eds.), *Clinical neuropsychology: Current status and applications*. New York: John Wiley, 1974.

Horton, A.M., Jr., Wedding, D., & Phay, A. Current perspective on assessment of and therapy for brain-damaged individuals. In C.J. Golden, S.S. Alcaparras, F. Strider & B. Graber (Eds.), *Applied techniques in behavioral medicine*. New York: Grune & Stratton, 1981.

Luria, A.R. & Majovski, L.V. Basic approaches used in American and Soviet clinical neuropsychology. *American Psychology*, 1977, *32*, 959–968.

6

SELECTED
NEUROPSYCHOLOGICAL
TESTS

The early history of clinical psychology was characterized by an avid search for the best test for assessing "organicity." This search was predicated on the naive assumption that brain damage could be treated as a unitary construct without regard for hemisphericity, lesion site, size, type, age and sex of subject, or any of a host of variables that mediate the expression of brain damage. This uniformity assumption myth was in part the outgrowth of Karl Lashley's research with lower organisms (where, in fact, brain tissue is largely undifferentiated) and his theories of cortical mass action and equipotentiality. In addition, psychologists had been extremely successful in developing tests to assess the construct of intelligence; it did not seem so much more difficult to assess the construct of brain damage.

Since Lashley's time, it has become exceedingly clear that no single test is adequate to top all of the variegated expressions of cerebral damage and that the single test has limitations even as a screening measure. This growing awareness led to the development of standardized batteries designed to survey the entire range of adaptive function. Two of these batteries—the Halstead–Reitan and the Luria–

Nebraska—are discussed in subsequent chapters. However, many neuropsychologists prefer to select their own tests on an *ad hoc* basis with time limitations and the relative severity of false-positive and false-negative diagnoses serving as the primary selection criteria. In addition, test selection may vary dramatically as a function of referral question; the patient with a CT-verified lesion may be given tests very different from those of the patient who presents as a diagnostic dilemma.

This chapter surveys some of the more popular and useful neuropsychological tests. As a heuristic device, we have categorized the tests into seven basic groups. We discuss each of these in turn with the goal of introducing the unfamiliar reader to the tests in question.

INTELLIGENCE

The assessment of intelligence is basic to the neuropsychological evaluation. It can be assessed in a rudimentary way during the mental status examination by asking questions that assess fund of information ("How far is it from Paris to New York?"), the ability to abstract (usually tested with proverb interpretation), similarities ("How are fear and hate alike?"), and by having the patient perform mental calculations and complete conceptual series (Straub & Black, 1977). With experience, and with proper respect for educational and cultural influences, this approach is generally adequate for classification into broad intellectual categories (e.g., superior, average, below average, retardation). However, beyond classification and in the absence of pathognomic signs, it provides little of neurodiagnostic utility.

With a slightly greater investment of the patient's time, it is possible to get a more accurate estimate of general intelligence with a test such as the Shipley Institute of Living Scale. The Shipley contains two subtests: vocabulary and conceptual thinking. The first is a straightforward measure of vocabulary; the latter requires that the patient complete a series of sequence patterns of increasing difficulty. The Shipley was initially designed to assess organicity in psychiatric patients; it was assumed that in cases of brain impairment, vocabulary scores would remain intact while ability in concept formation would deteriorate. While this basic premise is sound, subsequent research has demonstrated that the Shipley is not adequate for assessing brain damage (Lezak, 1976).

With patients who have not been exposed to traditional learning experiences and cultural mores, we will frequently use some other paper and pencil test that is less likely to be culturally biased. We find Cattell and Cattell's Culture–Fair Intelligence Test to be a good measure of Spearman's "g" (general or fluid intelligence). Raven's matrices will provide essentially the same information. Both of these tests are relatively brief and do not require the ongoing participation of the examiner. Both yield reliable IQ estimates and both are used in numerous neuropsychology laboratories. However, because each samples from only one domain, they are limited for diagnostic purposes.

To insure a comprehensive evaluation of intellectual abilities, it is necessary to individually administer one of the longer intelligence tests. Although a few older neuropsychologists still use the Stanford–Binet scales, it is clear that Wechsler's tests have assumed a premier position in American neuropsychology. We will discuss these tests in some detail because they are so widely used and because deficits in performance on the various subscales do have considerable neuropsychological significance. In addition, a widespread clinical "lore" has developed around these tests. Finally, the Wechsler tests are important because they form an integral part of the Halstead–Reitan Battery. However, we choose to discuss them here because of their wide general use by psychologists who do not use the other Halstead–Reitan tests.

Wechsler developed his tests while working as chief psychologist at Bellevue Psychiatric Hospital in New York City. His initial efforts were directed toward assessing adult intelligence in a more comprehensive manner than was available with the widely used Stanford–Binet scales. His work culminated in publication of the Wechsler–Bellevue (1939), which is still used by some neuropsychologists (e.g., Reitan) for research purposes. This test was extensively revised and standardized in the 1950s and was renamed the Wechsler Adult Intelligence Scale (WAIS). The new standardization sample was more culturally and geographically representative and within a few years the WAIS became the most widely used of the individually administered intelligence tests. More recently (1981) the WAIS has been revised and dated items have been deleted or modified; however, the revised WAIS (WAIS-R) is essentially the same test with about 80% of the items from the 1955 revision retained or only slightly modified (Wechsler, 1981).

Wechsler also developed similar intellectual scales for children. In 1949 he published the Wechsler Intelligence Scale for Children (WISC); this test was updated and renamed in 1974 and the revision (WISC-R) is widely used by developmental neuropsychologists and by specialists in learning disabilities. The WISC-R is normed for children between the ages of 6 and 16; WAIS-R norms are available for the age range 16 to 74. For younger children, Wechsler developed the Wechsler Preschool and Primary Test of Intelligence (WPPSI). This test is normed for children between the ages of 4 and 6½.

One of the primary changes made by Wechsler was to drop Binet's concept of mental age in favor of the concept of a deviation IQ. Simply stated, a person's IQ at any given time (age) is defined by his relative standing among his age peers (Matarrazo, 1972). Since performance on many of the WAIS subtests declines with age, a somewhat higher absolute level of performance is required in order for a younger person to earn an IQ equal to that of an older person. This use of deviation IQs obviated many of the problems inherent in the use of mental age to assess adult intelligence and deviation IQs were adapted for use with the 1960 revision of the Stanford-Binet scales.

Eleven subtests are included on the WAIS; the same subtests and format were retained for the WAIS-R. Other additional subtests were investigated but rejected. These included a test of level of aspiration (a variable that clearly interacts in important ways with intellectual ability) and a test of spatial ability (which turned out to be redundant with the Block Design subtest). In this volume, we discuss the neuropsychological implications of the WAIS subtests.

The WAIS tests are grouped into the two major categories of verbal and performance tests. The verbal tests include Information, Digit Span, Vocabulary, Arithmetic, Comprehension, and Similarities; the performance tests include Picture Completion, Picture Arrangement, Block Design, Object Assembly, and Digit Symbol. Each of these, both by itself and in the context of a neuropsychological battery, provides valuable information to the clinician.

The Information subtest is a well-validated measure of fund of information and long-term, remote memory. Scores tend to be most affected by dominant hemisphere injury; however, in general, the Information subtest is one of the Wechsler scales least likely to be affected by neurological insult or injury. We have seen patients who presented with massive lesions and yet retained relatively intact performance on this subtest. For this reason, Information (along with Vocabulary) will often serve as the best available gauge of premorbid intellectual ability.

Digit Span is almost universally included in intellectual assessment batteries (as well as most mental status examinations) and it forms an important part of the total WAIS picture. As administered with the WAIS, it is a test of immediate auditory memory. It is also one of the WAIS subtests most sensitive to brain damage (as well as anxiety). In a normal population, virtually all adults who are not brain damaged or retarded will be able to recall four digits forward and three backward with the average adult repeating six digits forward and five backward (Lezak, 1976). Our clinical experience suggests that this test has some utility in lateralizing lesions since right hemisphere damage may produce deficits in digits backward while digits forward remains relatively intact. This phenomenon is not consistently observed and is most likely related to the spatial aspect involved in transposition of digits.

The Vocabulary subtest correlates quite highly with the WAIS full-scale IQ and in itself serves as a good indicant of intellectual ability. It is most likely to be affected by dominant hemisphere injuries, but, in the nonaphasic patient, may remain high despite substantial impairment. Because the test is long and fairly tedious to score, and because the yield of specific neurodiagnostic information is low, some clinicians will omit this subtest and substitute a more specific test for aphasia (e.g., the Token test).

Arithmetic is a time subtest comprised of 14 items that tap arithmetic skill, logical reasoning, immediate memory, and concentration. The test is sensitive to brain impairment with dominant hemisphere lesions producing slightly more impairment.

The Comprehension subtest of the WAIS is a factorially complex task that assesses practical judgment, appreciation of social values and standards, and the ability to educe abstract principles. The test requires a fairly elaborate response from the subject (e.g., an explanation of the reason prescriptions are required before certain drugs can be purchased). This elaboration necessarily introduces some subjectivity in scoring; however, it also provides a rich source of clinical material that may prove invaluable to the diagnostician. Many neuropsychologists feel that this test is one of the best for distinguishing between psychiatric and neurological disorders.

The Similarities subtest requires that the patient identify the commonality that exists between two related stimulus words (e.g., praise and punishment). The test is an excellent indicator of general intellectual ability and it is not as susceptible to cultural and educational bias as some other verbal subtests (e.g., Information and Vocabulary). The test is one of the most sensitive predictors of damage to the dominant hemisphere, offering some support for Goldstein's position that brain impairment is most clearly present in those tests that assess "abstract attitude."

Each of the above tests are included in the calculations for determining verbal IQ. Five tests that are less dependent on verbal ability are used to determine performance IQ. The first of these is the Picture Completion subtest, a good predictor of general intelligence (especially at lower IQ levels) that is a relatively pure performance tests—that is, it is largely uncontaminated by verbal or visuospatial requirements. The test does not provide a great deal of specific neurodiagnostic information; however it may provide an excellent estimate of premorbid intellectual ability, especially in those cases where assessment of verbal IQ is confounded by the presence of aphasia. This is possible because the central idea (identification of a missing part) can be easily grasped with minimal amounts of verbal instruction and detailed responses are not required.

The Picture Arrangement subtest requires ability in comprehending a total situation (thematic perception) while not losing track of essential cues embedded in the pictures used. Some degree of anticipation and planning is also required if the cards are to be correctly sorted. This test is most sensitive to nondominant hemisphere damage; when extremely poor performance on Picture Arrangement is present in the absence of impaired performance on other WAIS subtests, one should consider the possibility of a focal right temporal lesion (Lezak, 1976).

The Block Design subtest is an adaptation of Kohs Block Test that provides considerable information about a patient's visuospatial ability. This test, which requires manipulating a set of red and white blocks so that the top pattern matches a stimulus card, also requires some degree of manual dexterity and psychomotor skill. The test is sensitive to the effects of brain damage in either hemisphere but is most depressed in cases of nondominant hemisphere injury. We believe it is the best available test for assessing spatial deficits and we will frequently include this test in our evaluations, even when a full WAIS is not being administered. Golden (1977, 1979) has suggested that the Block Design subtest is clinically useful in discriminating between schizophrenia and brain-damaged patients.

The Object Assembly subtest also taps visual–motor organization and the ability to form a meaningful spatial Gestalt given a set of individual elements. It is generally less sensitive to brain damage than the Block Design test; however, like Block Design, it is most sensitive to nondominant hemisphere lesions.

The Digit Symbol test, the last of the WAIS subtests, is quite important to the neuropsychologist insofar as it is the single subtest most sensitive to neurological damage. This results from the fact that an extremely wide range of cognitive functions are required for adequate performance, including new learning, immediate memory, sustained attention, motor speed, and visual–motor coordination. The test is affected by damage to either hemisphere and may be depressed even in the absence of any indicants of damage on the other WAIS scales.

Although originally designed to simply assess basic intellectual ability, it is clear that the data obtained from Wechsler's scales can be extremely useful diagnostically and that these tests form an important part of the neuropsychologists' set of tools. Wechsler himself popularized the concept of a deterioration quotient (DQ) based on the ratio of "hold" to "don't hold" scores. "Don't hold" scores were those subtests most susceptible to the effects of cerebral impairment. "Hold" tests were those tests least likely to be affected by cerebral insult (or age). Matarrazo (1972) has critiqued the available research on Wechsler's Deterioration Quotient and related actuarial approaches (e.g., Hewson ratios) and suggests that, in general, they have proven inadequate when used as simple decision rules for determining the presence of brain damage.

McFie (1975) has developed an extensive system that can be used to relate WAIS subscales to focal neurological deficits. McFie reports that while virtually all brain-damaged patients show decrements in Digit Symbol performance, specific patterns on the other scales characterize specific focal damage. For example, left frontal patients show marked deficits on Digit Span while right frontal cases perform most poorly on Picture Arrangement. Right temporal patients also show the greatest deficit on Picture Arrangement while left temporal patients perform poorly on Similarities and Digit Span. The right parietal patient is characterized by deficits on Block Design and Picture Arrangement, the left parietal patient by decrements in performance on Arithmetic, Digit Span, Block Design, and Similarities.

Another approach to lateralization—and one that has resulted in considerable controversy—is the use of the discrepancy index. This index is simply the difference between performance and verbal IQ. Matarrazo (1972) maintains that a 15-point discrepancy in either direction is clinically significant. Other researchers (e.g., Vega & Parsons, 1971) have maintained that depressed verbal scores are associated with left hemisphere lesions while depressed performance scores are more commonly found in patients with right hemisphere lesions. In contrast, Smith (1966) was unable to substantiate this relationship and claimed that brain damage to either hemisphere was most likely to affect performance IQ. Finally, Todd, Coolidge, and Satz (1977) failed to find significant differences between left and right hemisphere groups on the discrepancy index. Furthermore, the index could not differentiate the patients with diffuse damage from psychiatric controls. These authors report that "the Verbal IQ/Performance IQ discrepancy cannot be used as a diagnostic screening tool in those institutions in which both brain-damaged and psychiatric patients are seen" (p. 453). This finding, based on a sample of 355 clearly defined cases, is important because it runs contrary to a vast amount of clinical lore and to the everyday practice of most clinicians. Clearly, the relationship between neurological damage and verbal and performance IQ is a complex one dependent on a wide variety of factors including age and plasticity (the child's brain is still developing and functions are more diffusely represented in the cortex), extent of lesion (focal lesions are more apt to produce high discrepancies), and location (posterior lesions are more likely to produce the effect while frontal lesions in some cases do not even affect IQ). The discrepancy index offers the neuropsychologist relevant data in summary form; it should never be used in isolation as a sign of brain damage and it cannot replace a systematic review of subscale scores and a detailed analysis of specific test behavior.

MEMORY

The ability to store and retrieve memories is essential to the species and necessary for efficient daily functioning. It is important to the neuropsychologist because failure in memory is frequently the earliest sign of organic dysfunction. However, evaluation is complicated by the fact that patients with numerous disorders can present with a primary complaint of memory loss. Depressed patients in particular are apt to be misdiagnosed as cases of early dementia and a definitive diagnosis may be impossible without further observation. We have seen several patients who appeared clearly "organic" on psychological testing; however, the brain syndrome cleared after a judicious trial of tricyclics; this is *prima facie* evidence for a depressive etiology.

Assessment of memory is an important component of the mental status examination. First, the clinician will want to assess immediate memory with a test similar to the Digit Span subtest of the WAIS. Then recent memory will typically be assessed by having the patient recall three or four items (e.g., house, book, sewing machine) after a brief, interrupted delay. Finally, remote memory will be tested by asking the patient about historical events (e.g., who became president after Kennedy was shot). These questions require due consideration for the patient's educational and cultural background; however, they are to be preferred to questions that may be more personally relevant (e.g., "What year did you graduate from high school?") but impossible to substantiate.

One problem with the simple clinical evaluation described above is that the terms used are quite imprecise; a second problem is that the examination fails to sample an adequate array of memory abilities. Much more information is available from a test such as the Wechsler Memory Scale (WMS), which surveys a far more extensive range of memory abilities.

The Wechsler Memory Scale (WMS) was designed by David Wechsler (1945) and is frequently used to supplement the WAIS. The scale consists of seven subtests. The first, Personal and Current Information, asks some basic questions (e.g., age and year of birth). These are seldom missed; however, other questions require awareness of the names of public figures such as the governor and mayor. We have found that even well-educated subjects sometimes miss these items.

The second subscale assesses Orientation and consists of standard mental status items designed to tap orientation to time and place. With the popularity of calendar watches, increasing numbers of patients find themselves unable to specify the exact date. However, the fully oriented patient should be able to name the day of the week and at least approximate the date.

The third subtest is labeled Mental Control. This test requires that the patient count backward from 20 to 7, repeat the alphabet, and count from 1 to 40 by threes.

Subtest IV, Logical Memory, tests immediate recall of verbal ideas by having the patient repeat two fairly detailed stories. Subtest V requires that the patient repeat digits forward and backward; it is redundant with the Digit Span subtest of the WAIS and should not be repeated if the WAIS has already been administered.

The fifth subtest, Visual Reproduction, requires that the patient draw from memory several simple geometric figures. The final subtest, Associate Learning, assesses the ability to learn new material (paired associates) at two levels of difficulty. All six subtests are summed to produce a memory quotient (MQ) which can be compared to IQ results. Prigatano (1978) suggests that a short-term verbal memory deficit is likely in the patient with average or above average intelligence whose MQ is 12 or more points below full-scale IQ.

The Wechsler Memory Scale has been widely criticized because of inadequate normative data, a restricted age range, the failure to adequately assess nonverbal memory, and because memory quotient is so highly correlated with IQ scores in a nonamnesic population. The test may be sensitive to some left hemisphere lesions; however, with the exception of one subtest (Visual Reproduction), it is not useful in assessing the memory deficits associated with right hemisphere (temporal) lesions.

Russell (1975) has proposed a modification of the WAIS that uses only the Logical Memory and Visual Reproduction subtests to assess, respectively, verbal and nonverbal memory. This partially offsets the strong verbal bias present in the original WAIS and reduces the total testing time. In addition, a second administration of the test after ½ hour has elapsed allows for an adequate assessment of recent memory (vis à vis the immediate memory abilities assessed on the first presentation).

Additional options for the assessment of memory include the use of the memory scale of the Luria–Nebraska Battery and the various memory components of the Halstead–Reitan Battery (e.g., the memory component of the Tactile Performance Test and the last subscale of the Category Test). These are discussed in the chapters devoted to the respective batteries.

One final alternative should be mentioned. Corsi (1972) has designed a block-tapping test which is a spatial (right hemisphere) analog to the Digit Span Test. The test "appears to be the best available noninvasive test of right hemisphere hippocampal function" (Kolb & Whishaw, 1980, p. 321).

SPATIAL TESTS

Memory is a complex function bilaterally represented in the cerebral hemispheres. However, some tests of figural memory are of special significance to the neuropsychologist because of the insight they provide with regard to the integrity of the right cerebral hemisphere. We have lumped these instruments together under the rubric "spatial tests." Many of them figure importantly in the history of psychological testing.

The Bender Visual Motor Gestalt Test (Bender, 1938), more commonly referred to as simply "the Bender," has enjoyed a premier position in clinical psychology since the second World War, Designed initially to assess the maturation of perceptual motor functions in young children, the test soon came to be widely used with both children and adults as a measure of both personality and organicity. Numerous methods of administration and scoring the Bender have been proposed; these are reviewed in Golden (1979). Essentially, all of these methods are variations of a quite simple task in which the patient is required to copy nine different figures on a sheet of white paper. Neurological impairment is inferred from the presence of pathognomonic signs derived from Bender lore. These signs include rotation of individual designs, distortions in reproduction, overlapping designs, disproportionate components, use of circles or loops for dots, use of straight lines for curves, and perseverations (Small, 1980).

Loyalty to the Bender runs high, despite studies such as that of Goldberg (1959) demonstrating that hospital secretaries, psychology trainees, and doctoral level psychologists were all equally *inaccurate* in assessing brain damage using Bender protocols alone. In addition, the expert clinicians rated themselves as less confident about their judgments than did the secretaries, despite the fact that the clinicians worked with the Bender on a daily basis as a tool for assessing brain damage.

The Bender does appear to be a reasonably good test for assessing visuospatial difficulties and it is sensitive to right parietal lesions; in addition, rotations are often pathognomonic, occurring in right hemisphere cases about twice as often as in left hemisphere cases (Lezak, 1976). Our complaint is with those clinicians who use the test in a simplistic way as "screening for brain damage." It is clearly inadequate for that purpose.

A variation of the Bender–Gestalt was devised by Cantor in 1976. His method, called the Background Interference Procedure (BIP), involves two administrations of the test. The first is the normal procedure with responses drawn on a clean white sheet of paper. The second administration requires that the figures be drawn on special sheets covered with wavy lines (background interference). Those special forms have clean carbon sheets underneath; following administration, the confusing top sheets can be thrown away and performance on the two trials can be compared. The background interference is found to be especially disruptive for those patients with verifiable brain damage. More important, the BIP appears to be one of the few instruments useful in distinguishing between brain-damaged and schizophrenic patients (Heaton, 1978).

The Memory for Designs (MFD) test (Graham & Kendall, 1960) offers an alternative to the use of the Bender–Gestalt. The MFD consists of 15 geometric designs of increasing complexity. Each is shown to the patient for 5 seconds. The design is then removed and the patient is asked to reproduce the design. Errors are differentially weighted and a total error score is generated. The scoring system is quite strict and the test virtually never yields false positives (Lezak, 1976). Diagnostic accuracy is in the range of the Bender–Gestalt; this is not surprising since very similar functions are being tapped.

The Benton Visual Retention Test (BVRT) is another spatial test which is extremely popular among American neuropsychologists. This popularity is in part due to universal regard for Dr. Arthur Benton, one of the founding fathers of the neuropsychology movement. Benton's work at the University of Iowa has been instrumental in expanding our knowledge of brain–behavior relationships; in addition, Benton has developed dozens of neuropsychological tests. Of these, the BVRT is the best known and the most popular. The test consists of ten cards with multiple designs on each card. Three equivalent sets of cards are available; this allows for sequential testing without concern for the confounding effects of previous assessment with the same instrument. Norms are available for both adults and children; in addition, Benton has developed adjusted norms keyed to the patient's premorbid intellectual ability. Administration of the test is extremely flexible with the examiner selecting one of four basic testing procedures. In administration A, immediate memory is assessed by having the patient reproduce each card following a 10-second presentation. Administration B is identical except that a 5-

second exposure is given. Administration C is a copying test much like the Bender–Gestalt. Administration D is a test of delayed memory in which the patient is exposed to each stimulus card for 10 seconds and then required to delay responding for at least 15 seconds. Smith (1975) points out that the use of multiple stimulus items of the BVRT cards makes the test especially sensitive to homonymous hemianopsia and to unilateral spatial neglect. Both Smith (1975) and Golden (1981) recommend that the BVRT be used in lieu of the Bender when the goal of testing is assessment of organic deficits.

SENSORY–MOTOR TESTS

The sensory–motor evaluation of the patient begins when he or she walks into the office of a neurologist or neuropsychologist. Gait and expression should always be assessed for evidence of motor weakness. In addition, it is wise to shake hands with the patient; this establishes rapport and provides preliminary information about grip strength. The neurologist will proceed to conduct a detailed examination of the cranial nerves; this examination is described in detail in Chusid (1976) and is not discussed here. However, it is important to note that considerable overlap exists with the neuropsychological evaluation. The latter differs primarily in being more quantified, more concerned with higher cognitive functions, and in the use of structured tests to assess the abilities in question. For example, assessment of grip strength involves having the patient grasp and squeeze the fingers of the neurologist; the neuropsychologist is more likely to assess grip strength using a dynometer, knowing that there is a certain comfort in the precision of numbers.

It is possible to assess motor control by employing the finger tapping test developed by Halstead (1947). Nonimpaired individuals should be able to tap approximately 50 times in 10 seconds with the dominant hand; tapping with the nondominant hand is usually about 10% slower. It is important here to realize that the test can be used by itself as an excellent gauge of motor control. Comparison between the performance of the right and left hands provides valuable lateralization information; in addition, it is possible to partially localize focal lesions by comparing finger tapping with foot tapping. To the extent that foot tapping is impaired in the absence of significant finger tapping deficits, one suspects a superior medial lesion of the motor strip. More impaired finger tapping ability suggests a more inferior motor strip focus.

One of the more popular tests for assessing motor skill is the Purdue Pegboard Test. This test was initially designed for employment selection purposes; subsequent research has shown that it is effective in predicting lateralization of lesions (Vaughan & Costa, 1962). The test requires that the patient place as many pegs as possible in place as quickly as possible. Thirty-second trials are run with the left hand first, then with the right, then with both hands used simultaneously. The test is quick and provides an excellent index of manual dexterity.

The Wisconsin Grooved Pegboard Test provides similar information but requires slightly more time to administer. This pegboard differs from the Purdue in that it is considerably smaller and more portable. In addition, it requires finer motor control. Successful completion of the test requires that the patient place 25 grooved pegs in 25 randomly positioned slots; the groove in each slot requires that the peg be twisted before it will fit. Testing is done with each hand individually. Both total time required and number of pegs dropped are recorded for each hand.

The finger and foot tapping tests described above, as well as the Wisconsin Grooved Pegboard, comprise part of the Klove–Mathews Motor Steadiness Battery. In addition, this battery includes tests of maze coordination, vertical and horizontal groove steadiness, and static and resting steadiness. Data from each test are recorded by an electrical digital counter. Two scores are provided for each of the steadiness tests: number of contacts (e.g., amount of unsteadiness) and total duration of contact time. A "contact" occurs each time the metal stylus touches any of the various templates used in the tests.

Another test that has come out of the neuropsychology laboratory at the University of Wisconsion Center for the Health Sciences is the Klove–Mathews Sandpaper Test. The test was designed to assess tactile sensitivity to texture rather than form (Reitan & Davison, 1974) and provides a useful supplement to the usual tests for astereognosis. The subject's task is to arrange four sandpaper-covered blocks in order of roughness. Scoring is based on the time needed to complete the task and the accuracy of each hand.

A wide variety of other tests exist for assessing tactile, visual, and auditory sensation. The best of these are contained in the Sensory–Perceptual Exam of the Halstead–Reitan Battery and we discuss them in detail in Chapter 7.

PERSONALITY TESTS

There is a complex interaction between personality and cerebral integrity and the manifestations of each are shaped by the other. Two patients with very similar lesions may respond very differently due to premorbid personality differences; likewise, personality may change radically following cerebral insult or injury. However, psychology has not been able to develop personality tests that are successful in predicting large portions of behavioral variance and it appears that situations and circumstances are frequently better predictors than personality variables per se (Mischel, 1968). This is especially true in the case of the brain-damaged patient. Despite the poor showing of personality tests in general, many clinicians (frequently lacking skill in neuropsychological methods) have tried to adapt their training and talents to the problem of assessing the presence and extent of brain damage. Although a number of instruments have been tried, we will confine our discussion to the most popular of these, that is, the Rorschach Test and the Minnesota Multiphasic Personality Inventory (MMPI).

The well-known Rorschach method was developed by Hermann Rorschach, a Swiss psychiatrist, in the early 1920s. The test involves the individual presentation of a set of ten ink blots. Five of the blots are fully or partially colored; the remaining five are achromatic. The patient is expected to report what he or she sees in each blot. Since the ink blot is an unstructured and ambiguous stimulus, it is assumed that the subject will "project" his or her beliefs and feelings and that the response obtained will be a function of core personality structure. Although there is little empirical evidence supporting this belief, the test remains extremely popular among clinicians and is frequently included in comprehensive test batteries.

Piotrowski (1937) developed a scoring system for the Rorschach Test that is still used in inferring organicity from Rorschach protocols. The Piotrowski method is an actuarial approach in which the clinician looks for the presence of any of the following ten signs:

1. Fewer than 15 total responses
2. An average time per response greater than 1 minute
3. One or fewer movement responses
4. Simple naming of colors instead of forming color associations (e.g., a pink cloud)
5. Less than 70% of good form responses
6. Fewer than 25% popular responses
7. Perseveration of an idea across several ink blots
8. Impotency of response (i.e., recognition of the inadequacy of response while lacking ability to change it)
9. Perplexity of response (i.e., hesitancy and doubt)
10. The presence of automatic phrases

Piotrowski maintained that the presence of at least five signs was necessary before the patient could be labeled as brain damaged. Some studies have demonstrated that the Piotrowski signs are useful in discriminating brain-damaged subjects from controls; however, we wonder if the same discriminations could not have been made on the basis of a simple interview. To demonstrate the utility of any technique, it is necessary to show that the technique improves on simpler methodologies. It is insufficient to compare accuracy rates with chance predictions alone and then argue for the efficacy of the method. We find that this occurred in many of the early Rorschach studies. At any rate, it is clear that the Rorschach, and projective tests in general, are insufficient and inappropriate for neuropsychological assessment purposes.

Somewhat greater success results when predictions are made on the basis of objective personality tests. Of these, perhaps the best is the ubiquitous MMPI. This 556-item true–false questionnaire yields a profile consisting of t scores for 14 scales. Four of these are validity scales that provide basic information about the subjects approach to testing; the remaining 10 scales are clinical scales and compare the subject's response patterns to those of varied diagnostic groups. Like the WAIS, the MMPI should always be interpreted in terms of pattern analysis since the relationship between scales may be every bit as important as the elevation of the scales themselves.

A number of researchers have attempted to develop actuarial approaches to the prediction of brain damage from MMPI results. Hovey (1964) developed a test that is a model of parsimony in that predictions are made after examining the responses to five questions. A result of four or more responses in a specified direction suggests organicity. Unfortunately, the approach appears useful only in those cases where there is severe brain damage (Lezak, 1976) and what is most needed are tests that are sensitive to subtle and early signs of brain impairment.

Watson (1971b) developed a special MMPI scale that has shown some utility in separating hospitalized schizophrenics from brain-damaged patients. This $Sc-O$ scale consists of 80 items and is only applicable to male patients. Watson and Plemel (1978) devised the Psychiatric–Organic (P–O) Special Scale to compensate for deficiencies in the Sc–O scale and Horton and Wilson (1981) have conducted a successful cross-validation in a domiciliary setting.

Several early researchers devised caudality scales that attempt to use MMPI data to localize lesions in an anterior–posterior dimension. In general, it does not appear that the MMPI has any utility in localizing lesions in any dimension (Reitan, 1976).

In summary, it appears that the MMPI is sensitive to group differences between neurological and nonneurological patients and may be useful for research purposes. It has limited utility as a neuropsychological assessment instrument per se. However, we routinely administer this test to check for (1) psychiatric disturbance that may distort results of more reliable neuropsychological tests and (2) the extent of emotional and personality change following the development of a neurological disorder. In short, while personality tests may serve to supplement or extend the neuropsychological investigation, they are a poor replacement for specific neurodiagnostic tests and should always be treated as ancillary devices only.

MISCELLANEOUS TESTS

A number of tests popular in neuropsychology do not fit readily under the rubrics initially established. However, their use is too widespread for them to be ignored. In particular, we want to discuss the Stroop Color and Word Test, the Wisconsin Card Sorting Test, and the Token Test.

The Stroop Color and Word Test is a simple and easily administered test that consists of three cards that are read as quickly as possible by the patient. The first card requires simply the rapid reading of a series of color names. With the second card, the patient is required to rapidly name the colors of a series of letter Xs. Finally, the patient is presented with a card showing the color names from Card 1 printed in the various (and usually different) colors from Card 2. Here the patient must rapidly name the color of the ink each word is printed in while suppressing the natural inclination to read the words themselves (e.g., responding "red" to the word "blue" printed in red). This requirement for response inhibition on card three makes the Stroop especially sensitive to frontal disorders (Perret, 1974). Golden (1979) maintains that the test can also be used for purposes of lateralization and in the diagnosis of dyslexia.

Another excellent test for assessing frontal lobe deficits is the Wisconsin Card Sorting Test, which has been the basis of extensive research by Brenda Milner and her colleagues. The test requires that the patient match each card (in a deck of 64 cards) to 4 stimulus cards. Each card differs in terms of form, color, and number; correct matching can be made on the basis of any of these three categories. The examiner gives the patient verbal feedback about whether placement was correct after each match is made. What is unique about the test is the fact that the basis for correct classification changes without warning (after ten correct matches) and the patient must be flexible enough to change his behavior to meet the changing test requirements. Patients with frontal lobe lesions tend to perseverate on this task and may be unable to shift response strategies. Interestingly, they may be able to verbalize the fact that the previous strategy is no longer viable;

however, they continue to persist in the maladaptive response set. It appears that the neuroanatomical locus of this deficit is Brodmann's Area 9 in the left hemisphere (Kolb & Whishaw, 1980).

The Token Test (Boller & Vignolo, 1966) is another simple, inexpensive, and portable test that provides an excellent screening for aphasic difficulties. The test requires only a set of plastic or cardboard "tokens" (which can be constructed from available office supplies). The tokens vary in size, shape, and color. They are laid out before the patient who is required to respond to a number of commands of varying complexity. Those items that involve relational concepts appear especially sensitive (e.g., "Together with the yellow circle, take the blue circle"). This test is frequently used when the stimulus items for the Halstead–Wepman are not readily available.

Most clinical psychologists are eclectic in therapy and gravitate to "what works." Likewise, clinical neuropsychologists are apt to develop a set of favorite assessment tools with selection based on personal preference as much as documented diagnostic accuracy. While our review of neuropsychological tests was not exhaustive, it did include the most popular and most widely used tests in neuropsychology. Several of these can be judiciously combined to form a reasonably sound screening battery. However, if a comprehensive neuropsychological evaluation is desired (e.g., for litigation or rehabilitation planning), we recommend either the Halstead–Reitan or the Luria–Nebraska Neuropsychological batteries. Each is discussed in Chapters 7 and 8, respectively.

SUGGESTIONS FOR FURTHER READING

Benton, A.L., Hamsher, K.D., Varney, N.R., & Speen, O. *Contributions to neuropsychological assessment: A clinic manual.* New York: Oxford, 1983.

Golden, C.J. *Clinical interpretation of objective psychological tests.* New York: Grune & Stratton, 1979.

Horton, A.M., Jr. & Decker, E.B. Neuropsychological assessment of an adult minimal brain dysfunction: A case study. *Perceptual and Motor Skills,* 1981, *92,* 676–678.

Matarrazo, J. *Wechsler's measurement and appraisal of adult intelligence.* Baltimore: Williams & Wilkins, 1972.

McFie, J. *Assessment of organic intellectual impairment.* New York: Academic, 1975.

Butcher, J.N. (Ed.). *MMPI: Research developments and clinical applications.* New York: McGraw-Hill, 1969.

7

HALSTEAD–REITAN NEUROPSYCHOLOGICAL TEST BATTERY

While many clinicians opt to let the patient's behavior determine the selection of tests, many others have found it useful to adopt a standardized battery approach in which an identical set of tests is given to each patient, regardless of diagnosis or presenting complaint. This approach has the advantage of providing consistent levels of information for each patient and allows for a fairly comprehensive assessment of a wide variety of behaviors. In addition, it provides a stable information base for research purposes. However, it has the clear disadvantage of being inflexible and it may result in the collection of data that are unnecessary or, more serious, it may limit the imagination of the neuropsychologist and prevent investigation of more fertile areas that are not adequately assessed by the battery adopted.

In the United States, the battery approach is widely (and sometimes uncritically) accepted. Among the batteries available, the Halstead–Reitan is the most popular and is the battery most likely to be used in both medical and psychiatric settings. This popularity derives from the wide availability of workshop training in the Halstead–Reitan Battery and from the extensive research conducted by a variety of investigators demonstrating the general utility of this battery in separating brain-damaged patients from normal controls and, with somewhat less success, separating brain-damaged patients from psychiatric controls. Few other tests in neuropsychology have been studied so intensely or validated so well.

A variety of independent tests make up the Halstead–Reitan Battery. Most of these were developed in Halstead's laboratory at the University of Chicago; still others were added by Reitan (e.g., Trails A and B), who also deleted tests that were theoretically interesting but that failed to statistically discriminate between brain-damaged and normal subjects (e.g., Critical Flicker Frequency and the Time-Sense Test). The tests remaining include the Category Test, Tactual Performance Test, Speech Sounds Perception Test, Rhythm Test, Trails A and B, a Finger Oscillation Test (Tapping), the Reitan–Klove Sensory Perceptual Examination, the Reitan–Indiana Aphasia Examination, and the Lateral Dominance Examination. In addition, the Wechsler Adult Intelligence Test—Revised (WAIS-R) is included in the battery to assess general intellectual functions and some users include the Minnesota Multiphasic Personality Inventory (MMPI) to assess personality variables. Information from these tests is integrated with demographic variables (age, sex, education, etc.) and a personal interview with the patient. The wealth of data provided by the battery forms a complex mosaic that can provide considerable information about the patient when interpreted by a trained and experienced neuropsychologist.

Because of the wide use and popularity of the Halstead–Reitan Battery, we will discuss the major subtests in some detail. Some of these (e.g., Trails A and B) serve as excellent screening measures. For a more detailed discussion, the reader is referred to Golden, Osmon, Moses, and Berg's 1981 book, *Interpretation of the Halstead–Reitan Neuropsychological Test Battery: A Casebook Approach.*

THE CATEGORY TEST

The Category Test is a complex concept formation test that measures the patient's ability to deduce general principles from specific stimulus items projected on a screen. The adult version of the Category Test includes seven separate subtests and a total of 208 stimulus slides. The patient responds to each stimulus item by pulling one of four numbered switches. If a correct response is made, a bell rings; if one of the three incorrect switches is pulled, a buzzer will sound. Only one response is permitted per stimulus presentation. The patient is required to generate and test hypotheses and to use positive and negative feedback to modulate his or her response patterns.

Each subtest involves a single principle and considerable information is available from a qualitative analysis of category errors (e.g., perseverative, random, etc.). The last subtest does not have a single unifying principle; instead, the patient is required to remember the correct response for stimulus items that have already been presented. The test is frequently frustrating for the impaired patient and occasionally boring for the bright patient. There are no time limits for the test and the brain-damaged and obsessive patients frequently take longer than an hour to complete the test. A short form (120 items) has been proposed (Gregory, Paul, & Morrison, 1979); however, it has not been widely validated or adopted. Golden *et al.* (1981) suggest that the test be limited to 1 hour with scores prorated at that point.

Perhaps the major drawback to the Category Test is the fact that it is expensive and cumbersome. The test is not portable and cannot be conveniently administered at bedside. This problem is not so great when the booklet form of the test is given; this has just recently become available and offers a considerably less expensive alternative. There is still a need for a viewmaster version that can be easily held and conveniently administered.

The Category Test taps a wide variety of cognitive functions and is believed to be one of the Halstead–Reitan tests most sensitive to cerebral damage. Reitan recommends that a cutoff score of 50 errors be used; scores above 50 fell within the brain-impaired range.

>50 errors = impaired

TACTUAL PERFORMANCE TEST (TPT)

The Tactual Performance Test uses a modified Seguin–Goddard Form Board. In the adult version of this test, the blindfolded patient is required to place ten blocks into the appropriate spaces on the form board. The board is slanted at a 45° angle to the horizontal. The test is performed three times: first with the dominant hand, next with the nondominant hand, and, finally, with both hands working together. The time required for each trial is recorded along with the number of blocks correctly placed.

Following the last trial on the TPT, the form board is put away and the patient's blindfold removed. At this point the patient is asked to draw the board and as many blocks as he can remember in their correct location. Since the patient has not been forewarned of this requirement, the Memory and Localization components of this test provide excellent measures of incidental learning and spatial memory. Unfortunately, Reitan does not provide explicit scoring criteria for these tests and clinical judgment, however imprecise, determines the score. This is an important consideration since both scores are used in computing the impairment index and because the Memory component, along with the Category score, is frequently treated as an especially sensitive indicator of the presence of cerebral impairment.

The TPT requires the efficient integration of tactile and kinesthetic feedback, motor skill, spatial memory, and the abilty to acquire new skills in a novel learning situation. Differences between the performance of the left and right hands frequently provide valuable information relative to lateralization of damage; typically, the nondominant hand should be about one-third faster than the dominant hand because of practice effects. To the extent that either hand is markedly slow, one becomes concerned about the integrity of the contralateral hemisphere. This assumes, of course, that the slowness of one hand cannot be accounted for in terms of peripheral damage.

Reitan has suggested that a maximum of 15 minutes be allowed per trial. Others (e.g., Russell, Neuringer, & Goldstein, 1970) recommend that each trial be terminated at 10 minutes. This strategy shortens testing time considerably and reduces frustration in the patient who must remain blindfolded throughout the testing period. This last consideration becomes especially important when working with psychiatric patients who will frequently refuse to cooperate with the examiner's need to use a blindfold.

Reitan uses 15.7 minutes as the total time cutoff score for the TPT. Scores greater than 15.7 minutes fall within the brain-impaired range. Likewise, scores of five or less (correctly remembered) on the Memory component or four or less (correctly localized) on the Localization component are classified as suggestive of brain damage.

It is unfortunate that Reitan did not provide more precise normative data for the TPT since it is clear that both age and intelligence affect scores on this test.

SPEECH SOUNDS PERCEPTION TEST

The Speech Sounds Perception Test requires that the patient attend to 60 spoken (tape-recorded) stimulus words, all of which are variations of an "ee" sound formed by using different first and last consonants (e.g., teel, meer, weem). Each auditory stimulus item must be matched with the correct and corresponding visual stimulus (word) presented on a sheet with three other incorrect words. The patient must underline the correct alternative for each spoken syllable. The test requires clear auditory perception, the ability to sustain attention, and the ability to match auditory and visual stimuli. It assumes that the patient is at least semiliterate and does not suffer from marked hearing loss. Scores of eight or more errors are representative of the performance of patients with cerebral damage. Past research (e.g., Golden, 1978) suggests that this test is especially sensitive to damage in the left temporal area.

RHYTHM TEST

Halstead borrowed the Rhythm Test from the Seashore Tests of Musical Talent. The test involves presentation of 30 pairs of rhythmic beats that are sometimes identical and sometimes different; the patient's job is to keep up and to identify each pair as identical or different. Patients who cannot maintain attention or who lose their place during the testing procedure are penalized harshly because the test, once started, cannot be stopped, even if the patient does become confused. For this reason, psychiatric patients frequently perform poorly on the Rhythm Test. The test measures attention span, auditory memory, and rhythmic ability. While rhythmic ability alone cannot be ≥ 6 errors used for purposes of lateralization, poor performance is more common with right hemispheric lesions, especially when performance on the Speech Sounds Perception Test is intact (Golden *et al.*, 1981). Reitan maintains that six or more errors on this test places the patient's performance in the brain-damaged range.

TRAIL MAKING TEST

The Trail Making Test is a brief, portable and extremely useful neuropsychological screening instrument. The test consists of two parts labeled Trails A and Trails B. Trails A consists of 25 consecutively numbered circles that the patient connects by drawing a line through each element in the series. Trails B is a more complex task in which series of numbers (1–13) and letters (A–L) are present on the same page. The patient is required to work through the entire set alternately connecting numbers and letters (i.e., 1-A-2-B-3-C...) until the 25th circle is reached.

Brief samples of both Trails A and B are printed on the back of each test page. The patient works through these initially to insure his or her understanding of the test. In addition, the examiner must emphasize that the task is to be completed as rapidly as possible without making errors. In the event of a mistake in sequencing, the error is immediately pointed out and the patient continues the test from the point at which the error was first initiated. Timing continues during the correction period. The final score for both Trails A and Trails B is the total amount of time required to complete each task.

This test, like other good general predictors of brain damage, taps a wide range of neuropsychological skills, including letter and number recognition, visual scanning, mental flexibility, motor skill, and sequencing ability. Trails B, along with the Categories Test, TPT-Localization, and the impairment index, is considered one of the four best general indicants of cerebral dysfunction (Russell, Neuringer, & Goldstein, 1970). It is especially sensitive to left hemisphere injury, whereas Trails A requires more purely right hemisphere abilities. Golden (1979) suggests that part A indicates greater impairment if the score on part B is less than twice the score on part A, whereas part B indicates greater impairment when the score is more than three times the score on part A. Scores falling between these extremes are taken to indicate equivalent performance.

Mezzich and Moses (1980) have demonstrated that Trails B correlates quite highly ($r = .78$) with the average impairment rating, a summary index of performance on the Halstead–Reitan Battery. However, while it is an excellent screening measure, no test by itself is adequate to assess all the vagaries of behavior found in the brain-impaired population. For example, Orgel and McDonald (1967) found the Trail Making Test to be inadequate for differentiating between brain-damaged and psychiatric inpatients. In contrast, Goldstein and Neuringer (1966) found that a qualitative approach to interpretation of the Trail Making Test was 77% effective in making this difficult discrimination. These authors found that schizophrenics were more likely to produce error-free performances and bizarre or random patterns, and were more likely to abandon the task prior to completion. In contrast, brain-damaged patients were more likely to exhibit sequence binding (e.g., failure to alternate numbers and letters on part B).

Perhaps the most serious problem with the use of the Trail Making Test is that the cutting scores provided by Reitan (40 or more seconds on Trails A and 92 or more seconds on Trails B) result in a large number of false-positive diagnoses when testing older patients. Lezak (1976) suggests that Reitan's cutting scores are most appropriate for patients between 20 and 39 years of age. For older patients, we prefer the age-corrected cutting scores identified in Horton (1979d).

Finger Oscillation Test

The Finger Oscillation Test, also known as the Finger Tapping Test, is an excellent measure of fine motor control. The patient is required to tap a key as rapidly as possible. The key is attached to a counter that is reset after each trial. Finger tapping speed is assessed for the dominant hand first and then for the nondominant hand. The score for each hand is the average of five consecutive trials with patients given rest periods as needed. Additional trials are given if the patients performance is inconsistent (i.e., each trial must be within five taps of all other trials with the same hand to be acceptable).

The Finger Oscillation Test frequently provides valuable lateralization information when brain damage is present. In general, performance with the dominant hand can be expected to be about 10% better than performance with the nondominant hand. Of course, this applies only in those cases where there is no significant peripheral damage that could account for poor performance (e.g., injuries, neuropathy, arthritis). In addition, it is often useful to compare performance on the Finger Oscillation Test with performance on the Tactual Performance Test. To the extent that TPT performance is impaired in the absence of impaired finger tapping on the same side, one suspects increasing posterior involvement. To the extent that tapping speed is impaired with TPT performance intact, one suspects more focal involvement in the sensory–motor region.

REITAN–INDIANA APHASIA SCREENING TEST

The Reitan–Indiana Aphasia Screening Test is Reitan's modification of the Halstead–Wepman Aphasia Screening Test. It is a relatively brief and easily administered test that only requires a small booklet for presentation of the stimulus items. The test is designed to be sensitive to a wide variety of neuropsychological deficits including dynomia, dysgraphia, dyslexia, spelling dyspraxia, dyscalculia, central dysarthris, left–right confusion, and construction dyspraxia. While inadequate for a comprehensive assessment of language disorders, the Reitan–Indiana serves its purpose as a rapid screening measure and is an integral part of the Halstead–Reitan Battery. Interpretation typically consists of a qualitative analysis of the patient's errors; however, Russell, Nevringer, and Goldstein (1970) have proposed a useful scoring system that weights the various errors according to severity. Information with regard to lateralization of function is available from analysis of errors (e.g., errors in naming and spelling would suggest left hemisphere dysfunction; extreme difficulty in copying a Greek cross would imply a right hemisphere deficit).

REITAN–KLOVE SENSORY–PERCEPTUAL EXAMINATION

The tests in the Reitan–Klove Sensory–Perceptual Examination group parallel many of the measures that would be taken by a neurologist; however, they differ in being more quantitative, more detailed, and more standardized across examiners. Frequently, they provide invaluable information about the relative functioning of the two hemispheres by allowing detailed comparisons of sensory–perceptual function on each side of the body.

The first part of the examination tests for tactile, auditory, and visual dysfunction. Both unilateral and bilateral simultaneous presentations of stimuli are used. Failure to respond to unilateral stimulation is referred to as imperception. The consistent failure to perceive a stimulus on one side following bilateral simultaneous stimulation is referred to as suppression (or, in neurology, as extinction). While imperceptions occur for a variety of reasons, consistent suppressions in any modality are rare and serve as important pathognomonic signs, since suppressions are extremely rare in the absence of actual tissue damage. When tactile, auditory, or visual suppressions do occur, they imply damage to the primary projection areas of the parietal, temporal, and occipital lobes, respectively (Golden et al., 1981).

The tactile examination involves touching each hand while the patient sits with eyes closed. Contralateral hand–face combinations are also used. The auditory examination requires that the examiner stand behind the patient while briskly rubbing the fingers to produce an audible stimulus that the patient identifies as near the left ear, right ear, or both ears.

The visual examination is a crude but effective test for visual field deficits. The examiner sits in front of the patient, who is instructed to fixate on the examiner's nose. With arms extended at one of three levels (upper, middle, or lower), the examiner will make discrete finger movements and the patient will be requested to identify the side(s) where movement occurred. Psychiatric patients will sometimes perform poorly on sensory–perceptual tests because of their anxiety about being touched and/or not being able to see the examiner and will occasionally find it difficult to focus their attention on the examiner's nose.

The patient's ability to identify individual fingers following tactile stimulation is assessed with the test for finger agnosia. A more sensitive test for perceptual function is the Fingertip Number Writing Test. The examiner identifies the numbers that will be used (3,4,5, or 6) and the way each number will be formed. Then, with the patients' eyes closed, numbers are written in a standard sequence with four trials given for each finger of each hand.

The ability to recognize objects by touch alone (astereognosis) is assessed in a crude way by having the patient identify coins (a penny, nickel, and dime) with each hand. Although a standard part of the Halstead–Reitan Battery, we have not found this test useful in clinical practice. More relevant information with regard to astereognosis is available from the Tactile Form Recognition Test. Here, the patient is required to identify basic geometric shapes (a triangle, cross, circle, and square) on the basis of tactile cues alone. The patient points to one of the four figures on the face of the board to indicate the correct response; pointing rather than naming eliminates the likelihood of linguistic confounds that might contaminate the test. The latency of response is recorded for each presentation and frequently yields more information than the number of errors, since errors rarely occur on this test (Reitan, 1959).

REITAN–KLOVE LATERAL DOMINANCE EXAMINATION

The Lateral Dominance Examination is given to establish dominance for hand, foot, and eye. Information from these tests can frequently be correlated with other tests that compare the two sides of the body (e.g., Finger Oscillation and TPT). Handedness is determined by having the patient perform simple tasks that require only one hand, for example, signing his name or throwing an imaginary ball. Eyedness is determined by noting which eye is used for simple tasks such as looking through a telescope. In addition, the Miles ABC Test of Ocular Dominance is given. This test requires that the patient view ten stimulus items through V-shaped scopes that require monocular vision. The test is presented as a tool to assess visual acuity and most patients are unaware of the need for monocular vision. Finally, footedness is determined much like handedness: the patient demonstrates how he would kick a football and step on a bug; the examiner records which foot is used with each task.

As noted earlier, the Halstead–Reitan Battery also includes the WAIS-R and the MMPI. Many researchers and clinicians will supplement the battery with other tests; however, the basic Halstead–Reitan Battery consists of those tests described above.

Proposals to shorten the battery have been made by Golden (1976b) and Erickson, Calsyn, and Scheupback (1978). These abbreviated batteries eliminate the more time-consuming tests such as the Category Test and TPT and keep testing time to approximately 1 hour. Although these shorter versions are not popular, Wedding (1983) found that clinical judges were more accurate when classifying patients into major diagnostic groups (right damage, left damage, diffuse damage, schizophrenia, and normal control) using the shorter form proposed by Erickson. Judgments based on the entire Halstead–Reitan protocol were frequently inaccurate, probably because the judges gave undue weight to trivial variation in the larger data set.

It is argued that considerable training and experience are required to properly evaluate the completed Halstead–Reitan protocol. Reitan, in fact, has suggested that the training of the neuropsychologist should be just as intense as the training of the neurologist since both will be working in the same domain and with the same types of problems. In contrast, Goldstein, Deysach, and Kleinknecht (1973) found that very inexperienced clinicians, interpreting the Halstead–Reitan Battery, were more accurate than highly experienced clinical judges using traditional measures (e.g., the WAIS, MMPI, and Bender–Gestalt).

To avoid the problems of clinical judgment, several researchers have proposed various actuarial and statistical approaches to interpretation of the Halstead–Reitan Battery. Perhaps the premier actual approach is Halstead's Impairment Index. The impairment index is a summary score of brain impairment. The index can range from 0.0 (no evidence of brain damage) to 1.0 (evidence of severe brain damage). The score is actually a ratio formed by calculating the percentage of selected tests that fall in the brain-damaged range using Halstead's cutoff points. Although there is some variation in what tests go into calculating the index, most laboratories use the following seven tests (from Reitan, 1959):

Test	Normal range	Brain-damaged range
Tactual Performance Test		
Total time	15.6 and below	15.7 and above
Memory	6 and above	5 and below
Localization	5 and above	4 and below
Category Test	0-50 errors	51+ errors
Seashore Rhythm Test (errors)	4 and below	5 and above
Speech Sounds Perception Test (errors)	7 and below	8 and above
Finger Oscillation Test (worst hand)	51 and above	50 and below

The cutoff score for the impairment index is .40. Patients with a lower impairment index are classified as normal; patients with a higher index are assumed to have some degree of brain damage. Of course, with different patient groups, adjustments may be required. For example, in a state psychiatric hospital, many inpatients with no evidence of cerebral damage will have an impairment index in the range of .4 to .6; here a higher index would be used to lower the incidence of false positives. However, if the tests were given to a group of medical students, one would be concerned about those students earning scores of .3 to .4, despite the fact that these indices fell in the normal range.

One problem with the impairment index is the fact that its use of dichotomous cutoff scores wastes much potentially valuable data. For example, there is a world of difference between the patient who makes 51 errors on the Category Test and the patient who essentially responds at a chance level. However, no differentiation is made between these two when the index is calculated. To circumvent this problem, Phillip Rennick developed a method of rating the subtests of the Halstead–Reitan Battery on a 5-point scale where a score of 1 was normal, 0 was better than average, and 2, 3, and 4 represented mild, moderate, and severe impairment, respectively (Russell, Neuringer, & Goldstein, 1970). This standardization allowed comparison of subtests using a common metric. The Russell *et al.* rating equivalents for raw scores are reproduced in Table 7.1.

Table 7.1. The Russell, Neuringer, and Goldstein Rating Scale for Halstead–Reitan Scores (Revised Norms for Rating Equivalents of Raw Scores)

Test	Rating equivalents of raw scores					
	0	1	2	3	4	5
Average Impairment rating	0.00–1.00	1.01–1.35	1.36–2.00	2.01–2.85	2.86–3.50	3.51–5.00
Category errors[a]	≤25	26–52	53–75	76–105	106–131	132+
(TPT) Time Dominant hand	≤4.7	4.8–8.2	8.3–10	10 min and 9–5 blocks	10 min and 4–2 blocks	10 min and 1–0 blocks
Nondominant hand	≤2.6	2.7–4.5	4.6–6.1	6.2–8.8	8.9–10 and 10–6 blocks	10 min and 5–0 blocks
Both hands	≤1.5	1.6–2.7	2.8–3.7	3.8–5.2	5.3–10	10 min and 9–0 blocks
Total[a]	≤9.0	9.1–15.6	15.7–21	21.1–29.9	30 min and 14–30 blocks	30 min and 13–0 blocks
(TPT) Memory[a] (No. correct)	10–9	8–6	5–4	3–2	1	0
(TPT) Location[a] (No. correct)	10–7	6–5	4–3	2–1	0 and TPT Memory > 0	0 and TPT Memory = 0

Table 7.1. The Russell, Neuringer, and Goldstein Rating Scale for Halstead–Reitan Scores (Revised Norms for Rating Equivalents of Raw Scores) *(continued)*

	Rating equivalents of raw scores					
Test	0	1	2	3	4	5
Rhythm errors[a]	0–2	3–5	6–9	10–13	14–18	19+
Speech errors[a]	0–3	4–7	8–14	15–25	26–30	31+
Tapping (No.)						
Dom M	≥55	54–50	49–43	42–32	31–20	19–0
DOM F	≥51	50–46	45–39	38–28	27–16	15–0
Nondom M	≥49	48–44	43–37	36–26	25–14	13–0
Nondom F	≥45	44–40	39–33	32–22	21–10	9–0
Trails A (time)	≤19	20–33	34–48	49–62	63–86	87+
Trails B[a] (time)	≤57	58–87	88–123	124–186	187–275	276+
Aphasia[a] (errors)	0	1–6	7–15	16–25	26–40	41+
Spatial relations[a] (errors)	1	2–3	4–5	6–7	8–9	10–12

	0–4	5–12	13–30	31–50	51–80	81+
Perceptual[a] (errors)	0–4	5–12	13–30	31–50	51–80	81+
Visual suppression						
One eye	0	1	2	3	4	5
Two eyes	0	1–2	3–4	5–6	7–8	9–10
Heminaopia (count fields not eyes)	≥191	190–121	120–97	96–73	72–47	48–0
		(invalid if total number of functioning squares in both eyes is ≤96).				
Digit symbol[a] $(Av-1) = \dfrac{PA+PC+BD}{3}-1$	DS≥12 and ≤(Av-1)	DS≥12 and <(Av-1) or DS=9-11 DS=7-8 and ≥(Av-1)	DS=7-8 and <(Av-1) or DS=5-6 and ≥(Av-1)	DS=5-6 and <(Av-1) or DS=3-4 and ≥(Av-1)	DS=3-4 and <(Av-1) or DS=2-1 and ≥(Av-1)	DS=2-0 and <(Av-1)

Source: From Russell, E.W., Neuringer, C., and Goldstein, G. *Assessment of Brain Damage: A Neuropsychological Key Approach.* New York: John Wiley, 1970.
[a]These tests are the ones used in computing the average impairment rating.

A second change introduced by Rennick was the substitution of an average impairment rating (AIR) for Halstead's impairment index. The AIR is calculated by averaging the rated scores on 12 of the Halstead–Reitan tests: the Category Test, TPT (total) Time, Memory, and Localization, Rhythm Speech Sounds, Finger Oscillation Test (dominant hand), Trails B, Digit Symbol from WAIS, and rated scores for Aphasia and Spatial Relations. The cutting score of 1.55 is used to classify brain-damaged patients; patients with lower scores are classified as not brain impaired. The AIR can also be used to appraise severity of brain damage using the same classification system given for performance on individual tests.

The Rennick ratings and the average impairment rating are widely used today and offer a viable alternative to the use of the impairment index. Goldstein and Shelly (1972) have demonstrated that the AIR is as effective as discriminant functions in making the basic discrimination between brain-damaged and normal subjects. Perhaps even more important, however, is the fact that the rating scales provide much qualitative information while still allowing for convenient comparisons across tests.

Elbert Russell, working at the Topeka V.A., expanded Rennick's work and developed an actuarial approach using a series of keys similar to those used by biologists to classify plants and animals. These keys had an advantage in that little professional training was required for their application. Russell refined his system by developing a computer program that would make fairly specific predictions with regard to presence of brain damage, lateralization (left, right, or diffuse), and extent of lateralization. In addition, rudimentary predictions of process (congenital, static, or acute) are attempted.

A more ambitious program was developed by Finkelstein (1977). BRAIN 1 is a Fortran IV computer program which uses Halstead–Reitan summary score data to predict probability of brain damage, the presence or absence of recent tissue distinction, and the most likely neurological diagnosis. The program is quite sophisticated and uses multiple levels of inferences in making predictions (much the way a clinician would). These levels of inference include level of performance, left–right comparisons, patterns of performance, analysis of pathognomonic signs, and knowledge of base rates.

Unfortunately, few studies have assessed the utility of these computerized approaches to classification. One exception is the research of Anthony, Heaton, and Lehman (1980). This project was a large-scale and systematic comparison of the Russell program and Finkelstein's BRAIN 1. Unfortunately, the results suggest that while both programs can be used to predict presence or absence of brain damage, they are no more accurate in making this prediction than the more easily computed impairment index. Neither program is adequate to make the finer predictions of localization and process. These findings are essentially the same as those of Wedding (1983). However, as Anthony and his colleagues wisely point out, it is easier to criticize existing programs than to construct better ones and the studies of both Russell and Finkelstein are important first steps toward a more accurate computer prediction system.

The use of discriminant functions with the Halstead–Reitan Battery offers still another approach to classification and prediction. Discriminant function analysis is a statistical technique that can be used to predict discrete group membership in much the same way that regression analysis is used to predict position on a continuous scale. In a number of studies. Wheeler and his colleagues (Wheeler, 1963; Wheeler, Burke & Reitan, 1963; Wheeler & Reitan, 1963) demonstrated that discriminant functions, using Halstead–Reitan data as input variables, could effectively classify patients into left, right, and bilateral (diffuse) groups with a high degree of accuracy, exceeding the performance of every individual measure and out performing the impairment index. Ten to twenty percent shrinkage occurred with cross-validation; however, the functions still classified individuals into the appropriate groups with approximately 80% accuracy. Goldstein and Shelly, as documented in one article (1972), found that discriminant functions were no more accurate than the average impairment rating in predicting presence or absence of brain damage; however, in another study (1973) they demonstrated that the procedure was very effective in predicting lateralization of brain damage. Similar results were obtained by Swiercinsky and Warnock (1977).

It is likely that the upper limit of predictive accuracy for the Halstead–Reitan Battery—whether interpreted by computer or clinicians—is considerably less than 100%. This is especially true when working with a neuropsychiatric population. Perhaps the most cogent criticism of the Halstead–Reitan Battery is the fact that it frequently classifies psychiatric patients—especially chronic schizophrenics—as brain damaged when there is no objective evidence that true tissue destruction has occurred. Watson (1974) has been the most outspoken advocate of this position. Others (e.g., Levine & Fierstein, 1972; Stack & Phillips, 1970; Boll, 1974) have been far more successful using slightly different populations. The accuracy of classification appears to vary directly with the chronicity (and age) of the patient groups studied with older, more chronic patients highly likely to be classified as brain damaged. Of course these patients, or a significant proportion of them, may in fact be brain damaged. Heaton, Baade, and Johnson (1978) and Malec (1978) have reviewed this literature.

Slightly modified versions of the Halstead–Reitan Battery have been developed for testing children. The adult version is given to children 15 or over. Children between the ages of 9 and 14 are given essentially the same test with the Category Test and the Tactual Performance Test shortened and the Speech Sounds Perception Test slightly modified. For younger children (5–8) extensive modifications have been made. An electric finger tapper is used in lieu of the manual tapper used with adults and older children and a number of additional tests have been added. These are described in Reitan and Davison (1974).

Problems clearly exist with the Halstead–Reitan Battery. The necessary equipment is expensive and the battery itself is time consuming and tiring for patients. The equipment is not easily transported and it is difficult to test patients at bedside. Finally, interpretation of test results requires considerable experience and expertise. However, with all these shortcomings, the Halstead–Reitan Battery is still used because many clinicians have found that these tests offer an excellent survey of cognitive, sensory–perceptual, and motor functions that well serves the purposes of differential diagnosis and decision making in neuropsychology. Its use is supported by a wealth of research data, and many clinicians have learned to interpret the subtle nuances that can be so important in the inferential process. We anticipate that the battery will continue to be used over the coming years with clinicians adding individual tests that may supplement Halstead–Reitan results.

SUGGESTIONS FOR FURTHER READING

Boll, T.J. The Halstead–Reitan Neuropsychological Test Battery. In S.B. Filskov & T.J. Boll (Eds.), *Handbook of clinical neuropsychology.* New York: John Wiley, 1981.

Finlayson, M.A., Johnson, K.A., & Reitan, R. Relationship of the level of education to neuropsychological measures in brain-damaged and non-brain damaged adults. *Journal of Consulting and Clinical Psychology,* 1977, *45*, 536–540.

Golden, C.J., Osmon, D.C., Moses, J.A., & Berg, R.A. *Interpretation of the Halstead–Reitan Neuropsychological Test Battery.* New York: Grune & Stratton, 1981.

Reitan, R.M. Psychgological deficits resulting from cerebral lesions in man. In J.M. Warren & K.A. Akart (Eds.), *The frontal granular cortex and behavior.* New York: McGraw-Hill, 1964.

8

STANDARDIZED LURIA–NEBRASKA NEUROPSYCHOLOGICAL TEST BATTERY

The work of the Russian neuropsychologist Aleksandr Romanovich Luria (1902–1977) is highly respected by academic neuropsychologists and neurologists. However, prior to 1978 his writings had little impact on the practicing neuropsychologist. This occurred for a variety of reasons. Many of Luria's most important works were slow to be published and his research was not well known in the United States. In addition, Luria's methodology was highly qualitative and was in part based on his personal clinical acumen, developed after assessing literally thousands of brain-damaged patients. Unfortunately, few of us possess either Luria's wealth of experience or his genius for clinical description. Finally, Luria's approach to patient assessment was idiosyncratic and each individual patient was treated as a unique case that would necessarily require deviation from any sort of standardized protocol. This highly qualitative approach did not square well with the prevailing psychometric *Zietgeist* in this country or with the tradition of empirically derived and highly standardized tests such as the Wechsler–Bellevue and the Minnesota Multiphasic Personality Inventory (MMPI). The tests Luria used and his irregular way of using them were clearly much closer to behavioral neurology than to clinical neuropsychology. (This is not surprising given the fact that Luria was trained both as a neurologist and as a psychologist.)

Today there has been a resurgence of interest in Luria's work. Many of his books are selling well and at this time the interested student will have no difficulty gaining some appreciation of the breadth and depth of Luria's thought. For starters, we recommend *The Working Brain: An Introduction to Neuropsychology* (1973). The more serious student will want to read *Higher Cortical Functions in Man* (1980), a difficult but highly rewarding volume.

This resurgence of interest is due in part to the seminal work of Anne-Lise Christensen (1975). Christensen studied with Luria for three weeks in 1970 and developed a text and manual describing many of the specific tests used by Luria. These works were polished and an English version was prepared during a second visit to Luria's laboratory in 1972. Luria referred to Christensen's work as a vulgarization; however, he felt it was necessary and important enough for him to write the forward to the text.

Christensen's attempt at systemization (if not standardization) of Luria's work was an important first step in developing a set of tests that could be used by American neuropsychologists. She grouped related tests into conceptually meaningful categories (e.g., motor functions, visual functions, expressive speech) but did not provide scoring standards or normative data.

The second step was taken by Golden and his colleagues, who have pursued a programmatic series of studies culminating in publication of the Luria–Nebraska Neuropsychological Battery (Golden, Hammeke, & Purisch, 1978). The Luria–Nebraska Battery consists of 269 items that tap a wide variety of neuropsychological functions. The battery takes 2–3 hours to administer to a patient with average intelligence; somewhat longer testing times are required with a patient who is retarded or who suffers from serious brain impairment. Scoring is based on a variety of criteria that vary across individual items and include accuracy, speed, quality of response, latency of responses, trials to criterion, and number of responses made. Standards are provided so that the patient's responses to each item can be converted to an ordinal scale of 0, 1, or 2. Scores of 0 indicate that performance falls in the normal range; scores of 2 indicate that performance is in the brain-damaged range. A score of 1 suggests an intermediate response falling between the normative performance of brain-damaged and normal patients. These transformations are easily made since the normative data required to determine the scaled score on each item are given in the administration and scoring booklet and scoring can occur at the same time the test is administered (Golden, 1979b).

Following administration of the test, related items are grouped together to provide global indices of performance across 11 primary scales: Motor, Rhythm, Tactile, Visual, Receptive Speech, Excessive Speech, Writing, Reading, Math, Memory, and Intellectual Processes. In addition, three special scales are scored: the Pathognomonic Scale (used to indicate recency and severity of brain damage), and the Right and Left scales, used to predict lateralization of function. These special scales are comprised of items taken from the 11 basic scales and cannot be treated as statistically independent.

The first Luria–Nebraska Scale (Motor) is designed to assess a 1) Motor variety of simple and complex motor functions. The patient is required to perform varied motor acts (e.g., clenching each hand), reproduce the position of the left hand using the right hand (with eyes closed) and vice versa, imitate various motor acts, demonstrate oral praxis (e.g., chewing), draw from verbal instructions and from a model, and, finally, display evidence of speech regulation of motor acts (e.g., "If I knock hard, you knock gently, and if I knock gently, you knock hard"). The 51 items that make up the Motor Scale reflect pure motor abilities in varying degrees and patients without motor deficits may perform poorly on some items due to problems such as left–right confusion. However, *in toto* we feel this subtest nicely surveys a wide variety of motoric responses and offers useful information to the clinical neuropsychologist. If more information is needed (as it often is), we recommend that this subtest be supplemented with the Klove–Matthews Motor Steadiness Battery.

The second subtest, Rhythm, consists of 12 items that assess 2) Rhythm perception of pitch relationships, reproduction of musical melodies, evaluation of acoustic signals, and motor performance of rhythmic groups. It is somewhat shorter and more varied than the Rhythm Test of the Halstead–Reitan Battery and, interestingly, the two tests do not correlate highly (Golden *et al.*, 1981). A flaw common to both tests is the poor quality of the auditory stimuli presented to the patient.

The third Luria–Nebraska Subtest (Tactile) is designed to assess 3) Tactile higher cutaneous and kinesthetic functions. This scale consists of 22 items; 16 are devoted to cutaneous sensation (e.g., "Tell me where I'm touching you"), 2 to muscle and joint sensation, and 4 to stereognosis. The test is limited in that all items require a verbal response, confounding language and tactile functions. Because of this limitation, we sometimes supplement this scale with the Tactile Form Recognition Test from the Halstead–Reitan Battery since the latter test requires only that the patient point to the correct stimulus figure.

The Visual Scale is the fourth subtest and consists of 14 items that 4) Visual assess visual perception, spatial orientation, and intellectual operations in space. The patient is required to recognize and identify varied items and photographs of items, some of which are blurred, incomplete, out of focus, or overlapping. The scale includes several items that measure spatial abilities rather than simple visual skill and the subtest is best thought of as a general measure of visuospatial abilities. 5) Receptive Speech

Scales 5 and 6 purport to measure receptive and expressive speech. While useful as a heuristic device, this dichotomy does not do 6) Expressive Speech justice to the complexity of the organization of language in the brain or to current models in aphasia research (Spiers, 1981). Our concern here is not so much with the content of the subtests themselves; instead, we are concerned that elevated scores will be misinterpreted by naive and unsophisticated examiners and that the nomenclature employed will promulgate an antiquated concept of linguistic function.

The Receptive Speech Scale evaluates the patient's ability to comprehend and respond to spoken speech. Phonemic hearing, word comprehension, and appreciation of simple and complex logical grammatical structure are assessed. Unfortunately, speech comprehension is sometimes confounded with other neuropsychological skills (e.g., "If you hear 'ba,' please raise your right hand. If you hear 'pa,' please raise your left hand").

The 41 items on the Expressive Speech Scale assess the production of speech rather than its comprehension. The patient is expected to repeat speech sounds, words, series of words, and sentences given both as oral and as written stimulus items. In addition, dysnomia, fluency of speech, and verbal spontaneity are all assessed.

It is important to keep in mind that scales 5 and 6 offer at best a rough screening measure for language dysfunction and that comprehensive examinations for aphasia in themselves may require as much time as the entire Luria–Nebraska Battery. At least one report of misdiagnosis due to overreliance on these scales has been reported (Delis & Kaplan, 1981) and, in and of themselves, the 74 items on these two scales do not adequately serve to assess the variegated disorders of language that can occur with brain-damaged people.

Scales 7, 8, and 9 assess writing, reading, and arithmetic skills, respectively. Task requirements for the writing scale vary from very simple ("How many letters are there in 'cat'") to complex ("Write a few sentences about your main ideas on bringing up children"). This last question is scored for grammar, content, spelling, and total number of words written. The Reading Scale is a good measure of word recognition but totally fails to assess reading comprehension. The Arithmetic Scale assesses comprehension of numbers and skill in arithmetic operations. There are more items and the questions are simpler than those on the Arithmetic Subtest of the WAIS-R. Some items are included that have become standard parts of the mental status examination (e.g., serial sevens in which the patient is required to count backward from 100 to 58 by seven). *In toto*, the Arithmetic Scale appears to be a fairly good test for dyscalculia. However, it is important to note that this scale is the single subtest most likely to be affected by educational or cultural deprivation (Golden *et al.*, 1979).

The tenth subtest of the Luria–Nebraska Battery is devoted to memory functions. Although brief (13 items), the subtest surveys learning processes, sensory memory, and retention and retrieval of words, colors, sentences, and paragraphs. One problem with this subtest is that virtually all items assess immediate memory with little attention paid to remote or delayed memory. The interference tactics used (e.g., counting to 100 out loud) are too brief and do not allow for a comprehensive evaluation of mnestic processes. Once again, brevity precludes completeness and this scale must be supplemented if a more comprehensive evaluation is desired. We recommend that Russell's adaptation of the Weschler Memory Scale (discussed in Chapter 6) be used for this purpose.

The last of the 11 basic scales is Intellectual Processes. The 34 *11) Intellectual Processes* items on this scale require understanding of thematic pictures and texts, solving elementary arithmetic problems, and appreciation of language (e.g., word similarities, logical relationship, opposites, and analogies). The test does not correlate highly with the Wechsler Adult Intelligence Scale (Golden *et al.*, 1981) and correlations with other standardized tests (e.g., Raven's matrices) are not yet available.

The Pathognomonic scale brings together 34 items from all the *12) Pathognomonic* previous scales that are rarely missed by patients without brain damage. The scale serves to address the issue of presence of brain damage and, when present, offers an index of the severity (and recency) of tissue damage.

Likewise, the Right Hemisphere and Left Hemisphere scales are *13) Right Hemis* each based on 21 different items that reflect lateralized sensory or *14) Left Hemis* motor deficits. Poor performance on these scales is most likely to occur when damage directly involves the sensory–motor strip or adjacent areas. The items comprising each scale were selected on theoretical rather than empirical groups; however, preliminary validation results suggest that the scales are highly effective in discriminating between left and right focal injuries (Golden, Hammeke, & Purisch, 1980).

Once all scaled scores are calculated, they are plotted on a standardized and prenumbered grid so that T-score conversions can be easily made and interest-comparisons become possible. This grid is reproduced in Figure 8.1. Elevated scores (e.g., *t* scores greater than 70) on any of the scales indicate poor performance; the greater the deficit, the more elevated the score. However, performance is always related to a "critical level" (determined by the patient's age and education) rather than to absolute performance per se. The formula for calculating the critical level and the appropriate age and education tables are printed on the second page of each scoring booklet.

Golden (1979b) has provided a variety of rules for localizing brain damage with the Luria–Nebraska. He suggests that the Left Hemisphere and Right Hemisphere scales can be used to lateralize focal lesions in approximately 80% of cases. More detailed localization is also

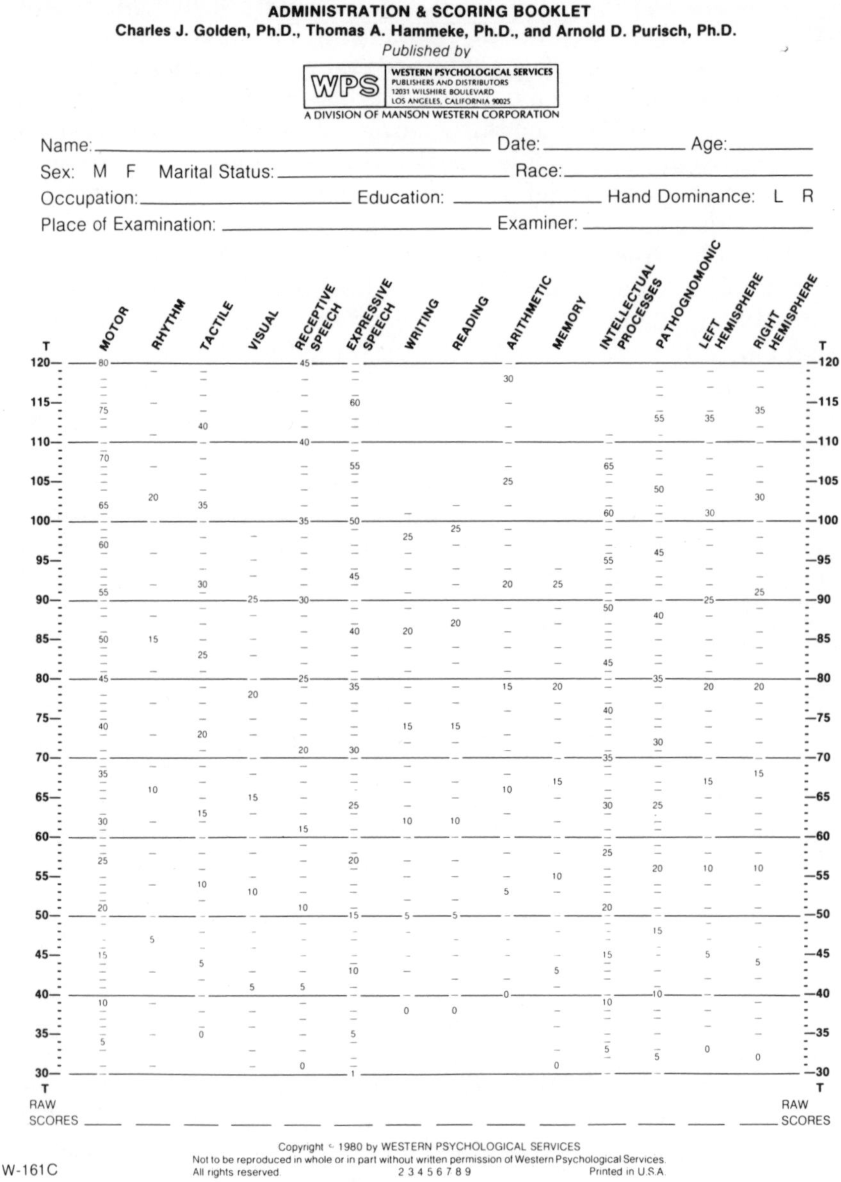

ADMINISTRATION & SCORING BOOKLET

Charles J. Golden, Ph.D., Thomas A. Hammeke, Ph.D., and Arnold D. Purisch, Ph.D.

Published by

WPS — WESTERN PSYCHOLOGICAL SERVICES
PUBLISHERS AND DISTRIBUTORS
12031 WILSHIRE BOULEVARD
LOS ANGELES, CALIFORNIA 90025
A DIVISION OF MANSON WESTERN CORPORATION

Name: _____ Date: _____ Age: _____

Sex: M F Marital Status: _____ Race: _____

Occupation: _____ Education: _____ Hand Dominance: L R

Place of Examination: _____ Examiner: _____

Figure 8.1. Luria–Nebraska Neuropsychological Battery Summary Sheet.

possible. For example, frontal injuries are apt to produce Motor Scale values more elevated than Tactile Scale values while left frontal patients score very high on the Pathognomonic Scale. Injuries to the parietal lobe show elevated tactile scores with injuries in the sensory–motor region producing marked differences between the Left and Right Hemisphere scales. More detailed examples of localization are presented by Golden, Hammeke, and Purisch (1980).

The Luria–Nebraska is currently being marketed by Western Psychological Services. It has been enthusiastically received by many psychologists as a briefer, less expensive alternative to the Halstead–Reitan Battery. However, several problems do exist with the battery, which has been criticized as a premature commercial enterprise (Adams, 1980) and as "organized and scored in such a manner that it does not adequately or comprehensively assess any major neuro-psychological function" (Spiers, 1981, p. 337). While we believe this criticism is unduly harsh, it is clear that the Luria–Nebraska is unsuited for testing aphasics, since complex verbal instructions are used and language skills are frequently employed to assess non-language functions such as naming an object placed in one's hand (Crosson & Warren, 1982). The test is clearly linguistically slanted with 32 of the 34 items on the Intellectual Processes scale requiring verbal comprehension. Of course, this same bias can be found in the work of Luria and is not surprising in a battery derived from his work.

Delis and Kaplan (1982) have presented a very instructive case history of a patient with fluent aphasia who appeared to be misdiag-nosed using a pure level of performance approach to interpretation of the Luria–Nebraska Battery. This critique appeared especially dev-astating given the stature of Dr. Edith Kaplan in aphasia research. However, Golden, Ariel, Moses, Wilkening, McKay & MacInnes (1982), in a move reminiscent of Marie's reexamination of the brain of Broca's patient, "Tan," reanalyzed both the neurological and neuro-psychological findings on this patient and pointed out that the original analysis was confounded by the fact that the patient's first language was Spanish, not English, and that considerable neurological evidence suggested the possibility of diffuse cortical damage (e.g., a history of chronic alcoholism, seizures, enlarged ventricles with bilateral atrophy, and possible evidence of an old left temporal–parietal infarct). The Golden *et al.* reanalysis stressed the importance of item pattern analysis (versus single-scale analysis) and used more current normative data to demonstrate that the Battery did in fact yield considerable information with regard to the patient in question.

Other criticisms can be leveled at the initial version of the Luria–Nebraska Battery. The designs used to test constructional apraxia are too simple and overlearned (Crossin, 1981). Many of the same stimulus items are repeatedly used across subtests, confounding the functions assessed with memory functions. In addition, testing materials for Form I are extremely cumbersome. The cards used were borrowed from Anne-Lise Christensen's *Luria Neuropsychological Investigations* and are not easily adapted for the Luria–Nebraska Battery. The test is frequently boring for patients who are not seriously impaired as well as for the examiners administering the test. Finally, we have frequently found that testing time can be as long as 3½ hours when working with patients with limited intellectual ability.

Golden and his colleagues have also been criticized for the misuse of statistical methods in their initial validation efforts. In particular, they have employed multiple *t* tests without regard for experiment-wise error rate and have conducted discriminant function analyses in which the number of variables exceeded the number of subjects. It is clear that their work has consistently emphasized criterion validity, perhaps at the expense of other validity issues. However, these criticisms pale in contrast to the wealth of data which has originated from Golden's lab and one is hard pressed to imagine a more prolific and productive researcher in clinical neuropsychology.

A number of validation studies are now appearing that support the utility of the Luria–Nebraska Battery for separating brain-damaged from normal subjects and, more importantly, brain-damaged from schizophrenic and mixed psychiatric patients. The test battery has been shown to predict localization of lesions (Golden *et al.*, 1981) as well as lateralization, and one study (Golden *et al.*, 1980) demonstrated that a set of three simple rules could accurately predict the presence of enlarged cerebral ventricles in young chronic schizophrenics. A similar study (Zelazowski *et al.*, in press) demonstrated the same effect in chronic alcoholics. While these results have largely come from Golden's laboratory, replication by independent investigators is expected to confirm and extend these findings.

For example, research results from the University of Mississippi Medical Center (Malloy & Webster, 1981) have confirmed the utility of the Luria–Nebraska Battery in separating true neurologic from "pseudoneurologic" patients, clearly a more demanding and more clinically relevant task than discriminating between brain-damaged and normal patients. Work by this same group (e.g., Webster & Dostrow, 1982) has also been directed toward the development of a decision tree approach to test administration in which individual tasks are grouped into functional hierarchies and "lower level" items are predicted to be correctly answered once the patient responds correctly to the first item in the hierarchy. This method permitted the omission of an average of 76 test items while still retaining an 87% hit rate in separating brain-damaged from normal controls.

Other recent studies have examined the relationship between the Luria–Nebraska Battery and other neuropsychological instruments. Golden *et al.* (1981) compared the Luria–Nebraska Battery and the Halstead–Reitan Battery using a sample of 48 brain-damaged and 60 normal patients. Discriminant analysis of the two batteries suggested that they were equivalent in predictive accuracy. Chelune (1982) reexamined the relationship between the two batteries and suggested that much of their common variance was due to overlap with WAIS IQ scores; however, this relationship is in part unjustly inflated because of the fact that postmorbid rather than premorbid IQ scores were used in the analysis (and postmorbid IQ will change due to the sensitivity of the WAIS as a neuropsychological measure).

McKay, Golden, Moses, Fishburne, and Wisniewski (1981) demonstrated that the Intelligence Scale of the Luria–Nebraska correlated highly with verbal, performance, and full-scale IQs (r's of -.84, -.74, and -.84, respectively on the WAIS). Similar results were obtained by Prifitera and Ryan (1981). Although the Luria–Nebraska will almost always underestimate IQs greater than 120 (since Luria–Nebraska intelligence scores are rarely less than a t score of 35), it does appear to be useful in predicting intellectual ability in the low and average range and performs at least as well as other brief tests of intelligence such as the Quick Test or Raven's Progressive matrices.

Golden has already begun to develop a children's version of the Luria–Nebraska that is being field tested as this volume goes to press. The children's version will closely parallel the adult version and will initially include 11 subtests (Motor, Rhythm, Tactile, Visual, Perceptive Speech, Expressive Language, Writing, Reading, Arithmetic, Memory, and Intelligence). It will be interesting to see if the children's version will be adopted with the same enthusiasm as the adult battery.

In summary, the work of Golden and his associates represents an important first step in standardizing Luria's method. While this effort necessarily involves some loss of the qualitative richness of an unstructured interview, the quantification of the Luria–Nebraska offers tremendous potential for research. We believe that the instrument could be improved by addition of test items sampling right hemisphere skills. Clinical utility is enhanced when the Luria–Nebraska is supplemented by additional tests such as the Wechsler Memory Scale, the Tactual Performance Test, or WAIS Block Design. In addition, we are somewhat concerned about glib interpretations made by untutored clinicians. We can envision someone as being "diagnosed" as having a Broca's aphasia on the basis of an elevated expressive speech scale in much the same way that inept clinicians diagnose schizophrenia solely on the basis of an elevated "Sc" score on the MMPI. However, cookbooks, if not abused, *are* useful and it is exciting to speculate that the Luria–Nebraska may engender the same wealth of research in neuropsychology that the MMPI engendered in personality assessment. Finally, we expect that the Luria–Nebraska will be revised as more data accrue and in response to criticism such as ours. In fact, a second version is currently being field tested. This "Form B" version is reported to address many of our concerns. Given the potential for revision, this test battery offers great promise as a neurodiagnostic instrument.

SUGGESTIONS FOR FURTHER READING

Adams, K. In search of Luria's battery: A false start. *Journal of Consulting and Clinical Psychology*, 1980, *48*, 511–516.

Golden, C.J. In reply to Adam's "In search of Luria's battery: A false start." *Journal of Consulting and Clinical Psychology*, 1980, *48*, 517–521.

Golden, C.J., Ariel, K.J., McKay, S.E., Wilkening, G.N., Wolf, B.D. & MacInno, W.D. The Luria-Nebraska Neuropsychological Battery: Theoretical orientation and comment. *Journal of Consulting and Clinical Psychology*, 1982, *50*, 291–300.

Golden, C.J., Hammeke, T.A., Purisch, A.D., Berg, R.A., Moses, J.A., Jr., Newlin, D.B., Wilkening, G.N. & Puenta, A.E. *Item interpretation of the Luria-Nebraska Neuropsychological Battery.* Lincoln: University of Nebraska, 1982.

Horton, A.M., Jr., Wedding, D., & Phay, A. Current perspectives on the assessment and therapy of the brain-damaged patient. In C.J. Golden, S.S. Alcaparras, F. Strider, & B. Graber (Eds.). *Applied techniques in behavioral medicine.* New York: Grune & Stratton, 1981.

9

BEHAVIORAL NEUROPSYCHOLOGY: THEORETICAL ISSUES

There are four principal subfields of neuropsychology: clinical neuropsychology, experimental neuropsychology, behavioral neurology and behavioral neuropsychology. The first three subfields are traditional areas of neuropsychology. Experimental neuropsychology is the analog of experimental psychology in the neurosciences. Behavioral neurology, despite its name, is scarcely behavioristic. Indeed, it is instead a quantitative, intuitive approach to neurological problems tied to a classical medical conception of neuropsychological phenomena.

At counterpoint to behavioral neurology is clinical neuropsychology, which is the application of knowledge of human brain–behavior relationships to clinical problems using psychometric quantitative procedures.

In contrast to the above, behavioral neuropsychology has only recently become recognized as a principal subfield of neuropsychology (Horton, Wedding, & Phay, 1981). Behavioral neuropsychology is defined as the application of behavior therapy techniques to problems of organically impaired patients while utilizing a neuropsychological assessment and intervention perspective (Horton, 1978). This treatment philosophy asserts that inclusion of data culled from neuropsychological assessment strategies is helpful in the formulation of hypotheses with regard to antecedent conditions (external or internal) for the observed phenomena of psychopathology and that a neuropsychological perspective may significantly enhance the ability of the behavior therapist to make accurate discriminations as to the etiology of patient behaviors. The formulation of a cogent plan of therapeutic intervention and its skillful implementation will be facilitated by an analysis of behavior deficits implicating impairment of higher cortical functioning (Horton, 1979a).

In this chapter, a number of issues relevant to behavioral neuropsychology will be considered. These issues include demographic epidemiological data, conceptual models, neurophysiological processes, and evaluation procedures. Each will be discussed from the perspective of possible contributions to behavioral neuropsychology and the therapy of brain-damaged patients.

DEMOGRAPHIC AND EPIDEMIOLOGICAL ISSUES

Demographic and epidemiological data provide compelling reasons for focusing attention on brain-damaged patients. One-fourth (25%) of mental hospital patients in the United States are diagnosed as having some sort of organic mental disorder (Segal, Boomer, & Bouthilet, 1975). Census figures suggest that the twin influences of the aging of the American population and serious alcohol abuse may dramatically increase the number of individuals diagnosed as having organic mental disorders (Lipowski, 1978).

Aging

The contribution of age to organic mental impairment is most significant. For individuals over the age of 65 (an often-used but arbitrary criterion for the elderly), organic mental disorders were almost two-fifths (38.2%) of all patient care episodes while schizophrenia and depressive disorders were each diagnosed in less than one-fifth (20%) of individuals over age 65. The proportion of the population over age 65 (22 to 23 million or 19% by present U.S. census figures) will at least double by the year 2030 (Horton, 1982) and the prevalence and incidence of organic mental disorders will be very significantly increased in the coming decades (Lipowski, 1978).

Alcoholism

Estimates of alcoholism and brain damage are quite similar to those for aging and brain damage. Alcoholism afflicts at least 5% of the United States population (no less than 9 million people) and all data indicate that each coming year will see more individuals suffering from alcoholism. At present alcoholism is the most common diagnosis among state hospital inpatients (Redick & Kellert, 1978).

With respect to brain damage and alcoholism, one thing is quite clear: chronic abuse of alcohol does cause brain damage (Tartar, 1975;

Miller, 1982). Numerous studies have demonstrated particular patterns of mental impairment secondary to alcoholism (Butters & Cermak, 1979). As the prevalence and incidence of alcoholism continue to increase, the number of individuals suffering organic mental disorders as a result of alcoholism will also dramatically grow. Thus, additional brain-damaged patients will be added to the lists of those suffering strokes, head injuries, and tumors.

CONCEPTUAL ISSUES

The intent of this section is to briefly review a number of theoretical concerns in rehabilitation with special attention to behavioral neuropsychology. At the conclusion of this section, some tentative attempts at integration will be offered. The three major perspectives to be addressed will be a behavioral theoretical rationale for including neuropsychological factors in treatment planning, the theoretical stance of A.R. Luria, and the rehabilitation model and procedures of L. Diller.

Behavioral Contributions

Several theoretical issues cloud the relationship between neuropsychological facts and behavioral methods. This discussion is divided into two parts to deal more accurately with these theoretical issues. Two major conceptual questions that may be identified are first, the theoretical relevance of neuropsychology to traditional behavioral conceptualizations, and second, how does neuropsychology interface with more contemporary views of behavioral assessment and treatment?

In reference to the first question, it is useful to describe the traditional behavioral model. From the very beginnings of the behavioral school in general psychology (Watson, 1913), there have been individuals within the operant conditioning camp who would maintain that human actions can be adequately accounted for in terms of a stimulus–response paradigm (S–R model). Adherents of this perspective strongly contend that unobservable factors (thoughts, images, etc.) are in no way necessary to fully explain the very complex behavior of human organisms (Skinner, 1938). The radical behaviorist perspective derogates the value of inferred variables and suggests that variables that are not observable stimuli or responses should be scrupulously avoided.

Indeed, there is some support for the viewpoint that the recent controversy over the inclusion of cognitive factors in the traditional behavioral model (Wilson, 1978) rests, at least partly, on the answer to the question of whether or not there are legitimate inferred variables in the functional analysis of behavior (Mahoney, 1974). Relating this to neuropsychology, there is a possibility that some might view knowledge of brain–behavior relationships as extraneous variables that are more likely to evoke problems than to ameliorate difficulties. To be sure, there is a superficial surface parallel between neuropsychological and cognitive perspectives in that both utilize inferred variables. Still, at the same time, there is a significant distinction.

Inferred variables can be divided into at least two fairly independent categories. These are intervening variables and hypothetical constructs (Craighead, Kazdin, & Mahoney, 1976). Intervening variables are purely theoretical creations. The functions they perform are conceptual in nature. Intervening variables such as thoughts or feelings have not been directly observed, yet behavior therapists in the cognitive mold often use thoughts and feelings to explain human behavior.

A hypothetical construct may be distinguished from an intervening variable because the former is usually more empirical or physical in function than the latter (Craighead, Kazdin, & Mahoney, 1976). A grossly oversimplified example of this distinction between intervening variables and hypothetical constructs is provided by considering the behavior of drawing a Greek Cross and explanations of the patient's failure to adequately perform this behavior. One intervening variable explanation would posit the patient's emotional state as a cause of poor performance. Conversely, the hypothetical construct explanation suggests possible impairment of the right parietal lobe of the brain. The major point is that hypothetical constructs can have neurophysiological referrents. Clearly, it is an advantage to know that the actual existence or nonexistence of the hypothetical construct can either be confirmed or denied. Computerized tomography, in the example above, could easily ascertain the structural integrity of the subject's right parietal lobe. If at some point thoughts and feelings can be objectively verified (by evoked potentials or some other neurodiagnostic method) then they will be classified as hypothetical constructs rather than intervening variables.

Since a neuropsychological perspective relies on hypothetical constructs, the inclusion of a neuropsychological perspective within the traditional behavioral model has implications dramatically different from the inclusion of a cognitive perspective. Without denigrating the clinical promise of cognitive interventions (Horton, 1978, 1979a) a clear distinction can still be drawn.

Given a historical perspective, the original decision to reject inferred variables from the functional analysis of behavior is understandable. At the time of Watson, neuropsychology was a totally undeveloped area of scientific and clinical interest. The benign neglect of neuropsychology could be explained in terms of the paucity of available contributions to research and clinical needs. However, drastic changes have come about in the last two decades. Without question, the knowledge base of brain–behavior relations has increased to a geometric pace (Davison, 1974). Research from Russia, France, Italy, and other countries has produced such impressive confirmation of the value of neuropsychological insights (Benton, 1967; Faglioni, Spinnler, & Vignolo, 1969; Golden, 1978; Hecaen & Ajuriaguerra, 1964; Luria, 1966) that it would be foolish to minimize its importance.

Contemporary behavior therapy is more amenable to utilizing inferred variables as legitimate concepts in the functional analysis of human behavior (Mahoney, 1974). Some writers see this as being the most significant trend in contemporary behavior therapy (Wilson, 1978). At the same time, the cognitive movement in behavior therapy has been the subject of great controversy and, indeed, there is a spirited ongoing debate with respect to the role of cognitive factors in behavior (Beck & Mahoney, 1979; Ellis, 1979; Lazarus, 1979; Wolpe, 1978). In the past, in some cases by default, behavior therapy has been largely defined in terms of particular techniques. While this state of affairs was directly in conflict with the intent and philosophy of its founder, Joseph Wolpe, M.D. (1958), there is considerable evidence it existed. Hayes and Zettle (1980), indicate that a technique such as self-monitoring would be regarded as "behavioral" while analysis of an MMPI would be "nonbehavioral." As might be reasonably expected, these "technical blinders" had a tendency to chaff the intellects of clinically creative behavior therapists and caused considerable disaffection. Possibly as a result of this situation, there is a movement among some behavior therapists to become more clinically sophisticated in their conceptual models (Horton, 1981).

A particularly clear and lucid description of this perspective has been proposed by Hayes and Zettle (1980). In a concise but conceptually faithful way, they distinguish between technical ("how to do X") and conceptual ("how to talk about doing X") aspects of clinical behavior therapy. The seminal point of their argument is that the conceptual rather than the technical dimensions should be the major focus of behavior therapy. The criterion for judging if a procedure is "behavioral" is whether it can be tested and discussed in terms of behavioral principles rather than in terms of its origin or topographical details. Thus, in a conceptual sense, sophisticated clinical behavioral assessment views the antecedents and consequences of an act with an eye on abstracting the *purpose* of the action, rather than listing physical details such as rate, frequency, intensity, and so on. Moreover, sophisticated clinical behavioral interventions, in a conceptual sense, seek to utilize methods that can be discussed in behavioral terms and that generate data that can be objectively assessed. Indeed, some assert that even insight-oriented procedures can best be conceptualized as "behavioral" using such a paradigm (Hayes & Zettle, 1980).

When behavioral assessment and therapy techniques are defined by the above conceptual criterion ("can talk about X"), clinical neuropsychological assessment instruments such as the Halstead–Reitan Neuropsychological Test Battery or the Luria–Nebraska Neuropsychological Test Battery can be included as "behavioral" assessment instruments. On the other hand, should behavior therapy be defined in a purely technical sense ("can do X"), then only a relatively limited group of classic behavior therapy instruments (such as fear survey inventories or self-monitoring sheets) will qualify. If one agrees that the true goal of behavior therapy is movement toward a "clinical science based upon clinical realities" (Hayes & Zettle, 1980) rather than a slavish adherence to traditional wisdom, then the multiple advantages of a conceptual viewpoint are self-evident. A neuropsychological perspective can rationally be integrated into an enlarged and clinically realistic behavioral paradigm. While the potential value of such a blend of neuropsychology and behaviorism in the professional arsenal or behavior therapists appears great, its true worth remains an empirical question, which should be objectively tested. Until such time as hard data from multiple sources can be obtained, conclusions can only be tentative.

Luria's Contribution

Luria's ideas with regard to neuropsychological therapy, like his clinical diagnostic methods, were based on his conceptual paradigm of neurobehavioral organization (Luria, 1966). Luria believed that human actions were performed as a result of different neural structures working as a functional system. The patient's unique mental and physical abilities as well as the specific requirements of the behavioral actions to be carried out determine which neural structures will be involved. This model forms the theoretical framework for Luria's neuroretraining methods.

Luria suggested that a local brain lesion will prevent the performance of behavioral actions, such as doing mental arithmetic or brushing one's teeth, by interrupting a functional system. An analogy can be seen by removing a tube from one's radio. A single part may be essential to the efficient functioning of the whole system. While the other tubes may be in excellent condition, a single defective one can prevent the radio from operating. In Luria's model, the method of rehabilitating the dysfunctional system is to rearrange the intact parts.

Three major ways of restoring functional behavioral performance were proposed by Luria in the case of local brain injury (Golden, 1978). It should be clearly understood that all three ways utilized a strong modality (or substitutional) approach (Horton, Wedding, & Phay, 1981); i.e., intact mental and physical structures are utilized in new ways to perform behavioral objectives.

The first of Luria's methods for restoring functional behavioral performance in the case of local brain injury rests on the notion of laterality. A brain region (i.e., temporal lobe, etc.) in one cerebral hemisphere will replace the functions of the same area in the other (damaged) cerebral hemisphere. An example of this method can be seen in melodic intonation therapy. If there is a local brain injury in the speech center of the left cerebral hemisphere, then it is possible that the unimpaired counterpart area in the right hemisphere, which is dominant for musical ability, can produce expressive language and in part compensate for speech defects (Albert, Sparks, & Helm, 1973).

The second of Luria's methods for restoring functional behavior in the case of local brain injury rests on the hierarchical distribution of function. More elementary systems in the human brain can compensate for deficits in higher cortical functioning. An illustration of this compensation can be illustrated by the task of distinguishing the phonemes "b" from "p" when this ability is lost due to a local brain injury. One way to regain the ability to distinguish these two phonemes is to use tactile feedback. Putting one's fingers on one's throat accomplishes this objective.

The third of Luria's methods for restoring functional behavior in the case of local brain injury also rests on hierarchical distribution of function in the human brain, but is the exact opposite of the second way. More specifically, just as intact lower centers can compensate for impaired higher centers, so can intact higher centers compensate for impaired lower centers. A particularly relevant illustration of this method was provided by Golden (1978), who gives the example of patients with motor area lesions. These individuals cannot tap their finger when requested to do so. By asking them to tap out their *age*, however, a higher (intact) center of the brain becomes involved and it is possible to accomplish the behavioral goal. In this case, making the task more intellectually complex facilitates performance.

Thus, all three of Luria's ways of restoring functional behavioral performance in the case of local brain injury rest on utilizing residual mental and physical structures. New functional systems are created that bypass impaired areas in order to produce the same behavioral performance that was customary previous to cerebral impairment. In all of these methods, the provision of clear and accurate feedback is essential (Golden, 1978).

Diller's Contribution

In the United States, the single individual most identified with the treatment of brain-injured patients is the rehabilitation neuropsychologist Leonard Diller. Over two decades, Diller has pioneered in the development of new methods to remediate perceptual and/or cognitive deficits secondary to brain injury. In recent years his colleague Yeuda Ben-Yishay, an Israeli neuropsychologist, has worked with him at the New York University Medical Center in the single most consistent and thorough program of research on remediating deficient areas of mental abilities and/or skills.

There are crucial distinctions between the methods of Luria and Diller. Luria's methods of remediating deficits secondary to local brain lesions concentrate on use of remaining intact brain areas. Luria uses the patient's strengths to compensate for weaknesses. There is no attempt to directly retrain the functions of the injured area. In contrast, Diller's paradigm, which had been termed cognitive retraining (Diller, 1976), concentrates on weaknesses. In other words, Diller attempts to directly address specific skill deficit areas (Horton, Wedding, & Phay, 1981).

The most central feature of Diller's contribution lies in the concept of the *rehabilitation task*. First, a skill that is defective and must be remediated is identified. Then a "task" is selected that includes both the single-impaired skill and also other skills that can be systematically varied. This task (or tasks) has a number of important properties. It must be capable of being analyzed in terms of both the stimulus properties that are inherent in it and also in terms of the response properties that are elicited by it (Diller, 1976). The skill and task must also have implications for normal self-care and vocational activities as well as brain–behavior relationships. By the careful and painstaking alteration of different parameters of task difficulty, the patient can be presented with precisely designed training experiences aimed at his or her level of perceptual and/or cognitive ability. A list of stimulus characteristics that can be modified for therapeutic effect would include (1) speed of presentation, (2) single or simultaneous presentation, (3) density of context, (4) orientation, (5) locus in space, (6) load, (7) type of materials, (8) sensory modality, (9) sensory context, (10) number of dimensions, (11) degree of anchoring, (12) concreteness versus abstractness, (13) options for responding, (14) size, (15) color, (16) relationships to other stimuli, (17) familiarity, (18) interest (based on need/history), and (19) movement (Diller, 1976). Response ch[...]teristics that can be modified for therapeutic effect include (1) sp[...] (2) duration, (3) feedback, (4) type of error (omission/commission, (5) rate, (6) initiation, and (7) nature of the error (Diller, 1976). As ca[...] be surmised, the planning of treatment becomes a rather complex affair.

Building on 20 years of research and clinical treatment with brain-injured patients, Diller and his fellow workers at New York University Medical Center have created a number of modular programs to retrain various perceptual and/or cognitive skills. For example, visuoconstructive abilities are retrained, in part, by using modified block design tasks while similarities items are used in the therapy of verbal abstract thinking. Both block design and similarities are, of course, subtests of the famous Wechsler Adult Intelligence Scale (WAIS). An important part of the training is the use of various specially designed mechanical devices to produce precise stimulus and response dimensions. Also, a recent addition to the overall program is the training of social skills by role playing in groups (Y. Ben-Yishay, pers. comm.).

A crucial factor in planning the sequence of modules is the need to first develop attention and concentration abilities. Without first gaining the ability to attend and be vigilant, training experiences have little impact.

Integration of Contributions

Truly effective therapy for the brain-damaged client/patient will have to involve a number of different approaches. Treatment should include both the psychometric task analysis and saturation cueing characteristic of the psychologist's approach (Diller's contribution). Also, to be most effective, treatment should include a neurological analysis to assess the focal point of the patient's deficit and to incorporate both awareness of the deficit and compensatory strategies (Luria's contribution). Moreover, a functional analysis of behavior will be useful to determine relevant stimulus–response dimensions as well as the effective uses of behavior modification and therapy techniques such a positive reinforcement, response–cost procedures (see Horton & Howe, 1981), cognitive restructuring, and systematic desensitization, among others. Such an amalgamation can produce publicly verifiable, objectively stated outcomes. With a modicum of luck, the therapeutic change would also generalize to new skills, tasks, and settings. As asserted by Diller and Gordon (1981a): "These approaches should be used in an ancillary rather than a competitive manner. All approaches require a sophisticated understanding of the patient and the condition. None can be applied in a simple mechanical way" (p. 725).

NEUROPHYSIOLOGICAL ISSUES

As suggested by Golden (1978) recovery of function (the Holy Grail of neuropsychological rehabilitation) of brain-injured individuals may occur in one of two ways. First, there may be a substitution of a compensatory strategy. To a large extent, this model follows Luria's work (1963) and has been discussed previously in this chapter. The second way by which recovery of function can proceed is through brain reorganization. Essentially, the remaining brain areas can take over new functions. This approach assumes that there is some ability to reorganize connections in the nervous system. This ability has been termed neuroplasticity (Jacobson, 1970). That there are environmental effects on the development of neural cell development is fairly well documented by anatomical, physiological, and biochemical evidence (Gazzaniga, Steen, & Volpe, 1979). Indeed, Rosenzweig's studies at the University of California at Berkeley are quite well known. Essentially, they demonstrate that, in rats, enriched environments produced brains that were heavier, had more glia cells, and contained different enzyme content. Rosenzweig (1980, p. 266) has detailed some of the most crucial findings from the animal literature:

1. An enriched environment (EC), which can loosely be compared to a therapy program, can compensate for certain brain lesions.
2. Two hours of EC per day is as effective as 24 hours of EC per day.
3. Socialization is not a substitute for EC.
4. Cortical lesions are not the only type of lesion that can be compensated for by EC; hippocampal lesions can also be compensated.
5. EC is effective in lesion compensation in adult as well as young rats. (p. 266)

Krech (1969) has argued that the most salient and instructive trend from this line of research is that simple stimulation is not enough and that the most effective way to develop the brain is through what he terms "species-specific enrichment experiences." The rat brain improves maximally from "freedom to roam around in a large object filled room." Krech (1969) hypothesizes this is because the rat has a "space-brain" rather than a lever-pressing brain or an arithmetic-reasoning brain. Krech maintains that human beings have language brains and that "language arts" will be the appropriate "species-specific enrichment experience" for humans.

At present, cogent arguments exist for the rejection of diaschisis and simple regeneration as long term neuronal mechanisms for recovery of function from brain injury (Wall, 1980). Diaschisis (i.e., functional recovery as a result of the reduction of edema) ceases to be a contributing factor as soon as 2 months postonset (Wall, 1980) and, technically, one may assert that the function was never truly lost, but rather obscured and hidden. With respect to regeneration, Lawrence and Stein (1978) have concluded that there is minimal relevance of regeneration sprouting to the recovery from brain damage. What does seem worthy of study is collateral sprouting and unmasking. Collateral sprouting is "sprouting from intact cells to a denervated region after some or all of its normal output has been destroyed" (Lawrence & Stein, 1978). Bach-y-Rita (1980) asserts that further studies will be necessary to clarify the importance of collateral sprouting in recovery from CNS lesions.

By contrast, unmasking is a much more attractive mechanism of recovery (Wall, 1981). Unmasking uses axons and synapses that are already existing in the brain but were not previously enlisted in the performance of the behavior under scrutiny. These can be called on when the previous brain system is no longer operative (Wall, 1980). In illustration, Bach-y-Rita (1981) suggests the analog of an interrupted telephone cable from New York to San Francisco. When the direct line is cut, calls can still be placed in a roundabout way (i.e., New York to Washington, D.C., to Denver to San Francisco.) Supposedly, if the functional demand is high this new system will become stronger and more efficient. Bach-y-Rita (1981) cites cat studies (Chow & Steward, 1972) and human research (Bach-y-Rita, 1980) to buttress his points.

In sum, it must be concluded that there is a scientific basis for neuroplasticity; however, the exact mechanisms of neuroplasticity remain unknown. As noted by Bach-y-Rita (1980), future research needs to address the neural mechanisms by which treatment influences recovery of function and demonstrates the effectiveness of particular treatment programs. While much has been accomplished, still more remains to be done before the mechanisms of neuroplasticity and its relationship to the effective and successful treatment of brain-injured patients can be meaningfully conceptualized.

EVALUATION ISSUES

It is perhaps more true of brain injury remediationism than any other area of neuropsychology that evaluation is sadly neglected. Golden (1978) has suggested that a key ingredient in this state of affairs is the complexity of the problems and processes involved. As it has almost become trite to say, brain–behavior relationships are incredibly complex and difficult to understand. Even in the most straightforward of situations, there is great difficulty in understanding neuropsychological concepts. For example, something as simple as a description of a lesion demands specification of laterality, localization, extent, type, chronicity, age of the patient, and premorbid level of functioning (Libet & Kilpatrick, 1974). When the myriad additional issues related to psychotherapy are included, the task becomes even more difficult. Notwithstanding this serious difficulty, evaluation in the area of behavioral neuropsychology is of paramount importance. Leaving issues of accountability aside for the moment, the major consideration of the patient's clinical needs demands a hardheaded empirical approach to evaluation. Within-subject designs have major advantages over group research in this area. For example, Diller, Ben-Yishan, Gerstman, Goodkin, Gordon, and Weinberg (1974) performed one study where subjects, because of their differing patterns of cerebral impairment, learned different skills from doing the *same task*. Within-subject (or what is somewhat incorrectly but more commonly called single-subject designs) have the potential to evaluate the ongoing effectiveness of therapy. Thus, single-subject designs can answer specific types of clinical questions such as: "Does a treatment work? Does one treatment work better than another, given that we already know they work? Does one treatment work, does another work, and which works better? Are there elements within a successful treatment that make it work? Does the client/patient prefer one treatment over another? Does a treatment work, and if it does, what part of it make it work? What level of treatment is optimal?" (Hayes, 1981). Because of their unique flexibility and their special contribution to behavioral neuropsychology, single-subject designs are discussed here. At the same time, however, the need for more classical between groups research is not denied. However, the paramount objective of rehabilitation neuropsychology is development of effective procedures for individual patients. Later, after the initial development of therapeutic procedures has been accomplished by single-subject designs, between-group experimental methods can be used to further validate and refine the parameters of behavior change.

A brief introduction to single-subject designs is presented in the hope of sparking additional clinical interest in these valuable procedures. Essentially, four types of single-subject designs are outlined. These are the reversal or ABAB design, the multiple baseline design, the changing criterion design, and the alternating treatments design.

Reversal Design (ABAB)

As asserted by Kazdin (1980): "The reversal design demonstrates the effect of the behavior modification program by alternating presentation and removal of the program over time" (p. 97).

Perhaps an example will make this design clearer. Suppose a brain-damaged patient has violent outbursts and physically attacks hospital staff. One possible behavior modification strategy would be to institute a time-out procedure (i.e., the patient goes to a quiet room for 5–10 minutes whenever he attacks staff). Figure 9.1 presents hypothetical data. In phase A, the baseline our client/patient averages is about 14 physical attacks per day over 5 days. In phase B, the time-out procedure is instituted and physical attacks drop dramatically. After 5 days, we return to baseline conditions to see if the intervention has a role in maintaining behavior change. In phase A₂, the time-out procedure is no longer in effect and physical attacks again go up to about 15 per day. In phase B₂, the time-out procedure is again put into operation. As a result, physical attacks decline. The crucial point is the demonstration that behavior changes when the intervention is in effect and returns to baseline levels when the intervention is no longer in effect. The more often this functional control of behavior is demonstrated, the greater logical reason to believe the intervention accounts for the behavior change (i.e., ABABABABAB, etc.).

One ethical and practical problem with the reversal (ABAB) design deserves mention. Often it is not possible, due to the nature of the problem, to allow the behavior to return to baseline levels. In the

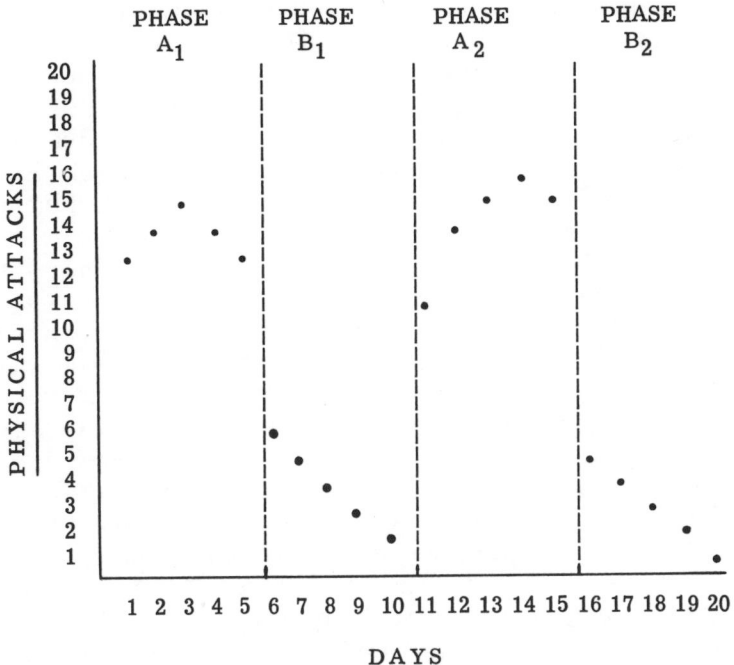

Figure 9.1.   Example of a reversal design (ABAB).

example in Figure 9.1, there is a danger to hospital staff from the physical attacks. Also, one could think of behaviors (i.e., face slapping, eye gouging, drug abuse) that are inimical to the patient and that ethically and practically preclude the use of a reversal design.

Multiple Baseline Design

As described by Kazdin (1978): "The multiple baseline design, used less frequently than the ABAB design, demonstrates the effect of the intervention without withdrawing treatment. In this design, the effect of the intervention is demonstrated by showing that behavior change accompanies introduction of the intervention at different points in time" (p. 631).

Baselines can be across behaviors, subjects, or settings. After stable baselines are achieved, the intervention is introduced in one condition at a time, with the other baselines serving as controls. Figure 9.2 gives hypothetical data for a multiple baseline design for three clients/patients all with the same problem as the case in Figure 9.1. The heavy dark line is the intervention. As can be seen, as the intervention (time-out) is introduced, the number of physical attacks on staff decreases. Other extraneous factors (time, maturating, etc.) causing the baselines to decrease are ruled out by the fact that the other baselines are not affected until the intervention is introduced.

A core assumption of the multiple baseline design is that the base lines are independent. The behaviors, subjects, or settings must not be related to each other in a causal manner. For example, if subject 2 saw what happened to subject 1 and decided to reduce his/her physical attacks to avoid the time-out contingency, the assumption of independence would be violated.

Recovery of function presents another potential problem with the multiple baseline in behavioral neuropsychology. Various neuropsychological functions will "spontaneously" recover for a period of time following brain surgery. (The purpose of therapy, of course, is to provide an increment of improvement over and above spontaneous or "natural" recovery of brain–behavior abilities.) What is less well known is that different neuropsychological abilities recover at different rates and not always in a steady fashion (Bach-y-Rita, 1981). While a full discussion of this complex area is precluded by space considerations as well as the scope of this section, one rule of thumb exists. As Tom Boll expresses it, the gross pattern of recovery is motor functions first, then language skills, and finally cognitive abilities. Boll, a Wisconsin native, describes cognition as "the last cow to come in the barn." Keeping that oversimplified and arbitrary pattern of neuropsychological recovery in mind (motor, language, cognition), one can

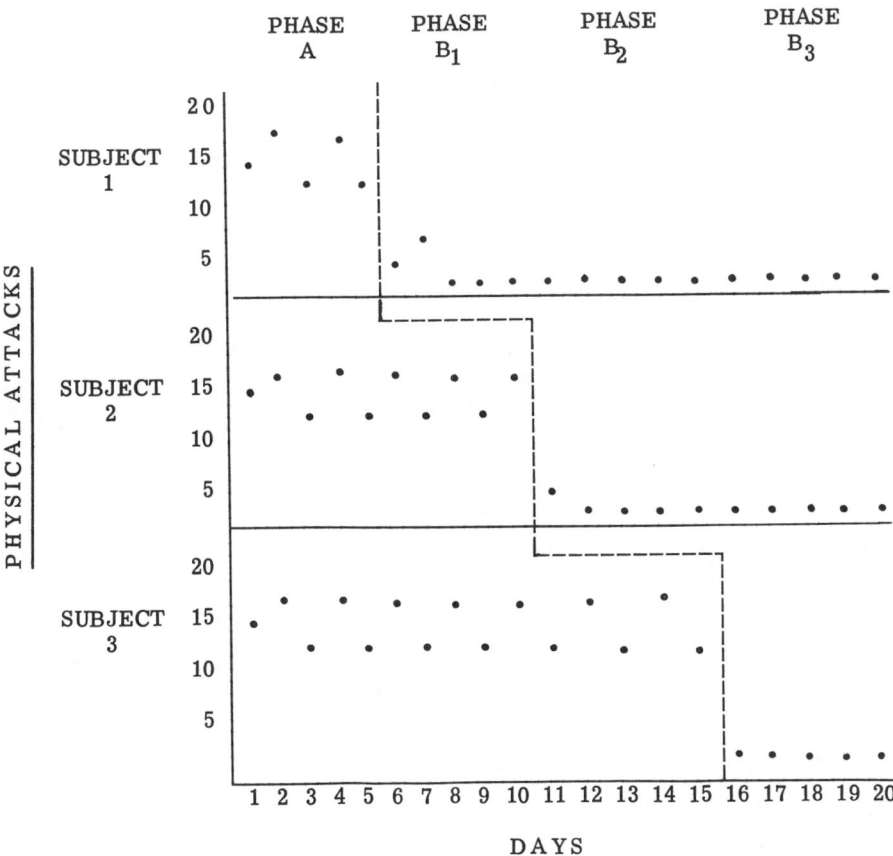

Figure 9.2.   Example of a multiple baseline design.

see that if a novice neuropsychologist designed a multiple baseline
study with a single brain-injured subject and used a motor measure
(finger tapping) for one baseline, a language measure (Reitan–Indiana
Aphasia Screening Test) for the second baseline, and a cognition
measure (Trail Making Test) for the third, then one could see how if the
intervention was applied in that sequence (i.e., motor first, then
language, and last cognition), then it would be possible to demonstrate
that a completely ineffective treatment showed changes over time as
the intervention was applied. Indeed, in one clinical neuropsychological assessment case, repeatedly evaluated at 3-month intervals over 2
years, the exact pattern proposed by Boll was shown—that is, motor
recovered at 6 months, language at about 1 year, and cognition at 2
years (Horton, unpublished data). No specific treatment effect over
and above the usual and customary rehabilitation was demonstrated.
Clearly, one must anticipate expected recovery patterns prior to
devising multiple baseline design studies with brain injured patients.

Changing Criterion Designs

Hayes (1981) has cogently described the logic of this design:

> If you arbitrarily specify the level that a given behavior must reach to achieve an outcome, and the behavior repeatedly and closely tracks these criteria, then the criteria are probably responsible. Typically, this element is used when the behavior can only change in one direction, either for ethical or practical reasons. (p. 198)

The degree to which the trend of the behavior change follows the arbitrarily set criteria is the logical warrant for assuming a relationship between the intervention and any behavior change. As Hayes (1981) points out, the limitation of the design is that "it is not always clear when observed behavior is tracking criteria shifts." Figure 9.3 demonstrates the use of a changing criterion design with the same clinical disorders utilized in Figures 9.1 and 9.2 (the heavy dark line is the intervention).

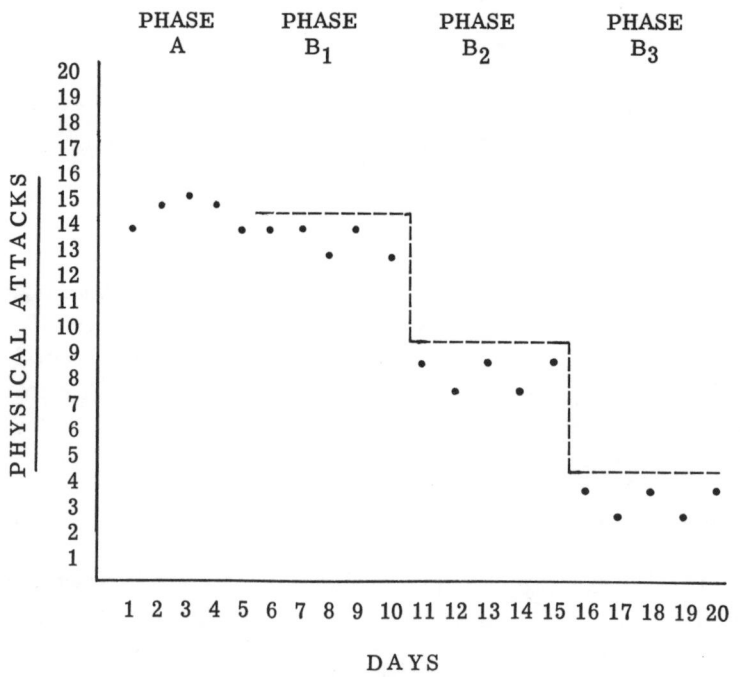

Figure 9.3.   Example of a changing criterion design.

Alternating Treatments Design

Barlow and Hayes (1979), in their classic discussion of the Alternating Treatments Design, note that:

> The basic feature of this design...is the fast alteration of two different treatments or conditions, each associated with a distinct and discriminative stimulus....Thus in the typical design, after a baseline period, two treatments (A and B) are administered, alternating with each other, and the effects on one behavior are observed....Conditions which might affect data other than treatments are counterbalanced as the experiment continues, such as time of day, therapist administering the treatment, or location of the treatment. (p. 200)

The essential point is that because other factors have been controlled for by counterbalancing, any differences between the individual patterns of the treatments would be a result of the specific treatment effect (Barlow & Hayes, 1979). An example of how this design might be applied may serve to clarify its parameters. Figure 9.4 deals with the same clinical disorder as in Figures 9.1, 9.2, and 9.3. Condition A refers to time-out contingencies and Condition B refers to

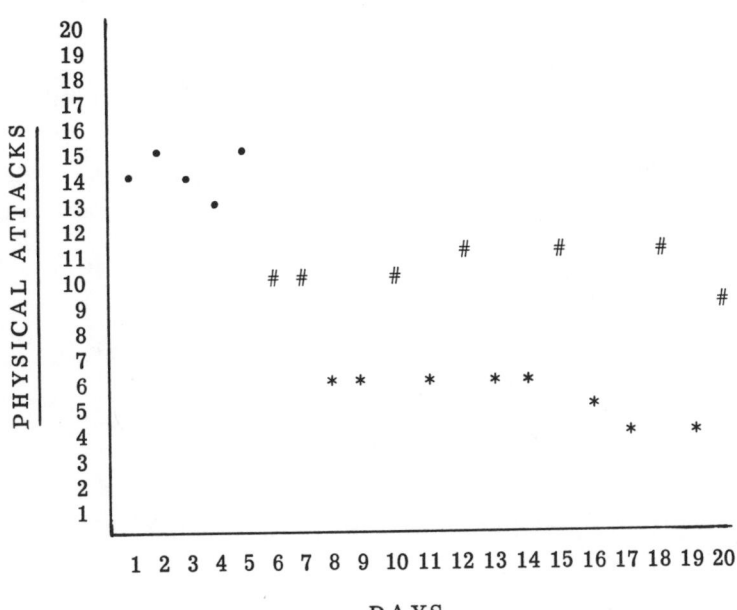

Figure 9.4.   Example of an alternating treatments design.

reinforcement of any other behavior by tokens redeemable for food, candy, and ride games. The first five dots represent a baseline condition. As can be seen, the B condition (*) is clearly more effective in controlling the client/patient's behavior than the A condition (#).

We believe that the single-subject methodology outlined above offers great potential for systematically assessing the efficiency of interventions applied for both management and rehabilitation of the brain-damaged patient. For example, the multiple baseline design might be effectively used by training a brain-impaired individual first in visual memory skills and then in auditory memory skills; if differences in performance covaried systematically with interventions it would suggest that the effects observed were due to training rather than simple spontaneous recovery of functions.

SUGGESTIONS FOR FURTHER READING

Bach-y-Rita, P. (Ed.) *Recovery of function: Theoretical considerations for brain injury rehabilitation.* Baltimore: University Park Press, 1980.

Bandura, A. Self-efficacy mechanism in human agency. *American Psychologist,* 1982, *37,* 122–147.

Diller, L. A model for cognitive re-training in rehabilitation. *The Clinical Psychologist,* 1976, *29,* 13–15.

Golden, C.J. *Diagnosis and rehabilitation in clinical neuropsychology.* Springfield, Ill.: Charles C. Thomas, 1978.

Hayes, S.C. Single case design and empirical clinical practice. *Journal of Consulting and Clinical Psychology,* 1981, *49,* 193–211.

Horton, A.M., Jr. Behavioral neuropsychology: A brief rationale. *The Behavior Therapist,* 1982, *5,* 100–102.

Kazdin, A.E. *Behavior modification in applied settings* (2nd Ed.). Homewood: Dorsey, 1980.

Luria, A.R. *Restoration of function after brain injury.* New York: Macmillan, 1963.

Rimm, D.C. & Masters, J.C. *Behavior therapy: Techniques and empirical findings* (2nd Ed.). New York: Academic, 1979.

10

BEHAVIORAL NEUROPSYCHOLOGY: PRACTICAL CONSIDERATIONS

INTRODUCTION

The major practical considerations relating to behavioral neuropsychology are patient factors, intervention assessment, treatment planning considerations, and behavior therapy approaches. Patient factors include age, emotional status, time since injury, residual neuropsychological abilities, and available social support. Our discussion of intervention assessment includes Lewinsohn's paradigm for assessing and treating brain-injured patients, and a process-analysis model drawn from the work of Bandura is outlined. Therapy planning is discussed on two levels. Some general considerations for the conduct of effective behavior change procedures are also discussed, and specific guidelines tied to structural neuropsychological aspects of the assessment process are outlined. Next, we explore some contemporary models of behavior therapy and describe three models of learning (classical conditioning, operant conditioning, cognitive learning).

Evidence for the effectiveness of behavioral treatment methods for brain-injured patients is also covered in the areas of voluntary movement, speech behavior, and cognitive functions.

CLIENT/PATIENT FACTORS

Multiple factors are important in planning treatment after brain injury. These factors include age, emotional status, time since injury, residual neuropsychological abilities, social supports available, and recovery pattern. Each of these is briefly discussed.

Age

In general, young people recover from brain injury more rapidly than older people (Golden, 1978). At the same time, however, the above relationship may be reversed in very young children—that is, in an immature brain, a lesion will have more serious consequences than the same lesion in a more fully developed brain (Johnson & Almi, 1978). However, brain plasticity has been demonstrated in persons as old as age 80 (Buell & Coleman, 1976), and age should not be used as a basis for denying treatment to the aged.

Emotional Status

The treatment of emotional, behavioral, and motivational problems is closely related, and brain injury will often produce emotional problems. While the exact effects depend on a number of factors including the site of injury (Meier, 1969), many brain-damaged patients have primary or secondary emotional difficulties. Symptoms can range from the well-known "catastrophic" reaction to severe depression and anxiety and may include extreme repression, denial, or a pervasive absence of self-regulation. An especially serious problem for the neuropsychologist is that emotional problems can destroy normal motivation to follow out a treatment program.

Selection of specific treatment programs should always be guided by the patient's overall condition (Golden, 1978). Low cognitive functioning individuals may need very heavily structured tangible reinforcement programs, while higher cognitive functioning individuals can be enlisted as allies in their own treatment and can be reinforced through intangible reinforcers (progress toward a subgoal, praise, attention, etc.).

Time since Injury

It is ideal for therapy to begin as soon as possible after brain injury. Human studies (e.g., Darley, 1975) have documented more recovery after early treatment. Some of these studies, however, have been criticized on the grounds that a certain amount of spontaneous recovery might well have been expected (Golden, 1978). Obviously, for ethical reasons, certain methodological features (i.e., control groups) cannot be used with humans. Given these constraints, at the present time available evidence supports the importance of early treatment.

Residual Neuropsychological Abilities

The greater the number of neuropsychological abilities that have been spared, the greater the probability of a significant spontaneous recovery. In addition, response to treatment following the brain injury will be more favorable (Golden, 1981). This relationship, of course, is mediated by considerations such as type of brain injury, laterality, localization of lesion, etc. President Reagan's Press Secretary, Mr. James Brady, was injured in what some term a "silent area" of the brain, the right frontal lobe, and thus his degree of impairment is subtle and less apparent than if the damage were to other brain sites. Conversely, in cases where injury to the brain occurs in the left temporal–parietal–occipital area, multiple deficits with complex verbal communication will arise.

Also, it should be observed that general measures of brain integrity serve as good prognostic indices of recovery. Meier (1974) has found that subtests of the Wechsler Adult Intelligence Scale (WAIS) and the Trail Making Test (TMT) can be helpful in this regard.

A related issue is the patient's global health status. If there are acute medical problems, the order of priorities is to first attend to these before starting treatment to remediate the adaptive behavior deficits secondary to cortical lesions (Lehmann, Delateur, Fowler, & Warren, 1975).

Available Social Supports

The most important factors determining whether or not a person will return to the community or remain in an institution are (1) a spouse and (2) a job (A. Hart, pers. comm.). A caring, loving, concerned family can provide a great deal of motivation for the brain-damaged patient and can elicit the sustained efforts needed to promote a good recovery. Indeed, often the availability of someone to supervise the patient on a daily basis is the deciding factor in community placement.

Therapy is often needed to allay concerns and to correct misconceptions with regard to the behavioral correlates of brain injury. Perhaps the most challenging and clearly the most emotionally rewarding work of the neuropsychologist is counseling the patient and his or her family. Counseling will frequently revolve around themes of guilt and helplessness (Golden, 1978).

Recovery Patterns

T.J. Boll (pers. comm.) has suggested in *very* general terms, that motor abilities recover from brain injury first, then language abilities, and finally cognitive functions. To a degree, this rule of thumb duplicates the developmental sequence. A child crawls and walks first, then he or she begins to say simple words and then talk and later the child begins to think and reason.

Time frames for these broad classes of neuropsychological abilities can also be gleaned from clinical lore. Very generally speaking, one would expect the majority of motor recovery to have been attained within 6 months after brain injury. This recovery is essentially spontaneous; however, a superb treatment program may extend this period of active recovery of motor function. Some motor functions are never regained. Rules of thumb for the return of language and cognitive functions are about 1 and 2 years, respectively. The senior author of this volume has followed selected cases and found this pattern to be reliable. Of course, these standards assume that the patient is not actively involved in a treatment program. It could be reasonably expected that active retraining methods will produce longer periods of active recovery.

Two more considerations should be mentioned. First, this general scheme can be modified by the usual parameters of brain injury (i.e., extent of lesion, localization, premorbid abilities, etc.). Second, the type of brain injury or dysfunction is particularly important for prognosticating recovery of function. Simply put, some sorts of brain disorders just do not get better, yet have predictable courses (multiple sclerosis, Parkinson's disease, Huntington's chorea, etc.). Clearly, the above-mentioned patterns of recovery will not apply to these neurological diseases.

INTERVENTION ASSESSMENT

It is important to clearly distinguish between assessment and classification since these two processes are often confused. Assessment refers to the *description* of a patient's thoughts, emotions, actions, and physiology (Lahey & Ciminero, 1980). This process utilizes interviews, direct behavioral observations, and various types of tests, at times including both biomedical (EEG, CT scan, etc.) and neuropsychological methods. Using the information gathered by the above methods, the second process is initiated. In classification, information is used to assign the patient's problem to one of several recognized categories. The person is defined as being a member of a class. The underlying assumption is that identifying the patient as a member of a class will yield valuable information in terms of conveying information, understanding the etiology of the disorder, selecting an appropriate treatment strategy, and making an accurate prognosis (Lahey & Ciminero, 1980). Assessment simply describes the disorder; classification assigns patients to conceptually meaningful groups. An example of this distinction might be seen in the neuropsychology of developmental reading disability (Pirozzolo, 1981). Reading processes can be described along a variety of dimensions, for example, visual, perceptual, attentional, and linguistic. Studies may examine eye movements or use other techniques to study various aspects of reading disability. This is assessment. How relevant this information is for treatment, however, rests on the utility of definable and relatively homogeneous groups with different treatment needs. Assigning persons to these groups is classification.

A justifiable criticism of clinical neuropsychology in the past has been its lack of relevance to remediation of adaptive behavior deficits secondary to brain injury (J. Singer, pers. comm.). Essentially, clinical neuropsychologists have devised test batteries to answer questions raised by neurologists, psychiatrists, and neurosurgeons. The most definitive current statement of what constitutes a clinical neuropsychological test battery has been advanced by the International Neuropsychological Society (INS) Task Force on Education, Accreditation, and Credentialing (1981). Its suggested test battery would include tests to assess each of the following areas: intellectual/cognitive, language, visual perceptual, memory (verbal and nonverbal), developmental status, achievement, and personality. This model is close to the one suggested by Reitan (1974) to assess similar domains: motor, sensory, psychomotor, intellectual, cognitive, language, spatial and temporal organization and integration, concept formation and abstraction abilities, speed, and power. Reitan's model is designed to meet neurological diagnostic needs, and the questions the battery was intended to answer are the determination of presence or absence of brain damage, lateralization of cortical deficits, localization of a focal lesion within a hemisphere, and neurological correlates of the psychometric pattern. While clinical neuropsychologists are, of course, quite able to give excellent answers to these questions, the advent of new sophisticated neuroradiological procedures such as CT and PETT scanning will diminish the general utility of neuropsychological localization methods (Heaton & Pendleton, 1981).

Neuropsychological test batteries will continue to answer clinical questions specific to remediation of adaptive behavioral deficits secondary to brain injury. At present, questions with respect to patient behavioral management and cognitive/perceptual/motor retraining are increasingly asked of clinical neuropsychologists by specialists working in rehabilitation medicine, alcoholism treatment programs, and nursing homes. However, clinical neuropsychologists often attempt to answer these questions with test batteries designed for and validated on neurological diagnostic criteria. There is a real need to reexamine many of the conceptual assumptions underlying the use of a test battery that was devised for one purpose and then applied to a quite different purpose. Although it appears that neuropsychological tests are sensitive to a wide range of human abilities and skills and thus are helpful in delineating a useful pattern of strengths and weaknesses (Heaton & Pendleton, 1981), the question still remains as to whether or not a test battery devised to answer essentially neurological questions can also both effectively and efficiently speak to remediation issues. It may be that the optimal neuropsychological test battery for planning treatment for brain-damaged patients is considerably different from the optimal neuropsychological test battery for differential neurological diagnostic issues.

A variety of paradigms for intervention assessment of the brain-damaged patient exist. These have been developed from longitudinal, cross-sectional, and behavioral perspectives and each model offers unique advantages and disadvantages.

Lewinsohn's Model

With his associates at the University of Oregon Neuropsychology Clinic, Peter Lewinsohn has done important clinical and research work (Lewinsohn, Danaher, & Kikel, 1977; Glasgow, Zeiss, Barrera, & Lewinsohn, 1977) investigating the remediation of memory deficits in brain-damaged individuals. In the course of this work, Lewinsohn has developed a useful paradigm for clinical work with brain-damaged people. It involves the following four steps (after Glasgow *et al.*, 1977):

1. General assessment of neuropsychological functioning
2. Specific assessment of neuropsychological functioning
3. Laboratory evaluation of intervention techniques
4. *In vivo* application of intervention techniques

General Assessment

The first step requires the use of standard neuropsychological assessment devices. For example, in the case of Ms. J., Glasgow and colleagues (1977) administered the WAIS and the Halstead–Reitan Neuropsychological Test Battery (HRNB) (Reitan & Davison, 1974) after an intake interview. This woman, who had received a concussion in an automobile accident 3½ years earlier and complained of school-related memory problems, earned a WAIS full-scale IQ of 114 and a Halsted Impairment Index of .25. The purpose of this first step is to obtain normative psychometrics and a global view of the patient's neuropsychological functioning.

Specific Assessment

The second step is to examine in detail the specific parameters of the patient's problem. In the case of Ms. J., selections from a reading skills training program of informational presentations and narrative prose were used to elucidate the actual dimensions of her semantic memory functions. To a degree, this step is very similar to a behavioral assessment of the patient's neuropsychological difficulty.

Laboratory Evaluation

In the third step, specific intervention techniques are introduced in the context of a controlled (or laboratory) setting. In the case of Ms. J., oral rehearsal and a study organization strategy (PQRST) were selected. Generalization efforts can be initiated after the demonstration of intervention effectiveness.

In Vivo Application

In the fourth and last step, application of the successful laboratory intervention to the real world is accomplished. In the case of Ms. J., this involved her applying the PQRST technique to her academic performance problems. Evaluation of the *in vivo* application was assessed by self-monitoring of negative and self-critical thoughts that were directly stimulated by her memory performance and also by her self-rating of recall of newspaper articles, immediately, 24 hours, and 7 days after reading. A final measure of outcome was that Ms. J. remained in school and enrolled for an increased number of credit hours. Thus, it can be seen that Lewinsohn's paradigm provides a framework for conceptualizing the longitudinal aspect of clinical behavioral therapy with brain-injured clients. Whereas the WAIS and HRNB were used with Ms. J., there is no reason this should always be the case. Rather, general assessment should be taken to mean the use of any quantitative neuropsychological measuring device. Indeed, it is possible to contemplate the use of neuroradiological devices (e.g., CT Scans) in this context with no conceptual difficulties. In the qualitative (or specific) assessment state, the same conceptual freedom should prevail. In order to elucidate the exact parameters of the patient's adaptive behavior deficits, considerable manipulation of stimulus–response dimensions may be necessary.

BEHAVIORAL ASSESSMENT

To a degree, the conceptual issues inherent in the Lewinsohn model overlap with recent thinking in behavioral assessment. A simple framework for task analysis in behavioral assessment is drawn from the work of Goldfried and Davison (1976), who discuss four types of variables associated with maladaptive behavior: (1) stimulus antecedents, (2) organismic variables, (3) response variables, and (4) consequent variables.

Stimulus Antecedents

It is important to realize that the environment plays an important role in determining behavior and to a large degree determines the success of coping effects. This is particularly critical when dealing with an individual who has some sort of perceptual, cognitive, or motor deficit.

Organismic Variables

On one hand, this category refers to various neuropsychological abilities that need to be assessed in an insightful manner. On the other hand, however, to just think of neuropsychological abilities in the classic sense of memory, abstraction, and concept formation fails to do this category justice. The behavior therapist working with brain-impaired patients must also consider patient expectations, attributions, and self-reinforcement standards (Goldfried & Davison, 1976).

Response Variables

In this category, the focus is on the patient's residual response abilities. If a brain-damaged individual is unable to comprehend verbal stimuli, it is futile to expect him or her to answer the telephone. Goldfried and Davison (1976) make the point that assessment of response variables should include situation-specific samples of the behavior under study as well as data concerning its duration, frequency, intensity, and magnitude. Moreover, a distinction between responses that are under autonomic nervous system control (respondents) and those traditionally seen as under voluntary control (operants) is also helpful.

Consequent Variables

The reinforcing or punishing consequences of actions play a role in determining whether or not the particular action will increase in frequency. Various parameters such as immediacy, type, content, and ratio of reinforcement to response are of critical importance for behavior initiation, rate, maintenance, and generalization.

The fact that a brain-damaged individual fails to perform an action does not mean he is incapable of performing the action. It could be he simply does not wish to perform the action because he is receiving more reinforcement for some other behavior. For example, one of the authors treated a man who had suffered massive frontal lobe damage as a result of an automobile accident and who subsequently refused to dress in street clothes. This refusal to don appropriate clothing had gone on for over 6 months. After it was found, however, that he had a desire for a particular brand of chewing tobacco, reinforcement contingencies were arranged and the man quite quickly began dressing appropriately. The ability to dress had been there all along but the proper incentive conditions were missing.

TREATMENT PLANNING

At this point in the development of behavioral neuropsychology, treatment planning is most appropriately labeled an art rather than a science. The present discussion focuses on general considerations in treatment planning. More detailed discussion of specific training strategies of neuropsychological deficits are available in other sources (Luria, 1963; Golden, 1981). The general considerations discussed include: (1) self-efficacy, (2) personality by treatment interactions, (3) resources, (4) intrusiveness to setting, and (5) aptitude by treatment interactions.

Self-efficacy

Bandura (1982) has advanced the idea that an individual's perceived effectiveness is an explanatory mechanism for therapeutic behavioral change. All behavior change methods that are successful work by creating and strengthening a person's conviction of personal effectiveness. This individual belief in self-effectiveness determines choice of activity as well as the amount and persistence of effort in the presence of aversive experiences. Essentially four sources of data shape self-mastery beliefs. These are successful personal behavioral performance, observed successful performance of others, states of physiological arousal, and verbal persuasion. Previous research by Bandura and his associates has demonstrated that successful personal behavioral performance appears to be the most powerful inducement for radical modification of self-efficacy beliefs. The implications of these ideas for treatment planning are straightforward.

Whenever possible, successful *in vivo* performance should be the focus of therapy with the brain-damaged patient. With the brain injured, providing prompt and salient behavioral feedback is often a difficult proposition. Wherever possible, devices or techniques to provide self-effectiveness feedback should be used. To a large degree, motivation for change is a function of both the reward or reinforcement for accomplishing an action and also the probability by which the individual assesses his/her likelihood of accomplishing the action or task successfully (i.e., Motivation = Reinforcement × Subjectively Assessed Probability of Success). Thus, it can be seen that influence of personal beliefs is a crucial process in treatment planning and must not be neglected.

Personality by Treatment Interaction

Personality by treatment interaction refers to patient character-istics that potentiate certain therapeutic methods. Goldfried and Davidson (1976) note difficulties with patients who are "brighter and more psychologically sophisticated" in reporting actual behavioral samples. They mention the great importance of knowing the patient's personal standards for self-reinforcement. An example of this particu-lar point may be found in a case described by Golden (1978). Essentially, a patient who had motor abilities within normal limits felt he was weak compared to his premorbid status. In order to attend to psychological needs a strength-building program was conducted that had the effect of improving the patient's emotional state and thus ensured considerable progress in the treatment of his more severe neuropsychological problems. In many cases, a major criterion for treatment planning is the ability to make quick progress. Early success has a major effect on building sustained motivation through the self-efficacy planning. As observed by Reynolds:

> The strength model is based on abilities which are sufficiently intact so as to subserve the successful accomplishment of the steps in the educational program, so that the interface between cognitive strengths (rather than weaknesses) determined from the assessment and the intervention strategy is the cornerstone of meaningfulness for the entire diagnostic-intervention process. (pp. 343–344)

Indeed, data from the work of Hartlage and his colleagues (Hartlage, 1975; Hartlage & Lucas, 1973) strongly attest to the worth of this approach to treatment planning.

BEHAVIORAL NEUROPSYCHOLOGY GUIDELINES

A modified table for identifying strengths has been developed by Heaton and Pendelton (1981) and is presented in Table 10.1.

How does one generate recommendations for the behavior therapy of brain-damaged patients from neuropsychological test results?

Table 10.1. Clinical Assessment of Daily Functioning[a]

Activity	Test	Impairment cutoff score
Vocational functioning	Average impairment index of HRNB	< 1.61
Conduct in routine and familiar everyday setting	Information and comprehension subtest of WAIS	$>$ Scaled score 7
Complex decision making and abstract activities	Category Test of HRNB	< 52 errors
Independent functioning in everyday situations	Category Test of HRNB	< 105 errors
Attention	Digit Span, Arithmetic, and Digit Symbol of WAIS	$>$ Scaled score 7
Cognitive efficiency and following detailed new procedures	Trail Making Test (part B) of HRNB	< 100 sec
General learning ability	Ingles Learning Task	< 20 trials
Semantic memory	Memory passages of RWMS	> 8
Figural memory	Visual reproduction of RWMS	> 8
Academic skills	Reitan–Indiana Aphasia Screening Test	< 6 errors
Perceptual–motor work	Spacial Relations Score of RIAST	< 5 errors
Fine manipulatory tasks	Tactual form recognition of HRNB	—
Fine motor	Grooved Peg Board and Finger Tapping Test of HRNB	—
Driving	Digit Span, Arithmetic, Digit Symbol, Block Design, and Object Assembly subtests of WAIS, Trail Making RIAST, Sensory–Perceptual Exam, Lateral Dominance Exam, Category Test of HRNB, and Visual Reproduction of RWMS	—

[a]After Heaton and Pendleton (1981).

Clearly, this is a difficult question. However, this problem can be initially conceptualized in terms of three primary dimensions (Meier, 1974). These are (1) left to right, (2) front to back, and (3) top to bottom. With respect to the cerebral cortex, these might be termed laterality, caudality, and dorsality. These terms are selected for the sake of convenience and are not intended to be of exact neuroanatomical significance or precision. These suggestions presuppose rather focal cortical lesions.

Laterality

On a clinical level, hemispheric specialization can provide a model for treatment planning. The two cerebral hemispheres process information in different ways. Assuming right handedness, the left hemisphere is logical and language oriented while the right hemisphere is intuitive and concerned with spatial aspects of stimuli. Modes of communication, therapy tasks, and therapeutic management may all be influenced by hemispheric mental asymmetry (Horton, Owens, & Hartlage, 1980). An operational example of how such a finding can influence therapy is illustrated by a case study from Horton (1979b) of a veteran who had sustained severe injury to the right cerebral hemisphere. The man had been referred for sexually touching unwilling females. Careful neuropsychological analysis of the case revealed that this veteran had only begun this socially inappropriate behavior after he had been assigned the task of assembling paper boxes in a sheltered workshop. Apparently, this touching behavior was used to escape a situation where the man was required to utilize his impaired visuospatial skills, which of course, were subserved by his severely impaired right cerebral hemisphere. Interestingly, when put in a controlled situation in the neurology ward of a medical center, the touching behavior extinguished rapidly.

Another example of how the relatively straightforward neuropsychological fact of lateralization may contribute to treatment planning may be gained from a brief consideration of educational intervention with school-aged children. Hartlage (1978) has outlined three mutually independent neuropsychological profiles that appear to have substantial validity both for diagnosis and for the prediction of the effectiveness of specific types of educational intervention (Table 10.2).

Fowler and Fordyce (1972) have also presented a number of excellent recommendations for behavioral management of the patient with lateralized brain damage. Their recommendations for the patient with left hemisphere brain damage are as follows:

1. Do not overestimate the patient's language comprehension abilities.
2. Use visual and tactual demonstrations to communicate.

Table 10.2. Basic Neuropsychological Profiles for Children

	Type I Child	Type II Child	Type III Child
Neuropsychological profile	Comparatively lower WISC-R verbal than performance IQ score with consistently lowered language ability (i.e., depressed ITPA and PPVT scores) relative to perceptual–motor skills (i.e., Bender–Gestalt or VMI)	Comparatively lower WISC-R performance than verbal IQ and consistently lowered perceptual–motor ability relative to language skills	No consistent pattern of WISC-R strength and weakness or clear superiority of either language or perceptual–motor abilities and skills
Neurological syndrome	Left hemisphere dysfunction	Right hemisphere dysfunction	Generalized cerebral dysfunction
Emotional correlates	Reserved, tentative, and uncertain of self-efficacy	Impulsive and uncritical of personal performance	Restless, irritable, and hyperactive

Table 10.2. Basic Neuropsychological Profiles for Children (continued)

	Type I Child	Type II Child	Type III Child
Educational intervention	Whole work or look–say reading programs and perceptually oriented instructional modes	Linguistic and aural instruction modes	Extreme structure and special placement
Prognosis	Persistent problem during academic career (after third grade) but relatively good adjustment in nonacademic pursuits	Difficulty in early school grades (K–2) but tend to do better in later elementary grades (3–6) with generally successful academic career	Little ultimate academic success

3. Simplify verbal communication and use adequate vocal volume.
4. Teach in small steps.
5. Give frequent feedback.

For right hemisphere brain damage, their suggestions are as follows:

1. Use verbal, linguistic cues rather than visual cues.
2. Provide clear vertical and horizontal visual reference points.
3. Teach in small steps with verbal cues.
4. Keep surroundings well lighted and give the patient extra room to move around.
5. Do not rely on the patient's self-estimate of his or her abilities.

With respect to unilateral neglect, the patient should be approached from the unaffected side and all stimuli should be presented from this side.

These suggestions only touch the surface of the many possible modifications that can be made in utilizing knowledge of laterality to aid in the selection of modes of communication, therapy tasks, and therapeutic behavioral management.

Caudality

A second more subtle distinction rooted in fundamental brain–behavior relationships that may have implications for behavior therapy is caudality of brain damage. The caudality of brain functioning is less often considered than laterality of brain functioning. Caudality refers to localization within the anterior–posterior dimension. There is some agreement that the frontal lobes involve the planning, execution, and verification of behavior while the posterior sections are more involved with the reception, integration, and analysis of sensory information from both the internal and external environment (Luria, 1966). Whether or not the prefrontal regions of the human brain have suffered impairment is of maximum clinical importance.

Brain impairment caudality can be translated into straightforward clinical therapeutic implications with little difficulty. The degree of novel problem solving that a patient will be capable of will depend on the pattern of spared and compromised frontal lobe abilities. Frequently, individuals with frontal lobe impairment may show deficits in self-management skills. Luria (1966) has commented on the very poor vocational rehabilitation prognosis of the patient with a frontal lobe lesion. Indeed, in the work setting of the first author, a number of cases have demonstrated that a brain-damaged patient with intact frontal lobes will display a much better behavioral adjustment than will the patient with frontal lobe impairment, even though the former patient may show more overall brain damage on clinical neuropsychological testing.

We have commented on Bandura's (1982) observation that a patient's self-rating of personal competence is an important predictor of response to treatment. One might speculate that a similar cognitive style measure would prove of some value in predicting the responses of brain-damaged individuals to behavior therapy. The first author has had some clinical success in using the items on the memory subtest of the Luria–Nebraska Neuropsychological Test Battery for assessing a patient's potential for personal *in vivo* problem solving.

The possible value of cognitive behavioral treatment strategies for frontal patients appears great. The use of self-instructional therapy to develop self-control (Meichembaum, 1977) with the brain injured is but a single area where future research efforts might be concentrated. In this regard, the first author has had clinical success in using the turtle technique (Schneider & Robin, 1976), a method for the self-control of impulsive behavior, to decrease temper outbursts of a brain-damaged adult male who had a locus of impairment in the right frontal area.

Consideration of caudality should not preclude the simultaneous consideration of laterality. A well-designed group study (Tucker, Shearer, & Murray, 1977) found evidence suggesting that hemispheric specialization interacts with cognitive behavioral techniques that employ either verbal self-instruction or coping imagery. The possible implications for clinical work are readily apparent. The study suggests that behavior therapists might best use self-instruction techniques with patients who primarily utilize the right hemisphere, while using coping imagery with patients who display a left hemisphere preference. Activation of the less frequently used hemisphere is recommended.

Dorsality

When there are cortical lesions there are often concomitant personality changes. It is also commonly observed that premorbidly controlled antisocial character traits of brain-damaged individuals are released after the onset of the brain injury. This syndrome might be explained by the triune brain model of Paul MacLean.

The issue of dorsality needs additional attention, as our current knowledge base is quite inadequate to generate many meaningful clinical suggestions. What can be offered, however, are some suggestions with respect to memory. Fowler and Fordyce (1972) offer the following suggestions for clinicians working with memory-impaired individuals:

1. Keep communications short and simple.
2. Establish a fixed routine.
3. Teach one step at a time.

4. Give repeated feedback through intact modalities.
5. Use memory aids such as written notes, instruction cards, and printed daily schedules.
6. Have the patient repeat, in his or her own words, any instructions given.
7. Have the patient *over*learn tasks.

CONCLUSION

The aforementioned materials were organized on the assumption that a blend of the behavioral and biomedical sciences holds significant promise in the treatment, management, and rehabilitation of the brain injured. As we have already observed, interest in and knowledge of brain–behavior relationships has increased geometrically in the past decade. Valid and reliable neurodiagnostic techniques, the result of collaborative behavioral/biomedical investigations, are now realities and the stage is set for a new era of clinical and research effort devoted to the generation of adequate, innovative solutions to the human welfare problems of brain-damaged people. This book has focused on this emerging area of psychological/neurological investigation. In particular, we have attempted to define a new speciality within the field of neuropsychology—behavioral neuropsychology.

The ultimate value of behavioral neuropsychology will rest on its ability to make significant contributions to the amelioration of the cognitive, affective, and behavioral difficulties of the brain-injured population. Of particular importance will be the issue of an appropriate interface with traditional systems of socialization and support. Our expectation, and hope, is that delineation of these considerations will be of value in the challenge to alleviate human distress and promote social well-being with those individuals who have suffered cerebral impairment.

In summary, it is premature to conclude that neuropsychology and behavior therapy have been entirely integrated. However, it is clear that early work on conceptual and empirical fronts has shown significant promise and we are excited about this emerging interface. We find ourselves in much the same position as the early biofeedback researchers and can only echo the words of Neil Miller at a similar juncture. Indeed, "we need to be cautious in what we claim but bold in what we try."

SUGGESTIONS FOR FURTHER READING

Ben-Yishay, Y., Diller, L., & Rattok, J. *Working approaches to remediation of cognitive deficits in brain damaged persons* (Rehabilitation Monograph no. 59). New York: New York University, Institute of Rehabilitative Medicine, 1978.

Hartlage, L.C. CLinical application of neuropsychological test data in a case study. *School Psychology Review*, 1981, *10*, 362–366.

Horton, A.M., Jr., Wedding, D., & Phay, A. Current perspectives on assessment of and therapy for brain-damaged individuals. In C.J. Golden, S.S. Alcaparras, F. Strider, & B. Graber (Eds.), *Applied techniques in behavioral medicine.* New York: Grune & Stratton, 1981.

Kennedy, R.W. & Kennedy, A. Absence of purposeful behavior: Issues in training the profoundly impaired elderly. In A.M. Horton, Jr. (Ed.), *Mental health interventions for the aging.* New York: Praeger, 1982.

11

CLINICAL
CASE STUDIES IN
NEUROPSYCHOLOGY

It is clear to us that reading about brain–behavior relationships is important and necessary but only a first step in the training of the clinical neuropsychologist. Many of the manifestations of brain impairment are subtle and elusive and cannot be easily described (e.g., *Witzelsucht*); however, some experience with patients displaying such disorders leaves students with lasting memories and a real appreciation for the clinical "feel" of the symptom. While we cannot provide the rich *in vivo* experiences that are so crucial, we do want to conclude this text with a number of case studies drawn from our own files and those of our colleagues. We are indebted to James Craine, William Tsushima, Paul Malloy, and Jeff Webster, all of whom contributed case material.

We have included samples of both the Halstead–Reitan Battery and the Luria–Nebraska Battery and, for a few patients, we have test results on each battery. We have included more examples of the Halstead–Reitan Battery because both authors have used it longer. Each Halstead–Reitan profile is presented on a standardized form utilizing the familiar 6-point coding system popularized by Russell, Neuringer, and Goldstein (1970). Essentially, the system converts performance on each Halstead–Reitan Battery subtest into a common ordinal metric in which 0 implies superior performance, 1 suggests performance falling in the average range, and scores of 2, 3, 4, and 5 imply respectively mild, moderate, severe, and extreme damage.

The Luria–Nebraska Battery scores are presented on the standard profile form included with the administration and scoring booklet. Profiles have been plotted and critical levels have been established and marked for each patient. Details that might identify the individuals involved have been omitted.

Following each presentation of neuropsychological data there is a brief description of the patient along with relevant medical studies. We suggest that the reader study the neuropsychological data first and attempt to draw your own conclusions regarding likelihood of cerebral impairment, lateralization, localization, etiology, and chronicity. You may find it useful to use the technique employed by Dr. Ralph Reitan—that is, rate each patient using a large sheet of white paper, listing general indices of brain impairment in the center with right and left localizing signs listed on the right and left side of the page. Only then should you read the page identifying the patient's problem.

THE CASE STUDIES

Neuropsychology Assessment

Patient Data: Name _____ A _____

Age: __44__ , Race: B (W) O, Sex: M (F)

Occupation: ___School Teacher___ Handedness: (R) L CR CL

Education: ___16 years___ Date of Testing: _____

Halstead's Neuropsychological Test Battery

Test	Raw Score	Rating
Category	68	0 1 ②3 4 5
T.P.T. Time	33.9	0 1 2 3 ④5
T.P.T. Memory	6	0①2 3 4 5
T.P.T. Location	0	0 1 2 3 ④5
Speech Perception	15	0 1 2③4 5
Rhythm	4	0①2 3 4 5
Tapping Speed	0 (N.G.)	0 1 2 3 4⑤
Halstead Impairment Index	0.7	
Average Impairment Rating	2.25	

Other Tests Sensitive to Cerebral Dysfunction

Name of Test	Raw Score	Rating
T.P.T. Dominant Hand (R)	13.6	0 1 2③4 5
T.P.T. Non Dominant Hand (R)	13.7	0 1 2 3 4⑤
~~Both~~ Hands (R)	6.7	0 1 2 3 ④5
Tapping Dominant Hand	57	⓪1 2 3 4 5
Tapping Non Dominant Hand	0	0 1 2 3 4⑤
Spacial Relations Score	4	0 1 ②3 4 5
Aphasia Score	0	⓪1 2 3 4 5
Trails A	70"	0 1 2 3 ④5
Trails B	116"	0 1②3 4 5
Perceptual Score	30	0 1②3 4 5
Digit Symbol Score	7	0①2 3 4 5
Grip Strength Dominant Hand	38.5 kg	
Grip Strength Non Dominant Hand	Unable	

Wechsler Adult Intelligence Scale

Subtest	Scaled Score		
Information	11	Digit Symbol	7
Comprehension	9	Picture Completion	7
Arithmetic	7	Block Design	7
Similarities	18	Picture Arrangement	6
Digit Span	9	Object Assembly	10
Vocabulary	13	Total Performance Score	—
Total Verbal Score	—	Performance I.Q.	88
Verbal I.Q.	107	Total Score	—
		Full Scale I.Q.	99

Comments

This patient has lost all function on the left side. The TPT was administered three times using the right hand only to assess learning across trials.

PATIENT A

This patient suffered a right cerebrovascular accident in the distribution of the right middle cerebral artery accompanied by a dense left hemiplegia at age 42. EEG was abnormal and was consistent with a vascular process involving the right cerebral hemisphere in the area of the middle cerebral artery. Brain scans demonstrated a "flip flop" of arterial venous circulation suggesting a thrombosis or embolism of the right middle cerebral artery. Computerized axial tomography of the brain demonstrated changes consistent with a cerebral infarction involving the right frontal–parietal area with a slight mass effect probably secondary to cerebral edema. All of the laboratory findings were consistent with a thrombosis or embolism of the right middle cerebral artery that would account for the patient's left hemiplegia.

Neuropsychological testing was performed 1½ years following the onset of the CVA. This patient had completed rehabilitation activities at that time and was able to walk with the use of a cane but her left arm was totally useless.

Neuropsychology Assessment

Patient Data: Name _____ B _____

Age: __41__ ,   Race: B (W) O,   Sex: (M) F

Occupation: __Commercial Fisherman__   Handedness: (R) L CR CL

Education: __10 years_____   Date of Testing: _____

Halstead's Neuropsychological Test Battery

Test	Raw Score	Rating
Category	85	0 1 2 ③ 4 5
T.P.T. Time	20.0	0 1 ② 3 4 5
T.P.T. Memory	7	0 ① 2 3 4 5
T.P.T. Location	5	0 ① 2 3 4 5
Speech Perception	25	0 1 2 ③ 4 5
Rhythm	5	0 ① 2 3 4 5
Tapping Speed	46	0 1 ② 3 4 5
Halstead Impairment Index	0.6	
Average Impairment Rating	1.67	

Other Tests Sensitive to Cerebral Dysfunction

Name of Test	Raw Score	Rating
T.P.T. Dominant Hand	7.8	0 1 ② 3 4 5
T.P.T. Non Dominant Hand	6.6	0 ① 2 3 4 5
Both Hands	5.6	0 1 2 ③ 4 5
Tapping Dominant Hand	46	0 1 ② 3 4 5
Tapping Non Dominant Hand	44	0 ① 2 3 4 5
Spacial Relations Score	3	0 ① 2 3 4 5
Aphasia Score	6	0 ① 2 3 4 5
Trails A	48"	0 1 ② 3 4 5
Trails B (2 errors)	165"	0 1 2 ③ 4 5
Perceptual Score	0	⓪ 1 2 3 4 5
Digit Symbol Score	7	0 1 ② 3 4 5
Grip Strength Dominant Hand	N.G.	
Grip Strength Non Dominant Hand		N.G.

Wechsler Adult Intelligence Scale

Subtest	Scaled Score		Scaled Score
Information	10	Digit Symbol	7
Comprehension	11	Picture Completion	10
Arithmetic	7	Block Design	9
Similarities	12	Picture Arrangement	9
Digit Span	10	Object Assembly	10
Vocabulary	9	Total Performance Score	—
Total Verbal Score	—	Performance I.Q.	99
Verbal I.Q.	99	Total Score	—
		Full Scale I.Q.	99

Comments

This patient performed very poorly on a mirror drawing task
and when asked to draw a clock. In addition, he has a great
deal of difficulty completing the Wisconsin Card Sorting Test.

PATIENT B

This man developed frontal sinusitis in early 1979 which ultimately resulted in a brain abcess. He had been treated with antibiotics and developed symptoms of headaches, nausea, vomiting, and coma. He had a positive spinal tap which documented meningitis as well as encephalitis. He then had a craniotomy, which included the drainage of a left frontal brain abcess. He subsequently had a ventricular peritonealostomy. His retromyogram demonstrated subacute neuropathic processes including multiple cervical routes bilaterally. Myelograms showed a complete blocking of the fourth thoracic level. He had a diagnosis of arachnoiditis by exclusion.

This patient demonstrated a typical frontal lobe affect and this presented problems in dealing with his rehabilitation. He also experienced problems with ataxia and had extremely poor balance.

Neuropsychology Assessment

Patient Data: Name _____ C _____

Age: __78__ ,   Race: B (W) O,   Sex: M (F)

Occupation: Dress Shop Owner _____   Handedness: (R) L CR CL

Education: College Graduate _____   Date of Testing: _____

Halstead's Neuropsychological Test Battery

Test	Raw Score	Rating
Category	78	0 1 2 ③ 4 5
T.P.T. Time	21.3	0 1 2 ③ 4 5
T.P.T. Memory	5	0 1 ② 3 4 5
T.P.T. Location	3	0 1 ② 3 4 5
Speech Perception	30	0 1 2 3 ④ 5
Rhythm	8	0 1 ② 3 4 5
Tapping Speed	0 (N.G.)	0 1 2 3 4 ⑤
Halstead Impairment Index	1.0	
Average Impairment Rating	3.25	

Other Tests Sensitive to Cerebral Dysfunction

Name of Test	Raw Score	Rating
T.P.T. (Left)	9.8	0 1 ② 3 4 5
T.P.T. Non Dominant Hand	7.0	0 1 2 ③ 4 5
Both Hands	4.5	0 1 2 ③ 4 5
Tapping Dominant Hand	0	0 1 2 3 4 ⑤
Tapping Non Dominant Hand	38	0 1 ② 3 4 5
Spacial Relations Score	4	0 1 ② 3 4 5
Aphasia Score	59	0 1 2 3 4 ⑤
Trails A	81"	0 1 2 3 ④ 5
Trails B (6 errors)	745"	0 1 2 3 4 ⑤
Perceptual Score	25	0 1 ② 3 4 5
Digit Symbol Score	3	0 1 2 3 ④ 5
Grip Strength Dominant Hand	N.G.	
Grip Strength Non Dominant Hand		N.G.

Wechsler Adult Intelligence Scale

Subtest	Scaled Score
Information	N.G.
Comprehension	"
Arithmetic	"
Similarities	"
Digit Span	"
Vocabulary	"
Total Verbal Score	"
Verbal I.Q.	"

Digit Symbol	3
Picture Completion	9
Block Design	9
Picture Arrangement	6
Object Assembly	9
Total Performance Score	—
Performance I.Q.	115
Total Score	—
Full Scale I.Q.	—

Comments

PATIENT C

This patient suffered a left hemisphere cerebrovascular accident approximately 8 months prior to testing. A right hemiparesis and aphasia resulted from this CVA; in addition, she has a history of hypertension and premature ventricular contractions. The latter condition was corrected by insertion of a pacemaker shortly after this woman's stroke. Recovery has continued since that time. It is interesting to note that this woman benefitted considerably from rehabilitation efforts, despite the severity of her stroke and her advanced age.

Neuropsychology Assessment

Patient Data: Name _____ D _____

Age: __30__ , Race: B (W) O, Sex: (M) F

Occupation: ___Policeman___ Handedness: (R) L CR CL

Education: ____14 years____ Date of Testing: _____

Halstead's Neuropsychological Test Battery

Test	Raw Score	Rating
Category	116	0 1 2 3 (4) 5
T.P.T. Time	30.0	0 1 2 3 4 (5)
T.P.T. Memory	4	0 1 (2) 3 4 5
T.P.T. Location	2	0 1 2 (3) 4 5
Speech Perception	7	0 (1) 2 3 4 5
Rhythm	5	0 (1) 2 3 4 5
Tapping Speed	41	0 1 (2) 3 4 5
Halstead Impairment Index	0.9	
Average Impairment Rating	1.83	

Other Tests Sensitive to Cerebral Dysfunction

Name of Test	Raw Score	Rating
T.P.T. Dominant Hand	10.0	0 1 2 3 4 (5)
T.P.T. Non Dominant Hand	10.0	0 1 2 3 4 (5)
Both Hands	10.0	0 1 2 3 4 (5)
Tapping Dominant Hand	5.8	(0) 1 2 3 4 5
Tapping Non Dominant Hand	41	0 1 (2) 3 4 5
Spacial Relations Score	2	0 (1) 2 3 4 5
Aphasia Score	0	(0) 1 2 3 4 5
Trails A	39"	0 1 (2) 3 4 5
Trails B	51"	(0) 1 2 3 4 5
Perceptual Score	17	0 1 (2) 3 4 5
Digit Symbol Score	7	0 (1) 2 3 4 5
Grip Strength Dominant Hand	59 kg	
Grip Strength Non Dominant Hand	46 kg	

Wechsler Adult Intelligence Scale

Subtest	Scaled Score		
Information	7	Digit Symbol	7
Comprehension	14	Picture Completion	6
Arithmetic	10	Block Design	8
Similarities	10	Picture Arrangement	6
Digit Span	14	Object Assembly	4
Vocabulary	10	Total Performance Score	—
Total Verbal Score	—	Performance I.Q.	76
Verbal I.Q.	104	Total Score	—
		Full Scale I.Q.	91

Comments

Discrepancy Index (VIQ – PIQ) = 28 points.

Each trial of the Tactual Performance Test was limited to 10 minutes. This patient was able to correctly place only one block with the right hand, one block with the left, and two blocks with both hands working together.

Patient D

This man suffered a gunshot wound to his head approximately 1 month prior to neuropsychological testing. The point of entry of the bullet was just above the right temple with the trajectory of the bullet being across the right frontal lobe. The bullet lodged behind the left eye. Surgery for removal of the bullet commenced within 1 hour after the injury occurred and on recovery this patient entered a physical and occupational therapy rehabilitation program.

Neuropsychology Assessment

Patient Data: Name _____ E _____

    Age: __33__ ,   Race: B (W) O,   Sex: M (F)

    Occupation:____School Teacher____   Handedness: (R) L CR CL

    Education: ____17 years____   Date of Testing: _____

Halstead's Neuropsychological Test Battery

Test	Raw Score	Rating
Category	110	0 1 2 3 ④ 5
T.P.T. Time	30.6	0 1 2 3 ④ 5
T.P.T. Memory	8	0 ① 2 3 4 5
T.P.T. Location	1	0 1 2 ③ 4 5
Speech Perception	12	0 1 ② 3 4 5
Rhythm	9	0 1 ② 3 4 5
Tapping Speed	32	0 1 2 ③ 4 5
Halstead Impairment Index	0.9	
Average Impairment Rating	2.33	

Other Tests Sensitive to Cerebral Dysfunction

Name of Test	Raw Score	Rating
T.P.T. Dominant Hand	9.3	0 1 ② 3 4 5
T.P.T. Non Dominant Hand	14.8	0 1 2 3 4 ⑤
Both Hands	6.5	0 1 2 3 ④ 5
Tapping Dominant Hand	41	0 1 ② 3 4 5
Tapping Non Dominant Hand	32	0 1 2 ③ 4 5
Spacial Relations Score	5	0 1 ② 3 4 5
Aphasia Score	0	⓪ 1 2 3 4 5
Trails A	91"	0 1 2 3 4 ⑤
Trails B	182"	0 1 2 ③ 4 5
Perceptual Score	10	0 ① 2 3 4 5
Digit Symbol Score	4	0 1 2 ③ 4 5
Grip Strength Dominant Hand	24 kg	
Grip Strength Non Dominant Hand	12 kg	

Wechsler Adult Intelligence Scale

Subtest	Scaled Score			
Information	9	Digit Symbol	4
Comprehension	12	Picture Completion	4
Arithmetic	11	Block Design	5
Similarities	11	Picture Arrangement	6
Digit Span	11	Object Assembly	4
Vocabulary	16	Total Performance Score	—
Total Verbal Score	—	Performance I.Q.	65
Verbal I.Q.	109	Total Score	—
		Full Scale I.Q.	90

Comments

Discrepancy Index (VIQ – PIQ) = 44 points

Wechsler Memory Quotient = 92

PATIENT E

Neuropsychological testing for this woman provides information on level of brain functions for a patient approximately 2 years after emergency brain surgery. An intracranial mass was partially removed from the posterior portion of the right cerebral hemisphere, followed by a series of radiation treatments. Her primary complaints at the time of testing were memory loss, spatial disorientation, a left visual field defect, and problems involving reading.

Neuropsychology Assessment

Patient Data: Name _____ F _____

Age: __48__ , Race: B W (O,) Sex: (M) F

Occupation: ____Foreman____ Handedness: (R) L CR CL

Education: ____14 years____ Date of Testing: _____

Halstead's Neuropsychological Test Battery

Test	Raw Score	Rating
Category	90	0 1 2③4 5
T.P.T. Time	26.0	0 1 2 3 4⑤
T.P.T. Memory	2	0 1 2③4 5
T.P.T. Location	0	0 1 2 3④5
Speech Perception	27	0 1 2 3④5
Rhythm	6	0 1②3 4 5
Tapping Speed	23	0 1 2 3④5
Halstead Impairment Index	1.0	
Average Impairment Rating	3.25	

Other Tests Sensitive to Cerebral Dysfunction

Name of Test	Raw Score	Rating
T.P.T. Dominant Hand	10.0	0 1 2③4 5
T.P.T. Non Dominant Hand	6.0	0 1 2 3 4⑤
Both Hands	10.0	0 1 2 3 4⑤
Tapping Dominant Hand	31	0 1 2 3④5
Tapping Non Dominant Hand	23	0 1 2 3④5
Spacial Relations Score	6	0 1 2③4 5
Aphasia Score	5	0①2 3 4 5
Trails A (3 errors)	233"	0 1 2 3 4⑤
Trails B (2 errors)	460"	0 1 2 3 4⑤
Perceptual Score	29	0 1②3 4 5
Digit Symbol Score	3	0 1 2③4 5
Grip Strength Dominant Hand	54 kg	
Grip Strength Non Dominant Hand	34 kg	

Wechsler Adult Intelligence Scale

Subtest	Scaled Score		
Information	9	Digit Symbol	3
Comprehension	6	Picture Completion	5
Arithmetic	5	Block Design	4
Similarities	4	Picture Arrangement	0
Digit Span	6	Object Assembly	2
Vocabulary	8	Total Performance Score	—
Total Verbal Score	—	Performance I.Q.	65
Verbal I.Q.	80	Total Score	—
		Full Scale I.Q.	72

Comments

PATIENT F

This 47-year-old male was brought to the emergency room following his sudden collapse while seated. On the basis of carotid arteriography, a diagnosis of left deep frontal hematoma was made. Neurological examination at bedside suggested bilateral deficits were present and neuropyschological evaluation was requested. Testing demonstrated right hemisphere deficits in addition to the known frontal damage. On the basis of these findings a CT scan was ordered that demonstrated extensive right parietal damage, presumably secondary to a severe anoxic episode that occurred at the time of his initial insult. A neurotraining program was initiated and this patient regained many of his earlier abilities.

Neuropsychology Assessment

Patient Data: Name _____ G _____

Age: _____ 43 _____   Race: B   W   O,   Sex: (M)   F

Occupation: _____ Unemployed _____   Handedness: (R)   L   CR   CL

Education: __ High School Graduate __   Date of Testing: _____

Halstead's Neuropsychological Test Battery

Test	Raw Score	Rating
Category	51	0 (1) 2 3 4 5
T.P.T. Time	17'44"	0 1 (2) 3 4 5
T.P.T. Memory	6	0 (1) 2 3 4 5
T.P.T. Location	3	0 1 (2) 3 4 5
Speech Perception	N.G.	0 1 2 3 4 5
Rhythm	10	0 1 2 (3) 4 5
Tapping Speed	12	0 1 2 3 4 (5)
Halstead Impairment Index	.83	
Average Impairment Rating	2.33	

Other Tests Sensitive to Cerebral Dysfunction

Name of Test	Raw Score	Rating
T.P.T. Dominant Hand	7'16"	0 (1) 2 3 4 5
T.P.T. Non Dominant Hand	7'2"	0 1 2 (3) 4 5
Both Hands	3'26"	0 1 (2) 3 4 5
Tapping Dominant Hand	15	0 1 2 3 4 (5)
Tapping Non Dominant Hand	12	0 1 2 3 4 (5)
Spacial Relations Score	—	0 1 2 3 4 5
Aphasia Score	—	0 1 2 3 4 5
Trails A	50"	0 1 2 (3) 4 5
Trails B	72"	0 (1) 2 3 4 5
Perceptual Score	—	0 1 2 3 4 5
Digit Symbol Score	—	0 1 2 3 4 5
Grip Strength Dominant Hand	54 kg	
Grip Strength Non Dominant Hand	62 kg	

Wechsler Adult Intelligence Scale

Subtest	Scaled Score		
Information	10	Digit Symbol	6
Comprehension	7	Picture Completion	8
Arithmetic	11	Block Design	14
Similarities	7	Picture Arrangement	6
Digit Span	7	Object Assembly	10
Vocabulary	5	Total Performance Score	—
Total Verbal Score	—	Performance I.Q.	97
Verbal I.Q.	87	Total Score	—
		Full Scale I.Q.	91

Comments

Wechsler Memory Quotient = 94

MMPI (T scores): Sc = 98; Hs = 95; Hy = 90; D = 85. (Valid Profile)

PATIENT G

This 43-year-old male suffered a stroke 2 years prior to testing that caused numbness and weakness on the left side of his body. Approximately 3 months prior to testing he had a second stroke that left his right side weak. In addition, he presented mild aphasic symptoms following the second stroke.

Neuropsychological testing revealed mild to moderate bilateral involvement of sensory, motor, and higher cognitive functions. MMPI results suggested considerable anxiety and depression and the expected somatic preoccupation. It was felt that this patient would show continued spontaneous recovery; he was counseled about realistic goals and objectives and was referred for psychiatric follow-up.

Neuropsychology Assessment

Patient Data: Name _____ H _____

Age: __58__ ,   Race: B (W) O,   Sex: (M) F

Occupation: ___Cost Estimator___   Handedness: (R) L   CR   CL

Education: ___12 years___   Date of Testing: _____

Halstead's Neuropsychological Test Battery

Test	Raw Score	Rating
Category	138	0 1 2 3 4 (5)
T.P.T. Time	—	0 1 2 3 4 5
T.P.T. Memory	—	0 1 2 3 4 5
T.P.T. Location	—	0 1 2 3 4 5
Speech Perception	—	0 1 2 3 4 5
Rhythm	—	0 1 2 3 4 5
Tapping Speed	39.6	0 1 2 (3) 4 5
Halstead Impairment Index		—
Average Impairment Rating		—

Other Tests Sensitive to Cerebral Dysfunction

Name of Test	Raw Score	Rating
T.P.T. Dominant Hand	—	0 1 2 3 4 5
T.P.T. Non Dominant Hand	—	0 1 2 3 4 5
Both Hands	—	0 1 2 3 4 5
Tapping Dominant Hand	39.6	0 1 2 (3) 4 5
Tapping Non Dominant Hand	11.5	0 1 2 3 4 (5)
Spacial Relations Score	10	0 1 2 3 4 (5)
Aphasia Score	5	0 (1) 2 3 4 5
Trails A	180	0 1 2 3 4 (5)
Trails B	N.G.	0 1 2 3 4 5
Perceptual Score	—	0 1 2 3 4 5
Digit Symbol Score	—	0 1 2 3 4 5
Grip Strength Dominant Hand	22 kg	
Grip Strength Non Dominant Hand	9½ kg	

Wechsler Adult Intelligence Scale

Subtest	Scaled Score		Scaled Score
Information	9	Digit Symbol	0
Comprehension	14	Picture Completion	8
Arithmetic	6	Block Design	0
Similarities	5	Picture Arrangement	0
Digit Span	7	Object Assembly	1
Vocabulary	10	Total Performance Score	9
Total Verbal Score	51	Performance I.Q.	63
Verbal I.Q.	95	Total Score	60
		Full Scale I.Q.	72

Comments

The Category score was prorated.

Evidence of dyscalculia and central dysarthria were present.

PATIENT H

This 58-year-old male had undergone a right temporal lobe biopsy for herpes encephalitis some months prior to testing. Neuropsychological testing revealed borderline intellectual functioning, severely impaired ability in abstraction and concept formation, a left homonymous hemianopsia, and a variety of aphasic symptoms. The pronounced discrepancy between verbal and performance IQ is lateralizing and suggests that this patient once functioned at a considerably higher level. His verbal skills allowed this patient to maintain a convincing verbal facade of personal competence and initially both family and staff had difficulty accepting the reality of this patient's marked behavioral deficits and the fact that he was clearly incompetent to manage his own affairs. This case illustrates the fact that a substantial amount of information can be gleaned from relatively minimal neuropsychological evaluation.

Neuropsychology Assessment

Patient Data: Name _____ I _____

Age: ___38___ ,   Race: B ⓦ O,   Sex: Ⓜ F

Occupation: _Former Aircraft Mechanic_   Handedness: Ⓡ L CR CL

Education: _____8 years_____   Date of Testing: _____

Halstead's Neuropsychological Test Battery

Test	Raw Score	Rating
Category	—	0 1 2 ③ 4 5
T.P.T. Time	—	0 1 2 3 ④ 5
T.P.T. Memory	—	0 1 2 ③ 4 5
T.P.T. Location	—	0 1 2 ③ 4 5
Speech Perception	—	0 1 2 ③ 4 5
Rhythm	—	0 ① 2 3 4 5
Tapping Speed	—	0 1 2 ③ 4 5
Halstead Impairment Index	.8	

Average Impairment Rating _____

Other Tests Sensitive to Cerebral Dysfunction

Name of Test	Raw Score	Rating
T.P.T. Dominant Hand	NA	0 1 2 3 4 5
T.P.T. Non Dominant Hand	NA	0 1 2 3 4 5
Both Hands	NA	0 1 2 3 4 5
Tapping Dominant Hand	NA	0 1 2 3 4 5
Tapping Non Dominant Hand	NA	0 1 2 3 4 5
Spacial Relations Score	NA	0 1 2 3 4 5
Aphasia Score	NA	0 1 2 3 4 5
Trails A	—	0 1 2 3 ④ 5
Trails B	—	0 1 2 3 ④ 5
Perceptual Score	NA	0 1 2 3 4 5
Digit Symbol Score	NA	0 1 2 3 4 5
Grip Strength Dominant Hand	NA	
Grip Strength Non Dominant Hand	NA	

Wechsler Adult Intelligence Scale

Subtest	Scaled Score		
Information	9	Digit Symbol	1
Comprehension	11	Picture Completion	8
Arithmetic	7	Block Design	5
Similarities	8	Picture Arrangement	6
Digit Span	7	Object Assembly	5
Vocabulary	10	Total Performance Score	25
Total Verbal Score	52	Performance I.Q.	72
Verbal I.Q.	92	Total Score	77
		Full Scale I.Q.	83

Comments

Not all tests administered

PATIENT I

This patient suffered a severe closed head injury that resulted in hospitalization for 2 years and caused a left hemiparesis. The accident had occurred 19 years prior to testing; the patient had been unemployed since the time of the accident.

Mr. "I" was referred because of his continuing tendency to touch females inappropriately. This behavior was offensive and resistent to intervention; the patient's participation in a vocational rehabilitation unit had been terminated because of this problem, which was attributed to his brain damage. Mild social punishment consistently delivered in a controlled environment (i.e., a neurology ward) proved adequate to suppress the inappropriate touching. Previously, female co-workers had ignored and/or tolerated the touching because the patient was "brain damaged." In addition, efforts were directed toward finding more appropriate, left-hemisphere-based rehabilitation activities commensurate with this patient's ability pattern and cognitive strengths.

Neuropsychology Assessment

Patient Data: Name _____ K _____

Age: __54__ , Race: B Ⓦ O,   Sex: Ⓜ F

Occupation: ___Credit Manager___   Handedness: Ⓡ L CR CL

Education: 18 (B.A. & M.B.A.)   Date of Testing: _____

Halstead's Neuropsychological Test Battery

Test	Raw Score	Rating
Category	104	0 1 2 ③ 4 5
T.P.T. Time	17.0	0 1 ② 3 4 5
T.P.T. Memory	8	0 ① 2 3 4 5
T.P.T. Location	2	0 1 2 ③ 4 5
Speech Perception	7	0 ① 2 3 4 5
Rhythm	4	0 ① 2 3 4 5
Tapping Speed	37	0 1 2 ③ 4 5
Halstead Impairment Index	0.5	

Other Tests Sensitive to Cerebral Dysfunction

Name of Test	Raw Score	Rating
T.P.T. Dominant Hand	8/10	0 1 2 3 4 ⑤
T.P.T. Non Dominant Hand	3.45	0 ① 2 3 4 5
Both Hands	3.20	0 1 ② 3 4 5
Tapping Dominant Hand	37	
Tapping Non Dominant Hand	35.6	0 1 2 ③ 4 5
Spacial Relations Score	4	0 1 ② 3 4 5
Aphasia Score	N.G.	0 1 2 3 4 5
Trails A	50"	0 1 2 ③ 4 5
Trails B	75"	0 ① 2 3 4 5
Perceptual Score	N.G.	0 1 2 3 4 5
Digit Symbol Score	8	0 1 ② 3 4 5
Grip Strength Dominant Hand	36 kg	
Grip Strength Non Dominant Hand	30 kg	

Wechsler Adult Intelligence Scale

Subtest	Scaled Score		
Information	17	Digit Symbol	8
Comprehension	19	Picture Completion	10
Arithmetic	13	Block Design	10
Similarities	11	Picture Arrangement	10
Digit Span	15	Object Assembly	7
Vocabulary	19	Total Performance Score	45
Total Verbal Score	94	Performance I.Q.	105
Verbal I.Q.	135	Total Score	139
		Full Scale I.Q.	124

Comments

244

PATIENT K

This 54-year-old male had obtained two degrees from a very prestigious Ivy League institution prior to a motor vehicle accident approximately 25 years prior to testing. He still experienced recurrent seizures at the time of testing and had not been employed since the accident.

WAIS results suggest considerable premorbid intellectual ability. The discrepancy index (30 points) is quite large and has some lateralizing value. Digit Symbol, the most sensitive WAIS indicator of cerebral dysfunction, was quite poor, as was performance on the Arithmetic and Similarities subtests. The impairment index of .5 suggests mild impairment of adaptive abilities is present.

This individual was referred for vocational rehabilitation that will be appropriately built around his excellent verbal skills. However, this patient will have a great deal of difficulty handling novel tasks. *In toto*, neuropsychological testing supports the rehabilitation potential of this patient and he is apt to benefit both cognitively and emotionally from an opportunity to resume working.

Luria-Nebraska Neuropsychological Battery

ADMINISTRATION & SCORING BOOKLET

by

Charles J. Golden, Ph.D., Thomas A. Hammeke, Ph.D., and Arnold D. Purisch, Ph.D.

Published by

WPS   WESTERN PSYCHOLOGICAL SERVICES
PUBLISHERS AND DISTRIBUTORS
12031 WILSHIRE BOULEVARD
LOS ANGELES, CALIFORNIA 90025
A DIVISION OF MANSON WESTERN CORPORATION

Name: **"L"** Date: _____ Age: **44**

Sex: M Ⓕ Marital Status: **Married** Race: **White**

Occupation: _____ Education: **12 th** Hand Dominance: L Ⓡ

Place of Examination: _____ Examiner: _____

	MOTOR	RHYTHM	TACTILE	VISUAL	RECEPTIVE SPEECH	EXPRESSIVE SPEECH	READING	WRITING	ARITHMETIC	MEMORY	INTELLIGENCE	PATHOGNOMONIC	LEFT HEMISPHERE	RIGHT HEMISPHERE
RAW SCORES	49	3	19	17	13	22	5	8	15	15	23	25	16	25

W-161C

246

PATIENT L

The patient was a 44-year-old, white female with a high school education. Her Luria–Nebraska Neuropsychological Battery performance produced eight scale scores above the brain-impairment cutoff line with the peak elevations occurring on motor in the right hemisphere scales. Also, scales most sensitive to the left hemisphere dysfunction (the Expressive, Receptive, Writing, Reading, and Intelligence scales) were all below her cutoff point for brain impairment. Qualitatively, her motor deficits involved poor motor control of the left hand, constructional dyspraxia and poor performance of bucolingual imitation. Her tactile deficits included reductions in pain, position, and fine touch sensitivity on the left arm. Also, deficits in stereognosis were noted on the left hand and graphesthesia was present bilaterally. On memory tests she missed all visual/nonverbal items and experienced difficulty on serial/verbal memory items and the interference memory tasks involving single words. Taken together, these results suggested the patient had sustained an extensive injury to the right hemisphere involving the right frontal, sensory motor, and parietal areas. The patient's pattern of deficits was most suggestive of an infarct to the right middle cerebral artery. It was also noted that the left hemisphere seemed somewhat compromised because of the patient's relatively high Memory and Pathognomonic Scale scores.

History revealed that 10 years prior to testing, this patient had suffered a right middle cerebral artery stroke from which she had shown substantial recovery. In the late 1970s she developed a seizure disorder and on evaluation she was found to have an abscess in the right frontal and temporal areas. The cyst was then surgically removed resulting in decreased seizure activity, but an increase in hemiparesis on the left side. At the time of testing, the patient's CT scan revealed atrophic right frontal and temporal lobes. An EEG performed at that time revealed marked slowing on the right hemisphere with frequency in the delta and theta ranges.

Luria-Nebraska Neuropsychological Battery

ADMINISTRATION & SCORING BOOKLET

Charles J. Golden, Ph.D., Thomas A. Hammeke, Ph.D., and Arnold D. Purisch, Ph.D.

Published by

WPS WESTERN PSYCHOLOGICAL SERVICES
PUBLISHERS AND DISTRIBUTORS
12011 WILSHIRE BOULEVARD
LOS ANGELES, CALIFORNIA 90025
A DIVISION OF MANSON WESTERN CORPORATION

Name: **"M"**   Date: Age: **31**

Sex: (M) F   Marital Status: **Married**   Race: **White**

Occupation: Education: **11 th**   Hand Dominance: L (R)

Place of Examination: Examiner:

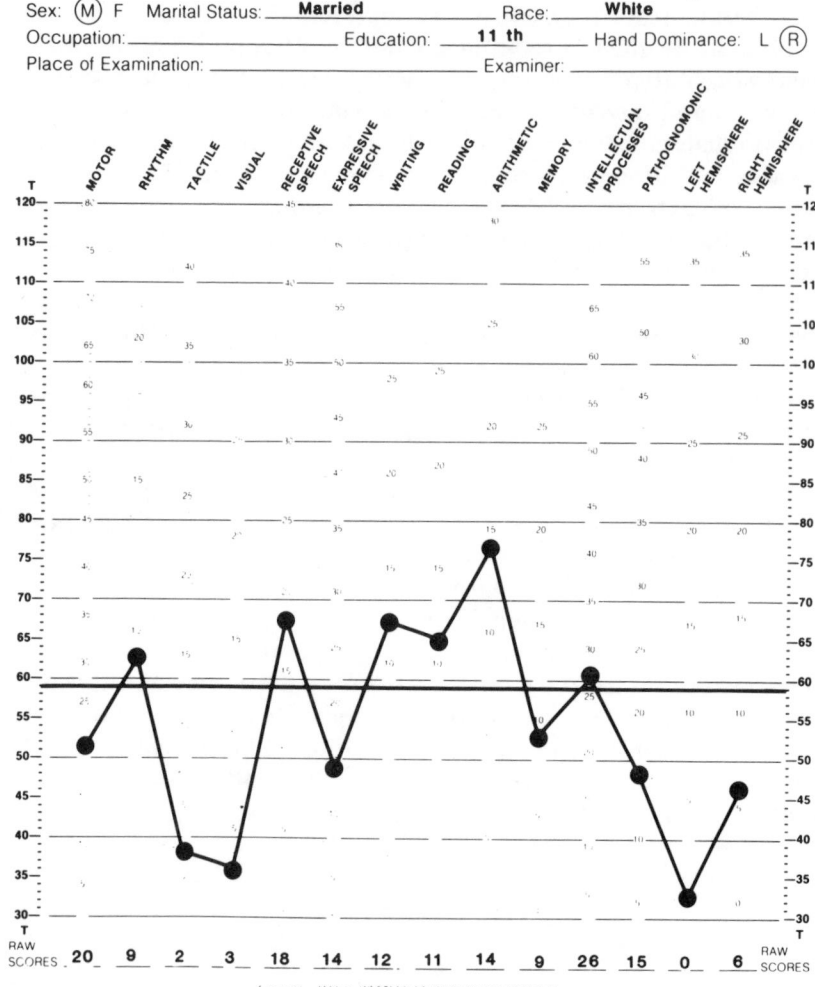

	MOTOR	RHYTHM	TACTILE	VISUAL	RECEPTIVE SPEECH	EXPRESSIVE SPEECH	WRITING	READING	ARITHMETIC	MEMORY	INTELLECTUAL PROCESSES	PATHOGNOMONIC	LEFT HEMISPHERE	RIGHT HEMISPHERE
RAW SCORES	20	9	2	3	18	14	12	11	14	9	26	15	0	6

W-161C

248

PATIENT M

This patient had suffered viral encephalitis in 1968 that resulted in seizure activity that was not well controlled by medication. The patient also had a history of depressive illness and periods of paranoid thinking. Neuropsychology was consulted to evaluate both the psychological and neuropsychological functioning of this patient.

On the Luria–Nebraska Neuropsychological Battery the patient had elevated scores on the Rhythm, Receptive Speech, Writing, Reading, Math, and Intelligence scales. Taken together, his Receptive, Writing, Reading, Math, and Intelligence elevations suggest the left hemisphere was more involved than the right. In addition, his low Motor and Tactile scores suggest that the sensory–motor zones of the left hemisphere are relatively intact. Elevations on Rhythm and Receptive Speech without elevations on the Expressive Speech Scale implicate the left temporal lobe. This is reinforced by the fact that the patient had considerable difficulty reproducing phonemic structures. It appears that this individual's present disorder is due to disruption in the left posterior temporal lobe. An EEG taken at the time of admission confirmed a focal dysfunction of the left temporal lobe.

Luria-Nebraska Neuropsychological Battery

ADMINISTRATION & SCORING BOOKLET

Charles J. Golden, Ph.D., Thomas A. Hammeke, Ph.D., and Arnold D. Purisch, Ph.D.

Published by

WPS WESTERN PSYCHOLOGICAL SERVICES
PUBLISHERS AND DISTRIBUTORS
1200 WILSHIRE BOULEVARD
LOS ANGELES CALIFORNIA 90025
A DIVISION OF MANSON WESTERN CORPORATION

Name: **"N"**   Date: _____   Age: **41**

Sex: (M) F   Marital Status: **Married**   Race: **Black**

Occupation: _____   Education: **14 years**   Hand Dominance: L (R)

Place of Examination: _____   Examiner: _____

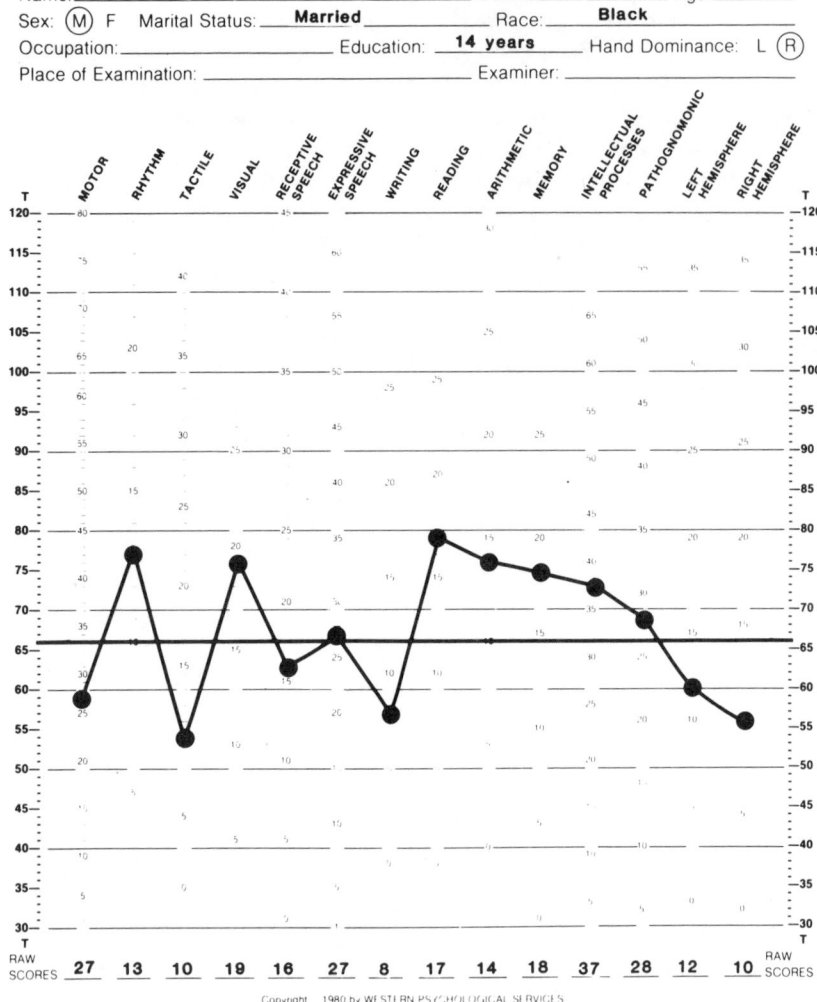

	MOTOR	RHYTHM	TACTILE	VISUAL	RECEPTIVE SPEECH	EXPRESSIVE SPEECH	WRITING	READING	ARITHMETIC	MEMORY	INTELLECTUAL PROCESSES	PATHOGNOMONIC	LEFT HEMISPHERE	RIGHT HEMISPHERE	
RAW SCORES	27	13	10	19	16	27	8	17	14	18	37	28	12	10	RAW SCORES

PATIENT N

This patient was a 41-year-old black male with a junior college education who was admitted to the stroke unit of the University of Mississippi Medical Center approximately 2 weeks after the onset of right-sided weakness. He became a diagnostic dilemma because of the absence of severe language deficits and because over his hospital stay he began to show some left-sided weakness. A Luria–Nebraska Neuropsychological Battery performed 1 week after his admission revealed multiple scale elevations. Pattern analysis and qualitative inspection suggested bilateral cortical involvement. In addition, his relatively better performance on the Tactile and Reading sections of the Luria–Nebraska suggested more anterior than posterioral cortical involvement. Finally, from a qualitative standpoint, many of his errors seemed to be attentionally based, suggesting that medial-based cortical areas were more impaired than lateral zones. This was further supported by the fact that his legs were significantly more impaired than his arms. The CT scan at the time of testing showed findings consistent with bilateral anterior celebral artery infarctions. Cerebral arteriography revealed marked stenosis of the prominant left anterior cerebral artery with delayed filling of several branches of both anterior cerebral arteries. Interestingly, an EEG done at the same time was within normal limits.

Luria-Nebraska Neuropsychological Battery

ADMINISTRATION & SCORING BOOKLET

Charles J. Golden, Ph.D., Thomas A. Hammeke, Ph.D., and Arnold D. Purisch, Ph.D.

Published by

WPS | WESTERN PSYCHOLOGICAL SERVICES
PUBLISHERS AND DISTRIBUTORS
12031 WILSHIRE BOULEVARD
LOS ANGELES, CALIFORNIA 90025

A DIVISION OF MANSON WESTERN CORPORATION

Name: **"O"** Date: _____ Age: **21**

Sex: (M) F   Marital Status: **Single** Race: **White**

Occupation: _____ Education: **10 years (GED)** Hand Dominance: L (R)

Place of Examination: _____ Examiner: _____

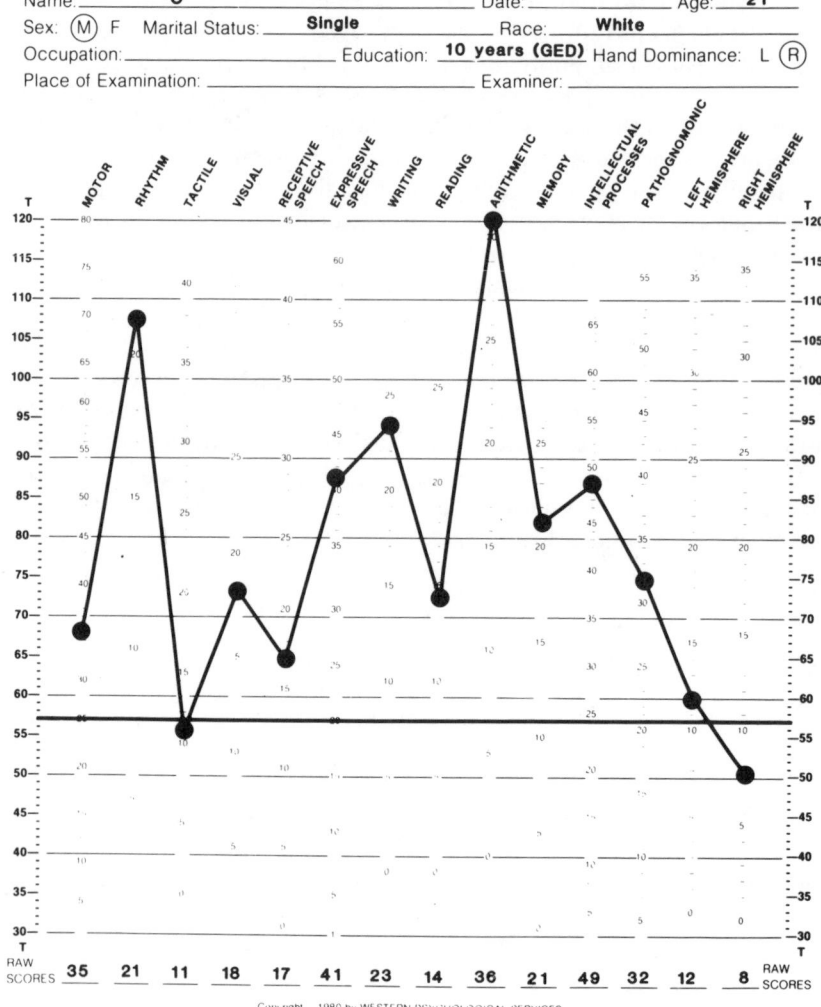

	MOTOR	RHYTHM	TACTILE	VISUAL	RECEPTIVE SPEECH	EXPRESSIVE SPEECH	WRITING	READING	ARITHMETIC	MEMORY	INTELLECTUAL PROCESSES	PATHOGNOMONIC	LEFT HEMISPHERE	RIGHT HEMISPHERE
RAW SCORES	35	21	11	18	17	41	23	14	36	21	49	32	12	8

W-161C

PATIENT O

This patient suffered from cerebral anoxia secondary to an attempted suicide by hanging 5 years earlier. Although clearly brain impaired, neuropsychological assessment was requested to establish this patient's potential for vocational rehabilitation.

Although virtually all scales fell within the brain-damaged range, especially poor performance was noted on the Arithmetic and Rhythm scales, probably due to the requirement for attention and sustained concentration. Motor, tactile, and receptive speech skills were relatively spared. The overall pattern of results suggests that patient O's performance has stabilized and that further deterioration of adaptive abilities is unlikely.

It is interesting to note that neither the Catagories Test nor Trails B could be completed by this patient. Damage is marked and diffuse and "O" will require close supervision in whatever activity he undertakes. However, his relatively good understanding of language and his eagerness to please suggest that he can benefit from rehabilitation efforts. The good receptive speech score coupled with the poor expressive speech score suggests that "O" will oftentimes know more than he can communicate. Remediation efforts are likely to be maximized when instruction can be combined with example (e.g., modeling with guided participation) so that this patient can capitalize on his stronger tactile and visual abilities.

Luria-Nebraska Neuropsychological Battery

ADMINISTRATION & SCORING BOOKLET

Charles J. Golden, Ph.D., Thomas A. Hammeke, Ph.D., and Arnold D. Purisch, Ph.D.

Published by

WPS WESTERN PSYCHOLOGICAL SERVICES
PUBLISHERS AND DISTRIBUTORS
12031 WILSHIRE BOULEVARD
LOS ANGELES, CALIFORNIA 90025
A DIVISION OF MANSON WESTERN CORPORATION

Name: __'P'__ Date: _____ Age: __54__

Sex: (M) F Marital Status: __Married__ Race: __White__

Occupation: _____ Education: __8th__ Hand Dominance: L (R)

Place of Examination: _____ Examiner: _____

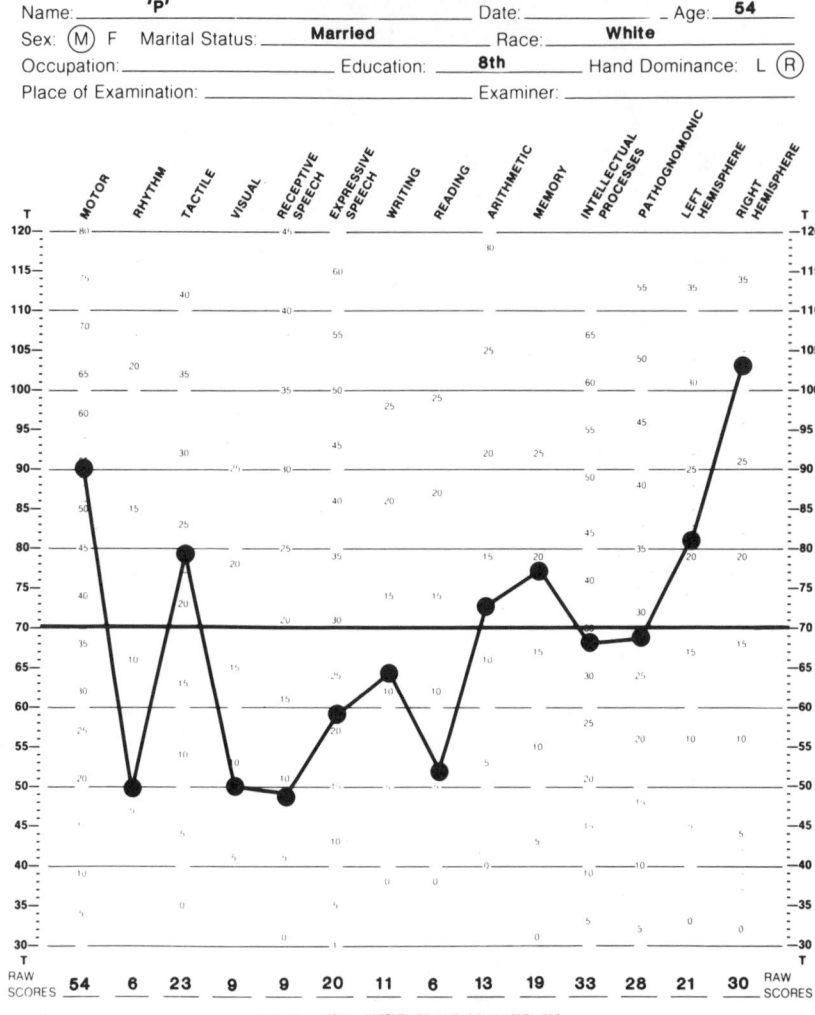

| RAW SCORES | 54 | 6 | 23 | 9 | 9 | 20 | 11 | 6 | 13 | 19 | 33 | 28 | 21 | 30 | RAW SCORES |

W-161C

PATIENT P

This patient was evaluated following his complaints of memory loss and anxiety while driving. Both unilateral and bilateral movement disorder were present and "P" demonstrated a left-sided auditory suppression with bilateral simultaneous stimulation. Bilateral tactile suppressions were present and touch, pressure, 2-point discrimination, and sterognosis were impaired. Visual functions, speech, writing, and reading were intact. Short-term verbal memory were severely impaired.

Mr. "P" presents a profile including both strengths (e.g., intact language functions and his ability to write, read, follow auditory commands, and speak without difficulty) and marked weaknesses (motor, tactile, and memory impairment). The left side of the body was consistently more impaired than the right.

CT evaluation showed evidence of an old, deep right hemisphere infarct. EEG was normal. An arteriogram revealed a completely occluded right anterior cerebral artery.

BIBLIOGRAPHY

Adams, J., & Kenny, T.J. Cross-validation of the Canter Background Interence Procedure in identifying children with cerebral dysfunction. *Journal of Consulting and Clinical Psychology*, 1982, *50*, 307–309.

Adams, K. Automated clinical interpretation of the neuropsychological battery: An ability based approach. (Doctoral dissertation, Wayne State University, 1974). *Dissertation Abstracts International*, 1974, 6085-B, (University Microfilms No. 75-13, 289).

Adams, K. In search of Luria's battery: A false start. *Journal of Consulting and Clinical Psychology*, 1980, *48*, 511–516.

Adams, R.L., Boalse, C., & Crain, C. Bias in neuropsychological test classification related to education, age and ethnicity. *Journal of Consulting and Clinical Psychology*, 1982, *50*, 143–145.

Agras, W.S., Kazdin, A.E., & Wilson, G.T. *Behavior therapy*. San Francisco: W.H. Freeman, 1979.

Albert, M.L. Geriatric neuropsychology. *Journal of Consulting and Clinical Psychology*, 1981, *49*, 835–850.

Albert, M.L., Sparks, R., & Helm, N. Melodic intonation therapy for aphasia. *Archives of Neurology*, 1973, *29*, 130–131.

American Psychiatric Association. *Diagnostic and statistical manual of mental disorders*, 3d ed. (DSM-III). Washington, D.C., 1980.

Anthony, W.Z., Heaton, R.K., & Lehman, R.A.W. An attempt to cross-validate two acturial systems for neuropsychological test interpretation. *Journal of Consulting and Clinical Psychology*, 1980, *48*, 317–326.

Bach-y-Rita, P. Brain plasticity as a basis for therapeutic procedures. In P. Bach-y-Rita (Ed.), *Recovery of function: Theoretical considerations for brain injury rehabilitation*. Baltimore: University Park Press, 1980. Pp. 225, 263.

Bakay, L., & Glasauer, F.E. *Head injury*. Boston: Little, Brown, 1980.

Balasubramanian & Ranamurthi, B. Sterestoxic amyglatomy in behavior disorders. *Confidia Neurological*, 1970, *32*, 367–377.

Bandura, A. Self-efficacy mechanism in human agency. *American Psychologist*, 1982, *37*, 122–147.

Barlow, D.H., & Hayes, S.C. Alternating treatment design: One strategy for comparing the effects of two treatments in a single subject. *Journal of Applied Behavior Analysis*, 1979, *12*, 199–210.

Barnes, G.W., & Lucas, G.J. Cerebral dysfunction versus psychogenesis in Halstead–Reitan tests. *Journal of Nervous and Mental Disease*, 1974, *158*, 50–60.

Barth, J.T., & Boll, T.J. Rehabilitation and treatment of central nervous system dysfunction: A behavioral medicine perspective. In C. Prokop & L. Bradley (Eds.), *Medical psychology: A new perspective.* New York: Academic Press, 1981.

Basso, A., Capitani, E., & Vignoloa, L.A. Influence of rehabilitation on language skills in aphasic patients: A controlled study. *Archives of Neurology*, 1979, *36*, 190–196.

Bastian, N.C. *Aphasia and other speed defects.* London: N.K. Lewis, 1898.

Beck, A., & Mahoney, M.J. Schools of thought. *American Psychologist*, 1979, *34*, 93–98.

Benbow, C.P., & Stanley, J.C. Sex differences in mathematical ability: Fact or artifact. *Science*, 1980, *210*, 1262–1264.

Bender, L.A. *Visual motor gestalt test and its clinical use.* American Orthopsychiatric Association Research Monograph, No. 3, New York: American Orthopsychiatric Association, 1938.

Benton, A.L. *Revised visual retention test manual.* New York: The Psychological Corporation, 1963.

Benton, A.L. Constructional apraxia and the minor hemisphere. *Confinia Neurologica*, 1967, *29*, 1–16.

Benton, A.L. Differential behavioral effects in frontal lobe disease. *Neuropsychologica*, 1968, *6*, 53–60.

Benton, A.L. Behavioral consequences of closed head injury. In G.L. Odom (Ed.), *Central nervous system trauma status report*, 1979, NINCDS, National Institutes of Health, Bethesda, 220–231.

Ben-Yishay, Y., Diller, L., & Rattok, J. A modular approach to optimizing orientation, psychomotor alertness and purposive behavior in severe head trauma patients. *Working approaches to remediation of cognitive deficits in brain damaged persons* (Rehabilitation Monograph No. 59). New York:

New York University Medicine Center, Institute of Rehabilitation Medicine, 1978. Pp. 63–67.

Ben-Yishay, Y., Diller, L., Gordon, W., & Gerstman, L. A modular approach to training in cognitive–perceptual integration (constructional skills) in brain injured people. *Working approaches to remediation of cognitive deficits in brain damaged persons* (Rehabilitation Monograph, No. 59). New York: New York University Medical Center, Institute of Rehabilitation Medicine, 1978. Pp. 107–132. (a)

Ben-Yishay, Y., Gordon, W., Diller, L., & Gerstman, L. A modular approach to training in eye-hand coordination with dexterity in brain injured people. *Working approaches to remediation of cognitive deficits in brain damaged persons* (Rehabilitation Monograph, No. 59). New York: New York University Medical Center, Institute of Rehabilitation Medicine, 1978. Pp. 68–106. (b)

Ben-Yishay, Y., Lakin, P., Ross, B., Rattok, J., Cohen, J., & Diller, L. A modular approach to training (verbal) abstract reasoning in traumatic head injured patients: Revised procedures. *Working approaches to remediation of cognitive deficits in brain damaged persons* (Rehabilitation Monograph, No. 61). New York: New York University Medical Center, Institute of Rehabilitation Medicine, 1980. Pp. 128–174. (a)

Ben-Yishay, Y., Lakin, P., Ross, B., Rattok, J., Cohen, J., & Diller, L. Developing a core "curriculum" for group-exercises designed for head trauma patients who are undergoing rehabilitation. *Working approaches to remediation of cognitive deficits in brain damaged persons* (Rehabilitation Monograph, No. 61). New York: New York University Medical Center, Institute of Rehabilitation Medicine, 1980. Pp. 175–235. (b)

Ben-Yishay, Y., Rattok, J., Ross, B., Lakin, P., Cohen, J., & Diller, L. A remedial "module" for the systematic amelioration of basic attentional disturbances in head trauma patients. *Working approaches to remediation of cognitive deficits in brain damaged persons* (Rehabilitation Monograph No. 61). New York: New York University Medical Center, Institute of Rehabilitation Medicine, 1980. Pp. 71–127. (c)

Ben-Yishay, Y., Piasetsky, E., & Diller, L. A modular approach to training (verbal) abstract thinking in brain injured people. *Working approaches to remediation of cognitive deficits in brain damaged persons* (Rehabilitation Monograph, No. 59). New York: New York University Medical Center, Institute of Rehabilitation Medicine, 1978. Pp. 133–153.

Ben-Yishay, Y., Rattok, J., & Diller, L. A clinical strategy for the systematic amelioration of attentional disturbances in severe head trauma patients. *Working approaches to remediation of cognitive deficits in brain damaged persons* (Rehabilitation Monograph No. 60). New York: New York

University Medical Center, Institute of Rehabilitation Medicine, 1979. Pp. 1–27.

Binet, A., & Simon, T. Methodes nouvelles pour le diagnostic du niveau intellectuel des anormaux. *L'Annee Psychologique*, 1905, *11*, 191–244.

Bizzi, E., & Schiller, P.H. Single unit activity in the _____. *Experimental Brain Research*, 1970, *10*, 131–158.

Blanchard, E.B., & Young, L.D. Clinical application of biofeedback training. *Archives of General Psychiatry*, 1974, *30*, 573–589.

Boll, T.J. Psychological differentiation of patients with schizophrenia vs. lateralized cerebrovascular, neoplastic, or traumatic brain disease. *Journal of Abnormal Psychology*, 1974, *83*, 456–458.

Boll, T.J. Diagnosing brain impairment. In B. Wolman (Ed.), *Diagnosis of mental disorders: A handbook*. New York: Plenum Press, 1978.

Botex, M.I., & Wertheim, N. Expressive aphasia and amnesia following right frontal lesion in a right-handed man. *Brain*, 1959, *82*, 186–197.

Bowden, D. The functional system: Keystone to Luria's neuropsychology. Paper presented at the American Psychological Associations annual convention, New York, 1966.

Braun, J.J., Meyer, P.M., & Meyer, D.R. Sparing of a brightness habit in rats following visual decortication. *Journal of Comparative and Physiological Psychology*, 1966, *61*, 79–82.

Buell, S.J., & Coleman, D.P. Dendritic growth in aged human brain and failure of growth in senile dementia. *Science*, 1976, *206*, 854–856.

Butters, N., & Brody, B.A. The role of the left parietal lobe in mediation of intra- and cross-model association. *Cortex*, 1969, *4*, 328–333.

Butters, N., & Cermak, L.S. *Alcoholic Korsakoff's syndrome*. New York: Academic Press, 1980.

Calsyn, D.A., O'Leary, M.R., & Chaney, E.F. Shortening the Category Test. *Journal of Consulting and Clinical Psychology*, 1980, *48*, 788–789.

Campbell, D.T., & Stanley, J.C. *Experimental and quasi-experimental designs for research*. Chicago: Rand McNally, 1963.

Canter, A.H. *The Canter Background Interference Procedure for the Bender Gestalt Test*. Nashville: Counselor Recordings, 1976.

Carter, L.T., Caruso, J.L., Languirand, M.A., & Bernard, M.A. Cognitive skill remediation in stroke and non-stroke elderly. *Critical Neuropsychology*, 1980, *2*, 109–113. (a)

Carter, L.T., Carouso, J.L., Languirand, M.A., & Bernard, M.A. *The thinking skills workbook: A cognitive skills remediation manual for adults.* Springfield, Ill.: Charles C. Thomas, 1980). (b)

Cartlidge, N.E.F., & Shaw, D.A. *Head injury.* London: W.B. Saunders, 1981.

Cattell, R.B. Theory of fluid and crystalized intelligence: A critical experiment. *Journal of Educational Psychology*, 1963, *54*, 1–22.

Chapman, L.F., & Wolff, H.G. The cerebral hemispheres and the highest integrative functions of man. *Archives of Neurology*, 1959, *1*, 357–424.

Charcot, J.M. *Clinical lectures on diseases of the nervous system*, Vol. 3. London: New Syclenhan Society, 1889.

Chelune, G.J. A re-examination of the relationship between the Luria–Nebraska and Halstead–Reitan Batteries: Overlap with WAIS. *Journal of Consulting and Clinical Psychology*, 1982, *50*, 578–580.

Chelune, G.J., & Edwards, P. Early brain lesions: Ontogenetic–environmental considerations. *Journal of Consulting and Clinical Psychology*, 1981, *49*, 777–790.

Chow, K.L., & Steward, D.L. Reversal of structural and functional effects of long-term visual deprivation. *Experimental Neurology*, 1972, *34*, 409–433.

Christensen, A. *Luria's neuropsychological investigation.* New York: Spectrum Press, 1975.

Chusid, J.G. *Correlative neuroanatomy and functional neurology.* Los Altos, Calif.: Lange, 1976.

Ciba Foundation Symposium 34. *Outcome of severe damage to the nervous system.* Amsterdam: Elsevier, 1975.

Cleeland, C.S. Biofeedback as a clinical tool: Its use with the neurologically impaired patient. In S.B. Filskov & T.J. Boll (Eds.), *Handbook of clinical neuropsychology.* New York: John Wiley, 1981.

Cleeland, C.S., Matthews, C.G., & Hopper, C.L. MMPI profiles in exacerbation and remission of multiple sclerosis. *Psychological Reports*, 1970, *27*, 373–375.

Cohen, J. A coefficient of agreement for nominal scales. *Educational and Psychological Measurement*, 1960, *20*, 37–46.

Comrose, J.H. The road from research to new diagnosis and therapy. *Science*, 1978, *200*, 931–937.

Connolly, C.J. *External morphology of the primate brain*. Springfield, Ill.: Charles C. Thomas, 1950.

Corkin, S. Tactually-guided maze learning in man: Effects of unilateral cortical excisions and bilateral hippocampul lesions. *Neuropsychologia*, 1965, *3*, 339–351.

Corkin, S. Acquisition of motor skill after bilateral medical temporal-lobe excision. *Neuropsychologia*, 1968, *6*, 255–265.

Corkin, S., Milner, B., & Taylor, L. Bilateral sensory loss after unilateral cerebral lesion in man. *Transactions of the American Neurological Association*, 1973, *98*, 118–132.

Corsi, P.M. Human memory and the medial temporal regions of the brain. Unpublished PhD thesis, McGill University, 1972.

Cotman, C.W. (Ed.). *Neuronal plasticity*. New York: Raven Press, 1978.

Courville, C.B. Coup-countracoup mechanism of cranial cerebral injuries. *Archives of Surgery*, 1942, *45*, 19–26.

Craig, P.L. Neuropsychological assessments in public psychiatric hospitals: The current state of the practice. *Clinical Neuropsychology*, 1979, *1*, 1–7.

Craighead, W.E., Kazdin, A.E., & Mahoney, M.J. *Behavior modification: Principles, issues and applications*. Boston: Houghton Mifflin, 1976.

Craine, J.F., & Gudeman, H.E. (Eds.). *The rehabilitation of brain functions: Principles, procedures, and techniques of neurotraining*. Springfield, Ill.: Charles C. Thomas, 1981.

Crosson, B., & Warren, R.L. Use of the Luria–Nebraska Neurological Battery in aphasia: A conceptual critique. *Journal of Consulting and Clinical Psychology*, 1982, *50*, 22–31.

Crovitz, H.F., Harvey, M.T., & Horn, R.W. Problems in the acquisition of imagery mnemonics: Three brain-damaged cases. *Cortex*, 1979, *15*, 225–234.

Dahlstrom, E.G. Recurrent issues in the development of the MMPI. In J.N. Butcher (Ed.), *MMPI: Research developments and clinical applications*. New York: McGraw-Hill, 1969.

Dahlstrom, L.G., & Walsh, G.J. *An MMPI Handbook.* Minneapolis: University of Minneapolis Press, 1960.

Darley, F.L. Treatment of acquired aphasia. In W.J. Friedlander (Ed.), *Advances in neurology,* Vol. 7. New York: Raven Pres, 1975.

Das, J.P., Kirb, J.R., & Jarmin, R.F. *Simultaneous and successive cognitive processes.* New York: Academic Press, 1979.

Davies, A.D.M. The influence of age on Trail Making Performance. *Journal of Clinical Psychology,* 1968, *24,* 96–100.

Davison, L.A. Introduction. In R.M. Reitan & L.A. Davison (Eds.), *Clinical neuropsychology: Current status and applications.* New York: John Wiley, 1974. Pp. 1–18.

Dawson, R.G. Recovery of function: Implications for theories of brain function. *Behavioral Biology,* 1973, *8,* 439–460.

Delis, D.D., & Kaplan, E. The assessment of aphasia with the Luria–Nebraska Neuropsychological Battery: A case critique. *Journal of Consulting and Clinical Psychology,* 1981, *50,* 32–39.

Denckla, M.B. Childhood learning disabilities. In K.M. Heilman & E. Valenstein (Eds.), *Clinical neuropsychology.* New York: Oxford University Press, 1979.

DeRenzi, E. Hemispheric asymmetry as evidenced by spatial disorder. In M. Kinsbourne (Ed.), *Asymmetrical function of the brain.* New York: Cambridge University Press, 1978.

DeWolfe, A.S. Differentiation of schizophrenia and brain damage with the WAIS. *Journal of Clinical Psychology,* 1971, *27,* 209–211.

DeWolfe, A.S., Barrell, R.P., Becker, B.C., & Spanner, F.E. Intellectual deficit in chronic schizophrenia and brain damage. *Journal of Consulting and Clinical Psychology,* 1971, *36,* 197–204.

Diamond, S.J., & Beaumont, G. *Hemisphere functions in the human brain.* New York: Halstead Press, 1974.

Diamond, J., & Miledi, R. A study of fetal and new-born rat muscle fibers. *Journal of Physiology,* 1962, *162,* 393–408.

Diller, L. A model for cognitive retraining in rehabilitation. *The Clinical Psychologist,* 1976, *29,* 13–15.

Diller, L., Ben-Yishay, Y., Gerstman, L.J., Goodkin, R., Gordon, W., & Weinberg, J. *Studies in cognition and rehabilitation in hemiplegia*

(Rehabilitation Monograph No. 50). New York: New York University Medical Center, Institute of Rehabilitation Medicine, 1974.

Diller, L., & Gordon, W.A. Rehabilitation and clinical neuropsychology. In S.B. Filskov & T.J. Boll (Eds.), *Handbook of clinical neuropsychology*. New York: John Wiley, 1981. (a)

Diller, L., & Gordon, W.A. Interventions for cognitive deficits in brain-injured adults. *Journal of Consulting and Clinical Psychology*, 1981, *49*, 822–834. (b)

Diller, L., Weinberg, J., Piasetsky, E., Ruckdeschel-Hibbard, M., Egelko, S., Scotzin, M., Conniotakis, J., & Gordon, W. Methods for the evaluation and treatment of the visual perceptual difficulties of right brain damaged individuals. *Supplement to 8th Annual Workshop for Rehabilitation Professionals*. New York: New York University Medical Center, Institute of Rehabilitation Medicine, 1980.

Dodrill, C.B. Sex differences on the Halstead–Reitan Neuropsychological Battery and in other neuropsychological measures. *Journal of Clinical Psychology*, 1979, *35*, 236–241.

Dodrill, C.B. Neuropsychology of epilepsy. In S.B. Filskov & T.J. Bolls (Eds.), *Handbook of clinical neuropsychology*. New York: John Wiley, 1981.

Drewe, E.A. An experimental investigation of Luria's theory on the effects of frontal lesions in man. *Neuropsychologia*, 1975, *13*, 421–429.

Dublin, A.F., French, B.N., & Rennick, J.N. Computed tomography in head trauma. *Radiology*, 1977, *122*, 365–369.

Duffy, F. Pharmacological reversal of deprivation amblyopia in the cat. Paper read at the 28th annual meeting of the American Academy of Neurology, Toronto, 1976.

Earle, K.M. Metastatic brain tumors. *Diseases of the Nervous System*, 1955, *16*, 86–93.

Elkind, D. Piagetian and psychometric conceptions of intelligence. *Harvard Educational Review*, 1969, *39*, 319–337.

Elliott, F.A. *Clinical neurology*. Philadelphia: W.B. Saunders, 1971.

Ellis, A. On Joseph Wolpe's espousal of cognitive–behavior therapy. *American Psychology*, 1979, *34*, 98–99.

Erickson, R.C., Calsyn, D.A., & Scheupback, C.S. Abbreviating the Halstead–Reitan neuropsychological test battery. *Journal of Clinical Psychology*, 1978, *4*, 925–926.

Faglioni, P., Spinnler, H., & Vignolo, L.A. Contrasting behavior of right and left hemisphere-damaged patients on a discriminative and a semantic task of auditory recognition. *Cortex*, 1969, *5*, 366–389.

Feuerstein, R. *Instrumental enrichment: An intervention program for cognitive modifiability*. Baltimore: University Park Press, 1980.

Field, J.H. *Epidemiology of head injury in England and Wales: With particular application to rehabilitation*. Leicester: Willsons, 1976.

Fields, F.R.J., & Fullerton, J.R. Differential assessment of chronic schizophrenia and brain damage using the Halstead Neuropsychology Test Battery. *Newsletter for Research in Mental Health and Behavioral Sciences*, 1975, *17*, 30–34.

Filskov, S.B., & Boll, T.J. (Eds.) *Handbook of clinical neuropsychology*. New York: John Wiley, 1981.

Filskov, S.B., & Goldstein, S.G. Diagnostic validity of the Halstead–Reitan neuropsychological battery. *Journal of Consulting and Clinical Psychology*, 1974, *42*, 382–388.

Finger, S. (Ed.) *Recovery from brain damage: Research and theory*. New York: Plenum Press, 1978.

Finkelstein, J.N. BRAIN: A computer program for interpretation of the Halstead–Reitan Neuropsychological Test Battery. (Doctoral dissertation, Columbia University, 1976) *Dissertation Abstracts International*, 1976, 5349-B. (University Microfilms No. 77-8864).

Finlayson, M.A., Johnson, K.A., & Reitan, R.M. Relationship of level of education to neuropsychological measures in brain-damaged and non-brain-damaged adults. *Journal of Consulting and Clinical Psychology*, 1977, *45*, 536–540.

Flor-Henry, P. Lateralized temporal-limbic dysfunction and psychology. *Annals of the New York Academy of Sciences*, 1976, *286*, 777–795.

Fowler, R.S., Jr., & Fordyce, W. Adapting care for brain damaged patients. *American Journal of Nursing*, 1972, *72*, 2056–2059.

Foxx, R.M., & Azrin, N.H. Restitution: A method of eliminating aggressive disruptive behavior of retarded and brain-damaged patients. *Behavior Research and Therapy*, 1972, *10*, 15–27.

Fredricks, R.S., & Finkel, P. Schizophrenic performance on the Halstead–Reitan Battery. *Journal of Clinical Psychology*, 1978, *34*, 26–30.

Gainotti, G. Emotional behavior and hemispheric side of lesion. *Cortex*, 1972, *8*, 41–50.

Gasparrini, B., & Satz, P. A treatment for memory problems in left hemisphere CVA patients. *Journal of Clinical Neuropsychology*, 1979, *1*, 137–150.

Gastant, H. The role of reticular formation in establishing conditioned reactions. In J. Jasper, L.D. Proctor, R.S. Knighton, W.C. Noshay, & R.C. Costello, (Eds.), *Reticular formation of the brain.* Boston: Little, Brown, 1958.

Gastaut, H. Clinical and electroencephalographical classification of epileptic seizures. *Epilepsia*, 1970, *11*, 102–113.

Gawler, J., Bull, J., DuBoulay, G., & Marshall, J. Computerized axial tomography in the normal EMI scan. *Journal of Neurology, Neurosurgical Psychiatry*, 1975, *38*, 935–940.

Gazzaniga, M.S. Determinants of cerebral recovery. In D.G. Stein, J.J. Rosen, & N. Butters (Eds.), *Plasticity and recovery of function in the central nervous system.* New York: Academic Press, 1974.

Gazzaniga, M.S. Consistency and diversity in brain organization. *Annals of the New York Academy of Science*, 1977, *299*, 415–423.

Gazzaniga, M.S. Is seeing believing: Notes on clinical recovery. In S. Finger (Ed.), *Recovery from brain damage: Research and theory.* New York: Plenum Press, 1978.

Gazzaniga, M.S., Glass, A.V., Saino, M.T., & Posner, J.B. Pure word deafness and hemispheric dynamics: A case history. *Cortex*, 1973, *9*, 136–149.

Gazzaniga, M.S., Steen, D., & Volpe, B.T. *Functional neuroscience*, New York: Harper & Row, 1979.

Geschwind, N. Disconnexion syndrome in animals and man. *Brain*, 1965, *88*, 237–294, 585–644.

Geschwind, N., & Levitsky, W. Human brain left–right asymmetries in temporal speech region. *Science*, 1968, *161*, 186–187.

Gianutsos, R., & Gianutsos, J. Rehabilitating the verbal recall of brain-injured patients by mnemonic training: An experimental demonstration using single-case methodology. *Journal of Clinical Neuropsychology*, 1979, *1*, 117–135.

Glasgow, R.E., Zeiss, R.A., Barrera, M., Jr., & Lewinsohn, P.M. Case studies on remediating memory deficits in brain damaged individuals. *Journal of Clinical Psychology*, 1977, *33*, 1049–1054.

Glick, S.D. Changes in drug sensitivity and mechanisms of functional recovery following brain damage. In D.G. Stein, J.J. Rosen, & N. Butters (Eds.), *Plasticity and recovery of function in the central nervous system*. New York: Academic Press, 1974.

Goldberg, L.R. The effectiveness of clinician's judgments: The diagnosis of organic brain damage from the Bender–Gestalt Test. *Journal of Consulting Psychology*, 1959, *23*, 25–33.

Golden, C.J. Identification of brain disorder by the Stroop Color and Word Test. *Journal of Clinical Psychology*, 1976, *32*, 654–658. (a)

Golden, C.J. The identification of brain damage by an abbreviated form of the Halstead–Reitan Neuropsychological Battery. *Journal of Clinical Psychology*, 1976, *32*, 821–829. (b)

Golden, C.J. The role of the psychologist in the training of the neurologically impaired. *Professional Psychology*, 1976, *8*, 579–584. (c)

Golden, C.J. Validity of the Halstead–Reitan Neuropsychological Battery in a mixed psychiatric and brain-injured population. *Journal of Consulting and Clinical Psychology*, 1977, *45*, 1043–1051.

Golden, C.J. *Diagnosis and rehabilitation in clinical neuropsychology*. Springfield, Ill.: Charles C. Thomas, 1978.

Golden, C.J. *Learning disabilities and brain dysfunction: An introduction for educators and parents*. Springfield, Ill.: Charles C. Thomas, 1979. (a)

Golden, C.J. *Clinical interpretation of objective psychological tests*. New York: Grune & Stratton, 1979. (b)

Golden, C.J. In reply to Adams' "In search of Luria's battery: A false start." *Journal of Consulting and Clinical Psychology*, 1980, *48*, 517–521.

Golden, C.J. *Diagnosis and rehabilitation in clinical neuropsychology* (2nd ed.). Springfield, Ill.: Charles C. Thomas, 1981.

Golden, C.J., Ariel, R.J., McKay, S.E., Wilkening, G.N., Wolf, B.A., & MacInnes, W.D. The Luria–Nebraska Neuropsychological Battery: Theoretical orientation and comment. *Journal of Consulting and Clinical Psychology*, 1982, *50*, 291–300. (a)

Golden, C.J., Ariel, R.J., Moses, J.A., Wilkening, G.N., McKay, S.E., & MacInnes, W.D. Analytic techniques in the interpretation of the Luria–Nebraska Neurological Battery. *Journal of Consulting and Clinical Psychology*, 1982, *50*, 40–48. (b)

Golden, C.J., Fross, K., & Graber, B. Split-half reliability and item consistency of the Luria–Nebraska Neuropsychological Battery. *Journal of Consulting and Clinical Psychology*, 1981, *49*, 304–305.

Golden, C.J., Graber, B., Coffman, J., Berg, R.A., Newlin, D.B., & Bloch, S. Structural brain deficits in schizophrenia. *Archives of General Psychiatry*, 1981, *38*, 1014–1017.

Golden, C.J., Graber, B., Moses, J.A., & Zatz, L. Differentiation of chronic schizophrenic with and without ventricular enlargement by the Luria–Nebraska Neuropsychological Battery. *International Journal of Neuroscience*, 1980, *11*, 131–138.

Golden, C.J., Gustavson, J.L., & Ariel, R. Correlations between the Luria–Nebraska and Halstead–Reitan Neuropsychological Batteries: Effects of partialing out education and post morbid intelligence. *Journal of Consulting and Clinical Psychology*, 1982, *50*, 770–771.

Golden, C.J., Hammeke, T., & Purisch, A.D. Diagnostic validity of a standardized neuropsychological battery derived from Luria's neuropsychological tests. *Journal of Consulting and Clinical Psychology*, 1978, *46*, 1258–1265.

Golden, C.J., Hammeke, T., & Purisch, A.D. *The Luria–Nebraska Neuropsychological Battery: Manual (Revised)*. Los Angeles: Western Psychological Services, 1980.

Golden, C.J., Kane, R., Sweet, J., Moses, J.A., Jr., Cardellino, J.P., Templeton, R.T., Vicente, P., Kennelly, D., & Graber, B. Relationship of the Halstead–Reitan Neuropsychological Battery to the Luria–Nebraska Neuropsychological Battery. *Journal of Consulting and Clinical Psychology*, 1981, *49*, 410–417.

Golden, C.J., Kuperman, S.K., MacInnes, W.D., & Moses, J.A. Cross validation of an abbreviated form of the Halstead Category Test. *Journal of Consulting and Clinical Psychology*, 1981, *49*, *606*–607.

Golden, C.J., MacInnes, W.D., Ariel, R.N., Ruedrich, S.L., Chu, C., Coffman, J.A., Graber, B., & Bloch, S. Cross-validation of the ability of the Luria–Nebraska Neuropsychological Battery to differentiate chronic schizophrenics with and without ventricular enlargement. *Journal of Consulting and Clinical Psychology*, 1982, *50*, 87–95.

Golden, C.J., Moses, J.A., Graber, B., & Berg, R. Objective clinical rules for

interpreting the Luria–Nebraska Neuropsychological Battery: Derivation, effectiveness, and validation. *Journal of Consulting and Clinical
Psychology*, 1981, *49*, 616–618.

Golden, C.J., Moses, J.A., Zelazowski, R.I., Graber, B., Zatzy, L.M., Horvath,
T.B., & Berger, P.A. Cerebral ventricular size and neuropsychological
impairment in young chronic schizophrenics. *Archives of General Psychiatry*, 1980, *37*, 619–623.

Golden, C.J., Osmon, D.C., Moses, J.A., & Berg, R.A. *Interpretations of the
Halstead–Reitan Neuropsychological Test Battery*. New York: Grune &
Stratton, 1981.

Goldfried, M.R., & Davidson, G.C. *Clinical behavior therapy*. New York: Holt,
Rinehart & Winston, 1976.

Goldstein, G. *Rehabilitation of the brain-damaged adult*. New York: Plenum
Press, 1983.

Goldstein, G., & Neuringer, C. Schizophrenia and organic signs of trail
making test. *Perceptual and Motor Skills*, 1966, *22*, 347–350.

Goldstein, G., & Shelly, C.H. Statistical and normative studies of the Halstead
Neuropsychological Test Battery relevant to a neuropsychiatric hospital
setting. *Perceptual and Motor Skills*, 1972, *34*, 603–620.

Goldstein, G., & Shelly, C.H. Univariate vs. multivariate analysis in neuropsychological test assessment of lateralized brain damage. *Cortex*, 1973,
9, 204–217.

Goldstein, K. *DieLokalisation in der grooshirnrinde*. In A. Bethe (Ed.)
Handbuch der normalen and pathologischen physiologie. Berlin:
Springer, 1927.

Goldstein, K. *The organism*. New York: American Book Co., 1939.

Goldstein, K. *After effects of brain injuries in war*. New York: Grune &
Stratton, 1942.

Goldstein, K. The mental change due to frontal lobe damage. *Journal of
Psychology*, 1944, *17*, 187–208.

Goldstein, K. *Language and language disorders*. New York: Grune & Stratton,
1948.

Goldstein, S.G., Deysach, R.E., & Kleinknecht, R.A. Effect of experience and
amount of information on identification of cerebral impairment. *Journal
of Consulting and Clinical Psychology*, 1973, *41*, 30–34.

Goodglass, H., & Kaplan, E. Assessment of cognitive deficit in the brain-injured patient. In M.S. Gazzaniga (Ed.), *Handbook of behavioral neurobiology 2: Neuropsychology.* New York: Plenum Press, 1979.

Goodman, L.S., & Gilman, A. (Eds.), *The small pharmacological basis of therapeutics,* (6th ed.). New York: Macmillan Publishing Company, Inc., 1980.

Graham, F.K., & Kendall, B.S. Memory-for Designs Test: Revised general manual. *Perceptual and Motor Skills, Monograph Supplement* (No. 2-VIII), 1960, *11,* 147–160.

Grant, I., Adams, K.M., Carlin, A.J., Rennick, P.M., Judd, L.L., & Schooff, K. The collaborative neuropsychological study of poly drug users. *Archives of General Psychiatry,* 1978, *35,* 1063–1074.

Grant, I., Mohns, L., Miller, M., & Reitan, R.M. A neuropsychological study of poly drug users. *Archives of General Psychiatry,* 1976, *33,* 973–978.

Gregory, R.J. Computerized interpretation of brain impairment tests: Preliminary results. *JSAS Catalog of Selected Documents in Psychology,* 1976, *6,* (MS. No. 1196).

Gregory, R.J., Paul, J.J., & Morrison, M.W. A short form of the Category Test for Adults. *Journal of Clinical Psychology,* 1979, *35,* 795–798.

Gudeman, H.E., Golden, C.J., & Craine, J.F. The role of neuropsychological evaluation in the rehabilitation of the brain-injured patient: A program in neurotraining. *JSAS catalog of selected documents in psychology,* 1978 (Ms. No. 1693).

Guilford, J.P. *The nature of human intelligence.* New York: McGraw-Hill, 1967.

Gur, R.E. Motoric laterality imbalance in schizophrenia: A possible concomitant of left hemispheric dysfunction. *Archives of General Psychiatry,* 1977, *34,* 33–37.

Gur, R.E. Left hemisphere dysfunction and left hemisphere over activation in schizophrenia, *Journal of Abnormal Psychology,* 1978, *87,* 226–238.

Halstead, W.C. *Brain and intelligence.* Chicago: University of Chicago Press, 1947.

Halstead, W.C., & Wepman, J.M. The Halstead–Wepman aphasia screening test. *Journal of Speech and Hearing Disorders,* 1949, *14,* 9–15.

Hartlage, L.C. Neuropsychological approaches to predicting outcome of remedial educational strategies for learning disabled children. *Pediatric Psychology*, 1975, *3*, 23–28.

Hartlage, L.C. Clinical application of neuropsychological test data in a case study. *School Psychology Review*, 1981, *10*, 362–366.

Hartlage, L.C., & Lucas, D.C. Group screening for reading disability in first grade children. *Journal of Learning Disabilities*, 1973, *6*, 48–52.

Hayes, S.C. Single case experimental design and empirical clinical practice. *Journal of Consulting and Clinical Psychology*, 1981, *49*, 193–211.

Hayes, S.C., & Zettle, R.D. On being behavioral, the technical and conceptual dimensions of behavioral assessment and therapy. *The Behavior Therapist*, 1980, *3*, 4–6.

Heath, R.G. Brain function and behavior. *Journal of Nervous and Mental Disease*, 1975, *16*, 159–166.

Heaton, R. The validity of neuropsychological evaluations in psychiatric settings. *Clinical Psychologist*, 1976, *29*, 10–11.

Heaton, R.K., Baade, L.E., & Johnson, K.L. Neuropsychological disorders in adults. *Psychological Bulletin*, 1978, *85*, 141–162.

Heaton, R.K., & Crowley, T.J. Effects of psychiatric disorders and their somatic treatments on neuropsychological test results. In S.B. Filskov & T.J. Boll (Eds.), *Handbook of clinical neuropsychology*. New York: John Wiley, 1981.

Heaton, R.K., & Pendleton, M.G. Use of neuropsychological tests to predict adult patients every day functioning. *Journal of Consulting and Clinical Psychology*, 1981, *49*, 807–821.

Heaton, R.K., Smith, H.H., Lehman, R.A.W., & Vogt, A.T. Prospects for taking believable deficits on neuropsychological testing. *Journal of Consulting and Clinical Psychology*, 1978, *46*, 892–900.

Hecaen, J., & Ajuriaguerra, J. *Left-handedness, manual superiority and cerebral dominance.* (E. Ponder, trans.). New York: Grune & Stratton, 1964.

Hecaen, J., & Albert, M.L. *Human neuropsychology.* New York: John Wiley, 1978.

Heilman, K.M., & Valenstein, E. (Eds.) *Clinical neuropsychology.* New York: Oxford University Press, 1979.

Heimberger, R.G., & Reitan, R.M. Easily administered test for lateralizing brain lesions. *Journal of Neurosurgery*, 1961, *18*, 301–312.

Horton, A.M., Jr. Behavioral neuropsychology: A tentative definition. *Behavioral Neuropsychology Newsletter*, 1978, *1*, 1–2.

Horton, A.M., Jr. Behavioral neuropsychology: Rationale and research, *Clinical Neuropsychology*, 1979, *1*(2), 20–23. (a)

Horton, A.M., Jr. Behavioral neuropsychology: A clinical case study, *Clinical Neuropsychology*, 1979, *1*(3), 20–23. (b)

Horton, A.M., Jr. Comment on effects of sex and anxiety on neuropsychological tests. *Journal of Consulting and Clinical Psychology*, 1979, *47*, 403. (c)

Horton, A.M., Jr. Some suggestions regarding the clinical interpretation of the trail making tests. *Clinical Neuropsychology*, 1979, *107*, 20–23.

Horton, A.M., Jr. The estimation of clinical significance: A brief note. *Psychological Reports*, 1980, *47*, 141–142.

Horton, A.M., Jr. Behavioral neuropsychology in the schools. *School Psychology Review*, 1981, *10*, 367–372.

Horton, A.M., Jr. Behavioral neuropsychology: A brief rationale. *The Behavioral Therapist*, 1982, *5*, 100–102.

Horton, A.M., Jr., & Decker, E.B. Neuropsychological assessment of an adult's minimal brain dysfunction: A case study. *Perceptual and Motor Skills*, 1981, *52*, 676–678.

Horton, A.M., Jr., & Howe, N.R. Behavioral neuropsychology and the traumatic brain-injured adult: A case study. Proceedings of the 5th annual post-graduate course on the rehabilitation of the brain-injured adult. Richmond: Virginia Commonwealth University, 1981. (Abstract)

Horton, A.M., Jr., Owens, R.C., & Hartlage, L.C. Neuropsychological assessment in private practice. Conversation hour sponsored by the American Society of Psychologist in Private Practice (ASPPP) at the 88th Annual Meeting of the American Psychological Association, Montreal, Canada, September, 1980.

Horton, A.M., Jr., & Sepsi, V.J. Neuropsychological assessment of attention deficit disorder, residual type: A case study. *Clinical Neuropsychology*, 1982, *4*, 108. (Abstract)

Horton, A.M., Jr., Wedding, D., & Phay, A. Current perspectives on assessment of and therapy for brain-damaged individuals. In C.J. Golden, S.S.

Alcaparras, F. Strider, & B. Graber (Eds.), *Applied techniques in behavioral medicine*. New York: Grune & Stratton, 1981.

Horton, A.M., Jr. & Wilson, F.M. Cross-validation of the psychiatric-organic (P.O.) special scale of the MMPI in a V.A. domiciling setting. *Clinical Neuropsychology*, 1981, *2*, 1–3.

Hovey, H.B. Brain lesions and five MMPI items. *Journal of Consulting Psychology*, 1964, *28*, 78–80.

Hubel, D.H., & Wiesel, T.N. Receptive fields of single neurons in the cat's striate cortex. *Journal of Physiology*, 1960, *150*, 91–104.

Huckman, M.S., Fox, J.H., & Ramsey, R.G. Computed tomography in the diagnosis of degenerative diseases of the brain. *Seminars in Roenterology*, 1977, *12*, 63–75.

Ince, L.P. *Behavior modification in rehabilitation medicine*. Springfield, Ill.: Charles C. Thomas, 1976.

Ingvar, D., & Franzen, G. Abnormalities of cerebral blood flow in patients with chronic schizophrenia. *Acta Psychiatrica Scandinavica*, 1974, *10*, 425–429.

International Neuropsychological Society (INS) Task Force Report on Education: Accreditation and Credentials 1971. *INS Bulletin*, 1981, September, 5–10.

Jacobs, L., Kinkel, W.R., & Heffrery, R.R. Autopsy correlations of computerized tomography: Experience with 6,000 CT scans. *Neurology*, 1976, *26*, 1111–1118.

Jacobson, E. *Progressive relaxation*. Chicago: University of Chicago Press, 1938.

Jennett, B., & Teasdale, G. *Management of head injuries*. Philadelphia: F.A. Davis, 1981.

Jerger, J., Lovering, L., & Wertz, M. Auditory disorder following bilaterial temporal lobe insult: Report of a case. *Journal of Speech and Hearing Disorders*, 1972, *37*, 523–531.

John, E.R. Neurometrics: Clinical applications of electrophysiology. In E.R. John & R.W. Thatcher (Eds.), *Functional Neuroscience*, Vol. 2. Hillsdale, N.J.: Lawrence Erlbaum Associates, 1977.

Johnson, B., & Almi, C.R. Age, brain damage, and performance. In S. Finger (Ed.), *Recovery from brain damage: Research and theory*. New York: Plenum Press, 1978.

Johnstone, E.C., Crowe, J.J., Frith, C.D., Husband, J., & Kreel, L. Cerebral ventricular size and cognitive impairment in chronic schizophrenia. *The Lancet*, 1976, *2*, 294–296.

Jones, M.K. Imagery as a mnemonic aid after temporal lobectomy: Contrast between material specific and generalized memory disorders. *Neuropsychologia*, 1974, *12*, 21–30.

Jouandet, M., & Gazzaniga, M.S. The frontal lobes. In M.S. Gazzaniga (Ed.), *Handbook of behavioral neurobiology*. New York: Plenum Press, 1979.

Kalat, J.W. *Biological psychology*. Belmont, Calif.: Wadsworth Publishing Company, 1981.

Kazdin, A.E. The application of operant techniques in treatment, rehabilitation, and education. In S.L. Garfield & A.E. Bergin (Eds.), *Handbook of psychotherapy and behavior change*, (2nd ed.). New York: John Wiley, 1978.

Kazdin, A.E. *Behavior modification in applied settings* (rev. ed.). Homewood, Ill.: Dorsey Press, 1980.

Keefe, F.J., & Surwit, R.S. Electromyographic bio-feedback: Behavioral treatment of neuromuscular disorders. *Journal of Behavioral Medicine*, 1978, *1*, 12–24.

Kertesz, A. Recovery and treatment. In K.H. Heilman & E. Valenstein (Eds.), *Clinical neuropsychology*. New York: Oxford University Press, 1979. Pp. 503–534.

Kiernan, R.J., & Matthews, C.G. Impairment index versus T-score averaging in neuropsychological assessment. *Journal of Consulting and Clinical Psychology*, 1976, *44*, 951.

Kiessler, D.J. Some myths of psychotherapy research and the search for a paradigm. *Psychological Bulletin*, 1966, *65*, 110–136.

Kimura, D. Speech lateralization in young children is determined by an auditory test. *Cortex*, 1963, *56*, 899–902.

Kimura, S.D. A card form of the Reitan-Modified Halstead Category Test. *Journal of Consulting and Clinical Psychology*, 1981, *49*, 145–146.

Kinsbourne, M., & Warrington, E.K. Disorders of spelling. *Journal of Neurology, Neurosurgery and Psychiatry*, 1964, *27*, 224–233.

Kliez, D.K. Neuropsychological evaluation in older persons. In M. Stormadt, D.C. Siegler, & M.F. Elias (Eds.), *The clinical psychology of aging*. New York: Plenum Press, 1978.

Klonoff, H., Fibiger, D.H., & Hutton, G.H. Neuropsychological patterns in chronic schizophrenia. *Journal of Nervous and Mental Disease*, 1970, *150*, 291–300.

Klonoff, H., & Paris, R. Immediate, short-term and residual effects of acute head injuries in children: Neuropsychological and neurological correlates. In R.M. Reitan & L.A. Davison (Eds.), *Clinical neuropsychology: Current status and application.* New York: John Wiley, 1974.

Kløve, H. Validation studies in adult clinical neuropsychology. In R.M. Reitan & L.A. Davison (Eds.), *Clinical neuropsychology: Current status and applications.* Washington, D.C.: Winston, 1974.

Kløve, H. & Cleeland, C.S. The relationship of neuropsychological impairment to other indices of severity of head injury. *Scandinavian Journal of Rehabilitation Medicine*, 1972, *4*, 55–60.

Kløve, W., & Matthews, C.G. Neuropsychological studies of patients with epilepsy. In R.M. Reitan & L.A. Davison (Eds.), *Clinical neuropsychology: Current status and applications.* New York: John Wiley, 1974.

Knopf, I.J. Attentional processes in children. Presidential address to the Southeastern Psychological Association Meeting, Washington, D.C., 1980.

Kolb, B., & Whishaw, I.Q. *Fundamentals of human neuropsychology.* San Francisco: W.H. Freeman, 1980.

Kolb, L.C. *Modern clinical psychiatry*, (9th ed.). Philadelphia: W.B. Saunders, 1977.

Kramer, H. Some observations on post-lobotomy patients. *Journal of Nervous and Mental Diseases*, 1955, *122*, 89–93.

Krech, D. Cortical localization of function. In L. Postman (Ed.), *Psychology in the making.* New York: Knopf, 1962.

Krech, D. Psychoneurobiochemeducation. *Phi Delta Kappa*, 1969, March, 209–219.

Lacher, D. *The MMPI: Clinical assessment and automated interpretation.* Los Angeles: Western Psychological Services, 1974.

Lacher, D., & Alexander, R.S. Veridicality of self-report: Replicated correlates of the Wiggins MMPI Content Scales. *Journal of Consulting and Clinical Psychology*, 1978, *46*, 1349–1356.

Lacks, P.B., Colbert, J., Harrow, M., & Levine, J. Further evidence concerning the diagnostic accuracy of the Halstead organic test battery. *Journal of Clinical Psychology*, 1970, *26*, 480–481.

Lahey, B.B., & Ciminero, A.R. *Maladaptive behavior.* Glenview, Ill.: Scott, Foresman, & Company, 1980.

Lakin, P., Ben-Yishay, Y., Rattok, J., Ross, B., Silver, S., Thomas, J.L., Hoofien, D., Fawzi, E.M., Hamza, M.H., & Diller, L. Special procedures for assessing aspects of interpersonal skills of head trauma patients undergoing rehabilitation. *Working approaches to remediation of cognitive deficits in brain damaged persons* (Rehabilitation Monograph No. 62). New York: New York University Medical Center, Institute of Rehabilitation Medicine, 1981. Pp. 68–102.

Lansdell, H. A general intellectual factor affected by temporal lobe dysfunction. *Journal of Clinical Psychology,* 1971, *27,* 182–184.

Lashley, K.S. *Brain mechanisms and intelligence.* Chicago: University of Chicago Press, 1929.

Lawrence, S., & Stein, D.G. Recovery after brain damage and the concept of localization of function. In S. Finger (Ed.), *Recovery from brain damage: Research and theory.* New York: Plenum Press, 1978. Pp. 369–407.

Lazarus, A.A. A matter of emphasis. *American Psychologist,* 1979, *34,* 100.

Ledwidge, B. Cognitive behavior modification: A step in the wrong direction? *Psychological Bulletin,* 1978, *85,* 353–375.

Leftoff, S. Perceptual retraining in an adult cerebral palsied patient: A case of deficit in cross modal equivalence. *Journal of Clinical Neuropsychology,* 1979, *1,* 227–241.

Leftoff, S. Learning functions for unilaterally brain damaged patients for serially and randomly ordered stimulus material: Analysis of retrieval strategies and their relationship to rehabilitation. *Journal of Clinical Neuropsychology,* 1981, *3,* 301–313.

Lehmann, J.F., Delateur, B.J., Fowler, R.S., & Warren, C.G. Stroke rehabilitation: Outcome and prediction. *Archives of Physical Medicine and Rehabilitation,* 1972, *56,* 383–392.

LeVere, T.E. Neural stability, sparing and behavioral recovery following brain damage. *Psychological Review,* 1975, *82,* 344–358.

Levin, H.S., Benton, A.L., & Grossman, R.G. *Neurobehavioral consequences of closed head injury.* New York: Oxford University Press, 1982.

Levine, J., & Feirstein, A. Differences in test performance between brain damaged, schizophrenic, and medical patients. *Journal of Consulting and Clinical Psychology,* 1972, *39,* 508–511.

Lewinsohn, P.M. *Psychological assessment of patients with brain injury.* Washington, D.C.: Division of Research, Department of Health, Education and Welfare, 1973.

Lewinsohn, P.M., Danaker, B.G., & Kikel, S. Visual imagery as a mnemonic aid for brain injured persons. *Journal of Consulting and Clinical Psychology*, 1977, *45*, 717–723.

Lewis, G., Golden, C.J., Moses, J.A., Jr., Osmon, D.C., Purisch, A.D., & Hammeke, T.A. Localization of cerebral dysfunction with a standardized version of Luria's Neuropsychological Battery. *Journal of Consulting and Clinical Psychology*, 1979, *47*, 1003–1019.

Lezak, M.D. *Neuropsychological assessment.* New York: Oxford University Press, 1976.

Libet, J.M., & Kilpatrick, D.G. Psychological evaluation. In P.M. Randel, L. McCurdy, W.S. Powell, D.C. Kilpatrick, & M.H. Keeler, *The psychiatry learning system*, (2nd ed.). Charleston: Medical University of South Carolina, 1974.

Lindzey, G., Hall, C., & Lothompson, R. *Psychology.* New York: Little, Brown, 1978.

Lipowski, A.J. Organic brain syndromes: A reformulation. *Comprehensive Psychiatry*, 1978, *19*, 309–322.

Lishman, W.A. *Organic psychiatry: The psychological consequences of cerebral disorder.* London: Blackwell Scientific Publications, 1978.

Liu, C.M., & Chambers, W.W. Intraspinal sprouting of doral root axons. *Archives of Neurology and Psychiatry*, 1958, *79*, 46–61.

Lockard, R.B. Reflections on the fall of comparative psychology: Is there a message for us all. *American Psychologist*, 1971, *26*, 168–179.

Lord, F.M. Cutting scores and errors of measurement. *Psychometrika*, 1962, *27*, 19–30.

Lubin, B., Wallis, R.R., & Pain, C. Patterns of psychological test usage in the United States: 1935–1967. *Professional Psychology*, 1971, *2*, 70–74.

Luria, A.R. *Restoration of function after brain injury.* New York: Macmillan, 1963.

Luria, A.R. *Higher cortical function in man* (B. Haigh, Trans.). New York: Basic Books, 1966.

Luria, A.R. *The working brain.* New York: Basic Books, 1973.

Luria, A.R. *Higher cortical functions in man.* New York: Basic Books, 1980.

Luria, A.R., & Homskaya, E.G. Disturbance of action control in frontal lobe lesions. In A.R. Luria (Ed.), *Human brain and psychological process.* New York: Harper & Row, 1966.

Luria, A.R., & Majovski, L.V. Basic approaches used in American and Soviet clinical neuropsychology. *American Psychologist,* 1977, *32,* 959–968.

Luria, A.R., Nayden, L.L. Tsvetkova, L.S., & Vinarskaya, E.N. Restoration of higher cortical function following local brain damage. In P.J. Vinken & G.W. Bryun (Eds.), *Handbook of clinical neurology,* Vol. 3. Amsterdam: North Holland Publishing Company, 1969. Pp. 368–433.

Lynch, W. The use of video games in rehabilitation. Presented at Conference on Models and Techniques of Cognitive Rehabilitation, Indianapolis, January 1981.

MacLean, L.D. *On the evolution of three mentalities.* Toronto: University of Toronto Press, 1973.

Mahoney, M.J. *Cognition and behavior modification.* Cambridge, Mass.: Ballinger, 1974.

Mahoney, M.J. *Scientist as the subject: The psychological imperative.* Cambridge, Mass.: Balinger, 1976.

Mahoney, M.J. Reflections on the cognitive learning trend in psychotherapy. *American Psychologist,* 1977, *32,* 5–13.

Malloy, P.F., & Webster, J.S. Detecting mild brain impairment using the Luria–Nebraska Neuropsychological Battery. *Journal of Consulting and Clinical Psychology,* 1981, *49, 768–770.*

Matarrazo, J. *Wechsler's measurement and appraisal of adult intelligence.* Baltimore: Williams & Wilkins, 1972.

Matthews, C.G. Applications of neuropsychological test methods to mentally retarded subjects. In R.M. Reitan & L.A. Davison (Eds.), *Clinical neuropsychology: Current status and applications.* New York: John Wiley, 1974.

Matthews, C.G., Cleeland, C.S., & Hooper, C.L. Neuropsychological patterns in multiple sclerosis. *Diseases of the Nervous System,* 1970, *31,* 161–120.

Matthews, C.G., Shaw, D.J., & Klove, H. Psychological test performance in neurological and pseudo-neurological subjects. *Cortex,* 1966, *2,* 244–248.

Mayo Clinic, *Clinical examinations in neurology.* Philadelphia: W.B. Saunders, 1976.

McFie, J. *Assessment of organic intellectual impairment.* New York: Academic Press, 1975.

McGlome, J. Sex differences in human-brain asymmetry: A critical survey. *Behavioral Brain,* 1980, *3,* 215–227.

McKay, S., & Golden, C.J. Empirical derivation of neuropsychological scales for the lateralization of brain damage using the Luria–Nebraska Neuropsychological Test Battery. *Clinical Neuropsychology,* 1979, *1,* 1–5.

McKay, S., Golden, S.C.J., Moses, J.A., Jr., Fishburne, F., & Wisniewski, A. Correlation of the Luria–Nebraska Neuropsychological Battery with the WAIS. *Journal of Consulting and Clinical Psychology,* 1981, *49,* 940–946.

McLardy, T. Memory function in hippocampal gyri. *International Journal of Neuroscience,* 1970, *1,* 113–117.

Meehl, P.E. *Clinical versus statistical prediction. A theoretical analysis and a review of the evidence.* Minneapolis: University of Minnesota Press, 1954.

Meehl, P.E. Schizotaxia, schizotypy, and schizophrenia. *American Psychologist,* 1962, *17,* 827–838.

Meehl, P.E., & Dahlstrom, W.G. Objective configural rules for discriminating psychotic from neurotic profiles. *Journal of Consulting Psychology,* 1960, *24,* 375–387.

Meichenbaum, D.H. *Cognitive behavior modification.* New York: Plenum Press, 1977.

Meier, M.J. The regional localization hypothesis and personality changes associated with focal cerebral lesions and ablations. In J.N. Butcher (Ed.), *MMPI: Research developments and clinical applications.* New York: McGraw-Hill, 1969.

Meier, M.J. Some challenges for clinical neuropsychology. In R.M. Reitan & L.A. Davison (Eds.), *Clinical neuropsychology: Current status and application.* New York: John Wiley, 1974.

Meier, M.J. Education for competency assurance in human neuropsychology: Antecedents, models, and directions. In S.B. Filskov & T.J. Boll (Eds.), *Handbook of clinical neuropsychology.* New York: John Wiley, 1981.

Meier, M.J., & French, L.A. Some personality correlates of unilateral and bilateral EEG abnormalities in psychomotor epileptics. *Journal of Clinical Psychology,* 1965, *21,* 3–9.

Meyer, J.S. Disordered neurotransmitter function. *Brain*, 1974, *97*, 655–664.

Meyers, P.I., & Hammill, D.D. *Methods for learning disorders*, (2nd ed.). New York: John Wiley, 1976.

Mezzich, J.E., & Moses, J.A. Efficient screening for brain-dysfunction. *Biological Psychiatry*, 1980, *15*, 333–337.

Miller, E. Psychological intervention in the management and rehabilitation of neurological impairment. *Behavior, Research, and Therapy*, 1980, *18*, 527–535.

Miller, W.R. Treating problem drinkers: What works. *The Behavior Therapist*, 1982, *5*, 15–18.

Milner, B. Psychological defects produced by temporal lobe excision. *Association for Research in Nervous and Mental Diseases*, 1958, *36*, 244–257.

Milner, B. Some effects of different brain lesion on card sorting: The role of the frontal lobes. *Archives of Neurology*, 1963, *4*, 90–100. (a)

Milner, B. Visually guided maze learning in man: Effects of bilateral hippocampal, bilateral frontal and unilateral cerebral lesions. *Neuropsychologia*, 1963, *3*, 317–338. (b)

Milner, B. Some effects of frontal lobectomy in man. In J.M. Warren & K. Akert (Eds.), *The frontal granular cortex and behavior*. New York: McGraw-Hill, 1964.

Milner, B. Memory and the temporal regions of the brain. In K.H. Pribram & D.E. Broadbent (Eds.), *Biology of memory*. New York: Academic Press, 1970.

Milner, B. Interhemispheric differences and psychological processes. *British Medical Bulletin*, 1971, *27*, 272–277.

Mischel, W. *Personality and assessment*. New York: John Wiley, 1968.

Morgan, W.P. A case of congenital word blunders. *British Medical Journal*, 1896, *2*, 1378.

Morrison, M.W., Gregory, R.J., & Paul, J.J. Reliability of the finger tapping test and a note on sex differences. *Perceptual and Motor Skills*, 1979, *48*, 139–142.

Mostofsky, D.I., & Balaschak, B.A. Psychobiological control of seizures. *Psychological Bulletin*, 1977, *84*, 723–750.

Mullan, S., & Penfield, W. Illusions of comparative interpretation and emotion. *Archives of Neurology and Psychiatry*, 1959, *81*, 269–275.

Murphy, S.T. Effects of a token economy program on self-care behaviors of neurologically impaired inpatients. *Journal of Behavior Therapy and Experimental Psychiatry*, 1976, *7*, 145–147.

Nalser, M.A., Gebhardt, C., & Levine, H.L. Decreased computerized tomography numbers in patients with presenile dementia. *Archives of Neurology*, 1980, *37*, 401–408.

National Head Injury Foundation, Inc. *The silent epidemic* (leaflet). Framingham, Mass., 1981.

National Institute of Neurological and Communicative Disorders and Stroke (NINCDS), 1976. In N.E.F. Cartlidge & D.A. Shaw (Eds.), *Head injury*. London: W.B. Saunders, 1981.

Nauta, W.J.H. Some brain structures and functions related to memory. *Neurosciences Research Progress Bulletin*, 1964, *2*, 1–20.

Nebes, R.W. Hemispheric specialization in commissurotomized man. *Psychological Bulletin*, 1974, *81*, 1–14.

Neiley, C. Color aphasia: A case report. *Cortex*, 1974, *10*, 388–402.

Newcombe, F., & Ratcliff, G. Long-term psychological consequences of cerebral trauma. In M.S. Gazzaniga (Ed.), *Handbook of behavioral neurobiology: Neuropsychology*, Vol. 2. New York: Plenum Press, 1979.

Noback, C.R., & Demarest, R.J. *The Human Nervous System*. New York: McGraw-Hill, 1981.

Orgel, S.A., & McDonald, R.D. An evaluation of the trail making test. *Journal of Consulting and Clinical Psychology*, 1967, *51*, 77–79.

Ornstein, R., Johnston, J., Herron, J., & Swencionis, C. Differential right hemispheric engagement in visuospatial tasks. *Neuropsychologia*, 1980, *18*, 49–64.

Parker, E.S., & Nobel, E.P. Alcohol consumption and cognitive functioning in social drinkers. *Journal of Studies on Alcohol*, 1977, *34*, 1224–1232.

Parsons, O.A., & Farr, S.P. The neuropsychology of alcohol and drug use. In S. Filskov and T. Boll (Eds.), *Handbook of Clinical Neuropsychology*, New York: John Wiley, 1981.

Patten, P.M. The ancient art of memory: Usefulness in treatment. *Archives of Neurology*, 1972, *26*, 25–31.

Penfield, W., & Milner, B. The memory deficit produced by bilateral lesions of the hippocampal zone. *Archives of Neurology and Psychiatry*, 1958, *79*, 475–497.

Perret, E. The left frontal lobe of man and the suppression of habitual responses in verbal categorical behavior. *Neuropsychologia*, 1974, *12*, 323–327.

Pincus, J.H., & Tucker, G.J. *Behavioral neurology.* New York: Oxford University Press, 1974.

Piotrowski, Z. The Rorschach inkblot method in organic disturbances of the central nervous system. *Journal of Nervous and Mental Disease*, 1937, *86*, 525–532.

Pirozzolo, F.J. Language and brain: Neuropsychological aspects of developmental reading disability. *School Psychology Review*, 1981, *10*, 350–355.

Pirozzolo, F.J., Campenella, D.J., Christensen, K., & Lawson-Kerr, K. Effects of cerebral dysfunction on neurolinguistic performance in children. *Journal of Consulting and Clinical Psychology*, 1981, *49*, 791–806.

Pirozzolo, F.J., & Wittrock, M. (Eds.) *Neuropsychological and cognitive processes.* New York: Academic Press, 1981.

Pribram, K.H. The primate frontal cortex: Executive of the brain. In K.H. Pribram and H.R. Luria (Eds.), *Psychophysiology of the frontal lobes.* New York: Academic Press, 1974.

Prifitera, A., & Ryan, J.J. Validity of the intellectual processes scale as a measure of adult intelligence. *Journal of Consulting and Clinical Psychology*, 1981, *49*, 755–756.

Prigantano, G.P., & Parsons, O.A. Relationship of age and education to Halstead test performance in different patient populations. *Journal of Consulting and Clinical Psychology*, 1976, *44*, 527–533.

Puchala, E., & Windle, W.F. The possibility of structural and functional restitution after spinal cord injury. A review. *Experimental Neurology*, 1977, *55*, 1–42.

Rattok, J., Thomas, J.L., Ben-Yishay, Y., Ross, B., Lakin, P., Silver, S., Hoffien, D., Fawzy, E.M., Hamza, M.H., & Diller, L. A remedial module for systematic training of traumatic head injured patients in the area of visual information processing. *Working approaches to remediation of cognitive deficits in brain damaged persons.* (Rehabilitation Monograph, No. 62). New York University Medical Center, Institute of Rehabilitation Medicine, 1981. Pp. 43–67.

Redich, R., & Kellert, S.R. Trends in American mental health. *American Journal of Psychiatry*, 1978, *135*, 1–12.

Reed, H.B.C., & Reitan, R.M. Intelligence test performance of brain damaged subjects with lateralized motor deficits. *Journal of Consulting Psychology*, 1963, *27*, 102–106.

Reitan, R.M. *Manual for administration of Neuropsychological Test Batteries for Adults and Children.* Neuropsychology Laboratory, University of Washington, privately published, undated.

Reitan, R.M. Validity of the trial making test as an indicator of organic brain damage. *Perceptual and Motor Skills*, 1958, *8*, 271–276.

Reitan, R.M. The effect of brain lesions on adaptive abilities in human beings. Unpublished manuscript, 1959.

Reitan, R.M. Psychological deficits resulting from cerebral lesions in man. In J.M. Warren & K.A. Akert (Eds.), *The frontal granular cortex and behavior.* New York: McGraw, 1964.

Reitan, R.M. A research program on the psychological effects of brain lesions in human beings. In N.R. Ellis (Ed.), *International review of research in mental retardation*, Vol. 1. New York: Academic Press, 1966.

Reitan, R.M. Psychological assessment of deficits associated with brain lesions in subjects with normal and subnormal intelligence. In J.S. Kehanne (Ed.), *Brain damage and mental retardation.* Springfield, Ill.: Charles C. Thomas, 1968.

Reitan, R.M. Sensorimotor functions, intelligence and cognition, and emotional status in subjects with cerebral lesions. *Perceptual and Motor Skills*, 1970, *31*, 275–284.

Reitan, R.M. Neurological and physiological bases of psychopathology. *Annual Review of Psychology*, 1976, *27*, 189–216.

Reitan, R.M., & Boll, T.J. Intellectional and cognitive functions in Parkinson's disease. *Journal of Consulting and Clinical Psychology*, 1971, *37*, 364–369.

Reitan, R.M., & Davison, L.A. (Eds.). *Clinical neuropsychology: Current status and application.* New York: John Wiley, 1974.

Reitan, R.M., Reed, J.C., & Dyken, M.L. Cognitive, psychomotor, and motor correlates of multiple sclerosis. *Journal of Nervous and Mental Disease*, 1971, *153*, 281–290.

Rincover, A., Newson, C.D., Lovaas, O.I., & Kocgel, R.L. Some motivational properties of sensory reinforcement in psychotic children. *Journal of Experimental Child Psychology*, 1977, *24*, 312–323.

Robert, D.R. Catatonia in the brain: A localization study. *International Journal of Neuropsychiatry*, 1965, *1*, 395–401.

Roberts, A.H. *Severe accidental head injury: An assessment of long-term prognosis.* London: Macmillan, 1979.

Rorer, L.G., & Davies, R.M. A base-rate boot-strap. *Journal of Consulting and Clinical Psychology*, 1982, *50*, 419–425.

Rosenbaum, M., Lipsitz, N., Abraham, J., & Najenson, T. A description of an intensive treatment project for the rehabilitation of severely brain-injured soldiers. *Scandinavian Journal of Rehabilitation Medicine*, 1978, *10*, 1–6.

Rosenblum, J.A. Human sexuality and cerebral cortex. *Diseases of the Nervous System*, 1974, *35*, 268–272.

Rosenthal, M., Bond, M.R., Miller, J.D., & Griffith, E.R. *Rehabilitation of the traumatic brain injured adult.* Philadelphia: F.A. Davis, 1982.

Rosenzweig, M.R. Animal models for effects of brain lesions and for rehabilitation. In P. Bach-y-Rita (Ed.), *Recovery of function: Theoretical considerations for brain injury rehabilitation.* Baltimore: University Park Press, 1980. Pp. 127–172.

Rosner, B.S. Brain functions. *Annual Review of Psychology*, 1970, *21*, 555–594.

Rosner, G. Recovery of function and localization of function in historical perspective. In D.G. Stein, J.J. Rosen, & N. Butters (Eds.), *Plasticity and recovery of function in the central nervous system.* New York: Academic Press, 1974. Pp. 1–30.

Royce, J.R., Yeudall, L.T., & Bock, C. Factor analytic studies of human brain damage: First and second-order factors and their correlates. *Multivariate Behavioral Research*, 1976, *11*, 381–418.

Russell, E.W. Validation of a brain damage versus schizophrenia MMPI key. *Journal of Clinical Psychology*, 1975, *31*, 659–661.

Russell, E.W., Neuringer, C., & Goldstein, G. *Assessment of brain damage: A neuropsychological key approach.* New York: John Wiley, 1970.

Russell, W.R., & Espir, M.L.E. *Traumatic aphasia.* London: Oxford University Press, 1961.

Sagan, C. *The dragons of Eden.* New York: Ballantine Books, 1977.

Salzinger, L., Feldman, R.S., & Portnoy, S. Training parents of brain-injured children in the use of operant conditioning procedures. *Behavior Therapy*, 1970, *1*, 4–32.

Sattler, J.M. *Assessment of children's intelligence*. Philadelphia: W.B. Saunders, 1974.

Sattler, J.M. Age effects on Wechsler Adult Intelligence Scale—Revised tests. *Journal of Consulting and Clinical Psychology*, 1982, *50*, 785–786.

Satz, P. A block rotation task: The application of multivariate and decision theory analysis for the prediction of organic brain disorder. *Psychological Monographs*, 1966, *80*, Whole #629.

Satz, P., & Fletcher, J.M. Emergent trends in neuropsychology: An overview. *Journal of Consulting and Clinical Psychology*, 1981, *49*, 851–865.

Sawyer, J. Measurement and prediction, clinical and statistical. *Psychological Bulletin*, 1966, *66*, 178–200.

Schacter, D.L., & Crovitz, H.F. Memory function after closed head injury: A review of the quantitative research. *Cortex*, 1977, *13*, 150–176.

Schneider, M., & Robin, H. The turtle technique: A method for self-control of impulsive behavior. In J.D. Krumboltz & C.E. Thorensen (Eds.), *Counseling methods*. New York: Holt, Rinehart & Winston, 1976.

Schorr, D., Bower, G.H., & Kiernas, R. Stimulus variables in the Block Design task. *Journal of Consulting and Clinical Psychology*, 1982, *50*, 479–487.

Schreiber, D.J., Goldman, H., Kleinman, K.L., Goldfader, P.R., & Snow, M. The relationship between independent neuropsychological and neurological detection and localization of cerebral impairment. *Journal of Nervous and Mental Disease*, 1976, *172*, 360–365.

Schwartz, G.E., & Beatry, J. *Biofeedback: Theory and research*. New York: Academic Press, 1977.

Scotti, G., & Spinner, H. Color imperception in unilateral hemispheric patients. *Journal of Neurology, Neurosurgery, and Psychiatry*, 1970, *33*, 22–41.

Scoville, W., & Milner, B. Loss of recent memory after bilateral hippocampal lesions. *Journal of Neurology, Neurosurgery and Psychiatry*, 1957, *20*, 11.

Segal, J., Boomer, D.S., & Bouthilet, L. *Research in the Service of Mental Health*, National Institute of Mental Health, 1975, DHEW Publication, 75–236.

Sexon, X., Deloche, G., Moulard, G., & Rovsselle, M. A computer-based therapy for the treatment of aphasic subjects with writing disorders, *Journal of Speech and Hearing Disorders*, 1980, *4*, 45–58.

Shure, G.H., & Halstead, W.C. Cerebral localization of intellectual processes. *Psychological Monographs*, 1958, *72*, Whole #465.

Simpson, C.D., & Vega, A. Unilateral brain damage and patterns of age-connected WAIS subtest scores. *Journal of Clinical Psychology*, 1971, *27*, 204–208.

Skinner, B.F. *The behavior of organisms*. New York: Appleton-Century-Crofts, 1938.

Skinner, B.F. *Science and human behavior*. Glencoe, Ill.: Free Press, 1953.

Small, I.F., Small, J.G., Milstein, V., & Moore, J.E. Neuropsychological observations with psychosis and somatic treatment. *Journal of Nervous and Mental Disease*, 1972, *155*, 6–13.

Small, L. *Neuropsychodiagnosis in psychotherapy*. New York: Brunner/ Mazel, 1980.

Smith, A. Verbal and nonverbal test performances of patients with "acute" lateralized brain lesions (tumors). *Journal of Nervous and Mental Disease*, 1966, *70*, 595–600.

Smith, A. Neuropsychological testing in neurological disorders. In W.J. Friedlander (Ed.), *Advances in neurology*, Vol. 7. New York: Raven Press, 1975.

Sperry, R.W. Cerebral organization and behavior. *Science*, 1961, *133*, 1949.

Spiers, P.A. Have they come to praise Luria or to bury him? The Luria–Nebraska Battery controversy. *Journal of Consulting and Clinical Psychology*, 1981, *49*, 331–341.

Spiers, P.A. The Luria–Nebraska Neurological Battery revisited: A theory in practice or just practicing? *Journal of Consulting and Clinical Psychology*, 1982, *50*, 301–306.

Spitzer, R.L., & Endicott, J. Can the computer assist clinicians in psychiatric diagnosis? *American Journal of Psychiatry*, 1974, *131*, 523–530.

Spitzer, R.L., Endicott, J., Cohen, J., & Fleiss, J.L. Constraints of the validity of computer diagnosis. *Archives of General Psychiatry*, 1974, *31*, 197–203.

Spitzer, R.L., Endicott, J., & Robins, E. *Research diagnostic criteria*. New York: Biometric Research, 1975.

Stack, J.T., & Phillips, A.R. Performance of normal, brain damaged, and schizophrenic patients on the Halstead–Reitain Neuropsychological Battery. *Newsletter for Research in Psychology*, 1970, *12*, 16–18.

Stein, D.G., Rosen, J.J., & Butters, N. *Plasticity and recovery of function in the central nervous system.* New York: Academic Press, 1974.

Stein, K.B. *Manual for the Symbol-Gestalt Test: A three-minute perceptual-motor test for brain damage*, (rev. ed.). Privately published by the author. Berkeley, Calif., 1970.

Sterman, M.B., & Friar, L. Suppression of seizures in an epileptic following sensory motor EEG feedback training. *Electroencephalography and Clinical Neurophysiology*, 1972, *33*, 89.

Straub, R.L., & Black, W. *The mental status examination in neurology.* Philadelphia: Davis, 1977.

Struss, D.T., & Trites, R.L. Classification of neurological status using multiple discriminant function analysis of neuropsychological test scores. *Journal of Consulting and Clinical Psychology*, 1977, *45*, 145.

Suchenwirth, R. *Pocketbook of Clinical Neurology.* Chicago: Year Book Medical Publishers, 1979.

Sufrin, E.M. The effects of a behavior modification treatment program on a neurologically handicapped population. Doctoral Dissertation, University of Southern California, 1975. Dissertation Abstracts, 1975, No. 75-28652.

Swiercinsky, D. *Manual for the adult neuropsychological evaluation.* Springfield, Ill.: Charles C. Thomas, 1979.

Swiercinsky, D., & Leigh, G. Comparison of neuropsychological data in the diagnosis of brain impairment with computerized tomography and other neuropsychological procedures. *Journal of Clinical Psychology*, 1979, *35*, 242–246.

Swiercinsky, D.P., & Warnock, J.K. Comparison of the neuropsychological key and discriminate analysis approach in predicting cerebral damage and localization. *Journal of Consulting and Clinical Psychology*, 1977, *45*, 808–814.

Swisher, L.P. Auditory intensity discrimination in patients with temporal lobe damage. *Cortex*, 1967, *3*, 179–186.

Tarter, R.E. Psychological deficit in chronic alcoholics: A preview. *International Journal of the Addictions*, 1975, *10*, 327–368.

Terman, L.M. A symposium. Intelligence and its measurement. *Journal of Educational Psychology*, 1921, *12*, 127–133.

Teuber, H.L. Space perception and its disturbances after brain injury in man. *Neuropsychologia*, 1963, *1*, 47–53.

Teuber, H.L. The riddle of frontal lobe function in man. In J.M. Warren & K. Akert (Eds.), *The frontal granular cortex and behavior.* New York: McGraw-Hill, 1964.

Todd, J., Coolridge, F., & Satz, P. The Wechsler Adult Intelligence Scale Index: A neuropsychological evaluation. *Journal of Consulting and Clinical Psychology*, 1977, *56*, 450–454.

Trexler, L. *Cognitive rehabilitation: Conceptualization and intervention.* New York: Plenum Press, 1982.

Tsushima, W.T., & Wedding, D. A comparison of the Halstead–Reitan Neuropsychological Battery and Computerized Tomography in the identification of brain disorders. *Journal of Nervous and Mental Disease*, 1979, *167*, 704–707.

Tucker, D.M.,. Sheaner, S.L., & Murray, J.D. Hemispheric specialization and cognitive behavior therapy. *Cognitive Therapy and Research*, 1977, *1*, 263–273.

Tuerk, L., Fish, I., & Ransohoff, J. Head injury. In S. Arieti (chief Ed.), *American handbook of psychiatry*, (2nd ed., Vol. 4). New York: Basic Books, 1975.

Turner, S.M., Hersen, M., & Bellack, A.S. Social skills training to teach pro-social behavior in an organically impaired and retarded patient. *Journal of Behavior Therapy and Experimental Psychiatry*, 1978, *9*, 253–258.

Vaughan, H.G., & Costa, L.D. Performance of patients with lateralized cerebral lesions II: Sensory and motor tests. *Journal of Nervous and Mental Disease*, 1962, *134*, 237–243.

Vega, A., & Parsons, O.A. Cross-validation of the Halstead–Reitan tests for brain damage. *Journal of Consulting Psychology*, 1967, *31*, 619–625.

von Monakow, C. *Die lokalisation im grosshirnrinde und der uabbau der funktion durch korticale.* Wiesbaden, FRG: J.F. Bergmann, 1914.

Wall, P.D. Mechanisms of plasticity of connection following change in mammalism nervous systems. In P. Bach-y-Rita (Ed.), *Recovery of function: Theoretical consultation for brain injury rehabilitation.* Baltimore: University Park Press, 1980.

Wall, P.D., & Werner, R. Physiology and anatomy of long ranging afferent fiber within the spinal cord. *Journal of Physiology*, 1976, *255*, 321–334.

Walsh, K.W. *Neuropsychology: A clinical approach.* New York: Churchill Livingston, 1978.

Ward, A.A., Jr., & Kennard, M.A. Effect of cholinergic drugs on recovery of function following lesions of the central nervous system. *Yale Journal of Biological Medicine*, 1942, *15*, 189–229.

Watson, C.G. Separation of brain damaged from schizophrenic patients by Reitan–Haltead Pattern analysis: An unsuccessful replication. *Psychological Reports*, 1971, *29*, 1343–1346. (a)

Watson, C.G. An MMPI scale to separate brain damaged from schizophrenic men. *Journal of Consulting and Clinical Psychology*, 1971, *36*, 121–125. (b)

Watson, C.G., & Plemel, D. An MMPI scale to separate brain-damaged from functional psychiatric patients in neuropsychiatric settings. *Journal of Consulting and Clinical Psychology*, 1978, *46*, 1127–1132.

Watson, C.G., Thomas, R.W., Anderson, D., & Felling, J. Differentiation of organics from schizophrenics at two chronicity levels by use of the Reitan–Halstead Organic Test Battery. *Journal of Consulting and Clinical Psychology*, 1968, *32*, 679–684.

Watson, C.W., & Kennard, M.A. The effect of anticonvulsant drugs on recovery of function following cerebral cortical lesions. *Journal of Neurophysiology*, 1945, *8*, 221–231.

Watson, J.B. Psychology as the behaviorist views it. *Psychological Review*, 1913, *20*, 158–177.

Webster, J.S., & Dostrow, V. Efficacy of a decision-free approach to the Luria–Nebraska Neuropsychological Battery. *Journal of Consulting and Clinical Psychology*, 1982, *50*, 313–315.

Wechsler, D. *The measurements and appraisal of adult intelligence*, (3rd ed.). Baltimore: Williams & Wilkins, 1944.

Wechsler, D. *The measurement and appraisal of adult intelligence*, (4th ed.). Baltimore: Williams & Wilkins, 1958.

Wechsler, D. *Wechsler Intelligence Scale for Children—Revised.* New York: Psychological Corporation, 1981.

Wedding, D. Clinical and statistical prediction in neuropsychology. *Clinical Neuropsychology*, in press.

Wedding, D., & Gudeman, H. Implications of computerized axial tomography for clinical neuropsychology. *Professional Psychology*, 1980, *11*, 32–35.

Weidelberg, E., & Stein, D.G. Functional recovery after lesions of the central nervous system. *Neurosciences Research Program Bulletin*, 1974, *12*, 191–303.

Weinberg, J., Diller, L., Gordon, W.A., Gerstman, L.J., Liebeman, A., Lakin, P., Hodges, G., & Eqrachi, O. Training sensory awareness and spatial organization in people with right brain damage. *Archives of Physical Medicine and Rehabilitation*, 1979, *60*, 460–477. (a)

Weinberg, J., Diller, L., Gordon, W.A., Gerstman, L.J., Liebman, A., Lakin, P., Hodges, G., & Eqrachi, O. Visual scanning training on reading-related tasks in acquired right brain damage. *Archives of Physical Medicine and Rehabilitation*, 1979, *58*, 480–486. (b)

Weinberger, D.R., Torrey, E.F., Neophytides, A.N., & Wyatt, R.J. Lateral cerebral ventricular enlargement in chronic schizophrenia. *Archives of General Psychiatry*, 1977, *36*, 735–739.

Wheeler, L.E., & Reitan, R.M. Discriminant functions applied to the problems of predicting cerebral damage from behavior tests: A cross validation study. *Perceptual and Motor Skills*, 1963, *16*, 681–701.

Wheeler, L.E. Complex behavioral indices weighted by linear discriminant function for the prediction of cerebral damage. *Perceptual and Motor Skills*, 1964, *19*, 907–923.

Wheeler, L.E., Burke, C., & Reitan, R.M. An application of discriminant functions to the problem of predicting brain damage using behavioral variables. *Perceptual and Motor Skills*, 1963, *16*, 417–440.

Wheeler, L.E., & Reitan, R.M. Presence and laterality of brain damage predicted from responses to a short aphasia screening test. *Perceptual and Motor Skills*, 1962, *15*, 783–799.

Wheeler, L.E., & Reitan, R.M. Discriminant functions applied to the problems of predicting cerebral damage from behavior tests: A cross validation study. *Perceptual and Motor Skills*, 1963, *16*, 681–701.

Wiggins, J.S. Substantive dimensions of self-report in the MMPI item pool. *Psychological Monographs*, 1966, *80*, Whole #630.

William, O. Man's temporal lobe. *Brain*, 1968, *91*, 639–651.

Williams, P.L., & Warwick, R. *Functional neuroanatomy of man.* Philadelphia: W.B. Saunders, 1975.

Wilson, G.T. On the much discussed nature of the term behavior therapy. *Behavior Therapy*, 1978, *9*, 89–98.

Wolpe, J. *Psychotherapy by reciprocal inhibition.* Stanford, Calif.: Stanford University Press, 1958.

Wolpe, J. Behavior therapy and its malcontents. I. Denial of its bases and psychodynamic fusinism. *Journal of Behavior Therapy and Experimental Psychiatry*, 1976, *7*, 1–5. (a)

Wolpe, J. Behavior therapy and its malcontents. II. Multimodel electicism, cognitive exclusivism and "exposure" empiricism. *Journal of Behavior Therapy and Experimental Psychiatry*, 1976, *7*, 109–116. (b)

Wolpe, J. Cognition and causation in human behavior and its therapy. *American Psychologist*, 1978, *33*, 437–446.

Zelazowski, R., Golden, C.J., Graber, B.B., Lose, I.L., Moses, J.A., Jr., Zatz, L.M., Stahl, S.M., Osmon, D.C., & Pfefferberm, A. The relationship of cerebralventricular size to impairment of the Luria–Nebraska Neuropsychological Battery in chronic alcoholics. *Journal of Studies on Alcohol*, in press.

Zimmerman, S.F., Whitmyer, J.W., & Fields, R.F. Factor analytic structure of the Wechsler Adult Intelligence Scale in patients with diffuse and lateralized cerebral dysfunction. *Journal of Clinical Psychology*, 1970, *26*, 462–465.

A

SUGGESTED GUIDELINES FOR
NEUROPSYCHOLOGY REFERRALS

In order to maximize the effectiveness of the staff neuropsychologist, the following referral suggestions are offered. Since there are a relatively large number of patients, a *conservative* approach to neuropsychology referrals would be appreciated. Providing high-quality services to those patients with clearly specificable needs is the preferred strategy.

GENERAL CONSIDERATIONS

1. Please remember that a distinction should be made between those requests appropriate for neurology and those appropriate for neuropsychology. When the question is one of an acute neuropathological disorder (e.g., neoplasm or cerebrovascular disorder), the consultation should *always* go to neurology. The neurologist, if necessary, may request a neuropsychology consultation. The area of expertise of the neuropsychologist is brain–behavior relationships. Questions with regard to the psychological effects of brain damage are most appropriate for neuropsychology.

2. Neuropsychology consultations are expensive in terms of both finances and professional time, since many hours of testing are involved. The generation of valid and reliable neuropsychological data is a time-consuming task and should be reserved for those cases where a clear contribution to patient care can be made.

3. Please remember that requests for neuropsychology consultations should be problem oriented. Vague requests such as "neuropsychological testing" or "evaluation please" should be avoided. It is ideal for the request to contain all important elements of a specific question or problem.

TYPES OF CONSULTATIONS

1. *Neuropsychological assessment.* These consultations would be most appropriate where a question of subtle cerebral dysfunction remained after negative brain scan, EEG, and so forth, or where psychological factors interact with a chronic neurological condition.

2. *Prognosis.* Neuropsychological testing can be useful in examining the effects of treatments affecting brain functioning and also in estimating the degree of recovery a patient is likely to show. This information can be helpful in counseling the patient and his or her family as well as in allocating limited rehabilitation resources.

3. *Behavioral neuropsychology.* In cases where a known OBS patient displays maladaptive behavior, the formulation of a cogent plan of therapeutic intervention and its skillful implementation can often be facilitated by an analysis of behavior deficits implicating impairment of higher cortical functioning. Specific suggestions for behavioral management can be generated from neuropsychological test data.

CONCLUSION

Your assistance in maximizing the clinical effectiveness of the staff neuropsychologist will be much appreciated.

B

Job Description for Clinical/Behavioral Neuropsychologists: Task Elements

Assessment

1. Make initial contact with the referred patient to obtain behavioral data in order to devise a tentative impression and to estimate probable needs for detailed psychometric evaluation using medical records, interviewing techniques, and brief screening tests (Mental Status Exam, Short Portable Mental Status Questionnaire, selected items from the Reitan–Indiana Aphasia Screening Test).

2. Take the case history by reviewing medical records and interviews with the patient, family and friends in order to summarize relevant medical, social, educational, vocational, avocational, and emotional variables of the patient's history using a standardized recording form (the neuropsychology screening questionnaire, the life history questionnaire, the Horton–Martinsburg mental status exam, the biomedical questionnaire, the Life-Style questionnaire, etc.). Knowledge of normal developmental patterns (medical, social, educational, vocational, avocational, and emotional), knowledge of psychopathology, medical disease processes, and deviant subcultures, and professional judgment gained through formal education and clinical experience are required.

3. Perform diagnostic evaluation of the patient's neuropsychological and behavioral functioning (motor, rhythm, tactile, visual, language, spatial relations, reading, writing, spelling, arithmetic, memory, intellectual and psychomotor abilities) in order to produce behavior data using visual (printed forms, gesture, objects, pictures, writing), auditory (live recorded), tactual (form boards, symbols traced on skin, objects, touch), and kinesthetic (movement of body parts, psychomotor tasks, pegboard, dynometer) stimuli manipulated

in contact with the patient as well as behavioral observations of the patient's functioning in selected settings.

4.   Record and score behavioral data produced by manipulation of visual, auditory, tactual, and kinesthetic stimuli in contact with the patient as well as behavior observations in order to produce raw data scores using standardized and informal recording forms (Halstead–Reitan Neuropsychological Battery, Minnesota Multiphasic Personality Inventory , Luria–Nebraska Neuropsychological Battery, Michigan Neuropsychological Battery, Rorschach Personality Test, and Rotter Incomplete Sentences) plus a variety of other clinical neuropsychology batteries composed to meet the unique needs of the patients and clinical profession judgment of normal, borderline, and impaired intellectual, personality behavior and neuropsychological functioning gained through formal education and clinical, counseling, and neuropsychological experience.

5.   Analyze and synthesize scores of data obtained from neuropsychological testing in order to integrate test findings into a coherent picture using knowledge of neuropathology (neoplasms, CVA, head trauma, MS, etc.) and psychopathology (depression, alcoholism, schizophrenia, etc.). Knowledge of the neuropsychological tests used, neuroanatomy and brain–behavior relationships, and formal education and clinical experience are required.

6.   Write a consultation report in order to describe the cognitive, neuropsychological, personality and behavioral functioning of the referred patient in terms of diagnosis, prognosis, treatment plan, recommendations for behavior management, patient education, vocational rehabilitation and placement using subjective and objective assessment tools, knowledge of diagnostic categories, prognostic variables, treatment parameters, behavior management, spatial suitabilities and requirements for patient education, vocational rehabilitation and placement, and etiological factors.

7.   Interpret diagnostic test results to other patient care team members in order to formulate patient treatment goals by participating in multidisciplinary team meetings using knowledge of normal behavior, personality theory and psychological and neuropsychological testing as well as personality assessment methods (MMPI, Rorschach, Behavioral Assessment, etc.).

THERAPY

1.   Provide patients with individual therapy in order that they may achieve more socially adaptable behavior patterns by using clinically accepted methods and procedures of interpersonal influence.

2.   Provide patients with group psychotherapy in order to assist them in developing adequate coping mechanisms that will improve their behavior by utilizing clinical skills based on knowledge of professionally sound ethical treatment modalities. This will be done using group dynamics and advanced group therapy skills gained through graduate and postdoctoral training and experience.

3.   Provide vocational rehabilitation counseling services to patients in order to develop appropriate goals commensurate with their attitudes, interests, and abilities by using interview, behavioral data, and psychometric devices such as personality, aptitude, career assessment and ability tests. Inferences generated from test data will be based on knowledge of complex diagnostic and treatment problems that was gained through graduate and postdoctoral training and experience.

4.   Provide patients with behavior therapy in order to teach them to eliminate unadaptive patterns of anxiety, learn adaptive behavioral skills and decrease antisocial behavior patterns using professionally accepted behavior therapy methods (instructions, modeling, desensitization, participant modeling, rational restructuring, imagery, covert sensitization, thought-stopping, positive reinforcement, response–cost procedures, self-monitoring, token economy, cognitive modeling, etc.), standardized and informal behavioral raters, and professional judgment gained through graduate and postdoctoral training and experience.

CONSULTATION

1.   Advise other patient care team members of accepted treatment modalities to be implemented in order to treat complex atypical problems that arise due to severe multihandicaps caused by psychological, neuropsychological, social and vocational maladjustments of long duration using acquired diagnostic and treatment skills and knowledge.

2.   Provide consultation to other psychology staff members in order to treat atypical treatment problems that arise concerning brain-damaged patients by using clinical skills and specialized knowledge of neuropsychology and clinical behavior therapy.

3.   Instruct other multidisciplinary health care staff members in neuropsychological theories, techniques (brain–behavior relationships, neuropsychological testing, and behavior modification) in order to promote smooth operation of the service and enhance present skills by lectures, seminars, workshops and/or demonstrations.

4. Schedule and conduct conferences with the patient's family members to discuss intellectual, neuropsychological behavioral, social, emotional, vocational, and personality problems, to provide emotional support, to familiarize facing change and to assist in the coordination of multidisciplinary care as needs arise using relevant handouts, clinical records, audiovisual materials, knowledge of normal and abnormal developmental patterns, awareness of intellectual, neuropsychological, behavior, social, emotional, vocational, and personality problems, brain–behavior relationships, counseling and psychotherapy techniques, group dynamics, and family therapy theory and skills all according with professional ethical principles, hospital procedures, and federal and state regulations.

5. Handling correspondence pertaining to patients in order to produce prompt notification of scheduled appointments, detailed history of previous therapy and evaluations, documents requested by outside agencies and correspondence from the patient that he/she could not produce or request by themselves.

RESEARCH

1. Investigate clinical problem areas (brain–behavior relationships, parameters of neuropsychological testing, personality, relationship of brain damage and behavior modification strategies). Describe, understand, and evaluate the relationship between variables and trace out causal sequences by using accepted research methods to properly design, collect, analyze, and report data.

ADMINISTRATION

1. Compare statistical information on patients to provide the information necessary to adequately allocate resources.

2. Conduct and monitor a hospital-wide neuropsychological laboratory, in order to provide patients with extremely complex neuropsychological and personality delineation of their cognitive abilities, adaptive capacities, and personality functioning.

3. Direct the word of psychology assistants in order that they perform their duties of assessing and treating the intellectual, neuropsychological, and personality abilities of patients. Use standardization and informal psychological/neuropsychological test and treatment forms, time sheets, and behavioral observations of the psychology assistant's work.

4. Maintain and upgrade test apparatus in the neuropsychology laboratory in order to maximize equipment lifetime and prevent breakage using instructional manuals and knowledge and experience gained through graduate and postdoctoral training and experiences.

EDUCATION/CONTINUING

Maintain knowledge of new research findings, equipment technology advances, and new techniques in administering treatment in order to provide state of the art neuropsychological, clinical, and counseling services by attending professional conventions, continuing education courses, and inservice training, and by reading relevant professional journals.

EDUCATION/TRAINING

1. Provide patients with information on the psychological aspects of their cognitive, emotional, and behavioral problems, in order to help them understand the complexity of their impairments by using lectures, visual materials, training exercises, and knowledge of goal attainment skills.

2. Provide supervision to clinical/counseling psychology practicum and internship students in order to increase and expand their level of clinical/counseling psychology competence through the use of demonstration, practice, and positive feedback using clinical/counseling and supervision skills.

3. Participate in hospital-sponsored administration of patient care programs in order to keep abreast of changing procedures, patient care technology, and new developments in areas of professional concern.

Name Index

SUBJECT INDEX

Communications
Deregulation

The Unleashing of America's Communications Industry

JEREMY TUNSTALL

Basil Blackwell

First published 1986

Basil Blackwell Ltd
108 Cowley Road, Oxford OX4 1JF, UK

Basil Blackwell Inc.
432 Park Avenue South, Suite 1505,
New York, NY 10016, USA

British Library Cataloguing in Publication Data

Tunstall, Jeremy
  Communications deregulation
  1. Communication and traffic——United States
  I. Title
  380.3'0973 HE203

  ISBN 0–631–14819–1

Library of Congress Cataloging in Publication Data

Tunstall, Jeremy.
  Communications deregulation.
  Bibliography: p.
  Includes index.
  1. Telecommunication—Law and legislation—United States. 2. Telecommunication policy—United States.
  I. Title.
  KF2765.T86   1986   343.73'0994   85–22983
  ISBN 0–631–14819–1   347.303994

Typeset by Photo-Graphics, Honiton, Devon
Printed in Great Britain by TJ Press Ltd, Padstow

Contents

PART V THE DEREGULATORY SHAKEOUT: EXPORTS, COMPETITION,
                LOCALISM, NEWS, POLICY

Acknowledgements

My thanks are due to City University for granting me sabbatical leave, and to the Economic and Social Research Council for granting me money to spend academic year 1983–4 in Washington DC. At George Washington University, four blocks from the White House, Christopher Sterling was the perfect academic host; as author, editor, former FCC employee, communications historian and proprietor of both *Communications Booknotes* and the Sterling Library, Chris is uniquely qualified to guide an ignorant foreigner. He provided invaluable advice and support in a congenial setting, and introduced me to such fresh delights as the Yellow Peril. He also read this book in very rough draft and reduced the errors of fact and interpretation by several hundred. Needless to say, however, the eccentric opinions are my responsibility, not his.

In Washington, Muriel and Joel Cantor were extremely generous with hospitality and manuscript advice. Jill Kasle, Paul Modic and Ellen Sterling were all consistently supportive.

Kurt and Gladys Lang swapped houses and allowed us to spend six happy summer weeks by the water's edge in Stonybrook, Long Island. Jackie McNally in La Jolla was also wonderfully generous, as were Diana and Rob Livesey in Columbus, Ohio.

In Washington, Leo Mondale and in London, Malcolm Brynin provided diligent and highly qualified assistance. This book was also read in manuscript by Chris Goodall, John Howkins, Wick Rowland, Dan Schiller and Colin Seymour-Ure. Few authors can have had the support of such an illustrious team of readers, and few manuscripts can have been more in need of such assistance.

My thanks go also to faculty and students at American University, Ball State, Carleton, Houston, Iowa, Illinois, McGill, Minnesota, MIT and Ohio State, upon whom some of these ideas were pretested.

Nearly a hundred busy people – mainly in Washington – agreed to be 'interviewed'; they almost all talked with considerable frankness and at some length. They represent the communications policy professionals of

Washington, an occupational community whose professional expertise has no equivalent elsewhere: Joseph Alegrett, Fritz Attaway, Richard Aurelio, David Aylward, Peter Barton, Dick Baxter, Robert Beecham, Marcie Behr, Jim Bouras, Les Brown, Martin Casey, Ward Chamberlin, Tom Cohen, Kathleen Criner, Roy Danish, Mimi Dawson, John Deviney, Lawrence DeVore, James Duffy, John Evans, Louis Frey, Edward Fritts, Joe Flaherty, Henry Geller, John Giles, Donald Graham, Susan Greene, Olga Grkavac, Robert Hadl, Paul Harris, William Harris, Annette Howe, Lucy Hummer, Martin Jacobs, John Kamp, Charles Kern, Jim Kilpatrick, Charles Kirudja, George Kohl, Erwin Krasnow, David Leach, Ken Leeson, Richard Levine, Bob Lewis, James McElveen, William McGowan, Frank Magid, Terry Maguire, Richard Mahler, Mary Jo Manning, Ron Martin, Mike Michaelson, Art Murphy, Fred Paine, Joseph Pelton, Robert Pepper, Dan Phythyon, Karen Possner, James Poteat, James Quello, Scott Rafferty, Carl Reber, Henry Rivera, John Rohrbeck, Bruce Russell, Anthony Rutkowski, John Saeman, Stewart Schley, Andrew Schwartzman, Lawrence Secrest, Chip Shooshan, Richard Simmons, Wallace Snyder, Richard Straus, Leonard Sussman, Eric Taub, Stephen Thompson, Donald Till, Lionel Van Deerlin, Donald Van Lenten, Christopher Vizas, Abbott Washburn, Fred Wertheimer, Don West, Reginald Westlake, Ronald Wheatley and Ward White.

Last, but not least, my thanks to Ruth Newton for typing so well from my worsening handwriting and to the exceptionally helpful staff of City University Library.

Abbreviations

ABC	American Broadcasting Corporation
ADAPSO	Association of Data Processing Service Organizations
ADI	Areas of Dominant Influence
AFP	Agence France Presse
ANIK	Canadian Communication Satellite ('Brother' in Eskimo)
ANPA	American Newspaper Publishers' Association
AP	Associated Press
AT	Advanced Technology
AT&T	American Telephone and Telegraph Company
ATC	American TV and Communications
BBC	British Broadcasting Corporation
BET	Black Entertainment Channel
BOC	Bell Operating Company
BUNCH	Burroughs, Univac, NCR, Control Data, and Honeywell. (The five non-IBM main frame companies)
CATV	Community Antenna Television
CBEMA	Computer and Business Equipment Manufacturers
CBN	Christian Broadcasting Network
CBS	Columbia Broadcasting System
CIA	Central Intelligence Agency
CNN	Cable News Network
COMSAT	Communications Satellite Corporation
CPE	Customer Premises Equipment
C-SPAN	Cable Satellite Public Affairs Network
CWA	Communications Workers of America
DBS	Direct Broadcasting by Satellite
DBSC	Direct Broadcast Satellite Corporation
DEC	Digital Equipment Corporation
DITI	Department of International Trade and Industry (proposed)
DOD	Department of Defense
ECOM	Electronic Computer Originated Mail
EDS	Electronic Data Systems
EEC	European Economic Community

EEOC	Equal Employment Opportunity Commission
EFT	Electronic Funds Transfer
EPA	Environmental Protection Agency
ESPN	Entertainment and Sports Programming Network
FCC	Federal Communications Commission
FDIC	Federal Deposit Insurance Corporation
FNN	Financial News Network
FTC	Federal Trade Commission
GAO	General Accounting Office
GE	General Electric
GM	General Motors
GTE	General Telephone
HBO	Home Box Office
HDTV	High Definition TV
IBM	International Business Machines
INMARSAT	International Maritime Satellite Organization
INTELSAT	International Telecommunications Satellite Organization
ISDN	Integrated Services Digital Network
ITT	International Telephone and Telegraph
ITU	International Telecommunications Union
JOA	Joint Operating Agreement
LAN	Local Area Network
LPTV	Low Power TV
MAC	Multiplexed Analogue Components
MCI	Microwave Communications Inc
MDS	Multipoint Distribution Service
MGM	Metro Goldwyn Mayer
MIT	Massachusetts Institute of Technology
MITI	Ministry of International Trade and Industry (Japan)
MMDS	Multichannel multipoint distribution service
MPAA	Motion Picture Association of America
MPEA	Motion Pictures Export Association
MSO	Multiple System Operator
NAB	National Association of Broadcasters
NARUC	National Association of Regulatory Utility Commissioners
NASA	National Aeronautics and Space Administration
NBC	National Broadcasting Company
NCR	National Cash Register
NCTA	National Cable TV Association
NEC	Nippon Electric Company
NRBA	National Radio Broadcasters' Association
NSA	National Security Agency
NTIA	National Telecommunications and Information Administration

NTT	Nippon Telephone and Telegraph
OECD	Organisation for Economic Cooperation and Development
OMB	Office of Management and Budget
OSHA	Occupational Safety and Health Administration
OTP	Office of Telecommunications Policy
PAC	Political Action Committee
PBS	Public Broadcasting Service
PBX	Private Branch Exchange
PPV	Pay per view
PTT	Postal, Telegraph and Telephone Authority
PUC	Public Utility Commission
RARC	Regional Administrative Radio Conference
RCA	Radio Corporation of America
SBS	Satellite Business Systems
SDI	Strategic Defense Initiative
SIG	Senior InterAgency Group
STC	Satellite TV Corporation
STV	Subscription TV
SMATV	Satellite-fed Master Antenna TV
TARPAC	TV and Radio Political Action Committee
TAT	Trans-Atlantic Telephone Cable
TCI	Telecommunications Inc.
TMC	The Movie Channel
UHF	Ultra high frequency
UN	United Nations
UNESCO	United Nations Educational, Scientific and Cultural Organization
UNIVAC	Universal Automatic Computer
UPI	United Press International
USCI	United Satellite Communications Inc.
USGPO	US Government Printing Office
USIA	United States Information Agency
VCR	Video cassette recorder
VHF	Very High Frequency
VOA	Voice of America
VSDA	Video Software Dealers Association
VSS	Video Satellite Systems
WARC	World Administrative Radio Conference
WIPO	World Intellectual Property Organization
WUI	Western Union International

For
Paul
Helena
Rebecca
Sylvia

PART I

Deregulation

1

Introduction

During the decade 1975–85, 'deregulation' came to be accepted by nearly everyone concerned with communications policy in the United States. But they all had their 'buts'. Some preferred other terms such as 'unregulation', and terms like 'prudent deregulation' were used by commercial interests, in favor of deregulation in general but hoping to secure a 'fair advantage' for their particular (in this case Hollywood) interests.

In communications policy 'deregulation' refers loosely to the repeal and rejection during the decade of 1975–85 of the regulations put into effect in the previous decade of 1965–75, largely during the Johnson and Nixon presidencies. Some of these regulations had been intended to get better television access for blacks and women. Deregulation also sought to protect the public interest by commercial competition, rather than by regulatory defense of the 'public interest'.

The pinnacle of deregulatory activity in communications perhaps occurred in January 1982, with two key decisions:

(1) *The divestiture of the old Bell/AT&T telephone company*. AT&T's vertical integration was removed by chopping off the local telephone systems (which served about 80 per cent of the US population) into what became seven new regional companies. AT&T was allowed to retain its dominant position in long-distance telephoning although in direct competition with such other long-distance companies as Microwave Communications Inc (MCI) and Sprint. AT&T was not free to expand from telephones into many aspects of data transmission and computers.

(2) *IBM*, the dominant computer company in both the US and the world, was released from a long-running antitrust case. Together with the entry of AT&T into computers, the IBM decision clearly signalled increasingly competitive conditions for all the lesser computer companies.

In addition to these two January 1982 decisions, deregulation made a major impact on other communications and mass media fields during 1975–85:

(3) *Space satellites* in 1975 were entering a period of radically reduced regulation, and this continued. In 1975 US space activities were still under the umbrella of NASA – a mixed military and civilian enterprise, but one strongly controlled by the federal government; by 1985 space had been opened up for commercial competition in telecommunications and television entertainment.

(4) *Cable television*, long held back as a potential threat to conventional television, experienced a rapid removal of constraints and explosive growth; Community Antenna Television (CATV) – a local system for boosting TV signals in areas of poor reception – was transformed into a national system of cable via satellite. In 1975 only one video satellite service was available; by 1985 this service, Home Box Office (HBO), had become a major force in Hollywood, and there were some 50 services – 'basic' and 'pay' – available via satellite to local cable operators. In 1974 about 13 per cent of US households had cable; by 1984 this had trebled to about 40 per cent. In late 1984 Congress passed deregulatory legislation which freed cable operators from nearly all constraints, and largely removed the threat of having their licenses rescinded.

(5) *Conventional radio* was somewhat similarly deregulated. Controls on content – such as minimum requirements for news and objectivity and maximum amounts of advertising and promotion – were removed; radio station managers now had almost no formal obligations, and de facto fairly secure tenure. Radio was positively encouraged to respond to commercial market forces and little else. During 1974–84 the number of licensed radio stations on the air in the US increased by 26 per cent to 9,577 in September 1984.

(6) *Conventional television* also experienced a major reduction in regulation, and the total removal of even self-regulation on maximum amounts of advertising. Licenses were extended from three to five years, and in practice became largely secure both from withdrawal and from expensive challenge. During 1974–84 the number of conventional TV stations also increased by 26 per cent to 1,180 local stations.

(7) *Low-power television*. By late 1984 some 300 new LPTV stations were on the air, with hundreds or thousands more to come. Similar to local translators or boosters, these are local stations operating within a small radius with a small audience, which are entirely free to explore the programming possibilities of local neighborhood television.

The decade 1975–85 saw the birth of numerous other novel services, in radio and television, in telecommunications, and in mixed areas. Two of the most dramatic are *direct broadcasting by satellite* (DBS) and *cellular mobile radio*, the first really effective and widespread car telephone system. We will consider these and other innovations later, but the important point here is that under deregulation new services and new technologies are encouraged; the general approach is to get new technologies out of the laboratory and into the marketplace as fast as possible. *New technologies in private hands are to be encouraged and regarded as innocent until proved guilty*; old, more cautious regulatory attitudes – with prime attention devoted to protecting existing services and technologies – have been rejected.

The free marketplace approach to new technologies even includes technical standards. Deregulation extends to not specifying official standards for new technologies, especially if the regulators think that official standards will impede market forces.

While there has been much fierce commercial and political infighting over deregulatory details whose financial implications often run into billions of dollars, there has also been a wider consensus gradually changing over the 1975–85 decade, one broadly shared by Republicans and Democrats, Congress and the courts. The main regulatory agencies in this area – the Federal Communications Commission (FCC) and the Federal Trade Commission (FTC) – have both, since around the mid-1970s, seen themselves as in the business of reducing the number of rules and regulations, and cutting back on red tape.

Some other broad assumptions are involved in this loose consensus:

(1) It is widely assumed that the 'electronics revolution' has made many former boundaries irrelevant. For example, old rules which kept the telephone companies out of selling computers and computing services are generally regarded as no longer viable, because modern telephone systems are built around computer switching systems. Similarly, satellites are, via cable, part of the mass media. Telecommunications can handle voice, video and data. It is thus widely agreed that communications is moving toward one huge 'playing field'.

(2) With these boundaries dissolved, it is also assumed that *antitrust constraints* must be relaxed; and, if bottlenecks of monopoly exist, the preferred procedure for removing them is by competition rather than regulation. A wave of mergers and acquisitions, such as happened in 1983–5, is a sign of market forces healthily at work.

(3) Similarly, it is believed that companies must be allowed to diversify into what once were separate fields but are no longer. Joint ventures and consortia are also necessary so that companies can share resources and technological expertise.

(4) *Competition has become international.* The giant playing field is not only nationwide but worldwide. Deregulatory orthodoxy has assumed that the best way to handle Japanese and West European protectionism is via competition in an open world marketplace.

2

Deregulation is Politicization

Deregulation does not take communications out of politics. On the contrary, to deregulate communications is to move it out of the government bureaucracy of regulation and throw it into the twin marketplaces of commerce and politics. The giant new communications field is a political field.

Having fewer rules is not the same as having no rules at all. The significance of the rules that remain is all the greater. But the abolition of some rules also makes the surviving rules seem more ambiguous and more vulnerable to alteration or abolition.

The consensus in US communications policy does not exist without tension. Indeed, the consensus is the current net result of current conflict. Alongside a loose consensus, there is commercial and ideological conflict of quite remarkable bitterness. Communications policy is fragmented between many Washington government agencies and commercial lobbies. Much of the conflict is within particular branches of government, within the Republican party, or within, for example, the broadcasting lobby.

Communications in many respects has become politics, and politics has become communications. Therefore communications policy is every bit as contentious, all-encompassing, obscure and fast-changing as US federal politics itself.

Communications deregulation had no neat beginning, and is unlikely to have a neat end. This study focuses primarily on the decade 1975–85, and in particular on the years of the first Reagan presidential term, January 1981 to January 1985.

TECHNOLOGY: TWO DECADES FORWARD/REGULATION:
TWO DECADES BACK

The communications revolution has two major dimensions – technology and regulation – but an infinity of details, regulations, markets and time-frames. There is the world electronics market, measured in hundreds of billions of dollars; but there are 'niche markets' for a thousand specialized products and services. Depending upon where one's gaze is directed, one can see either chaotic and massive change or not very much happening at all.

There are big changes for business users of telecommunications: some multinational banking or oil enterprises have advanced international, but intra-company, specially designed communications networks. But many private consumers have seen only relatively minor change. In 1984–5 the typical US family could still choose between only about 10 television channels, the same number that had been available to citizens of New York and Los Angeles for 20 years. And despite all the hype, most citizens have little or no sense of a communications revolution in either their home or their place of work.

Nevertheless, the twin revolutions in technology and regulation are indeed revolutionary, especially if one takes them together. It is the combination of running technology on 'fast forward' while running regulation on 'fast backward' that has produced the radical change. Or the image can be altered slightly to 'two steps forward and two steps back'.

In terms of technology there was a rapid advance in what was coming onto the public market in 1975–85. The old convention of keeping new technologies waiting in the wings for a decade or two was dropped. Thus, two decades' worth of new technology was let loose in a single decade.

At the same time the regulatory apparatus was being put back, and not just one decade back. A great deal of the Johnson–Nixon era regulation was indeed deliberately abolished; but the intention was not simply to return to 1974 or 1975, but rather, to go back to earlier decades, before the era of 'natural monopoly' in telephones or 'public service' goals in broadcasting. Policymakers explicitly looked back to the more competitive and chaotic days of the early twentieth century, before a phone and a TV set in every US home became the established norm, before 'universal service' was the goal of Ma Bell, and before the era of television as an all-singing and all-informing medium.

THE US AND COMMUNICATIONS AS NUMERO UNO

Behind the loose deregulatory consensus lie the twin assumptions that communications is becoming the number one industry in the world, and that the traditional position of the US as numero uno in all aspects of electronics/telecommunications/video/entertainment/computers/information technology is being challenged. A central purpose is to maintain both communications and the US as number one.

Japan and Europe have also increasingly recognized these as fields of exceptional importance, but there are special reasons for the US to be concerned. Communications and electronic high technology play a more central role in the US's view of itself than is the case with any other nation. Electronics was one of the first modern industries in which the US achieved preeminence; and in the 1980s it is, along with aircraft/aerospace and agriculture, one of only a few strategic industrial spheres in which the US can still claim to be the unambiguous world leader. Naturally the US does not relish the prospect of becoming the food-supplier to a numero uno Japan Inc.

Huge defense expenditure in part explains US leadership in electronics and telecommunications, space and aircraft. But the defense connection is two-way. No other nation is as dependent on telecommunications for the effective operation of its defense forces. The US requires telecommunications to control not only its submarines, but also its land-based military forces in Asia and Europe. The US military forces are thus the world leaders in international, intra-organizational, communications networks.

US domestic government is also extremely dependent on modern communications. Such federal agencies as the Census Bureau have long been in the forefront of data processing, and today the whole US tax system, for example, is heavily computerized. The federal government is by far the world's largest computer customer.

The preeminence of the US economy in general, and of US banking and financial services in particular, is also the result of modern communications. Wall Street is no longer confined to New York City; the world is moving toward a single stock market more or less continuously in session during the 24 hours, in Tokyo, New York and London. But Wall Street remains the chief center, and, just as the world currency has become the dollar, so the market floors of the unified world financial markets are electronic data networks, which show identical dollar data on similar screens simultaneously around the world.

Mass communications is another field in which the US wishes to maintain its world leadership of nearly a century. The US has increasing competitive difficulties with the hardware side of mass media, but it still reigns supreme in software/programming/culture and imagery.

There is one further vital communications field in which the US hopes to retain preeminence. This is the field of communications policy – in other words, deregulation. Deregulation involves inevitable elements of crudity, but it is also a rather sophisticated policy within a policy. Deregulation, it is believed, will sharpen the US competitive edge in the home market; but it will also, it is hoped – and not without evidence – appeal to the Japanese and to West Europeans, who, having imported the policy, will then be more than previously amenable to buying US hardware and software.

BIG, MEDIUM AND SMALL: IBM AND SILICON VALLEY AS MODELS

The rationale behind the twin IBM/AT&T decisions of January 1982 was to release IBM from domestic antitrust anxieties and at the same time to send AT&T into the world market as the other US super-company. (AT&T, as a regulated natural monopoly, had until 1982 largely kept out of world markets.)

Kenichi Ohmae, a managing partner in McKinsey's Tokyo office, posits guidelines for multinational competition. He argues that, to compete effectively, multinationals, and especially 'high-tech' companies, must operate in the US, Japan and Western Europe, and must be 'insiders' in all three locations, involved in investment, research, marketing and lobbying.[1] This certainly sounds like a description of IBM.

But the US is admired in the computer industry not only for the Big Blue qualities of the mammoth bureaucratic IBM; it is also admired, feared and copied for the apparently quite different qualities of innovation, venture capitalism and risk-taking exhibited in the Silicon Valley area to the south of San Francisco. Just as there are 'plug-compatible' copies of IBM computers, so also other areas in the US and around the world have tried to reproduce innovative communications capitalism in silicon glens, forests and ski resorts.

We will return later (chapter 7) to this marriage of IBM and Silicon Valley, but two quick points will be made here. Such a marriage between New York and northern California has quite a long history even in computers, and a longer history still in the entertainment industry. Over 60 years ago southern California took on the outlandish and frenzied task of creativity while head offices in New York controlled Hollywood from afar. Further, the US seems to be moving in computers and communications to not two, but four, levels of enterprise: first, a truly massive company (such as IBM or AT&T); second and third, large-medium and small-medium companies, typically with sales between ten and one billion dollars; and fourth, small companies proliferating in Silicon Valley. This is an unstable kind of structure under a deregulatory regime; but its very tensions, while painful for many or most people and enterprises, may perhaps give Americans an advantage over the Japanese and West Europeans. This is a highly competitive and also highly political kind of industrial system, in which cries of 'shake-out' and 'monopoly' are endemic.

HIGH TECH AS MARKET ENTRANT, IDEOLOGY AND QUAGMIRE

'High tech' is as vague a term as 'information technology', 'communications revolution' or 'deregulation', and, like these others, it belongs to salesmanship rather than technology. But it accurately conveys the equally vague, but important, 'machismo' quality which pervades policy and politics in these areas. High tech is, of course, associated with such traditional machismo areas as aerospace and defense.

In the US, high tech is often bracketed with 'market entry'. Both have a quality of ideological purity, 'as American as apple pie', but more dynamic and more virtuous. High tech has overtones of frontier ingenuity and getting a man on the moon before the Soviet Union.

Market entry is the point at which the wicked idea of monopoly is subverted, no matter that some will assert monopoly also to be as American as apple pie. The imagery of some new and high technology forcing itself into a previously closed market is potent indeed; the result is widely referred to as 'technology-driven' change. The sloganeering element in this is acknowledged, because most people who use such terms admit that 'technologist-driven' or 'company-driven' are more accurate.

The marketplace also features prominently in deregulatory ideology. Usually the market is seen as unitary. But in fact, in the mass media there is a market for advertising as well as for sales. In many telecommunications fields there are two rather different markets – business users and domestic households. Finally, there is the political and regulatory marketplace, from which for most communications services a license to operate has to be extracted; and in still regulated services there are service and rate restrictions to be observed. Moreover, this political marketplace is itself split between two very different entities – the national political marketplace of the federal agencies and the equally complex local political marketplace of state, city and county agencies and public utility commissions (PUCs). Thus there are five or six possible markets, which when paired make for a still greater number of possibilities. '*The*' marketplace is an abstraction with a high quotient of ideology.

Behind the values of 'high-tech marketplace entry' lie several traditional components. One is the Protestant ethic of hard work, achievement and entrepreneurial success; many high-tech entrepreneurs fit quite closely the mold of the workaholic, eccentric entrepreneur, who often has exotic political views as well. For 'high tech', you can usually read 'non-union'. Like early Hollywood, which relied on cheap land and Mexican labor, Silicon Valley does not relish unions; nor does the Texas electronics industry in Dallas and Austin, Cable News Network (CNN) in Atlanta or MCI in Washington DC.

But the ideological weighting of High Tech may lead to dangerous quagmires. In practice, high tech may need to be split into high, middle and low versions. Is not the really big payoff only in the middle and lower levels of high tech? Did not the Japanese have their big initial success by taking the really high tech of the US and Europe and manufacturing it cheaply and at high volumes and quality?

The ambition to export the high variety of high tech may lead to financial success but may also lead to huge imports of 'lower' varieties. For example, the US exports advanced computers, but imports a consumer version of an old American invention, the video cassette recorder (VCR), by the millions (and running to billions of dollars all told).

High tech can thus be said to have its export politics; but it may also have another, less anticipated kind of politics – *import* politics – the inevitable use of political pressure to obtain import quotas and other protectionist measures.

REAGANOMICS APPLIED TO COMMUNICATIONS?

The Reagan administration and 'Reaganomics' have certainly contributed; but communications deregulation predates Reagan's inauguration in January 1981 by several years. Moreover, it was the Democratic administration of President Carter which, in the late 1970s, gave communications deregulation its major political momentum.

Nevertheless, deregulation in general, and communications deregulation in particular, have been key goals of the radical New Right. The New Right has used the old mechanisms of the Kennedy–Johnson Democrats, many of whose causes were once funded by the Ford Foundation. The New Right has demonstrated that anything the Democrats could once do, it can do better and bigger. The New Right has more millionaires and more foundations; moreover, in the 1970s it developed new ways of raising money – notably by massive computerized direct mailing operations, whose leading exponent was Richard Viguerie; these operations used the US mails to trawl for cash throughout the entire nation, but especially in the South and West.

One use of this money was to pay many New Right economists and consultants, who produced studies hostile to most regulatory activity. AT&T increasingly found itself confronted with academic research in economics which challenged the supposed benefits of regulated natural monopolies. The American Enterprise Institute, the Heritage Foundation, the Georgetown Center for Strategic and International Studies and the Hoover Institution at Stanford were only a few of the scores of right-wing think tanks.[2] Recently, American academic political science – even more than economics – appears to have absorbed massive funding from these conservative sources, which have also spent heavily on publicizing their findings.

John S. Saloma III, in *Ominous Politics* (written in 1982–3), saw a coordinated 'labyrinth' of New Right groups subverting the Republican party with their money and ideological militancy. He pointed to links between right-wing academics, conservative think tanks and foundations, radical Political Action Committees (PACs), conservative television ministers, the Republican party in Congress, right-wing Democrats, some prominent black conservatives and conservative public-interest law firms. The extent and significance of such ties and coordination can inevitably be disputed.

Two interconnected aspects of the New Right, however, are especially significant for communications deregulation. One is that American business has geared itself up much more systematically in the last decade to influence politics, both via direct lobbying of politicians by chief executive officers and by such indirect routes as the mass media and PACs. The second is that the New Right, believing the media in the past to have been leftist, oppositionist and concerned with 'bad news values', has targeted the mass media as a key territory to be conquered, second only to direct political power itself.

The US Chamber of Commerce has predictably close ties with the Reagan administration, and many business PACs support the same politicians as the Chamber's PAC. The US Chamber of Commerce is also active in Cable television news, putting out its own pro-business 'Biznet' breakfast news show. Biznet's satellite facility was used by President Reagan in the 1982 election season for fund-raising speeches to groups of Republican businessmen across the country.

Numerous conservative, subsidized weeklies and monthlies now crowd the magazine racks. There has been funding for new right-wing student publications at major universities; several conservative media organizations, such as 'Accuracy in Media' and the Media Institute, are dedicated to exposing and opposing the supposed left-wing bias of the press and the TV networks. And a majority of the more widely syndicated newspaper columnists belong to the political right.[3] That these columnists are widely syndicated is largely, no doubt, due to public demand; but the preferences of conservative publishers can hardly be discounted.

Communications deregulation was launched not by the Republican right, but mainly by centrists and Democrats. However, it was seized upon with special zest by the radical Right, by the Reagan administration, and by those who saw it as a means of shifting both mass media and telecommunications to the political right.

MA BELL IS DEAD. LONG LIVE USA INC

Americans are fond of referring to 'Japan Inc', the alliance of large Japanese companies with the Ministry of International Trade (MITI); the US, of course, has nothing similar, so it is said. But, especially seen from another continent, there appears to be something that well deserves the name 'USA Inc' – a looser, more informal grouping than the Japanese version, but not necessarily any less effective.

Ma Bell/AT&T was always regarded by foreign state-owned telecommunications authorities as the nearest thing to an American Postal Telegraph & Telephone Authority (PTT). Thus AT&T has long dominated American delegations at Geneva involved in setting international standards. The divested AT&T is becoming much stronger *internationally* than it was before 1982. IBM has already been setting world computer standards for some years; and the two US news agencies have together given the world flow of news an American-accented version of objectivity.

Together with the US Department of Defense (DOD) and NASA, AT&T and IBM provide a huge reservoir of communications management talent. Many careers move between these organizations and out into other vital areas. For example, the Communications Satellite Corporation (COMSAT) has been heavily populated with executives of the Defense communications world. As NASA was cut back in the 1970s, its personnel moved into other key organizations, including the FCC, spreading space expertise more widely through USA Inc. Similarly, former IBM executives are to be found everywhere in communications, as well as in US business more widely.

NASA, AT&T, IBM and a few other large organizations have provided the US with an elite of communications executives who broadly share the deregulatory consensus. USA Inc appears to give the US many advantages in the depth, breadth and continuity of its combined business and technical expertise. But there may also be some disadvantages, such as that USA Inc, while a high-quality performer, also tends toward high prices. Low price was never a prime objective of the DOD; NASA did not get to the moon before 1970 by always insisting on the cheapest possible solution; AT&T was hardly encouraged to be a low-cost enterprise overall – its rates were regulated on a 'cost plus profit' basis, and the fulsomeness of its services was legendary. Nor was IBM a miserly operation; its systems claimed to be the most reliable, not the cheapest.

Some rivals – for example, MCI in long-distance competition with AT&T – showed that the job could be done much more cheaply. But the big battalions are still in a dominant position, and they may have evolved a USA Inc whose costs and prices are dangerously high.

CONGRESS IN CRISIS: COMMUNICATIONS, COMPUTERS, COMMERCIALIZATION

Not only is communications being further politicized under deregulation; politics itself is becoming more meshed into communications – both Congress itself and elections are now heavily computerized. Moreover, members of Congress from all political quarters acknowledge that campaign finance reforms have resulted in a Congress awash in PAC and other lobbying funds; some members of Congress freely admit that the raising of election funds has become their dominant concern, and that the public interest has declined as a motivating factor.[4]

Congress has become a bureaucracy with some 20,000 employees. Each member of the House has at least one staff member devoted to publicity, and a senator from a large state will have several. Including PR people attached to committees and subcommittees, there must be well over a thousand people on Capitol Hill pumping out material to the media; if free mailing activities are included, the publicity staff is much bigger. And of course the reason for members of the Senate and the House being obsessed with money is that money buys publicity.

Press, radio, television and direct mailing all come in both free and paid versions. In addition to printed releases for the press, there are electronic media releases in the form of tame interviews recorded within the premises of Congress and supplied free to stations back home. And members have the 'franking privilege', which allows incumbents to write direct to all their voters. The same facilities are used in paid versions, and again incumbents have a huge advantage because they find it much easier to raise money.

The two most expensive forms of paid publicity are computerized direct mail and paid advertising on television and radio. The ever increasing emphasis on these two items places politicians close to the core of the communications revolution. For both publicity and information, for both video and data, politics is becoming 'on-screen' activity.

Election spending is one of those numerous communications-related activities which is growing much faster than GNP and inflation combined. The first billion-dollar election was in 1980; the non-presidential elections of 1982 cost $1.2 billion.[5] Another big increase was seen in 1984. More money is spent because more money is being pumped in;

especially in the form of PAC money and the big 'soft money', expenditure of which subverts the legal spending limits for presidential candidates.[6]

Computerization is one of the relatively new developments which has raised expenditure and also the quantity both of publicity output from, and the flow of material into, congressional offices. The introduction of computers into Congress was first suggested by Senator Hubert Humphrey in 1964; but while the federal bureaucracy introduced computers on a large scale in the 1960s, Congress did not do so until the mid-1970s.[7] Computerization has had a major impact in at least three ways, all of which link Congress more closely with the communications industry. First, election campaigns for national office and Congress are now managed via computers. For a House election the computer can control expenditure, billing and scheduling, as well as various publicity functions.[8]

By the close of the 1984 presidential election, the Republican party's computer contained data from tracking surveys based on 1,000 interviews per day, many thousands of Democrat speeches and much else that was used on an almost hour-to-hour basis.[9] Second, computers have led to much more sophisticated mailing campaigns from congressional offices; separate mailings are now targeted at particular occupational groups or types of housing area, all names which the computer can recognize as Hispanic and so on. Third, the computer system is making data bases quickly available to congressional offices, and legislators hope that this will help them to keep up with the bureaucracy. The most used parts of these data bases seem to be the most obvious, such as abstracts from the *New York Times* and other leading newspapers and magazines.[10] This simply allows a speeding-up of the old process by which politicians' speeches came out of newspaper clippings.

Linked to these communications and computerization changes is the *commercialization* of Congress.[11] The very committee chairmen and major figures – such as Senator Dole – who benefit most from the inflows of money are often those who criticize the system most vociferously. Congressional committee members receive money from the PACs of the very industries and interests over which they supposedly exercise objective legislative oversight.[12] During 1979–84 the realtors' PAC gave money to 111 of the 119 current members of the four committees of most concern to realtors – the Senate Finance Committee, the Senate Banking, Housing and Urban Affairs Committee, the House Ways and Means Committee, and the House Banking, Finance and Urban Affairs Committee.[13] At least 54 pro-Israeli PACs give mainly to members of congressional Foreign Relations and Armed Services committees. They contributed heavily in 1984 to Paul Simon in his successful Illinois bid to unseat Charles Percy, the then chairman of the

Senate Foreign Relations Committee.[14] In 1982 the National Association of Broadcasters' TV and Radio PAC (TARPAC) gave to 18 members of
congressional committees involved in overseeing broadcasting; the
national cable TV Association's PAC gave to 15 members involved in
overseeing Cable television (mainly on the Commerce committees).[15]

Everyone is broadly agreed that such giving is legal and does not
constitute bribery, but also that it does not exactly ensure that justice
and objectivity are clearly demonstrated to the American public. Many
observers believe that these sleazy and near universal practices contribute to the public's estimation of Congress as a rather sleazy place –
although 'my own congressman is wonderful' remains a common belief.

Much attention is paid to extreme cases, such as the 1984 reelection of
Senator Jesse Helms in North Carolina, in which much of the $22-
million expenditure came from out of state.[16] About $5 million was
spent per contested US Senate seat in 1984. In some cases politicians
raise huge sums from industries related to their committee memberships. Senator David Durenberger of Minnesota used his membership of the Senate Finance Committee and his chairmanship of its
subcommittee on health to raise $3.1 million to fend off his millionaire
Democratic opponent in 1982. Much of the money came from PACS
related to the insurance, steel, airlines, gasohol, medical and oil
industries, and from pro-Israeli PACS.[17]

But in House elections the sums of money are typically only about
one tenth the size of those in Senate elections. Indeed, one of the sad
things about the House contributions is how small they are – many PAC
gifts are $1,000 or less. Some politicians insist that they cannot possibly
be bought for such paltry sums. But PACs in fact hunt in packs, and a
friendly attitude to a single industry can bring money from many
separate PACs. Moreover, PACs are not trying to swallow politicians
whole; all a PAC wants is to slice off a few ounces of a politician's surplus
integrity – at least the right to quick access when relevant legislation is at
a crucial juncture, and, if possible, one or two favorable votes out of the
hundreds which a congressman casts each year. Further, the giving of
money is only one of several interconnected activities – conventional
lobbying, the supplying of information and publicity, and inviting
politicians to speak at industry conferences for fees which supplement
their personal income.

These numerous gifts of between $500 and $5,000 constitute *commercialization* in a double sense. Politicians are seen in public to compromise their integrity on a routine, systematic basis. Second, these gifts
literally go to pay for *commercials* on radio and television.

LOBBIES AND INCUMBENTS: THE SEARCH FOR A FAIR
ADVANTAGE

The PAC phenomenon results from the alliance of organized lobbies with
political incumbents; Democrats get as much PAC support as Republicans (because PACs like incumbents, and over half of all congressional
incumbents in recent years have been Democrats). Such PAC support, of
course, in turn contributes to the fact that incumbents have an overwhelming tendency to be reelected.

Certainly in the communications policy field, the legislative battle has
increasingly been fought in recent years not between contending
political parties, but between contending lobbies – cable versus telephone or Hollywood versus the TV networks. Something rather similar
happens in the courts, where judges find themselves refereeing technical
contests between two commercial interests.

Lobbying has become a more elaborate business. The post-Watergate
reforms in Congress reduced the power of full-committee chairmen,
increased the significance of subcommittees (especially in the House)
and opened most committee meetings to the public. This means that
lobbyists now lobby individual legislators, and not simply key leadership
figures. In turn, this more systematic lobbying requires bigger resources,
and gives an additional advantage to the better-financed lobbies.

Some estimates put the size of the lobbying industry in Washington at
100,000 people. Lobbying now includes PACs, publicity and the involvement of chief executives; it is also directed at a wide range of executive
branch agencies besides Congress. It extends into the electoral process,
which itself is so complex legally as to resemble the tax system; election
campaigns now require the full-time employment of experts in election
law – both to evade the many traps and to locate the many loopholes.[18]

'All they want is a fair advantage', say politicians about lobbies. But
incumbent politicians are also looking for their own 'fair advantage'.
Electoral arrangements, including the aggressive pursuit and shameless
solicitation of PAC money, may look undignified and feel unpleasant to
incumbents. Their great attraction, however, is that they make most
challengers feel worse than merely undignified or embarrassed: they
make most challengers feel dead at the starting gate.

The major disadvantage for challengers is their radically less favorable access to both free and paid publicity. Incumbents, in general, can
much more easily attract financial support – so much so that a standard
tactic is to accumulate and then publicize a substantial 'war chest' early
in the primary election season; this may well persuade the strongest
challenger not to enter such an uneven contest.

TOWARDS AN ELECTRONIC FIRST AMENDMENT: THE BIRTH OF A SUPER-LOBBY

The lobbies of relevant industries have certainly played a very active part in communications deregulation. And simply because politicians are so vulnerable to media publicity, the media lobbies have long been unusually strong. The strength of the newspaper and broadcasting lobbies has in recent years been challenged by an aggressive cable lobby. Hollywood itself is no slouch at lobbying, and the old AT&T was thought by some to be a master of the lobbying art. More recently, the computer industry has moved (reluctantly at first) into systematic lobbying.

In the early 1980s a combined media lobby first appeared, with the objective of extending the First Amendment ('Congress shall make no law . . .') from the press to radio, TV and cable. This lobby was encouraged from within Congress by Senator Packwood, the Commerce Committee chairman (until he moved to chair the Finance Committee in 1985). The lobby insists that it is arbitrary to allow First Amendment freedoms only to the press; the case for the extension of such freedom to radio, TV and cable comes at least in part from newspaper companies that have moved into cable ownership.

Senator Packwood's bill was not supported by the Senate. The reason is well known. Incumbent politicians actually prefer the present restrictions on the electronic media (because in practice rules like 'fairness' and 'equal time' actually favor incumbents not challengers).

Nevertheless, the First Amendment coalition is a formidable one, and it seems probable that some kind of compromise will be reached, with judges (once again) broadly setting the rules. The 1984 deregulation of cable and Packwood's freedom of expression legislative efforts may be swinging public opinion.

A lobby of press, TV and cable alone is already, in terms of collective political strength, a super-lobby. If even *some* degree of electronic First Amendment evolves, this alone will be a massive piece of communications deregulation.

Waiting in the wings are IBM and AT&T, who may become more deeply involved in media ownership. If so, the First Amendment extension will become the focus of a truly powerful political lobby, and, since their competitors will complain, a truly powerful political conflict.

THE TAKEOVER OF MASS MEDIA AND NEWS

Communications deregulation involves the partial merging of the mass media into, and takeover by, telecommunications. Newspapers themselves are printed, and their news transmitted, electronically. The electronic media may become part of various two-way electronic services.

The marketplace principle, in practice, seems to involve breaking the media down into a number of more specialized markets within which more specific channels can be sold. Radio has already done this, followed by cable; the relative decline of general press media and the rise of specialist publications points in the same direction. Specific services must attract specific advertising or subsidy.

Subsidy itself seems to have become more political; the concept of the public-service subsidy is seen as political in a way that is hostile to deregulation. At the same time advertising has to be more fiercely fought for, because new media like cable offer fresh competition, and are willing to make 'commercial' compromises – for example, allowing advertisers to control editorial content.

In much of the post-1945 period the output of 'news' in the US has mildly flattered public taste. The services of Associated Press (AP) and United Press International (UPI), the network news, the newsmagazines and the local-monopoly dailies have all been a little more serious and less politically partisan than purely market forces might have dictated. But under deregulation the very concept of 'news' is challenged.

It is challenged from several directions. The telecommunications trends favor continuous streams of on-screen material in which the standard twentieth-century distinctions of an advertising/neutral news/comment kind are observed less and less. Words on screen and pictures on screen are both simply data derived from data bases, and no longer news derived from news source individuals.

News, never far removed from entertainment, also has to withstand fresh demands from that direction. The results are most noticeable on the big local television news. Even such relatively serious papers as the *Los Angeles Times* and the *Washington Post* make little attempt to offer a comprehensive national news service. The shape of things to come may be the *USA Today* marriage of the stodgy daily paper with the more colorful confections of *People* magazine, plus, of course, sports data.

News has gone through many changes in the last 200 years, and will not easily disappear. What is disappearing already, perhaps, is any general consensus as to what conventions of neutral news could or should be observed. News thus becomes doubly controversial – for what it reports, but also for the concept of news which it represents.

News executives and journalists, suspicious of attempted takeovers from various directions, may well further stir the controversy by the militancy of their defense. One controversy that has frequently brought American politicians and news executives into bitter conflict concerns the prediction of election results by TV networks while people are still voting in the western states. Politicians from western states are understandably resentful of a national mechanism dedicated to telling people the result while they are still lining up to vote. The TV network executives belligerently tell congressional committees that they cannot put a temporary embargo on information until a mutually agreed-upon release time, a claim that is threadbare because news executives do just this every day. That so much obtuseness and vitriol can surround such a relatively simple case illustrates how the concept of news itself comes to be seen as ideological claim-staking.

THE 50 PER CENT HAVE, 50 PER CENT HAVE NOT, PROBLEM

The tendency of communications deregulation is to the marketing of specialized, tailored services at cost, rather than the agglomeration of services into 'universal' or 'public-service' packages. With a wider range of services, each charged for separately, not every American can or will take every service. Some services are in any case only suitable for large organizations or the very rich.

But with many services and activities there is already a tendency for only about half the population to be reached. Only some take cable, and only some of these 'pay cable'. Newspaper reading remains a daily habit, albeit with a slowly declining percentage of the population; and voting itself is an activity in which about half the population does not participate – and more than half are nonvoters in nonpresidential years.

Some of the 50/50 trends are along lines of income and education. Others are regional – cities versus rural areas. Others are both regional and ethnic. The white middle-class suburbs already have more, and more effective, cable, TV, radio and newspaper choice than do the inner cities or the rural areas. Similar things seem likely for the telephone. At the same time the services become not only more specialized, but more politicized. Deregulated communications also offer channels for the preservation of minority languages and avenues for minority political education of a kind which some will inevitably see as an un-American version of citizenship.

Such trends promise political conflicts aplenty. In retrospect it may appear that the strength of consensual support for deregulation during the first Reagan administration partly derived from the fact that the US was first to taste the benefits, while some of the more divisive consequences were being postponed until late in the 1980s. The years 1982–4 were years of domestic growth. In 1984 alone, US computer sales grew by some 50 per cent.

Notes

1 Kenichi Ohmae, *Triad Power* (1985).
2 Alan L. Otten, 'Critics of the Hoover Institution Complain about Nature of Ties to Stanford University', *Wall Street Journal*, 26 June 1984.
3 David Shaw, 'Power of the Pundit is Fading', *Los Angeles Times*, 8 and 9 April 1984.
4 Elizabeth Drew, *Politics and Money* (1983). US Senate, 98th Congress, 1st Session, Hearings before the Committee on Rules and Administration, *Campaign Finance Reform Proposals of 1983*.
5 Herbert E. Alexander, *Financing the 1980 Election* (1983).
6 Brooks Johnson, 'Old-Time Politics: Loopholes allow flood of campaign giving by businesses, fat cats. A decade after Watergate, curbs almost disappear . . .', *Wall Street Journal*, 5 July 1984, pp. 1, 16.
7 Stephen E. Frantzich, *Computers in Congress* (1982), p. 137.
8 Rodney N. Smith, 'The new political machine', *Computer World*, 16 July 1984, pp. ID 19–25.
9 Jack Honomichl, 'Research acts as Reagan's eyes, ears', *Advertising Age*, 5 November 1984, pp. 1, 91.
10 Frantzich, *Computers in Congress*, pp. 152–3.
11 Judith Bender *et al.*, 'Making Congress Their Business', *Newsday*, 11 and 12 March 1984. Larry J. Sabato, *PAC Power* (1984).
12 John B. Oakes, 'The PAC-Man's Game: Eating Legislators', *New York Times*, 6 September 1984, p. A23. Dennis Farney, 'On Capitol Hill, Committee Assignments Can Influence Candidate's Fund-Raising', *Wall Street Journal*, 17 October 1984.
13 *Looking to Purchase or Rent*, a press release from Common Cause, 6 September 1984, p. 2.
14 'Study finds pro-Israeli PAC's active in '84 races', *New York Times*, 16 August 1984.
15 'Who Gets How Much', *Broadcasting*, 8 November 1982, p. 38.
16 Bill Peterson, 'North Carolina: lessons of a dirty campaign', *Washington Post, national weekly edition*, 3 December 1984, pp. 6–7.
17 'Top PAC Man: Sen. Durenberger got huge campaign gifts from firms he aided', *Wall Street Journal*, 24 April 1984, pp. 1, 25.
18 Thomas B. Edsall, 'Labyrinth of Laws Governing Election Funding', *Washington Post*, 27 November 1983, pp. A1, A16.

3

Deregulation: an Overview

REGULATORY TURBULENCE: FROM CITIZENS' RIGHTS TO BUSINESS SERVICES

Deregulation is as many sided a phenomenon as regulation. Since the Interstate Commerce Commission took on the regulation of the railroad natural monopoly in the 1880s, Congress has entrusted to a variety of federal agencies the regulation of various industries. The range of industries has been vast, and the dangers to be protected against have also been numerous. Thomas McGraw argues that the purposes have included disclosure and publicity, protection and cartelization, the reverse of the containment of monopoly, the promotion of supply for consumers and workers, and the legitimization of the capitalist order.[1]

Regulation has thus meant very different things to different industries – not surprisingly, since regulation is no less than a subspecies of law itself. Regulation has also tended to ebb and flow, giving each decade its particular regulatory character. The 1930s, for instance, saw the setting up of regulatory agencies which reflected such New Deal concerns as *stabilizing* prices. The FCC, established in 1934, and other agencies of this era were given significant independence and rather vague terms of reference. In later years such independent regulatory agencies were widely believed to have been captured by the industries they were supposed to regulate. The FCC had been captured by AT&T and the TV networks according to this argument. A Ralph Nader report, edited by Mark Green in 1971–3, saw the regulatory agencies as *The Monopoly Makers*.

The Nader group itself wanted not only *less* regulatory capture, but *more* effective regulation of industry and the environment in the public interest. Powerful groups pressing for both more and less regulation confronted each other for much of the 1970s, with the demand for less regulation in full flow by the late 1970s.

Some of the targets of the deregulators dated back to the New Deal and further, but in recent times their primary targets have been some of the Great Society social and civil rights legislation sponsored by

President Johnson in 1965 and subsequent years. More specifically, the targets were regulatory legislation enacted in 1967–73. The Clean Air Act of 1970 set up a new Environmental Protection Agency. Also established were the Occupational Safety and Health Administration, the Equal Employment Opportunity Commission, the National Highway Traffic Safety Commission, the Mining Enforcement and Safety Administration, and the Federal Energy Regulatory Commission. By 1980 these new agencies employed over 60,000 people and spent over $5 billion a year. The cost of their regulations to industry was variously estimated, but certainly ran into tens of billions of dollars.

Many industries found the environmental regulations especially burdensome and expensive. The legislation led to enormously complex litigation and the involvement of judges in highly technical questions.[2]

These specifically targeted agencies tended to adopt an aggressive regulatory style, and, far from being captured, they were typically seen by the affected industries as unremittingly hostile. But while these 'targeted' agencies were making the 1970s a decade of increasing regulation, other forces were already making the 1970s an era of deregulation. Opposition to red tape, bureaucracy and overregulation was given powerful support by President Ford when he took office in the late summer of 1974. At this point, getting rid of regulation had a strongly populist and consumerist flavor, and President Ford stressed the anti-inflationary possibilities of cutting regulated prices.

The greatest friction between the contending forces of more and less regulation came in the mid-1970s. The airline industry was a halfway case. In the winter of 1974–5 Senator Edward Kennedy became interested in the argument that the airlines were overregulated and controlled. In 1978 the Airline Deregulation Act was passed. The main benefits of airline deregulation went to regular users of flights between larger cities – that is, to business people, but also to other frequent travellers. There was a marked tendency for prices on less used routes to rise relative to prices on heavily used routes.

In the later 1970s deregulation swung away from a populist emphasis on providing better consumer services; arguments for general business efficiency which always co-existed with consumerist arguments, now became predominant. Of course, deregulation of financial services and long-distance telephoning do offer some benefits to individual consumers, but the main benefits go to companies and other bulk users. Other deregulatory efforts, in trucking and natural gas, for example, again offered some consumer benefits, but more business benefits.

This sea change in the mid-1970s gradually led toward a deregulatory consensus which saw much, if not most, regulation as guilty until proved innocent – not only the regulations of 1965–74, but also those of earlier periods such as the 1930s and going right back to the railroad regulation of the 1880s.

This consensus developed quite quickly during the Ford presidential years of 1974–6. It contained elements of post-Nixon and post-Vietnam disillusionment with Government; elements of a continuing move to the right in American politics, with hostility toward the trade unions, which had supported much of the 1967–73 legislation; increasing anxiety about Japanese competition; and a new mood in Congress favoring detailed and aggressive oversight of the executive branch and the regulatory agencies. This consensus was shared by presidents Ford, Carter and Reagan, by the majority of both Democrats and Republicans in Congress, by newly expanded congressional committee staffs full of investigatory zeal and eager to engage in Washington warfare, and by the courts. Many commentators point to the unanimity of economists' advice. Also added to the deregulatory consensus was the instinctive and simplistic antipathy of journalists for 'bureaucracy'.

Deregulation from 1970 to 1985 has involved a highly complex set of trends and events. Depending upon which industries, which agencies and which time periods are considered, very different conclusions can be, and have been, drawn.

The communications industry, like other industries caught up in all this, had its own peculiarities. Deregulation started earlier in communications than in most other industries; it really began with the 1968 Supreme Court 'Carterfone' decision which permitted non-AT&T telephones and customer equipment to be connected to the AT&T system. And in 1969 MCI won its original FCC permission to hook into the AT&T system. But despite these 1968–9 competitive beginnings, communications deregulation took well over a decade to arrive even partially. There are two very obvious reasons for this: firstly, AT&T was in such an exceptionally dominant position as a vertically integrated monopoly that its case was more difficult to resolve than were some of the others; second, the TV networks were another special case of exceptional industrial and political strength.

WASHINGTON: CITY OF LAWYERS, ECONOMISTS AND FASHIONS

US communications policy is given some coherence by the fact that, although it is made by forty different agencies and a dozen or more trade associations, nearly all the people who represent these organizations in policy discussions are lawyers. The number of lawyers in the US advances relentlessly toward a one million total, and there are more lawyers in Washington DC alone than in all but a very few entire countries. Even so, these familiar facts fail fully to prepare an outsider for the extent to which communications policy is made by an intellectual community of communications lawyers with offices in the downtown area, and of lawyer-politicians, lawyer-aides and lawyer-lobbyists with offices a mile or two east toward Capitol Hill. Even when some visiting team comes into town – they also tend to be lawyers – for example entertainment lawyers from Hollywood. Nor are the TV networks and AT&T slow to send legal reinforcements from New York City and New Jersey to back up their already strongly fortified legal outposts in Washington.

This is a high-priced legal location, and starting salaries in big Washington law firms compare with those paid on Wall Street. In part these high salaries can be explained in terms of the literally billions of dollars often at stake in FCC decisions and Washington court cases, as well as in congressional decisions. But there may also be a competitive machismo element between rival law firms involved.

Communications law is regulatory law, but it involves more than just law; as in other branches of law, much of the expertise is simply knowledge of how the wheels turn and of how inside know-how can be used to further progress. Communications law is infinitely complex and uncertain; it now potentially includes vast areas of high technology – and it certainly includes a range of agencies and authorities whose mandate is both large and vague. In each of the main arenas, any particular case, clause, law or appeal has to go through a whole series of stages. In Congress there are two Houses with up to a dozen committees and subcommittees in each that might claim jurisdiction over, say, a cable TV copyright proposal, and court decisions can always be, and often are, appealed. The FCC has to follow a prescribed series of quasi-legislative steps before it at long last reaches the rule-making stage. All this requires the full-time attention of lawyers. There is a sea of legal opinions, all of them written at fancy prices per hour; the lawyers also need to read the large weekly and daily trade press; and to do this, as well as to appear in court and at congressional hearings and FCC inquiries, they need to specialize. Lawyers specialize in TV license renewals, in First Amendment, in telephone rate cases and so on.

The language of US communications policy is primarily a legal language, which itself makes it impenetrable to most outsiders. However, the language has two additional admixtures, which further compound the difficulties. First, there is a strong element of utterly leaden language from telecommunications and engineering, to which has been added a further dose of free market economic theory and business school/accountancy jargon.

This unappetizing language is what you hear in the decidedly more appetizing restaurants between Dupont Circle and K Street, where the communications policy community has its offices. Its loyalty to this pleasant locality is understandable; and the community was seen in its most effective lobbying form when it was proposed to move the FCC headquarters some two miles west across the Potomac into a new office complex in Rosslyn. The proposal was defeated, and the FCC remains scattered among a number of buildings around 19th and M streets in the heart of Washington's restaurant quarter.[3]

Communications policy has always, of course, been heavily influenced by engineers. Phrases such as 'technology-driven' ignore the significance of professional engineering advice in communications and other fields. But in terms of deregulatory policy, a third group – economists – are widely believed to have taken Washington by storm in the last decade or two. It is pointed out that economists have acquired much control over the central running of the federal government via such bodies as the Office of Management and Budget (OMB) and the Council of Economic Advisers. Moreover, economists are now installed in the planning sections of most federal departments and agencies. The advice of these economists, both in communications and in general, seems from about 1975 onward to have been, with only a few exceptions, against regulation. One can argue as to whether the emergence of these free market economists was cause or effect of the swing to the right that resulted in, for example, the Nixon election landslide of 1972.

But certainly Washington is a city of fashions. The political climate changes every two years, and 1974 was a year of exceptional change. There was a huge expansion of congressional staffs, among whom was found a key deregulatory fervor. The staff of the House subcommittee on communications were of this kind from 1976 onward. Deregulation was the fashion, and the many different subtle shades of deregulation made it all the more attractive.

THE JAPANESE THREAT

Throughout the 1970–85 decade and a half of deregulation, a constant background factor has been American anxiety at the steadily increasing seriousness of the Japanese threat. Increasingly it has been recognized that two steeply rising graphs accompany this assault of the Rising Sun. One is the simple increase in scale of the Japanese threat, which was initially confined to a few products, but each year includes a broader range. The other has to do with the level of technology. Initially the Japanese can be seen to have targeted cameras, textiles and steel; then higher technologies such as cars, color TVs and VCRs; finally moving into classic high technology – advanced computers, biotechnology, space, aircraft and telecommunications. Increasingly American business spokesmen have said that the US cannot afford the one-sided and unfair free trade involved in this massive Japanese invasion of the US market while many Japanese markets are effectively closed to the US by nontariff barriers.[4]

One American analysis sees the key Japanese strategy as quick entry into the US domestic market at low price, an entry which seeks to deny US companies access to needed capital resources. The four-phase strategy is seen as consisting of:

(1) buying US research and development at bargain prices;
(2) Japanese industrial sectors targeted for major high-tech development all having access to capital at about half the interest rates effective in the US;
(3) the Japanese focusing less on *product* development and more on *manufacturing* development;
(4) Japan *de facto* protecting its home market, the second largest in the world, while it hones a new product into high quality/low price shape for world market entry.

By entering the US home market with low prices which are, in effect, subsidized, Japanese producers force American competition to cut prices below profit, which in turn denies them access to capital.[5]

The US deregulatory movement in general, and that in communications in particular, seems to have been heavily influenced by such analyses of the Japanese threat. There have been many incidents along the way, and, of course, particular industries have been demanding relief for many years. But in terms of high technology and communications, the year 1980–1 may perhaps be designated as Japanese Technological Panic Year USA. American observers began to recognize that Japan was about to take a leading position, for example, in some parts of the world semiconductor market.[6] This was a shock because, previously, US companies such as Texas Instruments had been far in the lead via massive DOD contracts.

This year also marked the arrival of the Reagan administration, full of businessmen from California, the state most familiar with Japanese industry. The Reagan administration appears to have decided, without any public announcement, to take a tougher line against Japan. Perhaps the major consequences of this new attitude were the twin AT&T and IBM decisions announced in January 1982, after one year of the Reagan administration. The thinking here seemed to be that the US had in IBM and AT&T two super-companies which should be unfettered from antitrust constraints and allowed to engage in uninhibited competition with Japan.

Paradoxically, however, the deregulation of AT&T, at least initially, opens up further prospects for Japan and others in the US domestic telecommunications industry. And deregulation thus quickly leads to demands for protection. 'Japan Runs Into America Inc' headlines were used to describe how in 1982 AT&T accepted its own, Western Electric, high bid for the major fiber-optic cable contract in the Northeast corridor, and rejected a lower bid from a Fujitsu-led consortium.[7]

But despite increasing pressure for selected protection, the American deregulatory stance toward Japan has in practice seemed to many American observers to increase still further the contrast between an open US market and a closed Japanese domestic market. Enormous efforts have gone into several specific efforts, such as securing some purchasing of American equipment by Nippon Telephone and Telegraph (NTT), the Japanese telephone authority; but the achievements have gone only a little beyond the token, especially in contrast to US purchases of Japanese telecommunications equipment.

The continuing lopsidedness of this trade relationship does not alter the fact that anxiety about Japan was an underlying factor in deregulation in general and telecommunications deregulation in particular. In the longer run, deregulation may make American industry and American telecommunications more competitive on the world market. But the initial experience tends to validate the criticism that American deregulation was not so much a carefully planned policy as a negative reaction, an instinctive nay-saying, to the previous drift of policy.

A SUMMARY OF COMMUNICATIONS DEREGULATION UNDER FOUR PRESIDENTS

Communications deregulation moved extremely slowly; in 16 years, from the first election of Nixon in 1968 to the reelection of Reagan in 1984, there was no comprehensive piece of communications legislation. This field was marked by even more than the usual amount of disputation between branches of government. This had a consequence familiar from American history, that the courts (and the Justice Department) played a big role in what communications deregulation did occur.

Although the impact of the presidents was mainly indirect (via their appointments) or unclear, the four presidential terms covering this period nevertheless roughly mark four phases which could also perhaps be described as walk, trot, canter and gallop.

(1) *The first Nixon years, 1969–72*, saw the first major examples of communications deregulation (although early stirrings can be traced back a decade earlier). Indeed the FCC's Carterfone decision in 1968, which allowed 'foreign' add-ons to AT&T telephones, was the beginning of a long series of AT&T defeats. In 1969 MCI was given FCC approval to

offer private-line services between St Louis and Chicago. Most important, however, was Nixon's appointment of Clay Whitehead to run an office of Telecommunications Policy (OTP) in the executive office of the president. Thus Nixon was the first major politician to recognize the need to take stock of new technologies and new playing fields. In practice, however, Nixon set back such initiatives by using OTP as a weapon in his feud with the news media.

⅄ (2) *The Nixon–Ford years, 1973–6*, were a phase of regulatory turbulence, with moves toward both more and less regulation. Administration and White House policy was virtually nonexistent in this Watergate period. The FCC was making encouraging noises in the direction of deregulating cable and telecommunications, but it was also defending AT&T and the networks and trying to cope with a flood tide of consumer demands for access, equal opportunity and fairness in broadcasting. In 1974 the Justice Department followed MCI in launching its own antitrust case against AT&T. Seeing the legal tide moving against it, AT&T aimed to clarify its position as a regulated monopoly by pushing through Congress legislation which would in effect turn the clock back to 1968 or before and would remove the irritating gnat bites of tiny rivals like MCI. This bill, The Consumer Communications Reform Act, was introduced in the House in March 1976, and was quickly dubbed by its opponents the 'Bell Bill'.

(3) *The Carter years, 1977–80*, saw the deregulatory pace quicken to a canter. In this phase the House of Representatives took the lead via its newly strengthened Communications Sub-Committee chaired by Lionel Van Deerlin (a Democrat from California). The Bell Bill reintroduced into the new Congress in 1977 received huge intitial support; but Van Deerlin and his Republican allies used parliamentary delaying tactics to kill it. They also reshaped the agenda, first by holding hearings on competition in telecommunications, and then by setting out to comprehensively rewrite the charter Communications Act of 1934. Separate 'rewrite' bills were presented in 1978, 1979 and 1980. None passed, but the interminable hearings transformed the communications landscape. AT&T's image was transformed from that of a benign and competent Ma Bell to a backward-looking, vindictive monopoly, out of kilter with the onrush of new technology.

This phase was marked also by active competition to take the lead in communications policymaking. The Senate set off in pursuit of rewrites, less comprehensive than those proposed in the House, but still massive. The FCC during the Carter years switched from resisting, to wholeheartedly pursuing, deregulation. In early 1978 an FCC decision was reversed in the US Court of Appeals, and MCI's Execunet service was allowed to enter general long-distance service in direct competition with AT&T. The FCC increasingly moved toward broadcast deregulation with sweeping decisions in radio and cable. In April 1980 came the FCC's

Computer II decision, allowing AT&T a partial escape from the regulatory straitjacket, by giving it permission to enter 'enhanced', or data
transmission, services via a separate subsidiary.

(4) *The first Reagan term, 1981–4*, saw deregulation accelerate to a
gallop, with Reagan's appointees at the FCC trying hard to set the pace.
The official policy of the main regulatory authority in communications
became deregulation. On 8 January 1982, twin Justice Department
announcements set IBM free from its antitrust case and proposed the
divestiture of AT&T's regional telephone companies. By August 1982
Judge Greene's Modified Final Judgement set out the plan for divestiture, which took effect on 1 January 1984. Congress continued to be
active in deregulation; in 1981 radio and TV station licenses were
extended to seven and five years respectively, a major move toward
broadcast deregulation. But Congress also on a number of occasions
restrained what it saw as the deregulatory impetuosity of Mark Fowler's
FCC. Finally, in the dying hours of preelection business in 1984, Congress
passed a comprehensive bill to deregulate cable; while giving cable huge
freedoms which it had long wanted, this bill also reflected the preference
of a major communications industry for some form of federal regulation
in place of fragmented and unpredictable local regulation.

Communications perhaps presents an example of deregulation which
is extreme in several respects: extreme in the length of time, 16 years,
taken to achieve even one major piece of deregulatory legislation, and
this only in cable TV; extreme in the strength of the lobbies from the
industries; extreme in the duration and intensity of conflict between the
branches of government and the numerous agencies involved; extreme
in the low profile of the White House and the high profiles of the courts
and the Justice Department; extreme in the extent to which, despite the
massed armies of contending lobbies, a small number of key personalities played vital roles: the ten people who occupied chairmanships of
importance – Wiley, Ferris and Fowler as FCC chairmen; Van Deerlin,
Wirth and Dingell as House Subcommittee and Commerce Committee
chairmen; Hollings, Goldwater and Packwood in equivalent Senate
chairmanships; and Charles Brown who took over in 1979 as chairmen
of AT&T; and William Baxter as assistant attorney general, and US
District Judge Harold S. Greene. These twelve men, the founding
fathers of communications deregulation, are a very mixed collection in
terms of previous careers and political orientation. All twelve, however,
had a streak of aggression and decisiveness, amounting sometimes to
arrogance, which seems to have been necessary to make any impression
on the paper mountains of communications policy in Washington.

Finally, communications deregulation was slow in coming, partly
because its consequences were recognized to be potentially extreme in

significance. By comparison, airlines deregulation, for example, has been a mere reshuffling of the competitive position between big, medium and small carriers. Communications deregulation is something much bigger – a leap into the dark, whose consequences have not been, and perhaps still cannot be, calculated.

CONGRESS VERSUS (SELECTED) LOBBIES AND AGENCIES

Critics of regulation had asserted that, typically, regulatory agencies were captured by industry lobbies: critics of Congress had asserted that members of the legislature were dominated by the urge to be reelected. Consequently, entrenched lobbies, in the absence of some major populist appeal to the electorate, could not be shifted.

But the deregulatory movement seemed to indicate the reverse. The post-Watergate reforms of 1975 and 1976 were significant here. New members demanded and obtained reforms. The deregulatory attack was often aimed not simply at a captured agency but at a trinity of industry, regulatory agency and associated trade unions. Divide-and-conquer tactics could be used between interests within an industry. In the case of trucking deregulation, the Teamsters Union was a major target; in the case of the airlines, major targets included not just the allocation of routes but the high salaries of pilots; in the case of telecommunications, the targets were not just the FCC and AT&T, but also the well-paid members of the Communications Workers of America (CWA).

This trinity of opponents – lobbies, regulatory agencies and unions – obviously interacted differently in different industries. In the cases of trucking and airlines, the trinity was shown to lack political potency. But in other cases it was more resilient. In communications this was certainly so. While abolition of the Civil Aeronautics Board was a realistic possibility, some body like the FCC seemed much harder to avoid. Both telecommunications and broadcasting had extremely strong traditions of craft unions based in traditional craft union centers such as New York, New Jersey and Hollywood. Moreover, both telecommunications and broadcasting had political clout. Thus they were able to regroup and to discover ways of making the post-Watergate reforms work in their favor. Both industries used the opening of committee hearings to observe – and then to lobby – individual subcommittee members, using more sophistication and going into greater detail. AT&T managed to lobby to death a deregulatory bill in Congress in 1982; and the National Association of Broadcasters (NAB) similarly killed broadcast deregulation legislation in the 1983–4 Congress.

AFTER DEREGULATION: THE BIG, THE SMALL AND THE SHAKEN OUT

It was suggested in chapter 2 that the IBM–Silicon Valley axis might be becoming a new model for American industry. If so, deregulation may be an effective mechanism for making that kind of innovative and competitive tension more widespread in the US economy.

US domestic airlines have certainly seen dramatic changes since the Airline Deregulation Act of 1978: numerous small new airlines were drawn into offering services on new routes; competition in prices and services became fierce; many airlines faced financial difficulty; huge pay and other cuts were negotiated with unions; and several of the larger carriers failed, as did dozens of the smaller ones. The big boys – notably United, American and Delta – fought back with discounts, sophisticated marketing and efficient use of hub cities such as Chicago and Atlanta. Common deregulatory consequences may include:

1 the two or three largest companies becoming larger and stronger;
2 companies immediately below this level facing severe difficulties, especially if they lack a serious long-term strategy;
3 much new and ferocious competition at the lower levels, as many such companies get shaken out, and those that survive develop a special relationship with one of the big boys – such as that between the small airlines which use United's facilities and feed traffic into United's hub at O'Hare in Chicago.[8]

Joel Bleeke argues that a key distinction must be made between managements which did and did not use the ample years of warning to plan a viable strategy. He believes that when deregulation finally arrives, some of the key new challenges may be the proliferation of new product/service combinations, the arrival of new low-cost producers and intensified introduction of new technology. Consequences of this keener competition may include excess capacity developing, severe price competition emerging in what were the most profitable regulated markets, industry entrants forcing drastic cost-cutting and staff reductions on established companies, less successful companies quickly starting to lose money, and many firms needing to invest just when their access to capital markets is worsening.[9]

This scenario is based on an analysis of deregulation's impact in stockbroking, airlines, trucking, railroads and business telecoms terminal equipment. Much of it seems to apply to computers – if one regards the IBM decision of January 1982 as the deregulation of that industry. But these observations seem to apply less generally to telecommunications and broadcasting, in part because such deregulation as has occurred has been relatively modest. In particular Bleeke's account underlines the exceptional strength of the seven divested ex-Bell Operating Companies (ex-BOCs), each of which continues to bestride a vast area of the US as a monopolist in local telephone service.

Although the impact of deregulation has been uneven, even in those relatively few industries which have been deregulated, those who dismiss the overall impact of deregulation on the US economy seem, nevertheless, to be dismissing too easily some major consequences. Several major industries have become much more competitive; regulatory agencies have become much more guardians of competition than guardians of the status quo; and trade unions representing some of America's most conspicuously highly paid workers – the teamsters, the communications workers and the airline pilots – have been severely mauled.

These changes have not taken place in isolation from the rest of the US economy. Indeed, the thrust of deregulation is to strip public service/public utility/regulated industries of their special status and to put them back into the mainstream of the economy. Meanwhile, in the mainstream, relationships between large and small companies have been changing. For example, the large car manufacturers have been reorganizing their suppliers into a more dependent and more Japanese-style pattern.

Finally, communications deregulation is doubly significant, because as the communications industry – telecommunications/computers/mass media – has moved to the economy's center stage, so also has it become exhibit number one of deregulation and the new competitiveness. Important communications deregulation questions remain. Will there be major changes in the ex-BOCs, the networks and Hollywood? What will be the longer-term consequences of telecommunications and cable deregulation?

As the communications industry becomes a flag-bearer for US industry and for deregulation, it also poses other, still broader questions. Is competition between the US and Japan leading to a convergence in industrial organization? Has deregulation already passed its peak? Are we about to witness a return to protectionism and more, not less, federal regulation?

Notes

1 Thomas K. McGraw, *Prophets of Regulation* (1984).
2 R. Shep Melnick, *Regulation and the Courts* (1983).
3 On lawyers in Washington, see John G. Kester, 'Are Lawyers becoming Public Enemy Number One?'. On lawyers and broadcasting policy, see 'The Washington lawyer: power behind the powers that be', *Broadcasting*, 10 June 1980, pp. 32–62.

4 'The US can no longer afford free trade', *Business Week*, 15 November 1982, p. 15.
5 Regis McKenna *et al.*, 'Industrial Policy and International Competition in High Technology' (1984).
6 Nico Hazewindus, *The US Microelectronics Industry* (1982), p. 101. Andrew Pollack, 'A Move into Microprocessors', *New York Times*, 6 September 1984, pp. D1, 6.
7 Edward Meadows, 'Japan Runs Into America Inc', *Fortune*, 22 March 1982.
8 'Small Airlines, in Competitive Squeeze, Are Linking with Big Carriers' Routes', *Wall Street Journal*, 31 July 1984, p. 10; Harlane S. Byrne, 'United and American Vie to Expand Share of Market at O'Hare Airport', *Wall Street Journal*, 27 August 1984, p. 15; Agis Salpukas, 'The Unfriendly Skies of Deregulation', *New York Times*, 11 March 1984, p. F4; 'Why so many airlines are dropping out of the crowded skies', *Business Week*, 17 December 1984, pp. 58–9.
9 Joel A. Bleeke, 'Deregulation: riding the rapids' (1983).

PART II

'Technology-driven'

4

Introduction

One of the most popular of all comments on the recent communications revolution is that deregulation was 'technology-driven'. But technology is itself invented, planned and developed by humans – indeed, the expression 'technologist led' has considerable validity. Even more simply, the new communications technology was invented and developed by a handful of organizations. If one defines the core of the revolution as a merging of space satellite technology, telecommunications and computers, then the new technology came mainly from NASA and COMSAT, AT&T and its Bell Labs, and IBM and other computer companies, with much of the initial funding coming from the DOD.

The DOD also played a key role in the US lead in the early 1980s in 'chip' technology, purchased in huge quantities from such companies as Texas Instruments. The national security interest in high technology is not new or recent. For example, RCA was brought into existence by the US Navy and the federal government, following lessons learned in 1914–18 about the military significance of radio. Before Japan Inc proved so successful at exporting in the 1950s, there had been a USA Inc policy of leadership in electronics; while the American leadership emphasized the importance of commercial exports, USA Inc also had strong overtones of scientific prestige and military leadership.

The key American high-tech organizations were all hybrid mixes of the commercial and the noncommercial. The old AT&T, the telephone monopoly, was the preeminent example of the peculiarly American notion of the 'common carrier'. Whereas in Europe the traditional way of handling utility and transport monopolies was direct public ownership, the US evolved the concepts of natural monopoly and common carrier. It also evolved a state-based pattern of public utility regulation of services, prices and profits, and at the national level an overseeing of commercial natural monopolies and common carriers by regulatory agencies. This model of the regulated natural monopoly was carried over from communication in the transportation sense into electronic communication, via the electric telegraph and the telephone into private radio and then public broadcast radio. In electronic communications regulation, 'common carrier' was taken to refer only to regulation of the *conduit* – the wires – and not the message that went down the wires , and when the 'wireless' came along, only the 'ether', the frequency, was regulated, and not what was said over the ether.

This pattern of public utility regulation/natural monopoly/common carrying/conduit licensing meant that the American communications range was gradually settled and fenced in; and though there was always dissension, the US evolved a distinctive regulatory tradition.

The technology, being man-made and pliant, could be made to conform to this pattern for a long time. A particular technology provided a particular kind of service under a particular regulatory regime. In return for the granting of natural monopoly status, or at least access to the severely limited radio spectrum, the regulated entities accepted the fact that they must keep to the straight-and-narrow within their particular regulatory fences. This was just like the railroads, which were confined by their regulatory regime to being in the railroad business; if the technology changed, that made no difference – a new technology like trucks on highways meant a separate regulatory regime across another sharply defined regulatory fence.

In 1950 electronic communications and mass media were all still quite neatly confined behind their regulatory fences. But in each case there were new technologies – which had often been pioneered in 1939–45 – which, as they emerged in the third quarter of the century, began to make the regulatory fencing look arbitrary and irrelevant (or 'bureaucratic'):

(1) *The common carrier* regime involved licensing of services, tariffs and profits by the FCC. Traditional services had gone down *wires* – the telegraph, then the telephone. Some newer technologies could be channelled into this regime – the Wirephoto services of news agencies. But after 1950 new technologies arrived which, some proponents argued, fitted the common carrier model much less well. While wires on poles were an established natural monopoly, microwave towers (capable of bouncing hundreds of phone calls to the next tower) looked more flexible, capable of many things, including perhaps even competition; and similarly with satellites, microwave towers out in space. And as telephone switching was increasingly done by computers, another fence began to look obsolete.

(2) *Private radio* services were also licensed by the FCC. The most traditional use was for emergency services such as fire, police and ambulance. In mid-century there was massive growth – for example, the use of radio in aviation. But there were industrial uses too – for example, in the oil industry, for talking to drilling crews and offshore rigs. The new technologies seemed to offer much more sophisticated industrial communication. But oil companies and others found themselves restricted in their use of microwave and irritated by private radio

regulation; they resented the need to buy telecommunications from a Ma Bell regulated in accordance with increasingly archaic assumptions.

(3) *Data*. The computer business was totally unregulated, and IBM's main anxieties were confined to antitrust legislation. Initially, computers were used for storing and processing vast files – for example, of Census data. Major applications in the commercial world included reservation systems. To run an airline reservation system required not only a computer and terminals, but also a means of communication between them. And the new technologies for data *transmission* included, once again, microwave and satellites.

(4) *Broadcasting* was initially licensed primarily in terms of a slot in the radio frequency band and for strength of signal. This minimal, 'traffic cop' role in relation to radio was largely carried over into television. But here again the same new technologies came into play – plus broadband cable (which threatened to destroy the frequency scarcity argument), the transistor and the VCR.

(5) *The press* differed from the others not only in lacking a regulatory regime, but also in having a severely worded 'nonregulation' regime, as laid out in the First Amendment. By mid-century, the press also was using electronic innovations – by 1950 both pictures and stories set in type could be sent around the country electronically by one news agency to a thousand daily newspapers. By the 1970s a computer storage revolution had occurred; journalists were using computer terminals. And by the 1980s newspapers were establishing national readerships via the same satellite systems used by all the other communications industries. The unfenced range of the press, and in particular its First Amendment freedom, was widely envied.

(6) *Video and film* also had no regulation apart from antitrust and other general laws. But the convergence of technologies had been evident even in the late 1920s when the *talkies* arrived with sound systems developed by AT&T. After 1950 film merged with television, and Hollywood was responsible for most TV programming. Later, video went via satellite, and broadband cable and the VCR evolved from 'industrial' studio use into a new, wild-card, unregulated medium – de facto partly exempt even from basic copyright law.

These new technologies mostly emerged during the Second World War, from the national war effort. *Computer* development was speeded up by cryptography; *microwave* technology came from radar; and *rockets* (for launching satellites) grew from the German V1s and V2s. In 1940 Bell Labs demonstrated stereophonic sound, and in 1948 unveiled the transistor – the beginning of miniaturization. During the 1940s these innovations all stayed behind the ordained fences. But as the 1950s moved on, and as new applications and new users emerged, the accumulating bulk of innovations began to spill over the fences.

5

Computers and Communications, Media and Money

Various forms of communications *convergence*, it is widely agreed, characterize the 1980s. The imagery itself varies – a single giant playing field, a single multipurpose work station wired into a single multipurpose network, or 'one stop communications shopping' – but it focuses primarily upon the convergence of two things, telecommunications and computers. This convergence is also seen as leading to a battle between the super-companies, AT&T and IBM, as AT&T diversifies into computers and IBM moves further into telecommunications.

Whether or not the IBM/AT&T battle goes beyond border skirmishes, the com/com convergence clearly exists. It promises to reach into almost every home and every workplace in the industrialized world.

But it may be wiser to view this convergence as *four-sided* – as including mass communications and also finance. It just happens that these latter fields provided some of the earliest – and still provide some of the best – applications for combined com/com. Com/com provides ways of shifting, processing and transporting large quantities of words, numbers and pictures. Newspapers are a prime source of words, and the financial/banking system of numbers, and the 1960s saw the early computerization of American newspapers and banks. These two areas have continued to be major examples of com/com. American newspapers are not only heavily computerized, but also now receive much of their word supply via satellite. The financial system is steadily moving away from paper transactions to electronic. Moreover, these two fields – newspapers and money – are themselves converging electronically, with AP–Dow Jones, for example, now being at the heart of both the news and the financial data markets.

In this giant convergence there are several long-term factors, just three of which will be mentioned here: defense, the microprocessor/small computer revolution and deregulation.

The com/com revolution began in the defense and military intelligence world, and much innovation continues to derive from there. It was first exhibited to the general public in the moon landings, and of course continues across the entire range of nuclear and nonnuclear military strategy. The urge to advance to ever more powerful mainframe computers, or supercomputers, comes mainly from the military.

In software too, certainly of the large system type, the military are crucial customers. Before Electronic Data Systems (EDS) was bought by General Motors (GM), it won mega-contracts from both the US Navy and Army.[1] The DOD is also centrally concerned in the development strategies of the entire US computer software business.

Com/com innovations, have typically trickled down into those parts of private industry most directly involved in DOD contracts, and then into the federal government – especially again the DOD and those government agencies closest to it.[2] In 1983 federal government agencies began to execute 'large office systems buys', some agencies were buying several thousand microcomputers with networking in mind.

The small computer revolution of the early 1980s was vital in the development of com/com because it led to a shift away from the hierarchical model of one mainframe computer with many terminals to more horizontal models featuring microcomputers capable of numerous functions besides talking to the mainframe.

Finally, *deregulation* – in its varied forms – gave com/com a distinct boost. The much celebrated Computer II decision dealt directly with the question of whether the still undivested AT&T should be allowed to add one com(munications) to the other com(puters). Computer II stated that AT&T could do this, but the device of a separate subsidiary was specified in order to guard against cross-subsidization and related antitrust sins.[3] The FCC in its Computer II decision (of April 1980) also deregulated terminal equipment.

Other deregulatory decisions had an equally explosive impact in the com/com area. The AT&T divestiture took further what earlier decisions allowing private networks and the opening up of domestic satellites had begun. Anyone could now play the network game, making anything talk to anything, with the help of telephone lines and a modem. Other FCC deregulatory decisions allowed further computer-telecommunications combinations to step into the marketplace; these included electronic mail, which enables one microcomputer (or word processor) to transmit a message into the memory of a separate remote computer for reading when the receiver so wishes, and cellular mobile radio, which involves a telephone in a car talking via a computer into the telecoms network. Also set free by deregulation were other com/com combinations, not least videotex.

Telecommunications and financial services deregulation occurred alongside each other. The Financial Deregulation and Monetary Control Act of 1980 was the centerpiece of efforts by banks to enter new financial areas – and of nonbanks to enter banking. Eager lawyers and electronic technology found numerous loopholes in the cumbersome and archaic system of bank regulation. Electronic Funds Transfer (EFT) soon allowed many billions of dollars per day to flash electronically through the gaping legal loopholes.

PUTTING NETS AROUND OFFICES AND FACTORIES

The ultimate noncommunications tower of Babel is a factory, office or company full of many different kinds of computer, each with its separate applications software, none of which can talk to the others. The opposite, and near universally desired, state is of a *network* within which large and small computers, terminals and word processors can communicate, using software which is largely or entirely interchangeable between machines. Of course, further specifications of the network vary according to the purpose in mind and the company operating the network.

Before the recent spread of microcomputers, one of the fastest-growing types of com/com was a company like Tymshare. This provided computer time-sharing, tax processing services, and, in Tymnet, a business-oriented data network using packet-switched technology. Subsequent developments removed much of the commercial appeal of Tymshare, but more companies – especially since the AT&T divestiture – are taking a much more active interest in designing their own communications networks.[4] They thus need fewer of the kinds of services provided by Tymshare, which in 1984 was bought by the aircraft manufacturer McDonnell–Douglas.

Some of the more dramatic examples of networking involve companies which build their communications systems around satellites. One such case is Citibank, which uses a Westar Satcom satellite to connect several buildings in New York City with facilities in Los Angeles, Denver, and Sioux Falls, South Dakota. Another company which relies heavily on satellite networking is the newspaper *USA Today*, whole pages being transmitted each day from Washington to printing plants around the country.

Efficient networks have been established within many different types of organizations, from airlines to supermarkets to retailers of spare parts for cars, but perhaps the most dramatic and controversial network possibilities lie in major manufacturing industry, such as car assembly. Both GM and Ford have made major efforts here.

Who would have predicted that GM would buy into both the satellite and the software business on a massive scale? But in 1984 it bought, for $2.5 billion, EDS, widely regarded as the leading software company in the US from the viewpoint of recent steady growth and even better prospects. And in 1985 GM bought Hughes Aircraft. EDS has specialized in systems integration, and has a unique record in winning huge contracts in three fields: in the processing of insurance medicaid claims; in banks, automatic clearinghouses and large companies, in which it has a 30 per cent growth record; and in federal government, where it has an even more dramatic growth record. Its first federal government contract was a $656-million 10-year contract to update the computer systems at 47 US Army bases, and included a training program for 60,000 US Army personnel. This was followed by other huge contracts for the US Navy and the US Postal Service.[5]

Why should GM want to buy a hotshot software company? For 30 years it had made no significant noncar industry acquisitions, but it changed its mind for three reasons:

1　Under its chairman Roger B. Smith, GM was planning a diversification into electronics; and this also led to GM's purchase in 1985 of Hughes Aircraft.
2　In its attempts to catch up with the Japanese, GM, one of the world's largest users of computers, was stuck with an internal data processing system plagued by too many computers that could not talk to each other.
3　GM was already committed to massive use of robots for auto assembly; and major bottlenecks were that robots 'cannot feel' or 'talk to each other' – that is, there was no systems integration.

GM thus saw EDS as a way both of improving its own production and of getting onto the rising computer software growth curve.[6]

What was there in this for EDS, one of the most flamboyant of US companies, a company based in Dallas and apparently dedicated to behaving like the *Dallas* of Hollywood? One reason why EDS could not refuse GM's offer may have been the chance it gave of putting an EDS/GM branding iron across a big slice of US manufacturing industry. For GM had already developed an elaborate 'Manufacturing Automation Protocol', which in effect set out to take away Digital Equipment Corporation's (DEC) leadership in machine and instrument control software.

The GM/EDS marriage implies that neither IBM nor AT&T will necessarily dominate in factory systems. Indeed, Ford's experience with AT&T's 'Advanced Communication System' produced little in the way of a working factory network, and much in the way of negative publicity.[7] Major car manufacturers may succeed in largely eliminating both paperwork and the use of outside telephone companies.

Although IBM hopes to play a major role in factory networks, its more traditional location in offices gives it special advantages in office automation. Although Wang has won the first (word processor) round in the office automation battle, it clearly had to expect the powerful challenge duly launched by IBM in 1984–5. But while Apple, Wang and others were all producing their Local Area Network (LAN) offerings, IBM, as often before, seemed to hold back. However, IBM's general plan of campaign is not hard to discern; within the protocol framework of its long-established 'Systems Network Architecture', its strategy stretched into the vital Private Branch Exchange (PBX) area with its purchase of Rolm, and in 1985 its deal with MCI brought IBM directly into long-distance telecommunications. Central to IBM's office automation strategy for the 1990s will be a small army of computers, supported by a large army of office applications software, capable of being linked upwards into IBM mainframes and downwards and sideways into large and small clusters of IBM microcomputers. Its strategy also includes a scheme for wiring buildings, in which twisted-pair wires – separate pairs for voice and data – extend into every office within the 'smart building', thus facilitating easy moves between offices.

The marriage of telecommunications and data processing within both office and factory points to yet another convergence, the blurring of distinctions between factory and office. In many manufacturing companies there is, of course, a significant office sector, and in such companies the prospect is of a single network encompassing robotics, word processing, electronic mail and cellular mobile phones, as well as keyboards, telephones, screens and computers.

One of the most obvious early examples of this merging of factory and office has been the American newspaper company. Once newspapers were primarily printing factories, with an adjoining, but sharply demarcated, editorial and advertising office. Now journalists have taken over the keyboarding/typesetting job once done by skilled compositors in the 'factory', and a single central computer links the previously separate sections.

'PERSONAL' COMMUNICATIONS

Prior to 1980 com/com mainly consisted of a terminal linked via a telephone line to a mainframe computer, the airline booking system being an early classic example. Since 1980 com/com has increasingly come to focus on the electronic work station, on which the worker can 'talk' not only to other microcomputers, but also to the company mainframe and the department microcomputer, and can use various kinds of software suitable for the organization's activities and also telephone or send data to his or her home.

All this has been facilitated by the deregulation of terminal equipment in 1980. Two other kinds of regulatory decision were involved in electronic mail and cellular mobile. Electronic mail offers a service not greatly different from telex, a keyboard-to-printer (teleprinter) style of telecommunications, which, conveniently for business, provides a hard copy of all messages. However, telex was not part of the AT&T empire, but belonged to that of Western Union. The US has long been behind Europe in telex, and the prevalence of microcomputers now favors electronic mail, which differs from telex in that the message, instead of being printed out on the receiving teleprinter, is stored in the receiving microcomputer until required by the recipient. Electronic mail has several competitors, including 'MCI mail', which was launched in 1983 with four levels of service, and was intended to compete with the courier services, rather than with the US Post Office, although typically flamboyant MCI advertising showed post offices undergoing demolition. However there was a real US Post Office involvement in the electronic mail business in the form of Electronic Computer Originated Mail (ECOM), which was fiercely attacked by its commercial competitors as a classic government monopoly illegally cross-subsidized by postal profits; thus electronic mail was squeezed between several regulatory regimes – the US Post Office, the hard copy 'record' carriers and the telephone carriers.

The office work station is supposedly being paralleled by the domestic 'electronic cottage' – just as you will hardly need to leave your desk in the office, so you will scarcely need to leave your home. The electronic cottage is as yet much less of a reality than the work station. But those who have a personal computer at work may also have one at home, or may commute clutching a portable. Studies to date tend to show that there is *some* truth in the idea that office workers will be able to work from home, but the main conclusion of this research is that most office workers will still need to visit their offices several times a week. Similarly, the domestic promise has some, but only some, reality. The electronic com/com gadgetry promises *fewer* visits to the bank and shops rather than none at all.

The two areas with the greatest possibility of delivering the electronic cottage are financial and mass media services. Before turning to these areas, however, we will take a brief glance at cellular mobile and paging devices. Both of these are personal gadgets – the cellular mobile phone in the car, the paging device carried in the pocket – and they each offer a potential impact both at work and at home; both can also alter commuting and travelling to the supermarket.

Cellular mobile had been around for a long time when it was finally given the FCC go-ahead in 1983. That it languished during the 1970s was partly because it posed an awkward regulatory problem. Here was a new technology which, at a time of AT&T monopoly, should logically have gone AT&T's way. Alternatively, there was an argument for a completely new monopoly on the model of the specialized (and monopoly) common carriers. Or there could be competition – but was cellular commercially strong enough to be able to bear direct competition? Eventually, in the early 1980s divestiture era, a compromise was agreed upon: competition between two (and only two) companies in each city market; one company in each case to be a telephone company and one a nontelephone company. Divestiture made this somewhat arbitrary decision more palatable because it was the regional ex-BOCs, and not AT&T, which inherited the largesse. In the top 30 markets the ex-BOCs got 23 of the telecoms licenses, and General Telephone (GTE) received a somewhat lavish 7.[8]

In the long run the new 'paging' devices may be as significant as the mobile phones. Newer versions of these pagers allow increasingly lengthy messages to be printed out. The whole business of sending and receiving messages is made vastly more efficient and flexible.

FINANCIAL DEREGULATION + COM/COM = VOLATILITY

The com/com electronic revolution has been one of several forces contributing to the volatile fortunes of the American banking and financial services industry in the late 1970s and early 1980s. The impact has been at several levels. At the customer/retail level, EFT has made possible the dispensing of cash from a machine. At the international level, com/com will make possible the New York–London–Tokyo world stock market which never sleeps; it has also enabled many billions of footloose dollars to race around the world each day, seeking and creating short-term currency fluctuations. Meanwhile, electronic banking allows several hundred billion dollars to pass back and forth instantaneously across the US on each banking day – as the banking system adjusts its balances for the day.

But as the millions and billions of dollars swoop electronically across the land, the underlying US banking system is a mess, marked by intransigent localism and state control, a vast superfluity of highly specialized and very small financial operations, and a system of regulation which is cumbersome, lax, arbitrary, overlegalized and underrespected to a degree extreme even by American standards. 'Safe as a bank' is not very safe, and banks are no longer highly rated as credit risks.

Electronic banking both reflects, and has itself contributed to, this rickety structure. First, there are too many banks at all levels, and these banks are allowed to do too few things. Main Street and the big-city skylines are dominated by local banks, which are heavily dependent on local industry, local politics and regulation for their survival. At the other extreme are the huge banks mainly on Wall Street, but also based in California and Chicago. It was a large Chicago bank, Continental Illinois, which in 1984 nearly went bankrupt, and had to be rescued by the apostles of bank deregulation.

While localism is still powerfully entrenched, several forces have sharpened competition and lowered bank earnings. The drop in inflation since the 1970s has shaken a financial system for which inflation had long been a godsend. The prospects for large safe loans to industry have dwindled as industry has turned away from banks as a source of finance. Consequently, American banks have run vast quantities of bad and dubious loans – not only to many of the world's most unreliable governments, but also many sleazy American businessmen unable to avoid bank borrowing.

Deregulation has also contributed here – in the form of the 1980 Act and other court and congressional decisions. The banking and related industries have become engulfed in political lobbying, and have also acquired legal expertise in evading the spirit, if not the letter, of the banking laws. Banks have struggled to move beyond banking, and meanwhile have ruthlessly divided their customers according to wealth and profit potential. The poor pay more and get served mostly by machines; the modestly affluent are allowed to stand in line and converse with a live teller; while the rich receive a luxury 'personal banking' service with generous inducements of various kinds.[9] This is what competition looks like in a semi-deregulated banking world of price competition for depositors and borrowers, although banks also want to operate in nonbanking pastures. The Savings and Loans (or 'Thrifts') are in dire trouble, in part because of their old habit of granting fixed-interest loans which are too low for latter-day high interest rates. The insurance business has also become more competitive and more risky.[10]

Much of the competitive action, however, has not come from these traditional, still regulated areas, but from the 'nonbank banks' – from stockbrokers like Merrill Lynch, from American Express and from department stores like Sears. These are the survivors of fierce competition, some of it from areas even further removed from banking. Communications companies on the whole have fared badly: Xerox, Control Data and RCA all made what turned out to be disastrous efforts to enter the world of financial services. A successful entrant like Merrill Lynch has had the huge advantage of being in finance but not in banking, and has thus been able to operate in all the states. American Express has moved from credit cards and travellers' checks into a wider range of financial services. And Sears has boldly attempted the one-stop financial shop, with banking, insurance, stockbroking and real estate available at adjoining counters within the Sears department store in the local shopping mall.

This has not happened without local commercial and political resistance. But Merrill Lynch, for example, plunged confidently into partnership with New York City in its support for the teleport, or 'satellite farm', on Staten Island.

Citicorp also has shown aggressive expansion both within New York and beyond. While linking up its various New York buildings to each other and to the new Staten Island facility by fiber optic,[11] Citicorp was also persuading the South Dakota legislature to change its laws so that it could escape interest-rate restrictions in New York and bring its credit card operations to Sioux Falls.[12] Since 1980 Citicorp has mounted a massive campaign to slip into as many foreign countries and as many states beyond New York as lawyers' ingenuity and political lobbying can make possible. The multiheaded federal regulatory system – the Federal Reserve, the Federal Deposit Insurance Corporation (FDIC) and the Comptroller of the Currency, plus Congress, the federal agencies and the states – has left many holes for the Citicorp legal battalions.

Crucial in the success of Citicorp in shaping bank deregulation in its own interests are the new means of electronic banking, symbolized by Citicorp's own satellite involvement. But the computer side of this is no less significant. Computers make possible the relentless and instantaneous operation of formula buying and formula selling; one set of lower quarterly earnings or one negative comment from a Wall Street specialist share analyst can immediately trigger selling instructions on computers in Hong Kong, London or Frankfurt. This was evident in the Continental Illinois crisis of 1984, which was fed by frighteningly sudden and massive panic selling not only in Chicago and New York, but in Europe and Asia.

On a more day-to-day domestic basis, increased competition and reduced brokerage charges have schooled many investors, large and small, in the virtues of aggressive portfolio management. Ironically, this 'fast forward' impact of electronic financial management has been exemplified especially clearly in the fate of computer stocks. A computer stock analyst like Steve McClellan gives as his first piece of advice, 'It never rains bad news, it pours', the implication of most of this advice being that immediately any bad news surfaces, you should sell any computer stock you have, because more bad news and continuing share price drops are coming.[13] Such advice as this, plus the opportunity to sell millions of shares literally by pressing a button, is both result and cause of Wall Street volatility in general, and of computer/hi-tech stocks in particular.

THE MERGING OF DATA, MASS COMMUNICATIONS AND COM/COM

Financial data – on screen, on satellite and on the move 24 hours a day – lies at the core of a giant merging, which includes the mass media. Financial data originate from and are still based in, *news* operations, such as AP–Dow Jones, the *Wall Street Journal*, Reuters news agency and a score of other financial publications.

The business of data bases and data transport leans heavily on data services such as Dow Jones and The Source (owned by Reader's Digest). The leading innovators in financial services also tend to have media connections. The Bank of America is a leader not only in electronic banking, but has been, and still is, a major funder of the Hollywood and international movie business. American Express made a big investment in Warner–Amex cable, in the hope of striking gold with cable TV and related banking-via-cable possibilities; that exercise was a costly failure, but a keen bank interest in cable remains.

Merrill Lynch played a very active part in the launch of cable television's Financial News Network (FNN), being a major initial investor, a major advertiser on FNN, certainly a major news source, and, while FNN was initially based in southern California, the location of FNN's New York office. This kind of involvement, like the US Chamber of Commerce's funding of a cable breakfast news show, reflects the perception that news has in the past been insufficiently pro-business.

TOWARD ONE-STOP COMMUNICATION

Videotex has seemed to offer the ultimate com/com service; but despite the electronic cottage imagery of the all-singing, all-dancing, multipurpose gadget attached to the domestic TV set, videotex has moved even more slowly in the US than Europe. Indeed, European and Canadian subsidized systems have contended to establish the US technical standards. In the US, although videotex is a combination computer terminal and telephone line, much of the early interest came from newspaper owners, anxious to protect their classified advertising.

However, the massive growth of personal computers in the US since 1983 increasingly makes a quite different kind of videotex solution possible; for example the IBM 3270 PC, launched in early 1984, offered more on-screen sophistication than previously available.

Increasingly, a date around 1990 looks to be when some major outcome can be expected. This turn-of-the-decade period may see the end of AT&T's seven-year itch to get into the electronic data business; it will also see a much wider diffusion of more sophisticated personal computers.

Certainly IBM's 1984 launches coincided with the increasing realization that financial data on screens had ceased to be a niche market – although 65 per cent dominated by the specialist Quotron company. Financial data could be the core, it now seemed, of a much wider video interactive system, stretching into financial services and home banking on the one hand, and beyond financial news into more general news and entertainment on the other. IBM involvement in two joint ventures illustrates these two sets of possibilities.

In March 1984 IBM and Merrill Lynch announced plans to compete against Quotron with an on-screen financial data offering to be called International MarketNet. A quarter of Quotron's existing market was indeed Merrill Lynch branch offices across the country and Quotron's market price fell somewhat more than a quarter on the day of the announcement. The rollout of the new service envisaged a pilot operation in Merrill Lynch's own offices in 1985, followed by availability to banks, thrifts, other brokers, insurance companies and ultimately the real estate market. After this, a limited form of the service might go to genuine *home* computer owners.[14] Later announcements indicated a fascinating variety of delivery systems:

1 over conventional telecommunications facilities (as in previous Videotex offerings);
2 via satellite dishes – in other words, a data service coming to the rescue of DBS;
3 via the Public Broadcasting Service (PBS), which reaches over 90 per cent of US homes. The service would utilize empty sections of the conventional TV signal, and pass via a special decoder onto the domestic (or office) TV screen. While a useful source of commercial funding to boost PBS's wilting finances, this mode of delivery seemed to offer unlimited marked possibilities.

The IBM alliance with Merrill Lynch was designed to prevent the British Reuters from extending its world market data dominance into the US domestic market. The IBM–Merrill Lynch linkup was in turn faced with other electronic data offerings from AT&T, Dow Jones, McGraw-Hill and Knight-Ridder. The ultimate winners of the electronic data competition seemed likely to come from a marriage of traditional data with specialist electronic delivery expertise.

Notes

1 Stephen T. McClellan, *The Coming Computer Industry Shakeout* (1984), pp. 142–3.
2 Charles Gularson and Cheryl Smith, 'The changing picture of federal office systems',

Computer World, 19 November 1984, pp. 1D/11–18.

3 Alan Pearce, 'A Masterful Decision', *Telecommunications*, June 1980, pp. 16, 21. US General Accounting Office, *Can the Federal Communications Commission Successfully Implement its Computer II Decision?* (1982). 'Court of Appeals ... upholds Commission 100% in Affirming Computer Inquiry II decision ...', *Telecommunications Reports*, 48, 15 November 1982, pp. 1–2, 4.

4 Bernard Gallagher, 'How Divestiture is Changing the Focus and Role of Today's Data Manager', *Communications News*, December 1984, p. 50.

5 McClellan, *The Coming Computer Industry Shakeout*, pp. 15–17, 137–45.

6 'GM's discussions with Electronic Data could signal a big push into new fields', *Wall Street Journal*, 21 May 1984. Urban C. Lehner and John Marcom, 'To battle the Japanese, GM is pushing boldly into computerization', *Wall Street Journal*, 9 July 1984.

7 Claudia Ricci, 'Missing Links: AT and T plan to market a computer network hits snags repeatedly', *Wall Street Journal*, 13 July 1984, pp. 1, 10. Darnon Davlin and Janet Guyon, 'GM's Planned Phone Network May Boost Effort to Autos More Efficiently', *Wall Street Journal* (Europe) 12 July 1985.

8 Colin Leinster, 'Mobile Phones: hot new industry'.

9 Daniel Hertzberg, 'US Banks Show Lack of Balance in fees for rich, poor customers', *Wall Street Journal* (Europe), 23 October 1984, pp. 11, 24.

10 Tim Carrington and Daniel Hertzberg, 'Money at Risk: Financial Institutions are showing strain of a decade of turmoil', *Wall Street Journal*, 5 September 1984, pp. 1, 28.

11 Michael A. Laviola, 'The Citibank Fiber-Optic Network', *Telecommunications*, February 1984, pp. 86–94.

12 'Citicorp: The battle for America', *The Economist*, 3 March 1984, pp. 77–8.

13 McClellan, *The Coming Computer Industry Shakeout*, pp. 323–4.

14 'Merrill Lynch joins IBM Venture', *New York Times*, 22 March 1984. Dennis Kneale and Scott Murray, 'Merrill Lynch and IBM unveil venture to deliver stock-quote data to IBM PCs', *Wall Street Journal*, 22 March 1984.

6

High-tech Machismo and the
Unfenced Communications Range

FROM STATIC REGULATED TECHNOLOGY TO DYNAMIC UNREGULATED TECHNOLOGY?

In writing about the old monopoly era of the US telephone industry and the more recent era of competition, Manley Irwin presented the schema shown in Table 6.1.

Under the old era of control, AT&T, via its effective monopoly of new technology obtained through Bell Labs, was able to control its entire market and political environment, and to proceed at its own pace, with its own technology, at its own cost-plus-profit, and in charge of its own destiny. During this time it concentrated – initially with reluctance, later with enthusiasm – on providing universal telephone service, and on subsidizing rural areas and local consumers through rate-averaging. It also continued to control its technological destiny by investing heavily in research, not only in the immediate area of telephones, but much more widely in electronics; it followed this aggressive research policy with an equally aggressive buying-up of other people's patents, and by maintaining a highly litigious watch over all potential encroachments.

In pursuit of technological security in telecommunications, AT&T made many of the basic discoveries in other areas of electronics. It also continued its long history of self-denial (and regulatory denial) by refraining from expansion into new fields. How then did its lose control of the technological battle and of its own destiny?

Judge Greene said that microwave spelled the death of a phone monopoly which was 'natural' only when telephone lines were strung between poles.[1] But other broader trends, dramatized by the Second World War, also played a part. Whereas before 1940 high-tech research and development was largely confined to a few dominant firms which could afford massive outlays, such as AT&T and RCA, after 1940 the federal government funded research on a scale that even AT&T could not match – the entire defense and aviation expenditure, the space program,

TABLE 6.1 An era of contrasts

Area	Era of control	Era of competition
Research and development	Electromechanical	Electronic
	Limited R & D base	Broad base
	Discretionary change	Accelerated change
	Limited substitutes	Expanding substitutes
	Domestic expertise	International expertise
	Crisp market boundaries	Softened market boundaries
Manufacturing	Narrow base of participation	Expanding base
	Product size: large	Product size: miniaturization increasing
	Product content: labor	Product content: capital
	Design cycle time: long	Design cycle time: short
	Product life: long	Product life: contracting
	Cost-plus pricing	Learning curve pricing
Facilities	Capital intensive; limited entry	Capital diversity; less entry restriction
	Cost of capital: prohibitive	Cost of capital: declining
	Depreciation life: long	Depreciation life: contracting
	Investment substitutes: limited	Investment substitutes: expanding
	Rate base accounting unquestioned	Rate base accounting inadequate
Services	No entry	Market entry
	Geographic separation	Geographic fusion
	Service boundaries clear	Service boundaries coalescing

Source: Manley R. Irwin, 'The American Telephone Industry', in Walter Adams (ed.), *The Structure of American Industry* (1982), p. 313.

and the huge flowering of university research, much of it also federally funded. Further, research and development became much more widely practised in a whole range of fast-growing new and related industries. In consequence there came to be many other companies, from outside telephones or mass media, which introduced their own new technologies and began to stake commercial and regulatory claims. And these new industries, such as aerospace, computers and office equipment systems, led to new generations of technology and new market entry coming onto the scene much more quickly and unpredictably.

Perhaps the key change was the simple fact of *growth*. The 1930s had a profoundly chilling effect on the entire telecoms/electronics world. Western Electric's peak sales year before the Depression was 1929, and in 1941 its sales were still below that point. But in 1942 it had a 44 per cent increase over 1941. From then on, such huge growth rates became common, not only within AT&T, but also among its rivals.

THE INTERNATIONAL DIMENSION: GEOGRAPHY

History and geography have given the US a special concern with communications of all kinds. The communications industries are themselves 'bi-coastal', split by a 3,000-mile gulf. The oil industry migrated to Alaska, and on stilts out into the Gulf of Mexico, and American industry has gone multinational. The US needs communications technologies which are efficient across both continents and oceans. The old British Empire staple of the ocean cable is a cumbersome means by which to talk to oil-drilling platforms. Geography has long favored radio communication or microwave, and the technology of many modern industries supports this.

Geography has also favored satellites. Many European distances are, or at least seem, too short to justify satellites. Europe also shares with Africa and the Middle East the same section of the equator, 15°W to 45°E, with some hundred countries squeezed into one-sixth of the world's available satellite slot space. But North America looks down (to the west of South America) on a vast expanse of empty Pacific, and the US, with Alaska and Hawaii staking claims far to the west, has *domestic* communications satellites spread (by international agreement) between 72°W and 143°W. The US shares with only some dozen north and central American countries one-fifth of the equator. Together with the USSR, the US seems to have been cast by favorable location, as well as area, into a role in space.

THE INTERNATIONAL DIMENSION: SECURITY AND BUSINESS

The DOD supports and reflects the national emphasis on far-flung communications. The US has long had military bases in Asia, Europe and elsewhere; it is thus, for both routine and war-readiness purposes, the ultimate multinational organization, continuously pumping data of many kinds through its world-circling data pipelines. The US military, especially at home, relies heavily on civilian communications, which means AT&T. The reason is obvious: AT&T's huge network is immensely flexible; in case of war or other emergency, it offers many alternative routes between Washington and Omaha, Nebraska, or between any other two points.

This is not to imply that all US communications are dominated by the military; the emphasis should probably be the other way around. The military are first among the clients of AT&T and IBM. There is much informal contact, and many military communications specialists enter the civilian industry. The influence cannot but have been important in the evolution of the consensus that the US must be number one in communications performance and innovation, no matter what it costs.

An important meeting point of civilian and security concerns is the vexed issue of high-tech exports, either legal or illegal, to the Soviet Union. Despite the bitterness caused by the practical application of official policy, there is little difference of opinion in the US on the validity of the overall goal.

It is also generally believed that US commercial enterprise abroad must be spearheaded by US leadership in all branches of communications – from Boeing aircraft to Hollywood movies, from NASA satellites to IBM computers. This general belief has been reinforced in recent years by the internationalization of the world's banking system and financial services.

COMPUTERS + TELECOMMUNICATIONS = THE TRANSFORMATION OF US BUSINESS

Given the far-flung geography of most large US companies, the central financial control, if not stock control, which allows continuous monitoring of many company locations and the supply of quarterly, indeed daily, financial numbers – all is only made possible by modern communications. But this is not simply a case of US business being technology-led. As Dan Schiller has demonstrated in *Telematics and Government* (1982), the marriage of computers and telecommunications in the service of US business was to a very large extent led by the US federal government. In the marriage of an unregulated, market-oriented, salesman-led industry like computers and a regulated technology-oriented, engineer-led company like AT&T, big business customers in the 1950s and 1960s found that AT&T was always the reluctant partner.

Just as telephones, along with typewriters, created the conditions necessary for the separation of the office in the downtown office district from the factory in the factory district in the 1890s, so after 1945 telecommunications enabled 'Detroit' to be spread nationwide. Industries which pioneered the marriage of computers and telecommunications in the 1950s and early 1960s were airlines, such as Eastern and United, which pioneered computer-based ticketing; retailers such as Sears, which needed a national system for credit, stock control and billing; railroads; oil companies with their numerous remote locations; the aerospace industry with its vast number of component suppliers; big manufacturing companies in heavy industries like chemicals and steel; and banks.

As these industries increasingly used computers-cum-telecoms as bases of the company's structural architecture, they found more and more to complain of in the services supplied by AT&T – services that were too concerned with the mass telephone market and not geared to intra-company communication; AT&T was oriented to voice traffic, leaving computers idle for untold, expensive seconds at a time. But the big companies were still dependent on AT&T, primarily for plain old telephone service. Nevertheless, despite the still comparatively small total size of the data traffic involved, big business obtained a compromise decision from the FCC: the FCC's lengthy 'Computer I' inquiry of 1966–71 finally concluded that communications and hybrid data services could go unregulated.

The big telecoms users, wielding high-tech and business efficiency arguments, had scored a useful tactical draw against AT&T. Technology was leading the FCC and AT&T; but technology was in the sense of the specialized organizational requirements of US national and multinational companies.[2] The technology was also being powerfully led by the numerous agencies of the US government which had been early and classic customers for the big early computers, linked to federal buildings and local offices across the continent.

PRODUCT CYCLE SPEED UP: THE SILICON VALLEYING OF
AMERICA

The whole advent of new technologies seems to be shifting from the measured tread of the old AT&T elephant to the pace of small computer and electronics companies with 25-year-old chief executives working 24 hours a day, searching for a market niche with the aid of a million-dollar ad campaign and a hundred-million-dollar bank loan. This may be the slightly overdramatized version of Silicon Valley presented by San Jose PR firms. But it had around 1980 a certain reality, and even the star status of Silicon Valley entrepreneurs is reminiscent of the early movie stars of United Artists in early Hollywood, who also played and directed all the parts, had huge bank loans and personal publicists.

The bank loans were a key factor, and present-day Silicon Valley innovation is a more risky bank investment than were the movies of Chaplin or Fairbanks. This need for high-risk, big-bucks financing has been partly met by the emergence in the US of the venture capital movement. Indeed, successful computer companies like Apple are prime examples of venture capital and financing paying off. Factors in the growth of the venture capital movement include the real prospect of very high returns, relaxations of capital gains tax in 1978, and a further loosening of financial rules which has allowed the big insurance fund investors to include ultrahigh risks in their portfolios.[3]

But the venture capital movement is there not merely to help the small innovative company; it is also there to help the banks, and increasingly to help the established giants like IBM. In return for their high-risk investment, the banks or industry giants not only get the chance of a high return; they also acquire intelligence about new developments, new products and new personnel. Such investment provides a means of incorporating bohemian originality and youthful arrogance in the portfolio, if not the offices, of such conservative buttoned-down companies as IBM, RCA or General Electric (GE).

One result is that the scenarios of shakeout, followed by renewed big-company dominance, may have already been played out financially before they happen in terms of overt company structure. The demise of yet another small computer, cable or software company may in some cases be little more than a big company calling, not merely the loans, but the entire small company itself into the major corporation's fold. Of course, this all has potential antitrust implications, and the increased stability of the big, established company must be placed against the potential scenario of shakeout followed by antitrust litigation.

Finally, the venture capital business, which is a key user of communications industry forecasting, must itself constitute one reason why such forecasts are an extreme case of the inaccuracy common in economic forecasting. The frenzied marketing assaults almost invite a faddish response of 'all aboard for this season's consumer electronic fad'; government regulations, court decisions, and competitors' strategies all switch with bewildering speed; and little is known about consumers, least of all their anxiety about jumping on the wrong technological bandwagon and ending up with quickly obsolete equipment.

But venture capital thinking itself is designed to take forecasts, based inevitably on projections of recent trends, and to drive a new highway at right angles across such projections. Or to change the metaphor, small high-risk innovators are in the niche-seeking business; they seek specialized niches too small and inaccessible for the big battalion to reach. But any sustained successful exploitation of a niche transforms it from a narrow niche into a broad pathway. Thus, it was only as the personal computer market seemed to turn sour and company failures multiplied, that IBM, the sure-footed elephant, trotted briskly into the marketplace.

CONSUMER PRICES: FREE FALL

A crucial uncertainty in the introduction of new technologies concerns prices which have often fallen many times faster than inflation has risen. Among the most familiar examples are the big computers of old, whose computing power is now available from a desk-top computer at less than 1 per cent of the original price. The silicon chip lies behind the former $500 calculator wristwatch now available for $5. Only slightly less familiar are the price drops in international telephone calls, resulting from the hundredfold capacity increase of later generations of communications satellites. Moreover, it is now possible to lease satellite channels on a 24-hour basis for not much more than is charged for 2 hours per day, which in turn costs what a few minutes of satellite time cost 20 years ago.

The recent hyperactivity in technological innovation results in part from companies anticipating the price drops which previously took perhaps a decade to fall the full distance. Now, by setting out to sell not a thousand, but a million units in the first year, you can concertina the entire price drop, and package it into the initial launch as key ingredient.

This 'shoot first' tactic has its most spectacular illustration in the chip industry – microprocessors and semiconductors – because this industry features cheap materials and a steep manufacturing 'learning curve'. Initially there is a high percentage of rejects, but with experience the proportion falls sharply, making possible a parallel sharp fall in prices. Similar scenarios also characterize a wide range of other fields, from the provision of satellite programming services in cable to the marketing of the latest type of telephone handset.

Western imagery reminds us that in any shoot-out positioning and timing are vital. Shooting first seems to offer the machismo company many possible benefits. Not least is the possibility of frightening off opponents before they have fired a shot.

SATELLITES VERSUS MICROWAVE VERSUS FIBER OPTICS

While the spectacular rises and falls of personal computer companies provide one compelling source of machismo imagery, there is no shortage of similar imagery from the most expensive and strategic of technologies.

Microwave was a technology which came to fruition in the 1950s; satellites had their most spectacular decade in the 1960s; and glass fiber optics is widely touted as *the* telecommunications technology of the 1980s. Some people predict that each may find its optimal applications – fiber optics for trunk routes, with microwave perhaps as the effective all-purpose flexible performer. As for satellites, they are the subject of widely divergent predictions.

But, in keeping with the trend toward greater speed of introduction and greater uncertainty, the biggest questions of all surround the explosively growing fiber-optic technology. Both the military and the FCC have been involved in its development; but important as these have been, fiber optics has been primarily a commercial development. AT&T (through its old subsidiary Western Electric) and Corning Glass each had about a third of the US market in 1983. Like other new technologies, fiber optics involves big initial investments by both manufacturers and customers. AT&T has been vital as a major manufacturer and customer. The big payoff in fiber optics lies partly in its high quality for voice, data and video alike, but, even more important, in its massive capacity. Fiber optics offers not just a broader highway, but a sudden leap onto a super-highway a hundred lanes wide. Or to put it another way, the traffic capacity of telecommunications is making such a huge leap forward that capacity is effectively approaching infinity.

But just as the promise is almost infinite, so also the uncertainty factor is vast – a set of interconnected uncertainties which may not be resolved before the 1990s. Initially the US had a number of advantages over Japan and all other countries. Fiber optics is genuinely high tech; and in addition to Corning Glass and AT&T, GTE – the largest telephone independent – was involved in the first telephone traffic use in 1977; thus there was an element of competition with cooperation.

The geography of the US has also been significant. The first contracts from AT&T and MCI were for the Northeast corridor from Boston to Richmond, Virginia; next came Los Angeles to San Franciso; and ultimately most of the major railroad routes across the continent seem destined to be laid with the glass cable. Following various phone–rail deals (such as MCI with Amtrak), some railroads decided to go it alone with fiber; in September 1984 Norfolk Southern and Santa Fe announced plans for an 8,000-mile fiber system capable of carrying 300,000 simultaneous voice transmissions.[4] Japan (and other fiber producers such as Siemens of Germany) lack these vast distances, and it is no accident that in 1983 the US still accounted for 85 per cent of world sales.

Nevertheless, Japan has indeed targeted this technology, and there is intense interest in how Japanese competition will play out in terms of volume and price. As elsewhere, US deregulation multiplies both the possibilities and the uncertainties. Deregulation has been kind to US fiber optics in removing any regulatory roadblocks to its early growth; no longer does the FCC try to protect the technological status quo. But deregulation has also offered hope to foreign competition. Indeed, MCI predictably steered clear of AT&T and its friends, and became a major purchaser of Japanese fiber optics for its initial Northeast corridor purchases.

The FCC responded to fiber optics and its uncertainties with its by now standard massive encouragement of new technologies. In the 1984 decision on the first fiber-optic Atlantic cable, there was indeed a strong element of technological machismo. It was pointed out to the FCC that during the remainder of the 1980s radically expanded INTELSAT satellite capacity would run well ahead of even the most bullish forecasts of demand. The fiber cable would compound a situation of massive overcapacity around 1990. Despite head-shaking by at least two of its five commissioners, the FCC, confronted with a yes or no vote on a crucial high-technology leadership project, voted for US leadership and consequent massive overcapacity. The French and British were happy to get contracts at their ends of the cable. AT&T duly received the lion's share of the massive contract, and thus of course acquired greatly improved chances of extending its leadership to many other glass fiber cables across the world's oceans.

In adopting this machismo posture, the FCC made the future look secure for AT&T. But it compounded the price and political uncertainties of the medium-term future for everyone else. While offering the prospect of further big price reductions not only in transatlantic phone calls, but also in TV transmissions and data hookups, the FCC's machismo must shake long-term confidence in satellites.

MACHISMO, INSECURITY AND MOTOROLA

Deregulation tends to be followed by the multiplication of new entrants, which in turn leads to a massive shakeout of small companies. But of course high-tech machismo also threatens the survival of established companies with sales in the low billions.

Even the most successful middle-size high-tech companies face an extremely unsure future. One example is Motorola, which in 1983–4 reached several pinnacles of success with new high-tech products. Motorola seemed to have made the none-too-common transition from one old technology to several new ones. Long a dominant name in car radios, it made its last car radio in December 1983, and became, with Texas Instruments and IBM (for its own use), one of the then three largest producers in the world of semiconductors. Also in 1983–4,

Motorola's very long wait before entering cellular mobile radio began to pay off in a big way. This superior car telephone system was invented by Bell Labs back in 1969, but was kept waiting in the wings by the FCC. Cellular offers greatly improved quality, and allows hundreds of thousands – rather than just thousands – of people to have car telephones.

At last, in 1983, the FCC gave the go-ahead, and produced rules which meant that existing phone companies (in practice, mainly the ex-BOCS) got one out of two cellular franchises in each city. Motorola had developed what the market regarded as about the best system, both the in-car telephones and the switching equipment that hands cars on from one transmitter cell to another within a city, and it did excellently in early sales.

Motorola was also in the high-tech lead in the development of portable two-way paging devices. Motorola received the accolade of having its pagers purchased in bulk by IBM and by NTT of Japan.[5]

Motorola also looked well placed to dominate the introduction of stereo sound to AM radio. This was another area in which the FCC dithered, giving a preliminary decision to Magnavox and later retracting. The FCC then left the contest open, but Delco, a division of GM and the largest domestic maker of radio sets, adopted the Motorola system, thus rendering it the probable effective standard.

Whether or not Motorola continues to make all the right decisions, it's easy to see that this company, exceptionally successful in 1983–4 in several highly competitive high-tech fields, will in each area have to face severe competitive threats from Japan, the US and elsewhere.

THE ISDN FUTURE: THROUGH A GLASS FIBER, DARKLY

Perhaps the ultimate example of technological change in the communications field is the Integrated Services Digital Network (ISDN). This is no less than a single communication pipeline for all communications, with tentacles stretching to every home, every office and every car, plane or person subscribing to what once was 'plain old telephone service'. ISDN, being digital, will be able to take voice, video, data, stereo, facsimile, electronic mail and anything else invented in the meanwhile. Nor is this some uncertain Star Wars notion of the future. The ISDN is already being built onto the present national and international telephone/telecom voice/video/data networks of today. Detailed planning was well advanced in a number of technical committees at the International Telecommunications Union (ITU) in Geneva before the year 1984 dawned.[6]

This extraordinary, yet tediously detailed, project incorporates in one giant envelope of both hope and menace the ironies, paradoxes and complex obscurities of technological innovation in communications. ISDN seems to be another project – like the atomic bomb or the NASA moon landing program – on which many brilliant minds have worked, but whose ultimate purpose or even immediate consequences nobody understands, and few have even seriously contemplated.

ISDN will be dominated by the dozen or so major telecommunications powers, with West Europe, Japan and the US in the lead. AT&T and IBM will be the two most important organizations involved. Was this why Charlie Brown had a glint in his eye as he announced the divestiture of the Bell regional companies in January 1982? Can anything prevent AT&T, the biggest of the telecoms giants – and the only one specializing in long-distance, multipurpose high-tech communications – from dominating the planning and execution of ISDN? Although the European PTTS and AT&T/IBM/ITT/FCC will supposedly be carrying out government policy, does anyone expect Washington to understand, let alone control, those committees beavering away in Geneva, or the multi-billion-dollar investments which follow?

Is this not going to be the biggest and best evidence that the real uses and usefulness of new technologies tend to be discovered only after they have been introduced? Finally, will not the ISDN, as it builds ever more certainly into a universal communications system, at the same time yet further exacerbate the surrounding uncertainty? Will not this ISDN octopus have a chilling effect on many other new technologies and potential investments?

The ISDN may be the ultimate in high-tech machismo, something which, although vast in scope and full of unknown consequences, is a practical engineering proposition, part of the remorseless competitive thrust for more advanced technology, and thus something which no industrial nation wants to be left out of. In the US, as in other participating countries, the arrival of ISDN requires a switch-over to digital – a high-tech version of the old Morse dots and dashes, which now allows all communication to be encoded in a single system of infinite simplicity and infinite capacity.

FROM BUSINESS TO CONSUMER MARKETS?

The American telephone system has two publics: business and domestic, which now generate approximately equal dollar revenue. This situation, which accounts for many policy dilemmas and much of the political excitement, has indeed resulted partly from the old AT&T accepting its natural monopoly obligation to take universal service to the great American public. This accomplishment of virtually universal service took about a hundred years.

Other communications markets are broadly following the telephone pattern, starting with businesses and business executives. Radio took an approximately similar route – industrial and military use before the takeoff around 1920 of a mass market for public radio broadcasting. Even the press in its early days was heavily oriented toward commercial and shipping news. Only the video media were an exception.

Today's most dynamic communications sector is data/information services/computing; part of its fast growth includes a tendency to jump more rapidly from the business to the domestic market than in the past. The personal computer for office/business use was quickly adapted by Apple and others for use in the home. But this demand had elements of faddism, and the search for a strong domestic market for computers or terminals will continue.

The question of consumer demand is also vital for such strategic developments as the ISDN. Clearly it may be convenient for a big company to pump all or most of its communications – financial data, purchasing, stock control, video and voice – down one digital data pipeline. But will a domestic household be happy to be attached for all its electronic needs by a single wire to the same giant pipeline? There will clearly be many political and privacy questions, besides purely marketing ones. And once again the technology will play both chicken and egg. Will the technology of privacy and consumer choice be able to outsmart the technology of integrated digital information?

One of the few certainties may be the continuing overlap volatility of business and consumer markets.

Notes

1 Lunch address to Practising Law Institute Conference, Implementing the AT&T Settlement, Shoreham Hotel, Washington DC. (1983).
2 Schiller, *Telematics and Government*, pp. 22–41.
3 Michael Schrage, 'Nation's High-Tech Engine fueled by Venture Capital', *Washington Post*, 20 May 1984, pp. G1–2, 8–10. 'It's the Morning After for Venture Capitalists', *Business Week*, 24 September 1984, pp. 82–3.
4 Sari Horwitz, '2 Railroads move into Fiber Optics', *Washington Post*, 13 September 1984, p. D1.
5 Motorola, *Annual Report*, 1983.
6 Anthony M. Rutkowski, 'ISDN: Designing the world's telecommunications networks', *Inter Media*, March 1983, pp. 14–23.

7

Unfencing Space: from International to Domestic Competition

INTELSAT: A CHALLENGE TO THE USSR AND AT&T

During his presidency of 1961–3, John Kennedy gave tremendous emphasis to space, including the manned moon landings. In addition he planned not only to rival the Soviet Union in space militarily, but also to make the US the world leader in civilian communications uses of space. This meant using space for two things in which the US was already a leader–television and telephones.

Initially, space was a purely international realm. Indeed, in 1962 all satellites still circled the world, and the geostationary, or parking, orbit had not yet been demonstrated. The major early use was for international telephone calls, and, while the transmission of television pictures across the Atlantic was more spectacular, it was a minor factor in use and earnings. But initially, TV via satellite was expensive and cumbersome, with one transmission filling up the entire capacity of the Intelsat I (Early Bird) satellite launched in 1965.

The goal of competition with the USSR, primarily in telephone traffic, was broadly successful. This goal was achieved via the International Telecommunications Satellite Organization (INTELSAT). Although other industrialized nothern countries (plus Australia) joined – indeed were vital for any international traffic – INTELSAT was initially owned 61 per cent by US interests.

Attached to this success was a double paradox. First, while *competing* with the Soviet Union (and to some extent Canada) in the civilian communications use of space, the US created a new domestic *monopoly* organization called COMSAT. In view of the early 61 per cent financial control, COMSAT became the operator of INTELSAT, and COMSAT/INTELSAT was de facto virtually a single organization.

In another paradox, the US government quite easily outplayed the USSR on the world telephone/communications stage, but had a much more difficult and indecisive struggle with its home telephone monopoly AT&T. Not only did INTELSAT and COMSAT overlap each other, but both also overlapped AT&T initially. The telephone giant was the leading owner of COMSAT, and the nonsatellite segments of international satellite calls also went primarily over AT&T's terrestrial facilities. Finally, AT&T also owned the lion's share of the main competing facilities, the under-ocean cables.

Since 1962 this three-sided relationship – INTELSAT/COMSAT/AT&T – has been the focus of US policy. For many years both foreign telecommunications authorities and US deregulators tried to prize the three apart. COMSAT's grip on INTELSAT was the first linkage to be weakened. But the total deregulation of domestic satellites took 22 years, until 1984.

The initial communications satellite system reflected not only the current state of the technology, but also the realities of AT&T's interests. The satellite system closely resembled the ocean cable arrangements, but transposed into space. Satellite 'gateways' were established – antennas in the form of vast dishes located in remote coastal areas, free (it was said) from the dangers of urban interference. The satellite itself had not only a low traffic capacity, but sent out only a weak signal. All this minimized any threat to AT&T. The weak signal/big dish architecture meant that gateways were expensive, and therefore limited in number. Most of the ultimate charge to telephone users was for the terrestrial leg, which meant that AT&T suffered little or no revenue loss.

Before looking at the 1962 legislation, it's worth recollecting just how dominant AT&T was in three relevant areas:

1 *international telecommunications* via ocean cable, in which AT&T had about an 80 per cent share, the remainder being spread between RCA, ITT and Western Union International (WUI);
2 *US domestic long-distance telephoning*, in which AT&T in 1962 had a 100 per cent monopoly;
3 *local US domestic telephones*, in which it had 80 per cent of the market, the other 20 per cent belonging to GTE and the other local independents.

This degree of AT&T dominance posed a dilemma, not only in satellites, but also in telecommunications: how to introduce competition, while preventing the dominant company from swallowing up its much smaller competitors. Or, in other words, how to reduce monopoly without increasing regulation?

PRESIDENT KENNEDY AND TELEPHONE POLITICS

The INTELSAT birth in the early 1960s was remarkably free of major conflict. The West Europeans reluctantly accepted the US initiative. Such effective opposition as occurred was largely in Washington, where the most vigorous opposition was from Democrats in both House and Senate, who saw the marriage of AT&T and the other major commercial carriers with the federal government in COMSAT as an unfortunate concession to both commerce and monopoly. Despite a filibuster in the Senate and hearings in a wide range of committees, the legislation moved quickly. Neither the State Department nor the DOD played very active roles. The telecommunications interests were much more active in their own self-protection, and they saw more quickly than the DOD such key distinctions as that between space and ground segments.[1]

However, in the light of later efforts at major legislation, perhaps the most remarkable aspect is the extent to which there was a clear national policy, which was first outlined by Kennedy in his State of the Union address ten days after his inauguration. Four months later, in the speech of 25 May 1961 in which he announced the goal of a man on the moon by 1970, Kennedy also called for the consolidation of American space leadership through an acceleration in the use of space satellites for international communication. Following this strong presidential lead, the Washington political process began to hum along in more or less civics textbook fashion. Congress took a very active, broadly constructive and clarifying role in modifying, but not radically altering, the presidential proposal. There was vigorous congressional opposition and some hard bargaining, but by Washington standards the delay was brief. The major industries lobbied vigorously, but were willing to settle for half. The complex bill was finally signed into law on 31 August 1962, some 15 months after the President's space speech.

There was a strong sense that this was an extension into a new sphere of tried and trusted policies. The US tradition of a regulated commercial enterprise, with rates, profits and areas of activity all under federal agency control, was being extended from the oceans into space. Space too was a not unfamiliar sphere, and this legislation followed on the lengthy post-Sputnik debate of the years 1957–60. The most severe rivalries in the US space effort had perhaps been those between the military services prior to 1957.

While John and Robert Kennedy and Lyndon Johnson are all gone, several of the key figures were still contributing to US communications policy more than two decades later. They included Newton Minow, then FCC chairman; Nicholas Katzenbach, then deputy attorney general; Robert McNamara, then Secretary of Defense; and Richard Colino, an early employee at COMSAT. The first two of these were active 20 years later in the interests of AT&T and IBM; and Richard Colino became head of INTELSAT in 1984. Joseph Charyk, who led COMSAT during its first 20 years, had previously been an assistant secretary of Defense under Eisenhower.

However, despite these careers stretching across decades of communications policy, there is also a sense in which the early COMSAT arrangements were seen as policies only for that decade of the 1960s. COMSAT and INTELSAT were actually conceived as part of the same policy that did indeed put men on the moon eight years after the 1961 speech. Parallel to the US technological achievement in reaching the moon was another dramatic demonstration of US technological and diplomatic clout – INTELSAT, a world telephone and television system in which the US and COMSAT were the hub, and behind which lay the showbiz of Hollywood and the peaceful technology of AT&T.

At the time, liberals saw this as an AT&T takeover; others were worried that AT&T would refuse to play ball in the compromise. AT&T itself could surely note several advantages – it was getting into a major new communications field, while largely deflecting any potential antitrust fears away from itself and onto COMSAT. The FCC was left with a lot of awkward regulatory detail, while AT&T was forging links around the world, not only with telecoms administrations, but with broadcast organizations and infant space industries. AT&T was also consolidating its status in the ITU and Geneva as the first among equals. While COMSAT might grow and wilt, the prospect for AT&T looked increasingly rosy.

THE COMSAT CONUNDRUM

COMSAT was the US national authority within INTELSAT; but initially it was more than that. COMSAT in the 1960s owned 61 per cent of the infant INTELSAT, and it was also the operator of a system which in other respects was an offshoot of NASA. COMSAT shared ownership of INTELSAT with the West Europeans, Japan, Canada and Australia, but one of the peculiarities of international communication is that it takes at least two countries even to make an international phone call. Foreign participation was initially about as minimal as such basic facts would allow.

COMSAT, it has been said, is the victim of its own success.[2] Two decades later, INTELSAT has long since taken over its own running, and COMSAT has become a strange and wayward symbol of the fragility of space communications and of the traditional American suspicion of any publicly regulated commercial enterprise which fails to establish an impregnable monopoly.

COMSAT, then, has suffered a double melt-down. As the US member of INTELSAT, it has gone from being the dominant owner and sole operator to being merely the largest owner (with under a quarter of the shares). But domestically also, COMSAT has ceased to be a pioneering organization, one which used to carry the American technological flag around the world. After two decades COMSAT has suffered a domestic melt-down, having diversified into a range of space activities other than INTELSAT – new enterprises that have proved to be extremely complex and financially risky. In 1984 COMSAT effectively pulled out of both Satellite Business Systems (SBS) and DBS.

But in early 1984, as AT&T was splitting into eight pieces, COMSAT was still profitably buoyed up by its 23 per cent share of INTELSAT's success. Inevitably, COMSAT was bitterly resented by the commercial firms trying to enter the expensive domain of space.

Deregulation has had its impact on COMSAT and on all US communications activities in space. But here, even more than elsewhere, the trends of the Carter and Reagan years are all part of a history that goes back to the initiatives of the Kennedy presidency. COMSAT was a stopgap device, recognized as initially necessary to get US space supremacy off the ground, but resented by the telecoms common carriers and soon the object already of antitrust suspicion. As a compromise between Government, AT&T and the other carriers, COMSAT was assigned a 'designated carrier' role; it was not itself allowed to supply services to end users, but was a 'carrier's carrier', a strange middleman whose role seemed increasingly to consist in presiding over a few small groups of large earth stations. As this small number of very big dishes itself became demystified – larger numbers of small dishes seeming better suited to user needs – COMSAT was accused of being a technologically archaic 1960s monopoly unfit for the new technologies and new competition of the 1980s.

COMSAT's history illustrates four additional generalizations about space, and about US space efforts in particular:

(1) Space communications is a very expensive game. Even COMSAT, which launched INTELSAT, may not be big enough. The capital sums involved are huge; the lead time before a return may be very lengthy, and while big profits are possible ultimately, they depend on luck and regulatory whim. It took NASA, the US government and the world's then largest company (AT&T) to get this show on the road in the early 1960s. In the 1980s the main players are the big boys of electronics and communications.

(2) The long lead times and the multiple uncertainties present at their birth mean that satellites are often not used in the way initially intended.

(3) Space satellites have played a key role in alerting the US and the world to so-called new technology. They have also been central to the breaking down of barriers of all kinds, not simply by making international phone calls cheaper and 'live by satellite' television commonplace, but by starting to dissolve boundaries between phone calls and TV programs, between mass media and data.

(4) This latter versatility was also cited by their supporters as the reason why satellites would survive the arrival of fiber optics. Satellite capacity expanded enormously – from 120 circuits on Intelsat I in the mid-1960s, for example, to 45,000 circuits on Intelsat VI in the mid-1980s – and this high capacity easily accommodates new uses like teleconferencing and the transmission of newspaper pages. Satellites are also suitable both for point-to-point (as in the original gateway-to-gateway INTELSAT configuration) and point-to-multipoint communication (as in distribution via satellite to thousands of local cable systems). Moreover, while AT&T encouraged people to think of satellites as suitable only for distances of thousands of miles, satellite in fact is quite economical for distances of a few hundred miles – in other words, for general long-distance US telephoning.

1965–72 TRENCH WARFARE ON DOMESTIC SATELLITE COMPETITION

For over seven years, from September 1965 to December 1972, a slogging battle was fought in Washington over the issue of US domestic communications satellites. The outcome, around the time of total domestic satellite (COMSAT) deregulation, is shown in Figure 7.1.

In 1984 there were seven separate organizations with domestic communications satellites operating commercially. This was more competition than most people foresaw at the time of the domsat policy battle. AT&T had only one satellite; COMSAT had its Comstar series; and two other satellite operators – RCA and Western Union – are two very familiar names in the history of US telecommunications. The only total newcomer is Hughes, although, as the premier satellite launching company, Hughes also was hardly an unknown quantity. The remaining company – SBS – started 1984 under the joint ownership of COMSAT, IBM and the Aetna life insurance company, but during 1984 COMSAT dropped out. (SBS was in turn descended from an MCI and Lockheed subsidiary.) Thus, while there was very genuine competition, it was competition between established corporate heavyweights which, given the initial costs, is hardly surprising.

As soon as the viability of INTELSAT has been demonstrated, the first demands for domestic satellites were heard. The transatlantic Early Bird inaugural two-way telecast occurred on 2 May 1965. In September of that year, ABC television applied to the FCC for a TV distribution satellite; this was a clear attack on AT&T and its high charges for television networking. The FCC cautiously returned the application to ABC 'without prejudice'. In March 1966 the FCC launched the first of a long series of satellite inquiries.

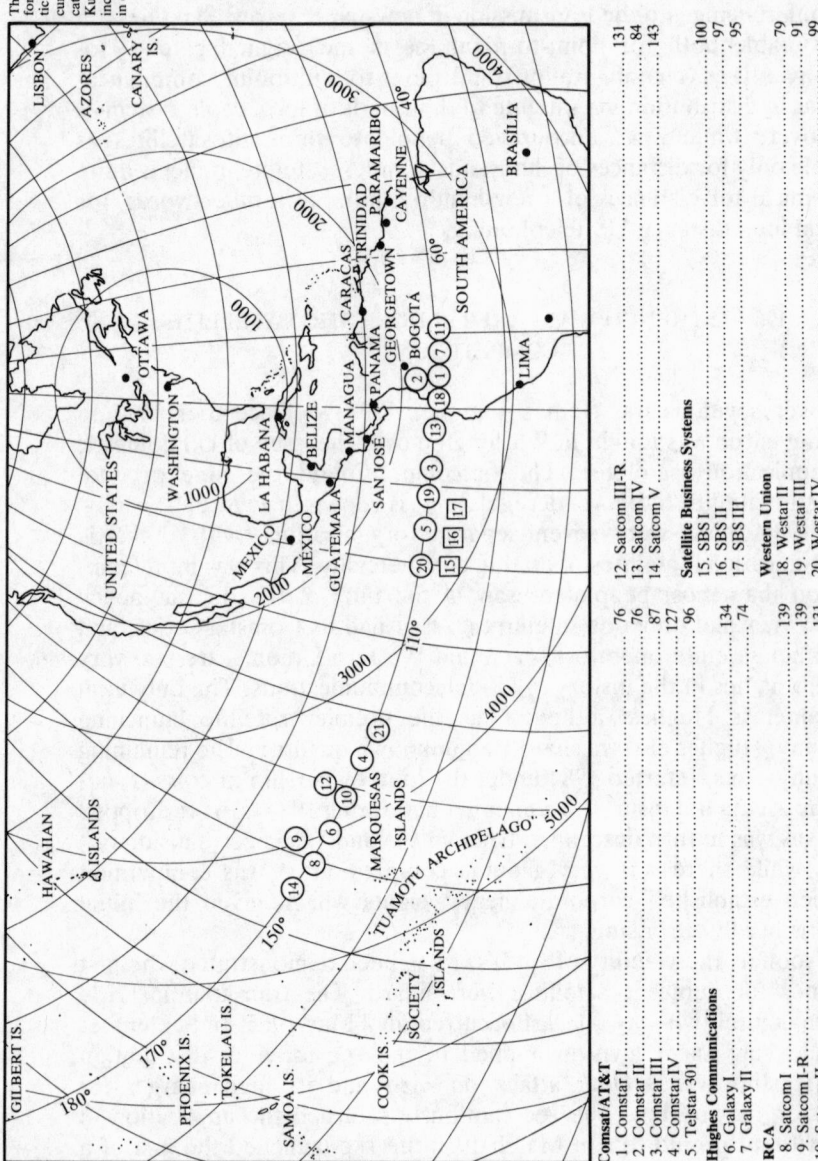

The map shows orbital slots for the United States domestic communications satellites currently in use. Circles indicate C-band and squares show Ku-band birds. The list below includes the orbital locations in degrees west longitude.

Comsat/AT&T

1. Comstar I	76
2. Comstar II	76
3. Comstar III	87
4. Comstar IV	127
5. Telstar 301	96

Hughes Communications

6. Galaxy I	134
7. Galaxy II	74

RCA

8. Satcom I	139
9. Satcom I-R	139
10. Satcom II	131
11. Satcom II-R	72
12. Satcom III-R	131
13. Satcom IV	84
14. Satcom V	143

Satellite Business Systems

15. SBS I	100
16. SBS II	97
17. SBS III	95

Western Union

18. Westar II	79
19. Westar III	91
20. Westar IV	99
21. Westar V	123

Figure 7.1 *US domestic communications satellites, April 1984.*

A major incident in this battle was the Johnson-appointed (Rostow) task force on telecommunications. In the closing days of the Johnson presidency, the task force produced a report calling for a domestic satellite system dominated by COMSAT. The new Nixon administration – principally Clay Whitehead and Dean Burch – wanted a more Republican and competitive solution. It was not until after almost four years of the Nixon presidency that the FCC at last reached its competitive domsat conclusion.

All along the FCC saw its problem as one of introducing domestic satellite competition without too seriously damaging (or annoying) AT&T. This was an almost impossible task, because satellites probably seemed to most Americans a 'naturally competitive' area, not one of natural monopoly. AT&T, aware of this, argued for some years that satellites were unsuitable for domestic use, and should be confined to international services.

The radio/TV networks were early antagonists of AT&T, correctly believing that satellites would offer a cheaper system of networking than AT&T's microwave towers. The networks were subsequently much sought after as potentially a key slice of the competitive satellite business. But the networks had their own interests to protect: they hoped to acquire their own satellite system, and thereby to stop the future possibility of cable via satellite.

Of the other directly interested companies, Hughes's motivations in the satellite hardware business were reinforced by its involvement with a major local cable operator; GTE wanted to reduce its dependence on AT&T; Lockheed and MCI had anti-AT&T motives and interests similar to Hughes; and COMSAT, of course, had hoped for dominance in domestic satellites.

A central dilemma – and not only for domsats – was that if all would-be players were allowed onto the field, the excessive level of competition might mean losses for all.[3]

Even after December 1972, the FCC domsat decision did not seem to amount to much. But eventually the FCC policy of moderately open access seemed to pay off. The first commercial satellite launches were made by Western Union in 1974 with Westar I and II. And soon domestic satellite slots were in short supply – before the anticipated glut eventually arrived in the 1980s.

1972–5: THE MARRIAGE WITH CABLE AND THE START OF
SPACE DEREGULATION

After ten years the trajectory of COMSAT and INTELSAT was going the predicted way. The roles of COMSAT and the US were declining, and

INTELSAT was steadily switching from a US model to something more resembling a UN model. The US could still pride itself on having designed the world's phone system or its space aspects. US industry was still getting nearly all the contracts to build INTELSAT's succeeding generations of more powerful satellites; and AT&T was still in a key position. In 1972 it was still true that COMSAT was really COMSAT/AT&T. AT&T still owned 29 per cent of COMSAT's shares, was still the dominant customer – using 60 per cent of all circuits leased by COMSAT, was also dominant in the rival technology of ocean cables and, finally, was a major hardware supplier (via its Western Electric subsidiary) to COMSAT.[4]

But in 1972, the whole political economy of space communications – and no less the popular imagery of space – was about to change. Space was going to be married to cable; the marriage of satellites and cable was going to produce a lusty child called Home Box Office, which, with other pay-cable offerings, was literally going to haul satellites down to earth with a new showbiz image in place of the high-tech remote imagery of AT&T-in-space. Pay-cable in turn would begin to drive the entire cable business; the resulting popularity of Hollywood-style high tech would also smooth the political path for the increasing transfer of space from the quasi-state enterprise COMSAT to unregulated commercial market entities.

Home Box Office (HBO) initially had no plans to use satellites. HBO first considered using the first (Westar I) bird, but plumped instead for the only other choice in 1975, RCA's Satcom I. Soon thereafter, an eccentric Atlanta businessman called Ted Turner had the bizarre idea that people in other cities might be interested in his local independent station, with its local Atlanta news and sport and its Hollywood reruns. Turner also chose the RCA satellite. By November 1979, RCA's Satcom I had 20 of its 24 transponders carrying cable-TV programming.

At this point it seemed that AT&T had suffered a big defeat, and COMSAT too had failed to switch out of international and into domestic space. It was the telecoms common carriers other than AT&T that the FCC had allowed into the domsat business. COMSAT was allowed into domsats, but the running had been made by RCA and Western Union, the latter making a giant leap indeed into space and away from its dying monopoly of telegrams.

Not unlike other fields of business, the new communications technologies offer the best financial prospects when the big financial investment can be recouped via a standardized service to several thousand outlets, terminals or antennae. Cable television offered just such a prospect. But, like other space applications, this is in some key respects a narrow field in which the winner may take all. There has been a tendency for all, or nearly all, of the cable programming to bunch up on one or two satellites. This follows from the simple fact that once a cable-operator's dish antenna is pointed at a particular satellite, he can pull down a dozen or more programming services without having to buy another dish antenna to point at another spot in the heavens. Thus, initially, the cablers all stacked up on Satcom I. After 1981 they all switched to its successor, Satcom III-R.[5] Subsequently the Hughes company successfully managed a diversification into satellites, and its Galaxy family of satellites has done well in the cable transmitting business.

THE DBS NIGHTMARE: BIG OUTLAY, FEW CUSTOMERS

Both the flexibility and the uncertainties of space satellites are illustrated by the American experience with DBS in the early 1980s. A satellite with a strong signal can send programming straight into a domestic TV receiver via a cheap roof dish antenna of about one meter diameter. But satellites are expensive, and even a one-meter dish retailed at several hundred dollars. The great unknown was whether a significant number of people would pay the rather high cost of subscribing to five extra DBS channels. The answer seemed to be no – certainly on the experience of 1980–4.

The first American DBS operator, United Satellite Communications Inc (USCI), began operations in November 1983, and just over a year later had only 9,000 subscribers to show against debts of $53 million. USCI's was a cheap DBS operation: it used a medium-powered Canadian ANIK ('brother' in Eskimo) satellite, rather than wait for a high-powered US one; at the launch only three of its five channels offered programming; the initial requirement was for a receiving dish larger than would be subsequently needed; and marketing, promotion and servicing were all inadequate. Within six months of its launch USCI humiliatingly failed to find any bank willing to lend it a stopgap $40 million.

USCI's DBS effort was shot down by various competing ways of delivering additional TV channels, and in particular by satellite-delivered cable services, which were being pumped into thousands of ongoing local cable systems on the ground. But unlike cable, DBS was forced to start big both in space and on the ground. Also unlike early cable, early DBS had competition not only from a now formidable cable industry itself, but from other systems – LPTV and VCRS as well as microwave Multipoint Distribution Service (MDS). It also had to compete with technology-buffs who equipped themselves with dishes of several meters and then pirated all of cable's satellite services.

By 1983–4, when USCI was launched, cable was already available to about two-thirds of all US homes. Cable offered more channels more cheaply, and was still growing fast. Thus, realistically, DBS could only aim at perhaps 15 per cent of the population – mainly in rural areas – and in 1983–4 seemed unlikely to sign up more than, say, 7 or 8 per cent of homes in the US. This was a marketing and servicing nightmare, for these were the very homes which all other services (not just electronic) found it unprofitable to service.

Only a small and decreasing proportion of cable systems offered as few as DBS's five or six new channels. But the most expensive and serious unknowns resided in some other rather important technical details. *Low-power* satellites (with 3-meter domestic dishes) offered break-even at perhaps one million homes; *high-power* satellites (allowing tiny, cheap 0.6-meter dishes) needed perhaps five million subscribers in order to break even. To compound this conundrum, most of the DBS aspirants proposed to start on low-power satellites, and then move on to high-power satellites later in the 1980s; this was likely to wreak havoc with both consumer confidence and overall financial viability. A related problem, again resulting from satellite flexibility, was that different DBS aspirants had quite different long-term aspirations. One system, for example, was basically trying to sell religion, while CBS saw in DBS a chance to promote its high-tech HDTV.

There were further problems about coverage areas. Most DBS aspirants planned to commence in the Northeast corner of the US and then, with one or more additional satellites, to transmit separate services to the Central, Mountain and Pacific time zones. As they rethought their particular zoning and rollout plans, the DBS aspirants came to favor different satellite locations. Despite many changes, the long-run favorite was a combination of two locations: one to the south of Mexico (to serve the eastern half of the US), one much further west toward Hawaii (to serve the western states).

But these 'flexibilities' were by no means all; there were others.

DBS: REGULATORY AND COMPETITIVE UNCERTAINTIES

These additional uncertainties had their separate foci. Neither excessive regulatory caution in the late 1970s nor excessive enthusiasm for DBS in the early 1980s stimulated any coherent FCC or other official view of DBS. The competitive uncertainty focused on COMSAT's urge to reduce its dependence on INTELSAT by diversifying into new domestic space ventures. COMSAT led the DBS charge, thereby encouraging others to follow close behind, just in case COMSAT should, after all, discover gold on remote rural rooftops.

DBS has a longish history.[6] It was first demonstrated as technically feasible in the 1960s. In 1971 a World Administrative Radio Conference

(WARC) assigned a frequency band to DBS. But at the 1977 WARC, at which slots were allocated to countries, the US played a leading role in persuading the ITU's Region 2 (America, North and South) not to allocate DBS slots just yet. This was deliberately postponed until a special regional conference for Region 2 to be held in the summer of 1983.

This six-year delay seemed like a mature and perceptive move. In 1977 DBS looked far away, and indeed by 1983 no DBS service yet existed anywhere in the world. However, in trying to avoid the European and Third World rigidity of allocating all the slots too far in advance, the US helped to introduce an opposite rigidity (a six-year delay) into its DBS. This allowed cable via satellite to get far ahead, and meant that by 1983 it seemed necessary to launch DBS with great urgency before cable entirely closed the door. In fact, the 1983 decisions for the American continent were not made (in Geneva) until mid-July; the USCI service was launched in Indianapolis on 15 November, just four months later.

The FCC had initiated an inquiry into DBS in October 1980, and the then FCC chairman Ferris showed more enthusiasm than most of his fellow commissioners. Only two months later, in December 1980, COMSAT's subsidiary, Satellite TV Corporation (STC), sent the FCC a voluminous application for permission to construct an experimental DBS system.

In early 1981 the broadcast industry in general, and the three networks in particular, denounced the COMSAT/STC proposal as an attempt to preempt the ITU 1983 decision and to give the latter's experimental system a commanding lead. Faced with the alternative of two and a half years of enforced indecision, the FCC gave a preliminary go-ahead not just to STC, but to a total of 13 applicants. This was to be an example of the new extreme deregulatory approach: the FCC would eventually allocate the slots, but the market could largely decide the runners, the technical standards and the service formats.

By late 1981 the field of DBS starters had shrunk to a mere eight. In addition to COMSAT/STC, there were CBS and RCA Americom, obviously trying to protect network and satellite turf, and Western Union, which also saw DBS as part of its overall satellite strategy. The remainder were Graphic Scanning, Direct Broadcast Satellite Corporation (DBSC), Video Satellite Systems (VSS) and USSB (the forerunner of USCI). The eight applicants' plans included a bewildering array of technical formats and service details, but all eight would offer between one and six new TV channels, a slimmed-down cable-style programming service.

COMSAT/STC was the front-runner. Its satellite experience was so extensive as to mean that, technically, its system carried complete conviction. Privately, however, COMSAT executives knew that they could easily fall down on programming, marketing and equipment servicing.

There was a steady barrage of psychological warfare between the contenders, and much discussion as to whether initial funding of $200 million was too high or whether $1 billion was too low.

In November 1982, all eight potential runners were still standing, and obtained FCC construction permits. COMSAT/STC made one more attempt to jump the July 1983 starting gun, but was held back. Finally, when in late summer 1983 the ITU slots were allocated, it was USCI that pushed past STC and launched its ill-prepared service. While STC and the others waited for the higher-powered satellites which would make roof dishes smaller and cheaper, USCI rushed ahead with a Canadian satellite already in orbit.

By October 1984, the field had been reduced from eight to four runners. Three of the strongest-looking runners – CBS, RCA and Western Union – had all withdrawn. And there was still only one system operating, and it, clearly, was in major difficulty. USCI was indeed experiencing the nightmare of big outlay and few customers.

In the fall of 1984 the DBS adventure turned into near total disaster. COMSAT's STC and USCI both desperately wanted partners, and eventually, despite previous hostile relations, they began merger talks. But after only a few weeks, COMSAT decided to withdraw entirely, and the early 1980s US effort in DBS had reached its terminal stage. This early 1980s' effort may, of course, subsequently appear analogous to the faltering early 1930s' efforts in television.

In view of technical advances, not least in the domestic reception sector, there may be some kind of late 1980s revival of DBS, perhaps in some kind of hybrid format with other modes of final delivery. In the meantime FCC deregulatory policy (and its interplay with Geneva ITU policy) was made to look wasteful, ineffectual and chaotic. Some hundreds of millions of dollars had been lost.[7] And finally, the 1983–4 disaster for DBS was on such a scale as to somewhat depress the entire business of space satellites.

EXIT COMSAT, ENTER IBM: SBS

In 1984 COMSAT pulled out not only from DBS but also from SBS, its satellite telecommunications system. COMSAT was thus both reflecting and contributing to the uncertainty which the deregulation of satellites had exacerbated. In early 1984, COMSAT itself had been involved as a US signatory and earth station provider to INTELSAT and the International Maritime Satellite Organization (INMARSAT); in COMSAT-General domestic communications satellites; in various specialized telecommunications manufacturing activities; in COMSAT laboratories; as full owner of STC, planning early entry to DBS, and as one-third owner of SBS. This was a wide and risky range, especially in that it included the AT&T-style burden of a major laboratory when its total revenues were less than 2 per cent of the current revenues of its partner, IBM.

And it seems to have been this latter kind of consideration which led to its pulling out from SBS. SBS was owned equally by COMSAT, IBM and Aetna Life. The intention was to use COMSAT satellite facilities to provide sophisticated total internal communications systems for large companies. But initially IBM sales people were prevented by the FCC from also selling SBS; and few of SBS's large customers seemed willing to commit their entire systems to SBS. As two remarkably acute articles by Jerome Lucas had predicted in early 1982, SBS's big customers were using SBS as just one of their communications resources. Lucas concluded that SBS would thus be in severe trouble, and that it would have to focus more heavily on the switched voice market – in other words, go into the long-distance telephone business against AT&T, MCI and Sprint.[8] All of this duly happened, and SBS began to offer its Skyline phone service to the general public. Moreover, as COMSAT withdrew, it was IBM which supplied the new chief executive. A year later IBM offered SBS to MCI as part of its new closer involvement with that long-distance telephone company. SBS thus seemed destined to offer satellite backup facilities to MCI's mainly fiber-optic network plans.

This perhaps explains the difficulties of a half-billion-dollar-revenue regulated company like COMSAT. Not only were there difficulties in trying to enter the big league of telecommunications; staying alive in its traditional leadership role in satellites no longer looked so easy either.

THE 1980S: SPACE DEREGULATION EQUALS GLUT?

The deregulation of domestic satellites was largely completed during the first Reagan administration. Small receive-only dishes suitable for pirate (unpaid) reception from satellites had been deregulated in 1979. They then went through the common price 'free fall' pattern. Whereas a common 1979 price for a small dish antenna was $50,000, five years later there had been a more than 90 per cent fall to $2,000 or $3,000. Sales forecasts of 60,000 new backyard dishes (and 60,000 new nonpaying customers) per month by 1985 were one of the sources of discouragement to DBS operators in 1984.

The FCC under Fowler made other satellite decisions parallel to those in DBS. For example, more satellite slots were made possible by an FCC decision to reduce the space between slots to only 2° in the high-power

Ku band. Domestic satellite services were completely deregulated in August 1984; operators could then alter rates and services without asking FCC permission.[9]

In April 1983 the FCC had authorized a massive new flock of satellites which would roughly double the total number by 1988. Nineteen new domestic satellites were authorized in the C and Ku bands. The new satellites' owners were to be RCA, SBS, Sprint, Western Union, Hughes, American Satellite and AT&T (one satellite only). Provisional approval was given to three other less well-heeled companies.

This decision had a precedent. An FCC decision under Ferris in 1980 had led to a doubling of satellite capacity by 1984. However, the FCC had then had in mind the experience of the late 1970s, when there was a scarcity of satellites, mainly due to the rapid growth of satellite-to-cable services.

But in 1983 the commission seemed to have less justification for its doubling decision. True, there was still growth in demand, but with video's extravagant bandwidth demands still predominating, and with cable-TV satellite services no longer increasing rapidly, the use of satellite transponders was growing only slowly. Between July 1983 and July 1984, the use of transponders did increase, but, with new capacity (as a result of the 1980 decision) still coming into effect, the total number of inactive C-band transponders rose from 107 to 145. Capacity was growing faster than demand, and in July 1984 40 per cent of all C-band transponders were inactive.[10] Moreover, the average 'active' transponder was active much less than 24 hours a day.

The prospect for the late 1980s is of satellite capacity doubling at just the same time that the full weight of fiber-optic cable is first experienced. The most spectacular of the new technologies, space satellites, seems likely to remain the most uncertain. And the uncertainties may continue to be exacerbated by the interaction of uncertain mass media demand for satellites and uncertain telecommunications demand, combined with inconsistent regulatory decisions on satellites.

Notes

1 Jonathan F. Galloway, *The Politics and Technology of Satellite Communications* (1972), pp. 47–73.
2 Alan Pearce, 'COMSAT: the perils of success', *Telecommunications*, March 1980, pp. 18, 29.
3 Michael E. Kinsley, *Outer Space and Inner Sanctums* (1976).
4 Galloway, *Satellite Communications*, p. 139.
5 'Satellites: tomorrow is here today', *Broadcasting*, 27 March 1978, pp. 57–68. 'Communications satellites: the birds are in full flight', *Broadcasting*, November 1979, pp. 36–47.
6 Dallas W. Smyth, 'Space Satellite Broadcasting: Threat or Promise?', *Journal of Broadcasting*, summer 1966, pp.191–8.

7 'The curtain's going up on DBS television's next frontier', *Broadcasting*, 15 September 1980, pp. 36–46. 'Down on DBS', *Broadcasting*, 9 February 1981, pp. 62–7. 'Good news, bad news in DBS spacerush', *Broadcasting*, 20 July 1981, pp. 23–7. Laura Landro, 'Satellite TV may not live up to promise', *Wall Street Journal*, 28 June 1982, p. 17. 'Where there once was one, now there are many', *Broadcasting*, 8 November 1982, pp. 40–1. John F. Clark, 'Proposed US Broadcasting-Satellite Systems', *ICEE Global Telecommunications Conference*, 29 November–2 December 1983, Miami. Michael Schrage, 'Murdoch, SBS sign $75 million agreement', *Washington Post*, 6 May 1983, p. D9. Lauro Landro, 'United Satellite Seeks $40 million in drive to expand direct-broadcast TV services', *Wall Street Journal*, 22 February 1982, p. 12. 'USCI reveals high cost of DBS', *Communications Daily*, 24 February 1984, pp. 1–2. Laura Landro, 'RCA backs away from plan to launch high-powered direct broadcast satellites', *Wall Street Journal*, 13 July 1984. Sally Russell, 'Stormy Weather for DBS', *Cable Vision*, 16 July 1984, pp. 31–4. 'Why Direct Satellite TV is down but not out', *Business Week*, 20 August 1984, p. 127. Albert R. Karr, 'Merger planned for Prudential, Comsat Units', *Wall Street Journal*, 5 September 1984. 'DBS ranks cut in half', *Broadcasting*, 15 October 1984, pp. 75–6. Jeanne Sadler and John Marcom, 'Comsat ends negotiations with Prudential on Venture', *Wall Street Journal* (Europe), 3 December 1984, p. 4.

8 Jerome Lucas, 'The Future of SBS', and 'The SBS User', *Telecom Insider*, January 1982, pp. 14–16; March, 1982, pp. 18–20.

9 'FCC stops regulating commercial satellites', *New York Times*, 9 August 1984, pp. D1, 4.

10 'Domsat operators cut the glut – somewhat'. *Communications Daily*, 7 August 1984, pp. 2–3.

8

The Two-Ace Policy Play: IBM and Competition

COMPUTERS: AN ALREADY UNREGULATED INDUSTRY

The computing industry differed from the other two major communications industries – telecommunications and space – because, unlike them, it had never been regulated by a federal agency. Nevertheless, prior to 1983, the dominant company pattern of the other two had indeed been repeated. While AT&T had fought its way into, and COMSAT had been awarded, regulated natural monopoly status, the computer industry had also produced its dominant company, IBM.

Computers, of course, were a post-1945 industry, and IBM did not achieve immediate dominance. However, IBM had run into antitrust problems in its pre-computer days, and it was only during the 1950s that it became dominant in computers. In 1965 it had a 65 per cent share in the computer market.[1] This was when computers were all mainframes, machines the size of one or more rooms. But even though this traditional end of the computer business has been relatively stagnant, IBM dominance has remained at about two-thirds for mainframes.

IBM's lawyers, like their opposite numbers at AT&T and COMSAT, have been kept busy. Of several significant antitrust cases, the most important was initiated by the Justice Department in the very last days of the Johnson administration, in January 1969. The case ran for exactly 13 years before it was dropped by the Justice Department on its famous day of decision (for both IBM and AT&T), 8 January 1982.

IBM's lawyers used classic delaying tactics. Much time was taken up with a government bid to show deliberate *intent* to monopolize the mainframe market with IBM 360 and 370 computers. Truly massive quantities of internal IBM documents were examined. Another legal battle, between IBM and Control Data, was settled in 1972, and the two sets of lawyers carried out a secret agreement to destroy their computerized file indexes to tens of millions of pages of each others' documents.

IBM's legal delaying tactics in the 1970s paid off for three reasons. First, IBM seems deliberately to have slowed down its competitive advance (or directed it more into foreign markets). Second, in the late 1970s the computer industry appeared to become much more competitive; Apple became an American legend, with revenues of $2.5 million in the year ending September 1977, $70 million in 1979 and $355 million in 1981. Apple was only one example of an explosion in growth, innovation and (it seemed) competition – and not only in Silicon Valley, but in other areas such as Texas. Finally, a fresh political wind arrived in the form of a Reagan administration preaching salvation through fierce competition. Moreover, it was an administration capable of the political sleight-of-hand of January 1982 which left the audience unsure as to what had really happened, but one which nevertheless produced a very large competitive rabbit, a soon-to-be-divested AT&T which might perhaps make a real competitive challenge to IBM.

Amid the various inconsistencies in this double decision were consistencies, in that the two decisions ensured that the computer and telecommunications industries would in future constitute much more similar, layered pyramids. In each case at least four levels would result:

1 at the top of the pyramid one dominant company – IBM dominating mainframes, and AT&T dominating long-distance telephone communication;

2 another level of eight or ten companies with revenues in 1982 of well over a billion dollars – primarily the divested AT&T operating companies in telecoms; the so-called BUNCH companies in computing (the competing mainframers: Burroughs, Sperry (UNIVAC), National Cash Register (NCR), Control Data, and Honeywell, plus a few others, such as Digital and the minicomputer success Hewlett-Packard);

3 in January 1982 there was another important group of fast-growing companies – in telecoms, such competing common carriers as MCI and Sprint, the larger local independents and some competing equipment suppliers; in computers, not only Apple, but other leading microcomputer companies, the new microprocessing chip producers and the larger software houses;

4 a final level of literally hundreds of companies offering specialized products and services in both telecommunications and computers.

By 1982 it could not be denied that the lower levels were seething with fresh competition. What was disputed was the significance of the different layers: could those at the top effectively dominate or eliminate those lower down? Also much disputed were the boundaries of the pyramids themselves. Opponents of IBM said that its 65–70 per cent dominance of mainframes led to vertical monopoly of the entire computer industry. Defenders of IBM stressed the growth of the new computer areas and the merging of computers with telecommunications; in its own, stated view, IBM operated on a playing field several times larger than mainframes, and thus its share of the field was not 65–70 per cent, but 15–20 per cent.

The Reagan Justice Department in effect accepted this latter argument, which was consistent with the consensus assumption that competition should be considered innocent until proved guilty.

In January 1982, then, IBM was free – for the moment, or at least for the Reagan duration. In 1982 it was still expected that Reagan would serve only one term. IBM's expectation that it would take three years to reassert its grip on an explosively changing industry probably explains in part its much more aggressive business tactics from January 1982 onward.

COMPUTER COMPETITION: AROUND $1 BILLION

Between $500 million and $5 billion in annual revenues there swirls furious competition; for many of these companies the goal is to be number two to IBM – in one of the main areas, such as mainframes, software, personal computers or disk drives.

Most of these companies are pursuing high-risk strategies, attempting to grow fast from a narrow base, battling with fierce competition; and, even if they succeed in becoming number two or three, these companies may still face the ultimate competitive test, a directly targeted onslaught from Big Blue, IBM itself.

Apple had sales of $583 million in 1982 and in 1984 reached $1.5 billion. But in April–June 1985 Apple experienced its first quarterly loss. Like other new members of the $1-billion sales club, Apple was pursuing a strategy that was uniquely its own, yet typical in being high-risk. Apple had decided to compete head to head with IBM, but without any IBM compatibility. Apple purchasers must lock themselves out of IBM's vast world of add-ons and software. But while the majority of even personal computer sales revenues came from office customers, Apple, with its laid-back, user-friendly, low-cost, computer-amateur image, faces an uphill battle against an IBM that is on its favorite competitive turf in supplying the *Fortune* 1,000 largest US companies.

Very rapid growth is perhaps the key feature of this competitive battle. A figure like 17 per cent annual growth, often quoted as IBM's target for the early 1980s, meant (if inflation were discounted) a doubling of revenue in four and a half years – no mean achievement since many prices were being cut at the same time. Figures twice as high were regarded as commonplace in fast-growth subfields, where growth rates of up to 100 per cent might be required in order to impress.

The micro revolution is the most dramatic area of such growth, and provides many recent examples of turbulent company histories. It has at least three main subareas, each of them growing and changing explosively. The *personal computer* field itself has seen spectacular changes; in 1980 three companies (Tandy, Apple and Commodore) had 83 per cent of the market, but by 1983 these three had slumped to only 30 per cent (and most of this was Apple's). In 1980 the four leading companies had 88 per cent of the market, but by 1983 four, different, leaders had only 60 per cent of the market. The second field of the micro revolution involved *semiconductors* themselves, another fiercely competitive and fast-moving business. And the third, *software* was becoming the key battleground, as buyers became more sophisticated, and insurgent software houses were forced to choose between IBM and Apple.

It was against this background of rapid growth and change that the BUNCH mainframe companies seemed to be becalmed in situations of slow or no growth in revenue and, typically, declines in profit. The BUNCH seemed to have made the classic business error in definition – thinking they were in the mainframe business, and failing to realize the opportunities for redefining themselves more widely. While in the late 1970s they had been many times larger than the micro insurgents, they now faced the prospect of being overtaken in the low-billions-per-year revenue league.

The *mini* companies were in somewhat better shape. Unlike the BUNCH, whose best days were the 1960s, the *mini* companies have had their best days with the minicomputer (really mid-size) revolution of the 1970s. DEC, Hewlett-Packard and Data General were some of the more successful and larger survivors in this category. At least another ten companies had at one time made a strong showing in minicomputers; some of these, such as Texas Instruments and Motorola, were still doing well in related subfields.

Taking the one-time major *mainframers* and the one-time major *minicomputer* companies, there were more than twenty companies all of whose computer prospects had dimmed or were dimming by the early 1980s. But clearly a fair number of these twenty were hoping for some kind of second-career revival.

Common to this change of fortunes are the twin phenomena of the *shortened life cycle* for both computer products and computer companies. Massive concentration on a single fast-growing product field makes possible spectacular results; but these results quickly attract heavyweight competition and price-cutting. If this cycle is also accompanied by a migration in consumer demand, it may lead along the path of Atari – the hot video games subsidiary of Warner – which went from sudden huge growth and profits to a loss of over $1.5 billion in 1983.

The venture capital revolution has contributed to both the up and down phases of this cycle. The venture capitalists' deliberate search for high-growth/high-risk prospects involves not only putting money generously and rapidly into hot prospects, but also ruthlessly and rapidly withdrawing it from cooling prospects.

These rapid changes in the external circumstances of many computer companies have also been accompanied by internal upheavals. Many start-up companies have resembled breakaway advertising agencies (or small film companies); but most have been launched by engineers, and one only has to imagine a hot Madison Avenue creative shop run by a still youthful engineer to realize that internal conflict and confrontation are likely to be endemic.

Many, perhaps most, computer and related companies have had founding father dependence problems. In the older companies these founding fathers have been self-made multimillionaires approaching retirement. William Norris, for example, remained chairman of Control Data into his seventies.[2] In the insurgent companies the founding fathers have tended to be self-made multimillionaires approaching age thirty. Neither category, it seems, finds taking advice very easy.

Computer companies, then, are often pretty chaotic places – long on prima donna engineers, stock options and burners of the midnight oil, but short on solid business efficiency and experience. A common solution is to bring in at the top an experienced marketing manager; this person is supposed not only to infuse much-needed marketing know-how, but to bring along some simple business competence as well. Some of these marketing managers have come from the soap or soft drinks business, others from IBM. In either case there is an infusion of a different kind of 'corporate culture', which may introduce more problems than it solves.

The revolution in *selling* is important. The old computer mainframe industry was far removed from marketing, either to the public or to middle management. Within a few years, the industry changed from the dominant IBM pattern of *leasing* to new patterns not only of aggressive selling to business customers, but of selling through department stores, computer store chains and large-scale advertising.

An ideal goal of this new marketing approach was to discover a niche market, big enough to be highly profitable, but too small to attract threatening competition. The least secure kind of niche market is one that IBM cannot possibly ignore, as Storage Technology learned the hard way. Storage Technology passed the $1-billion revenue mark in 1982, by specializing in data storage equipment for large computers. This meant making equipment primarily for IBM and IBM-compatible computers; but IBM was bound, one day, to think of doing the job itself. Knowing this, Storage Technology tried to diversify,[3] but instead found itself in 1984 seeking authority to reorganize under chapter eleven of the US Bankruptcy Act. Most niches are less vulnerable, but inevitably, the more attractive the niche, the less likely it is to stay that way for long.

MAJOR NEW PLAYERS: JAPAN INC, AT&T AND GM

Not only do niches attract new entrants, but so does the US computer industry itself. Perhaps the most feared and discussed of these have been the Japanese. The outcome here remains unclear, but the tactics of Japan Inc are clearly evident. The Japanese companies are aiming at joint ventures in general, and in particular for agreements with the mainframe BUNCH, and other old corporate hands of the US computer industry. One example is that of Nippon Electric Company (NEC) with Honeywell. The best-known arrangement of this kind is Fujitsu's large stake in Amdahl, which allows a Japanese and an American maker of IBM-compatible mainframes to combine their efforts. The departure of Gene Amdahl himself (to set up Trilogy) is said, however, to stem from, and illustrate, the special corporate culture problems posed when US founding father meets Japanese multinational.

AT&T remains another uncertain quantity. But, as we shall see in the next two chapters, its entry into the computer business is far from a token one. Until 1982 AT&T, through its Western Electric subsidiary, had dominated just one major computer market, that involving what were referred to as 'switches'.

Another interesting batch of new players are companies from other industries, such as GM and McDonnell Douglas. IBM must now face their competition, and perhaps competition of yet more major players from other industries in the future.

IBM'S RESPONSE: IF YOU CAN'T BEAT SILICON VALLEY, MARRY IT

Since January 1982 everyone has noticed a much more aggressive style in IBM behavior in many fields. But this change really predates 1982; IBM, well represented in the Carter administration, appears to have recognized in the late 1970s that the chances of a radical antitrust divestiture were declining. Prior to January 1982, IBM was just beginning to flex its muscles, but it was also lining up an army of new products and new practices with which to face the new conditions.

IBM had always been a *marketing* company, and it was perhaps this traditional orientation which, despite its buttoned-down, white-shirt, east coast, conservative corporate culture, enabled it to adapt to a completely new way of doing business. While the BUNCH companies turned their backs on the unwashed geniuses from Silicon Valley, IBM decided that, since it could not ignore the wayward westerners, it would have to marry them.

But, first, a brief reminder of what the main accusations had been against IBM in the 1969–72 antitrust case:[4]

(1) The hardware–software lock-in. Once a company had bought one IBM computer plus related software, it could not switch to another hardware supplier without also writing off expensive IBM software.

(2) Critics claimed that both the timing and the pricing of new models were aimed on occasion at killing the competition. In particular, IBM was accused of 'predatory' pricing, and of phantom products that existed only on paper, the announcement of which was calculated to confuse and penalize competitors.

(3) IBM used the classic devices of vertical and horizontal integration, it was said.

(4) Because of the strength of IBM and the link between its hardware and software, a common competitive tactic was to produce plug-compatible computers – essentially close, but not identical, copies which could operate with IBM software. These plug-compatibles were often cheaper and incorporated improvements on the IBM design. However, in the eyes of critics, this compatible market sector was further evidence of IBM dominance, which clearly left such companies vulnerable to the whims of IBM. For example, their product life cycle was shorter; moreover, by using the IBM standards and software, the compatible companies operated in effect as defenders of the IBM citadel, supporting IBM from without and obstructing direct competition.

But, especially since 1982, it has become even more common to see IBM as the ultimate exemplar of American management. Two business school authors have recounted the characteristics which they find in successful high-tech companies. Such companies typically must manage two conflicting trends – continuity and rapid change; often their histories show alternating periods of dogged continuity and dramatic change. The list of characteristics[5] is virtually a description of IBM:

1 Business focus. IBM's two themes of computers and other office equipment both focus on the business market.
2 Adaptability – again an obvious IBM characteristic.
3 Organizational cohesion.
4 Entrepreneurial culture. The authors here point to the case of Apple, and discuss the advantages of small intimate innovative corporate cultures. IBM has tried to adopt many of these small-company attributes.
5 A sense of integrity.
6 'Hands on' top management.

Following these general points, the present author now adds a list of specifically IBM characteristics in evidence during the years of newfound freedom, since 1982:

(1) IBM has altered its strategy in several forms of speedup. It has moved from mainly renting to mainly selling; at the same time, its truly massive profits have left resources available for many new tactical ventures.

(2) The whole rhythm of the company has accelerated toward a shorter product life cycle.

(3) IBM has geared up for the quick big volume its new approach requires, and has automated production.

(4) IBM has not only caught up in small computers, it has taken steps to make any future competitive 'break' of the kind once led by DEC and Apple much less likely to occur.

(5) IBM has set up internal versions of hot Silicon Valley innovative computer shops. These 'independent business units' were first used for robotics, educational software, telephone equipment and biomedical systems, among others.

(6) IBM is realistic about its mistakes; in 1985 it ceased production of its unsuccessful PC junior and, having failed in telecoms, bought into a successful telecoms company, MCI.

(7) More generally, IBM has lost any inhibitions it once had as regards setting technical standards. Only AT&T can compete.

(8) IBM has initiated an aggressive policy of investing in key areas such as semiconductor chips. Another important example is provided by the purchase of an avant-garde PBX (internal company) phone specialist; initially IBM chose the Canadian company Mitel, but later switched to Rolm. Companies like Intel (chips) and Rolm then receive massive IBM orders and massive prestige, but IBM remains free to move if it so wishes.

(9) While still making most of its own hardware, IBM was flexible enough to construct its first personal computers out of components largely made by outsiders. If one component (such as the keyboard) is unsatisfactory, this can be replaced.

(10) IBM used to discourage middlemen from trespassing on its market turf, but no longer. It now encourages middlemen, who buy a lot of equipment and package it for individual customers. Some also refurbish used computers.

(11) IBM has a special program for retail stores which allows customers to get answers to their queries.

(12) IBM isn't afraid to change its mind; in 1973 it left time-sharing but returned to it in 1982.

(13) IBM is interested in joint ventures for information delivery. It has joined with Merrill Lynch in one such, and with Sears and CBS in another.

(14) The introduction of small computers during 1981 was initially severely criticized in each and every detail. The criticisms were familiar: new IBM products of rather pedestrian quality, not especially cheap. But as the family of IBM baby computers grew in numbers and strength, comments tended to go to the other extreme: this was a team that was going to munch down Apple and all other competitors. Although the reception of the AT (Advanced Technology) small computer may have been overenthusiastic, this entire operation did reveal that IBM could make its marriage with Silicon Valley into a success story.

In IBM's 1985 deal with MCI, we again see some of its characteristic qualities. First, IBM rid itself of SBS, having evidently decided that SBS had no future on its own. Second, we see IBM cautiously trying a slice of (and taking a closer look at) MCI, the competing phone company. But third, IBM still retained the option of choosing at a later date whether IBM/MCI would confine itself mainly to data networks or whether it would also enter the voice/telephone business in a big way.

Notes

1 Robert Sobel, *IBM: Colossus in Transition* (1981), p. 162.
2 Richard Gibson, 'Control Data's slide raises doubts about its leadership', *Wall Street Journal* (Europe), 1 July 1985.
3 Karen Blumenthal, 'Storage Technology, in a slump, pins hope on new data device', *Wall Street Journal*, 16 August 1984, pp. 1, 14.
4 For a summary of the case against IBM, see Alan K. McAdams, 'The Computer Industry', in Adams (ed.), *American Industry*, pp. 249–97. A history of the IBM antitrust case is in Sobel, *IBM*.
5 Modesto A. Maidique and Robert H. Hayes, 'The Art of High-Technology Management', *Sloan Management Review*, vol. 25, no. 2, 1984, pp. 17–31.

9

Getting Ma Bell All Broken Up

A little still she strove, and much repented, and whispering
'I will ne'er consent' – consented.

Lord Byron, *Don Juan*

On 8 January 1982 the US Department of Justice and AT&T jointly
announced that they were terminating the case of US versus AT&T, which
had been running since 1974. AT&T would divest itself of the 22 local Bell
operating companies in which were located the majority of its one
million employees and the bulk of its revenue and profits. In return, it
would be free of the constraints of the Consent Decree of 1956, and
allowed to enter new businesses like computers.

At the press conference, according to reports, Charles Brown of AT&T
and William Baxter, the assistant US attorney general, themselves
seemed almost as startled as the journalists. The press's surprise was
based on several assumptions. The numerous antitrust cases against
AT&T had seemed as endless as the weather; but the Reagan administration – in office for just 12 months – appeared to be letting antitrust law
lapse in many cases, on the grounds that competition was international
these days.

True, the district court judge, one Harold Greene, had seemed to be
pushing the old case forward with fresh vigor. But insiders knew that the
judge had many problems in taking a strong line against AT&T. The
prosecution case was much more thinly justified than the case of the
defense; not only did AT&T have a small army of the best telecoms
lawyers, it also had a reasonable argument. The history of AT&T in the
last few decades was a history of monopoly, yes, but a legal monopoly,
because one regulated by the FCC as to profits, tariffs and services.
Further, it was subject to the 1956 Consent Decree, by which it had
agreed to keep out of such tempting new fields as data processing. In
January 1982, Judge Greene had still not heard most of AT&T's prepared
defense, and even this exceptionally self-assured judge must have been
uneasy at the prospect of single-handedly breaking up AT&T. There must

be unhappiness about a single judge making a decision with quite so many implications – not only economic, but also military and political. Such a decision would surely go to the Supreme Court, while the vast US telecommunications industry floundered in chaos. There was also the prospect of numerous subsequent cases, some about billion-dollar details.

Judge Greene, on the basis of his behavior immediately following the AT&T/Justice announcement, seems to have been in no less of a state of surprise and excitement than Brown and Baxter.

Adding to the mystery was the overt hostility of Brown to any such solution only a matter of weeks earlier. Even when hints that something important was about to happen began to trickle out during the days around Christmas 1981, these rumors of impending decision had to be weighed against the fact that Brown was on vacation first in Florida, then Colorado, while Baxter was skiing in Utah.

1934–65: AT&T'S LUCK, SKILL AND CAREFULLY CHAOTIC FINANCES

AT&T had many aspects and several names. 'The American Telephone and Telegraph Company' reflected its origins as a 'robber baron' monopolist from the late nineteenth century. 'Bell Telephone' reflected the successful rechannelling of the company's reputation into that of a scientific, competent natural monopoly dedicated to modest but secure dividends and high-quality service at bargain rates. 'Ma Bell' emphasized that AT&T was local and familiar – the telephone user could relate to his local Bell operating company.

AT&T had both the luck and the skill necessary for success in its two chosen spheres of business and politics. It was in politics at the federal and state levels, because its very existence, including its financial operation, was regulated. From 1934 it was regulated by the FCC, and also in most states by PUCs, which controlled the services offered and the rates charged for telephone calls within the state.

The biggest slice of luck, in retrospect, was that AT&T found itself in a business of steadily improving technology and scale economies, with only modest inflation. This meant that politically awkward telephone rate increases could largely be avoided, and on the rare occasions when customers heard about AT&T's rates changing, it was mostly because telephone prices were coming down.

In 1934 only about a quarter of American households had a telephone; this left room for a huge, benign expansion of a gadget and a system that peculiarly appealed to such American values as bigness, high technology and neighborliness. AT&T was able to succeed the railroads as benign builder of the nation. Indeed, the telephone map closely resembled the railroad map, because the wires ran alongside the tracks.

The American public was, with the help of much AT&T advertising, PR and massaging of statistics, lulled into believing that it had by far the world's best telephone system, a remarkable achievement in such a large and still thinly settled nation. In fact another, still more thinly populated nation, Sweden, has probably always had a better system (when measured by other than AT&T statistics); and other thinly peopled countries such as Canada and Finland are also to the fore. It seems to have been the countries whose phone services did not suffer in the Second World War that forged ahead (Denmark and Switzerland are other examples). But fortunately for AT&T, the foreign countries to which US tourists mainly went after 1945 – France, Germany, the UK, Italy, Japan and Spain – all fell behind in the 1940s and were, thereafter, a ready source of travellers' telephone horror tales.

In fact, the long-lines part of telephoning, as of railways, is the easy part. Also attractive from a commercial viewpoint is taking the phone to suburban households and exurban businesses; it is the thinly spread rural population which is hard to reach. The latter unattractive markets were largely outside AT&T's 80 per cent of US households. The remote rural areas were mostly served by independent companies, often literally mom and pop operations offering party-line and other low-quality, low-tech service at low prices. The extension of telephones into these areas after 1934 was largely financed by special federal subsidies.

The 1940s were a good period for AT&T in another way. The Second World War saw Bell come to the rescue of the military – with huge outputs of radar equipment, for example. Thereafter, AT&T retained several special relationships with the DOD, as provider of its basic US communications network (both over the public wires and in specially 'hardened' facilities) and through various high-tech offerings from Bell Labs, such as the original guidance mechanism for multiple targeting ballistic missiles. In the Eisenhower period, AT&T's active role in the Korean War was quoted as supporting evidence for dropping a new antitrust case. And AT&T's enemies were to complain that the Bell theme song was 'The Russians are Coming'.

Just how much was luck and how much skill in AT&T's financial practices may remain forever unknown. But AT&T evolved a system of financial control so complex, so muddled, so obscure that nobody seemed able to understand it. The important point was that AT&T operated in favorable financial circumstances. No matter that AT&T management itself was unable to fathom from which precise financial depths the profits came; no matter that a sizeable economics literature has been constructed on unreliable AT&T statistics. Regardless, state and federal regulators and politicians, who could not understand AT&T's

finances, for the most part were still willing to believe that voters were receiving good phone service at reasonable prices.

Most public utility commissioners were prepared to accept AT&T's word that it was heavily subsidizing *local* customer-voters. In a few areas – California was one – local commissioners beat down the Bell rates, and earned both the enmity of AT&T nationally and a genuine subsidy. Otherwise the subsidy card was one which AT&T could use in various ways, especially by telling small pockets of household subscribers that they were subsidized by business and long-distance telephoning. But in many cases the subsidies operated within categories. Some states were subsidized by others; the independent local companies were subsidized by AT&T; the affluent suburbs and small towns by the cities; national long-distance was subsidized by international; heavy routes (New York to Chicago) subsidized lighter routes of similar mileage (Poughkeepsie to Peoria); and the Western Electric manufacturing arm was subsidized by the local BOCs.

But the whole financial operation was swathed in a surfeit of detail and a lack of hard, bottom-line data. AT&T kept its financial details obscure for several reasons. First and foremost, its executives knew the bureaucratic truth that secrecy disarms opposition. Moreover, the brute fact of monopoly could be somewhat softened if the financial facts were shrouded in public service rhetoric. The defense obligations of AT&T were another excuse (here again the military were in some cases the subsidizers, while in others the subsidized receivers of AT&T's politically motivated largesse). Later, the whole computer issue was another reason for secrecy; AT&T had supposedly been regulated out of the computer business, but in fact the big 'switches', which were becoming central to the operation and the economics of the network, were computers made by AT&T's Western Electric subsidiary.

The obscurity of AT&T's financial detail was not entirely contrived. While federal and state regulators were interested, respectively, in long-distance and local calls – and whole separate companies within AT&T dealt with the two levels – in fact much of the investment resided in 'joint and common costs'. The big-city switches inevitably handled both local and long-distance traffic – indeed, switched one into the other – and thus any allocation of costs between the local BOCs and the central AT&T was bound to be arbitrary.

Paradoxically, despite AT&T's ambiguous attitude to financial detail, it was still very committed to quantitative goals. Instead of the usual financial criteria, Bell managers were expected to perform against a massive battery of measures – but measures calculated to impress the regulators and politicians, rather than to improve the profit figures. So Bell managers must perform against 'indexes' of performance, all explained in the company bible of 'Bell System Practices'.

AT&T personnel in general, and local managers in particular, were expected to engage in a vigorous and continuing campaign of community public relations. Managers were advised to put the company cash into the most politically influential banks, to employ the most prestigious local lawyers, to cultivate politicians before their initial election, to get to know the local newspaper editors. Bell managers should try to meet any customer's request with utmost speed; but in the case of anyone influential in local politics or business, the manager should try to anticipate requests.

AT&T was a regulation-driven, rather than financially-driven, company. Most senior people had entered the giant company after leaving high school or college, and had then worked their way to the top via Illinois Bell (as had Charles Brown) or one of the other units of the Bell organization. This inward-looking career structure, plus the peculiarity of AT&T being both a commercial business of legendary achievement and a government-regulated bureaucracy, seems to have endowed senior Bell management with a set of beliefs, uniformly and fiercely held, which can only be described as quasi-religious.

The Bell credo came in four parts, each part in keeping with an organization with such a weight and quality of engineering talent, well grounded in an activity of the company. All four parts of the credo were under severe challenge as the result of events immediately preceding the 8 January 1982 decision:

(1) A fierce belief in the sanctity of the *network*, the Bell 'long lines' in particular, stretching 3,000 miles from sea to shining sea, making up the world's largest single engineering project; but – and here the Bell managers did not expect outsiders to comprehend – this semisacred network must be treated with respect, almost reverence, because it was so intrinsically fragile. As the telephone systems of most other countries illustrated, the network was vulnerable to failures and inefficiencies of many kinds. It was the duty of Bell managers to keep their network clear and perfect, the equipment the best that humans could make; the Bell telephone must speak with truly Bell-like clarity. And the break must be absolutely minimal in any time of crisis or challenge. Even after a tornado or other natural disaster, service must be back in place within hours.

(2) Bell also had a strong belief in *local service*, both of which words were taken with a seriousness amounting to zealotry. Bell provided local telephone service to some 80 per cent of all US households, and a higher proportion of urban households. And service meant service: it meant being there at midnight with a skilled man and an expensive truck to fix a minor fault for a family that could have waited. Bell's armies of local service people across the land put to shame the paltry efforts of doctors

and all others claiming to render human service. And most of the Bell managers themselves had done house calls, had been up poles at times of year when the weather is hostile. Moreover, 'local' did not stop there: Bell managers were involved in local organizations, in the Chamber of Commerce, working for the good local causes. It was all part of the Bell priesthood.

(3) The Bell managers also had a strong belief in, and sense of, *national responsibility*. The network was not simply a triumph of human ingenuity and technical excellence: it was an American triumph. It was there for the nation as a resource, to help the economy of a vast and varied continent purr as smoothly as a Bell dial tone. It was there for the nation to talk to the nation; it was there in peace and in war. And increasingly after 1934, Bell managers came to combine the local and national principles in 'universal service'.

(4) Finally, Bell was dedicated, yes dedicated, to achieving *technical excellence*. Theirs was the ultimate in high quality and reliability. A Bell telephone should last for eternity; everything in the network was not just good quality, but the very best. Few companies in the world were quite so committed to scientific research and innovation. The whole life and talk of the vast company was engineering talk, improvements, patents, upgrading, the technological future.

But by the start of the 1980s, all four of these articles of faith were being challenged by an apparently uncaring and ungrateful US society.

First, the network had been under challenge for more than a decade. For example, MCI and other intruders had broken into the long-distance business, and were offering private-line and later public phone service, using, as AT&T described it, the tactic of skimming the cream off the thick (heavily used) routes. In addition, Bell had warned that the integrity of the network required that Bell make, or oversee the making of, all equipment attached to the network. But by the early 1980s, this had been ignored for some years: Americans could go out and buy phones of different colors and shapes that did fancy new tricks. Bell had always said that it must manufacture the phones, must install the phones and must determine what these phones would and would not do; moreover, Bell had insisted that phones would be for rent, not sale. The end of the network was the phone in the customer's hand, but the owner of the phone (as of the network) was Bell. Now, however, you could go down to Sears at the local shopping mall, pick up a phone of exotic shape and color, bring it home and plug it in yourself. This was more than a superficial change. Bell's advice had been ignored, and yet the network was still intact. Bell's advice was widely believed to have been not just false, but deliberately, self-seekingly false. Not only the integrity of the network, but the integrity of Bell was now in question.

Second, the local service concept especially was being challenged. Competition and price-cutting by other common carriers such as MCI and Sprint, must lead to lower profits and the loss of rate-averaged subsidies. Moreover, the whole thrust toward tighter accounting meant that those expensive local repair visits could less and less be justified. The effect of FCC deregulation and competition must be to drive prices toward costs, the Bell people said; the beneficiaries of such a change must be large businesses, and thus the losers must be small, local people, especially people living in nonurban areas and households with below-average income.

Third, the Bell managers felt that they and their sense of national responsibility had been exploited. They had agreed to be a national resource, a regulated monopoly; they had reluctantly consented to being kept out of many new fields (such as movies, satellites and foreign sales of hardware); they had exercised the full force of monopoly only in areas where their monopoly had been nationally sanctioned. In return, the Bell people thought, the main federal agencies had all been two-faced. The courts had let in the MCI competition and the new phone attachments. The FCC, supposedly in AT&T's pocket, had never really said where it stood: it had totally failed to stand up and be counted on the all-or-nothing issue of regulated monopoly in the public service. AT&T was helping the economy, providing services to the military, subsidizing rural areas and the local private user; it was doing all this by taking money from the cities, businesses and long-distance users. Yet the FCC, actively involved in running this Bell version of national responsibility via its regulatory activities, was unwilling to call a halt to changes which undermined its principles and would soon undermine its subsidies and the rest.

Fourth, Bell managers' belief in the value of technological innovation was no fantasy: it was grounded in Bell Labs, world-famous for basic research, Nobel prizes, and having made many, if not most, of the key discoveries in telecommunications and electronics in recent decades. The trend toward competition and assessment in terms of quarterly profit figures seemed to Bell managers likely, ultimately, to threaten this massive Bell subsidy to US technological innovation.

US society's apparently comprehensive rejection seems by the early 1980s to have added to the senior AT&T managers' credo a new element, part fatalism, part paranoia. This is powerfully expressed in a book called *Heritage and Destiny*, published in 1983, by Alvin von Auw, who had been vice-president/assistant to three chairmen of AT&T; the book is a 480-page cry of pain – a remarkable admixture of bitterness, eloquence and blinkered vision. As with so many Bell managers, von Auw joined the company when he graduated from college; he departed only upon his retirement 42 years later.

This tradition of career-long loyalty and lifelong job security rein-forced Bell's pseudo-religious and army-like qualities. It produced intense dedication and an equally intense inward-looking vision. All Bell managers had experience of an inexorably growing demand for plain old telephone service which dulled their sense of other marketing possibilities and public demands. A classic illustration was the Pic-turephone into which AT&T poured large sums in 1967–72. This particu-lar technological wonder that never was had one lethal weakness: it used the equivalent bandwidth of 250 telephone voice channels and was always going to remain prohibitively expensive.

1965–76: SLIPPING

Few politicians or commentators realized that by 1965 AT&T's relatively unchallenged position as a regulated natural monopoly was already starting to slip away. But those who did realize this included AT&T's own senior management, whose submerged paranoia surfaced as finger-in-the-dike imagery.

AT&T's monopoly as seen by outsiders, especially by business users of telecommunications, was a monopoly bulging ever more clumsily, both vertically and horizontally. Table 9.1 shows some of the ways in which that monopoly could be described:

Even this tabulation does not represent the full range of AT&T targets at which competitors and opponents could take aim. AT&T executives knew that their position in virtually all these sixteen categories was less secure than the formal regulated monopoly position might suggest.

But two of the most important early challenges were aimed at Customer Premises Equipment (CPE) and long-distance. Any electrician or hobbyist could take his home telephone apart and find quite a simple gadget, much simpler than a radio set. So, just as it would be absurd for RCA/NBC, say, to own all the nations' radio sets and lease these out, why should AT&T be allowed to own the domestic phones and get away with

TABLE 9.1   Four ways of describing AT&T's monopoly

Bell system	Hardware	Technology	Services
Bell Labs	Phones and CPE	Wires	Local
Western Electric	PBX	Microwave	Long-distance
AT&T long lines	Switches	Computers	Private-line
BOCS	Network	Satellites	International

making the great American public pay, in rental over the years, excessive sums of money? These were the challenging questions behind the Carterfone and Hushaphone cases. From the viewpoint of AT&T management, millions of US households and businesses were starting to nibble away at the roots of network integrity.

The long-distance challenge was even more disturbing, although initially it presented itself in the form of an obscure company called MCI wanting to run private-line business traffic the 300 miles between Chicago and St Louis. This challenge was more serious than the first Computer Inquiry itself, where the issue was the expansion of AT&T from voice into data, and from using computers as network switches into computers more generally.

The MCI decision of 1969 was recognized within the high command at AT&T as an attack of the utmost seriousness. And rightly so: MCI was to prove itself indeed the mouse which tripped the elephant. MCI's challenge had several disturbing aspects. In AT&T's eyes, it was pure heresy, because it challenged the sanctity of the network, and such a dangerous heresy demanded merciless suppression. MCI stood for Microwave Communications Inc, which underlined the hazards of this new technology. Born of radar, and capable of carrying voice, data and video, microwave was not an obviously 'natural monopoly' technology. Finally, MCI was threatening because its first customers, and obvious allies, were *business* users of telecommunications wanting cheap, bulk-rate facilities for everyday company communications. If the businessmen of St Louis and Chicago wanted thus to bypass the AT&T network, could the businessmen of the rest of the US be far behind? AT&T management saw all this, saw that it was bad, saw that MCI must die the death (see table 9.2).

The MCI challenge grew quickly; in 1971 the FCC opened up the key private-line area to other common carriers besides MCI. Meanwhile, MCI itself was after bigger game: it was determined to move from internal business telecommunications to the provision of general telephone service, and (with slightly doubtful legality) it used its Execunet offering as an entry to general long-distance telephoning. But MCI opened not only the competitive assault on AT&T, it also opened the legal assault; in March 1974 it chose the antitrust legal route, accusing AT&T of monopoly behavior in the sensitive private-line market. Eight months later the Department of Justice, responding to this implied rebuke of its own inactivity launched a much more comprehensive legal assault on the entire vertical monopoly structure of AT&T; seven years later this Justice case led to the AT&T Consent Decree.

Senior Bell management made a deliberate decision to kill MCI; MCI's chairman, Bill McGowan, subsequently revealed records of the relevant

TABLE 9.2 AT&T 1965–76

27 October 1965	FCC launches investigation of AT&T's charges and services.
15 September 1966	US Court of Appeals affirms FCC opinion: Telpak service rates are too low.
10 November 1966	FCC launches investigation of computer/communications overlap ('Computer Inquiry I').
27 June 1968	FCC's Carterfone decision: AT&T cannot outlaw customer-owned terminals.
14 August 1969	FCC allows MCI's Chicago–St Louis private-line service.
18 March 1971	FCC Computer Inquiry I forbids common carriers to offer data processing.
3 June 1971	FCC decision allows specialized common carriers to offer private-line services.
26 February 1973	AT&T proposes a de-averaged (Hi/Lo) private-line tariff; FCC will consider proposal.
30 July 1973	Senator Hart's antitrust subcommittee: specialized common carrier witnesses demand AT&T breakup.
20 September 1973	AT&T chairman John deButts's 'unusual obligation' speech to NARUC signals Bell fight back against recent 'experiments'.
6 March 1974	MCI files antitrust suit, asserting AT&T monopoly of private-line market.
22 October 1974	Chairman deButts calls on Congress to examine long-term telecommunications policy.
20 November 1974	Department of Justice files comprehensive antitrust suit, calling for AT&T divestiture of both Western Electric and at least some BOCs.
19 May 1975	AT&T challenges legality of MCI Execunet Service.
19 January 1976	FCC finds Hi/Lo tariff to be unlawful.
4 March 1976	With active AT&T support, the Consumer Communications Reform Act (HR.12323) is introduced in US House of Representatives. A similar bill (S.3192) quickly follows in the US Senate.
17 June 1976	Litton files against AT&T for monopolizing the PBX market.
28–30 September 1976	House Communications Subcommittee hearings on telecommunications competition effectively kill HR.12323, now known to opponents as the 'Bell Bill'.

Source: Alvin von Auw, *Heritage and Destiny* (1983), pp. 407–14.

meeting, which had been held in Key Largo, Florida. AT&T's determination to slay MCI surfaced on several occasions, such as:

(1) After almost three years of contemplation, the FCC in January 1976 disallowed Hi/Lo. The proposed Hi/Lo tariff would have waived the standard doctrine of rate averaging, allowing AT&T to underprice MCI on private lines.

(2) In John deButts's famous September 1973 'unusual obligation' speech to the National Association of Regulatory Utility Commissioners (NARUC), which was not merely a reaffirmation of AT&T public-service ideals, but a declaration of war on MCI.

(3) In deButts's October 1974 speech, which revealed his frustration with the creeping ad hoc decisions of the FCC and a determination to look instead to Congress for help.

(4) In AT&T's attempt in May 1975 to outlaw MCI's Execunet service, which nearly succeeded in destroying MCI.

(5) In its congressional assault, which began in March 1976, relying on its still excellent reputation in Congress, AT&T prevailed on friendly members to introduce 'Consumer Reform' legislation which, in fact, was designed in general to put the monopoly clock back to 1965, and in particular to render illegal MCI with all its offerings and imitators.

AT&T's consumer reform legislation attracted heavy congressional support initially, but in the longer run it was a massive and crucial mistake. Bill McGowan is probably correct in saying that in their Bell Bill effort to kill MCI, 'AT&T bet their company' and lost.[1] AT&T was entering upon nearly eight years of congressional trench warfare. No significant legislation survived these encounters, but neither did AT&T's reputation, nor indeed AT&T itself.

1976–80: THE BELL COALITION CRACKS

The last really good year for the old AT&T was 1980, mainly due to the landmark FCC decision, Computer Inquiry II, which went AT&T's way. Computer II promised at last to let AT&T out of what had increasingly become a straitjacket. Until then, AT&T had been kept on the communications side of an increasingly fictional divide between communications and data processing and transfer. It was required to set up an 'arm's-length' special subsidiary, which would also be allowed to sell telephone equipment. The FCC was allowing AT&T to establish a significant bridgehead in the data area, an area it was increasingly desperate to enter. Computer II was confirmed by the US Court of Appeals in Washington in late 1982. (It is in some respects best regarded as part of the AT&T case and the Consent Decree.)

But Computer II came in April, and in other respects 1980 was not a good year for AT&T. For example, only two months later, in June, MCI won its latest and largest case against AT&T; after trebling, the damages were $1.8 billion. AT&T of course appealed, this being not a decision that any company could take lightly. It was a double loss: a further eating away at the integrity of the AT&T monopoly, plus a huge sum of money.[2] But 1980 ended on an ambiguous note. After further legislative activity in the Senate and the House, Representative Lionel Van Deerlin, the man who had done so much to rewrite the telecoms agenda and to rewrite AT&T's image, went down to electoral defeat in November.

The November 1980 presidential victory of Ronald Reagan offered some hope that the antitrust case, now in its final stages of preparation, might be dropped. But this was a vain hope. In the late 1970s AT&T had lost its benign Ma Bell image, and regulated monopolies were now less popular. Moreover, AT&T, since its efforts to turn back the clock with the Bell Bill of 1976, had in fact succeeded in alienating nearly every major member of its once impregnable coalition.

The coalition in support of AT&T had included both parties in Congress, big business generally, the FCC, the local regulatory commissions, the DOD, the independent phone companies and the trade unions – led by the CWA. But first under President Ford, then in President Carter's term of 1977–80, this coalition fell apart. MCI fired the first shots, but AT&T was beaten by technology, inflation and politics. It proved increasingly difficult to control the technology, and inflation meant that AT&T was continually having to ask for, and increasingly to fight for, rate increases. Further, AT&T's leaders were defeated politically by failing to anticipate that repeated exposure to the glare of congressional committee hearings would steadily sap their strengths in lobbying, PR and financial sleight-of-hand.

A Congress that in 1976 was well disposed to Ma Bell was not impressed with AT&T's executives as witnesses. At first, congressmen were confused by AT&T's endless organizational intricacies and financial complexity; then they began to realize that part of the confusion was deliberate – designed to conceal the fact, for example, that poor inner cities subsidized affluent suburbs. Part of the confusion was all too genuine, on the other hand, since AT&T lacked an adequate accounting system and its own executives genuinely did not know at all precisely which activities were profitable and which subsidized.

Big Business was an equally vital constituency, not only because it provided Ma Bell with her biggest and best customers, but also because representatives of banks and other businesses sat on AT&T's national board, with local equivalents on the 22 regional BOC boards. Big business increasingly came to see Bell as technologically backward rather than innovatory, as reluctant to recognize business needs and sophistication in telecommunications, arrogant in response to criticism, paternalistic rather than competitive, self-seeking rather than public-spirited.

The FCC had always been friendly toward AT&T; but continual reversal of its decisions by the courts and Congress gradually needled the FCC into taking a more skeptical view of AT&T. The state regulators moved in a similar direction. Yet both FCC and PUCS still found AT&T a formidable challenge in terms of regulation. Increasingly, the regulators – especially the staff – saw themselves as unable to control an AT&T with too much money, lobbying power and monopoly clout, and too much engineering and legal sophistication. Increasingly, the FCC, frequently criticized by both courts and Congress, looked to both for leadership.

DOD support for maintaining the AT&T monopoly also seemed to crumble. The independent telephone companies, with the most obsolete and inadequate equipment, had a good case against AT&T.

AND THEN, 1981: GREENE'S TURF, BAXTER'S EYEBALLS, BROWN'S NIGHTMARE

Nineteen eighty-one might have been the year that AT&T was rescued by the new Republican administration; indeed, AT&T showed itself willing to accept a mildly competitive bill introduced by Republican Senator Packwood in April 1981. But while the newly arrived Republican deregulators in the White House and the FCC stayed silent, the foursome of the courts, the Justice Department, Congress and AT&T itself engaged in an every accelerating series of moves which led ultimately to the AT&T divestiture announcement eight days into 1982.

It began in the very first week of 1981. On 5 January, AT&T and Justice Department lawyers asked Judge Harold Greene for a postponement of the US versus AT&T trial. Two days later Greene denied the request; eight days after that the momentous trial began (see table 9.3). The case already dated from 1974, and had been delayed by the ill health (and later the death) of a previous judge. But in Harold Greene the case had acquired no ordinary judge; he was, by general consent, exceptionally able, fast-working, politically adept and decisive. His earlier connections with the Justice Department under Robert Kennedy, and his personal history as a Jewish refugee from Hitler's Germany, made Greene in some conservative eyes an extreme example of an 'activist' judge. Greene in fact was in the center of national politics – a strong believer in using antitrust laws to make American business more competitive. Greene had first been assigned to the case on 21 June 1978;

TABLE 9.3   The US versus AT&T case, 1981

AT&T	Courts	Justice	Congress	Defense
	7 January: Greene rejects postponement of US versus AT&T			
		20 February: Baxter nominated assistant attorney general		
	4 March: Recessed US versus AT&T case resumes			
				23 March: Weinberger urges case be dropped
			7 April: Senator Packwood introduces deregulatory bill S.898	
10 April: AT&T largely endorses S.898 bill		10 April: Baxter 'litigate ... to the eyeballs'		
	29 June: Litton wins suit against AT&T, awarded $276 million.			
	29 July: Greene refuses Justice request for delay to allow legislation			
	11 September: Greene denies dismissal: 'AT&T has violated anti- trust laws'			

TABLE 9.3 *cont.*

AT&T	Courts	Justice	Congress	Defense
			7 October: Senate passes S.898 by 90 to 4	
	26 October: Greene sets new schedule: verdict by July 1982			
			3 November: House sub-committee report on telecom-munications competition	
			10 December: Wirth's HR.5158 bill introduced, hostile to AT&T	
		3 December: Baxter: 'discussions have resumed on settlement'		

8 January 1982:
Justice Department and AT&T agreement: AT&T will divest itself of Bell operating companies.

Source: Alvin von Auw, *Heritage and Destiny* (1983), pp. 418–20.

by taking only 19 months to get 'the world's largest case' to trial, he was already breaking records.

All this was bad news for AT&T, which was using its tried and trusted legal tactics of massive legal forces, massive numbers of arguments and massive oversupply of documents. In two recent cases against MCI and Litton respectively, AT&T had supplied 12 million pages of documents of which the MCI and Litton lawyers had sifted out 2.5 million as possibly relevant. When asked for the same documents in the new case, AT&T

again offered the full 12 million. This issue itself then went to the US Supreme Court, which confirmed the sufficiency of the smaller quantity. Well aware of such AT&T tactics, which were backed by hundreds of AT&T lawyers and literally hundreds of millions of legal dollars, Judge Greene's own tactics were those of relentless speed and pressure.

A second exceptional personality crucially involved in the case was William Baxter, a former Stanford professor now in the number three job in Reagan's Justice Department. Baxter's views on antitrust were broadly similar to those of the Reagan administration, and Baxter had been involved in the tolerant antitrust line on IBM and in several other cases. But during Baxter's confirmation hearings, few observers noted the significance of two facts; first, that the attorney general and his number two were ineligible to handle the case because of previous dealings with AT&T, and second, that Baxter, who would thus be carrying the AT&T ball, had established views on AT&T – that it was an exception, a real monopoly with real neoclassical economic bottlenecks. Baxter was nominated on 20 February 1981.

Less than two months later, Assistant Attorney General Baxter, asked in a press conference to comment on a rumor that the US versus AT&T case was to be settled quietly, snapped out a remarkable statement: Baxter would 'litigate the suit to the eyeballs', the press stories said the next day. And, yes, Baxter confirmed the quote. This was the worst conceivable news for AT&T; it now faced the long-shot double disaster of not only a dynamic activist antitrust judge but also this California professor who had, it seemed, a strong case of the anti-AT&T disease.

The Baxter bombshell was all the more shocking because, even a few days earlier, the Reagan administration had looked to be so friendly. AT&T had endorsed Senate bill S.898; this bill, introduced by Senate Commerce Committee chairman Bob Packwood, appeared to be about the most favorable bill that AT&T could expect. The Packwood bill would largely deregulate the entire field of communications. But in return for added phone competition, AT&T would at least stay in one piece; it would (if the bill went AT&T's way) be able to compete without both hands tied behind its back; and, most important, it would be allowed to enter the communications/data/computer fields. Another reason for adopting a positive line toward this bill was that the inexperienced White House staff had already taken a look at telecommunications policy and decided to make its initial input via the experienced and conservative Senator Packwood. Another plus point for AT&T was that the new Defense Secretary, Casper Weinberger, already looking like the strong man of the first Reagan administration, had said on 23 March that the case against AT&T should be dropped for national security reasons.

Why, then, was it Baxter's statement in April that signalled the way events would turn out? Baxter, despite his junior ranking, played his cards well; in its first year the Reagan administration was in at least the usual state of initial confusion. One factor was that the Reagan White House was already in trouble for millionaire opulence and apparently letting business off too lightly; Jim Baker in the White House persuaded President Reagan that he needed at least one case which would show the electorate that he could be tough on antitrust. Baxter was also clearly the type who might resign (he resigned later after only three years in office), and his resignation – with perhaps more inflammatory, 'eyeballs'-style rhetoric – would be embarrassing. But Baxter's success lay perhaps in yet another unexpected twist. In the end, Baxter and the Justice Department persuaded AT&T and its boss Charles Brown to give in. Baxter was then able to upstage the entire Reagan administration by presenting not merely arguments, but the AT&T chief executive with surrender terms in hand.

AT&T's 'surrender' was, in turn, crucially influenced by a third unusual personality in an unusually favorable position to determine the outcome. Charles Brown had become chairman and chief executive of AT&T on 1 February 1979. He had quickly established himself as a much more flexible and future-oriented chief executive officer than his hard-line traditionalist predecessor John deButts. Brown's flexibility was illustrated when, in October 1981 he reluctantly accepted the Senate bill. Brown also seems to have been in a strong internal position within AT&T; if he and his chief legal advisers were to accept divestiture, it would be impossible for other senior AT&T managers to dissent.

But why did Brown agree? It seems that his views continued to change during 1981; he moved toward some kind of divestiture as it became increasingly clear that both Justice and Judge Greene were in tenacious pursuit. On the private antitrust case front the news continued to go from bad to worse. In late June AT&T had lost yet another major case, against Litton. AT&T was found to have violated the antitrust laws through a 1970s conspiracy to keep Litton out of the office switchboard market. Treble damages set at $267 million were added to AT&T's long list of legal losses; and Brown must have envisaged another disturbing list of legal defeats stretching into the future.

In July the Justice Department asked Greene to delay the case for 11 months, until midsummer of 1982, in the hope that the House might follow the Senate lead. This would mean in effect that the House had 11 months in which to pass its version of the Senate bill – not impossible, but, in view of the recent Van Deerlin rewrite attempts in the House, very far from a certainty. Judge Greene astutely refused the request, and the case continued. Indeed, in less than a week, in the steamy early days of August 1981, AT&T's defense began.

Presumably with the House response in mind, Baxter, speaking for Justice, said that the department would drop the case if strong legislation were passed to ensure genuine competition for other common carriers and other equipment suppliers. But, in effect indicating the kind of compromise required, Baxter's statement also underlined the difficulty of getting the Senate, the House, AT&T and the Justice Department all to agree on suitably strong legislation.

In September the court news became still worse: AT&T petitioned for the case to be dropped, and Greene refused yet again. But it was his language that was astonishing, going to the very borders of judicial rectitude, if not beyond: Greene's preliminary opinion was that AT&T had 'violated the antitrust laws in a number of ways over a lengthy period of time'. This did not leave much room for the imagination; Greene was signalling his total rejection of the reasonable-sounding argument that as a regulated entity AT&T was exempt from antitrust. It now seemed that AT&T's best tactical hope would be to attempt to batter down the none-too-well-prepared details of the prosecution case. But Greene, as usual, was skeptical and quick-footed, while still thorough on 'due process'. In late October, he set a new schedule. The massive AT&T testimony would be completed by January 1982, and the verdict would be in July 1982 at the latest; this latter date took note of the political fact that in an election year July is about the latest realistic deadline for legislation. But while a Senate–House compromise still looked highly uncertain, a negative verdict from Greene in the summer of 1982 looked highly probable.

During the fall and into the early winter of 1981, somewhat desultory discussions were being held between Baxter and AT&T's top lawyer, Howard Trienens. In these discussions the divestiture option was not very seriously considered initially, although it was being much more actively discussed in the higher reaches of AT&T. But then, once more, the bad news turned worse.

COUP DE GRACE: HR.5158

The final blow which broke the back of AT&T resistance was House Bill 5158, introduced on 10 December 1981 by Representative Timothy Wirth of Colorado. Only six days later, on 16 December 1981 (a Wednesday), AT&T lawyers told their Justice contacts that they would accept the Justice proposals.[3] Work on an agreement continued into the weekend, and on Monday 21 December the first draft of a divestiture agreement had been written. On 31 December the Justice Department announced that discussions with AT&T were in progress. The public announcement of divestiture was made by Baxter and Brown on 8 January. It had been only 29 days since Wirth's introduction of HR.5158.

Timothy Wirth was a young Colorado congressman, then little known to the general public. In early 1981 he had taken over as chairman of the House Telecommunications Subcommittee, following the defeat of Lionel Van Deerlin. Wirth was already well known to AT&T's leading lawyers and lobbyists; in the late 1970s, as a subcommittee member, he had not only exhibited an unusually quick understanding of telecommunications, but had already focused on *competition* as the key ingredient. In addition to powerfully independent views and a coldly articulate presentation, Wirth was about to show an acute sense of legislative timing. The subcommittee spent much of 1981 quietly holding hearings and accumulating evidence. On 11 September 1981 Wirth presided over the fifth and last day of subcommittee hearings on 'User Needs and Concerns in the Telecommunications Marketplace'. The title was modest enough, but almost all of some forty witnesses were highly critical of AT&T, and most of them represented either big or small businesses. These witnesses saw AT&T not as Ma Bell, but as a clumsy and vindictive monopolist insufficiently responsive to the needs of its business customers.

The Wirth subcommittee's second unpleasant surprise for AT&T came on 3 November, in the form a 435-page research report by the subcommittee majority (Democrat) staff entitled *Telecommunications in Transition: the status of competition in the telecommunications industry*. As connoisseurs of such documents, the AT&T lawyers could not fail to note the high quality of the report and its only thinly disguised hostility to AT&T. The volume was (and is) the only good summary of the competitive/monopoly position in US telecommunications up to 1981.

When the resultant bill, HR.5158, appeared on 10 December, it carried the devastating message that the congressional path was impassable, being blocked by most of the Republican and Democrat membership of the House subcommittee. AT&T and the Senate majority could not possibly accept the House bill because, while opening up competition, it did *not* free AT&T to enter new communications pastures; indeed it contained measures to prevent AT&T from cross-subsidizing its computer and communications activities with profits from the phone business. To AT&T legal eyes, this bill meant that, despite the Reagan victory and the Republican majority in the Senate with which AT&T could work, the House Republicans and Democrats had not been cured of their anti-AT&T stance of the late 1970s.

Faced with the prospect of endless indecisive legislative battles still to come in Congress, plus the prospect of a hostile verdict from Judge Greene appealed to the Supreme Court – with probably many other major court cases to follow – AT&T had to consider its long-term interests. Since 1973–4, all AT&T managers had been encouraged to study marketing texts, and all were familiar with the classic example of the railroads, which failed to recognize that they were in the transportation business. Clearly AT&T must not get stuck in its equivalent – namely plain old telephone service. Whatever the price, even divestiture, AT&T must boldly pursue the *communications* business.

And so AT&T, 29 days after the publication of the new House bill, was agreeing in public to a divestiture – a divestiture which assured a communications future, and also let go of the plainest and oldest (the local) parts of the telephone service. But Brown and the AT&T executives did this with sorrow in their hearts. Their predictions for the future showed the cold, calculating long-term economic view. Their damaged pride, their lost credo and their bitterness were expressed in their vengeful response to the House bill. They opposed HR.5158 with an otherwise irrational ferocity; they responded to the bipartisan House consensus with a lobby of unprecedented aggression, and by the ultimate crudity of filibuster they burned their legislative boats. AT&T now had no choice but to march with the Consent Decree.

JANUARY 1982–JANUARY 1984: DOING DIVESTITURE

Judge Greene appears to have been genuinely surprised by the Brown and Baxter statement of 8 January 1982. Although it was probably not the kind of divestiture that Greene himself favored, this clean, horizontal cutting off of the regional Bells held many advantages for Greene. The truly massive decision had been taken by others: the administration, elected only a year earlier had directly participated, and AT&T was 'consenting'. Greene's pressure had worked, and there had been no attempt at bluff-calling.

Greene was immediately faced with some delicate legal steps, since the existing (1956) consent decree was legally located in New Jersey and not in Washington DC. But Greene had both AT&T and the Justice Department with him. He was the judge that both Brown and Baxter now wanted; whatever they may have thought of his aggressive judicial style in 1981, by 1982 Greene's speed and decisiveness were what both AT&T and Justice wanted. The New Jersey legal knot was quickly untied, and Greene went to work.

The antitrust 'Tunney Act' at this stage did not allow changes in grand strategy, but it did require that a judge consider the public interest, and it allowed him to make modifications. Greene quickly set about this task. He was to hear 600 opinions, mainly from interested industrial parties. Perhaps the most important point was made by the FCC; having remained silent and uninvolved throughout 1981 in one of the biggest communications decisions of the century, the (Fowler) FCC approved the agreement in general. But it suggested to the judge that the ex-BOCs not be restricted to local phone service.

Having agreed in principle to divestiture and having supported Greene, AT&T had left the judge in a strong tactical position; Greene used this to the full, and his Modified Final Judgement gave AT&T a less favorable deal than had Baxter and Justice. Greene handed the highly profitable Yellow Page directories back to the ex-BOCs, even though, according to Baxter antimonopoly theory, the Yellow Pages belonged to the competitive, and thus AT&T long-distance side. Greene also calmed fears that AT&T would go into the *electronic* Yellow Page business; the newspaper publishers (ANPA) were especially worried that such an AT&T move would threaten their future, and Greene, who clearly wanted to avoid the enmity of the entire newspaper industry, let ANPA have its way – for seven years.

On 16 December 1982 AT&T made public its detailed blueprint for the breakup. AT&T claimed that it was off-loading to the regional companies about two-thirds of its one million employees, about three-quarters of its total assets ($145 billion in 1981) plus about half its revenue and profits.[4]

However, this is merely a summary of Judge Greene's activities in the first year (1982) of an extraordinary two-year interregnum. Two other events which occurred in the weeks immediately after 8 January 1982 may have been more important. On 19 February, just six weeks after the divestiture was announced, AT&T unveiled its plans for the BOCs after divestiture: the 22 Bell locals were to be grouped into seven regional companies, which now make up the familiar US telephone map. But the question remains: Did AT&T let go of the right pieces of the Bell empire?

Also following hard upon the 8 January divestiture announcement, a mere 18 days later, two House subcommittees began hearings. The subcommittees on telecommunications and monopolies held joint hearings on 26 January on the proposed antitrust settlements. Wirth's subcommittee then returned on 2 February to his HR.5158 bill, holding an exhaustive 12 days of hearings in February and March, the printed record of which runs to 2,700 pages. Wirth's view was that it was the duty of Congress to make major policy, and that a court-supervised divestiture was distinctly a second best. His subcommittee clearly agreed, voting 15–0 in favor of HR.5158 on 25 March. Despite this unanimous vote, AT&T stepped up its opposition to HR.5158, and succeeded in filibustering it to death in the full Commerce Committee.

The second phase of the divestiture process began in August 1982, when Judge Greene proposed his Modified Final Judgement, and both

AT&T and Justice quickly agreed. This phase perhaps closed on 10 December, at which time Greene announced a 110-day period for comment on AT&T's detailed plan.

The next phase closed on 8 July 1983, when Judge Green finally approved the AT&T blueprint.

The final phase culminated with a Supreme Court decision on 12 December 1983, affirming Judge Greene's ruling, and allowing the divestiture to take place three weeks later on 1 January 1984. While AT&T scrambled hard to complete the huge restructuring, the public issue which dominated this final phase was that of telephone costs in general, and access charges in particular. On this issue the House Democrats followed, and the Senate Republicans led, in the person of Senator Packwood with a bill (S.1660) to maintain universal telephone service. Telephone costs did indeed rise in 1984, but by nothing like the amounts predicted in late 1983. The about-to-be-independent BOCS asked for massive increases, but only much lower levels were granted. The FCC initially favored sizeable access charges (charged by the local companies to AT&T and other long-distance carriers, and then passed on to all customers); but the Senate Republicans forced a partial FCC retreat.

These telephone cost issues, and the political panic about them, reflected public ignorance, the chaotic regulatory conditions, and the fact that the two-year divestiture period had been dominated by legal considerations. The entire legal process indeed took up 23 of the available 24 months. The inevitable result was a decline in customer service and opinion polls that revealed a lack of public enthusiasm for the changes.

Another aspect of divestiture was that most of the action and all of the detailed planning revolved, once again, around AT&T. The senior management of AT&T was in a unique position; subject only to broad judicial umpiring, AT&T was given the task of designing not only its future self, but the futures of its former children and possible future rivals.

In the rush of events, including the fateful decisions of January and February 1982, AT&T may have mistakenly accepted the wrong kind of divestiture. The old Bell system had four levels, as shown in figure 9.1. The AT&T senior executives presumably thought – and sophisticated opinion in the industry largely agreed – that they had kept the best and most high-tech parts of the business. AT&T was keeping not only the pearl of Bell Labs, but Western Electric (including its capacity in microprocessors and computers) and the long-distance business. It was losing only the boring, low-tech BOCS, which would still be subject to tedious local regulation.

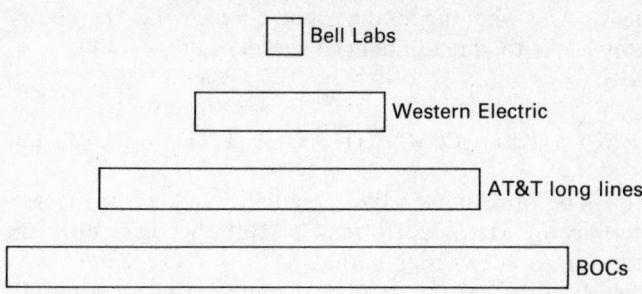

Figure 9.1 *The old AT&T*

But was not the AT&T high command accepting too easily what they had been reading in all those marketing textbooks? Even a slimmed down Bell Labs was likely to be a large and expensive pearl for a now much smaller AT&T; Western Electric was a high-cost sheltered producer, a commercial albatross. The industry which AT&T especially wanted to enter, computers and data, also happens to be an exceptionally competitive industry. The bulk of AT&T business would still be long-distance, and here again AT&T was a traditional, high-cost monopolist, destined to fight a bitter competitive battle.

The BOCS which AT&T was divesting itself of were all highly successful companies; moreover, at least during the transition period, they would still be regulated, and would thus be destined to struggle for years to break out of the restrictions imposed during divestiture. But, nevertheless, this was the great remaining area of Bell monopoly, and the management that would be running the BOCS was well suited to the task. Bell South, for example, was to be run by seven executives, all of whom had been in the Bell system for between 20 and 30 years.[5] In its first year of operations, Bell South earned over $1 billion, whereas the entire new AT&T earned only $1.38 billion. AT&T's earnings were only about one quarter those of the seven ex-BOCS.

The original Department of Justice antitrust action of 1974 had asked for the divestiture of Western Electric and some or all of AT&T's long lines from some or all of the BOCS. Was AT&T's decision to emphasize the computer business a mistake? Might not AT&T have done better to drop the entire albatross of Western Electric, while retaining all the BOCS and perhaps half the long lines? Of course, this latter choice would have required some AT&T senior managers to abolish their own jobs and to head back to places like Illinois and Atlanta. Moreover, it may never be possible to tell who made the right choice; the regulatory process inevitably seeks to spread financial success fairly evenly.

REGULATION + COMPETITION + POLITICS = TURBULENCE

In the days before January 1982, regulation added to the security and predictability of AT&T's performance. But the divestiture made little provision for an intervening period.

The implication was that the intervening period, before full telecommunications competition arrived, might comprise a decade or more. This lengthy period was implied by the maintenance of the seven new regional companies as regional monopolists, tightly regulated financially and severely restricted to telephone operations as their dominant activity. This decision may force the new regional BOCS to relive in the late 1980s and early 1990s the traumas experienced by AT&T a decade before – in particular with regard to the artificiality of the distinction between voice (telephone) and nonvoice (data and video) telecommunications. The scene was inevitably set for endless warfare between telecommunications companies, regulators (local and national), the courts and politicians (local and national). Certainly the legal profession will be a major beneficiary of these local telephone wars. Others – the public, the industry, the regulators – may find this reprise of the 1970s somewhat unfortunate.

In some other areas, the phasing-in of full, unregulated competition was quite rapid. In long-distance, AT&T was still totally dominant in January 1982; despite MCI's long struggle and the presence of GTE/Sprint, ITT, Allnet, US Telephone, SBS and many others, AT&T still received about 95 per cent of long-distance revenue in 1981. However, during the two-year divestiture period of 1982 and 1983 the competing carriers made big strides; and in 1984 AT&T took 'only' about 86 per cent of long-distance revenue.

This was worrying for AT&T as it entered the period for phasing in equal choice of long-distance carrier and equally easy dialling for all customers. Remarkably, neither the Modified Final Judgement nor the FCC nor the 'joint board' of FCC and local regulators had developed any ground rules for this much-anticipated event. The initial pattern in the 1984 'New Hampshire Primary' of telephone competition – Charleston, West Virginia – was for the local phone company to offer all its subscribers a long-distance choice, but to assign all nonchoosers to AT&T. The competing carriers obviously much preferred another system, used in a few early localities, of assigning nonchoosers to carriers in the same proportion as active choosers. According to which system was used, the outcome could be radically different; since the early proportion of 'nonvoters' was about half, one system awarded the competing carriers twice as many customers as the other. According to which system was allowed to prevail, the resulting AT&T long-distance market share by 1990 could be higher or lower by as much as 15 percentage points. AT&T's long-distance competitors lobbied furiously for the system which most favored them, and the FCC made a decision in that direction in June 1985. Leading competing carriers like MCI have some significant advantages in terms of somewhat lower costs and sharper management; MCI itself may also have the special advantage that the regulators may be reluctant to see its death, in view of its history as a brave flag-bearer for the principle of competition.

But AT&T has its own very considerable advantages, especially its reputation and its ability to reap advantages of scale in conditions of market growth and increasing productivity. Probably AT&T's best hope is for increasing revenue resulting from the overall market expanding faster than AT&T's share contracts. But this fairly obvious scenario has equally obvious uncertainties. Even if the telecommunications market expands less rapidly than the more ambitious forecasts indicate, it will still remain a rare example of a big and growing industry dominated by one rather old-fashioned company. This is an obvious challenge not only to the existing competing carriers, but also to other companies which may step forward to buy out any falterers. And the marriage with computers suggests that IBM/SBS/MCI may not be the only giant competitor. AT&T could find itself in competition with yet other giants, for example a US–Japanese computer-telecoms consortium.

Another key question is whether AT&T's executive structure and corporate culture will be able to withstand so many shocks from so many new directions. AT&T faces the same range of problems as do other carriers – such problems as 'bypassing' by major telecoms users setting up their own networks. But it also has many unique problems: it must attempt to *defend* its position in long-distance and in electronics manufacturing, while at the same time *attacking* international markets, engaging in joint ventures with foreign companies, as well as entering the computer and office automation fields. AT&T also faces the worrying prospect that several of its new enterprises could turn sour, just when the long-distance business falters in its role as a 'cash cow'.

Responding to these uncertainties, but also helping to exacerbate them, will be the FCC. That it will seek to prevent cross-subsidy and will continue to control services and monitor tariffs seems certain. But how far major regulation should continue – either in time or in breadth of application – will be a continuing focus of bitter debate and litigation. The FCC, like the courts and Congress, does not want to see the slimmed-down AT&T either too strong or too weak.

There lurks ahead yet another bundle of difficulties, perhaps in the early 1990s. For example, the seven-year moratorium on AT&T's entering the electronic Yellow Page business will run out then – leading perhaps to a stormy battle with the newspapers, which the latter may anticipate competitively in any of a number of possible ways. Moreover, by 1990 AT&T may well be quite deeply involved in competition with Bell regional companies, each of which by then may have increased in stature relative to its parent. Obvious foci of possible competition include not only data services and the sale of hardware, but intrastate and other intraregional long-distance initially awarded to AT&T. The BOCS quickly began to badger Judge Greene to let them into a wide range of other activities, and by the early 1990s these diversifications could threaten AT&T.

All trends and all forecasts are potentially self-disproving, because the regulators and courts will inevitably seek to trim any tendencies which they perceive as dangerous or excessive. Some forms of regulation could even be strengthened, but assuming that deregulation continues, the telecommunications field seems likely to be a prime example of the maxim: the fewer the rules, the more potent the rules that still exist.

Notes

1 William McGowan, interview with author, 15 March 1984.
2 Greatly lowered, however, by a subsequent court decision in 1985.
3 Interview with Richard Levine, attorney, Anti-Trust Division, Department of Justice, 13 September 1984.
4 'AT and T's 22 local units to get 75% of its assets at spin-off, filing says', *Wall Street Journal*, 16 December 1982, p. 3.
5 Annual Report, *Bell South* (1984), pp. 32–4.

PART III

'Setting the Media Free'

10

Introduction

In the US the main impact of the arrival of television had been experienced by 1960 – the redeployment of radio, the decline of Hollywood as movie capital and its rejuvenation as TV series capital, and the continuing strength of newspapers. But ever since 1960 there have been predictions of an imminent decline and fall of both television and newspapers as dominant vehicles for the established trinity of news, entertainment and advertising.

These 'Setting the Media Free' pages will consider how accurate such predictions have been, predictions which have become ever more strident with the twin revolutions of new technology and deregulation.

Predictions of cable via satellite and of an explosive growth in sales of VCRS had been made so often, that when HBO (in the late 1970s) and VCRS (1982 and after) suddenly did take off like rockets, most well-informed observers were taken by surprise. And even now, there is enormous variety in opinions as to the ultimate fate of cable and VCRS.

Most of the carefully phrased superlatives are backed by even more careful selections from industry-generated statistics. The national television networks, for example, have become adept at moaning to Congress that their audience is eroding rapidly, and nonnetwork offerings have recently trebled their slice of prime-time viewing, from 10 to something like 25 per cent. Meanwhile, the same networks have been telling Wall Street that all their vital signs of financial life are pointing steeply upward. Both claims have been true. The economic growth of the first Reagan term indeed increased the real (inflation-discounted) size of the media cake, helping both old and new media to grow quite substantially.

The impact of *deregulation* on the media has also been ambiguous. For example, some of the most significant deregulation has been in the old media – the abolition of most radio regulations, and the establishment of new independent (nonnetwork) TV stations in many more cities.

The deregulation of cable has been similarly full of ambiguity. The 1984 Act saw a fairly extensive deregulation of cable, but, like some previous cable decisions, the act was itself ambiguous. Much of it was aimed at altering the 1972 FCC decision, which had allowed cable to enter the major city markets, but only on a highly regulated basis.

The new media in general, and cable in particular perhaps, have been the subject of many 'blue skies' predictions – the wired nation, the interactive electronic home and local community access were simply going to blow away the New York networks. As these predictions failed to materialize on schedule, the deregulatory climate of around 1980 led to the famous 'alphabet soup' of new media technologies – STV, MDS, MMDS, DBS, SMATV, VCR, PPV and LPTV among others. We have already looked at DBS, and we will consider the others mainly in section 3.5 below, which deals primarily with VCR.

The main focus will be on the old technologies of *television* and radio, newspapers and magazines, plus just two 'new' technologies – cable and VCR. We will, therefore, be accepting the notion that the alphabet soup has, at least for the present, become cold. Noticeably, the most successful brand of alphabet soup, CATV, when it became successful lost its initials and was renamed 'cable'. The same seems to be happening with the VCR as it largely takes over the previously more encompassing title of home 'video'.

Cable, the electronic wild card of the 1960s and 1970s, has several similarities to the VCR, the electronic wild card of the 1980s. Both cable and VCRs feed primarily off old media, Hollywood movies in particular and recycled (or 'time-shifted') television fare in general. Both cable and VCRs give the viewer greater choice and greater flexibility – but the greater choice is mainly more of the same old favorites (such as sport, pop music and movies), and the greater flexibility involves mainly seeing these offerings at more suitable times and over longer periods. Both cable and the VCR suggest that many millions of Americans want something beyond 'free' – that is, advertising-supported – television; they are willing to pay extra to see material which carries less or no advertising and offers premium entertainment. But of course the revelation that Americans (like Europeans) are willing to pay for live sport and newish movies is a fairly modest one. Above all both cable and the VCR emphasize home delivery, the popularity of which was discovered by the newspapers a century ago.

The two old media of newspapers and television certainly predominate, their combined revenue being some five times that of cable and the VCR combined. However, cable, despite its still low advertising revenue, has overtaken both magazines and radio to become number three in revenue terms, now taking more than 10 per cent of combined media revenue. VCR rentals and sales of video cassettes received around 2.5 per cent of media revenue in 1984, but were already in hot pursuit of total theatrical movie revenues.

The VCR now takes the lead in dramatizing both the crisis of perpetual uncertainty and the theme that while all changes, all yet remains the same. Cable frightened broadcasters, programming suppliers and newspapers so much that they largely bought up cable – both as insurance and as an outlet for their surging cash flows.

The VCR business sees familiar Hollywood faces dominating its offerings, which are mainly entertainment; and the heavy recycling of daily soap operas, while pointing to the audience appeal of cheaper programming formats, is scarcely in line with futuristic blue skies predictions. Nevertheless, like cable, with its many new local operators of 1950–80, the VCR has revealed a new batch of mom and pop retailers, as well as some bigger brothers. But the really revolutionary aspects of the VCR are firstly, that it has become big media business without ever being regulated (unlike the press, movie, radio, TV and cable which, when they became sizeable industries, also attracted licensing and censorship), and second, that it seems to have been underestimated simply because in its mass form it was a foreign, Japanese gadget. This example, truly gigantic in dollar volume, emphasizes an important, and largely unanticipated, aspect of the new era of deregulation, or non-regulation: namely, that nonregulation opens the US market to massive foreign influence.

Both cable and the VCR emphasize that 'new' – or, at least, not previously applied – technology can be enormously important. But while the technology is new, the rest may remain much the same.

The new aspect of the new media consists largely in the same new technologies discussed previously – the converging technologies of computing, telecommunications, satellites and digitalization. These technologies primarily offer new means of instantaneous national distribution – one reason why the existing national media, such as TV networks, are presented with both new challenges and new opportunities.

But just as these new technologies both add to, and build upon, older technologies from the electric telegraph to microwave, so also the new media both expand and fall into other existing industrial patterns of production, wholesaling and retailing.

National production of media materials remains largely in Hollywood (movies, TV, recorded music) and Manhattan (news, advertising, finance).

Retailing and home delivery by newspapers, local radio and TV stations and theaters becomes in some respects more local and intimate: to more radio and TV stations are added the local cable company which, typically, has fewer customers and less annual revenue than a major supermarket. And to the cable company with less than 10,000 customers is added the video shop, and inevitably its big brother competitors, the supermarket and the video chains.

Wholesaling, always strong in an American media structure emphasizing both the local and the national, grows stronger still. The TV networks prosper, radio networks revive, and large newspaper chains acquire new links. The Hollywood majors continue their lengthy history, and are joined by a new boy on the block, HBO (which is dealt with mainly in chapter 13 on Hollywood).

Finally, we see the rapid emergence of another piece of alphabet soup, the subtly menacing initials, MSO, for multiple system operator. The leading MSOs already own hundreds of local cable systems. They may become the most controversial of all, because, as chains of local cable monopolies, their initials invite the redesignation 'monopoly system operators'; moreover, the prominence of other media interests in an MSO business, which is internally noncompetitive, invites such labels as 'cartel'.

11

Cable: Channel Profusion, Deregulation and Monopoly

THE PARADOX: CHANNEL PROFUSION AND MONOPOLY

The 1984 Cable Act largely deregulated cable, thus making it a showpiece for communications deregulation more generally. By 1984 the median cable subscriber had a choice of about 28 channels; but, paradoxically, the cable subscriber had no choice of cable company and no effective choice as to which 28 channels were offered. Nevertheless, the Cable Act justified allowing a regime of some 9,000 exclusive local cable franchises on the basis of competition from over-the-air broadcasting signals; if these were the usual minimum of four or five local television stations, then cable was held to have no monopoly. This, however, was a formula at odds with cable's history. The chaotic regulatory and policy history of cable before the FCC and Congress became involved had always in practice focused on allowing cable to bloom without damaging either national or local television; one of the few constant themes had been that cable should *complement*, not directly compete with, regular television.

This complementary development of TV and cable had indeed multiplied the number of channels provided. In 1960 the median US home could receive four channels, but by 1984 83 per cent of households received nine or more TV and cable channels combined. In 1984 only some 40 per cent of US homes had cable, but these were concentrated away from 30 largest cities, the urban areas most of which already had nine or more over-the-air TV channels.

There were many changes between cable's birth around 1948 and its deregulation in 1984. The early CATV systems carried at most three or four signals from the city over the hill, whereas some new systems of the mid-1980s boasted a capacity of 100 channels, and most have at least 30 programmed channels. The cable action has moved from rural valleys to the inner cities; regulation has largely moved from the township and county level to Washington; the impetus has moved from creating regulations to getting rid of regulations; the emphasis has changed from relaying conventional TV signals to offering original programming alternatives; cable has shifted away from the imitative competition of three similar general networks to the provision of numerous specialized theme channels, each seeking dominance in a separate market niche; it has evolved a new form of finance, viewer subscription, with advertising playing only a small part; for the local antenna on the local hilltop, cable has substituted its antennae out in space; from being a humble carrier seeking paths down the hillside and along small-town streets, cable has joined the mass media and seeks to enter the First Amendment's democratic elite.

These changes in cable have many consequences and implications for communications in general, and TV in particular. Cable has greatly increased the general competitive atmosphere; its history has emphasized – for anyone still in doubt – that, in addition to commercial competition, aggressive regulatory, legislative and court tactics are vital. Cable has also stressed the entertainment and commercial approach, while de-emphasizing 'public service'. In its fierce struggle to survive, cable has been willing to revert back to dubious practices not seen since the early days of television – in particular, seeking to win advertising by allowing advertisers to shape and make programming. Cable, in having to do much more programming with much less money, has also searched hard for new, cheap, but popular, programming formats.

There has been little serious attempt positively to design a national cable policy. Cable itself has grown up as a bizarre patchwork of several thousand franchises, each with a monopoly of a few square miles. This patchwork has no single architect or design team; rather, it is the result of warfare between a dozen trade lobbies and hundreds of cable franchise seekers. Franchising has taken the path of least resistance, and so also have both regulation and deregulation.

All the major lobbies have had their say, and cable has been squeezed into shapes which keep the major lobbies' core concerns largely untouched. The existing mass media, with old and new friends in local politics and business, have had a dominant influence. The telephone interests have achieved a satisfactory draw: no significant phone company involvement in cable, but also no cable involvement in the much larger telephone business.

Nationally, the early FCC concern was to protect the networks and the major new local independents. The networks have also achieved a draw: cable competes somewhat, but the most popular cable viewing is in fact the viewing of network signals, but with enhanced cable picture quality. The networks' owned-and-operated stations in five major markets have also been carried by cable into the regional hinterland, thus increasing audience size and advertising revenue. Hollywood has also achieved at least a draw: despite its extreme irritation at the success of HBO,

Hollywood has once again been confirmed, via cable, as the prime source of electronic entertainment.

Despite the many changes and the endless bitter lobbying, cable has some constants. It is a business requiring high initial investment, in that you have to put up a lot of wire before any money flows back; but in the long term, it is a strong cash-flow business. Cable began as a business of TV repair shops, but has long since become a management arena, stressing tax losses, accountancy and the efficient control of cash flow and debt.

Cable is still dominated by local systems. In its early days it was driven by hundreds, then thousands, of local system operators; today it is driven by about twenty multiple operators, the MSOs. The typical large MSO has some hundred small local systems, each one a local cable monopoly.

AND THE WINNER IS: THE MSO

By 1985 it was widely anticipated that the top ten MSOs, which already had half the total business, would eventually control 80 per cent or more. There were still a hundred companies with 40,000 or more subscribers and hundreds more with less. But by 1985 there were already seven MSOs with more than a million subscribers, which were increasingly the leaders.

Local system operators, whether small or large, predictably deny being monopolists. But they enjoy monopoly pricing, and increasingly are earning monopoly profits.

A subscriber may pay the local operator $10 per month for a 'basic tier' of perhaps 25 channels; of these 25, some 10 are 'must carries' (any regular TV signal receivable in the cable system's area must be carried on cable) and local access channels. The remaining 15 are dominated by satellite programmers, and for these 15 supposedly commercial channels the local system pays around $1.25, or less than 10 cents per channel per month. The local operator will also offer several 'pay' channels, and the typical household takes one of these for $10 a month. Of that $10, the local operator pays the supplier (such as HBO) between $4 and $6.

Of the $20 total that he receives from the subscriber, the small local operator will keep about $13, and the strong MSO may keep $15. Moreover, with a shift toward the 'basic' services, many local operators are further extending their share, and are keeping up to 80 per cent of what they collect from subscribers. (These are the reasons why satellite programmers are desperate to increase national advertising revenue, which they themselves can keep.)

If the fact that the retailer holds on to three-quarters of the customer's dollar is not a monopoly franchise, then what is a monopoly?

The 1984 Act's definition of competition in terms of the availability of broadcast TV turns a blind eye to an elementary fact of life. Broadcast TV lives solely off advertising. But cable, having very little advertising (see below), has acquired a monopoly of video *subscription* revenue.

Cable's great double act is that, first, it has found a new way to make American households pay $200 a year for video entertainment which was previously free, and second, that cable operators pocket up to $150 of that $200 subscription.

To this one might add a third triumph, especially of the MSOs. All the other players in the cable game are either so satisfied by their lobbying success or so frightened of MSO monopoly buying power, that they don't complain in public; even so, all the other players know that the MSOs are stealing the show.

1948–84: NONREGULATION, REGULATION, DEREGULATION

Although in some respects cable TV has been the first major piece of US communications to travel the deregulation road, as recently as 1972, the FCC was still heavily concerned to insist that cable was its to regulate, by issuing an elaborate set of rules – the 1972 Cable Television Report and Order.

The FCC's approach was defensive both of television in general, and of the independent station sector which it was actively encouraging. It was especially concerned with the case of San Diego, whose much canyoned local geography made it an early leader in cable; but the evidence from the mammoth Cox cable system was that San Diegans not only wanted clearer reception of local network affiliates, they also wanted signals imported from Los Angeles, 120 miles to the north. Since San Diego was a major market, and a city with a history, economy and atmosphere quite different from Los Angeles, this suggested that new independent stations in smaller cities than San Diego would also face fierce competition.

In 1972 fewer than 10 per cent of all US homes with television had cable. The 6 million subscribing households were fragmented into some 2,800 local systems; the typical local cable system in turn had 2,300 subscribers and provided less than a dozen channels. But by 1972 it was known that well-tried and cheap technology now made possible a coaxial cable carrying not 10 or 12, but 48 or more channels; moreover, established microwave technology meant that other TV signals could be brought in, not merely from the nearest big city, but from cities several hundred miles away. It was the real prospect of independent commercial stations being microwaved from the top fifty markets into all the other markets which made the FCC anxious to assert its authority, first over the microwave links, then over programming outflows.

In 1960 over two-thirds of the nation's established TV markets were still only receiving at most two of the three national networks. ABC was still far from being a fully established third national network. In this context, cable was seen first as extending the range of network TV signals, then as a fast-growing weed with unpredictable and possibly dire financial consequences for the struggling ABC network and the independent ultrahigh frequency stations (UHFS). But in addition to supporting these two struggling children, the FCC was also trying to establish its jurisdiction over cable.

As ever, the uncertainties of the courts and of the law were important. Did the FCC control the microwave links? Did it have the right to determine cable programming? What was the copyright position in the case of a distant signal transmitted to another market? In the 1960s, the courts broadly supported the FCC's jurisdiction and its insistence that cable stations carry all local TV stations. The US Supreme Court in 1968 held that carrying broadcast signals on cable did not infringe copyright law. Thus, local cable station operators did not have to pay for importing all those movies and sports events on UHF stations, which was a blow to FCC authority and policy in the UHF area.

It was against this legally uncertain background, with rapid change imminent and big dollar consequences implied, that the FCC introduced its 1972 attempt at a comprehensive policy and a set of rules. It was these 1972 rules, then, that the FCC began to 'deregulate' later in the 1970s, and most of which were either abolished or heavily modified by 1984.

The thrust of the FCC's Third Report and Order of 1972 was to build up cable as a new medium, under FCC regulation, supporting and extending television and bringing in distant signals; but it also encouraged cable to adopt a local and community aspect, to exist on a smaller and more intimate scale than either TV or radio. To achieve this latter aim the 1972 rules:

1 required cable systems in the top 100 markets to have at least 20 channels, two-way capacity, and four access channels, with 20 per cent of capacity for the use of the local people;
2 required the larger systems (over 3,500 homes) to make some of their own programming;
3 laid down a division of federal, state and local regulatory powers; while the FCC would oversee the technical standards and the architecture of the national system, individual stations would be under local control; in particular the franchising and refranchising

of local cable systems would, under FCC guidelines, be left to local political authorities.

As so often in US communications policy, there was little real policy, merely an adjustment of commercial and political interests. But in so far as there was an official vision of the future, it was an FCC vision; the FCC, without clearly articulating it, was in effect positioning cable to be the most *local* of what was now to be a trinity of TV, radio and cable. Cable was to be a variant of TV, but a much more local variant. It had to be controlled locally – the traditional and continuing burning issues having to do with taking cable down streets and across property. Local governments were already in control of this, the existing patchwork of very small stations creating a problem of literally thousands of fiercely competing franchise applicants, which the FCC lacked the resources to handle. Moreover, had the FCC tried to assert control over the issuing of local licenses, it would have faced the prospect of being mired in thousands of bitter local political squabbles, doubtless with hundreds of related court cases.

The FCC, recognizing these local realities, was merely suggesting – to the states, cities and counties – some guidelines for tidying up the political realities and sentiments which existed on the ground. No doubt local access channels also fitted well with popular political rhetoric, and increasingly with FCC habits and manners, circa 1970.

However, while this FCC strategy accorded with political reality at various levels, it did not accord with the economic, market or production realities of a new mass entertainment/communications medium. Who was going to install all those wires, sell all those subscriptions and supply all that programming? And who was going to supply the capital for a long-term and very large investment? There was a small blip on the slowly rising curve of cable subscribers in 1973–4. But this was temporary. The five-year period of 1975–80 was one of very slow growth: the Nielsen household penetration statistics rose from 12 per cent in 1974 to 19 per cent in 1979.

This very slow growth pattern was at last broken in 1979–82, and the cause was indisputably a truly massive surge in *pay-cable*. Throughout the later 1970s, pay-cable had been publicized as the savior of cable, the product-plus which made having cable worthwhile, on account of its new movies and other premium 'new' material.

Pay-cable, primarily HBO, solved, or helped to solve, all three cable industry problems. Programming? Pay-cable showed that it could deliver the goods via satellite. Companies willing to cable the nation and market the services? Yes, the industry's growth potential and market appeal were now there for all to see. Money? At last the banks could see their sums adding up: in response to their big investments, a strong answering cash flow had now been clearly demonstrated. Cable, which had once been seen by the banks as a less good investment than Argentina, Poland or Nigeria, was now elevated in loan status. Almost any group of businessmen with a license to cable a suburb also had in effect a license to obtain from a bank the necessary millions. The gold rush – perhaps more accurately the land grab – was on.

Cable's future was seemingly assured, but, despite local classified-style cable advertising, the *local* element was largely being lost. Not only was much of the money coming from national financial institutions, and the crucial new (and appealing) programming from Hollywood, New York and Atlanta, but the local system operators were going the way of the local drug store, into national chains.

The FCC's 1972 Report and Order was the result of numerous hearings and negotiations, in which Congress and President Nixon's OTP had also been involved. The final bargaining and compromises saw the failure of a suggestion that a significant proportion of local channels should be rented out to programmers on a shopping-mall basis; instead, local politicians and community organizations were assuaged with the prospect of one or two local access channels – destined, without finance, to be also without audience. Some 90 per cent of the channels were left under the control of the system operator, who was thus placed in a position similar to that of the only phone company or the only newspaper in town.

CABLE ADVERTISING WEAKNESS

In its early years, cable was not attractive to advertisers. The patchwork of small and fragmented areas made no sense to an advertising world built around city markets – which were basically TV station transmission areas, although they also coincided quite well with the reach of the major newspapers and the stronger city radio stations. Nor did the tiny cable areas have the virtue of being, like many small local newspapers, fitted to a particular shopping location. Not only did the cable areas lack marketing significance, but the proportion of the local public 'delivered' by any one channel was minute. Moreover, the early cable managers knew little or nothing about selling advertising. Consequently cable had – and still has – almost no local advertising.[1]

This advertising weakness was in other respects a strength. Cable has never appeared as a threat to the advertising revenue which fuels local TV, radio and press. This has also helped to keep the cable manager's sights on *subscription* as the almost sole form of revenue.

In the early 1980s, as some of the basic channels developed sizeable national audiences, they attracted some modest advertising attention.

But even the larger cable channels still had relatively little to offer as compared with regular TV networks. And the heavily specialized channels were probably less comprehensive vehicles than the relevant magazines. In order to attract advertisers, the larger cable channels offered lower prices per thousand for longer commercials and had some modest success. In 1984 the leaders in national cable advertising were such leading basic cable offerings as WTBS (superstation), ESPN (sports), MTV (music video), USA (entertainment) and CNN (news). In line with the still chaotic nature of cable advertising (and because discounting is rife), different services report quite different figures;[2] but these five, plus three more – CBN, Lifetime and Nickelodeon – probably accounted for over 90 per cent of national cable advertising revenue. But in 1984 the cable industry still drew only 6 per cent of its revenue from advertising, compared to 94 per cent from subscriptions.

SATELLITE PROGRAMMING SUPPLIERS: THE WINNERS, THE SUBSIDIZED AND THE SHAKEN OUT

As recently as summer 1976, only 15 per cent of American homes had cable, and the FCC and Congress were bitterly accusing each other of having bottled it up.[3] However, cable was about to escape.

HBO had a big initial impact when it took to satellite distribution in late 1975. (We will examine especially its impact on Hollywood and the networks in a later section.) HBO was almost literally a heavenly answer to the cable operator's prayers. At last from space came this miracle: programming with greater audience appeal than almost anything on regular TV – a feast of movies of all ages, but especially many almost new movies. By installing a by now somewhat cheaper dish behind the office, the cable operator had a single service for which subscribers were willing to pay about as much as for an entire basic tier of 20 or more channels. HBO gave cable the glamour it had long lacked – new movies have retained status; now cable was to do with movie deals, Wall Street, gossip in newspapers, high tech – and, most marvellous, was a veritable gusher of cash on an ongoing basis. HBO had proved wrong the 50-year-old adage that Americans would not pay for their daily fix of mass entertainment.

But HBO and the other pay and nonpay offerings must not blind us to the fact that this revolution, like much else in these fields, is a combination, a one-two punch. The other part of the combination was the *superstation* – in particular, the Atlanta UHF independent of Ted Turner, now WTBS, then WTCG, which went satellite in late 1976. Other superstations followed, but Turner's was, and is, the leader, the first big success of free or 'basic' cable. Ted Turner, by relentless promotion, has persuaded advertisers that his superstation is so big nationally as to constitute an alternative advertising buy (or backup) to one or more of the three national networks. With its movies and sports, Ted Turner's superstation has become so popular that it reaches some 97 per cent of all cable homes. Ted Turner has, of course, also pioneered with CNN, two versions of it – a long news (many discussions and interviews) and a short headlines video–radio news. This CNN venture has had many problems, but again it has characteristics which make local operators willing to pay. It is the first 24-hour video news show on earth; it is cable's class act, and one which cable operators like for the prestige which it confers, not least with politicians, but also with the up-market segmented audience which cable claims to be able to deliver to advertisers. Moreover, Turner has found that the whole package of WTBS/CNN/CNN HEADLINE has varied attractions, and it is sold in varying combinations at varying prices to cable systems.

At the start of 1985, there were some 55 national satellite video services available to a cable operator, which split into these categories:

1 Some 30 *basic* cable services, of which only the eleven shown in Table 3.1 received any significant revenue.
2 Four *superstations*, strongly led by WTBS of Atlanta, with the next, WGN of Chicago, well behind; these are all advertising-financed independents, counterprogramming against their local major market network stations, and then networked nationally via satellite.
3 *Pay-cable sevices*, in which HBO led a field of some 11, and for which consumers paid an average of about $9 per channel. The field was dominated by the HBO plus Cinemax (Time) stable versus the Showtime/Movie Channel (Hollywood) stable. These four accounted for about 90 per cent of pay subscriptions and revenue.
4 *Text services*, some nine of which were provided by AP, Reuters and others.

In addition to the above 55 national TV services there were some 24 *regional services*, offering mostly regional sports or religion, and some 7 *audio services*.

In each national category a handful of services absorbed most of the revenue. Thus, only about 7 or 8 of 30 basic channels – perhaps 2 pay channels, 1 superstation, and 2 or 3 text services – have a moderately secure future. Only about 14 of the 55 national channels have a strong chance of survival.

A greater number may well survive on subsidy; for example, the 6 religious stations among the basic 30 and the Silent Network (for the deaf) may survive by donations. Others may merge.

TABLE 11.1 Basic cable network revenues 1984–5
(in $ millions)

Network	Launch date	Content	1984 Adverti-sing	1984 Fee	1984 Total income	1985 Adverti-sing	1985 Fee	1985 Total income
WTBS	1976	Superstation	158	–	158	180	–	180
CNN	1980	News	52	40	92	64	50	114
ESPN	1979	Sport	58	10	68	72	30	102
Music TV	1981	Music video	52	10	62	83	17.5	100.5
USA	1980	Entertainment	42	6	48	50	8	58
Nickelodeon	1979	Children's	4.5	21.5	26	8.5	28	36.5
Christian Network	1981	Christian entertainment	26	–	26	39	–	39
Nashville	1983	Country music	18	–	18	28	–	28
Lifetime	1984	Health	8	3	11	15	4	19
FNN	1981	Financial news	11	–	11	14	–	14
The Weather Channel	1982	Weather	5	5	10	8	6	14
Satellite Program Network	1979	Hobbies, how-to	3	5	8	5	6	11
Totals			437.5	100.5	538	566.5	149.5	716

Source: Cable Vision, 10 September 1984, p. 100, based on estimates by Paul Kegan Associates.

In the meanwhile the successful formulae seem to be *broad* themes or *double themes* – such as Lifetime's mix of health and sex, or CBN's mix of westerns and other golden oldies with religion; even ESPN, the supposedly 24-hour sports network, carried a business news breakfast show (Biznet). The Black Entertainment Channel (BET) combines 'adult contemporary' music videos with black-oriented news, sports and talk. Such broad themes or combinations are also found in the two star performers: HBO offers live sport and adult concert fare in addition to newish movies, and WTBS offers the full TV range of entertainment, sport and TV reruns. These broad, winning formulae pose almost impossible challenges to the narrower and weaker satellite brethren.

The stronger of the satellite channels reveal that the traditional themes still have the strongest appeal: *movies* dominate not only HBO and the entire pay category, but are also a major draw in WTBS and CBN. *Music video* has been a huge audience success with MTV, and the Nashville network is only one of several imitators. *News*, *Weather* and *Sport*, all TV staples, are also strongly represented.

The ownership and financial characteristics of satellite offerings stress the need to do a lot with a little and the advantages which lie with a few strong ownerships. Of the $1.8 billion 1984 revenue of the satellite programming suppliers, well over a third went to *Time* Inc's HBO and Cinemax. About a quarter of all revenue went to the top five basic cable suppliers, with about half of that going to *Ted Turner*'s WTBS and CNN; most of the rest of the satellite revenue went to three other pay channels, all with *Hollywood* connections.

Other common financial characteristics include the following:

1 *free material*, whether it be music videos supplied free (to MTV, TNN or BET) or politics supplied free by the House of Representatives to C-SPAN (Cable-Satellite Public Affairs Network) or business news subsidized by the US Chamber of Commerce's Biznet;

2 *advertiser involvement*, as at ESPN, where a major food advertiser in pursuit of a healthy image (Nabisco) owns a slice of the sports cable offering;

3 *joint ventures* – for example, Time Inc, Paramount and MCA at the USA network;

4 *heavy involvement by the big battalions* – cable MSOs, the national TV networks and Hollywood;

5 *multiple ownership* – the sports-oriented ABC TV network owns most of the ESPN sports channel, and slices of Lifetime and of the Arts and Entertainment Service, for example, and Time Inc, Viacom and Warner Communications are each involved in three satellite efforts, Taft and Westinghouse in two.

Despite the thousands of local operators and the 55 national cable channels, just four companies – Time Inc, Turner Broadcasting, ABC and Warner–Amex earned nearly two-thirds of all national satellite programming revenue in 1984.

MSO: FROM COLUMBUS QUBE TO DENVER PLAIN VANILLA

The FCC has accepted, at least passively, the increasing dominance of MSOS, and it has seldom vetoed mergers between MSOS. By 1980 it was clear to all that about 15 large chains would dominate the ownership of local systems. The factors behind this are fairly familiar; there are some economies of scale – in management, in the purchasing of cable and other hardware, and especially in the acquisition of programming. Even more important was that, increasingly in the 1970s, those profitable businesses of newspapers and broadcasting saw cable as a natural for their strong cash flows and professional management resources. In the 1970s the cable industry also had a fair amount of political lobbying clout, in part because of its grass roots image; this, plus the support of press and broadcast investors, helped cable to retain its very favorable tax status.

A typical local operator with a system of 5,000 subscribers now finds himself with a business worth $5 million or more; the temptation offered by the MSO – to pay off all his debts and to retire him as a millionaire – has for some been hard to resist. The buying chain is often willing to pay above the odds, because it can see easy ways to boost the revenue, perhaps simply by introducing quite elementary marketing and office efficiency.

Not all the larger MSOS are national, although the top 15 typically have systems in many states. Some quite big systems have stuck to one major locality. An example is Heritage, the dominant company in Iowa. In late 1984 Heritage was the seventeenth largest MSO with 433,000 subscribers. In 1971 it had only 1,800 subscribers. But although predominant in Des Moines and other parts of Iowa, Heritage owns local systems in 14 other states. Much of its growth has been through acquisition. Its revenue passed $100 million in 1983, but when it first took HBO on its Des Moines system in 1976, its total revenue was less than $5 million. Heritage Communications (a name which indicates that its interests now lie beyond cable) was first listed on the New York Stock Exchange in 1982. Heritage's MBA managers stress their financial sophistication. They are justly proud of having got their sums right and of having avoided the hectic bidding for big-city franchises around 1980.[4]

No FCC commissioners seem to have taken much interest in the MSOS and where they might fit into US communications history. None seems to have realized that this very local industry would come to be dominated by national media conglomerates, and would see vertical links between a few programming suppliers and a few dominant chains of local monopoly systems.

Of course, it was not only the FCC that pursued policies and responded to lobbies in ways which had unintended local consequences. So also did local politicians, most notably in the largest cities, where they were responsible for the largest and final major round of franchising. By thinking big and demanding much, they ruled all but the largest companies out of the game. The big-city politicians ensured that the dominance of the large MSOS could only increase.

By 1979 the land grab was reaching fever pitch. Many cable managers were talking big and swallowing their own lies. As usual in a land grab, the fever was intensified by the shortage of unclaimed land. Only the big cities, mainly within the thirty largest markets, were left unfranchised, although in several cases the most affluent suburbs were gone. Nevertheless, the top 15 MSOS had long said that cable was to be the biggest and the best, and as leading consumers of their own propaganda, these prospectors knew that they needed more territory. Hence, they descended on the big cities, offering gifts. The big cities, seeing that they had a monopoly of the only significant unsettled lands in the entire US, knew quite well what to do: they raised the price still further.

The cities tended to think that while one coaxial cable with 48 channels was good, two cables with 112 channels would be better. The city was full of articulate politicians, minorities and universities, so give them perhaps a dozen access channels. The city was full of ghettos, so applicants would need to take on both poor areas and more affluent suburbs. Even so, one company should not be allowed to get away with those scale-efficiency arguments; the city would thus be split into several segments. Contributions to the local tax revenues would also be required, and perhaps a few choice public works (such as planting trees or supporting the city art gallery). The big MSOS gulped a little at such demands, and a few wise managements, such as Telecommunications Inc (TCI) and Heritage, decided to withdraw. Others saw that the whole process was getting even more outrageous as typical knee-in-the-groin city politics also came into play. Cable managers found numerous ways in which to help out big-city politicians with powers over the cable franchising process. Campaign contributions, consultancies, directorships and other largesse were showered on politicians. At least one prominent politician ended up in jail for accepting a bribe.

The most aggressive MSO – and the most successful at winning big city franchises – was Warner–Amex, an enterprise initially launched by

Warner Communications and later joined by American Express; Warner was the most successful Hollywood major of the late 1970s. All its main activities were prospering: its movies and recorded music did well, and the Atari acquisition did brilliantly. Steven Ross, Warner's chief executive, was Hollywood's most successful manager. Cable was another minor activity with promise of major success. The cities in the late 1970s and early 1980s were looking for the very best, and for a cable company not afraid to provide 100 channels, studios, local programming and state-of-the-art technology.

Warner and Warner–Amex were generous with all these, especially technology hyped in bravura Hollywood style. QUBE, the two-way 'interactive' system initially developed in Columbus, Ohio, had a seductive charm for the visitor. Cable is a frustrating thing to inspect, since there is little to see; but QUBE was the perfect franchise-winning gimmick. It had the conventional cable system's basic and pay tiers, but it also had some extras: five PPV movie channels; an unusually large amount of local, Columbus-made, programming – especially programming aimed at children and housewives; and the interactive capacity to allow viewers on three channels to 'touch in' answers to questions about products, public issues, persons or other programming just screened. This was a remarkably futuristic and fascinating combination; visitors took the one-hour plane trip back to New York very impressed with QUBE. Many hundreds wrote newspaper articles along 'I have seen the future, and it's interactive' lines. QUBE became world-famous. References to it in newspaper clippings and in academic footnotes are legion.

QUBE was a key part of the no-expense-spared assault on the cities. Warner–Amex acquired franchises in Columbus, Cincinnati, Chicago, Dallas, Pittsburgh and Milwaukee. The grand finale of the big cities courtship was to occur in the outer boroughs of New York City. Warner–Amex, after many contortions and extravagant promises, was the New York winner with the most desirable franchise areas in Queens and Brooklyn.

By 1983, however, Warner–Amex had become a symbol not of the profits, but of the losses which could be made in cable. American Express was little nearer to the reality, as opposed to the promise, of using cable for financial services. Both parent companies were making huge losses on cable; and Warner Communications was suffering the reverse experience of a few years before: Warner records were doing badly; Atari was a massive loser from the decline in video games; and now cable was also in major trouble. By 1983 Warner–Amex was trying to get out of at least some of the rash promises it had made in previous years. Defenders claimed that it had been unlucky with the recession and high interest rates; the less sympathetic argued that Warner–Amex had failed in every area of management: its promises were so lavish that no level of subscriber fees and no multiple purchasing of pay channels could ever had made the project profitable. QUBE, critics said, was a publicity gimmick; as technology, it was quickly obsolete, prone to breakdown and expensive to service; it was also based on the common, but mistaken, assumption that traditional cable systems could surpass the telephone as a realistic two-way medium. Some critics also questioned the entire strategy of trying to get big-city franchises: these franchises were indeed less valuable than the suburban ones, because the populations had low income and high mobility, while the existing TV provision was better and the costs of cabling (especially underground) radically higher. In any case, some critics believed, the big-city franchises would soon be available on more reasonable terms.

Rather than visit Columbus, the cable-oriented traveller would have done better to take a trip to Denver, Colorado. Denver is the home of perhaps the two most important MSOs – ATC and TCI. These two companies control 17 per cent of all US cable subscriptions. American TV and Communications (ATC) is the Time Inc MSO, and thus, along with HBO and Time's other video activities, a key part of the most powerful integrated cable company. Predictably for a Time Inc success story, ATC is comfortably housed, somewhat Ivy League and concerned with quality and being a good employer. When it issued its last separate company report in 1980, it had 120 local systems in 32 states.[5] Since then, it has pursued a policy of 'clustering' – trying to buy and sell local systems so as to have several adjacent systems, thereby enabling it to make marketing and other economies.

Cable's Denver history is especially entwined, however, with the life of one man, William Daniels. He entered the cable business in 1948, and since then nearly all of the key cable figures have worked with him as partners or managers. Daniels has also been involved in most of the major cable mergers; the Daniels company is the dominant cable broker. It also acts as a cable bank, and although he has sold most of his cable systems, Daniels is in the top thirty MSOs list.[6]

One of the many who worked with Daniels was John Malone, chief executive of TCI. Malone and his small group of managers, housed in a very modest office building in an outer Denver suburb, are the most admired and feared management in cable. Malone's plain vanilla cable is the opposite of Warner–Amex's. TCI is unusual in not being part of a communications conglomerate. Its management pursues its prime goals of high profits, acquisition and rapid growth with ruthless zeal. There is no interest in making programming, technical innovation or any other frills.

TCI specializes in rescue missions after cable companies get into trouble. Malone aides are despatched to inspect the ruins, and return with plans for surgery, economy, efficiency and more profits for the TCI bottom line. TCI's far-flung empire is run from Denver. Denver chooses all programming. Thought to be more efficient, such central buying allows TCI to exercise its full clout (10 per cent of all cable subscribers) in order to get programming at lower prices. Another economy is that TCI can provide its own, national programming guide; called *Cabletime* (and in *TV Digest* format), it had an immediate circulation of 3 million copies when it first came out. The distribution costs are negligible, because all mailings and transactions with subscribers are handled centrally.

While TCI does not believe in two-way addressability, it does believe in one-way. The new system means that a single computer center can control the details of over 3 million subscriptions – billings, mailings, connects and disconnects, changes between pay channels, discount packages and promotional offerings (HBO for a week's free trial). To some, this is a push-button fantasy or nightmare; for TCI, it is simply how total central control is made possible, and how it can deliver 'plain vanilla' (John Malone's phrase) cable at a brisk rate of profit and efficiency.[7]

TCI is an exception among the top ten cable MSOs – it alone is not part of a larger company involved in newspapers, television stations or Hollywood. TCI is controlled by its directors, and thus is free to pursue an aggressive acquisitions policy backed by tax write-offs and profits from its mature local systems. Nevertheless, it is probably just an extreme example of current consolidation and rationalization, and its takeover of Warner–Amex's franchise in Pittsburgh may become a landmark in cable history.

Pittsburgh was itself an extreme case of overbidding by Warner–Amex; Pittsburgh, which was won in 1978–9 with lavish promises, saw 20 per cent control go to minority groups, the construction of the 'most sophisticated' system in the US and quite massive losses. When TCI arrived in 1984 the Warner–Amex system had cost over $100 million to build and was losing $21 million annually on running costs of $43 million.

TCI quickly negotiated radical changes with the Pittsburgh city council. The minority investors were bought out; a new 15-year contract was signed – not the remaining 11 years of the old contract; two-way QUBE (losing over $5 million a year) was to be replaced with TCI's one-way addressable system; the number of programmed channels was cut from 63 to 44, and the number of local origin channels from 23 to 8; TCI would offer 3 price tiers of services rather than Warner–Amex's 5; in place of the QUBE equipment, subscribers would have a choice of 3 different terminals, 1 required for movies-on-demand channels; of 5 studios supplied for access producers, 2 would be closed, and the remaining 3 transferred to a separate nonprofit corporation; and a major production facility and a downtown institutional loop were also due for radical change. Finally, the Warner–Amex staff of 350 would eventually be cut to 150.[8]

TCI was lucky in that its renegotiation of the Pittsburgh contract coincided with congressional passage of the 1984 Cable Act, which weakened the city's powers. These two overlapping events may well mark an acceleration of the great cable shakeout. TCI – rather like IBM after the dropping of its antitrust case – seemed to grow even more aggressive. While MSO number one, TCI was smaller than the other cable leaders, all of which were conglomerates. However, it was entering the $500-million revenue league in 1985, and was entering joint ventures with various other companies, including Taft (a TV station owner).

While debunking most kinds of marketing and technological sophistication, TCI was a leader in developing a new style of cable which – deliberately avoiding the Warner–Amex hype – was in fact more technologically sophisticated. Despite discounting 'clustering', TCI was indeed starting to round up entire major urban areas; it already had most of the Pittsburgh suburbs, which with the city franchise included over 400,000 households, and was thus a very viable promotional/marketing proposition.

Perhaps more significant, TCI's one-way addressability seemed to offer an effective way of introducing some of the flexibility which the forthcoming battle with the VCR demands. Previous FCC insistence on focusing rate regulation on *basic* cable meant that cable overall had become stuck with a rigid on/off two-level proposition – a standard bunch of basics and a choice from a few pay services. The customer was faced with several $10-a-month yes or no choices; moreover, any channel change required one of those notoriously expensive home service visits to alter the converter. With addressability located back in the office, TCI could offer a much more a-la-carte type of service, with the leading basics now being sold separately for very modest amounts. But on top of this, TCI was also offering in Pittsburgh a movies-on-demand service: subscribers can 'rent' a film for one week from a monthly menu of eight, a type of offering that seeks to outshine and be more flexible than not only QUBE, but also HBO and the VCR.

THE 1984 CABLE ACT: MINIMAL REGULATION AT LAST

The Cable Telecommunications Act, which finally squeezed through Congress in October 1984, gave the cable industry most of what it most wanted. The Act shows what deregulation looks like in practice. What it provides, and what the communications industries want, is *minimal* legislation – minimal control over cable by the cities and the FCC, plus firm prohibitions against any general telephone company invasion.

The act was the outcome of four years of hearings and negotiations, although on several occasions in 1984 it looked to have less than a 50 per cent chance. The National Cable TV Association (NCTA) was lucky in that the negotiations coincided with the renegotiations in Pittsburgh and elsewhere. This put the NCTA's main opponents – the cities' and the mayors' national organizations – largely on the defensive. The NCTA had other good fortune in the late 1983 FCC Nevada decision, which limited rate regulation to basic tiers carrying local origin programming, and in a Supreme Court decision in 1984 supporting the FCC. Some NCTA members thought that these court decisions made comprehensive legislation unnecessary, but their doubts were finally suppressed. However, the frenzied late negotiations in September, and the House–Senate conference, left many clauses ambiguously worded. In effect the lobbies and Congress left many decisions to judges.

Nevertheless, the NCTA appears to have won the ten key rounds by about seven to three. Major cable industry wins are:

(1) Getting a bill at all, thereby removing the extraordinary chaos experienced especially by the MSOs. An MSO with 100 franchises previously had to confront almost 100 separate local sets of rules and personalities. As *Broadcasting* magazine put it: '... cable has been the most jerrymandered media landscape of them all, with no two jurisdictions marching to the same beat.'[9]

(2) The bill confirmed the local government right to renew franchises; but franchises cannot be denied 'unfairly', or if there has been 'reasonable' performance and 'substantial' compliance with initial undertakings. Even if a license renewal is denied, the cable operator must be paid market value. This seems to mean that franchise renewal is about 95 per cent certain, and there is no chance of losing the initial investment.

(3) After a two-year interim period (1985–6), all rate regulation was to be removed. This was a big win for NCTA, which had previously agreed to a four-year interim.

(4) Public pressure-group involvement in franchising will be minimal. The public was left with the right only to comment, not to be significantly involved.

(5) The NCTA also obtained only very weak equal opportunity provisions, despite demands for much stiffer requirements on the employment of minorities and women.

Several other major provisions were in effect draws:

(1) The franchising authority is allowed to charge the local operator a maximum 5 per cent fee on gross revenue.

(2) The bill tidied up a great many awkward legal problems with financial implications, including the privacy of records, obscene material (the *Playboy* channel and 'adult' movies) and its viewing by children, and provided quite severe federal penalties for theft of cable service.

(3) The idea that cable operators must be willing to lease channels into the control of independent programmers is accepted in the bill. Thus, 36–54 channel systems must be willing to lease up to 10 per cent of capacity. However, local operators are able to charge a commercial rate for this commercial practice.

(4) No cross-ownership is allowed by a broadcast station owner or a telephone company (with exceptions only in remote rural areas) operating in the franchise area. A local newspaper, however, is allowed to cross-own the local cable company (an extraordinary dual-monopoly concession achieved in late lobbying by the newspaper publishers).

There seems, to this author, to be only one clear city win, and this only for small cities. There will be deregulation only in markets with adequate broadcast competition (probably three TV network outlets plus one other TV station). This may mean that about a quarter of cable subscribers, mainly in traditional CATV-style remote areas, will remain regulated. But the spread of LPTV will presumably reduce this figure considerably.

AFTER DEREGULATION: TURBULENCE

The deregulation (or minimal regulation) of cable illustrates some of the strengths and weaknesses of this whole sphere of communications policymaking. The final negotiations were between a House–Senate team of subcommittee staffers and a cities–mayors team of local regulators. The Cable Association sat offstage, veto in hand.

This long drawn-out process frequently broke out in bitter public recriminations. Its ultimate achievement was to settle – or to refer to judicial decision – most of the burning issues of the current and recent regulatory chaos. What the process largely failed to do was to protect against the turbulence ahead.

Less than a year after the 1984 Act the Federal Court of Appeals struck down the rule that cable operators 'must carry' all local television signals. This was a blow to television stations and would enable, especially smaller capacity, cable systems to offer more programming choice.

It should not have been hard to see that by early 1987, when rate controls would be largely lifted, the cable industry would be vulnerable to accusations of monopoly profit. Wall Street analysts quickly noted that rate deregulation would lead to greatly increased cash flow, notably by placing increased charges on basic services (the great bulk of which money stays with local operators).[10]

By 1987 nearly all of the major construction will be completed, and the main concern will be the marketing task of raising household penetration levels along already cabled streets. Even relatively modest increases here (such as raising an urban system from 40 to 50 per cent penetration) will provide huge additional boosts to cash flow.

Asked about these imminent gushers of cash, cable managers tend to confirm the flow, but say that they will continue to put the cash into expensive system upgrading. However, even in 1984, only 26 per cent of subscribers had as few as 21 channels; and 25 per cent had 36 channels or more. Already in 1984 the median cable household had about 28 channels.[11] This median figure must soon rise to well above 30 channels, since all new systems have higher capacity. And with the developing shakeout, plus the flexibilities of addressability, systems with 30–40 channels will not be in severe need of upgrading.

The more successful independent and multiple system operators can look toward 1990 across an increasingly huge pile of cash. This will probably give an extra boost to the shakeout, since the more aggressive MSOs will be able to buy and buy.

But various significant others are certain to be a trifle envious. The stronger satellite programmers will insist on being paid more by the MSOs. This may speed up the shakeout among programmers. Moreover, some of the shaken out will surely be unable to resist pointing to the monopoly trends among – and links between – satellite programmers and MSOs.

A number of delicate issues seem likely to spill out of the closet in which they were firmly constrained while the 1984 Act was being negotiated. These include:

1 the monopoly status of the incumbent local operator, which will be asserted by losers at refranchising exercises;
2 the fact that as MSOs find ways of extracting even higher percentages from programming, the makers of programming – both Hollywood and the satellite suppliers – will have a motive not only for raising yet again the copyright issue, but for uttering the 'monopoly' battle cry;
3 the likelihood that cable operators, having done better in the 1984 Act on money matters than on First Amendment principles, will increasingly assert their right to editorialize, to report, and to share the constitutional privileges of print.

Finally, the embarrassingly high cash flows of some MSOs will give added emphasis to all the big questions about the giant single new playing field. High cash flows will seek new outlets in other communications areas. Similarly, the promise of such profitable operations will attract the envy, and in some cases, the participation, of other communications companies, not least the telephone companies. Moreover its privileged tax position, which has fuelled so much cable growth, may be in danger.

Notes

1 Ronald B. Kaatz, *Cable: An Advertiser's Guide to the New Electronic Media* (1982).
2 For example, Paul Kagan, the Cable TV Advertising Bureau and *Advertising Age* in its 6 December 1984 Special Report on Cable TV.
3 Ronald P. Kriss, 'Cable TV: the bottled up Medium', *Columbia Journalism Review*, July–August 1976, pp. 26–68.
4 Heritage Communications Inc, *1982 Annual Report*.
5 ATC, *Financial and Operational Highlights* (1980).
6 Feature supplement on 'Twenty-Fifth Anniversary, Daniels & Associates', *Cable Vision*, 25 July 1983, pp. 36–64. 'Setting the Table', *CableVision*, 11 January 1982. 'Big spending demands dictate MSO financing', *Cable Age*, 19 April 1982. Tom Marinkovich, 'A closer look', *Cable Age*, 6 February 1984. Paul Maxwell, 'Bill Daniels: First of the Pioneers ... and still crusading', *CableVision*, 8 May 1978. Jim Duffy, 'Cable Capital: Bill Daniels has made Denver No. 1 in cable-TV industry', *Denver Post*, 15 August 1982. Randy Welch, 'Bill Daniels: the builder of cable empires', *Channels*, January–February 1985, pp. 45–52.
7 On TCI, see Madeline Hardart, 'Empire building, brick by brick', *CableVision*, 13 February 1984, pp. 34–43; Joe Boyle, 'TCI's John Malone talks of strategies in Cable TV', *Multichannel News*, 11 June 1984, p. 15; 'The surprising success stories in cable television', *Business Week*, 12 November 1984, pp. 82–4; and Victoria Gits, 'The Plain Vanilla Juggernaut', *CableVision*, 18 March 1985, pp. 28–33.
8 'TCI makes Pittsburgh an offer', *Broadcasting*, 2 July 1984, p. 78. 'TCI's Pittsburgh plans: kill QUBE, cut channels', *CableVision*, July 1984, pp. 18–9. 'TCI exec outlines program to regain Pittsburgh system's financial health', *CableVision*, 12 November 1984, pp. 34–5.
9 'Cable's Cliffhanger', *Broadcasting*, 1 October 1984, p. 106.
10 'Wall Street Analyst predicts sharp rise in cable stock values', *Multi-Channel News*, 26 November 1984, pp. 1, 40.
11 *CableVision*, 19 November 1984, p. 44.

12

The Broadcast Networks Tremble

The financial and regulatory fate of American television and radio stations rests upon one basic fact of life – a license to broadcast on a certain frequency, more-or-less permanently, and thus on a property-like basis. Ever since the 1950s any TV station manager who could stay out of jail had about a 99 per cent chance of retaining his license to operate; in most (but not all) cases TV stations produced profits – and were sold for sums – out of proportion to the physical value of the studios, offices and other fixed plant. Radio was much more varied and competitive; but most TV licenses provided effective title to a buoyant cash flow, if not a cash gusher.

In US radio and television, the late 1970s resembled both the late 1960s and late 1950s in most respects. The networks remained the dominant single force, but dependent on Hollywood production houses, the Madison Avenue advertising industry and the three network affiliates based in each of the one hundred most populous city regions' markets.

One of the few really major changes in the entire decade of the 1970s was the rise of the ABC network. In 1970 the competition was still between NBC and CBS; but during the decade, ABC steadily advanced until, by the end of the decade, it at last began to win the ratings battle.

It was nevertheless the ABC network which on 18 March 1985 announced that it was to be bought by Capital Cities, a much smaller, but more profitable and diversified, media company. It had been during ABC's commercially triumphant coverage of the Los Angeles Olympic Games in August 1984 that rumors and stories had begun to circulate about the imminent takeover of ABC.[1] There had been a previous, unsuccessful attempt by ITT, but this was before ABC's years of success. Now ABC's share price fluctuated rapidly, apparently illustrating a new and broader element of vulnerability in the fortunes of a television network. One month later, in April 1985, Ted Turner produced his unorthodox bid for CBS.

The strong deregulatory trend in Washington since 1980 was the key change. Congress, the Courts, the White House and the FCC itself by 1985 all opposed the FCC's 1970s policy of freezing the network status quo. Networks were now free to accept a friendly bid, as did ABC with the Capital Cities bid. CBS was also free to defeat the hostile Turner bid as both the FCC and a federal court ruled on 31 July 1985. But at least five different markets, upon which ABC's and the other networks' fortunes depended, were each exhibiting a quite new degree of volatility by 1985.

In the 1984–5 new programming season, ABC was suffering doubly in the *audience market*. The combined network prime-time audience share was continuing its early 1980s pattern by sinking about three percentage points a year; but ABC was being hit the worst, falling back into its third ratings place of a decade earlier.

It was also suffering in the *programming market*; the glitzy fantasy shows of Aaron Spelling, such as *Love Boat*, *Dynasty*, *Hotel* and *T. J. Hooker*, seemed no longer to have the audience appeal of a few years back, and ABC was having trouble striking a new seam of profitable fantasy in the Hollywood hills.

It was still doing well in the *advertising market*, and 1984 was a successful year for TV advertising in general. Nevertheless, the declining ratings must imply longer-term problems, especially with cable at last beginning a steep ascent in advertising revenue (from a very low base).

Also active was the *television station market*; the two-year period 1983–4 saw 143 television stations change hands, more than in the previous four years together. Combined radio and TV station transactions in 1983–4 totalled almost $5 billion.[2]

Yet another market both reflecting and creating volatility was the *stock market*. The new volatility led to predictions of takeovers and much buying and selling of large blocks of broadcasting stock. In general, Wall Street viewed broadcast stations as commercial entities not earning up to their full potential; broadcast companies were thought to be undervalued in relation to their assets – classic takeover material.

Most important, the networks faced a much more uncertain *political/ regulatory* climate. For three decades, politicians and regulators had feared the power of the three networks which programmed up to 90 per cent of the American public's television viewing. Such rules and regulations as existed, while irritating to the networks, had basically protected their dominance. But in the early 1980s, quite modest deregulation further exacerbated the new volatility. ABC became vulnerable to takeover in part because of the traditional pattern of regulating constriction followed by relaxation. Moreover, the confirmation of this and other mergers was also uncertain, and itself rested upon FCC and Justice Department approval.

ABC: AN EXTREME CASE OF VULNERABILITY

ABC was the most obviously vulnerable major broadcasting company. As figure 12.1 shows, ABC obtained 89 per cent of its revenue (and all of its profit) from its broadcasting networks and stations. Capital Cities' revenue was only 25 per cent of ABC's in 1984; but Capital Cities was much more diversified, with revenue coming more equally from magazines, newspapers and broadcasting.

Most important, ABC's net income was only 5.3 per cent of revenue, while Capital Cities' net income was 15.2 per cent of revenue. Capital Cities' broadcasting operations were also exceptionally profitable.

ABC's management had long been attempting to diversify out of such dependence on broadcasting; but they were hemmed in by FCC rules forbidding, for example, the ownership of local cable systems by a group. ABC's sole moderately successful diversification was into publishing. But its several efforts in the satellite-to-cable programming business had produced losses rather than profits; the Satellite News Channel, the Arts and Entertainment Channel and Lifetime had all been loss-makers. Only ESPN promised ultimate success – but this sports-oriented network was not exactly a major diversification for sports-oriented ABC.

The other major, related problem seemed to be ABC's own management and organization. ABC was the only network one of whose founding fathers was still active; 79-year-old Leonard Goldensen was still ABC's chairman, and in agreeing to sell ABC to a company one-quarter its size, he was not only choosing his successor (Thomas Murphy of Capital Cities), he was also deliberately not making the choice from within ABC. CBS's top 34 executives at the time were each averaging $360,000 in salaries, bonuses and 'other cash payments',[3] and ABC's top management was said to be even more bloated.

ABC had previously given 'commercial' television new meaning, allowing 14 minutes of advertising and promotion per hour during the 1984 Olympics.[4] But one clear lesson of its 1985 surrender was that ABC had nevertheless not been commercial enough, or profit-oriented enough. Capital Cities was able to step forward with a confidence based on a remarkable management record of both revenue and profit increasing at around 19–20 per cent per annum. It was regarded on Wall Street as having about the most financially effective management in broadcasting. It was dedicated to cutting waste and costs, while raising revenue and profits. The merger proposal was interesting in another way. ABC was being taken over by a company most of whose revenues came from newspapers and magazines.

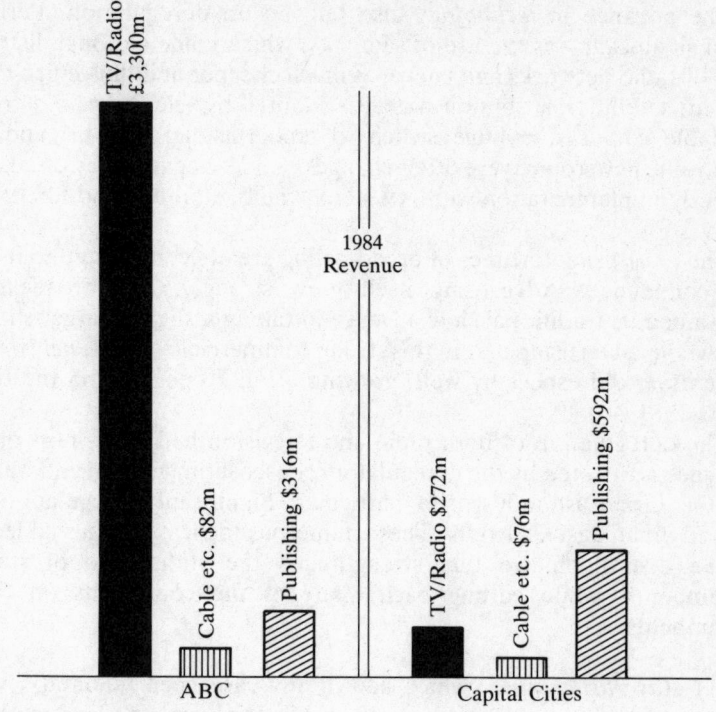

Figure 12.1 *David swallows Goliath: ABC and Capital Cities 1984 revenues.*
(Source: Wall Street Journal, 20 March, 1985).

RADIO/TV DEREGULATION FLOATS ON TECHNOLOGY AND ADVERTISING

Significant deregulation of radio took place in 1980,and, after much Washington infighting, the FCC gave television deregulation a major impetus in 1984. The obvious difference was the much larger number of radio stations. A typical market – half the people live in larger, half in smaller population areas – then has 700,000 or 800,000 *households*, or about 2 million people living within the radius of the main TV signals. In this size of city – Phoenix, Portland (Oregon), San Diego or Cincinnati – there are at least 20 local radio stations, but usually only 5 TV stations. The TV choice in such a representative city is usually three network affiliates, one commercial independent and one public station. Thus the competitive argument for extending deregulation to television had to rest partly on the spread of cable.

The advance in *technology* also buoyed up deregulation. Perhaps most significant was the use of satellites, which made national distribution of radio networks and packages much cheaper and thus much more varied; satellite distribution was also adopted by television. Electronic portable cameras, a huge switch to tape (instead of film) and the electronic newsroom were other changes. Under active policy discussion or early implementation were AM stereo radio, stereo sound for TV and HDTV.

The *advertising* fortunes of broadcasting greatly contributed to industry confidence. Advertising itself grew strongly, and broadcasting continued its traditional slow advance in taking a slightly larger slice of the whole advertising pie. In this strong commercial context, *network TV advertising* did especially well, growing a full 50 per cent in the three years 1981–4.

The deregulation of both radio and television had gone most of the distance advocated by the deregulatory consensus in general and wanted by the broadcast industry in particular. Significant deregulation occurred on at least six fronts. These numerous tactical changes added up to an overall change that strengthened the status quo of station incumbents, while cutting back many of the constraints on those incumbents:

(1) *Advertising* rules, which had in any case been voluntary, were removed, leaving no constraints on either the number of minutes per hour or the spillover of paid advertising into programming.

(2) *Content* rules, operated by the FCC, had specified a minimum of 5 per cent information, 5 per cent local and a total of at least 10 per cent nonentertainment programming. The multiplicity not only of stations but also of 'news' and 'talk' programming was quoted as justification for abolishing these content rules. In addition, stations were largely relieved of the traditional task of logging what they had broadcast.

(3) *Ownership rules* of several kinds were relaxed. The number of stations allowed to a single owner increased, in particular from 5 to 12 very high frequency (VHF) television stations. 'Attribution' rules were relaxed so that an individual could own up to 5 per cent of a media company before being defined as an 'owner'. This provision alone stimulated stock market activity, because it allowed a major investor simultaneously to pursue several possible takeover targets. The period for which a station must be owned before it could be resold was reduced. And cross-ownership rules, which from 1970 to 1982 forbid broadcast ownership in cable, were relaxed.

(4) *Franchise renewal* procedures were heavily modified in favor of incumbents. Not only were the duration of incumbency extended and the programming requirements reduced, but so were the opportunities

for threatening a costly franchise battle, which in turn could be used to extract public service or minority employment concessions.

(5) *More stations* were licensed, especially more independent commercial TV stations, but also hundreds more radio stations. This was potentially an unattractive increase in competition for incumbents, but was made palatable, even welcome, when placed alongside the extended group ownership provisions.

(6) *Equal opportunity* provisions for ethnic minorities and women were in general cut back. Ethnic minorities still owned less than 2 per cent of the broadcasting station industry. One major irritation to broadcasters – 'ascertainment' of minority community provision, depending on elaborate interviewing and documentation – was removed.

FROM THREE TO TWENTY: NETWORKS AND MAJOR MARKETS

CBS, ABC and NBC remain as the only three full-fledged TV and radio networks; each still owns a VHF television station in each of the three main urban markets of New York, Los Angeles and Chicago. This three-times-three formula of owned-and-operated TV stations is still the core of the US broadcast system.

What has happened is not so much the decline of three networks or three markets but the addition to them of another 15 or 18 *networking* operations and another 15 or 18 massive urban markets. In both networking and urban markets, to the top three has now been added the *top twenty*.

Deregulation in broadcasting is justified in terms of this increased competition, and broadcast deregulation itself furthers the trend toward a top-twenty pattern of dominance. Especially crucial is the new 12/12/12 rule, allowing one company to own 12 each of AM, FM and TV stations up to a maximum direct coverage of 25 per cent of the US population.

The Capital Cities/ABC merger was the first major test case of how this new pattern would develop. There might be 20 *networking operations*, but it would be possible for them to be merged within a much smaller number of *organizations*. Capital Cities was itself the fifth largest broadcasting company by revenue, and obviously if mergers of two top companies are to be allowed, the effective number of dominant organizations must shrink.

The biggest new *networking* phenomenon has of course been cable; as discussed previously, the number of satellite-to-cable offerings is much higher than the 6, or at most 10, apparently viable organizations. In addition, PBS makes networked programming available in most larger markets.

In 1984–5 three broadcast networks each reached some 98 per cent of households. Five cable networks (ESPN, CNN, USA, CBN and MTV) reached at least 25 per cent of all households, and at least that proportion also received HBO or one of the other film channels. Adding 3 commercial networks, 1 PBS and 6 cable totals 10 networks. To these must be added four other relevant developments:

(1) *The independent stations* have become an extremely important part of the US television scene; in 1970, independents were confined to larger markets, but by 1984, they were much more widely spread, picking up about a quarter of both the total TV audience and total advertising revenue. Especially strong in the early evening, 'counter-programming' entertainment against network and affiliate news shows, the independent stations collectively were as strong as, or stronger than, a regular TV network. Cable was important in enhancing poor UHF reception and carrying the independent signals beyond the core market area.

(2) The *superstation*, notably Ted Turner's Atlanta-based WTBS, was an independent carried by satellite across the continent. In 1984–5 it was already reaching more than a third of all US homes, and was beginning to establish itself in Madison Avenue as a backup network advertising buy.

(3) The *syndication* of programming had expanded enormously, especially in order to fill the requirements of the independents, but also because the former supplies of Hollywood network series available for 'stripping' (5 episodes per week) were tending to dry up. Stripping requires a minimum of 65 shows (13 weeks), but this depends on a network run of at least 3 seasons. Syndication has boomed partly because advertising-rich independents can now afford to pay network-level Hollywood prices; the market is also younger, meaning that some shows dropped by the networks can still prosper in syndication. While independents all dip into the same supplies of syndicated offerings, the independent station has great *flexibility* in terms of scheduling and local audience tastes.

(4) *Major groups of stations*, perhaps most important of all, have become active in syndication. In 1984 Metromedia's stations reached 20 per cent of US homes, and another three groups had stations reaching between 10 and 20 per cent of all US homes. Obviously these groups, either singly or collectively, could, in partnership with programming syndicators, form the core of quasi-networking arrangements.

The major groups also, of course, tend to have their stations in the larger markets. While in 1984 the 3 networks together owned and operated 9 TV stations in New York, Los Angeles and Chicago, the top 10 groups (including the 3 networks) owned 17 stations in these 3 key markets. The top 10 groups also owned 29 stations in the top 8 Nielsen markets.

The top 20 'markets' reflect a post-1945 phenomenon, the emergence of huge new sprawling urban areas, especially in the South and the West, including Dallas–Fort Worth, Houston, Miami, Atlanta, Seattle–Tacoma, Tampa–St Petersburg, Denver and Sacramento–Stockton. These 'areas of dominant influence' (or ADIS) are cities defined as markets in general, media markets in particular.

The top 20 markets include just over two-fifths of the US population, but that proportion understates their slice of the national TV audience. Their audience is bigger because exurban cable companies must carry their signals, because of the superstations, and because many cable systems carry other independent stations from two or three hundred miles away. Regional syndication of sports programming has the same effect; and when Metromedia engages in syndication, it must think first of its own stations in New York, Los Angeles, Chicago, Boston and Washington DC.

The new 12/12/12 rule, with its 25 per cent maximum clause, is a crucial new ingredient in top-twenty trends in networking and in dominant national markets. Table 12.1 shows the national position before the 12/12/12 rule and also indicates that the Capital Cities/ABC merger exceeded the 25 per cent limit by less than 2 per cent. That such a merger was allowed – subject to the relatively minor required trimming – gave a green light to other mergers within the top 20 ownerships. Such mergers could notionally reduce the top 20 station ownerships of 1984 to a mere 8. Perhaps a more practical possibility might be 12 or 13 station groups – that is, the 3 old networks plus about 10 large groups increasingly involved in quasi networking.

The market forces certainly seem to point in that direction. The big question is what the regulatory process will allow, and that uncertainty contributes to the wider volatility of broadcasting.

RADIO: MEDIA DEREGULATION, EXHIBIT ONE

In world communications terms, domestic US radio provides an ultimate example of media saturation: the average US household owns five or six functioning radios, making radio the only bedroom/kitchen/car medium; the number of radio stations passed 1,000 in 1946, 5,000 in 1963 and is now around 10,000.

The arrival of television destroyed radio as a premier national medium and transformed it into a local, fragmented, background service. As radio came to offer largely national hit music, plus local

Setting the Media Free

TABLE 12.1 TV station groups by net weekly circulation, 1 January 1984

Group owner	Rank 1983	1984	No. of stations	Net weekly household circulation	Percentage of US TV households
Metromedia	3	1	7	16,675,400	19.9
ABC	2	2	5	15,869,100	18.9
CBS	1	3	5	15,790,500	18.8
NBC	4	4	5	15,108,200	18.0
Tribune Co. Broadcasting	5	5	5	13,757,800	16.4
Westinghouse	6	6	6	9,291,000	11.1
RKO General	7	7	3	8,994,200	10.7
Storer	8	8	7	7,644,700	9.1
Gaylord	10	9	7	6,873,600	8.2
Taft	13	10	7	6,787,200	8.1
Capital Cities	12	11	6	6,276,700	7.5
Cox	11	12	6	6,102,100	7.3
Gannett	18	13	6	5,458,700	6.5
Hearst	14	14	5	4,627,200	5.5
Scripps–Howard	15	15	6	4,559,200	5.4
Times–Mirror	17	16	7	4,296,700	5.1
Post–Newsweek	16	17	4	4,244,000	5.1
Lin	33	18	7	3,970,400	4.7
Meredith	23	19	7	3,935,600	4.7
A. H. Belo	42	20	5	3,905,900	4.7

Source: Herbert H. Howard, *Group and Cross Media Ownership of Television Stations: 1984*, Washington: NAB, 1984, p. 15.

chatter and advertising, regulation from Washington became increasingly without meaning or substance.

Most FCC regulations in fact consisted of roundabout attempts if not to mandate particular serious content, then at least to require minimal amounts of local and nonentertainment material. Such efforts peaked in the 1970s with FCC attempts to impose minimal requirements of equal opportunity on radio, policed by elaborate logging of output and documented ascertainment of local community leader approval. But such efforts were largely token and ineffectual. Even FCC requirements that a station stick to its agreed programming format were ludicrous and impracticable. Labels such as Rock, Album-Oriented Rock, Top 40, Adult Contemporary, Contemporary Hit Radio alternated from time to time, but each is deliberately vague. Requirements such as a few per cent of local or nonentertainment material were also meaningless when the requirement could be met by a disk jockey reading out the station's morning mail.

Well before the deregulation debates of the late 1970s, radio was variously regarded as the leading example of both the virtues and the vices of multiple voices in the media marketplace. With 20 or 30 choices on the dial, radio did indeed provide some impressive market achievements – minority-owned stations, all news stations and, as FM advanced in the 1970s, a superior sound quality for a dazzling choice of popular hit music. But critics were already comparing US radio with junk food – 20 different kinds of fast food, but no nourishing meals – and pointing to the plethora of local advertisements and 'announcements' against the lack of local substance.

The deregulation of radio occurred in several stages. In 1980–1, just before the arrival of the Reagan appointees, the FCC proposed the formal abolition of most content restraints on radio. An early Reagan budget measure in 1981 extended radio licenses to seven years, which, together with the other relaxations, meant a 99 per cent chance of license renewal. With voluntary constraints on amounts of advertising being also declared illegal constraints on trade, the main remaining regulations referred to what had always been the one and only key issue – the ownership of radio stations. Thus the FCC's 1984 extension of the 7/7/7 rule to a 12/12/12 rule allows one company to have 12 FM and 12 AM stations was the most important of all radio deregulation measures. ABC, for example, already owned radio stations in New York, Los Angeles, Chicago, Washington, Houston, San Francisco and Detroit, and it was now free to buy stations in the remaining 5 of the top 12 markets.

By 1980 the radio industry had much experience of adjusting to other media; it was now having to adjust to cable, much of whose cheaper programming (music videos, nationwide phone-ins) was really radio with pictures. According to FCC statistics, in 1980 over 2,000 radio stations were losing money. One key to radio station operation was keeping costs to a minimum. According to an NAB study released in 1984, the typical radio station had revenues of $540,000 and employed 14 full-time staff, mainly in general administration and in selling local advertising. At most, only 5 or 6 staff voices would ever be heard on the air, despite 24-hour operation. Even in bigger markets, the large amount of competition meant that a few stations tended to dominate in audience and revenue numbers; they did this by having the strongest transmission signals, by employing local celebrity 'personalities' or journalists, and by expensive promotion. But even leading stations in many markets used largely or entirely prerecorded material.

Nevertheless, despite the spartan economics of most stations, US radio is in several respects the world's most pervasive mass medium. Americans 'listen' to radio for some three and a half hours each day, nearly as much as they 'view' television. Over half of what they hear is music, and radio's (and TV's) stars are *the* superstars of the moment. At least 20 per cent of all radio is advertising, totalling almost $6 billion in 1984.

Radio is also much the most pervasive dispenser of news. The all-news stations are confined to a few major markets, and are sustained by a high audience proportion of senior executive males, who interest advertisers. But in the typical market, the average FM station runs 85 minutes of news per 24 hours, or 3½ minutes per hour. Ninety per cent of stations admit to using news wire services as a primary source. And radio news, not TV or newspapers, is the most frequently and universally received form of news for the US population. Typical adults who watch network news three times a week and read a daily paper four or five days a week, listen to radio news three or four times a day. Few studies exist of this phenomenon, which is perhaps 700 million times a day broad, but less than 5 minutes deep. Radio news may well be the most headline-oriented and most violent of all major forms of news; these quick fixes of news several times a day dwarf in their huge numbers all other communications – apart from those other several-times-a-day quick fixes, the nation's daily telephone calls.

The steadily increasing number of radio stations, the deregulation of radio and television, plus the appearance of additional video media, have made yet more competitive the already fierce competition for radio advertising. In 1984 radio still received some 7 per cent of all advertising expenditure, the same figure as throughout the 1970s.[5]

Radio's attempts to survive the additional competition inevitably turned to new ways of providing attractive music and other programming. And this meant more *networking*, especially since satellite transmission enables the national broadcast networks to operate more cheaply and to meet FM standards of sound quality. ABC blossomed into no less than 7 separately targeted additional radio networks (with FCC deregulatory permission); a new league table of radio networks emerged, with multiple-networking efforts from ABC, CBS and NBC, taking 10 or so of the top dozen places. ABC was in 1984 claiming 1,744 radio station affiliates and NBC and CBS have both been following in ABC's footsteps.

But a small local station, which is not a network affiliate, now has several different sorts of *syndication packages* available from a fast-growing new breed of suppliers. Westwood One and Drake–Chenault in Los Angeles and Clayton–Webster in St Louis are leaders among at least 50 companies which syndicate radio programming nationally; these companies are not confined to greater Los Angeles and New York, but are liberally spread around Dallas, Boston, St Louis, Chicago, Detroit and other top-twenty markets. The services they supply include the following:

1 entire 24-hour music services in the major music formats, with gaps left for local station commercials;
2 daily blocks of material targeted for particular times of day or night;
3 weekly specials, featuring interviews with current hit musicians, sports, religion and other features;
4 very short inserts, usually between 1½ and 3½ minutes, of humor, politics, business/finance news, leisure, hobby, travel or automotive talk, many of which are provided by newspapers, business magazines or hobby publications;
5 celebrity interview programming, syndicated by major stations.

Reliable information about the sales and use of these syndication packages is not available (or, if it is, has a suspect promotional ring), but many local stations undoubtedly use this material some, most or nearly all the time. Much of the material is bartered for free inserted advertising spots; other services are supplied for a few hundred dollars a month to smaller market stations. For $1,000 a month a station manager may be able to fill up a couple of hours a day, making it possible to program a 24-hour station for very modest sums. A syndicator with several such services selling to several hundred stations can still collect two or three million dollars a year.

Deregulated radio is thus even more prevalent, more nationwide, more fragmented and more unknown in its basic details than was the case before deregulation and before satellites (in fact most radio syndication is still done on tape).

Radio provides ever greater quantities of FM popular music; black voices are getting a much better hearing in 'adult contemporary' and more generally; radio is especially good at reaching young people, who are light users of both newspapers and television. Radio can be brilliantly local, especially regarding weather or emergencies. It is also extraordinarily flexible in pursuit of novel formats for delivering audiences to advertisers.

But this hyperflexibility is also a major weakness. Formats change with dizzying speed; most people have little idea of the full range available; many young people now stick to FM and never try AM; nearly everyone sticks to their two or three favorite channels; and the supposedly most intimate medium is dominated by hype, promotion, cynicism and plain old advertising for many minutes per hour.

Paradoxically, the most specifically targeted and specialized medium is also the medium that jumbles everything up together, so that the listener has difficulty telling apart the music, news, views and advertising. Much is not what it seems to be; the 'local' programming may come from 2,000 miles away; both music and talk tend to be free publicity for music groups, authors or other self-promoters; the views tend to be rabid; and phone-ins often offer voyeuristic excursions into unstable minds. The news itself is suspect: what presents itself as news may also be a plug for a business magazine or a particular company. Even the fast 'genuine' news, at which radio can be so brilliant, is too often not only undiluted mayhem and murder, but plain old self-promotion by your friendly, local police PR person.

Deregulated radio certainly exhibits plenty of both virtues and vices. Whether the prevailing commercialism and fragmentation, the extremes of local and national, flatter or insult the market approach is a matter of opinion. What is not a matter of opinion is that radio deregulation received little opposition from politicians. The typical House of Representatives district contains about 25 radio stations, and for the House member, local radio is a gold mine of free 30-second messages once an hour on the hour. For the radio station, the politician is a friend at court, and a source of free, but virtuous, 'live from Washington' material.

Radio's strengths are well known to politicians; Ronald Reagan was a radio star both before and after he was a movie star. But in terms of hard data, radio as a medium is unknown and becoming more so. Most radio audience figures – above and below 1 per cent – are statistically worse than dubious. Deregulation has actually exacerbated the uncertainty by requiring less documentation. This does simplify and cheapen radio station management, but in terms of documenting deregulation, it leaves a data gap and suggests at best a lack of confidence in deregulation.

NETWORKS FOR EVER?

Both regulation and deregulation were heavily concerned with the central position of the three networks in the American broadcasting system. Nevertheless, regulation did not directly address the network system, regulation being angled toward licensing *stations* and possible *competitors*; its most immediate impact on the networks were certain negative constraints ensuring that the networks did not excessively dominate the Hollywood suppliers and their local affiliates, and restricting network entry into such other local media market activities as newspapers and cable.

Deregulation, also, did not directly address the networks as such. With backs turned, Congress and the FCC directed their gaze primarily at other aspects of the media, old and new, meanwhile looking nervously over their shoulders to see what impact all this was having on the networks.

The three networks which evolved from this regime of indirect rule were quite different in their corporate makeup. RCA was the senior operation, a diversified electronics company, now into new hardware areas such as satellites, with about *one-quarter* of its revenue coming from its NBC broadcasting subsidiary. CBS was next in seniority, and for some years has drawn about *one-half* its revenues from broadcasting; CBS's other major revenue areas have been CBS records and publishing. Finally, ABC, the junior network company, was, after selling its movie theater interests, about 90 per cent involved in broadcasting.

Even though regulation did not force the networks into a standard mould, nevertheless, through its scrutiny in general and its restrictions on media diversification in particular, it may have made all three network companies more cautious and slow-footed than comparable companies in neighboring fields.

Certainly all three networks were going through diversification problems when deregulation arrived in the 1970s. RCA's difficulties were perhaps common to other large electronics companies, but its NBC network languished in third ratings place for a decade.

CBS was generally regarded as the most commercially successful of the networks; its TV network had long been either in first place or a very close second to ABC. CBS's other great success was in records. But in the early 1980s, CBS's diversification efforts were fairly disastrous; DBS, video games, cable arts programming and moviemaking were four areas in which CBS lost money. CBS was perhaps the network most interested in new technology, but any payoff from HDTV, videotex and others still seems a long way off. These uncertainties prompted Ted Turner's brash 'junk bond' takeover bid in 1985; essentially Turner would have sold off all the non-TV diversifications in order to finance ownership of the TV network.

Are there any other factors common to the networks which might give clues to their future destiny?

Outsiders, including Capital Cities, are inclined to see one common network fault as an inability to control costs. The networks operate primarily in New York and Los Angeles, and these are also the locations of their most profitable activities, their two leading owned-and-operated TV stations. These locations may lie behind several relevant common factors. All three networks have suffered from *founding father* problems, and in the case of RCA founding father and son problems. All three networks have been located not simply in high-cost cities, but confronted there by a constellation of organizations adept at acquiring high rates of pay; these are the craft unions, creative guilds and performers' talent agencies which ensure that if profits rise, so too does the cost of production.

Perhaps there is something about organizations which straddle the twin fantasy industries of Sunset Boulevard and Madison Avenue which makes it difficult for them fully to develop their commercial assets. Certainly there is a remarkable rigidity and ineptness in the networks' attitudes to Washington, which tend to confirm politicians' prejudices as to the networks' excessive power and insufferable arrogance.

The networks seemed destined to follow the path of other communications giants: increasing gross revenue, but a declining share of a growing total market. Just as AT&T and IBM planned to handle this problem by diversification, so also the networks' futures seem to depend partly on their success in diversification. And this in turn will depend heavily upon the regulatory decisions of FCC, the Justice Department, the courts and Congress.

PBS, MARKETPLACE EXCEPTIONS AND IDEOLOGICAL SLIPPERY SLOPES

Deregulation in the mass media, as in telecommunications, has been supported most of the way by a consensus. The consensus has broken down only over the issue of 'exceptions' to the generally approved marketplace principle. Most exceptions quoted are the same as in telecoms: does the competitive media marketplace fully provide for ethnic minorities, for the rural, for the elderly? In broadcasting there is also the issue of children's and/or educational output.

Here the consensus breaks down, and in the early 1980s the overall impact was that subsidized support and legal provision for such exceptions were cut. One of the four FCC commissioners who voted to remove all specific requirements for children's programming told this writer that marketplace forces would not in fact fill the gap; nevertheless, it was necessary to vote against requiring provision for children, because any vote for it would lead down the 'slippery slope' to government-dictated content. Such a response is honest. But in placing marketplace principle before the admitted needs of children, it pleads guilty to the opposing charge of 'ideology'. The trade paper *Variety* headlined this story: 'Fowler's FCC tells kids to get lost'.[6] In this, the uncompromising deregulators have damaged their own cause, confounded common sense, presented a ludicrous portrait of decent television for children as the onrush of tyranny, inflamed the opposition and thus ensured that the issue will not go away.

This is another vast topic, and public radio and public television have been through some anxious times. Some of the key 'market exception' developments in the broadcast deregulation saga have been as follows:

(1) In 1981 the Reagan administration proposed to cut back severely on federal funding for public broadcasting; these cuts were gradually restored by Congress. There were two Reagan presidential vetoes in 1984 of federal funding for the Corporation for Public Broadcasting. These interventions by the Reagan administration were seen within PBS as its worst crisis since President Nixon's funding veto of June 1972. Public television survived with roughly level funding in 1985 against a background of rising costs.

(2) National Public Radio went through a separate financial crisis – of overspending and near bankruptcy; but with a change in leadership, it began to make payments on a lifesaving loan from the Corporation for Public Broadcasting.

(3) Various developments in cable are relevant. By late 1984 the Black Entertainment Channel (BET) was the seventeenth-largest 'basic' cable offering, reaching 8 million households. Nickelodeon, a children's basic cable service, was the seventh largest cable service, reaching 20 million homes (about 24 per cent of all TV households). Both BET and Nickelodeon were entertainment-oriented services run on a commercial basis. Rock videos and interviews (BET) and cartoons and comedy (Nickelodeon) were the main offerings.

(4) LPTV was advocated by the FCC and others as suitable for ownership by, and programming to, ethnic minorities. But in practice, LPTV stations are normal repeater stations, carrying a major TV signal into an area of otherwise weak reception. However, they are now licensed to carry some local programming for the local audience. LPTV thus seems more relevant to mountain communities in Alaska or Colorado than to black communities in Alabama or Chicago.

(5) *Lottery procedures* were introduced by the FCC for LPTV and other new franchises. In these lotteries – and contrary to FCC chairman Mark Fowler's wishes – minority applicants were each given two shakes of the dice.

(6) In the *Cable Deregulation Act of 1984*, the main equal opportunity provisions were deleted at a very late stage in the bargaining. Radio deregulation also occurred with little special provision for minorities, and none at all for children.

Representative Timothy Wirth and other members of the House Communications Subcommittee attempted, in their House version of television deregulation, to add several provisions to ensure programming aimed at children, minorities, the elderly and local audiences generally. In effect, the Wirth bill proposed a trade-off: the broadcasters would get significant deregulation (including considerable security of license tenure), but in return they would have to provide minimum amounts of programming specifically for exceptional groups. The details were to be complex and FCC-administered, but the legislation would require commercial stations to put on something like one hour per day of children's programming, with other significant amounts of minority, elderly and local interest programming. NAB eventually denounced this proposal as more regulatory than deregulatory, and the legislation died.

The US was thus left with PBS still the major provider of material for marketplace exceptions. But PBS is a remarkable patchwork of intentions and of compromises which leave its overall mission unclear. Figure 12.2 shows the 1982 funding picture which confronted the Reagan administration in 1981. Total federal funding was about $200 million, and so it was to remain, despite much turf warfare.

PBS funding still betrays its educational origins before the Second World War. It later developed with the help of two major foundations: the Ford Foundation which contributed much of the early money, and the Carnegie Corporation which funded and published two famous reports which are landmarks in PBS history. From this history have emerged three major paradoxes:

First, a PBS system which some believe is supposed to assist the poor and uneducated in fact continues to have an audience skewed toward the affluent and the well-educated. In early 1984, 65 per cent of all US college graduates watched at least once a week, against 49 per cent in the least-educated category. The strongest predictors of PBS viewing are a higher education, an income of over $30,000, being middle-aged (35–64) and being a pay-cable subscriber.[7]

Second, PBS supposedly has local community aspects, and is funded more by state and local than by federal government. But in practice the cost of television programming and economies of scale mean that PBS has relatively little local programming; some 80 per cent of its national output is made in either New York or Boston. Most of the remainder comes from Pittsburgh, Philadelphia or Washington DC (whence many performers in fact commute from New York) or is made at the PBS stations in Los Angeles and San Francisco.

Third, PBS, in keeping with its educational origin, maintains an emphasis on culture and public affairs/documentary programming. But these types of programming are among the most expensive, and thus PBS tends to use recorded stage performances, and has, over the years,

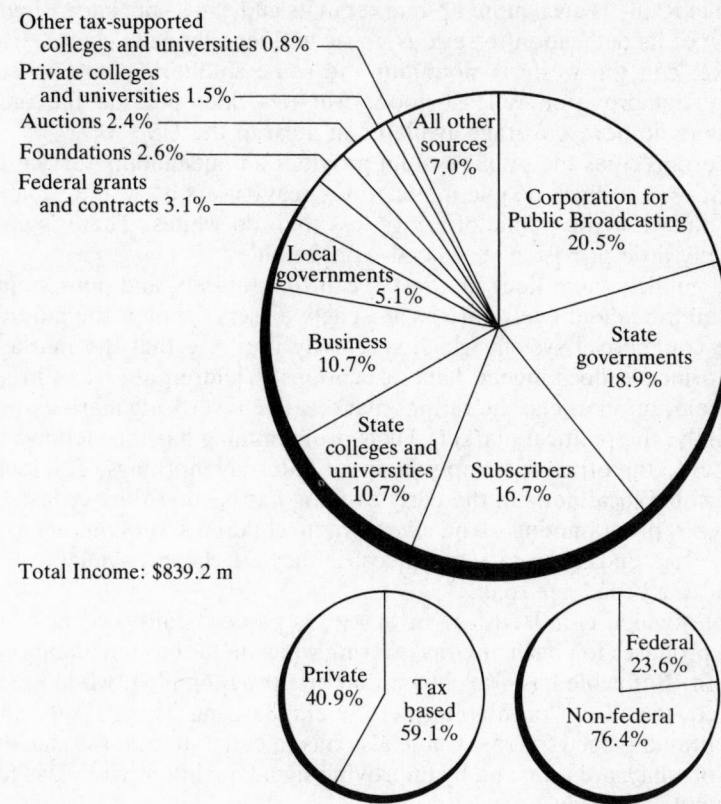

Other tax-supported
colleges and universities 0.8%
Private colleges
and universities 1.5%
Auctions 2.4%
Foundations 2.6%
Federal grants
and contracts 3.1%

All other
sources
7.0%

Corporation for
Public Broadcasting
20.5%

Local
governments
5.1%

Business
10.7%

State
governments
18.9%

State
colleges and
universities
10.7%

Subscribers
16.7%

Total Income: $839.2 m

Private
40.9%

Tax
based
59.1%

Federal
23.6%

Non-federal
76.4%

Figure 12.2 *Sources of Public Broadcasting Income during fiscal year 1982.*
(*Source*: *Corporation for Public Broadcasting Policy Planning and Development, June 1983.*)

imported much of its material from the BBC and from the British Commercial TV companies. And when, in September 1983, PBS launched a one-hour version of its MacNeil/Lehrer news, the service relied overwhelmingly on in-studio interviews. Thus, a television service funded by the federal government and some of the largest US corporations puts on the kind of programming one might expect from one of the world's smaller and poorer nations. The weaknesses of the network system – grossly inadequate coverage of the outside world and a general failure to reflect the richness of US life, politics and culture – are found also in the PBS system, which reflects, but does not repair, the commercial system's inadequacies.

Public Radio is even more up-market in its audience – not surprisingly in view of its dedication to serious music and lengthy news shows. It is also weak in the western mountain and some southern states, where commercial provision is least good. But NPR does provide the only serious radio news coverage available in most of the US.

In certain cities the public system provides an outstanding service to minorities, but black people in general – heavy users of TV and radio – listen and view the public offerings less than do whites. There is also relatively little provision specifically for the elderly.

The public system does the best it can for children, and households with children under twelve are its most active users. But it is the failures of the commercial system which so clearly illustrate that the market-place principle does indeed have exceptions. Children are weak in all three relevant markets: the ratings market, the advertising market and, especially, the political market. Their programming has thus tended to shrink into the otherwise empty hours of Saturday mornings. The local stations' big local news in the early evening has been at the expense of children's programming. And even when children's programming is screened, it tends to be cartoons, because they are cheaply available and appeal to a broad age-span.

Cable, which is indeed a rival to PBS, is paradoxically also an ally. Cable promises to poach any PBS offering which holds out the likelihood of profit. But cable has also shown that arts programming, while much admired, is still not profitable, thereby emphasizing its suitability and the continuing need for PBS. Cable also has to carry all local PBS signals, many of which are UHF, and by improving signal quality provides PBS for once with a 'subsidy'.

Meanwhile PBS stumbles on in genteel poverty – an underfunded service for up-market audiences, and a service which fills the gaps without taking away advertising from the commercial system or signi-ficant subscriptions from cable.

ALAS, POOR NETWORKS

American broadcasting grew increasingly competitive in the 1970s, and new technologies, combined with deregulation, make it still more competitive now. This heightened competition, especially in radio, does indeed have some uncanny resemblances to the specialist fast-food business.

But there are comparisons even closer at hand, and from the television business itself. Multichannel television was pioneered in several Latin American countries while the US was still severely limited to two and a half national networks.

The New York networks were not believed when they said that the business was already very competitive and very expensive. The conventional wisdom among management critics is that the networks in recent years have made inadequate profits, with costs too high and assets underutilized, and have thus had insufficient funds for diversification and become vulnerable to takeover.

The networks complain that they lack the funds to put on adequate children's programming, say, and that they would also lack the clout to make their affiliates transmit such programming. This is true. The networks are caught in a trap by the regulations that remain, by antitrust sanctions against any restrictive gentleman's agreements, and by the insatiable appetite of the William Morris talent agency for commission income.

Alas, poor networks. Yes, poor indeed. They thought they were in the entertainment business, the merchandising of fantasy. Now they discover, rather late in the day, that they are in fact in the millionaire business; nearly everyone who appears frequently on prime-time television – that great A team of actors, artistes, authors, anchors, athletes and agents – is either a millionaire already, or well on the way to becoming one. No wonder the network executives on Madison Avenue and Sunset Boulevard also want to join the team. No wonder, too, that the networks tremble.

But when networks tremble, plenty of others get the shakes. The networks may or may not recover. It may all depend on whether they can return to a time of fewer millionaires and more regulations.

Notes

1 Anise Wallace, 'Turning Out Broadcasting Stocks', *New York Times*, 12 August 1984.
2 'Changing Hands 1984', *Broadcasting*, 28 January 1985, pp. 45–71.
3 'Salaries, stock, for CBS toppers listed in proxy', *Variety*, 20 March 1985, pp. 2, 130.
4 David Bergmann, 'Gold, Goodwill . . . and Money', *Variety*, 22 August 1984, p. 89.
5 Christopher H. Sterling, *Electronic Media* (1984), p. 85.
6 *Variety*, 28 December 1983, p. 25.
7 US Senate Subcommittee on Communications, *Corporation for Public Broadcasting Authorization: Hearings on S.2436*, 26 March 1984, p. 25.

13

Imprudent Hollywood: Deregulated and Defenestrated

Ever since the late 1940s and the court-ordered breaking of the old movie cartel, Hollywood has been one of the most genuinely competitive parts of the US communications industry. After the TV programming industry moved west in the 1950s, Hollywood found itself during the 1960s in two main businesses; after 1970 three others were added.

First, Hollywood continued to supply *movies to theaters*; although Hollywood no longer owned the theater chains, it did still control the key middle man function ('distribution'), both in the US and to a large extent around the world, and it still got quite a good financial deal, receiving up to half of what a theater took at the box office.

Second, Hollywood was in the *television business*. TV rights for movies commanded high fees and, although the New York networks dominated the commissioning of TV series, an FCC decision in 1972 confirmed that Hollywood should retain control of TV syndication – subsequent TV showings – which could produce huge windfall profits.

But in the 1970s, Hollywood became the location of a third entertainment production business – *recorded music*. Although financial control tended to remain in New York, recorded music also brought new money and power to Hollywood studios and producers.

Around 1980 it was predicted that the 'new media' would bring additional production businesses to Hollywood.[1] The Hollywood companies made many elaborate deals and entered into many joint ventures in their attempts to get into the home video business. The *Wall Street Journal* published a chart showing the numerous linkages,[2] which was remarkably similar to one of those Marxist charts which shows that all capitalists sleep in the same bed.

While Hollywood was engaging in its favorite art form, the complex paper deal, two new production industries were indeed being established, but both on terms much less favorable to Hollywood than it had ever previously accepted.

So, fourth, Hollywood found itself in the business of *pay-cable* movie supplier. This was far from a commercial bonanza, however, HBO quickly became a dominant force in pay-cable, with over half the action; it emerged as a new hybrid – in part a fourth television network, in part the newest and most powerful Hollywood distributor. However you described it, the most vital and most painful fact was that Hollywood kept only about 20 per cent of what the HBO subscriber paid to the local cable company.

Moreover, pay-cable exposure increasingly eroded the audience figures when the same movies were shown subsequently on prime-time network television; thus, in the early 1980s, the networks paid less for movies – $3 million, for example, instead of the previous $5 million – and overall Hollywood received little additional money from this brave new medium.

Hollywood also became, fifth, the main supplier of *pre-recorded video-cassette* material for playing on VCRs. But here again Hollywood received a bad deal. Whether the cassettes are rented or sold, Hollywood gets only about 20 per cent of what the customer pays at the local video store.

Thus Hollywood, the first deregulated sector of the mass media, has failed to achieve much financial benefit from the deregulation of cable and from the new, unregulated VCR business.

Hollywood has become ever more complex and difficult to describe. One crude, but realistic, perspective presents Hollywood as a pyramid. At the very top level are the three New York networks, CBS, NBC and ABC. HBO shows signs of having vaulted quickly up to this highest level; and the video distribution business may be doing the same.

The Hollywood 'majors' are only on the second level in their own industry. Six major companies – Paramount, Warner, MCA–Universal, Columbia, MGM/United Artists and Fox – have a remarkably traditional set of names, suggesting continuity and stability. There is continuity in that these companies operate a 'full service' studio – each has typically a large slice of west Los Angeles real estate with extensive studio and office plant capable of producing batches of both feature movies and weekly television series. However, these six Hollywood majors are indeed highly competitive, and most recent years have seen at least one of the majors sold to a new conglomerate owner. Columbia, MGM, United Artists and Fox have been bought, sold and merged with especial frequency.

Further down the Hollywood pyramid are the larger independent companies, which typically make a few movies or a few TV series each year. But even the successful ones, such as Orion in movies and Lorimar in TV series, are insecure. Beneath this are several hundred much smaller companies – often a lone producer turned entrepreneur – which are typically handling a single movie and/or a 'pilot' for a possible TV series.

This Hollywood pyramid is very hierarchical; it is about money, power, prestige, security and chances of success. The higher up the pyramid, the more of each.

Apart from pyramid imagery another Hollywood favorite in recent years has been the 'window' perspective. For the antiquated notion of a movie release pattern has now been substituted a series of windows – a movie property is licensed for a carefully controlled sequence of markets and publics; a typical sequence of windows for a movie deal made in 1984–5 was:

1 theaters, the first, and for Hollywood still much the most lucrative, window, which lasts some months; next, three 'new' windows:
2 home video, both renting and buying;
3 PPV cable, available on a minority of local cable systems;
4 'nontheatrical' markets, such as hotels, airlines and oilrigs;
5 pay-cable – HBO and its competitors – which get the movies next, showing them repeatedly as 'new movie of the month' and then less intensively for several subsequent months;
6 network prime-time television showings, beginning two or three years after initial release;
7 pay-cable, for a second showing of a movie now four or five years old;
8 television syndication, in which the now old movie is sold off to the highest bidder in each local market, often an independent TV station;
9 'basic' cable.

All this window work clearly makes Hollywood movie contracts even more of a lawyer's paradise than before. But all the window clauses and window talk cannot put Hollywood back together again, or conceal the crude fact that two brash youngsters initialled HBO and VCR have thrown Hollywood out of the window, thus reviving the practice of defenestration, which helped to launch the Thirty Years' War in seventeenth-century Europe.

Yet another image portrays Hollywood as a chessboard; down one side of the board are eight (or so) release windows. Down the other are eight types of Hollywood product – full theatrical movies, made-for-TV movies, television series, TV miniseries, TV docudramas, live sport, audio for records and tape and music videos. On this 8-by-8 chessboard there are alternate regulated and unregulated (black and white) squares.

HOLLYWOOD'S DILEMMAS: COMPETITION, COST
INFLATION, DEREGULATION

If the New York networks have a problem of controlling costs, Hollywood is a worse case of the same problem; this is primarily because Hollywood is indeed too internally competitive for its own health. Paradoxically, its high-cost problem – especially in the form of lavish salaries for both stars and executives – creates the impression that Hollywood thrives on competition. Its lavish ways seem to proclaim that Hollywood requires no regulatory protection.

In the Carter and Reagan years, Hollywood has found itself receiving little regulatory relief from any branch of government. Some of the main decisions affecting Hollywood have been:

(1) The FCC's 1983 attempt to allow the networks back into television syndication, which was successfully blocked by lobbying in Washington and the support of President Reagan. The Hollywood committee which coordinated this effort argued for 'prudent deregulation', but all Hollywood achieved was an extension of the status quo.

(2) The FCC's extension of the station ownership rule to 12 TV stations and up to 25 per cent of the US population, which was opposed by Hollywood in 1984–5, but unsuccessfully. Whether the networks or the independent station groups benefited the most, Hollywood's bargaining strength was hardly likely to improve.

(3) A series of court decisions, in which various studio groupings were forbidden in 1980 and 1981 – on antitrust grounds – from setting up a consortium to attack HBO's dominance in pay-cable. The courts were in effect asked to decide whether HBO or Hollywood was trying harder to monopolize pay-TV, and Hollywood was prevented from pursuing its 'monopolistic' goal.

(4) The famous Sony–Betamax case, which confirmed the right of the citizen to VCR record programming without having to pay copyright fees, and was thus another loss for Hollywood.

Hollywood's cost-inflation problem has many aspects, but the most visible, that of star salaries, is indeed important. To a significant extent, stars and their agents drive the industry; when superstars want 10 per cent of the gross (theater receipts), and many actors earn more than $1 million per picture, it's not surprising that feature film budgets tend to exceed $10 million.

Similar escalation occurs in TV series. If the series is a success, all the Hollywood agents can see that those other agents on Madison Avenue are paying $100,000 for a 30-second commercial, and that the series stars have a chance to 'negotiate up'. Actors have agents, writers and directors have guilds, and everyone else has a trade union.

The Hollywood bargaining style is flamboyant and aggressive. The actors' agents set the pace, and have also established the norm that everyone always wants more and is prepared to go beyond all reasonable limits to get it. Actors and producers also want to own their products, and, since some such independents earn huge profits (while most fail), success in studio management in turn leads to demands for million-dollar bonuses on top of rather generous salaries.

Thus Hollywood is always calculating what a 'property' will earn – if the movie is a super-success, or if the TV series hits the syndication jackpot in six years' time. It thus adopts 'deficit financing'.

Much speculation concerns whether the industry really needs to be encamped around the expensive hillsides of west Los Angeles. But the core reasons remain: Hollywood has to be, first, where the entertainment talents have their main permanent residences, and, second, where the investment in full-service studios and specialist backup facilities exists.

The studios, despite their names and plants having been there for decades, are still relatively fragile enterprises. One piece of supporting evidence for this is the predominant pattern of the studio as a subsidiary within a conglomerate – Paramount as part of Gulf and Western, Columbia as a subsidiary of Coca-Cola. The studios make some money by renting out their sound-stages, offices and back lots to independent producers; they also act as bankers and distributors for those below them on the Hollywood pyramid. But most studios' fortunes in any one year typically ride on the backs of a very few high-risk enterprises. Each season a studio may release 15 movies, but its big hopes ride on just one or two; so also with its record interests, where one super-hit album is enough to transform an entire annual balance sheet. And each spring sees the networks ordering perhaps 60 'pilot' films for potential TV series, of which few will become series that last even a year.

Studios still gamble heavily each year on a few movies and a few TV series, and revenue can roller-coaster from year to year; in successive years from 1980 to 1984 MCA–Universal's share of US theatrical film rentals was 20, 14, 30, 13 and 8 per cent.[3] Sometimes theatrical and TV earnings rise and fall together; between the 1979/80 and 1984/5 TV seasons, Fox's share of theatrical movie earnings rose from 13 to 21 per cent and then declined to 10 per cent, while roughly in parallel, its prime-time TV series hours rose from 2 to 6½, then declined to 3½ hours per week. It was at this latter point, early in 1985, that Rupert Murdoch stepped in with finance for the ailing Fox company.

Hollywood studios are asset-rich: their back libraries have endless earning potential, their back lots are choice real estate, and their studios have eager customers in a time of booming production. Thus they tend to be worth more dead than alive, and the studio name lives on as one of the assets purchased by the new owner. The biggest asset, however, is the library of the studio's past film output. And with the new network turbulence a studio like MGM was especially attractive to a new network, like Ted Turner with his WTBS super-station.[4]

Hollywood has found itself trying to sell single properties, and has lost its old direct pipeline to its own, as of pre-1950, cartel-controlled local theaters. In theater movies, still the source of Hollywood's biggest market and highest margins, the studio has to market each movie separately. Consequently, enormous sums are spent on promoting the product in other media (a job which the local theater once largely did); the number of major films also tends to creep up to unrealistic heights in each boom, which in turn requires more promotional expenditure and brings a lower chance of success. No wonder that moviemakers try to emulate James Bond movies and *Star Wars* with sequels; movies in general have become novelty products, accompanied by high risk and high promotion cost.

The tendency toward excess product is yet another example of a failing which derives at least in part from fear of antitrust action. As prosperity grew in the early 1980s, the total number of Hollywood feature films grew from 300 to more than 400 in 1984, and the number of feature movies with a major distributor grew from around 110 a year toward 150. Meanwhile studio bottom lines shrank, especially in comparison with those of the more sheltered press companies. Several of the new moves most menacing to Hollywood came from plain old press dominance/monopoly – Capital Cities and ABC, Murdoch and Twentieth Century Fox, and of course Time Inc, whose press profits had fuelled HBO.

HBO CHURNS ONWARD

HBO had its first great success via satellite in 1975; the Ali–Frazier heavyweight boxing contest was transmitted from the Philippines via satellite to just two cable systems – one ATC owned in Jackson, Mississippi, and a United Artists Columbia cablevision system in Florida.[5] Subscribers came forward in droves, and 4 months later, 28 cable systems had applied for satellite reception of HBO. In less than 2 years, it was available on 350 systems in 45 states, and was reaching 700,000 customers.

By the early 1980s HBO already had a dazzling list of achievements. First of these was its high level of profitability. HBO had in effect completed an end run around the entire Hollywood system. It had found a fresh way of getting new movies to customers. It quickly became a Hollywood major distributor, with an entirely new exhibition circuit in the form of, first hundreds, then thousands, of local cable systems, each with its receiving dish antenna.

HBO executives had shown once again that Hollywood is slow to recognize major new developments in its own business. HBO had exploited Hollywood rivalries by going to each company and signing up the right to show its movies within months of initial theatrical release. Later, when Hollywood got together to defeat the intruder, HBO won in court, painting Hollywood with the old cartel brush. HBO began to bypass the big studios and sign up directly with independent producers; it also started to end-run Hollywood's lengthy art form, the movie deal. Instead of the script, casting and finance preliminaries, the endless meetings with agents, packagers and stars, the rewriting of the script for the umpteenth time, HBO's brash young men had been given authority by Time Inc to bargain and sign all at a single meeting. Quite quickly these aggressive and successful ways of operating – accompanied by the continued rocket-like ascent of HBO's vital numbers – began to throw a new light on all existing Hollywood practices: were any of them really necessary? The next nasty blow was that, as HBO grew, it started to use its bargaining strength to pay less per household reached. The existing competition in pay-cable was of little use; HBO had more than half the market. HBO offered less per subscriber reached, but more in absolute terms, than the opposition. It was a type of offer you couldn't refuse, but you could and did resent. The young men from Time Inc acquired a reputation for arrogance, for being bad winners – hardly a novelty in Hollywood, to be sure; they became scapegoats for the real dictators behind the scenes, the MSOS.

HBO has since run into all kinds of problems. Perhaps the most fundamental is that pay-cable suffers from a particularly severe case of the cable disease called 'churn'. The rate of churn is something like 3½ per cent per month; in other words, of 100 subscribers HBO may have had in January, about 40 will have cancelled by Christmas, nearly half of them being people moving house. But the remainder must be influenced by a simple fact: when you first get HBO, it is a double novelty. It has a batch of recent movies, whose reviews you can remember reading in the last 12 months, and there are also specials from entertainment and sport. But HBO also keeps rerunning other, older secondary product. Inevitably the new subscriber is unfamiliar with the initial offerings – the choice of fresh films every evening at 6, 8, 10 and 12. However, after three months or so, he has seen all those he wants to see. Now HBO's prime offering is just five or six new films a month, half of which may not appeal to his taste. This author subscribed to HBO for four months and then became part of the churn statistics.

Another problem was that the initial Nielsen cable semiannual survey almost certainly grossly overestimated the subscriber numbers – for example, in June 1983 Nielsen reported that 18.3 million households had HBO, when HBO itself claimed only 12.5 million. Part of this may have been due to piracy – another cross for HBO – but part was due to bad sampling. Later the Nielsen figure came down toward HBO's own, with unfair stories about an HBO decline. This was doubly unfortunate for HBO, because a real weakening in its growth did begin around June 1983. This was almost certainly due to the growth of home video.

Nevertheless, HBO has driven ahead in its characteristic relentless style. Despite much conflict with Hollywood, HBO is still getting new movies from all the majors except Paramount. It is still carrying boxing fights and other specials. It has moved decisively into making its own movies in partnership with others. HBO is involved in the entire output of Orion, the leading Hollywood independent. It is also involved in Tri-Star with Columbia and CBS. It has made a joint-financing movie deal with Metromedia, the TV station group. It is a partner with Paramount and Universal, in ownership of the USA cable network, even though these are perhaps its two leading enemies in Hollywood. It has funded series of documentaries from independent producers on sensational subjects – e.g. 'When Women Kill'. It is strongly interested in PPV. Finally, it is selling video cassettes of its own movies.

HBO's strategy appears to be to become a new kind of movie and entertainment distributor/packager which actively seeks out and finances projects, but which also uses what, by old Hollywood conventions, are modern and exotic patterns of delivery. HBO is taking a lead in the new game of sequencing windows around a very large quantity of properties which it partly or wholly controls.[6]

Once again it has been that old partnership of the US Justice Department and the federal courts which has dominated policy in the new field of pay-cable-TV. Other pay-cable companies were involved as well, but basically the battle lines were drawn between HBO, which always had more than half the pay-cable business, and various Hollywood groups trying to form their own pay-cable company. This Hollywood grand alliance would adopt the familiar old tactics of trying to round up the best product and deny it to HBO.

The question became one of how many Hollywood majors could combine together to go into pay-cable without being forbidden on antitrust grounds. The first two efforts included four, then three, Hollywood majors, and each was judged a constraint of trade. Finally, a more modest merger was allowed, but one too modest to pose a significant threat to HBO. The three episodes were as follows:

(1) Four movie majors – Fox, Paramount, MCA–Universal and Col-

umbia – combined in 1980 to form a pay-cable network named Premiere.[7] Also involved was a lot of Getty oil money. Premiere would get first pay-cable rights to all films distributed by all four of these movie majors. Only after a further 9 months would these movies be licensed to other pay-cablers, including HBO. HBO complained to Justice, which subsequently won in US District Court.

(2) The next effort involved beefing up one of the other pay-cable companies, namely The Movie Channel. TMC was already owned by the Warner–Amex cable combine. The new proposal was for two of the Premiere four, Paramount and MCA–Universal, to combine with Warner and American Express as a new foursome ownership; this had the advantage of only three Hollywood majors supporting an existing pay-cabler. This merger involving half the Hollywood majors was also opposed by Justice and forbidden in court in the summer of 1983.

(3) A third proposal was for a merger of the two weak pay-cable companies, TMC and Showtime (owned by the TV syndicator Viacom). The combined Showtime/TMC would thus have the support of Viacom and American Express, but of only one movie major, Warner. The Justice Department agreed, and the merger took place.

Later in 1983 and 1984 a series of new agreements were signed, which constitute in effect a truce until the late 1980s. The most important agreement was signed by Paramount (widely regarded as the most astute Hollywood management) and the new Showtime-TMC. This agreement sold all pay-cable rights of Paramount movies to Showtime/TMC for five years. Meanwhile HBO, through other agreements, acquired rights to the bulk of future non-Paramount movies, including those of arch-enemy Universal.

While relishing all the gossip about a slowdown in HBO growth, Hollywood was still anxious. As one senior Hollywood executive said to this author: 'First we created one monster in HBO. Have we now simply created a second monster in Showtime/TMC?'

Meanwhile, pay-cable in general, and HBO in particular, still seem to have many cards to play. The slow migration of premium sport to pay-cable and the connection between HBO and its own local MSO have unexploited potential. In general, HBO has problems which others might well relish.

The pay-cable phenomenon, moreover, shows Hollywood being outplayed by two new forces; the local cable operators and HBO between them take 80 per cent, while Hollywood gets only about 20 cents of the consumer's dollar.[8] In being outplayed by these two forces, Hollywood showed that it had failed to grasp the significance of a new technology – satellites – and its deregulation in the early 1970s.

THE NETWORKS WIN PRIME TIME, HOLLYWOOD WINS SYNDICATION

The networks have the upper hand over Hollywood in prime-time programming. Hollywood supplies each year about 23 episodes of a series which can be shown twice; the prices paid are up to $20 million for 23 action adventure full hours, about $8 million for 23 situation comedy half-hours. In addition, $3 million is paid typically for a theatrical movie, $2.5 million for a made-for-TV movie. These prices tend to be a little below the real cost to the studio, including overheads.

But in syndication, Hollywood wins. The big gold mine is a popular series which has amassed 100 episodes, and can often be syndicated for more than its previous network earnings. The other kind of syndication programming is the make cheap/sell dear formula found in game shows; a week's worth of five game show episodes can be made for the mere pittance of $120,000 and syndicated for much, much more.

Overall this can be regarded as a draw; certainly Hollywood gets a better deal than it does in pay-cable. The deal depends heavily on a 1972 Consent Decree in which the networks agreed, albeit with some small exceptions and anomalies, not to buy syndication rights from Hollywood, but only to buy the rights to the two initial prime-time showings. This leaves the network evening news (and a few other shows such as *Sixty Minutes* on CBS) as the few lone offerings either in or just before prime time which are made by the networks. The great bulk of the network prime-time schedule is made in Hollywood.

The FCC made a tentative decision in early August 1983 to partially relax these constraints. The FCC did not propose initially, in fact, to allow the networks to syndicate prime-time programming. But it did propose to remove most of the surrounding constraints:

1 The networks could own or syndicate made-for-TV and theatrical movies.
2 They would be allowed to acquire ownership and/or syndication rights in all programming outside prime time.
3 This freedom would extend to all daytime programming.
4 Networks could also control all foreign rights and syndication.

Finally, the FCC proposed to 'sunset' all remaining rules by 1990 – that is, there would be no renewal of any constraints in 1990.[9]

Initially, the relevant parts of the Reagan administration, Commerce and Justice, applauded this as a sound deregulatory initiative by the FCC. Hollywood in its various forms created a Committee for Prudent Deregulation, orchestrated by Jack Valenti and the Motion Picture

Association of America's (MPAA) Washington office. Movie lawyers, accompanied by selected movie stars, went calling on Capitol Hill, presenting Hollywood as David and the networks as Goliath.

Congressional investigation started, with yet more lawyers and movie stars. Hollywood began to win. President Reagan summoned his former aide, FCC chairman Mark Fowler, to the White House for a discussion. Commerce and Justice quickly changed their minds. Facing White House and congressional pressure, the FCC in its turn agreed to a delay. Negotiations took place between Hollywood and the networks, during which the networks scaled down their demands. Hollywood remained adamant. Finally, in March 1984, a group of 20 senators, led by Senate Communications Subcommittee chairman Barry Goldwater, asked the FCC for a two-year delay.

For the moment Valenti and prudent deregulation (Hollywood style) seemed to have won.

THEATERS AND MOVIES: MORE MEANS LESS FOR HOLLYWOOD

The theatrical showing of movies remains Hollywood's most lucrative market, primarily because of takings of around 40 per cent of the box office; the domestic US box office in 1984 took about $4 billion.

In the early 1980s, most of the US theater business's vital signs looked healthy. Between 1980 and 1984 admissions rose by 17 per cent, and the box office gross by 47 per cent; the number of screens was also expanding quite rapidly.

However, all this expansion was not good for Hollywood, because it spelled glut. Studio-released films' average *cost* of production rose by 54 per cent during 1980–4, somewhat faster than the gross box office take.

As a glut of new films emerged, the studios handed the exhibition trade a stronger negotiating position; between 1981 and 1984 the Hollywood companies' share of the box office take slipped from 44 to 38 per cent. At the same time Hollywood's old staple, the foreign box office, was in bad financial shape.

The theater owners, who a few years ago had been begging for more films, now found themselves in a strong position, with stable box office demand and a wider choice of movies to show. The multiplex theater, often in a shopping mall, has many marketing advantages, including flexibility and the chance to allow local taste to focus upon a choice of current films. And while Hollywood's distribution function is still important, some strong new theater chains, plus the multiscreen style of exhibition, have taken away some of the distributors' clout.

Thus deregulation (especially of cable), by opening up other film markets, has contributed to the worsening of Hollywood's position in its traditional, and still its best, market.

Notes

1 Jeremy Tunstall and David Walker, *Media Made in California* (New York: Oxford University Press, 1981), p. 197.
2 Stephen J. Sansweet, 'Movie, TV firms building alliances to take advantage of home video', *Wall Street Journal*, 26 March 1982, p. 29.
3 *Variety*, 16 January, 1985.
4 Ray Loynd, 'Turner Awaits Financing on MGM Deal', *Variety*, 14 August 1985. pp. 3, 24.
5 'Bird is in hand for pay cable', *Broadcasting*, 6 October 1975, p. 26.
6 Jonathan Black, 'The man who started Television II', *Channels*, December–January 1981-2. Tony Schwartz, 'Hollywood debates HBO role in film financing', *New York Times*, 7 July 1982, p. C19. 'Ferocious rivalry develops in pay services for cable TV', *Wall Street Journal*, 12 August 1982, p. 21. 'How HBO dominates pay-TV', *Business Week*, 14 September 1982, p. 64. 'HBO's dominant role in pay-TV field faces increasing challenges', *Wall Street Journal*, 8 November 1982, p. 24. Tom Shales, 'HBO', *Washington Post*, 17 April 1983, pp. L1-3. Kathryn Harris, 'Battle for control of the movie pipeline: pay TV vs. the studios', *Los Angeles Times*, 27 September 1982. 'HBO's Biondi outlines plans for expansion with Hollywood', *Broadcasting*, 30 April 1984, p. 130. 'Fuchs and Collins on the record: "We're all in this together"', *CableVision*, 10 December 1984, pp. 36–50.
7 Pamela G. Hollie, 'Hollywood offers Pay-TV challenge', *New York Times*, 29 April 1980, p. D1. Charles Schreger, 'Stage set for Pay TV legal fray', *Los Angeles Times*, 29 August 1980. 'Waiting for Goettel: Will Justice's first stone break Premiere's window?', *CableVision*, 1 December 1980, pp. 88–96. Tony Schwartz, 'Court Halts Pay-TV Network', *New York Times*, 1 January 1981, pp. B1, 35.
8 With volume discount, a system operator with over 100,000 subscribers who charges subscribers $10 pays HBO $4.12 per subscriber. This leaves 41% to be divided between HBO and Hollywood. *HBO: Rates and Services Information*, dated 1983, supplied 1984.
9 'Networks win financial interest, syndication battle', *Broadcasting*, 8 August 1983, pp. 27–30.

14

VCR: Uncertainty Fast Forward

The VCR, like cable, arrived on a big scale in the US later than it did in some other countries. Nevertheless, when it finally arrived with a bang in 1984 (7.6 million VCRs were sold in that year), its numbers sailed past those for personal computers and HBO subscribers. The VCR surge was seen in many lights – as the greatest media invention since television, or the most superficial fad since video games.

Perhaps it was, and is, the very prevalence of uncertainty which the VCR best reflects, exacerbates, and thus symbolizes. The VCR is versatile: it can record and play back pornographic movies, family wedding pictures and operas, either soap or grand.

It symbolizes Hollywood's continuing inability to get its act together. And here the new entrepreneurs who stole the show from under Hollywood's nose were not the Manhattan media folk from Time Inc but the mom and pop team which switched to video retailing from dry cleaning or the corner grocery shop.

This bottom-up marketing success indeed says something not only about Hollywood's inadequacies when it comes to marketing, but also about the weaknesses of American big business itself at this supposedly American art.

While the software at least is American-made, initially by the pornographic, nonstudio industry in Hollywood, the hardware is overwhelmingly Japanese. The VCR machine is a symbol of the assault by the Japanese electronics industry.

The VCR machine is actually an American invention, but it is a Japanese industrial mass-market product. This may represent a new trend. Once, new hardware was invented in Europe, refined and mass-produced in the US, then reexported to Europe. In the new era, the US plays the old role of Europe.

The impact of the VCR in the US is both especially large and especially unpredictable, because it entered fairly late into a US marketplace already full of much new technology and many new entertainment channels. Perhaps the VCR and the entertainment-filled cassette represent the dominant principle of the entertainment media, the music model of novelty. In many respects this is the exact reverse of the computer market. In computers customers want 'user-friendliness', efficiency and above all reliability; in entertainment the customers may want some familiarity, but they also crave novelty. If this is so, then IBM is in the right business, and people connected with the VCR, both its hardware and software, presumably, face an unsettling and uncertain time in an industry which deliberately sets out to contradict predictions and to refute expensively generated forecasts.

THE SONY–BETAMAX CASE, 1976–84

1984 was the year of the VCR in the US, primarily because on 17 January the Supreme Court found VCR home copying innocent by a vote of five to four. Thus was the cassette recorder deregulated by court action – probably deregulated beyond recall, because few politicians will want to reassert copyright protection in a way that will penalize so many voters' leisure pursuits.

The case had begun over seven years before. In November 1976, when the VCR was still very far from the mass market, MCA–Universal and Disney had filed suit against the Sony (Betamax–distributed) VCR. In 1979 US District Court Judge Warren J. Ferguson, in Los Angeles, had four d the VCR innocent. However, his decision was reversed on appeal in San Francisco in October 1981.[1]

At that stage there were some 3 million households with VCRs. Over two years later, when the Supreme Court reversed the Appeals Court, there were some 9 million. In fact, the rate of growth did not alter much, with sales nearly doubling in each year of the early 1980s.

However, the law's delays may account in part for Hollywood's hesitance; Hollywood's policy was to protect copyright before trying to boost sales. Paradoxically, therefore, the law's delays may have helped Main Street market forces to operate 'in secret' before their considerable development came to national attention.

The early history of the VCR consists of two clear phases, both lacking in respectability. The first was dominated by pornography – cheap to produce, expensive to buy. High prices – $79.95 and the like – continued into the second phase, in which conventional Hollywood *movies* came to predominate; retailers in the US – as in Europe – began to rent movies for a few dollars. But this advance from pornography was also into an area of doubtful legality. Did the copyright-holder retain any royalty interests beyond the 'first sale' to the retailer? As to the behavior of the home consumer, was he or she entitled to rent a cassette without an additional copyright payment? And, second, was he or she legally entitled to record (mainly Hollywood material again) from television?

The Sony–Betamax decision of January 1984 settled these issues in favor of the home consumer. The decision marked – even if it did not cause – the maturing of a third phase, a wider range of cassette materials, going beyond movies into such areas as do-it-yourself and music video.

In both retail sale and rental terms, movies continued to be the prime product. Indeed 1984 saw major advances in the marketing of movies, notably by Paramount with popular movies retailing at $24.95. Paramount thus indicated a middle way between the super-expensive and super-cheap sales strategy. The super-expensive strategy encouraged sales only to retailers, who then rented the cassettes; thus the sales figure was only a few per cent of the size of the market actually reached. The super-cheap pricing strategy (analogous to the mass-market paperback) meant very little for Hollywood, given the 20 per cent or so margins now well established. The $24.95 price provided at least $5 for Hollywood, and was analogous to a higher-priced paperback strategy. Disney's major 'classics' feature films at $29.95 for the 1985 Christmas market was another important precedent.

Meanwhile, the third phase seemed to indicate that besides movies, the main sales and rental appeal would be how-to, children's and music videos (presumably a few dominant genres). But what else? That was a question to be answered in the next phase. In the meantime, while pornography sank in percentage terms, it continued to sell and rent at premium prices, and in view of its low production cost still plays an important role in keeping the now respectable video industry profitable.

THE ZAPPY AUDIENCE: BUY/RENT/TIME-SHIFT

In 1984 the VCR achieved recognition not only from *Time*, *Newsweek* and the US Supreme Court, but also from A. C. Nielsen, the marketing and television research company.

The VCR was especially strong among above-average-income residents of metropolitan counties. The rather small Nielsen sample failed to pick up heavy use among minorities, although heavy VCR use among Hispanics must already have existed.

The biggest single use is the well-known one of *time-shifting* – seeing prime-time programming at other times, but also daytime programming. Daily soap opera serials were the most popular specific programming; obviously any serial that appears five times a week has five chances to feature in a consumer survey. But this popularity of cheaply made serials may be good news beyond video – for example, in cable.

Time-shifting also involves a shift in the composition of the social group which views. The lone viewing already common in multiset TV households is further encouraged; but the VCR also makes possible the party watching pornography, children's fare, recycled soaps or the family's special weekend movie show.

The motive which the video industry will presumably most wish to foster is that of collection.

COMPLEMENTARY OR ANTAGONISTIC?

The biggest initial casualty of the VCR appears to have been the video disk – attractive to copyright-holders because it could not be copied, but for customers too lacking in versatility. However, even this may be reversed, especially if a disk system with recording capability arrives.

Several relationships continue to be controversial, and this may be because the VCR is partly a plus and partly a minus. For example, the VCR is a rival of pay-cable, but pay-cable is also a source of new movies to copy. Similarly with movie theaters, the VCR probably discourages some attendance, while also rekindling the movie habit for some people.

PPV, and its relationship to VCR, is also causing much anxiety, but it could be a draw or a plus for PPV via cable. LPTV is another question mark. Since some LPTV stations have settled upon music video as the best available cheap programming formula, the relationship here may depend on the wider relationship between audio and video.

Perhaps the two key questions are whether the VCR will be married to audio and/or to the camera. Music video will presumably take over some of the territory of audio records/tapes and of radio, but will these media become mere loudspeaker extensions of music video?

Equally large and puzzling are questions about the camera and VCR. Clearly one appeal of the VCR is its ability to show home movies, to play back family weddings and meetings, to perform as a video postcard. This VCR function has knocked down many of the barriers between the television industry and the camera/photographic industry, which inevitably further multiplies the uncertainties.

ZAPPING THE COMMERCIALS

Opinions differ also as to whether advertising will need to worry about the zapping of commercials by VCR owners. The first Nielsen survey reported that this occurred on a substantial scale – 36 per cent of respondents said that they 'usually' (three-quarters or more of the time) used the 'stop' or 'pause' features to delete commercials.[2] Including those who zapped less frequently, this seemed to add up to 40 per cent or more of commercials being deleted. Whether or not some consumers exaggerated their anticommercial behavior, some advertisers clearly were worried.[3]

There are plenty of signs that both consumers and VCR equipment will get more sophisticated at zapping. A VCR add-on gadget already exists which can automatically recognize commercials – by the dip to a black screen before the break – and delete them, and its price can be expected to drop from its initial high level of $399.

Another prediction is that the advertising world will think up its own responses. Indeed, it already has responses available, such as sponsorship, quickie ten-second commercials in the pauses between items in a 60-second news flash, and other ways of burying commercials deeply in the content of programming. Such practices in turn may produce further consequences, thereby making for yet more uncertainty.

CERTAINTY ZAPPED

The VCR is not just a wild card; it seems likely to be a rogue that will deal a whole handful of wild cards, which in turn points toward a very chancy game of poker.

Nobody can predict the outcome. Even the future shape of the VCR industry is extremely uncertain, at both the wholesale and retail levels. Some element of exclusivity seems probable. But whose exclusivity will it be? No major video retailer will want to control all the fastest porno action, but it might like to have exclusive local rights to certain popular family movies; since supermarkets are among the few retail outlets that many Americans visit frequently, they might seem uniquely suited to cassette collection and return. But there are other possibilities: gas stations, department stores and the plain old video chain store in the local shopping mall.

Exclusivity may make the video business more like the movie business, in which theaters have long held exclusive local rights to movies. Such exclusivity, of course, is as American as apple pie – and so is the accompanying accusation of monopoly. Here the story may return to the courts and Congress.

But the future of regulation is the ultimate uncertainty.

Notes

1 'VCRs lose legal round on copyright', *Broadcasting*, 26 October 1981.
2 'Getting a fix on how they're using all those VCRs', *Broadcasting*, 7 May 1984, pp. 74–5.
3 'Zapping is happening', *Advertising Age*, 26 November 1984, p. 16.

15

The Electronic Press

Although the US press has supposedly been unregulated since its earliest days, it has actually been heavily influenced by communications deregulation. And while the newspaper has supposedly been surpassed by television as the main source of news, the American newspaper in fact remains the main source of news. Although circulation has indeed fallen relative to population, the American newspaper is still alive and reasonably well.

American newspapers operate primarily on advertising revenue, and this source of revenue has remained stable. Indeed, ever since 1965, the proportion of advertising revenue going to daily newspapers has remained at around 27 or 28 per cent; and to magazines and radio, at around 6 or 7 per cent each; only television has advanced, but only to around 22 per cent – well behind daily newspapers and far behind all newspapers and magazines combined.

Nevertheless, some major changes have occurred. Total daily sales of newspapers have remained approximately stationary, while population has steadily increased; the proportion of households *not* buying a daily paper has increased steadily, by at least 1 per cent per year. But these households not taking a daily paper are mainly the increasing number of single-person, nonmarried couple, black and Hispanic households.

The daily newspaper has become more middle-class, middle-income and middle-aged; in line with increasing seriousness, the proportion of morning dailies has increased, and fewer afternoon papers have survived. Many urban dailies have died, and some of their readers have lost the newspaper habit, but successful new dailies have begun in the middle-class suburbs. The most highly educated and the highest-income households buy about twice as many daily papers as the lowest-educated and lowest-income households.[1]

As US newspapers have moved into the suburbs and moved up-market, the resultant average product has become more serious, being aimed above the middle point because there are more affluent readers and more advertising above the middle point. The newspapers now flatter public taste somewhat, just as US television somewhat insults it –

exactly the opposite of the United Kingdom. Filling the demand for more popular 'newspapers', tabloid weekly publications like the *National Enquirer* and *The Star* have increased circulation.

Many of the central trends of the US press are encapsulated in the huge commercial success of the massive Sunday editions, which in many cases account for 40 per cent of total revenue, four times that of one daily edition. These Sunday papers are, of course, packed with supplements, consumer features and prodigal quantities of advertising, with preprinted coupons now especially evident; they are short on news and long on feature/magazine material.

The Sunday editions are especially prominent with the larger newspapers, and they are one way in which the strong have tended to get stronger.[2] Other ways include acquisition, the decline in competition and the increase in monopoly. Between 1976 and 1984 the top 20 newspaper groups' combined total increased – from 326 to 461 daily papers. A few large cities besides New York still have vigorous head-to-head competition – Chicago, Detroit, Denver, Boston and Dallas being leading examples – but in most of the top 50 cities such competition as exists is either token or controlled by a special exemption from the antitrust laws.

The antitrust laws are the main form of 'regulation' which affects newspapers, and it is indicative of the newspaper industry's past and present political clout that it has such a remarkable exemption: remarkable because this industry earns high profits. In 1983, for example, 27 public traded newspaper companies had a total operating income of $1,701 billion – 18 per cent of revenue.[3]

New technology has affected the press in several ways. First, when newspaper printing went electronic in the late 1960s and the 1970s, very large savings were made in skilled labor. Second, the deregulation of satellites has assisted the *national* spread of some previously local dailies. Third, news agencies have been transformed, but embarrassingly, UPI has become a casualty.

On balance, these new technological influences have contributed to the decline in competition and to the dominant monopoly trend. The need to purchase new electronic plant was in many cases the occasion for a family ownership to settle its squabbles by selling out to one of the big chains. New plant, once purchased, has encouraged 24-hour production, or morning and evening editions of the same daily.

But there are some countervailing tendencies. The new printing technology has made entry much cheaper, and there has been a growth in the quantity and quality of free weekly 'shoppers', which give some small dailies real competition. The magazine field also continues to be fiercely competitive.

METROPOLITAN AND SUBURBAN NEWSPAPER MONOPOLY ISSUES

There are at least four major antitrust provisions which strongly influence the predominant US pattern of very limited daily newspaper competition at both the city and suburban levels.

First, and most important, is the *Joint Operating Agreement*, based on a limited exemption from antitrust laws and intended to preserve editorial competition, but not business competition. The Newspaper Preservation Act of 1970 was intended to avoid the otherwise imminent death of the weaker of two competing dailies in a single city. There are some 25 Joint Operating Agreements (JOA), mainly in cities which are among the 60 largest though not among the 15 largest. The largest daily involved in such an agreement is the morning *San Francisco Chronicle*, with a sale of over 500,000. Its agreement is with the afternoon *San Francisco Examiner*; the two papers share printing plant, business departments and circulation vans, and offer a combined advertising rate, but they continue to have separate editorial staffs.

The legislation which allowed this kind of arrangement produced bitter congressional controversy and lengthy hearings, especially in the Senate. Critics claimed that this law was special-interest legislation to protect the profits of publishers and their political clout. But there was also an element of experiment. Would the papers survive, and would the editorially separate voices remain so? In most cases the answer to both questions has been yes.

The legislation, originally called The Failing Newspaper Bill, passed in 1970 under a new name, the Newspaper Preservation Act. At the time there were 22 agreements involving 44 daily papers. There have been remarkably few changes in the picture in the last 15 years.[4] In most cases the weaker paper has tended to get weaker, especially if it was an afternoon one. But the economies of joint operation and smaller staff, and the fact that these have been buoyant times for newspapers have meant that most JOA papers have prospered, and that both have made more profit than either would have done with competition.

In some cases, however, the dominant partner has grown restless. If it is the morning paper, it may now prefer to go it alone; if it is the afternoon paper, it may want to switch to the morning. The agreements vary, but they tend to be lengthy – in some cases dividing up the profits on a fixed formula for up to 50 years from the date of agreement.

The JOA which has attracted the most attention in recent times was one in St Louis, where an unsuccessful attempt was made to close down the afternoon and money-losing *Globe Democrat*.[5] In another case, two dailies in Seattle wanted to form a JOA but were resisted by the (Baxter) Justice Department. However, the US Supreme Court thought otherwise. These events leave the Newspaper Preservation Act and the JOA in almost as ambiguous a state as they were 15 years ago.

A second major example of antitrust rulings is almost equally important. It concerns competition between often quite large dailies and small free 'shoppers'. The general thrust of judicial opinion has been that very aggressive attempts to grab advertising from a shopper are 'predatory', and thus illegal. Competition at some 'reasonable' level, somewhere below the 100 per cent death threat, is legally acceptable. Newspaper executives these days spend a lot of time thinking about 'total market coverage' – less politely, delivering junk mail to all households, including those which do not subscribe to the daily; and many thoughts about this are focused on just how aggressively low you can set your prices in the junk mail delivery business without triggering judicial antitrust wrath.

A third antitrust legal doctrine asserts that major metropolitan newspapers should not be allowed to own suburban dailies in the same city region; the *Los Angeles Times* was prohibited from buying a suburban daily in Orange county on the grounds that this would reduce competition.

A fourth provision, developed partly by the FCC and partly by the courts, has forbidden *cross-ownership* of newspapers and broadcast or cable outlets by one ownership in the same media market.

One obvious, if unintended, consequence of these latter provisions has been to limit dominance within a single region and to divert groups such as Times–Mirror toward national ambitions. Times–Mirror has indeed become a national force, owning major dailies in Dallas and Denver, and, with Long Island's *Newsday* and three dailies in Connecticut, it is now the dominant owner on the affluent eastern side of the New York megalopolis.

A second unintended consequence of discouraging the acquisition of suburban dailies by metropolitan dailies has been to encourage a daily like the *Los Angeles Times* to adopt localized editions and printing plants; the *Los Angeles Times* now sells in a market which stretches 200 miles, from Santa Barbara to San Diego. The dominance of one newspaper in an area which contains more than half of California's population thus also makes the paper a predominant influence in the politics of the nation's largest state.

ADVERTISING: NEWSPAPERS VERSUS THE US POSTAL SERVICE AND THE FCC

US daily newspapers, which get over 85 per cent of their advertising *locally*, have reached an accommodation with television, which gets over 70 per cent of its advertising from *national* advertisers. But the newspaper industry is extremely concerned, first about junk mail, and second about the ultimate possibility of Yellow Page and other forms of advertising migrating to the telephone companies.

Decisions of the US Postal Service (advised by the independent Postal Rate Commission) have always affected both newspapers and magazines. Newly important, however, are the commission's third-class mail pricing decisions, because these are the Post Office's prices for delivering junk mail. One estimate is that 142 billion pieces of coupon advertising were delivered to US households in 1983. About one-third of these coupons reach householders folded into Sunday newspapers. But the US Post Office is in a strong competitive position; in many inner cities the metropolitan newspaper has a low household penetration, and many suburban areas are shared with suburban dailies, meaning less than 50 per cent household penetration over most of the circulation area. In order to compete with the Post Office's 100 per cent household coverage, the newspaper resorts to total market coverage tactics such as giving away a free sheet (plus coupon inserts) to households which do not subscribe to the daily or Sunday newspaper.

The newspaper is thus placed in the uncomfortable position of delivering a paid-for newspaper to one house but a free sheet to the house next door; the newspaper also faces the embarrassing prospect of being seen primarily as a deliverer of advertising, with news as an optional extra. The US Postal Service may be the butt of many jokes, but to newspaper industry managers and lawyers, the Post Office looks like a formidable adversary.

Newspapers are also heavily affected by a second regulatory body, the FCC. The AT&T settlement recognized newspapers' fears and lobbying by forbidding AT&T from entering the electronic Yellow Page business for seven years. But in the long run there will be a whole range of electronic services which could carry advertising, and the FCC has become involved in such issues. As the great deregulator of the electronic media, the FCC can also seem to the newspaper world as the advocate of new technologies which are hungry for life-giving advertising revenues.

SATELLITE DEREGULATION = US NATIONAL PRESS

The deregulation of satellites in the early 1970s has made possible the emergence of a national daily press. Satellite distribution to regional printing centers is radically cheaper and more efficient than the previous terrestrial technology. Thus the new electronic technologies which have indirectly played a part in the drift to local daily monopoly are now helping to provide national competition for those local monopolies.

The *Wall Street Journal* was the pioneer in satellite distribution, which it began to use in 1974. It had printed a separate western edition in San Francisco since 1929, and this edition was separately set over a teletypesetter system. Gradually the *Wall Street Journal* increased its number of regional printings and its total sales. But the introduction of satellites speeded up the existing nationwide expansion. In 1977 it was already printing in 10 plants; 6 new printing plants were introduced in 1981–2 – in Ohio, Pennsylvania, Iowa, Texas, Georgia and North Carolina – bringing the total to 17, and soon taking the circulation to over 2 million.[6]

Second into this satellite game was the *New York Times*: in 1984, with sales around one million, it opened its fifth sub-printing plant in Austin, Texas, to add to four others in northern and southern California, Chicago and Florida.

More dramatic, and potentially the most significant in terms of possibly confirming the trend to a national daily press, was the launch, also via satellite, of *USA Today* in the fall of 1982. This was no satellite distribution of an established New York publication. *USA Today* was a publication born for the space age. It was not designed for the elite audiences of the *Wall Street Journal* and the *New York Times*; it was designed to sell initially from street boxes, and to look unlike any other paper. It succeeded in this with color printing of high technical quality, used with editorial flamboyance. *USA Today* is edited to be read in all states; its weather and its sports reporting are acknowledged to be outstanding. Its numerous charts and graphs assume that readers are numerate. The stories are brief. The most remarkable aspect is the launching of such a massive and risky enterprise with the certainty of huge early losses. Losses of the order of $100 million per year were made possible by monopoly, Gannett's chain of (then) 87 small dailies.

An interesting addition to the satellite club is the *Christian Science Monitor*, with four regional plants now converted to satellite technology.[7]

But *USA Today* is the key case because it illustrates the enormous determination and effort required to succeed in such a venture. This was no cautious rollout to a series of regional elites, stock market investors and exiled New Yorkers. *USA Today* faced horrendous problems in all main departments. Editorially it was aiming to use a style familiar in newsmagazines but unknown in dailies; in terms of sales, its inevitably thinly spread and fluctuating readership was a nightmare, compared with delivery to every second house in a few selected suburbs. Above all, *USA Today* was certain to have advertising problems, because there is no established supply of mass-market daily newspaper advertising, and a daily lacks the 'shelf life' and solidity of a weekly newsmagazine.[8]

Such a paper, if and when it becomes a success, may be a mammoth one. With a sale of several million, all the above minuses will become pluses, imitators will follow, and advertising will be plentiful. But several hundred million dollars will have been invested, illustrating that, though satellite transmission itself may be cheap, the overall exercise of a popular American national daily is a task beyond all but the very richest newspaper chains.

Moreover, 'popular' may be a misnomer. *USA Today* made a decision to go to a sale price of 50 cents in late 1985. This is not a popular paper in the old tabloid or European sense. It is much more of a daily newsmagazine aimed primarily at 'baby boomers' born in the 1950s and 1960s and belonging to the top half of the population in income and education.

UPI'S DECLINE

UPI's decline can be traced back at least two decades,[9] and the death of UPI was predicted by this author in 1979. If the efforts to revive UPI ultimately fail, it will leave AP as the only American general news agency, thus raising the century-old issue of AP monopoly; this would be an embarrassing outcome for the US at home, and even more so abroad.

UPI's problems are well known. The most basic difficulty lies in the decline of newspaper competition. Typical American cities used to have competing ownerships which took competing news agency services. By 1980 both AP and UPI distributed their services via satellite into dish antennae at the newspaper's plant; and both also transmitted over these satellite facilities the numerous specialized supplemental services now available. UPI was thus carrying some of the very services that were threatening its life.

American newspapers, as well as local radio and TV stations, are still enormously dependent on agency news, not only for national and international events, but also for intrastate news. But this need is now largely met by AP, whose new computer technology spews 1,200 words per minute into newsrooms across the land. The service is much more sophisticated than in the past: wire editors can now choose from their screen which stories to receive and which to reject, and there are many more specialist and feature stories available.

AP is a cooperative controlled by the US newspapers, and it has always been regarded as the more accurate and indispensable of the news services. UPI was owned by Scripps–Howard until 1982, when it was finally sold after many years of losing money. Both AP and UPI were relatively slow to respond to the new possibilities of diversification into electronic data. The British agency Reuters had pioneered in this field throughout the 1970s, and by the early 1980s had surpassed AP in revenues to become a new sort of financial data agency. It was not so much direct competition from Reuters as AP's response to Reuters' moves which gradually eroded UPI's position. Less dramatically than Reuters, AP nevertheless succeeded in steadily diversifying into a wide range of mainly financial news services in league with the Dow Jones/*Wall Street Journal* company; these two, with Telerate, also have plans to compete more actively against Reuters for the lush international market for on-screen financial data. Whereas AP in 1983 for the first time received less than half its revenue from its member US newspapers,[10] UPI's cutbacks have led to its discarding most of its diversification efforts. In 1984 it sold its international picture service to Reuters, which had been considering buying up the whole of UPI for several years.

While UPI was losing abroad, it was also losing at home, as a more aggressive AP has followed Reuters' lead. AP had increasingly dominated agency news service to all the larger groups and newspapers. Between 1976 and 1984, AP's 'member' newspapers went from 70 to 90 per cent of US daily circulation.[11]

THE PRESS BIG TEN CONSOLIDATE

In recent years some 10 organizations have come increasingly to dominate all aspects of the American press. These are:

1 AP, the main carrier of news;
2 Time Inc, much the biggest magazine company with three of the six financially leading publications – *Time*, *People* and *Sports Illustrated*;
3 Knight–Ridder, owner of four major dailies in Miami, Detroit, San Jose and Philadelphia;
4 Gannett, owner of the biggest chain of small dailies plus *USA Today*;
5 Times–Mirror, owner of *Los Angeles Times* and major dailies in Denver, Dallas and Long Island;
6 Advance (Newhouse), a big group of mainly small dailies and big magazines;
7 Tribune, the *Chicago Tribune* group, also owners of the New York *Daily News* and the *Daily News* of northwest Los Angeles;
8 The *New York Times* group;

9 Dow Jones, owners of the *Wall Street Journal* and various financial
   data services;
10 The *Washington Post* group, also owners of *Newsweek*.

These 10 press organizations are steadily increasing their economic
and political power. While television may elect the president, these
organizations dominate the overall news system which is the lifeblood of
Congress, government and politics. The 10 organizations have indeed
diversified into broadcasting and cable, and their growth there plus their
growth within the press exceeds the very slow comparative decline of
the press.

These 10 organizations dominate the press financially. Most of them
in 1985 had annual revenues above $1 billion, and the larger ones were
pushing past $2 billion. In 1984, a banner year for the press, Gannett,
despite its *USA Today* losses, had net earnings of $224 million on
revenue of $1.96 billion.

Overall, these big ten of the press are exposed to only moderate
amounts of competition. The Tribune group, which experiences tough
competition from Murdoch's News America in both New York and
Chicago, is an exception. Both the *Washington Post* and the *Los
Angeles Times* have the perfect situation of direct competition from a
commercially feeble opponent – the *Washington Times* and the *Los
Angeles Herald Examiner*, respectively.[12] Even in relatively competitive
New York, the *New York Times* has no direct competition as a
heavyweight general metropolitan daily.

There is a somewhat clublike quality about these 10 press groups, and
one of its expressions is the disdain heaped on Rupert Murdoch's
relatively modest excursions into old-time competitive slugging. There
are many cooperative ventures, both of a general and of a particular
nature. These organizations have at last agreed on advertising standards
which allow a uniform advertising agency insertion into any daily paper.
They jointly dominate, and partly own, AP.

The *Los Angeles Times* and *Washington Post* jointly operate a news
service which goes to over 200 dailies, mainly just below the largest size.
This service includes material from the two principals' junior partner
dailies, from the *Guardian* (London) and from the French and German
national news agencies – in fact nearly all the material a medium-sized
daily needs in addition to AP. The *New York Times* has a similarly widely
used syndication service. The top 10 together with AP, indirectly through
their syndication and directly via their own local and satellite sales,
dominate the entire news flow in the US.

These organizations together own all the leading publications, including *Time* and *Newsweek* (one remaining area of real, if imitative,

competition). They are located in all the major cities, and between them dominate the flow of news out of these cities. Individual papers, notably the *Los Angeles Times* and *New York Times*, are also the dominant news voices affecting the state politics of the largest states in the union.

The slow but steady advance of these big 10 organizations can be seen in three important areas. First, when a prestige publication comes up for sale – not the losing competitor daily which Rupert Murdoch usually pursues – these groups are the leading prospective purchasers. For example, in 1985 the *Des Moines Register* was sold; this paper has often been listed as one of the 10 best in the US, is internationally known as a voice of the farmbelt, and, as the only paper which sells in all 99 counties of Iowa, its national political importance has increased with Iowa's recent prominence as an 'early' state in presidential elections. The bidding was carried on by the Tribune Company, the *Washington Post* company and Hearst (trying hard to retrieve its former status in the top 10). And the winner was Gannett, which paid $200 million, nearly twice Dow Jones's opening offer. Later in 1985 Gannett also bought the 667,000 daily circulation *Detroit News*, the tenth largest US daily sale; this raised Gannett's total daily sale to 5.5 million.[13]

A second obvious area of continuing expansion is the data business. Dow Jones, in various permutations with the *Wall Street Journal* and AP, is easily the leading supplier of news/data/financial information on screens. The leading videotex experimenters are Knight–Ridder and Times–Mirror.

Third, there are the US news organizations which operate abroad – the *Wall Street Journal* now has Asian and European printings. Members of this club control the *International Herald Tribune*; the *New York Times* and the *Los Angeles Times/Washington Post* services sell around the world; and the news-based data bank business is also led on the world scene by Dow Jones.

THE FUTURE OF THE PRESS

We will return to some of the political and regulatory issues surrounding the press, news, and the First Amendment, in the concluding section of the book.

But clearly this $30-billion-revenue industry (in 1984) is far from dead, and is destined to remain a key player on the information and communications playing field.

Notes

1 Leo Bogart, *Press and Public* (1981), pp. 56–7.
2 'Newspapers: Studying Sunday Successes', *Advertising Age*, 24 January 1985, pp. 13–43.

3 'Analysis of newspaper performance', *Editor and Publisher*, 5 January 1985, p. 20.
4 Randy Brubaker, 'The Newspaper Preservation Act' (1982).
5 John Curley, 'Globe Democrat's fate to be decided at meeting today', *Wall Street Journal*, 9 January 1984. Michael Asikoff, 'Gluck trying to spin Globe into safe orbit in St Louis', *Washington Post*, 29 January 1984, pp. G1-2. B. G. Yovovich, 'Media's mystery whiz kid', *Advertising Age*, 3 May 1984, pp. M6-7.
6 Jerry M. Rosenberg, *Inside The Wall Street Journal* (1982), pp. 214-25.
7 'Adapting to Satellites', *Editor and Publisher*, 13 October 1984, p. 38.
8 John Morton, 'USA Today's Ad-versity', *Washington Journalism Review*, September 1984, p. 18.
9 Oliver Boyd Barrett, *The International News Agencies* (1980).
10 Vernon A. Guidry, 'Minding the wire; Lou Boccardi and the Associated Press', *Washington Journalism Review*, May 1984, pp. 21-8, 56.
11 'Fuller turns over the reins', *Editor and Publisher*, 5 January 1985, pp. 44, 55.
12 The *Herald Examiner*'s circulation in 1984 was 22 per cent that of the *Los Angeles Times*, but the *Herald Examiner*'s share of advertising would have been considerably smaller.
13 'A big bucks deal', *Editor and Publisher*, 9 February 1985, pp. 12-13. Laura Landro, 'Allen Neuharth's Urge to Merge Aggrandizes Gannett's Operations', *Wall Street Journal* (Europe) 13 September 1985, pp. 1, 8.

PART IV

Hyperactive Policy Fragmentation, DC

16

Introduction

In subsequent pages the Washington politics of deregulation are directly confronted, and the separate policymaking activities of five major areas of Washington power are considered: the administration in power in the White House, Congress, the courts, the relevant federal agencies – primarily the FCC – and the lobbies.

Policymaking is fragmented between – and also within – these five areas. Within each, a policy has to pass through a number of stages, votes or decisions. To emerge from the 'administration', a decision in fact needs to pass through several agencies – for example, Commerce, State and Defense – before winning approval at several points within the White House. Similarly, there are multiple stages within Congress – several subcommittees and main committees in both the House and the Senate before either body can vote; then reconciliation of rival versions. In the courts, major cases can, and usually do, drag on for years, passing from federal district court to US Court of Appeals to the US Supreme Court. In the FCC area there is also a multistage process, in which elements of both the administrative/bureaucratic and the judicial processes are combined; from an initial FCC 'Notice of Inquiry' to a final FCC rule-making can, and often does, take several years. Fifth, the 'lobby' arena is itself very far from simple; there are many lobbies both between different industries and within single industries. The telephone lobby is engaged both in civil warfare within the telephone business and in warfare against, for example, the broadcasting and/or cable interests.

There are many ways of counting exactly how many stages or votes or decisions are involved in establishing a new communications policy; but the number is somewhere between a dozen and a hundred, depending on the case and the method of counting. Policymaking fragmentatation is reflected in many things, including a tendency for descriptive metaphors to become mixed, if not mangled. But imagery such as a horse race with many jumps or numerous bites at an apple (any one bite being enough to stop a new measure) is referring to the same thing.

Given this basic Washington system, there are two major types of generalization or theory about what drives Washington policymaking –

a pluralist view of several contending forces, or a view which sees one branch or area of government as predominant. In Washington politics generally, this issue surfaces in arguments about presidential versus congressional supremacy. In communications politics the issue also surfaces in arguments about FCC supremacy. For example, it was often argued in the decades following its birth in 1934 that the FCC, via its close relationship with AT&T, RCA and a few other companies, dominated US communications policy.

COMMUNICATIONS POLICY AS AN ENDLESS BELT

The Politics of Broadcast Regulation has become an established work in its field, and has sold well on college campuses. At the time of publication of its third edition, in 1982, the senior author, Erwin Krasnow, was the popular and able general counsel of the NAB. This study takes a pluralist/functionalist view, in which broadcast regulation is said to be determined by six entities – the FCC, industry, citizens' groups, the courts, the White House and, last but not least, Congress.

While an instructive and useful introduction, the Krasnow study, however, is inadequate and mistaken in its general conclusions. It focuses on case studies; although some of these follow issues through 15 or more years of evolution, they are collectively misleading, nevertheless. The case studies focus too heavily on a medium time-frame, and the 1982 edition concentrates too heavily on the 1970s; it thus overestimates the long-run importance of citizens' groups (most of whose 1970s achievements were already being rapidly unravelled by 1982). This edition also underplays several other major trends already evident by 1982 – for example, it underplays the revolutionary extent of *technological* change, the comprehensive nature of *regulation*, the radical (and often unanticipated) consequences of *market* openings, and it almost entirely ignores the *internationalization* of communications and of communications policymaking. Arguably these trends were less dramatic in broadcasting than elsewhere, but this raises the issue of whether broadcasting policy can any longer be understood apart from its telecommunications context.

The Krasnow approach of focusing on four or five case studies within broadcasting only has the unfortunate effect of arbitrarily narrowing its vision, and thus losing the crucial broadening-out of the communications playing field. This approach also leads to a false historical perspective. Policymaking is seen as a number of separate cases in which various parties, including citizens' groups, have their say and exercise their share of influence.

But communications policymaking needs to be seen in a wider context, and in a longer historical time-frame. The deregulatory efforts of around 1980 need to be seen as part of a century-long regulatory struggle – as Thomas McGraw, the Harvard business school historian, sees them in his *Prophets of Regulation*.

Rather than as a series of separate case studies, communications policymaking should perhaps be seen as an endless belt, something which goes on all the time, and whose endlessness and ever increasing breadth ensures that those with the greatest breadth and depth of resources and expertise will succeed.

LOBBY VERSUS LOBBY: THE KEY STRUGGLE

In the opinion of this author, the lobbies have nearly always been the key determinant of communications policy. The initials AT&T, ITT, RCA, CBS, ABC and IBM are all better known to the American public than FCC – and this public perception corresponds to the reality. Indeed, it follows from a broadly *commercial* system that the forces of commerce must be in the lead. And this deliberate emphasis in the US system has been further underlined by deregulation.

However, both US communications tradition and the recent deregulatory emphasis on marketplace competition not only point toward lobbies as the key locus of power, but also provide for a contest between lobbies. Recent telephone policy has largely consisted of a battle between AT&T, the dominant *provider* of telephone sevice, and the rest of big business, the leading *users* of telephone service. Broadcasting policy has largely consisted in recent years of a battle between the television industry and cable interests.

The intermingling of political, technological and market forces, so characteristic of recent communications policymaking, favors the commercial lobbies. A basic strength of industrial lobbies is that they operate on a continuing basis in all relevant spheres; they not only respond to technological change, but actually fund and create such change; they operate in the marketplace; they pursue their interests through the administration, Congress and the FCC by lobbying and negotiating, and they employ expensive teams of lawyers who, on a continuing basis, beaver away in the courts at lobbying by litigation.

It is also the commercial interests which are redrawing the boundaries and the communications map itself. But this redrawing and redefinition, which further exacerbate existing fragmentation between Washington agencies, in practice involves the policy world's acceptance of new industry definitions.

The increasing complexity of technological, financial and market detail also derives from commercial interests, and poses problems of understanding in all three branches of government; politicians and aides in the White House, the State Department or Congress, inevitably appear amateurish, short-term and internally fragmented when confronted by industry spokesmen and experts. Judges, normally untrained in technology or economics, and usually well past the first flush of youth, are inevitably aware of their own lack of expertise. And even the supposedly technically expert agency the FCC has to spread its nearly 2,000 personnel over so many areas that its experts in the relevant fields tend to be younger, less qualified, less experienced – and especially far less numerous – than the industry experts.

Of course, each branch of government develops some depth of expertise and professional talent. But the relevant senior White House personnel and the senior communications office-holders in administration agencies were replaced several times during the Nixon–Ford–Carter–Reagan era of deregulation. In Congress, the House Telecommunications Subcommittee, for example, developed some real expertise, but this was quite fragilely based upon a handful of able young subcommittee staffers.

Certain judges and certain courts in Washington also develop some expertise, but this is limited. And at the FCC, while files bulge with massive documentation, many of the key personnel, including the commissioners themselves, opt for the Washington revolving door, often after remarkably brief stays.

INTERNATIONALIZATION OF POLICY

Communications policymaking has long been heavily influenced by international considerations, and US communications foreign policy has in turn been heavily influenced by the major commercial interests. For example, US delegations engaged at the ITU in Geneva in negotiating with national telecoms authorities from other countries, have in fact consisted mainly of AT&T personnel.

For many decades, new communications technologies in the US have been boosted in their early years in line with a consensual national goal of communications superiority. The Washington-supported booms in canals, railroads and the electric telegraph established a tradition which, in the twentieth century with radio, took on a sharper focus of strategic interest and would-be superiority. And in consequence the railroad frenzy has been followed by radio, film, talkie, telephone, television and other frenzies. The US tendency toward lavish early expenditure, leading to overcapacity but also world leadership, is evident in space, domestic satellites, and the massive efforts involved in US-led under-ocean fiber-optic cables seem likely to cause over-capacity by the late 1980s.

The increasingly international nature of communications policy has many aspects, one of the least ambiguous of which is the superiority of major multinational companies in these areas, when compared with Washington agencies. International communications policy is the full-time task of only a few dozen government employees in Washington and not a single FCC commissioner. In contrast, IBM alone employs 100,000 people in Europe.

THE LOBBIES CONTEND, WASHINGTON REFEREES

Washington policymaking in general, and perhaps communications policymaking in particular, tends toward the model of a legal argument between competing lobbies which is fought out before a succession of other lawyers engaged in various judicial and quasi-judicial roles.

Thus a bill before Congress may be bitterly contested through numerous committee and subcommittee sessions, but the contest tends to be between two or more lobbies while the congressional committee members sit in judgement and from time to time deliver majority verdicts on contentious clauses. Similarly, the various executive branch agencies, as well as the various offices within the White House, deliver their verdicts after being lobbied by the same lobbying teams. Something rather similar happens at the FCC, which has its own quasi-judicial procedures, and where the commissioners ultimately deliver their own majority verdict. And of course the courts are often involved, too, with a real judge or judges again choosing between legally deployed lobbies; here it is especially clear that the judge/referees have little knowledge of their own and require the material supplied by one lobby as the wherewithal for investigating the competing lobby.

Sometimes the lobbies may be foreign interests – either a single country such as Japan or many foreign governments lobbying on behalf of INTELSAT or UNESCO. On other occasions the lobbies are actually politicians or public appointees, such as the cities, mayors and local utility commissioners involved in the battles against the cable trade associations, which is what led to the cable legislation of 1984.

Whatever the lobby, the lobbying process is much the same. Most lobbies are either trade associations or single companies, and their tools are teams of their own lawyers, reinforced for various specialist purposes from the Washington law factories, and backed up by further platoons of consultants, economists, market researchers, public relations personnel, PACs and direct mailings to the constituents of key 'referees'. Most of all, lobbying involves stamina, insight and judgement, which in turn means money.

17

White House Stealth, Administrative Fragmentation

The last US president to pursue communications policy with vigor was Nixon, but his often farsighted telecommunications policies were sunk by his attack on the media during the Watergate era of 1973–4.

Subsequent presidents seem to have drawn the conclusion that communications policymaking is a trap to be avoided, a White House no-go area. Thus communications deregulation during the Ford, Carter and Reagan presidencies took place with only passive acquiesence from the White House. And this partly explains the slow and haphazard evolution of deregulation in communications, which has depended upon a consensus slowly emerging from turf warfare between numerous outposts of Washington power.

Other governments in the Western world experience somewhat similar problems of fragmentation; this cannot be avoided entirely, because communications cuts across so many potentially conflicting goals and interests of government – publicity and secrecy, commerce and culture, defense and diplomacy, high technology and free trade.

All these common democratic dilemmas are also present in the US, but there they tend to take on an extreme form, not least because the US has traditionally seen communications as of unique importance. The First Amendment to the US Constitution inhibits media policy in general and press legislation in particular. The media are even more jealously observed by US than by other democratic politicians, because of their exceptional dominance in election campaigns. The role of government is unusually weak, and the role of commercial interests unusually strong in telecommunications, and this also inhibits policy-making.

Throughout the twentieth century, the US attempted to be the world leader, especially in all aspects of radio and other electronic communication. In addition, the special importance of defense spending (and within defense of communications) has made the Pentagon more salient in communications policy than are its equivalents in Europe.

The inevitable rivalry over communications power takes place within a system which in any case gives special emphasis to the separation of powers; moreover, the Nixon legacy means that the common method of resolving Washington rivalries – a strong presidential initiative leading to a deal with Congress – is not available.

These tendencies toward extreme fragmentation were further exacerbated under President Reagan. It has become ever more evident that communications, old and new, dominate elections, electoral finance and, increasingly, politics itself. Moreover, communications is ever more evidently the number one industry in the US and the world; consequently, not only does every elected politician covet its plants in his constituency, but at least twenty agencies in Washington contend to be number one in at least some aspects of America's number one political and industrial activity. The turf fights are about something which is real: the turf in question is strategic. Meanwhile, the incumbent in the White House was not only another Californian conservative Republican, especially reluctant to evoke any echoes of Nixon, he was also the first authentic media president – a Hollywood actor, who quickly in 1981 showed great communicator skills in winning congressional votes. As such, he was naturally reluctant to adopt an aggressive stance which could have led to his being dubbed the Citizen Kane or Louis B. Mayer of communications policy.

The White House in fact has considerable powers, especially in being able to make key appointments in most of the relevant policy agencies. These powers, according to a list drawn up at the time of Reagan's 1980 election, include the following:

(1) The White House can initiate legislation to rewrite or to amend the 1934 Communications Act.

(2) It can quietly exert pressure on the FCC.

(3) The president nominates all the members of the FCC and the top officials of the main federal departments involved in communications policy, such as Justice, State, Commerce and Defense. The president also nominates the relevant judges at all three levels – federal district courts, courts of appeal, and the US Supreme Court.

(4) The White House has a close involvement in defense and internal security aspects of telecommunications.

(5) The White House usually has a close relationship with the Office of the Trade Representative in the Executive Office of the President – on, for example, the issue of telecommunications trade and the Japanese electronics challenge.

(6) Through its control of economic policy and through other bodies such as the President's Council of Economic Advisers, the White House can push general policies such as deregulation, as well as more specific policies such as cable deregulation.

(7) Finally, the White House is a key user of telecommunications and broadcasting.[1]

President Reagan, predictably, chose to use most of these powers with caution, if not stealth. His major initiative was in making appointments – at the Cabinet level, to key second-level positions (for example, within the Commerce Department) and to the regulatory agencies, especially the FCC and FTC. These appointments gave overwhelming preference to people with right-wing – and highly deregulatory – views; but this did not attract special attention, since such appointments normally reflect a president's ideological position.

The general White House oversight of economic and budgetary policy was also important. Especially significant here was the salience given to the OMB under David Stockman. Although to some supply-siders Stockman was a highly placed traitor, his role as the regulator of the regulators led to a reduction in the federal funds going to communications policy in the early Reagan presidency.[2] The FCC, the FTC and the National Telecommunications and Information Administration (NTIA) in the Department of Commerce all suffered from Stockman's fierce budget-cutting. This budget-cutting was a powerful encouragement to deregulation: agencies solved the problem of covering a growing territory with a shrinking staff by simply abolishing some of their previous tasks.

These budget cuts were identified with Stockman, however, and were not peculiar to communications policy. They were part of the budgetary/ financial frenzy of 1981, and were perhaps the most overt White House involvement in communications policy. The cuts policy also extended to international organizations, and was one factor leading to US withdrawal from UNESCO at the end of 1984.

Meanwhile President Reagan's own overt and ideological interventions in communications policy were confined to occasional lapses, in areas which did not carry major political risks. On two occasions in 1984, he vetoed the authorization for the Corporation for Public Broadcasting. On another occasion, in 1983, he intervened on the side of Hollywood and against the TV networks on the syndication issue. He also pressed successfully for big increases in the budget of the United States Information Agency (USIA), and put old California friend Charles Wick in charge there.

On the big issues – the divestiture of AT&T, the 'freeing' of IBM, the deregulation of radio and TV and cable legislation – Reagan kept a low profile. Nevertheless, this low profile included White House approval for the Justice Department actions on AT&T and IBM. It also allowed the deregulatory running to be made by the Republican appointees in the federal agencies and by the Republican leadership in the Senate.

CONFLICTING GOALS: STRATEGIC, TRADE, DEREGULATION

One of the consequences of this deliberately low-profile performance by the White House was that the consensus goal of deregulation continued to cut across a wide range of other goals, agencies and turf. This was most evident in the sphere of *international* communications policy, because the White House carries the main responsibility for coordinating domestic and foreign policy, and because previous international communications policy initiatives, such as the Kennedy space policy, were achieved by vigorous White House leadership. But both Carter and Reagan made little or no attempt to resolve the conflicts between strategic (Pentagon), diplomatic (State Department) and trade (Commerce Department) goals.

Under the first Reagan administration, an additional small unit was set up within the State Department to deal with communications policy. The head of this unit was Diana Lady Dougan, and her official titles were revealing – 'Ambassador' and 'Coordinator for International Communication and Information Policy'. This was the official place to go for a statement on the goals of external communications policy, which, according to Dougan, were to:

1 promote an environment in which ideas and information can flow more freely among nations;
2 ensure the continued technological and economic strength and leadership of the US in this field;
3 ensure our national security and strategic communication capabilities;
4 encourage international commerce of all kinds through the efficient and innovative use of communication resources; and
5 expand the information access and communications capabilities of developing countries.

Regarding how these goals may be reached, Dougan has this to say: 'These objectives can be most effectively achieved by relying whenever possible on free enterprise, competition and free trade with a minimum of direct government regulation.'[3] This rather confused set of policies – some pursued with belligerence, others quietly suggested as being the wave of the future – might also drawn attention to a final, but key, paradox in US communications policy: that it was the policy of the US to export not merely communications goods, services and images, but also communications policies. US communications policy involved a delicate balancing act – persuading other nations that deregulation was beneficial to them as well as to the US.

Meanwhile there were two major foci of communications policy even within the State Department: first, the Office of International Communications Policy (in the Bureau of Economic and Business Affairs); and second, Diana Dougan's 'Co-ordinator' office, reporting to the under secretary for security assistance, science and technology. Obviously the military uses of communications interest the US Department of Defense, which is a heavy user of AT&T's long lines, as well as of the space shuttle. And other Washington agencies, notably the National Security Agency (NSA), are at the forefront of the computer/telecoms revolution. NSA was said to have a budget of around $10 billion a year even at the start of the Reagan administration.[4] The NSA, CIA, NASA, COMSAT and DOD have made the Washington beltway the Silicon Valley of military high tech.

The most notorious example of DOD involvement in civilian high tech was of course its fierce opposition to 'strategic' high-tech exports to the Soviet Union. The DOD managed to block the export of many categories of computers and other high-tech equipment which could have defense applications. Some critics complain that this went absurdly far.

A former US ambassador to Sweden has said that, even in the Carter years, about half his time was taken up with issues of technology transfer. He is very skeptical about sanctions, however, and offers these reasons as to why the US attempt to stop the USSR–Western Europe gas pipeline was inept:

> The reasons are easy to see: (a) our demands quite literally are taken as interference in the internal affairs of allies and trading partners; (b) our position is severely undercut by our insistence that we be allowed to continue grain sales to the Russians; and (c) there are serious doubts by both academic and business leaders, despite official reports that the problem is actually severe enough to warrant the restriction of exchange of scientific issues or the free exchange of manufactured goods. One aspect of the overall effect of this is that we have managed to do to our alliance what the Soviets could not accomplish – help fracture it and subject it to the worst strains since World War II.[5]

While the DOD has tried to pay attention to some of the worst and most annoying details of its highly un-deregulatory policies (with some relaxations in early 1985), new high-tech challenges keep appearing. For example, it has become possible to send computer software over conventional voice/data telecommunications facilities. So the DOD decided that it would have to 'listen in' – by setting up computer tracking arrangements – on entire categories of overseas telecommunications traffic. This DOD decision, which became widely known in Washington in 1983–4, naturally caused some embarrassment in the Department of State, whose diplomats found such listening in not exactly in line with their goal of free flow. And although State agreed to a compromise with Defense, some such monitoring is certainly in place.[6]

The US government subsidizes the high tech/computer/telecoms field on a massive scale. If aircraft, navy, military space, NASA, NSA and AT&T electronics defense expenditures are combined, they must run into tens of billions of dollars per year. Clearly this expenditure in pursuit of military and intelligence leadership is known to West Europeans, Brazilians and Japanese, and does not encourage them to accept US criticisms of 'subsidies' and 'nontariff trade barriers'.

Why has Japan been allowed to operate what most Americans regard as a protectionist policy at home, while exporting massive quantities of electronics and other hardware to the open markets of its trade partners? Part of the explanation must be strategic: the Washington perception that it is better to let Japan dump goods in the West rather than trade heavily with the USSR and China. Thus one of the main beneficiaries of AT&T divestment has been Japanese industry.

Such is the vagueness of the goals and so great is the contention between different agencies that examples can be quoted to support almost any thesis. Many projects combine several goals. For example, NASA in the Reagan years had the three goals of scientific research, commercial operation for profit and secret defense work; and these different goals seemed to have been combined with at least some success in the space shuttle. But other cases, notably DOD-inspired restrictions on strategic exports, have merely convinced even ideologically friendly politicians in other countries that military arguments were being used as a cover for US commercial objectives.

CONFLICTING AGENCIES: COMMERCE AND STATE

The overall declared Reagan policy was to cut bureaucracy in Washington. The larger economic departments – Treasury, Transport and Agriculture – all wielded much more clout than did the small Department of Commerce. Within Commerce, the NTIA itself was one of the weaker sections, and thus suffered even greater cuts. Many of the expert communications staff were either fired or left the NTIA to go to other government agencies or into private practice and industry. Those who remained found that the new head of the NTIA was to be a certain Bernard Wunder, who had an appropriate track record as a senior Republican aide to the Senate Commerce Committee, but who as an administrator was a failure.

Wunder resigned early in 1983, but not before the General Accounting Office (congressional watchdog/auditing body) had produced a critical report on the NTIA. One element of miniscandal in the GAO report indicated President Reagan's real assessment of the NTIA's importance. A senior official from the NTIA, the GAO reported, had accompanied President Reagan on two trips to his California ranch in the summer of 1982. The senior official in question, Dennis LeBlanc, was a former policeman and had been a member of Reagan's bodyguard when he was California's governor; as such he had contributed valuable handiwork around the Reagan ranch. After Reagan's victory, LeBlanc had joined the White House staff and then been given a $58,000 job at the NTIA. However, the GAO discovered that when LeBlanc accompanied the president to the Santa Barbara ranch, there were no discussions of NTIA or communications policy. LeBlanc admitted that his duties continued to be the performance of any chores the president asked him to do around the ranch.

The Wunder period at the NTIA lasted less than two years. Policy activity was minimal; for example, the NTIA's filings with the FCC were down from 80 in 1980 to only 11 in 1981. The main activity seems to have been people walking out of the door.

The Bernie Wunder shambles may at last have been seen in the White House as something which needed attention. The next appointment as head of the NTIA was David Markey; confirmed by the Senate only in July 1983, Markey quickly reversed the rapid decline of the NTIA and reestablished it as indeed the main administration focus of communications policy. A list of some of Markey's activities in his first year makes the point. Under Markey, the NTIA supported the idea of competition for INTELSAT, opposed the 'universal service' phone legislation but was also critical of the FCC access charge decision, took part in ITU meetings on ISDN, supported the Senate (but not the House) cable deregulation bill, took an active interest in the cable–telco issue, favored the House Tauke–Tauzin broadcast deregulation bill, and initially argued for the networks and the FCC, and against Hollywood, on financial interest/syndication. Markey also successfully beefed up the NTIA's performance in international communications, and got some NTIA budget cuts restored.[7]

Nevertheless, NTIA/Commerce, while supposedly in charge of domestic communications policy, still had to contend with the FCC, whose responsibilities for regulation had in fact also increasingly led it into policy areas. And in international communications policy NTIA/Commerce confronted the State Department.

International communications policy has been the central task of only a handful of people in Washington. And a major, if not *the* major, activity of these people in both 1983 and 1984 seemed to involve a turf war as to their own responsibilities and powers.

One turf war was fought with the State Department and Commerce as the principal protagonists. Since the Carter administration, the position has been that the Commerce Department is the principal agency dealing with communications, including its foreign aspects; but that on matters of purely international communications, the foreign policy agency, the State Department, must be supreme. These arrangements continued into the Reagan years until it was decided to expand the State Department effort; in May 1983 Diana Dougan began work as the coordinator for international communication and information policy. This amounted to little more than adding a few people to the section of State which had previously carried these responsibilities. Dougan was executive secretary to the Senior Interagency Group (or SIG) on international communications and information policy. Chairman of this committee was William Schneider, under secretary for security assistance, science and technology at State. Represented on SIG were:

Department of Commerce (NTIA)
Bureau for International Broadcasting
OMB
USIA
National Security Council
Department of State
NASA
DOD
US Trade Representative
Agency for International Development (part of State)
Office of Science and Technology Policy
CIA
the FCC, as an observer

The main conflict appeared to be between Schneider and Dougan at State, and Commerce Department Secretary Malcolm Baldridge and NTIA boss David Markey, but there was certainly conflict within the State Department too. The turf war also reflected other enduring features of the Washington landscape. There was an element of House versus Senate. Dante Fascell, chairman of the House Foreign Relations Committee, was a strong advocate of a strong State Department lead in this field. Fascell had long pressed this view, and the Dougan appointment was a watered-down version of his demands. But the Fascell view was actively opposed by Senator Barry Goldwater, who had introduced legislation (S.999) calling for an Office of Special Representative in the executive office of the President – a new, more narrowly defined version of the old Nixon OTP. There were yet other congressional champions for yet other bureaucratic solutions: John Dingell and Timothy Wirth both wanted responsibility to go to the Commerce Department, where, of course, it would just happen to fall under the purview of their House committee and subcommittee. Needless to say, Senator Packwood was not without a solution that would just happen to give him a more direct role – indeed, it would have shared executive control with Congress.

A further indication that this was a power play involving the entire communications policy establishment was the lack of any clear differences on policy between State and Commerce; they fought on several current issues – INTELSAT, COMSAT and training for telecommunications development – but their positions differed very little. The conflict was punctuated by agreements in 1983 and again in late 1984. But the White House used the Commerce–State dispute as an excuse for holding up for nearly two years a decision on licensing international telecoms competition with INTELSAT. And the Senate leadership in 1984 used the dispute as an excuse for keeping the Dougan office in State understaffed and underfunded.

At the same time, there was support in 1983 in the Senate Governmental Affairs Committee (Bill S.121) and elsewhere for a new Cabinet-level Department of Trade. This proposal has recurred in various forms for some years, and was brought up again in early 1985 by a presidential Commission on Industrial Competitiveness chaired by John Young. Some proposals merely call for a bringing together of Commerce and the US Trade Representative's Office. Other versions call for a Department of International Trade and Industry (DITI) modelled on the Japanese MITI. But the US has nothing comparable to the Japanese, or even the European, tradition of industrial policy. Moreover, the agency conflicts merely reflect Washington political realities, a confusing set of goals and a White House still conscious of the Nixon legacy.

OTP: NATIONAL TELECOMMUNICATIONS ACQUIRES A NIXON IMAGE

Even had Nixon's communications policy initiatives not become mixed in Watergate, there should certainly have been other difficulties. But Nixon's timing in setting up OTP in 1970 was good. There was a sense that the space policy momentum of the Kennedy period had been lost under Johnson, who, although strongly interested in space, was also (through his wife) the owner of a major TV station in Austin, Texas, and thus believed to favor the broadcasting status quo.

Nevertheless, Johnson set up a Task Force on Communications Policy in August 1967, which reported at the very end of his presidency in December 1968. Its chairman was Eugene Rostow, and the report suggested that there should be a single focus of policy in the executive branch, but left open its precise location.[8]

Nixon decided to establish such a focus, the OTP, and to locate it in the executive office of the president. It was in fact located for most of its life at 1880 G Street, a block away from the old executive office building. Most of OTP's functions were similar to those of its predecessor, the Office of Telecommunications Management: advising the president on telecommunications, coordinating the government's own telecommunications activities, allocating the government share of the radio frequency among government and commercial users. What was new in OTP, indicated in the change in its title from 'management' to 'policy', was that it was to become the spokesman for the executive branch in the broad area of policy formulation, and before Congress and the FCC. The OTP was to oversee both government and commercial telecommunications, and it had a specific duty to pursue long-range policy development.

The first director was Clay Whitehead, at the time only 31 years old. He held higher degrees in electrical engineering and management from MIT; he had worked in the Rand think tank in Santa Monica, and had been a White House aide from the start of the Nixon presidency in 1969. One of Whitehead's jobs in the White House had been to draw up a plan for the very office of which he then became director. The task thrust upon Whitehead was a difficult, if not impossible one: to formulate a national telecommunications policy with little help from others, and then to sell it to Congress, the FCC and, most important, President Nixon. Senator Pastore in effect acknowledged the immense difficulties, when, in hearings, he kept asking Whitehead how long it would take to present a new set of communications policies.

Late 1970 and all 1971 were a honeymoon period for the rather academic young man now placed on a political hotspot. Studies were initiated, mainly in telecommunications rather than mass media. Some commentators began to refer to Whitehead by titles such as 'czar without a czardom'. Similar skepticism came from State, Defense, the FCC and other agencies with communications powers. Although Whitehead made a habit of saying that he spoke with the authority of the president, Washington gossip asserted that Whitehead spoke largely for himself, although as one well acquainted with White House policies. But Whitehead lacked the experience and the top-level contacts in the White House that might have enabled him to breathe life into the senior policy-coordinator idea. He also lacked the policy proposals to take up a broad leadership role. His idea of the merging of mass communications and telecommunications was an avant-garde one for the time, and it did not translate easily into policy proposals. Whitehead's staff did begin to produce some research reports, however, especially on telecommunications.

Perhaps the high point of Whitehead's career was his chairmanship of a 1973–4 Cabinet Committee on Cable Television, which produced an early call for less regulation, and which anticipated much further thinking on cable. But to fulfil the initial Nixonian promise, Whitehead would have needed to produce a number of such reports, and to have seen them taken up by Congress and the FCC.

By 1972, OTP's honeymoon was over, mainly due to Whitehead's involvement in the White House campaign against the media. Most of Whitehead's ideas seem to have flowed from a set of conservative convictions parallel to those of Nixon. Moreover, Whitehead clearly regarded telecommunications policy as worthy of careful research, while he favored sweeping assertions and condemnation of the mass media. During 1972, the year of the presidential election and the Watergate break-in (June), Nixon pursued a policy of keeping the TV networks off balance. In April 1972 an antitrust suit was filed against the three TV networks by the Justice Department (under John Mitchell); this suit had been ready in 1970, and the timing was thus political.[9]

Clay Whitehead and the OTP became centrally involved in these tactics, which were fairly transparently designed to discourage network criticism of a president who was heading toward a re-election landslide in November. Less than two months before election day, Whitehead made a speech in San Francisco in which he supported the current Screen Actors' Guild position that the networks were carrying too many reruns of old TV shows. Whitehead's speech was based on a major study of the topic by OTP, but the threat remained clear: that the White House would support the employment arguments of the Hollywood unions in favor of more original production, which in turn would cut into network profits.[10]

It was in a speech in Indianapolis, a few weeks after the November 1972 reelection of Nixon, that Whitehead finally attracted the full force of anti-Nixon sentiment from both the networks and Capitol Hill. Paradoxically, the speech offered the networks the kind of deregulatory relaxation of constraints which they ultimately achieved only a decade later. Whitehead suggested the extension of TV licenses to five years (from three), called for provisions which could have made successful license challenges much more difficult, and demanded the prohibition of any FCC attempt to impose quantified standards for programming. However, Whitehead's speech also included passages of (then) Vice-President Agnew-style rhetoric, accusing the network news people of being an eastern liberal elite who dispensed gossip instead of news. The negative effect of such remarks on Whitehead's reputation in Congress was soon apparent. In February 1978 he was mercilessly grilled in Senate hearings by his former patron Senator Pastore. Similar views came loud and clear from the House, and the Indianapolis speech was denounced by the Democrat chairman of the House Communications Subcommittee.

The criticism was that Whitehead, having set out to launch a high-level national effort toward an agreed set of communications policy goals, had allowed himself to be used by President Nixon in his Watergate defensive skirmishes with the media. But Whitehead had never received major presidential support. On the other hand, his OTP did not produce enough reports or proposals to constitute a major presidential communications policy initiative.

Nixon may have been correct in setting up a high-level think tank attached to the White House, although he did little to resolve the inevitable rivalry between an OTP linked to the White House and the much larger FCC linked to the Congress.

Whitehead deserves some credit for what he accomplished, despite being led astray by the political rhetoric of his White House masters. He produced both broadcast deregulation proposals and a license renewal bill. His Cabinet Committee on Cable Television pointed the way toward subsequent court and FCC relaxation of constraints on cable; he also achieved significant broadcast industry approval. White advocating the Nixon position that Public Broadcasting was becoming too much like an additional (liberal) national network, Whitehead did help to breathe some new life into the grass roots of public broadcasting. OTP played a major part in unleashing the domestic satellite business. It was also influential with its emphasis on commercial participation, even in international space efforts. In radio spectrum management, it was instrumental in the development of a large third slice of the spectrum, no longer exclusively governmental, but shared between government and private sector.[11]

The OTP lingered on after Nixon's resignation in August 1974, although Whitehead left OTP the following month. It was only finally laid to rest in 1978, by President Carter, who played a prime part in establishing the post-Watergate orthodoxy that communications grand strategies are a political no-go area for the White House. Carter avoided the numerous opportunities for intervention provided by the 1977–80 succession of attempts to rewrite the 1934 Communications Act.

The OTP closure decision was not made until the second year of Carter's term. Communications policy, mainly the inescapable minimum of government spectrum management, was returned to its previous location in the Commerce Department. Within Commerce, a new body, the NTIA, was set up early in 1978 under an assistant secretary of commerce, Henry Geller, who had previously been chief counsel at the FCC. Geller, later regarded as the intellectual guru of the field, was already a connoisseur of communications policy in a somewhat academic, law professor way. In general Geller lent his technical, legal and political expertise to the effort of Lionel Van Deerlin to rewrite the 1934 Act, but he was prepared to let Van Deerlin run with the ball.

Henry Geller was, at last, the qualified man in the right place – someone capable of grasping the full complexity of what was happening, and of persuading others to his viewpoint, rather than alienating them. But Geller, having previously been involved at the FCC in drafting some of the most interventionist efforts of that body to influence television content, was by the time of his reign at NTIA swinging more and more toward an absolutist First Amendment emphasis and against any such interventionism. Indeed, Geller placed his main emphasis on telecommunications, and played a key role in persuading the Democratic Party establishment that the AT&T monopoly must be broken.

Carter was in no hurry to put the new NTIA arrangements into effect. Geller began formally as a 'consultant', and received job confirmation only after a year and a half of the Carter presidency. Geller's efforts continued to focus on educating and persuading others across a broad range of detail. In addition to numerous appearances during the congressional rewrite exercise, Geller's NTIA forcefully expressed its views in FCC proceeding after proceeding.

ADMINISTRATION POLICYMAKERS: AIDES, AMATEURS AND PROFESSIONALS

Henry Geller was unusual as a senior administration communications policymaker in that he was qualified for the job. He had previously been the FCC's top lawyer; but most of the usually quite young men who occupy senior FCC positions subsequently become communications attorney/lobbyists, thus ensuring that the lobbyists are better qualified than the administrators. To put it even more bluntly: Henry Geller was unusual among senior communications lawyers in being, apparently, relatively uninterested in money.

Since most of the best-qualified communications policy talent goes off to work for the commercial lobbies, from whence are administration policymakers drawn? The most common career background is that of political aide. All the senior communications policy people put in place by the Reagan administration in 1981–3 were conservatives, most of whom had worked on the personal staff of Republicans in Congress or for Republican candidates in the 1980 election. A key gathering point was the Reagan transition team, which several had joined in the closing weeks of 1980.

In the past, some of the more significant 'amateurs' in communications policy had been academic lawyers – for example, Eugene Rostow, a former Yale law professor and a senior appointee in the State

Department, whom President Johnson had chosen to head the Task Force on Communications Policy in 1967–8. Rostow's ignorance of communications policy, and his preoccupation with his senior State Department post, may well have been reasons for Johnson's choice; nevertheless, the Rostow report is an important landmark. Another academic lawyer, Baxter from Stanford, was indeed the unanticipated star of communications policy in the early Reagan years; Baxter's success in obtaining approval for breaking up AT&T overshadows the efforts of, for example, the 2,000 people at the FCC.

Apart from domestic telecommunications, the most challenging areas of policy are international, and the Reagan appointees in these areas have been especially inadequate. The USIA, with its dual experience in communications and diplomacy, had in the past attracted and held plenty of policy talent. But Reagan's choice to head the USIA, his old California pal Charles Wick, was one of the most inept and inadequate of all the senior Reagan appointments. Under Wick, the USIA budget rapidly increased, but Wick was repeatedly in political trouble for various Nixon-like tendencies, including his habit (illegal in some states) of taping telephone calls without the other persons's permission.

Another Reagan international communications appointee was clearly inadequate: Diana Lady Dougan, whose lack of experience in both communications and diplomacy made her task of policy coordination at the State Department exceedingly difficult; it was all too easy for turf-fight opponents to point out that her appointment depended upon her local Republican connections in Colorado.

The three key domestic communications policy posts were assigned to three youngish conservatives, all with personal ties to the Reagan White House. The most difficult of these three jobs, that of chairman of the FCC, was, once again, given to the least able and least qualified of the three, namely Mark Fowler (see chapter 20). Somewhat more qualified but no less conservative, was James C. Miller III as chairman of the FTC. (In 1985 Miller succeeded David Stockman as Director of OMB.)

The best qualified of the Reagan appointees also had the easiest of the major communications policy jobs: the politically fairly sheltered role of heading the NTIA within the Commerce Department. David Markey, who took on the job in 1983, had, compared to Fowler, a much better law background (clerk to two judges), better political experience – almost ten years on the staffs of a Republican governor (Agnew) and two US senators – and better communications policy experience, having worked for more than six years as a lobbyist for NAB. Markey's Senate confirmation hearings took place on his forty-third birthday, and the value of his lengthy experience soon became evident.[12]

The pervasive presence of inexperienced political appointees in senior policy positions, of course, made it easier for the better-qualified industry lawyer/lobbyists to succeed. Another consequence of such appointments, plus the budgetary turmoil of 1981–2, was that many experienced civil servants were themselves on the move, or at best playing little part in making policy.

Within agencies presided over by political appointees aged around forty was a second level of agency departmental heads – often aged only around thirty – whose main qualifications were their conservative political beliefs and connections.

All the Reagan communications appointees compared unfavorably in terms of ability and independence of mind with a professional like Henry Geller or a talented aide such as Clay Whitehead, who entered communications policy via Nixon's campaign for the 1968 Republican nomination.

WHAT'S GOOD FOR AMERICA: UNESCO AND ITU

The Reagan administration which arrived in 1981 saw the ITU and UNESCO in a trebly critical light: they were both UN agencies and thus naturally prone to the ills of bureaucracy; they were both governmental organizations in need of deregulation; and they were communications organizations threatened by the combined votes of the small Third World nations.

One Reagan administration assumption implied that the US could both weaken the agencies through deregulation while at the same time strengthening US leadership. The second assumption was that the Western nations in general, and the US in particular, were underrepresented in UN staff numbers; while this was true of UNESCO, in the more important ITU, the US in 1981 contributed 7 per cent of the funding but had 9 per cent of the staff.[13]

This public criticism of Third World influence was accompanied in private by additional criticism of France. UNESCO was based in Paris and ITU in Geneva, another French-speaking city. Both organizations have acquired some of the flavor of their base cities; the ITU was for a long time staffed by Swiss, and still has an atmosphere of Swiss efficiency. UNESCO has strong overtones not only of France, but of francophone Africa; a number of key UNESCO and ITU figures come from such former French territories as Tunisia and Senegal. The French-language theme carries over also into US communications relations with Canada.[14]

In late December 1983, the State Department announced that in 12 months the US would pull out of UNESCO. Many reasons were given for this much-predicted decision: that the UNESCO bureaucracy was excessive; that its management was dictatorial, rigid and given to cronyism; that UNESCO had too many lengthy ideological discussions and spent too little time ministering to the world's poor; and that UNESCO suffered from too many financial perks and too much budgetary irresponsibility. All these points were probably true, but exactly the same criticisms are also made by congressmen about the US Congress and the FCC, among other bodies.

The real reasons for leaving UNESCO were, firstly, there was a desire in Washington to hit back at the supposed humiliation of the US in various forums, and UNESCO was chosen as the agency which the US could leave least painfully. Second, there was US hostility to several UNESCO policies and practices, but in particular to UNESCO criticism of the Western news media. The third US reason for leaving UNESCO was the belief that it had come under the control of a clique of francophone Africans hostile to the US. This criticism focused especially on the UNESCO director general, Mr M'Bow of Senegal. His predecessor had been a Frenchman, and these two French-speaking chief executives, based in Paris, seem to have established a fairly dictatorial management style.

Within the US, while many leading press voices continued their anti-UNESCO line, other voices were much less sure. For example, the House Committee on Foreign Affairs sent a staff study mission to Paris which returned with a balanced verdict which leaned somewhat toward UNESCO. This report criticized UNESCO but it also sharply criticized the conduct of US policy in relation to UNESCO. The US, it said, has given too much weight to bilateral diplomacy; US diplomatic personnel have sometimes been inadequate; 'politicization' charges against UNESCO are exaggerated; the US decision to withdraw has been badly timed; and so on.[15]

The US had been responsible for making the free flow of news and communication central to UNESCO at its birth. The Third World had declared this to be a dated and transparently exploitative idea. But it should have been possible for the US to come up with some suitably renovated and diplomatic version of 'free flow' and 'deregulation'. The news agencies, which are central to the debate, have in fact long made compromises with the full range of political regimes around the world. But that is the way of the worldly, low-profile news agencies.

By 1982 there were some Washington whispers to the effect that the US might leave not only UNESCO, but also ITU. Since 1977 the US had had a series of uncomfortable ITU experiences, and the big Nairobi conference in 1982 was the most uncomfortable of all.

The 1982 conference happened to coincide with the Israeli invasion of Lebanon; the plenipotentiary conference, the least frequent and most elevated of ITU's many conferences, was nearly wrecked by a bitter battle over an Algerian resolution calling for the expulsion of Israel. Ten days of debate were given over to the issue – something quite unprecedented: in its more than century-long history, ITU had always stuck to the technological detail of spectrum, standards and services.

The US had suffered a defeat in the opening contest at Nairobi over the choosing of a new secretary general. The contest was between the incumbent, M. Mili of Tunisia (with a reputation for autocratic and ineffective management similar to that of M'Bow at UNESCO), and the Australian incumbent deputy secretary general, Richard Butler. The US ineptly supported the Tunisian incumbent, who was in fact defeated by Butler. Butler already had the reputation of being the most know-ledgeable expert on all aspects of ITU's complex activities; he had also shown his political savvy by openly campaigning for votes through visits to Third World countries. Although the US delegation opposed him, Butler was in fact a blessing in disguise for the US.[16]

The conference also accepted a British compromise, which allowed the majority to condemn Israel but without expulsion. After these two crises, the Nairobi conference returned to something more like standard ITU practice – an obsession with engineering consensus and a horror of politics.

In the following year, 1983, the US emerged much more comfortably from a Regional Administrative Radio Conference (RARC) on DBS space slots for the American continent. After some initial Canadian hard bargaining the US, Canada, Mexico and Cuba played prominent roles in finding acceptable compromises. Even though the circumstances were already favorable, some credit should probably go to US preparation and leadership. In particular, one cannot overlook the fact that chair-man of the 1983 US delegation, Abbott Washburn, was a man of great experience, both as an FCC commissioner and internationally, via his long experience in USIA/VOA. Washburn was an Eisenhower Republican, a moderate deregulator, who, while still at the FCC, had opposed some early positions taken by Mark Fowler. Washburn was the kind of charming, articulate and slightly old-world American that foreigners tend to admire. His report on the conference is extremely positive in almost all respects;[17] it is dated 31 October 1983, only weeks before the sharply contrasting decision to leave UNESCO.

DEREGULATORY GLOBAL TALK: INTELSAT AND FIBER CABLES

In November 1984 President Reagan made a long-anticipated announcement of his support for satellite systems, which would provide some competition for INTELSAT, the international satellite cooperative.

Several dilemmas and paradoxes complicated this decision. INTELSAT was seen from within the deregulatory consensus as an international version of Ma Bell; but on the Bell analogy, INTELSAT was only the 'long lines' part of Bell; the 'local' companies internationally are the national phone administrations, who have so contrived the charges as to make the land links the part of the system which charges monopoly prices.

But AT&T is more directly involved in both INTELSAT and ocean cables, and it can be accused of the classic monopoly sin of cross-subsidizing between the two. Paradoxically, the Reagan deregulatory thrust toward more capacity and more competition in both satellites and under-ocean cables may indeed strengthen American leadership in both technologies. However, ocean cables may be a more serious threat to INTELSAT than the new, small, competing satellite carriers, and thus AT&T's dominance in cables may lead to a strengthening of monopoly rather than competition.

In terms of communications policy and diplomacy, the prospect of competition for INTELSAT has tended to leave the US as a minority of one, with the UK sitting on the fence. As an exercise in persuading the world to accept deregulation, this piece of communications diplomacy has been distinctly confrontational.

Most US arguments against INTELSAT assume that it is a monopoly, and that it must go the way of AT&T. INTELSAT is owned by its users, but most of these are monopoly telecoms administrations in Europe and around the world; thus INTELSAT is not only a carriers' carrier, it is also a monopolists' monopoly. INTELSAT's numerous defenders in the rest of the world, as well as its few rather hesitant defenders in the US, say that 'monopoly' is a gross misnomer. In addition to ocean cables, there is some international phone competition over land by microwave (as in Europe), and over middle distances via regional satellites: for example, the Arabs and the Indonesians and their neighbors, already have regional satellites, and others are coming in Europe and elsewhere.

The defenders of INTELSAT also insist that their system is neither a monopoly nor a cartel, but a *cooperative*. Ownership (with minor exceptions) is proportional to usage, which gives the US the biggest ownership slice, with the UK second, and the other OECD countries plus the odd Saudi Arabia and Brazil having the only other significant holdings. This is one international organization which is indeed controlled by a dozen of the richer and older Western nations; but Third World nations also belong in big numbers, although most have only a fraction of 1 per cent of the equity.

Unfortunately for INTELSAT, the cooperative argument seems to carry little weight in Washington. In the US, 'cooperative' lacks that European glow of the virtuous small entrepreneur. INTELSAT would have been wiser to describe itself as a 'condominium', a term which summons up in US minds such virtuous concepts as real estate, capital gains and get-up-and-go.

Since its creation by John and Robert Kennedy in the early 1960s, INTELSAT has gone through many changes. Near-total US dominance – in ownership, management, NASA sponsorship and cold war prehistory – has long since evolved into mere US leadership. Leadership consists of some 23 per cent of the traffic and the equity, the location of INTELSAT in Washington DC, and only a few exceptions to total US dominance so far in the supply of launchers, space vehicles and tracking systems. In 1984 a US citizen, Richard Colino, took over from the Chilean incumbent as chief executive.

There have been changes in the capacity of the system, big price drops, vastly increased usage. INTELSAT's ability to pump the World Football Cup or the Olympics round the world to audiences of a billion people has come to seem routine. It's all a long way from the small, technically crude and uncertain beginnings. In the early days it was not even clear that the geostationary parking of satellites was possible.

In one crucial respect INTELSAT is a product of the 1960s: this is the basic architecture of the world system. The concept is of satellites parked over the Atlantic, Pacific and Indian oceans. Following from this, and talking to the satellite above, is the big earth station, a massive and expensive dish placed often in a coastal or other remote location. On the INTELSAT map of the world, it is possible to mark in all these giant dishes. Domestically these become 'gateways'; in the US all the gateways are on the two main coasts, looking to the satellites of the particular ocean.

In order to make a phone call from, say, Detroit to London, you have to make three linked calls: an AT&T call from Detroit to a COMSAT earth station in Andover, Maine; then the space segment up to an INTELSAT satellite parked between Brazil and Africa; then the third segment, which runs from a British Telecom giant dish at Goonhilly Downs in Southwest England to London, a final 300-mile land link.

This system was valid and effective in the 1960s, but looked increasingly archaic in the early 1980s. The two terrestrial sections at present account for the great bulk of the charge to the user. The system could be redesigned in any one of a number of ways; but an obvious point made by critics is that many more cities and companies should be allowed to have their own local gateways.

INTELSAT may or may not be delivering the right service, but what it *is* delivering has fallen so dramatically in price as to justify the term 'free fall prices'; with a little exaggeration, one can say that the INTELSAT space segment of an international phone call is to all intents and purposes *free*. The two terrestrial links account for about 90 per cent of all costs, the satellite space segment only about 10 per cent. Even with rapid inflation over the last 20 years, INTELSAT has repeatedly cut its prices. In real terms of stable money value, INTELSAT proudly claims that its prices in the 1980s are about 5 or 6 per cent of its prices 20 years ago.

This spectacular price fall has been achieved by a massive reaping of scale economies. Traffic has expanded rapidly: during 1971–83, at an annual average of 23 per cent, which is a doubling in volume every three and a half years. Indeed, it is figures like these which have whet the appetites of other people in the US.

Almost all the high-tech contracts have gone to Hughes and other US companies. In effect, the US space industry has been subsidized by an international body. Going beyond the purely financial and vaguely realpolitik arguments, INTELSAT and most of its members had another argument, a legal one: that under the INTELSAT operating agreement, member governments had agreed not to set up competing services. There has been the prospect of INTELSAT going to court both in the US and internationally.

The first of the would-be US competitors to reveal its plans was Orion. It was immediately possible to see that getting into competition with INTELSAT was not a cheap activity. Orion would provide customized transatlantic satellite service to large international corporate users. It would put up the satellite system, but would then sell or long-lease transponders to corporate customers on a condominium basis. Orion would simply undertake to keep the satellite operational, and provide backup space vehicles, insurance and so on.

Orion saw the capital cost of this system as being $215 million. It offered the conventional arrangement of one backup satellite in space and a third on the ground.[18] The Orion application was dated March 1983; it was destined to remain on the table for many months. One of the originators of the Orion application, Christopher Vizas, had worked as a Senate staffer, and the application was carefully drafted to appeal to current deregulatory sentiment. All the key people in Congress came out in support, and the 12 agencies in SIG also agreed, including Commerce and State. Only White House approval was required for the FCC to move. But the Orion application stalled at the White House for most of calendar year 1984.

Orion was perhaps unfortunate in getting bound up in the turf wars between Commerce and State: even though both agreed on Orion, they insisted on saying so in separate documents. At one point Diana Dougan's office at State jumped the gun by sending out a background briefing to all US embassies abroad on an imminent White House decision – one that remained imminent for many more weeks.

The fair political winds which the Orion proposal encountered brought out several more would-be competitors; each had slightly different things to offer, but the general strategy of 'noncompetitive' services predominated. The one big name among the new applicants was RCA, which offered its Americom satellite. One deviant voice was International Relay, which wanted to compete on the link-in to INTELSAT, by way of a Chicago ground station in competition with COMSAT. The number of competitors posed a new problem: Was there room for one Orion, let alone six? One consultant's report suggested that even two new services would both lose money, because they would be too small to reap the full economies of scale.

Meanwhile, in 1984, the FCC approved the TAT-8 transatlantic fiber-optic cable, with AT&T as the leading participant, and with twin cables offering a capacity of 40,000 simultaneous phone calls or circuits. Despite cries of future overcapacity, the FCC again went for expansion and competition when, in 1985, it approved a US–British twin ocean cable, a joint venture between a US consortium and the British company Cable and Wireless.

The INTELSAT dispute involved many complexities and unknowns, but surely no more than did the original decisions of the early 1960s. In the setting up of INTELSAT there had been compromises, and, despite some acrimony, a remarkable degree of common purpose within both the US and the world. The issue of competition with INTELSAT in the early 1980s was treated quite differently by the Reagan White House, which seemed more concerned to sort out the dispute between State and Commerce (despite their agreement in this case) than to pay attention to the criticisms of the world community. Certainly this international issue was addressed mainly from a domestic viewpoint, and an interesting novelty was the sight of INTELSAT openly lobbying in Congress and elsewhere in traditional Washington turf-war style.

The passivity of the White House in international as well as domestic communications policy has had the effect of transferring the belligerent style of Washington policy fragmentation onto the international scene. The majority of the world's nations, whether in UNESCO or INTELSAT, are treated by the White House like the striking air traffic controllers in 1981.

Deregulation, both in communications and more generally, takes many forms; but in presidential communications policy it seems to mean passivity or stealth – at the very least, always keeping a low profile. The White House may be active behind the political scenes, but for public consumption it seems to interpret deregulation not merely as getting rid of regulation, but as ceasing to make policy altogether.

However, while the White House tolerates turf warfare and belligerance, diplomacy and policymaking do not vanish entirely. The corporate big battalions cultivate diplomacy, compromise and policy while the White House turns its back.

Notes

1 Alan Pearce, 'Telecom Policy and the White House', *Telecommunications*, November 1980, p. 16.
2 Paul Craig Roberts, *The Supply-Side Revolution* (1984).
3 Diana Lady Dougan, prepared statement, 19 October 1983. US Senate, *International Communication and Information Policy*. Hearings before the Subcommittee on Arms

Control, Oceans, International Operations and Environment of the Committee on Foreign Relations. p. 17.

4 James Bamford, *The Puzzle Palace* (1982).

5 Rodney Kennedy-Minott, 'Technology Transfer: an overview', *Telecommunications*, May 1983, p. 16.

6 Interview, by this author, with State Department source.

7 Two-part interview with David Markey in *Communications Daily*, 20 and 21 December 1983. 'A strong voice, an even hand', *Broadcasting*, 5 March 1984, p. 95.

8 Eugene V. Rostow (chairman), *Final Report: President's Task Force on Communications Policy* (1968).

9 'Antitrust or Distrust?', *New York Times*, 18 April 1972, p. 46.

10 'The President takes sides against network re-runs', *Broadcasting*, 12 September 1972, pp. 12–14.

11 'A beleaguered Whitehead and battered OTP', *Broadcasting*, 17 September 1973, pp. 16–17. 'Cable report: Will it live as legacy of Whitehead?', *Broadcasting*, 4 February 1974, pp. 19–20. James Miller, 'Policy Planning and Technocratic power: the significance of OTP', *Journal of Communications*, 32, winter 1982, pp. 53–60. Idem, 'The President's Advocate: OTP and Broadcast Issues', *Journal of Broadcasting*, 26, summer 1982, pp. 625–39.

12 US Senate. Hearings before the Committee on Commerce, Science and Transportation. *Nominations – Federal Maritime Commission and Department of Commerce* (1983), pp. 8–15.

13 Heritage Foundation, *Americans at the UN: an endangered species*, 14 February 1983, p. 6.

14 This language point is made by James Ebel, one of the US's most experienced representatives at international conferences on satellite policy, in 'The World according to Ebel', *Broadcasting*, 7 June 1982, p. 62.

15 US House of Representatives, Committee on Foreign Affairs, *U.S. Withdrawal from UNESCO* (1984). Leonard R. Sussman, 'Evaluation of UNESCO's Commission IV Action on Issues regarding the flow of mass communications', 17 November 1983.

16 According to one account, the US supported Mr. Mili because of 'his perceived lack of concern' about less developed country issues. Leslie Milk and Allen Weinstein, 'United States Participation in the International Telecomunications Union', Center for Strategic and International Studies, Georgetown University, 1984, p. 29.

17 US Department of State, *Report of the United States Delegation to the ITU region 2 Administrative Radio Conference on the Broadcasting Satellite Service* (1983).

18 *Application of Orion Satellite Corporation for an International Satellite System*. Before the FCC. March 1983. pp. I-11-12.

18

Congress: Much Action, Few Acts

Congress potentially has enormous power, especially in a field like communications which induces extreme White House caution. But the legislative branch, despite the salience of communications policy in recent years, has passed very little new communications law. Whereas executive branch involvement in communications policymaking founders in administrative fragmentation and White House passivity, Congress has seen much communications legislation proposed by its members, and endlessly discussed in committee, only to see almost all of it fail to pass into law.

The old Washington adage that it's relatively easy to stop something happening is extremely noticeable on Capitol Hill. Many laws are proposed, but, after lobbies have had their say in hearings and elsewhere, few bills succeed in going the full distance, past all the numerous legislative veto points.

During the 1975–85 decade of the Ford, Carter and first Reagan presidential terms, communications moved from being regarded as one of the most boring to one of the most challenging legislative areas. By 1985 the Telecommunications Subcommittee of the House of Representatives had reached the unusually large number of 24 members. But despite this popularity, the extent of legislative achievement remained small. Indeed, during this decade, only two communications legislative measures of importance passed Congress. One was an extension of radio and TV station license periods, which was tacked onto a compendium budget measure in the early Reagan days in 1981; the second was the Cable Bill which just squeezed through into law in the dying hours of Congress in late 1984.

The paucity of laws passed contrasts with the flood of legislative activity. In every year between 1976 and 1984 there were major pieces of communications legislation before Congress, but nearly all of them were defeated. And the Communications Act of 1934, passed before television, let alone space satellites and computers had arrived, remains the basic law governing a vast area. Despite many attempts to reform or rewrite the Communications Act, the legislative outcome has been merely to stick Band-Aids on its antiquated bulk.

The other side of congressional inability to pass communications legislation is, of course, the proven ability of organized lobbies to prevent the passage of most communications legislation.

Legislative activity focuses upon one or more communications lobbies, and is concentrated in a few subcommittees and committees in Congress. Typically, legislation is introduced in the early months of a two-year congressional session, and goes into the relevant subcommittees of the House and the Senate. The lobbying battle which then takes place often adopts the form of an artillery duel in which massive fire power is deployed repeatedly on the narrow front of a few detailed sentences in the proposed legislation. This concentration of firepower often occurs for reasons of lobbying machismo or chairmanly tactics, rather than for reasons of major substance.

The congressional committee system has been grossly inadequate in recent years in what is supposedly the legislative branch's main business, namely the writing of legislation. The committee system has also ignored many important strategic issues in domestic and, even more so, in international communications policy.

But the congressional committee system has been extremely successful in eliciting information in its endless hearings, and at shaping a broad agenda and a loose consensus in communications deregulation. While Congress has been an ineffective branch of government in terms of its legislative role, it has, nevertheless, been a leader in communications policy over most of the years 1975–85.

While largely unable to perform its formal role, it has managed to influence, and even to assume the roles of, the executive and judicial branches. In struggles with the executive to control the FCC, Congress largely succeeded, first in baiting the Carter FCC into action, and second in making the Reagan FCC realize that it was indeed a 'creature of Congress'; this was done by control of the FCC budget, by frequent appropriations and oversight hearings, and by firing warning congressional votes across the FCC's bows.

Congress has also enormously influenced the performance of the courts on communications issues; the judges in general, and Judge Greene, the divester of AT&T, in particular, in searching for reasonable standards and a national consensus, have looked toward Congress for guidance. On major issues, laws have in effect been vetoed in Congress by lobbies, only to be passed subsequently by judges in the courts. This has been possible because, despite shelf upon shelf of congressional hearings, it is relatively easy at any one time to discover where the congressional consensus has got to; the latest case of FCC evidence on the Hill and the opening statements of individual legislators indicate clearly where the deregulatory consensus now is. A conscientious judge, wishing to give voice to the public will and policy consensus, can search in vain amid the executive branch fragmentation; but judges can, and do, cut-and-paste current congressional wordings into court decisions.

THE DYNAMICS OF LEGISLATIVE IMMOBILITY

As a legislative area, communications reflects most of the major trends in the US Congress in the post-Nixon era. The truism is valid that members of Congress have two major concerns – getting reelected and building a power base. Both concerns are present in the sheer quantity of bills introduced, something like 15 bills per House member per 2-year Congress. Depending on the definition of communications, there must be between 100 and 200 communications bills per session. Some of these are little more than press releases aimed at the folks back home.

The election time lost in the second year and the large number of hoops which successful legislation must jump both argue for a brisk legislative pace in the first year. And so, for example, by 21 July 1983, only six months into the ninety-eighth Congress, the Wirth–Dingell bill, one of numerous Universal Telephone Service Preservation bills, was the three thousand, six hundred and twenty-first bill to be introduced that year.

The fragmented nature of Congress – every member a chairman of something, each subcommittee with its fiercely defended turf – contributed to the fragmentation of communications policy. For example, while the FCC and NTIA were responsible to the Communications Subcommittee, other major communications policy players belonged elsewhere. In both House and Senate, intricate copyright issues affecting computer software and semiconductor protection belong to subcommittees of the main judiciary committee, whereas issues of competition and antitrust go to another judiciary subcommittee. International telecommunications is of interest to the Foreign Relations committees. Other wider communications issues cross the jurisdictions of Armed Services and Science committees.

While communications is a multi-issue, involving more than a dozen subcommittees, communications continues to enter all levels of the political arena in single-issue guise. No politician wants to be dubbed by an opponent 'the candidate who doubled your phone bill' or 'the man who voted for cable pornography'. Indeed, politicans seek the opposite of such labels, and launch bills to provide suitable evidence to the electorate.

In AT&T this legislative area possessed perhaps the most formidable single-organization commercial lobby of all time. The strength of industrial lobbies in this field is unusual – in part because mass media publicity is the central nervous system of politics. But the communications revolution/deregulation/new technology trends have cast lobbies in the role of opponents; for example, the nimble-footed and much admired cable lobby against the heavyweight champ AT&T. In some legislative episodes, the legislators have sat in the stands and watched the lobbyists fight it out to a compromise; only when the lobbies have reached their own compromise have the legislators become active again – and by this time the congressional two-year term is often too far advanced for anything except to try again in the next Congress.

Nevertheless, the obvious inefficiencies of Congress, the frenetic immobility, do produce a lot of legislative experience and knowledge. The present system of (approximately) seniority plus merit produces main committee chairmen of both ability and experience; these chairmen, endowed by the system with very considerable power, are a good match for the chief executives of large organizations, and more than a match for the commissioners on regulatory commissions. A commerce committee chairman, compared with the appointed chairman of the FCC, is likely to be someone of considerably greater ability and experience. Although he lacks the 2,000-person bureaucracy of an FCC, he has many sources of intelligence which are his to deploy – his personal staff, the main committee staff and a subcommittee staff as well.

But there must always be the agony of Sisyphus: the legislator forever pushing his legislation up the slopes of Capitol Hill, only to watch it roll down again. All members of Congress occasionally vent their frustrations on the young staff members who inevitably do much of the work; or frustrations can be expressed collectively in measures like Senate Bill S.1080, which in 1983 sought to clip the wings of all the regulatory agencies.

COMMITTEE AND SUBCOMMITTEE POWER

Lionel Van Deerlin, in the course of a succession of attempts to entirely rewrite the old Communications Act of 1934, failed each time to get a new act through Congress; but while he thus failed to rewrite the law, he was much more successful at rewriting the agenda.

The nature of the Washington policy consensus obviously meant that Van Deerlin was only one of many people involved. But he was the right man in the right place at the right time. The House Subcommittee on Communications was the place where the action was focused in the years 1976–80. Van Deerlin became chairman of the subcommittee in April 1976. His political qualifications were excellent: he had already been on the subcommittee for ten years, and was thus familiar with both mass media and telecommunications. He was a Democrat with broadly liberal social views, but favored more conservative market ideas in economics and communications. He was a man of charm and modesty, also a man of shining integrity – above the rather sleazy financial behavior which is such a curse of the US Congress, so nobody ever thought of accusing him of being in this for some quick electoral bucks.

His entry to the field was via journalism; even more significant, his roots were in Southern California journalism, having been prominent in both print and electronic journalism in San Diego. The then far right-wing Copley newspaper management disliked him not least because, as a Newspaper Guild local spokesman, he had negotiated the first $100-a-week contract in San Diego journalism. San Diego, surrounded by a bowl of mountains, had also been a pioneer in big cable systems, and Van Deerlin decided early that the TV networks were on a downward slide. He was also much more aware than most politicians of the methods and realities of Hollywood; Van Deerlin was born in Los Angeles in 1914 and attended the University of Southern California, where he edited the campus daily.[1] In 1934 he was reporting the Los Angeles Olympics.

In launching his rewrite effort, Van Deerlin made good use of this early exposure to show business publicity. His device for attracting the attention of AT&T and the FCC was to demand the breakup of both, as was proposed in the 1978 bill. He was also aware of the slow drip effect of daily publicity and repetition. During the rewrite war, the House subcommittee held 95 days of hearings and took evidence from more than 1,200 witnesses. Even then, the general media carried fairly little material; but the trade press was awash in coverage, and the word slowly seeped out via the communications policy community into Congress more generally.

Despite his extensive experience, despite a real quota of political guile, and despite an exceptionally quick mind and self-deprecating wit, Van Deerlin retained a slight air of innocence, even naivety. He had the journalist's combination of cynicism and optimism. He was surprised when, toward the end, some of his liberal Democrat colleagues jumped off the sinking rewrite ship, even though there had been signals aplenty. But perhaps only a man with exceptional personal qualities plus a touch of naivety would have taken on such an apparently hopeless task. His achievement, he said, was to take 'a thousand-to-one shot and turn it into a fifteen-to-one shot'.[2]

Van Deerlin landed in the chair of the House subcommittee at the right time in several respects. It was the year 1976, in which the post-Watergate reforms were taking effect. Power was being removed from committee chairmen and given to subcommittee chairmen. In 1977 there was a big swing to the Democrats, and the subcommittee's expanded membership saw Van Deerlin heading a total of 10 Democrats, with only 4 Republicans. Perhaps more important was that, for the first time, the House subcommittee had a large and able staff team. The previous chairman, Torbert Macdonald, had had a minute staff consisting of a young lawyer called Harry (Chip) Shooshan III. During Macdonald's long terminal illness, Shooshan had devoted his energies to becoming an expert in the subcommittee's broad area of competence. Here was another one of the select few who had a deep understanding of both telecoms and mass media policy. Shooshan was to be the young inquisitor in the endless hearings, while Van Deerlin for long periods sat quietly fingering his spectacles or interjecting the occasional joke.

The Democratic majority in the House endowed the subcommittee with a sizeable staff; Van Deerlin and Shooshan acquired a team of very young and able staffers. It was like a seminar of bright postgraduates presided over by a young teaching assistant (Shooshan) and a benign professor (Van Deerlin) who decided to take on AT&T, the networks, IBM and anyone else who might come over the horizon. The rewrite of the 1934 Act made a class project large enough in scope to keep them all busy. The staffers began work on a sort of telecommunications policy textbook, later to be called *The Options Papers*. This was the first of Van Deerlin's several coups de theatre.

Meanwhile, he was also gathering support among subcommittee members. He devoted special attention to wooing the Republicans; in particular, a Florida Republican House member, Louis Frey, Jr, was to be his trusted ally and legislative cosponsor. It was Louis Frey who first used the Band-Aid imagery to describe the weaknesses of fragmented policymaking: you could put a Band-Aid over some portion of communications policy, but this always led to a new distortion popping out elsewhere.

The congressional approach to communications policy was inevitably altered by the 1980 elections, which produced not only a Republican president but a Republican majority in the Senate. The lineup thus tended to become the Senate plus the administration versus the still Democratic House. The Senate tended to get big majorities for deregulatory measures, while the House took much longer haggling over somewhat similar deregulatory bills with various additional saving clauses.

But nearly as important as the party changes in 1981 were the new chairmen and their political personalities. All four – Goldwater, Packwood, Wirth and Dingell – were political mavericks and originals in the classic Washington style. All were a strange mixture ideologically, their views explicable in terms of electoral factors back home mixed with Washington power-base building.

Senator Barry Goldwater took over in 1981 as chairman of the Senate Subcommittee on Communications. One reason why the subcommittee was relatively inactive was Senator Goldwater's other committee obligations:

in 1983–4 he was chairman of the Senate Intelligence Committee; a member of Armed Services, and its Tactical Warfare (chairman), Preparedness and Strategic and Theater Nuclear Forces subcommittees; on the Senate Commerce, Science and Transportation Committee, and also on the Communications (chairman), Aviation and Science, Technology and Space subcommittees; and, being from Arizona, on the Indian Affairs Committee. The Communications Subcommittee was not a popular choice in a Republican Senate predominantly concerned with defense and finance, budget and the US economy. Nevertheless, Goldwater was active and successful in communications legislation. His views, once considered eccentric, now seemed conventional. He was in close and regular touch with the White House, but was also prominent among those conservatives who, while deregulating telecommunications and broadcasting, openly regretted the disappointing results.

In keeping with the usual Senate way of doing things, more communications business is conducted in full committee than subcommittee. In 1981–4, the committee was chaired by Senator Bob Packwood of Oregon. Overall, Packwood was a conservative Republican, but one of quite considerable independence. The NAB followed his lead, rather than the reverse. In some respects he was the ultra-deregulator, the proponent of freedom of expression legislation, initially seen as a rewrite of the First Amendment. Packwood wanted to repair the founding fathers' unfortunate lapse in not including the electronic media – along with religion, speech and press – as entitled to special protection. Needless to say, he was a big man on all kinds of deregulation. Well, almost: not, it seemed, when the FCC and AT&T were about to raise telephone bills in January 1984. His state of Oregon is the kind of place which still faces big increases in rural phone rates unless some remedy can be found. Packwood also was not consistently a friend of the White House, and made little attempt to hide his own White House ambitions. His relations with his fellow Republican senators, including Goldwater, were intermittently frosty. Although the Senate Commerce Committee had 17 members, its communications hearings for four years tended to consist of Packwood sitting alone – the single most formidable and powerful communications deregulator at work.

The two House communications chairmen were another fascinating couple. Timothy Wirth in 1981 succeeded the defeated Lionel Van Deerlin as chairman of the House subcommittee. The subcommittee continued its by now nearly decade-long eminence as the leading public forum for communications policymaking; the level of knowledge, expertise and commitment on the part of staff and members, both Republicans and Democrats, was impressive. The subcommittee saw itself as a restraining force on the excesses of deregulatory enthusiasm elsewhere in communications policymaking. The House subcommittee's mandate is telecommunications, consumer protection and finance. In 1984 it had a staff of some 18 people – huge compared with the staff of ten years earlier. Its 1984 Budget Justification ran to 73 single-spaced pages.

Wirth was first elected as one of the Watergate babes in 1974. He served six years on the subcommittee prior to becoming its chairman. Wirth's district is Boulder, Colorado, the high-tech and campus city at the foot of the mountains near Denver. Wirth was a leading Gary Hart supporter in the 1984 Democratic primaries, and like him is a neo-liberal 'Atari Democrat'. In addition to having the classic mountain-state concern for the environment, Wirth was an advocate of high tech in general and cable in particular; some saw him as a spokesman for the Denver cable lobby. Wirth saw cable as competition for the big, potentially bad forces in communications. He was indeed the politician most feared and hated by both AT&T and the networks. Wirth was another formidably well equipped politician, with higher degrees from Stanford and Harvard and key Washington experience. Good-looking and articulate almost to excess, the trade press could find nothing worse to accuse him of than arrogance.[3] Wirth was also an accomplished legislative tactician, having learned from a master of the trade, one John Dingell.

The House Committee on Energy and Commerce became known in Washington as 'The Committee',[4] and its chairman, John Dingell, as '*The* committee chairman'. Not long ago the commerce committees of both House and Senate were relatively quiet and sleepy, with small staffs quite inadequate for overseeing such vast tracts of the US industry and economy; a 1975 investigation from the Ralph Nader stable had little difficulty in showing that both commerce committees were fairly ineffectual.[5] Since then, staffs and expertise have increased, and the commerce subcommittees are chaired by some aggressive legislators. Henry Waxman, for example, used his chairmanship of the Health and Environment Subcommittee to become a major figure not only in the environmental movement but in the Democratic party.

If the House Commerce Subcommittee chairmen were forceful neo-liberals, John Dingell was a neo-baron. Dingell came to the chairmanship in 1981, partly on the strength of his role in stopping energy from migrating into a separate committee, as a House ad hoc committee on committees had demanded. Now a re-formed Committee on Energy and Commerce oversaw the commanding heights of US industry – oil, gas, telecommunications, car manufacture and much else. Dingell was yet another maverick, a latter-day Michigan version of Lyndon Johnson, a wheeler-dealer liberal Democrat who happened to be against both gun control and clean air – Dingell's House district being near Detroit, he preferred cars to clean air.[6]

In the Ninety-seventh Congress (1981–2) the Commerce Committee sat for 998 hours on 310 days and considered 876 bills. It published 52,548 pages of material. It reported out only 55 bills and failed to achieve its two main legislative goals – Wirth's attempt to clip AT&T's wings and an amendment to the Clean Air Act put forward by Waxman. Much time was consumed on the Reagan budget revolution of 1981–2.

Behind the neo-Kennedy front of Wirth, there always lurked also the neo-LBJ figure of John Dingell, enemy of the Reagan White House, relentless prosecutor of corruption in the EPA, and one of the few real barons in Congress.

THE 1976 BELL BILL, AND THE 1978, 1979 AND 1980 REWRITE ATTEMPTS

The heavy congressional action of the deregulatory decade began with an innocent-sounding bill called the Consumer Communications Reform Act of 1976. This measure was quickly dubbed by its enemies the 'Bell Bill', because AT&T's lawyers drafted it, and because it attempted to put the clock back by eliminating the still small MCI and other at that time modest encroachments of telecoms competition. In 1976 AT&T still had its benign Ma Bell image almost intact and, although the bill was drafted in deliberately extreme, if not belligerent, form, 189 members, almost half the entire House membership, signed as cosponsors.

It was at this point – with subcommittee chairman Macdonald just deceased from cancer, and the traditional communications policy leader, Senator John Pastore, about to retire – that Van Deerlin and Frey had to use their skills and procedural guile in order to delay, and thus kill, the Bell Bill. Van Deerlin delayed for six months, and then announced hearings, not on the Bell Bill, but on telecommunications competition; Frey pronounced on the utopian idea of rewriting the 1934 Act; and young Colorado Democrat Tim Wirth introduced his own counter-Bell pro-competition bill. Thus the Bell Bill ran out of time.

Table 18.1 shows in summary the two major attempts to rewrite the entire Communications Act of 1934. By 1979 the Senate was coming back into the game. S.611, introduced by Senator Hollings, Democrat chairman of the Senate Communications Subcommittee, was fairly similar to Van Deerlin HR.3333 but the rival bill introduced by Goldwater, the ranking Republican Senator on the subcommittee, differed from the other two bills in that Goldwater was unwilling to exact the price of a spectrum use fee in return for deregulating broadcasting.

TABLE 18.1   The Van Deerlin rewrite era in Congress, 1976–80

Year	House of Representatives	Senate	FCC
1976	HR.12323 The Bell Bill	Senate Bell Bill S.3192	
1977	*The Options Papers*		September Ferris became chairman
1978	HR.13015 (Van Deerlin & Frey) Rewrite One		
1979	HR.3333 (Van Deerlin & Collins) Rewrite Two	S.611 (Hollings) S.622 (Gold-water)	Starts to pursue de-regulation actively
1980	HR.6121 (Van Deerlin) Rewrite Three	S.2827	May, Computer II decision

By 1980 Van Deerlin had dropped the idea of a general rewrite and was following Senator Hollings's suggestion of a rewrite 'merely' of the telecommunications section of the 1934 Act. Thus 1980 saw the major focus on AT&T, which was given further prominence by the FCC's landmark *Computer II* decision; Computer II allowed AT&T and other regulated common carriers to enter unregulated areas such as data transmission, as long as this was done within an 'arms-length' separate subsidiary. Computer II was a sign that Van Deerlin's initiatives were increasingly stirring the FCC into action. Computer II also sowed the seeds of further decisions on AT&T: it eroded the competitive barrier on one side by allowing AT&T into fresh pastures, but it also, by implication, raised the issue of allowing other phone companies to enter further into AT&T pastures. Moreover, by drawing yet another unenforceable de-marcation line around AT&T, the FCC also prepared the way for yet further attempts at clarification.

But the first and crucial coup de theatre was *The Options Papers*, released by the House Communications Subcommittee in April 1977.[7] *The Options Papers* consist of a succession of chapters covering the whole range of broadcasting, common carriers, international telecom-munications, cable, land mobile radio and privacy. Each chapter discusses several alternative policies for that particular field, with, in many cases, further sublists of neatly balanced advantages and dis-advantages. This avalanche of 'neutral' advice strongly implied, first, that new technology had by 1977 created a sizeable number of policy options; second, that the status quo represented one rather arbitrary choice from the range available.

Despite the numerous changes which have occurred in the meantime – many presaged in the *Options Papers* – these 1977 ideas still read quite well. The opening chapter challenged the FCC practice on comparative license renewal as being slow and inefficient, preferring the use of some market mechanism such as lottery or auction. The next chapter suggested that there were at least four different possible regulatory strategies in the case of broadcasting alone: the license option, the lease, the public utility and, finally, the access or quasi common carrier option.

On domestic common carrier policy the *Options Papers* pointed to two key questions: 'What portion of the joint costs of the local telephone network shall be assigned to the interstate jurisdiction?' and 'What is the boundary between regulated monopoly markets and other markets, and under what conditions will regulated monopolists be allowed to cross the border?' (pp. 367, 417).

The chapter on international telecommunications was equally to the point. US foreign telecoms are characterized by a whole series of arbitrary distinctions – from ocean cable (in the hands of AT&T *et al.*) to the world cartel of INTELSAT in the satellite field. US international telecoms is split into an arbitrary set of compartments (video, voice, data), and when a new service arises, a new monopoly carrier is created – thus *facsimile* appears and is awarded to a new purpose-built monopoly carrier called Graphnet; there is also a complete lack of fit between the European monopoly PTTS and the peculiar regulated cartels and minimonopolies of the US. Cable television was seen in the *Options Papers* as yet another area of confusion; cable is part common carrier and part broadcaster, thus belonging to two different regulatory regimes. In addition to having a split personality within the FCC, cable is also regulated by local governments at various levels.

A later chapter listed a dozen possible locations for telecoms policy in the Washington bureaucracy, one of which involved the often suggested option of taking all the telecoms responsibilities currently fragmented across some 40 separate federal agencies and placing them in a single Department of Telecommunications.

When the first rewrite bill appeared the next year, 1978, it did not include many of the *Options Papers'* options, and thus some industry sighs of relief were in order. However, the proposals in HR.13015 did include replacement of the FCC and a radical transformation of AT&T by the excision of Western Electric, its giant manufacturing arm.

The unusually lengthy hearings in the House of Representatives on *The Communications Act of 1978* opened on 12 hot days in July–August. Thus began the long procession of witnesses – the commissioners of the

FCC, the heads of the main telecommunications enterprises and many more. Most witnesses politely applauded the subcommittee for its wisdom in holding the hearings and for the vision of some of its proposals. Witnesses typically had strong reservations, however, about the particular fate indicated for themselves and their interests. The witnesses' relentless pursuit of what Van Deerlin called 'a fair advantage' augured badly for the legislative outcome; but the same distinguished witnesses' happiness about deregulation and competition, for others and in general, helped to legitimize competitive ideas which until recently would have seemed radical and unworldly.

Van Deerlin, Frey and Shooshan saw themselves as being involved in a series of trade-offs. They would take on all the industry lobbies at the same time and would offer each lobby a trade-off, the most basic trade-off being: you can be deregulated, but in return, you, like all the others, must also accept more competition.

Broadcasters 'hate competition more than they hate regulation' was one Van Deerlin explanation as to why the NAB came out in full opposition to the rewrite. But this is not the whole story; Van Deerlin's tactics on broadcasting were quite subtle. He himself was a strong believer in getting rid of irritating content restrictions such as equal time and fairness; obviously the NAB agreed. Van Deerlin was also against the whole business of comparative license renewal proceedings if the current licensee was challenged. He was in favor of awarding licenses more or less permanently; and in the case of radio this would be done immediately, thus tactically driving a decisive wedge between the TV membership and the radio membership of the NAB. But in return for this concession, Van Deerlin was also demanding a pound of flesh in the form of a 'spectrum use fee'; in return for permanent tenure, the licensees would have to pay for the privilege of using the scarce resource. Although the proposed 1978 total of $267 million may not have looked large to outsiders, at the time it would have been enough to fund both the FCC and Public Broadcasting. The fee system seemed to fall especially heavily in the biggest markets, and thus on the networks.[8] The broadcasters also objected for a mixture of other reasons, including their reluctance to cede the argument that, despite the First Amendment, they could be charged a fee; once this principle was accepted, the modest initial fee, which many smaller stations would pay, could rise. The stick-and-carrot approach meant that the broadcasters tasted the carrot, but thought they could have the carrot without the stick. If even a liberal Democrat like Van Deerlin could consider offering complete deregulation, might it not be possible to take this part of the trade-off without paying the price? This argument also gained support when in 1979, the second rewrite indicated a sharply reduced level of spectrum use fees.

Similar thoughts were prevalent in other fields. AT&T was also offered a trade-off: in return for loss of parts of its phone monopoly, it would be allowed to compete in the previously forbidden areas of computing and data transmission. The 1978 rewrite would have exacted the divestiture of Western Electric as the price. Next year, in the second rewrite, Van Deerlin lowered the price, allowing AT&T to keep its manufacturing arm, and only requiring it to accept such competition as the expansion of rival long-distance phone companies. By 1979 the trade-off presented to AT&T had altered again. But while the HR.6121 trade-offs now achieved 13 to 1 support in the House subcommittee, AT&T was still dubious.

The trade-off for the cable TV industry was that cable would win almost total deregulation, but at the price of no longer having an automatic right to retransmit distant broadcast signals locally. Since bringing in distant signals from larger cities had been so crucial to its rise, the cable industry strongly objected. Perhaps they too thought that they could have the carrot without the stick.

In retrospect, AT&T might have been wise to accept the third rewrite of 1980, because this bill (HR.6121) involved far fewer concessions than AT&T subsequently made in the Consent Decree of January 1982. In fact, AT&T had a fairly easy time sinking HR.6121. One highly placed friend in the House, Peter Rodino, was all it took. Rodino, as a long-time Representative from AT&T's second home state of New Jersey, was a natural ally. When the third rewrite came out of the Communications Subcommittee, Rodino pulled rank as chairman of the House Judiciary Committee, asking the House Speaker to refer the bill to his committee for a look at its antitrust aspects. The Judiciary Subcommittee on Monopolies (also chaired by Rodino) held two days of hearings that September. Its subsequent opinion was negative, and rewrite number three was dead.[9]

Another problem for Van Deerlin was that his opposite number in the Senate, 'Fritz' Hollings, was less dedicated to the total rewrite approach, and that, while he liked the idea of rewriting just the telecommunications part of the 1934 Act, he had higher priorities as a senior Senate figure with other more important (to him) chairmanships. Moreover, Hollings also had two upcoming elections on his mind; in 1980 he was running for reelection to the US Senate, and was already preparing for his presidential bid of 1984.

The other key Senate member with whom Van Deerlin established some, but not quite enough, rapport was Barry Goldwater. Goldwater and Hollings had almost reached an agreement in 1979. And had Van Deerlin been willing to drop the not very large (in dollar terms) spectrum use fee, he might have had Goldwater's support, thus making for a bipartisan subcommittee front in both House and Senate. But the spectrum use fee was the minimum condition that Van Deerlin's Democratic colleagues on the House subcommittee would accept in return for broadcast deregulation. And this was only part of the difficulty Van Deerlin had in carrying with him his fellow Democrats on the subcommittee. When the key period for the comprehensive second rewrite came in early summer of 1979 – as the bill came for markup and forwarding to the full Commerce Committee – Democratic support was fading. The Republicans stuck with Van Deerlin, but the Democrats found themselves assailed by an alliance of industry lobbies and citizens' groups, the latter proclaiming that the rewrite was giving away the store to the lobbies, while hazarding universal phone service, citizen access, public broadcasting and equal employment opportunity. Van Deerlin claims to have been surprised by this populist outburst. But he should not have been. Tim Wirth, for example, had all along been a critic of the total rewrite concept as too large and cumbersome for success, and there were others.

Van Deerlin was defeated in San Diego in November 1980, in part because he had taken his district too much for granted. His successful opponent further reduced Van Deerlin's sinking chances with a grossly dishonest mailing five days before the election. In an envelope that superficially resembled a Bell one (the front had a telephone logo, the back a US area-code map), there was an official-looking message which stated that Van Deerlin's phone legislation would double San Diego phone bills.[10] Van Deerlin, unlike the true media politician with financial reserves available for a return advertising blast at the last moment, could make no effective reply. But Van Deerlin had rewritten the agenda of the national communications debate, and his ideas will also be influential in countries far from San Diego.

1981, REAGAN'S YEAR: THE SCENE IS SET

In retrospect, the high tide of communications deregulatory fervor may be seen to have occurred in 1981. This was the year in which the Republicans took control of the White House and the Senate; with right-wing conservatives installed at Commerce, the FCC and elsewhere, the relatively strong minority position of Republicans in the House was the crucial limit to legislative possibilities. The White House and nearly everyone else calculated (accurately) that, without Reagan's coattails, the House would swing back in a more Democrat direction in November 1982. The new White House staff initially focused its prime attention on a radical Reaganization of the federal budget. Its plans for many other things, communications deregulation included, were relatively vague and unformed.

One of the most important deregulatory moves, the extension of radio and TV station licenses to seven and five years respectively, was actually passed as part of a last-minute compendium budget measure in late July of 1981. But the Commerce Department was in the midst of a shambles of budget-cutting, as was the FCC, at a time when the Republicans had their best chance of pushing through a comprehensive set of communications policies. In the Senate, Packwood wheeled out his legislation with tactically correct briskness; but Packwood, too, fumed at the delay and political ineptness displayed by the White House. Dingell and Wirth held Packwood to a draw on the broadcast/ budget negotiations, and then in late 1981 began to stake out their defensive positions.

January 1982 saw the announcement of the AT&T divestiture. By now the schedule for the next three Reagan years was largely set, and any subsequent deregulatory initiatives were of less than strategic significance. So 1981 was the year, and some of the main events were as follows:

(1) On 7 April Senator Packwood introduced S.898, the Telecommunications Competition and Deregulation Bill. This measure would allow extensive competition, but it involved no divestiture, and it allowed Bell to offer unregulated services.

(2) On 2 June a hearings session on S.898, chaired by Packwood, was told that administration witnesses would not be appearing to testify. Packwood angrily denounced this lack of White House readiness.

(3) In early June, Packwood decided to throw all his current broadcasting deregulatory bills into the mammoth compendium budget bill. These bills included S.601 to extend station licenses; S.821 to turn the FCC from a permanent agency to one requiring legislative renewal every three years; and measures on Public Broadcasting finance and on technical standards. This package was accepted by the full Commerce Committee and, with yet more broadcast items added, passed the full Senate by 55 to 40.

(4) Several weeks later the Senate–House conference stage was reached. Although S.601, the license renewal measure, was Goldwater's, the conference negotiation was left entirely to Packwood. For the House, Dingell held all the Democratic votes, but Wirth was also present. Negotiations consumed the entire weekend of July 25–26 and ran into Monday. The final compromise included extended license terms, PBS funding and permission for the FCC to use a lottery. All other broadcast provisions were struck out. This package became part of the new budget law.

(5) On 7 October the Senate's telecommunications bill was passed, by 90 to 4. Wirth announced that his House version of the bill would differ in many aspects.

(6) On 10 December Wirth's House version, HR.5158, was introduced, and it was much less favorable to AT&T. (This was the move that speeded up AT&T's acceptance of divestiture.)

(7) A few days earlier, Dingell had announced his general opposition to further deregulation and his belief in broadcasting as a public service.

AT&T WINS ONE AND LOSES ONE

In 1982 the old AT&T used its lobbying resources to the full, and managed to kill a House telecommunications bill which it disliked. But when the next major congressional test arose, this time concerning the about-to-be-divested AT&T, the FCC and AT&T suffered a major defeat over the issue of access charges and the maintenance of universal telephone service.

In the first place the Senate has passed on 7 October 1981 a bill (S.898) which gave AT&T the kind of deregulation it could accept. But the surprisingly easy passage of this rather pro-AT&T measure through the Senate was not to be matched in the House. The only recently installed subcommittee chairman, Tim Wirth, had already established a track record on AT&T; his position emphasized both making AT&T compete and also retaining regulation against cross-subsidy and predatory competition.

The first unveiling of this bill, on 8 December 1981, had been one unpleasant surprise for AT&T. A second surprise was that despite the 8 January 1982 divestiture announcement, Wirth refused to drop his bill, arguing that it was the task of Congress, not the courts and the Justice Department, to set national policy. In the House hearings on the Wirth bill, AT&T made its strong opposition very clear. But an even bigger surprise was to follow. The bill came out of the subcommittee with all 15 members voting 'against AT&T' as AT&T saw it. Alvin Von Auw's approved 'reflections' record these events in language whose superficial coolness does not mask the bitter resentment:

March 25 (1982)	The House telecommunications subcommittee approves by 15–0 vote a version of HR.5158 that would isolate Long Lines as a separate subsidiary, impose handicaps and restrictions on telephone network services and activities required by the marketplace after divestiture, give Yellow Pages to the divested companies along with existing customer premises equipment and keep AT and T out of information service markets.
March 25	Mr Brown [AT&T chief executive] urges employees and stockholders to express their views on HR.5158 to their elected representatives.

April 21   At annual meeting in April, Mr. Brown tells share
                    owners that HR.5158 would restrict the Bell System
                    and provoke years more of litigation, uncertainty
                    and regulatory snarl.[11]

From 25 March to 27 July AT&T mounted four months of lobbying which
some observers say was one of the most intensive efforts ever seen on
Capitol Hill. AT&T activated its three million stockholders and one
million employees; it placed 'HR.5158 is a Wrong Number' advertisements in 150 leading newspapers. The CWA, after a favorable labor
settlement, also campaigned for AT&T. The phone company was accused
of allowing employees to use company stationery and postage meters.
Some Bell local companies put anti-HR.5158 fliers in the monthly
phone-bill envelope. Some individual congressmen are said to have
received as many as 20,000 letters.

But that was only part one of the campaign, because the bill still
seemed likely to clear the full Commerce Committee with a big vote.
And an easy majority was in store in the full House.[12] However, AT&T
found a filibusterer in Tom Corcoran, an Illinois Republican whose
district south of Chicago included thousands of Western Electric and
Bell Labs employees. Corcoran repeatedly used such tactics as insisting
that the clerk read his 100-page amendments (supplied by AT&T) in full.
By such tactics Corcoran, largely alone, talked the bill to death in the
full Commerce Committee.[13]

AT&T certainly won this congressional battle, but at the cost of strong
resentment of their legislative tactics. One consequence may have been
the high level of bipartisan support for universal telephone legislation a
year later. The FCC itself initially delayed its access charges from 1
January 1984 to 3 April, under strong pressure from Congress. But the
full House passed its universal phone legislation in November 1983.

More remarkable, perhaps, was that Packwood's S.1660 Universal
Phone Bill caused such a stir in the Senate. This was a complex measure
from the Senate's great communications deregulator which proposed a
complex set of subsidies for locations where long-distance costs were
above average; ironically, not only did this bill interfere with market
forces by subsidy, but it also attempted to cut back on that other market
phenomenon of bypass. This was Packwood the populist senator from
the mountainous Northwest. The White House was hostile to this
measure (as to the House one), and there was a sharp split between
Goldwater and Packwood. The Packwood bill was only narrowly
defeated, 44 to 40, suggesting a far from smooth ride for both AT&T and
the FCC in the Senate in the future.

The universal phone legislation saw some old partnerships renewed,
especially that of AT&T and the FCC. But some interesting new partnerships also emerged. Against the legislation was the entire telephone

lobby – not only AT&T, but MCI and GTE – and the entire New Jersey congressional delegation. In favor of the bills were all the public interest groups, the elderly, the police and most of the PUCS, as well as both Dingell and Packwood.

Here for the first time was a telecommunications bill on which members of Congress went in fear of voter retribution. Something had to be done. It was – by Senator Dole, who with 33 other senators, mostly Republicans, called on the FCC to delay its residential and single-line small business end user charges until 1985.

BROADCAST DEREGULATION: SLOWLY, SLOWLY

Senator Packwood's decision to grab what broadcast deregulation he could get in the early months of the Reagan presidency in 1981 was shown by subsequent events to have been a wise one. Broadcast deregulation had received no further legislative support by the end of 1984. Although, on at least two occasions, in spring of 1983 and spring of 1984, it looked to some legislators as if the House would accept the Senate's lead.

Certainly the Senate was in the lead throughout 1981 and 1982. After the budget measures of summer 1981, supporters of broadcast deregulation in the Senate took all the items dropped at the House – Senate conference and made these the basis of a new bill. This was Senator Howard Cannon's (a conservative Nevada Democrat) S.1629, which passed the Commerce Committee in December 1981. There was then some delay – over the old question of New Jersey and Delaware both lacking a commercial VHF TV station but the bill finally passed the Senate on 31 March 1982. This bill confirmed the FCC's almost total deregulation of radio, and, by abolishing comparative renewal, made both radio and TV station license renewal virtually automatic.

In the House, Wirth and Dingell were waiting to see what the Senate would finally produce; their preference for a very cautious consideration of any further broadcast moves looked increasingly reasonable during 1982, the year of the extraordinary AT&T lobby and filibuster. Nevertheless, the prospects for some House movement in the following year looked quite good. Indeed James Broyhill (Republican from North Carolina), the ranking Republican on the House Commerce Committee, introduced measures (HR.5584/5) which went beyond the Senate position. Even more significant, Al Swift, Democratic House member from Washington State, introduced into the House the measure already passed in the Senate.

In early 1983, in the new Congress, House prospects for broadcast deregulation continued to look rosy. A bipartisan bill was introduced by

Billy Tauzin and Tom Tauke, respectively Louisiana Democrat and Iowa Republican. At this point over half the House membership indicated their support for the Tauke–Tauzin bill. However, it failed to pass. The Tauke–Tauzin tactics were to make an end run around Wirth's subcommittee obstruction, and to use the popularity of deregulation, plus the lobbying support of NAB and the networks, to get the measure past the full Commerce Committee. The initial idea was naive, however; after his recent experiences with AT&T, Wirth was unlikely to take kindly to these aggressive tactics. The end run also depended on Dingell's choosing to support the NAB and the broadcast lobby, rather than his independent-minded subcommitee chairman. Dingell's initial silence was incorrectly read as indecision; it was simply Dingell using standard delaying tactics before placing his crucial support firmly behind Wirth. It was, in fact, the Tauke–Tauzin NAB lobby that was indecisive. Faced with the prospect of a bitter battle with Dingell and Wirth, Tauke and Tauzin agreed to negotiate; this wasted most of the rest of 1983, and allowed Wirth to regain control of the situation and of the legislation.

Wirth's tactics, like those of all cautious deregulators, were to demand some public interest quid pro quo in return. Up to this point Wirth had been demanding a spectrum use fee; now, in negotiation with Tauke and Tauzin, he agreed to drop the fee (which was anathema to all broadcast lobbyists); instead, he agreed to a different kind of public interest safeguard – namely, some kind of quantified quota of serious programming (such as a certain number of hours per week) to be required in return for deregulation. The notorious difficulties of framing broadcasting legislation containing legal quantification should have been a warning as to what Wirth was doing. To revert back to the football metaphor, rather than being end-run, Wirth was himself wrong-footing the entire opposing defense. For Wirth agreed to use Al Swift's deregulation-cum-quantification measure as a new basis. This move pulled Swift back onto the Wirth team. Meanwhile, the House subcommittee staff doggedly began to prepare the quantification exercise by sending out questionnaires to 1,000 radio stations. NAB naively fell into the trap by opposing such committee snooping. This simply created more of the very delay which was Wirth's goal.

The entire broadcast lobby began to reveal that it suffered from a bad case of deregulatory fragmentation. There was little leadership, coordination, or tactical insight in what had looked like a powerful coalition. Tauke and Tauzin in the House, Packwood in the Senate, Fowler at the FCC, the networks and the radio industry all showed themselves more interested in their own narrow concerns than in easing broadcast deregulation through an initially favorable House of Representatives.

Compared with Senator Packwood's decisiveness and success in a few weeks in summer 1981, this lobbying battle was a shambles of two years' duration. Packwood himself hardly helped the cause by his vigorous pursuit of freedom of expression and his determination to throw away the fairness and equal time provisions which most members of Congress wanted to keep. It was Packwood, also, who bluntly accused the NAB of being unable to lobby its way out of a paper bag in the House.

The NAB leadership at the time was in a state of disarray. A very inexperienced Southern small-town broadcaster, Eddie Fritts, was trying to establish himself as its new and credible president; he was also attempting to give the NAB a more aggressive profile. But more experienced observers of the Washington scene correctly foretold the outcome. *Broadcasting* magazine, normally a pro-NAB voice, was on several occasions distinctly skeptical, and despite its hostility to Wirth, neatly described the NAB's tactics as 'Wirth-less'.

In addition to being ineptly led, broadcasting was also exhibiting its familiar internal splits. The small-station radio trade association NRBA infuriated many fellow lobbyists by actually accepting the idea of a small spectrum fee; at this time the larger group TV owners were setting up a separate trade body. Meanwhile the TV networks were giving higher priority to their financial interest/syndication battle – a network effort which not only led to defeat at the hands of Hollywood, but was also a reminder to many members of Congress of how much they had always disliked the networks.

Yet further disarray came from the direction of the FCC. Mark Fowler's support for the NAB inevitably left the FCC open to the accusation that a supposedly neutral federal agency was once again aligning itself as part of a greedy commercial lobby. Eddie Fritts and Mark Fowler were also vulnerable to characterization as a pair of politically naive, brash, small-town southern radio advertising salesmen who were now trying to hustle the Congress of the US into a crude giveaway of a public trust.

After the failure of 1983 negotiations, they continued in a desultory way into 1984. Once again the NAB attempted to go around the Wirth subcommittee to the full committee; this time it was exasperated by Wirth gradually raising his demands again – now including a special children's time quota for all TV stations, and (in league with Leland of Texas) new equal employment demands. But the NAB's faith in Dingell's willingness to undermine Wirth was shown yet again to be mistaken. The final blow was struck by Packwood, who disapproved of the current state of the Tauke–Tauzin–NAB bill (HR.2382). Packwood, with typical bluntness, ordered the NAB to drop the bill.[14] This last unkind cut showed that the supposedly all-powerful NAB had managed completely to misread the intentions of all three of the key communications policy players in Congress.

Broadcast deregulation legislation was now effectively dead for 1984, and the year's remaining moves consisted of staking out starting positions for 1985.

CABLE: THE ONE MAJOR PIECE OF DEREGULATORY LEGISLATION

On 11 October 1984 the final conference version of a major bill to deregulate cable passed both Senate and House; later the same evening Congress adjourned for the biennial election. This bill, which just scraped through in the last hours, was the only comprehensive piece of communications deregulation to become law in the entire four years 1981–4.

Why did this legislation succeed, where so much other communications legislation had failed? The answer seems to be that, despite some initial appearances to the contrary, all four communications barons in Congress were in favor of bringing some legislative order into the quite exceptional chaos of cable regulation. Certainly they had some difference. As was usual during the years 1981–4, the Senate Republican barons, Goldwater and Packwood, were out in front with a sweeping set of deregulatory proposals which their fellow senators saw as relatively noncontroversial. The House waited for the Senate to take the lead; and again, as usual, there was some friction between Dingell and Wirth, although this time Wirth was strongly for deregulation, whereas Dingell, with his big-city liberal background, tended to side with the cities and mayors against the cable industry. However Dingell's opposition was in part a ritual exercise for constituency consumption. Dingell early made clear to the National League of Cities that he would not block the legislation in the House Commerce Committee.

Even with the active or passive support of these four barons, it still took cable deregulation 31 months to become law; and throughout that time the prospects roller-coasted frequently. The problem for the legislators was not disagreement among themselves – even between two Senate conservative Republicans and two House liberal Democrats – nor was it, on this occasion, one of the politicians being persecuted and undermined by the lobbies. The main problem was that the politicians did not wish to go ahead without the agreement both of the cities and the cable industry; much of the pressure in fact consisted of key politicians trying to force agreement both among and between the cities and the cable industry.

The original Goldwater bill (S.2172) took from March 1982 to June 1983 to pass the Senate by 87 to 9. Under its later designation of S.66, the Senate bill was highly deregulatory: while franchise renewal was not automatic, the rather vague wording suggested that license nonrenewal would be about as uncommon as it had been in television; and the fee charged by a franchising authority could not exceed 5 per cent of revenue, which matched existing FCC rules.

In the ebb and flow of negotiation, many important middle-range details kept altering shape, but all versions of the legislation gave cable franchise-holders a high degree of programming and financial autonomy. The main problems in this cable legislation saga occurred after the House hearings began in May 1983. For the next year and a half the legislation went through many crises. But two were especially severe, both involving splits within one of the main camps.

One major crisis occurred in November–December 1983, when the National League of Cities disowned what its own negotiators had agreed upon with the NCTA. And only a few months later, in the spring of 1984, the NCTA, accused by the cities of having stolen the show, began to complain that the legislation offered little or nothing that could not be acquired by other means. The NCTA was buoyed up by the belief that if the legislation failed, then the FCC would go ahead and deregulate anyway. In addition, several court decisions around this time favored cable, and seemed to amount to de facto deregulation. The cable industry may also have thought that as a result of the Warner–Amex debacle, the cities were being forced to behave more reasonably. For such reasons, the NCTA started in August 1984 to campaign against the bill it had previously supported.

Throughout September 1984, the Cable Bill's fate hung in the balance. Full-page advertisements – for and against, bitter and statesman-like – blossomed in the cable trade papers. AT&T fought its common carrier corner against cable incursions. Mickey Leland of Texas increased his demands in the equal opportunity area. John Malone, Mr Plain Vanilla Cable of Denver, suddenly threw his weight behind the bill as essential to the long-term stability of the industry. And John Dingell left it to the very last moment to get off the fence; he then bludgeoned, bullied, threatened, begged and cursed the cable executives. And with this bravura display of baronial clout, the serfs finally agreed to accept the bill.

That a cable bill which attracted so much strategic support, such tactical finesse, and so much good luck only just scraped through, shows how hard it is for communications legislation to go all the way – and just how absolute a lobby veto can be.

Notes

1 'Van Deerlin: Making a Difference', *Broadcasting*, 7 May 1979, pp. 39–50.
2 Three interviews with Lionel Van Deerlin, all in San Diego, in June 1979 and twice in April 1984.

3 Two-part interview with Timothy Wirth, *Communications Daily*, 8 and 9 February 1984, pp. 2–6, 3–5. 'Tim Wirth: Boulder's Voice in Congress', *Boulder Winter Guide*, 1983–4, pp. 7–9. 'The Congressman and the Achilles Heel', *Broadcasting*, 17 October 1983, pp. 42–54.

4 This was the title given to a series of investigative articles by David Maraniss on the House Commerce Committee – for example, 'Leaders tailor panels for productivity', *Washington Post*, 22 May 1983, pp. A1–A8; 'Power Play: Chairman's gavel crushes gas decontrol vote', *Washington Post*, 20 November 1983, pp. A1–A9; 'Hard questions in Acid-rain control are who benefits and who must pay', *Washington Post*, 29 January 1984, pp. A1–A6.

5 David E. Price, *The Commerce Committees* (1975); see especially chapter 5, 'Communications', pp. 212–51.

6 Dennis Farney, 'Gunning for game is the favorite sport of Rep. John Dingell', *Wall Street Journal*, 17 November 1983, pp. 1, 27.

7 US House of Representatives, Subcommittee on Communications of the Committee on Interstate and Foreign Commerce, *Options Papers prepared by the Staff for Use by the Subcommittee on Communications* (1977).

8 Six VHF stations in New York would each have had to pay $7.7 million, eating up the bulk of their profit. In the tenth market, Dallas–Forth Worth, four VHF stations would each have had to pay $1.7 million, equalling 25 per cent of annual profits. In market number 60, Knoxville, Tennessee, two VHF stations would have each paid $328,000, equalling 17 per cent of profits.

9 US House of Representatives, 96th Congress, 2nd Session Committee on the Judiciary, *Telecommunications Act of 1980. Adverse Report Together With Additional and Supplemental Views*. (To accompany HR.6121).

10 A copy of this mailing was shown to the author by Lionel Van Deerlin in April of 1984.

11 Auw, *Heritage and Destiny*, pp. 420–1.

12 'Telecom Insider poll reveals that AT and T is losing fight to kill HR.5158', *Telecom Insider*, June 1982, p. 1.

13 David Maraniss, 'How AT and T got Hill to hang up on a reform bill', *Washington Post*, 6 October 1983, pp. A1, A2.

14 'Packwood warns NAB to avoid House dereg bill – or else', *Broadcasting*, 2 April 1984.

19

The FCC: Regulation in Fragments

The FCC may appear, especially as seen from other countries, to be the engine that drives US communications policy, and recently as the leader in communications deregulation. Such an impression, however, is mistaken. The key communications policymakers in Congress are fond of reminding the FCC that it is a creature of Congress, and they speak only the truth.

The FCC is indeed a creature of, or a football for, all the main branches of government. Its commissioners are appointed by the president, and they continue to look to the executive branch for ideological guidance. In some respects the FCC is subordinate to the Commerce Department's NTIA; the latter is in strategic charge of the whole radio spectrum, while the FCC allocates only its nonmilitary frequencies.

The FCC is also beholden to the courts; indeed its decisions, like those of other regulatory agencies, can be, and frequently are, appealed to the US Court of Appeals in Washington. And the FCC is also beholden to the commercial lobbies – it has long been quite cautious, for example, about disagreeing with AT&T or the TV networks.

The FCC comes into conflict with, and tends to be slapped down by, all these major branches of government, in part because it has such a wide range of functions, which include elements of the administrative, the judicial and the legislative.

Its *administrative* activities include administering the Communications Act of 1934; it processes applications, forms and permits by the thousand.

Its *quasi-judicial* functions include making choices between competing applicants for the scarce slots in the radio spectrum, and setting technical standards. Moreover, it still presides over AT&T activities by vetting its services and prices.

Its *quasi-legislative* functions include promulgating what are virtually new laws to cover new services and new technologies.

In carrying out these functions, which incorporate bits of all the three main branches of government, the FCC also has its own legalistic rules of procedure, with set periods of 90 or 120 days allowed for commenting on its proposals, and so on.

In addition, the FCC has a certain ideological makeup. The Reagan appointees were chosen for their ideological rectitude and, given the many conflicting allegiances, it should not be too surprising perhaps that the Reagan FCC by 1983 had elevated deregulation from a means to an end, some said to a theology.

But therein lies another dilemma. The more quiescent the FCC, the more the three branches of government let it alone. But the higher the FCC's profile – and it has been high ever since the civil rights movement of the 1960s – the more likely it is to be slapped down, particularly by Congress.

Nearly three years into the Reagan presidency, the *Wall Street Journal* ran a series of articles on 'the rule slashers', one of which was headed 'In Rush to Deregulate, FCC Outpaces Others, Pleasing the Industry'.[1] But the biggest pieces of deregulation, such as the AT&T divestiture, were not the work of the FCC. Moreover, the possibilities for pleasing all the competing industries were not great – for example, cable's gain tended to be broadcasting's loss.

Nevertheless, as the *Wall Street Journal* article also stated, the Reagan FCC chairman, Mark Fowler, had become known by some as the 'Mad Monk of Deregulation'. The 'mad' was earned partly by Fowler's willingness to say slightly outrageous things in press interviews. But the title also sums up a characteristic FCC form of hyperactivity. The Fowler approach was to 'unregulate' as much as possible, in part to create such a flood of decisions that at least some would get past the vetoes of Congress and the courts. For the FCC under Fowler, getting rid of regulations was partly a matter of free market ideology, and partly an administrative device to cope with a burgeoning mountain of bureaucratic chores at a time of staff- and budget-cutting.

With a staff of nearly 2,000, the FCC is asked not only to oversee its old fields of telephone and broadcasting, now bigger and more complex themselves, but also to manage the domestic side of the radio spectrum, to be responsible for space satellites, and to make decisions about under-ocean international cables. Further, it is increasingly involved in a myriad of international problems – a whole new vast field of electronics/high-tech trade and diplomacy; and it also impinges on the whole world of computers and data flow – notionally, at least, influencing the extent to which AT&T gets into battle with IBM. More generally, the FCC is involved in the crucial merging of telephone and computer; it also has such other matters to consider as cable, DBS and the ISDN.

In each of these areas the FCC has quite limited authority in practice. In most cases a small segment of its total personnel confront a much bigger and more powerful commercial entity. In other cases, such as satellite policy, where the FCC has formal power to license domestic satellite services, the matter is of interest to such Washington heavyweights as the DOD and NASA.

Asked to regulate in detail some of the most complex and fast-changing issues of our time – satellites above, cables below, what children see on TV, technical standards for many new technologies – the FCC has dutifully established a quasi-judicial set of procedures, which are also (like the fields they cover) complex and fast-moving, or at least fast to accumulate freshly minted subregulations. Then, having piled up this mountain of rules in the sixties and early seventies, the FCC in the mid-seventies began slowly to dismantle the system and to throw away as many rules as possible.

THE FCC AS A CREATURE OF CONGRESS

Unlike his two predecessors as FCC chairmen, both of whom had experience working as congressional staffers, Mark Fowler, when appointed in 1981, had no experience or knowledge of Congress. And for his first two years at least, he was in continual conflict with Congress. Part of this, however, was due to the fact that from 1981 onward the Republicans controlled the Senate, while the Democrats still controlled the House. Fowler tended to side with ideological friends in the Senate and then get caught up in the conflict between the Senate and the House.

However, there was also an element of the Fowler FCC thinking that it could somehow stampede the House Democrats into accepting more deregulation than they really wanted. A somewhat similar mistake had recently been made, in a different ideological direction, at the FTC. Michael Pertschuk had headed the Senate Commerce Committee staff, and had pursued the liberal Democratic pro-consumer policies of its leadership up to 1978. At this point Pertschuk was appointed to the post of chairman of the FTC, where he attempted to continue the same liberal activist pro-consumer policies. However, the 1978 elections led to a major turnover in membership of the Senate Commerce Committee. Pertschuk ran into aggressive opposition from the new membership, which no longer favored a hard consumerist line against breakfast cereal manufacturers and funeral directors. The result was a sequence of unsettling and humiliating retreats forced upon the FTC's new chairman; indeed, a new phrase was coined to describe his unpleasant experiences – 'to be Pertschuked', which, loosely translated, means to learn the hard way what it means to be a creature of Congress. Pertschuk has described his experience with splendid insider insights and self-deprecating humor in his book *Revolt Against Revolution*. Two more detached students analyzed the same events and find no mystery, only continuity. The FTC (like the FCC) follows congressional opinion; the turbulence at the FTC in 1979–80 was caused by a change in the congressional leadership and the reluctance of an ex-Senate staffer FTC chairman to accept this.[2]

How does an agency like the FTC or FCC follow congressional opinion? Given the Packwood/Goldwater/Dingell/Wirth differences of opinion within and between the relevant committees in 1981–4, there were some problems of detailed interpretation. But basically the congressional committees had all the power, and were quite prepared to use it. Formal appearance on Capitol Hill in general, and appropriations hearings in particular, left little doubt that the FCC was beholden for its existence to Congress. In addition there is a day-to-day flood of public statements, speeches, comments and briefings of *Communications Daily* and other trade publications. Moreover, the congressional personal and subcommittee staffs are constantly in touch with the personal staffs of FCC commissioners, as well as with FCC bureau chiefs and others. This flow cannot but delineate where the lines of disagreement lie and roughly where a negotiated consensus might be sought.

After the turbulence of 1981, even the exceptionally ideological Fowler FCC slowly came to recognize that the consequences of trying to bypass either communications subcommittee were likely to be painful. And increasingly, decisions reached in public discussion at meetings of the FCC commissioners had not only been rehearsed previously among the commissioners, but had already been agreed upon by the key players in Congress. A 1984 example, which showed this FCC learning process still at work, was the decision to extend TV station ownership rules. In 1984 the FCC unilaterally changed its old rule of a maximum of 7 to a new figure of 12 stations. However, in early August it yielded to congressional opposition; Wirth introduced legislation in the House specifically forbidding the FCC move, and a similar bill was being prepared in the Senate. Four months later the FCC commissioners voted on, and accepted, a revised version of the new rules which added another maximum figure – no TV group's stations were to reach more than 25 per cent of the US population. This compromise was orchestrated by Wirth and the House subcommittee staff, with the active involvement of Senator Pete Wilson of California, who, although not on the Senate Commerce Committee, was a close friend of Hollywood.[3] In July 1985 the FCC was prompted by senators from five rural states to inquire into how it should handle hostile broadcasting takeover bids.

THE REGULATIONS ACCUMULATE: EARLY 1960S TO EARLY 1970S

The FCC during the 1960s in effect had a policy of protecting its major friends – AT&T and the networks – while giving some very modest encouragement to the new boys on the block, such as the competing phone companies, specialized carriers and also CATV.

But in addition to the quantitative change – the rapid increase in the numbers of licenses – the 1960s also saw a qualitative change, which was perhaps best signalled by Newton Minow, the Kennedy FCC chairman, who focused national attention on the low quality of US TV programming. By describing television as 'a vast wasteland', Minow was pointing to the content of TV, an area sometimes believed to be out of First Amendment bounds. This and other events in the 1960s – not least the civil rights movement and the Vietnam War – focused attention on such questions as the number of black faces and the selection of war footage seen on television.

Even if not much else happened, there was a great increase in meetings, hearings, and confrontations on these citizens', equal opportunity and access issues. For a time the FCC was almost transformed into a PR organization first, and a mass media and telecoms regulator second. This period is perceptively and amusingly described in *Reluctant Regulators*, by Barry Cole and Mal Oettinger.

Regulation of content always had to be approached indirectly, and certainly required more regulation to achieve less result or an unintended result: for example, the FCC's 1970 Prime-Time Access rule, while intended to open up a slot alongside the national news for half an hour of good local programming, in fact led to a bonanza in game shows syndicated from Hollywood.

But there was indeed a proliferation of regulations bordering the forbidden area. One prominent example was broadcast 'ascertainment' – an elaborate and ever increasing list of organizations whose leaders a TV or radio station manager must formally interview for the purpose of ascertaining their views on their local communities' issues and needs. The increasing complexity of ascertainment sent station managers into a quiet rage. In 1976 the FCC amended its regulations to identify 19 local categories that broadcasters should consider as significant local groups. In 1980, with radio deregulation now well advanced, the FCC was clarifying its ascertainment list yet again, this time including the handicapped and homosexuals.[4]

DEREGULATION BEGINS: WILEY SLOW, FERRIS FURIOUSLY

Richard Wiley, FCC chairman 1974–7, saw himself as not simply the first chairman who really went out and listened to the people, but also as the first of the deregulators. In retrospect, he is perhaps a transitional figure who contained the flood of new regulations and began to plan for an opposite movement.

It was under Charles E. Ferris, Carter's FCC chairman (1977–81) that deregulation began. Ferris's term of office saw the Van Deerlin rewrite efforts. The commissioners did indeed respond wonderfully to the 1977 Van Deerlin suggestion that they should be abolished. There were major decisions aimed at comprehensively deregulating cable and radio. Although there had been FCC economists before, a new wave arrived in 1979, with all five professional positions in the Office of Plans and Policy occupied by economists.[5]

A sharp illustration of what deregulation meant occurred in early 1980, when the FCC unveiled its proposed new broadcast license renewal application form to replace the old forms, which were 21 pages long for TV stations. The new 'form' was postcard-size and included just five questions, four of which required applicants to check a 'yes' box. The FCC claimed that the new forms would cut industry form-filling time of 300,000 hours by two-thirds.

In his last two years, goaded by Congress, and perhaps glimpsing his window of opportunity fast closing with President Carter's sinking popularity, Ferris took up his new cause of deregulation with almost frenzied enthusiasm. Such a frenzy is not uncommon among FCC chairmen, who normally get off to a slow start during the first year of a new presidency, and then have to wait for new allies and votes to appear.

By 1980 Ferris was saying nearly all the things that Fowler was to make sound typically Reaganite two years later. But Ferris wanted to retain structural regulation, whereas Fowler's innovation was to demand deregulation without any conditions or quid pro quo.

MARK FOWLER AND FCC COMMISSIONER COMPETENCE

Mark Fowler became President Reagan's FCC chairman in May 1981; he is a classic illustration of the weaknesses of the FCC commissioner system. His main strengths lay in an outgoing personality and an ideological bent in line with that of the Reagan team. His political assets were his connections formed during the 1976 and 1980 Reagan election campaigns; he had the loyalty of an election supporter, rather than the political savvy found in the other kind of political aide, the Capitol Hill staffer used to the long haul of legislative politics. Fowler himself said on the occasion of his swearing-in that he owed the job to Charles Wick, Reagan's close personal buddy and his inept head of the USIA.[6]

It was only after a string of jobs in small radio stations in southern states, including work as a salesman of advertising time, that Mark Fowler went to law school; his academic performance there was distinctly average, and has thus been the subject of snobbish comment from the many Washington lawyers who performed well at better law schools. More seriously, Fowler's one major piece of relevant experience, in broadcasting, seemed to have taught him little; in his numerous interviews with the trade press, his most frequent comment about broadcasting was that he wanted broadcasters to be able to welcome the FCC as a friend rather than fear it as a policeman. His more general comments on broadcasting were banal. He had a law degree, but he lacked what by 1981 was clearly the single most important qualification for an FCC chairman – some knowledge of telecommunications and the new technologies.

Nevertheless, Fowler 'hit the ground running' in May 1981 and immediately began to set his stamp on the FCC; within weeks he was able to shuffle his conservative choices into a majority of the top staff jobs, and within months a strong Fowler–Reaganite majority was also in place among the commissioners. Fowler had been prominently involved in the Reagan transition team's plans for the regulatory agencies, and he quickly announced a set of five goals, which, with minor changes, were suitable for any Reagan appointee as chairman of any regulatory commission:

1 creation of an unregulated marketplace for telecommunications;
2 elimination of unnecessary rules, regulations and policies;
3 a prime emphasis on the provision of services and service choices to the public;
4 the promotion of international communications in the interests of US commercial, defense and foreign policy;
5 the maintenance and extension of freedom of speech and of the press.

Fowler was able to make several key staff changes, because several key senior slots were vacant, and it is the chairman's prerogative to take the initiative in filling such posts. During his first few days in office Fowler was able to choose for the FCC a new general counsel, Stephen Sharp, who had graduated from the University of Virginia law school only eight years earlier and came from the Reagan transition team for the FCC. Fowler also chose new chiefs of the Office of Plans and Policy, the Cable TV Bureau and the Common Carrier Bureau. All four of these senior staff appointees were young conservative lawyers with some experience of communications law. The typical Fowler FCC senior staffer was in his thirties, with a good but not dazzling academic law background and some years of communications law experience, but little other experience apart from involvement in conservative politics.

The strengths of such senior staffers under Fowler's leadership were a powerful common commitment to carrying deregulation further and faster than had the previous Democratic team, and the fact that they had allies elsewhere in the administration, the White House, and the Republican majority in the Senate. The weaknesses of such a team were equally apparent: although by no means lacking in intelligence, ability and experience, these young Reaganite lawyers simply had less intelligence, less ability and less experience than, for example, the senior lawyers at AT&T and NAB. In addition, their national political experience – mainly in the Reagan election and transition teams – did not prepare them for handling either the Democratic majority in the House of Representatives, or even the Republican minority. The House was certain to be the legislative sticking point; but although the members of the House Communications Subcommittee shared at least some of Fowler's enthusiasm for deregulation, no serious attempt was made to evolve a common set of goals. Fowler quickly became involved in a highly combative relationship with Wirth, chairman of the House Communications Subcommittee. Although Fowler won some tactical victories, Wirth held the strategic cards – not least, control of the FCC's budget. Fowler was also up against a man of intellect and political finesse, with a much surer grasp of communications technology and policy; so when Fowler rushed into a series of acrimonious public confrontations, Wirth had little difficulty in painting him as a hyperactive and somewhat mindless zealot.

One of the dangers of being FCC chairman is that most of the people you meet are beholden to you; many senior people from AT&T, the networks and the Washington law firms had a low opinion of Fowler, but did not voice it. What was said at House hearings, however, was what many others were thinking.

'The business of selecting FCC commissioners has for years been little more than an exercise in political patronage', write Cole and Oettinger, after summarizing the qualifications of the 16 commissioners who were in office in the years 1970–7.[7] But, if any change can be detected between the Burch and Wiley commissions and that of Fowler, it is that the quality of the commissioners seems to have fallen still further.

The 1970–7 commissioners follow the traditional pattern; nearly all had a highly placed political patron, often a senior senator. Very few had previous special knowledge of telecommunications. But nearly half seem to have been people of some ability and with some strong relevant experience. Kenneth Cox was an able lawyer, an ex-chief of the FCC broadcasting bureau and Senate staffer. Nicholas Johnson was an energetic populist maverick. Dean Burch, once campaign manager to Barry Goldwater, was a man of obvious ability and integrity, with a successful legal career behind him. Glen Robinson was an able academic lawyer, who became known to politicians on the basis of law review articles. Abbott Washburn was for some years deputy director of

USIA, and later a successful telecommunications diplomat. Joe Fogarty had legal and Senate Commerce Committee staff experience, and the then rare insight that there was a need to learn about telecommunications. Finally, Richard Wiley had been FCC general counsel, and was clearly an able lawyer.

The above do not seem too unimpressive a collection, especially when compared with the Reagan–Fowler team in its full 1984 flowering. James Quello was an undistinguished holdover from the Wiley FCC, his main background having been in broadcast station management. Mimi Dawson had been a senior staffer to Senator Packwood, then Republican chairman of Senate Commerce Committee – a classic background indeed. Henry Rivera was the first Hispanic commissioner; a young conservative Democrat lawyer from New Mexico, he became the quiet rebel of the Fowler Commission. The fifth seat remained empty for some time, but was eventually filled by Dennis R. Patrick, at 32 a surplus Reagan White House staffer, who had law-clerked for William Clark, a California friend of Reagan and later US Secretary of Interior.

The 1982 reduction from seven to five commissioners made it less easy to have at least one commissioner with some specialist understanding of, for example, space satellites. The way in which this seven-to-five reduction occurred also underlines the raw politics involved. It was quite simply a neat solution to a political problem. The White House wanted Stephen Sharp, then FCC general counsel, to become a new commissioner. But Packwood, chairman of the Senate Commerce Committee, blocked the nomination because of a previous agreement with Senator Ted Stevens of Alaska who had his own favorite candidate. The compromise was to eliminate the empty seat plus another that was just falling vacant, and thereby to reduce the total to the five found on most other regulatory commissions. Such a reduction had long been discussed, and it might not have been a problem for a commission of five strongly qualified individuals; but the Fowler commission was surely one of the weakest ever, and the small number of five covering such a vast field merely underscored its inadequacies.

DEREGULATION AS DOGMA

The FCC's predecessor, the Federal Radio Commission (1927–34) was responsible only for radio. The new body, the FCC, was set up in 1934 to regulate not only radio but also telecommunications. For many years it was the political importance, first of radio, then of television, which was salient. The FCC was run by seven commissioners, nominated by the president and confirmed by the Senate. Not more than four could belong to one party. In the early years when the Democrats were in control of Congress, President Roosevelt was able to establish a run of Democratic chairmen. And ever since, a new FCC chairman has been appointed who is of the party of the incoming president. Eisenhower appointed the first Republican; Kennedy appointed one of Adlai Stevenson's staff, Newton Minow. Nixon appointed two Republican chairmen, Burch and Wiley; Carter's man was Ferris, and Reagan's was Fowler. One exception to this list of same-party appointments was President Johnson's reappointment of the previous Republican FCC chairman, Rosel Hyde; Johnson made this exception not out of farsighted concern, but because he wanted an FCC chairman who would not disturb the Johnson broadcast properties in Austin, Texas.

Most new FCC commissioners, since 1934, have in fact been propelled into the job by a highly placed political friend, usually in the Senate or the White House. It also helps to have no political enemies. Many FCC commissioners have come from the election staff and/or personal staff of a prominent politician. Naturally they continue to belong to a political friendship network in Washington, and may subsequently go on to other political posts – Dean Burch, for example, went from the FCC chairmanship to a senior post in Nixon's White House. But many commissioners simply return to the industry they have regulated, at a greatly increased salary. Becoming an FCC commissioner is a boost to a career, and a reward for political loyalty.

None of this is very shocking. But the sight of these middle-level political operatives presiding, in semijudicial style, over the nation's telecommunications does have a certain lack of conviction. Its rather doubtful legitimacy seems to encourage the interference of Congress and the courts. Indeed, nearly every major FCC decision is challenged and reconsidered, often at some length by the commission itself, followed by the courts, Congress or both.

And while the FCC has these powerful people – the president, senators and judges – hovering over it, the FCC also has problems with those down below whom it is supposedly regulating and controlling. For the FCC, since its earliest days, has had to deal with two troublesome entities – AT&T and the broadcast networks.

Commentators and ex-staff members of the FCC have noted that, throughout its history, the commission has always spent most, perhaps two-thirds, of its time on broadcast issues. Broadcasting is interesting, glamorous, hasn't changed too much since the early 1950s and isn't too difficult to understand. The same cannot be said for telecommunications. The telephone business seems to have been regarded by nearly all FCC commissioners as rather dull, too economically intricate and technical, impervious to outside investigation, and best left in the very capable hands of Ma Bell. When Joseph Fogarty became a commissioner in 1976, his decision to specialize in telecommunications was almost unprecedented.

Of course the FCC, whose staff numbers have hovered around or below 2,000 in recent years, has a large professional staff of engineers as well as lawyers. They mostly fall into two categories – first, young lawyers and engineers recently out of graduate school; second, people who have served at least five years and expect to stay in the FCC until their retirement. For both categories, it must indeed have seemed a forbidding task to try seriously to take on AT&T, whose lawyers, engineers, scientists and economists were much better paid, more numerous and much better qualified. AT&T's scientists included Nobel prizewinners; AT&T always seemed to retain as consultants a high proportion of America's most distinguished economists; and the in-house engineers were running the US phone system. The in-house lawyers had legendary reputations for their ruthless pursuit of regulatory and political advantage. Moreover, even if you could beat the smart guys from AT&T, would Congress or the courts – or even the FCC commissioners – back you up?

Consequently, for many years the task of the FCC was seen as being mainly to sort out quarrels *within* broadcasting and within telecommunications – between the networks, the affiliates and the program suppliers; and to maintain the status quo between AT&T and the local independents which had some 15 per cent of the phone business.

FEWER POLICIES, MORE LOTTERIES

The politically appointed and short-stay commissioners, thrust into a technical revolution within a political minefield, are not encouraged to think policy thoughts. They are encouraged to be efficient expediters of business, to handle the flood of material that comes in the mail, to keep the administrative wheels moving. And there is safety in detail: grand designs can be challenged by Congress and farsighted plans can be dismissed by the industry, but the pursuit of bureaucratic detail is, in any government enterprise, shielded from view.

It was the explosion of technologies other than cable and the expansion of traditional broadcasting which strained the FCC – both its judicial neutrality and its administrative resources. The FCC was faced with the problem of awarding licenses in a short period of time for hundreds of new TV stations, hundreds of cellular mobile radio systems, thousands of new radio stations and thousands of LPTV stations. For example, in 1980 the FCC invited applications for LPTV licenses, and received more than 5,000 applications. Almost all of these were competing applications, which meant that, should the FCC use its full panoply of procedures and hearings for 'comparing' the rival applicants, it would take years (if not decades) to allocate all the licenses.[8] In 1983 there were 16,000 applications, many of them 60 or 70 pages long, for multichannel multipoint distribution service (MMDS).

What came to the FCC's rescue was the lottery; the first LPTV lottery was held in September 1983, and other lottery rounds soon followed. The lottery idea had been discussed for some years. In the Van Deerlin era the question had been posed perhaps slightly tongue in cheek: Are the traditional procedures any better than a lottery? Both the FCC and Congress can lay claim to having first taken the lottery seriously. The FCC voted to use a lottery in an FM radio comparative hearing in May 1980, and the lottery featured in an FCC budget provision from Congress in July 1981. The FCC complained that the congressional plan was unworkable, but the scheme was finally modified and put into effect.

The lottery solves the administrative resources problem; it also absolves the FCC from differentiating between numerous very similar applications. It acknowledges the inability of the FCC meaningfully to carry out its quasi-judicial function. It also accepts that in an era of deregulation, it is even less possible than previously to hold license applicants to promises.

The lottery, as a national device, removes much of the local element that might seem to justify LPTV or MMDS. It rejects excellence, demanding only adequacy. In practice, the winner takes all – either the right to keep the franchise for ever, or alternatively, the right to sell after one year to the highest bidder, a de facto comparative renewal based on the sole criterion of dollars. All this the Fowler FCC accepted and would defend as simple realism and market rationality.

But the lottery solution to the quasi-judicial dilemma is also an example of a procedure, based on political and administrative compromise, which was such a radical departure from the past as to virtually guarantee awkward unforeseen consequences. In the case of LPTV it was not even anticipated that, while ethnic small entrepreneurs might feature among the applicants, the big battalions would also be on the march. Surprisingly, it came as a surprise to the FCC when Sears, the nation's largest retailer, bid for 141 low-power stations. The lottery may solve some problems and create others. But it also marks the FCC's admission that it cannot continue to perform its full quasi-judicial role. The FCC has moved out of the role of referee at the big match, and has repositioned itself as the croupier at a set of narrow, well-lit gaming tables.

UNREGULATING TECHNICAL STANDARDS

In cellular mobile radio the technology was largely invented by AT&T; indeed, Bell Labs invented, and AT&T had patented, many of the technologies which became standard not only in telephones and telecommunications but throughout the electronics fields. However, the FCC had also come to play an increasing part in decisions regarding their application. It had not always been quick to do so, however, and FM radio was delayed for this very reason.

The emerging FCC policy, broadly shared by other agencies in Washington, has been not only to let a thousand technologies bloom, but to allow each technology to encompass a marketplace battle to resolve the issue of technical standards. Certainly this traditional role of the FCC, like the others, has become harder to maintain with wisdom and conviction. But once again the FCC has been shown to combine indecision with dogmatism. The DBS standard was a case in point. Here was a technology in which the US had decided to bide its time at the 1977 RARC. Consequently, the Europeans and Japanese were more advanced when, at the regional RARC in summer 1983 dealing with the Western Hemisphere, the US finally acquired its DBS slots in space. The US could choose between the standards already available, which included the German–French one, the British MAC system and high-definition standards from Japan and from CBS. But the FCC initially seemed to wash its hands of the whole idea of interfering with the market forces.

The FCC has also stepped aside from standard setting in AM stereo and teletex. This is a remarkably dubious way of making decisions, and the effect may yet be to leave the US entirely out of some new technologies. No decision at all is the ultimate in perverse regulatory behavior; in some cases almost any decision would be more welcome than none, to all parties, in which case the lottery would surely make more sense than this bizarre species of technological Darwinism.

FCC: SCHOOL FOR LOBBYISTS

The FCC is, most obviously, a Washington bureaucracy of about 2,000 people which processes many thousands of applications a year. Its four major bureaus employ well over half its personnel; these are the Mass Media Bureau (previously, broadcast and cable were separate), Common Carrier, Private Radio and Field Operations. The FCC's biggest bureaucratic problem in the 1980s has concerned how these bureaus can handle a big increase in applications while conforming to the huge budget cuts which passed Congress in 1981. It was planned that personnel should drop from more than 2,000 to less than 1,600, but in fact the cuts were less severe, or were balanced out by increases for fresh activities.

A GAO report in 1983 presented some fairly horrendous figures. In 1982 the Mass Media Bureau received more than 7,000 applications (which included LPTV); the Private Radio Bureau had 280,000 applications; and the Common Carrier Bureau had 8,400 applications for point-to-point microwave, with other massive increases for satellite facilities, for example.[9]

The Office of Managing Director is the only other large group of employees at the FCC. But important areas with significant numbers include the commissioners' own offices and staffs; the Office of Science and Technology; the Office of General Counsel; and, matching these nests of engineers and lawyers, the relatively new Office of Plans and Policy – the economists.

It has often been remarked that the FCC fails to generate its own data, and is too dependent on other people's facts and figures. It is especially dependent on AT&T and the networks, and appears to be much less skeptical of network data than a Madison Avenue advertising agency would be, and less skeptical of AT&T data than a large commercial user of telecommunications would be.

The FCC has also made the situation worse by deliberately dropping many of its requirements for factual reporting in broadcast and cable. The FCC produces documents, reports and articles on a prodigal scale, but most often these are legal opinions, or extremely abstract conservative economic theorizing. The worst failing of the FCC in the factual area lies in its accounting efforts. In 1983 GAO found that the FCC was still using an accounting method first adopted in 1935. The FCC was not capable of conducting effective financial monitoring in the key controversial area of telephone company costs; it could not ascertain how AT&T allocated costs between regulated and unregulated activities, and whether there was a cross-subsidy. Nor could it hope to do so for at least another three years.[10]

None of this is too surprising, especially if one considers another de facto function of the FCC. It is a training school for communications lawyer-bureaucrats. There are two predominant categories of FCC employees. First, there are many women, mostly youngish and mostly black – the clerks, typists and secretaries. The only other big category are men, mostly youngish lawyers wearing white shirts and dark suits. It is the latter who are making use of the FCC's unrivalled educational facilities. After three or four years at the FCC, a young lawyer may expect to enter one of the big Washington law firms, to work in a major communications corporation as a lawyer or lobbyist, or to plunge into the growing state-level industry of communications policy.

Having worked for three or four years at the FCC enhances a young lawyer's employment and salary prospects. Now he knows his way around the regulatory world. Much communications law requires, rather than legal expertise, simply familiarity with persons and procedures inside the FCC bureaucracy.

Although the FCC pays quite well, the networks, AT&T, and other major commercial players obviously pay much better. Thus for an ambitious young lawyer, job movement is a one-way trip out of the FCC – unless perhaps he is asked to return, still young, to one of the FCC's top jobs, such as bureau chief. Apart from this, the FCC is training talent which will be harvested by other players in the communication policy game.

Notes

1 *Wall Street Journal*, 7 December 1983, pp. 1, 22.
2 Barry Weingast and Mark J. Moran, 'Bureaucratic Discretion or Congressional Control?' (1983).
3 Jeanne Adler, 'FCC postpones ownership rules on TV stations', *Wall Street Journal*, 10 August 1984. 'The real FCC stands up', *Broadcasting*, 31 December 1984, p. 138.
4 'The "others" in ascertainment get more recognition', *Broadcasting*, 19 March 1980, p. 72.
5 'FCC's Cornell: Nobody loves a Critic', *Broadcasting*, 15 January 1979.
6 'Taking up the reins of power', *Broadcasting*, 25 May 1981.
7 Barry Cole and Mal Oettinger, *Reluctant Regulators* (1978), p. 22.
8 Margaret Garrard Warner and Laura Landro, 'FCC swamped with applications for new low-power TV stations', *Wall Street Journal*, 30 October 1981, pp. 11, 15.
9 Report by the Comptroller General, *FCC Can Further Improve Its Licensing Activities* (1983).
10 US GAO, *Status of Federal Communications Commission Efforts to Allocate Costs Between Telephone Companies' Regulated and Unregulated Activities* (1983).

20

The Courts Decide, Indecisively

The courts indeed play a large part in the American system of government. In the case of communications policy there is the shining example of Judge Harold Greene, the lone judge who fearlessly broke up the world's largest company and in subsequent months continued to pour out well-argued – and above all, decisive – pronouncements on some of the remaining billion-dollar details.

But such an account is misleading. The judiciary may be especially important in the US system. The administration keeps its head down in order to avoid Watergate bricks; Congress is stalled by the strength of internal vetoes and lobbies; the FCC barks loudly, but learns not to bite the congressional hand that feeds it. All this leaves a lot of partly digested decisions, which are then referred to the courts. FCC decisions are very frequently referred to the US Court of Appeals in Washington.

But the judges, on the whole, do not fearlessly, farsightedly, and with clarion call, then proceed to pronounce what shall be the policy of the US in these difficult and complex matters. On the contrary, the judges proceed with great caution; they are careful to present themselves as interpreting 'what Congress really meant', and as giving expression to a national consensus which had almost surfaced already.

Judges do not typically pronounce what US policy shall be; on the contrary, they choose between what two sides present to them in court on a particular past issue or issues, sometimes the past of several years ago. Cases can be appealed and then go to the Supreme Court; sometimes they go back down the line to a junior court again. The MCI case against AT&T dealt with a relatively narrow topic – monopolization of the inter-city private-line telephone market. The case was filed in March 1974; in June 1980 a jury awarded MCI $1.8 billion in damages; but eleven years after the case began, evidence was still being heard in a Chicago court. Eventually, in 1985, the damages were severely cut.

Communications cases present judges and juries with appalling difficulties. The basic law was enacted in 1934 when most of the present-day technologies did not yet exist; the legal status of several of the relevant entities is uncertain – the FCC, the First Amendment and the DOD are among the landmarks shrouded in legal mist. The judge who tries a complex communications case ideally needs a knowledge not only of the law but also of engineering and economics as well.

Where, on the Washington, or national, scene, do we find people with a good overall grasp of communications policy? There are several places: first, at the FCC among some of the senior staff; second, at the NTIA, in the Commerce Department; also in Congress among the members and staff of the two communications subcommittees. These are just four locations, and in each case the knowledge resides in a smallish number of people, a team or group of complementary specialists. Here one finds mainly lawyers, but also economists, engineers, politicians and the occasional ex-journalist or ex-professor. Often a lawyer sits in an office next to an engineer, and in some cases a single person is both.

In addition to these four Washington enclaves of policy expertise there are others. Among the communications law specialists of relevant major law firms in Washington and New York, such expertise exists – perhaps twenty lawyers all specializing in different aspects of communications law. Finally, such expertise exists in some of the largest companies which span the communications business – AT&T, IBM, RCA and others.

Communications policy is so complex, so many-sided, spread around so many industries, services and agencies, that mastering it has become a team game. It's not a game that one player can play any more and expect to win.

So what happens to the judges? While the effective communications teams, like American football teams, can call upon specialists and reserves, the judge is out there all alone. While the policy teams feature young players, some of whom specialize in computers or engineering or economics, the judge is usually one elderly man with a minimal legal staff. Moreover, very few, if any, judges are specialists in communications law. Even Judge Greene was totally concerned with telecommunications and AT&T only for a relatively short time; in 1984, while still handling a steady flow of important telecommunications cases, many dealing with the diversification of ex-BOCs, Judge Greene was spending most of his time on nontelecoms cases.[1]

The solution of judges to the problem of being the lone individual on a playing field dominated by teams is very simple. He plays the role of referee between the two teams involved in the contest. The teams play the game, and deploy the expertise and the arguments; he sits there and blows the whistle. This has the advantage of producing a result. It has certain other obvious disadvantages – at least if one is under the illusion that judges are then in a position to make policy or express a complex consensus.

JUDGE GREENE AND AT&T

Judge Harold Greene of the US District Court in Washington, DC, has dramatized and personalized the role of the judiciary in communications deregulation. We have discussed the central role he played – along with William Baxter of the Justice Department and Charles Brown of AT&T – in the divestiture. The exact part played by each man (and by others such as Tim Wirth in the House) may well be long debated. But it seems that Greene's aggressive judicial style, his heavy judicial hints and his refusal to grant the administration's request for delay were major factors in convincing the AT&T high command to seek peace.

Greene has some other major (and minor) claims to deregulatory fame. As the telecommunications expert on the Washington DC bench, Greene was assigned a long series of cases dealing with the detailed application of his Modified Final Judgement. Some of the 'details' were of the billion-dollar variety, many of them in fact being major issues posed by the seven ex-BOCS; for example, all seven companies wanted to broaden out into conglomerates, whereas Greene was determined to make them focus predominantly on providing telephone service.

Greene was also the judge involved in another important consent decree, in the takeover of the second competing long-distance phone company, Sprint (Southern Pacific Communications), by GTE, the giant of the old independents.

The complete deregulation of television advertising is another, highly controversial, achievement of Greene. His initial 1982 court decision was that the NAB code, which allowed the advertising of only a single product in one 30-second ad, was clearly in restraint of trade and designed by broadcasters in order to sell more advertising time. Greene's characteristically strongly worded opinion was taken by NAB to mean that the whole code must lapse. And thus there are now no restrictions on any of the key parameters of TV advertising, such as the number of minutes allowed per hour.

Running through these decisions of Greene can be seen the common theme of antitrust. Also present in each case is his 'take charge' approach. And in several interviews and speeches, following the AT&T decisions, Greene pointed to an implicit consensus that existed between the FCC, Commerce, Justice and Congress, to which he was in effect simply giving the previously missing imprimatur of law. In these statements Greene sketched a distinctive view of the AT&T policy problem: that technology, especially microwave, had made telecoms competition inevitable; that AT&T was not playing its rightful leadership role on the world scene; that the FCC lacked the expertise and political clout effectively to regulate AT&T.

THE SONY–BETAMAX CASE AND THE SUPREME COURT

The Sony–Betamax case was quite quick by some standards. Starting in a US district court in Los Angeles in 1979, it finished up with a Supreme Court decision in early 1984, taking less than five years to make the entire trip, including a visit to the US Court of Appeals in San Francisco in 1981.

Much of the legal difficulty focused on the fact that although there was a fairly recent Copyright Act, passed in 1976, it did not mention the videotaping situation first raised in the case just three years later.

The majority in the Supreme Court quoted such evidence as that most film use of VCRs was simply to record them off the air for time-shifting. The majority of judges said that Congress might well want to legislate on this in the future, but that meanwhile it was not the court's task to enforce laws which Congress had not yet passed.

This was, like many cases, both unique and typical. It was unique because it arose from a new piece of technological gadgetry and the case obviously had vast implications, affecting millions of people and billions of dollars. However, it was typical in being a straight fight between two lobbies – the Hollywood moviemaking industry and the electronics hardware interests.

The referee in this case was a team of nine Supreme Court justices, who duly split five to four. They must have found these new gadgets puzzling indeed. Chief Justice Burger was 76 at the time, and a majority of the justices – five out of nine again – had passed their seventy-fifth birthdays.

These elderly judges could not have been collectively more indecisive than their five to four vote shows, and here they were considering a problem of vast complexity as just one more quick case. They were, in a word, judges – elderly, frail, puzzled and neither well qualified to, nor much wishing to, make communications policy.

It has been argued that the more expert District of Columbia Appeals Court promulgates something like telecommunications policy by judicial decree. But in fact this court has tended to tread fairly carefully, and several studies show that it has upheld the FCC more often than it has reversed it. Between 1958 and 1971 the Court of Appeals reversed the FCC in only 69 out of 185 cases, some 37 per cent. On the whole, it has tended to defer to the superior technical expertise of the FCC.[2]

ANTITRUST: THE DOMINANT THEME IN US
COMMUNICATIONS POLICY HISTORY

Communications antitrust concerns predate 'deregulation' by decades. Indeed, much of the 'regulation' which the deregulators have been seeking to remove was first placed there in order to control or tame monopolistic tendencies.

The news agency field has an antitrust history dating back to the 1890s; in more recent times there was the Newspaper Preservation Act of 1970. In telecommunications the Bell monopoly's lengthy history does not stand alone; the electric telegraph monopoly of Western Union predates it.

Nearly as old is the propensity of the movie industry to become a cartel; this happened initially while the film industry was still on the east coast, and the move west was motivated partly by a hope of escaping cartel control. Hollywood, of course, was found to be a cartel in the famous mid-century case, and the theater chains were forcibly sold off (a precursor of what was to happen 30 years later to the retail end of Bell).

The history of the networks is in part an antitrust history. The dominant company, RCA/NBC, was broken up; and more recently major antitrust inhibitions have been apparent, as for example in the proposed ITT takeover of ABC in 1966–7. IBM's history is also heavily peppered with antitrust concerns. Indeed, the criticism in recent times that customers are 'locked in' by their software purchases was anticipated by earlier focus on the punched cards – early software with some hard monopoly implications.

THE COURTS AND COMMUNICATIONS

We will recapitulate just briefly the main outlines of court involvement in these areas during the recent era of deregulation:

(1) The *press* has continued to be an active antitrust field, especially in the battle for local advertising, with newspapers getting into trouble for 'predatory' attacks on small free newspapers. The decline and fall of UPI also meant that the old AP monopoly problem has not disappeared.

(2) In *telecommunications* antitrust concerns remain salient. Both the long-distance and the local markets have the continuing experience of dominant companies.

(3) *Hollywood* in recent times has also been slapped down on antitrust grounds, for its attempts to build a strong enough pay-cable cartel to blow HBO out of the sky.

(4) IBM has been out of immediate antitrust trouble since January 1982 in the US and since August 1984 in Europe; but it remains so dominant that the possibility, or probability, of yet further antitrust challenges remains.

(5) And in the *video cassette/VCR* field the courts have played a vital role, yet again; here, of course, it was on copyright grounds that the Hollywood companies made their challenge – in the Sony–Betamax case.

(6) Finally, *cable* has had major antitrust court cases in the pay-cable supply end of the business; but as the mergers proceed among MSOs, the setting of some kind of antitrust limit – some as yet undetermined total of hundreds of natural local monopolies which will be said to add up to an unnaturally large MSO – seems more and more probable.

The deregulatory fervor of Congress and the FCC has led to many new players stepping onto the playing field. At the same time, there has been some dismantling of boundaries between different playing fields – for example, AT&T and IBM both now operate in computers and long distance telecommunications. Meanwhile, this bigger new playing field has itself moved into a more prominent position in both the national economy *and* national politics.

As the players cross boundaries, so also will the antitrust issues. Antitrust issues in communications are acquiring new complexities: for example, in addition to the old dimension of vertical or horizontal monopoly, there are now dimensions which cross previously separate industries; and there are also added international complexities.

Some of the developing antitrust questions will be the old questions now applied to new industries. Should IBM be allowed to maintain its degree of vertical control in hardware, software, production, marketing and retailing? Are any of the new kinds of diversification contrary to antitrust law? For example, does it matter if the biggest car company (GM) also owns one of the largest computer software companies (EDS)? What is the antitrust position in relation to those consortia which are so common in new enterprises spanning previously separate fields? Does it matter if Sears, IBM and CBS run a videotex company? What happens if, eventually, the long-distance phone business can sustain only one or two competitors with AT&T, or if the early phase of price-cutting is later reversed? There are many delicate issues in software/copyright – not least, news, sport, advertising and financial data – which again will be much more difficult than in the past. To take one example, are there any limits to the allowable combined market share of Dow Jones, AP–Dow Jones and the *Wall Street Journal*?

One of the traditional boundaries that has been kept intact to date, but which cannot survive for ever, is the boundary between the First Amendment and antitrust. Ted Turner, for example, has already claimed that the FCC's 'must carry' rules are illegal under the First Amendment, because they impinge on the editorial rights of cable operators. This assertion puts the broadcasters and their trade association in an extremely difficult position. The 'must carry' rules are vital to the position of broadcasters, and enable the conventional TV networks and stations to have the bulk of the audience time even in cable households. But in some cases these rules are keeping out Turner's satellite offerings. The NAB is also, along with the newspaper and cable trade associations, a key leader of the alliance in favor of Senator Packwood's freedom of expression proposals, and of extending full First Amendment autonomy to electronic media. Here is a tangle of immense complexity, and a set of issues which will be fought with true ferocity.

LITIGATION AS COMPETITION, LAWYERS AS LOBBYISTS

For American communications companies the courtroom is one of the familiar arenas of commercial competition. For example, quite a common way of penalizing a breakaway start-up company in Silicon Valley is to sue it; the executives of a small new company may find their early weeks dominated by a court case, and the courtroom may be as far as the new company goes.[3]

And just as there is little difference between litigation and commercial competition, so also there is often not much difference between being a company lawyer and a company lobbyist.

What the US legal system is totally unqualified to do is to make policy. Nevertheless, in the absence of alternatives, judges do find themselves making – or presiding over the making of – policy.

Judge Greene, when discussing AT&T, frequently stressed that the slimmed-down AT&T should be a national and international commercial success. But most judges are better at looking backward than forward; and while Greene showed himself to be a master of AT&T's commercial past, he was less adept at grasping its commercial present and future. The Modified Final Judgement was a charter for *importers* of telecommunications equipment.

The Sony–Betamax decision was also a charter for importers – this time of Japanese VCRs.

Notes

1 Linda Greenhouse, 'Judge in Bell case defends his role under Tunney Act', *New York Times*, 12 September 1982, p. D14. Caroline E. Mayer, 'Greene rejects credit, blame for Bell break-up', *Washington Post*, 27 November 1983, p. H1. Robert E. Taylor, 'Judge Harold Greene finds reputation tied closely to AT and T case', *Wall Street Journal*, 8 December 1983, pp. 1, 21. 'US District Judge Greene defends AT and T divestiture in his first public speech', *Communications Daily*, 12 December 1983, pp. 3–4. David Myers, 'Greene has no apologies on "inevitable" Bell break-up' *Computerworld*, 2 July 1984, pp. 17–18. Caroline E. Mayer and Peter Behr, 'Greene: No Regrets about AT and T Break-up', *Washington Post*, 2 December 1984, pp. F1, 3.
2 Ron Garay, 'The FCC and the US Court of Appeals: Telecommunications policy by Judicial decree?', *Journal of Broadcasting*, 23:3 (Summer 1979), pp. 301–18.
3 Erik Larson, 'Modem operandi: In High-Tech Industry, New Firms often get Fast Trip to Courtroom', *Wall Street Journal*, 14 August 1984, pp. 1, 14.

21

Lobbying as Dominant Policymaking Mode

It is difficult to imagine a political system which gives more weight to lobbying than does that in Washington. And within the Washington system few policy areas are more sensitive to lobbying than the communications policy area.

The separation of powers, explicitly stated in the Constitution, sees policy as a consensus emerging via checks and balances. This system, given the huge multiplication in terms of support staff and issue complexity, in practice is a system which elevates lobbying into the dominant policy mode.

This does not necessarily mean that the biggest company or industry always wins. But policy wins are the result of lobbying battles fought between contending interests – battles which are often fought through multiple episodes, and adjudicated by the relevant politicians, regulators and judges in the various branches of government.

Lobbying expands to match the number of persons who are available to be lobbied. As congressional staffs have become much larger in the last decade, they have become junior adjudicators working on behalf of their bosses, the elected politicians. As these large staffs become de facto a lower bench of 'judges', the lobbying staffs expand to be able to cover all the newly relevant personnel.

There is a family congruence between lawyer-policymakers, draft laws to be bargained and lobbying. They encompass a single career path and a single field of activity. It is a well-populated and well-paid field, because the issues being lobbied involve such large dollar figures. Because there are so many policymaking places and people, lobbying is a team game, and sometimes a game with several, linked teams playing different roles. A team of 15 or 20 lobbyists, together with their related expenses, may cost several million dollars a year; but one apparently modest lobbying win – perhaps the rewording of a particular sentence in a bill before Congress – can have consequences worth a hundred, or a thousand, times as much.

Communications policymaking is especially strongly dominated by lobbying, due to a few familiar facts. First, politicians depend on the media for reelection, and are thus especially sensitive to phone calls from, or discussions with, newspaper publishers and station managers in their constituencies. Second, the information technology industry, having acquired a unique reputation for commercial dynamism, carries great constituency clout – prestige, employment and government contracts.

A third familiar characteristic of this broad policy area is the paradox of little legislation combined with a massive policy shift. This paradox leaves a wide scope for lobbying.

Most policymaking activity in and around Congress, the FCC and the administration is lobbying. The ordinary activity of lobbying is no more than modified by frequent excursions to the courts. Litigation is lobbying carried on by slightly different means in a more formal setting; then the lobbying teams return to their usual task of lobbying without end, Amen.

LOBBY POWER IN COMMUNICATIONS POLICY

Since, typically, lobbies are primarily engaged in fighting other lobbies, there are as many lobby losses as wins. But there have been few recent wins for legislators: nearly all their major pieces of legislation have failed. On the other hand, most of the main policy decisions can quite realistically be described as a win for a particular industry or interest. Domestic satellite deregulation was a win for aerospace interests. The AT&T divestiture was a win for telecommunications large users and for the competing carriers. The extension of TV licenses in 1981 was a win for NAB. The syndication/financial interest decision was a win for Hollywood. Only the cable legislation of 1984 was a trifle ambiguous: Wirth got his bill, and the cities and mayors acquiesced, but the largest winner was still the local cable operators' lobby.

Legislation tends to be complex and general, and thus engaged in an unequal contest with lobbying, which is typically simpler and more specific; lobbying focuses all its firepower on limited objectives, such as deleting two or three sections of a piece of proposed legislation. Both the legislation and the lobby are backed by a team; but the legislative team – a subcommittee and its staff – is trying to satisfy a wide range of interests, whereas the lobbying team is often supporting a position which has near universal support within its interest group.

Lobbies are powerful primarily because they can reward or punish decision-makers. A lobby can provide insurance against unpleasant surprises from a particular quarter; the lobbyist in effect guarantees that if he is accommodated, then there will be no opposition from the interest he represents. Lobbies also provide positive help, the simplest kind being financial support from PACS, of which a single industry may have many. Lobbies can also provide expertise, information and warnings about unexpected repercussions; the lawyer-lobbyist of experience can suggest solutions which meet his clients' needs but are also consistent with the legislator's goals.

Punishment is the other side of the coin. Lobbyists negotiate against the implied threat that they can, if need be, make waves. In particular, a powerful lobby can make waves in the politician's home constituency: the media can threaten opposition and negative publicity; other interests can orchestrate mailing and phone campaigns to the politician's office. Lobby punishment may be most effective when directed at politicians who are only marginally concerned; such lobby opposition may not shake the legislation's sponsorship by subcommittee members, but it may change enough votes in the main committee to kill any chance of enactment. Main committee members are threatened with grass roots hostility on an issue about which they perhaps know little and care less.

The presence of lobbies holding such vetoes means that most politicians' instinct most of the time is to avoid policies opposed by truly powerful lobbies. Following from this is the equally common assumption that the way to handle powerful lobbies is to talk to them and to discover their minimum requirements. It is the job, typically, of staff members to search out these minimum requirements, and to seek their inclusion in the next draft of the proposed legislation.

These communications lobbies are a clear example of how some of the campaign finance and open government ('sunshine' laws) reforms of the post-Watergate period have strengthened, not weakened, lobbying. The opening-up of the meetings of congressional committees and regulatory agencies has simplified the lobbyists' job; now they go along and observe not merely the votes, but the arguments and the interplay. At the FCC the commissioners can be seen in conjunction with senior staff members; one of the latter typically makes a presentation (which will normally have been agreed upon in advance, at least by the FCC chairman), and the commissioners then spend some time on questions and comments, before formally voting. At congressional hearings and FCC meetings, especially if there are large financial implications, there is often standing room only; and the people who have arrived early and filled the seats are mostly lobbyist-lawyers. After attending a few such meetings, any lobbyist can begin to get a sense of where the lobbying possibilities lie; just being there two or three times a week will soon build up in the lobbyist's head, as well as in his files, an extensive data bank of material on each public player.

Lobbying has become highly professionalized, of course, and there has been a shakeout of the public interest lobbies of the 1970s; the few which have survived, such as Common Cause and Ralph Nader's group, are in turn professionally expert and ruthlessly selective in choosing very specific issues on which to mass their expert firepower. The communications lobbies are typical in being involved in issues which require specialist expertise, but they are perhaps a little unusual in the extent to which they combine legal, economic and technical engineering expertise with the ability to cause a stir back in Main Street, USA.

Several of the communications lobbies deal with issues which can not only be projected in populist form – hands off your local radio station, or your universal phone service – but can also play in every congressional district across the country. However, although virtually all Americans consume the mass media and use telephones, it is the managerial gatekeepers in these fields who are activated, if and when the Washington lobby seeks to demonstrate to Congress its grass roots clout. The standard procedure is that the lobby alerts its local gatekeepers, and these people then phone, write or visit the congressman. If the shaking-the-grass-roots operation works as it should, every member of the House or the subcommittee or the Commerce Committee receives urgent messages from newspaper publishers, TV and radio station managers, or local telephone managers – whichever the case may be – from his home district.

LOBBYING AS TEAM WORK AND PROCESS

Lobbying is most typically based on trade associations and on individual companies. A successful trade association lobby will orchestrate the lobbying effort of the individual companies' own lobbyists. The lobbying effort may include PACs and advertising. Consultant firms are retained, and their reports are adroitly released at key points in the negotiations; engineers' and economists' reports are the most common in communications.

The lobbying process takes place on several levels. The hearings in Congress and before the FCC are merely the tip of the iceberg; these hearings have typically been rehearsed previously in private meetings or in quiet coaching sessions. During the various Bell bills, rewrites and telecommunications bills of 1976–81, evidence was given to Senate and House hearings by 59 different AT&T witnesses. But, according to Alvin von Auw's pro-AT&T view, 'What changed minds, corporate and Congressional, was an intense and almost continuous process of negotiations in which, alternately, the Bell System and its competitors pressed on the members of Congress – or, more often, their staffs – their opposed views of how the industry should be structured.'[1]

Lobbying, then, goes on and on. Repeat visits and repeat negotiations make up the prevailing phenomenon of repeat lobbying. The more they are in politicians' offices, the more they talk to the staff, the more they engage in late-night negotiating sessions, the more the lobbyists behave like – and become – insiders. For this reason also, lobbyists' employers happily pay several hundred dollars a time for them to visit politicians' fund-raisers; perhaps the slight whiff of sleaziness brings the lobbyist into the position of coconspirator with the politician-recipient. Certainly for the few hundred dollars entry fee to a small gathering, the lobbyist buys a few minutes access, not just to the staffers, but to the politician in person.

Lobbying teams, such as trade associations, also often hire temporary support from one or more of the high-priced specialist lobbying firms in Washington. This extends the lobby's range, and reaches other politicians besides its usual friends. Handling the politicians themselves require contacts, knowledge and experience. But some lobbying is of a more foot-slogging nature – for example, counting votes, or passing the word as to who did vote, or will vote, how.

THE BIG BROTHER LOBBIES

AT&T probably took lobbying to excessive lengths, and thus frightened or antagonized some of the very people it was trying to influence. In its pre-divestiture days, AT&T had a designated intermediary with every single member of Congress. AT&T managers had always been encouraged, or directed, to join local business, charitable and voluntary organizations. Typically, then, when a new member of the US House of Representatives was elected, there would be one or more local AT&T managers who had known the aspiring politician in earlier days. Indeed, one of these managers might well have been designated as contact man even before the new US Representative was elected, and very likely, would already have smoothed the way – for example, by getting especially quick and favorably priced telephone service into the election campaign headquarters. Later, this designated contact would appear at least annually in the politician's office on Capitol Hill. Congressional lobbying was part of the executive development program for rising Bell managers. During the unusual legislative activity around 1980, these managers were seen more and more frequently. At key legislative moments, members of Congress would find the Bell contact assigned to them spending whole days hovering in the outer office, laying polite siege to the legislator.

Another company whose lobbying activities are legendary is IBM. But IBM's lobbying has long differed from that of AT&T, in that IBM has lobbied with more finesse, flexibility and sense of direction. Some of its lobbying effort goes through CBEMA and ADAPSO (the hardware and software trade associations).

The NAB is less given to overkill than was the old AT&T. Like other lobbies, it has a state-level apparatus, which the Washington office can trigger by placing 50 phone calls. The leading broadcasters in each state are then supposed to telephone the offices of their US Senators and/or Representatives. The typical senator has some 20 TV and some 160 radio stations in his state; the Representative has perhaps 4 or 5 TV stations and 20 radio stations. If even a fraction of this number do indeed make a phone call to Washington, the phone calls are unlikely to be ignored.

Of course, there are other ways in which politicians meet the major media managers of their districts. For example, during election campaigns each main candidate will be asked into local newspaper offices and questioned, probably by managers and journalists, including senior editorial-page personnel. An endorsement may follow. Any politician's staff member who collects the press clippings each day during a campaign can see how vital these are – not only directly, but also indirectly, by shaping what the electronic media report. There are indications that press interests relatively rarely get involved in active Washington lobbying; except in the occasional cross-media issue, the FCC is of no interest to them. Certainly the location chosen by ANPA, a pleasant exurban setting in Reston, Virginia, is closer to Dulles International Airport than to Capitol Hill. ANPA gives the impression of an organization more concerned with the mid- and long-term future of newspapers – what kind of videotex, what ultimate substitute for paper as a material – than with short-term activities such as chasing legislators down corridors.

Different again is the style of MPAA. This is located some three blocks from the White House, and Jack Valenti specializes in appropriately Hollywood flourishes; one of these is the exclusive sneak preview – guests are invited for a little food and drink plus the showing of a not-yet-released movie in the MPAA's viewing theater. Valenti also has a way of upstaging other lobbyists by appearing at Washington hearings in the lead role, with Hollywood superstars playing cameo supporting roles.

Other umbrella lobbies can be important on particular issues. For example, the American Electrical Association has a vast membership from the electronics industry, and may be influential on electronic trade issues.

Meanwhile each technological innovation brings its new lobbies and coalition of lobbies. There is a coalition of lobbies concerned with copyright; videotex, LPTV and the Video Software Dealers (VSDA) all have their trade associations.

COMMUNICATIONS SUPER-LOBBYISTS AND OTHERS

Even within communications lobbying, lobbyists usually concentrate on part of the territory. Most lobbyists are lawyers, but some are PR people, engineers, or ex-staffers from Capitol Hill (who are also often lawyers).

Some super-lobbyists have a wider, generalist approach, and the most obvious examples of these in 1985 were the three men who had been FCC chairmen in the years 1969–81: Burch, Wiley and Ferris. Burch (FCC chairman 1969–74) had close ties to the Reagan–Bush 1984 campaign, having been involved, for example, in negotiations over the Reagan–Mondale television debates. In 1984 also, Burch was named as chairman of the US delegation to the 1985 WARC on satellites. But Burch still found time in 1983–4 to represent the Association of Independent TV Stations in the lobbying battle against Hollywood over financial interest/syndication.

Richard Wiley, FCC chairman 1974–7, was subsequently regarded as perhaps the number one communications lobbyist. He was a founding partner in the law/lobbying firm of Wiley and Rein, which in turn was well populated with Wiley's associates and former staff members. Wiley's clients in 1984–5 included ANPA, CBS, INTELSAT, COMSAT, GTE, the NAB and Xerox. On behalf of several of these clients, Wiley had lobbied against AT&T.

Charles Ferris (FCC chairman 1977–81) also had a whole range of law/lobbying clients. Ferris's lengthy senior staff experience on Capitol Hill was reflected in three political clients – the Democratic National Committee and the Democratic leaderships in both House and Senate; other Ferris clients included GTE, Western Union, McClatchy Newspapers (of California) and Turner Broadcasting.

An example of a lobbying firm which offers more specialist lobbying skills was Patton, Boggs and Blow, whose clients included ABC, NCTA, MCI, and nine US subsidiaries of Japanese manufacturers of videotape recorders. One partner, Thomas H. Boggs, Jr, came from a Louisiana political family, and specialized in flamboyant high-profile lobbying. Boggs was a major figure (on behalf of Mars) in the sugar advertising lobby's defeat of the 1979–80 attempts by the FTC to control advertising to children. But Boggs's partner, James O'Hara, specialized in the very different area of parliamentary rules and procedure in Congress. In this connection he was a key specialist player in the cable lobby's legislative win in 1984.

Another major lobbying firm with a distinctive image was that of Wexler, Reynolds, Harrison and Schule. Wexler and Reynolds were perhaps the two most prominent women lobbyists in Washington, Wexler having worked in the Carter White House and Reynolds having worked for Governor Ronald Reagan. In 1984 Anne Wexler was employed as a special adviser by Democratic vice-presidential candidate Geraldine Ferraro; but Wexler was also active, for example, on behalf of the cable lobby, especially in handling the mayors, who had fallen within the orbit of her public liaison post under President Carter.[2]

AN EXAMPLE OF LOBBIES IN CONFLICT: THE NEWSPAPER OWNERS DEFEAT AT&T

In addition to losing the strategic battles of the late 1970s, AT&T also suffered some tactical defeats after the divestiture announcement of January 1982. One example, which also illustrates the common phenomenon of policy being made via a conflict between two powerful lobbies, concerned the issue of whether AT&T should be allowed into electronic publishing in general, and into electronic Yellow Pages in particular.

ANPA appears almost to have forgotten how to lobby; its last major lobby effort was more than a decade earlier, on the Newspaper Preservation Act. Nevertheless, eventually ANPA was rewarded, when Judge Greene did indeed alter the Justice Department position and in his Modified Final Judgement required that AT&T stay out of this field for seven years. Here is part of the sequence of events as reported to ANPA members by their chief counsel Terry Maguire:

(1) Early 1980: ANPA identifies problems with legislation to rewrite the Communications Act; mainly that it doesn't protect adequately against AT&T's becoming an electronic publisher.

(2) 5 May 1980: FCC issues Computer II decision. AT&T may offer information services through a subsidiary, starting in 1983. ANPA and others appeal.

(3) 31 July 1980: House Commerce Committee passes HR.6121 with amendment by Rep. Timothy Wirth prohibiting AT&T from electronic publishing over its own lines.

(4) 4 February 1981: ANPA Board of Directors adopts ANPA Telecommunications Statement of Principle.

(5) 3 September 1981: US District Court Judge Vincent P. Biunno in Newark rules that 1956 consent decree does not prevent AT&T from entering computer-based information field (as Computer II decision allows).

(6) 7 October 1981: Senate passes telecommunications bill (S.898) by vote of 90–4. Amendment prohibits AT&T from electronic publishing over its own lines.

(7) 10 December 1981: House Telecommunications Subcommittee Chairman Wirth introduces HR.5158. Prevents AT&T from electronic publishing over its own facilities.

(8) 8 January 1982: Justice Department, AT&T announce tentative settlement of antitrust suit. Allows 'national' AT&T to enter electronic publishing, but prohibits 'spun off' local phone companies from doing so.

(9) 25 March 1982: House Telecommunciations Subcommittee unanimously approves HR.5158 which, contrary to proposed antitrust settlement, prohibits not only local operating companies, but also national AT&T, from electronic publishing.

(10) 20 July 1982: Wirth abandons HR.5158, saying there is not enough time for passage in the 97th Congress. Blames delay on AT&T lobbying campaign of 'fear and distortion'.

(11) 11 August 1982: US District Court Judge Harold H. Greene, presiding over antitrust trial says he will approve settlement if, among other things, parties agree that AT&T may not serve as information publisher over its own lines for at least seven years.

(12) 24 August 1982: AT&T, Justice Department agree to Greene's changes. Greene signs new consent decree in which 'diversity principle' becomes law.

During this two-year period ANPA, one of the few lobbies which is so powerful that it seldom needs to actually engage in much serious lobbying, steadily polished its rather rusty lobbying skills. Initially somewhat embarrassed at actually asking for favors, by 1982 ANPA had developed a vigorous lobbying style. Major east coast newspaper publishers, including Katharine Graham of the Washington Post Company, paid lobbying calls at key Washington points, especially the White House and Congress. In the House, Timothy Wirth, in pursuit of his marathon contest with AT&T, proved an early and crucial ally; and the anti-AT&T provisions were one of several House modifications which were quickly echoed in Judge Greene's Modified Final Judgement.

The success of the ANPA lobby has some similarities to the success of the NCTA lobby, leading up to its legislative win of 1984. In both cases we see a powerful communications lobby, able to attract the attention of almost all members of Congress, using its lobbying assets in a contest against a powerful opposing lobby. Each communications lobby had a fairly uniform set of goals – in one case to stop AT&T's entry into electronic publishing, in the cable case to cut back city and local government powers over cable.

There were some differences in style. ANPA includes in its membership major figures well known to politicians, and these publishers were thrown directly into lobbying activity. The cable lobby does not have equivalents to these well-known publishers, but the NCTA leadership compensated for this by using as many as a dozen specialist lobbying firms for tapping different skills and reaching different constituencies. The cable lobby, in its lobbying battles of the 1970s, up to its 1984 triumph, earned the reputation of being the most sophisticated of the Washington communications lobbies. Some of this success is surely due to skilled leadership, but some of it may derive from two other factors. Compared with the NAB, for example, the cable lobby had to fight for its very survival. Second, as an organization of small, local monopoly cable suppliers, it had a common focus on the financial concerns of license renewals and fees and of the tariffs to be charged to consumers.

The successes of the newspaper publishers and the cable operators – and the far from total failure of AT&T – contrast with the decline of the citizens' lobby, which seemed in the 1970s on the verge of major success. The citizens' lobby, or the 'Broadcast Reform Movement', lacked certain qualities which appeared increasingly necessary for lobbying success as the deregulatory pace of the 1970s quickened in the early 1980s. The Broadcast Reform Movement:

1 lacked any sharply defined goals and allowed itself to be fobbed off with FCC regulations which protected or buttressed the status quo;
2 was a loose coalition of voluntary citizens' groups, lacking the discipline and coherence necessary for an effective lobby;
3 failed to employ the carefully controlled team of lobbying professionals required for success;
4 lacked the several million dollars per year, which is the minimum for mounting an effective Washington lobby.[3]

INTERNATIONAL COMMUNICATIONS LOBBYING

In the era of deregulation, international issues have become more significant, and communications lobbying more prevalent. It should, then, be no surprise that at least three different forms of international communications lobbying have become much more active.

First, US companies now take a much more active and direct part in international lobbying and communications policymaking; this happens both because of the increased importance of international telecommunications in general, and because of the increasingly commercial emphasis of American representation within the ITU. ITU business has long been conducted in numerous conferences and committees which consume many man-years of negotiating time, conferences often lasting five or six weeks. The mode of approach is consensus and endless discussion in order, if possible, to achieve unanimity. This work (and domestic preparation for it) has become almost a full-time occupation for many senior postal ministry and PTT officials in other countries. The US, lacking a PTT, inevitably handed over much of the task of ITU telephone tariff and regulation detail to AT&T. Only a small part of US involvement in ITU is handled wholly by government – mainly the high-level and infrequent plenipotentiary and administrative council meetings. About half of US involvement is entirely in the private sector, and something under half is handled by mixed government and private-sector teams.[4]

But, of course, private-sector involvement takes different forms according to the organization in question. In the case of Hollywood, a trade association type of body, the Motion Picture Export Association (MPEA), negotiates directly with foreign governments. In the case of the World Intellectual Property Organization (WIPO), based in Geneva, the private-sector involvement is of book publishers' associations and the like. In the case of UNESCO the private sector involved a whole range – academics, the culture industry and news media orgnizations. In the case of ITU, the private sector means AT&T, IBM and other major telecommunications and electronics companies.

The largest US representation to the ITU has always been from AT&T. But now, AT&T is not merely a US version of a domestic telecommunications authority; it is both more commercially minded, and for the first time interested in exporting its own hardware, as well as its services. Inevitably, commercial sales activities must become entangled in diplomacy and lobbying, both within the US delegation itself and within the prime foreign markets which surround the ITU's headquarters in Geneva.

When, during the Reagan administration, consideration was given to leaving both ITU and UNESCO, some private-sector elements naturally carried more clout than others. To put it very simply, AT&T, IBM and the industry lobbies were horrified at the prospect of leaving an organization vital to their multinational operations, so the US stayed in ITU. But with regard to UNESCO, the cultural people and academics wanted to stay in, while the newspaper publishers and journalists, crying Third World censorship, wanted out. Since journalists and their publishers have more clout in Washington than do academics and cultural bureaucrats, the US therefore decided to leave UNESCO.

But, perhaps more significantly, Geneva has become the focus of a new kind of policy and commercial international lobbying. The ITU agenda is the world's telecommunications agenda, not just for new hardware, but for new policies and standards, and that agenda is influenced by US diplomacy and technology more than by any other single factor. And these US demands are in turn not merely suggested by, but directly negotiated by, senior personnel from AT&T, IBM and other companies. US delegations to the ITU in Geneva constitute a new kind of super-lobby in action.

Second, INTELSAT provides an example of an international communications lobby operating in the reverse direction. And INTELSAT's new director general, Richard Colino, by his frenetic lobbying did more than enough in 1984 to deserve the title of international communications lobbyist of the year. Colino was the first US citizen to become the chief executive of INTELSAT. His had been a classic Washington communications career: a lawyer, graduate of the FCC training school (attorney adviser, FCC Common Carrier Bureau 1962–4), then a long-time employee of COMSAT, he had then spent 1979–83 in the US commercial communications world. Colino, therefore, had known INTELSAT from its earliest days, had followed satellite technology for over 20 years, and had also known Washington for the same length of time. In January 1984 Colino hit the ground running, and quickly organized a vigorous lobbying defense. A lobbying firm was employed – one which included previously prominent political figures – and foreign governmental members of INTELSAT were orchestrated in a vigorous letter-writing campaign to Congress.[5] Friendly politicians also initiated several bills in INTELSAT's interest. In addition, INTELSAT began launching a wide range of new services for business, which were promoted by professional PR people with conservative political contacts.

A third, newly prominent type of international lobbying is that conducted by Japanese electronics firms. Japanese industry and government spent $19.9 million in 1984 on lobbying, public relations and legal services – much the highest of any foreign lobby. But the real total was several times higher. Much pro-Japanese lobbying in Washington is carried on by native US surrogates, such as associations of importers and dealers and by US subsidiaries of Japanese companies.[6]

All three types of international communications lobbying are far from new, but all three have rapidly expanded, and seem likely to expand further.

LOBBYING AS DOMINANT POLICYMAKING MODE

Sometimes communications lobbying in Washington is taken to absurd lengths. In the 1982 legislative encounter between those in favor and those against a copyright fee to be paid for home videotaping, each lobby marshalled a former FCC chairman. The Hollywood (pro-copyright fee) group had Dean Burch; the anti-fee group had Charles Ferris. The Hollywood group employed three former congressmen, while the other side had four. The Hollywood group had at least five senior people from the then recent Carter administration; the anti-fee lobby also had several. The two sides between them employed 17 Washington law firms, 13 consulting firms and several PR firms. Also involved in addition to the Carter people, were senior members of the Kennedy, Johnson, Nixon and Ford administrations.[7]

Why so much lobbying firepower? There are several reasons: the sums of money at stake, the fear of losing, and a desire to deny the best lobbying talent to the opposing lobby. But another reason is that the legislators like and rely on lobbies in so many ways.

We even find full committee chairmen encouraging lobbies to lobby with greater force. Senator Packwood in 1983–4 told a number of lobbies with an interest in First Amendment extension that unless they lobbied more aggressively he would drop his legislation. John Dingell certainly advised the National League of Cities to lobby harder in its contest with the cable interest on cable deregulation. For committee chairmen with much business to transact, it can save a lot of time if the lobbies bash each other's heads (rather than the chairman's) and come up with a compromise. But the active involvement of lobbies also satisfies the political needs of those members of a committee who are less familiar with the complex detail; these politicians want to avoid any unpleasant electoral surprises, and if they can be told that the two main and opposing relevant lobbies have agreed, then the resulting legislation is less likely to lead to a political ambush.

But there are also some major disadvantages to allowing lobbying to become the predominant political mode. One of the most obvious disadvantages of allowing lobbies to write their own wording into a bill, and to agreeing on compromise wordings which are essentially meaningless, is that the resulting laws are a mass of contradictions and obscurity. Some laws are deliberately scrambled into a mess which judges are then left to interpret; one batch of lawyers deliberately creates more work both for itself and for other lawyers.

Another unfortunate consequence is the subordination of professional expertise and objectivity to commercial lobbying expediency. Not only are communications lawyers paid a fee to plead a case, but the same thing happens to economists and others claiming communications expertise. Expertise, preferably esoteric enough to convey an air of mystery and distance, becomes a saleable commodity, part of the mobile weaponry of lobbying. Truly objective and genuinely independent expertise is drowned in waves of public relations handouts and carefully staged public appearances at hearings.

The lobbyists have become the foot soldiers of communications policy: the suppliers of research, phone calls, and letter-writing campaigns, as well as the carriers of rumor, the financiers of political campaigns, the bush telegraph of the political tribes.

Sometimes the lobbyists seem to be the performers and the politicians the spectators; at other times the roles are reversed. But, at least in a field like communications policy, elected politicians seem to perform precariously atop a giant pyramid of policymakers; the policy pyramid consists mainly of staff members who respond to lobbying and lobbyists who respond to their paymasters. One can argue as to how far the trend has gone. But communications policy is decreasingly influenced by citizens complaining about their telephones or television; it is increasingly established through various kinds of lobbying in which organized interests predominate.

The centrality of lobbying results from the separation of powers and the fragmentation of policy. But lobbying, by focusing such heavy artillery on such narrow fronts of interest, contributes to the phenomenon of policy fragmentation.

Deregulation has increased the significance not only of the marketplace, but of the political arena. Politicization may also have increased the importance of politicians, as against bureaucrats, in the making of communications policy. However, if deregulation has increased the power of politicians, it has also disproportionately increased the importance of lobbying, lobbyists and commercial interests of all kinds.

Notes

1 Auw, *Heritage and Destiny*, p. 100.
2 Much of the above paragraphs is derived from 'The Lobbyists', *Broadcasting*, 25 February 1985, pp. 45–60.
3 Willard D. Rowland, Jr, *The Illusion of Fulfillment* (1982).
4 A. M. Rutkowski, 'The International Telecommunications Union and the United States', *Telecommunications*, October 1983, p. 40.
5 Elizabeth Tucker, 'Down-to-Earth Lobbying over Communication in Space', *Washington Post*, national weekly edition, 1 April 1985, p. 14. 'All the world's his stage', *Broadcasting*, 12 November 1984, p. 99.
6 Eduardo Lachica, 'Japanese Lobby Haul in the U.S. to Counter Big Protectionist Push', *Wall Street Journal* (Europe), 26 August 1985, pp. 1, 7.
7 Howie Kurtz, 'Chariots for hire', *Washington Post*, 4 July 1982, p. B1.

PART V

The Deregulatory Shakeout: Exports, Competition, Localism, News, Policy

PART V

The Deregulatory Strikeout: Experts, Competition, Localism, News, Policy

22

Deregulation versus Policy

'Deregulation' and 'communications' both have many definitions. But whatever else US communications deregulation may be, it is not a policy. The word 'deregulation' suggests undoing things, and communications deregulation in the US has indeed meant the piecemeal abolition of previous regulations and fragments of policy.

When dire consequences have been predicted, the reply of the deregulators has in effect been, wait and see. Deregulation has favored giving competition a chance to show its virtues, allowing private enterprise an opportunity to show that it is indeed superior to governmental enterprise or control. Some pieces of deregulation have, more accurately, been pieces of interim regulation – for example, AT&T being prohibited in the Modified Final Judgement of 1983 from offering electronic Yellow Pages for seven years. Indeed, 1990 has been either openly stated, or tacitly implied, as a date by which wait-and-see may lead to some kind of tidying-up process, some kind of second phase of deregulation.

Deciding whether communications deregulation has been a success or failure will, of course, itself be contentious – because communications deregulation lacks not only an agreed-upon definition, but also an agreed-upon goal. These difficulties are inevitably present in the following attempt to sketch out a brief scorecard of successes and failures for communications 'policy' in the years 1970–85. The scorecard considers US national successes and failures on the world scene, the consequences for domestic US business and industry, and finally the consequences for the US domestic public.

(1) *The domestic space satellite deregulation* of the 1970s was, in retrospect, a major US success, strengthening its international lead in satellites; domsat policy strengthened the US aerospace industry and launched new specialist hardware companies. The domestic public also benefited via improved telephone service, satellite-fed video entertainment and new employment opportunities.

(2) *Video deregulation* helped to confirm US international dominance in entertainment, but it also led to massive additional importing of video cassette hardware, mainly from Japan. All the domestic entertainment industries benefited – Hollywood, broadcasting and cable. The US public got some (at least) more programming choices; the employment consequences were complex, but favorable overall.

(3) *The divestiture of AT&T* was a US success in some respects: it greatly stimulated competition, innovation and telecommunications investment, and in its wake AT&T redefined itself to include an export goal. An obvious failure of the divestiture was that the newly independent ex-BOCS (themselves perhaps the major long-term 'successes') quickly sucked in large quantities of telecoms hardware imports. For US business the divestiture was a somewhat mixed blessing, but in general it promised more choice and lower prices for business telecommunications. For the US public the divestiture caused dislocation, and made local calls more expensive, but promised cheaper long-distance calls.

(4) *The nondivestiture of IBM* has been a US success in that IBM's national and international dominance has been confirmed and increased by its more aggressive commercial approach. However, IBM's strength has weakened the rest of the US computer industry, and perhaps therefore indirectly aided the Japanese industry in the world and within the US. For domestic US business generally, the IBM events have probably contributed to better computer service at decreasing cost. For the US public, IBM has forced its microcomputer competitors to cut prices.

(5) *Fiber optics*: The AT&T divestiture and decisions on fiber-optic ocean cables have contributed to US dominance in a key new technology which fits neatly with US geography and history. The US decisions are likely to precipitate a crisis of massive overcapacity, a consequence of which some policymakers were well aware. For domestic US industry this looks like a major win, since it promises greatly increased (digital) communications efficiency at radically lower prices. For the US domestic public also, overcapacity may lead to long-distance phone calls, via fiber-optic cable or space satellite, at flat rates regardless of distance.

(6) *Data services*. US free-flow policies, despite the awkward term 'transborder data flow', have largely been a success, leading to US dominance in nearly all aspects of data management and provision; these policies have greatly assisted the aggressive worldwide expansion of the major New York banks. However, 'free flow' has also contributed to excessive international financial volatility, whose consequences are complex but include international suspicion of US behavior and motives. For domestic US businesses the data revolution provides significant international advantages. The skeptical response to early videotex offerings suggests that as yet there are few major consequences for the US public.

(7) *US versus Japan*. Stated US government policies of breaking down Japanese nontariff trade barriers in general, and those affecting telecommunications products in particular, have been fragmented and indecisive in execution, and have been accompanied by rising US electronics trade deficits. However, a US political success may be indicated by the Japanese decision to 'privatize' its telecommunications, and more generally by the sharpening of US competitiveness that has resulted from competing against Japan. Some US industries have suffered severely from the competition, of course, while others (such as IBM) compete successfully around the world, as well as in Japan. Japanese involvement in the US mainframe computer industry may be a domestic weakness, as well as making for total US–Japanese dominance against the world. The domestic US public may have suffered in employment terms, but has benefited from policy failure in terms of improved product choice and lower prices.

(8) *US versus USSR*. The US communications lead over the Soviet Union was already large, and may have been strengthened by deregulation. Paradoxically, however, the main failure in this area appears to lie in strategic exports policy, in which US regulations have been strengthened. These policies smack of closing the door after the horse has departed. In Europe especially, such policies are widely seen as the use of military and diplomatic persuasion to establish unilateral commercial advantage. US industries appear to have lost markets (especially in Eastern Europe). Benefits to the US domestic public are claimed, but not easily demonstrated.

EXPORTING DEREGULATION, IMPORTING CONSEQUENCES

It has long been one of the core assumptions of the deregulators that the US needed not only to deregulate its own communications, but also to persuade its main trading partners to deregulate their own industries. In some cases, such as international airlines or telecommunications, deregulation can occur only if other nations agree. But in all cases the US task has been to persuade other nations, mainly the OECD nations in Europe and Japan, that deregulation will benefit everyone. The thought has often been expressed publicly in Washington that, given the fragmented nature of US policymaking, general international deregulation will benefit all, but especially the US.

By 1985 the goal of exporting the practice of deregulation was achieving some success in a number of fields, including international airlines and international banking. Europe was by 1985 also slowly advancing into multichannel commercial television. And the most dramatic evidence of success was the decision by both Japan and the UK to move their telecommunications systems in a commercial direction.

But in communications trade itself, the main American successes were in fields in which the relevant US industries had already been doing well for decades. The MPEA was continuing its dominance of video entertainment export earnings. The US was still playing a focal role in international telephone calls – via AT&T and via US leadership of INTELSAT.

In the telecoms and computer fields, the two most remarkable US performers had long been IBM and ITT, but their success, while continuing, was also somewhat ambiguous.

In the early 1980s IBM earned almost half its total revenue abroad, and about one-quarter in Western Europe alone. In 1984, when these European revenues were about $10 billion, IBM settled its long-running case with the commission of the European Economic Community (EEC). IBM made a few concessions, but these were seen by the US press as merely token.[1] The reasons for the modesty of Europe's final demands are revealing: IBM is a major employer and a major exporter from the EEC to other countries; further, IBM, as the biggest computer manufacturer in each of the main European countries, plays a major part in each country's claim to high technology, to having a computer industry. Europe was clearly worried by IBM's somewhat dubious claim that it might move its European production elsewhere. Finally, the ultimate reason for fear of IBM is that each West European government and economy is heavily dependent on IBM hardware and software for many of its central and sensitive operations. These arguments point to IBM Europe as possessing quite breathtaking power; and IBM Europe's successful negotiation of its EEC difficulties shows a commercial lobby directly engaged in big-league diplomacy. It may also be that IBM's being 'let free' in Europe was assisted by its having earlier been 'let free' in Washington. However, what was good for IBM and its shareholders on such a large scale was good for the US only on a more modest scale. The IBM strategy of foreign manufacture means that its direct assistance to the US balance of payments is relatively small, and in fact in 1984 was less than the negative effect of Japanese VCR imports.

The other great US overseas success was ITT, the company which long ago took over AT&T's foreign activities. In 1984 ITT was still the foreign legionnaire of US telecommunications, but it was reorganizing itself, and in so doing retreating from the world market in an attempt to grasp the new domestic US competitive opportunities offered by the Bell breakup. This reappraisal was provoked by increasing hostility by a number of governments in Latin America and Europe.

ITT's and IBM's experience should perhaps have raised some questions as to whether it was realistic to expect AT&T to become a significant exporter. For this was indeed an increasingly resonant theme in the rewrite/divestiture debates of 1977–82: AT&T should stop being a cosy domestic monopolist and should get off its backside and go out to bat on the world stage for the US.

The most obvious consequence of the January 1982 divestiture decision was that by 1984 foreign companies such as Northern Telecom (Canada), Ericsson (Sweden) and Fujitsu (Japan) were moving on from their previous achievements in the US PBX market to become major suppliers to the ambitious investment activities of the ex-BOCs. The constituent parts of the old Bell system quickly became major importers, without becoming significant hardware exporters.

It may be that deregulation in other countries will ultimately benefit US communications exports. British deregulation did provide some such indications. But in 1985 it was unclear both as to how far such international deregulation might go, and as to how far it would benefit the US; for example, European countries might open their telecommunications markets, but only to other European companies.

Ambiguity marks not only the prospects for the future, but also the experience of the past. US government *military* policy in the 1950s and 1960s was responsible for much of the early development of the American semiconductor industry. But subsequently this US military involvement looked less large, and Japanese government policy became more instrumental in expanding the industry.[2] Furthermore, US military policy put a major effort into reducing computer exports, for strategic reasons.

Against this background, a desire to grasp the technological lead once more, by another massive infusion of military/space spending, was clearly one motivation behind President Reagan's adoption of the Strategic Defense Initiative (SDI) or Star Wars program. Requiring a huge and wide-ranging research program, Star Wars research and development would ultimately spill over into civilian applications. But this strand of military spending is very far from a brisk piece of free marketeering or a quick flurry of cancelled regulations.

FROM REGULATED TO UNREGULATED MONOPOLY?

The AT&T divestiture, which came into effect on 1 January 1984, has several claims to being the single most important event in US communications deregulation. The divestiture supposedly did at least three important things: it paved the way for *competition*; it broke down the false distinction between telecommunications and data; and it rejected the notion of natural or inevitable monopoly. Some skeptics argued that both IBM and AT&T had histories of antitrust, as do most large American industries, and consequently, that it was easy to predict an evolution of competition, via excess capacity, price-cutting and shakeout, into a new phase of monopoly. Both proponents and opponents of divestiture were astonishingly vague as to what they expected – indeed, some were too busy fighting over the divorce settlement – but there was a widespread expectation that the competitive phase would last only a few years. Maybe it would be possible to see the outcome sometime around 1990; meanwhile the Justice Department would keep its usual watch on monopolistic tendencies.

In retrospect the task given to Judge Harold Greene, of dividing the local from the national, was an almost impossible one, when in the very nature of a modern telephone system, the two met in the twin forms of large switch/computers and 'joint and common costs'. So much attention was devoted to this conundrum that little time was left to consider how competition might actually work. A scheme was devised by the FCC (and adopted by most city governments) for introducing consumers, market by market, to the notion that they could now choose either AT&T or one of its long-distance competitors. The form of questioning initially used in most localities grossly favored the incumbent AT&T. And within just under 18 months, MCI was already seeking to form an alliance with IBM; the only other powerful, long-distance competitor, Sprint, already belonged to the independent giant GTE.

Thus by 26 June 1985 telephone competition, as it had been known for a year and a half, was already at an end. The ferociously competitive MCI, 'the company which took on AT&T and won', was seeking an alliance with the computer giant. There were still scores of other small companies (mostly re-sellers of AT&T capacity) offering long-distance service. But the strategic consolidation was already underway.

The IBM–MCI moves were interesting also because they were typical of so much else that had happened in the first 18 months after 1 January 1984. In almost every communications area, mergers and consolidation had been occurring. In addition to IBM and AT&T's own acquisitions, there had been further concentration in the press; while UPI sank, AP was left as the only major news (and now also data) agency; within a few months, two of the three TV networks and the biggest nonnetwork group had been the subject of takeover bids; a cable bill had been passed confirming local cable monopolies, and the leading cable company, TCI, was becoming ever more aggressive in its acquisitions. Videotex was shaping up to be dominated by groupings of industry leaders. GM had bought not only a leading computer software company, EDS, but also in Hughes the leader in space vehicles.

Critics had forecast that the merging of communications and computers, together with international moves toward an ISDN, would lead to AT&T and IBM dividing up the vast new playing field between them. In view of these obvious dangers, and the equally obvious warnings, the confidence of the deregulators in the invisible hand of Adam Smith was remarkable. Many of the events which occurred after January 1984 made the script look more as if not A. Smith, but K. Marx, was writing it.

Even the most elementary aspects of post-divestiture competition and of ex-BOC monopoly were left unclear. This lack of clarity itself contributed to the uncertainty, and added to the already considerable problems of MCI, Apple and other illustrious start-ups of the previous two decades. The uncertainty took many forms – but not least, at a time of high interest rates, it hardly helped in the raising of capital for expansion.

LOST LOCALISM?

Deregulation opens up possibilities for many new services at the local level, but, despite this increase in local possibilities, what is offered tends to be ever more national. The ultralocal LPTV station may well focus its programming on music videos, just as the ultralocal cable station's audience uses it almost entirely to watch nationally satellited entertainment.

The AT&T divestiture created seven regional Bell holding companies, but no sooner had these companies come into existence than they unveiled their plans to diversify into almost every conceivable kind of communications activity aross the country and across the world; and although Judge Greene resisted, national expansion looked like their eventual destiny. Similarly with data offerings, early US videotex systems launched by newspapers (to protect their advertising) offered mainly local information. But the indications were that the early demand was for information mainly from national newspaper data banks, and that the most promising future data providers would be other national entities, such as department store chains.

There are several very simple reasons for the general trend against localism in communications. The most obvious is that national services offer economies of scale; moreover, as the 'natural' market size increases, deregulation's emphasis is toward the commercial, and away from various kinds of federally and state-regulated subsidies for local services.

A second new factor is equally familiar. New technologies, such as satellite, are no longer distance-sensitive; it costs the same to send a signal 20 miles, 200 miles or 2,000 miles. And even where rates are charged according to distance, as in telecommunications, this is also where the biggest price cuts will come.

Third, there is a tendency for intermediary levels to be eliminated between individual customer or household and the distant or national supplier. This household–national relationship is symbolized by the backyard or roof dish antenna, but exists in many other areas. A future symbol of this phenomenon may be the personal paging or messaging device linked to a national telecommunications carrier. But already, many Americans are sitting in front of similar screens which carry customized selections from a similar lengthy *national* menu of offerings.

Fourth, local media advertising is stronger than local news. Local advertising in the US is not only plentiful but highly profitable, both for local newspapers and local TV and radio stations. This profitability, however, depends on juxtaposing local editorial and programming which have audience appeal but do not eat up too much advertising revenue. This is done via a number of familiar formulae, which typically involve 'news' that is easy or free to collect; the local weather, local professional sports and local crime news are all facilitated by interested parties. So also is local political news. Breathless live news coverage often depends on friendly sports, police or political PR personnel. But the other formula involving 'local' news is to insert offerings which may look vaguely local, but are in fact supplied nationally, whether by satellite or by mail – advice on your garden, sex life or diet; national news with regional slanting; national features followed by local letters or phone-ins; national authors, actors, musicians or other celebrities in town tonight to plug their latest book, movie or song.

This is all in line with a long American tradition, noted by de Tocqueville and others over the last 150 years, that the super-local and the super-national have an affinity in American life. In recent times *communications* has been ever more about networks, and *politics* has been ever more about lobbies; in both cases local entities are orchestrated to deliver a national sound, and communications deregulation feeds on, and encourages, both tendencies.

NEWS AS AN OBSOLETE CONCEPT?

Communications deregulation both reflects and encourages a number of tendencies which, together, threaten the traditional concept of 'news'. Of course, 'news' has always spanned a multitude of activities, sinful and otherwise; moreover, each succeeding generation has had its news values, redefinitions and the like.

Nevertheless, the current threat to news is indeed unprecedented, because current multichannel capacity favors narrowly defined and financed streams of specialized material targeted at specific audiences. In particular, the trend toward digitalization and the vastly increased speed and capacity of transmission and storage seem to favor a redefinition of news in terms of data, information and data banks.

Each generation tends to look back to a previous one as the golden age. Nevertheless, the 1950s and 1960s may have been the two golden decades in 200 years of US news history. At this stage television was still exerting a benign effect on the press; competition existed between newspapers and television, but newspapers still retained easily the biggest share of advertising. In 1961 newspaper competition still existed in the 61 larger city markets where most Americans lived. But around 1960, competition was mostly on a 2 + 2 + 2 basis – two competing dailies in a typical medium-sized city, only two effective TV network news operations (NBC and CBS) and two national news agencies (AP and UPI).

Around 1960, news maintained its separate identity. News was demarcated quite sharply from *advertising*; news included *entertainment*, but the latter only invaded news in modest quantities; news media carried *opinion*, but made an attempt to label it as such – indeed, 1960 was the height of the syndicated column, and columns tended to be somewhat to the political left of the newspaper's publisher. News was separate from the *news sources* which supplied the news. News included *data*, especially in the traditional form of stock market prices, but such data was edited and contextualized. *Journalists* and reporters played a prominent or dominant part in the operation of news. And finally, news was typically shaped via competition, but only quite limited competition.

The 'two sides' reporting of news was widely followed and practised in particular by the news agencies. In the 1960 presidential election, the two major candidates, Nixon and Kennedy, received broadly equal coverage in the press and on television. Indeed, the Communications Act of 1959 seemed to represent a reasonable compromise between flexibility and fairness; the 1959 Act, which exempted news programming from equal-time requirements, nevertheless was widely believed to have codified the fairness doctrine, and to have required an opportunity for conflicting views. Given the very limited amount of television news and politics available around 1959–60, this was widely seen as a reasonable compromise with the general First Amendment principle of 'no law' on the press.

However, nearly all the assumptions of the 1950s and 1960s about the nature of news have been put in question by developments since then, and especially by the transition from limited competition to a more recent pattern of pockets of monopoly surrounded by fierce and unlimited competition.

A fundamental challenge was posed by the emergence of the 'big local news' on television in the early 1970s. Big slabs of local news in the early evening, before the national network news, challenged all the previous assumptions. In particular, this big local news was driven by *advertising*; such local programming was potentially highly profitable, because the local station kept all the revenue, without the network taking a large share. Immediately, the big local news made all kinds of concessions to advertisers, in particular by using 'consumer' features about food, homes, leisure and the like. Second, the big local news did not simply include some *entertainment*, it offered an entertainment show in a news format; anchor 'personalities' were employed, and their sometimes stumbling attempts to be entertaining quickly earned the label 'happy talk news'. Attempts to exclude, or at least to label opinion were largely dropped. Much of this expanded local news was highly dependent on news sources. Journalists and reporters were often subordinate to anchor persons with little news experience. The atmosphere, especially in the largest markets, was ferociously competitive, more like the tabloid press of the 1920s, as independent stations battled against the local news offerings of the network owned-and-operated stations or affiliates.

The big local news has steadily evolved since the early 1970s, and it has become even more successful in audience terms. The availability (via satellite) of more and more national news and feature offerings has enabled the big local news to cream off the top few national stories and to combine these with local disasters, murders, consumer experiences, weather and sport.

More recently, and especially since 1980, deregulatory policies have led to an explosion of additional news offerings, the most dramatic example being CNN, the 24-hour Turner video news offering which began in June 1980. However, these news offerings have found themselves operating in extremely competitive and financially lean circumstances, and they have been forced to make major concessions. Leading examples are the 'business news' programs and inserts; PBS played a major pioneering role here but the cable industry, especially after 1980, increasingly took up the running. In late 1983 there were five competing national daily video business news offerings of at least half an hour with breakfast-time the favorite scheduling. A Media Institute document listed 29 separate 'Business, Financial and Economic News Programs' nationally available to cable, TV and radio; these varied from the then 12 hour offering of Financial News Network to several 60 second radio insert services. In July 1985 one daily offering, 'Business Times', folded, but CNN stepped in with its breakfast business news show, keeping the total at six daily half hour video news shows.[3] These business news satellite offerings differ from anything previously labelled as news on either network or local TV news. These shows are friendly, indeed obsequious, towards business in a style previously more familiar in sport; as in sports coverage there is a powerful impetus to attract advertising, subsidy and cheap or free material. Such support varies from direct origination by the US Chamber of Commerce to 'news' shows which are really promotions for financial publications, financial services companies or the selling of real estate. The boundaries once observed between news, data, advertising, entertainment and editorial are blurred into an overall business boosterism.

CBS and NBC, of course, no longer operate a comfortable duopoly of national video news. In the 1970s ABC became a major news force. The big local news shows are now the major competition. But the cable offerings are also significant. CNN's 1985 decision to go for a much softer, entertainment style of 24-hour news, modelled on the network breakfast news shows, as it eagerly told Madison Avenue,[4] was an indication of where the competitive pressures were leading. The networks news shows, which never had top ratings, suffered quite serious audience losses in the early 1980s.[5] The networks do not feel they either can, or should, make the same concessions as their smaller rivals, but their willingness to pay million-dollar-plus salaries to anchor persons, such as Dan Rather, reveals their anxieties. So also does the network tactic of offering additional doses of national news outside the usual 7–7.30 p.m. time band.

By the 1980s the newspaper press was also in a somewhat less confident mood. Since 1970 it has compensated for a slowdown in sales as against population by extracting more and more advertising from less and less competitive local markets. Between 1970 and 1984, daily newspaper sales increased by just 2 per cent, while metric tons of newsprint consumption went up by 51 per cent. Some of this fattening was accounted for by Sunday newspapers, which by 1983 were on an average 68 per cent advertising.[6]

All these changes leave the elite daily press of the major cities as the only major remaining guardians of traditional news and news values. Most of these elite papers have increased in recent years in sales and/or quality. But even here there is a major threat to news: if 'news' does indeed become redefined as 'data' or 'information', the elite press is the most likely place for this to happen. And what has already happened in the news agency field could be an indication of things to come. As UPI slowly faded, AP, the now monopoly general news agency, was already profitably engaged with Dow Jones in selling a data and news service. The Dow Jones News Retrieval service passed the 150,000-customer threshold in mid-1984, and began to move into significant profitability. This was the same service which US Secretary of State George Shultz used for quick updates, and as a way of keeping foreign desk officers on their toes.[7]

Initially, of course, the elite daily newspapers see data and information retrieval as a source of additional revenue and/or as a defensive move against subsequent competition from telephone companies, IBM or other communications revolutionaries. But if and when such data services achieve mass market penetration onto millions of home and office screens, the sums of money involved may dwarf what can be obtained from selling news as traditionally defined.

These threats to, or new definitions of, news pose many important and delicate issues. But the main public debate has taken the form of a lobbying battle between entrenched interests. Broadly the battle has consisted of the electronic media versus the politicians. The electronic media, led by the ambitious Senator Packwood, have been campaigning to abolish the fairness doctrine and to extend the First Amendment to broadcasting, cable and other electronic media. On the opposing side are the majority of politicians, who like the existing arrangements of fairness and equal time applied to the electronic media, because news values and television news in practice favor political incumbents against challengers. Both sides have lined up their supporters for an ongoing battle. The incumbent politicians have the support of the remnants of the old liberal activist media critics of the 1970s. The electronic media have the support of most journalists, for whom an extension of the First Amendment would mean an extension of professional autonomy. CBS and other electronic media interests have funded a Frank Stanton Professorship of First Amendment at Harvard University.

There is certainly plenty to be studied. And as a member of the Harvard Law Faculty has pointed out, some kind of compromise seems necessary between the absolutes of First Amendment freedom and the legitimate concerns which exist in a modern society about the unregulated introduction of new mass media technologies.[8]

POLITICIANS AND LOBBYISTS

American communications policy has previously been made via gladiatorial combats of lobby versus lobby; this lobby combat has been judged by teams of Washington adjudicators, themselves in competition with each other. The recent phase of deregulation, together with the increased policy salience of IBM and AT&T, means that, if no major changes occur in policymaking, this lobby mode will continue. Policy in perhaps the world's most sophisticated and important industry will be made by two teams of lobbyist-lawyers, while Washington's various branches of government spectate and intermittently adjudicate.

But deregulation not only throws policy into the commercial arena, it also implies that while the role of bureaucrats should be smaller, that of politicians should be greater. In the last decade, politicians on relevant congressional committees have taken up the challenge; but the task is too great, and the obstructions within Congress too severe.

The AT&T divestiture has left the seven ex-BOCS in much the same position as AT&T a decade or more earlier. Unless the ground rules are changed, this area promises interminable battles, with lawyers as prime beneficiaries. These regional problems require national attention.

The executive is the branch of the federal government which has most obviously failed here. Occupants of the White House cannot, and surely need not, continue to regard communications policy as a no-go area haunted by the ghost of Richard Nixon.

If the executive cannot, or will not, recognize the need for more effective and considered national policymaking, then perhaps the commercial lobbies themselves may need to lobby in effect to reduce their own power. As communications and communications policy becomes ever more international, it is not ultimately in the interest of IBM and AT&T, or of Hollywood and the TV networks, that they should appear to be more powerful than the government of the United States.

Notes

1 *New York Times*, 3 and 6 August 1984, and *Wall Street Journal*, 3 August 1984.
2 Daniel I. Okimoto *et al.*, *Competitive Edge* (1984), pp. 78–133.
3 Timothy E. Schellardt, 'US Business to Unveil TV Network Soon, Raising Fears of Unfair Clout in Lobbying', *Wall Street Journal*, 13 April 1982, p. 14. 'The Fifth Estate is Bullish on Business News, *Broadcasting*, 15 August 1983, pp. 41–54. The Media Institute, 'Business, Financial and Economic News Programs', Washington, DC: The Media Institute, November 1983. Mark Hosenball, 'FNN Heads for Profits after Shaky Start', *Multichannel News*, 18 June 1984, pp. 1, 30–6. 'Effort to raise funds fails; "Business Times" canceled', *CableVision*, 1 July 1985, p. 22.
4 'CNN: Features in the Future', *Advertising Age*, 21 January 1985, pp. 1, 82.
5 'Why TV News has been losing its audience', *Business Week*, 16 April 1984, pp. 137–41.
6 ANPA, *Facts About Newspapers: '85*.
7 'Secretary of State consults news retrieval service', *Editor and Publisher*, 27 October 1984, p. 31.
8 Mario L. Baeza, 'Safeguarding the First Amendment in the Telecommunications Era'.

Bibliography

BOOKS AND ARTICLES

Adams, Walter (ed). *The Structure of American Industry*, 6th edn, New York: Macmillan, 1982.

Alexander, Herbert E. *Financing the 1980 Election*. Lexington, Mass.: Lexington Books, 1983.

Auerback, Lewis. 'The Distinction between Carriage and Content', *Telecommunications Policy*, March 1981, pp. 3–11.

Auw, Alvin von. *Heritage and Destiny: Reflections on the Bell System in Transition*. New York: Praeger, 1983.

Avery, Robert and Pepper, Robert. 'Interconnection Reconnection'. In *The Politics of Interconnection: a history of public television at the national level*. Washington: NAB, 1979.

Babyak, Gregory R., Jackson, Charles I. and Shooshan, Harry M., III. 'Legacy of Legislation: How the Courts and Commissions are Influenced by Legislative Proposals'. Draft, March 1984.

Baeza, Mario L. 'Safeguarding the First Amendment in the Telecommunications Era'. *Harvard Law Review*, vol. 97, no. 2, pp. 584–96.

Bagdikian, Ben H. 'Congress and the Media: partners in propaganda'. *Columbia Journalism Review*, January–February, 1974, pp. 3–10.

——. *The Media Monopoly*. Boston: Beacon Press, 1983.

Baldwin, Thomas and McVoy, D. Stevens. *Cable Communication*. Englewood Cliffs, NJ: Prentice-Hall, 1983.

Ball, Howard (ed). *Federal Administrative Agencies*. Englewood Cliffs, NJ: Prentice-Hall, 1984.

Bardack, Eugene and Kagan, Robert A. *Going by the Book: the problem of regulatory unreasonableness*. Philadelphia: Temple University Press, 1982.

Beck, Kirsten. *Cultivating the Wasteland*. New York: American Council of the Arts, 1983.

Becker, Lee B., Dunwoody, Sharon and Rafaeli, Sheizaf. 'Cable's Impact on Use of Other News Media'. *Journal of Broadcasting*, vol. 27, no. 2, spring 1983, pp. 127–40.

Bernstein, Jeremy. *Three Degrees Above Zero: Bell Labs in the Information Age*. New York: Charles Scribner's, 1984.

Besen, Stanley M. and Johnson, Leland L. *An Analysis of the Federal Communication Commission's Group Ownership Rules*. Santa Monica, Calif.: Rand Corporation, 1984.

Black, Norman. 'The Deregulation Revolution', *Channels*, September–October, 1984, pp. 52–6.

Bleeke, Joel A. 'Deregulation: riding the rapids'. *The McKinsey Quarterly*, summer 1983, pp. 18–36.

Bogart, Leo. *Press and Public*. Hillsdale, NY: Lawrence Erlbaum, 1981.

Bolter, Walter G. 'Entering the Information Age Without a Communications Policy'. *Telecom Insider*, October 1982, pp. 7–14.

——, Duvall, Jerry B., Kelsey, Fred J. and McConnaughey, James W. *Telecommunications Policy for the 1980s: The Transition to Competition*. Englewood Cliffs, NJ: Prentice-Hall, 1984.

Botein, Michael and Rice, David M. (eds). *Network Television and the Public Interest*. Lexington, Mass.: Lexington Books, 1980.

Bouras, James. Remarks at WIPO's 'Worldwide Forum on the Piracy of Sound and Audiovisual Recordings', held in Geneva, 26 March 1981. New York: MPAA.

Boyd-Barrett, Oliver. *The International News Agencies*. Beverly Hill: Sage; London: Constable, 1980.

Brenner, Daniel L. and Rivers, William L. (eds). *Free But Regulated: Conflicting Traditions in Media Law*. Ames, Iowa State University Press, 1982.

Breyer, Stephen. *Regulation and Its Reform*. Cambridge, Mass.: Harvard University Press, 1982.

Brock, Gerald W. *The Telecommunications Industry: the Dynamics of Market Structure*. Cambridge, Mass.: Harvard University Press, 1981.

Brooks, John. *Telephone: the First Hundred Years*. New York: Harper and Row, 1975.

Brooks, Thomas R. *Communications Workers of America*. New York: Mason/Charter, 1977.

Brotman, Stuart N. 'Judicial Review of the FCC: The Developing Legacy of Greater Boston', *Journal of Communication*, vol. 30, no. 1, winter 1980, pp. 31–6.

Brown, Charles. Address at the National Press Club, Washington DC, 6 December 1983.

Brown, Les. 'Reagan and the Unseen Network', *Channels*, October–November, 1981, pp. 17–18.

Brubaker, Randy. 'The Newspaper Preservation Act: How It Affects Diversity in the Newspaper Industry'. *Journal of Communication Inquiry*, vol. 7, no. 2, winter 1982, pp. 91–104.

Burnham, David. *The Rise of the Computer State*. New York: Random House, 1983.

Cantor, Muriel and Cantor, Joel. 'Regulation and Special Interests: the politics of broadcasting in the United States'. In Raymond Kuhn (ed), *Broadcasting in Crisis*. London: Croom Helm, 1985.

Cargill, Thomas F. and Garcia, Gillian G. *Financial Deregulation and Monetary Control*. Stanford University, Hoover Institution Press, 1982.

Carnegie Commission on Educational Television. *Public Television: A Program For Action*. New York: Harper and Row, 1967.

Carnegie Commission on the Future of Public Broadcasting. *A Public Trust*. New York: Bantam Books, 1979.

Carron, Andrew S. 'Banking on Change: the Reorganization of Financial Regulation', *The Brookings Review*, spring 1984, pp. 12–21.

Cater, Douglass and Nyhan, Michael J. (eds). *The Future of Public Broadcasting*, New York: Praeger, 1976.

Chamberlin, Bill F. and Brown, Charlene J. (eds). *The First Amendment Reconsidered*. New York: Longman, 1982.

Clarke, Peter and Evans, Susan H. *Covering Campaigns: Journalism in Congressional Elections*. Stanford University Press, 1983.

Coates, Vary T. and Finn, Bernard. *A Retrospective Technology Assessment: Submarine Telegraphy. The Transatlantic Cable of 1866*. San Francisco Press, 1979.

Cohen, Marvin S. 'Airline Deregulation: a model for the '80s'. *Journal of Contemporary Business*, vol. 9, no. 2, 1980, pp. 41–7.

Cole, Barry and Oettinger, Mal. *Reluctant Regulators: The FCC and the Broadcast Audience*. Reading, Mass.: Addison-Wesley, 1978.

Common Cause. *People Against PACS*. Washington, DC: Common Cause, 1983.

Compaine, Benjamin M. (ed). *Understanding New Media*. Cambridge, Mass.: Ballinger, 1984.

Connor, Charles D. 'MDS Television in the Eighties: Video Cops and Video Robbers'. *Communications and the Law*, vol. 6, no. 1, February 1984, pp. 45–58.

Cornell, Nina W. and Webbink, Douglas W. 'The Present Direction of the FCC: an Appraisal'. *American Economic Review*, vol. 73, no. 2, 1983, pp. 194–7.

Cowan, Geoffrey. *See No Evil*. New York: Simon and Schuster, 1979.

Cox, Kenneth A. 'Does the FCC Really Do Anything?' *Journal of Broadcasting*, vol. 11, no. 2, summer 1967, pp. 97–113.

Creager, Stephen E. 'Airline Deregulation and Airport Regulation'. *Yale Law Journal*, vol. 93, no. 2, December 1983, pp. 319–39.

Criner, Kathleen and Wilson, Jane. *Telecommunications: A Review and Update*. Reston, Virginia: ANPA, 1983.

Dale, Richard. *The Regulation of International Banking*. Cambridge: Woodhead-Faulkner, 1984.

Danielian, N. R. *AT and T: The Story of Industrial Conquest*. Vanguard Press, 1939. Reprint, New York: Arno Press, 1974.

Davidson, Roger H. and Oleszek, Walter J. *Congress and Its Members*. Washington DC: Congressional Quarterly Press, 1981.

Davidson, William H. *The Amazing Race: Winning the Technorivalry with Japan*. New York: John Wiley, 1984.

Derthick, Martha and Quirk, Paul. *The Politics of Deregulation*. Draft. Washington DC: The Brookings Institution, 1984.

de Sola Pool, Ithiel. *Forecasting the Telephone: a retrospective technology assessment*. Norwood, NJ: Ablex, 1983.

——. *Technologies of Freedom*. Cambridge, Mass.: Belknap/Harvard University Press, 1983.

Dizard, Wilson P. *The Coming Information Age*. New York: Longman, 1982.

Drew, Elizabeth. *Politics and Money: the new road to corruption*. New York: Macmillan, 1983.

Emery, Edwin and Emery, Michael. *The Press and America*, 5th ed. Englewood Cliffs, NJ: Prentice-Hall, 1984.

Ergas, Henry and Okayama, Jun (eds). *Changing Market Structures in Telecommunications*. Amsterdam: North-Holland, 1984.

Etzioni, Amitai. *Capital Corruption: the new attack on American Democracy*. San Diego: Harcourt Brace Jovanovich, 1984.

Evans, David S. (ed). *Breaking Up Bell*. New York: North-Holland, 1983.

Feigenbaum, Edward A. and McCorduck, Pamela. *The Fifth Generation: Artificial Intelligence and Japan's Computer Challenge to the World*. London: Pan Books, 1984.

Feketukuty, Geza and Aronson, John D. 'The World Information Economy'. Paper for conference at McGill University on *Policy Issues in the Canadian– American Information Sector*, 1983.

Fishman, Katharine D. *The Computer Establishment*. New York: McGraw-Hill, 1982.

Flammang, Robert A. *US Programs that Impede US Export Competitiveness: the Regulatory Environment*. US Export Competitiveness Project, Center for Strategic and International Studies, Georgetown University, Washington DC, 1980.

Foote, Susan B. 'SMR Forum: Changing Regulatory Strategies – What Managers Should Know about Federal Preemption'. *Sloan Management Review*, vol. 26, no. 1, fall 1984, pp. 69–72.

Ford, Frederick W. 'The Meaning of the "Public Interest, Convenience or Necessity"'. *Journal of Broadcasting*, summer 1961, pp. 205–18.

Fowler, Mark S. 'Broadcast Unregulation in the 1980s'. *Television Quarterly*, vol. 19, no. 1, spring 1982, pp. 12–18.

——. "Congress Shall Make No Law ...". *Channels*, September–October, 1982.

——. 'The Public's Interest'. *Communications and the Law*, vol. 4, no. 1, winter 1982, pp. 51–8.

——. 'The Boom Goes Bust, the Bust Goes Boom'. *Communications and the Law*, vol. 6, no. 3, June 1984, pp. 23–9.

—— and Brenner, Daniel L. 'A Marketplace Approach to Broadcast Regulation'. *Texas Law Review*, vol. 60, no. 2, February 1982, pp. 1–51.

Frantzich, Stephen E. *Computers in Congress*. Beverly Hills: Sage, 1982.

Freiberger, Paul and Swaine, Michael. *Fire in the Valley: the making of the personal computer*. Berkeley: Osborne/McGraw Hill, 1984.

Fund for the City of New York. *The Wired Island*. New York, 1973.

Gabel, Richard. 'The early competitive era in telephone communication, 1893–1920'. *Law and Contemporary Problems*, vol. 34, no. 2, spring 1969, pp. 340–59.

Galloway, Jonathan F. *The Politics and Technology of Satellite Communications*. Lexington, Mass.: Lexington Books, 1972.

Gandy, Oscar H., Jr. *Beyond Agenda Setting: Information Subsidies and Public Policy*. Norwood, NJ: Ablex, 1982.

——, Espinosa, Paul and Ordoyer, Janusz A. (eds). *Proceedings from the Tenth Annual Telecommunications Policy Research Conference*. Norwood, NJ: Ablex, 1983.

Ganley, Oswald H. and Ganley, Gladys D. *International Implications of United States Communications and Information Resources*. Cambridge, Mass.: Harvard University Program on Information Resources Policy, 1981.

Gans, Herbert J. *Deciding What's News*. New York: Pantheon; London: Constable, 1980.

Garay, Ronald. 'The FCC and the US Court of Appeals: Telecommunications Policy by Judicial Decree?'. *Journal of Broadcasting*, vol. 23, no. 2, summer 1979, pp. 301–18.

——. *Congressional Television: a legislative History.* Westport, Conn.: Greenwood Press, 1984.

Geller, Henry. 'The Role of Future Regulation: Licensing, System Allocation, Content, Access, Common Carrier and Rates'. Telecommunication Conference April 13–15, 1984.

—— and Barron, Ira. 'The AT & T Settlement: Painting a black and white picture of a shaded world'. *Telecom Insider*, July 1982, pp. 4–7.

Gerbner, George and Siefert, Marsha. (eds). *World Communications: a handbook.* New York: Longman, 1984.

Glenn, Robin Day. *Financing of United States Exports of Telecommunications Equipment.* Washington, DC: Georgetown University Law Center, 1982.

——. *Legal Issues Affecting Licensing of TV programs in the European Economic Community.* Washington DC: Georgetown University Law Center, 1983.

Goulden, Joseph C. *Monopoly.* New York: Pocket Books, 1970.

Graber, Doris A. (ed). *Media Power in Politics.* Washington DC: Congressional Quarterly, 1984.

Grangé, Jean Louis. (ed). *Satellite and Computer Communications.* Amsterdam: North-Holland, 1983.

Green, Mark J. (ed). *The Monopoly Makers.* New York: Grossman, 1973.

——. *Who Runs Congress?* 4th edn. New York: Dell, 1984.

Greenberg, Bradley S., Burgoon, Michael, Burgoon, Judee F. and Korzenny, Felipe. *Mexican Americans and the Mass Media.* Norwood, NJ: Ablex, 1983.

Greene, Judge Harold H. 'Modification of Final Judgement'. *United States v. Western Electric Co and American Telephone and Telegraph Co.* District Court for the District of Columbia, 24 August 1982.

Gregory, Gene. *Japanese Electronics Technology: Enterprise and Innovation.* Tokyo: The Japan Times, 1985.

Grunwald, Joseph and Flamm, Kenneth. *The Global Factory: foreign assembly in international trade.* Washington DC: The Brookings Institution, 1985.

Haight, Timothy R. (ed). *Telecommunications Policy and the Citizen: Public Interest Perspectives on the Communications Act Rewrite.* New York: Praeger, 1979.

Hambrecht, William. 'Venture Capital and the Growth of Silicon Valley'. *California Management Review*, vol. 26, no. 2, winter 1984, pp. 74–81.

Hansen, Allen. *USIA: Public Diplomacy in the Computer Age.* New York: Praeger, 1984.

Hanson, Dirk. *The New Alchemists: Silicon Valley and the micro-electronics revolution.* New York: Avon, 1983.

Harnett, Bertram. *Law, Lawyers and Laymen.* San Diego: Harcourt Brace Jovanovich, 1984.

Hazewindus, Nico. *The US Microelectronics Industry.* New York: Pergamon, 1982.

Horsfield, Peter G. *Religious Television: the American Experience.* New York: Longman, 1984.

Howard, Herbert H. *Group and Cross Media Ownership of Television Stations: 1984.* Washington, DC: NAB, 1984.

—— and Kievman, Michael S. *Radio and TV Programming.* Columbus, Ohio: Grid Publishing, 1983.

Jackson, Charles, Shooshan, Harry M. III and Wilson, Jane L. *Newspapers and*

Videotex: How free a press? St Petersburg, Fla.: Modern Media Institute, 1981.

Jackson, Kay Charles. *The Influence of the United States Court of Appeals for the District of Columbia on Federal Policy in Broadcast Regulation, 1929–71.* New York: Arno reprint, 1979.

Jacobson, Robert. 'Designing the Information Environment'. Paper at Twelfth Annual Telecommunications Policy Research Conference, Airlie, Virginia, April 1984.

James, Beverley. 'Economic Democracy and Restructuring the Press'. *The Journal of Communication Inquiry*, vol. 6, no. 2, winter 1981, pp. 119–29.

Jansky, Donald and Jeruchim, Michael. *Communications Satellites in Geostationary Orbit.* Dedham, Mass.: Artech House, 1983.

Jassem, Harvey C. 'An examination of self-regulation of Broadcasting'. *Communications and the Law*, vol. 5, no. 3, spring 1983, pp. 51–64.

Johnson, Mark. 'Technological Abundance and the Future of Video Delivery System Regulation'. *Communications and the Law*, vol. 5, no. 4, fall 1983, pp. 51–65. ·

Johnson, Nicholas. 'A New Fidelity to the Regulatory Ideal'. *Georgetown Law Journal*, vol. 59, 1971, pp. 869–908.

Jones, William H and Anderson, Laird. *The Newspaper Business.* A 12-part series published by the *Washington Post* in July–August 1977.

Jonquieres, Guy de and Betts, Paul. *America's Communications Revolution.* A 9-part series published by the London *Financial Times* in January 1983.

Kaatz, Ronald B. *Cable: an Advertiser's Guide to the New Electronic Media.* Chicago: Crain Books, 1982.

Kahn, Frank. 'Economic Regulation of Broadcasting as a Utility'. *Journal of Broadcasting*, spring 1963, pp. 97–112.

—— (ed). *Documents of American Broadcasting.* 4th edn. Englewood Cliffs, NJ: Prentice-Hall, 1984.

Kalmanir, Karen A. 'A Strange Animal: the FCC and Broadcast EEO'. *Communications and the Law*, vol. 6, no. 2, April 1984, pp. 25–46.

Kareken, John H. 'The First Step in Bank Deregulation: What about the FDIC?'. *American Economic Review*, vol. 73, no. 2, 1983, pp. 198–203.

Katzmann, Robert A. *Regulatory Bureaucracy: the Federal Trade Commission and Antitrust Policy.* Cambridge, Mass.: MIT Press, 1980.

Kerr, Elaine B. and Hiltz, Starr Roxanne. *Computer-Mediated Communication Systems.* New York: Academic Press, 1982.

Kessler, Lauren. *The Dissident Press.* Beverly Hills: Sage, 1984.

Kester, John G. 'Are Lawyers Becoming Public Enemy Number One?'. *The Washingtonian*, February 1984, pp. 114–18, 138–41.

Kildou, Judith Tegger. *Intelsat: Policy-Maker's Dilemma.* Lexington, Mass.: Lexington Books, 1973.

Kinsley, Michael E. *Outer Space and Inner Sanctums: Government, Business and Satellite Communication.* New York: John Wiley, 1976.

Kittross, John M. (ed). *Administration of American Telecommunications Policy.* 2 vols. Reprint. New York: Arno Press, 1980.

Kleinfield, Sonny. *The Biggest Company on Earth: a profile of AT&T.* New York: Holt, Rinehart and Winston, 1981.

Krasnow, Erwin G. and Bentley J. Geoffrey. *Buying or Building a Broadcast Station.* Washington, DC: NAB, 1982.

——, Longley, Lawrence D. and Terry, Herbert A. *The Politics of Broadcast Regulation*. 3rd edn. New York: St Martin's Press, 1982.

Krugman, Dean M. and Reid, Leonard N. 'The "Public Interest" as defined by FCC policy makers'. *Journal of Broadcasting*, vol. 24, no. 3, summer 1980, pp. 311–25.

Labunski, Richard E. *The First Amendment Under Siege: the politics of broadcast regulation*. Westport, Conn.: Greenwood Press, 1981.

Lancaster, Kathleen Landis. *International Telecommunications*. Lexington, Mass.: Lexington Books, 1982.

Lang, Gladys Engel and Lang, Kurt. *Politics and Television Re-Viewed*. Beverly Hills: Sage, 1984.

—— and ——. *The Battle for Public Opinion: the President, the Press and the Polls during Watergate*. New York: Columbia University Press, 1983.

Lawrence, John Shelton and Timberg, Bernard (eds). *Fair Use and Free Inquiry: copyright law and the new media*. Norwood, NJ: Ablex, 1980.

LeDuc, Don R. *Cable Television and the FCC: A crisis in media control*. Philadelphia: Temple University Press, 1973.

Legates, John C. *Telecommunications Costs and Prices in the United States – an overview*. Cambridge, Mass.: Harvard University Program on Information Resources Policy, 1982.

Leinster, Colin. 'Mobile Phones: hot new industry'. *Fortune*, 6 August 1984, pp. 108–13.

Lempert, Larry. 'AT&T Lawyers Prepare to Confront a Changing World'. *Legal Times of Washington*, 8 February 1982, p. 40.

Levin, Harvey J. *Fact and Fancy in Television Regulation: An economic study of policy alternatives*. New York: Russell Sage Foundation, 1980.

Levine, Henry. 'Smart Buildings Come of Age'. *Telematics*, vol. 1, no. 2, June 1984, pp. 1–2, 8–11.

Levy, Jonathan D. 'Competition and Diversity: a framework for Analysis'. Paper read at Twelfth Annual Telecommunications Policy Research Conference, Airlie, Virginia, April 1984.

Lewin, Leonard (ed). *Telecommunications: an interdisciplinary text*. Dedham, Mass.: Artech House, 1984.

Lieb, Charles H. 'The Sony Betamax Case – Winds of Change?' *Communications and the Law*, vol. 4, no. 2, spring 1982, pp. 17–22.

Litan, Robert E. and Nordhaus, William D. *Reforming Federal Regulation*. New Haven: Yale University Press, 1983.

Litman, Barry R. *The Vertical Structure of the Television Broadcasting Industry: the coalescence of power*. Lansing, Mich.: Michigan State University Graduate School of Business Administration, 1979.

Lucoff, Manny. *Telecommunications Management and Policy: Who Governs?* Association for Education in Journalism: Journalism Monographs, 51, 1977.

——. 'The Rise and Fall of the Third Rewrite'. *Journal of Communication*, vol. 30, no. 3, summer 1980, pp. 47–53.

McClellan, Stephen T. *The Coming Computer Industry Shakeout*. New York: John Wiley, 1984.

McGarrity, John. *Implementing Access Charges: Stakeholders and Options*. Cambridge, Mass.: Harvard University Program on Information Resources Policy, 1983.

McGill University Centre for Study of Regulated Industries, *Policy Issues in the Canadian–American Information Sector*. Montreal, 1984.

McGraw, Thomas. *Prophets of Regulation*. Cambridge, Mass.: Belknap/Harvard University Press, 1984.

McKenna, Regis, Borrus, Michael and Cohen, Stephen. 'Industrial Policy and International Competition in High Technology'. *California Management Review*, vol. 26, no. 2, winter 1984, pp. 15–24.

McLean, Mick (ed). *The Japanese Electronics Challenge*. London: Frances Pinter, 1982.

McMahon, Robert Sears. *Federal Regulation of the Radio and Television Broadcast Industry in the United States, 1927–59*. New York: Arno Press, 1979.

Macy, John W., Jr. *To Irrigate a Wasteland*. Berkeley: University of California Press, 1974.

Magnant, Robert S. *Domestic Satellite: An FCC Giant Step*. Boulder, Colo.: Westview Press, 1976.

Maguire, W. Terry. 'How the Diversity Principle became the law of the land'. *Presstime* (ANPA), October 1982, pp. 22–6.

Malbin, Michael J. *Unelected Representatives: Congressional staff and the future of representative government*. New York: Basic Books, 1980.

Manning, Willard G. and Owen, Bruce M. 'Television Rivalry and Network Power'. *Public Policy*, vol. 24, no. 1, winter 1976, pp. 33–57.

Matusow, Barbara. 'When Push Comes to Shove'. *Channels*, August–September 1981, pp. 33–9.

——. *The Evening Stars*. New York: Ballantine, 1984.

Mayer, Martin. *The Money Bazaars*. New York: E. P. Dutton, 1984.

Melnick, R. Shep. *Regulation and the Courts: the case of the Clean Air Act*. Washington, DC: The Brookings Institution, 1983.

——. 'Deadlines, Common Sense, and Cynicism'. *The Brookings Review*, fall 1983, pp. 21–4.

Melvern, Linda, Anning, Nick and Hebditch, David. *Techno-Bandits*. Boston: Houghton Mifflin, 1984.

Meyer, John R., Wilson, Robert W., Baughcum, M. Alan, Burton, Ellen and Caouette, Louis. *The Economics of Competition in the Telecommunications Industry*. Cambridge, Mass.: Oelgeschlager, Gunn and Hain, 1980.

Miller, James. 'The President's Advocate: OTP and Broadcast Issues'. *Journal of Broadcasting*, vol. 26, no. 3, summer 1982, pp. 625–39.

Milk, Leslie and Weinstein, Allen. *United States Participation in the International Telecommunications Union*. Washington, DC: Georgetown University Center for Strategic and International Studies, 1984.

Minow, Newton N. *Equal Time*. Atheneum, 1964.

Moritz, Michael. *The Little Kingdom: the private story of Apple Computers*. New York: William Murrow, 1984.

Morris, Roy L. 'Making it as an interexchange carrier after Divestiture: Having the Right Stuff'. Paper presented at 'Telecommunications in the Post-Divestiture Environment' seminar at Scanticon–Princeton Conference Center, April 1984.

Mosco, Vincent and Wasko, Janet (eds). *The Critical Communications Review. Volume II: Changing Patterns of Communications Control*. Norwood, NJ: Ablex, 1984.

NAB, *Opportunities in Communications Law*. Washington, DC: NAB Legal Department, July 1983.

Nadel, Mark and Noam, Eli (eds). *The Economics of Direct Broadcast Satellites*

(DBS): an Anthology. New York: Columbia University, Graduate School of Business.

Naisbitt, John. *Megatrends*. New York: Warner Books, 1982.

National Research Council, Office of International Affairs, *International Competition in Advanced Technology: Decisions for America*. Washington, DC: National Academy Press, 1983.

Noam, Eli M. 'Towards an Integrated Communications Market: overcoming the local monopoly of cable television'. *Federal Communications Law Journal*, vol. 34, no. 2, 1983, pp. 209–57.

——. *'Monopoly and Productivity in Cable Television'*. New York: Columbia University Graduate School of Business, 1984.

Noll, Roger G., Peck, Merton, J. and McGowan, John J. *Economic Aspects of Television Regulation*. Washington, DC: The Brookings Institution, 1973.

OECD. *Telecommunications: pressures and policies for change*. Paris: OECD, 1983.

Oettinger, Anthony G. and Weinhaus, Carol L. *The Once and Future Telephone Plant and Costs: at the heart of debates*. Cambridge, Mass.: Harvard University Program on Information Resources Policy, 1983.

—— and ——. *Federal/State Costing Methods: who controls the dollars*. Cambridge, Mass.: Harvard University Program on Information Resources Policy, 1984.

Ohmae, Keniche. *Triad Power: the coming shape of global competition*. New York: The Free Press, Macmillan, 1985.

Okimoto, Daniel L., Sugano, Takno and Weinstein, Franklin B. *Competitive Edge: the semi-conductor industry in the US and Japan*. Stanford University Press, 1984.

Orion Satellite Corporation, *Application for an International Communications Satellite System*. Before the Federal Communications Commission, 1983.

Owen, Bruce M. and Manning, Willard G., Jr. *The Television Rivalry Game*. Stanford University Department of Economics, 1973.

—— and Braeutigam, Ronald. *The Regulation Game: strategic use of the administrative process*. Cambridge, Mass.: Ballinger, 1978.

Pascale, Richard Tanner and Athos, Anthony G. *The Art of Japanese Management*. London: Penguin Books, 1982.

Pearce, Alan. 'Congressional Influence evident in Judge Greene's "Admirable" terms for AT&T antitrust suit settlement'. *Telecom Insider*, September 1982, pp. 1–4.

Pelton, Joseph. *Global Talk*. Brighton: Harvester Press, 1981.

Pertschuk, Michael. *Revolt Against Regulation: the rise and fall of the consumer movement*. Berkeley: University of California Press, 1982.

Peters, Charles. *How Washington Really Works*. Reading, Mass.: Addison-Wesley, 1980.

Poole, Robert W., Jr (ed). *Instead of Regulation*. Lexington, Mass.: Lexington Books, 1982.

Powers, Ron. *Supertube: The Rise of Television Sports*. New York: Coward-McCann, 1984.

Practising Law Institute, *Antitrust, the Media and the New Technology*. New York: PLI, 1981.

——. *Current Developments in Copyright Law 1982*. New York: PLI, 1982.

——. *Legal and Business Aspects of the Magazine Industry 1982*. New York: PLI, 1982.

——. *Legal and Business Aspects of the Advertising Industry 1982*. New York: PLI, 1982.

——. *After the AT&T Settlement: The New Telecommunications Era*. New York: PLI, 1982.

——. *Cable Television in a New Era*. New York: PLI, 1983.

——. *Implementing the AT&T Settlement: The New Telecommunications Era*. New York: PLI, 1983.

Preece, Robert S. and Morris, Roy L. 'A Roadmap for Deregulating AT&T'. Paper read at Eleventh Annual Telecommunications Policy Research Conference, April 1983.

Price, David E. *The Commerce Committees*. New York: Grossman, 1975.

Reagan, Ronald. 'Remarks of the President at the Presidential Proclamation Signing Ceremony for World Communications Year 1983'. The White House, 16 December 1982.

Redman, Eric. *The Dance of Legislation*. New York: Simon and Schuster, 1973.

Rice, Jean (ed). *Cable TV Renewals and Refranchising*. Washington, DC: Communications Press, 1983.

Rice, Ronald E. and associates. *The New Media: communication, research and technology*. Beverly Hills: Sage, 1984.

Ritchie, David. *Space War*. New York: New American Library, 1983.

Roberts, Paul Craig. *The Supply-Side Revolution: an insider's account of policymaking in Washington*. Cambridge, Mass.: Harvard University Press, 1984.

Rogers, Everett M. and Larsen, Judith K. *Silicon Valley Fever: growth of high-technology culture*. New York: Basic Books, 1984.

Roman, James W. *Cablemania: the Cable Television Sourcebook*. Englewood Cliffs, NJ: Prentice-Hall, 1983.

Rosenberg, Jerry M. *Inside the Wall Street Journal*. New York: Macmillan, 1982.

Rowan, Ford. *Broadcast Fairness: Doctrine, Practice, Prospects*. New York: Longman, 1984.

Rowland, Willard D., Jr. *The Illusion of Fulfillment: the Broadcast Reform Movement*. Association for Education in Journalism and Mass Communications: Journalism Monographs, 97, 1982.

——. 'The Continuing Crisis in American Public Telecommunication: the historic pattern of disenfranchisement'. Paper read at Twelfth Annual Telecommunications Policy Research Conference, Airlie, Virginia, April 1984.

Rubin, Michael Rogers (ed). *Information Economics and Policy in the United States*. Littleton, Colo.: Libraries Unlimited, 1983.

Sabato, Larry J. *The Rise of Political Consultants*. New York: Basic Books, 1981.

——. *PAC Power: inside the world of Political Action Committees*. New York: W. W. Norton, 1984.

Saloma, John S. III. *Ominous Politics: the new Conservative Labyrinth*. New York: Hill and Wang, 1984.

Salvaggio, Jerry L. 'Social Problems of Information Societies: the US and Japanese Experiences'. *Telecommunications Policy*, September 1983, pp. 228–42.

Sampson, Anthony. *The Sovereign State: the secret history of ITT*. London: Coronet, 1974.

Saunders, Robert J., Warford, Jeremy J. and Wellenius, Bjorn. *Telecommunications and Economic Development*. Baltimore: Johns Hopkins University Press, for the World Bank, 1983.

Schement, Jorge Reina, Guttierrez, Felix and Sirbu, Marvin A., Jr (eds). *Telecommunications Policy Handbook*. New York: Praeger, 1982.

Schiller, Dan. *Telematics and Government*. Norwood, NJ: Ablex, 1982.

Schiller, Herbert I. *Information and the Crisis Economy*, Norwood, NJ: Ablex, 1984.

Seldes, George. *Lords of the Press*. New York: Julian Messner, 1938.

Shaw, David. *Press Watch*. New York: Macmillan, 1984.

Shelp, Ronald Kent. *Beyond Industrialization: Ascendancy of the Global Service Economy*. New York: Praeger, 1981.

Shooshan, Harry M. III (ed), *Disconnecting Bell: the impact of the AT&T Divestiture*. New York: Pergamon, 1984.

Sigel, Efrem. *The Future of Videotext*. White Plains, NY: Knowledge Industry Publications, 1983.

Simmons, Steven J. *The Fairness Doctrine and the Media*. Berkeley: University of California Press, 1978.

Simon, Michael E. 'Government Regulation: adding up the cost', *Journal of Contemporary Business*, vol. 9, no. 2, 1980, pp. 5–16.

Singh, Indu B. (ed). *Telecommunications in the Year 2000*. Norwood, NJ: Ablex, 1983.

Slack, Jennifer Daryl. *Communications Technologies and Society*. Norwood, NJ: Ablex, 1984.

Sloan Commission Report. *On the Cable: the television of abundance*. New York: McGraw-Hill, 1971.

Sobel, Robert. *IBM: Colossus in Transition*. New York: Bantam, 1983.

Spear, Joseph C. *Presidents and the Press: the Nixon Legacy*. Cambridge, Mass.: MIT Press, 1984.

Spector, Phillip L. 'Ma Bell's Children Grow Up', *Telematics*, vol. 1, no. 1, May 1984, pp. 1–6.

Sperry, Robert. 'A Selected Bibliography of Works on the FCC and OTP: 1970–1973'. *Journal of Broadcasting*, vol. 18, no. 1, winter 1975, pp. 55–112.

Sterling, Christopher H. *Electronic Media: a guide to trends in broadcasting and newer technologies 1920–1983*. Praeger, 1984.

—— (ed), *International Telecommunications and Information Policy*. Washington, DC: Communications Press, 1984.

Stern, Jill Abeshouse, Krasnow, Erwin G. and Senkowski, R. Michael, 'The New Video Marketplace and the Search for a Coherent Regulatory Philosophy'. *Catholic University Law Review*, vol. 32, no. 3, spring 1983, pp. 529–602.

Stevens, John D. *Shaping the First Amendment*. Beverly Hills: Sage, 1982.

Straus, Richard (ed). *Communications and International Trade*. Washington, DC: US National Committee of the International Institute of Communications, 1982.

Stubblebine, William Craig and Willett, Thomas D. *Reaganomics: a mid-term report*. San Francisco: Institute for Contemporary Studies, 1983.

Terrou, Fernand and Solal, Lucien. *Legislation for Press, Film and Radio*. Paris: UNESCO, 1951.

Thomas, Sari (ed). *Studies in Mass Communication and Technology*, vol. 1. Norwood, NJ: Ablex, 1984.

Tolchin, Susan J. and Tolchin, Martin. *Dismantling America: the rush to deregulate.* Boston: Houghton Mifflin, 1983.

Toman, William J. 'Local Regulation of Cable: the Boulder Cases'. *Communications and the Law*, vol. 5, no. 2, spring 1983, pp. 39–50.

Trebing, Harry M. 'Common Carrier Regulation – the Silent Crisis'. *Law and Contemporary Problems*, vol. 34, spring 1969, pp. 299–329.

Trent, Judith S. and Friedenberg, Robert V. *Political Campaign Communication.* New York: Praeger, 1983.

Tsoukalis, Loukas (ed). *The Political Economy of International Money.* London: Sage, 1985.

Tunstall, Jeremy. *The Media Are American.* London: Constable; New York: Columbia University Press, 1977.

—— and Walker, David. *Media Made in California* New York: Oxford University Press, 1981.

Tunstall, W. Brooke. *Disconnecting Parties: managing the Bell system break-up: an inside view.* New York: McGraw-Hill, 1985.

Turkle, Sherry. *The Second Self: Computers and the human spirit.* New York: Simon and Schuster, 1984.

Uttal, Bro. 'Is IBM playing too tough?'. *Fortune*, 10 December 1984, pp. 82–5.

Walker, Orville C. Jr. and Rudelius, William. 'Ascertaining Programming needs of "Voiceless" community groups. *Journal of Broadcasting*, vol. 20, no. 1, winter 1976, pp. 89–99.

Weil, Ulric. *Information Systems in the 80s.* Englewood Cliffs, NJ: Prentice-Hall, 1982.

Weingast, Barry R. and Moran, Mark J. 'Bureaucratic Discretion or Congressional Control? Regulatory Policymaking by the Federal Trade Commission', *Journal of Political Economy*, vol. 91, no. 5, pp. 765–93.

Wertheimer, Fred and Huwa, Randy. 'Campaign Finance Reforms: Past Accomplishments, Future Challenges'. *New York University Review of Law and Social Change*, vol. 10, no. 1, 1980–81, pp. 43–65.

Wigand, Rolf T. 'Local Communication and Communication Research: An American Perspective'. In Michael Burgoon (ed), *Communication Yearbook 5*, pp. 189–217. Beverly Hills: Sage, 1982.

Wilcox, Clair and Shepherd, William G. *Public Policies Toward Business.* 5th edn. Homewood, Ill.: Richard D. Irwin, 1975.

Will, Thomas E. *Telecommunications Structure and Management in the Executive Branch of Government.* Boulder, Colo.: Westview, 1978.

Williams, Frederick. *The Communications Revolution.* Beverly Hills: Sage, 1982.

Williams, Wenmouth. 'Impact of Commissioner Background on FCC decisions: 1962–1975'. *Journal of Broadcasting*, vol. 20, no. 2, spring 1976, pp. 239–60.

Wilson, James Q. (ed). *The Politics of Regulation.* New York: Basic Books, 1980.

Winston, Brian. 'The Prison of Freedom: reality and myth in American telecommunications regulatory policy'. Paper read at Manchester University Broadcasting Symposium, March 1983.

Yurow, Jane H. (ed). *Issues in International Telecommunications Policy: a sourcebook.* Washington, DC: George Washington University Center for Telecommunications Studies, 1983.

Zuckman, Harvey I. and Gaynes, Martin J. *Mass Communications Law.* 2nd edn. St Paul, Minn.: West Publishing, 1982.

US GOVERNMENT PUBLICATIONS

US Senate, 90th Congress, 1st and 2nd Sessions. Hearings before the Subcommittee on Antitrust and Monopoly of the Committee on the Judiciary, on S.1312, *The Failing Newspaper Act.* Parts 1–7. US Government Printing Office (USGPO), 1968 and 1969.

US Senate, 94th Congress, 2nd Session. Committee Print for the Use of the Committee on Commerce. *Appointments to the Regulatory Agencies: the Federal Communications Commission and the Federal Trade Commission.* USGPO, April 1976.

US Senate, 97th Congress, 2nd Session. Hearings before the Committee on Commerce, Science and Transportation, on *Freedom of Expression.* 28, 30 September and 19 November 1982. Serial no: 97–130. USGPO, 1983.

US Senate, 97th Congress, 2nd Session. Hearings before the Committee on Commerce, Science and Transportation, on *Cable Television Regulation.* 18 January and 16 February 1982. Part 1. Serial no: 97–97. USGPO, 1982.

US Senate, 97th Congress, 2nd Session. Hearings before the Subcommittee on Communications of the Committee on Commerce, Science and Transportation, on S.2172, *Cable Television Regulation.* 26–28 April 1982. Part 2. Serial no: 97–97. USGPO, 1982.

US Senate, 97th Congress, 1st Session. Hearing before the Subcommittee on Communications of the Committee on Commerce, Science and Transportation, on S.271, *International Record Carrier Competition Act of 1981.* 18 February 1981. Serial no: 97–5. USGPO, 1981.

US Senate, 97th Congress, 2nd Session. Hearings before the Subcommittee on Communications of the Committee on Commerce, Science and Transportation, on S.2469, *International Telecommunications Deregulation Act of 1982.* 14, 15 and 17 June 1982. Serial no: 97–126. USGPO, 1982.

US Senate, 97th Congress, 1st Session. Hearings before the Subcommittee on Communications of the Committee on Commerce, Science and Transportation, on S.601, *TV Licensing and Renewal Act of 1981.* 23 and 30 March 1981. Serial no: 97–33. USGPO, 1981.

US Senate, 97th Congress, 1st Session. Hearings before the Subcommittee on Communications of the Committee on Commerce, Science and Transportation, on S.720, *Public Telecommunications Act of 1981.* 6 and 8 April 1981. Serial no: 97–32. USGPO, 1981.

US Senate, 97th Congress, 2nd Session. Hearing before the Subcommittee for Consumers of the Committee on Commerce, Science and Transportation, on *FTC's Authority Over Deceptive Advertising.* 22 July 1982. Serial no: 97–134. USGPO, 1982.

US Senate, 97th Congress, 2nd Session. Hearing before the Subcommittee on International Trade and the Subcommittee on Taxation and Debt Management of the Committee on Finance, on S.2051 and S.2058, *Trade in Services.* 14 May 1982. USGPO, 1982.

US Senate, 97th Congress, 2nd Session. Hearings before the Permanent Subcommittee on Investigations of the Committee on Governmental Affairs. *Transfer of United States High Technology to the Soviet Union and Soviet Bloc Nations.* 4, 5, 6, 11 and 12 May 1982. USGPO, 1982.

US Senate, 97th Congress, 1st and 2nd Sessions. Hearings before the Committee on the Judiciary, on S.1758, *Copyright Infringements (Audio and Video*

Recorders). 30 November 1981 and 21 April 1982. Serial no: J–97–84. USGPO, 1982.

US Senate and House of Representatives, 98th Congress, 1st Session. Joint Hearings before the Committee on Commerce, Science and Transportation, US Senate, and the Committee on Energy and Commerce, House of Representatives, on S.1660 and HR. 3621, *Universal Telephone Service Preservation Act of 1983.* 28 and 29 July 1983. Serial no: 98–30 (Senate) and 98–39 (House). USGPO, 1983.

US Senate, 98th Congress, 1st Session. Hearings before the Committee on Commerce, Science and Transportation. *Nominations – Federal Maritime Commission and Department of Commerce.* Robert Setrkian (FMC) 12 May and David J. Markey (Commerce) 25 July 1983. Serial no: 98–26. USGPO, 1983.

US Senate, 98th Congress, 1st Session. Committee on Commerce, Science and Transportation. *Long-Range Goals in International Telecommunications and Information: an outline for United States Policy.* 11 March 1983. USGPO, 1983.

US Senate, 98th Congress, 1st Session. Hearing before the Committee on Commerce, Science and Transportation on *Local Telephone Rates.* 29 August 1983. Serial no: 98–36. USGPO, 1983.

US Senate, 98th Congress, 1st Session. Report, together with minority views, of the Committee on Commerce, Science and Transportation, on S.1660, *Universal Telephone Service Preservation Act of 1983.* Report no: 98–270. USGPO, 1983.

US Senate, 98th Congress, 1st Session. Committee on Commerce, Science and Transportation. *Print and Electronic Media: The Case for First Amendment Parity.* Committee Print: 98–50. USGPO, 1983.

US Senate, 98th Congress, 2nd Session. Hearings before the Committee on Commerce, Science and Transportation. *Freedom of Expression Act of 1983.* 30 January and 1 and 8 February 1984. Serial no: 98–62. USGPO, 1984.

US Senate, 98th Congress, 1st Session. Report, together with minority views, of the Committee on Commerce, Science and Transportation on S.66, *Cable and Telecommunications Act of 1983.* USGPO, 1983.

US Senate, 98th Congress, 1st Session. Hearings before the Subcommittee on Communciations of the Committee on Commerce, Science and Transportation, on S.1707, *Competition in Television Production Act.* 2 and 4 November 1983. Serial no: 98–53. USGPO, 1984.

US Senate, 98th Congress, 1st Session. Hearings before the Subcommittee on Communications of the Committee on Commerce, Science and Transportation, on S.607, *FCC Authorization,* 9 March 1983. Serial no: 98–14. USGPO, 1983.

US Senate, 98th Congress, 1st Session. Hearings before the Subcommittee on Communication of the Committee on Commerce, Science and Transportation, on S.66, *Cable Telecommunications Act of 1983.* 16 and 17 February 1983. Serial no. 98–11. USGPO, 1983.

US Senate, 98th Congress, 2nd Session. Hearing before the Subcommittee on Communications of the Committee on Commerce, Science and Transportation, on S.2436, *Corporation for Public Broadcasting Authorization,* 26 March 1984. Serial no: 98–65. USGPO, 1984.

US Senate, 98th Congress, 2nd Session. Hearings before the Subcommittee on Communications of the Committee on Commerce, Science and Transportation, on S.880, *Daytime Broadcasting Issues*. 3 and 14 April 1984. Serial no: 98–39. USGPO, 1984.

US Senate, 98th Congress, 1st Session. Hearings before the Subcommittee on Science, Technology and Space of the Committee on Commerce, Science and Transportation, on S.1286, *Role of Technology in Promoting Industrial Competitiveness*. 23 November and 6 and 7 December 1983. Serial no: 98–29, part 2. USGPO, 1984.

US Senate, 98th Congress, 1st Session. A Report prepared for the Committee on Foreign Relations by The Congressional Research Service, Library of Congress. *International Telecommunications and Information Policy: Selected Issues for the 1980s*. USGPO, 1983.

US Senate, 98th Congress, 1st Session. Hearings before the Subcommittee on Arms Control, Oceans, International Operations and Environment of the Committee on Foreign Relations. *International Communication and Information Policy*. S.HRG 98–483. USGPO, 1983.

US Senate, 98th Congress, 1st Session. Hearings before the Committee on Rules and Administration. *Campaign Finance Reform Proposals of 1983*. 26 and 27 January, 17 May and 29 September 1983. USGPO, 1983.

House of Representatives, 95th Congress, 1st Session. Subcommittee on Communications of the Committee on Interstate and Foreign Commerce. *Options Papers prepared by the Staff for Use by the Subcommittee*. Committee Print: 95–13. USGPO, 1977.

House of Representatives, 95th Congress, 2nd Session. Hearings before the Subcommittee on Communications of the Committee on Interstate and Foreign Commerce, on HR.13015, *The Communications Act of 1978*. 18 July–28 September. Volumes I–IV. Serial no: 95–194/8. USGPO, 1978–9.

House of Representatives, 96th Congress, 1st Session. Hearings before the Subcommittee on Communications of the Committee on Interstate and Foreign Commerce, on HR.3333, *The Communications Act of 1979*. Vol. 1, Part 1. 1–4 April and 8 May 1979. Serial no: 96–121. USGPO, 1980.

House of Representatives, 96th Congress, 2nd Session. Hearings before the Subcommittee on Monopolies and Commercial Law of the Committee on the Judiciary on HR.6121, *Telecommunications Act of 1980*. 9 and 16 September 1980. Serial no: 69. USGPO, 1981.

House of Representatives, 96th Congress, 2nd Session. Committee on the Judiciary, Adverse Report, together with additional and supplemental views on HR.6121, *Telecommunications Act of 1980*. USGPO, 1980.

House of Representatives, 96th Congress, 2nd Session. Report by the Committee on Government Operations, *International Information Flow: Forging a New Framework*. House Report no: 96–1535. USGPO, 1980.

House of Representatives, 97th Congress, 1st Session. Hearings before the Subcommittee on Telecommunications, Consumer Protection and Finance of the Committee on Energy and Commerce. *Public Broadcasting Oversight of 1981*. 25 and 26 March 1981. Serial no: 97–3. USGPO, 1981.

House of Representatives, 97th Congress, 1st Session. Hearings before the Subcommittee on Telecommunications, Consumer Protection and Finance of the Committee on Energy and Commerce, on HR. 3238 and HR.2774, *Public Broadcasting Amendments Act of 1981*. 28 and 29 April 1981. Serial no: 97–12. USGPO, 1981.

House of Representatives, 97th Congress, 1st Session. Hearing before the Subcommittee on Telecommunications, Consumer Protection and Finance of the Committee on Energy and Commerce, on HR.3240, 1891, 3239 and 1801, *FCC and NTIA Authorization for 1981*. 30 April 1981. Serial no: 97–51. USGPO, 1981.

House of Representatives, 97th Congress, 1st Session. Hearings before the Subcommittee on Telecommunications, Consumer Protection and Finance of the Committee on Energy and Commerce. *Diversity of Information*. 15 and 23 September 1981. Serial no: 97–57. USGPO, 1981.

House of Representatives, 97th Congress, 1st Session. Hearings before the Subcommittee on Telecommunications, Consumer Protection and Finance of the Committee on Energy and Commerce. *Telecommunications and Information Products and Services in International Trade*. 29 April and 22 July 1981. Serial no: 97–59. USGPO, 1981.

House of Representatives, 97th Congress, 1st Session. Hearings before the Subcommittee on Telecommunications, Consumer Protection and Finance of the Committee on Energy and Commerce. *User Needs and Concerns in Telecommunications Marketplace*. 23, 24 June, 18, 19 August and 11 September 1981. Serial no: 97–60. USGPO, 1982.

House of Representatives, 97th Congress, 1st Session. Hearings before the Subcommittee on Telecommunications, Consumer Protection and Finance of the Committee on Energy and Commerce. *Telecommunications Miscellaneous – Part 1*. 9, 16 June and 23 and 28 July 1981. Serial no: 97–64. USGPO, 1981.

House of Representatives, 97th Congress, 1st Session. Hearing before the Subcommittee on Telecommunications, Consumer Protection and Finance of the Committee on Energy and Commerce, in HR.4726, 4780 and 4781, *Broadcast Reform Proposals*. 2 December 1981. Serial no: 97–76. USGPO, 1982.

House of Representatives, 97th Congress, 1st Session. Hearing before the Subcommittee on Telecommunications, Consumer Protection and Finance and the Subcommittee on Oversight and Investigations of the Committee on Energy and Commerce. *FCC Regulation of Common Carriers*. 24 September 1981. Serial no: 97–78. USGPO, 1982.

House of Representatives, 97th Congress, 1st Session. Hearing before the Subcommittee on Telecommunications, Consumer Protection and Finance of the Committee on Energy and Commerce. *Satellite Communications/Direct Broadcast Satellites*. 15 December 1981. Serial no: 97–81. USGPO, 1982.

House of Representatives, 97th Congress, 1st Session. Hearing before the Subcommittee on Telecommunications, Consumer Protection and Finance of the Committee on Energy and Commerce. *Telecommunications and Its Impact on the New England Economy*. 5 October 1981. Serial no: 97–82. USGPO, 1982.

House of Representatives, 97th Congress, 1st Session. Hearing before the Subcommittee on Telecommunications, Consumer Protection and Finance of the Committee on Energy and Commerce. *Record Carrier Competition Act of 1981*. 15 October 1981. Serial no: 97–83. USGPO, 1982.

House of Representatives, 97th Congress, 2nd Session. Joint Hearings before the Subcommittee on Telecommunications, Consumer Protection and Finance of the Committee on Energy and Commerce and the Subcommittee on Monopolies and Commercial Law of the Committee on the Judiciary. *Proposed Antitrust Settlement of US v AT&T*. 26 and 28 January 1982. Serial no: 97–116 (Commerce) and 35 (Judiciary).

312   *Bibliography*

House of Representatives, 97th Congress, 2nd Session. Hearings before the Subcommittee on Telecommunications, Consumer Protection and Finance of the Committee on Energy and Commerce, on HR.5158, *Telecommunications Act of 1982 Parts 1–3.* 2, 9, 11, 17, 18, 23, 24, 26 February and 3, 4, 9 and 10 March 1982. Serial no: 97–119/120/121. 3 volumes. USGPO, 1982.

House of Representatives, 97th Congress, 2nd Session. Hearing before the Subcommittee on Telecommunications, Consumer Protection and Finance of the Committee on Energy and Commerce, on HR.5427, *Radio Broadcasting to Cuba.* 10 May 1982. Serial no: 97–127. USGPO, 1982.

House of Representatives, 97th Congress, 2nd Session. Hearing before the Subcommittee on Telecommunications, Consumer Protection and Finance of the Committee on Energy and Commerce. *Cable Franchise Investigation: Local Participation.* 8 March 1982. Serial no: 97–137. USGPO, 1982.

House of Representatives, 97th Congress, 2nd Session. Hearing before the Subcommittee on Telecommunications, Consumer Protection and Finance of the Committee on Energy and Commerce. *Financial Crisis Confronting Public Broadcasting.* 11 March 1982. Serial no: 97–139. USGPO, 1982.

House of Representatives, 97th Congress, 2nd Session. Hearing before the Subcommittee on Telecommunications, Consumer Protection and Finance of the Committee on Energy and Commerce, on HR.4726, 5242, 5584, 5585 and 5752, *Broadcast Regulation Reform Proposals.* 6 May 1982. Serial no: 97–140. USGPO, 1982.

House of Representatives, 97th Congress, 2nd Session. Oversight Hearings before the Subcommittee on Telecommunications, Consumer Protection and Finance of the Committee on Energy and Commerce. *Broadcast, Mass Media, and Common Carrier Issues.* 1 December 1982. Serial no: 97–185. USGPO, 1983.

House of Representatives, 97th Congress, 1st Session. A Report by the Majority Staff of the Subcommittee on Telecommunications, Consumer Protection and Finance of the Committee on Energy and Commerce. *Telecommunications in Transition: The Status of Competition in the Telecommunications Industry.* Committee Print: 97–V. USGPO, 1981.

House of Representatives, 97th Congress, 1st Session. Hearing before the Subcommittee on Trade of the Committee on Ways and Means. *Trade in Services and Trade in High Technology Products.* 24 May 1982. Serial no: 97–60. USGPO, 1982.

House of Representatives, 97th Congress, 1st Session. Hearing before a Subcommittee of the Committee on Government Operations. *International Broadcasting: Direct Broadcasting Satellites.* 23 October 1981. USGPO, 1981.

House of Representatives, 97th Congress, 2nd Session. Hearings before the Subcommittee on Courts, Civil Liberties and the Administration of Justice of the Committee on the Judiciary, on HR.4783, 4784, 4808, 5250, 5488 and 5705, *Home Recording of Copyrighted Works.* 12, 13, 14 April, 24 June, 11 August and 22 and 23 September 1982. Serial no: 97, Part 1. USGPO, 1982.

House of Representatives, 98th Congress, 1st Session. Hearing before the Subcommittee on Telecommunications, Consumer Protection and Finance of the Committee on Energy and Commerce. *Children and Television.* 16 March 1983. Serial no: 98–3. USGPO, 1983.

House of Representatives, 98th Congress, 1st Session. Hearing before the Subcommittee on Telecommunications, Consumer Protection and Finance of the Committee on Energy and Commerce. *Prospects for Universal Telephone Service*. 22 March 1983. Serial no: 98–11. USGPO, 1983.

House of Representatives, 98th Congress, 1st Session. Hearing before the Subcommittee on Telecommunications, Consumer Protection and Finance of the Committee on Energy and Commerce, on HR.2755, *FCC Authorization Legislation – Oversight*. 19 April 1983. Serial no: 98–25. USGPO, 1983.

House of Representatives, 98th Congress, 1st Session. Hearing before the Subcommittee on Telecommunications, Consumer Protection and Finance of the Committee on Energy and Commerce. *International Trade Issues in Telecommunications and Related Industries*. 23 March 1983. Serial no: 98–36. USGPO, 1984.

House of Representatives, 98th Congress, 1st Session. Hearing before the Subcommittee on Telecommunications, Consumer Protection and Finance of the Committee on Energy and Commerce. *Broadcast Regulation: Quantifying the Public Interest Standard*. 24 May 1983. Serial no: 98–61. USGPO, 1983.

House of Representatives, 98th Congress, 1st Session. Hearings before the Subcommittee on Telecommunications, Consumer Protection and Finance of the Committee on Energy and Commerce, on HR.4103, 4229 and 4299, *Options for Cable Legislation*. 25 May, 22 June and 3 November 1983.

House of Representatives, 98th Congress, 1st Session. Hearings before the Subcommittee on Telecommunications, Consumer Protection and Finance of the Committee on Energy and Commerce, on HR.4103, 4229 and 4299, *Options for Cable Television*, 25 May, 22 June and 3 November 1983. Serial no: 98–73. USGPO, 1984.

House of Representatives, 98th Congress, 1st Session. Hearing before the Subcommittee on Telecommunications, Consumer Protection and Finance of the Committee on Energy and Commerce. *Impact of Recent FCC Decisions on Telephone Service*. 17 December 1983. Serial no: 98–88. USGPO, 1984.

House of Representatives, 98th Congress, 1st Session. Hearing before the Subcommittee on Telecommunications, Consumer Protecton and Finance of the Committee on Energy and Commerce. *Financial Deregulation in New York State*. 14 December 1983. Serial no 98–90. USGPO, 1980.

House of Representatives, 98th Congress, 2nd Session. Hearings before the Subcommittee on Telecommunications, Consumer Protection and Finance of the Committee on Energy and Commerce. *Early Election Projection: The Iowa Experience*. 27 February 1984. Serial no: 98–92. USGPO, 1984.

House of Representatives, 98th Congress, 1st session. Hearings before the Subcommittee on Telecommunications, Consumer Protection and Finance of the Committee on Energy and Commerce. *Minority Participation in the Media*. 19 and 23 September 1983. Serial no: 98–93. USGPO, 1984.

House of Representatives, 98th Congress, 1st Session. Hearings before the Subcommittee on Telecommunications, Consumer Protection and Finance of the Committee on Energy and Commerce, on HR.2250, *Financial Interest and Syndication Rules*. 1 June and 1 August 1983. Serial no: 98–96. USGPO, 1984.

House of Representatives, 98th Congress, 1st Session. Hearings before the Subcommittee on Telecommunications, Consumer Protection and Finance of the Committee on Energy and Commerce. *Broadcast Regulation Reform*. 4 August and 6 October 1983. Serial no: 98–99. USGPO, 1984.

House of Representatives, 98th Congress, 2nd Session. Hearing before the

Subcommittee on Telecommunications, Consumer Protection and Finance of the Committee on Energy and Commerce. *Nippon Telephone & Telegraph Procurement Agreement.* 7 March 1984. Serial no: 98–100. USGPO, 1984.

House of Representatives, 98th Congress, 2nd Session. Hearing before the Subcommittee on Telecommunications, Consumer Protection and Finance of the Committee on Energy and Commerce. *Federal Communications Commission Oversight.* 8 February 1984. Serial no: 98–106. USGPO, 1984.

House of Representatives, 98th Congress, 2nd Session. Hearing before the Subcommittee on Commerce, Transportation and Tourism of the Committee on Energy and Commerce. *Oversight of FTC Law Enforcement.* 22 February 1984. Serial no: 98–123. USGPO, 1984.

US General Accounting Office. Report to the Congress by the Comptroller General of the United States. *Legislative and Regulatory Actions Needed to Deal With a Changing Domestic Telecommunications Industry.* CED–81–136. 24 September 1981.

US General Accounting Office. *Can the Federal Communications Commission Successfully Implement Its Computer II Decision?* CED–82–38. 29 January 1982.

US General Accounting Office Report to the Chairman, Subcommittee on Government Information and Individual Rights, House Committee on Government Operations. *The Federal Communications Commission's International Telecommunications Activities.* CED–82–77. 19 April 1982.

US General Accounting Office. Report by the Comptroller General of the United States to the Chairman, Subcommittee on Government Information, Justice and Agriculture, Committee on Government Operations, House of Representatives. *FCC Needs to Monitor a Changing International Telecommunications Market.* GAO/RCED–83–92. 14 March 1983.

US General Accounting Office. Report by the Comptroller General of the United States. *FCC Can Further Improve Its Licensing Activities.* GAO/RCED–83–90. 26 April 1983.

US General Accounting Office. A Study by the Staff. *Computer Technology at IRS: Present and Planned.* GAO/GGD–83–103. 1 September 1983.

US General Accounting Office. Report to the Honorable Ernest F. Hollings, United States Senate. *Status of Federal Communications Commission Efforts to Allocate Costs Between Telephone Companies' Regulated and Unregulated Activities.* GAO/RCED–83–235. 2 September 1983.

US General Accounting Office. *Assessment of Bilateral Telecommunications Agreements with Japan.* GAO/NSIAD–84–2. 7 October 1983.

US General Accounting Office. Report by the Comptroller General of the United States to the Chairman, Committee on Government Operations, House of Representatives. *Implications of Joint NASA/DoD Participation in Space Shuttle Operations.* GAO/NSIAD–84–13. 7 November 1983.

US Department of Commerce, International Trade Administration. *An Assessment of US Competitiveness in High Technology Industries.* February 1983.

US Department of Commerce, International Trade Administration, *High Technology Industries: The Telecommunications Industry.* April 1983.

US Department of Commerce, National Telecommunications and Information Administration. *Telecommunication Policies in Seventeen Countries: Prospects for Future Competitive Access.* NTIA–CR–83–24. May 1983.

US Department of Commerce, International Trade Administration. *A Competi-*

tive Assessment of the US Data Processing Services Industry. December 1984.

US Department of Commerce, International Trade Administration. *A Competitive Assessment of the US Software Industry*. December 1984.

Congress of the United States, Office of Technology Assessment. *Computer-Based National Information Systems: Technology and Public Policy issues*. OTA–CIT–146. September 1981.

US Department of State, *Report of the United States Delegation to the ITU Region 2 Administrative Radio Conference on the Broadcasting Satellite Service*, Geneva, 13 June–17 July 1983. Submitted by Abbott Washburn, chairman, US delegation.

United States International Trade Commission, *Changes in the US Telecommunications Industry and the Impact on US Telecommunications Trade*. Report to the Committee on Finance, US Senate. June 1984.

Rostow, Eugene (chairman). *Final Report: President's Task Force on Communications Policy*. 7 December 1968 (established pursuant to the president's message on communications policy, 14 August 1967).

Quello, James H. (chairman). *Final Report: Temporary Commission on Alternative Financing for Public Telecommunications*. A report to the Congress of the United States, 1983.

Index

[redacted]

LIVING AMERICA SERIES

BUILDING our

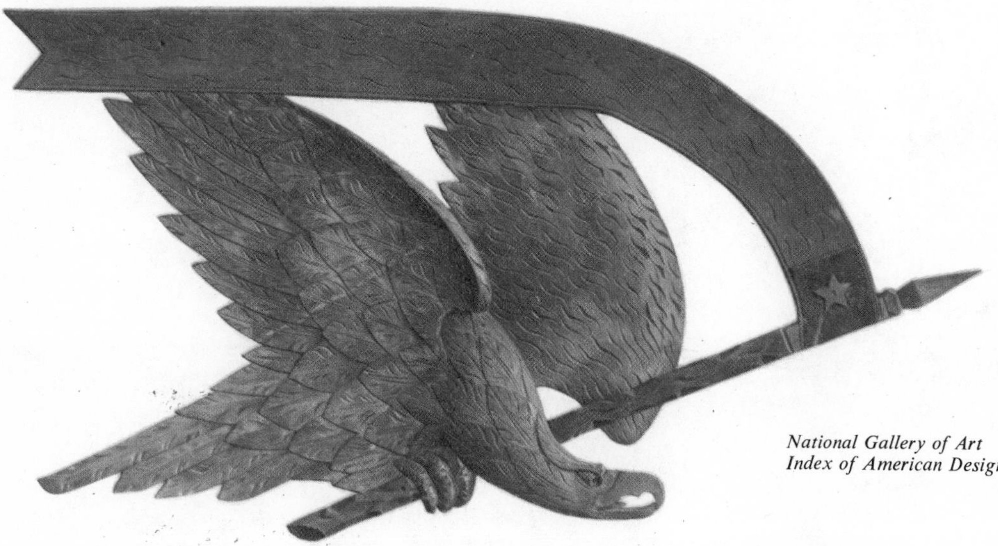

National Gallery of Art
Index of American Design

DEMOCRACY

Vanza Devereaux

COAUTHOR AND RESEARCH CONSULTANT
Homer Ferris Aker

CURRICULUM CONSULTANT
Chester D. Babcock
Assistant Superintendent in Charge of Curriculum and Instruction
State of Washington

SAN FRANCISCO   HARR WAGNER PUBLISHING COMPANY

COVER PHOTOGRAPH: *Jacqueline Altstaetter*

CONTENTS

Unit Two THE FOUNDATION of AMERICAN DEMOCRACY

UNIT FOUR   HOW a DEMOCRATIC GOVERNMENT SERVES the PEOPLE

CHARTS

An Introduction to Free Government

AN INTRODUCTION TO

FREE GOVERNMENT

YOU are living in a country that stands for freedom and the ideals of democracy. You are fortunate! Many young people throughout the world do not have this privilege. In many parts of the world those stirring words, *life, liberty, and the pursuit of happiness,* have no meaning for the people.

Your heritage of freedom came to you from the earliest days of history. Time and again men fought for freedom and the right to guide their own lives. Time and again they fought to establish the beginnings of democracy.

The American colonists suffered great hardships to win independence. They fought to establish a free government in the New World.

This free government is yours. This country is yours.

The determined minutemen were among the first Americans to shed their blood for liberty.

Griffin—FPG

2

Independence Hall in Philadelphia has been called the birthplace of American liberty.

In a few short years you will be among the men and women who will govern our nation. You will share responsibility for its growth and progress.

How can your responsibility be carried out? Today you are an apprentice citizen in a free democracy. *An apprentice is a person who is learning to perform a task.* In your home, your school, and in your country you are learning to become a good citizen. You are preparing to take your place as a citizen of a democratic country.

There are many ways in which you can become a good citizen. You can obey and respect the laws of your country, your state, and your community. You can respect the rights, the property, and the opinions of others. You can accept your share of responsibility in your home, your school, and your community. You can love and respect your flag and the ideals of democracy.

But you must do even more! To love and to respect your country, you must understand the principles upon which it has been built. You must learn to know and appreciate its goals. You must learn how to safeguard it and to keep it free.

A good citizen is an informed citizen. An informed citizen knows what is going on in the world today. He understands his nation's position among the other nations of the world. He follows the actions and policies of elected officials. He observes how those acts and policies affect his welfare and the welfare of the nation.

An informed citizen also has a background of knowledge. Against his background of knowledge he judges the events of today. Against his understanding of the past he builds an understanding of his country and of our changing times.

Building Our Democracy will help you to understand how freedom and democracy came to you. It will show you how your free government serves you, and how you can help to preserve your government. It will help you to become a truly informed citizen. It will help you to make your country even better than it is today!

3

The search for religious liberty brought the Pilgrims to America. For it they endured great hardship.

Ewing Galloway

". . . conceived in liberty and dedicated to the proposition that all men are created equal."

WHAT IS A FREE GOVERNMENT?

People in all parts of the world live under some form of government. Many of them are happy, others are not. For a people to be truly happy, their government must be a government "of the people, by the people, for the people." It must be a free government.

The government of the United States *is* a free government. It is a government built upon the belief that the individual is important—that it is his right to be free. It was planned as a government of, by, and for free men.

A government can serve the people or it can be their master. Americans believe that the purpose of government is to serve the people. They believe that the people themselves should control their government. They be-

4

lieve that a government should protect the rights of life, liberty, and the pursuit of happiness. Only in this way can a people be truly free!

The government of the United States is called a *representative democracy*. In a democracy the people are free to work out their problems in their own way. They are free to help determine the policies of their government. It is true they choose representatives to do the actual work of governing, but the representatives are elected to serve the people. The people have the right to nominate candidates for public office. They have the right to vote for any candidates they choose. *By voting, the people choose the men who make our laws and many of the men who carry out the laws.*

The elected officials may appoint other officials to help them, but the power is left in the hands of the people. If the government fails to serve the needs of the people, the people can vote to change officials. They can elect officials who *will* see that their rights and privileges are protected.

Our plan of government is a written document called The Constitution of the United States. The preamble to the Constitution begins with the words, "We, the people of the United States . . ."

It is *we, the people*, who give Congress the right to make the laws for the nation.

It is *we, the people*, who give the President and his helpers the right to carry out the laws.

It is *we, the people*, who give our courts the right to judge our laws and to see that justice is done.

In a free government all the people are important. They control their own destinies and the actions of their government. The government serves the people—it does not rule them. Ours is a free government!

Many countries in the world today do not have free governments. These countries are called *totalitarian* countries. They are run by *dictators*. In a totalitarian country the people have little to say about their govern-

Nowak—FPG

The Washington Monument, honoring our first Chief Executive, faces the nation's Capitol. A grassy mall, several blocks long, connects the two landmarks. Both are symbols of our great democracy.

Ewing Galloway

ment and the way it operates. The country is governed by a small group of privileged men. These men have complete power over the government and over the people.

The State owns and runs the farms, the businesses, and the industries. The people work for the State and not for themselves. They do not know what individual freedom means. They have few rights and privileges. They vote, but they are not free to choose the candidates who run for office. The leaders choose the candidates and tell the people how to vote. The people dare not oppose them.

In the United States the leaders of the government rule for the benefit of the people. They consider the needs and the wishes of the people. In a totalitarian country the personal needs and liberties of the people are not considered. The leaders do not ask, "Can the State (government) be of service to you and your family?" They simply say, "You and your family belong to the State. We will tell you what to do."

The people of the United States would not enjoy life

Freedom includes respect for the rights and opinions of others. American students work together in harmony and freedom.

6

under totalitarian conditions. The United States as a nation has always been free. It will continue to be free. *The American people will not allow their freedom to be taken away from them!*

THE MEANING OF FREEDOM

The real meaning of freedom is often misunderstood. There are some who will say, "Freedom is the right to do whatever I wish to do, whenever I wish to do it." This is not true. If everyone were free to do exactly as he wished, *no one would be free.*

Suppose a boy has been saving his money to buy a new bicycle. He has delivered papers and cut lawns to earn money. He has given up many pleasures to save his money. Finally he has enough to buy the wanted bicycle. He is very proud and decides to ride the bicycle to school.

On the way to school he meets another boy who also wants a bicycle. If this boy were free to do anything he wished, he might take the bicycle and ride away with it.

Willinger—FPG

Freedom and democracy are as important in sport as in government. They are based on the principle of fair play.

7

Would this be freedom for the boy who had worked to buy the bicycle? Should not the boy who owned the bicycle have the right to enjoy using it?

True freedom does not mean the right to do whatever one chooses regardless of the rights of others!

If the pupils in a schoolroom do not care about the rights and the desires of their classmates, little can be accomplished. Suppose some pupils wish to sing, others wish to study, others to play ball, others to rehearse a play—all in the same room at the same time. No one then can really accomplish his purpose. *To have freedom in a schoolroom, each pupil must learn to understand and to respect the rights of his classmates.*

How can freedom in the classroom be accomplished? All pupils are free to think. They are free to choose and to decide what is best for the majority, as well as for the individual. When a student can do this, he has learned one of the first lessons in both freedom and democracy. When he can accept the decision of the class in a sportsmanlike manner, he has learned one of the first lessons in being a true American.

To have freedom and to be a good American, there are other lessons every person must learn. Each one must learn to make decisions for himself. He must learn to think, to judge facts carefully, and to make intelligent decisions. He must learn to improve his own behavior. *He must learn to become a responsible member of his home, his school, and his town.* Only then will he be ready to take his place as a worthy citizen in a free and democratic country. Only then will be be able to say:

I am an American. A free American
Free to speak—without fear
Free to worship God in my own way
Free to stand for what I think right
Free to oppose what I believe wrong
Free to choose those who govern my country.
This heritage of Freedom I pledge to uphold
For myself and all mankind.

THE AMERICAN HERITAGE FOUNDATION

Above the portico of the Supreme Court are engraved the words, "Equal justice under law." This is one of the principles on which our democracy is built.

Zehrt—FPG

8

Ewing Galloway

In 1789 our land was a place of small cities, farms, and wilderness. Today it is a land of industry and skyscrapers. Yet the plan of government prepared in 1789 has served us well through all the changes.

YOUR HERITAGE OF FREEDOM

In the National Archives Building in Washington, D. C., are two glass-topped marble cases. Each evening the marble cases are lowered into one of the strongest safes in the world. Each morning they are raised from the safe and placed on display on the main floor of the building.

Inside the marble display cases are three documents that are part of your heritage of freedom. The documents are written by hand in the spelling and style of colonial days. The parchment on which they are written

Give me your tired, your poor, your huddled masses yearning to breathe free, the wretched refuse of your teeming shore. Send these, the homeless, tempest-tossed, to me. I lift my lamp beside the golden door!

is crinkled and yellowed with age. The ink is faded, but the documents themselves are priceless.

They are handled carefully and guarded cautiously. The glass-topped cases in which they rest are airtight and filled with helium gas to preserve the documents. But the documents are neither stored nor hidden away! They belong to *you* and to all the other people in America. They are precious reminders of the liberty, equality, and free government that have come to you from the past.

What are these valuable documents? Why do Americans honor and cherish them? Why are they guarded so carefully? In back and above the two display cases are engraved the words

THE

DECLARATION OF INDEPENDENCE

THE

CONSTITUTION

OF THE

UNITED STATES OF AMERICA

AND THE

BILL OF RIGHTS

The Declaration of Independence proclaimed to the world that the colonists had declared themselves free and independent from England. The Constitution is the plan of government written by the freedom-loving Americans who established our great nation. *It is the fundamental rules and laws by which our country is governed.* The Bill of Rights is the first Ten Amendments to the Constitution. These Amendments safeguard the personal rights and freedom of the American people.

Today the United States is one of the truly great nations of the world. It is a great nation because it is based upon the ideals of liberty, justice, and self-government. The Constitution, *our national plan of government*, was written over one hundred seventy years

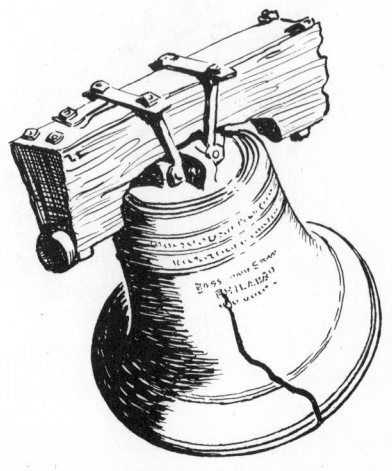

ago. It is still our basis for good government! It still protects the rights and liberties of every man, woman, and child in this country.

Building Our Democracy is the story of the Declaration of Independence, the Constitution of the United States, and the Bill of Rights. It is the story of how your city, county, state, and national governments affect the daily life of every citizen. It is the story of men and women who were willing to sacrifice and to fight that you might enjoy the privileges of living in a free country. The story of the struggles and the sacrifices made by these men and women will help you to understand and to appreciate the fight for freedom. It will help you to appreciate the truly great heritage they have given you. When you understand and appreciate this heritage you will want to know how to do your part in preserving the ideals of freedom!

UNIT ONE

The Background of American Democracy

THE BACKGROUND of AMERICAN DEMOCRACY

The United States is a republic. In a republic *the people* hold the power of government. They rule by choosing representatives to make their laws and to see that the laws are obeyed. They rule by voting on important measures that will affect their city, state, and nation. The ballot box and the *right to vote* are symbols of each man's right to take part in his own government. They are symbols that the people really control the government. In a republic the elected representatives are responsible *to the people*. If they do not govern as the people wish, the people will elect other representatives.

The republic of the United States is also called a democracy. But in America the word "democracy" has a special meaning. In some countries the leaders speak of the "people's democracy." They do not mean democracy as we know it! In a "people's democracy" the people give up their rights to the State. The government is then run for the benefit of the State. The rules and laws are made by a few leaders, not by representatives of the people. The individual citizen is no longer important. He works only for the progress and glory of the State.

Under American democracy the individual *is* important. There is no privileged class in America—*all men are free*. The government exists to help each and every citizen live a happy and a worthwhile life. In America, democracy means a government *of* the people, *by* the people, and *for* the people. It means a free government controlled by a free people.

Today we know the privileges of living under a free government. But men have not always known this freedom. In this unit you will read about man's long struggle for freedom. You will read how it forms the background for American democracy. There are four topics in this unit.

THE WILL TO BE FREE
DEMOCRACY BEGINS IN THE NEW WORLD
THE COLONIES BECOME FREE AND INDEPENDENT
A NEW NATION—THE UNITED STATES OF AMERICA

As you study these topics think about the men and women who made your freedom possible. Think about the reasons they were willing to fight and die for freedom. Think about how precious the right of freedom really is. Think how important it is to remember that

Eternal vigilance is the price of freedom.

14

The Will To Be Free

FREEDOM has not always been the law of the land. But it has always been the desire of courageous men and women. The struggle to be free began many, many years ago. It is still going on today!

The people in the past were much the same as the people of today. They had the same feelings, the same desires, and the same ambitions. The people of the United States believe that every man has the right to *life, liberty, and the pursuit of happiness.* Other men, throughout the ages, have believed in these same ideals and privileges. They did not use the words *life, liberty, and the pursuit of happiness.* But the goals toward which they struggled were the same.

The Right to Life

The right to live was a never-ending problem for early man. In an uncivilized world death walked with him at every step. Fierce animals stalked his path. The task of getting food was difficult and dangerous. It was not easy to find shelter and protection for his family.

In those days it was easier to starve than to find food. It was easier to die than to live. But early man wanted to live. He wanted to find food, to obtain clothing, and to make a home for his family. These desires urged him to conquer a world that was still savage. To gain the right to live he fought fiercely and courageously.

People today want the same right to live. Each and every man wants the right to live without fear. He wants to know that he will always have the right to feed, clothe, and house his family.

The struggle for the right to live has been going on ever since time began. It has continued as men learned to live and work and play together. It will go on forever. The desire to be free from hunger and fear can never be crushed.

The Right to Liberty

The right to live is not enough! Man longs for other things. He seeks a better and richer life. A slave can live. His master gives him food, clothes, and a place to sleep. Yet he is not satisfied. He would rather go hungry and be free. If he were free, he would have the right to guide his own life. He would be free to think and to choose for himself.

The Right to the Pursuit of Happiness

The desires for life and liberty have urged men on to accomplish many things. The desire for happiness has been equally important. As men sought happiness, they developed a better way of life. Pictures were painted. Music was composed. Books were written. Men invented machines to help them ease the drudgery of work. They invented automobiles, radios, telephones, television sets, and many other things to make life more pleasant. People wanted not only to have life, but to enjoy it.

Life, liberty, and the pursuit of happiness might be called the great desires of man.

It was the desire for freedom that led the Pilgrims across the Atlantic Ocean. It was the desire to live their own lives that moved the colonists to seek independence from England. It was the desire for *life, liberty, and the pursuit of happiness* that guided the men who wrote the Constitution of the United States.

But the story of democracy did not begin in America. Egyptian slaves who rebelled against their masters were a part of the story. The ancient Greeks and Romans were another part. Each of them established a form of democratic government. Each of them contributed something to the democracy we know today. But the people

Below is the scene of a Roman military triumph. Marcus Claudius Marcellus, a great Roman general, returns from killing the leader of the Gauls in 223 B.C. These men did not hesitate to fight for their beliefs.

P.I.P.

who really gave us the pattern for American freedom were the English.

The Magna Carta

Over seven hundred years ago King John succeeded to the throne of England. He was one of the most unpopular monarchs in all English history. He was cruel and greedy. He oppressed the clergy and the nobles. He forced severe hardships upon the common folk.

Taxes had been heavy in England. King John increased them and collected them more frequently. He called the barons to arms although there was no war. He kept the men waiting until they paid to go home. During his reign even religious services were discontinued for a time.

In 1213 a group of bishops and barons met to discuss what should be done. Angrily they related their grievances. "People have been starved in prison," they cried. "They have been imprisoned and killed without trial. The king has taken our lands without payment. He has seized the estates of widows and children. All the rights and liberties of free men are being taken away from us."

There were established laws in England. The barons and bishops decided to force the king to abide by them. Stephen Langton was Archbishop of Canterbury. He helped the men make a list of the rights and liberties they demanded. This was the first written "bill of rights" in English history. It is called the Great Charter, or the Magna Carta.

When King John first heard the terms of the Magna Carta he became very angry.

P.I.P.

The bishops and the barons met with King John in a meadow at Runnymede, England. They forced him to accept the terms of the Magna Carta.

"I will not sign such a paper," he stormed. But the determined barons and bishops would not be refused. On June 15, 1215, they met with the king. They forced him to attach the royal seal to the Great Charter and to accept its terms.

The Magna Carta is one of the most important documents in English history. It proved that a king could not disregard the rights of the people. It proved that he could be forced to rule more justly. It also limited the powers of the king. This gave the people an opportunity to secure other rights and privileges.

During the reign of King Charles I Parliament passed the Petition of Right. The king was forced to accept it. Later King Charles I was beheaded.

Englishmen Gain Other Rights

Four hundred years later, Parliament forced other important rights from an unwilling king. King Charles I tried to rule England as a dictator. He dissolved two Parliaments and tried to impose his own will on the people of England. He ordered various persons to lend him money. When some of them refused, he threw them into prison. He compelled English families to provide food and shelter for his soldiers. Many of the soldiers were rough and uncouth. They did not respect the rights of the people with whom they lived.

In King Charles's third Parliament were men who were not in sympathy with the king. In 1628 they passed a bill called the Petition of Right. They forced the king to sign it. The Petition of Right said that

1) the king could not force anyone to lend him money without the consent of Parliament;

2) he could not imprison men without just cause;

3) soldiers could not be housed in private homes without the consent of the owner; and

4) citizens could not be forced to accept military laws in time of peace.

The Petition of Right gave Englishmen new liberties, but they were still not free. They had to go on fighting tyrants for many years. King Charles was tried by a military court and ordered beheaded. His son, Prince Charles, was banished from England. Then Parliament and Oliver Cromwell, a general in the army, ruled England as a dictatorship. The government they forced upon the people was called the Commonwealth government.

After the death of Cromwell, his son Richard ruled for a time. But the Commonwealth government was not successful. Finally, Prince Charles was recalled to England and crowned as King Charles II.

One of the important events during the reign of Charles II was the passage of the *Habeas Corpus Act*. The Habeas Corpus Act became a law in 1679. Under that law a person could not be put in prison and kept

there without a trial. He had to be brought before a judge within a certain length of time. Then the judge, not the king, reviewed the case. He decided whether the prisoner before him should be held for trial or discharged.

When Charles II died, James, Duke of York, became King James II of England. (It was he who gave New York its name.) King James did many things which displeased Parliament and the British people. Finally Parliament demanded that King James give up his throne.

King James had a daughter, Mary, who lived in Holland. She and her husband, William, ruled a province there. Important leaders in Parliament asked William and Mary to become King and Queen of England. They agreed. William and his army marched into London, and King James fled to France. In 1689 William and Mary were crowned King and Queen of England. Even before their coronation they were forced to agree that certain rights belonged to the people and to Parliament. These rights are known as the Bill of Rights.

The Bill of Rights gave Parliament freedom of speech in all its sessions. It forbade courts to inflict cruel punishments. It forbade excessive fines or excessive bail. It said that jurors should be freely chosen. It gave the people the right to petition the king if they felt they were being treated unjustly. The Bill of Rights named the powers that belonged to the people and Parliament. It listed the rights that were taken away from the king.

The Magna Carta, the Petition of Right, and the Bill of Rights are often called "the Bible of English liberties." They were the foundation upon which English democracy was built.

To the people of England they are very important. They are also important to us. The colonists who came to the New World brought their love of freedom with them. This love of freedom inspired them to fight for independence. It guided them in writing our Constitution—the plan of government that gives us the rights and privileges we enjoy today.

P.I.P

King William and Queen Mary accepted the Bill of Rights in 1689, shortly before their coronation. Later, this document was to become part of the pattern for democracy in the New World.

Things to Do

1. The dates given in this topic are to be used for cross reference. While you are reading about the struggle for independence in America, turn back and see what was happening in England at the same time.
2. Make a class time line entitled, "The Time Line of Freedom in the Old World." Begin with primitive man, who first sought freedom from fear, death, and starvation. Include the struggles of the ancient Egyptians, Greeks, and Romans. (You will need to use encyclopedias and other reference books.) Bring the English struggle for liberty down even farther than the Bill of Rights. Save your time line for later reference.
3. Make a list of countries which are now democracies. Write a short article explaining why you think nations progress under democratic governments.
4. Make charts for your schoolroom illustrating the different steps in the struggle for freedom. Use pictures illustrating the fight for freedom in our own country.
5. Find out all you can about the phrase *habeas corpus*. Be ready to describe some situations in which it is used today. Tell why the Habeas Corpus Act was such an important milestone in the history of freedom.

Questions to Answer

1. During the Second World War the Magna Carta was sent to the United States for safekeeping. There is also a copy of the Magna Carta in the United States. Can you tell where it is kept? Why are the people of the United States interested in the Great Charter?
2. Are there any people in the world today who once had freedom but have lost it? Bring to school a newspaper or magazine article which tells about these people.
3. What are some of the things you do every day that were made possible because the people of yesterday gained the right to *life*?
4. What are some of the things you do every day that depend upon the right to *liberty*?
5. Name some of the things that give you *happiness*. How did the English barons help you to have these things?
6. Why is the Magna Carta so important to Englishmen? Was it a part of their struggle for freedom? Why?
7. Which do you think people appreciate more: the things that are given to them or the things they have to work for? Do you think that men who have had to fight for freedom appreciate it more than those who have not had to fight or work for it?

8. Do people still have to fight for any of the rights in the English Bill of Rights? Name countries where there is no freedom of speech; where jurors are not freely chosen; and where people do not have the right to petition the government if they feel they are being treated unjustly.

A Written Exercise

Copy and complete the following sentences:
1. We received the pattern for our freedom from_____.
2. The people of England disliked King John because_____.
3. The three great desires of man are_____.
4. The Magna Carta demanded that the king_____.
5. Parliament passed the Petition of Right because the king was forcing the English people to_____.
6. Two of the rights given to the people by the Petition of Right were
_____.
7. The Habeas Corpus Act stopped the practice of_____.
8. The Bill of Rights made laws more important than_____.
9. Some of the rights listed in the Bill of Rights were_____.
10. "The Bible of English liberties" is the foundation upon which____
_____.

Words to Study Before You Read the Next Topic

resentful	compact	boycotted
Continental Congress	treaties	tyranny
sincerely	survive	delegates
shirking	responsibilities	violated

Democracy Begins in the New World

THE *Mayflower* lay anchored in Cape Cod Harbor. The long, long journey across the Atlantic was over. The little band of Pilgrims looked out upon the shores of the new land. They were both joyous and fearful. They were far away from all that they had known. What would they find in the New World? Would they find freedom and the right to live their lives in their own way? Or would they find more suffering, hardships, and tyranny?

The leaders of the group were worried. The discomforts of the long journey had made many of the men resentful. They talked of rebelling against their leaders. The leaders knew they must act and act quickly to bring peace to the group.

The Mayflower Compact

All the men on board the ship were called into the cabin of the *Mayflower*. "Even a small group of people must have a government," said the leaders. "We have come to a new and unfriendly world. The winter will be difficult. We must build houses and protect ourselves from the Indians. But we cannot do these things unless we band together. We shall all perish unless we understand that each man's welfare is important. None of us will survive unless we work together for the good of each other and the good of the colony."

There was a great deal of discussion. Finally the men realized that their leaders were right. No man could hope to find liberty alone. They must all work together. To work together successfully they needed a set of rules. *They needed to make laws and abide by them.*

The agreement to do this was put into a document drawn up in the little cabin of the *Mayflower*. This document was named the Mayflower Compact. Under the terms of the Compact the people were to make their own laws. They were to choose their own officers to enforce the laws. They promised to work with one another to conquer the wilderness. They agreed to preserve order in their colony and to establish a form of government that would give justice to all.

This part of the Compact shows how wisely the Pilgrim leaders planned. It shows how well they foresaw the needs of the colony.

In the name of God, Amen. We whose names are underwritten, the loyall subjects of our dread soveraigne . . . King James . . . having undertaken . . . to plant the first colonie in the Northerne parts of Virginia, doe . . . solemnly & mutually . . . combine ourselves together into a civill body polotick, for our better ordering & preservation & furtherance of the ends aforesaid; and by vertue hearof to enacte . . . such just and equall lawes . . . as shall be thought most meete & convenient for the generall good of the Colonie, unto which we promise all due submission and obedience. . . .

A Colony
Is Established

During that first winter the Pilgrims suffered almost unbelievable hardships, but they stayed in America. They lived their lives in their own way. They held elections and passed new laws that were needed. They punished all persons who violated the laws.

The Pilgrim leaders made treaties with the Indians. They bought land and distributed it among the colonists. They guaranteed to everyone the right to worship God as he pleased.

The Pilgrims wanted justice for everyone. They believed in equal rights and equal duties. *They began the first American colony founded upon the right of the people to govern themselves.*

Other colonists were also settling along the Atlantic seaboard. They all helped to conquer the dangers of the new land. They all fought to gain their independence. They all helped to establish the beginnings of American democracy.

The Pilgrims drew up a plan for self-government. They agreed to live by majority rule until a permanent government was established. Below are some signatures that appeared on the Mayflower Compact.

P.I.P.

543

Factors Contributing to the Development of Democracy in the English Colonies

Charters were made attractive to encourage colonists to go to the New World

The rugged life in America made the colonists feel equal

In the New World there were still protests against religious rule

There were also protests against Royal Governors who tried to force their rule on the people

Many of our democratic traditions were brought over from England

In New England the church was controlled by the congregation. "Rule by the people" was carried over into town government

A New Fight for Freedom

In time, the long, cold winters of starving were over. The colonists had made friends with the Indians. They had cleared lands, cultivated farms, and built roads. Life was not so comfortable in America as in England, but the colonists were satisfied. They were happy with their progress.

English colonists had lived in America for more than 150 years. They had seen their colonies grow and prosper. They loved their new land, but this did not mean they had forsaken England. They were still proud to be Englishmen.

But there were leaders in England who felt that the colonists were shirking their responsibilities. The cost of the French and Indian War had been heavy. It was also expensive to keep English soldiers stationed in America to protect the colonists from the Indians. Taxpayers in England did not want to bear the whole expense. "Let the colonists pay their share," they grumbled.

To Parliament and the king, this seemed reasonable. They began to tax the colonies in various ways. Some of the colonists protested. "We do not object to paying our share of the cost of the war," they said. "We do not object to helping pay for soldiers stationed here. But we are not represented in Parliament. We do not help to make the laws. We will not pay taxes until we are represented. Taxation without representation is tyranny."

Parliament and the king would not listen. Instead, Parliament passed a new tax—the Stamp Tax. Stamps, costing from a half penny to several shillings, were required on various papers. Newspapers, licenses, leases, advertisements, and many kinds of legal papers had to have stamps. Even bills of lading were to be stamped.

The colonists were up in arms. First the merchants organized to protest the Stamp Act. They were soon joined by lawyers, bankers, newspaper men, and even clergymen. Under their leadership, the colonists refused to buy the stamps! They boycotted English goods. English businessmen protested to Parliament. The Stamp Act was repealed.

Then Parliament passed a tax on trade. Again the colonists refused to buy English

Representative government on the new continent began with the Virginia Legislature of 1619. Twenty-two burgesses were elected.

Bettmann Archive

P.I.P.

On a cold December night, a group of Boston colonists disguised themselves as Mohawk Indians. They climbed aboard the tea ships and threw the tea into the water. Then they disappeared into the darkness.

goods. Some of them made their own or went without.

Finally, Parliament repealed the tax on everything but tea. Colonial tempers quieted. For a time there was peace between England and the colonies.

Then the British government made a mistake. It gave the Dutch East India Company the sole right to sell tea in the colonies.

Again the colonial merchants were angered. In Charleston, no one bought the tea. New York and Philadelphia shipped the tea cargoes back to England. In Boston,

men dressed as Indians boarded tea ships. They dumped all the tea into the harbor. The king was furious. He closed the port of Boston to all trade with the outside world. He took away the Massachusetts charter. General Gage, commander of the British troops at Boston, was made governor of the colony.

The First Continental Congress

The colonies had often quarreled among themselves, but they rallied to the support of Boston. From nearly every one of the

thirteen colonies came supplies and offers of help. But a permanent solution was needed.

Everyone began to demand action. A group of colonists gathered in Williamsburg, Virginia. "Let us organize a congress!" they said. "Let representatives from all the colonies decide the rights and the duties of colonists!"

In 1774 the First Continental Congress met in Philadelphia. All the colonies except Georgia sent delegates. The delegates were sincere and honest men. Their farms, their jobs, and their personal pleasures had been put aside. They had left their homes and their families. Many of them had traveled for weeks over rough and dusty roads. They were tired, but personal discomfort mattered little. The freedom of the colonies was threatened.

Many important men took part in the First Continental Congress. Among them were George Washington, John Adams, Samuel Adams, and Patrick Henry. All were true patriots, giving freely of their time, and paying their own expenses.

The Work of the First Continental Congress

Some of the delegates to the Congress were still loyal to the king. They hoped the trouble with England could be settled peaceably. Other delegates believed that the colonists should take a firm stand. Hot-tempered Patrick Henry declared in effect, "There are no longer Virginians, Pennsylvanians, New Yorkers, or New Englanders. We are all Americans." He urged the congress to stand firm.

This first Congress remained in session two months. For many hours each day the delegates debated. Finally they agreed to take a strong stand. A petition to the king was drawn up. The petition listed the ways in which the colonists' rights had been abused. It demanded that the laws against Massachusetts be repealed. It declared that the colonists had the right to govern themselves.

Then the First Continental Congress adjourned. The fifty-five members of the Congress agreed to wait six months. If conditions had not improved within that time, they would meet again.

Patrick Henry urged the colonies to fight against England. "Is life so dear, or peace so sweet," he asked, "as to be purchased at the price of chains and slavery? Forbid it, Almighty God! I know not what course others may take, but as for me, give me liberty, or give me death."

FPG

The Colonists Begin
to Think of Independence

Until now *independence* had been a secret and almost forbidden word in the colonies. But colonial thought was changing. The colonists were beginning to think of themselves as Americans, not as Englishmen. Peace was desirable, but not at the price of oppression.

A few months after the close of the First Continental Congress, Patrick Henry began to urge the colonists to prepare for war. Sincerely he pleaded with his fellow countrymen. "Why stand we here idle?" he asked them. "Is life so dear, or peace so sweet, as to be purchased at the price of chains and slavery?"

At first, talk of independence was hushed and solemn. Women whispered it at quilting bees. Men in the fields, following homemade plows, spoke guardedly of it to one another. But gradually the *desire for freedom* grew stronger and stronger. Men began to speak more freely of independence. In churches and inns the question began to be discussed openly. "Let us declare our independence," people said. Hope for peace was growing dim.

Then came the Battle of Lexington! After the fighting was over, eight Americans were dead, and ten were wounded.

War had come to the colonies. The old, old battle for freedom was beginning anew. The struggle of common people against rulers who sought to take away their rights was smoldering. A new call went out to the Continental Congress.

If there could be no peace without oppression, there must be preparation for war!

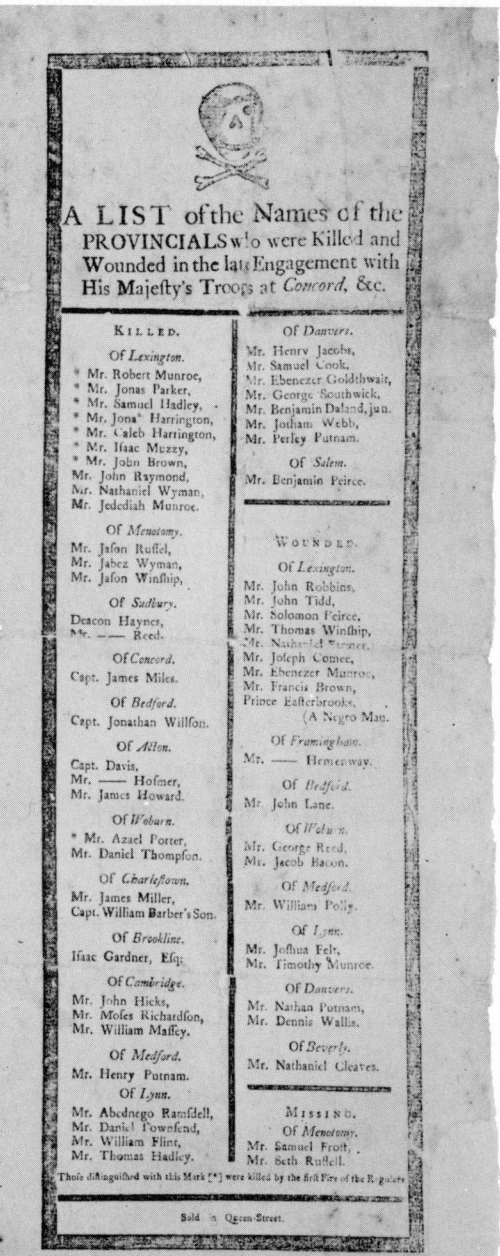

After the bloodshed at Lexington and Concord, the colonists were filled with rage at England. While the battle was still fresh in their memories, the people called for a meeting of the Second Continental Congress.

Things to Do

1. Dramatize the signing of the Mayflower Compact.
2. Hold a town meeting in protest against taxation without representation. Draft a set of resolutions that a group of colonists might have sent to England.
3. Write an editorial about the work of the First Continental Congress.
4. Find words or phrases in the Mayflower Compact that help to prove it was the beginning of a democratic form of government.
5. Find out all you can about George III. Would you say that he was a dictator? Prepare a list of reasons for your answer.

Questions to Answer

1. Why was the Mayflower Compact necessary?
2. What made the Mayflower Compact democratic?
3. Why do you think the American colonies waited for over 150 years before rebelling against England?
4. In what ways were the taxes passed by Parliament a threat to the colonists?

A Written Exercise

Copy each of the following sentences, using only the lettered word or phrase that makes the statement correct.
1. The Pilgrims came to the New World seeking
   a) fame and fortune.
   b) freedom and the right to live their lives in their own way.
2. The Mayflower Compact was
   a) the agreement the Pilgrims made to pay their passage on the ship.
   b) the written permission given the Pilgrims to settle in the New World.
   c) a set of laws and rules by which the colony in the New World was to be governed.
3. The Mayflower Compact was made by
   a) the captain of the ship.
   b) the leaders who were to govern the colony.
   c) all the men on board the *Mayflower.*
4. The most important reason the colonists rebelled against the king and Parliament was that
   a) Parliament and the king imposed taxes on them.
   b) they had to buy goods made in England.
   c) they were not represented in Parliament.

5. The First Continental Congress was composed of men
    a) appointed by the king.
    b) paid by the colonists to demand justice from the king.
    c) meeting at their own expense because they believed in freedom and justice.
6. The First Continental Congress sent the king a petition which
    a) declared the loyalty of the colonies to England.
    b) declared that the colonies have the right to govern themselves.

Words to Study Before You Read the Next Topic

majority	sacrifices	Declaration of Independence
efficient	massive	Articles of Confederation

The Colonies Become Free and Independent

ON May 10, 1775, the Second Continental Congress met in Philadelphia. Each colony was represented in the Congress and each colony had one vote. The Congress was still divided. Only a small majority of delegates favored independence. The leaders of independence did not try to force a break with England. They realized it was not yet time. Congress wrote a message to the king. The message said the colonists were still loyal, but they wanted the right to carry on their own government.

The delegates were divided on the question of independence. But they all agreed on one thing. They all wanted freedom and liberty for the colonies. Accordingly, they appointed George Washington commander in chief of any and all troops raised for the defense of American liberty.

Independence Is Proposed

Richard Henry Lee was the delegate from Virginia. On June 7, 1776, he rose solemnly before the Congress. As he arose, a hushed silence came over the room. Some of the delegates knew he had been instructed to present the question of independence. They wondered what would happen. In a clear, strong voice Lee began to read from a piece of paper he held in his hand. The words rang out strong and clear in the quiet room. "Resolved that these United Colonies are, and of right ought to be, free and independent states."

When Lee finished reading, he turned to his fellow delegates. "Why do we delay?" was the text of his suggestion. "Why do we still debate this important question? Let us instead declare our independence. Let us form on this continent a new republic. Let this new nation establish peace and order and bring happiness to all."

The delegates hesitated. This was not a time to act hastily. There must be time for discussion and careful thinking. The men debated the question frankly and honestly. Some of them sent messages to their home colonies asking what the people wished them to do. Others went home themselves to talk with the people and to listen to their opinions. Then Thomas Jefferson was appointed chairman of a committee to draft a written declaration.

The Declaration of Independence

Thomas Jefferson was one of America's truly great men. He was chosen to write the first draft of *The Declaration of Independence*. That document is as important to Americans as the Magna Carta is to Englishmen. It is, in a very real sense, the cornerstone of our democracy.

In discussions of what should go into the document, the words "life, liberty, and property" were often heard. But Jefferson was more interested in people than in property. His words *life, liberty, and the pursuit of happiness* established the pattern for our American way of life.

First Jefferson wrote a draft of the Declaration. He gave the draft to Benjamin Franklin and John Adams for corrections and suggestions. Then the document was copied on parchment. The parchment copy was presented to the Congress. Congress made a few other changes. Then on July 4, 1776, the Congress formally adopted the Declaration of Independence.

The Declaration united the colonies more truly than they had ever been united before. True, many colonists remained loyal to the king. They still believed that the mother country and the colonies could work out their differences. The loyalists were outnumbered, however. The colonies organized for war.

The Colonists Work and Sacrifice for Freedom

The War for Independence was not a war of well-trained soldiers and massive war machines. It was a war of the people. It was a war in which men, women, and children joined. It was a war in which all groups made sacrifices for the cause of freedom.

Men who were wealthy gave freely of their fortunes. Other men offered what little they could spare. Soldiers gave their lives on the field of battle. Women and children worked so men could fight. Even freedom-loving Frenchmen sent soldiers to help the American cause.

The British lost nearly half their men in three bloody charges before they won the Battle of Bunker Hill. It was in this battle that the New England troops proved they could fight. They waited for the enemy until they saw "the whites of their eyes."

Ewing Galloway

Jefferson, with help from Franklin and Adams, wrote the Declaration of Independence. But ideas from Thomas Paine's pamphlet, *Common Sense*, were also a part of this document.

33

Weaknesses of the U. S. Government under the Articles of Confederation

Could ask States for money ... BUT could not levy taxes

Could make treaties ... BUT could not enforce them

Could plan for army ... BUT could not draft the troops

Could protest foreign duties ... BUT could not set up uniform U. S. tariff

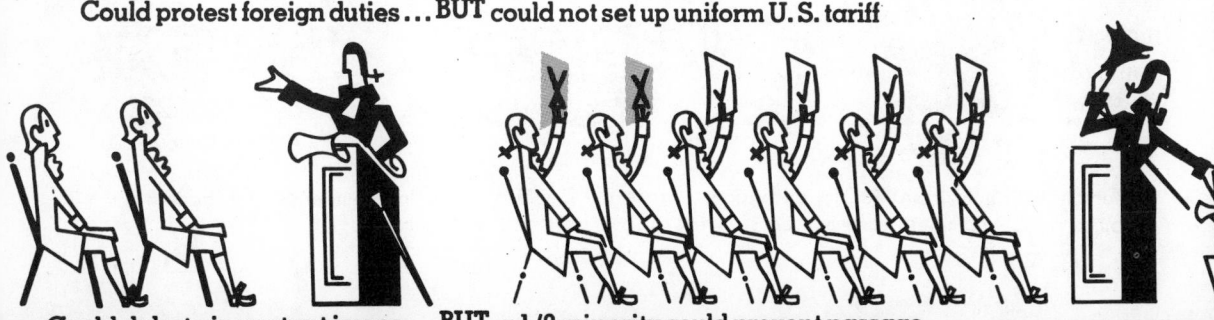

Could debate important issues ... BUT a 1/3 minority could prevent passage

In October, 1781, the English under General Cornwallis were finally defeated. American and French troops, under General Washington, trapped Cornwallis at Yorktown. The English general was forced to surrender. This marked the end of the fighting in the War for Independence.

Finally, Washington forced the British to surrender. In 1783 the colonies became free and independent.

The War for Independence was over. Another chapter in the long struggle for freedom had been written. Once more a people had rebelled against unjust rule. Once more faith and courage had won. Once more a people had earned the right to guide their lives in their own way. Would the people use that precious right wisely?

The Articles of Confederation

After the thirteen colonies declared themselves free, they established their own state governments. They also created a union of states. The constitution for the union of states was called the Articles of Confederation. Under the Articles of Confederation there was a Congress much like the Continental Congress. The states sent delegates to this Congress. Nevertheless, each state still considered itself "free, separate, and independent."

Congress was supposed to govern the country, but it lacked the necessary powers. For instance, it was not given the power to enforce laws. It had no power to collect taxes. It could *ask* the states for money, but most of the states were slow in paying. Some even refused. Times were hard. Property values had fallen after the war. The state governments had little enough money.

Metropolitan Museum of Art, Bequest of Charles Allen Munn

They did not see how necessary it was to pay taxes to the national government. Soon there was no money to apply on the war debt. There was no money with which to pay the soldiers. There was no money even for the ordinary day-to-day work of the federal government.

In addition, many states ignored the laws passed by Congress. Others began to quarrel over state boundaries. There was a feeling of unrest and rebellion throughout the country. Congress was having almost as much trouble as the king had had. *What could be done?* A few leaders realized that an efficient federal government should be created before it was too late.

Things to Do

1. Dramatize the scene in Congress when independence was proposed.
2. Make a chart comparing the provisions of the Magna Carta with those of the Declaration of Independence.
3. Read about the life of Thomas Jefferson. Make a brief report to the class.
4. Write a newspaper editorial explaining how colonial men, women, and children helped fight the war for freedom.
5. You are a member of the Congress under the Articles of Confederation. Write a letter telling about the difficulties of the Congress.
6. Read the Articles of Confederation. Discuss its advantages and disadvantages. Make suggestions that would have improved it.
7. Explain why the colonists made George Washington commander in chief of the colonial armies while they were still loyal to the king.

Questions to Answer

1. What was the difference between *American freedom and liberty* and *American independence from England*?
2. Did anyone force the colonists to declare their independence from England? How did they decide to do so? Did they make their decision in a democratic way?
3. Does it not seem strange that England, a much stronger nation than the colonies, lost the War for Independence? Why do you think the colonists were willing to fight in the war while many of the people of England were not?
4. Why were the states at first unwilling to support a central government?
5. What were some of the problems that the new Congress "inherited" from England?

A Written Exercise

Copy and complete the following sentences:
1. The delegates to the Second Continental Congress were divided on the question of declaring themselves independent of England, but they were not divided on the question of_____.
2. Independence was proposed in Congress by_____.
3. The Declaration of Independence was written by_____.
4. It was corrected by_____.
5. The Declaration of Independence was adopted on_____.
6. The Articles of Confederation proved inadequate because_____.

36

7. Before they could progress and be truly united, the states had to learn to_____.

8. Under the Articles of Confederation, Congress could levy taxes but it could not_____.

Words to Study Before You Read the Next Topic

preside	ratify	draft	adjourned
representation	revise	legislative	validity
executive	unanimously	judicial	distinguished

A New Nation—the United States of America

WISE leaders realized that a stable federal government was necessary. The states were quarreling about such things as the right to use the rivers. The new nation was in danger of destroying both its strength and its freedom.

The Virginia legislature suggested having an interstate convention. It was hoped that such a convention could at least settle problems of commerce.

Not all the states were willing to take part. However, in September, 1786, delegates from five states met at Annapolis, Maryland. They began to discuss the regulation of commerce. The more they talked, the more one thing became clear. Commerce was too big a subject to be handled by itself. It involved many things that could not be decided by so small a group. The delegates made a bold suggestion.

"What we need is a convention of delegates from all the states," they said. "The delegates must be given authority to revise the Articles of Confederation." This proposal was sent to the Congress of the Confederation. The Congress resolved that such a convention should be held.

The Constitutional Convention

The Constitutional Convention met in Philadelphia on May 25, 1787. The delegates met in the same building in which the Declaration of Independence had been signed. They chose George Washington to preside over their meeting. It was a distinguished gathering. Each state had sent some of its wisest, most talented, and most patriotic men to the Convention.

When the Convention first opened, the delegates tried to revise the Articles of Confederation. But they soon realized this was a hopeless task. It would be much better to create a new national government.

Creating a New Government

Fortunately for the new government, its creation was entrusted to some able and brilliant men. George Washington was one.

The delegates to the Constitutional Convention met in Independence Hall, the same building in which the Declaration of Independence had been signed. Here the business of preserving the peace was begun.

His fellow Virginian, George Mason, was another. Others included Benjamin Franklin, Alexander Hamilton, Gouverneur Morris, Robert Morris, and James Madison. There were fifty-five delegates to the Constitutional Convention. The youngest was twenty-seven years old, the eldest eighty-one. Nine of the delegates were foreign-born. All of them wanted the best for the new nation. But not all of them agreed as to what that "best" might be.

The work of the delegates was at no time easy. The Convention was nearly wrecked by the struggle between the large states and the small states. Many questions were debated hotly. Should there be a strong federal government? Should each state have an equal number of votes?

The larger states wanted representation based upon the number of people living in each state. "Equal numbers of people should have equal representation," they contended. "It is not right that five hundred people should have the same representation as five thousand people."

The smaller states were equally firm in

39

Franklin urged the Constitutional Convention to "proceed with a spirit of 'give and take.'"

their demand. "Each state must have equal representation," they said. "We will not agree to union if the larger states are to have all the power."

The arguments became very heated. For a time it seemed as if the Convention might be forced to disband. Then Benjamin Franklin, a very old and very wise man, addressed his fellow delegates. "This is not a time to disagree," was the text of his plea. "If a man is building a board table and the edges of the planks do not fit, he does not throw the planks away. He takes a little from this side and a little from the other side until he has a good joint.

"We must do the same. This Convention must proceed with a spirit of 'give and take.' Each side must be willing to part with some of its demands and appreciate the demands of the other side. Only in this way will we be able to establish a plan of government suitable to all the people."

Agreement was finally reached. It was decided that Congress should consist of two houses, the Senate and the House of Representatives. *Each state, regardless of size, was to have two members in the Senate. Membership in the House of Representatives was to be based upon population.* The more people living in a state, the more representatives it would have. This satisfied both the large and the small states.

The New Government Begins to Take Shape

As the hot summer days went slowly by, the new government began to take shape. The men worked sincerely and continuously. They studied all known governments for suggestions that might help them. They found no government in all history that they wished to copy exactly. But they learned what things to avoid. They learned that any government, to preserve freedom, must divide and balance the powers of government.

The members of the Constitutional Convention provided for three branches of government. They are the legislative

branch, the executive branch, and the judicial branch. The legislative branch is the Congress. The executive branch is the President and the various departments and agencies under his jurisdiction. The judicial branch is the Supreme Court of the United States and the lower federal courts.

The legislative branch passes the laws. The executive branch carries out the laws. The judicial branch interprets the laws or judges the validity of any law that is questioned.

Each branch has definite work to do, yet none is entirely independent of the others. A bill passed by Congress cannot become a law unless it is signed by the President, or repassed over his veto. A treaty proposed by the President cannot become effective until it is approved by a two-thirds majority of the Senate. A law passed by Congress and signed by the President cannot be enforced if the Supreme Court rules that it is not in keeping with the meaning of the Constitution.

The Splendid Work of the Convention

It is doubtful whether any member of the Constitutional Convention realized what a splendid work had been accomplished when the Constitution was written. It is doubtful whether any man realized that the Constitution would become the ideal by which good government is measured. Here was a group of men representing all sections of a struggling young republic. They had no thought of receiving payment or of becoming national heroes. They were working of their own free will, because they realized their country was in danger.

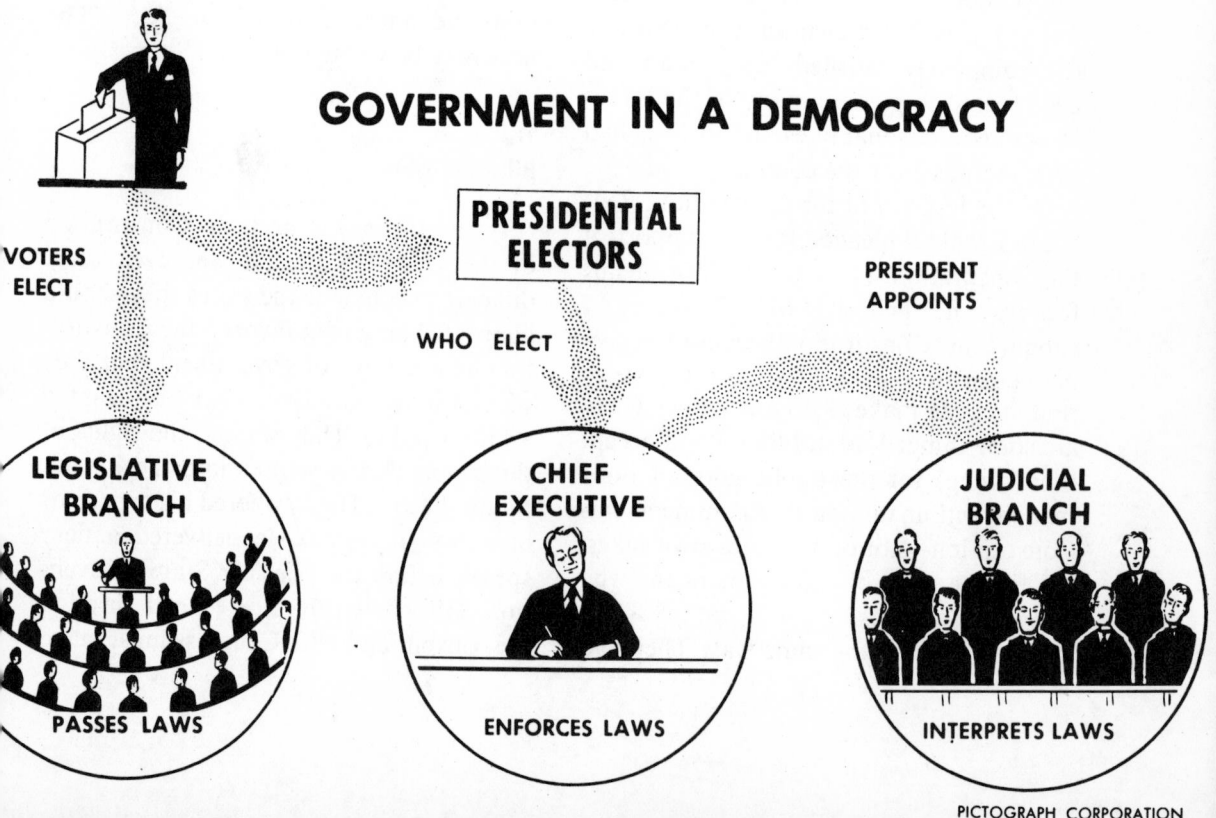

GOVERNMENT IN A DEMOCRACY

PRESIDENTIAL ELECTORS

VOTERS ELECT

PRESIDENT APPOINTS

WHO ELECT

LEGISLATIVE BRANCH

CHIEF EXECUTIVE

JUDICIAL BRANCH

PASSES LAWS

ENFORCES LAWS

INTERPRETS LAWS

Bettmann Archive

None of the delegates was entirely satisfied with the Constitution. Yet all were willing to compromise for the sake of a united nation.

The men toiled constantly from June until September. By the middle of September the plan of government had been completed. It was read to the members of the Convention. The members listened attentively, but with little enthusiasm. No one felt completely satisfied. Each man had been forced to give up many of the things he wanted. Personal likes and dislikes had been sacrificed for the common good.

On the last day of the Convention, Benjamin Franklin pleaded for the support of the Constitution. These words illustrate his feelings and beliefs. "Mr. President, I support this Constitution because I expect no better. It may be the best Constitution men can make; I do not know. There are some things I do not like. I will accept those things for the public good. I hope that we will unanimously recommend this Constitution—not only for our own sakes, but for the good of those Americans who may come after us."

Other men felt the same way. They had worked long and hard. They had planned the best form of government they could devise for present and future needs. Thirty-nine members, delegates from twelve states, signed the Constitution. Then it was sent to the Congress of the Confederation. It was recommended that Congress ask state conventions to approve the new federal Constitution. The delegates to the state conventions were to be chosen by the people of the states. When nine of the thirteen states had accepted the Constitution, it was to be put into operation. It was to become the foundation for the new democratic government of the United States of America.

Before the Convention adjourned, George Washington made an earnest speech. He expressed his hope that the Constitution would be adopted by the states. "If the states do not accept this Constitution, we may never have another opportunity to draft one in peace," he said in effect. "The next may be written in blood."

The Bill of Rights

It was not easy to draft the Constitution of the United States. It was even more difficult to convince the states they should adopt it. Many men favored the Constitution as a pattern of government, but they wanted more than that. They also wanted a bill of rights. They wanted the rights of the people clearly written into the Constitution. Patrick Henry offered his own draft of a bill of rights. He delivered a fiery speech before the Virginia State Convention. His powerful voice echoed through the convention hall. "Congress must make

no laws interfering with the freedom of religion, freedom of speech, or freedom of the press. It must recognize the right of the people to peaceful assembly, trial by jury, security against search and seizure. . . ."

For a while it seemed impossible to get nine states to accept the Constitution without a bill of rights. Finally, nine months after it was written, New Hampshire became the ninth state to ratify it. Rhode Island did not sign until the spring of 1790. Most of the states signed with the understanding that there would be a bill of rights.

The first national Congress met in New York in 1789. The delegates to the Congress knew that the people wanted a bill of rights. Even so, they hesitated to pass one.

But men who have fought and sacrificed for freedom are not easily discouraged. People throughout the colonies refused to accept a government that did not protect their personal liberties. Finally their determined battle was won. James Madison, a member of Congress, proposed a series of amendments to the Constitution. Ten amendments were passed by Congress and ratified by the states. In 1791 they became a part of the Constitution. These ten amendments are called the Bill of Rights.

The first Congress of the new nation met in 1789 at Federal Hall in New York City.

New York Public Library

A New Nation— the United States of America

A new plan of government had been adopted by the thirteen states. The three branches of the federal government checked and balanced one another. There was balance between the state and the federal governments. There was balance between the large states and the small states. There was balance between personal liberty and lawful order.

From bitter hours of struggle, from long days when it seemed as though the cause of freedom might be lost forever, the new nation had emerged. It was destined to survive and prosper and become a leader among nations. It is our own beloved United States of America.

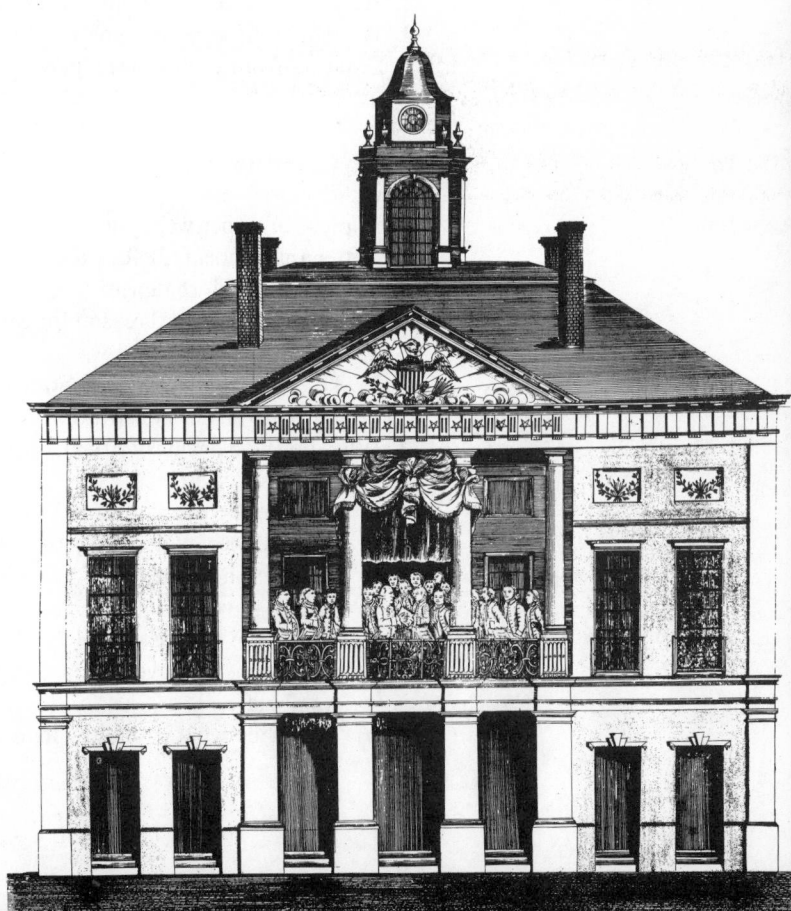

Things to Do

1. Write a conversation that might have taken place between two members of the Constitutional Convention. One may be a delegate from one of the larger states, the other a delegate from a small state.
2. Make an illustrated map showing some of the conditions in the thirteen states that might have accounted for the differences of opinion among the delegates.
3. Write a newspaper story telling the people that the Constitution has been adopted and that George Washington has been chosen the first president of the United States. Write an editorial explaining why George Washington will make a good president.
4. Tell why the members of the Constitutional Convention planned for three branches of government.

Questions to Answer

1. Did the Constitutional Convention work out a plan of government in a democratic manner? Explain your answer.
2. Why was the Bill of Rights necessary?
3. What may have been some of the reasons it was decided to have two Senators from each state, regardless of size?

A Written Exercise

On a piece of paper write the numbers 1 through 6. After number 1, write the letter that appears before the phrase which answers the question. Do the same with each sentence.

1. What was the original reason for calling the Constitutional Convention?
   a) To elect a president.
   b) To revise the Articles of Confederation.
   c) To write a new constitution.
2. Why did the delegates to the Constitutional Convention decide to write a new constitution?
   a) Because the people wanted to be entirely free from England.
   b) Because the smaller states did not like the Articles of Confederation.
   c) Because the Articles of Confederation did not establish a stable federal government.
3. What was the greatest problem of the Constitutional Convention?
   a) To establish a government that would satisfy both the large and the small states.
   b) To decide what should be included in the Bill of Rights.

c) To create a stable federal government that would also protect the rights of the states.

4. Which of the following helped to create greater harmony in the Constitutional Convention?
   a) Defining the powers of Congress.
   b) Providing that amendments would become law when approved by three fourths of the states.
   c) Establishing a two-house legislature representing both the states and the people.

5. The Bill of Rights was passed to protect the personal rights and liberties of the people from unfair treatment by which of the following?
   a) The state governments.
   b) Government agencies.
   c) The federal government.

6. Which of the following is the legislative branch of the federal government?
   a) The President and the executive departments under him.
   b) The Congress of the United States.
   c) The Supreme Court and the lower federal courts.

Words to Study Before You Read the Next Topic

acquire	anniversary	render
entitled	naturalization	legislatures
destroyed	abolished	quartered
imposed	unalienable	endowed

UNIT SUMMARY

You are living in a free country. You enjoy certain precious rights. Among them are the rights to *life, liberty, and the pursuit of happiness.* These rights did not come to you by chance. They came to you because men in the past have worked, struggled, and died for freedom.

Early man rebelled against cruel masters. The people of England struggled to gain new freedoms through the Magna Carta, the Petition of Right, and the Bill of Rights. The colonists braved the dangers of the New World and fought to establish an independent and free nation. They wrote the Constitution and the Bill of Rights to help preserve this free nation.

The freedom you enjoy today took long centuries to achieve. It is yours, *but to keep your freedom you must guard it.* As you finish this unit think about man's long struggle for freedom. Think about the sacrifices that have been made to give you a free government. Talk about the things you can do to guard and to preserve your freedom and the freedom of your country.

UNIT TWO

The Foundation of American Democracy

THE FOUNDATION of AMERICAN DEMOCRACY

Architects have a saying that "a building is only as strong as its foundation." This is true. A tall skyscraper requires a stronger and a deeper foundation than a small home or building.

At one time the United States was a weak union of thirteen states. Today it is a strong nation of fifty states. It has grown strong because its foundation is strong. In this unit you will read about *The Foundation of American Democracy*. You will read about the firm foundation on which our government is built. The topics in the unit are:

> THE DECLARATION OF INDEPENDENCE
> THE DECLARATION OF INDEPENDENCE IS ADOPTED
> THE CONSTITUTION OF THE UNITED STATES
> TO FORM A MORE PERFECT UNION
> TO ESTABLISH JUSTICE
> TO INSURE DOMESTIC TRANQUILITY
> TO PROVIDE FOR THE COMMON DEFENSE
> TO PROMOTE THE GENERAL WELFARE
> AMENDMENTS TO THE CONSTITUTION

The Declaration of Independence, the Constitution, and the Bill of Rights are the documents upon which our way of life is founded. Study these great documents. Discover how they form the strong foundation on which our way of life stands firm.

The Declaration of Independence

THOMAS JEFFERSON was only thirty-three years old when he wrote the Declaration of Independence. But without realizing it, he had been preparing for that great task for many years. As a student at William and Mary College, he had read widely. He had studied law. He had pleaded the cases of many clients who had been treated unjustly. He had often read, studied, and thought about fair and just government. He had talked with the other colonists about independence. He had weighed their ideas and his own. He had read and reread a Virginia Declaration of Rights drawn up by his friend, George Mason. Sincerely and earnestly he had searched for the soundest thoughts.

When Jefferson was chosen to draft the Declaration of Independence, he had definite goals in mind. He wanted the Declaration to express man's desire for freedom. He wanted to make very clear the reasons why such a declaration was necessary. To know how well he succeeded, you have only to give a little thought to the stirring words that came from his quill pen.

The following is an imaginary conversation in a classroom. The words of the teacher which are in italic type are the words of the Declaration of Independence. The rest of the conversation explains the Declaration in more simple language.

MR. DAVIS: Each year the people of the United States celebrate the Fourth of July. As you know, that is the anniversary of the adoption of the Declaration of Independence. Throughout the land there are many patriotic celebrations. Flags fly proudly in the breeze. Bands play stirring music. The Declaration of Independence is sometimes read aloud. You may have heard these famous words. Do you understand their meaning?

KATHRYN: I don't, Mr. Davis. I didn't think young people needed to understand them.

MR. DAVIS: You are quite wrong, Kathryn. The Declaration of Independence has a meaning for all young people. It is not just for adults to understand and appreciate. The Declaration of Independence made possible the American way of life. If the colonists had not declared themselves independent from England, the Constitution could not have been written.

I am going to read most of the Declaration to you. As I read each part we will discuss it for a while. We will try to put it in our own words.

When, in the course of human events, it becomes necessary for one people to dissolve the political bands which have connected them with another, and to assume among the powers of the earth, the separate and equal station to which the laws of nature and of nature's God entitle them, a decent respect to the opinions of mankind requires that they should declare the causes which impel them to the separation.

DEANNA: I believe I can explain that, Mr. Davis. When it becomes necessary for one people to separate from another, they should be willing to state their reasons for doing so.

MR. DAVIS: Yes. The colonists felt that the time had come for them to break their ties with England. They believed that the colonies were entitled to a "separate and equal station" among the nations of the earth. They believed that the "laws of nature and of nature's God" gave every man the right to live his life in his own way. Since England had not allowed the colonists to do this, they wanted to establish a separate nation. They respected the opinions of other people and of other nations. For this reason the colonists decided to explain to the world why they wished independence. The Declaration of Independence gave their reasons for declaring themselves independent from England.

Unalienable Rights of All Men

MR. DAVIS: *We hold these truths to be self-evident: That all men are created equal; that they are endowed by their Creator with certain unalienable rights; that among these are life, liberty, and the pursuit of happiness.*

RICHARD: May I explain that? The fact that men are born equal should require no proof. God gave to them certain rights that should not be taken away from them. Three of these rights are life, liberty, and the pursuit of happiness.

MR. DAVIS: The colonists believed that all men are born with equal rights and common desires. They are not only born with them—they have the right to try to

To the PUBLIC.

THE Senfe of the City relative to the Landing the India Company's Tea, being fignified to Captain Lockyer, by the Committee, neverthelefs, it is the Defire of a Number of the Citizens, that at his Departure from hence, he fhould fee, with his own Eyes, their Deteftation of the Meafures purfued by the Miniftry and the India Company, to enflave this Country. This will be declared by the Convention of the People at his Departure from this City; which will be on next Saturday Morning, about nine o'Clock, when no Doubt, every Friend to this Country will attend. The Bells will give the Notice about an Hour before he embarks from Murray's Wharf.

By Order of the COMMITTEE.

NEW YORK, April 21ft, 1774.

The Tea Act was one of the unfair laws that caused the colonists to rebel. This law threatened all colonial business with unfair competition with goods from England. Above is a public notice asking colonists to show their "detestation of the measures pursued" by England.

fulfill them. The colonists considered life, liberty, and the pursuit of happiness the most important of man's desires. They were willing to fight for these rights.

Purpose of Governments

MR. DAVIS: *That, to secure these rights, governments are instituted among men, deriving their just powers from the consent of the governed; that, whenever any form of government becomes destructive of these ends, it is the right of the people to alter or to abolish it, and to institute new government, laying its foundation on such principles, and organizing its powers in such form as to them shall seem most likely to effect their safety and happiness.*

BRUCE: I know what that means. Men form governments to help them secure the rights to life, liberty, and the pursuit of happiness. A government should receive its powers from the people. Whenever a government does not protect the rights of the people, the people should be able to change it.

MR. DAVIS: The colonists believed a government should be a government of the people. If the colonies had been represented in London, perhaps the colonists would not have been so dissatisfied.

JEAN: Just think! If they had not been dissatisfied, we might still be ruled by a king!

MR. DAVIS: *Prudence, indeed, will dictate that governments long established*

should not be changed for light and transient causes; and accordingly all experience hath shown that mankind are more disposed to suffer while evils are sufferable, than to right themselves by abolishing the forms to which they are accustomed.

BOB: I'm not sure what every word in that paragraph means, but I think I can explain the ideas. It is not wise to change a government for unimportant causes. It is not wise to overthrow a government for causes that will soon pass away. Men do not like to change their government. They prefer to suffer evils as long as the evils are bearable.

Necessity for Change of Government

MR. DAVIS: *Such has been the patient sufferance of these colonies; and such is now the necessity which constrains them to alter their former systems of government. The history of the present King of Great Britain is a history of repeated injuries and usurpations, all having in direct object the establishment of an absolute tyranny over these states. To prove this, let facts be submitted to a candid world.*

CHARLES: May I explain that? The colonies had suffered long and patiently. They had suffered so long they considered it necessary to change their government. The King of England had seized power that did not belong to him. He had tried to establish a tyranny over the colonies. To prove this, the colonists were willing to submit the facts to the whole world.

MR. DAVIS: The colonists believed they had good cause to establish a new government, but they desired to be fair. They wanted the world to know the facts and to judge them honestly.

Abuses by the King

MR. DAVIS: *He has refused his assent to laws the most wholesome and necessary for the public good.*

He has forbidden his governors to pass laws of immediate and pressing importance, unless suspended in their operation till his assent should be obtained; and, when so suspended, he has utterly neglected to attend to them.

He has refused to pass other laws for the accommodation of large districts of people, unless those people would relinquish the right of representation in the legislature—a right inestimable to them, and formidable to tyrants only.

JAMES: That is not hard to explain. The king has refused to approve laws that would have helped the people. He has refused to permit his governors to enforce laws without his approval. Much-needed laws have been passed by the legislatures. The king has neglected either to approve or to disapprove them. Even after laws were passed by the legislatures, they were not effective.

He has refused to approve laws for large districts of people unless the people agreed to give up all right of representation in the legislatures. The right of representation is very valuable to the people. Only a king who is a tyrant need be afraid of it.

MR. DAVIS: That is quite true, James. The colonists had their own legislatures. They also knew that the first principle of a government by the people is the right

of representation. No country can be truly democratic unless the people, through their representatives, control their own government.

More
Unfair Practices

MR. DAVIS: *He has called together legislative bodies at places unusual, uncomfortable, and distant from the depository of their public records, for the sole purpose of fatiguing them into compliance with his measures.*

ANN: The king has called the assemblies together at unusual places. He has called them together at places uncomfortable and far distant from the places where the public records are kept. He has tried to make the assemblymen so tired they would agree with whatever he wished to do.

MR. DAVIS: *He has dissolved representative houses repeatedly, for opposing, with manly firmness, his invasions on the rights of the people.*

He has refused, for a long time after such dissolutions, to cause others to be elected, whereby the legislative powers, incapable of annihilation, have returned to the people at large for their exercise; the state remaining, in the meantime, exposed to all the dangers of invasion from without and convulsions within.

RICHARD: The king has abolished colonial assemblies again and again because they have opposed him. He has refused for

These stamps, like those pictured on page 56, are examples of those the English government required to be placed on colonial documents.

Bettmann Archive

a long time to allow other assemblies to be elected. The colonists have tried to govern themselves without legislatures. In the meantime the colonies have been exposed to danger. The colonists could have done little if an enemy had tried to invade their shores. They could not even have stopped disturbances at home.

MR. DAVIS: *He has endeavored to prevent the population of these states; for that purpose obstructing the laws for naturalization of foreigners, refusing to pass others to encourage their migrations hither, and raising the conditions of new appropriations of lands.*

CAROL: The king has tried to prevent the growth of the colonies. He has refused to approve naturalization laws. He has refused to encourage people to come to the colonies. He has made it difficult to acquire new land.

Local Justice Obstructed

MR. DAVIS: *He has obstructed the administration of justice, by refusing his assent to laws for establishing judiciary powers.*

He has made judges dependent on his will alone for the tenure of their offices, and the amount and payment of their salaries.

There were no friendly policemen in colonial cities. The king's soldiers enforced the king's rules . . . not always justly or politely.

JAMES: The king has refused to approve laws establishing free courts. He fixes the salaries of judges. He can appoint or remove judges as he likes.

BOB: A judge who depended upon the king for his position and his salary would not dare to oppose the king's wishes. He would render decisions in favor of the king instead of the people, wouldn't he?

MR. DAVIS: I'm afraid he might, Bob. That made things difficult for the colonists.

He has erected a multitude of new offices and sent hither swarms of officers to harass our people and eat out their substance.

He has kept among us in times of peace, standing armies, without the consent of our legislatures.

FPG

By ORDER OF HIS EXCELLENCY

Sir William Howe, K. B.

General and Commander in Chief, &c. &c. &c.

PROCLAMATION.

I DO hereby give Notice to the Inhabitants of the City of Philadelphia and its Environs, it is the Order of His Excellency, that " No Person whatever, living " within the said City and its Environs, shall appear in " the Streets between the Beating of the Tattoo, at Half " an Hour after Eight o'Clock in the Evening, and the " Revellie in the Morning, without Lanthorns: And all " who shall be found abroad, within the Time aforesaid, " will be liable to be examined by the Patroles, and con- " fined, unless they shall give a satisfactory Account of " themselves." And I do hereby enjoin and require the Inhabitants, and all others residing in the said City and its Environs, to pay strict Obedience to the said Order, and govern themselves accordingly.

Given under my Hand at Philadelphia, this 9th Day of January, in the Eighteenth Year of His Majesty's Reign. JOS. GALLOWAY, Superintendent-General.

He has affected to render the military independent of, and superior to, the civil power.

LOUISE: The king has created many new offices. He has sent many officers to the colonies. These officers have annoyed the people. It has been very expensive for the colonists to support all these officers. Even in times of peace the king has kept standing armies in the colonies. The armies have not been approved by the colonial legislatures. The king has tried to make the army the supreme power in the colonies without the consent of the people or of their colonial legislatures.

RICHARD: The king probably thought a large standing army would keep the colonists from rebelling.

MR. DAVIS: You are probably right, Richard. But man's desire for freedom lies deep. It cannot be destroyed by kings or soldiers.

Imposed Laws and Practices

MR. DAVIS: *He has combined with others to subject us to a jurisdiction foreign to our constitution and unacknowledged by our laws, giving his assent to their acts of pretended legislation:*

For quartering large bodies of armed troops among us;

For protecting them, by a mock trial, from punishment for any murders which they should commit on the inhabitants of these states;

For cutting off our trade with all parts of the world;

For imposing taxes on us without our consent;

Bettmann Archive

Colonists in all walks of life angrily protested the Stamp Act.

For depriving us, in many cases, of the benefits of trial by jury;

For transporting us beyond seas, to be tried for pretended offenses.

JEAN: The first line you read says, "He has combined with others." What "others" does this mean, Mr. Davis?

MR. DAVIS: Undoubtedly the British Parliament, Jean. But the writers of the Declaration did not wish to recognize Parliament even by mentioning its name.

JEAN: I understand. The king and Parliament have tried to force the colonists to live under laws they did not make. The Parliament has pretended to make laws for the good of the colonies and the king has approved them.

Under the laws, large armies have been quartered among the colonists. The soldiers have murdered some of the colonists. They have been protected by mock trials.

JAMES: The king has cut off colonial trade with all parts of the world. He has imposed taxes upon the colonists without their consent.

55

Many times he has not allowed the colonists to be tried by a jury of their fellow countrymen. He has accused colonists of offenses they did not commit. He has had these colonists shipped back to England to be tried.

BOB: Why should the colonists be sent to England to be tried for crimes they did not commit?

MR. DAVIS: They shouldn't, Bob. Englishmen had fought before for the right of a fair trial by jury. Most of the colonists were English, and they were ready to fight for this same right again.

There is one thing we must remember, though. Not all kings are unjust. Neither are all officials in a democracy necessarily good. But in a democracy the people can change their officials by the use of the ballot. They can replace undesirable officials with others who are sincerely interested in the welfare of the people they serve. Under most other forms of government, the people cannot do that. They have to fight for their rights.

The people of England have fought for their rights many times. Today the British Parliament is elected by the people. The king or queen is loved and honored, but Parliament governs Great Britain.

So far we have discussed about half the Declaration of Independence. When we have finished the other half, you will have a better picture of the situation. You will understand why the colonists declared their independence. You will understand why they were willing to make sacrifices to attain freedom.

Bettmann Archive

Things to Do

1. Take a large sheet of plain drawing paper. Burn the edges to give it an antique appearance (your art teacher will show you how). Make your own Declaration of Independence. In your own words write on the paper the reasons the colonists declared their independence from England. Make the paper large enough to include the other reasons you will read about in the next topic.
2. Form the class into a colonial convention. Discuss the first half of the Declaration of Independence that has been presented for approval.
3. Give a short talk on "What the Declaration of Independence Means to Me."
4. Read more about the life of Thomas Jefferson. Make a report to the class.
5. Choose five of the reasons given for separation. Compare the colonial grievances with those suffered by people in totalitarian countries today.

Questions to Answer

1. Why is the Declaration of Independence an important document to Americans?
2. Do you agree with the purpose of government as explained in the Declaration? Does it present a democratic point of view? Explain your answer.
3. Did the people in England have any part in governing themselves at this time?
4. Not everyone in England was in sympathy with the king and against the colonists. Why do you think this was so?
5. Do you think the difficulties between England and the colonies could have been solved another way? Explain.
6. Was it unjust to send accused colonists to England for trial? Give reasons for your answer.

A Written Exercise

Copy and complete the following sentences so that the statements will be true:

1. The colonists wrote the Declaration of Independence because they wanted the world to know_____.
2. The colonists believed the "laws of nature and nature's God" entitled them to_____.
3. The colonists were willing to fight for the right to_____.

4. The colonists believed that if a government did not protect the rights of the people, the people should_____.
5. It is not wise to overthrow a government for_____.
6. The courts of the king failed to establish justice because they_____.
7. Some of the injustices imposed on the colonists by the king were_____.
8. The colonists did not like to be sent to England for trial because_____.

Words to Study Before You Read the Next Topic

commerce	generosity	condemn
allegiance	pledge	injustices
dedicated	ravaged	suspended

The Declaration of Independence Is Adopted

MR. DAVIS: *For abolishing the free system of English laws in a neighboring province, establishing therein an arbitrary government, and enlarging its boundaries, so as to render it at once an example and fit instrument for introducing the same absolute rule into these colonies;*

For taking away our charters, abolishing our most valuable laws, and altering, fundamentally, the forms of our governments.

For suspending our own legislatures, and declaring themselves invested with power to legislate for us in all cases whatsoever.

CAROL: The king has done away with the free system of English laws in Canada. He has set up a dictatorship there and will try to do the same in the colonies.

KATHRYN: He has taken away the charters of the colonies. He has done away with valuable laws and changed forms of government in the colonies. He has suspended legislatures, giving himself and Parliament the power to make colonial laws.

More Grievances

MR. DAVIS: *He has abdicated government here, by declaring us out of his protection and waging war against us.*

He has plundered our seas, ravaged our coasts, burnt our towns, and destroyed the lives of our people.

He is at this time transporting large armies of foreign mercenaries to complete the works of death, desolation, and tyranny already begun with circumstances of cruelty and perfidy scarcely paralleled in the most barbarous ages, and totally unworthy the head of a civilized nation.

He has constrained our fellow citizens, taken captive on the high seas, to bear arms against their country, to become the executioners of their friends and brethren, or to fall themselves by their hands.

MARION: He has given up his right to rule the colonies by refusing to protect them and by waging war against them.

KATHRYN: The king has sent his men to rob colonial ships. They have attacked colonial seacoasts and burned colonial towns. They have even murdered people.

ANN: The king is sending over large armies of hired soldiers. These hired armies will finish the destruction already begun. The colonists have suffered great cruelties. The king has broken his promises. His actions have shown him unfit to be the ruler of a civilized country.

BOB: The king has captured colonial citizens on the high seas. He has forced them to fight against their own colonies. He has forced them to kill their friends and their brothers or be killed themselves.

Tyrant Unfit to Rule a Free People

MR. DAVIS: *He has excited domestic insurrections amongst us, and has endeavored to bring on the inhabitants of our frontiers the merciless Indian savages, whose known rule of warfare is an undistinguished destruction of all ages, sexes, and conditions.*

In every stage of these oppressions we have petitioned for redress in the most humble terms; our repeated petitions have been answered only by repeated injury.

A prince whose character is thus marked by every act which may define a tyrant is unfit to be the ruler of a free people.

DEANNA: The king has tried to get colonists to rebel against the colonies. He has encouraged Indians to attack the people living on the frontiers. These Indians destroy men, women, and children without mercy.

RICHARD: Again and again the colonists have asked the king to correct these injustices. They have asked him politely and humbly. The only answers they have received from him have been more injustices. His actions toward the colonies have shown him to be a tyrant. Anyone who acts like a tyrant is not fit to be the ruler of a free people.

MR. DAVIS: The dictionary defines a tyrant as "one who exercises power cruelly or unjustly." The colonists felt that the king and Parliament were tyrannical.

Appeal to the English People

MR. DAVIS: *Nor have we been wanting in our attentions to our British brethren. We have warned them, from time to time, of attempts by their legislature to extend an unwarrantable jurisdiction over us. We have reminded them of the circumstances of our emigration and settlement here.*

JEAN: The colonists had told the English people what Parliament was trying to do. They had reminded the British people that most of the colonists had come to the New World to seek freedom and peace.

MR. DAVIS: The colonists felt that the actions of Parliament and the king were not the actions of the British people. They had appealed directly to the people. They had tried to make the English understand how unjustly the colonies had been treated.

Forced to Separate from England

MR. DAVIS: *We have appealed to their native justice and magnanimity; and we have conjured them, by the ties of our common kindred, to disavow these usurpations, which would inevitably interrupt our connections and correspondence. They, too, have been deaf to the voice of justice and of consanguinity. We must, therefore, acquiesce in the necessity which denounces our separation, and hold them, as we hold the rest of mankind, enemies in war; in peace, friends.*

RICHARD: The colonists appealed to the British sense of justice. They appealed to the generosity of the British people. They reminded them that the colonists and the people of England had the same forefathers. They asked the British people to

Thomas Jefferson here presents his draft of the Declaration of Independence to the Congress.
Standing near him are the other members of the committee appointed to write the Declaration.

Ewing Galloway

American government is dedicated to the people. Because courageous colonists declared their rights, this typical American family is enjoying life, liberty, and the pursuit of happiness.

condemn the actions of the king. But the people did not listen. They seemed to be completely indifferent. Finally the colonists decided to separate from England, even at the risk of war.

MR. DAVIS: The colonists were naturally disappointed when the English people did not answer their plea. Still I believe that many of them understood. Jefferson wrote into the Declaration that the colonists must accept the necessity of the separation. This might have been a way of saying to the English people, "We understand your

feelings. We are not angry with you. Still we have no choice except to regard you now as enemies."

We Declare Ourselves Free and Independent

MR. DAVIS: The most inspiring part of the Declaration is the last paragraph. That is where the colonists declare themselves free and independent. Richard, you and Bob may explain this part of the Declaration. Try to explain it as a colonist might have done.

We, therefore, the representatives of the United States of America, in General Congress assembled, appealing to the Supreme Judge of the world for the rectitude of our intentions, do, in the name and by authority of the good people of these colonies, solemnly publish and declare that these united colonies are, and of right ought to be, free and independent states; that they are absolved from all allegiance to the British Crown, and that all political connection between them and the state of Great Britain is, and ought to be, totally dissolved; and that, as free and independent states, they have full power to levy war, conclude peace, contract alliances, establish commerce, and to do all other acts and things which independent states may of right do. And, for the support of this declaration, with a firm reliance on the protection of Divine Providence, we mutually pledge to each other our lives, our fortunes, and our sacred honor.

RICHARD: We, the representatives of the United States, are assembled in General Congress. We ask Almighty God to bless what we are about to do. In the name of all the colonists we declare the colonies are,

as they should be, free and independent states.

BOB: The colonies no longer owe allegiance to the British Crown. All connection between them and Great Britain has ended. They are free and independent states. As such, they have the power to declare and to wage war. They can make peace. They can enter into pacts and treaties. They can carry on commerce. They can do everything else that free and independent states have the right to do.

Not forgetting our trust in God, we promise to support this Declaration. Upon our sacred honor we pledge our lives and our fortunes to the cause of freedom.

MR. DAVIS: What a truly great moment it was! The colonists had declared themselves free and independent from England.

They had proposed a government that received its powers from "the consent of the governed." If they won their independence, they would be free to establish a government based on liberty and equality for all men.

To support the Declaration they pledged their lives and their fortunes. On their "sacred honor" they promised all they held dear to the cause of freedom. They believed that with the help of Almighty God they would not fail.

They did not fail! Out of their courage to fight for independence came the beginnings of a great nation. Out of their deep belief in the rights of free men came a new government—a government dedicated to give all people the right of *life, liberty, and the pursuit of happiness.*

AMERICA'S IMPRESSIVE PRODUCTION RECORD

With only 6% of the world population, we have rolled up this share of world output and ownership

POPULATION 6%

GRAIN PRODUCTION 21%

RAILROAD MILEAGE 29%

MEAT PRODUCTION 30%

COAL PRODUCTION 34%

NATIONAL INCOMES (World total) 42%

ELECTRIC POWER PRODUCTION 43%

STEEL PRODUCTION 45%

OIL PRODUCTION 51%

TELEPHONE INSTALLATIONS 58%

AUTO REGISTRATIONS 69%

From "*A Visual History of the United States,*" by Harold U. Faulkner & Graphics Institute

Things to Do

1. Write a letter to a friend in England explaining the views of the colonists concerning the actions of the king and Parliament. As an Englishman, write an answer to the letter expressing your sympathy with the colonial cause, but explaining why you feel you can do little about it.
2. Finish the Declaration of Independence you started to make after you studied the last topic.
3. Suppose you had been one of the men who signed the Declaration of Independence. Choose one of the signers and put yourself in his place. As that person, write a letter to a friend explaining why you signed the Declaration.
4. Not every colonist supported the Declaration of Independence. Those who remained loyal to the king were called loyalists. Put yourself in the place of such a person. Write a letter to a friend explaining why you honestly believe the Declaration to have been a mistake.
5. Organize several class committees to study the kind of government the British people had in 1776 and the type of government they have today. Write committee reports on the growth of democracy in England.

Questions to Answer

1. Which in your opinion was the most important reason the colonists gave for their separation from England? Why?
2. Why did the colonists claim the king had already given up his right to rule the colonies?
3. How would you describe a tyrant? Make a list of the characteristics of a tyrant. Name some of the tyrants in history.
4. The king encouraged the Indians to attack the colonists living on the frontiers. Would you hold the king or the Indians responsible for the attacks?
5. Do you think the colonists regretted being forced to call the English people their enemies? What is meant by "common ancestry"?
6. Suppose the colonists had lost the War for Independence. Do you think the king would have abused them even more? Do you think this occurred to any of the colonists?

A Written Exercise

Copy and complete the following sentences.
1. The colonists complained of the government the king had set up in the province of_____.

2. They were afraid the king would use that government as_____.
3. The colonists objected to the king's hiring of_____.
4. The king encouraged the Indians to_____.
5. The signers of the Declaration of Independence said that the colonies ought to be_____.

Words to Study Before You Read the Next Topic

traditions	amendments	posterity
political	tranquility	preamble
complex	flexible	fundamental
interpretations	function	signifies

The Constitution of the United States

THE Declaration of Independence is very important to us. It signifies the beginning of our free nation and our American way of life. The Constitution of the United States is even more important. *The Constitution is our written plan of government. Congress follows that fundamental plan in passing the federal laws by which we are governed.*

American democracy is built upon an understanding of one another's rights. One way to preserve these rights is to make rules or laws and choose leaders to enforce them.

When people, as a group, make rules of conduct and enforce their rules, they have a form of government. A small group of people may have a very simple form of government. A larger group must have a more complex form.

Government Is All around You

The first government a child knows is the one in the home. To live and work happily together, a family must make rules and abide by them. Members of the family must be on time for meals. They must keep their own possessions in place. They must be polite and pleasant to one another. They must do many other things for the good of the family group. The father and the mother are the leaders of the family government. It is their duty and their right to see that family rules are obeyed.

The organization of the Boy Scouts of America is another example of government. There are many *laws and rules* of scouting that must be obeyed by members of this organization. There are also many *officials* to see that the laws are obeyed.

Two things are necessary in any government. First, the *laws* that govern people in the group, town, city, state, or nation. Second, the men, or the *officials*, who enforce these laws.

Everyone who has belonged to any organization realizes the need for laws and leaders. If the members of an organization need rules, what about the people who live together in a city?

The people in a large city depend upon one another for many things. One man could not provide schools, churches, libraries, playgrounds, or a water system for his family. People in a city must work together to enjoy these advantages. To help them work and live together they make

city *laws*. City laws are usually called *ordinances*. City officials are elected to enforce the ordinances.

People also work together to form a state government and to make state laws. They elect a governor and other state officials to enforce the state laws. The people of a nation elect representatives to make laws for the entire nation. Officials are chosen to enforce those laws.

The Constitution is the plan of government for our nation. It is a good plan of government. It has safeguarded freedom in the United States for many years.

The Constitution Provides for Growth and Change

Since the Constitution was adopted, there have been many changes in the United States. A weak union of thirteen states has grown into a powerful nation of fifty states. Many small towns have grown into great cities. The invention of machinery has changed small shops into vast factories. The nation's resources have made it wealthy. Modern science has changed the way of living for every man, woman, and child.

The men who wrote the Constitution

The Boy Scouts are on an overnight hiking trip. They are enjoying themselves. They are also obeying certain democratic rules laid down by Boy Scout officials. These rules give them a form of government.

Ewing Galloway

HOW OUR GOVERNMENT MEETS CHANGING CONDITIONS

BY AMENDMENTS TO THE CONSTITUTION

FIRST TEN AMENDMENTS

OTHER AMENDMENTS

BY INTERPRETATIONS OF THE SUPREME COURT

BY NEW CUSTOMS DEVELOPED BY THE PEOPLE

PRESIDENT'S
CABINET

BY WIRE AND LETTER
INFLUENCING CONGRESS

PARTY SYSTEM

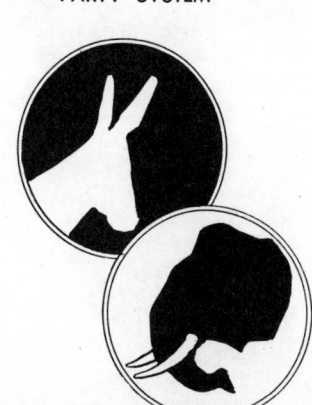

MARCEL GUILLIAMS

could not foresee such great changes, but they planned well. They made the Constitution serve their own needs. *They also planned to make it serve as the foundation for good government no matter how much the country changed.*

A plan of government must be stable. It must also be flexible, to allow for growth and change. If it is not, it will soon be discarded. The Constitution of the United States is as workable today as when it was written. How is this possible?

There are two ways in which the Constitution meets the changing needs of the nation.

1) Amendments are added to the Constitution.

2) The Supreme Court of the United States interprets the Constitution as it applies to changing conditions.

Customs, traditions, and unwritten laws also help our government serve the changing needs of the people.

Amendments That Have Been Added to the Constitution

The Bill of Rights was the first group of amendments to be added to the Constitution. From time to time, other amendments have been added. The Thirteenth Amendment abolished slavery. The Fifteenth Amendment said that no citizen could be denied the right to vote because of race or color, or because he had been a slave. The Seventeenth Amendment gave the people of the states the right to elect Senators. Before this, Senators had been elected by the state legislatures. The Nineteenth Amendment gave women the right to vote.

Together there have been twenty-three amendments added to the Constitution. They have been added because of public demand or because of public need.

The Supreme Court Interprets the Constitution

The Supreme Court of the United States is sometimes called the guardian of the Constitution. The Court is often asked to decide whether a law is *constitutional* or *unconstitutional*. A law that is *constitutional* is in keeping with the meaning of the Constitution. An *unconstitutional* law is not.

In the early days of the nation the Supreme Court used little of its authority. Today it is often asked to interpret laws passed by Congress. These interpretations apply to many things that were unknown to the men who wrote the Constitution. Some of these things are: railroads, airplanes, and buses; radio and television networks; telegraph and telephone lines.

Traditions and Unwritten Laws

The United States is a young nation. Even so, we have developed a number of important customs and traditions. These customs and traditions are not a part of our written Constitution, but they help the government to function more efficiently. They have become a part of our way of governing.

The Constitution does not provide for political parties in the United States. Yet the Republican Party and the Democratic Party have become very strong. Custom has made two or more political parties an unwritten part of our way of life.

The ringing of the Liberty Bell announced to the people of Philadelphia that the Declaration of Independence had been approved by Congress. The news soon spread to Boston and New York.

The Constitution does not say that the President must appoint a Cabinet. It suggests that he might find it advisable to secure written opinions from the heads of departments. George Washington was President of the young republic during difficult times. He wanted more than the written opinions of the department heads. He called them into conference. Soon he began to hold regular meetings. The department heads became a *Cabinet*, which advised the President.

In George Washington's time three regular departments were represented in the Cabinet. Today there are ten. But Washington's custom of calling the heads of the departments into conference continues today. The practice of holding Cabinet meetings has become an "unwritten law."

Traditions and customs are established *by the people*. If a custom is broken, it is broken through the will of the people. The Constitution originally said that a President should serve for a term of four years. It did not say *how many terms* he might serve. George Washington refused to become President for a third time. Thomas Jefferson also refused. It became a tradition to serve no more than two terms of four years each. But Franklin Roosevelt was elected for a third and then a fourth term. The tradition was broken because *the majority of the people wished to keep the same President*.

Later the people wanted to return to the old tradition. In 1951 the Twenty-second Amendment was added to the Constitution. This amendment says that no person shall be elected to the office of President more than *twice*. It also says he cannot be elected more than *once* if he has served more than two years of a term to which someone else had been elected. This is an example of how constitutional amendments express the will of the people.

The Constitution of the United States

The preamble to the Constitution expresses the hopes of the men who wrote it. It tells the goals they wished to achieve.

PREAMBLE TO THE CONSTITUTION

We the people of the United States, in order to form a more perfect union, establish justice, insure domestic tranquility, provide for the common defense, promote the general welfare, and secure the blessings of liberty to ourselves and our posterity, do ordain and establish this Constitution for the United States of America.

Notice the opening words in the introduction to our plan of government. *We the people!* Those words point up the American approach to government. The *people* decide what is to be done. The *people* set about building our democracy.

Nor did the framers of the Constitution mean just the people who were living in their time. Look at the words *secure the blessings of liberty to ourselves and our posterity.* Those words reach out—to our own day and beyond. They make it clear that the Constitution, which is based on the goals listed in the Preamble, is for the equal benefit of all Americans, for all time.

Our discussion of the Constitution will be based upon these goals: to *form a more perfect union, establish justice, insure domestic tranquility, provide for the common defense, promote the general welfare.* Some sections of the Constitution relate to one goal, some to more than one. In this book, the sections are not discussed in the order in which they appear in the Constitution. They are discussed in the order of the Preamble goals to which they are most closely related.

The Constitution, just as it was approved and signed, can be seen today in the rotunda of the National Archives. The reproduction shown here gives you a good idea of the original.

Things to Do

1. Hold class meetings to plan a class constitution. Decide upon your goals. Decide how the goals can best be achieved. Appoint a committee to do the actual writing. Then meet to discuss and vote on each provision as written.
2. Read again the preamble to the Constitution of the United States. Pretend you are a member of the Constitutional Convention. Choose one of the reasons given for drawing up the Constitution. Write a letter to a friend at home about that reason. Explain why you think it is an ideal or a goal of good government.
3. Organize the class into committees. Find out how the idea that the President should serve only two terms became a tradition. Find out how the tradition was broken, and how it later became part of the Constitution. Make committee reports to the class.
4. Make an illustrated chart showing some of the most important traditions and customs that have developed in the United States.
5. You are entertaining a friend from a foreign country. Explain to him how the Supreme Court helps a growing nation meet its needs.

Questions to Answer

1. When a plan of government is being established, what are two important things to consider?
2. Why is it necessary to establish a plan of government that will provide for growth and change?
3. Why can we say that the Constitution has proved worthy to remain our plan of government?
4. What is a constitutional law? What is an unconstitutional law? Can you think of some examples of each?
5. What is the fundamental basis the Supreme Court uses when judging a law? Why is this good for the nation?
6. Are there any traditions or customs that have developed in your town, your school, or your home? How did they develop?
7. What is an unwritten law?
8. Do you know of any customs or unwritten laws which have become written laws? Name them.
9. What do you consider the main goal around which the Constitution was written? Put this goal in your own words. Explain what it means to your way of living.
10. Is the preamble to the Constitution as important to us today as it was to the Americans who lived when it was written? Give reasons for your answer.

11. How can we keep the preamble to the Constitution alive today? What can we do to help keep its promises of *justice, domestic tranquility, welfare, defense, liberty*?

A Written Exercise

Copy and complete the following sentences, using as many words as you wish.

1. Two things necessary to any good government are_____.
2. The plan of government for the United States is the_____.
3. Three ways in which our government meets the changing needs of the nation are_____.
4. A constitutional law is_____.
5. An unconstitutional law is_____.
6. A law is declared constitutional or unconstitutional by the_____.
7. The President chooses a Cabinet in order to_____.
8. To work, play, and live together successfully groups of people must make rules and_____.

Words to Study Before You Read the Next Topic

House of Representatives	fiscal	inaugurated
presidential electors	Senate	succession
apportionment	census	adherence

To Form a More Perfect Union

HOW could the delegates to the Constitutional Convention plan a *more perfect union*? They had to keep in mind three things. First, they had to form a national government in which all the states would work together as a team. Second, they had to make sure that the government would be a government of and by the people. Third, they had to give to everyone the rights to *life, liberty, and the pursuit of happiness.*

The task was not easy. The federal government had to be given authority over national problems; the state governments authority over state problems. At the same time the state and federal governments had to protect the rights of each individual citizen. *Within the framework of the Constitution*, the national government, state governments, and individual citizens had to work together.

The Congress

A Congress consisting of two houses was planned. The House of Representatives was planned as *the house of the people*. The Senate was planned as *the house representing the states*. In the Senate each state, whether large or small, was to have two Senators. In the House, the number of representatives was based upon the number of people living in each state. States with more people had more representatives. In this way both the states and the people would have equal representation.

The makers of the Constitution believed this plan would work. It would create a happier feeling between the people in large states and those in smaller states. It would help to *form a more perfect union.*

The Constitution limits the kinds of laws that the national government can make. But the law-making powers that the national government does have are given to Congress. Individuals or departments may suggest laws. Only Congress can pass them. *The Congress of the United States consists of two houses, the Senate and the House of Representatives.*

The House of Representatives

The House of Representatives is composed of congressmen elected every two years. They are elected by the people of the state they represent. A Representative must be at least twenty-five years old. He must

Ewing Galloway

Graceful symbol of our national unity is the White House, home of the President and his family.

SENATORS

MUST BE 30 YEARS OLD

TWO ELECTED FROM
EACH STATE

ELECTED FOR 6 YEARS

MUST HAVE BEEN
UNITED STATES CITIZEN
FOR 9 YEARS

ELECTED BY DIRECT VOTE SINCE
THE 17th AMENDMENT

REPRESENTATIVES

MUST BE 25 YEARS OLD

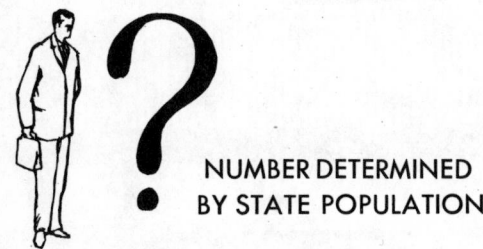

NUMBER DETERMINED
BY STATE POPULATION

ELECTED FOR 2 YEARS

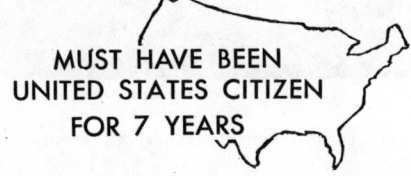

MUST HAVE BEEN
UNITED STATES CITIZEN
FOR 7 YEARS

ELECTED BY DIRECT VOTE

MARCEL GUILLIAMS

live in the state he represents. He must have been a citizen of the United States for seven years.

The number of Representatives from each state is determined by the population of the state. In this way the *people* of the nation are represented. The states having more people have more Representatives in Congress. The states having fewer people have fewer Representatives. Each state, however small, is entitled to at least one Representative.

Representatives are elected every two years. Frequent elections keep the Representatives in close touch with the voters. That means they will be more likely to understand and abide by the will of the people. They know what will happen if the people decide that their interests are not being served. They will soon vote to change Representatives!

The first House of Representatives was composed of 65 members. In 1929 Congress set the permanent membership at 435. When Alaska and Hawaii became states, there were 437 members until the 1960 census. Then a new apportionment was made on the basis of 435 members.

Sometimes a Representative dies, resigns, or is expelled from office. Then the governor of the state usually calls a special election to choose a new Representative. If a regular election is to be held in the near future, the governor may wait for the election. *He never appoints a Representative.*

Officers of the House of Representatives

Any organization must have officers and leaders to guide its activities. *The House of Representatives elects its officers.* One elected officer is the Speaker. He presides at all meetings. He also has the right to vote on all questions.

If there are more Republicans than Democrats in the House of Representatives, the Republican Party is the *majority party.* If there are more Democrats than Republicans, the Democratic Party is the *majority party.*

The Speaker of the House is always a member of the majority party. He probably wields more influence than any other federal official except the President. Indeed, if the President and Vice-President should die in office, the Speaker would become the President.

The House also elects other officers. It elects its own Sergeant at Arms, Clerk, Doorkeeper, Postmaster, and Chaplain. These are not members of Congress, but their election is controlled by the majority party.

The Sergeant at Arms keeps order in the House. The Clerk keeps a record of the activities of the House. The Chaplain opens each meeting with prayer.

The Senate

The Senate of the United States is composed of Senators. Every state has two Senators in the Senate. Each Senator has one vote. He serves for six years. A Senator must be at least thirty years old. He must live in the state from which he is elected. He must have been a citizen of the United States for nine years.

The Constitution originally said that Senators should be chosen by the state

THE HOUSE OF REPRESENTATIVES

THE VOTERS ELECT REPRESENTATIVES EVERY 2 YEARS

MEMBERS OF THE HOUSE REPRESENT THE DISTRICTS WITHIN THE STATE

REPRESENTATIVES ARE ELECTED THE FIRST TUESDAY AFTER THE FIRST MONDAY IN NOVEMBER IN EVEN-NUMBERED YEARS

legislatures. In 1913 the *Seventeenth Amendment was added to the Constitution. It allowed the people to elect their own U. S. Senators.*

Each Senator is elected for *six years*. Yet senatorial elections are held *every two years*. The Constitution stated that the first Senate should be divided into three groups. The Senators of the first group were to serve for two years. The Senators of the second group were to serve for four years. The Senators of the third group were to serve for six years.

After two years, the first group went out of office. Senators chosen for six years took their places. Next the four-year Senators completed their terms of office. Senators chosen for six years took *their* places. In another two years the Senators who served for six years completed their terms. They had to be replaced or chosen again.

The result is that now one third of the Senators are elected every two years, but all Senators serve for six years. This is an advantage. Two thirds of the Senators are always experienced. One third have been in recent touch with the voters.

When a Senate seat becomes vacant, the governor of the state usually calls a special election. In the meantime, the state law may allow him to make a temporary appointment. The temporary appointee may serve until a new Senator is elected.

Officers of the Senate

The House elects its own chairman, but the Senate does not. The Constitution says that *the Vice-President of the United States shall be the president of the Senate.*

MARCEL GUILLIAMS

The Vice-President presides over the Senate, but he is not a member of the Senate. He cannot enter into the debate on any question. Neither can he vote, except in case of a tie. The Vice-President usually attends Cabinet meetings. He is considered a link between the President and the Senate. He helps present the views of the President to the Senate. He also presents the views of the Senate to the President.

The Senate does not elect its president. However, it does choose other important officers. A new Senate convenes every two years. At this time it elects a temporary president. Another title for the Senator so elected is *president pro tempore*. The temporary president presides in the absence of the Vice-President or if the Vice-President becomes President.

The Senate, like the House, elects other officers. It elects a Secretary, Chief Clerk, Executive Clerk, Sergeant at Arms, Doorkeeper, and Chaplain. The officers chosen are members of the majority party.

Election and Assembly

The election of Representatives and Senators is held in the even-numbered years. It is held in each state on the first Tuesday following the first Monday in November. The Constitution does not say that Senators and Representatives have to be elected on that day. Maine, for instance, used to hold elections in September. Since 1957, however, Election Day in Maine has been the same as in the other states.

In states entitled to more than one Representative, the state is divided into districts. *A Representative is chosen from each*

ONLY ONE THIRD OF THE SENATORS ARE ELECTED EVERY 2 YEARS

MEMBERS OF THE SENATE REPRESENT THE STATES

SENATORS ARE ELECTED THE FIRST TUESDAY AFTER THE FIRST MONDAY IN NOVEMBER IN EVEN-NUMBERED YEARS

79

MARCEL GUILLIAMS

district. In this way a person living in a small city has as much voice in his government as a person living in a large city.

The Congress that met in 1789 was named the First Congress. The life of each Congress is two years. Thus, from 1963 to 1965 the Eighty-eighth Congress will be in office.

The Constitution says that *Congress shall assemble at least once a year.* At first the Constitution set the opening meeting for the first Monday in December. Congress still meets once a year, but the opening date was changed by the Twentieth Amendment. Congress now convenes, or assembles, in regular session on the third day of January. In addition, the President may call the Congress into special session at any time.

The President of the United States

The members of the Constitutional Convention worked long and hard to *form a more perfect union.* They created a Congress to make the laws for the nation. Then came the question, "Who shall enforce the laws passed by the Congress?"

The power to enforce the laws passed by Congress is given to the President of the United States. The President is the executive head of the government. His term of office is four years. A Vice-President is elected at the same time the President is elected. His term of office is also four years. The Vice-President becomes President if the President dies or is removed from office.

The delegates realized they must give one man power to enforce the laws. But they did not wish to give him too much power. They did not want to let him make himself a king or a dictator. For this reason they limited the term of office of the President to four years. They believed that if a President had to be elected every four years, no man could become a dictator.

At first the President was selected by *presidential electors.* Each state was allowed as many electors as it had Senators and Representatives. A state with two Senators and thirteen Representatives had fifteen presidential electors. A state with two Senators and twenty Representatives had twenty-two electors. *The people voted for the electors.* Then the electors met together. They *selected* the man they thought most capable of heading the nation.

The President is still chosen by electors. Each state still has as many electors as it has Senators and Representatives. But today the election procedure is quite different. *This part of the Constitution has been changed by tradition, or custom.*

Today each political party holds a national convention. Delegates to the convention nominate party candidates for President and Vice-President. Then the party organizations in each state select presidential electors. The names of the party's candidates for President and Vice-President are usually listed on the state ballot. Under their names are the names of the presidential electors who will vote for them.

The people vote only for the electors. They usually know beforehand which candidate each elector will name. The people vote for the electors in November. The electors meet in December and elect the President and Vice-President.

ELECTION OF PRESIDENT AND VICE-PRESIDENT

REPUBLICAN PARTY

NOMINATES CANDIDATES FOR

PRESIDENT

and

VICE-PRESIDENT

DEMOCRATIC PARTY

NOMINATES CANDIDATES FOR

PRESIDENT

and

VICE-PRESIDENT

SELECT

REPUBLICAN ELECTORS

DEMOCRATIC ELECTORS

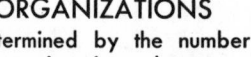

THE STATE PARTY ORGANIZATIONS
Number of electors is determined by the number of Senators and Representatives in each state.

THE PEOPLE

VOTE FOR THE

ELECTORS

WHO WILL VOTE FOR

PRESIDENT

and

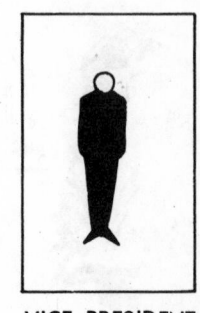

VICE-PRESIDENT

THE PEOPLE VOTE EVERY 4 YEARS FOR ELECTORS

THE PRESIDENT OF THE UNITED STATES

TERM OF OFFICE 4 YEARS

MUST BE A NATIVE-BORN CITIZEN

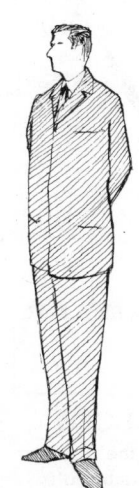

MUST BE AT LEAST
35 YEARS OF AGE

MUST HAVE RESIDED IN THE UNITED STATES FOR 14 YEARS

MARCEL GUILLIAMS

The President must be at least thirty-five years old. He must have lived in the United States for fourteen years. He must be a native-born citizen. He cannot be a naturalized citizen.

A native-born citizen is a person born in the United States, its territories, or possessions. He may also be a person who is born of American parents in a foreign country or on the high seas.

What happens if both the President and Vice-President die or are unable to continue in office? Congress passed the Presidential Succession Act to handle that problem. Government officials would succeed to the presidency in this order: Speaker of the House, President Pro Tempore of the Senate, Secretary of State, Secretary of the Treasury, Secretary of Defense, Attorney General, Postmaster General, Secretary of the Interior, Secretary of Agriculture, Secretary of Commerce, and Secretary of Labor.

A President-elect might die before he takes office. If this happens, the Vice-President-elect becomes President.

The day on which the President takes office is called Inaugural Day. Until 1936 the President was inaugurated on March 4, following his election. Then the Twentieth Amendment was passed. *The Twentieth Amendment says that the President shall take office on January 20, following his election.*

The Chief Justice of the Supreme Court administers the oath of office to the President. The President places his hand on the Bible and then repeats the following oath: "I do solemnly swear (or affirm) that I will faithfully execute the Office of President of the United States, and will to the best of my ability, preserve, protect and defend the Constitution of the United States." Then he adds, "So help me God." Placing the hand on the Bible and saying "So help me God" are both traditions.

After the President repeats the oath of office, he gives a speech. It is called the inaugural address. The inaugural address is broadcast over the radio and televised. Millions of people listen to the inaugural program on the radio. Millions hear and see it on television. All over the world, people have an opportunity to hear and see the new President of the United States.

Until 1873 the President's salary was $25,000 a year. In 1873 it was increased to $50,000. In 1909 it was increased to $75,000, and $25,000 a year traveling expenses were added. In 1948 it was increased again. *Today the President receives a yearly salary of $100,000. His expense allowance is $50,000. He also gets an allowance for travel and entertainment not to exceed $40,000. The Vice-President receives a yearly salary of $35,000, plus $10,000 for expenses.*

The White House is the official residence of the President and his family. Here the President lives and carries on his executive duties while he is in Washington. The White House was first occupied by President John Adams, in 1800. It has been rebuilt and renovated several times. Even today, however, it still has much of the original architecture. Many of the original furnishings are still there.

The first floor of the White House contains elaborate rooms for state affairs. There are smaller rooms for private dinners and receptions. The second and third floors are for the President, his family, and his guests.

83

SUCCESSION TO THE PRESIDENCY

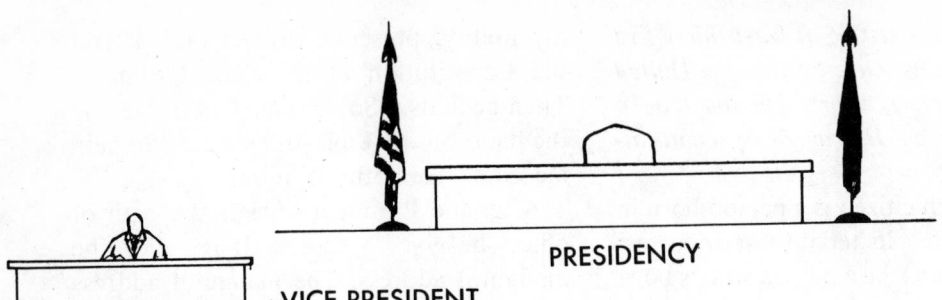

PRESIDENCY

VICE-PRESIDENT

SPEAKER OF THE HOUSE

The Secretaries of Agriculture, Commerce, and Labor are also included in the succession. They follow the Secretary of the Interior in the order named.

PRESIDENT PRO TEM
OF SENATE

SECRETARY OF STATE

SECRETARY OF THE TREASURY

SECRETARY OF DEFENSE

ATTORNEY GENERAL

POSTMASTER GENERAL

SECRETARY
OF THE INTERIOR

84

No branch of our government is completely independent. The framers of the Constitution formed a careful system of checks and balances. For instance, the President can make treaties with other nations. A treaty is not valid, however, until the Senate has approved it by a two-thirds vote. All important appointments made by the President must also have Senate approval.

The President selects ambassadors to foreign countries, federal judges, and Cabinet members. He appoints officers of the armed forces. He names postmasters in the larger cities. These are some of the most important of many appointments. In some cases he must divide appointments between members of both major parties.

The President's Cabinet

To aid the President, Congress has created ten regular departments. *The President, with the approval of the Senate, appoints the heads of these departments.* The heads of these departments make up the President's Cabinet.

The Department of State

The Department of State has charge of the foreign affairs of the nation. It protects our interests in any part of the world. It sees that treaties, trade agreements, and international law are carried out. It issues passports to citizens of the United States

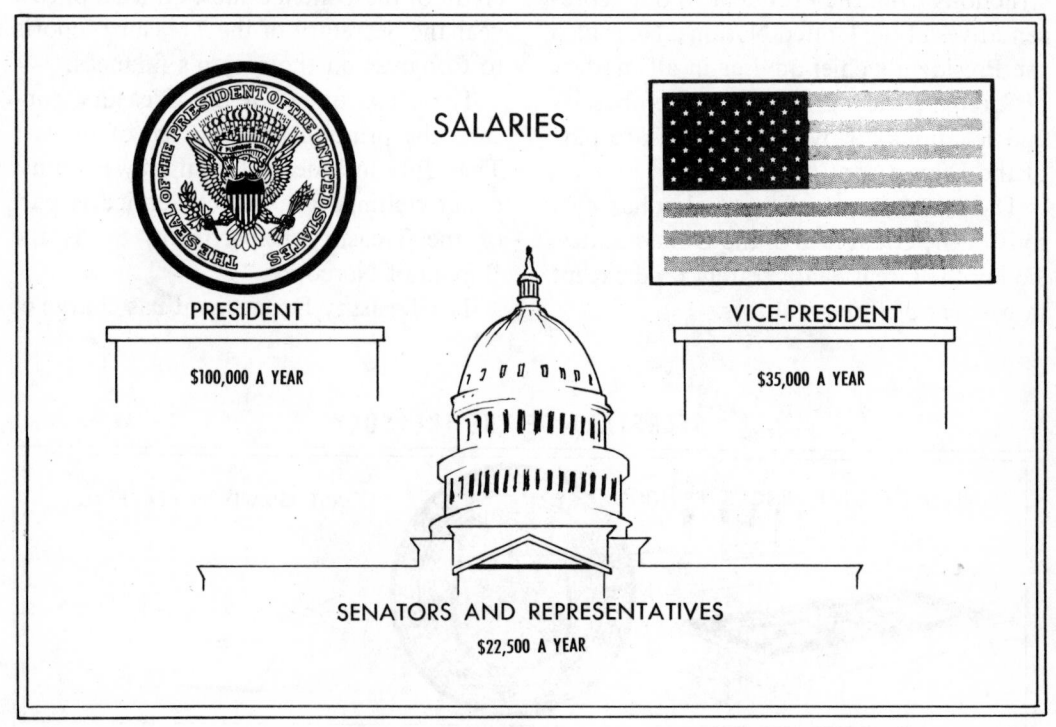

SALARIES

PRESIDENT

$100,000 A YEAR

VICE-PRESIDENT

$35,000 A YEAR

SENATORS AND REPRESENTATIVES

$22,500 A YEAR

MARCEL GUILLIAMS

SECRETARY OF STATE

who wish to travel in foreign countries. It issues visas, or visitors' permits, to foreigners who want to visit the United States. It arranges for artists and students from other countries to visit us. It also arranges for American artists and students to go abroad. The Secretary of State carries instructions from the President to our representatives at the United Nations. He is also the President's chief adviser in all matters of foreign policy. United States embassies and legations all over the world are part of the Department of State.

The Department of State also has custody of the Great Seal of the United States. Today the Great Seal is rarely used except in matters of foreign affairs.

The Department of the Treasury

The Department of the Treasury has charge of the nation's finances. The Secretary of the Treasury and his assistants supervise the collection of taxes. They arrange for the borrowing of money on the credit of the United States. At least once a year the Secretary of the Treasury reports to Congress on the nation's finances.

The Department of the Treasury controls the printing and coinage of money. That duty includes enforcing laws against counterfeiting. The Secret Service is part of the Treasury Department. So is the Bureau of Narcotics.

The Treasury Department has charge of

SECRETARY OF THE TREASURY

BUREAU OF ENGRAVING & PRINTING   COAST GUARD IN PEACETIME

MARCEL GUILLIAMS

the construction of public buildings owned by the government. It has charge of the Bureau of Engraving and Printing. It directs the Coast Guard, except in time of war. In wartime, the Coast Guard is considered as part of the Navy. It is then under the direction of the Department of Defense.

The Secretary of the Treasury is the head of the Treasury Department. But he is not the Treasurer of the United States. That is a separate office. The office was established in 1789. It became part of the Fiscal Service of the Treasury in 1940. The Treasurer of the United States acts as the banker for the entire government. He collects the money, pays out the money, and accounts for the money. He is in charge of borrowing money for government use, and of paying principal and interest on the public debt. Government checks are drawn on the Treasurer of the United States, not on the Secretary of the Treasury.

The Department of Defense

The Department of Defense sees that the military establishments of the nation are maintained. It has charge of the enlisting and the equipping of men in the Army, the Navy, the Marines, and the Air Force. It makes contracts for supplies. It arranges for the transportation of our armed forces. It sees that the nation has military, air, and naval fortifications to defend our seacoasts, harbors, and cities. The Department maintains navy yards, airfields, and army posts. It superintends the upkeep, the operation, and protection of the Panama Canal. It also has charge of improving our waterways.

The Department of Defense superintends the training of our armed forces. It has charge of the United States Military Academy (West Point), the National War College, and Industrial College of the Armed Forces (Washington). It has charge of the Naval Academy at Annapolis and the Air Force Academy at Colorado Springs. It supervises the administrative work of the Court of Military Appeals.

The Secretary of Defense works closely with the heads of all branches of the armed forces. He tries to keep their work from overlapping. He tries to keep all the armed services working together as a team.

SECRETARY OF DEFENSE

ARMY U.S. ARMY AIR FORCE USAF NAVY

IMMIGRATION LAWS

FEDERAL BUREAU OF INVESTIGATION

ATTORNEY GENERAL

The Department of Justice

The Department of Justice has charge of the legal affairs of the nation. The head of the Department is the Attorney General. The Attorney General prosecutes offenders who break the federal laws. He advises the President on legal affairs when requested to do so. The heads of departments may also consult him.

The Attorney General conducts cases before the Supreme Court. He supervises the work of the United States district attorneys and marshals. The work of the Federal Bureau of Investigation (FBI) is under his direction.

The Department also administers the naturalization and immigration laws of the nation.

The Post Office Department

The first Postmaster General was Benjamin Franklin. He was appointed in 1775, under the Continental Congress. The foundation for much of our present-day postal system was planned by Franklin. In his day there were few post offices. Now there are nearly thirty-six thousand!

Article I of the Constitution gave Congress the power to "establish Post Offices and post Roads." The first Postmaster General under the Constitution was appointed in 1789. It was not until forty years

POSTMASTER GENERAL

MARCEL GUILLIAMS

later, however, that the Postmaster General became a member of the President's cabinet. Today he is listed as eighth in the order of succession to the Presidency.

The Postmaster General has charge of one of the largest businesses in the world. He makes arrangements for the transportation and delivery of tons of mail each day. He enters into postal agreements with foreign countries. He decides what new issues of postage stamps should be brought out, and when. To help him carry out his duties and responsibilities, the Postmaster General has more than 500,000 employees.

The Department of the Interior

The Department of the Interior has charge of our public lands. It supervises Indian affairs, national parks, and some of our territories and possessions.

This Department has many different offices and bureaus. The Bureau of Land Management surveys, manages, buys, and disposes of public lands. The Bureau of Reclamation develops irrigation and drainage projects.

The Geological Survey investigates water supplies and sources of electric power. It supervises oil, gas, and mining operations on public lands. It is always looking for more natural resources. When new sources are found, they are shown on geological survey maps.

The Fish and Wild Life Service helps to conserve and increase different kinds of wild life. The Office of Indian Affairs supervises all matters relating to Indian tribes—their land, money, supplies, and schools. The Bureau of Mines surveys mineral resources. It also tries to improve health and safety conditions in mines.

The Department of Agriculture

The Department of Agriculture helps to improve the farming industry. The Department has many bureaus. The Bureau of Animal Industry fights animal diseases. The Bureau of Plant Industry searches for ways to improve crops. One bureau fights insect pests. Another studies the problems of grading, inspecting, and marketing farm products.

SECRETARY OF THE INTERIOR

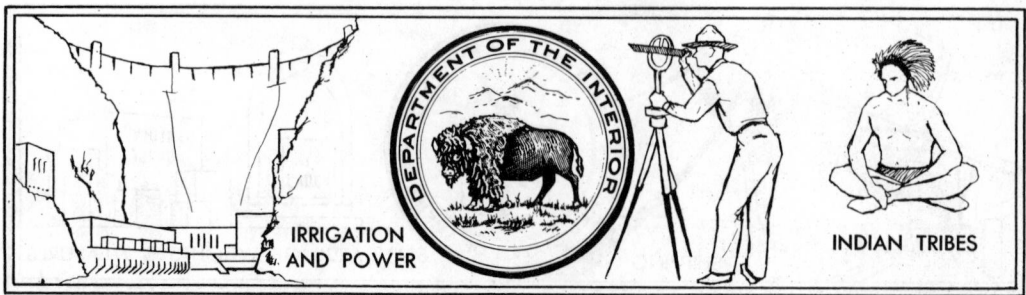

IRRIGATION AND POWER

INDIAN TRIBES

SCIENTIFIC FARMING

PEST CONTROL

SECRETARY OF AGRICULTURE

The Forest Service and the Soil Conservation Service are also important divisions of the Department of Agriculture.

The Department of Commerce

The Secretary of Commerce is interested in everything affecting commerce. He tries to promote and improve manufacturing, shipping, fisheries, and transportation. The Department supervises the Lighthouse Service. It inspects steamships. It has charge of the licensing of merchant ships and the licensing of air pilots. It registers and supervises airplanes used in business. It collects information relating to foreign and domestic commerce. It also supervises the taking of the census every ten years.

The Patent Office and the Bureau of Standards, which fixes the standards of weights and measures, also belong to this Department. Weather forecasts and storm warnings are this Department's responsibility. It is this Department, too, that supervises the spending of federal funds for highway improvement.

The Department of Labor

The purpose of the Department of Labor is to promote the welfare of the workers, or wage earners, of the United States. The Department tries to improve working conditions. It tries to open up opportunities

SECRETARY OF COMMERCE

SHIPPING

1 POUND

BLOCK GAUGE

STANDARDS OF WEIGHTS & MEASURES

CHILD LABOR LAWS

SECRETARY OF LABOR

for employment, especially for the physically handicapped. It helps set up apprentice and training programs. It also helps to settle disputes between workers and employers.

The Department investigates the welfare of women and children in industry. It sees that the laws to protect them are enforced. It also gathers and publishes material about labor problems.

The Department of Health, Education, and Welfare

The Department was established to promote the general welfare in the fields of health, education, and economic security. The Public Health Service helps protect and improve the health of the people. The Office of Education helps to improve our schools.

The Social Security Administration administers Federal Old-Age and Survivors Insurance. It approves state plans for aid to needy people. The blind, the aged, the permanently disabled, and dependent children receive such aid.

The Office of Vocational Rehabilitation works with the states to teach handicapped persons useful occupations. The Food and Drug Administration sees that federal laws concerning certain foods and drugs are carried out. It tries to see that all products covered by these laws are pure. It makes sure the products are labeled truthfully.

SECRETARY OF HEALTH, EDUCATION, AND WELFARE

The Ten
Departments

The heads of these ten regular departments make up the President's Cabinet. Cabinet meetings are held once or twice a week. Each member reports on the affairs of the nation relating to his department. The President uses this information as a basis for decisions.

Independent
Agencies

Some national problems require specialized agencies to deal with them. These special agencies are in the executive branch of the government. They are not under any of the ten regular departments, however. Instead of being headed by a secretary, the independent agency is usually administered by a *board* or a *commission*. The board or commission members are appointed by the President. But they are not members of his Cabinet.

Among the most important of the independent agencies is the Atomic Energy Commission. Another is the Federal Reserve System, which supervises banking operations throughout the country. The General Services Administration is the "housekeeping" department of the government. It buys and sells and leases government buildings. It sees that they are kept clean and in good repair. It buys needed supplies for government use. It sells equipment no longer being used.

The Securities and Exchange Commission was set up to protect the public against unfair dealings in the field of financial investments. The U.S. Civil Service Commission has charge of selecting people to work for the government. Another independent agency is the Veterans Administration. It carries out all the laws which give benefits to veterans and their families.

There are many other independent agencies in the executive branch of our huge government. Those mentioned here are just a few of the important ones.

The Constitution,
the Supreme Law of the Nation

The Constitution is the supreme law of the United States. Next in order come treaties and federal laws, state constitutions, state laws, and local or city laws. The judges in all states are bound by the Constitution, regardless of the state laws.

The Supreme Court may declare that any law made by Congress is unconstitutional. It may declare unconstitutional any state law that conflicts with the meaning of the Constitution. It may declare unconstitutional any law that conflicts with other laws or treaties made under the Constitution. An unconstitutional law cannot be enforced.

All state and federal officers must take an oath to support the Constitution. The Constitution clearly states that no officer shall be made to pass a religious test of any kind. A few states ask their officeholders to declare their faith in God. No state requires adherence to any one religion.

The members of the Constitutional Convention wanted a strong and united national government. They declared the Constitution supreme over any state or any state law. They believed that only in this way could they *form a more perfect union.* Only in this way could they create a truly united nation.

Things to Do

1. As a group of citizens, hold a meeting to try to find candidates for vacancies in the House of Representatives and the Senate. Discuss the qualifications needed for each office. Consider age, citizenship, occupation, and the kind of person needed.

2. Draw a diagram showing the organization of the House of Representatives. (Speaker of the House, Sergeant at Arms, Doorkeeper, Chaplain, Clerk, etc.) Draw a companion diagram illustrating the organization of the Senate.

3. You are the governor of a state from which a Representative in Congress has recently died. You receive a letter from a voter, asking how the vacant seat will be filled. Answer the letter. Explain to him how a Senate vacancy is filled also.

4. Some Americans believe we could adopt a better method of electing a President. Write down what such a method might be. List the ways in which it would be better than the present plan.

5. Find out the exact duties of the Doorkeeper of the House of Representatives. Find out who occupies that post at the present time.

6. The Federal Trade Commission and the Federal Communications Commission are both independent agencies. Choose one of them to study. What are the purposes and duties of the commission? Who heads it? Where was it established? Why do you think it became necessary to establish it? Can you find a magazine story or news article referring to the work of the commission?

Questions to Answer

1. Which department in the government issues passports?
2. Which department is most concerned with our natural resources?
3. Suppose you are a U.S. Marine. Which member of the President's Cabinet has final responsibility for directing your activities?
4. How does the Speaker of the House attain that position?
5. Who was the first Postmaster General?

A Written Exercise

Copy and complete the following sentences, using as many words or phrases as you choose.
1. The Constitution grants all lawmaking powers to_____.
2. The two houses of Congress are_____.
3. The Constitution established two houses of Congress because_____.

4. The number of Representatives from each state is determined by
_____.

5. The number of Senators from each state is_____.
6. A Senator is elected for_____.
7. The presiding officer of the Senate is_____.
8. The Vice-President does not have a vote in the Senate unless_____.
9. The life of each Congress is_____.
10. Congress convenes in regular session on_____.

Words to Study Before You Read the Next Topic

consuls	continuously	filibuster	infringement
impeachment	abuse	slander	ambassadors
navigable	evidence	reprieve	unconstitutional

To Establish Justice

IT is difficult to separate the various goals of the Constitution. The makers of the Constitution tried to *form a more perfect union*. Yet one of the most important ways to form a more perfect union was to *establish justice*. Establishing justice was a *means* toward forming a more perfect union. It was also an important goal, or *end*, in itself. This topic will discuss ways in which the Constitution seeks to establish justice, but these are not the only ways. Almost every section of the Constitution helps to establish justice in some form.

The Power of Impeachment

Most government officials are honest and hard-working. Sometimes there may be one who is not. Even some President of the United States might prove unworthy of his high office. The Constitution protects the people against dishonest officials. The President or any federal officer who does not carry out his duties in an honorable way may be *impeached*. That means he may be charged with wrongdoing.

The evidence against an official accused of wrongdoing must first be presented to the House of Representatives. The House considers the evidence. If it seems to justify a trial, the House places formal charges against the official. *The charges are then presented to the Senate. When the official is tried, the Vice-President presides at the trial. The House of Representatives conducts the trial. The Senate sits as a court to judge the evidence.*

If the President of the United States is on trial, the Chief Justice of the Supreme Court presides. The Vice-President does not preside because he might have a personal interest in the impeachment. If the President were impeached and found guilty, the Vice-President would become President.

Since the adoption of the Constitution, thirteen federal officials have had impeachment charges brought against them. Eleven have been impeached and brought to trial in the Senate. Four have been found guilty and removed from office.

The Senate can remove the convicted men from office. It can forbid them to hold any government office. It does not have the power to punish them after their removal. The men can be tried in other courts, however.

Other Laws That Help to Establish Justice

Each house is the judge of the elections and the qualifications of its own members. Neither house shall proceed with business unless it has a quorum.

Occasionally the election of a congress-man may be in doubt. Several times Congress has refused to seat elected members whose elections were thought to be unfair. Either house may refuse to seat a member-elect if a majority votes against him.

A *quorum* is the number of Senators or Representatives needed to proceed with

IMPEACHMENT PROCEEDINGS

Impeachment proceedings must originate in the House of Representatives.

If the House believes the evidence justifies a trial, formal charges are made.

The formal charges are then sent to the Senate.

HOW THE PROSECUTION IS CONDUCTED

The Vice-President presides unless the impeachment charges are against the President.

The Senate sits as the jury.

Then the Chief Justice of the Supreme Court presides.

The House prosecutes.

business. In the Senate fifty-one members make a quorum. In the House of Representatives two hundred eighteen are needed. In other words, a *majority* of the membership is needed for a quorum. Sometimes there is important legislation to be passed and a quorum is not present. When that happens, the Sergeant at Arms may compel absent members to attend.

Each house has the right to punish its own members for disorderly conduct. Each house may make its own rules of order. The House of Representatives is larger than the Senate. It has found more need for laws and rules. One of the most important laws in the House limits the debate of each member. In other words, no one is allowed to speak longer than one hour. This rule is enforced unless all members of the House consent to let a member speak longer.

The Senate does not have a rule governing the length of speeches. However, sixteen members may petition that a debate be closed. The Senate votes on the petition. A two-thirds vote may close the debate on any measure. This is called the *closure rule*, or *cloture rule*. Even after the closure rule is in force, the debate continues for a time. Each Senator is allowed one hour in debate before a vote is taken on that measure.

Once in a while a Senator may abuse his right of debate. He may *filibuster*, or talk continuously, to prevent the passage of a bill. A filibuster in the Senate may be very unfair. A bill proposed by one house must also pass the other house before it can become a law. Even one Senator might prevent the passage of a much-needed law if he chose to carry on a filibuster.

The Constitution states that *during the regular session of Congress neither house may adjourn for more than three days without the consent of the other.* This helps the two houses work together as one Congress.

A congressman cannot be arrested while Congress is in session, except for a serious crime. This is to protect a congressman. With this rule, no one can arrest him for a minor offense to keep him from voting.

Senators and Representatives have complete freedom of speech while they are on the floor of Congress. This is not true of speeches made outside of Congress. It is not true of anything published outside of Congress. Outside of Congress, a congressman may be sued for slander or libel just as any other citizen.

The Constitution gives privileges to the congressmen. It also puts restrictions upon them. During the time for which they are elected, *Senators and Representatives cannot be appointed to any civil office they have helped to create. They cannot be appointed to any civil office in which they have helped to increase the salary. They cannot hold any other federal office so long as they remain in Congress.*

Representatives and Senators are paid by the federal government. Each receives a salary of $22,500 a year and a $2,500 tax-free expense allowance. The Representative who is elected Speaker of the House receives a $35,000 yearly salary and $10,000 for expenses.

Federal Courts to Establish Justice

The final judge of all federal laws in the United States is the Supreme Court of the United States. The Court is composed of a

RULES GOVERNING HOUSES OF CONGRESS

SENATE

51 Senators make
a quorum

HOUSE

218 Representatives
make a quorum

HOUSE and SENATE

Both must pass a bill before
it can become a law

SENATE

A two-thirds vote limits debate
to one hour

HOUSE

One hour limit of debate
for each member

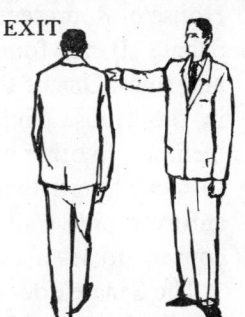

HOUSE and SENATE

A two-thirds vote may expel
a member from either house

MARCEL GUILLIAMS

Chief Justice and eight associate justices. The justices are appointed by the President, with the approval of the Senate.

To relieve the Supreme Court of some of its burden, Congress created a system of lower federal courts. These include United States District Courts, United States Courts of Appeals, a Court of Customs and Patent Appeals, and a Court of Claims.

The United States District Courts are trial courts. There is at least one such district court in each state. Some states have as many as four. These federal courts handle cases that involve the Constitution,

the laws of Congress, and treaties with foreign countries. Federal courts sit in judgment on disputes that arise on the high seas or upon navigable waters. If a crime has been committed on the seas, the accused person is brought before the United States District Court nearest the place where he is landed.

Any court may decide whether a law is constitutional or unconstitutional. If the decision is questioned, it may be appealed. The federal appeals courts have authority to review most decisions of the U.S. District Courts. Sometimes, only the Supreme

RULES GOVERNING MEMBERS OF CONGRESS

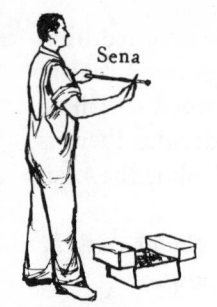

NEITHER
...nators nor Representatives
...ay hold any other office

NEITHER
house of Congress may adjourn
for more than three days without
the consent of the other

NEITHER
a Senator nor Representative
may be arrested during a session
except for a serious crime

...OUSE and SENATE
...h houses may approve or
...st the election of members

NEITHER
a Senator nor Representative
may be appointed to
an office he helped to create

HOUSE and SENATE
Both Senators and Representatives
have complete freedom of
speech on the floor of Congress

MARCEL GUILLIAMS

Court itself has that authority. The Supreme Court also reviews many decisions of federal appeals courts or state supreme courts that are appealed to it. The Supreme Court hears the appeal, then makes its decision by a majority vote. Cases involving ambassadors, public ministers, consuls, or states are brought directly to the Supreme Court. In any case, the decision of the Supreme Court of the United States is final.

The Court of Customs and Patent Appeals is just what its name implies. It decides questions relating to customs duties on imported products. It also considers cases of infringement of trademarks or patents.

The Court of Claims judges most civil claims against the United States government. *A civil claim is a claim that asks money for the violation of a personal right.* Such a claim might arise from work done for the government under a contract. If a person feels his rights have been violated by the federal government, he may take his case to the Court of Claims. If the Court directs payment, Congress votes the necessary money to pay the claim.

One protection against tyranny is the right of a trial by jury. The framers of the Constitution realized this. They wrote into the Constitution that *all criminal cases tried in federal courts shall be tried by a jury, except in cases of impeachment. They shall be tried in the state where the crime was committed.*

The men who wrote the Constitution were determined to *establish justice.* Federal judges and Supreme Court justices are appointed for life. They cannot be removed from office unless impeached by the House and found guilty by the Senate.

A federal judge does not depend upon the wishes of men in government. He cannot lose his office because he makes a decision that does not please someone.

The makers of the Constitution wanted the highest courts of the land to guarantee justice to all. That is why they made a judge's term of office depend on his good behavior.

The Writ of Habeas Corpus

There are many provisions in the Constitution which establish justice. *The Constitution states that every person is entitled to a writ of habeas corpus.* A writ of habeas corpus is a legal paper. It prevents a person from being held in jail without a proper charge against him.

"Habeas corpus" is a Latin term. It means "that you have the body." The writ is a court order. It directs an officer of the law to bring an arrested person *immediately* into court.

The person is then told the reason for his arrest. The judge listens to his story and to the story of the men who arrested him. If the judge decides there is good reason to hold the man, he is returned to jail to wait for trial. If the judge decides there is not enough reason to hold him, the man is released.

No person in the United States may be held in prison without just cause.

More Laws to Establish Justice

The Constitution states that Congress cannot pass a bill of attainder. A bill of attainder would allow officials to punish a man without giving him a trial. Congress is also prohibited from passing any *ex post facto* law. An ex post facto law makes punishable an act committed before the law was passed. *The Constitution protects every citizen of the United States against bills of attainder and ex post facto laws.*

The President has the power to grant pardons or reprieves to persons convicted of offenses against federal laws. He can grant reprieves and pardons for offenses committed in the District of Columbia and certain territories of the United States. He cannot, however, pardon or reprieve any person convicted on impeachment charges.

A reprieve means a temporary delay in carrying out the sentence of a prisoner. Suppose a man convicted of a crime is sentenced to be executed on a certain date. The morning he is to be executed he receives a thirty-day reprieve. This means that his execution will be delayed for thirty days.

A pardon frees a prisoner from his sentence. It restores to him all his rights as a citizen.

Things to Do

1. On the blackboard write some of the rules by which Congress is governed. Choose one of the rules and explain it.
2. Make a list of reasons why jury trials in federal cases help to establish justice. List reasons why you think the Constitution requires trials to be held near the place where the crime was committed.
3. As a class, write a letter to the lawyers' club or bar association in your county. Invite them to send one of their members to address your class. Indicate that you are particularly interested in hearing about cases that involve
   a) the writ of habeas corpus;
   b) ex post facto laws;
   c) an appeal to the Supreme Court of the United States;
   d) the U.S. Court of Claims.
4. Write a short story illustrating the injustice of a bill of attainder.
5. Try to find, by doing research at the library, one occasion on which Congress held impeachment hearings. What were the results? Prepare a report of your findings.
6. Try to find a newspaper or magazine account of a filibuster. Bring it to class. In your own words, describe the filibuster process. Tell whether one man must talk constantly, or whether he can find ways to rest without ending the filibuster.

Questions to Answer

1. What number of pupils in your room would constitute a quorum?
2. How do you think a certain kind of law came to be known as *ex post facto*?
3. What is the difference between a reprieve and a pardon?
4. What is the exact meaning of each of these words: Representative; Senator; congressman?
5. Do you think a filibuster is a good thing or a bad thing? Give reasons for your answer.

A Written Exercise

Copy each of the following sentences, using only the lettered word or phrase that makes the sentence correct.
1. The impeachment trial of a President is presided over by
   a) the President of the Senate.
   b) the Chief Justice of the Supreme Court.

2. When a man has been found guilty of an impeachment charge, the Senate has the power to
   a) remove him from office.
   b) punish him according to the seriousness of his crime.
3. Either house in Congress can refuse to seat a new member
   a) if the President requests it.
   b) if a majority of the house votes against the new member.
   c) if the Supreme Court feels he is not worthy of holding office.
4. A quorum in Congress is
   a) a majority of the members of either house.
   b) one hundred Senators or Representatives.
5. Each house in Congress is governed by laws made by
   a) the President.
   b) the Supreme Court.
   c) its own members.
6. During the regular sessions of Congress, neither house may recess without the consent of the other for more than
   a) three days.
   b) five days.
   c) one week.
7. Representatives and Senators are paid by
   a) the state in which they live.
   b) the federal government.
8. The number of judges in the Supreme Court is
   a) seven.
   b) nine.
   c) ten.
9. A writ of habeas corpus is
   a) the written decision of the judge.
   b) a court order that demands an immediate hearing for a person accused of a crime.
   c) a written warrant for the arrest of a person accused of a crime.

Words to Study Before You Read the Next Topic

Congressional Record	annulling	certificate
alien	alliance	bankruptcy
provision	impairing	currency

To Insure Domestic Tranquility

THE third goal of the preamble is to *insure domestic tranquility*. Domestic tranquility means peace within the nation. A people happy within their own country will fight to keep their homes and their way of life. They will not seek war. The framers of the Constitution knew that peace was important to their new nation. They knew that it would not last unless its people were at peace with one another. They put into the Constitution provisions which they believed would keep peace and harmony.

Laws That Insure Domestic Peace

In a democracy it is important that the people understand the laws by which they are governed. When they understand the laws they are more willing to obey them. They are more likely to understand their responsibility for helping to build good government.

Each house in Congress keeps a journal of its daily proceedings. The account of the proceedings is printed in the Congressional Record. In addition, at the end of every session of Congress each house publishes a complete history of the bills and resolutions which have come before it.

These publications are found in most public libraries. Anyone can order his own copies by writing to the Superintendent of Documents, Washington, D.C.

The provision requiring Congress to print a record of all its actions is wise and just. It reminds Congress that the people are really the judges of good government.

The Constitution states that no duty shall be laid on articles exported from any state. The men who wrote the Constitution knew that, to keep peace, all states must have equal rights. The Constitution forbids any state to tax articles brought in from other states. This law builds trade between the states. It also helps to create a feeling of friendliness.

There is another provision that helps to keep peace among the states. *In states which have seaports or river ports, the ports are governed by the same rules of commerce. The duties in every port are the same. No vessel going to or from a port in one state is required to pay duty in a port in any other state.* In the early days some seaports tried to draw trade by charging low duties. The Constitution stopped that. It made duties the same everywhere. *It gave every seaport the same opportunity.* This provision of the

Constitution encouraged trade between the states. People who trade together have an added reason for getting along together.

The Constitution also states that *no title of nobility shall be granted in the United States. No person holding any office of trust under the United States government can accept a present, an office, a title, or a decoration from any foreign country without the consent of Congress.* This may not seem so important today. When the Constitution was written, however, that provision helped to create faith in the new government.

Restrictions upon the States

The makers of the Constitution knew that the federal government must be stronger than the state governments. For this reason they wrote into the Constitution certain restrictions upon the states.

No state may enter into any treaty, alliance, or confederation. If the states were allowed to make treaties or alliances, the nation would be in danger. The United States is a powerful country. Yet one state making an alliance with an enemy could undermine the strength of the whole nation.

No state may pass a law impairing the obligation of a contract. When people sign a contract, each signer promises to do certain things. But sometimes conditions change. One party may tire of the bargain and want it changed. At one time the states could pass laws which allowed them to change or cancel contracts. They cannot do this now.

No state may grant any title of nobility. No state may pass a bill of attainder.

No state may pass an ex post facto law.

No state may coin money or issue paper money.

No state may impose duties on imports or exports, except what may be necessary to pay the cost of state inspection. Even then all such laws are subject to revision and control by Congress. Any money left over after state expenses are paid must be turned over to the United States Treasury.

No state shall, without the consent of Congress: lay a duty on the tonnage (or carrying capacity) of a vessel; keep troops or ships of war in time of peace; enter into any agreement or compact with another state or a foreign power; engage in war unless actually invaded, or when in such immediate danger that there is not time for the federal government to act.

There was a reason for each of the restrictions upon the states. Why do you think the writers of the Constitution would not allow the states to keep troops or ships of war? They wanted to encourage the people to count on the federal government for protection. All the restrictions were planned to help the states to work together and unite as one nation.

Other State Provisions

Besides having restrictions put upon them, the states retained certain rights and privileges. *Under the Constitution every state has equal rank. The laws, trials, and legal records of any state must be held in good faith in all other states.*

Suppose a man is sued in the State of California. Judgment is brought against him for $10,000. Suppose the man wishes

104

STATE RESTRICTIONS UNDER THE CONSTITUTION

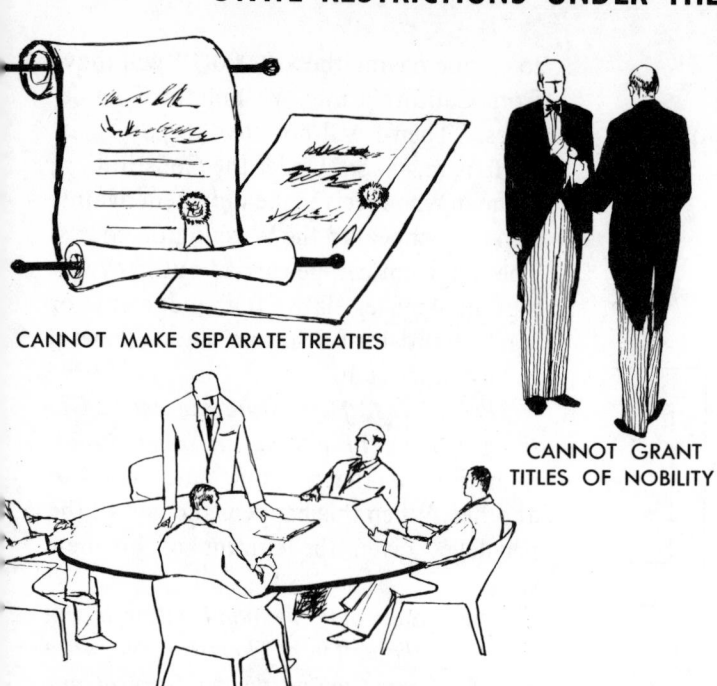

CANNOT MAKE SEPARATE TREATIES

CANNOT GRANT
TITLES OF NOBILITY

CANNOT PASS
LAWS ANNULLING OBLIGATIONS

CANNOT PASS AN EX POST FACTO LAW

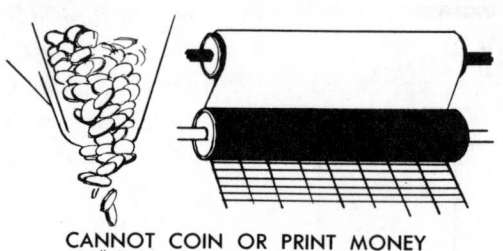

CANNOT PASS A BILL OF ATTAINDER

CANNOT COIN OR PRINT MONEY

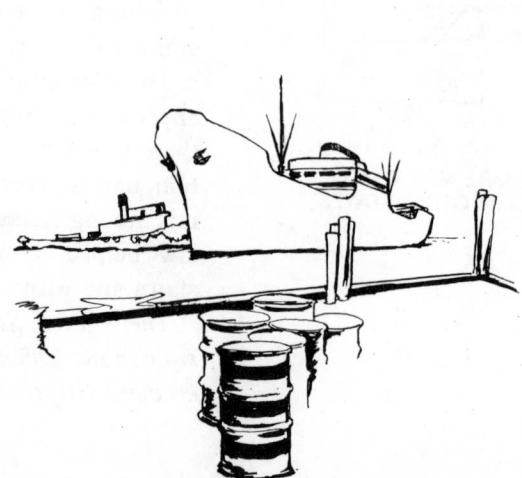

CANNOT ENGAGE IN
RATE WAR UNLESS INVADED

CANNOT LEVY
PORT OR TONNAGE DUTIES

CANNOT
MAINTAIN ARMED FORCES

MARCEL GUILLIAMS

LAWS OF ONE STATE MUST BE
RESPECTED IN OTHER STATES

STATE LINE

CITIZENS FROM ONE STATE MAY ENJOY
CITIZENSHIP PRIVILEGES IN OTHER STATES

to escape paying the $10,000. "I will move from California into Washington," he decides. "Then I will not have to pay."

He is mistaken. Under the Constitution, the men who received the judgment against him may appeal to the Washington courts. The judgment can be carried out in Washington. Any legislative act, judgment, or legal record lawful in one state is lawful in any other state.

The citizens of any state are entitled to the privileges of citizens in other states. Sometimes a citizen of one state moves to another. When this happens, he has all the privileges given the citizens of his new state.

New states may be admitted into the Union by the action of Congress. No state may be formed within the territory of another state without the consent of the state legislature and the Congress. No new state may be formed by the joining of two or more states without the consent of the state legislatures and the Congress. Not even parts of states may join together without the consent of both the state and the federal governments.

Maine separated from Massachusetts and became a state in 1820. This was possible because the Massachusetts lawmakers and the Congress both gave their consent.

The Constitution requires Congress to approve new states. If it had not done so, there might have been disputes over state boundaries. There might have been quarrels among states and parts of states. This law helped to keep peace between the states and within the nation.

The United States guarantees to every state in the Union a republican form of government. It protects each state against in-

vasion. It protects each against violence from its own citizens, if the state legislature so requests. If the legislature is not in session, the governor may make the request.

A government in which *the people rule through their chosen representatives* is a republican form of government. It is sometimes called a democratic form of government, or a democracy. A democratic form of government does not mean that the nation is governed by the Democratic Party. A republican form of government does not mean that the nation is governed by the Republican Party. *A democracy, or a republic, is a government controlled by the people. The people's representatives form the policies of the nation.*

If one state or a group of states should try to set up a dictatorship, the federal government would step in. It would force the state to remain a part of the nation.

This has never happened in the United States. However, the government has protected states against invasion. In 1817 federal troops protected Georgia from invading Indians. In 1845 troops were sent into Texas. The U.S. troops prevented Mexican troops from occupying territory claimed by both Texas and Mexico.

Sometimes a governor or a legislature feels that a situation in a state is out of control. Either may ask that federal troops be called in to prevent violence.

Other Laws to Promote Tranquility

Congress shall establish a uniform rule of naturalization. Naturalization is the process by which an alien (or foreigner) becomes a citizen of the United States.

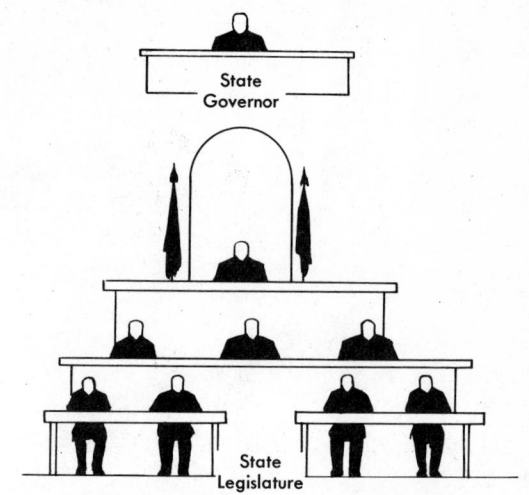

STATES ARE ALLOWED TO ESTABLISH THEIR OWN STATE GOVERNMENTS

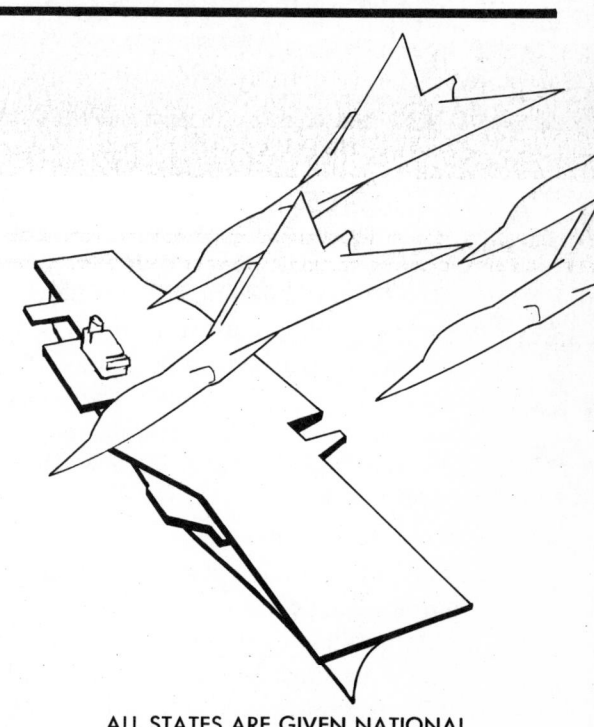

ALL STATES ARE GIVEN NATIONAL PROTECTION

FPG

Dollar bills are printed in large sheets. Here the sheets are being counted automatically.

To become a citizen, an alien must have lived here continuously for five years. If he, or she, is married to a United States citizen, three years is enough. The alien goes first to an office of the Naturalization Service. With him he takes people who can testify to the length of time he has lived here. He also takes two persons who can testify he is of good moral character. Then he files his petition to become a citizen.

After filing, he studies to take an examination in English, United States history and government. While he is studying, the Service checks to see that he is eligible to become a citizen. If so, he is notified of the date he may take his examination.

If he passes the examination, he appears in court. A member of the Naturalization Service recommends that he be made a citizen. If the court approves, the alien takes the oath of citizenship. He pledges to support the Constitution and the laws of the United States. Then he receives his certificate of naturalization. The certificate makes him a citizen. It also makes his minor children citizens.

Congress shall establish uniform laws regarding bankruptcy. There was a time when a person who could not pay his debts could be thrown into prison. This cannot happen today. A person who cannot pay his debts may seek relief under the bankruptcy laws of the nation. Most of his property is divided among those to whom he owes money. Then he is released from his debts.

Congress has the power to coin money and to regulate its value. This is one of the most important powers of the Congress. If each state had a different system of currency, confusion would result. The nation could not be truly united.

The federal government coins silver, copper, and other metals. It issues paper money and certificates. The coins are minted in Denver and Philadelphia. The paper money is printed by the Bureau of Printing and Engraving in Washington, D.C. It is guaranteed in part by gold and silver deposits in the Treasury. The rest is guaranteed by government securities. Paper money is the government's promise to pay.

Congress fixes the standard of weights and measures. It is easy to understand why the federal government controls weights and measures. If there were no standard of distance, there might be disputes over land boundaries. If there were no standard of

weights and measures, there might be quarrels over things bought and sold. These standards help to keep peace among both states and individuals. To carry out this provision of the Constitution, Congress created a Bureau of Standards in Washington. The Bureau established standards for measuring weight, distance, temperature, volume, and many other things.

The Constitution says that *Congress shall provide punishment for any person who counterfeits the securities or the current coin of the United States.* "Current coin" is coin that is now legal tender.

Counterfeiting means making imitation coins or paper money and using them as real money. Counterfeiting is both a federal and a state offense. A convicted counterfeiter may be sentenced to as many as fifteen years in prison. He may be fined as much as $5,000.

There are many provisions in the Constitution which help to create and preserve harmony. Without harmony no nation can progress, no people can be happy. Harmony within the nation has helped the United States become a world power. It has helped the people work together to build a better future. The men who wrote the Constitution were wise in their choice of goals. *To insure domestic tranquility* is one of the most important goals mentioned in the preamble.

CONGRESS CONTROLS THE COINAGE AND PRINTING OF MONEY

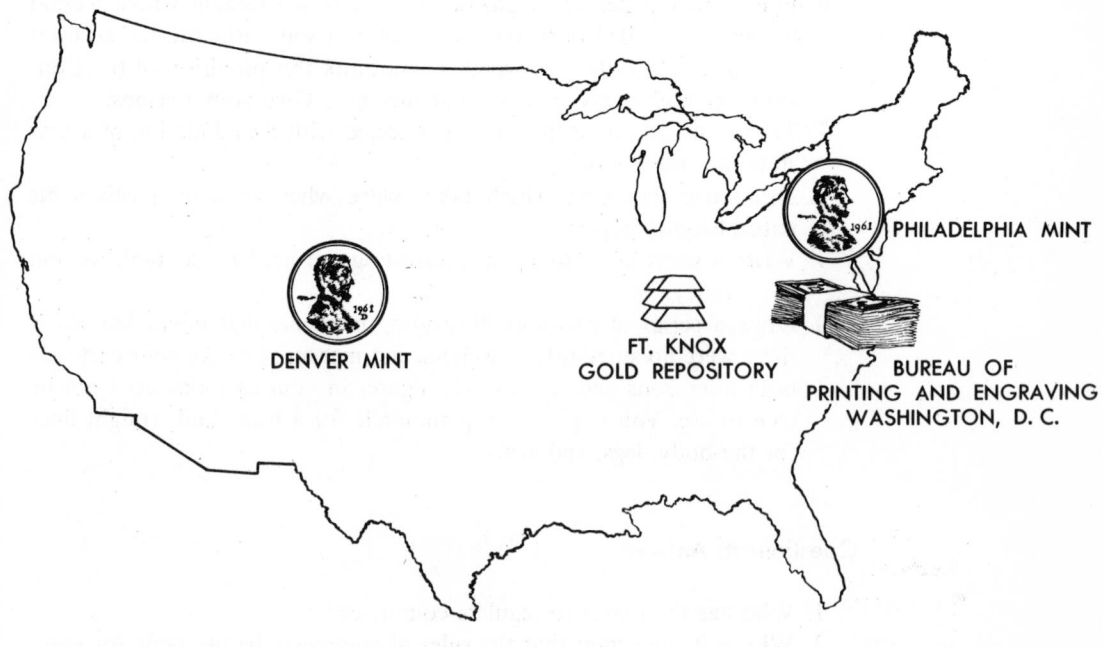

PHILADELPHIA MINT

DENVER MINT

FT. KNOX
GOLD REPOSITORY

BUREAU OF
PRINTING AND ENGRAVING
WASHINGTON, D. C.

MARCEL GUILLIAMS

Things to Do

1. Get a copy of the Congressional Record. Read and discuss it in class. Tell why you think it is necessary for the people of the United States to know what their representatives are doing.
2. The Constitution forbids a tax on articles exported from one state to another. It makes every port in the nation subject to the same rules of commerce. Give a short talk explaining how this encouraged commerce between the states. Write a short paragraph explaining how it helped the nation to be at peace.
3. Why do you think the Constitution prohibits government officials from accepting presents, titles, or decorations from any foreign country without the consent of Congress? Could such acceptance harm the interests of the United States today? How?
4. The framers of the Constitution felt it very important to put into the Constitution a provision denying any state the right to enter into a treaty, alliance, or a confederation. Is this provision still important today? Write a class play showing what might happen if your own state entered into an agreement with a foreign power.
5. Why is it important that every state have equal rank under the Constitution? Try to find an example showing how a legislative act considered lawful in one state is accepted as lawful in another state.
6. Find a newspaper or magazine account of a situation where federal troops were called in to restore order in a state. Rewrite the account in your own words. Tell whether you think this provision of the Constitution was wisely used in that instance. Give your reasons.
7. Try to find an interesting story connected with the admission of a new state into the Union.
8. Dramatize the scene which takes place when an alien receives his naturalization papers.
9. Write a short story or poem illustrating the need for a stable system of currency.
10. Draw a series of cartoons illustrating incidents that might happen if there were no standards of weights and measures. Make your cartoons both humorous and serious. The figures in your cartoons need not be true to life. You might use a plain circle for a head, and straight lines for the body, legs, and arms.

Questions to Answer

1. Who has the power to regulate commerce?
2. Why is it important that the rules of commerce be the same for every state?

3. What is meant by a republican form of government?
4. How can an alien become a naturalized citizen of the United States?
5. Why do you think the makers of the Constitution put a law about bankruptcy into the Constitution?
6. Who has the power to coin and regulate the value of money in the United States?
7. Who created the Bureau of Standards?
8. Why is it dangerous for the welfare of the nation to have counterfeit money in circulation?

A Written Exercise

On a piece of paper write the numbers 1 through 7. After number 1, write the letter that appears before the phrase which makes the statement correct. Do the same with each number.

1. The Congressional Record is a written record of
   a) the order in which bills come before Congress.
   b) the names of the lobbyists who have worked for a bill passed by Congress.
   c) the bills that have been read by title in the Senate.
   d) the debates, motions, speeches, and votes of the congressmen.
2. Under the Constitution no state has the power to
   a) levy taxes.
   b) maintain a militia.
   c) make treaties with foreign nations.
   d) establish a system of public education without the consent of Congress.
3. The Constitution gives the power to admit new states into the Union to
   a) the Senate.
   b) the Secretary of State.
   c) the Congress.
   d) the President.
4. A new state may be formed within the boundary of another state if
   a) the people living in the area sign a petition asking that a new state be formed.
   b) the governor and the state legislature agree that a new state should be formed.
   c) the state legislature and the Congress of the United States both consent.
5. To become a naturalized citizen, one of the things a person must do is
   a) prove that he is able to support himself and his family.
   b) promise to obey our laws.
   c) reside in the United States for eight years.

6. Under the Constitution the states are allowed to
   a) coin and issue money.
   b) pass bills of attainder.
   c) pass laws impairing the obligation of a contract.
   d) maintain a militia.
   e) grant titles of nobility.
7. The Constitution guarantees to each state
   a) the right to levy a tax on articles exported from other states.
   b) a republican form of government.
   c) the right to regulate interstate commerce.

Words to Study Before You Read the Next Topic

regulations	penalty	commissioners
maintain	witnesses	District of Columbia
militia	arsenals	circumstantial

To Provide for the Common Defense

IF the states were to share and share alike, they needed common safeguards. Danger to one state meant danger to the nation. The Pilgrims had won their fight for the right to live in the New World because they had all worked together. The states must also work together, but *people can work together better if they feel secure.*

To "provide for the common defense" was an important task to the planners of the Constitution.

Crimes upon the High Seas

The Constitution gives Congress the power to define and to punish piracy and other crimes upon the high seas. It gives Congress the power to punish persons who break laws agreed to by all nations.

In peacetime each country has the authority over all ocean waters near its shores. Beyond these coastal waters the ocean is called the high seas. The high seas are open to all nations on equal terms.

Piracy is robbery taking place on the high seas. It is an offense against the laws of all nations. The usual penalty for piracy is life imprisonment.

On the high seas other serious crimes *aboard United States ships* are also subject to our federal laws. A ship flying the flag of the United States must obey the laws of the American government. It must obey American laws even though it may be on the high seas or in foreign waters.

The United States must have authority over the waters around its shores. If it did not, the country would always be in danger. The nation could not protect its interests upon the high seas. It could not remain a world power.

Declaration of War

Congress may declare war and make rules concerning captures on land and water.

It is right that only Congress, *the representatives of the people,* should have the power to declare war. The declaration of war is one of the most important steps ever taken by any country. It is a step too important to be trusted to any one man.

A declaration of war should be the will of the people. It should be made only when our honor, freedom, and way of life are threatened.

Only then will people be willing to fight to protect their homes and their country. *In the United States, war may be declared by both houses of Congress. Such a step must also be approved by the President.*

Congress has made a set of rules governing captures on land and water. These regulations are in keeping with the Constitution. They must be obeyed by the Army, the Navy, and the Air Force.

The Armed Forces

Congress has the power to raise and support armies. It can vote money for that purpose for a period of two years.

Congress decides how large the standing army shall be. It then votes money to care for the soldiers for two years, or until the next Congress takes office. The President and the Department of Defense send recommendations to Congress. They make suggestions about the size of the army needed. Congress may or may not act upon these suggestions.

The Constitution also says that *Congress shall provide and maintain a navy.* The United States has two long coastlines. It has a large world trade. Our flag flies on islands in many parts of the world. An army alone cannot defend our coastlines, our islands, and our interests in other parts of the world. A navy is a very necessary part of the nation's defense at any time. *The Congress must also vote money to maintain the Navy.*

Congress provides and maintains an army, navy, and air force. *It makes rules governing these armed forces.* Congress represents the people. Thus, the *people* control the armed forces of the United States. No man, or group of men, can establish a military dictatorship in the United States.

In addition to the regular armed forces, each state has a National Guard. The

P.I.P.

These young men are students at the United States Naval Academy at Annapolis, Maryland. Such students are called *midshipmen*.

114

National Guard is a reserve military organization. Its main job is to protect the state during times of local emergency. In time of war the Guard may become a part of the regular army.

The National Guard is organized and trained under the supervision of the Department of Defense. Congress provides part of the money to care for the National Guard. The rest is provided by the state.

Each state may also have a *state guard*. This state guard has different names in various states. In times of danger the President calls the National Guard to serve the nation. It is then that the state guard may serve *within the state*. The state guard never serves outside its own state.

The President is commander in chief of the Army, the Navy, and the Air Force. He is also commander in chief of the state militias when the militia is called into the active service of the nation. In time of war the President takes command of all the nation's armed forces.

The President does not have the power to declare war. Once war is declared, however, he commands the armed forces.

Treason against the United States

The Constitution defines treason as: (1) levying war against the United States; or (2) giving aid or comfort to any persons or any nation that are enemies of the United States.

The crime of treason is a very serious one. The framers of the Constitution wanted to protect the United States against treason. They also wanted to protect the people from being wrongly convicted of treason.

They did not want anyone to be convicted on circumstantial evidence alone. For that reason, they made special rules for treason trials.

Under the Constitution, one of two things must happen before a person can be convicted of treason. He may be convicted if two witnesses saw him commit a treasonable act. He may be convicted if he confesses his crime in open court. In no other ways can a person be found guilty of treason against the United States.

The punishment for treason may be death. It *must* be not less than five years in prison and a fine of $10,000. A person found guilty of treason can never again hold a government office. He loses his citizenship. He also loses any rights he might have as a veteran.

The Constitution gives Congress the power to decide the punishment for treason. It also states clearly that only the convicted person shall be punished. An innocent member of the guilty person's family cannot be punished.

Lands over Which Congress Has Complete Control

Congress has complete control over the District of Columbia. It has control over any land where there are federal forts, arsenals, docks, or government buildings.

The Constitution gave Congress complete control over the future seat of government of the United States. New York was the first seat of government. Then Philadelphia became government headquarters. In 1800 the city of Washington in the District of Columbia became the capital. The District of Columbia has been

under the control of Congress ever since.

Residents of the District of Columbia do not have a voice in their government. They cannot vote for their local officials. But they can vote for the President and Vice-President of the United States. The District is governed by a board of three commissioners. Two of the commissioners are appointed by the President, with the approval of the Senate. They must be residents of the District. The third commissioner must be an Army engineer. He, too, is appointed by the President. The District is not represented in Congress.

The government owns much land throughout the nation. All sites for arsenals, lighthouses, post offices, military airfields, and navy yards belong to the government. These lands are under the direct control of Congress. This is another way in which the writers of the Constitution planned for the *common defense*.

Lighthouses, like this one located on the "rockbound coast" of Maine, are built on federal property.

Things to Do

1. Make a collection of pictures illustrating the life of men and women in one branch of the armed forces.
2. Find some pictures of government-owned sites of land throughout the nation. Name at least three reasons why you believe the federal government should control these lands.
3. Make a poster or a chart illustrating the difference between treason in the United States and in a totalitarian country. Include in your poster or chart the effect of treason on a man's family in the United States and in a country ruled by a dictator.
4. The House and the Senate each have a *standing committee* to handle matters pertaining to the District of Columbia. By doing some research at the library, find out more about standing committees in Congress. Why are they necessary? How are they selected? What are the names of some of them? Make a report to the class.

Questions to Answer

1. What is piracy?
2. What do we mean by the high seas?
3. How is war declared in the United States?
4. What is the difference between the National Guard and the state militia?
5. Why do you think the framers of the Constitution said Congress could vote money for the armed forces for only two years?
6. Why do you think the residents of the District of Columbia were not allowed to vote in either local or national elections? In what way did the Twenty-third Amendment change this situation?
7. What are some of the public land sites which are owned by the government? Why is it necessary or wise that these sites be owned by the government?
8. Does the property of a man convicted of treason against the United States become the property of the government?

A Written Exercise

Copy and complete the following sentences.
1. In the United States, the commander in chief of the armed forces is_____.
2. Treason is defined in the Constitution as_____.

3. A treason conviction requires the testimony of_____.
4. Residents of the District of Columbia cannot_____.
5. The family of a person convicted of treason against the United States is_____.

Words to Study Before You Read the Next Topic

conveniences   intrastate   interstate
appropriation   enacted   adaptable
bonds   emergency   frontier
dredge   veto   resolution

To Promote the General Welfare

THE last goal of the Constitution is also important. *To promote the general welfare* is to consider the needs of all the people. It is to provide things that will make the people healthy, happy, and prosperous.

Many sections of the Constitution help to promote the welfare of the people. One of the most important has to do with taxes. It says that *Congress, the representatives of the people, shall have the right to levy and collect taxes, duties, imposts, and excises to pay the debts and provide for the common defense and welfare of the country. All duties, imposts, and excises shall be the same throughout the nation.* Duties, imposts, and excises are different forms of taxes which may be levied.

At first glance, it may not seem that paying taxes helps keep people healthy, happy, or prosperous. Many people object to taxes. But the purpose of a tax is to collect money to support the various branches of the government. The nation as a whole benefits from taxes. The country is improved through the use of taxes. All people share alike in the improvements. They all benefit from good roads and mail service. They all benefit from national defense and other things that taxes make possible.

Tax money is used to take care of all the nation's needs. But sometimes the tax money is not enough. The nation may be faced with an emergency or a great danger. In such times the government must often raise money quickly. When that happens, *Congress has the power to borrow money on the credit of the United States.* The Secretary of the Treasury may make suggestions as to how the money shall be raised. Congress makes the final decision.

The government usually borrows money by issuing and selling bonds. In time of war it may sell bonds and stamps. The government also issues bonds in peacetime. Anyone who buys a government bond, either in time of war or in peace, lends the government money for a certain length of time. When the money is due, the government repays it with interest.

A person who lends the government money has no fear that his money will not be repaid. He knows that the government of the United States has been, and will continue to be, a stable government. He knows that his money will be repaid when the loan is due.

There are other sections of the Constitution that help to promote the welfare of

119

the people. *Congress has the power to regulate commerce with foreign nations, among the states, and with the Indian tribes.*

Commerce includes all forms of transportation on land, by water, and in the air. It includes the movement of messages, goods, and persons. Telegraphs, telephones, radio and television networks, and other means of communication are a part of commerce. So are railroads, buses, airplanes, and other means of transportation.

Commerce that begins and ends within the borders of a state is called *intrastate commerce*. It is controlled by the state. Commerce that crosses a state border is called *interstate commerce*. It is controlled by the federal government.

Under the *interstate clause*, Congress can regulate the sale of goods between states. It can forbid the sale of harmful drugs from one state to another. It can see that diseased cattle are not sent across a state border. It can prevent the shipment of impure foods across state lines.

Under this clause Congress can also build lighthouses, dredge rivers and waterways, and build flood controls. It can aid the development of transportation and communication. This clause is small but it is very important. It has done much to improve business and living conditions. It has done much to promote the welfare of the nation.

Other Provisions for the Welfare of the People

Congress shall provide for the establishment of post offices and post roads. Post

CONGRESS HAS THE POWER TO REGULATE BOTH FOREIGN AND INTERSTATE COMMERCE

SUPERVISION OF INDIAN TRIBES

FOOD AND DRUG REGULATION

FLOOD CONTROL

MAINTENANCE OF WATERWAYS

LIVESTOCK INSPECTION

LIGHTHOUSE CONTROL

MARCEL GUILLIAMS

offices and other aids to communication are not only conveniences; they are necessities. A nation without a good system of communication will not grow and develop. It will not remain united.

While the nations in Europe were forming, there were few means of communication. It was difficult to travel from one country to another. People did not know much about their neighbors across the river or over the mountain. They developed different languages and different customs. People with the same languages and customs naturally grouped together. They formed their own systems of government. They became little republics or small kingdoms.

In the United States it was quite different. The pioneers who opened up the new territory to the west wanted to keep in touch with friends and relatives back home. They wanted to be able to write to them.

As the frontier pushed westward, means of communication were developed. *Through communication* the bond between the hardy pioneers and the people in the east was maintained. This bond kept the pioneers interested in the affairs of the young nation. It made them want to join the Union once their territory was developed.

The delegates to the Constitutional Convention had to look far into the future. They had to ask themselves, "Will all the vast territory to the west ever be colonized? If so, will it remain one big nation?" Many men who attended the Convention believed that it would. They realized how important it was to establish a good system of communication. It was important to the people at home. It was important to the

Ewing Galloway

The United States Postal Service is one of the largest businesses in the world today.

pioneers opening up the vast new wilderness. It was a problem too important to be left to chance. They assigned the task to Congress.

Congress has performed its task well. The United States has one of the best systems of communication in the world.

The Constitution also says that *Congress shall promote the progress of science and useful arts. It shall protect authors and inventors by granting them patents and copyrights.*

The encouragement of arts and sciences is an important part of the American way

121

of life. Through patent and copyright laws, the government has tried to protect inventors and authors. It has tried to encourage inventors to invent new and more useful things. It has tried to encourage authors to create good literature for our education and enjoyment.

A *patent* is a grant given to a person who invents something. It gives him, for seventeen years, the *sole right* to make, use, and sell his discovery in the United States, or in any territory flying our flag. Anyone else who manufactures the article without permission from the inventor may be sued for damages.

The *copyright law* protects authors, composers, publishers, and artists. It protects their books, magazines, newspapers, lectures, plays, musical compositions, maps, works of art, drawings, photographs, illustrations, and motion pictures. No one else is allowed to copy their works for twenty-eight years, without special permission. To do so, could bring a very heavy penalty.

A patent or copyright may be renewed once. If the person who holds the original patent or copyright dies, his heirs may renew it.

Guarding the Public Purse Strings

Money cannot be drawn from the public treasury unless Congress votes a definite appropriation. A regular statement must be published from time to time. It must give an account of the money taken in and the money spent.

Congress has full control of the purse strings of the nation. Congress alone can order the spending of money. The President may ask Congress for money to be spent for the good of the nation. Congress itself must appropriate, or vote, the money before it can be touched. The Treasury Department issues a statement at the close of each day's business.

The men who wrote the Constitution believed that no one man should be allowed to impose taxes upon the people. They believed that the people should pay only those taxes voted by their representatives. They believed that the people, *through their representatives*, should decide how the tax money should be spent. The people

elect congressmen. They can see from the daily financial statement of the United States Treasury how Congress is spending their money. As nearly as possible, *the people of the United States control the purse strings of the nation.*

The President Helps to Promote the General Welfare

The Constitution states that the President shall (1) *from time to time, give Congress information about the condition of the country,* and (2) *recommend the passage of such laws as he thinks are necessary for the welfare of the nation.*

U.S. Army

The President delivers a message to Congress at the beginning of each regular session of Congress. This message is often called the "State of the Union" message. In it the President discusses the most important national problems. He may suggest ways to solve these problems. Today millions of people hear or read the President's message. Thousands of them may let the President know that they agree or disagree with him.

The President also sends or delivers other messages to the Congress while it is in session. These messages usually concern national problems that have arisen. The President explains the problems. He may recommend that Congress pass laws to deal with the situation.

Sometimes an important problem arises while Congress is not in session. *The President may then call a special session of the Congress.* The President does not often need to do so. Nevertheless, the provision is a wise one. It makes it possible for the government to provide at all times for any emergency.

The President also formally receives heads of state, ambassadors, and public ministers from other countries. He appoints and consults with our own ambassadors and ministers. He commissions, or authorizes the Defense Department to commission, all of the officers of the United States Army, Navy, and Air Force. He and his administrative assistants see that all laws passed by Congress are carried out.

The "hat throw" is a traditional part of graduation day activities at the United States Military Academy, West Point, New York.

123

Lawmaking Promotes
the General Welfare

Any bill to raise money must originate in the House of Representatives. Later the Senate may propose amendments to such bills. Bills to promote the general welfare may originate in either house.

After any bill is approved by one house, it must be sent to the other house. If it is passed by both houses, it is sent to the President for his approval.

If the President approves a bill, he signs it. If he does not approve a bill he returns it, with his objections, to the house where it originated. That house records the objections of the President in its journal and reconsiders the bill. If, after reconsideration, the bill is again passed by a two-thirds vote, it is sent to the other house. If the second house also passes the bill by a two-thirds vote, it becomes a law without the President's signature.

When a bill is reconsidered, the votes in both houses must be "yeas" and "nays." The names of the persons voting for and against the bill must be entered in the journal, both in the Senate and in the House.

If a bill is not returned by the President within ten days (Sundays excepted) after it is presented to him, the bill becomes a law, unless Congress adjourns before the ten days have passed. If Congress adjourns before the ten days are up, the bill does not become a law unless the President signs it.

All these rules regarding legislation are written into the Constitution. Including them was another way in which the framers of the Constitution safeguarded our welfare. No law can be imposed upon the people by any one man or any one group of men. To become a law, a bill must go through the democratic process outlined in the Constitution.

How a Bill
Becomes a Law

The Constitution sets forth the *rules* for enacting laws. Congress, through the years, has worked out lawmaking *procedures*. The procedures are in keeping with the Constitutional provisions.

Hundreds of bills are introduced in every session of Congress. Most of them are never enacted into law. Each one, however, must go through certain steps.

Let us say a Representative decides to introduce a bill. He may first call the Legislative Counsel. The Counsel will help him put his thoughts into legislative language.

When the bill has been drafted, the Representative places it in a box on the desk of the Clerk of the House. This is called "putting the bill in the hopper." The Clerk gives each bill a number. The numbered bills are sent to the Government Printing Office and printed. The next step is to refer the printed bill to the appropriate congressional committee.

A Senator who wishes to introduce a bill may simply stand and wait to be recognized. The president of the Senate recognizes him by saying, "The Senator from ....," naming the Senator's state. The Senator may then introduce several bills at once and ask that they all be referred to appropriate committees. None of the bills, of course, can be bills to raise money.

Each house has a number of regular, or standing, committees. From time to time

HOW A BILL IN CONGRESS BECOMES A LAW

Bill is introduced in House and referred to appropriate committee.

It may be reported out with or without change —or it may be shelved.

Rules ("traffic") Committee may delay bill—or even pigeonhole it indefinitely.

House then debates the bill. If it is passed (with or without revision) bill is sent to the Senate.

If a majority of members of the House sign a petition requesting it, bill can bypass committee and come up for vote.

Senate committee considers bill, may shelve it or report it out to the floor.

If Senate passes bill and it differs from House version, it goes to conference.

Conference may adopt a compromise. This is submitted to both houses.

If he signs, bill becomes law; if he vetoes, both Houses can override by two-thirds majority.

If both houses accept the compromise, the bill goes to President for signature.

PICTOGRAPH CORPORATION

125

both houses create additional special committees. Often bills in either house are introduced by a committee chairman.

Each committee studies and discusses as many bills as it can. When it has reached a decision regarding the merits of a bill, it prepares a report. If the majority report is favorable, the bill with the committee's recommendation is sent back to the House where it originated. It is placed on a calendar and scheduled for consideration by the entire chamber.

When a committee fails to report on a measure, it is usually the end of the measure. It is said to have "died in committee." Occasionally a majority of the members of the House of Representatives may sign a petition and force a bill out of committee. This is rarely done in the House and never in the Senate.

After a committee has sent a bill back to the House or Senate, the measure is open for debate. If, after debate, it is passed by a majority in that house, it is sent to the other house. If it is passed by a majority there, too, it is sent to the President for his approval.

If one house changes a bill that is sent to it, the bill must be sent back to the original house. If the original house does not agree to the changes, a conference committee is appointed. The conference committee is composed of members of both houses. The conference committee adjusts the parts of the bill that are questioned. Then the bill is returned to both houses for approval. If it is approved by both houses, it is sent to the President.

The President must sign or veto each bill as it is. He cannot veto parts of the bill and sign other parts. He must approve or veto the complete bill. If he vetoes a bill, he must return it to the house where it originated. He must send with it a written statement of his objections.

A vetoed bill may still become a law, provided Congress repasses it. If it is repassed by a two-thirds majority in each house, it becomes a law without the approval of the President.

The President must return a bill within ten days or it becomes a law. That gives the President time to study the bill. It does not permit him to hold up the passage of a needed law.

It sometimes happens that Congress adjourns before the ten-day period (excepting Sundays) has passed. In that case, the bill does not become a law *unless the President signs it*. If the President does not sign, it dies by what is known as a "pocket veto."

After a bill has been approved by both houses of Congress and signed by the President, it is turned over to the General Services Administration. There it is given a serial number. The number is preceded by the letters "P.L.," which stand for "Public Law." At the end of each session of Congress, all the new laws are published. Even before that time, copies of them may be obtained from the Government Printing Office.

The Constitution avoids giving too much power to any one branch of the government. It provides for a system of checks and balances. Thus, Congress must send legislation to the President for approval. That gives the President a check on Congress. But that check is balanced by another. Congress, in turn, can pass laws over the President's veto—but only when two thirds of the Congress approve.

The Constitution states that *any resolution, order, or vote of both houses must be sent to the President for approval*. This has been taken to mean any resolution, order, or vote *having the force of law*. A resolution of sympathy, for example, does not need the President's approval. But a declaration of war needs such approval. It has the same meaning as a law.

Congress Controls
the Territories of the United States

Congress has the power to make all needful regulations governing territories and dependencies of the United States. In other words, our national government is concerned with the general welfare of people in our territories and dependencies. In most cases, this concern has had very happy results. All the lands that were once territories of the United States have now become states. Alaska and Hawaii were territories until 1959. Each elected its own legislature, but territorial governors were appointed by the President. Now that Alaska and Hawaii are states, the people elect their own officials.

The United States still has many dependencies, however. These include Guam, Wake Island, the Midway Islands, and American Samoa. The Virgin Islands, the Panama Canal and the Canal Zone, and Puerto Rico are dependencies, too. Most of these dependencies were acquired by treaties of one kind or another. Guam, for instance, was ceded to the United States by Spain in 1898. A treaty with the Republic of Panama gave the United States jurisdiction over the Canal Zone.

With the Virgin Islands, however, the story was different. They were formerly called the Danish West Indies. We bought them from Denmark for twenty-five million dollars. Their inhabitants have been United States citizens since 1927.

In the Virgin Islands and in Guam, the governor is appointed by the President of the United States. Puerto Rico, however, has almost complete home rule. All officials are elected by the Puerto Ricans. Puerto Rico sends one delegate to Congress. He can serve on congressional committees. He can take part in debates. He cannot, however, vote on any question.

The other dependencies are governed in various ways, as determined by Congress. The Department of the Interior is charged with administering some of them.

The United States also has a hand in administering certain other lands. In 1945 representatives from fifty countries met in San Francisco. After two months of discussion of world problems, they organized the United Nations. They hoped that this new organization would help the governments of the world maintain peace and promote the welfare of people everywhere. One thing the organization did was to set up the International Trusteeship System. This operates under the direction of a Trusteeship Council. The Trusteeship Council is the guardian of the Non-Self-Governing Territories. Its goal is to safeguard the rights and privileges of the people in these territories. It also tries to prepare the people to be ready to govern themselves. The United States is a member of the United Nations and of its Trusteeship Council. As such, the United States serves as trustee of some groups of islands in the Pacific. These are the Carolinas, the Marshalls, and all the Marianas except Guam.

HOW AMENDMENTS TO THE CONSTITUTION ARE PROPOSED

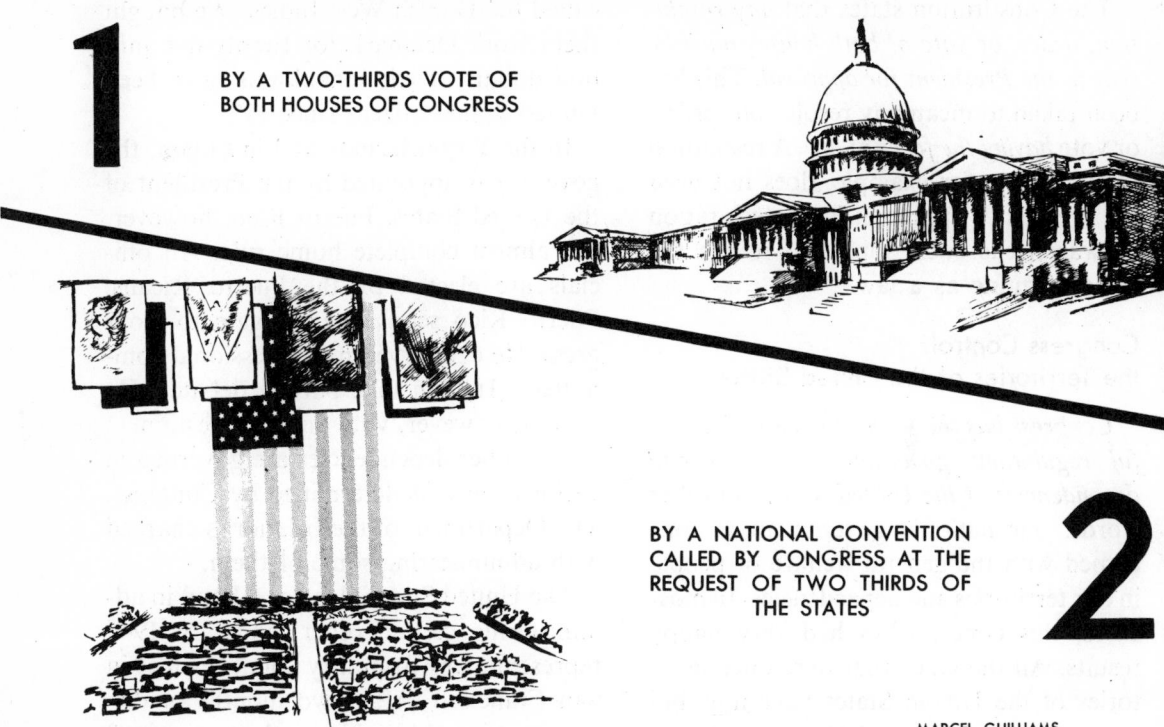

1 BY A TWO-THIRDS VOTE OF BOTH HOUSES OF CONGRESS

2 BY A NATIONAL CONVENTION CALLED BY CONGRESS AT THE REQUEST OF TWO THIRDS OF THE STATES

MARCEL GUILLIAMS

The trusteeship is a protective type of relationship. Its principal purpose is to help the dependent countries develop their resources and eventually become independent or self-governing. Until these goals are reached, the trustee country has full power to make and administer the laws, maintain the courts, and establish military bases in the area.

The "Elastic Clause" of the Constitution

The framers of the Constitution were wise and farsighted men. They realized that they could not foresee the developments of the future. Yet they wanted to provide for the welfare of the people at all times. To do that, they had to make the Constitution adaptable. One way in which they tried to accomplish that was through what is called the "Elastic Clause." That is the name given to the last paragraph of Section 8, Article I. It gives Congress power to make all the laws necessary to carry out the provisions of the Constitution. It has sometimes been used as the basis for passing laws not directly authorized by other sections of the Constitution.

Because of the "Elastic Clause," the Constitution has had to be amended only twenty-three times through all our changing history. Even that possibility was provided for by the men who wrote the Constitution. They prescribed the steps by which the Constitution could be amended when necessary.

128

HOW AMENDMENTS TO THE CONSTITUTION ARE APPROVED

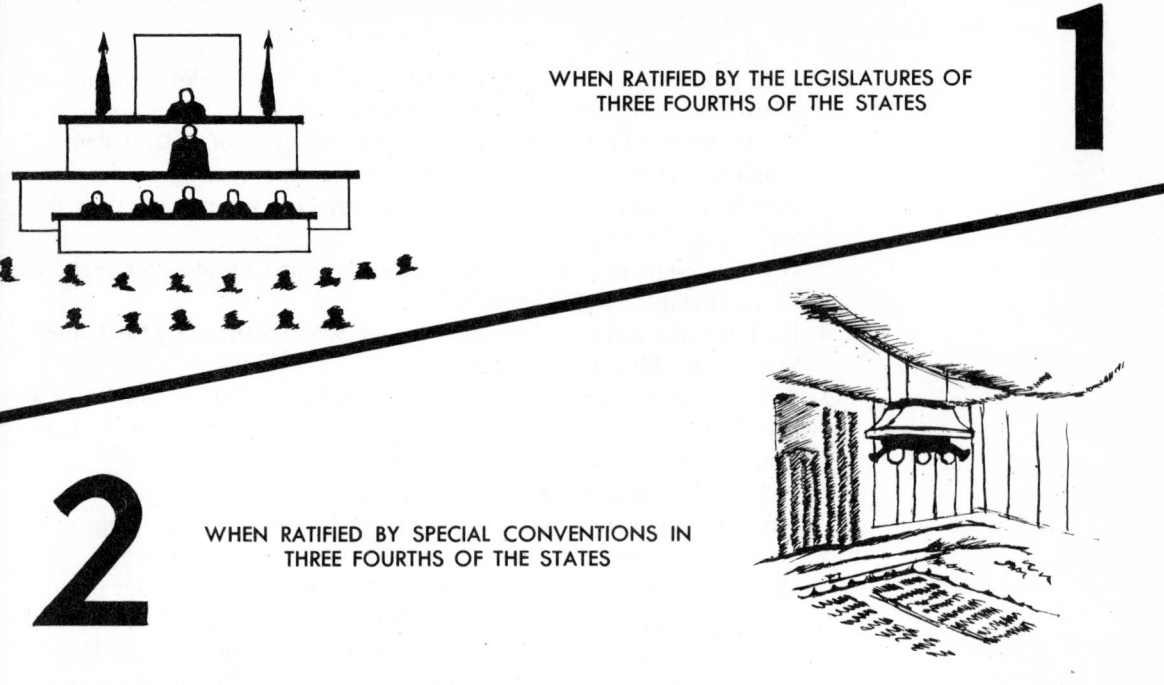

WHEN RATIFIED BY THE LEGISLATURES OF
THREE FOURTHS OF THE STATES

1

2

WHEN RATIFIED BY SPECIAL CONVENTIONS IN
THREE FOURTHS OF THE STATES

MARCEL GUILLIAMS

Ways in Which the Constitution May Be Amended

Amendments to the Constitution may be proposed:

1) *By a two-thirds vote of both houses of Congress.*
2) *By a convention called at the request of two thirds of the states.*

Amendments may become laws in two ways:

1) *When ratified by the legislatures of three fourths of the states.*
2) *When ratified by special conventions in three fourths of the states.*

An amendment to the Constitution has never been proposed by a national convention. The amendments have always

been proposed by Congress and ratified by the states. The twenty-three amendments will be discussed in the next topic.

The Foundation of Good Government

Since the Constitution was written, great changes have taken place. In the early days most of the people were farmers. Today the United States is highly industrialized. The Machine Age and the Atomic Age have changed our ways of living.

The government, too, has changed. It grows and expands as the nation does. But, through all the changes, the foundation of our free government will always be the *Constitution of the United States.*

Things to Do

1. Find a newspaper or magazine account of an example of government control of interstate commerce. Summarize the account in your own words. State whether or not you think this type of federal control promotes the general welfare. Give your reasons.
2. Give a one-minute radio talk entitled, "A Democracy Considers the Welfare of the People."
3. Give a one-minute talk entitled, "A Dictatorship Considers the Welfare of the Dictator and His Agents."
4. Find or make pictures illustrating the services performed by the United States Post Office Department.
5. Pretend you are a member of the Constitutional Convention. Write a letter to a friend explaining why you believe the Congress should have control of the purse strings of the nation.
6. Pretend your class is the Congress of the United States. Draft a resolution which would need to be sent to the President for approval. Draft a resolution which would not need the President's approval.
7. Choose a bill passed at the last session of Congress. Appoint one person to order a copy of the bill from the Government Printing Office. Appoint another person to order a copy of the public law into which the bill developed. Select part of the class to be Senators. The others may be Representatives. Choose a congressional committee from each group. Act out the steps that took place from the introduction of the bill to its passage. Keep a record of the proceedings. Such a record is known in Congress as the *legislative history* of a measure.
8. Give an example of a transaction involving interstate commerce. Give an example of a transaction involving intrastate commerce.

Questions to Answer

1. Who levies the taxes paid by the people of the United States? Is this a democratic procedure? Give reasons for your answer.
2. The Constitution includes a special provision regarding revenue bills. What is the provision? Why do you think the framers of the Constitution included it?
3. Would you say that the provision regarding revenue bills has any effect on the general welfare? Give reasons for your answer.
4. What are some of the things that contributed to the development of communications in this country?
5. Why do you think the framers of the Constitution considered it necessary to encourage writers and inventors?
6. What is the difference between a copyright and a patent?

A Written Exercise

Some of the following sentences are true. Some of them are false. Copy on another piece of paper only those sentences that you believe to be true. After each sentence you write, put down the number of the section of the Constitution on which it is based.

1. The President's Cabinet provides for the establishment of post offices and other means of communication.
2. A government can function without the power to raise money.
3. The President has the power to levy taxes.
4. The President has the power to borrow money on the credit of the United States if he has the approval of the Secretary of the Treasury.
5. A patent gives the government of the United States the right to manufacture the patented article.
6. The patent and copyright laws encourage inventors, scientists, and artists to create new and better things for the education and enjoyment of the people.
7. The Secretary of the Treasury decides how the tax money shall be spent.
8. The President recommends to Congress the passage of laws he deems necessary for the welfare of the people.
9. The Department of Justice is responsible for seeing that the laws made by Congress are enforced.
10. A bill must be passed by both houses of Congress before it can be sent to the President for his approval.
11. A Senator may rise in the Senate and announce his intention of introducing a bill.
12. If a bill which has passed the House of Representatives is changed in the Senate, it must be sent back to the House.
13. The President may veto parts of a bill and approve other parts of it.
14. A vetoed bill becomes a law if Congress repasses it by a two-thirds vote in each house.
15. The Congress appoints the governor of a territory.

Words to Study Before You Read the Next Topic

waive	suffrage	warrant
totalitarian	indictment	jeopardy
redress	specific	denying

The Bill of Rights
and Other Amendments to the Constitution

Our Constitution has withstood the test of time. It has proved to be a wise and stable document. At the time it was written, however, many people had honest doubts about it.

The writers of the Constitution wanted to be sure the people generally approved their work. They also wanted the Constitution to have a fair chance. They sent it to each of the thirteen states. Each state elected a group of men to study its provisions. But it was not necessary for all the thirteen states to approve. Article VII of the Constitution provided that approval by nine states would be enough.

There were many arguments in the various states. Some people felt that the national government would have too much power. They were afraid that the rights of individual states would be endangered.

Throughout the colonies, men made speeches against ratification. They warned that the Constitution might make possible an American monarchy. They said the President might become powerful enough to make himself a king.

People in favor of the Constitution had to quiet these fears. "There is little danger that such a thing could happen," they countered. "The Constitution is a democratic plan of government. If it does not safeguard the rights of the states and the people, it can be amended. The Constitution itself provides for additions, or amendments."

Some supporters of the Constitution drew up a group of suggested amendments. The amendments provided safeguards for certain specific rights. These included the rights to religious freedom, freedom of speech, and freedom of the press. Most state constitutions guaranteed such rights and liberties. With similar *national* guarantees in prospect, the Constitution became acceptable to most people. It was ratified in 1788.

In 1789, ten amendments to the Constitution were formally proposed. They became effective two years later. Those ten amendments are dear to the hearts of Americans. They form what we proudly call our *Bill of Rights*.

The Bill of Rights is part of the Constitution of the United States. It is also a symbol of our personal freedom. Throughout the years it has protected the rights and

Some Highlights of the Bill of Rights

Freedom of Religion

Freedom of Speech

Freedom from unreasonable searches

Right to assemble

Right to petition

Right to jury trial and counsel

Right to summon witnesses

No illegal loss of liberty

No excessive bail or fines

Just compensation for property

From "*A Visual History of the United States.*" by Harold U. Faulkner & Graphics Institute: Abelard-Schuman.

privileges of all Americans. *It has helped to make possible our American way of life.*

The First Amendment

The First Amendment to the Constitution states that the federal government shall guarantee certain rights. These are *freedom of religion, freedom of speech, freedom of the press, the right to peaceful assembly, and the right to petition the government if wrongfully treated.* Congress cannot, at any time, pass laws that will take away these rights. It cannot pass laws that will modify or interfere with any of them.

Many countries have an official religion.

The United States does not. This First Amendment says that none may ever be established. Each American remains free to worship as he sees fit. The citizens of our new nation felt very strongly on this subject. Many of their forebears had come to this country solely to find religious liberty. Little wonder this guarantee was the first provision in the first amendment to our Constitution.

In a totalitarian country the press is controlled by the government. Newspapers and magazines are allowed to print only what government leaders want the people to know. Many people know they are not reading the truth in government-controlled

The first provision of the First Amendment to our Constitution guarantees freedom of worship to all Americans.

newspapers. But what can they do about it? They do not know how to learn the facts.

In the United States newspapers and magazines are free to print the news as it happens. They are free to criticize the government. They may criticize the policies of government leaders. They are free to express their own ideas of how the government should be run.

The people are free to read all newspapers, magazines, and books. They are free to read the opinions of different men and women. They are free to think for themselves and form their own opinions.

Radio and television stations are free, too. The term *freedom of the press* applies to them also. They are free to report all the news. All the people are free to listen to their reports.

The freedom of the press is never limited except in time of war. Then it is sometimes necessary to keep certain news from being published. If it were published, it might help the enemy. In time of peace, however, the freedom of the press is not restrained.

Freedom of speech is another cherished right. Americans like to discuss the policies of their government. The leaders of the nation know this. It makes them more careful. It reminds the leaders that they are really responsible to the people. It helps them to govern the nation according to the will of the people.

The right to assemble peacefully is another important right. A dictator takes that right away from his people. He does not want them to meet and exchange ideas. He does not want them to get together. They might decide on ways to improve the government! This is one of the basic differences between the United States and totalitarian countries.

Another difference lies in our Constitutional right to petition the government for redress of wrongs. If our government takes an action that we think is unfair to us, we

can protest. We can draw up a petition. We can say, "We have a grievance. We have been wrongfully treated by the government. We want the government to do something about it." Such a thing could not happen in a totalitarian country. There, no matter what the government does, the people cannot object. If they did, they might even lose their lives.

The Second Amendment

The Second Amendment was very important in the early days of the nation. It still gives us a right we would not wish to lose. *It gives the people the right to organize state militias.*

The colonists had suffered at the hands of the king's soldiers. Patrick Henry had warned that they might some day be in danger from a President's army. They wanted to protect themselves. Such protection is no longer considered necessary. Congress protects the rights of all the people of all the states. In the early days, however, the Second Amendment was needed. It was one of the proposed changes that quieted objections to the Constitution.

The Third Amendment

This is another amendment that seems of little value today. Nevertheless, it gave the people of the new nation a feeling of security. In colonial days the king's soldiers could be quartered in private homes. Many of the colonists suffered great hardships at their hands. They did not want such a thing to happen again. They wanted the Constitution to definitely forbid it. The Third Amendment does so. It says that, *in peacetime, no soldier can be quartered in a private home without the owner's consent. Even in wartime, if such quartering is necessary, it must be arranged in a lawful manner.*

The Fourth Amendment

The Fourth Amendment also guards the homes of the people. *No officer of the federal government may search a person's home without a warrant. He may not take anything from a person's home without a warrant. He cannot arrest a person without a warrant. The warrant must describe the place to be searched. It must describe the person or things to be seized. It can be issued only when there is enough evidence to justify the search or seizure. The evidence must be sworn to before the public official who issues the warrant.*

In some countries officials of the government may go into a man's house at will. They may take his property or even his life. In the United States, the poor man's home is just as secure as the home of the rich man. Neither may be searched without a warrant. A federal officer who enters a home without a warrant may be treated as an intruder.

Most states have similar laws. State laws prevent *local* and *state* officials from entering a man's home without a warrant.

The Fifth Amendment

The Fifth Amendment secures other rights for the people. They are very important rights. They have to do with liberty and freedom.

135

First, *to be tried for a serious crime, a person must be charged by a grand jury.* A grand jury is a group of citizens summoned by law to hear evidence against an accused person. There are twenty-three persons, or *jurors*, on a federal grand jury. The jurors are chosen by lot. They swear to judge all evidence fairly.

These are the usual steps in trying a serious crime.

1) The grand jury weighs the evidence against the accused person. It declares whether or not he should be held for trial. *It does not decide his guilt or innocence.* Perhaps the grand jury believes there is enough evidence against the accused person to hold him for trial. If so, it returns a formal charge against him. This formal charge is called an *indictment*. If there is not enough evidence, the jury says so. It returns what is called a *no-bill*. That means the jury is bringing no charges against the accused.

2) If the accused is indicted, he goes to trial. In the courtroom he appears before a trial jury. The trial jury is made up of twelve persons. It is usually called a petit jury. The petit jury listens to the evidence presented at the trial. It then decides whether the accused person is innocent or guilty.

3) If the verdict is guilty, the case goes to the judge for sentence.

The Fifth Amendment protects an accused person in other ways. *A person who has been tried and found innocent cannot be tried again for the same offense.* The amendment says he cannot "be twice put in jeopardy." This is a wise provision.

Without it, an innocent man might be held in prison for months or years. When one trial was over, a new one could be ordered. Even if a man were let out of prison he could not live in peace. He would always live in fear of being brought to trial again.

Another provision of the Fifth Amendment says that *no person may be compelled to testify against himself.* The United States is one of the few countries in the world where this is true. But the colonists had learned a very important lesson. Many of them had been accused of crimes they had not committed. They had been beaten and treated cruelly to make them confess. When they had confessed, they had been punished for crimes someone else had committed. The men who wrote the Fifth Amendment wanted to make certain this could not happen again. Juries and judges in the United States must judge a person's guilt or innocence on the evidence presented. *Evidence obtained by force or unfair means cannot be used in court.*

In some parts of the world, military courts may try civilians. This does not happen in the United States. Men and women in the armed forces may be tried in military courts. Such a court is called a court-martial. Under the Fifth Amendment, however, *civilians cannot be tried in military courts.* Civil courts insure justice for the people of the United States.

The Fifth Amendment also contains a special provision to safeguard other freedoms. It says *no one can be deprived of life, liberty, or property without due process of law. Due process of law* means according to the established law of the land. A man's life cannot be taken unless he has been

legally condemned. He cannot be kept in prison "without due process."

The government does have the right to take private property when it is needed for public use. This governmental right is called the right of eminent domain. *When eminent domain is used, the due process of law must be followed.* If the person owning the property and the government do not agree upon the price to be paid, a hearing is held. Each side presents its case. A fair price is decided upon. The government takes the land and pays the owner the price set by the court.

Suppose there is a town in the United States that has grown very rapidly. The old schoolhouse is run-down. It is too small to accommodate all the pupils. School district officials decide to build a new school. They look for a piece of property. The town is small. There is only one suitable site on which to build. The board offers the owner a certain sum for his land. The man refuses to sell.

The school district board and the townspeople urge him to reconsider. Will he not sell for the good of all the people? The man finally agrees to sell his land. Then he names his price. It is far more than the real value of the land. This is not fair to the school district nor to the taxpayers!

The school district board may use the right of eminent domain. In some states the board must appeal to a court for the right to take the man's property. If the court decides the land is necessary for public use, a fair price is set on the property. Then the school district board takes

The amount of money to be paid to property owners in eminent domain cases is frequently decided by a jury. Sometimes a special group of officials study the evidence and make the decision.

Every American is entitled to a fair trial, even in the matter of minor traffic violations. He has the right to be tried by a jury of fair-minded citizens, unless he waives a jury trial.

the land. It pays the man the price set by the court.

Federal, state, and local governments all have the right of eminent domain. Under the Fifth Amendment, however, this right must be carefully used. *No private property may be taken unless it is necessary for the public good. Any property so taken must be paid for in full value.*

The Sixth Amendment

The Sixth Amendment guarantees to every man the right to a speedy public trial by jury. It says the accused person must be tried in the district where the crime was committed. It gives him the right to know the charges against him. He can face the witnesses who testify against him. He can summon witnesses in his defense. He can employ a lawyer to defend him. If he cannot afford a lawyer, the government will provide one.

A fair and speedy trial is one of the first rights a dictator takes away from his people. He may pretend to give them a fair trial, but it is only a pretense. The courts are not courts of the people. They are courts of the dictator. The accused person may be given the right to hire a lawyer to

defend him. This does not help much. They both know that even the lawyer dare not oppose the dictator.

In the United States all citizens have the right to a fair and speedy trial. This means that no one can be held in prison unjustly. It means that everyone accused of a crime has the right to defend himself. He has the right to be tried by a jury. He cannot be thrown into jail simply because he is disliked by some government official.

The Seventh Amendment

Not all trials involve crimes. Two persons may disagree about their rights in a contract, for instance. If the people live in different states, trial may be held in federal court. It is called a civil trial.

The Seventh Amendment has to do with these civil cases only. It says that in all such cases a jury trial must be available, with one exception. If the amount involved is twenty dollars or less, no jury is necessary. A judge can decide the case. In actual practice, both parties may agree to waive their right to a jury. That is their privilege. If either party wants a jury, however, the Seventh Amendment guarantees that one will be provided.

Most states have laws similar to the Seventh Amendment. Some states also have a Small Claims Court in certain cities. In these courts the judge hears and decides cases in which the sum involved does not exceed a certain amount set by law.

The Eighth Amendment

The English Bill of Rights was drawn up about a hundred years before ours. The Eighth Amendment, however, borrows some of the wording of the English document. It says: *Excessive bail shall not be required, nor excessive fines imposed, nor cruel and unusual punishments inflicted.*

A person is often let out of jail upon payment of bail. Bail is the security given for his release. The prisoner says, "I will leave this money with the court as security. I will return and face trial. Otherwise I would forfeit all this money."

A person accused of a very serious crime may be refused bail. When bail is allowed, its amount is usually based on the seriousness of the crime. The more serious the crime, the higher the bail. But even if the bail is high, it must not be *excessive*.

Early English kings set bail very high. Few men could pay for their release from prison while waiting for trial. The kings also imposed heavy fines for small offenses. The Eighth Amendment forbids any federal court to impose an excessive fine or an excessive bail.

Most states have similar laws. They do not permit *state* courts to impose excessive fines or excessive bail.

The Ninth Amendment

The Constitution spells out many rights. It could not list every right that belonged to the people. Still, those unlisted rights had to be protected. The Ninth Amendment provides that protection. It says in effect: *The fact that a right is not listed in the Constitution does not mean it does not exist.* This was reassuring to the people of the new nation. It meant that no part of their power could be taken away from

them. They could enjoy any rights they might establish by law.

The Tenth Amendment

The Tenth Amendment does not define the rights of the people. It gives suggested rights to the states. The federal government has only those powers which have been given to it by the Constitution. The tenth amendment says: *The powers not delegated to the United States by the Constitution, nor prohibited by it to the states, are reserved to the states respectively, or to the people.*

Our Code of Freedom

The Bill of Rights is the code of freedom for the American people. It is their guarantee that the rights of each individual will be protected. It is their heritage from freedom-loving forefathers. So long as the Bill of Rights remains a part of the supreme law of the land each citizen is free. He has the right to demand and to receive justice.

The most important papers and documents of our history are kept safe in the National Archives, Washington, D.C. Inscriptions outside the building read: *What is past is prologue. Study the past.*

Ewing Galloway

He has the right to live his own life. He knows that his personal safety and freedom are protected.

The Bill of Rights is not only an American privilege. It is an American ideal. It must always remain so! It must always remain the basis for true personal freedom and liberty in the United States. But we must not take it for granted. *Every citizen must do his part to guard and defend it.*

Other Amendments

The Bill of Rights is the first ten amendments to our Constitution. They were all adopted at one time, in 1791. Since then there have been only thirteen additional amendments. This is truly a remarkable record, considering how much the world has changed. It shows how stable our Constitution is—how well and how wisely our forefathers planned.

Most people are familiar with the provisions of the Bill of Rights. They are not so familiar with the other amendments. Yet each amendment has its own importance. Each one was carefully considered by the Congress, the people, and the state legislatures. Each one went through the long and democratic process prescribed by the Constitution. Only one has ever been repealed. It was repealed through the same process as an amendment is adopted.

The Eleventh Amendment

The framers of the Constitution wanted to define clearly the powers of the federal courts. They listed the various kinds of cases that federal courts can handle. The list included controversies "between a state and citizens of another state."

After a few years, some of the states became disturbed about that provision. "It's not fair," was a common complaint. "If a citizen of one state wants to sue another state, that should be his privilege. But his suit should be brought in the courts of the state that is being sued. He should not be allowed to use the federal courts for that purpose."

To make it quite clear, the Eleventh Amendment was passed. It says that *suit against a state cannot be brought in federal court by citizens of another state. Citizens or subjects of foreign countries cannot bring a state into federal court either.*

The Twelfth Amendment

In national elections that are held today the people vote for electors. The electors then vote for a President and Vice-President. This was not true originally. Before the Twelfth Amendment was passed, the electors simply voted for candidates. They did not indicate which candidate was for which office. The candidate who received the greatest number of votes became President. The candidate who received the next greatest number of votes became Vice-President. In case of a tie vote, the House of Representatives voted to break the tie.

Such a situation occurred in the election of 1800. All of the electors voted for Thomas Jefferson and Aaron Burr. This made a tie vote. Most of the electors wanted Jefferson to become President, but they had no power to elect him. When the House voted to break the tie, Burr came

very close to being chosen. This worried many people. They decided something should be done.

The Twelfth Amendment was adopted in 1804. This amendment changed the confusing situation. *It provided that the electors use two separate ballots. One ballot is for the office of President. The other ballot is for the office of Vice-President.*

The Thirteenth Amendment

This is the amendment that made slavery illegal in the United States. President Lincoln announced in 1863 that the slaves were freed in all states still fighting against the Union. His proclamation did not have the force of law, however. Slavery was not entirely abolished until 1865 when the Thirteenth Amendment was adopted. This amendment *abolishes slavery forever in the United States and its territories. It also gives Congress the power to pass any laws that are needed to enforce the amendment.*

The Fourteenth Amendment

Simply being declared "free" did not put the slaves on an equal footing with other Americans. *The Fourteenth Amendment was passed to ensure all the privileges of citizenship to all Americans.* It defines citizenship as follows: *All persons born or naturalized in the United States, and subject to the jurisdiction thereof, are citizens of the United States and of the state wherein they reside.* It says *that no state shall interfere with the rights of any citizen. No state shall deny to any citizen the equal protection of the laws.*

The Fifth Amendment says that no person may be deprived of life, liberty, or property without due process of law. This amendment applies specifically to the federal government. The Fourteenth Amendment applies to the state governments. It says that *no state may deprive any person of life, liberty, or property without due process of law.*

The Fourteenth Amendment also changed part of Article I of the Constitution. The number of Representatives a state could send to Congress depended on its population. But in the past a slave had counted as only three-fifths of a person. The Fourteenth Amendment says *all the people (except untaxed Indians) must be counted.* It also provides a penalty for any state denying voting rights to any of its 21-year-old male citizens. The penalty prescribed is a reduction in the number of Representatives a state may send to Congress.

There are other provisions in the Fourteenth Amendment. They were included to cover special situations arising after the War Between the States. They have little application to our lives today. The definition of citizenship, however, is still extremely important. The provision that all citizens should be treated equally is also important. The clause that guarantees "due process of law" in all the states is another precious right of the people.

The Fifteenth Amendment

The states make most of their own laws regarding voting. Some of them may require payment of a poll tax. Others may

demand that a voter pass certain written tests. The Fifteenth Amendment, however, puts some restrictions on both state and federal voting laws. It says *no one can be denied the right to vote because of race, color, or previous condition of servitude.*

The Sixteenth Amendment

After the adoption of the Fifteenth Amendment, forty-three years passed without further changes. Then, in 1913, the income tax amendment was adopted.

Congress had once passed a law taxing incomes. The Supreme Court said the law was unconstitutional. According to the Constitution, direct taxes had to be levied against the states on a population basis.

The cost of government had become very high. More money had to be raised. If the Constitution prohibited an income tax, then it might be necessary to change the Constitution. An amendment seemed to be the only answer.

The Sixteenth Amendment gives Congress the power *to levy and collect taxes on income from whatever source derived. Such taxes do not have to be apportioned among the states nor based on population figures.* Most of the revenue of the United States now comes from income taxes.

The Seventeenth Amendment

Originally, under Article I of the Constitution, United States Senators were chosen by state legislators. Often the legislators could not agree. While they argued, Senate seats were left vacant. The Seventeenth Amendment corrected that situation. It provides that *Senators shall be elected by the people.* It also provides that *a state legislature may authorize the governor of the state to make temporary appointments to the Senate.* If a vacancy occurs, the governor may call a special election. He may choose to wait for the next regular election. In either case, he may be empowered to appoint someone to serve until an election is held.

The Eighteenth Amendment

This amendment prohibited the manufacture and sale of intoxicating liquors. It was approved in 1919. In 1933 the Twenty-first Amendment repealed it.

The Nineteenth Amendment

Until 1920 the influence of women on American politics was largely indirect. Many of them may have persuaded their husbands to vote one way or another, but they did not have suffrage, or the right to vote. Some states had passed laws allowing women to vote in local and state elections. But, in national elections, women could not cast ballots.

The role of women in other phases of American life had become increasingly important. During World War I many women had handled jobs previously done by men. There seemed to be no logical reason for denying them the right to vote.

The women themselves began to organize. They stated their position fearlessly, in the face of abuse and ridicule. At last their efforts were rewarded. The Nineteenth Amendment was passed. It provides

that *neither state nor nation can deny any citizen the right to vote on account of sex.*

The Twentieth Amendment

When the Constitution was written, there was neither telephone nor telegraph. There was no radio or television. It took weeks for the results of an election to reach all the people. It might also take weeks for the persons elected to reach the capital. With these things in mind, the framers of the Constitution chose March 4 as Inaugural Day. This left plenty of time between Election Day and the day of taking office.

In modern times, however, that long delay following November elections was unnecessary. It was also undesirable. The outgoing President was in a difficult position. So were the defeated congressmen. They were no longer the people's chosen representatives. Such hold-over officials were known as "lame ducks." The Twentieth Amendment is known as the "Lame Duck Amendment."

The Twentieth Amendment provides that *the terms of the President and the Vice-President shall end at noon on January 20.* This means January 20 of the year following the national election. The new presidential term starts at the same time.

The same amendment directs *Congress to assemble at least once a year, normally on January 3.* If January 3 falls on Sunday, however, Congress usually meets on January 4. Congressional terms begin on the same day.

The Twentieth Amendment contains another important provision. If the President should die, the Vice-President would succeed him. Until the Twentieth Amendment was passed, however, there was no provision for a successor if the Vice-President, too, should die. The Twentieth Amendment *gave Congress the power to establish rules for presidential succession.*

The Twenty-first Amendment

This repealed the Eighteenth or Prohibition Amendment on a national basis. It does permit the states to have prohibition laws, however.

The Twenty-second Amendment

Until 1940, no President had ever been elected more than twice. Then Franklin Roosevelt was elected for a third and a fourth term. The Twenty-second Amendment, adopted in 1951, prohibits such long service. *A President may now serve only two terms. If he serves more than two years of someone else's term, he may serve only one term of his own.*

The Twenty-third Amendment

The Twenty-third Amendment gives permanent residents of the District of Columbia the right to vote in national elections. The District will have three electoral votes —the number allowed the six least populous states. The people will vote for the electors just as people living in states vote for presidential electors. The electors will then meet in the District and vote for President and Vice-President.

The amendment does not give the District statehood, nor change the local form of government.

CONSTITUTIONAL GOVERNMENT IN THE UNITED STATES

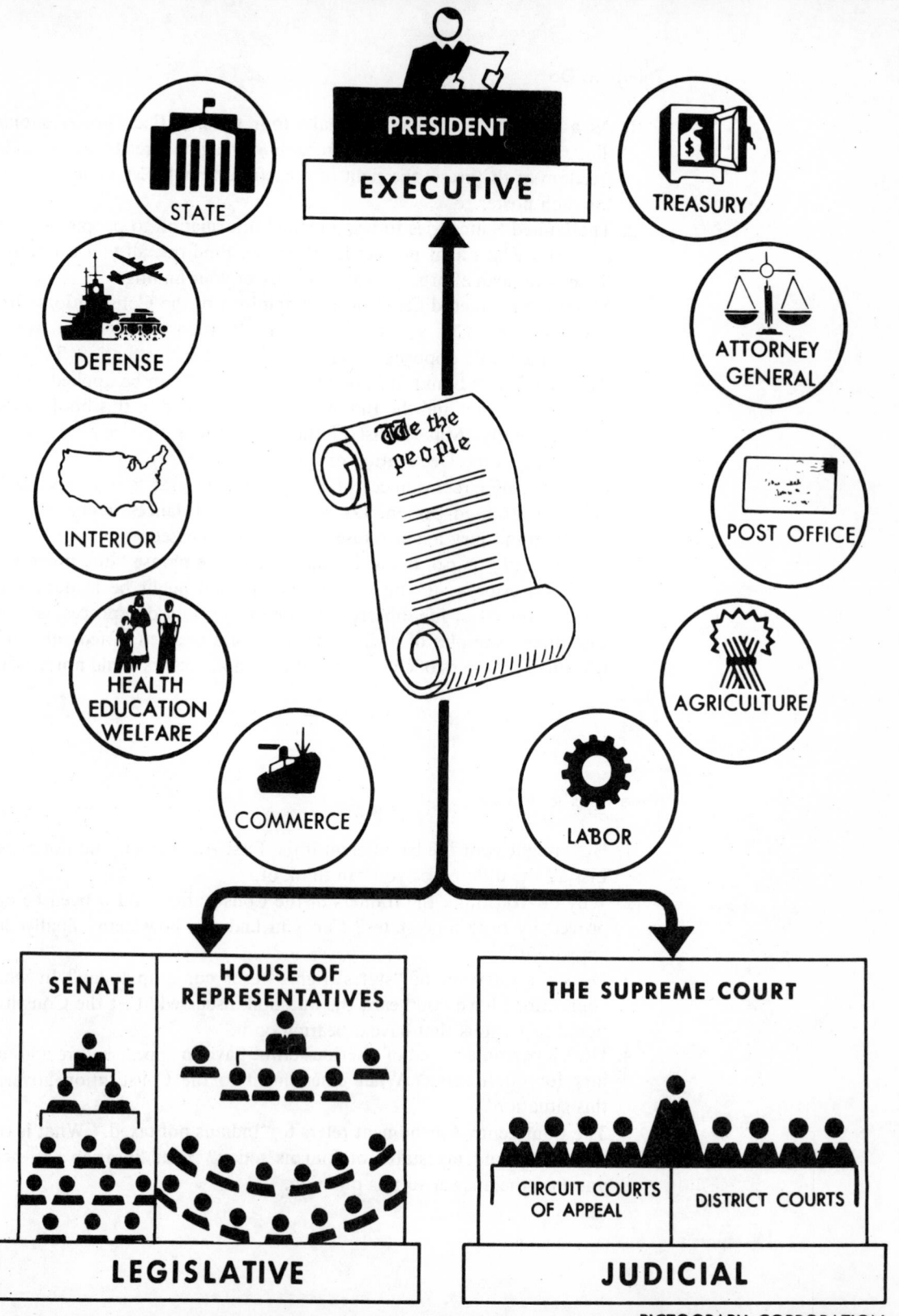

PICTOGRAPH CORPORATION

Things to Do

1. As a class project, plan and make four posters. Each poster should illustrate one of the following: freedom of religion; freedom of speech; freedom of the press; the right of peaceful assembly. Make up a motto for each poster.
2. The United States tries to bring factual information to people of other countries who might not get it otherwise. Find out all you can about these American efforts. Prepare a report of your findings.
3. Many honest men differed in their opinions of the Constitution when it was written. Can you think of some situations today about which sincere men hold opposite views? Describe one such situation. Tell how Patrick Henry's brand of "good sportsmanship" can be applied today.
4. The Constitution and the Bill of Rights are printed in this book. Read them carefully. Make a list of those provisions that remind you of something in the Declaration of Independence.
5. List a set of circumstances under which a federal grand jury might indict an accused person. List a set of circumstances under which a federal grand jury might refuse to indict the accused.
6. Find out all you can about the meaning of the phrase "due process of law." Describe a situation in which a person might be in danger of being deprived of life, liberty, or property without due process of law.
7. List three examples of civil suits that would be tried in federal court. List three examples of civil suits that the federal courts could not handle.

Questions to Answer

1. How might your life be different if the First Amendment did not exist? List all the differences you can think of.
2. Why do you think the framers of the Constitution said it need be approved by only nine states? Can you find out how many finally did approve it?
3. Does the question of "states' rights" ever come up today? In what connections have you heard the question discussed? List the Constitutional provisions that have a bearing on it.
4. Does a person accused of a serious crime have to appear before a grand jury for questioning? What amendment to the Constitution governs this situation?
5. The Fourteenth Amendment refers to "Indians not taxed." What is the citizenship and tax status of Indians today? Your librarian can help you find the answer to this question.

6. What are some kinds of federal taxes other than income taxes?
7. What is the line of Presidential succession that Congress has established? By what authority did Congress establish it?
8. What is the difference between a grand jury and a petit jury? Why do you think they are called *grand* and *petit*?
9. Can you think of any kind of an amendment that would improve our present Constitution? Do you think any future amendments will be necessary? Give reasons for your answer.

A Written Exercise

Copy and complete the following statements. You may use as many words and sentences as you need.
1. Freedom of speech is necessary to a democracy because_____.
2. A court-martial is a_____.
3. Soldiers accused of wrongdoing are tried_____.
4. The governor of a state may fill a vacancy in the United States Senate by_____.
5. The governor of a state may fill a vacancy in the United States House of Representatives by_____.
6. The Eighth Amendment protects citizens of the United States by_____.
7. The Bill of Rights consists of_____.
8. The Bill of Rights was added to the Constitution because_____.
9. These steps are followed in bringing to justice any person accused of a crime:_____.
10. One example of how Americans use their right of peaceful assembly is_____.

Words to Study Before You Read the Next Topic

prosecuting	surveyor	revenues
boroughs	incorporated	coroner
registrar	moderator	inquest
similar	parish	mortgages

UNIT SUMMARY

In this unit you have been reminded of how the Declaration of Independence came into being. You have seen how the Declaration of Independence paved the way for the Constitution. You have observed the grievances in the Declaration reflected as safeguards in the Constitution. You have realized how necessary is the Constitution to our free way of government. You have analyzed many of the ways in which the Bill of Rights and later amendments help protect our freedom.

These great documents provide a strong foundation. They are the sturdy rocks on which our nation is still building. Think of the courage and the foresight of the men who wrote these documents. Remember that many of them were young men. They recognized early in life their responsibilities toward the general welfare.

Remember that the young men and women of today can follow in those footsteps. They can . . . they must . . . protect and build upon our American foundation of freedom.

UNIT THREE

A Panorama of American Government

A PANORAMA of AMERICAN GOVERNMENT

A panorama is a picture, or a view, of many things seen at once. From a great height one can look down upon mountains and valleys, farms and forests. All are part of one huge picture. Each fits into the pattern of the landscape.

This unit, *A Panorama of American Government*, is that kind of an over-all picture. It is a picture of the various parts of our government. Government in the United States is more than just the government in Washington. It is also the government in towns, cities, counties, and states. It includes government officials. It includes the government workers in every part of the nation. In this unit you will see how each phase fits into the whole picture. The topics in this unit are:

COUNTY, TOWNSHIP, AND VILLAGE GOVERNMENT
CITY GOVERNMENT
STATE GOVERNMENT
A VISIT TO WASHINGTON
HOW THE GOVERNMENT IS FINANCED
A PRESIDENTIAL ELECTION

As you study these topics, you will notice that our government is divided into many parts. Each part is important in itself. It is also a necessary part of the whole scheme. Find out how the different branches of government work. Find out how they co-operate with one another. There are many variations in local government throughout our nation. Nevertheless they share a common goal. Every branch of our government exists to preserve our freedoms. They all work together to help keep our nation a wonderful place in which to live!

County, Township, and Village Government

TOM stood looking at the statue of Abraham Lincoln. Shadows played about the rugged, kindly eyes. It was nearly dusk, yet the shadows seemed touched with gold. Tom studied the statue reverently. "You really believed in government 'of the people, by the people, for the people,' didn't you?" He was thinking the words so intently he said them half aloud.

"Pretty impressive figure, isn't he?"

Tom jumped at the sound of the voice behind him. He had thought he was alone in the great memorial.

"Pretty impressive indeed," he agreed. He stepped aside to make room for the young Marine officer who had joined him.

" 'Of the people, by the people, for the people.' Sometimes you get to thinking they are just words," the young man said soberly. "Seeing him looking down at you like this, though, you *know* they have real meaning. You really realize what a great man he was."

"That's right," said Tom. "I've been thinking about Lincoln a lot lately. We've been studying about government in school. It could be rather a dull subject—all laws and rules and office buildings. When you think about it the way Lincoln did, though,

it gets exciting. 'Government of the people.' That means *us*. President Lincoln was talking about *us*."

The officer smiled. "Of course he was. He had a gift for putting ideas in human terms. I can almost hear him telling you about democracy and self-government."

"What do you think he would have said?" Tom's eyes searched the massive, placid face of the statue as if to read an answer there.

"First of all, he probably would have said, 'What's your name, son?' "

"The same as Jefferson's." The boy grinned as he spoke, but it was a very proud grin!

"Well, then," the Marine went on, "Lincoln might have said something like this. 'Tom, the government is your friend and neighbor. It is a good friend and neighbor. It has many helpers throughout the country. Some of the helpers work for the federal government. Millions of others work in town, city, county, and state governments. They include mayors and city councilmen. Some are policemen or firemen or public health officials. They are all the people who keep the wheels of government turning smoothly. They live in every

Mr. Lincoln said, "This country, with its institutions, belongs to the people who inhabit it."

town, city, and county in the United States. They are symbols of a nation that is *governed by the people.*' "

Tom's next question came rapidly. "And suppose I said, 'Mr. Lincoln, what do these government helpers do?' "

"I think Mr. Lincoln would answer clearly. He would say, 'They build the roads over which Americans travel. They test the food to be eaten in American homes. They see that milk is sweet and clean. They distribute mail even into the far corners of the nation. They sweep the streets of big cities. They put out harmful fires. They protect people from danger. They measure the wind. They forecast storms and fair weather.' "

"And if I said, 'Is that all, Mr. Lincoln?' "

"He would answer, 'No, Tom. They bring pure, clean water into American homes. They take care of people who have no homes. They comfort the sick and the weary. They take care of the blind and the underprivileged. They teach the children and the youth of America. They are librarians, teachers, nurses, judges, soldiers, sailors, and truck drivers. Among them is just about every kind of worker you could think of. Their work reaches into every home in this great land. They touch the life of every boy and girl, every man and woman in this country. They are America!' "

Tom's eyes were bright. "And I would answer, 'Mr. Lincoln, I know you are right. They try to help everyone in the United States enjoy *life, liberty, and the pursuit of happiness.*' "

The officer was thoughtful for a moment. Then he said, "Yes, Tom, but I believe Mr. Lincoln might add another thought. He might add that the individual must also help himself. Every American has a duty toward his government, just as the government has a duty toward the individual. *The government and the individual must work together. Only in that way can there be true freedom for all.*"

———————

There are various branches of government in the United States. There is the *federal* government. There are *state* governments. There are *county* governments. There are the governments of *cities, towns,* and *villages.* These governments work alone, yet they all co-operate with one another. They all help make the United States a democracy.

The federal government passes laws for the general welfare of the nation. The state government passes laws for the general good of the state. The city and county governments pass laws to meet the needs of their particular communities.

John Smith walks on paved streets in his home town. He sends his children to public schools. His family enjoys pure drinking water, public playgrounds, public libraries, and many other conveniences. *Who makes it possible for them to enjoy these things?* It is their local government. Local governments furnish street lights. They furnish police and fire protection, health protection, and many other things that touch the everyday lives of the American people.

Democracy means government "of the people, by the people, for the people." In all local governments the *government is close to the people.* The people have more opportunity to take part in local government. They have more opportunity to

watch democracy work. They have more opportunity to help it work successfully.

County Governments

There were counties in this country long before there were states. The colonies had counties. States were formed from groups of counties. A county is a very important unit of government. For one thing, it serves as the principal link between state and municipal governments. It offers an easy means through which towns and cities can work together.

Some counties in the United States are very large, others are small. San Bernardino County in California is the largest county in the United States. The very smallest county is in the state of Virginia. The state legislature in each state except Louisiana divides the state into counties. Louisiana is divided into parishes. In this sense, a *parish* serves the same purpose as a county.

County governments perform many services. Here are some of the duties probably carried out by your county government.

1) Taking charge of local elections and helping to conduct state and national elections.
2) Maintaining courts to establish and administer justice.
3) Keeping official records of births, deaths, and marriages that take place in the county.
4) Keeping copies of important documents such as deeds, title papers, mortgages, judgments of law courts, and wills.

5) Helping to care for the county poor, the aged, and the orphaned.
6) Helping to prevent the spread of disease, and building and maintaining county hospitals.
7) Helping to build and repair roads, underpasses, overpasses, and bridges within the county.
8) Helping to maintain good schools for the pupils who live in rural areas.

Not all counties in the United States have the same type of government. However, they all follow patterns that are similar. Most counties throughout the nation elect similar officials. The principal governing body is usually a *board of supervisors,* or commissioners. Other officials include a *sheriff*; a *county treasurer*; a *county clerk*; a *district attorney*; an *assessor and collector of taxes*; a *surveyor*; a *coroner*; a *recorder*; a *county judge*; and a *county superintendent of schools.*

The County Board of Supervisors

The board of supervisors is the legislative body of the county government. It makes all the county laws. It is also responsible for constructing and maintaining county roads and bridges. It decides on other county improvements and lets the contracts for them.

Most counties have such institutions as county hospitals and homes for the aged. The board of supervisors makes rules for the operation of such institutions. It often employs or appoints county officials. It also sets the tax rate for the county and supervises elections.

There are usually three, five, or seven

County officials help citizens find any specific information they may need regarding such things as births, deaths, marriages, or titles to property in the county.

members on the board of supervisors. There are some exceptions. In Rhode Island the county sheriff takes the place of the board of supervisors. In Georgia a board of commissioners (or a single commissioner) of roads and revenues is the legislative body.

In many counties, the board of supervisors heads the *executive* branch of the county government. The chiefs of the various departments are directly responsible to the board of supervisors.

In a few counties, the board of supervisors appoints a county manager. The county manager directs the affairs of the county government. He must see that the laws of the county are enforced. He must see that all departments of the county government function efficiently. Some of the county officials are appointed by him. He

must always be prepared to tell the board of supervisors how each department is functioning.

The County Sheriff

It is the duty of the county sheriff to see that the laws of the county are enforced. He is responsible for maintaining order in the county, *outside of city limits*. He supervises the care of prisoners in the county jail. He is authorized to make arrests and to carry out orders of the county courts.

In some of the larger counties the sheriff has deputy sheriffs to help him. He also receives assistance from the state police. Most sheriffs work very closely with the state police.

The County Treasurer

The county treasurer takes care of the money belonging to the county. He receives the taxes and fees paid to the county. In some states county treasurers are authorized to collect state taxes paid by citizens of their counties.

When the county supervisors authorize payment of a bill, the county treasurer pays it. He also pays bills or wages that are authorized by law. The county treasurer handles thousands of dollars of public money each year. Like other government officials who handle public money, he must be under heavy bond. The bond is much the same as an insurance policy. If for some reason the public money is misused or lost, the bonding company stands the loss.

Ewing Galloway

In this county seat, the county offices and the city offices occupy the same building. The county seat is the "capital" of the county.

The County Clerk

The county clerk is sometimes called the county recorder. It is his duty to keep the official records of the county. In some counties he issues naturalization papers, marriage licenses, and other licenses. He may also serve as secretary to the board of supervisors.

The District Attorney

In some states the district attorney is called the *prosecuting attorney* or the *county attorney*. One of his important duties is to prosecute persons who break the

criminal laws of the state or county. Violations of municipal laws are handled by the local officers in the towns and cities.

The district attorney gives advice about law to county officials. He both prosecutes and defends court cases. For example, he might conduct two cases in court the same day. In one case a man might sue the county because of an injury he received. He might say the injury was caused because the county failed to repair a certain bridge. The district attorney would *defend* the interests of the county. In the other case a man might be accused of murder. The district attorney would *prosecute* the man who had been accused.

The district attorney must always protect the public interest. He must be sure that all the county officials work for the welfare of the people. Suppose he suspects a public official of being dishonest or of failing to perform his duty. In such a case, the district attorney asks the grand jury to investigate. If the grand jury finds enough evidence against the suspected official, it brings charges. The district attorney then prosecutes the case before a petit jury.

In some counties there is also an official known as the *public defender*. Sometimes a person accused of a crime cannot afford to hire a lawyer. The public defender must defend a person without charge.

The County
Superintendent of Schools

In most states there are county superintendents of schools. A county superintendent may be elected by the people. He may be selected by the county board of education. In a few places he may be given a civil service appointment for life. Usually the county superintendent is in charge of all the small schools in the county. Larger schools are generally supervised by town or city officials.

The official who administers the oath of office to the county superintendent might make a little speech. He might say, "The small schools of this county are now under your supervision. You must see that they are good schools. If you need help, you may appoint supervisors to help you. It will be your duty and theirs to visit these schools. You must help the teachers in any way you can.

"You are to advise school boards on the selection of teachers. You will help them choose books and school equipment. Help them plan their school programs of studies. You must also require reports from teachers concerning the schools and the attendance of pupils. You must ask the school boards for an accounting of how they spend public money. You must see that the money is spent wisely and well. The people of the county must receive full measure for the money they spend for education."

The County
Coroner

The county coroner investigates all questionable deaths. He holds an inquest if it seems that a crime has been committed. The following imaginary story will illustrate the work of a county coroner.

Mr. Benson lived three miles out in the country. He often walked to the neighboring village to visit with friends and relatives. One evening he failed to return home.

Three days later his body was found in a canal.

At first everyone believed Mr. Benson had accidentally fallen into the canal. Then the county coroner arrived. "It is true this may have been an accident," he said. "But we cannot be sure. The cause of death is unknown. We must have an investigation to determine the real cause."

The coroner called in doctors to examine the body. The doctors found that Mr. Benson had not drowned. He was dead before his body was in the water. This proved that Mr. Benson had not accidentally fallen into the canal. How had he met his death?

The coroner summoned a jury. An inquest was held. *The inquest was the meeting of the jurors to determine the cause of death.* The jurors listened to the testimony of the doctors. They listened to other witnesses. Then they retired into another room to reach a verdict. The verdict was "death at the hands of a person or persons unknown."

After the inquest, the coroner turned the evidence over to the district attorney. The district attorney and the sheriff worked together to solve the crime. They finally found the guilty person. They brought him into court, where he was tried and sentenced.

The county coroner had found the real cause of Mr. Benson's death. Without his services, a murderer might have gone free!

The County Recorder

The county recorder is sometimes the county clerk. Also, he is sometimes called the registrar of deeds. He records all deeds to real estate. A deed is an official paper showing ownership of land and permanent improvements upon land. The county recorder also records mortgages on real estate and other property. It is very important that his records be kept carefully and accurately.

The officials discussed are not the only county officials. They are only some of the most important ones. Nearly all of them are elected by the people. It is their duty to see that the welfare of the people is protected.

The Town Meeting

The United States is a democratic country. But there are two kinds of democracy. One kind is usually called *pure* democracy. The other is called *indirect* or *representative* democracy. In a pure democracy, the people handle everything themselves. They meet together to make laws and levy taxes. They meet together to make decisions about all kinds of public business. In a representative democracy, also, the people control the government. The day-to-day work of passing laws and making decisions, however, is carried on by their elected representatives. There has been very little pure democracy in this country since early colonial days. In those days the business of government was carried on at town meetings.

Most of the early colonists settled in groups. They built their homes around a meetinghouse. The meetinghouse was used for worship. It was used for other purposes as well. Whenever the group had problems

HOW COLONIAL TOWN GOVERNMENT WORKED

Citizens make the laws
in Town Meeting

LEGISLATIVE BRANCH

Citizens elect officials
and selectmen to
enforce laws

EXECUTIVE BRANCH

Citizens elect judges
and court officers to
decide what laws mean

JUDICIAL BRANCH

to discuss, they met in their meetinghouse. They met there to make new laws and to choose new leaders. Such a gathering was called a town meeting. It was usually attended by everyone in town.

Even in those days some governmental powers were delegated. At the town meeting the people chose officers to govern them during the coming year. They first chose *selectmen*. The selectmen were given the authority to decide some of the town problems themselves. They did not always have to call the people together in a town meeting.

The people also chose other officers. Some of them were a clerk, a constable, a hogreeve, a fence viewer, and an overseer of chimneys.

As the nation grew westward, it became harder for people to meet together. County and city governments began to take the place of the town meeting. Today town meetings are held in only a few places, most of them in New England.

In those few places a form of town meeting is still held once a year. The problems for the coming year are discussed. If necessary, the selectmen may also call other meetings from time to time.

Notice is sent out some days in advance of each meeting. The notice tells what business is to be discussed. In this way each person has time to think about the problems.

The meeting is presided over by a chairman, or *moderator*. Many different opinions may be expressed by the citizens present. Sometimes a decision cannot be reached in one meeting. Then the meeting is adjourned to a later date.

The town meeting is an example of pure democracy at work. Such meetings train citizens to take part in their own government. It also makes any dishonesty in government easier to detect. But the town

Ewing Galloway

At town meetings everyone is free to express his own opinion of the matters being discussed. Each voter is his own representative. He participates directly in government.

160

meeting does not meet the needs of large cities. So many people cannot successfully meet in one room to discuss their problems. It is usually better for the people to select officials to represent them.

Town-meeting governments are not all exactly alike. Most of them, however, have a number of officers. The selectmen— three, five, seven, or nine—are chosen by popular vote. Their duties are similar to those of the mayor and city council in a small city. Other important officers in a town-meeting government are *treasurer, auditor, clerk, superintendent of schools, a school committee, chief of police, board of health*, and *a planning board*.

Whatever form town government takes, it has important work to do. The duties vary widely. They include enforcing health laws and providing public transportation. Recording births and deaths in the township is an important task. So is helping the poor. Police and fire protection must be provided. Public parks and public libraries must be established and maintained. Even though they elect others to do these things for them, the townspeople should not lose interest. Each person's stake in his town government is as great as it ever was. Each one should follow its activities as closely as if town meetings were still the order of the day.

The Government of Villages and Small Cities

To people who live in rural sections, county government is very important. The county government makes it possible for all the people in the county to work together. It provides common protection even for people who may live miles apart. In *villages*, however, people are grouped more closely together. They need a different form of government.

Villages are really small towns or cities. In the eastern states they are sometimes called *boroughs*. As you enter a village you may see a sign bearing the village name. Underneath the name you may see the word "Unincorporated" or "Incorporated." Many villages or small towns are *incorporated. This means that the state has granted them certain powers of self-government.*

How does a village become incorporated? Imagine a small farming community in the Middle West. The community is under the rule of the county government. As the years go by, the community grows. It becomes more thickly populated. The people notice neighboring towns, where their friends and relatives live. "The people in an incorporated town have more advantages than we have," they may say to one another. "Their streets are paved. They have street lights. They have a sewerage system and garbage collection. The county government cannot provide these things for us. It cannot tax the other people in the county for something that will not benefit them directly."

In order to get the things they want, the people may decide to incorporate. They apply to the state for the right to govern themselves as a town or village. The state allows them to incorporate and gives them some form of home rule. This gives the people of the village the right to tax themselves to pay for the conveniences they desire.

This is a typical peaceful, prosperous New England village of the present day. Proud of their democratic heritage, the people who live here keep in close touch with their local government.

This story of one village is typical of many others. As soon as a village is incorporated, it usually begins to change. New streets and sidewalks are built. Better street lights are installed. Water systems and drainage systems are built. An incorporated village usually provides a better school system than that furnished by the county. It gives the townspeople better police and fire protection. It builds public libraries and public playgrounds.

An incorporated village has its own public officials. They are usually the councilmen, or trustees; a mayor; a clerk; a treasurer; a chief of police; a health officer; and a justice of the peace. The council is the *lawmaking* body of the village. It has the power to make laws, or *ordinances*, for the village. It appoints officers to help the mayor govern the town. The mayor is the chief *executive* officer of the village. It is his duty to see that the town ordinances are carried out. The justice of the peace is the *judicial* officer of the village. It is his duty to try minor cases.

The other officers assist the mayor and the town council. They all work for the welfare of the people. Councilmen are usually elected by the people for a term of one or two years. The mayor, too, is elected for a term of one or two years. In most places the justice of the peace is elected, too.

The people in a small town or village know one another as friends and neighbors. This should help them work together for the common good of the community. But even in a small village, the people must be careful whom they choose to govern them. Honest and efficient leaders will help the community to grow and progress. They will give the people many advantages that inefficient leaders cannot give them.

At every level of democratic government, each person's vote is important. Elections have been decided by one vote. This is especially true in towns and villages. There are not very many voters in a town or village. As a result, every vote cast carries a great deal of weight. It is important to be well informed about matters of local government. It is important to vote intelligently in local elections. The outcome may affect your welfare as much as the results of state or national elections.

Things to Do

1. Make a list of the things you have done today. Show in what way government has affected each of them.
2. Try to make a list of ten things you do each day that are not affected by any phase of government. Check your list with those of other members of the class.
3. Learn the organization of government in your own county. Make a chart that will illustrate the work of the different county officers.
4. Pretend you are a county superintendent of schools. Keep a diary of your activities for a week.
5. You are living in a small community that is governed by the county. Write a short newspaper article explaining why you believe your community would progress faster if it were an incorporated city.
6. If you live in a small city, visit your city hall. Find out the names of the city officers and their duties.
7. Divide the class into four voting districts. Elect a town mayor. Then hold meetings of the citizens in each district. Let each group elect a representative to the town council. Decide what actions the councilmen should propose. Hold a meeting of the mayor and the council. Each councilman will present the action his district wants. Then the whole class, or meeting, can discuss the merits of each proposal. Adopt the proposal that is judged best for the welfare of the entire group.
8: Try to find an example of an election that was decided by a very few votes.

Questions to Answer

1. What is the main purpose of local governments?
2. Is your county governed by a county board of supervisors? What are the duties of a supervisor?
3. What are some of the duties of the county sheriff? Write these duties on the blackboard.
4. What is a bond? Why do you think the county treasurer is under a heavy bond? Are there other public officials under bond?
5. What kind of licenses does your county clerk issue?
6. Have you heard of a recent case prosecuted by your district attorney? Talk about it in class.
7. Can an honest district attorney influence other county officials to be more trustworthy and efficient? Why and how?
8. Why do the county coroner, the county sheriff, and the district attorney often work together? Do you think it is important to have a county coroner? Why?

9. How did town meetings originate?
10. What are the advantages and disadvantages of the town-meeting form of government?
11. What is the legislative body of a small town? Who heads the executive branch? Who is the judicial officer of a small town government?

A Written Exercise

Copy and complete the following sentences, using as many words as you choose.

1. Local governments usually provide the following services for the people: street lights, _____.
2. Some of the duties of the county board of supervisors are_____.
3. The sheriff is responsible for_____.
4. The district attorney must see that public officials_____.
5. The chief duty of the district attorney is to prosecute_____.
6. The county superintendent of schools is responsible for_____.
7. The county coroner investigates_____.
8. The county recorder records_____.
9. A town meeting is said to be true democracy at work because_____.
10. One disadvantage of a town-meeting government is_____.
11. An incorporated town grows faster than an unincorporated town because_____.
12. The lawmaking body of a village is_____.
13. An incorporated village is one that has_____.
14. The executive officer of a village is_____.
15. The judicial officer of a village is_____.
16. It is important to choose honest city officials because_____.
17. If a man is accused of a crime and has no money to pay a lawyer, his rights will be protected by_____.

Words to Study Before You Read the Next Topic

municipality	receded	quarantine
commission	corrupt	contagious
museums	sanitation	zoning
purified	viaducts	residential

TOPIC TWO

City Government

A *municipality* is a village, town, or city that has been granted the right to make and enforce its own local laws. Smaller municipalities are called villages or towns. Larger municipalities are cities.

In some states, a community must have a population of ten thousand to be called a city. In other states, communities with a population of only a few hundred may be incorporated as cities.

In all of the states, all of the people living in cities have some form of self-government. It is granted to them by the state legislature. They choose their own city officials. They make their own city laws. *They must do so, however, according to the laws of the state. They must abide by the provisions of the charter granted them by the legislature.*

Some states have laws which say that all cities must form the same kind of government. Other states divide the cities into classes according to size. Cities of the same class must establish the same form of government. In other states larger cities may choose their own form of government. The legislature decides the kind of government smaller cities may establish.

Three Forms of City Government

The first local governments were town-meeting governments. Soon many cities in our country became too large to be governed by town meetings. There were problems to be decided every day, if the cities were to grow and progress. People were demanding more and more services from their local governments.

"We want a police force," some of the people said. "We want policemen to protect the life and property of every citizen. We want them to enforce the laws of the city."

"We want an efficient fire department," said others. "Firemen are needed to protect the life and property of citizens from destruction by fire."

"We want our city to provide a pure water supply," was another demand.

The list of needs seemed endless. "The city is growing larger. Some of us do not

have means of transportation. It is difficult for us to go from one part of the city to another. We would like the city to provide some means of transportation."

"We want better lighting for the streets in the residential sections of our city."

"The city should build and maintain public parks and playgrounds for the children."

"We need art galleries, museums, and libraries. The city should build these for the enjoyment and the education of everyone."

"The health of our citizens should be protected. The city should establish sanitation rules and regulations. It should build public health clinics. We must try to see that every citizen stays strong and healthy."

And so it went. Americans wanted their city governments to perform more and more important services for them. In an attempt to provide these services three important forms of local government developed. One is the *mayor-council* type. Another is the *commission* type of government. The third is the *city-manager* type of government.

The Mayor-Council
Form of Government

The *mayor-council* type of city government is a very old one. It is patterned after the federal and the state governments. The council is the *lawmaking* branch of the city government. The mayor is the chief officer of the *executive* branch. Both the mayor and the council are elected by the people.

Under the mayor-council plan the council makes the laws and appropriates money. The mayor sees that the laws are carried out. He sees that the money appropriated is spent for the benefit of the people. The mayor usually appoints most of the other city officials. He must be very careful in his choices. It is he who is finally responsible to the people for good government.

The Commission
Type of Government

A good example of the *commission* type of government is the one used in Galveston, Texas. In 1900 a great tidal wave swept over a large part of Galveston. When the waters receded, five thousand people had lost their lives. The once thriving city was almost in ruins.

To handle the giant task of rebuilding the city, the Texas legislature appointed a commission of experts. The commission was given the power to pass and enforce any law necessary to rebuild the city. No one expected this form of government to become permanent. However, it was very successful in rebuilding Galveston. Since then the commission plan has been adopted by several other cities.

In most forms of commission government, five commissioners are elected by the people. These commissioners take the place of the mayor and the city council. *They make the laws and also see that the laws are carried out.* The power to govern the city is in their hands. Each commissioner is assigned to one department such as public works, public safety, or streets. Each commissioner appoints his own assistants.

The commission type of government can be very successful. It will be successful if

MAYOR-COUNCIL TYPE OF CITY GOVERNMENT

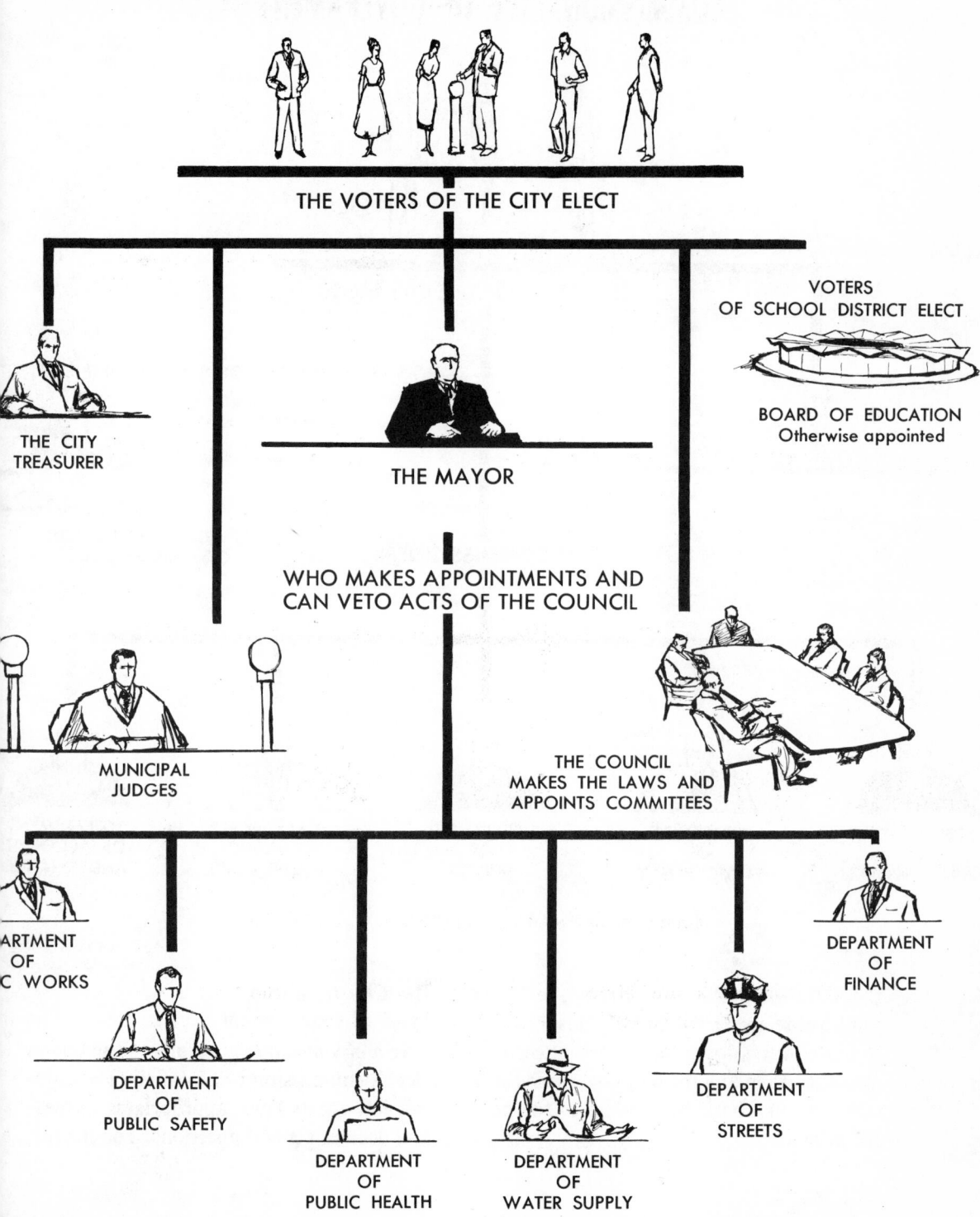

THE VOTERS OF THE CITY ELECT

THE CITY TREASURER

THE MAYOR

VOTERS OF SCHOOL DISTRICT ELECT

BOARD OF EDUCATION
Otherwise appointed

WHO MAKES APPOINTMENTS AND CAN VETO ACTS OF THE COUNCIL

MUNICIPAL JUDGES

THE COUNCIL MAKES THE LAWS AND APPOINTS COMMITTEES

ARTMENT OF C WORKS

DEPARTMENT OF PUBLIC SAFETY

DEPARTMENT OF PUBLIC HEALTH

DEPARTMENT OF WATER SUPPLY

DEPARTMENT OF STREETS

DEPARTMENT OF FINANCE

MARCEL GUILLIAMS

COMMISSION TYPE OF GOVERNMENT

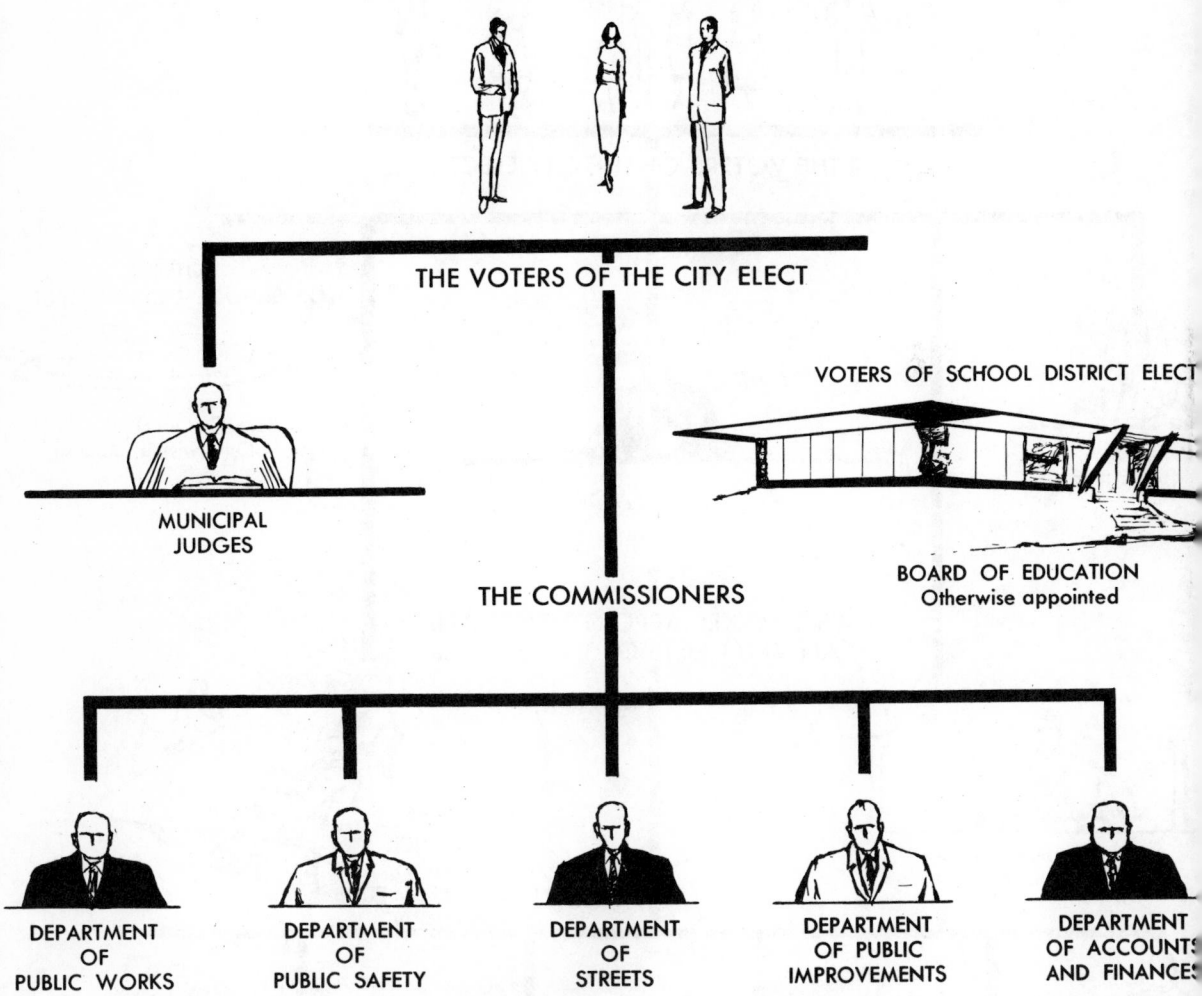

THE VOTERS OF THE CITY ELECT

VOTERS OF SCHOOL DISTRICT ELECT

MUNICIPAL
JUDGES

THE COMMISSIONERS

BOARD OF EDUCATION
Otherwise appointed

DEPARTMENT
OF
PUBLIC WORKS

DEPARTMENT
OF
PUBLIC SAFETY

DEPARTMENT
OF
STREETS

DEPARTMENT
OF PUBLIC
IMPROVEMENTS

DEPARTMENT
OF ACCOUNTS
AND FINANCES

Each commissioner appoints his own assistants

MARCEL GUILLIAMS

the commissioners are honest, efficient public officials. It will be very unsuccessful if the commissioners are not honest and efficient. As in any form of government the officials must have the welfare of the people at heart.

The City-Manager Type of Government

In a *city-manager* government the voters elect a commission or a council. The commission enacts laws, appropriates money, and decides general questions. The mayor,

CITY-MANAGER TYPE OF GOVERNMENT

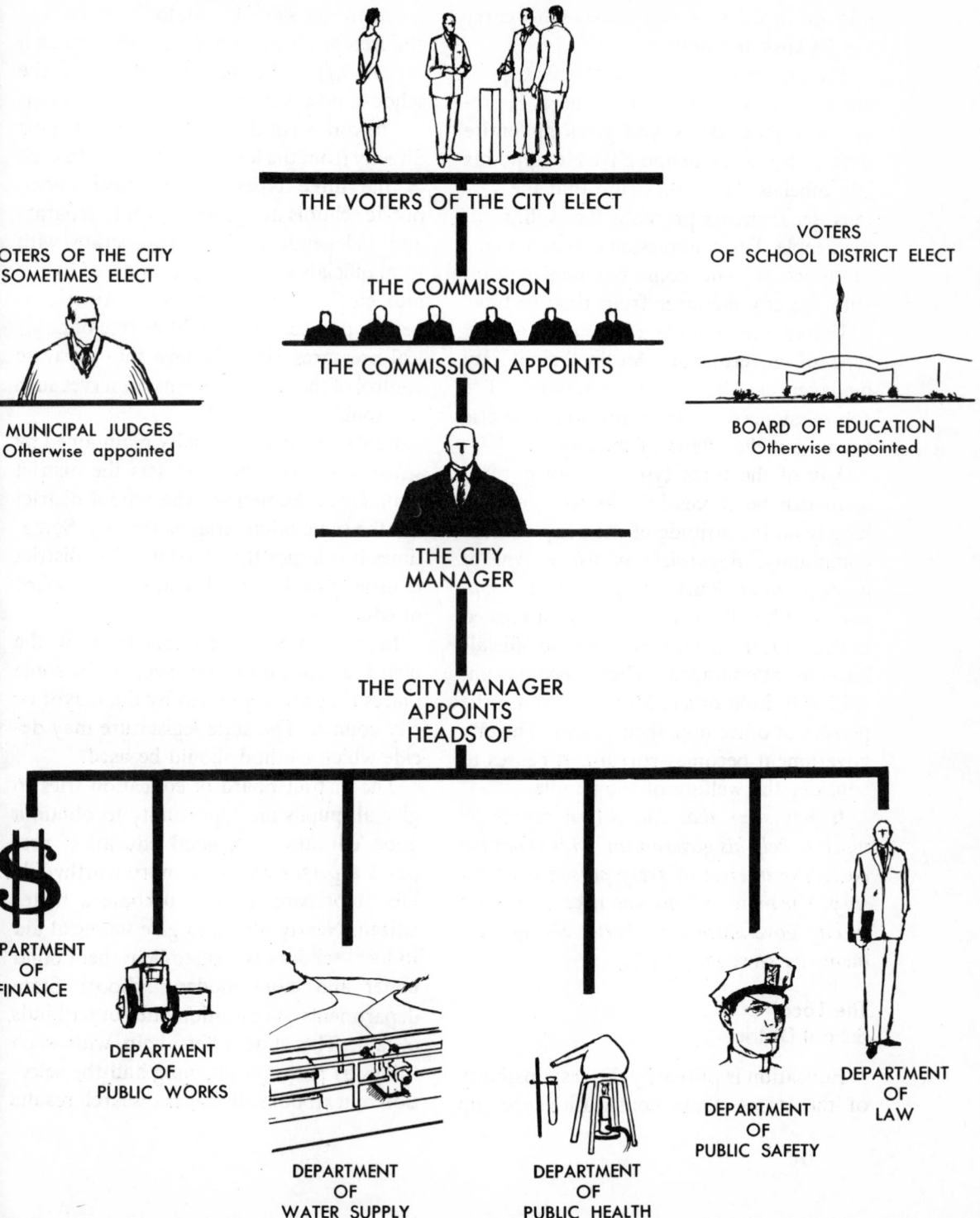

THE VOTERS OF THE CITY ELECT

THE COMMISSION

THE COMMISSION APPOINTS

OTERS OF THE CITY
SOMETIMES ELECT

MUNICIPAL JUDGES
Otherwise appointed

VOTERS
OF SCHOOL DISTRICT ELECT

BOARD OF EDUCATION
Otherwise appointed

THE CITY
MANAGER

THE CITY MANAGER
APPOINTS
HEADS OF

EPARTMENT
OF
FINANCE

DEPARTMENT
OF
PUBLIC WORKS

DEPARTMENT
OF
WATER SUPPLY

DEPARTMENT
OF
PUBLIC HEALTH

DEPARTMENT
OF
PUBLIC SAFETY

DEPARTMENT
OF
LAW

MARCEL GUILLIAMS

if there is one, has little power. The commission *appoints a city manager* to carry out its laws and policies.

The city manager is usually an experienced businessman or an engineer. He receives a good salary and gives his entire time to the work of the city. He appoints city officials. He makes sure that the various departments promote the welfare of the people. The commission acts as a board of directors. The commissioners consult with the city manager from time to time.

There is one advantage in a city-manager type of government. An inefficient city manager can be readily dismissed. The commissioners can then hire someone else to manage the affairs of the city.

Any of the three types of city government can be successful. Success depends largely on the attitude of the people in the community. *Regardless of which type of government is chosen, the people must support it.* When the people are not interested in their government, honest public officials become discouraged. They become unwilling to hold office. Men who abuse the powers of office take their places. The city government becomes corrupt. It ceases to consider the welfare of the people.

It may seem that one citizen cannot do much to help his government. This is not the case. The interest of every person is necessary. The more citizens who take an interest in city government, the better the government can serve the people.

The Local School District

Education is primarily the responsibility of the states. State constitutions set up certain standards and rules for the establishment of schools. State laws require children to go to school until they reach a certain age. The actual control of the schools, however, is usually a local matter.

The control of the schools does not come directly from the local government. In each of the three types of city government, public schools are generally quite separate and independent. They co-operate with local officials but are not dominated by the municipal government. Most Americans believe that schools should be free of political pressures. They believe that separate control of the school systems preserves such freedom.

Public schools are usually maintained by *school districts*. The state sets the district boundaries. Sometimes the school district has the same boundaries as the city. Sometimes it is larger than the city. The district is usually under the direction of a board of education.

In most places, the members of the board of education are elected. In some places they are appointed by the mayor or city council. The state legislature may decide which method should be used.

The district board of education tries to give all pupils an opportunity to obtain a good education. A good education prepares a person to live a more worthwhile life. It prepares him to become a better citizen. Nearly all states give financial aid to local school districts to help them build better and more modern schools. State departments of education offer other kinds of aid. The state offers help with such things as program planning and the selection of textbooks. It makes research results

available to school districts. The federal government also helps. Under the National Defense Education Act, school districts can ask financial aid for certain purposes. But neither the state nor the federal government dictates school policy. This is determined by local school boards.

Services of a City Government

City dwellers want their city government to provide them with many services. One important service is the provision of a fresh, pure water supply. This requires the building of waterworks. The water must be pumped, filtered, and purified. It must be piped into homes and buildings. Sometimes a city must pipe the water supply from lakes or rivers many miles away.

Cities also employ experts to examine food that is prepared for sale. They have experts who inspect dairy farms, markets, factories, restaurants, and bakeries. These experts all help to keep the people healthy and well fed.

Nearly every city has a department of health. The city health officials keep a record of births and deaths in the city. They quarantine persons who have contagious diseases. They teach people how to prevent disease and how to remain well and healthy. Many cities also have public hospitals and clinics. These hospitals and clinics care for people who cannot afford to pay for other medical care.

City governments remove trash and garbage and clean the streets. They build and repair bridges, streets, viaducts, and underpasses. They light the city streets and mark them with names and numbers. They main-

Ewing Galloway

Among the important city documents in this fireproof vault are the signed originals of city laws and ordinances.

tain police and fire departments for the protection of the people. They build libraries, parks, and community swimming pools. They support museums and art galleries for the pleasure and education of the citizens.

Cities also try to plan for the future. They plan new public buildings. They try to improve certain districts of the city. They pass zoning laws. Zoning laws help keep factories and office buildings from the residential parts of the town. Cities do many, many things to help their citizens live together happily and peacefully.

Things to Do

1. Make an illustrated chart showing some of the things a city government does for the people of the city.
2. Make a list of the things you can do to co-operate with the city officials.
3. Make a chart showing the organization of your municipal government. Show the names of the officials now in office.
4. What are some of the laws in your state regarding the establishment of municipal governments?
5. Write a newspaper editorial expressing your opinion as to whether your form of local government is the best one for your community. Be sure to give your reasons. Support your reasons with facts and figures.
6. With all class members voting, choose a form of government for your classroom.
7. Select candidates for office in your classroom government and conduct an election campaign.
8. When the election is over, present your new officials with a list of projects you think they should consider for classroom betterment.

Questions to Answer

1. What qualities do you think are desirable in a city official? Why?
2. Do you know of a recent city ordinance that was passed by your city council? How did the council pass it? Why was it passed?
3. Why is an inefficient city government expensive?
4. Do you think it is necessary for cities to establish and maintain parks? Give reasons for your opinion.
5. What is the source of the water used in your community? What is done to insure its purity?
6. Why is it necessary to keep records of births and deaths in your community?
7. In what ways is your community planning for the future?
8. Your local government performs many services for you. How are these services financed?

A Written Exercise

Copy and complete the following statements. Use as many words and sentences as you wish.

1. Most city governments provide these services for the people: street lighting; _____.
2. The three kinds of city government are_____.

3. The commission type of city government became prominent in_____.
4. No city government will work efficiently unless_____.
5. In the city-manager type of government the manager is chosen on the basis of_____.
6. Public schools are usually maintained by_____.

Words to Study Before You Read the Next Topic

appellate	circuit	handicapped
deceased	resources	fertile
probate	universities	conservation
juvenile	orphans	municipal

TOPIC THREE

State Government

THE first purpose of any state government is to provide peace and order. Beyond that, the state government helps protect the rights to which its citizens are entitled. To this end, all state governments perform many services for the people. Some of these services are listed below.

1) Guarding the health of the people.
2) Providing for the education of the people.
3) Helping to care for those in need.
4) Improving transportation within the state.
5) Protecting the forests, mineral deposits, and other natural resources of the state.
6) Protecting the lives and property of all citizens.
7) Regulating many kinds of business within the state.
8) Improving the living and working conditions of the people.

Each state has a group of officials who help to protect the health of the people. Some of these officials examine the qualifications of doctors, nurses, druggists, and others. If these persons are qualified, the state issues licenses entitling them to work. They join in the fight against disease and death.

The states also maintain hospitals. There are hospitals for both the mentally and physically ill. State inspectors see to it that these hospitals are properly maintained.

Other state health officials examine foods and drugs. They test to be sure the foods and drugs are safe to use. Every state has laws that forbid the sale of harmful drugs. Every state has laws against selling impure or spoiled food. Most of the states have laws which say that dairy cattle must be inspected. If the cattle are found to be diseased, they are destroyed. State health officials try in many ways to prevent the spread of disease. They try to keep all the people as healthy and happy as possible.

State governments also help to educate the people. They provide some state schools and help to support other public schools. All states have laws that require children to attend school until they reach a certain age. State school officials help to decide what courses of study shall be used in the schools. In some states they decide what textbooks shall be used in the public schools.

The first great state university was founded in Virginia in 1825. Now all the states have their own universities and state colleges. The state college campus shown here is in Iowa.

Sometimes a community cannot raise enough money to build the schools it needs. In that case, some state money may be allotted to help with the construction. States also maintain state colleges and universities. Sometimes they provide schools for special purposes. In one, housewives may learn how to manage a home. In another, workmen might learn trades and crafts. There are some state schools where farmers can learn better methods of farming. Sometimes a person trained in one trade has to give it up. Perhaps illness or an accident makes it impossible for him to do that kind of work any longer. Most states help such a person to learn another trade. They would help him to help himself to earn a living.

States build and repair state roads. They help pay the cost of building and repairing county and township roads. State governments work with the national government in planning, building, and paying for national highways.

States employ highway patrol officers to enforce the state traffic laws. They issue licenses to the owners of cars and trucks. In most states a person cannot drive any motor vehicle unless he has received a driver's license. To get a driver's license, a person must pass certain tests. He must prove that he is capable of driving intelligently, skillfully, and courteously.

Nearly all states have speed laws for automobiles. They have other rules as well for highway safety. A very common one is that railway crossings must be guarded by gates or signal lights.

The state helps to pay for those city streets or freeways that form part of the state highway system.

California State Department of Public Works

States usually help to care for citizens who cannot take care of themselves. They build and operate homes for orphans and crippled children. They provide homes for the needy aged, and schools for the deaf and the blind.

For many years the people of the United States did nothing to conserve the country's natural resources. Today both state and federal governments try to stop this waste. They set aside timberlands for state and national forests. They plant young trees to replace those that have been cut down.

To make their states better places in which to live, state governments perform many services.

1) They protect birds and wild animals.
2) They try to teach farmers how to keep the soil fertile.
3) They try to prevent the washing away of fertile soil.
4) They provide for the proper use of water power in rivers and streams.
5) They regulate the removal of oil, coal, and other minerals from the ground.
6) They bring waters from rivers and lakes to irrigate dry lands.
7) They create and manage state and national parks.

States also supervise and inspect working conditions in mines, factories, and other places. They make rules for railroad companies and other transportation lines. They supervise gas, water, telephone, telegraph, and electric companies. They pass laws regulating the number of hours women and children may work.

State governments perform many, many services. They work with local governments and with the federal government to promote the general welfare.

Redwood Empire Association

The northward-flowing Eel River courses through a beautiful, wooded state park in California.

The Organization of State Governments

Each state has a constitution. The constitution is the state's plan of government. The state government does not receive its powers from the federal government. *State powers come directly from the people of the state.* The people may put any provision they choose into their state constitution. The only restriction is that state laws must *not conflict with any provision in the Constitution of the United States.*

State constitutions are very much like the federal Constitution. Each provides for a governor. The governor has the same position in the state as the President has in the nation. Each state except Nebraska

177

This is the lower house of a state legislature while in session. The aisle separates political parties.

has a two-house legislature, just as our national government has. Each state has a system of courts. The courts, too, correspond roughly to our federal courts. The state supreme court is the highest court in every state, except New York. In New York the highest court is the Court of Appeals.

Some of the state constitutions are amended frequently. Generally amendments are approved by the direct vote of the people.

State Legislatures

The state legislature is the lawmaking, or *legislative*, body of the state government. It serves the same purpose in the state as Congress does in the nation. *The state legislature sees that the state constitution serves the needs of the people.* As the needs of the people and the state change, the state legislature changes old laws. It makes new laws, to fit the changing times.

All of the state legislatures except

Nebraska have two houses. The upper house is called the *senate*. The lower house is called the *house of representatives*, or the *assembly*. Senators and assemblymen are elected by the people. The number varies in each state. The smallest house of representatives has thirty-five members. The largest house has four hundred. The smallest senate has seventeen members. The largest senate has sixty-seven.

In Nebraska the state constitution was amended in 1934 to provide for a *unicameral*, or one-house, legislature. The amendment says that the legislature shall be a one-house group with from thirty to fifty members. The exact number was set at forty-three.

In most states the state senators are elected for four years. State representatives are usually elected for two years. In a few states both serve two years, and in a few others both serve four years. The senators and representatives are elected from counties or districts within the state.

The Duties of the State Legislatures

State senators and representatives or assemblymen are all called legislators. Their main duty is to pass laws. They are expected to pass laws that safeguard the rights of the people. They are expected to promote the welfare of the state.

The people say to their legislators, "Go to the state capital. Look after our interests there. Make laws that will protect us from dishonest persons and from criminals. We want laws that will protect us against theft and robbery. We want laws that will protect us against accidents at work. Make laws that will provide good working conditions. See that our state laws protect us against dishonest businessmen."

There are already thousands of laws in every state. Still the people ask for changes and additions.

"Give us health laws that will protect us against epidemics," they may say. "Give us laws that provide for the inspection of milk. Give us laws to protect us on the highways and at railroad crossings. Protect us against personal and property damage.

"Provide for the blind, the deaf, the poor, and the children who are orphans. Give us good hospitals for the people suffering from mental diseases. Give us training schools for the mentally handicapped. Give us institutions where boys and girls who have broken the law can learn right from wrong. Pass laws that will help them become good citizens.

"Control and regulate such public utilities as electric, gas, telephone, water, and transportation service. Establish rates for these services so we will not be charged unfair prices. Inspect our state banks from time to time. We want to be sure that our savings are secure. Inspect other corporations that handle money invested by the public. Give us a good educational system for our children. Examine state budget requests carefully before you approve them.

"Protect our game and other wild life. Pass laws that will protect our scenery and our state parks. Help protect the farmer against loss from plant disease and other causes."

These are some of the responsibilities placed upon the state legislatures by the

people. The people who elect the legislators have a responsibility, too. *It is the voters' responsibility to choose efficient men to govern the state.*

How State Laws Are Introduced and Passed

Each house in the state legislature chooses its own officers. Each conducts its business according to parliamentary law. In many of the states the lieutenant governor presides over the senate. The officer who presides over the lower house is known as the *speaker.*

Any member of either house may introduce a bill. Some states have a department to help the legislators prepare their bills. After a bill has been introduced, it is read by title. To *read by title* means to state the purposes and the object of the bill. After reading, it is given a number and ordered to be printed.

In some states all bills to raise money must originate in the lower house. Other bills may be introduced in either house. There are usually hundreds of bills introduced at each session of the legislature. Each legislator could not study every bill. Instead, committees are appointed to study the different bills. These committees are very important. They may combine several bills into one. They may change or alter a bill. If they believe a bill is unwise, they may even "kill" it. In that case, the bill never reaches the calendar. The *calendar* is the schedule of bills to come before the legislature.

In all states except Nebraska a bill must pass each house of the legislature separately. If it is passed by both houses, it is

Spivak—FPG

State public health nurses visit homes and schools. They help people who are ill, but they are equally concerned with preventing illness. They are concerned with both mental and physical health.

sent to the governor for his approval. If the governor signs it, it becomes a law. However, the governor may veto the bill. In most states a bill that has been vetoed by the governor may become a law anyway. It becomes a law if it is repassed by a two-thirds majority of each house.

The State Executive Department

Every one of our fifty states has a governor. Governors are elected by the voters for terms of from two to four years. It is the governor's duty to see that the state laws are carried out. He has control over the state police. In time of peace he also has control over the state militia. He may

call the legislature into special session at any time he believes it is necessary. He may call a special session to consider emergency laws he thinks are needed.

The governor has a great deal of influence over the legislature. He can send messages to the houses recommending some bills and disapproving others. He can veto bills passed by the state legislature. The relationship between a governor and the legislature is like that between the President and Congress.

If the governor believes a certain bill should be passed, he may call in the press. He may say to the reporters, "Bring this bill to the attention of the public. Discuss it in your newspapers and magazines. Ask the people to write to their legislators, urging them to pass the bill." By arousing public opinion, the governor can sometimes speed the passing of much-needed laws.

The governor of any state has many powers and duties. Perhaps his most important power is the right to appoint public officials. He appoints heads of various departments. He appoints members of state boards such as the tax board, the board of education, and the board of public utilities. If he makes wise appointments, the interests of the people will be safeguarded. If he makes unwise appointments, the state government will not serve the needs of the people.

The governor is the chief executive officer of the state. Most state constitutions also provide for an *executive department*. Other officers of the executive department include the *lieutenant governor* and the *secretary of state*. The *state auditor*, the

state treasurer, and the *state superintendent of public instruction* are also part of the executive department. The governor does not have any legal power over these officers. Their powers and duties are usually listed in the state constitution.

State Agencies

In most states the legislature meets only for short periods of time every two years. Yet the work of the state government must go on day after day. The public schools of the state must be kept open. The public health must be guarded. Roads must be built and repaired. Police protection must be given the citizens. Prisons, state hospitals, and other state institutions must be maintained.

How is this done? Many of the services of the state government are performed by state boards or state departments. Some of the most common boards are the tax board, the board of education, and the public utilities board. Some of the most common departments are agriculture, education, finance, and employment. There are also departments responsible for state prisons, charities, hospitals, roads, and public health. Some departments are concerned only with the conservation of state resources. From time to time, if the need arises, new departments are created.

Many of the people working for these boards and departments are *state civil service* employees. That means they have passed certain qualifying tests. It means that their salaries and certain of their working conditions are prescribed by state law. It is important to have efficient civil service

employees. The success of the state government depends to a great extent on their work.

State Courts

Each state has its own system of courts. In most states they are of two types: (1) *trial* courts and (2) *appellate* courts. The trial courts are also called lower courts. They are courts in which cases are first considered, or *tried*. The appellate courts are those to which cases decided in the lower courts may be *appealed*.

The legislature has the power to create the lower trial courts. The legislature also decides how many such courts there shall be. It decides where such courts will be located.

There are various kinds of trial courts. They include justices' courts, police courts, and municipal courts. These courts try cases involving small sums of money and minor offenses.

The more important trial courts are county courts. They are usually called *circuit courts, district courts*, or *superior courts*. These courts hear *civil* cases, or cases between private parties. They also try *criminal* cases in which the state prosecutes a person accused of a serious crime. The circuit courts or superior courts are principally trial courts. They may also have the power, however, to decide appeals from lower trial courts.

In addition to the regular trial courts there are special courts for special purposes. The *probate court* settles the estates of deceased persons. It orders their property distributed as directed in their wills. If there is no will, the court distributes the estate among the rightful heirs.

The *juvenile court* cares for neglected or abandoned children. It handles the cases of children who are accused of wrongdoing. It protects the rights of children who are brought into court.

The appellate courts are higher than the trial courts. First a case is tried in a trial court and a decision given. Then the losing party may *appeal* the case to an appellate court. He may say that he feels the decision is unfair. The appellate court usually consists of three, five, seven, or nine judges. These judges study the record of what took place in the trial court. They hear arguments from attorneys on both sides. Then they make their decision. If the appellate judges decide the trial court was right, they *affirm*, or approve, its decision. If they believe the trial court was wrong, they *reverse*, or *modify*, the decision. The case may be sent back for a new trial.

Most of the states have one highest court of appeals. It is usually called the *state supreme court*. The supreme court reviews cases that are appealed from the lower courts. The decision of the supreme court is final unless the question involves the Constitution, federal law, or treaties of the United States. Then the case may be appealed to the United States Supreme Court.

Judges of state courts are usually elected by the people. Sometimes a vacancy occurs during a judge's term of office. When that happens, a new judge may be appointed. The appointment may be made by the governor or another officer having this power.

STATE COURTS

STATE SUPREME COURT
Highest State Appellate Court

INTERMEDIATE APPELLATE COURTS

PROBATE COURTS
Trial Courts

CIRCUIT or SUPERIOR COURTS
Trial Courts, and Appellate Courts
for Justices' Courts

**JUVENILE
COURTS**
Trial Courts

JUSTICES' and CITY COURTS
Trial Courts

MARCEL GUILLIAMS

Things to Do

1. Try to find an example of co-operation between your state government and the federal government. Write a short report for the class.
2. Make a chart of the executive department of your state government. Show the names of the people now holding the executive positions.
3. Arrange to visit a county, district, or city court. Make a report to the class.
4. Explain the work of the governor of the state. Write a newspaper editorial entitled, "A Good Governor Should Have These Qualifications."

Questions to Answer

1. What are some advantages of a *bicameral*, or two-house, legislature? What are some of its disadvantages?
2. How often and for what period does your state legislature meet?
3. Can you think of any situation in your district that should be called to the attention of your legislators? How would you go about directing their attention to such a situation?
4. Who is the state senator from your district? Who is the representative or assemblyman? Do you know of a bill that either has introduced in the state legislature? What do you think were the reasons for introducing the bill?
5. How many members are there in your own state legislature? How many senators? How many representatives?
6. Within a few years you will be voting for state legislators. What qualifications will you look for in the candidates?
7. How does your state constitution resemble the federal Constitution? What are some of the ways in which it differs?
8. What responsibilities will you, as a voter, have with respect to your state government?

A Written Exercise

On a piece of paper write the numbers 1 through 5. After number 1, write the letter that appears before the phrase which makes the sentence correct. Do the same with each number.

1. The chief executive officer of the state government is
   a) the attorney general.
   b) the governor.
   c) the chief justice of the state supreme court.

2. The only state having a one-house legislature is
   a) Rhode Island.
   b) Kentucky.
   c) Nebraska.
3. Courts that review cases appealed from other courts are called
   a) trial courts.
   b) appellate courts.
   c) district courts.
4. In the state legislature the calendar is
   a) the time of year the legislature convenes.
   b) the days of the week the senators and assemblymen work.
   c) the schedule of bills to come before the legislature.
5. Probate courts were established to
   a) protect the rights of children who are brought into court.
   b) settle the estates of deceased persons.
   c) decide cases that have been appealed from other courts.

Words to Study Before You Read the Next Topic

concessions	smuggling	dissenting	engrossed
schedule	concurring	tack	sponsored
minority	delegation	confers	pending

A Visit to Washington

IT is a great honor to be chosen President of the United States. But being President is a difficult and wearing task. Even in normal times the President has little time to think of his own personal affairs. His days and most of his evenings are taken up with the affairs of the nation. In time of war or national emergency there are very few hours he can call his own.

The President has several secretaries. One is his appointment secretary. That secretary's main duty is making appointments for the President. The appointment secretary must also try to see that appointments begin and end on schedule.

These might be the President's activities on a typical day.

9:00 The Senator from Oklahoma calls to discuss plans for a government project in his state.

9:30 The President confers with a committee investigating the production of defense materials.

10:00 The President holds a news conference to inform reporters of important national and world developments.

10:30 The ambassador from England calls to discuss plans for cooperation between his country and the United States.

11:30 The Secretary of Agriculture calls to discuss the nation's agricultural industry.

12:00 The President has lunch with the Vice-President, the Speaker of the House, and other political leaders of both houses. They discuss important legislation that is pending in the Senate and the House of Representatives.

1:00 A delegation of congressmen arrive at the White House to be present when the President signs an important bill they sponsored.

1:30 The President receives ambassadors from Canada and Mexico.

2:00 The President reads his mail, which has been carefully sorted by his secretaries.

3:00 The President receives a labor delegation proposing a way to improve labor-management relations.

4:00 The President confers with his Army, Navy, and Air Force chiefs concerning new developments in warfare.

5:00 The working day is over, but the President discusses national problems with some of his advisers.

8:00 The President delivers a television address.

9:00 It is time for the President to rest, but he talks with a member of his Cabinet regarding problems in that department.

11:00 The President retires for the night, still thinking about the problems of the nation.

The President is a very busy man. He is the head of the largest organization in the nation—the federal government. He and his helpers work long hours. All the services of the government are in their charge. The growth and progress of the nation are in their hands.

A Glimpse at Congress

Congressmen also work long hours. They have a double responsibility. They are directly responsible to the people of their own state. They also have an obligation to the nation. A congressman must try to satisfy the people of his own district. He must also be fair to the rest of the nation.

The following imaginary story will illustrate part of the work of Senators and Representatives. The *aid-to-education bill* referred to in the story is not a real bill. Congress has passed aid-to-education bills, but this is not one of them.

Suppose that one of the Representatives from Colorado is named Curtis Howard. Suppose that Mr. Howard has been in the House for many years. His secretary, Miss Burton, has worked for him much of that time. She knows many of the rules and customs of the Congress as well as he does. One morning she hands him a large basket of mail. "The people at home are worried about the shortage of schools," she says. "Every day you get letters asking that Congress do something about it."

"Congress is worrying about the problem, too," replies Congressman Howard. "The people in all states are becoming insistent. We must act soon. I think I shall introduce a bill calling for some kind of federal aid. Will you go to the Library of Congress and find all the material you can that will help me in writing the bill? Bring me any books, magazine articles, or newspaper editorials you can find on the subject."

Miss Burton asked for help from the *Legislative Reference Service* in the Library of Congress. It took many hours to gather the material Congressman Howard wanted. He studied it very carefully. Then he held conferences with other people who were also studying the problem. Finally he felt he was ready to introduce the bill.

Before a bill can be introduced it must be put into the proper legal form. Congressman Howard took his bill to the *Office of Legislative Counsel*. In this office an expert hired by the Speaker of the House helped him prepare his bill correctly.

Then Congressman Howard took his bill to the House. He arrived just as the Sergeant at Arms was placing the mace at the

right of the Speaker's platform. The mace is a symbol of authority. It is placed in position as a sign that the House is in session. Then the chaplain arose. He opened the meeting with a prayer. After the prayer, the journal of the proceedings of the previous day was read and approved. Then it was time for the business of the day.

Before finding a seat, Congressman Howard walked up to the desk of the House clerk. He placed a copy of his bill in the large box on the desk. Then he went to sit with friends on his side of the aisle. (In the House, Democrats sit on the Speaker's right. Republicans sit to his left.) He knew that the clerk would give his bill a number. He knew that the numbered bill would be printed that very night. Printed copies of it would be available the next morning.

Lobbyists are often invited to appear at committee hearings to express their views for or against a bill under consideration. Most hearings are open to the public. Anyone interested may come to listen.

Ewing Galloway

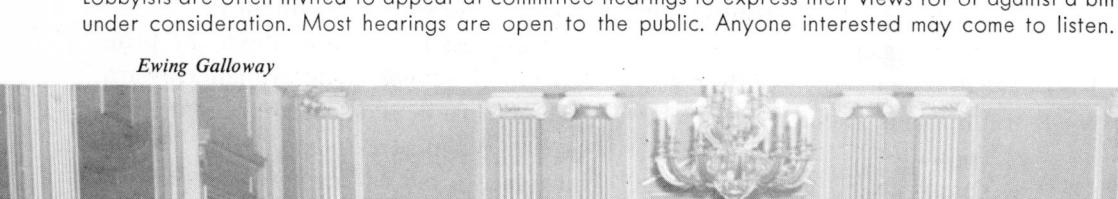

The bill was numbered H.R. 9999. "H.R." stands for "House of Representatives." The number meant that 9998 other House bills had already been introduced during that session of Congress. When other congressmen spoke of the bill they might refer to it by number. Many of them might call it simply "the Howard Bill."

The next day the Howard Bill was printed by title in the *Congressional Record*. Then the House Parliamentarian referred it to the proper committee for study. The committee members studied the bill very carefully. Should they "kill it in committee"? Or should they present it to the House for consideration? The committees "kill" many bills that are sent to them. They send only about one out of every ten bills to the House floor. The aid-to-education bill was considered very important. There would be many people in favor of it. There would be many others who would not like it. What was the fair thing to do? What would promote the welfare of the majority of the people?

The committee held public hearings upon the bill. The committee members sat around a long table. They listened to the people who appeared before them. Some of the people were private citizens, interested in their children's schooling. Some were educators. Some were officials of government agencies interested in the problems involved. Some were from labor organizations. Some represented taxpayers' associations. Many of the people argued in favor of the bill. Others were strongly opposed to it. The committee members questioned the speakers very carefully. They wanted to understand thoroughly all sides of the problem.

After the hearings, the committee again studied the bill. The committee members discussed the reactions of the people. The committee could recommend the bill by giving a favorable report to the House. They could recommend changes or amendments. Or they could "kill" the bill by not reporting upon it at all.

Congressman Howard's Bill was too important to kill. Yet many of the committee members did not believe that it would solve the problem. They suggested some amendments and additional provisions. Then they reported favorably upon it. The bill was placed on the calendar. Bills are called for debate in the order in which they appear on the calendar.

Lobbying

Congressman Howard, as well as many other Representatives, began to receive floods of mail. They also received telegrams and telephone calls from people interested in the bill. Many of them expressed enthusiasm for the bill. Others condemned it. The lobbyists in Washington had been busy.

Lobbyists are men and women who work for some special group or organization. Each lobbyist tries to get congressmen to vote for bills favoring the interests of his group. He tries to influence them against bills harmful to those interests. This is called *lobbying*.

Nearly every large organization in the United States has lobbyists in Washington. The lobbyists watch closely all bills that are introduced in Congress. If a bill threatens the interests of their group, they go to work. They try in many different ways to

get congressmen to vote against the measure. They do all they can to defeat the bill.

Lobbyists not only work *against* certain bills. They also try to have certain bills passed. Sometimes they even draft a bill and persuade a congressman to introduce it. Then they urge the other Senators and Representatives to vote for it. They work hard to try to get the bill passed.

Lobbying can be both good and bad. Sometimes lobbyists help Congress to understand how the people really feel about a bill. Sometimes they are thinking only of their own special interests. This is another reason why voters should be cautious and well informed. They must be careful to elect lawmakers who are honest, trustworthy, and capable.

The Bill
in the House

The first reading of a bill is called "reading by title." Today it is not really a reading at all. Simply *printing* it by title in the *Congressional Record* is sufficient. Next comes consideration in the House. At that point the bill is open to amendment.

The day came for consideration and general debate on the Howard Bill. The congressmen who disliked the bill were prepared to speak against it. If they felt this would not prevent its passage, they would try another approach. They would offer amendments that would take the strength out of the bill. Congressman Howard, on the other hand, was prepared to defend his bill.

With great force, congressmen argued for and against the bill. Some of them wanted to talk for more than an hour. The House has a rule about that, however. To talk longer than an hour, a congressman must have the unanimous consent of the House. Such consent was not given to anyone speaking on the Howard Bill.

Then amendments were offered and argued about. Those arguments were limited to five minutes each. The amendments were voted on and defeated.

All this time, there were private arguments and conversations going on. The big House chamber was a noisy place. Finally the Speaker rapped his gavel for silence. "Shall the bill be engrossed and read a third time?"

All those congressmen in favor said "Aye." There were several " nays," too, but the " ayes" were in the majority. Only the title of the bill was read. Any member could have asked that it be read in full. No one did, though. They were all familiar with its contents.

Then the Speaker called for a vote on passage of the bill. That time it was impossible to tell whether there were more "ayes" or "nays." A congressman from Utah stood up and said "Mr. Speaker." When he was recognized he said, "I ask for a division." This meant he wanted a standing vote on the bill. Any member may make such a request. First those in favor of the bill were asked to stand up and be counted. Then those opposed stood up. The first group was larger. The bill had passed!

A Threat
of Filibuster

Now Congressman Howard's Bill was sent to the Senate. There, too, it was

LOBBYING

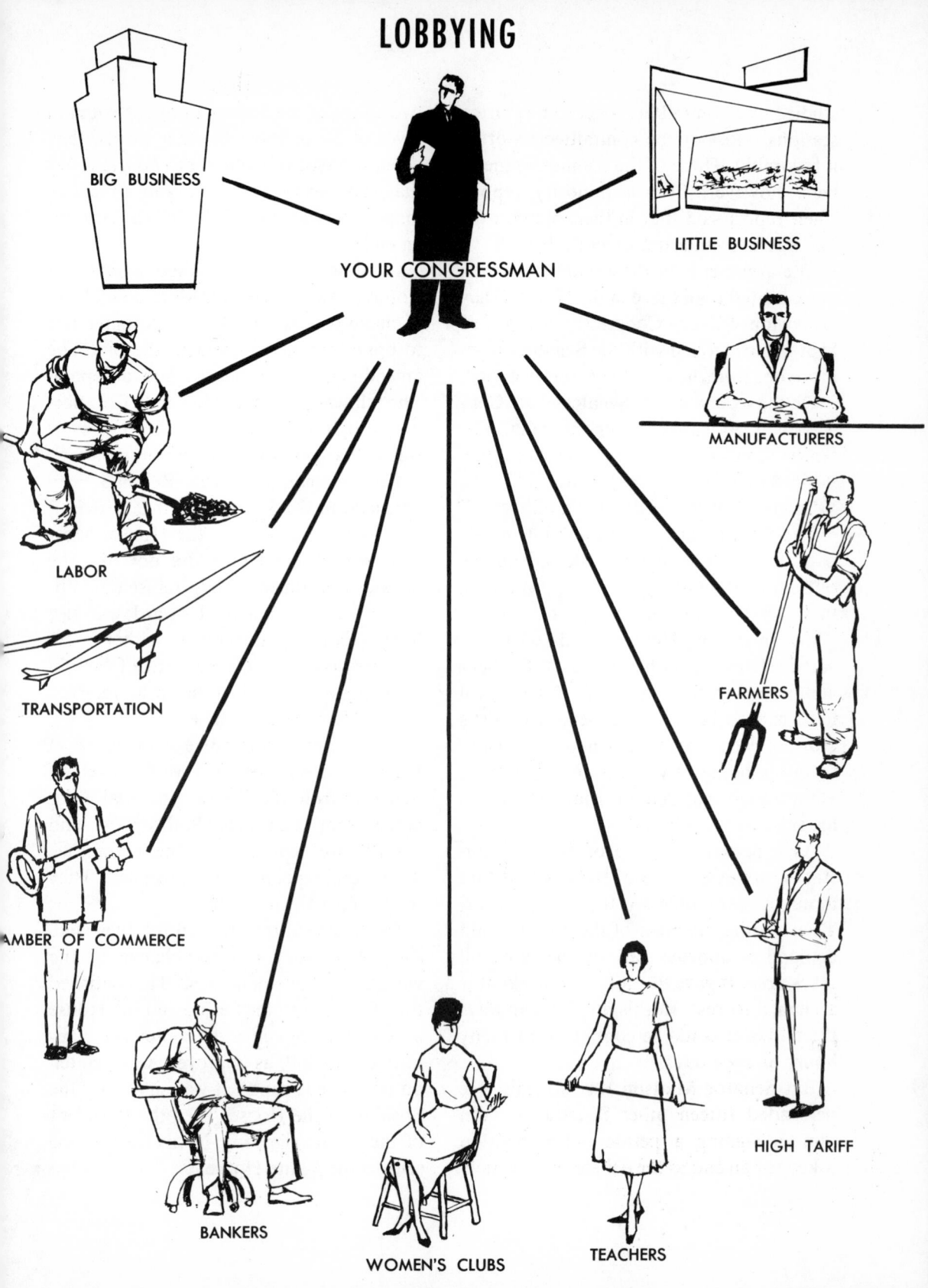

BIG BUSINESS

YOUR CONGRESSMAN

LITTLE BUSINESS

LABOR

TRANSPORTATION

MANUFACTURERS

FARMERS

AMBER OF COMMERCE

HIGH TARIFF

BANKERS

WOMEN'S CLUBS

TEACHERS

MARCEL GUILLIAMS

studied by a committee. After some stormy sessions, most of the committee reported it favorably. Three of the committee members, however, filed a minority report. Their report said that in their opinion the bill was unsound and unworkable.

The arguments in the Senate were even more heated than those in the House. They lasted longer, too. Congressman Howard kept in close touch with the Senators from his state. Both he and they were worried.

On the second day of Senate debate Congressman Howard's telephone rang. The senior Senator from Colorado was calling. "It looks bad, Curt," the Senator told him. "I'm afraid we're headed for a filibuster."

The Senate places no time limit on debate. Senators sometimes take advantage of this fact. By talking on and on for hours, they can delay or prevent a vote.

Congressman Howard did what he could. He called all his friends in the Senate and asked for their help. But the real fight had to be led by a Senator. Curtis Howard was glad that Senator Mattson, from his home town, was an able leader. He was glad that Senator Mattson was on his side.

As expected, a group of Senators did start a filibuster. One of them would talk more or less aimlessly for a few hours. Then another member of the group would demand a quorum call. A quorum call takes time. It gave the filibustering Senator a chance to rest. In this and similar ways the filibuster could be continued for many hours or even days.

But Senator Mattson was not idle. He persuaded fifteen other Senators to join him in signing a petition. The petition asked for an end to the debate. Fortunately two thirds of the Senators present voted in favor of the petition. In other words, they voted in favor of *cloture*, or *closure*. After that, no Senator was allowed to speak longer than an hour. The debate came to an end.

In return for getting votes in favor of cloture, however, Senator Mattson had had to make concessions. He had to agree not to oppose an amendment to the bill. The amendment was proposed and accepted. The bill was passed as amended. That part of the fight was over. The bill, however, was still a long way from becoming a law.

Congressman Howard's Bill had been amended in the Senate. For that reason it had to be sent back to the House. Most members of the House did not like the Senate amendment. They refused to approve it. Congressman Howard was not happy about the amendment, either. Nevertheless he wanted some form of his bill to be passed. He asked that it be referred to a conference committee.

A conference committee is made up of ten or fourteen people. Five or seven of them are from the House. An equal number is from the Senate. Both "pros" and "cons" are represented. The committee discusses the points of disagreement. They try to settle the differences.

In the case of the Howard Bill they were successful. They made a change in the wording of the amendment. That satisfied the House. Both the Senate and the House accepted the report of the conference committee. The bill, as approved, was printed on parchment paper. It was signed by the Speaker of the House. Then the President of the Senate signed it. It was ready to be sent to the White House.

The President of the United States may address a joint session of Congress on matters of great importance to the nation. A joint session may also be called when the two houses disagree on a bill.

The End
and the Beginning

As it happened, the President was in agreement with Congressman Howard. He was happy to sign the Howard Bill. In fact, he invited the congressman to his office to watch the signing. Then the President gave a present to proud Curtis Howard. He gave him the pen with which the Howard Bill was signed.

Some three months had gone by since the Howard Bill had become H.R. 9999. Now it was sent to the General Services Administration and given a different number. It became P.L. 239. It was at last a public law.

This was the end of the arguments and the discussions. This was the end of the disagreements and the compromises. In another sense it was only a beginning. But the burden now no longer lay with Congressman Howard or Senator Mattson. From now on, unless the law should be repealed, the burden belonged to the President. Whoever he might be, the President of the United States throughout the years

THE FEDERAL COURTS

THE SUPREME COURT

CIRCUIT COURT
OF APPEALS

DISTRICT COURTS

COURT OF
CLAIMS

COURT OF CUSTOMS
& PATENT APPEALS

CUSTOMS
COURT

would be concerned with the bill introduced by Congressman Howard. Through all the years he would have to see that it was respected and obeyed. He would have to see that it was carried out in all its details. The bill by Congressman Howard had become a law of the land.

This is an imaginary story of how a bill might become a law. It illustrates how many of the nation's laws are made. It shows that members of Congress do not have an easy time. Their lives are interesting, but full of responsibility. A congressman must devote many hours of his time to a study of the nation's problems. He must forget his own interests. He must work for the good of all the people.

When a congressman fails to do this, the fault lies with the people. *It is the duty of the people to elect congressmen worthy of the office. It is the duty of the people to see that their representatives in Washington live up to the ideals of a democratic government.*

The Federal Courts of the United States

To establish justice in the United States, a system of federal courts was created. The highest federal court is the *Supreme Court of the United States*. The next highest federal courts are the *United States Courts of Appeals*. The lowest federal courts are the *United States District Courts*.

There is at least one federal district court in every state. States that are thickly populated have two or more courts. The courts are presided over by judges appointed by the President, with the approval of the Senate. The number of judges in each court varies, depending upon the number of cases tried by the court. Kidnaping, counterfeiting, mail robbery, smuggling, and violations of other federal laws are tried in the United States District Courts. Cases that involve more than one state or citizens of different states may also be tried in the United States District Courts.

For judicial purposes, the United States, with its dependencies, is divided into eleven *circuits*. Each circuit covers several states. The Ninth Circuit, for instance, includes nine states, plus Guam. In each circuit there are several United States District Courts and one United States Court of Appeals. The judges of the United States Court of Appeals review decisions of the United States District Courts in that circuit. They listen to arguments by attorneys for both sides. They study the printed record. Then they may approve the decision of the District Court. On the other hand, they may not. Instead they may reverse the decision. They may even send the case back to be tried all over again.

Cases from the United States Courts of Appeals may be appealed to the Supreme Court. *This is especially true if there is a question as to whether the decision is constitutional.* The Supreme Court also hears cases appealed directly from the federal district courts and from the highest state courts.

The Supreme Court of the United States

The Supreme Court of the United States convenes every weekday, except Saturdays and holidays, from October until June. The day's session begins at noon. It lasts

During the months the Supreme Court is in session, each Monday is "opinion day." That is the day on which the justices announce whatever opinions they have reached with respect to the cases before them.

throughout most of the afternoon. The lawyers who are to appear have sent in briefs well in advance. A brief is a short statement covering the main points in a legal argument. Each justice has had a chance to study the briefs. In the courtroom the lawyers present their arguments orally and in greater detail. The justices may ask them questions about certain points. Later the justices hold a closed session to discuss the case. Then the Chief Justice calls for a vote. The majority vote of the justices is the decision of the Court.

The decision of the Court is made public in a statement that gives reasons for the decision. This statement is called an *opinion*.

Sometimes a justice agrees with the decision but not with the reasons given. If so, he may write a statement of his own. In it he gives *his* reasons for agreeing with the decision. This statement is called a *concurring opinion*.

One or more justices who disagree with the decision of the court may also write an opinion. It, too, is presented to the public. This is called a *dissenting opinion*.

The nine justices of the Supreme Court are appointed by the President. The Senate must approve each appointment. The justices serve for life, unless they prove unworthy of their high office.

Congress, the President, Cabinet members, and judges all help to carry on the work of the nation. It is their duty to see that the nation progresses. It is their duty to see that no provision of the Constitution is violated. It is their duty to see that every citizen is accorded the rights of a democratic government.

Things to Do

1. Gather newspaper items that tell about some of the activities of the President. Make up a day's schedule for the President.
2. As a class project make a chart that will illustrate some of the duties of a congressman.
3. Divide the class into a Senate group and a House group. Each group may choose a subject on which they think legislation would be a good thing. The subject may be one either of school or national interest. Select one member of each group to draft a bill on the subject chosen. Carry each bill through all its legislative steps, to enactment or defeat.
4. Review the material you have read about how a bill becomes a law. Prepare five test questions on this material.
5. Dramatize an interview between a congressman and a lobbyist. The subject may be one of the bills you are considering in class. If you wish, it may be a bill that has actually been introduced this year in Congress.

Questions to Answer

1. In the imaginary story, the President signed the Howard Bill. What other course could he have followed?
2. What special service does the Library of Congress offer Senators and Representatives? What are some of the other services performed by the Library of Congress? Your school librarian may help you with this.
3. You know that Senators and Representatives are busy people. Do you think voters should add to their duties by writing letters to them? Give reasons for your answer.
4. What groups can you name who have lobbyists in Washington to protect their interests?
5. What is a filibuster? If you belonged to the Senate would you be in favor of introducing a rule that would forbid filibustering? Why?
6. Lawyers have a saying, "Today's dissent is tomorrow's law." What do you think this means?

A Written Exercise

In the following sentences only one of the phrases makes the sentence correct. Copy each sentence, using only the correct ending.
1. A Supreme Court decision is made public in a statement called
   a) an argument.
   b) an opinion.
   c) a brief.

2. To kill a bill in committee means to
   a) alter or change the bill.
   b) lay it aside for a certain length of time.
   c) refuse to report it to the house where it originated.
3. Lobbyists are
   a) men or women who spend most of their time in the lobby of a hotel.
   b) persons who try to influence the actions of the lawmakers.
4. The cloture rule in the Senate is a rule whereby
   a) a session of Congress may be brought to a close.
   b) two thirds of the Senators may vote to limit the debate on any subject to one hour for each Senator.
5. The dissenting opinions of the justices of the Supreme Court are
   a) the opinions of justices who disagree with a favorable vote.
   b) the opinions of justices who disagree with the majority vote of the Court.

Words to Study Before You Read the Next Topic

compulsory	license	franchise	assessment
inheritance	commodity	corporation	dividends
luxuries	investments	heirs	estate

How the Government Is Financed

WHO *pays the cost of a democratic government?* In a democracy the people pay the cost of their own government.

How do the people pay the expenses of their government? They pay the expenses of their government through the payment of taxes.

What are taxes? Taxes are compulsory payments of money to the government. They are for the purpose of maintaining the different branches of local, state, and federal government.

Why are taxes compulsory? Taxes are compulsory so that all citizens will share in the cost of government.

Why Taxes Are Necessary

It takes billions of dollars each year to maintain government in the United States. The different branches of the government are like business establishments. They cannot operate without money. If the people refused to pay taxes for any length of time, there would be no government. A government cannot function *unless the people pay for the services they receive.*

No man could provide his family with all the benefits they receive from the taxes he pays. Suppose he had to pave the street in front of his house! Or provide his own water and electric light systems! Imagine each man having to keep his own fire engine in the garage! Or hiring policemen to guard his property night and day. Suppose he had to build his own school building, buy textbooks, and hire teachers to teach his children. Suppose he had to light the streets at night or establish his own post-office system!

These are but a few of the many services our government provides. Every citizen receives many benefits from the government. The government builds streets and roads. It operates schools and maintains public parks and playgrounds. It develops water and power systems. It collects garbage and digs sewers. It provides fire and police protection. The government establishes hospitals and provides institutions for the handicapped. It maintains state and national parks. Almost everything a person does is influenced by the benefits he receives from good government!

The few cents you pay for a stamp does not cover the cost of sending a letter across the country. Taxes help pay for our mail service.

Ewing Galloway

How can the government provide benefits for the people? It can provide them in only one way. It must tax the people to pay for the services performed by the government. In a democracy each person must pay his just and full share of taxes. Only if he does, can the various branches of government continue to serve all the people. Only then can the government continue to *promote the welfare* of the nation.

Why the Costs of Government Increase

The costs of government are higher today than they were one hundred years ago. Good schools cost more than poor schools; good roads more than poor roads. Lighted streets cost more than dark streets. It costs more to draw water from a faucet than to carry it from a spring. It is more expensive to live in a modern home than it was to live in a log cabin.

The pioneers who were struggling to build homes in the wilderness did not pay taxes. Neither did they enjoy the comforts and advantages that Americans enjoy today. As the nation progressed, taxes increased. People were no longer content to live as their forefathers had lived. They wanted richer, fuller lives. The more advantages they wanted, the more tax money was needed. The leaders of the government tried to give the people the advantages they wished. They also tried to divide up the taxes. They tried to be sure that each person would pay his just and equal share.

Everyone Pays Taxes

The people of the United States pay taxes to federal, state, and local governments. In the early days land and property

represented most of the nation's wealth. At that time the tax on property was the common method of local taxation. Later, much of America's wealth was invested in business and factories. The landowners began to feel they should not carry the whole burden. "There should be some way to tax business," they said. "Why not tax those people who have large incomes?"

The leaders of the government realized that the landowners were right. They began to study other methods of taxation. Today there are many different forms of taxation in the United States. Everyone, whether he is rich or poor, whether he owns property or not, pays taxes.

There are two kinds of taxes—*direct* taxes and *indirect* taxes. When a direct tax is levied, *the taxpayer pays the cost of the tax himself.* He knows exactly how much tax is being collected and why. When an indirect tax is levied, *the taxpayer shifts part or all of the cost to others.* Often the person who pays the indirect tax does not know how much he is paying. He may not even know he is paying a tax.

Property taxes and income taxes are good examples of the direct tax. Indirect taxes, or hidden taxes, are usually included in the price of something. Manufacturers add the tax they pay to the cost of the commodity they sell. *The person who buys the commodity really pays the indirect, or hidden, tax.*

Federal Sources of Revenue

The federal government performs many services for the people of the nation. These services must be paid for through taxes.

The following are some of the most important sources of federal revenue.

1) *Income taxes.* An income tax is a tax on a person's earnings. Those earnings may be in any of several forms. They may be salary or wages. They may be dividends or interest on investments. They may be in the form of rent from property the person owns. Wherever the earnings come from, all the income over a certain amount is taxed. Even winnings from a lottery or a television quiz show are taxable. Persons with large incomes pay at a higher rate than persons with smaller incomes.

2) *Estate taxes.* If a person leaves a large estate, a tax is charged against it. The tax is collected before the estate is divided among the heirs.

3) *Customs taxes.* The United States collects taxes on goods brought in from foreign countries. Such a tax is called a tariff, or customs tax.

4) *Other taxes.* The government collects large sums of money in what are called excise. taxes. Excise taxes are those levied on the manufacture and sale of certain products. Some of the products are cigarettes, matches, drugs, jewelry, and chewing gum. The government also collects a tax on tickets for theaters and other forms of amusement.

5) *Corporation taxes.* Business corporations pay annual taxes based on the amount of their net profits.

6) *Toll on ships.* The federal government charges a toll on ships that pass through the Panama Canal.

State Sources of Revenue

The state governments also receive money from many different sources. These are some of the sources.

1) *Income taxes.* Most states have income tax laws very much like those of the federal government. The rate of income tax varies from state to state.
2) *Property taxes.* Property taxes are of two kinds. Some are levied against *real property*, which includes land and buildings. They are sometimes called real estate taxes. *Personal property* taxes are levied against such things as furniture and electrical appliances. The tax is based on the value of whatever is being taxed.
3) *Inheritance taxes.* An inheritance tax is a tax on the value of the property a person inherits. It is also called an estate tax.
4) *Corporation taxes.* These are taxes on the net profits of a corporation.
5) *Franchise taxes.* A franchise tax is a tax on companies whose business requires the use of highways or public property. Such companies include railroads, electric and gas companies, streetcar, truck, and bus companies. These companies must pay for the privilege of using public property.
6) *Gasoline taxes.* The motorist pays a tax on each gallon of gasoline he buys.
7) *Sales taxes.* Most states collect a tax on articles bought and sold in the state. Some states also charge a tax on theater tickets and other luxuries.
8) *Use taxes.* Some states impose a use tax on things used in the state, even though they were bought elsewhere.
9) *Fines.* Persons convicted of breaking state laws are fined.
10) *License fees.* Professional persons such as dentists, doctors, and nurses pay license fees. Barbers, beauty shop operators, and other workers who serve the public must also pay license fees. Owners and operators of automobiles, trucks, buses, and motorcycles pay license fees. Persons who sell liquors and tobacco products also pay license fees. Fees are also collected for hunting and fishing licenses.

Local Sources of Revenue

Cities, towns, and counties collect money to pay the costs of local government. The following are some of the most common sources of local revenue.

1) *Property taxes.* These correspond with state property taxes. The rate varies from one location to another.
2) *Franchise taxes.* These are like state franchise taxes, but on a local level.
3) *Fines.* Persons who break the laws of the city, town, or county are fined.
4) *Special assessments.* An assessment is a charge on the property in a certain district. It may be levied to pay for special services to the people of that district. It may be levied to pay for public improvements that increase the value of the property. It is often necessary to levy assessments for paving streets, or for putting in water lines or street lights.

Would the People Be Satisfied If There Were No Taxes?

In the early days of our country, the tax picture was confused. You have read about the Articles of Confederation. You know that they gave the government power to levy taxes. But levying taxes was not enough. Taxes have to be collected. The Confederation was not authorized to force collection. Many people refused to pay. The new nation nearly went bankrupt.

The Constitution of the United States corrected that situation. It gave to Congress the power to "lay and collect taxes."

The states, too, have power to levy and collect taxes. The states, in turn, have delegated some of their taxing powers to local governments. Thus, the federal, state, and local governments are all assured of enough money to operate. The people know what taxes they are expected to pay. They know that the tax burden is divided among all the people. They know that taxes finance the governmental services we receive.

Some persons object to paying taxes. They feel they would be more prosperous if there were no taxes. But would they? Look at the petition on the next page. Would you be willing to sign it?

VERNMENT INCOME AND EXPENDITURES

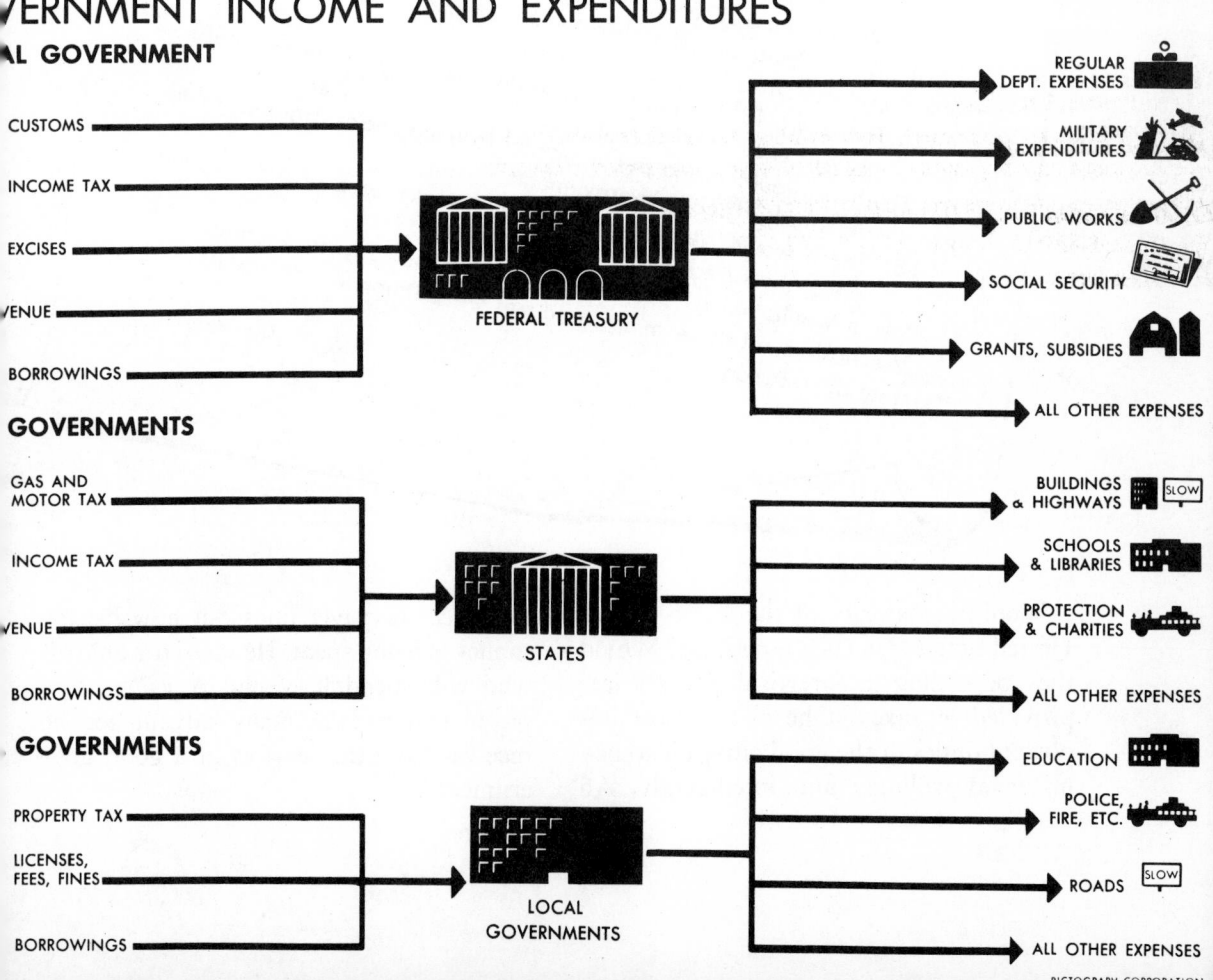

AL GOVERNMENT

CUSTOMS
INCOME TAX
EXCISES
VENUE
BORROWINGS

FEDERAL TREASURY

REGULAR DEPT. EXPENSES
MILITARY EXPENDITURES
PUBLIC WORKS
SOCIAL SECURITY
GRANTS, SUBSIDIES
ALL OTHER EXPENSES

GOVERNMENTS

GAS AND MOTOR TAX
INCOME TAX
VENUE
BORROWINGS

STATES

BUILDINGS & HIGHWAYS
SCHOOLS & LIBRARIES
PROTECTION & CHARITIES
ALL OTHER EXPENSES

GOVERNMENTS

PROPERTY TAX
LICENSES, FEES, FINES
BORROWINGS

LOCAL GOVERNMENTS

EDUCATION
POLICE, FIRE, ETC.
ROADS
ALL OTHER EXPENSES

PICTOGRAPH CORPORATION

To the Leaders of Our Government:

We, the voters of Our Town, want you to end all forms of taxation. We know that the taxes are used to pay for the services we receive from the government. We are willing to sacrifice those services. We know the following would be true.

1) Our property would not be protected by law.
2) There would be no public schools for our children.
3) We would not be protected against contagious diseases.
4) There would be no public school classes for adults.
5) Our food would not be inspected by government inspectors. (We would not know whether it was wholesome or unfit for use.)
6) Our water supply would not be fresh and pure.
7) Our garbage would not be removed unless we disposed of it ourselves.
8) We might not have enough water to use in our homes or to fight fires.
9) There would be no jails for criminals, or courts where accused persons could receive justice.
10) There would be no policemen or firemen to protect our lives and our property.
11) There would be no public parks, public libraries, or public playgrounds.
12) There would be no public money to build roads, bridges, or to make other public improvements.
13) There would be no public money to take care of the sick, the poor, the aged, and the handicapped.
14) It would not be safe to travel from one town to another.

We realize all these things, and yet we petition you to abolish the system of taxation.

The Voters

Would a majority of the voters in the United States sign such a petition? Would they be willing to forego all the services provided by taxes? One of the most important duties of the good citizen is to pay his taxes willingly and intelligently. An *intelligent* taxpayer finds out how his tax money is being spent. He votes for officials who will spend it wisely. A *willing* taxpayer realizes the many advantages he receives from the services of a good government.

Things to Do

1. There is much discussion these days as to whether sales taxes or income taxes are the more democratic. Discuss the subject generally in class. Then choose two debating teams. Each team may appoint a committee to help them do research. Set a date for a debate on the question, "Resolved: That sales taxes are more democratic than income taxes." The captains of the teams may toss a coin to decide which will take the negative side.

2. Give a short radio talk explaining why it is necessary for people to pay taxes.

3. Dramatize a conversation in which one person objects to paying taxes of any kind and the other person believes it is the duty of every citizen to pay his taxes willingly and intelligently.

4. There are many newspaper and magazine articles on hidden taxes. Try to find one and bring it to school, or report your findings to the class.

5. Try to find out how the taxpayer's dollar is divided among the different public services in your community. Make a chart showing your findings.

Questions to Answer

1. What are some of the things you enjoy at public expense? Do you think that the government should add other things to this list? Do you think the government should drop some of the things from this list? Discuss each of your answers in class.

2. What is the real estate tax rate in your community? What does it average per family?

3. Is there any service you would like to have discontinued so that taxes could be reduced in your community? By how much could taxes be reduced if such a service were dropped?

4. Does your community need any additional services? Does it need any additional facilities, such as parks or schools? How much would they cost? How much more would the average family have to pay in taxes if these needed services or facilities were added? (Some of the officials of your local government may be able to help you answer these questions. After the class has decided what information you want, select someone to call on the officials or write them a letter.)

5. Do you think an inheritance tax is a just tax? Why?

6. Arrange to visit your city hall. Find the names of some of the companies that pay a franchise tax to your town or city. Why do they pay a franchise tax?

7. Has your town or city levied a special assessment tax recently? Who had to pay the tax? Why?

8. If you knew you were going to have to give up some of the privileges you enjoy that are paid for by tax money, which would you be willing to give up first? List ten services of the government in the order in which you would be willing to give them up.

A Written Exercise

Some of the following sentences are true; others are not. Copy the true sentences.
1. Taxes are voluntary payments of money to the government.
2. Everyone must pay taxes so that all citizens will share in the cost of government.
3. If the people refused to pay taxes for any length of time, the government could not function.
4. A man could provide for himself all the benefits he receives from taxation.
5. Tax money helps to provide public schools, public parks and playgrounds, good roads, public libraries, public hospitals, garbage collection, mail delivery, water systems, and street lights.
6. There are many Americans who do not pay taxes of any kind.

Words to Study Before You Read the Next Topic

eligible	nonpartisan	controversial	demonstration
precinct	candidates	campaign	ineligible
registration	integrity	electors	literacy

A Presidential Election

THERE is nothing in the Constitution of the United States about political conventions. The Constitution does not even talk about political parties. Yet political parties and conventions have become an important, exciting part of our way of life. Every four years, each of the major political parties holds a convention. At this gathering, the party chooses its candidates for President and Vice-President of the United States.

The two major political parties in the United States began to develop soon after Washington became President. Alexander Hamilton was Secretary of the Treasury. Thomas Jefferson was Secretary of State. The two men did not agree upon some of the problems that faced the new nation.

Among other things, Hamilton believed in a strong federal government. He wanted the government to promote manufacturing and commerce. He felt that well-educated men were better able to guide the new government.

Thomas Jefferson believed the federal government should not become too strong. He disliked Hamilton's plans for promoting manufacturing and commerce. He wanted the country to remain an agricultural nation. He liked people and believed that all men were capable of governing.

Before long each man had many followers who shared his views. Jefferson's party was first called the Republican Party, later the Democratic-Republican Party. Still later, in Andrew Jackson's time, it became the Democratic Party—the same Democratic Party we know today.

Hamilton's party was first known as the Federalist Party. As time went on it, too, had several names. When Lincoln ran for President, it was called the Republican Party. It is still known by that name.

Today anyone who wishes to hold office usually seeks election through his party. Sometimes a candidate seeks election on a *nonpartisan* ticket. A nonpartisan ticket means that the candidate runs for office without the help of any party. The candidate claims he does not belong to either party. He claims he is free to do whatever he thinks is best, regardless of party politics.

In state and national elections the party system is considered the best method of

choosing candidates. Each party tries to choose its best men to run for office.

Perhaps the most interesting and exciting election is the national election. Almost as soon as one presidential election is over, plans are begun for the next convention. Cities all over the country offer to be hosts. They offer to pay a large part of the convention expenses. Sometimes the city that makes the best financial offer is chosen. Sometimes the choice is a city with the best convention hall or the most hotel rooms. Each party sends more than a thousand delegates to its convention. In addition, every convention attracts hundreds of other interested people. There are radio, television, and newspaper reporters. Each hopeful candidate brings a staff of willing workers. Most important political figures, whether or not they are delegates, try to be in town.

Ewing Galloway

Each party selects a certain number of delegates from each state. Sometimes the party's state executive committee chooses delegates. Sometimes they are chosen at state conventions of the party. Other states hold primary elections to choose them. Some state groups instruct their delegates to vote for a certain candidate at the convention. Other state groups simply send the delegates to the convention. Once there, the delegates are free to use their own judgment.

A National Convention

National political conventions are held in the summer of a presidential election year. Microphones and broadcasting booths are set up in the convention hall. Television cameras are brought in. The voter, at

Ours is the only country where presidential candidates are chosen at national political conventions.

around their state banners, settle back to listen to the keynote speech.

The keynote speech, given by an important leader, is a general statement of party beliefs. Even while the keynoter is speaking, however, political dealings are being arranged. On the convention floor, in nearby restaurants, in hotel rooms, delegates are talking. Workers for one man try to get delegates to vote for him. Some states have a "favorite son" candidate. They ask other state delegations to vote for him, at least on the first ballot. Often, state delegations may caucus. That means they act rather like football players in a huddle. They meet quickly to decide what their next move will be.

The keynote speech is usually followed by wild clapping. A permanent chairman may be chosen by the delegates. Not much other work is done on that day, however.

The next day some party committee chairmen give their reports. Some of these may not be of great interest to all the delegates. To keep the delegates from getting bored, entertainers may be brought in. They may perform between reports from the committee chairman.

One committee report, however, usually

home in his living room, will have a ringside seat. He may know more of what goes on at the convention than the delegates do, or the people in the visitors' gallery.

Most conventions are somewhat alike. A temporary chairman is chosen. He calls the convention to order. A famous singer leads the delegates in singing "The Star-Spangled Banner." A religious leader says a prayer. Then the delegates, grouped

interests everyone. That is the report of the Platform Committee. The committee recommends the stand the party should take on controversial issues. Sometimes the delegates disagree among themselves about these matters. They may vote not to follow the committee's ideas. Then the platform has to be written over to make it acceptable to the majority.

The third day is the most exciting. The states may now nominate candidates. As the chairman calls the name of a state, the head of the delegation answers. He may simply say, "Alabama passes." Or he may say, "Alabama's governor wishes to place a name in nomination." If that happens, the roll call stops while the Alabaman makes a nominating speech. The speech is followed by a noisy demonstration for the man named. Then there are other speeches, seconding that nomination. It may be a long time before the chairman calls the name of the next state on the list.

Sometimes a state may not pass. It does not ask permission to place a name before the convention. The chairman of the state delegation may say something like this: "The great state of Illinois wishes at this time to give the floor to our sister state, Wisconsin." This gives Wisconsin an earlier chance to place a name in nomination. Otherwise, Wisconsin would have to wait until almost the end of the roll call.

The Wisconsin nomination sets off another political demonstration. Bands play. Delegates march around the hall. Banners wave. Balloons soar. Signs with the candidate's name and picture bob up and down. There is a great deal of noise for a few minutes. Then the chairman's gavel brings back order. The order lasts, of course, only until a seconding speech is made. Then the demonstrations start again.

When every state delegation has had a chance to speak, the voting starts. This, too, is done by roll call of the states.

In order to win his party's nomination, a candidate must get a majority of the delegates' votes. Some state delegations have more votes than others. It is important for a candidate to win New York, California, and Pennsylvania. The number of votes is more important than the number of states that support him.

Occasionally a candidate is nominated on the first ballot. Sometimes the balloting goes on for days. At last, however, enough votes are swung in one direction or another. One candidate becomes his party's choice. No matter how hard they fought his nomination, all delegates are expected to back him now.

Choosing a vice-presidential candidate follows the same lines. Finally, the tired delegates go home. But neither they nor their candidates will have much time to rest. Within a few short weeks campaigning will begin. All members of the candidates' political party will work hard.

The campaign is carried on right to the eve of election. Then the matter is in the hands of the people. They vote by secret ballot. Their votes decide who will be the next President of the United States.

The government of the United States has been a good government. It must be kept a good government. It will be kept so by honest and hard-working public officials. It is the duty of the people to elect such men. *The integrity of government can be preserved only if the people take an interest in the welfare of their nation.*

Before every election the candidates and their supporters try to talk to as many voters as possible.

The Electoral College

Americans do not vote directly for President or Vice-President. The Constitution itself sets out the voting procedure for choosing these officers. It calls for the selection of presidential electors. The electors, in turn, cast ballots for President and Vice-President.

To many people this seems a roundabout way to hold an election. Dozens of congressmen have tried to change the procedure. None have succeeded.

Each political party in each state chooses a slate of electors. The number of electors equals the number of Senators and Representatives the state has. On election day the voter casts his ballot for the electors of his choice. In some states, the names of the presidential and vice-presidential candidates are not even on the ballot. Only the electors' names are listed.

There is no law that says the electors must vote for their party's nominee. In practice, however, they usually do. When a voter casts his ballot for a group of electors, he feels that the electors are his

messengers. He gives them his vote. They deliver his vote to the candidate their party has nominated.

New York has the greatest number of electoral votes. Pennsylvania and California are next in line. Then comes Illinois. Ohio and Texas follow close behind. Every candidate wants to win the electoral votes in those states. He needs a majority of all the electoral votes in order to win the election.

The presidential election is held on the first Tuesday after the first Monday in November. Usually by the next day everyone in the country knows which candidate has won. He is not really elected yet. The electors meet on the first Monday after the second Wednesday in December. They vote for their party's candidates. The votes are counted. A report is sent to the President of the Senate. On January 6 Congress counts the electoral votes. Only then does the election result become official!

Election Day

The voters of the United States vote by secret ballot. The voter goes alone into a booth and marks his ballot. Then he folds it and puts it into a locked box. The names of the candidates (or the electors) are printed on the ballot. The voter may vote for anyone he chooses. No one knows for whom he has voted.

In some of the larger cities voting machines are used. On a machine, the voter presses the lever opposite the name of the candidate for whom he wishes to vote. The machine records his vote and no one sees the way he voted.

To be eligible to vote, a person must have reached an age decided by state law (usually twenty-one years); must be a citizen of the United States; must not be a convict; in some states, must be able to pass a literacy test; and must be registered in his state. The residence requirement varies from state to state. In one state, a voter must have lived in the state for a year, in the county for ninety days, and in the district, or precinct, for fifty-four days.

In most of the states *anyone who wishes to vote must register* before a certain date in the year. To register, the voter gives his name and address and declares that he is eligible to vote. He also gives the precinct, or district, in which he lives. Then workers in the office of the Registrar of Voters check the names and list the qualified voters by district.

On election day the list of qualified voters for each district is given to the election board of the district. When a person votes, his name is checked on the list. That is to make sure that no one votes twice in the same election. The registration lists also make it impossible for a voter to vote in more than one district. Anyone may ask to see the registration lists. Any evidence of a dishonest registration is carefully investigated. The lists prevent ineligible persons from voting.

The secret ballot is a precious heritage. It is a privilege, denied to millions in many parts of the world. It is a privilege that every American would do well to use. Only through use can it be kept alive. Only through its use—faithful, intelligent, and informed—can democracy itself survive in our beloved land.

Throughout history men have fought for self-government. The right to vote is a precious heritage.

Things to Do

1. Find out how electors are chosen in your state.
2. You are backing a candidate who is running for public office. Send a telegram to a friend urging him to vote for your candidate.
3. Write one sentence or a short paragraph about each of the following words or phrases: national convention, registration of voters, nonpartisan ticket, secret ballot, party platform, political party, election campaign.
4. Obtain a sample ballot and discuss it in class.
5. Conduct an election in your classroom. Nominate candidates, appoint election officials, have an election campaign, make ballots and ballot boxes, and prepare a registered voters' list.
6. Find magazine accounts of the most recent national convention of either party. On the basis of those accounts, dramatize a national convention.
7. Arrange for a debate on the question, "Resolved: That the President and Vice-President should be elected directly, by popular vote."

Questions to Answer

1. Why are elections important in a democracy?
2. If you are a member of a certain party, should you always vote for the party candidates? Explain your answer.
3. What are some of the ways in which a citizen can become a more intelligent voter?
4. Do you think a national convention is a democratic way of choosing candidates for President and Vice-President?
5. Why are the people to blame if the government is not a good government?

A Written Exercise

Copy and complete the following statements. Use as many words and sentences as you wish. You may have to do some research at the library to make your statements meaningful.

1. State delegates to a national convention are chosen_____.
2. State delegates to a national convention may caucus in order to _____.
3. The two-party system in American politics came about_____.
4. In order to be represented on the ballot a political party must_____.
5. A person who wishes to take an active part in politics should begin by_____.

Words to Study Before You Read the Next Topic

volunteer	inflammable	rigid
valves	identification	teletype
extinguishers	revive	laboratories
suffocated	desperate	fire traps

UNIT SUMMARY

In *A Panorama of American Government* you have read about the various branches of government in the United States. You have studied the organization of each branch. You have seen how each one serves the needs of the country and of the people. The federal government looks after the welfare of the nation as a whole. The state government looks after the interests of the people of the state. The city and county governments look after the everyday needs of the citizens of the community.

Each of the different branches of government has a definite plan in the pattern of our democracy. None would be complete without the others. To have a truly united nation, all the branches must work together to uphold the principles of our government.

Think of some of the ways in which the federal government, the state government, and your local government help to make you a happier and a more useful citizen. Talk about why you believe the branches of government must work together to make the pattern of our government complete.

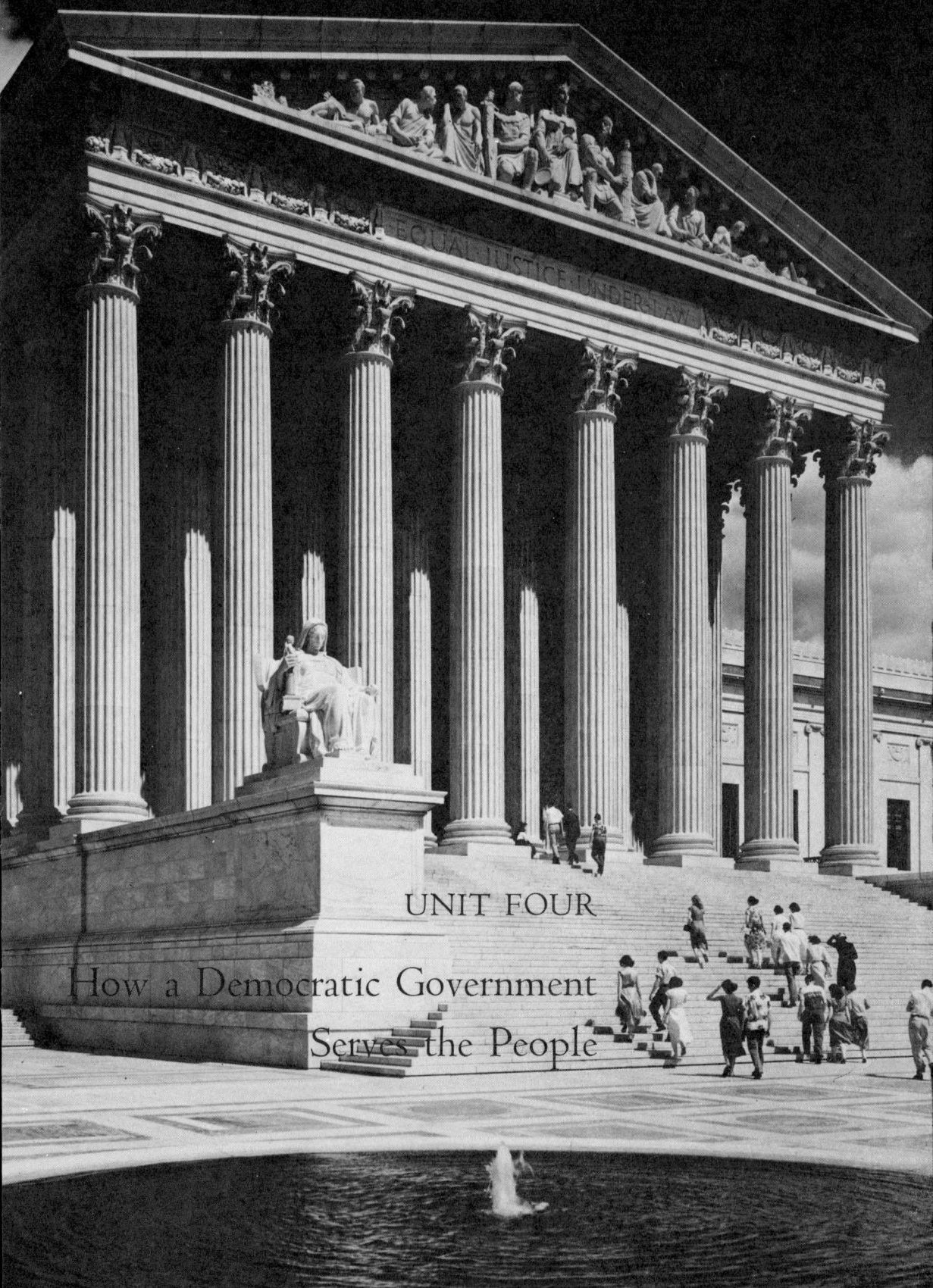

UNIT FOUR

How a Democratic Government
Serves the People

HOW a DEMOCRATIC GOVERNMENT SERVES the PEOPLE

Life, liberty, and the pursuit of happiness are unalienable rights that belong to everyone. This famous phrase from the Declaration of Independence helped inspire the colonists to win their independence. It served as a model for the men who wrote the Constitution and the Bill of Rights. *Our government was planned to further and to protect these rights for all the people.*

In this unit you will read how the government protects and furthers these rights. The topics in this unit are:

HOW THE GOVERNMENT PROTECTS THE LIFE OF ITS CITIZENS
OTHER WAYS OF PROTECTING LIFE
HOW THE GOVERNMENT FURTHER SAFEGUARDS LIFE
LIBERTY IN A DEMOCRACY
DEMOCRACY AND THE PURSUIT OF HAPPINESS
MORE PROBLEMS AND THE PURSUIT OF HAPPINESS
THE PURSUIT OF HAPPINESS TODAY AND TOMORROW

As you study this unit, notice in how many ways the government helps you and every other citizen of the United States to enjoy the rights to *life, liberty, and the pursuit of happiness.*

TOPIC ONE

How the Government
Protects the Life of Its Citizens

EVERY three minutes a home or a building burns in some town or city in the United States! It has been said that the buildings burned in one year could line both sides of a street reaching from Chicago to New York. This is a terrible loss. In addition, *six thousand persons are burned to death each year.* Think what would happen if there were no fire departments! Thousands more people would be burned to death. The buildings destroyed would reach from New York to San Francisco!

Fighting fires is one way in which the government protects the life of its citizens. Nearly every city government in the United States has a fire department. Nearly every town and county government has a fire department. The protection of life and property from fire is one of the important duties of local governments.

Causes
of Fires

A good citizen would not knowingly do anything that would cause another person to lose his life. A good citizen would not knowingly destroy another's property. Yet most of the fires in the United States are caused by carelessness. Many persons who believe themselves good citizens may start fires. They let small children play with matches. They go into the forests and leave their campfires smoldering. They throw lighted matches, cigars, or cigarettes into piles of rubbish, dry leaves, or dry grass. Any of these things may cause a damaging fire—*because someone was not careful and thoughtful.*

About ninety-five per cent of the fires in the United States could have been prevented. Sometimes gasoline or kerosene is used to start a fire quickly. This may cause an explosion. Oily rags are not thrown away. Many times they catch fire. People leave their houses and forget to shut off their gas heaters or stoves. They forget to turn off electric irons. They are not careful when cleaning clothes with gasoline or cleaning fluid.

The careless person who starts the fire is not always the one who is hurt. Fires started through carelessness often spread to the property of others. A carelessly dropped match may start a fire that will burn half a dozen buildings. Many people may be trapped in the burning buildings.

219

They may lose their lives or be hurt through no fault of their own.

The man who dropped the match may go home never knowing what he has done. He may be unaware that he has caused thousands of dollars' worth of damage and the loss of several lives. *Just one person's carelessness may hurt many innocent persons.*

The Prevention of Fires

Every large city in the nation has a good fire department. The prevention of fires is one of the duties of this department. In some cities the department hires a man called the *fire prevention engineer.* Other cities have fire wardens or fire marshals. Sometimes the fire prevention engineer is the fire warden or the fire marshal.

The fire prevention engineer has many duties. He must carry out rules governing the building and repairing of houses, garages, factories, stores, and office buildings. He must see that these buildings are planned to prevent fires.

His department must check the electrical wiring in new buildings. It must inspect gas and water mains, theaters, and other public buildings. In some cities the department

has the power to condemn old buildings that are firetraps.

The department looks at buildings where inflammable things such as paints, varnishes, or gasoline are stored. It makes sure these buildings are not overcrowded. It checks to be sure the exits are not blocked. It often asks the city council to pass laws to help prevent fires.

Many cities have passed laws forcing owners to make buildings and factories as nearly fireproof as possible. Fire extinguishers must be kept in all parts of the buildings. In some places sprinkler systems must be installed. A sprinkler system has a number of nozzles set into the ceiling a certain distance apart. On each nozzle is a

Firemen work at all hours and in all kinds of weather.

valve. The valves are connected with water pipes and are covered with a metal that melts easily. If a fire starts in the building, the heat melts the metal in the valve. As soon as the metal melts, the water pipes open. Water is sprinkled onto the fire below. At the same time a fire alarm is set off. This type of sprinkler system puts out many fires that occur in buildings that are empty at night.

The prevention of fires is the duty of every citizen in the United States. Everyone can help by being careful. Even after fire has started, there are things a person can do to help. Perhaps the most important is to stay calm. A calm person has a much better chance to escape from a burning building than a person who gets excited. It would help, too, if everyone learned how to give first aid.

Each year there are many fires in homes. One great danger from these fires is that people may be suffocated. Like any other form of warm air, heat and smoke tend to rise. If a fire breaks out in the lower floors of a building, people sleeping upstairs may suffocate. Stairways leading to upstairs bedrooms should always be closed off by doors.

If a person suspects there is fire beyond a closed door, he should feel the door. If it feels hot, he should not open it. If, after feeling the door, he is still not sure, he may open the door carefully. If it opens out, he must brace himself against it. He should open it just a little. Otherwise, heated air and smoke may rush out and smother him.

The fire department in every town does much to prevent fires. Still, it needs the help of all the citizens.

The Fire Department at Work

In the early days, volunteer bucket brigades were formed to fight fires. Whenever there was a fire, men and boys came running from all parts of town. They were all carrying buckets. They formed a line from the burning building to the nearest water. The buckets were filled with water. They were passed rapidly from one person to another until they reached the end of the line. Then they were grabbed by the fire fighters. These men dashed the water onto the fire. Then the buckets were sent back to be refilled.

These brigades tried to protect the homes of everyone. Still, the loss from fire was high. As cities grew, new means of fighting fires were found. Today nearly every community has a fire department. It protects the homes and property of everyone. In some of the smaller towns there are still volunteer firemen who give their services free. In the larger cities the firemen are paid.

The firemen in the cities are required to pass many examinations. They must be intelligent. They must be physically fit and strong. They must go to schools and take classes in fire fighting. In the schools they learn how to fight fires in the most efficient ways possible. They learn how to rescue persons from burning buildings. They are taught how to revive those overcome by smoke. They learn how to give first aid.

The fireman of today does not depend upon a bucket of water to fight a fire. Efficient, modern equipment has taken the place of buckets. A hook-and-ladder truck and a pumping engine are usually sent to

There are few things more terrifying than a forest fire out of control. There are few things that cause more damage. A large percentage of forest fires are caused by carelessness.

fires. If the building is very tall, a water tower is also sent. A water tower looks a little like a derrick. It is placed opposite an upper window. It pours water through the window onto the fire. A high-pressure water tower can send eight tons of water a minute into a burning building. Even this much water would not put out an oil fire, however. It would only make the fire spread. Foam and waterfog are used to put out oil fires.

Large cities require more fire-fighting equipment than smaller communities. It is harder to fight a fire in a tall skyscraper than in a one-story dwelling in a small town. The chief of the fire department, or the fire prevention engineer, studies the needs of his community. He asks the city council to buy fire-fighting equipment his firemen need. Along the water fronts, fires are fought by fireboats, as well as by fire trucks.

Fire is very useful to man, but it can also be very dangerous. There are far too many fires in the United States today. There are far too many people killed or burned. There is too much property loss from fire. Most of the damage is caused by carelessness. Fires are carelessly started or are left to burn without being watched. *Every good citizen will do his best to see that no fire damage results from his thoughtlessness.*

The Police Department

Another department of government which protects the lives of Americans is the police department. Policemen do many things to make the life of the average American safer and more pleasant. They stand long, wearisome hours directing traffic. They patrol the streets. They protect the life and property of the people on their beats. They detect all sorts of crimes. They guard school children who are crossing the streets. They direct strangers, courteously and pleasantly.

If children are lost, policemen direct them to their homes. Sometimes they take them to the police station until their parents can be located. Policemen keep people from going near burning buildings. They see that property owners remove snow and ice from slippery pavements.

If a sudden danger arises, a policeman

faces the danger fearlessly. If he must capture a desperate bandit, he does not think only of his own safety. He thinks of others whose lives might be endangered.

The best policeman is not always the one who captures the most criminals. He is not always the one who makes the most arrests. A good policeman is interested in stopping crime as well as in punishing it. He often advises people about laws. He tries to help them obey the laws. People should remember this. They should think of the policeman as a friend. They should respect and help him in every way.

In small towns the chief of police or the constable is usually elected by the people.

Policemen are appointed. In the larger cities policemen must pass rigid examinations. They must keep physically fit. In some states they must study criminal law. Some of them must learn fingerprinting and identification. They must learn how to give first aid. They even have to know how to make emergency car repairs. They must learn to look at everything very carefully in case they have to report on it later. They also must be expert marksmen.

The Organization of Police Departments

During colonial days there were no police departments. Even cities did not have

Policemen often risk their lives to prevent crime. These policemen are trying to capture a gunman.

United Press International

policemen. Today nearly every city and town in the United States has some kind of police department. The chief of police is the "commander in chief" of the policemen under him. If the police force is large, it is organized rather like an army. The patrolmen are the privates of the police force. The officers over them are police sergeants, lieutenants, and captains.

The police captains are in charge of police districts, or precincts, in each town. There are two kinds of policemen—the policemen who wear uniforms and the "plain-clothes" detectives. The plain-clothes detectives are sometimes called the scouts of the police force.

To protect the community both day and night, the police force is divided into three shifts. The actual working day is usually eight hours. Often a policeman works much longer. If he is pursuing a criminal, he may not stop simply because he has already worked his shift. In times of emergency a policeman may go without food or sleep for many hours.

The American people go about their work and play, knowing that their government is protecting them at all times. Day and night, policemen patrol their beats. They are alert for signs of danger.

If a policeman needs help, he can reach police headquarters by using the telephone signal boxes on city streets. He can also talk with headquarters or other policemen by using his car radio. Over these radios the policemen can receive messages from

The "property room" of a big city police department often has a special section just for bicycles. Boys and girls whose bicycles have been lost or stolen sometimes find them here.

Los Angeles Police Department

headquarters. Most of them can also send messages to headquarters and to policemen in other cars. Radios have helped the police capture many criminals. A policeman with a radio can receive word of a crime almost as soon as it has been committed. He can get to the scene much faster than if he had to wait for the message to reach him in some other way.

Large cities have many special services within their police departments. They have mounted police and traffic officers. Some of them have helicopters at their disposal. They have health squads and radio squads. They have pickpocket squads and homicide squads. Men on the homicide squads are expert in solving murder cases. Some cities have policewomen. They usually work with women or children. Many cities have police surgeons. They care for emergency cases and accident victims.

Sometimes men commit a crime and then escape in a high-powered car. Descriptions of the criminals are sent over the teletype, a telegraph typewriter, to policemen in many states. The bandits can then be captured wherever they go. Fingerprinting has also proved a great aid to the men who enforce the law.

Many large police departments have laboratories where blood stains can be identified. An expert can tell whether a spot of blood is human or animal blood. He can tell which blood type it is.

Some experts can also identify a person's handwriting, even though he tries to disguise it. Other experts can identify hair, cigarette ashes, or particles of clothing. Still others can tell whether a bullet was fired from a certain gun. Clues can be detected even in tiny particles of dirt.

Co-operation between Police Departments

City police departments are very important. *County*, *state*, and *federal* police are also important. The sheriff and his men enforce the laws throughout the county. The state policemen protect rural areas and patrol highways. The federal police agencies, such as the FBI, may work anywhere in the nation. They may make arrests, however, only when a federal law is broken.

The different police departments all work together. Imagine what might happen if they did not! Suppose a group of bandits committed a bank robbery, stealing thousands of dollars and killing two of the bank employees. Suppose the city police heard the alarm and gave chase. Suppose they could follow the bandits only to the city limits and then had to stop! If they could not find a county officer and notify him of the crime, the trail might end.

But suppose the county officers did see the bandits in time to take up the trail. Suppose they were closing in on the criminals. Then suddenly they came to the county line! The bandits would escape unless state officers happened to see them.

Then suppose the state officers could go no farther than the state line. If there were no federal police standing by, the bandits would go free!

Fortunately, this is not what happens. It is true that city, county, and state officers usually stay within their own boundaries. Nevertheless, most states have passed laws so the different police departments can co-operate. Some states also have agreements whereby the police of one state may pursue a criminal into another state, if necessary.

Things to Do

1. Arrange to visit a large store or factory to see what fire precautions have been taken.
2. Collect newspaper or magazine accounts of fires. See how many are reported in a month. Figure up the losses. Keep an account of how many of the fires were started through someone's carelessness.
3. Visit your fire department and see what kind of equipment they use. Ask what you might do to aid fire control.
4. Make charts showing how fires may be started through carelessness.
5. Policemen and firemen perform important services. Set a date for a class discussion about choosing a career as a fireman or policeman. Appoint a committee to gather information about such things as hours, salaries, and working conditions and bring the facts to the discussion.
6. Make a set of rules that might be called, "Fire Prevention Rules." Check to see how many of them you obey.
7. Arrange to visit your local police department. Ask to see how fingerprints are made. See if the department uses other modern methods of detecting and preventing crimes.
8. Invite a member of the police force to talk to the class about what citizens can do to help prevent crime.
9. Form committees to investigate what is being done in your school about (1) fire prevention and (2) law and order. Form permanent class committees to co-operate in these matters.

Questions to Answer

1. How may innocent persons be injured by a fire caused through someone's carelessness?
2. How can a camper be certain his campfire is out?
3. Name some of the causes of fire. How can fires from these causes be prevented?
4. What are some of the duties of a fire prevention engineer?
5. Name ways in which a community can help to prevent fires in homes, in schools, and elsewhere.
6. Why is the work of a policeman often dangerous?
7. Why do you think policemen are required to pass examinations?
8. Name some ways in which scientists and inventors have helped the policemen of today.
9. Find stories about criminals who have been captured by the police. How did the police catch them? Did more than one police department co-operate to solve the crime?

10. How many policemen and firemen does your community have? How does that compare with the size of the population? Do you feel that the police and fire departments are large enough?

A Written Exercise

Complete correctly the following statements, using as many words and sentences as you choose.
1. A house or building burns in the United States every_____.
2. Most of the fires in the United States are caused by_____.
3. Some of the common causes of fire are_____.
4. Some of the duties of a fire prevention engineer are_____.
5. If one suspects there is a fire, it is best to_____.
6. Some different kinds of fire-fighting equipment are_____.
7. During a fire everyone should_____.
8. It is important to help prevent fires because_____.

Words to Study Before You Read the Next Topic

espionage	reckless	blackmailing	slum
disloyal	eliminated	pedestrians	hazards
disadvantage	reform	sabotaged	intersections

TOPIC TWO

Other Ways of Protecting Life

NEWSPAPER stories often use the letters FBI. These letters mean the *Federal Bureau of Investigation*. The men who work for the Federal Bureau of Investigation are one unit of the federal police. They are the most highly trained law-enforcement officers in the country. They have many duties. They look into cases of *espionage*, or spying on the military activities of the United States. They go to work when government property is *sabotaged*, or willfully destroyed. They look into the activities of persons they think might be disloyal to our form of government.

The FBI arrests people who have broken federal laws. Such laws include the National Stolen Property Act, the Federal Kidnaping Act, and the Motor Vehicle Act. Persons who take stolen property or stolen automobiles across a state line break a *federal* law. Anyone who takes a kidnaped person across a state line violates the Federal Kidnaping Act. Once a federal offense is suspected, the FBI men swing into action. They do not stop at the state borders. They trail the suspected criminals night and day. They follow them from city to city and from state to state until they capture them.

The FBI investigates robberies of national banks and banks insured by the federal government. It looks into blackmailing. It even looks into dishonest voting. The FBI does not prosecute the criminals it catches. It has the authority only to investigate crimes and to arrest persons suspected of federal offenses. It turns the evidence and the arrested persons over to the Department of Justice.

Even the worst criminals live in fear of the FBI. There is an old saying that the Royal Canadian Mounted Police "always get their man." This is also true of the FBI. They are among the best police officers in the world!

It is not easy to become a part of the federal police. To receive an appointment as an FBI officer, a man must be between the ages of twenty-five and forty. He must have a college degree in law or accounting. (In some cases the degree may be in science or languages.) He must be in excellent health. When he is appointed to the FBI he is trained in the lastest methods

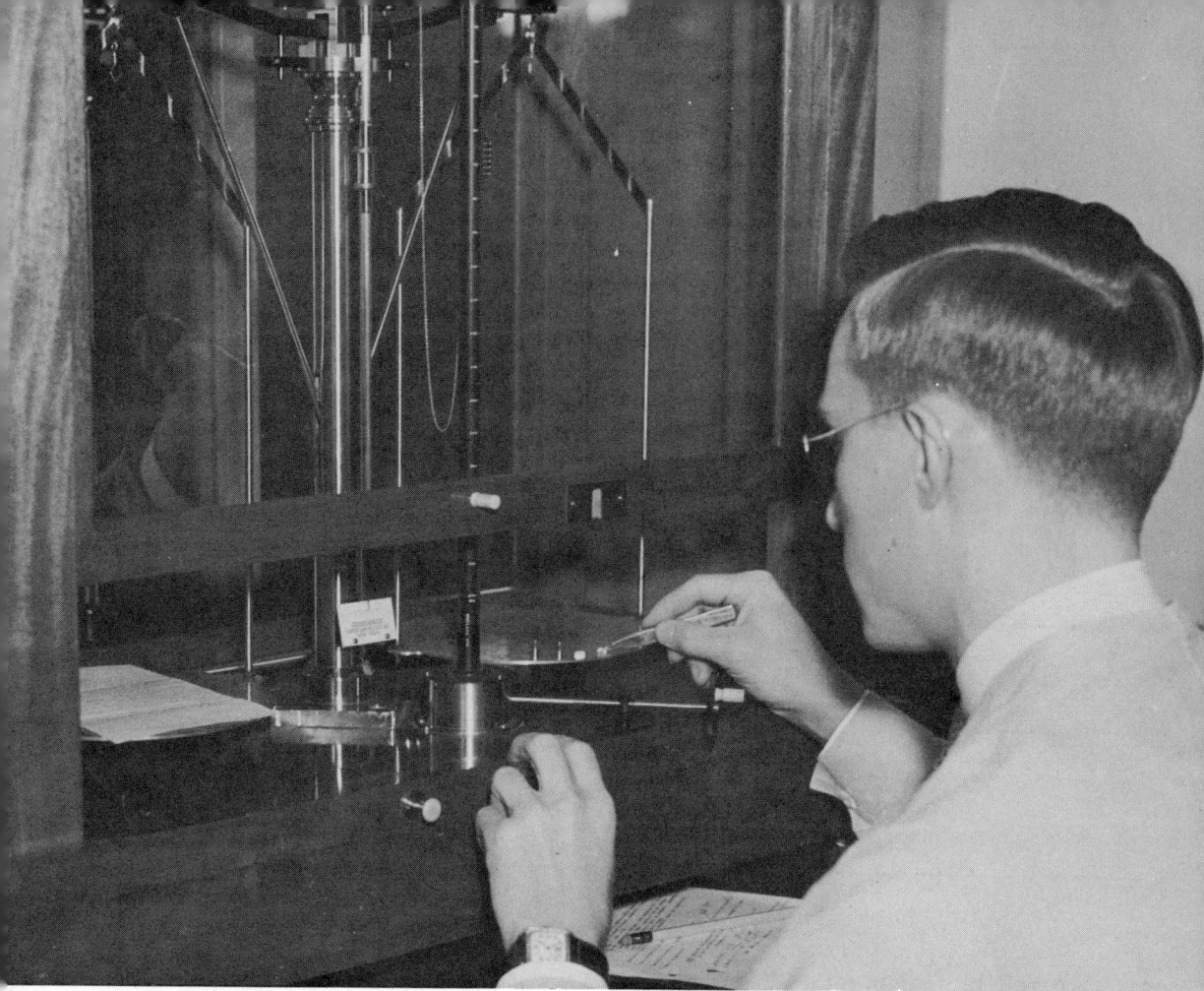

One duty of FBI laboratory technicians is to determine whether certain documents are false or genuine. The examiner shown here is weighing paper. This is one step in his investigation.

of crime detection and investigation. He is also trained to become an expert in the use of firearms. A criminal who attempts to "shoot it out" with an FBI man is at a disadvantage. There are few criminals as quick and as clever with a gun as the FBI men.

The crime laboratory of the FBI is one of the best in the world. In one part of the laboratory there are millions of fingerprints. Many of them are the fingerprints of criminals. Every day thousands of fingerprints are sent to the laboratory for comparison. Suppose police in a small town in Idaho are working on a murder case. They find fingerprints on the murder weapon. Do the fingerprints match any of those in the files of the FBI? The Idaho police can soon find out. Suppose a policeman in California finds a man who has been badly hurt. No one knows who he is. Are his fingerprints on file in Washington? The police officers simply send the fingerprints to the FBI.

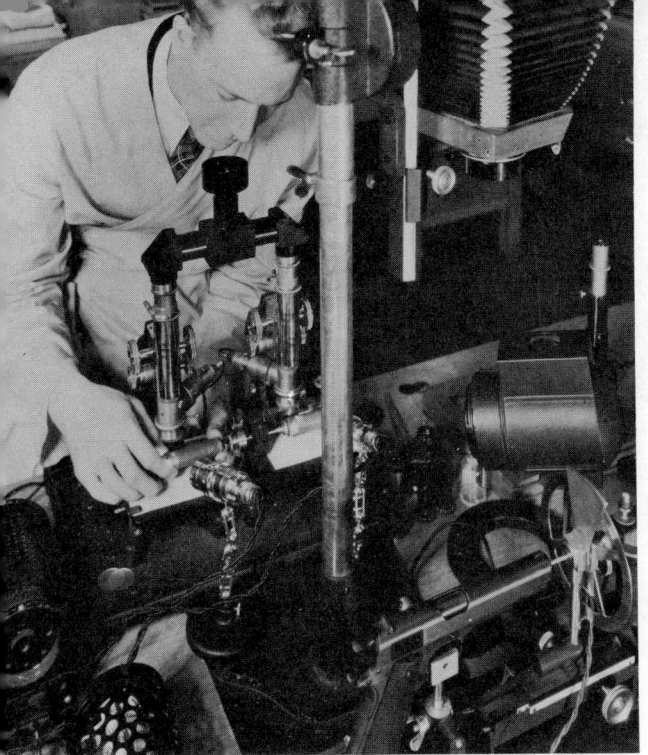

Ewing Galloway

This FBI expert is trying to determine whether two particular bullets were fired by the same gun

How can one set of fingerprints be compared with the thousands and thousands on file in the laboratory? An operator receives a set of fingerprints for comparison. He does not take first one card and then another out of the files and examine them. If he did, the task might take years to complete. There are more than one hundred million fingerprints on file.

The comparison of fingerprints is done entirely by machine. The machine seems almost human. The operator examines the fingerprints sent to him for comparison. He notes their general characteristics. He sets certain dials on his machine. Then he goes to the files where *similar* types of fingerprints are kept. He begins feeding the machine thousands of finger-printed cards. When the right card comes along, it pops out! The machine stops. The task is complete.

Law-enforcement officers throughout the country may send anything they wish to this laboratory for identification. The FBI men can tell if a bullet was shot from a certain gun. They can tell if the soil on a man's shoe came from a certain garden or patch of ground. They can take tiny pieces of skin from under the fingernails of a dead person who has scratched his attacker. They can tell if that skin came from the body of the person accused of the murder. They can tell if a thread came from a certain piece of cloth. They can tell if ashes came from a certain fire and what kind of ashes they are. Experts in the FBI laboratory help solve many baffling crimes.

The FBI men are among the most courageous police officers in the world. They are among the most efficient. They have done much to protect the lives of their fellow Americans.

Crime and Its Prevention

The cost of crime in the United States is very high. *America's crime bill is half as much as the schools of the nation spend for education.* Yet Mr. Average American often shrugs his shoulders and says, "Crime has nothing to do with me. I am a law-abiding citizen." But the cost of crime is his concern. He pays for it through taxes. Also, his automobile may be stolen. His house may be burglarized. Someone may even take his life or the life of one of his family. It is not enough to be a law-abiding citizen. *Mr. Average American must help to prevent others from committing crimes.*

230

It would be hard to say just why there is so much crime in the United States. A study of police records shows that most crimes happen in slum areas. Poverty may be one of the causes of crime.

Men and women who have studied the problem believe that some of the causes lie in the home and the community. They believe that society should find the causes of crime. They believe that those causes should be destroyed. Many communities are trying to solve the problem. They are trying to build better housing in crowded and unsanitary areas. They try to help unemployed men find jobs.

Many areas are building parks, public playgrounds, and gymnasiums. People can spend their leisure time pleasantly and profitably in such places. They are less likely to break the law. Many states are building clinics and hospitals. Mentally ill persons who might break the law can go to them for treatment.

Many cities are trying to overcome conditions that lead children to break the law. They are building playgrounds for children. They build athletic fields, libraries, and club houses. Some schools have special teachers who visit the homes. They try to help children who are having trouble.

There are men and women who devote their lives to helping unfortunate boys and girls. These understanding counselors help boys and girls decide what they want in life and how to achieve it.

Ewing Galloway

Many patients in federal hospitals are taught new trades. In this picture the young man is learning mechanical drawing.

Many police departments have officers who study the problems of boys and girls. These officers are always ready to help young people in trouble They try to help the young people "go straight." They give these boys and girls an opportunity to change. They try to help all boys and girls become good citizens.

Before long all public schools may be teaching the prevention of crime. Citizens may become aroused over the crime problem. They may insist that all government officials be honest and hardworking. They may insist that the people who do break laws be given swift but *just* sentences.

Law-abiding citizens will insist that public officials enforce all laws. They will set a good example for those around them by obeying traffic laws, health laws, and safety laws. They will make it clear that *there is nothing "smart" about breaking any law*.

Modern Prisons

There are federal prisons and state prisons. There are city and county prisons. City and county prisons are often called jails.

Persons convicted of serious federal offenses are sent to federal prisons. State prisons are for criminals who have committed serious offenses against the state. City and county jails are for people who have committed less serious offenses. They also house prisoners waiting to be tried or taken to other prisons.

Today, more and more people believe that a prison should not be just a place of punishment. It should be a place to reform a criminal. In some modern prisons a prisoner is given a chance to change. He is

treated with respect as long as he obeys the rules. He is given a clean bed and good food. He has a chance to study and to learn a trade.

When his work is done, he may go to the prison library. He may have a recreation period on the athletic field. In many prisons the prisoners have baseball and football teams. They put out prison newspapers. They may watch motion pictures and television. Some prisons have farms and dairy barns. There the prisoners may study modern methods of farming and dairying. The prisoner is closely guarded. At the same time he is allowed to try to remake his life.

Not all prisons have such good conditions. Not all prison officials believe that a criminal can change. Many of them believe that criminals should be sent to prison quickly. They believe all law-breakers should be given long sentences.

Just what will solve America's crime problem is not known. Many men are studying crime prevention. They will keep on studying it. Perhaps in the future they will learn how to stop crime. They may learn new and better ways to protect life and property.

Life Can Be Safer

Not long ago the National Safety Council released some frightening figures. Nearly one hundred thousand people in the United States lose their lives through accidents each year! Over fourteen thousand children are killed in accidents! Sixteen thousand workmen in different industries lose their lives! There are over one hundred deaths a day from accidents involving motor vehicles! The cost of accidents in the United States is over seven billion dollars a year!

This loss of life and property is far too high. It would be impossible to prevent all accidents. Still, many of them could be avoided. Many people are needlessly killed in their own homes. Falls cause most of the home injuries. People fall in the bathtub. They fall down stairs. They fall on freshly waxed floors. With care and caution, many of these falls could be avoided. A baby reaches for a shiny kettle on the stove. The kettle is filled with boiling water. The water splashes over and scalds the baby. A mother is burned when the gasoline with which she is cleaning clothes explodes. Fumes from gas stoves kill many persons. Sometimes leaking gas pipes allow deadly gas to escape into the house.

Many mothers are afraid their children will catch contagious diseases. *Accidents kill far more children each year than diseases do!* One good sign is that fewer children are hurt in accidents today than were hurt a few years ago. This may be the result of safety campaigns in schools. In many schools large posters warn children to be careful when they cross the streets.

In some schools safety patrols are chosen. The safety patrols guard street crossings near the school. They direct traffic. They help children cross the streets safely. ,

Early Americans had little machinery. As the years passed, many kinds of machines were invented. The invention of machinery multiplied the number of accidents in industries. Thousands of workmen were killed in factories and mines. Many

more were injured. This loss of life was a big problem for the nation to solve.

To prevent accidents in industry, safety laws were passed. Factory and mine owners said, "We will hire speakers to tell workmen how to stop accidents. We will give prizes for the best safety records. We will find men to design safer machinery. We will ask them to cover wheels and moving parts. We will put guards on our saws and other dangerous machinery."

Many factories have done everything possible to protect the lives of their workers. The workers must do their part by being careful at all times. There are fewer fatal accidents than there used to be. There are still far too many!

Traffic Accidents

Traffic accidents take a great many lives every year. Traffic accidents happen because someone is careless. Many of the accidents happen because the driver is going too fast. Sometimes a careless person starts across the street without first looking both ways. Other pedestrians are killed crossing the street in the middle of a block. Persons who walk along the highways are in danger of being hit by speeding autos. *If a person must walk along a highway, he should face the oncoming cars.* Children who chase balls in the streets are often hurt. It is also very dangerous to catch rides on passing trucks.

Loss of life is too great a price to pay for carelessness. Both drivers and pedestrians must be careful at all times.

The Prevention of Traffic Accidents

How can traffic accidents be prevented?

First, drivers and pedestrians must realize it is their duty to avoid accidents. It is their duty to follow safety rules.

Second, traffic laws must be strictly enforced. Reckless and drunken drivers must be punished severely.

Third, communities must help. They should build wide streets and highways. Every city should have a good system of traffic lights. Underpasses and overpasses should be built to prevent accidents at railroad crossings and busy intersections. Night driving in cities should be made safer by well-lighted streets. Highways should be clearly marked with signs.

Last, there should be more safety campaigns. Safety campaigns among drivers and pedestrians will bring down the number of traffic accidents. They will bring down the number of accidental deaths.

Making Land, Sea, and Air Travel Safer

Water transportation is considered the safest form of travel. Occasionally a large steamer sinks at sea. However, such tragedies do not happen often. The government makes sure all ships are seaworthy. Each modern vessel carries good fire-fighting equipment. Many of the new vessels in the merchant marine are nearly fireproof. Government boats patrol the seas. They report icebergs and other hazards. Ships can radio for help when they are in trouble.

When railway trains first traveled across the country, there were many accidents. Trains crashed into one another. Locomotives were derailed. Engines blew up. Bridges fell apart. Then safety campaigns were begun throughout the country. Wooden cars, which caught fire easily, were

Airports use highly specialized equipment to keep their air passengers safe. This is the control tower of an airport. From here, men can observe flying conditions and communicate with airplane pilots.

replaced by steel cars. Roadbeds were rebuilt to make them safer. Warning signs were placed at crossings. Block signals were invented. In the block-signal system, the track is divided into parts called blocks. A train cannot leave one block until the signal on the next block shows green. The green light means "all clear."

The invention of the air brake made train travel much safer. Air brakes make it possible to stop trains quickly. This helps to avoid accidents. Many communities have eliminated dangerous grade crossings. This, too, is a very important safety measure.

The airplane is the newest and fastest form of travel. At first it, too, was dangerous. Then the airplane manufacturers, the airlines, and the government worked together to make flying safer. Today airlines hire only experienced, capable pilots. Planes are checked carefully before they leave the ground. In the air, the pilots keep in touch with airports by radio. Sometimes radio beams are used to guide airplanes. Radio also keeps them on their courses. Modern planes can fly high enough to avoid much bad weather. Accurate and frequent weather reports also help make flying safer.

235

Things to Do

1. Illustrate in any way you choose the old saying, "Crime does not pay."
2. Gather pictures and make charts that will illustrate the work of the FBI. Find newspaper stories about the FBI.
3. List five factors you think might contribute to the reformation of a criminal.
4. Make charts, cartoons, or sketches illustrating some of the things you think might cause crime in the United States. You will be able to get many suggestions from newspapers and news magazines.
5. Read more about modern prisons. Tell the class some of the most interesting things you read.
6. Plan a safety campaign for your school and your community.
7. Make an illustrated chart that will show how accidents are caused through carelessness.
8. Check your home or school for conditions that might cause accidents.
9. List at least five rules a good driver always follows.
10. Study traffic problems in your community. Form committees to study (1) volume of traffic, (2) parking problems, and (3) safety measures needed to prevent accidents.

Questions to Answer

1. Why do you think legal training is useful to an FBI man?
2. Should everyone have his fingerprints taken? Why?
3. If the cost of crime were reduced in the United States, how would it help the average citizen?
4. If you were a prison official, would you try to reform a criminal or would you give him severe treatment? Why?
5. Name some of the reasons why so many accidents happen in the home. What could you do to help eliminate accidents in your own home?

A Written Exercise

Copy and complete the following sentences. Use as many words or sentences as you wish.
1. To work for the FBI, a man must _____.
2. Some ways to prevent crime include_____.
3. Some of the causes of crime are_____.
4. In some of the modern prisons a prisoner is_____.
5. Many accidents in the home are caused by_____.

6. Some of the things that may be done to help prevent accidents are_____.

7. Traffic accidents may be reduced by_____.

Words to Study Before You Read the Next Topic

tuberculosis	contaminated	adhesive	pollution
vaccinated	chlorine	aeration	injection
research	antitoxin	comply	nourishing
sanitarium	pharmacists	epidemics	pasteurized

How the Government Further Safeguards Life

GOVERNMENT officials are not only the officials who work in Washington. There are public officials throughout the country. Every day these officials do many things to safeguard the life and health of every American.

It is estimated that the average worker in the United States loses two weeks of work each year because of sickness. The loss in industry due to sickness is nearly a billion dollars each year. A healthy citizen is usually a good citizen. A healthy worker is usually a good worker. Many forms of sickness can be prevented with proper care. The government is spending large sums of money each year to prevent sickness, to save lives, and to improve the health of many people.

A few years ago the White House Conference on Child Health and Protection found a great amount of sickness among school children. "Sick days" are lost days. Anything that can be done to prevent sickness is worth while. To try to prevent it, many schools have a school doctor and dentist. Most schools have school nurses. Doctors, dentists, and nurses all help to protect the health of boys and girls in school.

In the fall the doctor gives each student an examination. If he finds a student who is ill, he sends him to the family doctor. Sometimes the student cannot afford to pay for medical treatment. In that case, the school doctor tries to arrange to have the work done free.

The school dentist also examines each pupil. If he finds decayed teeth, he asks the pupil to have them filled. If the pupil cannot afford to do so, the dentist may send him to some community agency. The agency will arrange to have the child's teeth filled.

The school nurse tests the eyes and the ears of each pupil. Parents are notified if a child needs glasses. Some pupils may be hard of hearing. The nurse will suggest to the teacher that those children sit near the front of the room. Parents are also notified so they may take the child to a doctor.

There are many contagious diseases. Today, however, there are very few epidemics. Many diseases are prevented through the use of vaccine or antitoxin.

Most pupils today have been vaccinated against smallpox. Most of them have also been given diphtheria antitoxin. At one time these diseases took a high toll of life. Today smallpox is almost unheard of and diphtheria cases are few.

The city board of health takes measures to prevent all epidemics. Occasionally, though, a serious epidemic does break out. Suppose an epidemic of typhoid fever breaks out in a town. Persons suffering from typhoid fever may contaminate food if they touch it. The typhoid germ is taken into the body of the person who eats that food. Contaminated milk and water are the main sources which spread the disease. Unclean fruits, vegetables, and other foods may also spread the germs.

There are a few persons who carry the germs in their bodies, even after they have recovered from the disease. These persons are called *typhoid carriers*. A carrier may contaminate food he handles and thus spread the disease. For this reason every person who has had typhoid fever should be examined carefully. If he is a carrier, he should not be allowed to touch food that is to be eaten by others.

If an epidemic of typhoid does break out, the city board of health rechecks the water supply. Even though the water is filtered and purified, chlorine may be added to it. Chlorine is a chemical that kills the germs in water. It does change the taste of the water slightly. Most people do not mind the taste. They realize their health is being protected by the chlorine.

After the water supply has been checked, other tests are made. Dairies are reinspected to make sure they are sanitary. People are urged to buy only pasteurized milk. Fruit, vegetable, and fish markets are reinspected. Usually, the disease is brought under control within a short time.

Health authorities are also learning to control tuberculosis, another dread disease. Most cases of tuberculosis can be cured if they are discovered early. To help discover the disease in its early stages, many city health departments have mobile X-ray machines. The machines can be moved from one place to another. They take small, inexpensive pictures of the chest and lungs.

From these pictures the doctor can usually tell if a person has tuberculosis. If there is a doubt, the person is given some tests. One is the *tuberculin*, or patch, test. A small patch is fastened between the shoulder blades with adhesive tape. The patch contains a special substance. It will cause the skin around it to turn red if the patient has any tuberculosis germs in his body. An *interdermal* test may also be given. For this test, a substance is injected into the arm. If the skin around the injection turns red, the test is positive. Neither of these results necessarily means the person has tuberculosis.

Larger X-ray pictures are also taken. If the tests are positive, and the large X-ray picture indicates tuberculosis, the doctor can be almost sure the patient has the disease.

If a person does have tuberculosis, he may be sent to a sanitarium for treatment. In the sanitarium he rests many hours a day. He receives plenty of nourishing food. He is given medical treatment. With rest and modern treatment, most patients can soon return to their homes. Most of them will soon be leading normal lives again.

City
Health Services

Most of our large cities have good health departments. Even the smaller cities are beginning to understand the need for city health services. The board of health is usually headed by a doctor or a sanitary engineer. Nurses and laboratory technicians are employed. Food factories, packing plants, bakeries, markets, and restaurants are inspected. Milk and water supplies are also tested. The health department tries in every way possible to combat disease. If an epidemic threatens the city, the board of health may decide to close the schools. They may also close theaters and other public places where large numbers of people gather. When the danger has passed, these places are again opened to the public.

These doctors are "reading" a patient's chest X-ray to determine whether he has tuberculosis.

Ewing Galloway

Many cities employ nurses to visit people who cannot afford to pay for medical care. The city nurse usually has many families to visit. She can spend but a short time with each one. Even so, she saves many lives. She helps many persons to be happier and healthier.

In the past, many poor people died because they could not afford to pay for medical care. Today cities maintain free clinics for those who cannot pay for medical care. Some cities also maintain baby clinics. Mothers may take their children there for examination and care. The city board of health in most cities wages war constantly upon sickness and disease. It tries to make the city a cleaner, safer place in which to live.

No one can be healthy unless he breathes plenty of clean fresh air. Some cities have laws against pollution of the air. The laws say that chimneys must be built so that as little smoke, dust, and harmful fumes escape into the air as possible. They prescribe building standards for houses, too. They may say that houses must be built so they will receive good ventilation and plenty of sunlight.

Cities also require hotels and rooming houses to be clean and sanitary. The owner of a hotel or rooming house must comply with the city health regulations. Otherwise he will lose his permit to operate the business.

City zoning also helps to make a community a healthful place in which to live. Most cities have separate zones for family dwellings and apartment houses. Places of business and industrial plants are likely to be confined to another part of town. That helps to keep the residential districts clean

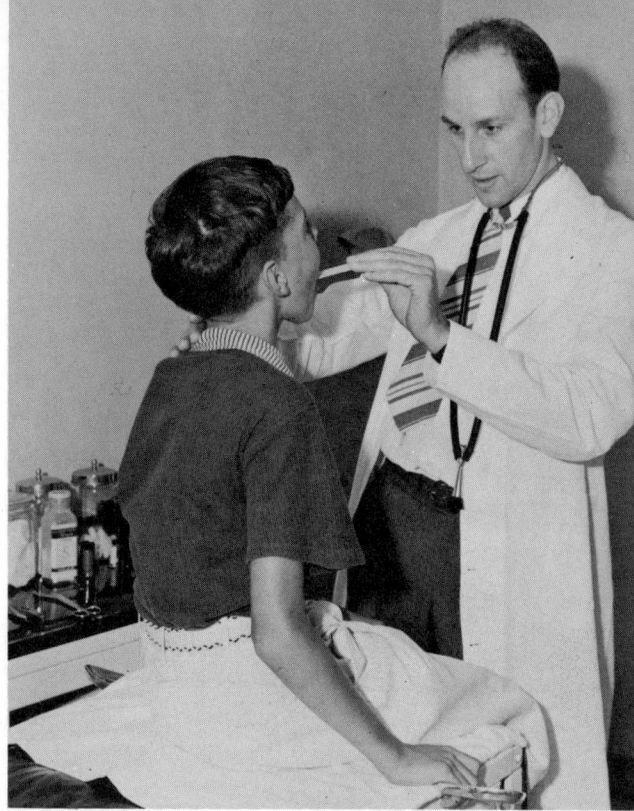

United States Public Health Service

Regular health examinations help prevent serious illness by revealing disease in its early stages. Some children have them annually.

and free from smoke. Zoning laws may also prevent houses from being built too close together. They may require each house to receive sunlight and fresh air.

Zoning laws would be of little value if the city were not clean. Clean streets, clean alleys, and clean yards make a city more beautiful. They also make it more healthful. All large cities, and many smaller ones, collect garbage and clean their streets regularly. The health boards ask citizens not to allow rubbish to collect in back yards. They ask them to destroy breeding places for rats, mosquitoes, and flies.

To keep citizens healthy, cities also provide a supply of pure water. Science has

241

"All work and no play make Jack a dull boy" goes the old saying. Outdoor play is necessary for both physical and mental health.

found that impure water is one of the chief sources of sickness. Cities, towns, and even rural areas try to provide an abundant supply of clean water. Most cities and towns get their water supply from nearby lakes and rivers. Others have to pipe the water for many miles. There are various ways of purifying the water. Some cities build filtration and aeration plants. Filtration helps to purify the water. Aeration removes unpleasant tastes and odors. It gives the water a fresher and more natural taste.

Parks and public playgrounds, too, have helped Americans to be healthy. Even in crowded cities, people can enjoy clean, fresh air in the parks. They can rest or play games. Recreation refreshes minds and bodies. Public-spirited citizens and city officials realize this. They have helped to provide attractive places where people can relax and find enjoyment. City governments have done much to help citizens live happier, healthier lives!

State Health Services

Every state in the nation has a department of public health. Through this and other agencies the state helps to protect the health of its citizens. Most states carry on five forms of health work.

1) *Sanitary control.* All states have laws regarding sanitation. The laws have to do with water and milk supplies. They govern the preparation and handling of food. They prescribe standards for plumbing, sewerage, and the disposal of refuse.

   Many states inspect the sanitary conditions where certain types of work are done. Barbershops and beauty parlors, for example, must conform to standards of cleanliness prescribed by state laws.

2) *Disease control.* The state health department tries to prevent, check, and stamp out various diseases. The department can take drastic steps to control an epidemic. They can even close schools, factories, offices, stores, and theaters, if necessary.

3) *Licensing of health workers and others.* Persons doing work which may affect the public health must pass examinations. Only if they pass can

they obtain licenses to practice. This applies to such persons as physicians, pharmacists, dentists, opticians, and nurses. Various state boards consider the qualifications of these persons. If the board decides a person is qualified, the state gives him a license.

Barbers and beauty operators must also pass examinations. They, too, must receive licenses before they can carry on their work. There are many other occupations that require licensing by the state.

4) *Promoting and safeguarding public health*. Many states operate hospitals, tuberculosis sanitariums, and special laboratories. The laboratories cooperate with doctors and health authorities throughout the state. Suppose a local doctor suspects a child has diphtheria. He can send a culture from the child's throat to the state laboratory. The laboratory workers will examine the culture. They can soon tell the doctor whether or not the child has the disease.

Many state departments of health distribute vaccines and antitoxins. Some of these are diphtheria antitoxin, smallpox vaccine, and rabies vaccine. Some state health departments also furnish anti-polio vaccine.

5) *Research and education*. Many states have state medical schools and state research laboratories. They carry on the work of discovering the cause, cure, and prevention of disease.

The state department of health also publishes pamphlets concerning public health. It distributes them to every town, city, and county in the state.

American Meat Institute

You often see a government stamp on the meat you buy. Meat is graded and stamped only after careful examination by a government inspector. Here you see some graded meat being stamped.

The Federal Government Also Provides Health Services

The health laws of the states and of the federal government are for our protection. Without them, a person might buy ground meat mixed with sawdust. He might buy imitation strawberry preserves mixed with grass seeds colored to look like strawberry seeds. He might buy foods that were colored with a poisonous coloring matter. He might buy a patent medicine that was nothing but colored water.

The Pure Food and Drug Act was passed by Congress in 1906. It prohibits interstate shipments of impure foods and drugs. In 1938 the Act was enlarged. Its name was changed to the Food, Drug, and

Cosmetic Act. Under the new act, impure foods, drugs, or cosmetics cannot be sold in interstate commerce. The act also forbids false advertising. Labels must be correct. A buyer who reads the label will know what ingredients have been used.

Patent medicine bottles or containers must also be correctly labeled. They must tell the name and amount of each substance that is in the medicine. Failure to give this information may bring a heavy federal fine and a long prison term. The Food, Drug, and Cosmetic Act also regulates the sale of drugs. It helps protect people against drugs that might be dangerous.

The federal government protects the people of the nation against the introduction of diseases from foreign countries. It helps to prevent the spread of disease from state to state. It helps provide money for state and local health programs. It carries on research work to discover the causes and cures of various diseases.

There are many things the government does to protect the health of its citizens. City, county, state, and federal health agencies all co-operate. They all try to improve the health of the American people. They all help to safeguard the life of every citizen!

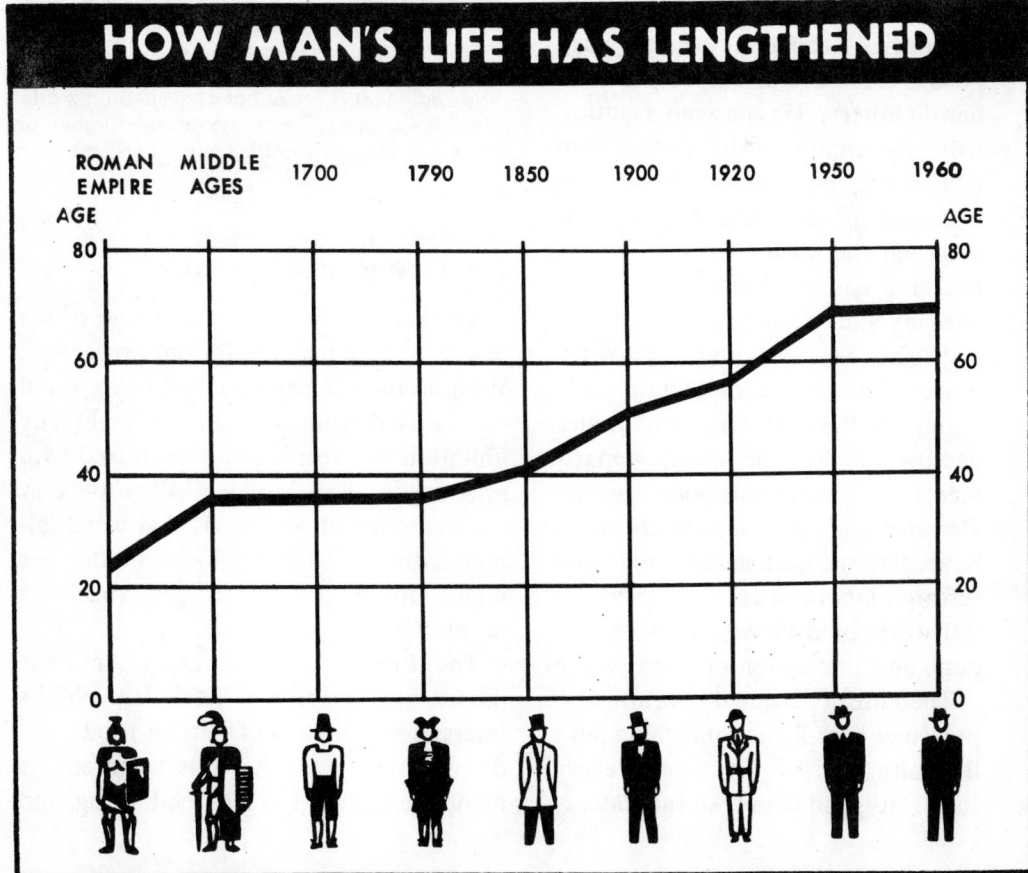

HOW MAN'S LIFE HAS LENGTHENED

ROMAN EMPIRE | MIDDLE AGES | 1700 | 1790 | 1850 | 1900 | 1920 | 1950 | 1960

CHART BY GRAPHICS INSTITUTE, N.Y.C.

Things to Do

1. Draw sketches or cartoons that will illustrate the work of some government agency that tries to protect health.
2. Make an illustrated chart showing the things your city, town, or county does to protect you against disease.
3. As a class project, arrange visits to the water plant, the garbage and sewage disposal plant, a dairy, and a meat market. Each student should write his own report on the visit.
4. Write an editorial for a newspaper explaining why the government is interested in the health of its citizens.
5. Find pictures that will illustrate the work of the state department of health.
6. As a class project, prepare a TV program of interesting things that might have happened in connection with the Food, Drug, and Cosmetic Act.
7. Pretend you are doing one of the kinds of work listed below. Write an essay on what you do to protect public health. Here is the suggested list: doctor; dentist; schoolteacher; optician; public school nurse; X-ray technician; pharmacist; research worker; sanitary engineer; park gardener; playground supervisor; barber; beauty operator; dairy worker; garbage collector; chemist.
8. In some communities a chemical substance, a *fluoride*, is added to the drinking water. Some people favor fluoridation of water as a preventive of tooth decay. Others are against fluoridation. Have a class discussion of the subject. Choose two teams to do research. Set a date for a debate on the question, "Resolved: That our community should practice fluoridation of water."

Questions to Answer

1. What is zoning? How can it affect health?
2. Does your community have or expect a smog problem? Why is smog considered a health problem?
3. Do you know of any way in which a city board of health helped to stamp out an epidemic of disease? If so, tell the class about it.
4. What are some ways in which your food is protected against contamination?
5. How does your town or city dispose of its garbage?
6. Where does your water supply come from?
7. Has the health record of the United States improved or deteriorated within the last fifty years? Why?
8. What are some of the sources of air and water pollution?

A Written Exercise

Copy and complete the following statements. Use as many words or sentences as you wish.

1. Smallpox can be prevented by _____.
2. Diphtheria can be prevented through the use of _____.
3. Chlorine is a _____.
4. To keep citizens healthy the government inspects _____.
5. City zoning laws prevent _____.
6. People should use the services of the mobile X-ray units in their community because _____.
7. Public parks and playgrounds have helped the people to become healthier because _____.
8. Some services of the state health department are _____.
9. Some of the services performed by the federal health department are _____.
10. Science has helped to prevent disease by _____.

Words to Study Before You Read the Next Topic

| minimum | phases | patronize | intolerance |
| budget | picket | radical | gymnasium |

Liberty in a Democracy

THE Constitution and the Bill of Rights are the foundation upon which our free society is built. They are the basis for much of the liberty we enjoy. The right of free speech, freedom of the press, and peaceful assembly are important rights to the American people. Equally important are their *homes, free schools, churches,* and the *right* to choose their own occupations.

Homes, schools, and churches share many worthwhile aims. They all seek understanding, truth, and wisdom. They all seek to make each citizen a credit to his country and to his God. They all seek to make him a happy, healthy citizen *from childhood to old age.*

The American Home

A child is born. His parents give him warm clothes, good food, and a home. They give him love, security, and companionship. They teach him to live happily with his own family. As he grows, his parents teach him to get along with his playmates. They teach him to do tasks that boys of his own age should be able to do. They teach him to be honest and dependable.

A child who lives happily with his family will get along well with his playmates. He will get along well with people outside the home. A child who learns how to act properly at home has an advantage. Many things are more easily learned at home. Courtesy and good table manners, for instance, are easy to learn. A child who learns them at home gets along better than a child who does not. Household tasks, too, are easy to learn at home. A girl who learns them, a few at a time, will be a better homemaker when she grows up. A boy who works is fortunate, too. He will find it easier to earn a living and be a useful citizen when he is a man.

The homes of today are not like the homes of yesterday. When our nation was young, there was very little machinery. There were few of what we call "service industries." Each family took care of its own needs. Today machines do much of the work that used to be done in the home.

The home is no longer a place where the family must depend upon itself alone. But the spirit of family life is still the same.

It is still the duty of the home to take care of boys and girls. They must be helped to grow up with strong, healthy bodies. The home must teach them the difference between right and wrong. It must teach them how to live peaceably and happily with others.

Unfortunately, families do not always do these things. Some fathers do not earn enough money to buy proper food for their children. They do not earn enough money to rent or to buy comfortable homes. They cannot pay for proper medical care. Sometimes a mother does not know how to take care of her family properly. She does not know how to teach them to become good citizens.

Americans believe that everyone should have the opportunity to live a normal, happy, and *useful* life. Children from underprivileged homes do not have the same opportunity as other boys and girls. What can be done to make American homes the kind of homes that will produce better citizens?

The government has tried to help families that cannot support themselves. It tries to make low-cost housing available. It has passed laws to provide better working conditions for workmen. It has established minimum wages for the workers. A *minimum* wage is the *lowest* wage that may be paid by law.

These things all help. But perhaps the best way to have better homes and better citizens is through education. Parents must learn how to guide their children intelligently. Boys must learn how to earn money and how to spend it wisely. Girls must learn homemaking and how to budget the family income. Both boys and girls must learn that it is important to live happily with other members of the family. It is important to get along well with people outside the family.

The Right of Free Worship

The church is an important factor in the growth of individuals and of a nation. There are many churches in the United States. The government did not build these churches. It does not regulate the services that are held in them. The people of the United States are allowed to build any kind of church they choose. They are allowed to worship in that church in any manner they wish.

The government does not decide which church its citizens shall join. It does not support any church through taxation. The American people have religious freedom. They may join any faith they choose.

More than half of the American people are members of a church. The churches reach everyone in the nation. All churches try to teach people to live better lives. They try to teach people to be more honest and courageous. They try to teach them to be true to their God and to their country.

Good citizens must remember that religious freedom is a right of all Americans. Good citizens have a duty to keep this right for all. Sometimes persons in one church look down upon people in other churches. *This is not democracy*. There should be no intolerance nor ill feeling among religious groups. Whatever their religious views, they are all Americans.

Ewing Galloway

Each family must train its young people for useful lives. This girl is learning to be a homemaker.

Members of every church have helped the United States fight for liberty. Members of every church have helped the nation to progress in times of peace. The Constitution honors the religious faith of all churches. All churches and all religious faiths should work together for the betterment of the people and of the nation.

Education for All

Democracy is the result of long years of struggle. The public school system of the United States is also the result of struggle. A century and a half ago anyone who proposed free education for all the people was considered radical. In most states, the well-to-do families sent their children to private schools. Some of them hired tutors to teach their children at home. Poor people could not do that. Some children of the poor attended free charity schools. But about half of all the children in the nation went uneducated. In 1850, there were about a million Americans who could neither read nor write!

The American people have always been progressive and independent. They realized the need of education for all. America was a land of opportunity. To make the most of its opportunities, the people needed education. Without education, they could not even understand and appreciate democracy.

During the 1800's many people began to urge free education for all pupils. "The United States is supposed to be governed by all the people," they said. "How can a nation be governed by people who are not educated? Everyone should have an opportunity to go to school. The schools should be maintained by public money."

At first there were protests and objections by many people. "Why should we pay

Today nearly every girl and boy in the U.S. can attend a public school.

taxes to support public schools?" they said. But thoughtful men were not swayed by their objections. "The nation will not endure," they said, "unless the people are educated. The people must understand their government. They must have the knowledge to make it a better government. How can a nation progress if most of its citizens cannot read or write?"

Little by little the idea of free education became acceptable to all the people. Public elementary schools were established in every state. At the same time there was a demand for free public high schools. The first free public high school was opened in Boston in 1821. Then high schools were opened in other parts of the country.

Today nearly every boy and girl in the United States can attend a free public school. Our public school system is the largest in the world. It is not conducted for profit, but is supported by public tax money. It is run by the people, for the people. It helps to keep America great.

Modern Schools

Many schools have motion-picture equipment, radios, phonographs, and television sets. Some of them have cafeterias. Some of them have manual-training shops, airy gymnasiums, and well-equipped outdoor playgrounds. In the early public schools of America, the boys and girls were taught reading, writing, and arithmetic. In the modern schools they are taught many additional subjects. They are taught how to appreciate good music, good art, and good literature. They learn scientific principles and principles of government.

They learn how to sing, to paint, to write stories, and to act in plays. They learn to know the world about them. They visit and study factories in operation. They examine different departments of their city government, and other phases of community life. They build and make things in school. They conduct safety and health campaigns. They prepare to live as grown-up members of society.

The schools of the nation have improved year after year. Still there are many problems to be solved. Ways must be found to help children who still go to school in poorly equipped one-room schools. Some rural communities have joined together and formed one large school district. They have pooled their money and built a larger, more modern school building. They have equipped it with the conveniences found in modern city schools. They have bought new books, maps, and other equipment. They have hired more teachers and offered more subjects to the pupils. They have provided school buses. They are doing everything they can to help the pupils obtain a good education.

Most of the money for school purposes comes from taxes on property. Some property is more valuable than other property. In school districts where property is valuable, more money can be raised. If school money came only from local property taxes, children in the poorer districts would suffer. They could not have such good schools as the children in the wealthier districts. Some states provide the same amount of money for each pupil or teacher whether a district is rich or poor. Other states give the poorer districts more state aid than the wealthier districts. Many people believe

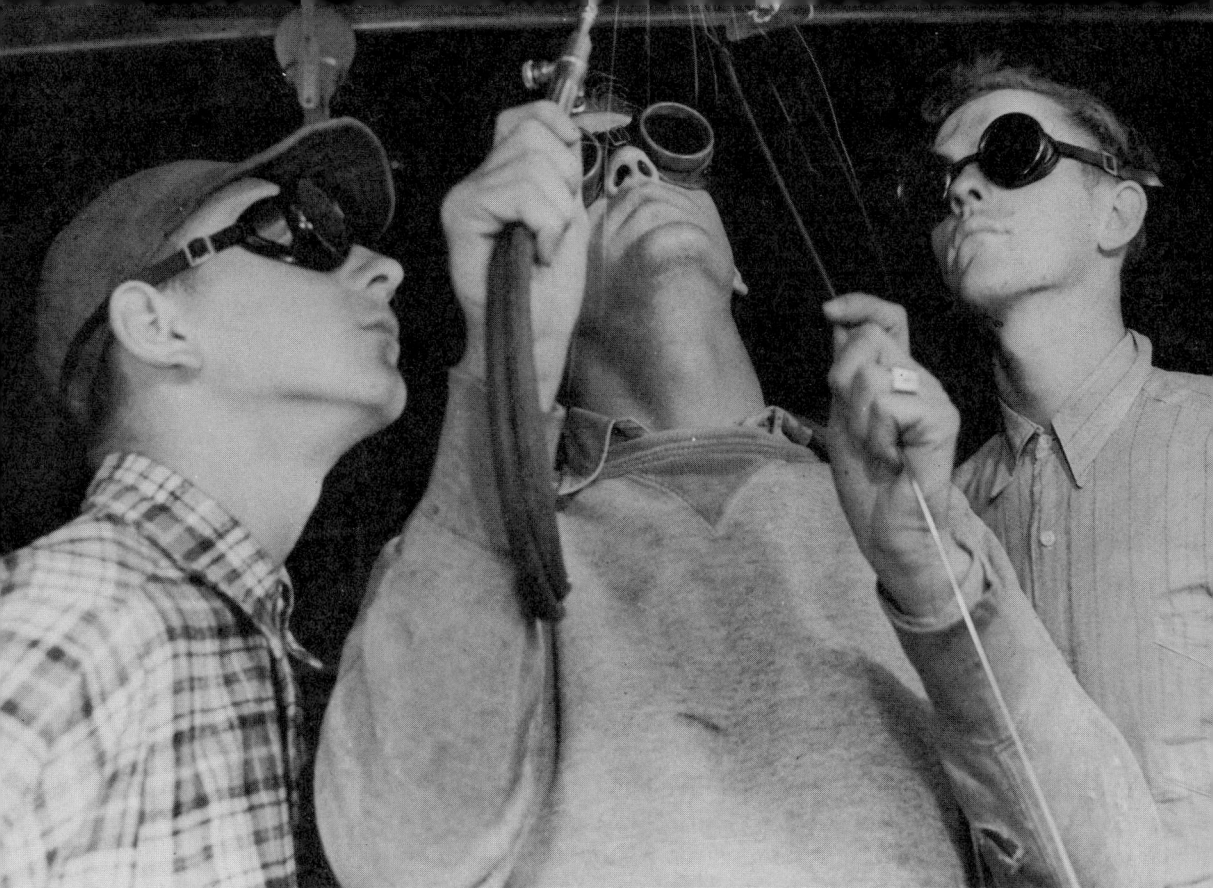

United States Information Service

Millions of young Americans attend vocational, or trade, schools. These boys are learning the difficult art of overhead welding. When they have finished their courses they hope to go to work in the aircraft industry. Note the safety glasses worn by instructor and students.

that some such plan should be adopted for the nation. Others are not sure what role the federal government should play in education. But each year the schools of the nation improve. Some day the American ideal may be completely realized. Some day every boy and girl in the nation may truly have an equal opportunity for education.

The Right to Choose One's Occupation

In some countries in the world a king's son becomes a king. The son of a carpenter becomes a carpenter. A jeweler's son goes into his father's business whether or not he wants to. In such countries it is the custom for sons to follow in their fathers' footsteps. The sons cannot choose a different vocation. They cannot rise above the position of their parents.

Young people in our country do not have to follow the same kind of work as their parents. Each person has the right to choose the kind of work he would like to do. Not everyone, of course, can afford to train for the kind of work he would like to do. But the government and other groups

try hard to help him realize his ambition.

Many men whose parents were poor are wealthy today. Many men whose fathers were farmers or tradesmen are now professional men. Many men whose fathers were professional men are now tradesmen or farmers. In the United States anyone may seek any kind of work he chooses. He may seek it in any part of the country.

The Workers Organize

The working day in shops and factories used to be from twelve to fourteen hours. Children worked as many hours as adults did. Mines, shops, and factories were often dangerous places to work. Then workers began to join organizations to better their working conditions. These organizations are called *labor unions.*

The labor unions have asked for laws that would not allow children to work. They have asked for minimum-wage laws. They have asked for limits on the number of hours a worker could be asked to work each day and each week. They have tried to protect workers from unsanitary and dangerous conditions. The labor unions have done many things to improve working conditions for the average workman. In doing so, they have helped to raise the standard of living in America. But they also have made demands which seem unfair to some people.

In any industry there are two important factors. There are the people who supply the money, or the *capital*, to operate the industry. There are also the workers, or *labor*. Workmen could not work without the factories, machinery, and raw materials

supplied by capital. The factory owners could not operate their businesses without the workers. *Each is dependent upon the other.*

Disagreements between Employers and Employees

There are many disagreements between employers and employees. Often the workers make demands which the employers feel are unfair. The employers refuse to meet the demands. When this happens, the workers may call a strike. They may refuse to work until the employer meets their demands. Sometimes they picket his shop. By that means, they try to keep other workmen from going there. They try to persuade the public not to patronize the employer.

When such a disagreement arises, the owner sometimes closes his business. Strikers, too, often close down factories or stop transportation. A great many people, in addition to the strikers and employers, suffer.

For this reason, the federal government and many of the states created boards to help settle labor troubles. When a dispute arises, employers and employees may come before the board. Each side presents its problems. The board studies the complaints and the demands of each side. Then it does all it can to help the workers and the employers agree upon a settlement. It tries to find a solution that is fair to both sides.

What Is the Solution?

It would not be fair for the working man to have all the advantages. Neither would it be fair for the employer to be favored.

This is a democracy. Both employees and employers have rights. The employer should try to understand the problems of the men who work for him. The working man should try to understand the problems of the employer.

Employers need laborers. Laborers need someone to provide work for them. Employers must make some profit on the money they have put in to their businesses. Workers must receive a decent living wage. They must have good working conditions. Both sides must work together for the greatest good of the country.

ORGANIZED LABOR: A GROWING FACTOR IN U. S. LIFE

1915 — UNION HALL — 2,500,000

1920 — UNION HALL — 5,000,000

1930 — UNION HALL — 3,400,000

1940 — UNION HALL — 8,500,000

1950 — UNION HALL — 16,000,000

1960 — UNION HALL — 18,100,000

GRAPHICS INSTITUTE

Things to Do

1. Draw cartoons or sketches showing how the home, the school, and the church teach young people to become better citizens.
2. Choose a famous American who came from a poor family. Write a short biography. Compare the famous American's position with that of his parents.
3. List ways in which your school helps to prepare you to become a good citizen.
4. Dramatize or describe a scene that might take place before a labor-management board.
5. Find stories that show how people of different faiths work together for a common cause.
6. Gather information about the kind of schools famous men and women have attended. Find out about the schooling of notable teachers, scientists, inventors, industrialists, and writers. Find out about the schooling of three presidents of the United States. In each case, try to show how education influenced the person's life.
7. Write a letter to your parents. Tell them what occupation you would like to train for. Tell why you chose that occupation.
8. Visit a factory or packing plant. Find out about working conditions. How many hours does each person work? Is he paid on a piecework or an hourly basis? What safety measures have been installed to guard against accidents? What special benefits do the workers have?

Questions to Answer

1. Do you believe that children who live in the country are happier than children whose homes are in the city? Why? What are the advantages of a city home? What are the advantages of a country home? What makes a happy home?
2. How can the home help to develop good citizens?
3. Can a boy or girl help to make his home a happier place in which to live? How?
4. What was the population of the nation in 1850? What percentage of the population could not read or write? What is that percentage now? Your librarian can help you find the answers.
5. How has the government tried to help families that cannot support themselves?
6. What are some of the services that used to be performed in the home that are now available elsewhere? What are some of our "service industries"?
7. What is the average American wage? How does it affect our economy?

A Written Exercise

Complete each of these statements correctly in two different ways.
1. The duty of the family is to
   a)
   b)
2. Parents provide their children with
   a)
   b)
3. Parents should teach their children
   a)
   b)
4. Homes, schools, and churches all try to
   a)
   b)
5. Some parents cannot take care of their children properly because
   a)
   b)
6. Some advantages provided by modern schools are
   a)
   b)
7. Free public education is an advantage because
   a)
   b)
8. A person belonging to one church should not look down on a person belonging to another church because
   a)
   b)
9. Workers in the United States are free to
   a)
   b)
10. Employers and employees should agree because
    a)
    b)

Words to Study Before You Read the Next Topic

Braille	conduction	converse	infantile paralysis
symbols	artificial	vibrations	vocation
contrary	institutions	emotional	supplement

Democracy and the Pursuit of Happiness

WHEN Thomas Jefferson wrote the words *life, liberty, and the pursuit of happiness,* he was not thinking of one person or one group of persons. He was thinking of all the people. Jefferson liked people. He believed in them. He wanted to see everyone have equal opportunity.

Jefferson's ideals have become a part of our American way of life. Our democratic government seeks to establish equality and justice for all people. It seeks to give everyone an opportunity to live a happy and worthwhile life.

There are many ways in which the government protects our rights to *life* and *liberty*. There are also many ways in which it helps us seek *happiness*. To most people, a happy life means a busy, useful life. It means helping others attain worthy and meaningful goals.

Our government is not content with giving part of the people the right to seek happiness. *It tries to help everyone who is willing to help himself.* It tries to help each citizen become a useful and worthy member of a free society.

Helping the Blind

In the United States there are a number of schools where skilled instructors train guide dogs. Each dog is trained to lead a blind person. The dog acts as the blind person's "eyes." With the dog's help, the blind person can do many things as well as people with sight. The dog has a special harness with a leash. The blind person holds the leash so that he can follow the dog. The dog has been trained to avoid obstacles and to stop at curbs and steps.

The blind persons attend the same training school. The blind person and the dog train together for about a month. The dog learns to understand his master. The master learns to understand the signals the dog gives him.

Once they understand each other, the dog can lead his master through heavy traffic. Together they can ride on elevators or on buses. The dog will lead the man around low-hanging obstacles and other dangerous things. The dog has even been taught to disobey his master if the need

257

arises. He will not knowingly lead his master into danger no matter how many times his master may give him a command.

Seeing-eye dogs and guide dogs have helped many blind persons to find happiness. Schools for the blind have also brought happiness to many persons who cannot see. Most of these schools are maintained by the state governments. Many of them have some teachers who are blind. A blind teacher may understand, better than a person with sight, the needs and feelings of a blind pupil. Sighted persons who train guide dogs are required to remain blindfolded for days or weeks. This helps the sighted person understand the problems of the blind.

Dogs to be trained as guides for the blind are carefully tested and selected. German shepherd dogs are among the best adapted for this work.

Ewing Galloway

Louis Braille was a famous Frenchman who was blind. He invented a system of reading and writing for people who cannot see. His system is called the Braille method. It is made up of sixty-three combinations of raised dots. Letters, punctuation marks, numbers, and musical symbols are written in raised dots. A blind person learns to read these dots by passing his fingertips over them.

Through their fingertips, blind persons read many books and magazines. Several companies in the United States print books and magazines in Braille. These are distributed to libraries for the blind. Blind persons may order books from these libraries. The government pays the postage.

The blind also learn to write. They use a sharp pointed instrument called a stylus. A piece of paper is put into a frame which holds it firm and smooth. Then the blind person punches Braille dots into the paper with the stylus.

Some schools have typewriters with Braille keys. The machine punches raised dots on the paper. A blind person who uses a Braille typewriter can often type as rapidly as a sighted person.

Schools for the blind use "talking books." These are entire books which have been recorded on phonograph records. When a person tires of reading Braille, he can hear recordings of the world's best books. He can also listen to the radio. News broadcasts, plays, concerts, and speeches help him to keep in touch with the rest of the world.

Schools for the blind help the blind adjust to their handicap. The students learn to develop their senses of touch and hearing. These help take the place of their

Many of the world's greatest books are now available in Braille editions for the blind to read.

sight. First, a blind person learns to walk, care for himself, and read Braille. Then he may learn a vocation.

Most vocations were once thought to be closed to the blind. Yet, in recent years, many blind people have mastered skills that allow them to work alongside sighted workers. Many blind people learn new trades. Others return to jobs they had before they were blinded.

Blind students also enjoy physical education periods. They learn to play baseball and basketball. They have track meets with other schools for the blind. They run the fifty-yard dash by following strings stretched along the track! They can follow the ball on a basketball court by listening to the sound it makes as it bounces. Blind people develop many skills that seem amazing to the sighted.

The Government Helps

There are over one hundred thousand blind persons in the United States. About half of these people did not become blind until they were past middle age. It would be fortunate if they could all support themselves, but this is not the case. Workshops for the blind have been established and blind men and women do some kinds of work in certain factories. This takes care of part of the blind. The government helps to take care of others. Under the Federal Social Security Act the federal government helps the states care for the blind. It matches the amount of money spent by the state to care for blind persons not in institutions. Usually this does not equal the expenses of the blind person. But it helps to supplement what he earns himself and makes him happier and more secure.

What Can Be Done to Prevent Blindness

One of the tragedies of blindness is that three out of four cases could have been prevented. *Three out of four blind persons would still have sight had it not been for someone's carelessness!*

Some childhood diseases cause blindness if the child is not given good care. Accidents also cause many cases of blindness. Workmen set off explosives without protecting their eyes from flying particles. Children play with firecrackers and other explosives. Hunters are careless with their guns. Factory owners put safety devices on their machinery, but many men ignore these devices. They lose their sight as a result.

Many things are being done to help reduce the amount of blindness. Campaigns to teach workmen to protect their eyes while doing dangerous work are carried on in many plants and factories. Educational material concerning proper lighting is available to the public. Some schools have sight-saving classes. In these classes students with poor eyesight are given special attention. They also study from books with very large type.

When one has good eyesight, it is not easy to imagine a world of darkness. No price is too great to pay for the joy of normal sight!

Help for the Deaf

There are many deaf persons living in the United States today. These people can never lead completely normal lives. However, a deaf person is not so greatly handicapped as a person who is blind. He has more opportunity for work than a blind man has. Not so many occupations are closed to the deaf as are closed to the blind.

The government has done many things to help the deaf. In nearly every state there is a state school for the deaf. Deaf children cannot learn by imitating speech as other children do. *They must be taught to speak.* Schools for the deaf also teach lip reading. The deaf are taught to understand what a person is saying by watching the movements of his lips. Many deaf children also learn to recognize tones. They learn to get sounds through conduction. First, they group around a piano. Their hands touch the instrument. As the piano is played, the deaf children feel the vibrations through their fingertips. After a few months of

training, many pupils can place their hands on the piano and recognize the tune that is being played. This training helps them in learning to sing.

A deaf child may not be entirely deaf. In that case the teachers try to help him make use of the hearing that he has. They use the organ and harmonica to teach him rhythm. He also learns how to recognize tones.

Teachers in the schools for the deaf are patient and skillful. They teach pupils how to use their lips, their tongues, and their teeth to make sounds. The pupils watch the teachers' lips, tongues, and teeth. They feel the movements of the teachers' faces and throats. Gradually the pupils learn how to make sounds. In some cases the children learn to converse by using the sign language. A person who learns to "talk" with his hands can converse with others who know the sign language. It is an international language. American children who learn it could converse with Swedish or French children.

State schools for the deaf also teach students a vocation. Many deaf persons learn how to type. Others learn to use adding machines and other office equipment. Girls study dress designing and dressmaking. They make pottery and baskets. Boys are taught farming, woodworking, weaving, or any of several trades. Nine out of ten students who graduate from a school for the deaf are able to earn a living and support themselves. The government, by establishing schools for these people, helps protect their rights. It helps protect their right to the *pursuit of happiness.*

Help for the Crippled

In the United States there are many men, women, and children who are crippled. Some were born crippled. Accidents and diseases have crippled others. Some of them

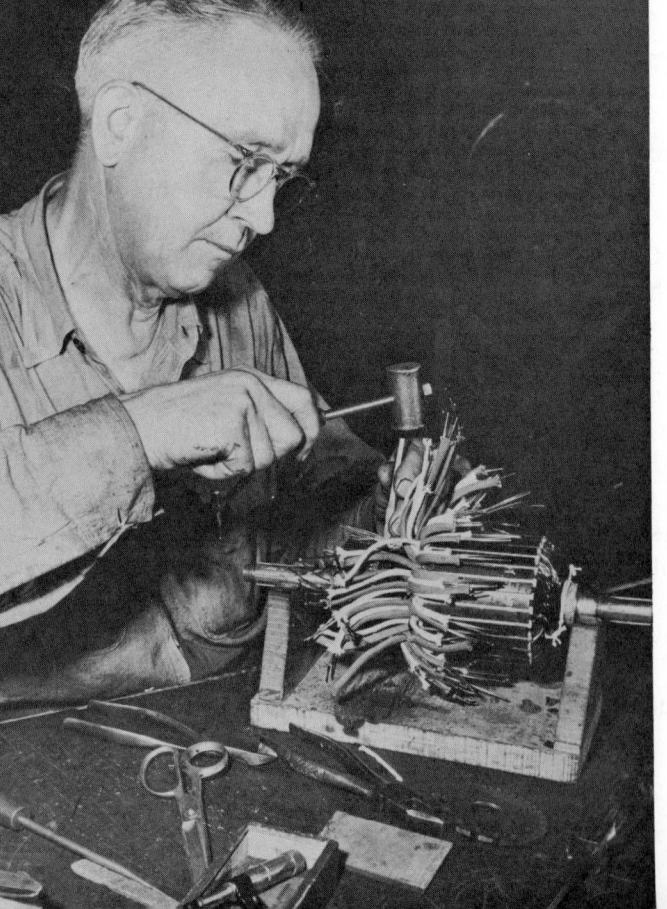

With proper training, many deaf workers are able to find types of employment where deafness is no real handicap.

Today nearly every state provides schools to help the deaf lead normal lives. These deaf children are learning about rhythm. They clap when they hear a special high-pitched sound on their earphones.

have been crippled in the service of our country.

Some children have deformities because they do not live in the right way. Children need proper food and sunlight. They need fresh air and exercise. Rickets, a bone disease, is common where housing is poor. The children there do not get enough sunlight or food. Another disease that cripples children is tuberculosis of the bone. Another is infantile paralysis, or polio.

While disease cripples many persons, accidents cripple many others. Falls from high places, automobile accidents, and accidents in factories and mines, all take their toll.

What is being done to prevent accidents and to help persons who are already crippled? The federal government helps the state government. Together they try to provide medical care for crippled children. They teach crippled workmen new occupations. Then these workmen can make their own living. Many cities, too, provide treatment for cripples. In many places the community hospital has a section devoted to the treatment of cripples. There are doctors on the staff who only treat crippling diseases. They know what to do for crippled patients. They know how to cure them if there is a chance for recovery.

Civic organizations often provide care for needy crippled men, women, and children. They pay for operations. They donate

money to pay for hospital care, or to buy braces and artificial limbs. Some organizations maintain hospitals which specialize in the treatment of crippled children.

Many communities provide schools for crippled children. In these schools pupils are taught to exercise and strengthen weakened muscles. They are given special diets and medical treatment. They are also given an education. They study all the subjects taught in regular schools. In addition, many of them learn typing and other office skills. Some of them learn to draw, or to make and repair jewelry. These skills help them to become self-supporting. Many later go to college and learn professions.

But the treatment of cripples is not enough! People must also try to prevent crippling accidents. Some dedicated scientists devote their lives to research for the prevention and cure of crippling diseases. They should have the encouragement and co-operation of every citizen.

Aid for the Mentally Handicapped

Every state builds and maintains institutions for the mentally retarded. Those who cannot care for themselves are kept in hospitals. Those who are able to follow simple directions go to state schools.

Some of these people learn to care for farm animals. Some learn to raise farm produce. Some may make brooms, rugs, and other articles. Others are taught to operate machines. They can learn to work at anything that does not require great mental skill. Many of the retarded leave the schools and return to their homes after they have learned to perform simple tasks.

The Mentally Ill

There are many persons who are physically ill. There are also many persons who are mentally ill. If a person has appendicitis, heart trouble, or pneumonia, he calls a doctor. If he is mentally ill, he should see a doctor, also. Mental illness is not a disgrace. It is a misfortune. But, happily, many forms of it can be cured.

City, county, state, and federal government health agencies all try to help persons who are mentally ill. Sometimes a case of mental illness is caused by worry, grief, or disease. When that is true, those in charge try to remove the cause.

Each year thousands of mentally ill persons are being restored to health. Many community hospitals have divisions where mental patients can receive treatment. Other hospitals have mental clinics. There patients may be examined and receive recommendations for treatment. Very often a patient who is not too ill receives treatment while he continues his ordinary work.

Mental Health

A sound body and well-adjusted emotional behavior should be the goals of every American. To achieve these ideals, many schools teach mental hygiene. Mental health is as important as physical health. The teachers try to teach pupils good mental habits as well as good physical habits. They try to discourage habits that might lead to mental illness. *Wholesome ways of thinking and good habits of emotional behavior are the foundation of mental health and good citizenship.*

Things to Do

1. Find stories of handicapped persons who have overcome their handi-
   caps and become useful members of society. Tell one of these stories
   in your own words.
2. Read the life story of Helen Keller. Be prepared to discuss the story
   in class.
3. Find pictures of state institutions for the handicapped. Tell the class
   any interesting information you know about them.
4. Memorize the poem by Edna St. Vincent Millay entitled, "A Visit to
   the Asylum." Put into your own words the story the poem tells.
5. Find out and make a list of some of the things your school or city does
   to help the handicapped. Find out if there is any way in which members
   of your class could be of assistance.
6. Try to find a book written in Braille. Bring it to school and let the other
   members of your class look at it.
7. If there is a guide-dog training center near you, invite one of the trainers
   to give a demonstration at your school.
8. Find out all you can about the way guide dogs are trained to pass
   obedience tests.

Questions to Answer

1. Do you think the government should try to help handicapped persons?
   Why?
2. What are some of the causes of blindness? Is there anything that can
   be done to eliminate these causes?
3. What is the Braille system of reading and writing?
4. What kinds of work can blind persons perform?
5. If you had a relative who was deaf, would you suggest that he be sent
   to a state school for the deaf? Would he be better off in the school or
   at home? Explain your answer.
6. Do you know of a cripple who earns his own living? How has he overcome his handicap? What character traits does his success indicate?

A Written Exercise

Copy each clause and add two or more phrases to make a true sentence.
1. In schools for the blind, the blind persons learn_____.
2. Blind persons of today can live happier lives because_____.
3. Some of the causes of blindness are_____.
4. Blindness might be reduced by_____.

5. In schools for the deaf, pupils are taught_____.
6. Society has tried to help crippled persons by_____.
7. Persons are often crippled because of_____.
8. Schools for crippled children teach_____.

Words to Study Before You Read the Next Topic

prevalent	depression	dependent	retirement
tenement	air conditioning	guarantee	poverty
disability	pension	annuity	insulated

More Problems and the Pursuit of Happiness

THE American standard of living is higher than the standard of living in most of the world. American housing is among the best in the world. Most Americans feel that good housing is part of the *pursuit of happiness*.

As good as our housing is, however, there is room for improvement. Many persons in the United States still live in homes that are neither clean nor comfortable. Big cities still have far too many dirty tenements. In nearly every town there is a place where people live in shacks.

It is easy to say, "Other people's homes have nothing to do with me!" But substandard housing has something to do with all of us. Poor housing brings problems that touch everyone. Tenement houses bring disease. Tuberculosis thrives in the crowded slum districts. Rickets, the bone disease which cripples hundreds of children, is also prevalent in the slums. Where many families are crowded into dirty homes, disease spreads quickly. Everyone is in danger. Thousands of dollars of tax money are spent each year to stop diseases that are the result of poor housing and overcrowding.

Crime also grows in the slums. There is more crime in the slum sections of a large city than in any other part of the community. Slum neighborhoods take more of the police department's time. They take greater watchfulness on the part of the fire department.

The government has done many things to aid the handicapped. It has done much to make life more pleasant for them. There are other Americans, not physically or mentally handicapped, who need help. These include the slum-dwellers. It is true that many of these people are not good citizens. But it is hard to judge them fairly. If they lived in better homes, they might be happier. Their ideas about life might change. They might become good citizens.

Americans have solved many problems. Many more must be solved. Slum clearance is one on which many communities are now working. Low-cost housing within the reach of all Americans has become an American goal.

Some Things
That Are Being Done

Private construction companies open up hundreds of new subdivisions each year. The subdivisions are usually on the outskirts of town—where there is plenty of sunshine and fresh air. The houses built in the subdivisions are modern and attractive. Many of them have built-in stoves and refrigerators. They have good heat and good lighting. Families buy the houses with a small down payment. They pay the balance in monthly payments that seem like rent.

The federal government is helping to solve the housing problem. The government has created a mutual mortgage insurance fund. It is handled by the Federal Housing Administration. Many families have been able to buy homes with Federal Housing Administration loans. These FHA loans are obtained through banks or other lending institutions.

A person wishing to buy a home goes to a bank. He asks for an FHA loan. The bank checks the man's credit rating and his ability to repay the loan. Then a man from the bank looks the home over very carefully. He wants to be sure that its value justifies the loan. If the bank feels that the loan will be approved, it submits the application to the FHA.

The FHA officials also look at the home. They, too, consider the man's credit rating and his ability to repay the loan. If they find that the FHA requirements have been met, they approve the application. The bank then makes the loan.

The loan carries a fairly low rate of interest. It is repaid in monthly payments over a long period of years. The monthly payments include interest, taxes, and fire insurance. Also included is a small fee paid to the mutual mortgage insurance fund to guarantee the loan.

Another government agency, the Veterans' Administration, helps war veterans to build or buy homes. The loans are obtained from private lending institutions, after approval by the Veterans' Administration. The Veterans' Administration guarantees a certain part of each loan to the lending institution.

The government has also built a number of low-rent housing projects. The houses are rented to families with very small incomes. Other things are also being done. New housing projects are being built by both private industry and the government. Families are able to buy inexpensive ready-made houses. The ready-made houses are produced in great quantities. Some are fireproofed and insulated against heat and cold. Some have air conditioning that will cool them in the summer and warm them in the winter. Some of these houses are so inexpensive that families with very low incomes can afford them.

The housing situation is a big problem. But the people of the United States have solved many big problems. They want to solve this one, too. People who have comfortable housing are likely to be better, happier citizens. Comfortable housing is part of the *pursuit of happiness*.

The Unemployment
Problem

It has often been said, "If a man really wants to work, he can find a job." For many years Americans believed this to be

Kaiser Services
Government and private industry, working together, are trying to make it possible for all American families to buy or rent comfortable housing.

true. During the depression after 1929, however, people began to change their minds. Almost overnight, men were thrown out of work through no fault of their own. The whole nation was affected. Most of the people who were out of work looked for work. But business and industry were almost at a standstill. There were not enough jobs to go around.

Local relief agencies have always helped the unemployed and underprivileged. Community Chest organizations, the churches, the Red Cross, and other organizations did all they could. They gave money, food, and clothes to needy families. They sheltered those who were temporarily without homes. But the depression lasted a long time. The burden became too heavy for the communities to bear.

Congress, realizing it was a national problem, set up a number of relief organizations. These national agencies worked with local, state, and federal groups. They helped to relieve some suffering. But this relief was not enough. A new plan had to be worked out for the future. Out of the need for such a plan came the Social Security Act.

Social Security

The Social Security Act was passed by Congress in 1935. It has been changed several times since then. The main purpose of the law is to *prevent* persons from becoming needy. It also helps to provide aid for certain classes of needy persons.

The Social Security Act helps the states provide: (1) unemployment insurance; (2) aid to the needy aged; (3) aid for dependent children; (4) aid to the needy blind; (5) services to help protect the health of children and mothers; (6) help for needy children; (7) treatment for crippled children; (8) public health services; (9) ways of teaching handicapped persons how to earn a living. *It also provides for federal Old-Age and Survivors Insurance.*

Unemployment and Disability Insurance

The Social Security Act paved the way for states to set up unemployment insurance programs. Under the Act, the federal government agreed to share the cost of *running* the state programs. Unemployment *benefits* come from a tax paid by employers. In some states employees also pay.

Every state now has an unemployment insurance plan. The plans are not all alike. In some states an unemployed worker receives as much as $55 a week. In other states he receives much less. The insurance is usually paid for twenty to twenty-six weeks, if necessary. However, the worker must have been employed a certain length of time to be able to receive it. His unemployment must last a certain time before he can start drawing benefit payments.

Sickness or disability insurance is also paid in some states. It is paid to insured workers who are not able to work because they are sick or disabled. In most states having such a plan, the employees help to pay for it.

Old-Age and Survivors Insurance

The Old-Age and Survivors Insurance program is one of the most important parts

of the Social Security Act. It helps many old people live their remaining years free from worry.

A worker insured under the Social Security Act can look forward to a retirement income. He will get that income as a matter of right, not of charity. Another name for this income is *annuity*. It is like an annuity paid under a private insurance policy. Women workers can receive it when they become sixty-two. Men must reach age sixty-five. The amount of the income depends upon the number of years the worker has paid into the fund. It also depends on the amount of his earnings. An extra sum is paid to the worker's wife if she is over sixty-five. Part of the amount of the annuity is also paid to each of his dependent children under eighteen.

Sometimes a person insured under the Old-Age and Survivors Insurance dies before retirement. Then the widow or widower and the children under eighteen receive monthly payments. There is also a cash death payment. No income taxes have to be paid on Social Security benefits.

When the Social Security Act was first passed, it insured only workers in commercial or industrial jobs. Later amendments changed this. Now almost everyone who works for wages or a salary is insured. Even farmers and other self-employed people are included, provided they earn $400 a year. Employers and employees each pay three and one-half per cent Social Security tax on a worker's earnings. Only the first

$4,800 of a person's yearly earnings are taxed. The tax rate is scheduled to rise to a total of eight per cent in 1966. It will rise to nine per cent three years later.

Unfortunately, many persons were already aged when the Social Security Act was passed. Many of them had no means of support. They lived in fear of going hungry. The Social Security Act made state pensions possible for these needy people. The federal government agreed to pay half the costs of any old-age pension plan that state governments should establish. Old people can qualify for a pension without having paid money into the pension fund. In order to qualify, however, they must prove that they are in need. No such "means test" exists under the Social Security Old-Age and Survivors Insurance

Ewing Galloway

Millions of elderly Americans are enjoying comfortable retirement. Old-Age and Survivors Insurance payments help to make this possible.

270

plan. By now most aged people can receive Social Security annuities, based on former earnings. In 1959 old-age benefits of about ten billion dollars were being paid each year. They were being paid to some thirteen and a half million old people!

It is hoped that the Social Security Act and similar measures will help prevent depressions. Old-age and unemployment insurance are sometimes called *economic cushions*. They *cushion* declines in our economy. Even if business should be at a low ebb, buying power would not stop. The old people and the unemployed would not become public burdens. They would keep their buying power to some degree. Their guaranteed incomes would help the United States avoid a severe depression.

Help for Needy Children

There was a time when some dependent children were placed in children's homes or in boarding schools. Others were placed in foster homes. The state paid for each child's board and room. Some of these children were half-orphans whose fathers had died. Others came from families which the father had deserted.

Many of the children were happy in foster homes. They were loved and given good care. But the mothers often grieved because they could not keep their children at home. Finally the welfare workers suggested a solution. "Some of the children are better off in foster homes," they said. "Others should be at home with their mothers. The state should help support *worthy* mothers so they could have their children at home with them."

The Social Security Act established aid for states adopting this plan. The state and county governments provide so much a month for each needy child under a certain age. The federal government adds to that sum. This is a happy arrangement for children who need to be at home with their mothers.

Misfortune and the Pursuit of Happiness

In a democracy every person should have an opportunity to earn a good life. He should have a good home. He should be able to buy newspapers, books, and magazines. He should have dental and medical care. He should have good food and the chance to go to school. He should also have some healthful recreation. A good American does not want charity. *He wants to work. He wants to earn these things.*

But sometimes a family experiences illness, unemployment, or other misfortunes. A man cannot earn enough to feed and to clothe his family properly. He cannot earn enough to give his family the advantages they should have in a free society.

The various branches of government have done many things to help the situation. They have provided aid for the handicapped and payments to dependent children. They have made provisions for old age, disability, and unemployment. All these things have helped. *But the problem is still up to the individual citizen.* He must learn how to work and how to apply his knowledge. He must learn how to manage his income and provide for emergencies. Then he truly will become a *happier* and a better citizen!

Things to Do

1. Form committees to study housing in your community. Discuss improvements that would help the whole community.
2. Make a study of the Social Security Act. There was a great deal of controversy about it before its passage. Look up some of the arguments against its passage. Have any of those arguments proved to be correct?
3. Find out some of the names of the social agencies in your community. Explain what they do to help people.
4. Certain groups, such as railroad and government workers, have their own retirement plans. Compare one such plan (the Railroad Retirement Act, for instance) with the Social Security Act. Decide whether or not you think it is wise to have separate plans. Prepare to support your opinion.
5. Compare American standards of living with living standards in any one of the following countries: China; Denmark; Italy; Germany; Spain; Sweden; Russia. Base your comparisons on such things as housing, health protection, educational opportunities, and working conditions.

Questions to Answer

1. Do you think the American people should try to solve the problem of poverty? Why?
2. What are some of the things that have been done to improve the housing conditions of the nation?
3. What do you think is the connection between the Social Security Act and the *pursuit of happiness*?
4. What is meant by "aid to dependent children"?
5. What is the difference between an old-age annuity and an old-age pension?
6. How does poor housing in another part of town affect your *pursuit of happiness*?

A Written Exercise

Copy and complete the following statements. You may use as many words and sentences as you wish.
1. The standard of living in the United States is_____.
2. The happiness of children is important to a nation because_____.
3. Federal Old-Age Insurance is important to the nation as well as the individual because_____.
4. Some communities are improving housing conditions by_____.
5. A country's standard of living is measured by such things as_____.

Words to Study Before You Read the Next Topic

reforested	levees	erosion	replenish
relaxation	rotate	slaughtered	refuges
humus	topsoil	reservoirs	assets

The Pursuit of Happiness
Today and Tomorrow

"ALL work and no play makes Jack a dull boy." All work and no play also makes Jack an unhappy boy. Play and health are closely related.

It is not study alone that makes a boy or girl grow physically and mentally. The boy or girl who plays is usually more alert mentally. He is usually stronger physically. Games help to develop self-control, courage, and honesty. They develop quick judgment and co-operation. A boy who makes a quick decision in football or baseball is training himself to think rapidly. A player who obeys the leader of his team is learning to co-operate with teammates. He is learning to play and to work successfully with others. Play is very valuable if it is the right kind of play.

Success in life is often measured by the amount of money a man makes, but too often he makes money only to find that he has lost his health or his happiness. Unless he has learned to relax and use his leisure time wisely, his money will not bring him true happiness.

Wholesome Recreation

Not all boys and girls enjoy the same sports. They do not all enjoy the same kinds of recreation. This is also true of adults. But in the United States, there are many, many interesting things to do. There are hobbies and recreations to please everyone.

Recreation does not necessarily mean playing games. For adults, recreation is a change from the work of the day. Some people find recreation in outdoor play. Others like to read books or magazines. Others like to go to the theater or to concerts. Clubs, museums, and libraries attract still others.

There is a public library in nearly every city in the United States. The libraries offer many services. They have books printed in foreign languages. They have books printed in Braille for the blind. Some of the city libraries circulate music, motion pictures, and picture slides.

Santa Fe Railway

Among America's many wonderful recreational areas is the magnificent Grand Canyon in Arizona.

There are also county libraries and state libraries for public use. Many state libraries have extension departments. Persons can write to the state library for books. In some states, bookmobiles make regular trips to areas where there are no public libraries.

The public libraries provide many hours of pleasure. But for persons who want outdoor recreation, there are also opportunities. Schools have well-equipped playgrounds and gymnasiums. Nearly every city has a public park and playground. Cities also provide tennis courts, and baseball and softball fields. Many of them have croquet courts, volleyball courts, and swimming pools. A few have golf courses, bowling alleys, and polo fields. In the larger cities there are usually zoos and botanical gardens.

People throughout the country find recreation and relaxation in travel. Nowhere in the world is there more beautiful and varied scenery than in the United States. We have mountains and lakes and valleys and deserts. We have seashores and plains. Our state and national parks are among the most beautiful in the world. Each year thousands of people enjoy these magnificent works of nature.

Transportation and Communication

Imagine waking up some morning to find that all transportation and communication had been stopped! Imagine what would happen if there were no telephones, telegraph lines, or mail service. Imagine getting along without radios, newspapers, or magazines. Imagine what would happen if there were no means of transportation.

Picnicking is a favorite American pastime. Wise picnickers carefully follow rules and regulations.

Ewing Galloway

In a short time food supplies would be gone. There would be no oil or coal for fuel. Factories would have to close for lack of raw materials. Men would be thrown out of work. There would be untold suffering. The life of the nation really depends upon its transportation and communication.

The American people have become accustomed to the finest means of transportation. They have become accustomed to excellent mail service. Telephones, radios, television, and telegraph services are taken for granted. So are newspapers, magazines, books, and other means of communication. Americans are so used to all these things that they often fail to appreciate them. They do not realize how hard it would be to get along without these services. They do not realize how much these services have helped Americans in their *pursuit of happiness.*

What of Tomorrow?

The people of the United States have many things to make life pleasant. Since colonial times the resources of the nation have been developed. There have been many new inventions. Citizens have been given more opportunity both for work and for play. But what of the future? Will the nation continue to improve? Will the United States always be a good place in which to live?

When the settlers came to the New World they found a land rich in natural resources. Natural resources are forests, water, fertile soils, minerals, coal, and other gifts of nature. Then the building of America began! Forests were cleared and homes were built. Highways, stores, and cities took the place of the prairies, the forests, and the rich meadow lands. Men worked with a will, but not with foresight. It seemed that the resources of the new land would never be exhausted. "America will always be rich," the settlers reasoned. "There are few people and many resources."

But the population of the nation *increased* steadily. The resources *decreased.* The United States is still rich in natural resources, but there is serious danger. The nation is not yet two hundred years old. Yet almost one third of many of the nation's resources have been used. Many of them have been wasted. What will happen in the future if Americans continue to be wasteful?

Conserving the Farm Lands

It takes nature from five hundred to a thousand years to make an inch of fertile topsoil. Yet, every year, hundreds of tons of topsoil are lost from the farm lands of the United States. Much of this loss is due to poor farming methods. Sometimes farmers plow their fields and leave a layer of loose soil on top. The rains wash away this loose soil. Winds blow it to far distant places. The land is no longer good for farming. *This wearing away of the land by wind and rain is called erosion.*

Erosion has ruined thousands of acres of farm land. Other things, too, have made land unproductive. Each crop needs different plant foods from the soil. Some farmers grow the same crop year after

year. In time, the plant foods needed for that crop are gone. It is necessary to fertilize the soil and replace the lost plant food. If these things are not done, the land becomes useless.

Reclaiming the Land

Acre after acre of good farming land was ruined. Finally experts in the Department of Agriculture began to study the problem. They taught farmers how to rebuild worn-out land. They showed them how to farm so that the land would not be worn away by erosion.

To the farmers with eroded land the experts said, "Plow *around* instead of up the hillsides. Terrace your fields. The terraces and the furrows will act as dams. They will hold the water and let it seep into the ground. Plant strips of grass or clover here and there on your sloping fields. The grass and clover will catch the soil that has been washed down.

"To prevent the washed-out gullies from becoming deeper, you can build check dams of brush or stone. When the water rushes down the gully, the check dams will hold it. Much of the valuable topsoil will be saved. You might also plant trees along the tops of the hills. When the trees grow, their roots will help to hold the soil together."

The experts also had advice for farmers

The U.S. Soil Conservation Service tries to help farmers prevent this kind of soil erosion. It also tries to help them avoid serious drought by conserving water resources.

Ewing Galloway

with worn-out land. "You must build up your soil by using fertilizer," they said. "You must not plant the same crop year after year. You must rotate your crops. Plant corn one year and wheat the next. Then plant clover or some grass which will add humus to the soil. If you rotate your crops in this way, your land will become rich and fertile again."

Conservation of soil is not the only problem. Bugs, lice, gophers, and wild animals constantly attack growing crops. The farmer must destroy these enemies. Otherwise they will destroy his crops.

The government employed scientists to study these problems, too. The scientists taught the farmers how to kill bugs and insects with poison sprays that would not harm the plants. They taught them how to cure plant diseases. They taught them efficient ways to kill animals that destroy crops and livestock. Science has helped the farmer greatly. Science has taught him how to grow better and more profitable crops.

Other
Conservation Needs

Water power is one of the most valuable assets of the nation. The people of our country are now trying to make the best possible use of it. This was not true in the past. Many rivers now furnish great amounts of water power. Channels have been deepened and many rivers made navigable. To prevent floods, engineers have deepened rivers so that the flood waters can be carried away. They have constructed levees along riverbanks. They have built earth and concrete dams to check the flood

International Harvester Company

Scientific knowledge and modern farm machinery both help the farmer conserve resources. This bean rancher is carefully using a disk plow.

waters. They have built large storage reservoirs. They have done many other things to prevent the disastrous floods.

When the settlers came to the New World, much of the land was covered with forests. Many of these forests have been destroyed. Trees have been cut down four times as fast as new ones can grow! In the early days settlers burned the forests to clear the land for crops and homes. Later, the lumber companies cut down many of the finest trees and destroyed others.

To save the forests, the government was forced to take action. Today, large sections of timberland are protected. Many of them have been made national forests. The cutting of timber in these areas is closely supervised. Only a certain number of trees is

OUR FORESTS YESTERDAY AND TODAY

U.S. FORESTS IN 1620

ORIGINAL FORESTS

BRUSH, ET

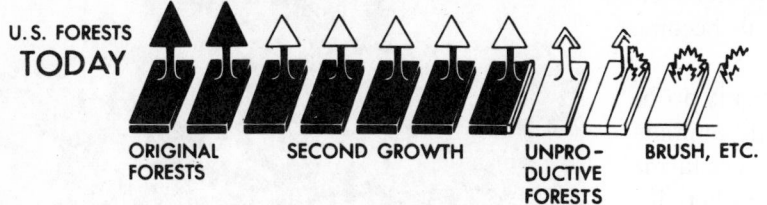

U.S. FORESTS TODAY

ORIGINAL FORESTS   SECOND GROWTH   UNPRO-DUCTIVE FORESTS   BRUSH, ETC.

EACH UNIT REPRESENTS 50 MILLION ACRES

PICTOGRAPH CORPORATIC

cut each year. Lumber companies, too, are helping to conserve the nation's trees. They have changed their methods of cutting timber. They are careful to protect young trees. Both the government and private companies plant trees in areas that have been burned or destroyed in some way.

The United States Forest Service has done much valuable work in protecting the forests. It has reforested many areas. It has fought insects that have attacked the trees. It has built roads into forests so that forest fires could be fought more successfully. States, also, have established forest reserves. State and federal forest reserves now total millions of acres of forest land.

More Conservation

At one time thousands of buffalo roamed the plains of the United States. Hunters slaughtered them. Most of the buffalo were killed merely for the sport of it. They were not needed for food. One after another, the great herds were wiped out by thoughtless hunters. Only a few of the great beasts were left.

The story of other kinds of wild life was much the same. Finally, true lovers of nature came to the rescue. "We must protect our animals, our birds, and our fish," they said. "We must make the public understand the seriousness of the situation. We must urge Congress and the state legislatures to pass laws that will protect our wild life."

Their efforts were successful. Laws for the protection of game were passed by the state and federal governments. Now game animals and birds can be hunted for only a short time each season. A limit is also set on the amount of game a person may shoot. Anyone who kills more game birds or animals than the law allows is subject to a heavy fine. So is a person who kills game out of season. Some game-law violations can result in prison sentences.

The government also helps protect our

fish supply. Trout, bass, and other fish are raised in state and federal fish hatcheries. When the fish are grown, they are planted in streams and rivers.

The state and federal governments have provided many breeding and feeding grounds for wild life. Game refuges are scattered throughout the parks and forests of the nation. However, *the government alone cannot solve the problem of conserving wild life.* Hunters, farmers, and others must also do their part. Everyone must help protect the game and other wild life in our country.

The conservation of forests and wild life is a great problem, but it is not a hopeless one. It is possible to plant new trees. It is possible to replenish the wild life of the country. Conservation of minerals is more serious. When the mineral resources of the country are gone, they can never be replaced. When the petroleum or oil is gone, there will be no more.

In the past, Americans wasted these resources. Only the best grades of ore were used. Only ore easily obtained was mined. As soon as a shaft became hard to mine, it was abandoned. Some of the mine shafts caved in, burying thousands of tons of valuable ore. Petroleum, too, was wasted.

Today experts are studying the problems of conservation. Local and federal governments try to regulate the mining of minerals and the pumping of oil. But the problem can not be solved by government alone. It can best be solved by the people.

The American people are beginning to realize the serious need for conservation. They are beginning to ask that our resources be fully protected by law. They are beginning to see how important it is for all citizens to obey conservation laws. A nation without natural resources could not long survive. Natural resources are necessary to the *pursuit of happiness*—tomorrow as well as today.

Government game protection began just in time to save the once plentiful buffalo from extinction.

Ewing Galloway

Things to Do

1. In any way you choose, show how play or recreation has (1) a character-building value and (2) a health-building value.
2. Choose any one of our natural resources to study. You may choose trees, or oil, or uranium, or fish, or anything you wish. Read books and magazine articles. Find out whether Americans have ever wasted that resource. Find out whether it is being wasted now. If it is being conserved now, find out what means are used to conserve it. Prepare a report of your findings.
3. Make a travelogue of pictures of our national parks.
4. Gather facts about erosion and soil conditions in your region. Find out what is being done to improve conditions.
5. Make a list of some of the things that have been done to conserve our natural resources.
6. The United States had one President in particular who helped the cause of conservation. Find out his name. As a class project, prepare a television program dramatizing some of the things he did for conservation.

Questions to Answer

1. What are some of the ways in which careless people endanger our natural resources? How can we stop this waste?
2. What kinds of public recreation do you have in your community? Do they have anything to do with natural resources?
3. What does forest conservation have to do with soil conservation? with water conservation?
4. What does the word *conservation* mean to you?
5. What connection is there between conservation of natural resources and the *pursuit of happiness*? Discuss this question in class.
6. What natural resources does your state have? Are any conservation measures concerning them under discussion in your state?
7. Who are your representatives in the state legislature? Can you find out how they have voted on conservation measures of any kind?

A Written Exercise

Copy and complete the following statements. Use as many words or sentences as you wish.
1. The advantages of having a hobby are_____.
2. Natural resources that can be replaced as we use them include

_____.

3. Natural resources that cannot be replaced include_____.
4. The things in this room that come from some natural resource include_____.
5. I can help to conserve the natural resources of our nation by_____.

Words to Study Before You Read the Next Topic

stimulants	frugality	temperance	punctual
proprietor	perseverance	personality	industrious
distinguish	excel	conscience	moderation

UNIT SUMMARY

There are many ways in which our government protects the *life* and *liberty* of everyone living in the United States. There are many ways in which it gives people the right to the *pursuit of happiness*. The government serves the people well. Each year the words written by Thomas Jefferson take on new meaning. They will take on a still greater meaning when each and every citizen also does his part. The government and the people, working together, will find even better ways to make *life, liberty, and the pursuit of happiness* a living example for all free people.

UNIT FIVE

The Duties of a Citizen in a Democracy

THE DUTIES of a CITIZEN in a DEMOCRACY

There are two things that make a student a valuable member of any group. The group may be a football squad or a debating team. It may be any other kind of team or group. In any of them, a student is valuable if he does his task well. He is valuable if he co-operates with the group. To put it another way, to be a valuable member of any group, one must be able to do his own work efficiently. He must be able, at the same time, to work successfully with others.

This is also true of the citizen in a democracy. He must be a good citizen in his home, in school, and at work. He must co-operate with those around him. Only in this way can he further the interests of his city, state, and nation.

In this unit you will study about *The Duties of a Citizen in a Democracy*. You will discover ways in which each citizen can do his part to make democracy really work. The topics in this unit are:

PREPARING TO BECOME A USEFUL CITIZEN
OTHER DUTIES OF A GOOD CITIZEN
THE FUTURE IS YOUR RESPONSIBILITY

As you study this unit think about the things you can do to make yourself a better citizen. Think about the ways in which every citizen can help his government serve the needs of the people.

Preparing to Become a Useful Citizen

THERE is an old proverb that goes something like this: "A chain is only as strong as its weakest link." This proverb might well be applied to a democracy. It might well be said, "A democracy is only as strong as its individual citizens. A democracy cannot grow and progress unless its individual citizens also grow and progress."

A democracy is a government of the people. The phrase *the people* does not mean only those who are public officials. It means each and every citizen in the nation. To make a democracy strong, each citizen must first make himself strong. He must make himself strong physically, mentally, and morally.

Building Better Bodies

Good health is usually a matter of training from early childhood on through life. Physicians today try to *prevent* disease as well as cure it. This should be the aim of every individual citizen. If a person forms good health habits while he is young, his battle for health is half won. *Good health habits, established in youth, make a man a healthier and more useful citizen.*

Cleanliness is a good habit to establish early in life. Soap and water should be used freely and often. Teeth should be brushed twice a day—once just before bedtime. Fingernails should be kept clean. The hair and scalp should be washed thoroughly and frequently. Each individual should have his own towel and washcloth. He should also keep his clothes clean.

Wholesome food should be eaten at each meal. A wholesome diet includes plenty of milk, meat, eggs, fresh fruits, whole-wheat bread, cereals, and fresh vegetables. The food should be eaten slowly and chewed well.

Refreshing sleep is also necessary for good health. Young people should have at least eight or nine hours of sleep each night. A person should sleep with the windows open to insure an abundant supply of fresh air.

Proper exercise will also help to build a strong body and an alert mind. Each person should spend at least one hour out of doors each day exercising pleasantly and moderately.

Good posture is necessary to good health. To help build a strong body, free from disease, one should stand, walk, and sit erect.

Plenty of pure, fresh water should be taken daily. Most people need from six to eight glasses a day. All young people should have at least one pint of milk each day. They should not drink stimulants such as tea or coffee. Neither should they drink alcoholic liquors. Fruit juices are refreshing and healthful. A daily glass of orange juice will help to build a stronger and better body.

Recreation is an important part of the health program. It is as important to play as it is to eat and sleep. There are many pleasant forms of recreation that help to refresh tired bodies. Everyone should learn to enjoy at least one outdoor sport.

Building Mental Health

Good health means more than just physical strength and well-being. Good health involves the complete self. It means well-adjusted emotional behavior, as well as physical strength and fitness.

Fresh air, good food, exercise, and the proper rest are important physical needs. *Emotional and social needs are just as important to good health.* The ability to work and play with others—even one's happiness in life—depends upon his emotional needs.

Three important emotional and social needs are listed below:

1) *Acceptance.* Everyone needs to feel that he is an accepted member of a group. He needs to feel that he is "one of them."

2) *Affection.* Everyone needs to feel that he is loved. Everyone needs a loving family, and friends who like him.

3) *Achievement.* Everyone needs to feel that the things he does are worth while. From time to time he needs to feel that he has done some one thing unusually well.

When a person realizes the importance of these needs, he will understand himself, his family, and his friends better. He will learn to consider their feelings. He will adjust more quickly to their needs and desires. When he does this, his own emotional and social needs will be more easily fulfilled. *He will develop a greater feeling of security.* This feeling of security will help him to be more successful in whatever he tries to do. It will help him to be happier and better adjusted.

It is true that there are times when everything seems to go wrong. Everyone becomes unhappy sometimes over things that seem of little importance to others. Try to understand when another person feels that way. By understanding why others act as they do, a person can often avoid quarrels and unhappy situations. This does not mean that he should avoid responsibility. *The well-adjusted person accepts responsibility and faces his problems squarely.* He tries to solve his problems so that the solution will mean happiness to himself and to others. He knows that each difficult problem he solves helps him to solve better his next problem.

Learning to Know One's Self

Everyone should learn to know himself, his interests, and his abilities. When he does, he will find it easier to choose a life's work. If he feels he can succeed, working

Ewing Galloway

Cleanliness and good grooming are habits that should begin early in childhood. They are essential to good health. Proper food, sleep, exercise, posture, and recreation all contribute to the body's well-being.

Through group and community activities, young people learn to understand other people. Such companionship is vital to a happy life.

toward his chosen goal will make work both meaningful and satisfying.

Success in life also depends upon a person's ability to work with others. Learning to live with others means learning to live with one's self.

As a person learns to understand his own emotions and his actions, he grows in self-control. As he grows in self-control, he finds more happiness in working and playing with others. He becomes more understanding of their thoughts and actions. He learns to understand and to help them, rather than to criticize.

Mental and emotional health are largely built in associations with other people. If a person wishes to have good mental health, he should take an interest in the things that are happening around him. He should enjoy people. He should try to understand their actions as well as his own actions. In this way he will be laying the foundation for a happy and a more successful life.

Here is a little list of reminders some people have found helpful. Some people copy this little list and keep it where they can read it often.

Cy La Tour

MYSELF AND I

I must live with my neighbors, and they must live with me, but most of all I must live with myself.

A neighbor may move away. If he has disagreeable qualities, he takes them with him.

My own disagreeable qualities I must live with forever, or overcome them; and I *can* overcome most of them.

I must be firm enough to stand on my own feet so that I am not ashamed of myself, yet friendly and agreeable enough to get along well with my neighbors.

Developing a Good Moral Character

A sound body and sound emotional health are worthy goals, but they are not complete without moral fitness. It takes all three to make a worth-while citizen.

It is very important to the welfare of the nation that its citizens be of good moral character. *It is just as important to the citizens themselves.* No person can be truly happy if he knows that he has broken the rules of good conduct. An interesting item appeared in a newspaper not long ago.

SOMEWHERE IN TEXAS—The proprietor of a small grocery store in the north end of town was surprised when he opened a strange-looking letter this morning. It contained three one-dollar bills, a worn leather billfold, and a note which read:

"Dear Sir: When I was in your store two years ago, I took this billfold without paying for it. My conscience has hurt me ever since. The billfold is worn out, but please accept this money to buy a new one."

The proprietor of the store did not know who had taken the billfold. The man would never have been punished for it. But he could not live with himself. He could not be happy knowing that he had taken something which did not belong to him!

Qualities That Distinguish a Good Moral Character

What are some of the things that distinguish a person of good moral character? First of all, he is honest and truthful. He is truthful in dealing with his parents, his teachers, and his friends. He is able to overcome temptation. He plays fair. He does not cheat anyone. He does not break the laws of the home, the school, or the nation.

Another quality of a good moral character is dependability. A dependable person can be relied upon to keep his word. He does his work in the best way he knows how. He finishes his work on time. He is not late for an appointment. He does not fail to keep a promise.

A person of good character is also industrious. An industrious person keeps at his work steadily until he has finished it. Even if he has a distasteful task to perform, he performs it to the best of his ability. He puts his work and his duties before pleasure.

Courage is another quality of a man with good character. A man who has courage is not afraid to stand for what he thinks is right. He is not afraid to become the champion of those weaker than himself. Even though his companions may drift into a life of crime, he takes the path of law and order. He has the courage to stand on his own feet.

Self-control is another virtue of a good character. The man of good character does not lose his temper easily. He is a good loser and a good winner. If he wins he does not boast. If he loses he does not complain. He controls his emotions and his actions. He does not willfully hurt anyone by word or action.

There are also many other qualities that mark the man of good character. He has perseverance and good judgment. He is tolerant and sincere. He is clean-living and clean-thinking. He is a good citizen.

Developing a Good Personality

Character and personality are sometimes taken to have the same meaning. They are closely connected, it is true. But one may have a good character without having a good personality. Character might be said to be those qualities that make a man a good citizen or a poor citizen. Personality is one's whole make-up. It is all the traits he has. It includes those things that make up his character. It also includes the things that make other people like or dislike him.

Benjamin Franklin listed the virtues which he felt everyone should cultivate. These virtues are: *temperance, silence, order, resolution, frugality, industry, sincerity, justice, moderation, cleanliness, tranquility, chastity*, and *humility*. These are all desirable qualities, but present-day Americans might wish to add others. Unselfishness, loyalty, tact, tolerance, friendliness, enthusiasm, open-mindedness, initiative, and perseverance might be added to the list. These and many other things make up one's personality.

Character, appearance, education and training, manners and habits are all a part of one's personality. Likes and dislikes, actions, and secret ambitions affect one's personality, too. A good personality is a priceless possession. It influences a person's whole life. If one is not liked by his business associates, he will not get along well in the business world. If he does not have friends, he will miss much enjoyment.

It is very important for everyone to try to improve his personality. The following questions may show you how to improve your own personality.

PERSONALITY QUESTIONS

1) Do you make friends readily? If not, how can you learn to be more friendly?
2) Are you interested in other people? Are you interested in the things they like to do? Do you ever sacrifice your own interests for the interests of someone else?
3) Do you carry on a conversation easily?
4) Do you remember names as well as faces?
5) Do you smile easily?

Groups such as this Hi-Y Club of the Y.M.C.A. aid young people in developing full personalities.

Ewing Galloway

Club sports activities can be fun! These boys are riding the ski lift to the mountain at Squaw Valley.

6) Do you make others feel that they are appreciated?

7) If a sincere criticism is offered for your own good, do you accept it graciously? Do you act upon it? Do you become stubborn and contrary? Do you take the criticism as a joke?

8) If you were seeking employment, might you be turned down because of carelessness in your speech?

9) Do you know the difference between pretended courtesy and real courtesy?

10) Are your clothes clean and attractive? Do you realize that attractive clothes do not need to be expensive clothes?

11) How are your manners at home, at school, at a party, on the street, or when making an introduction?

12) Are you loyal to your friends, your teachers, your home, your school, your community, and your country?

13) Are you tolerant? Do you look down upon those who do not have the same opportunities you have?

14) Are you tactful? Can you tell someone an unpleasant truth without hurting his feelings? Do you know how to get along with your teachers, your friends, your parents, and those with whom you work?

Ewing Galloway

Many girls enjoy helping to make their homes pleasant. This girl is going to surprise her family with a cake.

15) Are you open-minded? Will you listen to the other person's story? Or do you make up your mind in advance that he is wrong? Do you think he is wrong because his ideas differ from yours? Are you willing to learn something new?

These questions may help you to understand what sort of person you are. They may help you to improve your personality. If they do, your life will be happier and more useful.

Your Obligation to Your Home

The home, the school, and the community do many things for you each day. You, in turn, have a duty to them. *What are some of the things you can do to accept your share of responsibility in the home?*

Your parents make many sacrifices for you. You should love, respect, and obey them. You should be willing to co-operate with them in doing tasks about the home. You should do your share of the work without complaining.

You should be cheerful around home. Everyone will enjoy your company more if you are pleasant. You should be thoughtful of your parents. You should be considerate of your brothers and sisters.

There should be a spirit of "give and take" in the home, just as there is in a democracy. Each member of your family has his own interests. In addition there are interests that all of you can share. Your mother and father are the leaders of the family. Accept their suggestions willingly when you can. When you cannot do so willingly, talk the matter over with them. Perhaps you can convince them that your way is better.

Each member of the family should have certain tasks to perform about the home. You should not expect your father and mother to do all the work. They should have time for their own pleasures.

Your Obligation to Your School

Each student should support the ideals and the activities of his school. He should remember that it is not only the athlete who is loyal to his school. A pupil who has a good scholarship record is showing true school spirit. A student who has a good citizenship record is also displaying school spirit.

Scholarship, citizenship, and sports each

have a place in the school. To excel in sports is no more important than good scholarship or good citizenship. Sports can teach students to become better citizens, but only *if they teach good sportsmanship*.

SOME THINGS TO REMEMBER ABOUT GOOD SPORTSMANSHIP

1) The spectator at the game represents his school just as truly as does the athlete who plays on the team.
2) The decisions of the officials who referee the game should be accepted without question. The officials should not be hissed or booed.
3) Every student should disapprove of rough or unfair play by *anyone representing his school*.
4) Every student should realize that the reputation of the school is more important than a ball game *won through unfair play*.
5) Good playing or good sportsmanship on the part of the player on the opposite team should be applauded.
6) A team should be cheered even when it is losing.
7) Every student should encourage fair play and the proper school spirit in the classroom, in the auditorium, and throughout the school building.

OTHER CHARACTERISTICS OF A GOOD SCHOOL CITIZEN

1) A good school citizen will know and obey the rules and regulations of the school.
2) A good school citizen prepares his lessons carefully. He respects the wishes of the teacher.
3) A good school citizen is punctual. He is never late to school nor absent from school unless it is absolutely necessary. He is quiet and respectful in the schoolroom.
4) He is honest in his school work. He is willing to accept his share of responsibility.
5) He respects the property of others. He cares for school property as he would care for his own.
6) He does not litter the schoolroom nor the schoolyard with trash. He keeps his desk neat and clean.
7) A good school citizen is polite to teachers and classmates. He tries in every way possible to further the good name of the school.

Your Obligation to Your Community

The growing citizen has a duty to his home and to his school. He also has a duty to his community. He can do a number of things to make it a better place in which to live.
1) He can keep the streets clean. He need not throw trash or papers onto the streets. He can keep them until he finds a trash container.
2) He can obey the laws of the city. He can co-operate with city officials in making the town a safe and healthful place in which to live.
3) He can be fair in his dealings with his neighbors.
4) He can be loyal to his community and take part in community affairs. He can help the relief agencies in the community to take care of the needy.

Your community, your home, and your school are what you make them. If you live up to the ideals of good citizenship you can make them good places in which to work and to play.

Things to Do

1. Make a list of the things you can do to make your community a better place in which to live.
2. After you have answered the fifteen "personality questions," reread your answers thoughtfully. Then write a short, honest paragraph about your shortcomings and how you can correct them.
3. Write a list of the qualities you like in your friends. Do not at any time mention names.
4. Make a list of the things you can do around home to make your home more pleasant.

Questions to Answer

1. What makes a good citizen in the home, in the school, and in the community?
2. What are the advantages of developing a pleasant personality?
3. Do you know the difference between character and reputation? Why is it important to have a good reputation as well as a good character? Does the company you keep affect your reputation, your character, or both?
4. Why do you think self-control is one of the requisites of good mental health?
5. Explain why you think that facing your problems squarely will help to build mental health.
6. Is the teacher who lets you "get by" easily really playing fair with you? Discuss this question in class.

A Written Exercise

Copy and complete each sentence.
1. It is important to protect your health because_____.
2. Cleanliness promotes good health by_____.
3. Wholesome food should be eaten because_____.
4. To refresh tired bodies everyone should_____.
5. Two rules to remember when exercising are_____.
6. Good posture is necessary if one is going to_____.
7. Two important things to remember about recreation are_____.
8. One cannot think clearly if he is_____.
9. A person can help to build sound mental health by_____.
10. It is important for a person to develop a good moral character be-cause_____.

11. Some qualities that make good character are_____.
12. Some of the things that make up personality are_____.
13. To be a good citizen at home you should_____.
14. To be a good citizen at school you should_____.
15. To be a good citizen in the community you should_____.

Words to Study Before You Read the Next Topic

ventilation   receptacle   gist   disaster

Other Duties of a Good Citizen

Do unto others as you would have others do unto you. This Golden Rule was written many hundreds of years ago. It is still a good motto for present-day Americans. The Golden Rule might well be called the Rule of Good Citizenship.

There are many ways in which the Golden Rule should be followed. One of the most important has to do with respect for the rights of others.

Respect for the Rights of Others

A new student in a school may be talked about by other pupils. Unkind things may be said, even before the new student has had a chance to become acquainted. This is not fair. It is not living up to the rules of good citizenship. Everyone has a right to expect others to judge him fairly. In turn, they have a right to expect fair judgment from him.

It is difficult to judge another person's actions. One does not know what he would do if he were placed in the same position. Before you judge a person, try to understand him. Do not pass judgment hastily. Be open-minded. Respect his rights as you would expect him to respect yours!

You expect your teachers to obey the rules and regulations of the school. They have a right to expect you to obey them, too. You expect policemen to enforce the laws of the city, state, and nation. They have a right to expect you to obey them. You expect the city board of health to enforce the health laws for your protection. They have a right to expect you to obey the laws.

There are many, many examples of respect for the rights of others. Suppose your neighbor wishes to borrow your fountain pen. She keeps it longer than is necessary. When she returns it, the point is bent. The next day you notice she has a book you have been wanting to read. You ask her to lend it to you. She refuses. This is not following the Golden Rule.

A person should not ask to borrow another's property if he does not wish to lend his own property.

He should return borrowed property promptly.

He should return it in good condition.

He should not make a habit of borrowing.

Mr. A. works in a factory. One morning he is late starting for work. As he backs

Good citizenship can be taught in the schoolroom. Learning to share information, working in groups, and helping others may be among the first steps a student takes toward becoming a responsible citizen.

out of his driveway, his car crushes some flowers his neighbor has planted. Mr. A. shrugs his shoulders and goes on. As he comes to a stop sign, he swerves. In his hurry he bumps into a car parked along the curb. The owner of the car has not seen the accident, so Mr. A. drives on. At noon he goes to a nearby park to eat his lunch. He throws the papers from his lunch on the ground although there is a wastepaper receptacle near by. Then he takes out his pocket knife. He whittles the edge of the bench he is sitting on. Judging from his actions, Mr. A. is not a good citizen.

A good citizen respects the property of others. It makes no difference whether it is personal or public property. He also has a right to expect that others will respect his property.

Another way to respect the rights of others is to develop a spirit of "live and let live." In the world today, there are people who are persecuted because of their race or religion. This is not democracy! Democracy respects the rights of all peoples.

There should be no ill feeling based on differences of race, religion, or opinion. Everyone has a right to his own opinions

and ideas. Because they may differ from yours is no indication that they are wrong. Even if they are wrong, be tolerant of them. If a person is honestly trying to do what is right, be tolerant of his mistakes. Tolerance and kindness in your dealings with other people will help to make the world a better place.

A good citizen should also be willing to do the right thing, even if it is inconvenient. He should be polite. He should have patience with those who cannot perform tasks so efficiently as he can. He should appreciate the talents of others. In turn, he has a right to expect these same attitudes from others.

It is surprising how often the Golden Rule can be applied to citizenship. Perhaps some day all the peoples of the world will learn to live by this wise counsel: *Do unto others as you would have others do unto you.*

Improving Yourself

The first duty of every citizen is to make himself worthy to be called an American. Your duties are not the same as the duties of adult citizens. Your duties are more concerned with preparation than theirs. You are preparing to become the men and women who will govern the nation in the future.

Securing an education is one of your

Finding an enjoyable hobby for his leisure hours is a valuable part of a young person's education.

Ewing Galloway

most important duties to your country. This does not mean that you are just to attend school. It means that you should make your time there as valuable as possible. Your teachers will teach you many things. You will learn other things through study and observation. Make it a practice to discuss what you learn. Discussion will help you remember it. The student who develops good study habits learns rapidly. He accomplishes one of his first duties as a good citizen.

Improving Your Study Habits

PHYSICAL FITNESS

1) Eat plenty of wholesome food to keep your body strong and your mind alert.
2) If studying causes eyestrain, wear glasses or check the light by which you are reading.
3) If you become tired while studying, a little physical exercise may clear your mind and refresh your body. Then you can study more efficiently.

CONCENTRATION

1) Begin your work promptly.
2) Do not begin by looking around. Do not let your mind wander.
3) Read a paragraph or a chapter through as you would a story. Get the gist of the material.
4) Reread the material for the main points and the supporting details.
5) Outline your notes if necessary.
6) Develop regular habits of work, both as to time and place.
7) Study at least fifteen minutes at a time.
8) Develop an interest in what you are studying.

GOOD WORKING CONDITIONS

1) Keep your study materials organized. Do not scatter them so you are forced to hunt for material when you need it.
2) Always have good light when you are studying.
3) Try to keep the temperature of the room at about 68°F.
4) Study in a quiet room.
5) Study in a room with plenty of fresh air and ventilation.
6) Study at a desk or table.
7) Do not try to study in a room where a television show is in progress.

A SELF-ANALYSIS

1) Should I use the dictionary more?
2) Should I make wider use of reference books?
3) How can I make use of short study periods?
4) How can I improve my reading habits?
5) How can I increase and improve my vocabulary?
6) Do I review what I have previously studied?
7) Am I learning to apply the information I gain through study?
8) Do I try to put into my own words the material I have studied?

To improve your study habits is to improve your knowledge. A good citizen keeps himself informed. He knows what is going on in the world. He does not bury his head in the sand of his own interests. He does not say, "I am not concerned with what other people are doing." He knows he is a part of society. As a member of society he must take his part in the pattern of life and government.

LOST—Somewhere between sunrise and sunset, two golden hours, each set with sixty brilliant minutes. No reward is offered, as they are gone forever.

Students, as well as men and women, waste many precious hours of time each day. Use your leisure time profitably. Do not sit and dream. Read a good book or a good magazine. Play a game that will help to improve your health and refresh your mind. *Use your leisure time for self-improvement.*

Other Duties of a Good Citizen

There are persons who complain that public officials are not performing their duties efficiently. It is true that some of them are not. The people who complain, however, are often those who refuse to go to the polls and vote. There is only one way in which the American people can really control their government. That one way is through the use of the ballot.

When a voter knows a public official is dishonest, he should work for that official's defeat at the polls. He should vote for someone to take that official's place. *Each voter should make certain that the candidate he supports is an honest, law-abiding citizen. Each voter should also be sure to vote for measures that will promote the public welfare.*

Citizens should pay taxes willingly and intelligently. A good citizen will know *why* he pays taxes. He will ask *how* the tax money is used. He will see that it is spent honestly and for the welfare of the people.

Holding office is another important duty of the good citizen. Too often men of real ability say, "I do not wish to hold office.

The public criticizes everything one does. No one seems to appreciate how much time a public official gives to his duties." This only leaves the way clear for less honest or able persons to be elected.

Suppose no one wished to hold public office of any kind. The nation would soon be in a sad state of affairs. If a person is qualified to hold public office he should not refuse to do so. He should offer to accept his share of responsibility. Once in office, he should do his work as efficiently as possible. If he does, he has a right to expect his fellow citizens to express their appreciation of his work. They should show him they are sincerely grateful to honest and efficient officials.

Another duty of a good citizen is to *serve on juries*. It is important to stamp out crime in the United States. Unless intelligent, objective citizens are willing to serve on juries, this cannot be done. Some people who serve on juries may be influenced by flattery or favors. They may vote to release a prisoner regardless of the crime he has committed. Others may be swayed too much by the oratory of lawyers. They may let their emotions decide the guilt or innocence of the accused person. It is both a duty and a privilege to serve honestly and intelligently as a juror.

Good citizens must also be honest and intelligent witnesses. The jury listens to witnesses on both sides of a case. It is very important that these witnesses tell the truth, the whole truth, and nothing but the truth. No man should be punished because someone testifies against him falsely. Neither should a criminal be allowed to escape punishment because no one will

testify against him. We must be honest, willing witnesses when called upon. Only then can we expect our government and our officers to protect us and our property.

A good citizen does his part. In a democracy there is work for everyone. In times of emergency, all citizens should give wholeheartedly of their time, money, and efforts. If a disaster strikes your community, do not say, "I was fortunate. My property was not damaged. None of my family was hurt. Why should I be interested?" Help in any way you can. Next time you may not be so fortunate. You may need the help of someone just as someone needs your help now. Support the worthy organizations that are trying to aid the unfortunate. Donate your time and your money. *Do your part, no matter how small!*

Today complex farm machines help farmers use their soil to full capacity without harming the land.

Caterpillar Tractor Company

Help your firemen, your policemen, and your health officials. Help all public officials who are working for the good of the community. *Obey the laws.* Report law violations immediately. No one can do exactly as he wishes. There must be laws to protect the rights of all. If the laws are unjust or unnecessary, they can be changed. As long as they remain the laws of the nation, they must be obeyed.

Conserving the Nation's Resources

Our country has a wealth of natural resources. Because of its natural resources, it can give its citizens more advantages than can many other nations. But it can continue to do so only if all of us help conserve those precious natural resources.

Nature has been kind to the United States. Nature gave us our tall forests and our abundant game and wild life. Nature gave us valuable minerals, oil, and water power. All these helped to make the nation great. *These resources must not be wasted.*

Conservation means the *wise use* of resources. Nature took millions of years to provide us with coal and oil. If we are not careful, these resources may be wasted in a few years. No form of use *which permits waste* is conservation. Some of our natural resources that are wasted today cannot be replaced for fifty years or more. Many others can never be replaced!

The citizen who believes in his country will use all resources wisely. He will teach others to understand and appreciate their value. He will practice conservation at all times. Only thus can his country continue to be one of the great nations of the world.

Things to Do

1. As a class project, write a play showing what can happen as a result of making too hasty a judgment about someone.
2. Have a mock trial. Suppose two boys have had a collision with their bicycles. One is suing the other for damages. The boy being sued says the accident was not his fault. Choose a lawyer for each boy. Choose pupils to be witnesses on both sides. Elect a judge. The rest of the class can serve as jurors. Judge and jury will listen to the evidence. The judge will instruct the jury as to what they must consider in reaching a decision. After the jury has decided the case, the judge will (1) decide the amount of damages that must be paid, or (2) dismiss the case.
3. For at least two weeks, follow closely all the rules listed in the section called "Improving Your Study Habits." At the end of that time write a report describing
   a) the place in which you studied;
   b) the times at which you studied, noting the exact times you started and stopped each day;
   c) the way you organized your work;
   d) the difference between this method and your former way of studying.
4. You have read the story of Mr. A. and his destructive ride to work. Write a story of Mr. B., a good citizen, on his way to work.

Questions to Answer

1. Why are the actions of people like Mr. A. important to you?
2. What are some of the advantages of improving your study habits?
3. How can you be of help to public officials in your community?
4. What are some of the natural resources for which your state is famous?
5. What are some of the things that you, as an individual, can do to help conserve our country's natural resources?

A Written Exercise

There are several ways to complete correctly each of the following statements. Complete each statement in two different ways.
1. A person who wishes to borrow another's property should
   a)
   b)
2. You should obey the laws of the city, state, and nation because
   a)
   b)

3. You should improve your study habits because
   a)
   b)
4. It is a civic duty to be an intelligent witness because
   a)
   b)
5. Honest and intelligent citizens must be willing to serve on juries because
   a)
   b)
6. To have a spirit of tolerance means to
   a)
   b)
7. To pay taxes willingly and intelligently one must
   a)
   b)
8. You can use your leisure time wisely by
   a)
   b)

Words to Study Before You Read the Next Topic

indignant	self-conceit	contradicting
defile	self-reliance	menace
humanity	ridicule	slipshod

The Future Is Your Responsibility

IN the past one hundred fifty years the United States has grown rapidly. Each year it has become a better place in which to live. Today the people of our nation are among the best housed people in the world. They are among the best fed and the best clothed. Most of them are truly enjoying the right to *life, liberty, and the pursuit of happiness.*

There were many problems to be solved before this was true. There are many more still to be solved. You boys and girls will soon be men and women. It will be your task to solve these problems. You must not only keep the United States as good a country as it is today—you must make it a better country.

In Defense of Democracy

The Constitution of the United States has stood the test of time. The government established under it has served the nation well. The people in our country enjoy advantages that most of the people in the world do not have. *They enjoy these advantages under a democratic government.* It will not be your task to change that form of government. It will be your task to improve upon it, but *within the tested framework of the Constitution.*

In your schoolwork you often make mistakes. You learn by making mistakes and correcting them. This is also true of a democracy. In the past, many mistakes have been made. People have learned through these mistakes. The people who govern us today may make mistakes. We must learn through their mistakes to build a better and more useful government. It would be unwise to condemn a government because of a few failures. It would be far more sensible to let the failures guide us toward a better future.

A ball player does not quit the game because he throws a wild ball or fans out at the plate. To play without mistakes is not the main purpose of the game. Many ball games have been won in spite of the players' mistakes. Many ball teams have been improved because players learned to correct their mistakes.

A democracy cannot be judged by its mistakes alone. It must be judged by the goal toward which it is working. It must be judged by the progress it makes toward that goal. Soon you will be governing the United States. When that time comes, establish worthy goals and work toward them. Profit by every mistake, your own or others'. If you do, the nation of your day will continue to move forward. It will continue to be a land of rising standards and increasing opportunities.

Be a Good American

An honest and efficient government should be your highest aim when you take over the task of governing America. Perhaps you will become an official of the government. If so, you must understand your obligation to the men and women who voted for you. You must play fair with them. You must use public money wisely. You must see that your office is run honestly and efficiently. You must make certain you live up to the true meaning of Americanism. You must conduct yourself according to the principles and purposes of the Constitution.

You must always remain worthy of your public office. Help others to do the same. Teach those around you to vote for honest, law-abiding officials. Teach them to live up to the laws of our country honestly and fairly.

Perhaps you will not serve in the government directly. Perhaps your role will be that of a voter. In many ways this role is even more important. It carries with it great responsibility. First of all, you must be an *informed voter*. Second, you must *use your vote*. Third, you must *show your appreciation* of honest and efficient public workers. You must make it very clear that you *want good government*. You must refuse to tolerate public waste and inefficiency. Finally, you must *live up to the ideals of good government yourself*. You must *be a good American*!

There are many definitions of a good American. Perhaps there is none more clear than the definition given in *The Code of the Good American*, by William J. Hutchins.

This boy is learning to be a good farmer and a good citizen through competition in the 4-H Club.

4-H Clubs

THE CODE OF THE GOOD AMERICAN*

Citizens who are good Americans try to become strong and useful, worthy of their nation, that our country may become ever greater and better. Therefore, they obey the laws of right living which the best Americans have always obeyed.

THE LAW OF SELF-CONTROL

Those who best control themselves can best serve their country.

I will control my *tongue*, and will not allow it to speak mean, vulgar, or profane words. I will think before I speak. I will tell the truth and nothing but the truth.

I will control my *temper*, and will not get angry when people or things displease me. Even when indignant against wrong and contradicting falsehood, I will keep my self-control.

I will control my *thoughts*. I will not allow a foolish wish to spoil a wise purpose.

I will control my *actions*. I will be careful and thrifty, and insist on doing right.

I will not ridicule nor defile the character of another; I will keep my self-respect and help others to keep theirs.

THE LAW OF GOOD HEALTH

The welfare of our country depends upon those who are physically fit for their daily work. Therefore:

I will try to take such food, sleep, and exercise as will keep me always in good health.

I will keep my clothes, my body, and my mind clean.

I will avoid those habits which would harm me.

I will make, and, I will try never to break, those habits which will help me.

I will protect the health of others. I will try to guard their safety as well as my own.

I will grow strong and skillful.

THE LAW OF KINDNESS

In America those who are different must live in the same communities. We are of many different sorts, but we are one great people. Every unkindness hurts the common life; every kindness helps. Therefore:

I will be kind in all my thoughts. I will bear no spites or grudges. I will never despise anybody.

I will be kind in my speech. I will never gossip and I will not speak unkindly of anyone. Words may wound or heal.

I will be kind in my acts.

I will not selfishly insist on having my own way.

I will be polite; rude people are not good Americans.

I will not make unnecessary trouble for those who work for me, or forget to be grateful.

I will be careful of other people's things.

I will do my best to prevent cruelty, and will give help to those in need.

*From *The American Citizens' Handbook*, arranged by Joy Elmer Morgan, and published by The National Education Association of the United States, Washington, D.C.

THE LAW OF SPORTSMANSHIP

Clean play increases and trains one's strength and courage and helps one to be more useful to one's country. Sportsmanship helps one to be a gentleman, a lady. Therefore:

I will not cheat, nor will I play for keeps or for money. If I should not play fair, the loser would lose the fun of the game, the winner would lose his self-respect, and the game itself would become a mean and often cruel business.

I will treat my opponents with courtesy, and trust them if they deserve it. I will be friendly.

If I play in a group game, I will not play for my own glory, but for the success of my team and the fun of the game.

I will be a good loser or a generous winner.

In my work as well as in my play, I will be sportsmanlike, generous, fair, honorable.

THE LAW OF SELF-RELIANCE

Self-conceit is foolish, but self-reliance is necessary to citizens who would be strong and useful.

I will gladly listen to the advice of older and wiser people; I will respect the wishes of those who love and care for me, and who know life and me better than I. I will develop independence and wisdom to think for myself, act for myself,

according to what seems right and fair and wise.

I will not be afraid of being laughed at when I am right.

I will not be afraid of doing right when the crowd does wrong.

When in danger, trouble, or pain, I will be brave. A coward does not make a good American.

THE LAW OF DUTY

The shirker and the willing idler live upon others. They burden fellow citizens unfairly with work. They do not take their share for their country's good.

I will try to find out what my duty is as a good American, and my duty I will do, whether it is easy or hard. What it is my duty to do I can do.

THE LAW OF RELIABILITY

Our country grows great and good as her citizens are able more fully to trust one another. Therefore:

I will be honest, in word and in act. I will not lie, sneak, or pretend.

I will not do wrong in the hope of not being found out. I cannot hide the truth from myself and cannot often hide it from others.

I will not injure the property of others.

I will not take without permission what does not belong to me. A thief is a menace to me and others.

I will do promptly what I have promised to do. If I have made a foolish promise, I will at once confess my mistake, and will try to make good any harm which my mistake may have caused.

I will so speak and act that people will find it easier to trust one another.

The Law of Truth

I will be slow to believe suspicions lest I do injustice. I will avoid hasty opinions lest I be mistaken as to facts.

I will stand by the truth regardless of my likes and dislikes, and scorn the temptation to lie for myself or friends. I will not keep the truth from those who have a right to it.

I will hunt for proof, and be accurate as to what I see and hear.

I will learn to think, that I may discover new truth.

The Law of Good Workmanship

The welfare of our country depends upon those who have learned to do in the right way the work that makes civilization possible. Therefore:

I will get the best possible education, and learn all that I can as a preparation for the time when I am grown up and at my life work. I will invent and make things better if I can.

I will take real interest in work, and will not be satisfied to do slipshod or merely passable work. I will form the habit of good work and keep alert. Mistakes and blunders cause hardships, sometimes disaster, and spoil success.

I will make the right thing in the right way to give it value and beauty, even when no one else sees or praises me. When I have done my best, I will not envy those who have done better, or have received larger reward. Envy spoils the work and the worker.

The Law of Teamwork

One alone could not build a city or a great railroad. One alone would find it hard to build a bridge. That I may have bread, people have made plows and threshing machines, have built mills and have mined coal, have made stoves and have kept stores. As people learn better how to work together, the welfare of our country is advanced.

In whatever work I do with others, I will do my part and will encourage others to do their part, promptly and quickly.

I will help to keep in order the things which we use in our work. When things are out of place, they are often in the way, and sometimes they are hard to find.

In all my work with others, I will be cheerful. Cheerlessness depresses all the workers and injures all the work.

When I have received money for my work, I will be neither a miser nor a spendthrift. I will save or spend as one of the friendly workers of America.

The Law of Loyalty

If our America is to become ever greater and better, her citizens must be loyal, devotedly faithful, in every relation of life; full of courage and regardful of their honor.

I will be loyal to my family. In loyalty I will gladly obey my parents, or those who are in their place, and show them gratitude. I will do my best to help each member of my family to strength and usefulness.

I will be loyal to my school. In loyalty

I will obey and help other pupils to obey those rules which further the good of all.

I will be loyal to my town, my state, my country. In loyalty I will respect and help others to respect their laws and their courts of justice.

I will be loyal to humanity and civilization. In loyalty I will do my best to help the friendly relations of our country with every other country, and to give to everyone in every land the best possible chance. I will seek truth and wisdom. I will work, and achieve if I can, some good for the civilization into which I have been born.

If I try simply to be loyal to my family, I may be disloyal to my school. If I try simply to be loyal to my school, I may be disloyal to my town, my state, and my country. If I try simply to be loyal to my town, state, and country, I may be disloyal to humanity. I will try above all things else to be loyal to humanity; then I shall surely be loyal to my country, my state, and my town, to my school, and to my family. This loyalty to humanity will keep me faithful to civilization.

He who obeys the law of loyalty obeys all of the other ten laws of the Good American.

THE GROWTH OF DEMOCRACY IN AMERICA

A COLONY IN 1640

LEGAL BASE	EXECUTIVE POWER	LEGISLATIVE POWER	RESTRICTED VOTE

THE ROYAL CHARTER	GOVERNOR APPOINTED BY KING OR PROPRIETOR	COLONIAL ASSEMBLY ELECTED BY VOTERS	RELIGIOUS, PROPERTY, RACIAL, AND SEX RESTRICTIONS

THE UNITED STATES IN 1789

LEGAL BASE	EXECUTIVE POWER	LEGISLATIVE POWER	RESTRICTED VOTE

THE CONSTITUTION	PRESIDENT INDIRECTLY ELECTED	REPRESENTATIVES DIRECTLY ELECTED — SENATORS INDIRECTLY ELECTED	PROPERTY, RACIAL, AND SEX RESTRICTIONS

THE UNITED STATES IN 1850

LEGAL BASE	EXECUTIVE POWER	LEGISLATIVE POWER	RESTRICTED VOTE

THE CONSTITUTION	PRESIDENT DIRECTLY ELECTED – ELECTORAL COLLEGE AND POPULAR VOTE SYSTEM	REPRESENTATIVES DIRECTLY ELECTED — SENATORS INDIRECTLY ELECTED	RACIAL AND SEX RESTRICTIONS

THE UNITED STATES TODAY

LEGAL BASE	EXECUTIVE POWER	LEGISLATIVE POWER	UNIVERSAL VOTE

THE CONSTITUTION	PRESIDENT DIRECTLY ELECTED — ELECTORAL COLLEGE AND POPULAR VOTE SYSTEM	REPRESENTATIVES AND SENATORS DIRECTLY ELECTED	ADULT CITIZENS

Chart by Graphics Institute, N.Y.C.

Many a famous American started his career with the responsibility of a newspaper-carrier job.

Your Responsibility

As an American citizen you have been given a rich heritage from the past. You have received the wisdom of the ages written in books. You have the right to freedom of speech and freedom of religion. You enjoy freedom of the press. You are protected by the Constitution and the Bill of Rights. You have an inspiring example in the lives of the early Americans who did so much to make this country great. You have a share in the vast resources of one of the richest nations on earth.

But the task of building the United States is not yet complete. As an American you cannot say, "I will leave that task to my neighbor. He is more capable than I." You have a part to play just as truly as your neighbor has. He may have one kind of talent. You may have another. Simply by carrying out the duties of a good citizen, you can help to build democracy. One vote in an election may make an important difference. One voice on a jury may insure justice. *Your part in building democracy is a vital one, even though it may seem small to you.*

No nation has ever been made great because its citizens merely wished it to become great. Dreams and hopes are not fulfilled through idle wishing. They are made real *through work*. It takes work to turn the wheels of industry. It takes work to till the soil. It takes work to build homes.

Nothing truly great has ever been accomplished without work. America has become great because the colonists were willing to work. They worked to conquer the wilderness of the New World. It has become great because the pioneers were not afraid to work. They worked to break the trails to the West. They worked to settle and to build the West. America has become great because men like these have made great plans and have *worked* to carry them out.

Be proud of your country—you have a right to be! *But let your pride be real.* Let it be a deep pride in the ideals of democracy and Americanism. Let it be a pride that will inspire you to keep the good that has come to you from the past. Let it inspire you to improve upon the past. Let it lead you on to build an ever better and better America.

Things to Do

1. Write a newspaper editorial entitled, "In Defense of Democracy."
2. Draw up a code of honesty for public officials.
3. Discuss each of the laws of a good American as explained in *The Code of a Good American*, by William J. Hutchins.
4. Write a paper entitled, "My Responsibility to the Future."

Questions to Answer

1. What advantages do you enjoy today that were not enjoyed by the boys and girls of early America?
2. Why is individual honesty in government so important?
3. How can you help to promote honesty in government?

A Written Exercise

Copy and complete the following sentences. You may use as many words or phrases as you choose.

1. It is my task not only to leave the United States as good a country as it is today, but it is also my task to_____.
2. A democracy cannot be judged only by its mistakes; it must be judged by_____.
3. Public officials who are dishonest should_____.
4. When I am grown I can help to eliminate dishonesty in public office by_____.
5. As a citizen of the United States I have received from the past_____.
6. A democratic, or a republican, form of government is a good government because_____.

UNIT SUMMARY

The United States is one of the great countries of the world. It is a great country because its people have the right to *life, liberty, and the pursuit of happiness*. It is a great country because its government is a government "of the people, by the people, for the people."

In this book you have read many things about the story of American democracy. You have read how it began after long years of struggle. You have read how it developed because men believed in freedom and justice for all.

You have studied our plan of government—the Constitution and the Bill of Rights. You have learned how these great documents protect the rights and personal liberties of everyone. You have read about many of the ways in which a democratic government serves the people. You have read how good citizens serve both themselves and their country.

The government of the United States is only part of the plan of our democracy. The other part of the plan is *you, the citizen.* You and your government work together in Building Our Democracy.

The unanimous Declaration of the thirteen united States of America.

WHEN, in the Course of human events, it becomes necessary for one people to dissolve the political bands which have connected them with another, and to assume among the powers of the earth, the separate and equal station to which the Laws of Nature and of Nature's God entitle them, a decent respect to the opinions of mankind requires that they should declare the causes which impel them to the separation.—We hold these truths to be self-evident, that all men are created equal, that they are endowed by their Creator with certain unalienable Rights, that among these are Life, Liberty and the pursuit of Happiness.—That to secure these rights, Governments are instituted among Men, deriving their just powers from the consent of the governed.—That whenever any Form of Government becomes destructive of these ends, it is the Right of the People to alter or to abolish it, and to institute new Government, laying its foundation on such principles and organizing its powers in such form, as to them shall seem most likely to effect their Safety and Happiness. Prudence, indeed, will dictate that Governments long established should not be changed for light and transient causes; and accordingly all experience hath shewn, that mankind are more disposed to suffer, while evils are sufferable, than to right themselves by abolishing the forms to which they are accustomed. But when a long train of abuses and usurpations, pursuing invariably the same Object evinces a design to reduce them under absolute Despotism, it is their right, it is their duty, to throw off such Government, and to provide new Guards for their future security.

—Such has been the patient sufferance of these Colonies; and such is now the necessity which constrains them to alter their former Systems of Government. The history of the present King of Great Britain is a history of repeated injuries and usurpations, all having in direct object the establishment of an absolute Tyranny over these States. To prove this, let Facts be submitted to a candid world.—He has refused his Assent to Laws, the most wholesome and necessary for the public good.—He has forbidden his Governors to pass Laws of immediate and pressing importance, unless suspended in their operation till his Assent should be obtained; and when so suspended, he has utterly neglected to attend to them.— He has refused to pass other Laws for the accommodation of large districts of people, unless those people would relinquish the right of Representation in the Legislature, a right inestimable to them and formidable to tyrants only.—He has called together legislative bodies at places unusual, uncomfortable, and distant from the depository of their public Records, for the sole purpose of fatiguing them into compliance with his measures.—He has dissolved Representative Houses repeatedly, for opposing with manly firmness his invasions on the rights of the people.—He has refused for a long time, after such dissolutions, to cause others to be elected; whereby the Legislative powers, incapable of Annihilation, have returned to the People at large for their exercise; the State remaining in the mean time exposed to all the dangers of invasion from without, and convulsions within.—He has endeavored to prevent the population of

these States; for that purpose obstructing the Laws for Naturalization of Foreigners; refusing to pass others to encourage their migrations hither, and raising the conditions of new Appropriations of Lands.—He has obstructed the Administration of Justice, by refusing his Assent to Laws for establishing Judiciary powers.—He has made Judges dependent on his Will alone, for the tenure of their offices, and the amount and payment of their salaries. —He has erected a multitude of New Offices, and sent hither swarms of Officers to harass our people, and eat out their substance.—He has kept among us, in times of peace, Standing Armies without the Consent of our legislatures.—He has affected to render the Military independent of and superior to the Civil power.—He has combined with others to subject us to a jurisdiction foreign to our constitution, and unacknowledged by our laws; giving his Assent to their Acts of pretended Legislation:—For quartering large bodies of armed troops among us:—For protecting them, by a mock Trial, from punishment for any Murders which they should commit on the Inhabitants of these States:—For cutting off our Trade with all parts of the world:— For imposing Taxes on us without our Consent:—For depriving us in many cases, of the benefits of Trial by Jury:—For transporting us beyond Seas to be tried for pretended offences:—For abolishing the free System of English Laws in a neighboring Province, establishing therein an Arbitrary government, and enlarging its Boundaries so as to render it at once an example and fit instrument for introducing the same absolute rule into these Colonies:—For taking away our Charters, abolishing our most valuable Laws, and altering fundamentally the Forms of our Governments:—For suspending our own Legislatures, and declaring themselves invested with power to legislate for us in all cases whatsoever.—He has abdicated Government here, by

declaring us out of his Protection and waging War against us.—He has plundered our seas, ravaged our Coasts, burnt our towns, and destroyed the lives of our people.—He is at this time transporting large Armies of foreign Mercenaries to compleat the works of death, desolation and tyranny, already begun with circumstances of Cruelty & perfidy scarcely paralleled in the most barbarous ages, and totally unworthy the Head of a civilized nation.—He has constrained our fellow Citizens taken Captive on the high Seas to bear Arms against their Country, to become the executioners of their friends and Brethren, or to fall themselves by their Hands.—He has excited domestic insurrections amongst us, and has endeavored to bring on the inhabitants of our frontiers, the merciless Indian Savages, whose known rule of warfare, is an undistinguished destruction of all ages, sexes and conditions. In every stage of these Oppressions We have Petitioned for Redress in the most humble terms: Our repeated Petitions have been answered only by repeated injury. A Prince, whose character is thus marked by every act which may define a Tyrant, is unfit to be the ruler of a free people. Nor have We been wanting in attentions to our British brethren. We have warned them from time to time of attempts by their legislature to extend an unwarrantable jurisdiction over us. We have reminded them of the circumstances of our emigration and settlement here. We have appealed to their native justice and magnanimity, and we have conjured them by the ties of our common kindred to disavow these usurpations, which, would inevitably interrupt our connections and correspondence. They too have been deaf to the voice of justice and of consanguinity. We must, therefore, acquiesce in the necessity, which denounces our Separation, and hold them, as we hold the rest of mankind, Enemies in War, in Peace Friends.—

We, therefore, the Representatives of the

united States of America, in General Congress, Assembled, appealing to the Supreme Judge of the world for the rectitude of our intentions, do, in the Name, and by Authority of the good People of these Colonies, solemnly publish and declare, That these United Colonies are, and of Right ought to be Free and Independent States; that they are Absolved from all Allegiance to the British Crown, and that all political connection between them and the State of Great Britain, is and ought to be totally dissolved; and that as Free and Independent States, they have full Power to levy War, conclude Peace, contract Alliances, establish Commerce, and to do all other Acts and Things which Independent States may of right do.—

And for the support of this Declaration, with a firm reliance on the protection of divine Providence, we mutually pledge to each other our Lives, our Fortunes and our sacred Honor.

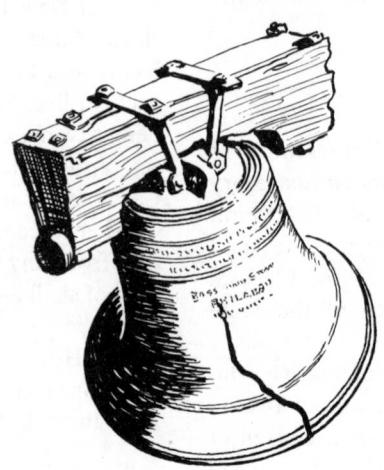

$We\ the\ People$ of the United States, in Order to form a more perfect Union, establish Justice, insure domestic Tranquility, provide for the common defence, promote the general Welfare, and secure the Blessings of Liberty to ourselves and our Posterity, do ordain and establish this Constitution for the United States of America.

ARTICLE 1

Legislative Department*

Section 1. All legislative Powers herein granted shall be vested in a Congress of the United States, which shall consist of a Senate and House of Representatives.

House of Representatives

Section 2. The House of Representatives shall be composed of Members chosen every second Year by the People of the several States, and the Electors in each State shall have the Qualifications requisite for Electors of the most numerous Branch of the State Legislature.

No Person shall be a Representative who shall not have attained to the age of twenty five Years, and been seven Years a Citizen of the United States, and who shall not, when elected, be an Inhabitant of that State in which he shall be chosen.

Representatives and direct Taxes shall be apportioned among the several States which may be included within this Union, according to their respective Numbers, which shall be determined by adding to the whole Number of free Persons, including those bound to Service for a Term of Years, and excluding Indians not taxed, three fifths of all other Persons. The actual Enumeration shall be made within three Years after the first Meeting of the Congress of the United States, and within every subsequent Term of ten Years, in such Manner as they shall by Law direct. The Number of Representatives shall not exceed one for every thirty Thousand, but each State shall have at Least one Representative; and until such enumeration shall be made, the State of New Hampshire shall be entitled to chuse three, Massachusetts eight, Rhode-Island and Providence Plantations one, Connecticut five, New-York six, New Jersey four, Pennsylvania eight, Delaware one, Maryland six, Virginia ten, North Carolina five, South Carolina five, and Georgia three.

When vacancies happen in the Representation from any State, the Executive Authority thereof shall issue Writs of Election to fill such Vacancies.

The House of Representatives shall chuse their Speaker and other Officers; and shall have the sole Power of Impeachment.

The Senate

Section 3. The Senate of the United States shall be composed of two Senators from each State, chosen by the Legislature thereof, for six Years; and each Senator shall have one Vote.

Immediately after they shall be assembled in Consequence of the first Election, they shall be divided as equally as may be into three Classes. The Seats of the Senators of the first Class shall be vacated at the Expiration of the second Year, of the second Class at the Expiration of the fourth Year, and of the third Class at the Expiration of the sixth Year, so that one third may be chosen every second

---

* Italicized sideheads, inserted to aid teachers and students, are not a part of the Constitution.

year; and if Vacancies happen by Resignation, or otherwise, during the Recess of the Legislature of any State, the Executive thereof may make temporary Appointments until the next Meeting of the Legislature, which shall then fill such Vacancies.

No Person shall be a Senator who shall not have attained to the Age of thirty Years, and been nine Years a Citizen of the United States, and who shall not, when elected, be an Inhabitant of that State for which he shall be chosen.

The Vice President of the United States shall be President of the Senate, but shall have no Vote, unless they be equally divided.

The Senate shall chuse their other Officers, and also a President pro tempore, in the Absence of the Vice President, or when he shall exercise the Office of President of the United States.

The Senate shall have the sole Power to try all Impeachments. When sitting for that Purpose, they shall be on Oath or Affirmation. When the President of the United States is tried the Chief Justice shall preside: And no Person shall be convicted without the Concurrence of two thirds of the Members present.

Judgment in Cases of Impeachment shall not extend further than to removal from Office, and disqualification to hold and enjoy any Office of honor, Trust or Profit under the United States: but the Party convicted shall nevertheless be liable and subject to Indictment, Trial, Judgment and Punishment, according to Law.

Organization of Congress

Section 4. The Times, Places and Manner of holding Elections for Senators and Representatives, shall be prescribed in each State by the Legislature thereof; but the Congress may at any time by Law make or alter such Regulations, except as to the Places of chusing Senators.

The Congress shall assemble at least once in every Year, and such Meeting shall be on the first Monday in December, unless they shall by Law appoint a different Day.

Section 5. Each House shall be the Judge of the Elections, Returns and Qualifications of its own Members, and a Majority of each shall constitute a Quorum to do Business; but a smaller Number may adjourn from day to day, and may be authorized to compel the Attendance of absent Members, in such Manner, and under such Penalties as each House may provide.

Each House may determine the Rules of its Proceedings, punish its Members for disorderly Behaviour, and, with the Concurrence of two thirds, expel a Member.

Each House shall keep a Journal of its Proceedings, and from time to time publish the same, excepting such Parts as may in their Judgment require Secrecy; and the Yeas and Nays of the Members of either House on any question shall, at the Desire of one fifth of those Present, be entered on the Journal.

Neither House, during the Session of Congress, shall, without the Consent of the other, adjourn for more than three days, nor to any other Place than that in which the two Houses shall be sitting.

Section 6. The Senators and Representatives shall receive a Compensation for their Services, to be ascertained by Law, and paid out of the Treasury of the United States. They shall in all Cases, except Treason, Felony and Breach of the Peace, be privileged from Arrest during their Attendance at the Session of their respective Houses, and in going to and returning from the same; and for any Speech or Debate in either House, they shall not be questioned in any other Place.

No Senator or Representative shall, during the Time for which he was elected, be appointed to any civil Office under the Authority of the United States, which shall have been

created, or the Emoluments whereof shall have been encreased during such time; and no Person holding any Office under the United States, shall be a Member of either House during his Continuance in Office.

Section 7. All Bills for raising Revenue shall originate in the House of Representatives; but the Senate may propose or concur with Amendments as on other Bills.

Every Bill which shall have passed the House of Representatives and the Senate, shall, before it become a Law, be presented to the President of the United States; If he approve he shall sign it, but if not he shall return it, with his Objections to that House in which it shall have originated, who shall enter the Objections at large on their Journal, and proceed to reconsider it. If after such Reconsideration two thirds of that House shall agree to pass the Bill, it shall be sent, together with the Objections, to the other House, by which it shall likewise be reconsidered, and if approved by two thirds of that House, it shall become a Law. But in all such Cases the Votes of both Houses shall be determined by yeas and Nays, and the Names of the Persons voting for and against the Bill shall be entered on the Journal of each House respectively. If any Bill shall not be returned by the President within ten Days (Sundays excepted) after it shall have been presented to him, the Same shall be a Law, in like Manner as if he had signed it, unless the Congress by their Adjournment prevent its Return, in which Case it shall not be a Law.

Every Order, Resolution, or Vote to which the Concurrence of the Senate and House of Representatives may be necessary (except on a question of Adjournment) shall be presented to the President of the United States; and before the Same shall take Effect, shall be approved by him, or being disapproved by him, shall be repassed by two thirds of the Senate and House of Representatives, according to the Rules and Limitations prescribed in the Case of a Bill.

Powers of Congress

Section 8. The Congress shall have Power To lay and collect Taxes, Duties, Imposts and Excises, to pay the Debts and provide for the common Defence and general Welfare of the United States; but all Duties, Imposts and Excises shall be uniform throughout the United States;

To borrow Money on the credit of the United States;

To regulate Commerce with foreign Nations, and among the several States, and with the Indian Tribes;

To establish an uniform Rule of Naturalization, and uniform Laws on the subject of Bankruptcies throughout the United States;

To coin Money, regulate the Value thereof, and of foreign Coin, and fix the Standard of Weights and Measures;

To provide for the Punishment of counterfeiting the Securities and current Coin of the United States;

To establish Post Offices and post Roads;

To promote the Progress of Science and useful Arts, by securing for limited Times to Authors and Inventors the exclusive Right to their respective Writings and Discoveries;

To constitute Tribunals inferior to the supreme Court;

To define and punish Piracies and Felonies committed on the high Seas, and Offences against the Law of Nations;

To declare War, grant Letters of Marque and Reprisal, and make Rules concerning Captures on Land and Water;

To raise and support Armies, but no Appropriation of Money to that Use shall be for a longer Term than two Years;

To provide and maintain a Navy;

To make Rules for the Government and Regulation of the land and naval Forces;

To provide for calling forth the Militia to execute the Laws of the Union, suppress Insurrections and repel Invasions;

To provide for organizing, arming, and disciplining, the Militia, and for governing such Part of them as may be employed in the Service of the United States, reserving to the States respectively, the Appointment of the Officers, and the Authority of training the Militia according to the discipline prescribed by Congress;

To exercise exclusive Legislation in all Cases whatsoever, over such District (not exceeding ten Miles square) as may, by Cession of Particular States, and the Acceptance of Congress, become the Seat of the Government of the United States, and to exercise like Authority over all Places purchased by the Consent of the Legislature of the State in which the Same shall be, for the Erection of Forts, Magazines, Arsenals, dock-Yards, and other needful Buildings;—And

To make all Laws which shall be necessary and proper for carrying into Execution the foregoing Powers, and all other Powers vested by this Constitution in the Government of the United States, or in any Department or Officer thereof.

Restrictions, State and Federal

Section 9. The Migration or Importation of such Persons as any of the States now existing shall think proper to admit, shall not be prohibited by the Congress prior to the Year one thousand eight hundred and eight, but a Tax or duty may be imposed on such Importation, not exceeding ten dollars for each Person.

The Privilege of the Writ of Habeas Corpus shall not be suspended, unless when in Cases of Rebellion or Invasion the public Safety may require it.

No Bill of Attainder or ex post facto Law shall be passed.

No Capitation, or other direct, Tax shall be laid, unless in Proportion to the Census or Enumeration herein before directed to be taken.

No Tax or Duty shall be laid on Articles exported from any State.

No Preference shall be given by any Regulation of Commerce or Revenue to the Ports of one State over those of another; nor shall Vessels bound to, or from, one State, be obliged to enter, clear or pay Duties in another.

No Money shall be drawn from the Treasury, but in Consequence of Appropriations made by Law; and a regular Statement and Account of the Receipts and Expenditures of all public Money shall be published from time to time.

No title of Nobility shall be granted by the United States: And no Person holding any Office of Profit or Trust under them, shall, without the Consent of the Congress, accept of any present, Emolument, Office, or Title, of any kind whatever, from any King, Prince, or foreign State.

Section 10. No State shall enter into any Treaty, Alliance, or Confederation; grant Letters of Marque and Reprisal; coin Money; emit Bills of Credit; make any Thing but gold and silver Coin a Tender in Payment of Debts; pass any Bill of Attainder, ex post facto Law, or Law impairing the Obligation of Contracts, or grant any Title of Nobility.

No State shall, without the Consent of the Congress, lay any Imposts or Duties on Imports or Exports, except what may be absolutely necessary for executing it's inspection Laws: and the net Produce of all Duties and Imposts, laid by any State on Imports or Exports, shall be for the Use of the Treasury of the United States; and all such Laws shall be subject to the Revision and Controul of the Congress.

No State shall, without the Consent of Congress, lay any Duty of Tonnage, keep

Troops, or Ships of War in time of Peace, enter into any Agreement or Compact with another State, or with a foreign Power, or engage in War, unless actually invaded, or in such imminent Danger as will not admit of delay.

ARTICLE II

The Executive Department

Section 1. The executive Power shall be vested in a President of the United States of America. He shall hold his Office during the Term of four Years, and, together with the Vice President, chosen for the same Term, be elected, as follows

Election of President

Each State shall appoint, in such Manner as the Legislature thereof may direct, a Number of Electors, equal to the whole Number of Senators and Representatives to which the State may be entitled in the Congress: but no Senator or Representative, or Person holding an Office of Trust or Profit under the United States, shall be appointed an Elector.

The Electors shall meet in their respective States, and vote by Ballot for two Persons, of whom one at least shall not be an Inhabitant of the same State with themselves. And they shall make a List of all the Persons voted for, and of the Number of Votes for each; which List they shall sign and certify, and transmit sealed to the Seat of the Government of the United States, directed to the President of the Senate. The President of the Senate shall, in the Presence of the Senate and House of Representatives, open all the Certificates, and the Votes shall then be counted. The Person having the greatest Number of Votes shall be the President, if such Number be a Majority of the whole Number of Electors appointed; and if there be more than one who have such Majority, and have an equal Number of Votes, then the House of Representatives shall immediately chuse by Ballot one of them for President; and if no Person have a Majority, then from the five highest on the List the said House shall in like Manner chuse the President. But in chusing the President, the Votes shall be taken by States, the Representation from each State having one Vote; A quorum for this Purpose shall consist of a Member or Members from two thirds of the States, and a Majority of all the States shall be necessary to a Choice. In every Case, after the Choice of the President, the Person having the greatest Number of Votes of the Electors shall be the Vice President. But if there should remain two or more who have equal Votes, the Senate shall chuse from them by Ballot the Vice President.

The Congress may determine the Time of chusing the Electors, and the Day on which they shall give their Votes; which Day shall be the same throughout the United States.

No Person except a natural born Citizen, or a Citizen of the United States, at the time of the Adoption of this Constitution, shall be eligible to the Office of President; neither shall any person be eligible to that Office who shall not have attained to the Age of thirty five Years, and been fourteen Years a Resident within the United States.

In Case of the Removal of the President from Office, or of his Death, Resignation, or Inability to discharge the Powers and Duties of the said Office, the Same shall devolve on the Vice President, and the Congress may by Law provide for the Case of Removal, Death, Resignation or Inability, both of the President and Vice President, declaring what Officer shall then act as President, and such Officer shall act accordingly, until the Disability be removed, or a President shall be elected.

The President shall, at stated Times, receive

for his Services, a Compensation, which shall neither be encreased nor diminished during the Period for which he shall have been elected, and he shall not receive within that Period any other Emolument from the United States, or any of them.

Before he enter on the Execution of his Office, he shall take the following Oath or Affirmation:

"I do solemnly swear (or affirm) that I will faithfully execute the Office of President of the United States, and will to the best of my Ability, preserve, protect and defend the Constitution of the United States."

Duties and Powers of President

Section 2. The President shall be Commander in Chief of the Army and Navy of the United States, and of the Militia of the several States, when called into the actual Service of the United States; he may require the Opinion, in writing, of the principal Officer in each of the executive Departments, upon any Subject relating to the Duties of their respective Offices, and he shall have Power to grant Reprieves and Pardons for Offences against the United States, except in Cases of Impeachment.

He shall have Power, by and with the Advice and Consent of the Senate, to make Treaties, provided two thirds of the Senators present concur; and he shall nominate, and by and with the Advice and Consent of the Senate, shall appoint Ambassadors, other public Ministers and Consuls, Judges of the supreme Court, and all other Officers of the United States, whose Appointments are not herein otherwise provided for, and which shall be established by Law: but the Congress may by Law vest the Appointment of such inferior Officers, as they think proper, in the President alone, in the Courts of Law, or in the Heads of Departments.

The President shall have Power to fill up all Vacancies that may happen during the Recess of the Senate, by granting Commissions which shall expire at the End of their next Session.

Section 3. He shall from time to time give to the Congress Information of the State of the Union, and recommend to their Consideration such Measures as he shall judge necesary and expedient; he may, on extraordinary Occasions, convene both Houses, or either of them, and in Case of Disagreement between them, with Respect to the Time of Adjournment, he may adjourn them to such Time as he shall think proper; he shall receive Ambassadors and other public Ministers; he shall take Care that the Laws be faithfully executed, and shall Commission all the Officers of the United States.

Removal of Federal Officials

Section 4. The President, Vice President and all civil Officers of the United States, shall be removed from Office on Impeachment for, and Conviction of, Treason, Bribery, or other high Crimes and Misdemeanors.

ARTICLE III

The Judicial Department

Section 1. The judicial Power of the United States, shall be vested in one supreme Court, and in such inferior Courts as the Congress may from time to time ordain and establish. The Judges, both of the supreme and inferior Courts, shall hold their Offices during good Behaviour, and shall, at stated Times, receive for their Services, a Compensation, which shall not be diminished during their Continuance in Office.

Section 2. The judicial Power shall extend to all Cases, in Law and Equity, arising under

this Constitution, the Laws of the United States, and Treaties made, or which shall be made, under their Authority;—to all Cases affecting Ambassadors, other public Ministers and Consuls;—to all Cases of admiralty and maritime Jurisdiction;—to Controversies to which the United States shall be a Party;—to Controversies between two or more States;—between a State and Citizens of another State;—between Citizens of different States;—between Citizens of the same State claiming Lands under Grants of different States, and between a State, or the Citizens thereof, and foreign States, Citizens or Subjects.

In all Cases affecting Ambassadors, other public Ministers and Consuls, and those in which a State shall be a Party, the supreme Court shall have original Jurisdiction. In all the other Cases before mentioned, the supreme Court shall have appellate Jurisdiction, both as to Law and Fact, with such Exceptions, and under such Regulations as the Congress shall make.

The Trial of all Crimes, except in Cases of Impeachment, shall be by Jury; and such Trial shall be held in the State where the said Crimes shall have been committed; but when not committed within any State, the Trial shall be at such Place or Places as the Congress may by Law have directed.

Section 3. Treason against the United States, shall consist only in levying War against them, or in adhering to their Enemies, giving them Aid and Comfort. No Person shall be convicted of Treason unless on the Testimony of two Witnesses to the same overt Act, or on Confession in open Court.

The Congress shall have Power to declare the Punishment of Treason, but no Attainder of Treason shall work Corruption of Blood, or Forfeiture except during the Life of the Person attainted.

ARTICLE IV

States' Relations to One Another

Section 1. Full Faith and Credit shall be given in each State to the public Acts, Records, and judicial Proceedings of every other State. And the Congress may by general Laws prescribe the Manner in which such Acts, Records and Proceedings shall be proved, and the Effect thereof.

Section 2. The Citizens of each State shall be entitled to all Privileges and Immunities of Citizens in the several States.

A Person charged in any State with Treason, Felony, or other Crime, who shall flee from Justice, and be found in another State, shall on Demand of the executive Authority of the State from which he fled, be delivered up, to be removed to the State having Jurisdiction of the Crime.

No Person held to Service or Labour in one State, under the Laws thereof, escaping into another, shall, in Consequence of any Law or Regulation therein, be discharged from such Service or Labour, but shall be delivered up on Claim of the Party to whom such Service or Labour may be due.

New States and Territories

Section 3. New States may be admitted by the Congress into this Union; but no new State shall be formed or erected within the Jurisdiction of any other State; nor any State be formed by the Junction of two or more States, or Parts of States, without the Consent of the Legislatures of the States concerned as well as of the Congress.

The Congress shall have Power to dispose of and make all needful Rules and Regulations respecting the Territory or other Property belonging to the United States; and

nothing in this Constitution shall be so construed as to Prejudice any Claims of the United States, or of any particular State.

Section 4. The United States shall guarantee to every State in this Union a Republican Form of Government, and shall protect each of them against Invasion; and on Application of the Legislature, or of the Executive (when the Legislature cannot be convened) against domestic Violence.

ARTICLE V

Amending the Constitution

The Congress, whenever two thirds of both Houses shall deem it necessary, shall propose Amendments to this Constitution, or, on the Application of the Legislatures of two thirds of the several States, shall call a Convention for proposing Amendments, which, in either Case, shall be valid to all Intents and Purposes, as Part of this Constitution, when ratified by the Legislatures of three fourths of the several States, or by Conventions in three fourths thereof, as the one or the other Mode of Ratification may be proposed by the Congress; Provided that no Amendment which may be made prior to the Year One thousand eight hundred and eight shall in any Manner affect the first and fourth Clauses in the Ninth Section of the first Article; and that no State, without its Consent, shall be deprived of its equal Suffrage in the Senate.

ARTICLE VI

Debts of the United States

All Debts contracted and Engagements entered into, before the Adoption of this Constitution, shall be as valid against the United States under this Constitution, as under the Confederation.

Supremacy of Federal Government

This Constitution, and the Laws of the United States which shall be made in Pursuance thereof; and all Treaties made, or which shall be made, under the Authority of the United States, shall be the supreme Law of the Land; and the Judges in every State shall be bound thereby, any Thing in the Constitution or Laws of any State to the Contrary notwithstanding.

The Senators and Representatives before mentioned, and the Members of the several State Legislatures, and all executive and judicial Officers, both of the United States and of the several States, shall be bound by Oath or Affirmation, to support this Constitution; but no religious Test shall ever be required as a Qualification to any Office or public Trust under the United States.

ARTICLE VII

The Ratification of the Conventions of nine States, shall be sufficient for the Establishment of this Constitution between the States so ratifying the Same.

done in Convention by the Unanimous Consent of the States present the Seventeenth Day of September in the Year of our Lord one thousand seven hundred and Eighty seven and of the Independence of the United States of America the Twelfth In witness whereof We have hereunto subscribed our Names,

GO. WASHINGTON,
Presidt. and Deputy from Virginia.

AMENDMENTS to the CONSTITUTION*

Amendment 1

Congress shall make no law respecting an establishment of religion, or prohibiting the free exercise thereof; or abridging the freedom of speech, or of the press; or the right of the people peaceably to assemble, and to petition the Government for a redress of grievances.

Amendment 2

A well regulated Militia, being necessary to the security of a free State, the right of the people to keep and bear Arms, shall not be infringed.

Amendment 3

No Soldier shall, in time of peace be quartered in any house, without the consent of the Owner, nor in time of war, but in a manner to be prescribed by law.

Amendment 4

The right of the people to be secure in their persons, houses, papers, and effects, against unreasonable searches and seizures, shall not be violated, and no Warrants shall issue, but, upon probable cause, supported by Oath or affirmation, and particularly describing the place to be searched, and the persons or things to be seized.

Amendment 5

No person shall be held to answer for a capital, or otherwise infamous crime, unless on a presentment or indictment of a Grand Jury, except in cases arising in the land or naval forces, or in the Militia, when in actual service in time of War or public danger; nor shall any person be subject for the same offence to be twice put in jeopardy of life or limb; nor shall be compelled in any criminal case to be a witness against himself, nor be deprived of life, liberty, or property, without due process of law; nor shall private property be taken for public use, without just compensation.

Amendment 6

In all criminal prosecutions, the accused shall enjoy the right to a speedy and public trial, by an impartial jury of the State and district wherein the crime shall have been committed, which district shall have been previously ascertained by law, and to be informed of the nature and cause of the accusation; to be confronted with the witnesses against him; to have compulsory process for obtaining witnesses in his favor, and to have the Assistance of Counsel for his defence.

Amendment 7

In Suits at common law, where the value in controversy shall exceed twenty dollars, the right of trial by jury shall be preserved, and no fact tried by a jury, shall be otherwise reexamined in any Court of the United States, than according to the rules of the common law.

Amendment 8

Excessive bail shall not be required, nor excessive fines imposed, nor cruel and unusual punishments inflicted.

Amendment 9

The enumeration in the Constitution, of certain rights, shall not be construed to deny or disparage others retained by the people.

* The first Ten Amendments were adopted December 15, 1791, and form what is known as the Bill of Rights.

Amendment 10

The powers not delegated to the United States by the Constitution, nor prohibited by it to the States, are reserved to the States respectively, or to the people.

Amendment 11
(adopted January 8, 1798)

The Judicial power of the United States shall not be construed to extend to any suit in law or equity, commenced or prosecuted against one of the United States by Citizens of another State, or by Citizens or Subjects of any Foreign State.

Amendment 12
(adopted September 25, 1804)

The Electors shall meet in their respective states and vote by ballot for President and Vice-President, one of whom, at least, shall not be an inhabitant of the same state with themselves; they shall name in their ballots the person voted for as President, and in distinct ballots the person voted for as Vice-President, and they shall make distinct lists of all persons voted for as President, and of all persons voted for as Vice-President, and of the number of votes for each, which lists they shall sign and certify, and transmit sealed to the seat of the government of the United States, directed to the President of the Senate; —The President of the Senate shall, in the presence of the Senate and House of Representatives, open all the certificates and the votes shall then be counted;—The person having the greatest number of votes for President, shall be the President, if such number be a majority of the whole number of Electors appointed; and if no person have such majority, then from the persons having the highest numbers not exceeding three on the list of those voted for as President, the House of Representatives shall choose immediately, by ballot, the President. But in choosing the President, the votes shall be taken by states, the representation from each state having one vote; a quorum for this purpose shall consist of a member or members from two-thirds of the states, and a majority of all the states shall be necessary to a choice. And if the House of Representatives shall not choose a President whenever the right of choice shall devolve upon them, before the fourth day of March next following, then the Vice-President shall act as President, as in the case of the death or other constitutional disability of the President —The person having the greatest number of votes as Vice-President, shall be the Vice-President, if such number be a majority of the whole number of Electors appointed, and if no person have a majority, then from the two highest numbers on the list, the Senate shall choose the Vice-President; a quorum for the purpose shall consist of two-thirds of the whole number of Senators, and a majority of the whole number shall be necessary to a choice. But no person constitutionally ineligible to the office of President shall be eligible to that of Vice-President of the United States.

Amendment 13
(adopted December 18, 1865)

Section 1. Neither slavery nor involuntary servitude, except as a punishment for crime whereof the party shall have been duly convicted, shall exist within the United States, or any place subject to their jurisdiction.

Section 2. Congress shall have power to enforce this article by appropriate legislation.

Amendment 14
(adopted July 28, 1868)

Section 1. All persons born or naturalized in the United States and subject to the jurisdiction thereof, are citizens of the United

States and of the State wherein they reside. No State shall make or enforce any law which shall abridge the privileges or immunities of citizens of the United States; nor shall any State deprive any person of life, liberty, or property, without due process of law; nor deny to any person within its jurisdiction the equal protection of the laws.

Section 2. Representatives shall be apportioned among the several States according to their respective numbers, counting the whole number of persons in each State, excluding Indians not taxed. But when the right to vote at any election for the choice of electors for President and Vice President of the United States, Representatives in Congress, the Executive and Judicial officers of a State, or the members of the Legislature thereof, is denied to any of the male inhabitants of such State, being twenty-one years of age, and citizens of the United States, or in any way abridged, except for participation in rebellion, or other crime, the basis of representation therein shall be reduced in the proportion which the number of such male citizens shall bear to the whole number of male citizens twenty-one years of age in such State.

Section 3. No person shall be a Senator or Representative in Congress, or elector of President and Vice President, or hold any office, civil or military, under the United States, or under any State, who, having previously taken an oath, as a member of Congress, or as an officer of the United States, or as a member of any State legislature, or as an executive or judicial officer of any State, to support the Constitution of the United States, shall have engaged in insurrection or rebellion against the same, or given aid or comfort to the enemies thereof. But Congress may by a vote of two-thirds of each House, remove such disability.

Section 4. The validity of the public debt of the United States, authorized by law, including debts incurred for payment of pensions and bounties for services in suppressing insurrection or rebellion, shall not be questioned. But neither the United States nor any State shall assume or pay any debt or obligation incurred in aid of insurrection or rebellion against the United States, or any claim for the loss or emancipation of any slave; but all such debts, obligations and claims shall be held illegal and void.

Section 5. The Congress shall have power to enforce, by appropriate legislation, the provisions of this article.

Amendment 15
(*adopted March 30, 1870*)

Section 1. The right of citizens of the United States to vote shall not be denied or abridged by the United States or by any State on account of race, color, or previous condition of servitude.

Section 2. The Congress shall have power to enforce this article by appropriate legislation.

Amendment 16
(*adopted February 25, 1913*)

The Congress shall have power to lay and collect taxes on incomes, from whatever source derived, without apportionment among the several States, and without regard to any census or enumeration.

Amendment 17
(*adopted May 31, 1913*)

The Senate of the United States shall be composed of two Senators from each State, elected by the people thereof, for six years; and each Senator shall have one vote. The electors in each State shall have the qualifications requisite for electors of the most numerous branch of the State legislatures.

When vacancies happen in the representation of any State in the Senate, the executive authority of such State shall issue writs of election to fill such vacancies: *Provided*, That the legislature of any State may empower the executive thereof to make temporary appointments until the people fill the vacancies by election as the legislature may direct.

This amendment shall not be so construed as to affect the election or term of any Senator chosen before it becomes valid as part of the Constitution.

Amendment 18
(*adopted January 29, 1919*)

Section 1. After one year from the ratification of this article the manufacture, sale, or transportation of intoxicating liquors within, the importation thereof into, or the exportation thereof from the United States and all territory subject to the jurisdiction thereof for beverage purposes is hereby prohibited.
· *Section* 2. The Congress and the several States shall have concurrent power to enforce this article by appropriate legislation.

Section 3. This article shall be inoperative unless it shall have been ratified as an amendment to the Constitution by the legislatures of the several States, as provided in the Constitution, within seven years from the date of the submission hereof to the States by the Congress.

Amendment 19
(*adopted August 26, 1920*)

The right of citizens of the United States to vote shall not be denied or abridged by the United States or by any State on account of sex.

Congress shall have power to enforce this article by appropriate legislation.

Amendment 20
(*adopted February 6, 1933*)

Section 1. The terms of the President and Vice President shall end at noon on the 20th day of January, and the terms of Senators and Representatives at noon on the 3d day of January, of the years in which such terms would have ended if this article had not been ratified; and the terms of their successors shall then begin.

Section 2. The Congress shall assemble at least once every year, and such meeting shall begin at noon on the 3d day of January, unless they shall by law appoint a different day.

Section 3. If, at the time fixed for the beginning of the term of the President, the President elect shall have died, the Vice President elect shall become President. If a President shall not have been chosen before the time fixed for the beginning of his term, or if the President elect shall have failed to qualify, then the Vice President elect shall act as President until a President shall have qualified; and the Congress may by law provide for the case wherein neither a President elect nor a Vice President elect shall have qualified, declaring who shall then act as President, or the manner in which one who is to act shall be selected, and such person shall act accordingly until a President or Vice President shall have qualified.

Section 4. The Congress may by law provide for the case of the death of any of the persons from whom the House of Representatives may choose a President whenever the right of choice shall have devolved upon them, and for the case of the death of any of the persons from whom the Senate may choose a Vice President whenever the right of choice shall have devolved upon them.

Section 5. Sections 1 and 2 shall take effect on the 15th day of October following the ratification of this article.

Section 6. This article shall be inoperative unless it shall have been ratified as an amendment to the Constitution by the legislatures of three-fourths of the several States within seven years from the date of its submission.

Amendment 21
(*adopted December 5, 1933*)

Section 1. The eighteenth article of amendment to the Constitution of the United States is hereby repealed.

Section 2. The transportation or importation into any State, Territory, or possession of the United States for delivery or use therein of intoxicating liquors, in violation of the laws thereof, is hereby prohibited.

Section 3. This article shall be inoperative unless it shall have been ratified as an amendment to the Constitution by conventions in the several States, as provided in the Constitution, within seven years from the date of the submission hereof to the States by the Congress.

Amendment 22
(*adopted March 1, 1951*)

Section 1. No person shall be elected to the office of the President more than twice, and no person who has held the office of President, or acted as President, for more than two years of a term to which some other person was elected President shall be elected to the office of the President more than once. But this Article shall not apply to any person holding the office of President when this Article was proposed by the Congress, and shall not prevent any person who may be holding the office of President, or acting as President, during the term within which this Article becomes operative from holding the office of President or acting as President during the remainder of such term.

Section 2. This Article shall be inoperative unless it shall have been ratified as an amendment to the Constitution by the legislatures of three-fourths of the several States within seven years from the date of its submission to the States by the Congress.

Amendment 23
(*adopted March 29, 1961*)

Section 1. The District constituting the seat of Government of the United States shall appoint in such manner as the Congress may direct:

A number of electors of President and Vice President equal to the whole number of Senators and Representatives in Congress to which the District would be entitled if it were a State, but in no event more than the least populous State; they shall be in addition to those appointed by the States, but they shall be considered, for the purposes of the election of President and Vice President, to be electors appointed by a State; and they shall meet in the District and perform such duties as provided by the twelfth article of amendment.

Section 2. The Congress shall have power to enforce this article by appropriate legislation.

The Grand Union Flag

The Bennington Flag

The Story of Our Flag

The first Stars and Stripes

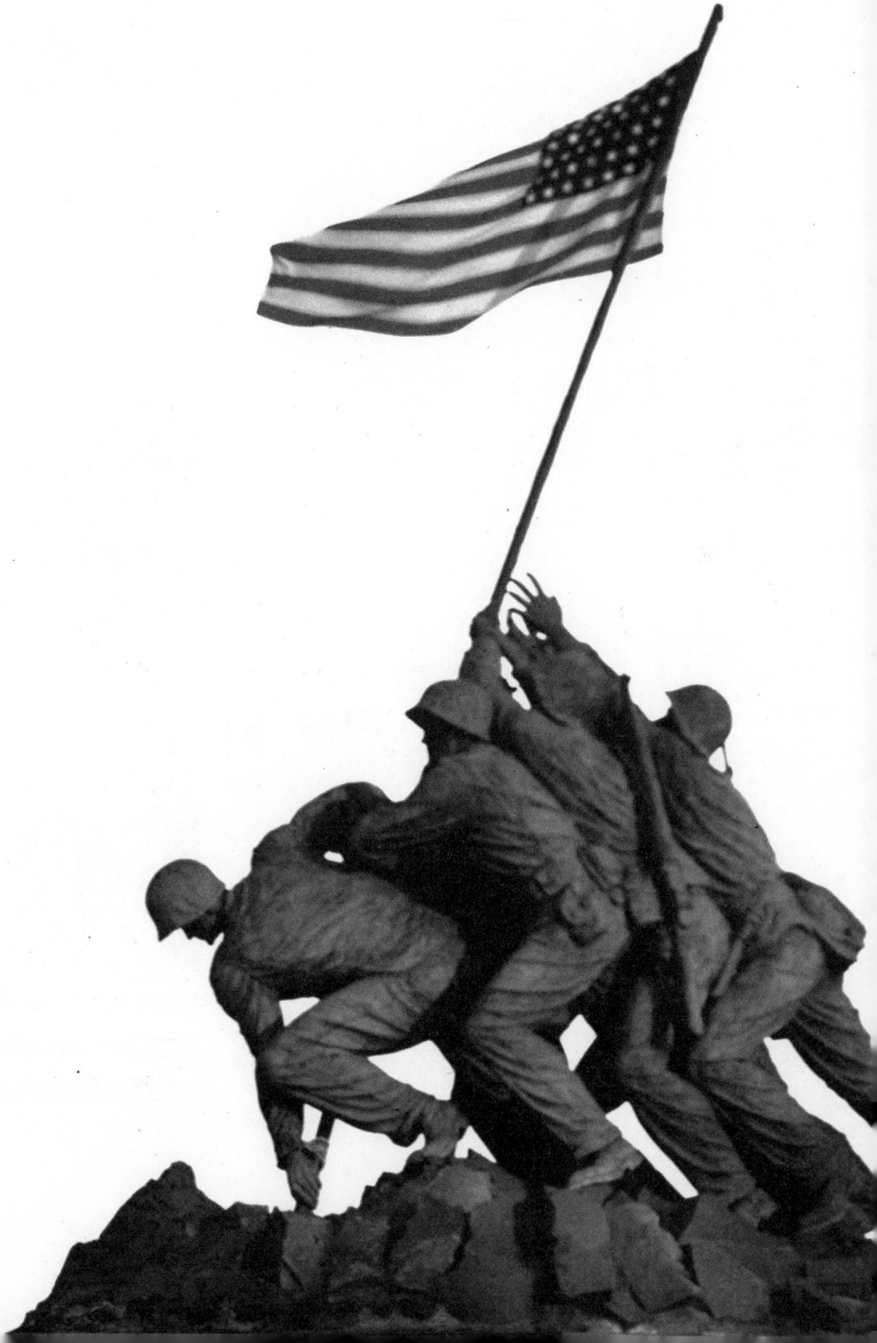

THE STORY OF
OUR FLAG

F ROM time immemorial, flags have served as symbols of men's beliefs. One of the earliest flags we know about was used by a group of Persians in 800 B.C. The Persians were in revolt against a dictator. The flag they followed was only a blacksmith's apron, flying from a staff. To the Persians, however, the apron was a solemn symbol. It was an emblem of their shared belief in liberty.

Our beloved and beautiful Star-Spangled Banner is a symbol of liberty, too. It is a symbol of liberty because Americans have made it so. It will remain a symbol of liberty only so long as Americans keep it so.

President Woodrow Wilson once spoke of the responsibilities we bear to our country's flag. This is part of what he said. "This flag, which we honor and under which we serve, is the emblem of our unity, our power,

This monument in the National Cemetery at Arlington, Virginia, preserves in bronze a famous photograph made at Iwo Jima.

our thought and purpose as a nation. It has no other character than that which we give it from generation to generation. The choices are ours."

Each of the original thirteen colonies had its own flag. Most of them reflected in some way the colonists' life in the new land. Their designs included anchors and pine trees, rattlesnakes and beavers. Many of them bore mottoes. "Hope" was one motto. "Liberty" was another. One very famous one was "Don't tread on me."

In 1776, however, the colonies united for a common cause. The symbol of their unity was the *Grand Union* flag. It was the direct ancestor of our Stars and Stripes. It had thirteen stripes, alternating red and white. Thirteen stars gleamed white against a field of blue.

The Grand Union flag flew first at Cambridge, Massachusetts on January 2, 1776. It was not until June 14 of the next year that Congress adopted it as a national emblem. June 14 is still celebrated as Flag Day, the birthday of our flag.

This "star-spangled banner" was the emblem of the Continental Army. George Washington, leader of the army, described the design of the flag. This is what he said. "We take the stars from heaven, the red from our mother country, separating it by white stripes, thus showing that we have separated from her, and the white stripes shall go down to posterity representing liberty."

Much later, when the Revolution was over, Kentucky and Vermont became states in the Union. Some people wanted a stripe and a star added to the flag for each new state. Others thought further ahead. "There will be many new states in our Union," they said. "We cannot go on adding a stripe for every one. Our flag will get too big to handle. Let's just add a star instead."

Congress agreed. Through the years, each new state has had its star. Alaska brought the number of stars to forty-nine. Hawaii made the total fifty. But the number of stripes is still thirteen . . . a permanent reminder of the original colonies.

"Hats off! The flag is passing by!"
This line from a famous poem, "The Flag Goes By,"
catches some of the pride and excitement of a parade.

HOW TO DISPLAY THE FLAG

In 1922 representatives from more than sixty organizations met in Washington. They adopted a code of etiquette to help Americans show the proper respect for their flag. Later the code was approved by Congress, and it became Public Law Number 829. Some of the most important regulations under this law are given below.

1. The flag should be displayed only from sunrise to sunset unless different hours are designated by the proper authority. It should be displayed on all state and national holidays, and on historic or special occasions. On public buildings the flag should be displayed every day if the weather permits. The flag should be hoisted briskly and lowered slowly.

2. When carried in a procession with another flag or flags, the Flag of the United States should

be on the marching right or, if there is a line of other flags, carried in front of the center of that line.

3. When displayed with another flag against a wall, the Flag of the United States should be on the right, the flag's own right. If the staffs of the flags are crossed, the staff of Old Glory should be in front of the staff of the other flag.

4. When the flags of states or cities, or the pennants of societies, are flown from the same halyard with the Stars and Stripes, the Flag of the United States should always be at the top. When the flags are flown from adjoining staffs, the Flag of the United States should be hoisted first and lowered last.

5. When the flags of two or more nations are displayed, they should be of equal size. They should be flown from separate staffs of the same height. International usage does not allow the flag of one nation to be placed above that of another nation in time of peace.

6. When the flag is displayed at an angle from the window sill, balcony, or front of a building, the union of the flag should go clear to the head of the staff unless the flag is at half-mast. The union of the flag is the white stars on the blue field.

7. When the flag is not flown from a staff, it should be displayed flat. If it is placed upon the wall, the union should be uppermost and to the flag's right. When the flag is displayed in a window, it should be displayed in the same way, that is, with the union or field of blue to the left of the observer in the street.

In a group, our country's flag should be centered, or at the highest point.

Our nation's flag always flies above any city, state, or organization flag that is on the same staff. If such lesser flags are flown from adjoining staffs, the U.S. flag is hoisted first, lowered last:

8. When displayed over the middle of the street, the flag should be hung with the union at the top. In an east and west street the union should be to the north. It should be to the east in a north and south street.

9. When used on a speaker's platform, the flag should be displayed on the wall above and behind the speaker. If it is flown from a staff, the flag should always be to the speaker's right.

10. The flag should form a distinctive feature of the ceremony of unveiling a statue or monument, but it should never be used as the covering for the statue or monument.

11. When the flag is flown at half-mast, it is first hoisted to the peak and then lowered to a half-staff position. It is again raised to the peak before it is lowered for the night. The flag flown at half-mast signifies a time of mourning.

12. When the flag is used to cover a casket, it should be placed with the union at the head and over the left shoulder. The flag is not lowered into the grave nor allowed to touch the ground.

13. When the flag is displayed in church, it should be placed at the right of the congregation. If it is in the minister's pulpit, it should be placed at the right of the minister.

14. When a flag is worn out, it should not be cast aside or used in any way that is disrespectful to the colors. It should be completely destroyed in private.

Sometimes the flag is displayed flat against a wall or in a window. In that case, the flag is placed so that the *union*, or field of stars, is uppermost and to the flag's own right, that is, to the observer's left.

When an important public official dies, flags are flown at half-mast as a sign of mourning. In such cases, the flag is raised all the way to the top of the mast first, then lowered to the halfway point.

The rules of flag etiquette you have just read should be observed by every American. There are also other things that you, as boys and girls, can do to show respect for your country's flag.

Never allow *anyone* to show disrespect for the Flag of the United States. Do not allow the flag to touch the ground or to trail in the water.

Do not dip the flag to any person or to any thing. Do not display the flag with the union down except as a signal of distress.

Do not use the flag as drapery. Use red, white, and blue bunting when you wish to drape the colors in any form whatsoever.

Do not mar or deface the flag in any way. Do not place lettering, advertising, or an emblem upon the flag. Do not use the flag as part of a costume.

Do not use, store, or display the flag in such a manner that it can be easily soiled or damaged.

I pledge allegiance to the Flag of the United States of America and to the Republic for which it stands; one Nation under God, indivisible, with liberty and justice for all.

FLAG PHOTOGRAPHS: *Madison Devlin*

Teachers should take advantage of every opportunity to have pupils use the index.
This is an important social studies skill.

Index

INDEX

A

B

C

M

N

O

P

State: Department of, 85–86; secretary of, 83, 86, 181
State agencies, 181–82
State government, 174–82: agencies, 181–82; courts, 182; laws, 179–80; legislature, 178–80; officials, 180–81; services, 174–77, 242–43
State guard, 115, 135
States: commerce among, 103–04; restrictions on, 104; rights of, 104–07, 140
Succession to office, 83, 144
Superintendent of schools, 157, 181
Supreme Court, 41, 69, 92, 97–100, 143, 195–96

T

Tax board, 181
Taxes, 55, 86, 119, 143, 199–204: collection of, 156, 203; direct and indirect, 201; expenditure of, 122–23, 156; payment of, 201; reasons for, 199–200
Territories, 127–28
Town meeting, 158–61, 165
Traffic regulation, 176
Transportation, 234–35, 276–77
Treason, 115
Treasurer, county, 156
Treasurer of the United States, 87
Treasury: Department of, 86–87, 122; secretary of, 86–87, 119
Treaties, 104
Trusteeship Council, of United Nations, 127–28

U

Unalienable rights, 50–51
Unemployment, 268–69: insurance, 269
United Nations, 127–28

V

Veterans Administration, 92, 267
Veto: by governor, 181; by president, 41, 126
Vice-President, 78–80, 95, 210
Village government, 153, 161–62
Virgin Islands, 127
Virginia Declaration of Rights, 49
Vocational Rehabilitation, Office of, 91
Voters, 212

W

Wake Island, 127
War, declaration of, 113–14, 115, 127
War for Independence, 32, 35
Washington, George, 27, 31, 35, 38, 42, 70
Water supply, 171, 241–42, 279
Waterways, 279
Weights and measures, 108–09
White House, 83
Wild life, conservation of, 177, 280–81
Women: right to vote, 143; working conditions, 177
Writ of Habeas Corpus, 100

Z

Zoning laws, 171, 241

FIRST GRAPHICS

Manners Matter

TITLES IN THIS SET:

the
deeper
genome

*Why there
is more to the
human genome
than meets
the eye*

JOHN PARRINGTON

UNIVERSITY PRESS

OXFORD

UNIVERSITY PRESS

Great Clarendon Street, Oxford, OX2 6DP,
United Kingdom

Oxford University Press is a department of the University of Oxford.
It furthers the University's objective of excellence in research, scholarship,
and education by publishing worldwide. Oxford is a registered trade mark of
Oxford University Press in the UK and in certain other countries

© John Parrington 2015

The moral rights of the author have been asserted

First Edition published in 2015

Impression: 1

Published in the United States of America by Oxford University Press
198 Madison Avenue, New York, NY 10016, United States of America

British Library Cataloguing in Publication Data
Data available

Library of Congress Control Number: 2014957585

ISBN 978–0–19–968873–9

Printed in Great Britain by
Clays Ltd, St Ives plc

ACKNOWLEDGEMENTS

I would like to thank a number of people who have helped bring this book to fruition. I owe particular thanks to Latha Menon, my editor at Oxford University Press, who was both firm in her suggestions about where the text needed modifying, and encouraging where she felt it did not. I would also like to thank Emma Ma and Jenny Nugee of the OUP editorial team, for their help on a multitude of practical matters, and Elizabeth Stone at Bourchier Limited for her meticulous copy-editing of the book. I gained some very valuable insights and suggestions for modifications to the text from a number of people who read my original proposal and various drafts of the book, namely Guida Ruas and Martin Empson, together with four anonymous reviewers. I also owe many thanks to Anthony Morgan for producing the photo for the book cover. For their excellent assistance with marketing and publicity I would like to thank Phil Henderson and Kate Farquhar-Thomson of OUP, as well as Jonathan Wood of the Oxford University Press Office. I would also like to thank Kate Gilks of OUP and Andrew Hawkey for their skill and expertise in proof-reading and compiling the index. I am very grateful to friends and colleagues who have indulged my many queries and speculations about matters relating to the genome during the writing of this book, as well as providing very helpful feedback and suggestions. Finally, I owe special thanks to my family, who have provided me with love throughout the writing and production of this book, and put up with the many hours spent researching and writing when it cut into our time spent together as a family.

CONTENTS

INTRODUCTION

How the Genome Lost Its Junk

'Sit down before fact as a little child, be prepared to give up every precon-
ceived notion, follow humbly wherever and to whatever abysses nature leads,
or you shall learn nothing.'
                                                                    Thomas Huxley

'What is a scientist after all? It is a curious person looking through a keyhole,
the keyhole of nature, trying to know what's going on.'   *Jacques Cousteau*

It was on the morning of 5 September 2012 that I first heard about the death of
'junk' DNA. I was sitting at a desk at *The Times* newspaper in London; to one side,
through huge windows, I could see the Thames, Tower Bridge—which all summer had been sporting the Olympic and Paralympic symbols—and beyond that
the Shard, the London Eye, and other famous landmarks. Above me, in the open-
plan building occupied by Rupert Murdoch's News International company, was
the floor occupied by the *Sun*, with its huge, framed past front pages with headlines like 'Up Yours Delors!' and 'Sling Your Hook!', references to European
Commission President Jacques Delors and radical Muslim cleric Abu Hamza,
respectively. At the time the *Sun* was embroiled in a major investigation into its
alleged use of illegal phone tapping.[1] Although it was 9.30 a.m. the offices were still
largely empty; the deceptive lack of activity was contradicted, however, by the influx
of messages in my e-mail inbox from other journalists, pitching ideas to the editors
for the day's stories even as they travelled to work by the Underground or rail.

Although I'd been working at *The Times* for over a month, my position funded
by a British Science Association Media Fellowship,[2] I still felt a bit of an imposter,
perhaps because the day-to-day activities of being a journalist were so different

1

compared to my normal role as a biologist and lecturer at Oxford University. One particular difference was the tempo; while in my regular job I may spend months, even years, gathering data for a study and presenting it for publication, submitting the manuscript to a journal, and then spending more time battling with anonymous reviewers who can either damn the whole study with a dismissive word or demand further data, here the pace of publication was very different.

So a typical day at *The Times* began by scouring Eureka Alert and other websites that gather together the latest press releases, funding announcements, and other news from the world of science.[3] This would form the basis of my day's pitch to the news editors, which typically would consist of two, maybe three, stories I thought might compete with other news from the world of politics, economics, sport, and scandal. After anxiously waiting while the editors had their mid-morning meeting, I would hopefully get the go-ahead to write 600 words on one topic, 400 on another, all to be submitted to the news desk by 3 or 4 p.m. to have any chance of making the printed paper. Around me, kick-started into life by similar demands, the office was now a whirring hub of activity as everything became subsumed towards a central goal—the production of the next day's news. If I had written well, and, as important, proved lucky against competing news items, I might see one or two of my articles online by early evening. However, the real test of how well I was doing would be seeing a piece that I'd written appear in next day's print edition. And then, like rubbing clean a slate, the next day kicked off exactly the same way.

This morning, however, it was clear something odd was afoot. Over a dozen different press releases had appeared on Eureka Alert, all from different research institutions, but all mentioning ENCODE—an acronym for ENCyclopedia of DNA Elements. As I read further, I learnt the reason for this sudden burst of information: ENCODE was the culmination of almost a decade's research involving 442 scientists from 32 institutions and costing $288 million.[4] And its claims seemed as big as its budget. So while the original Human Genome Project provided the sequence of letters that make up the DNA code, ENCODE appeared to have gone substantially further and told us what all these different letters actually do. Perhaps most exciting was its claim to have solved one of the biggest conundrums in biology: this is the fact that our genes, which supposedly define us as a species, but also distinguish you or I or anyone else on the planet from each other, make up only 2 per cent of our DNA. The other 98 per cent had been

written off as 'junk'; however, this raised the question of why our cells should spend vital energy replicating and storing something with no function. The existence of so much junk DNA had also featured heavily in debates between evolutionists and creationists, for why would any creator design a genome in which only 2 per cent actually works?

Now, as I read though, I found that ENCODE's new findings, all synchronized to appear simultaneously in 30 linked publications, had a new and excitingly different take on this matter. By scanning through the whole genome rather than just the genes, and using multiple, cutting-edge approaches to measure biochemical activity, ENCODE had come to the startling conclusion that, far from being junk, as much as 80 per cent of these disregarded parts of the genome had an important function. Indeed, for Ewan Birney of the European Molecular Biology Laboratory near Cambridge, the charismatic spokesperson of the project, this was probably an underestimate, since it was 'likely that 80 percent will go to 100 percent. We don't really have any large chunks of redundant DNA.'[5] The path-breaking nature of the project was emphasized by another ENCODE researcher, John Stamatoyannopoulos of Washington University in Seattle, who predicted that the findings would 'change the way a lot of concepts are written about and presented in textbooks'.[6] Perhaps most excitingly for a general audience, ENCODE also claimed that its findings were casting important new light on links between the genome and common diseases such as heart disease, diabetes, auto-immune conditions, and mental disorders like schizophrenia.[6]

Clearly, this seemed like big science at its best, and, as such, I co-wrote a story with Tom Whipple for *The Times*, in which we spelled out the study's implications. It appeared in the following day's paper entitled 'Rummage through "junk" DNA finds vital material'.[7] Similar positive assessments of the new findings appeared in media outlets across the world, all of which repeated the project's main conclusion that the idea of 'junk' DNA had been overturned by the discovery that as much as 80 per cent of the genome had an important function.[8,9,10] This was also the message from serious science journals such as *Nature* and *Science*, with the latter headlining the discovery 'ENCODE project writes eulogy for junk DNA'.[11]

By the end of my six-week placement at *The Times*, I'd published a total of twenty-two stories and features, on topics ranging from why chocolate is addictive, the discovery of the oldest tooth filling in history, and whether becoming a eunuch would make men live longer, to the burning question of whether a

potential super-volcano is lurking under the city of Naples.[12] But the story that most resonated for me on a personal level was the ENCODE findings. I resolved to find out more about their implications, not just for my own research, but also with regard to the much bigger question of how our genomes define us both as a species and as individuals. Most intriguing was the controversy that erupted a little while after the ENCODE findings were published. So an article published in the journal *Genome Biology and Evolution* in February 2013, attacked the findings in a vitriolic tone not normally associated with scientific debate, or at least not in the pages of an academic journal.[13] According to the article, the claims of ENCODE were 'absurd', its statistics 'horrible', and it was 'the work of people who know nothing about evolutionary biology'. And in a subsequent interview, lead author, Dan Graur of Houston University, said 'this is not the work of scientists. This is the work of a group of badly trained technicians.'[14] A central criticism was that ENCODE researchers had confused activity with functionality. 'Just because a piece of DNA has biological activity does not mean it has an important function in a cell,' said Graur. 'Most of the human genome is devoid of function and these people are wrong to say otherwise.'[14]

In contrast, there was the view of John Mattick of the Garvan Institute of Medical Research in Sydney, who argued that the ENCODE leaders were, if anything, too conservative in their claims, and that the findings showed 'we have misunderstood the nature of genetic programming for the past 50 years'.[15] Another proponent of this view, Evelyn Fox Keller of the Massachusetts Institute of Technology, believes recent 'genomic science has changed the very meaning of the term, turning the genome into an entity far richer, more complex, and more powerful—simultaneously both more and less—than the pre-genomic genome, in ways that require us to rework our understanding of the relation between genes, genomes and genetics'.[16]

So who is right? I resolved to find out, and this book is partly a result of that quest. However, while my interest in writing this book began with ENCODE, it has subsequently grown to encompass a much wider field of enquiry, all relating to the topic—how do our genomes make us human? This is a question that often comes up in the lectures and tutorials I give to medical and biology students at Oxford University in which we discuss the genetics of disease; for instance, why are some people more susceptible to certain disorders than others? But it also flows from a long-standing personal interest in what distinguishes humans as a

species, but also as individuals. Unfortunately, for some time now I've been dissatisfied with the available explanations as to how our human genomes work, on the one hand to distinguish us from other species on the planet, and on the other to create the unique mix of personality, capabilities, needs, desires, and susceptibility to illnesses and disorders, that define us as individuals.

As a child, I remember being fascinated by my parents' copy of *The Naked Ape*, by Desmond Morris. This book became a publishing sensation in the 1970s with its claim that modern human behaviour and society was largely rooted in instincts that had evolved in the Stone Age.[17] There was a problem though, in that Morris's take on prehistoric life was about as accurate as the 1950s cartoon *The Flintstones*, or the '60s film *One Million Years* BC starring Raquel Welch. However, what *The Naked Ape* lacked in authenticity was more than compensated by its numerous references to sex, which, to someone just reaching puberty, were almost as alluring as Welch's animal skin bikini. For a teenage boy just starting to worry about my attractiveness to the opposite sex, being told that humans not only have the largest brain compared to body size, but also the largest penis, making them the 'sexiest primate alive',[18] was sweet music to my fragile ego. Meanwhile, learning that humans' fleshy ear lobes, unique to our species, are erogenous zones, or that women's breasts are an important sexual signalling device rather than simply providing milk for babies,[19] was definitely something for my newly hormone-stimulated brain to chew over. And finally, Morris's claim that monogamy evolved so that men out hunting could trust their mates were not having sex with other men, and that human 'nakedness' helped intensify pair-bonding by increasing sensory pleasures,[19] were all food for thought to a teenage mind.

Unfortunately, as scientific fact such claims were about as substantial as Welch's bikini, although they could possibly be excused by a lack of understanding of human evolution and its molecular and cellular basis at this time. Yet what is surprising is how little many 'biological' explanations of human behaviour and society have changed since the 1970s. Take, for example, a recent book about human culture by Mark Pagel of Reading University, which moves in a few pages from self-sacrifice in amoeboid slime moulds to what Pagel calls a 'helping gene' that codes 'for an emotion that disposes people to be friendly'.[20] This sounds quite nice except this helping gene's influence only extends to people of the same nation; towards other national groups it becomes the 'jingoism' or 'xenophobia' gene. The author ends by saying 'next time you feel that warm nationalistic pride

at the sound of your national anthem or the news of one of your country's soldiers' valour, think of the amoebae!'[21]

One problem with this argument is its assumption that all members of a nation state behave in a similarly patriotic manner. So it fails to explain why millions of people in Britain opposed their government and marched against the recent wars in Iraq and Afghanistan.[22] But a more fundamental difficulty is that the proposed 'gene', which somehow manages to combine both nice and nasty characteristics, is a complete figment of the author's imagination. And, lest this be seen as an isolated incident, I could point to a range of other examples in which single genes are said to determine intelligence, personality, and even men's supposed unwillingness to do the ironing, without scientific evidence to back up such claims. In fact, for all the lip service paid to genetics in such accounts, the 'gene' here might as well be made of green cheese given the lack of any real attempt to engage with actual molecular mechanisms rooted in the real genome.

Actually, this is not quite true. The claim that homosexuality is due to a 'gay' gene, which made headlines across the world in 2003, was based on a study published in the prestigious journal *Science*. Evidence was presented that gay men had specific differences in a region on the X chromosome, Xq28, that was claimed to be linked to their homosexuality, and passed down through the mother.[23] What followed was a huge debate about the implications of the discovery. In the gay community itself reactions ranged from fears that screening programmes might identify and abort 'gay foetuses' on the basis of their possession of the gene, to those who thought the discovery would scientifically 'legitimize' homosexuality and therefore help end gay oppression, although this ignores the fact that the clear biological basis of skin colour has not prevented oppression based on this difference.[24] Such was the publicity around the discovery that a T-shirt with the slogan 'Xq28—thanks for the genes, Mom!' became a popular item in many gay bookstores. Missing from much of the coverage, however, was that what had been discovered was not an actual gene but merely an association with a DNA region on the X chromosome. And two decades later, the authors have failed to identify such a gene, while attempts to reproduce the findings by others have been equally negative, leading to suspicions that the original 'discovery' was just a statistical artefact.[25]

Such failed attempts aside, one undoubted reason for the popularity of accounts of human behaviour and society that make no attempt to engage with

actual molecular mechanisms, is that they tell entertaining 'just-so' stories about human evolution without having to bear scrutiny as to whether such stories are actually true. In this sense, as science journalist Tim Radford has noted, the 'gene' here is not so much a real object as a 'metaphor, an analogy, an "as if", a useful way of thinking about how behaviours, strategies and responses might have emerged'.[26] Now while I'm all for metaphors as a way of making complicated scientific concepts comprehensible, a problem arises when these get in the way of a true understanding of the material basis of nature. Taking an example from the physical sciences, the initial model of the atom proposed by Ernest Rutherford in 1911 pictured it as a miniature solar system, with electrons orbiting the nucleus just as our own planet orbits the Sun; however, subsequent studies showed that this metaphor was far too simplistic. Surprisingly, in the biological sciences far too many popular accounts are still anchored in an old-fashioned view of genes that either sees them as abstract units with no material form, or if they do acknowledge this link, subscribe to the crude picture of genes as 'beads on a string', discrete and isolated entities on each chromosome.

In contrast, while in this book there will be plenty of speculation about the link between genes and what it means to be human, my aim will be to make sure this is always backed up with evidence of real molecular mechanisms based on the most cutting-edge studies of the genome. Here, though, we face a problem. While key individuals involved in the Human Genome Project, such as Sir John Sulston of the Sanger Institute near Cambridge, promised that, 'for the first time we are going to hold in our hands the set of instructions to make a human being',[27] and British Science Minister Lord Sainsbury said 'we now have the possibility of achieving all we ever hoped for from medicine',[27] the reality has been rather different. So when scientists sought to use the genome to identify links between differences in the DNA code and common disorders like heart disease, diabetes, and mental conditions like schizophrenia, bipolar disorder, and autism, the problem was not finding genetic links to these disorders but rather the astounding number of these.[28,29] Instead of identifying just a few strong genetic links with each condition, as had been commonly predicted, scores or even hundreds of such links have been made, with each only apparently contributing a tiny amount to the chance of succumbing to these disorders. Such findings seem to mock the idea that we can find meaningful, and useful, links between our genomes and such conditions, and if true for disease, surely it must be more so for other aspects of being human,

such as our unique personalities and capabilities. This has led one critic of the genome project—neuroscientist Steven Rose of the Open University—to argue that 'they said this was the greatest achievement since landing a man on the moon. One even said it ranked with the discovery of the wheel. And yet none of this cornucopia of benefits has come out of it.'[30] Another critic, bioethicist Tom Shakespeare of Newcastle University, has said 'we share 51 percent of our genes with yeast and 98 percent with chimpanzees—it is not genetics that makes us human'.[27]

In this book, my aim is to find a middle way between the view that the complexities of the human condition can be reduced to simple, hypothetical 'genes' without any mechanistic underpinning, and the opposite view that sees things as far more complex, yet rejects the idea that we have learned anything useful from the genome project, about both the diseases that afflict us as a species, and what it means to be human. In so doing, I will be drawing on many years of experience studying genes and how they function. In my quest to understand how cellular signals regulate important bodily processes, I have isolated and characterized novel genes and studied their functional properties in a test tube and in cultured cells, but also what happens when their activity is inhibited or altered in a living animal. This has allowed me to appreciate the power, but also limitations, of the so-called 'reductionist' approach to biology.

Such an approach aims to understand complex biological systems by dissecting them into their constituent parts, or as Francis Crick, co-discover of the DNA double helix put it, 'to explain all biology in terms of physics and chemistry'.[31] The power of this approach was demonstrated to me when my colleagues and I used it to show that a single gene codes for a protein in the sperm which triggers the chemical signal in the egg that stimulates embryo development.[32,33] However, while studying the role of genes in the living organism, I have also increasingly come to realize the complexity of their behaviour. A common method for studying how genes work and their function within the body is to breed animals in which the action of a particular gene is inhibited by genetic engineering, thus creating a 'knockout' mouse.[34] Such animals have become very important 'models' of human disease. Yet, surprisingly, in many cases abolishing a gene's activity has little effect on the whole organism, or leads to opposite or very different effects than predicted based on its properties in a test tube or in cells in a culture dish. Such unexpected findings are often said to be due to

'compensation' by other genes during embryo development but this is really just a hand-waving gesture to convey the fact we often know very little about why particular genomic manipulations have unforeseen effects.[31] What these findings do suggest is that while isolating the effects of one gene from others in the body can lead to important insights, ultimately, gene action can only be properly understood as part of a wider whole. And if true for a mouse how much more so for humans, with our complex behaviour and culture driven by social innovation as much as by biology.

So does this mean that attempts to find genetic links to the complexities of human behaviour and society are doomed to failure? In this book I intend to show this is far from the case, but I also want to challenge some long-held assumptions in biology: one being the idea that genes can be treated in isolation, and also the very definition of what we mean by a gene. To do this I will not only explore what the ENCODE findings have to tell us about this question, but also investigate what I believe is a more general shift taking place in our perception of the genome and how it works. Importantly, this shift is based on new technologies that mean that, rather than studying single genes in isolation as previously, we can now observe changes in the activity of the genome as a whole.[35] This analysis can extend both to a whole organ like the human brain, but also allows us to study how genes are switched on and off, in real time, in a living cell, something undreamed of only a few years ago.[36]

Based on the findings emerging from the use of such technologies, I will look at important new developments like the increasing recognition that, far from simply being a linear code, the genome only really makes sense as a 3D entity.[37] Moreover, this 3D entity dynamically changes in response to signals originating both from within, and outside, the cell. Another important development is the recognition that RNA, DNA's chemical cousin, plays a far more important role in the cell and organism than previously thought.[38] So instead of simply being a messenger between DNA and proteins—the building blocks of the body—RNA is proving to have a multitude of other key roles, and on a much vaster scale than could have been imagined. Finally, new evidence is emerging that, far from being a fixed DNA 'blueprint', the genome proper is a complex entity that includes proteins, and both the DNA and these proteins can be chemically modified in a far more rapid, and reversible, fashion than suspected.[39] This makes the genome exquisitely sensitive to signals from the environment, and challenges the idea that

life is merely a one-way flow of information from DNA to organism. Perhaps most surprisingly, the genome's status as a structurally stable unit is being called into question, with evidence that certain genomic elements have an ability to move about, sometimes to the detriment of normal cellular function, but also acting as a new source of genome function.[40,41,42]

Excitingly, while the significance of such phenomena for long-term evolutionary change remains controversial, there is increasing evidence that these newly recognized features of the genome may have played a fundamental role in the emergence of *Homo sapiens* as a unique species with self-conscious awareness and the power to transform its environment in a way that sets it apart from all other life forms on the planet.[43] This focus on human beings will be an important theme of this book, for although I will show how studies on organisms ranging from the humble bacterium to our closest living animal cousins, chimpanzees, have transformed our understanding of human biology, ultimately it is with our own species that I will be most concerned. And I will be aided in this task by the fact we can now study the genomes not just of living primates, but also extinct proto-human species like Neanderthals.[44,45] In addition, it is becoming increasingly feasible to determine the complete DNA sequence of genomes, as well as chemical modifications of this DNA and its associated proteins, from large numbers of living human beings.[46]

Before tackling these important new reconsiderations about the genome though, I first want to take us back in time to look at how scientists came to understand how living things appeared on Earth, what led to the diversity of life we see around us, and how genes and genomes mediate this process. In so doing we will reach back into the lives and times of famous scientists like Darwin and Mendel, but also lesser known figures whose theories and findings have nevertheless enriched our view of the cell and organism. Having thus developed a secure foundation based on what, until recently, constituted the 'orthodoxy' in this area of science, we will examine how this orthodox view is currently being challenged. Using such new information we will seek to understand what this can tell us about abnormalities of the human condition, not just 'single-gene' disorders, but also more common disturbances, such as heart disease and diabetes, and also mental conditions like schizophrenia and bipolar disorder, that afflict millions of people across the world. In particular, we will investigate whether the genetic complexity that appears to underlie these disorders mean that attempts to

identify new methods of diagnosis and treatment are fatally flawed, or if there is a path to a new understanding of these conditions despite this complexity. Finally, we will explore how such new understanding of the genome is being used to address a key remaining question for humanity, namely what is so special about our own species that led us to such a primary position on Earth. With all that in mind, it's time to begin our quest. But first, a personal question—do you feel lucky?

1

THE INHERITORS

'Every individual alive today, even the very highest, is to be derived in an unbroken line from the first and lowest forms.'   *August Weismann*

'If we didn't have genetic mutations, we wouldn't have us. You need error to open the door to the adjacent possible.'   *Steven Johnson*

Do you ever feel you could use a little extra luck? Most of us can remember missed opportunities when a helping hand from chance wouldn't have gone amiss. Of course, winners in life are often said to make their own luck, but the popularity of lotteries across the world is proof of the hope that great fortune might nevertheless turn up out of the blue with minimal effort. Unfortunately, at odds of 14 million to one, you're four times more likely to be killed by a lightning strike, and seven times more likely to die falling out of bed than become a lottery multi-millionaire.[47] But what if I told you that you're already a winner at odds that, in comparison to a lottery win, would make the latter seem as certain as the sun rising each morning?[48] To calculate just how lucky you are, first consider the chance that accompanied your mother and father meeting and deciding to have a child, estimated at one in 20,000. Then there's the good fortune that, of the four trillion sperm a man generates in his lifetime, and the 100,000 eggs a woman produces, the pair that gave rise to you happened to come together. But really we're only getting started when we consider the unlikeliness of your existence. For we must also consider an even more implausible chain of events, namely that each of your ancestors lived to reproductive age throughout the 3.7 billion years since life began on Earth. As such, the unlikeliness of your birth comes to about 1 in $10^{2,685,000}$, or putting it another way, it's as unlikely as the people in central London getting together, each with a trillion-sided dice, and all rolling the same number.

All of which means you are extraordinarily lucky to be here. But before you get too carried away, you should also know you share similar good fortune with all the other living things on Earth. That's not just the other seven billion human beings, but also the nine million other species on our planet. I'm not even going to try and calculate the total number of organisms on Earth, but the fact that in your guts alone there are 100 trillion bacteria, should give a sense of the scale we're talking about. And yet, like you, each individual organism on the planet came into being through an extraordinarily lucky set of events. Yet there's something even more fundamental than good fortune that you share with all these organisms, and that's a common ancestry. From the mighty elephant to the minuscule flu virus, all of life is, in a sense, our cousins.

This view of life—that undirected blind chance led to each individual organism being alive today on Earth, and also that we share a common ancestry—was famously proposed by Charles Darwin in *The Origin of Species* in 1859.[49] Following his trip around the world on the HMS *Beagle*, and stimulated by the diverse life forms he had seen on the trip, Darwin concluded that there was no necessary requirement for a supernatural creator to have produced the multitude of species on our planet—instead this could be explained by a driving force he termed 'natural selection'. This required both that populations of species varied in their size, shape, and capabilities, and new environmental pressures acted upon these variants to ensure 'survival of the fittest'. Although this phrase conjures up the image of nature as 'red in tooth and claw', Darwin was careful to point out that although 'two canine animals, in a time of dearth, may be truly said to struggle with each other which shall get food and live', the fight to survive is equally valid for 'a plant on the edge of a desert [struggling] for life against the drought'.[50] Another important aspect of the theory is that for such survival to have any consequence for future generations, survivors must pass on their attributes to their offspring, who then represent a more significant proportion of the population. To see how natural selection works, consider giraffes: while their ancestors had shorter necks, a few animals with slightly longer necks would have had a survival advantage in being able to access the highest leaves on the trees. Through selection over generations, these variants came to predominate. Eventually, such differences can lead to the birth of a new species.

In fact, Darwin was not the only person who had this crucial insight—so did Alfred Russel Wallace. Unlike the wealthy, university-educated Darwin, Wallace

began working for a living at 13 years old, first as a builder's apprentice, later by collecting biological specimens and selling them to collectors. Wallace was also a socialist who continued promoting his radical views until his death at the ripe old age of 90.[51] However, despite these differences, Wallace reached the same conclusions about the evolutionary process as Darwin through a remarkably similar route. Importantly, he had the same crucial exposure to an extraordinary number of species and their variants during his travels around South America and what is now Indonesia, as Darwin had on the HMS *Beagle*. Moreover, Wallace arrived at the idea of a struggle for existence being the driving force for evolution after reading Thomas Malthus's *An Essay on the Principle of Population*, exactly as Darwin had years earlier. In 1798 Malthus proposed that famine and disease were an inevitable feature of human society, since, while food supply only increased linearly, populations grew in an explosive, exponential fashion. In particular, he believed that the 'lower orders' were primarily to blame in the latter respect, being too inclined to have children.[52] Many critics, then and subsequently, have pointed to flaws in Malthus's reasoning, such as the fact he ignored the likelihood of technological advances in food production.[52] An additional flaw was his disregard for the possibility of birth control, which, ironically, he detested.[52]

However, as a stimulus to the idea of natural selection, Malthus's arguments were central to the development of both Darwin's and Wallace's thought. In Wallace's case, it was in 1858, while fighting a malarial fever in Ternate, Indonesia, that he recalled Malthus's arguments and realized a struggle for scarce resources could provide a mechanism for evolution.[53] In the mid-nineteenth century it was still highly risky to advocate a view of life's origins that left no requirement for God. Although Darwin developed his own version of natural selection as early as 1838, he held back from publishing this, partly out of an obsessive desire to work out every last little theoretical detail, but also out of fear of how going public would affect his respectable position in society.[54] Wallace had no such qualms, and in June 1858 he wrote to Darwin with an outline of his new idea, and a request to review his theory and then send it to the geologist Charles Lyell, who, ironically, had been secretly urging Darwin to publish his work.[53] For Darwin, the letter arrived like a bombshell, for, as he observed to Lyell, 'if Wallace had my manuscript sketch written out in 1842, he could not have made a better short abstract!...So all my originality, whatever it may amount to, will be smashed.'[55]

Instead, a compromise was arranged by Lyell and others in the scientific establishment, whereby both men's views on the subject were presented at a meeting of the Linnean Society in London in July 1858.[54] Neither Darwin nor Wallace attended this, the former being ill and the latter still in Indonesia, and the meeting drew surprisingly little attention at the time. Instead, it was the best-selling *Origin of Species*, published in November 1859, that both introduced the theory to a wider public, and ensured its primary association with Darwin. However, another reason for the relative lack of public recognition of Wallace's contribution may also be his unwillingness to follow the theory through to its logical conclusion and apply it to the origin of human consciousness. So while Darwin did this in 1871 in *The Descent of Man*, where he proposed that humans are 'descended from a hairy, tailed quadruped, probably arboreal in its habits',[56] Wallace appealed to supernatural mechanisms to explain humanity's unique mental attributes. In some ways, Wallace was too sophisticated for his own good. At a time when even the liberal Darwin could view the native peoples of the countries he visited as 'degraded savages', Wallace argued that all human beings are essentially equal.[57] Indeed, he counterposed the morality of the 'primitive' people he encountered to the 'social barbarism' of Victorian England, and their harmonious coexistence with nature to the environmental destruction being wreaked by the Industrial Revolution.

This positive view of human potential led Wallace to wonder why, if the complexities of the human mind were a product of blind chance, people living in primitive settings had the same mental capabilities as those in the civilized world. To him, this implied that the great part of human intelligence in such an environment went unused. To explain this conundrum, Wallace concluded that 'some higher intelligence directed the process by which the human race was developed',[58] much to the dismay of Darwin, who told Wallace, 'I hope you have not murdered too completely your own and my child!'[59] So it was that Darwin, the bourgeois gentleman, proved more revolutionary than Wallace, the socialist.

Despite its success, the theory of natural selection as expounded by either Darwin or Wallace faced a major problem: the lack of a proper explanation for how new characteristics are passed down to offspring so that those more appropriate for survival in a new environment come to predominate. At this time, human offspring, like animals or plants, were known to share many characteristics with their parents,

whether in looks, abilities, or temperament, but this was thought to occur through a mixing of the parents' blood, an idea espoused by ancient Greek philosopher Aristotle,[60] and which underlies the still-used phrase 'blood relations'. Aristotle's view that offspring inherit characteristics from their parents by their mother's menstrual blood combining with their father's semen (which he considered a purified form of blood), may seem ridiculous now but it fitted the observations he could make with the limited experimental tools available.[60] However, the idea that inheritance was passed down in this way posed problems for evolutionary theory, for such mixing would dilute any new characteristics that arose. This problem plagued Darwin until his death.

Yet ironically, the problem of inheritance had, unknown to Darwin, been solved in his lifetime by Gregor Mendel.[61] Mendel's experiments on inheritance in pea plants at St Thomas's Abbey, Brno, now in the Czech Republic, first showed that characteristics like height, colour, and shape are passed down to offspring according to precise mathematical rules, and his work helped complete the puzzle that had baffled Darwin. Of crucial importance was Mendel's conclusion that an organism's inherited characteristics are determined by discrete 'factors', later termed genes. This was hugely important for evolutionary theory, for such discrete elements could be passed down to offspring without their effect being diluted by mixing. Mendel's work implied that, for any particular characteristic, there are two copies of each genetic determinant, one inherited from the father, one from the mother (see Figure 1). In 'dominant' situations, only one copy of a gene variant is needed to determine the characteristic, whilst in 'recessive' situations, both copies are required. While Mendel only studied peas, the mathematical rules he established explain the inheritance of human disorders like cystic fibrosis or Huntington's disorder, these being recessive and dominant respectively, so that we still use these rules to predict the likelihood of someone inheriting them.[62]

Mendel realized the potential general significance of his findings, saying 'I am convinced that it will not be long before the whole world acknowledges the results of my work.'[61] Instead, despite being published less than a decade after *The Origin of Species*, the importance of Mendel's findings lay unrecognized until they were rediscovered in 1900, Mendel having died in 1884. Quite why their value for evolutionary theory was not recognized sooner remains a matter of debate. Some have pointed to the fact the findings were published in the local

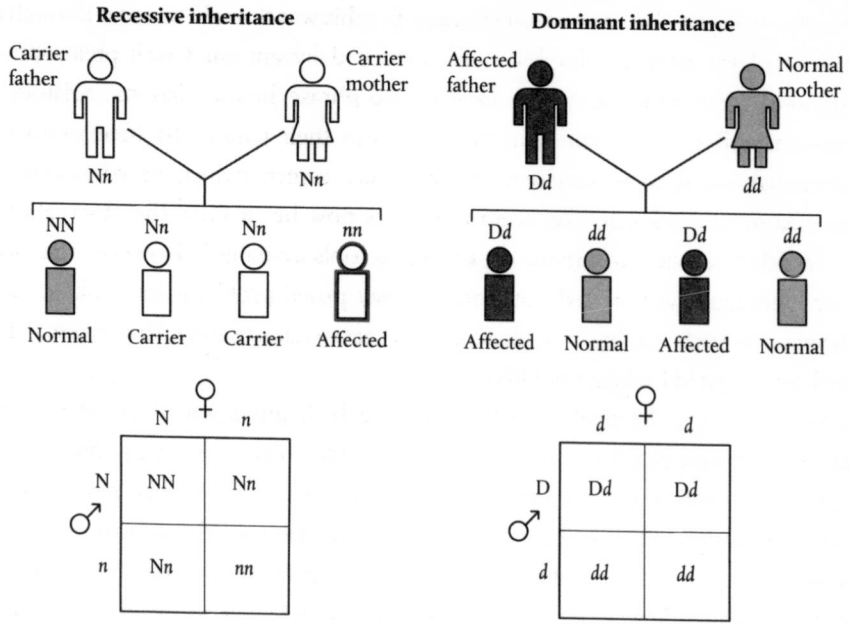

Figure 1. Mendel's patterns of inheritance

journal of the Brno Natural History Society; however, this journal was sent out to libraries across Europe and Mendel himself tried to interest leading international botanists in his work, albeit without success.[61] Another explanation is that the mathematical rigour Mendel applied to inheritance was too advanced for its time, biologists in those days being used to qualitative, not quantitative, explanations of nature.[63] Whatever the exact reason for their initial obscurity, the value of Mendel's findings was finally recognized more than thirty years after they first appeared in print, by Hugo de Vries, Carl Correns, and Erich von Tschermak, scientists coming to similar conclusions themselves.[64] It would be nice to say Mendel's prior claim to fame was acknowledged fairly and ungrudgingly, however, de Vries originally seems to have tried to pass off Mendel's insights as his own, only to be rumbled by Correns.[64] Such are the temptations of immortality, albeit of the scientific variety.

Given that Wallace lived for thirteen years after the rediscovery of Mendel's findings, one might have expected him to welcome this major theoretical link that had eluded him and Darwin. Yet, up to his death, Wallace remained unconvinced of its importance.[65] His scepticism was partly due to the fact that de Vries linked

Mendelism to his own view that changes in species occurred in leaps, which he explicitly counterposed to the gradualism that both Darwin and Wallace espoused. In addition, Wallace viewed the rigidity of Mendel's 'laws' as antagonistic to the plasticity he saw as central to evolution, noting that Mendel's factors 'are transmitted without variation, and therefore, except by the rarest of accidents, can never become adapted to ever varying conditions'.[65] It was a good point but neglected the crucial role of mutations: changes in genes that affect their function.

A proper recognition of the role of mutations in evolution awaited the work of Thomas Morgan, who, early in the twentieth century at Columbia University, New York, systematically identified and characterized these genetic changes in what became a central 'model' organism for genetics—the fruitfly.[66] Morgan was initially sceptical about both Darwinism and Mendelism, being more influenced by de Vries's theory that evolution was driven by dramatic changes affecting the whole body plan of the organism far more rapidly than could be accounted for by natural selection.[67] This idea was based upon de Vries's discoveries of new forms of the primrose plant. In fact, we now know these were due to genome duplications in these plants, with little general relevance for normal evolution. However, they inspired Morgan to go looking for mutations in animals. He first studied rodents, but then, realizing they reproduced far too slowly for identification of the molecules of inheritance, Morgan turned to fruitflies, because their short generation span, and the fact they can be kept in a milk bottle with some banana to keep them happy, meant they were ideal for scientific studies.[68] From 1907 onwards, he and his co-workers spent many hours searching for naturally occurring mutations.[69] At first it seemed a fruitless task and one designed to drive the team bananas, leading Morgan to exclaim, 'There's two years' work wasted. I have been breeding those flies for all that time and have got nothing out of it!'[66]

However, in April 1910 the team made a breakthrough. In one of the bottles was a fly with white eyes rather than the normal red ones.[68] Further analysis showed that this was recessive, while red eyes were dominant, in line with Mendel's laws. There was a complication though, for this particular characteristic showed an unusual pattern not identified by Mendel, being generally only present in males.[69] So what could be the material basis for this difference? The answer eventually came from one of those occurrences in science when two lines of investigation fortuitously converge. Although Mendel's findings were only rediscovered in 1900, in the intervening period major discoveries were still being made

18

relating to the material basis of inheritance. By this time it was recognized that cells divided to form other cells, and that hereditary information was stored in their central nucleus. But that still left unanswered how that information was distributed during cell division to each daughter cell formed during this process. The answer came from Walther Flemming of Kiel University, Germany, in 1878. In the late nineteenth century Germany led the world in the production of new chemical dyes for the textile industry, and some scientists realized these dyes could also be used to stain cellular structures. Flemming used this method to study cell division.[70] By using dyes to both stain the cell's components and 'fix' the cell at a particular stage in the process, Flemming identified tiny condensed threads that formed in the nucleus during a stage of cell division that he named mitosis, after the Greek for thread. The threads were named chromosomes, Greek for 'coloured bodies', reflecting their discovery with the aid of dyes.

Flemming demonstrated that chromosome pairs are first duplicated during cell division, the pairs then subsequently segregating into the two daughter cells.[70] The obvious analogy with inheritance convinced many scientists that chromosomes must play a crucial role in this process. This was demonstrated experimentally in 1889 by Theodor Boveri, working at the Stazione Zoologica in Naples, who showed that chromosomes are required for embryo development to occur.[71] And in 1905, just before Morgan's discovery of sex-linked mutations, Nettie Stevens and Edmund Wilson showed that cells of male and female flies could be distinguished by females having two copies of the X chromosome, while males have one X and one Y chromosome.[72] Despite previously opposing the idea of chromosomes being agents of inheritance, based on his belief that passive observations were no substitute for direct experimentation, Morgan realized his findings must mean the gene for the red eye colour resided on the X chromosome, white eyes being an 'X-linked' recessive disorder.

We now recognize this pattern of inheritance in human disorders like haemophilia, Duchenne muscular dystrophy, and red–green colour blindness. While standard recessive disorders require both copies of a gene to be faulty since males only have one X chromosome, in X-linked disorders a single faulty copy can cause the disease. This is why it is very rare to find women with such disorders; instead, human females 'carry' these diseases to the next generation of males, as Queen Victoria did when she passed on haemophilia to many royal males in Europe.[73] In the fly experiments, however, a few white-eyed females were

detected, and in such proportions that confirmed they must have two faulty copies of the gene associated with red eyes. So, despite his initial scepticism about the link between chromosomes and inheritance, Morgan had himself provided the first experimental evidence for this link.[74] And indeed, in a rare moment of generalization on his part, this extreme empiricist now proposed that all genes must reside on chromosomes. Finally a connection had been made between Mendel's abstract 'factors' and real cellular entities within the cell.

A further major step forward came with the discovery by Morgan's colleague, Hermann Muller, that treating flies with X-rays greatly increased the chance of their offspring becoming mutants.[75] This was the first demonstration of the dangers of radiation, and Muller would build a career highlighting these dangers for human beings. But it also allowed Morgan's lab to dramatically increase the numbers of available mutants, and to create flies with multiple mutations and then compare their inheritance.[76] This led to some unexpected findings. Mendel's laws predicted that inheritance of each characteristic should be completely independent from the next,[61] but that those on the same chromosome should be inherited together, and this was found to be the case in most of the fly studies.

Puzzlingly though, while some mutations on the same chromosome stayed 'linked' in this way, others became separated, and the degree to which this happened varied. Seeking an explanation for these strange findings, Morgan was intrigued to learn of an observation made in 1909 by Frans Janssens at Leuven University, Belgium; he had been studying the segregation of chromosomes during the formation of eggs and sperm.[77] Normal cell division—mitosis—involves, first, the duplication of a cell's genetic material, and then equal segregation of this to each daughter cell, which are therefore exact copies of the parent cell (see Figure 2). But eggs and sperm only contain half the genetic material of a normal cell, because there is no duplication, only segregation. However, what Janssens found when studying this process, named 'meiosis' from the Greek for lessening, was that, before splitting, each chromosome pair became twisted together and even appeared to exchange segments with each other.[77] Morgan realized that this 'crossing over' explained why some characteristics were more linked than others. If the genes on a chromosome are like beads on a string, the closer two genes are together, the more likely the chance of remaining together during crossing over.

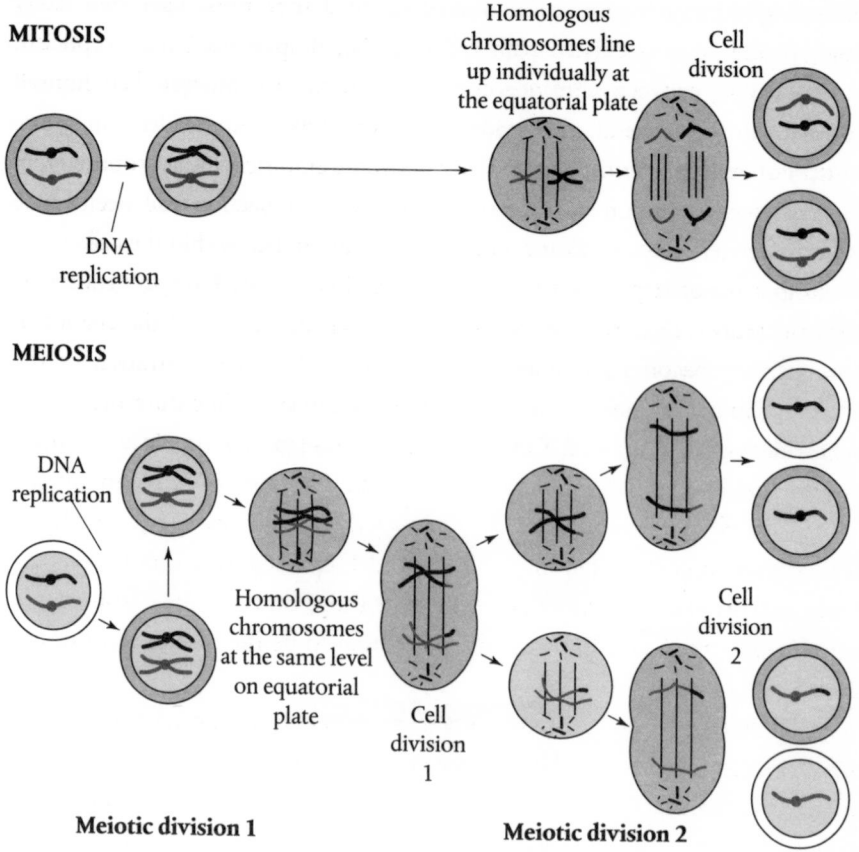

Figure 2. Mitosis and meiosis

This insight led to the first genetic 'map'. Remarkably, Alfred Sturtevant, who first proposed such a map, was only an undergraduate student when he came up with this idea.[68] Sturtevant had been so inspired by Morgan's lectures he asked if he could work in the latter's lab. Morgan was happy to take gifted students under his wing and Sturtevant became fully integrated into the lab even as he studied for his degree. As further inspiration for an ambitious student, Morgan's lab was one of the first in which students were treated as colleagues and encouraged to be co-authors or even sole authors of papers.[78] Such democracy was unusual given that the model at this time was the 'German research university, in which the Geheim-rat, the great scientific leader, ordered the hierarchy of his subordinates'.[68] Instead, in Morgan's lab, 'each carried on his own experiments, but each knew exactly what the others were doing, and each new result was freely discussed'.[79]

Musing one evening about the linkage phenomenon, Sturtevant realized that 'the variations in the strength of linkage already attributed by Morgan to difference in the spatial separation of the gene offered the possibility of determining sequence in the linear dimensions of a chromosome. I went home and spent most of the night (to the neglect of my undergraduate homework) in producing the first chromosome map.'[68] Crucially, knowing the linkage frequencies for at least three characteristics would allow not only the order of the genes associated with these characteristics on the chromosome to be known, but also their relative distances from each other (see Figure 3).[78] As well as revolutionizing experimental genetics, this discovery paved the way for genetically mapping human characteristics, including diseases. The pioneering nature of Morgan's research was acknowledged in 1933 with a Nobel Prize; notably, he shared the prize money

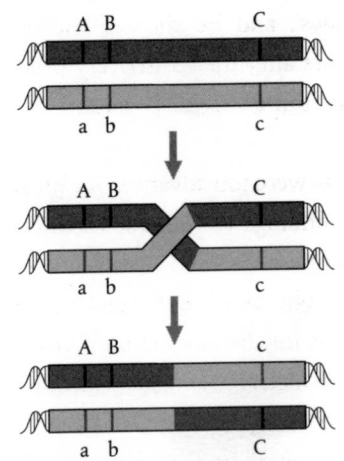

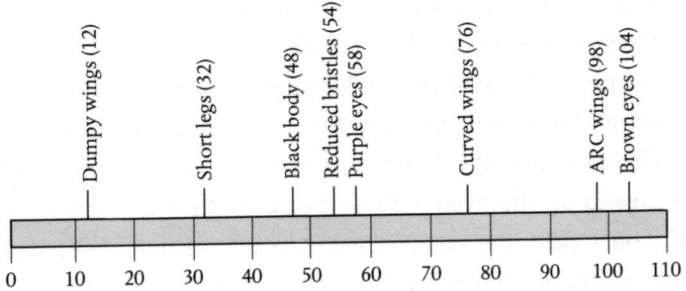

Figure 3. Crossing over and genetic map

with Sturtevant and another student, Calvin Bridges.[68] Muller also received a Nobel Prize for his discovery of the mutagenic properties of radiation, in 1946.[75] Only a year before this, in 1945, the atomic bombs dropped in Japan had demonstrated the devastating effects of radiation on the human body.

The first human disease shown to follow a Mendelian pattern of inheritance was alkaptonuria, a defect in metabolism associated with early-onset arthritis and heart disease, but whose most visible symptom is a tendency to produce black urine. Its inheritance pattern was first identified in 1902 by Archibald Garrod, a physician whose bedside manner was said to be limited to interest in his patient's urine samples.[80] But while he might have lacked interpersonal skills, Garrod played a key role in advancing the scientific basis of medicine. For him, science was 'a way of searching out by observation, trial and classification; whether the phenomena investigated be the outcome of human activities, or of the more direct workings of nature's laws', and he showed the power of this approach by recognizing, just two years after the rediscovery of Mendel's work, that alkapto-nuria displayed the very same recessive pattern of inheritance shown by the latter's pea plants.[80]

In fact, Garrod's insights were too advanced for most biologists and clinicians at that time; they saw his findings as relevant for this one odd disorder, but not generally applicable to human disease.[80] Instead, it was only in the 1920s, when Ronald Fisher, Sewall Wright, and J. B. S. Haldane began independently seeking mathematical explanations for the inheritance patterns in human populations by reference to the laws that Mendel had established, that the union between Darwinism and Mendelism could be considered secure.[81] Not everyone was enamoured of this approach, evolutionary biologist Ernst Mayr likening it to comparing 'the genetic contents of a population to a bag full of colored beans. Mutation was the exchange of one kind of bean for another...To consider genes as independent units is meaningless from the physiological as well as the evolutionary viewpoint.'[82] Haldane agreed that such 'beanbag genetics' were based on many unrealistic 'simplifying assumptions', namely that the characteristics being studied followed simple Mendelian rules, mating was random, and populations could be treated as effectively infinite; however, he also maintained that this approach could yield important quantitative information about the incidence and spread of disease, and, indeed, other characteristics in a human or animal population.[83]

23

Another major step forward in genetics was the demonstration by George Beadle and Edward Tatum of Stanford University that genes and enzymes were directly connected. It was while listening to a seminar by Tatum in 1941 in which the latter posed the question 'What do genes do?' while also discussing cellular biochemistry, that Beadle suddenly realized how to connect the two issues. Observing Tatum writing sequences of reactions on the blackboard, Beadle 'suddenly realized how stupid we had been all these years...instead of looking for reactions by enzymes controlled by known genes, why not look for genes that control already known chemical reactions? We might then expect to find mutations characterized by an inability to synthesize essential diffusible substances such as vitamins, amino acids and other building blocks of the cell's protoplasm.'[84] A former student of Morgan, Beadle persuaded Tatum that the best way to investigate this issue was to use an even simpler organism than the fly—a bread mould called *Neurospora*—whose biochemistry was well worked out. By using X-rays to create mutants in this species, then studying which biochemical pathways were defective, in only a few months Beadle and Tatum showed that mutants segregating in a Mendelian fashion affected specific enzymes in these pathways. This suggested each gene is used to produce a single protein, and resulted in a Nobel Prize for Beadle and Tatum in 1958.

What was remarkable about Mendel's pioneering work in establishing the principle of genes as discrete entities; the extension of this principle by Morgan, Beadle, and Tatum experimentally, and Garrod clinically; and its mathematical underpinning by Haldane and colleagues, was that all this had been achieved despite the molecular basis of genes remaining unknown. For geneticist Richard Goldschmidt, reflecting back on this era in 1950, it was such a leap forward in science as to rank alongside 'the explanation of the movements of the celestial bodies by Kepler, Copernicus, and Newton; Galileo's experiments inaugurating the age of inductive science, and Darwin's establishment of the theory of evolution'.[68] Yet as the 1950s began, and post-war austerity gave way to the post-war boom and the new music of rock 'n' roll, the molecular foundation of this new genetics remained far from clear, almost a century after Mendel's breakthrough. This state of affairs was, however, about to change in a way that would first strengthen the modern synthesis, but eventually come to challenge it, with the discovery that the genetic material was deoxyribonucleic acid, more popularly known as DNA.

2

LIFE AS A CODE

'Science moves with the spirit of an adventure characterized both by youthful arrogance and by the belief that the truth, once found, would be simple as well as pretty.'
Jim Watson

'The human genome consists of about 3.3 billion base pairs...0.8 gigabytes of information, or about what you can fit on a CD. With a microwave radio transmitter, you could beam that amount of information into space in a few minutes, and have it travel to anyone at light speed.'
Seth Shostak

We're so used to thinking of DNA as the blueprint of life that it's easy to forget how resistant many biologists were to this idea at first. DNA was discovered by Swiss scientist Friedrich Miescher as early as 1869, through his interest in identifying the biochemical components of the cell nucleus. Miescher made the discovery while studying with the biochemist Felix Hoppe-Seyler in Tübingen, Germany. Like something out of a Frankenstein film, Hoppe-Seyler's lab was based in a medieval former royal castle; Hoppe-Seyler occupied the former laundry room while Miescher worked in the old kitchen.[85] Hoppe-Seyler wanted to catalogue the chemicals in blood, and had already studied red blood cells, so Miescher was given the task of looking at white blood cells. This proved fortuitous since these cells have a very prominent nucleus, and it was while studying this that Miescher identified DNA as a central component and set out to purify it. Fortunately, or unfortunately depending on your point of view, a ready supply of white blood cells was available from pus in surgical bandages collected at a local hospital. Every day a hospital orderly delivered these gruesome items which Miescher smelled to determine which were the freshest. But 'driven by a demon', he threw himself into the task and following a year's hard work he had a sample of pure DNA.[85]

Miescher predicted that DNA would soon 'prove tantamount in importance to proteins'.[86] However, despite a major clue as to the physiological role of the molecule being its exclusive location on chromosomes, DNA was not thought complex enough to carry the hereditary information. Instead, proteins, also abundant in chromosomes for reasons we'll explore later, seemed much more suited to this role.[86] Proteins were, after all, at this time being identified as life's 'building blocks'. We now know proteins form the primary cellular structures, but also catalyse chemical reactions, and control transport into and within the cell. To carry out such multiple roles, proteins come in many shapes and sizes, a feature made possible by the 20 different amino acids, each with its own individual character, of which these molecules are built. The multiple ways in which amino acids can be combined produces the dizzying diversity of protein types (see Figure 4). Proteins can be long, thin, and fibrous like collagen, with a higher tensile strength than steel, which it imparts to bones or cartilage, or soluble and globular like haemoglobin, which carries oxygen around the body. It was hardly odd then to assume that since proteins are the building blocks of life, they would also be its instruction manual.

In contrast, DNA seemed a far simpler and less interesting molecule. In contrast to proteins, the units of DNA come in just four varieties. A unit of DNA is called a nucleotide and consists of three parts. The first is a deoxyribose sugar, which

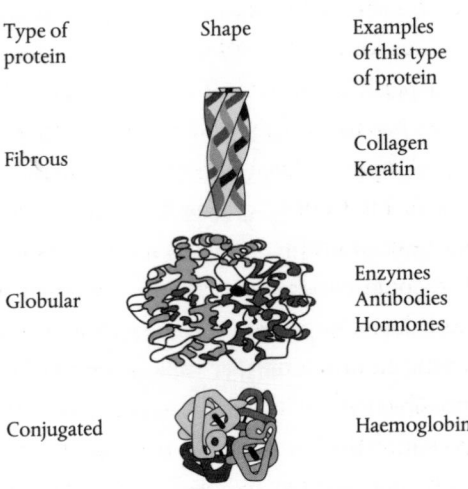

Type of protein	Shape	Examples of this type of protein
Fibrous		Collagen Keratin
Globular		Enzymes Antibodies Hormones
Conjugated		Haemoglobin

Figure 4. Different types of proteins

forms a pentagon, in contrast to the hexagonal glucose. The second is a phosphate, which joins the units to each other, such that a DNA chain is said to have a 'sugar phosphate backbone'. The third is a nitrogenous base; this part varies, being either adenine, guanine, cytosine, or thymine, although nowadays these are generally abbreviated simply to A, G, C, and T. While proteins vary in shape and size, DNA is a long, thin molecule that just goes on and on. Since the bases themselves didn't appear that different chemically, and Phoebus Levene, a chemist at the Rockefeller Institute in New York, had proposed that the sequence of bases was an endless repetition of ACGT, it wasn't at all clear how this apparently boring molecule could do anything significant at all.[87] So, as late as the mid-twentieth century, a commonly held view was that, despite being a central component of chromosomes, 'DNA could only be some sort of structural stiffening, the laundry cardboard in the shirt, the wooden stretcher behind the Rembrandt, since the genetic material would have to be protein.'[87] This scepticism was such that even when clear evidence emerged that DNA was the molecule of inheritance, it was disregarded by most biologists. However, nature has a habit of asserting itself despite the intentions of the scientists studying it. This was certainly true for Oswald Avery, also at the Rockefeller, who in 1944 began studying transmission of heredity in bacteria as a way of identifying the molecule responsible.

Previously, Fred Griffith of the British Ministry of Health had shown, in 1928, that bacteria could swop particular characteristics in the bacterial equivalent of sex, these being then transmitted to future generations. It was a discovery with major future implications for the study of genetics, but at the time its significance was barely recognized, partly because of Griffith's extremely shy nature.[88] On one occasion, his colleagues had to virtually kidnap him and drive him to a conference where he'd been invited to speak. Even once there, he mumbled his way through some obscure aspect of his studies, and made no mention of his key finding. Avery, however, did hear about the findings, and he reasoned that the process Griffith had identified could be used to study the molecular basis of heredity by eliminating each individual component of the bacteria, to see how this affected transmission of genetic information. Particularly important was the fact that transmission was possible even with dead bacteria. Avery thus destroyed, first, the sugar molecules coating the bacteria, then the proteins, then their RNA. None of this affected transmission, until finally the bacterial DNA was destroyed, upon which the ability to pass on genetic information ceased.[88]

Yet even this apparently clear-cut result failed to sway many biologists. It didn't help that Avery was ultra-cautious in his report of the study, concluding that 'it is of course possible that the biological activity ... is not an inherent property of the nucleic acid but is due to minute amounts of some other substance', something seized upon by those who believed that proteins were the agents of inheritance, and therefore must be the contaminating factor.[89] In addition, Avery's findings left unresolved how the apparently simple DNA could be life's blueprint. Max Delbrück of the California Institute of Technology observed later that Avery's findings clashed strongly with the belief that 'DNA was a stupid substance, a tetranucleotide which couldn't do anything specific'.[89]

One person unconvinced by Avery's findings and the claims for DNA's importance was Alfred Hershey, of Cold Spring Harbor Laboratory.[90] In 1952 he decided to further test the matter using a type of virus called bacteriophage, or phage for short. Phage infect bacteria, proving there is some truth in Jonathan Swift's claim that 'a flea has smaller fleas that on him prey; and these have smaller still to bite 'em, and so proceed *ad infinitum*'.[91] Studies of phage under the electron microscope by Thomas Anderson at Cold Spring Harbor had recently revealed that the phage never entered the bacterium during an infection; instead, it remained on the host cell's surface. This suggested that it acted like a hypodermic needle to inject the hereditary molecule into the bacterium; this then took over the cellular machinery in order to create new viruses. Hershey realized that, by labelling the viral DNA and protein with radioactive phosphorus and sulphur respectively, it should be possible to determine which had entered the bacterium.[90] One technical obstacle remained for Hershey and his assistant Martha Chase, and that was finding a way to separate the bacteria and phage after infection. Having tried 'various grinding arrangements, with results that weren't very encouraging', Hershey and Chase decided to use a simple kitchen blender. This device, more generally used for making Mai Tais, mojitos, and other cocktail party drinks of the 1950s, efficiently removed phage from the bacteria without rupturing the latter. With this tool, Hershey and Chase showed conclusively that the viral DNA, not its protein, entered the bacterium. Even faced with this apparently incontrovertible evidence, Hershey initially had trouble accepting the result, telling the audience to which he first presented the findings that 'I don't believe in that DNA'.[90] The problem was that it still remained unclear how such a boring molecule as DNA could act as the hereditary molecule.

Instead, it was only when Jim Watson and Francis Crick, working at Cambridge University, unveiled their model of the famous double helix structure of DNA, that it finally became clear how the molecule could function in such a way. Watson and Crick's discovery, published in *Nature* in April 1953, is rightly seen as the starting point of a revolution in how humans view life and their own species. Thanks to Watson's own frank and somewhat scurrilous account in his book *The Double Helix*, this discovery has become famous for showing that brilliant insight and dubious practices can triumph over the sort of plodding, painstaking construction of theories, based upon a careful examination of experimental data, often held up as an example of the scientific process.[92] A precocious child, Watson began studying biology at the University of Chicago, his native city, aged only 15. There he was seduced by genetics and applied to do a PhD at Indiana University in 1947 because of its association with Hermann Muller.[93] But already the study of fruitfly genetics was looking jaded in comparison to new directions, such as the use of bacteriophage. Consequently, Watson began his PhD studies with Salvador Luria and Max Delbrück, pre-war refugees from fascist regimes in Italy and Germany respectively, who were now establishing themselves as masters of this new field of research.[93] Only two years into studying for his PhD, Watson decided that 'I wanted to find the structure of DNA; that is, DNA was going to be my objective.'[94] Comparing the quest to the fever that had gripped his nation a half century earlier and led thousands to brave all in the Yukon region in Alaska, Watson claimed 'DNA was my gold rush'.[95]

Realizing that the best place to achieve his objective was in England, where structural analysis of biological molecules was, at that time, amongst the best in the world, Watson joined the Cavendish Laboratory in Cambridge, presided over by Sir Lawrence Bragg. Although, in Watson's book, Bragg is portrayed as a stuffy administrator, more likely to be at his London club than doing any actual science,[96] in fact the latter had already distinguished himself by solving the first ever molecular structure, that of NaCl or common salt, in 1912, and so became the youngest person to win a Nobel Prize at the age of 25.[97] The key to Bragg's success was a technique called X-ray crystallography, which works by firing a beam of X-rays at a crystal of the molecule under investigation; the scattering of this beam in response to the atoms it encounters is used to build up a picture of the structure of the molecule.[97] At the Cavendish this technique was primarily being used to solve the 3D structure of a protein, haemoglobin, while, due to an arrangement

with the Medical Research Council, analysis of DNA was being carried out at the Randall Institute, King's College London, by Maurice Wilkins and Rosalind Franklin.[98] However, such minor details would soon prove less important than Watson's thirst to get to the goal first. It also helped that he found an ideal partner at the Cavendish in Francis Crick. At this point Crick appeared to be the opposite of precocious, since, although 35 years old, he hadn't even completed a PhD. Yet over the next decade Crick would prove to have one of the sharpest minds in twentieth-century science.

An important factor in Watson and Crick's favour was that the research effort at the Randall Institute was seriously undermined by the inability of Wilkins and Franklin to work together. The seeds of this schism were sown by John Randall himself, one of the creators of radar, who after the war was given funds to use physics to solve key questions in biology.[99] Randall led both Wilkins and Franklin to believe they would be leading the effort to determine DNA's structure, and, coupled with a clash of two quite different personalities, this led to a rapid falling-out.[99] One of the greatest travesties in the discovery of the DNA double helix was that Watson and Crick obtained a crucial piece of unpublished experimental data from Rosalind Franklin without her knowledge.[100] That this data was shown to Watson by Wilkins, unbeknown to Franklin, is now recognized as one of science history's more glaring injustices. Wilkins has his own version of events, which stresses Franklin's prickly character,[101] but it is hard not to view the way Franklin was marginalized at King's as linked to her gender. So she was barred from lunching with her male colleagues,[102] and the nicknames many called her— 'Rosy', the 'Dark Lady'—show that it was not just Watson at this time who treated her in a sexist manner. Yet these features of the discovery should not detract from the brilliance of Watson and Crick's insight when their model-building strategy, which had been largely dismissed by Franklin and Wilkins, led them to the double helix structure.[103] In this respect the pair were undoubtedly helped by DNA having 'molecule of life' written all over it, so much so that, on Saturday, 28 February 1953, when they finally resolved the structure, Crick told everyone within earshot, at their subsequent celebration at the Eagle pub in Cambridge, that he and Watson had discovered the 'secret of life'.[104]

The first major revelation of the double helix structure was showing the way in which the molecule is capable of self-replication. We've seen that nucleotides come in four varieties, defined by the bases adenine, cytosine, guanine, and

thymine, or A, C, G, T for short. Watson and Crick proposed that the two strands of the double helix were held together by an attraction of A for T, and G for C, these paired bases occupying the space within the helix-like steps in a spiral staircase (see Figure 5). So famous is this iconic structure now that Martin Kemp, an art historian at Oxford University, recently called it 'the Mona Lisa of modern science'.[105] Scientifically, the structure made sense of a previous discovery by Erwin Chargaff of Columbia University, New York, whose chemical analysis of DNA in 1952 showed that A and T occurred in equal amounts, as did G and C.[106] Chargaff himself thought Watson and Crick were a couple of cowboys on the make, after an encounter in which the pair showed their ignorance about the chemical structures of the nucleotide bases.[107] A decade after Watson and Crick's discovery, his opinion of them hadn't improved, as shown by his comment that 'molecular biology is essentially the practice of biochemistry without a license'.[108] Yet their structure made sense of Chargaff's findings in a way that had eluded him.

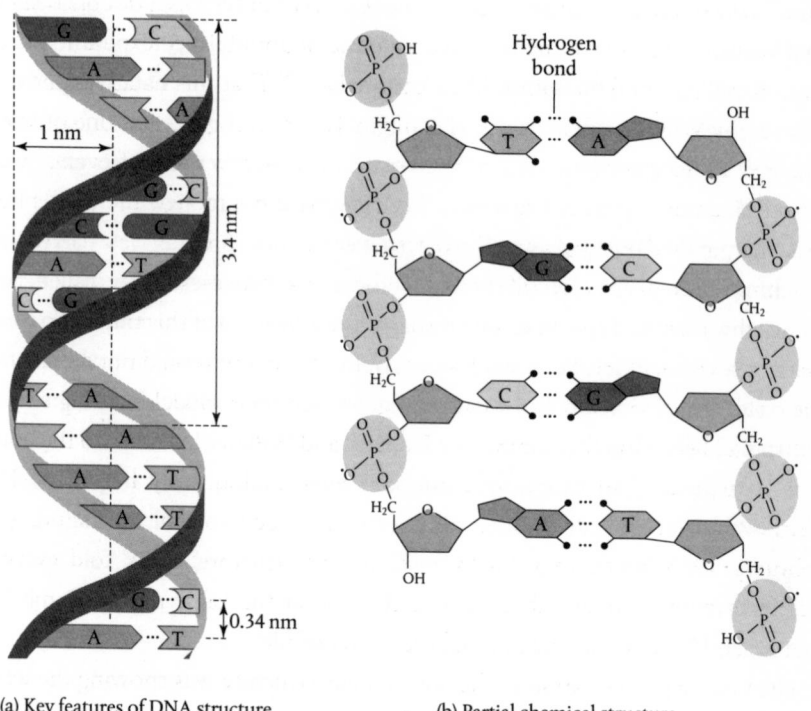

(a) Key features of DNA structure   (b) Partial chemical structure

Figure 5. Structure of DNA showing double helix and base pairing

That AT and GC 'base pairing' might be centrally linked to how DNA replicated itself, was suggested by one of the most famous cryptic comments in science, when, in Watson and Crick's *Nature* paper, they said 'it has not escaped our notice that the specific pairing we have postulated immediately suggests a possible copying mechanism for the genetic material'.[109] Indeed, their follow-up paper, also published in *Nature*, proposed a form of replication they named 'semi-conservative', that involved the two strands splitting apart during each cell division, and forming the template for another mirror-image strand to be formed from each.[110] Another less likely possibility was that the double helix did not split into two during replication but instead another new molecule formed alongside it—'conservative' replication.

One person for whom Watson and Crick's discovery had life-changing importance was an Oxford University PhD student, Sydney Brenner, who would later play a major role in solving the genetic code and many other fundamental problems of biology. He recalled how having been told that the structure of DNA had probably been solved by two people in Cambridge, Francis Crick and Jim Watson, 'I went to Cambridge and saw the model and met Francis and Jim. It was the most exciting day of my life. The double helix was a revelatory experience; for me, everything fell into place and my future scientific life was decided there and then.'[111] Not everyone was as convinced though, for, as Brenner also noted, 'when the paper appeared a few weeks later, it was not well received by the establishment, composed largely of professional biochemists. They could not see, at the time, how profoundly it would change their subject by offering us a framework for studying the chemistry of biological information.' This may account for the delay in Watson, Crick, and Wilkins being awarded a Nobel Prize for the discovery, which finally happened in 1962. Whether Rosalind Franklin should also share the prize was never posed, due to her death in 1958 aged only 38, from cancer possibly induced by the X-rays she had been exposed to in her work.[112]

For the scientists who grasped the importance of the double helix discovery, there was much work to be done. Brenner later gave a sense of the excitement among those involved, when he noted that 'many have gone on to do important scientific work but all remember those wonderful times when we and our science were young and our excitement in meeting new challenges knew no bounds'.[113] A first important task was to confirm experimentally whether DNA replication

occurred semi-conservatively or by the alternative conservative route. This question was answered by a study in 1958 by Matthew Meselson and Frank Stahl, often called 'the most beautiful experiment in biology' for its elegant simplicity. Meselson and Stahl met in the summer of 1954 as visiting graduate students at the Marine Biological Laboratory at Woods Hole, Massachusetts, where Watson and Crick were both giving guest lectures. Inspired by the talks and fired up by discussions over numerous gin martinis, the two decided to tackle this key question with the latest experimental techniques.[114] Since DNA contains nitrogen, which naturally occurs in two 'isotopic' forms, ^{14}N and ^{15}N, Meselson and Stahl used a new technique called density gradient centrifugation to distinguish DNA molecules containing the heavy and light isotopes.[115] Bacteria were grown in a broth containing ^{15}N for several generations, then transferred to one containing ^{14}N. By removing bacteria at various points and analysing their DNA, Meselson and Stahl showed that, after a single replication, the bacterial DNA had a density halfway between the high and low forms, exactly as expected of semi-conservative but not of conservative replication; the latter of which would have led to equal amounts of DNA of the higher and lower densities, but none of intermediate status. In 1956 the enzyme that carries out DNA replication—DNA polymerase—was isolated and characterized by Arthur Kornberg of Washington University, Saint Louis, which led to him being awarded a Nobel Prize in 1959.[116]

Yet while the DNA structure immediately suggested its likely mechanism of replication, there seemed nothing inherent in it to show how its information was translated into the biochemical processes of a cell or organism. The key was surely proteins, the building blocks of the cell and organism. But how could a linear sequence of DNA nucleotides code for the multiple shapes and sizes of different proteins? A vital clue was supplied by Fred Sanger, also in Cambridge, who was working on a method to identify the sequence of amino acids in a protein. A trained chemist, Sanger devised ways to mark the amino acid at the end of a protein chain and also break the chain into overlapping fragments.[117] He applied this technique to insulin, one of the few pure proteins available, due to its use by diabetics. Prior to Sanger's investigations, it was known that the proportion of different amino acids in a particular protein was specific to that protein, but the order in which they were strung together was thought to be random. However, in work that led to him being awarded a Nobel Prize in 1958, Sanger showed that every insulin molecule had the same unvarying sequence.[118] This raised the

exciting possibility that since DNA also had a linear sequence, there might be a connection between this and the sequence of amino acids. The question was how the two could be connected.

Surprisingly, the first step in solving this mystery came not from a biologist, but a theoretical physicist, George Gamow, a refugee from Stalin's Russia, now based at the George Washington University, Washington DC. Gamow had played a key role in developing the 'Big Bang' theory of the origin of the universe.[119] Commenting on the timescale of the universe Gamow observed that 'it took less than an hour to make the atoms, a few 100 million years to make the stars and planets, but five billion years to make man!'[120] Perhaps it was a wish to understand what happened in those several billion years that led to an interest in Watson and Crick's new structure and its relevance for life, for Gamow began sending the two scientists letters outlining how a DNA code might operate.[121]

Initially dismissing him as a crazy stalker, Watson and Crick quickly realized Gamow had important insights to share. Gamow suggested that overlapping triplets of DNA bases specified a single amino acid, with the DNA acting as a direct template for the growing protein chain.[119] His view was that on each base a cavity must exist complementary in shape to part of an amino acid, so providing a mechanism for how a linear chain of nucleotides could code for one of amino acids. But there were problems with this model from the start. One was that proteins were known to be made not in the cell's nucleus, where DNA is located, but in the surrounding cytoplasm.[122] In fact, even removing the nucleus from a cell had no immediate effect on the speed at which proteins were made. These facts were hard to square with DNA acting as a direct template for protein synthesis.

What seemed necessary, therefore, was an intermediary between DNA and proteins. An obvious candidate was DNA's chemical cousin, RNA, known to be present in both nucleus and cytoplasm. RNA differs from DNA in that its units are ribonucleotides not deoxyribonucleotides, and it contains uracil, usually abbreviated to U, instead of the thymine found in DNA. In addition, RNA usually occurs as a single strand, unlike double-stranded DNA. Finally, while DNA stretches for the length of a whole chromosome, RNA occurs as much smaller fragments. So could RNA be acting as a go-between, ferrying information from DNA to proteins? This idea was strengthened by the discovery of RNA polymerase, an enzyme that catalyses the production of RNA from DNA.[123] But it still remained

unclear how a nucleotide code, albeit one contained within RNA, could be transformed into one based upon amino acids.

In principle, Gamow's idea of overlapping nucleotide triplets acting as the template for an amino acid chain could apply to RNA as much as to DNA. But there were other problems with the model emerging, since it predicted that many pairs of amino acids would never be found next to each other in proteins. Yet as more proteins were sequenced, it became clear that any combination of amino acids was possible.[124] It was also very difficult to imagine how RNA could act as the direct template for protein synthesis in the way Gamow had envisaged for DNA, with the shape of the individual bases directly determining the sequence of the growing protein chain. Instead, in 1955, Crick proposed a radically different model, whereby amino acids were ferried to the point of protein synthesis by 'adaptor' molecules, which he suggested could themselves be some type of RNA.[125]

Crick's proposal was subsequently confirmed by Paul Zamecnik and colleagues at Massachusetts General Hospital, Boston. Zamecnik was a clinician who became interested in how cells regulate growth, and why this process seemed defective in some of his patients.[126] This led him to try and identify all the cellular components required for generation of proteins. A major step forward came with his discovery that a 'cell-free' extract of rat liver could still generate proteins if supplied with amino acids.[126] Plying this system with radioactively labelled amino acids or RNA in order to identify their respective roles in the synthesis process, Zamecnik noticed that, 'strangely enough, the RNA fraction was labelled from the amino acid precursor. In spite of careful washing procedures, the amino acid remained tightly bound to the RNA.' Finding that the specifically bound RNA molecules were of low molecular weight, Zamecnik realized they must be the adaptors Crick had proposed, and he named them transfer RNA, or tRNA for short. Subsequently, he showed there were twenty types of tRNA, one for each amino acid. But there was more to come, for he also demonstrated that proteins were manufactured in a huge molecular structure he called the ribosome, a complex of both proteins and another type of RNA, ribosomal RNA or rRNA.[126]

An unresolved issue remained, however. If the ribosome was the structure upon which proteins were made, and tRNAs the molecules that ferried amino acids to it, this failed to explain how the DNA code in the nucleus was subsequently translated into a protein sequence in the cytoplasm. Some intermediary

must presumably carry the code from the nucleus to the cytoplasmic ribosomes, but what was its molecular identity? Watson and Crick initially proposed that rRNA itself fulfilled this role, with a unique version of one of these molecules being specific for each different protein. However, analysis of rRNA revealed it to be uniform in its sequence and very stable, not the qualities expected of the predicted transient intermediary. Instead, it was only with the discovery of a third type of RNA, by Sydney Brenner and colleagues, that the pieces of the puzzle finally fell into place.

Brenner was from a poor Jewish family in Johannesburg, his parents having immigrated to South Africa from the Baltic States.[127] His father, a shoemaker, spoke English, Yiddish, Russian, Afrikaans, and Zulu, but was illiterate, and it was an elderly neighbour who taught Brenner to read fluently before the age of 4, using the newspapers that served as a tablecloth in her house. A child prodigy, Brenner enrolled at the University of the Witwatersrand at the age of 15 and published his first scientific paper at 18. As we've mentioned already, Brenner was a PhD student in Oxford when he heard about Watson and Crick's great discovery and went personally to view their model. As he noted later, 'the moment I saw the model and heard about the complementing base pairs I realized that it was the key to understanding all the problems in biology we had found intractable—it was the birth of molecular biology'.[128] In 1960, Brenner decided to try and directly investigate the nature of the RNA intermediary with Matthew Meselson, whom we've already mentioned, and French geneticist Francois Jacob, whom we'll mention again shortly.[129] Brenner was intrigued by a report he had read of a study published in 1956, which showed that, at the height of a bacteriophage infection, there was a transient increase in an RNA with the same proportion of bases as the viral DNA. He suddenly realized that the transient RNA intermediary might reveal itself much more visibly during a bacteriophage infection because of the way the virus took over the workings of the cell.

To test this idea, Brenner, Meselson, and Jacob, at Meselson's laboratory at the California Institute of Technology, Pasadena, infected bacteria with the virus and, at the same time, added radioactively labelled phosphate to the media that bathed them.[130] The idea was to use the same density centrifugation method Meselson and Stahl had used to study DNA replication to identify the elusive messenger. But the ribosomes kept falling apart in the centrifuge, and for weeks it proved impossible to get things to work as planned. The frustration was, however,

tempered by frequent trips to the beach, during which play was combined with intense discussions about how to overcome the block.[129] Finally, after trying a variety of conditions, the three experimenters detected a newly formed radioactive RNA associated with ribosomes, indicating it was linked to protein production. The intermediary had been found and was christened messenger RNA, or mRNA.[129]

These combined studies showed mRNA is produced in the nucleus as a single-stranded copy of the DNA code, with a distinct mRNA for each protein-coding gene. The tRNAs play a dual role, on the one hand bringing a specific amino acid to the ribosome, on the other recognizing the sequence of bases that specifies that amino acid in the RNA (and DNA) code (see Figure 6). The puzzle was almost complete; it only required the code to be cracked. Gamow had suggested a triplet code but did this match reality? In 1961, an ingenious approach was devised by Crick and Brenner to test this idea. Using chemicals to mutate DNA, they found they could insert or remove bases in phage DNA.[131] If they removed or added one or two bases the effects upon the virus were catastrophic; however, if three were

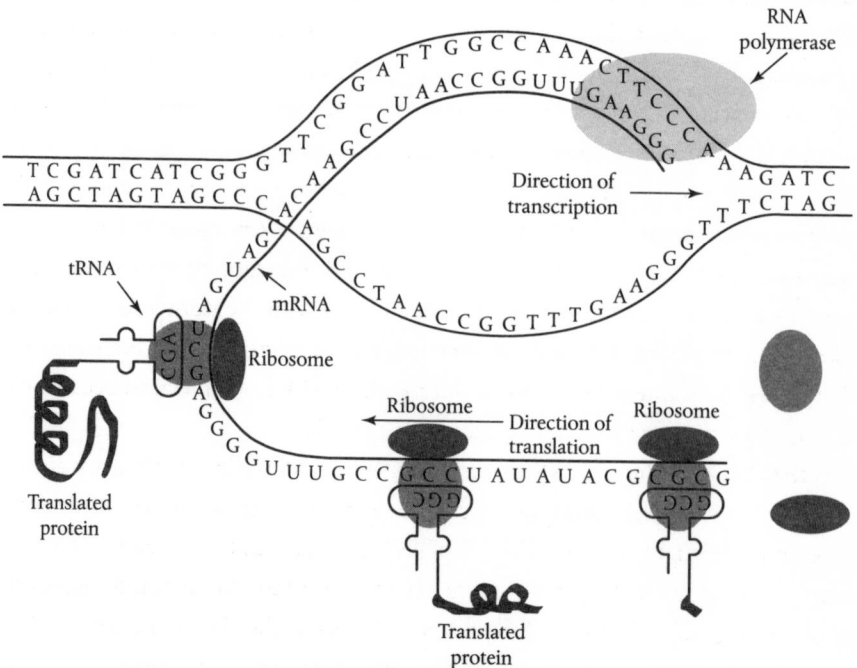

Figure 6. The linked processes of transcription and translation in bacteria

removed or added, there was little effect. This suggested each amino acid was coded by a triplet of bases, since adding or removing one or two bases caused a 'frameshift' in a three-letter word code, scrambling the meaning of the code beyond the mutation. In contrast, adding or removing three bases only altered a single amino acid. This still left the crucial issue of which triplets coded for which amino acid. This problem was solved by Marshall Nirenberg and his assistant Johann Matthaei at the National Institutes of Health in Maryland, who showed that an artificial RNA consisting of multiple U bases generated a protein consisting solely of phenylalanine, implying that UUU specified this amino acid.[132] Similar studies identified every other triplet sequences, or codons, that specify the twenty different amino acids, as well as where the protein starts and stops (see Figure 7). Nirenberg received a Nobel Prize for his discovery in 1973.

These findings showed Gamow was right to propose a triplet code but wrong to suggest it overlapped. Moreover, each amino acid could be specified by more than one triplet, making it a redundant code. The discovery of the genetic code signalled the primacy of the new discipline of molecular biology. Central to this was Crick's claim that life is a one-way flow of information from DNA to RNA to

Second letter

First letter		U	C	A	G	Third letter
U	U	UUU UUC } Phe UUA UUG } Leu	UCU UCC UCA UCG } Ser	UAU UAC } Tyr **UAA Stop** **UAG Stop**	UGU UGC } Cys **UGA Stop** UGG Trp	U C A G
	C	CUU CUC CUA CUG } Leu	CCU CCC CCA CCG } Pro	CAU CAC } His CAA CAG } Gln	CGU CGC CGA CGG } Arg	U C A G
	A	AUU AUC AUA } Ile **AUG Met**	ACU ACC ACA ACG } Thr	AAU AAC } Asn AAA AAG } Lys	AGU AGC } Ser AGA AGG } Arg	U C A G
	G	GUU GUC GUA GUG } Val	GCU GCC GCA GCG } Ala	GAU GAC } Asp GAA GAG } Glu	GGU GGC GGA GGG } Gly	U C A G

Figure 7. The triplet genetic code

protein—the 'central dogma of molecular biology'. He later claimed not to have realized 'dogma' meant a belief that cannot be doubted, and to have really meant a 'grand hypothesis'.[133] In fact, in his future theorizing Crick often proved far from dogmatic, but rather someone who, when solving scientific problems, learned 'how not to be confused by the details and that is a sort of boldness, and how to make oversimplifying hypotheses—and how to test them, and how to discard them without getting too enamoured of them'.[134]

There was undoubtedly a boldness in Crick's claim for the primacy of DNA, since the central dogma was centrally aimed at the biochemists who had dominated cell biology for over a hundred years. Such scientists saw the cell as a network of interacting chemical reactions, 'a subtle flux of materials and energy', all of it regulated by those ubiquitous proteins. However, they failed to explain how this related to the genetic material; therefore, what better way to distinguish molecular biology from biochemistry, than by asserting that however varied and complicated the actions of proteins are within the cell, ultimately they are merely slaves of the DNA code? Watson and Crick, and the scientists who flocked to their banner after the discovery of the double helix, saw this as a necessary step to undermine the old order that, in their view, blocked the path to a proper understanding of how life works. And in many respects they were right. However, from the outset there were some fundamental flaws in this new way of looking at life.

The view of life as the unravelling of a digital code has been expressed most forcibly by Sydney Brenner: 'If you say to me here is a hand, here is an eye, how do you make a hand or an eye, then I must say that it is necessary to know the programme; to know it in machine language which is molecular language; to know it so that one can tell a computer to generate a set of procedures for growing a hand, or an eye.'[135] Yet how true is the proposal that information only flows in a one-way direction from DNA to RNA to proteins? A lot depends on the definition of information. The proposal that DNA fulfils its role as the hereditary molecule by acting as a linear code, now led to it being compared to the blueprint of a building or machine. But even a blueprint must be read by an architect or engineer, so what was the equivalent for DNA? In fact, we now recognize that the cellular environment in which the DNA resides is crucial to unlocking its potential; and just how important this environment is, was shown by a startling discovery made by John Gurdon at Oxford University in 1962, just as the genetic code was being deciphered.

Gurdon serves as an example that future scientific success cannot always be gauged from school results, since he came last in biology out of the 250 boys in his year group at Eton College. As such, his teacher's assessment that 'he has ideas about becoming a scientist; on his present showing this is quite ridiculous' was harsh but at least appeared to have a factual basis.[136] Condemned this way, Gurdon reluctantly applied to do Classics at Oxford; however, at the last minute he was allowed to change to zoology, although only because a mistake had been made filling places in this subject and additional students were needed to fill the gap. Yet despite his teacher's criticisms Gurdon displayed an aptitude for experiments that led to him being offered a PhD project by Oxford biologist Michael Fischberg.[137]

Gurdon's somewhat ambitious project was to explore how DNA information in the nucleus of a fertilized egg can give rise to the multitude of distinctive cell types in an adult, this process being known as differentiation. As early as 1893, the German scientist August Weismann, most famously known for his distinction between the sex cells—sperm and eggs—and the remaining 'somatic' cells that populate the different organs and tissues of the body, had proposed that as embryonic cells differentiate into specialized cell types like nerve, muscle, heart, or liver, their hereditary material is progressively cast off or permanently inactivated, so that they become incapable of specifying anything other than that particular cell type.[138] Such was the dogma, but Gurdon decided to test whether differentiation was really irreversible by taking a nucleus from a differentiated frog cell, and seeing what happened when this was transplanted into an egg with its own nucleus removed. In fact, Robert Briggs and Thomas King of the Institute for Cancer Research, Philadelphia, had already shown that a nucleus from an early frog embryo—a blastula—triggered development when transplanted into an egg.[137] However, they had not tested the potential of nuclei from later stages of development when Gurdon began his experiments. Remarkably, Gurdon found that even nuclei from fully differentiated frog cells were capable of beginning embryo development anew, and generating a whole new fertile male or female frog.

This finding went so much against accepted dogma that, according to Gurdon, 'it took nearly 10 years for the major result to be accepted'.[139] Moreover, in an extension of their earlier experiments, Briggs and King subsequently failed to achieve successful development with nuclei from any later stage of development than the blastula. As Gurdon himself later acknowledged, it was therefore 'entirely reasonable for the sceptics to say, well these well-established people have already

done this experiment and here's a graduate student from Europe who is disagree-ing with them, why should we pay attention to that?'[139] Acceptance finally came, however, and Gurdon's demonstration that the cloning of adult animals was possible would eventually culminate in the cloning of Dolly the sheep by Ian Wilmut and Keith Campbell of the Roslin Institute, Edinburgh. This discovery would have to wait another thirty years due to greater difficulties in 'reprogram-ming' the nucleus of a differentiated mammalian cell compared to that of a frog, but this, and the demonstration by Shinya Yamanaka of Kyoto University that ordinary skin cells could be reprogrammed simply by changing the cellular environment, led to the eventual belated award of a Nobel Prize to Gurdon, together with Yamanaka, in 2012. Importantly, Gurdon's findings had shown, for the first time, that the passive potential of a genome to hold information can be distinguished from the active ability of that information to code for life's processes. And how this activation of the genome's potential is accomplished is the question to which we will turn in Chapter 3.

3

SWITCHES AND SIGNALS

'Scientific advances often come from uncovering a hitherto unseen aspect of things as a result, not so much of using new instruments, but rather of looking at objects from a different angle.' *Francois Jacob*

'In science, self-satisfaction is death. It is the restlessness, anxiety, dissatisfaction, agony of mind that nourishes science.' *Jacques Monod*

In science, as in life, sometimes it's the little things that count. Whether it be the apocryphal apple that landed on Newton's head and started him thinking about the laws of gravity, or the bread mould that blocked bacterial growth and led to Fleming's discovery of penicillin, apparently simple starting points can lead to the most profound scientific conclusions. One phenomenon initially deemed uninteresting but which turned out to be key to how the potential of the genome is unlocked, is how bacteria grow in a broth containing two different sugars—glucose and lactose. Rather than growing and dividing in a continuous manner, the bacteria grow rapidly initially but then their growth stalls briefly, after which they embark upon another burst of growth and division before this too comes to an end. This feature of bacterial growth was first noticed by Jacques Monod, a PhD student at the Sorbonne University in Paris, in 1941.[140] Monod was a late starter to a scientific career, being one of those infuriating individuals who excel in everything they do to such an extent that they find it difficult to make a choice. So his skills at music, as well as science, had his family seriously debating whether 'Jacques is going to be a new Pasteur, or a new Beethoven?'[141] Having finally decided to follow the scientific route, Monod's quest to explain the bacterial phenomenon he called 'diauxy', from the Greek for two growth phases, would occupy the rest of his career and eventually lead to a model of how genes are

switched on or off that is broadly applicable to our own genomes. Yet, initially, Monod's studies were viewed as unimportant by other academics, with the head of his own laboratory confiding to one of his PhD examiners that 'Monod's work is of no interest to the Sorbonne'.[142]

However, Monod was not a person easily deterred by adverse circumstances. In occupied France, one could accept the Nazi presence, or fight it. Monod chose the latter route, despite being heavily involved in searching for a scientific explanation for the biological phenomenon he had discovered. Joining the French Resistance in 1942, a year later he became its Chief of Staff, the three previous occupiers of this post having disappeared without trace into the hands of the Gestapo.[143] Yet Monod did not suffer this fate—despite having to go underground at one point after individuals in his resistance 'cell' were captured—and he distinguished himself on multiple occasions in the fight against the Nazis. It was Monod who arranged parachute drops of weapons, railway and bridge bombings, and mail interceptions in preparation for the Allied invasion of France, and he also drafted the appeal to Parisian citizens to mount the barricades before the arrival of Allied forces into the city in 1944. Despite his military exploits, Monod somehow managed to continue with his studies; indeed, at times the two coincided, as when he hid vital resistance documents in the hollow leg bones of a giraffe skeleton outside his laboratory, this being one of the zoological specimens on display in the department.[144]

Still seeking to explain the two phases of bacterial growth he had observed, Monod speculated that this represented a switch from the metabolism of glucose to that of lactose. Somehow glucose must suppress the metabolism of the other sugar, but how remained a mystery. Monod's initial suggestion was that there must be some change in the conformations of the catalytic proteins—also known as enzymes—that carried out the metabolism of the two sugars. But another possibility presented itself in 1944 when he read an article in the travelling US army library which he had access to through his contacts with American soldiers, about Avery's discovery of the link between DNA and inheritance.[145] Could it be that the switch was due not to a change in the enzyme that metabolized lactose, but activation of the gene that coded for the enzyme, with the latter only being produced following such gene activation? If so, studying the switch might lead to important insights into how genes were switched on and off. Confirmation that the lactose metabolizing enzyme was being newly synthesized came when

Monod, now working at the Pasteur Institute in Paris, produced an antibody that detected the protein. This showed that the enzyme—now termed beta-galactosidase, or beta-gal for short—was only generated once all the glucose had been used up.[140] Somehow, this loss must send a signal to the cell that activated the gene coding for beta-gal. But could such a process be studied? Monod realized he needed to move from biochemistry to genetics. Luckily, he was now coming into contact with scientists who could help him make this transition.

In particular, a young Jewish scientist called Francois Jacob began working with Monod. Jacob had also played a heroic role fighting the Nazis, working first for the resistance and then participating in the D-Day landings.[146] Indeed, he was almost killed during the latter action after being hit by over a hundred pieces of shrapnel from a German air bomb; these permanently damaged his right side, including his hand, and put an end to his dream of becoming a surgeon. But medicine's loss was science's gain, for after the war Jacob began to forge a talented career as a geneticist. By the time he began working with Monod, he had already acquired great skill, not only in creating bacterial mutants but also in carrying out genetic crosses that previously had only been thought possible with multicellular organisms like fruitflies and mice. He did this by making use of the phenomenon of bacterial sex first identified by Griffith. In addition, Jacob proved an ideal partner in more than technical skills. According to Monod, Jacob was 'much more intuitive than I am; and I'm more of a strict logician than he is'.[147] In this sense, the combination of two quite different temperaments proved a potent mixture, just as had been the case for Watson and Crick, which shows that such partnerships can be as valuable in science as in music, with its Lennon and McCartney, or Jagger and Richards.

Isolation of mutants defective in the metabolism of lactose and the use of bacterial sex to carry out genetic crosses allowed Jacob and Monod to establish functional relationships between the different genes regulating the metabolism of this sugar. Importantly, they established a distinction between 'structural' genes—those coding for the enzymes that carried out the metabolism of lactose—and the 'regulatory' genes that coded for proteins which acted as switches to turn the structural genes on or off.[140] Another important discovery was that the beta-gal gene is switched on simultaneously with two others coding for proteins involved in lactose utilization. This co-regulation of proteins involved in the same metabolic process would turn out to be true of other bacterial genes. The unit of

clustered lactose-metabolizing genes was christened the 'lac operon', and the term operon was soon used to define all clusters of co-regulated genes with a common function.[140]

A key moment in identifying how the lac operon was regulated was Jacob and Monod's isolation of a mutant whose lactose-metabolizing genes were always turned on, even in the absence of lactose. This suggested a defect in a protein that normally bound at the start of the lac operon and prevented it being turned on, or expressed. However, in the presence of lactose the protein lost its attachment and this allowed expression. This protein became known as the 'lac repressor', and established the idea that proteins could regulate the expression of genes.[140] Undoubtedly, the most unexpected aspect of the discovery was the demonstration that the interaction between the repressor and the gene it controlled was so direct. Jacob and Monod had assumed that the repression acted in some general fashion on the protein synthesis machinery. That this was not the case was truly exciting because, until then, as Monod put it, 'the gene was something in the minds of people—especially of my generation—which was as inaccessible, by definition, as the material of the galaxies'.[148] His and Jacob's demonstration that the gene was a tangible entity that could be turned on and off like a light switch was therefore a major revelation, and resulted in a Nobel Prize for both men in 1965.

This type of regulation was termed 'negative' because it involves the lifting of repression by an inhibitory protein that normally blocks gene expression. Excitingly, it also helped explain why, in certain cases of infection of bacteria by bacteriophages, the virus remained dormant, or 'lysogenic', until a stimulus, such as UV light, triggered expression of its genes. As Jacob put it, 'the analogy between [lactose repression] and immunity of lysogenic cells is such that we can hardly escape the assumption that immunity also corresponds to the presence of a repressor in the cytoplasm of lysogenic cells'.[149] Subsequent studies showed this was the case, with UV light triggering destruction of this repressor. Ironically, this phenomenon had been studied by André Lwoff, head of the Pasteur Institute, for some years.[150] So the two adjoining laboratories had essentially been studying the same molecular process without knowing it! Lwoff shared the Nobel Prize with Jacob and Monod for this discovery.

But was negative regulation sufficient to account for all instances of control of gene expression? Certainly Jacob and Monod thought so, but in the mid-1960s Ellis Englesberg and colleagues at the University of California, studying an operon

controlling metabolism of a different sugar, arabinose, presented evidence that positive regulation played an equally important role.[151] Despite this claim being based upon sound experimental data, it was initially dismissed by Monod, and for years Englesberg had trouble publishing his findings.[152] Yet Monod ought to have welcomed other forms of gene regulation, because one aspect of the phenomenon that had originally stimulated his interest remained a mystery. So although the discovery of the lac repressor explained why lactose stimulated expression of the lac operon, it left it unclear why, in a mixture of glucose and lactose, this expression only kicked off when all the glucose had been used up.[140] This dominance of glucose over lactose was named the 'glucose effect', but the model of gene regulation based solely upon the lac repressor provided no explanation for why such an effect should occur.

However, in 1965, a biochemist called Earl Sutherland showed that levels of a chemical called cyclic AMP, or cAMP, increase when glucose levels are low. We shall hear more about Sutherland and cAMP shortly, but for now it's enough to note that his finding excited the interest of two scientists studying the lac operon—Ira Pastan at the National Institutes of Health in Washington, and Agnes Ullmann, who worked at the Pasteur Institute alongside Jacob and Monod—who both immediately recognized it as a possible explanation for the glucose effect. Ullmann owed Monod a huge personal debt, for in 1960 he helped smuggle her out of her native Hungary where she was a dissident against the Stalinist regime and under threat of imprisonment after her role in the failed 1956 revolution.[153] Although Monod had been a member of the French Communist Party during the war, his later hatred of what he saw as the 'ideological terrorism' of Stalinism meant that he was willing to help. Using expertise learned in the French Resistance, Monod smuggled Ullmann and her husband across the tightly controlled Hungarian border and into Austria, hidden underneath a bathtub in a compartment of a pull-along camping trailer.[153] Now, however, she was about to challenge his view that negative regulation was the only mechanism controlling gene expression.

Independently, Pastan and Ullmann tested whether increasing cAMP levels artificially in bacteria in a mixture of glucose and lactose could activate the lac operon, and found that indeed it did.[154] This finding suggested that cAMP must work through an as yet unidentified regulatory protein. The search for this protein, by both Pastan and Jonathan Beckwith of Harvard University, eventually

culminated in the discovery of what became known as the cAMP activator protein, or CAP.[154] Further studies showed that CAP was a positive regulator of exactly the type that Englesberg had proposed. Now, belatedly, the significance of his findings was recognized, and here, finally, was an explanation for Monod's original observation. In the presence of both sugars, initially only glucose is metabolized because its presence inhibits the activation of the CAP protein and therefore expression of the lac operon. But once the glucose is used up, the CAP protein is activated and the presence of lactose means the repressor does not inhibit expression of the lac operon (see Figure 8).[154]

So Monod's initial observation of a quirky feature of bacterial growth had led to the establishment of the fundamental principles by which gene expression in bacteria is regulated. Ironically, he was now offered the Chair of Biochemistry at the Sorbonne, the institution which had previously judged his studies as being 'of no interest'.[155] In fact, Jacob and Monod's discovery went even further than the recognition of how genes are turned on or off, for during his studies Monod stumbled upon another key biological process that would turn out to be central to

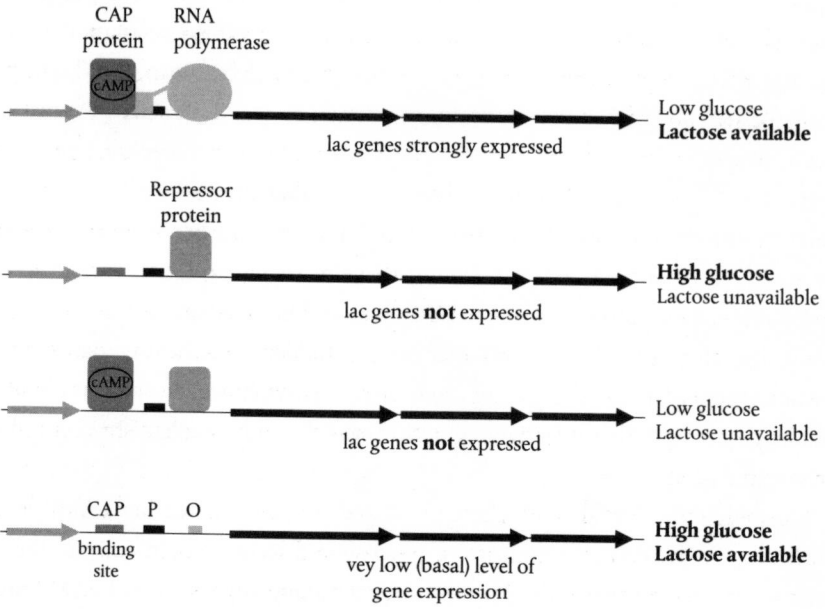

Figure 8. The lac operon showing negative and positive mechanisms of control of gene expression

how enzymes, and indeed proteins in general, respond to changes in their environment. What he had recognized was, that for lactose to exert its effects upon the lac repressor so rapidly, it must physically interact with the protein somehow. Moreover, cAMP must interact with the CAP protein in a similar fashion. Recognizing the importance of the discovery, Monod announced to a startled Agnes Ullmann that he had discovered 'the second secret of life'. Later Ullmann recalled that 'I was quite alarmed by this unexpected revelation and asked him if he needed a glass of whisky. After the second or maybe the third glass, he explained the discovery, which he had already given a name: "allostery".'[156]

Allosteric regulators act on enzymes at a site distinct from their catalytic centre. Instead, they influence their target's activity by altering its 3D structure, a 'conformational change' that alters the shape of the catalytic centre by action at a distance (see Figure 9). Just as allosteric regulation of metabolism is as important for our own cells as for bacteria, so the studies of gene regulation in bacteria pioneered by Jacob and Monod have proven highly relevant for complex

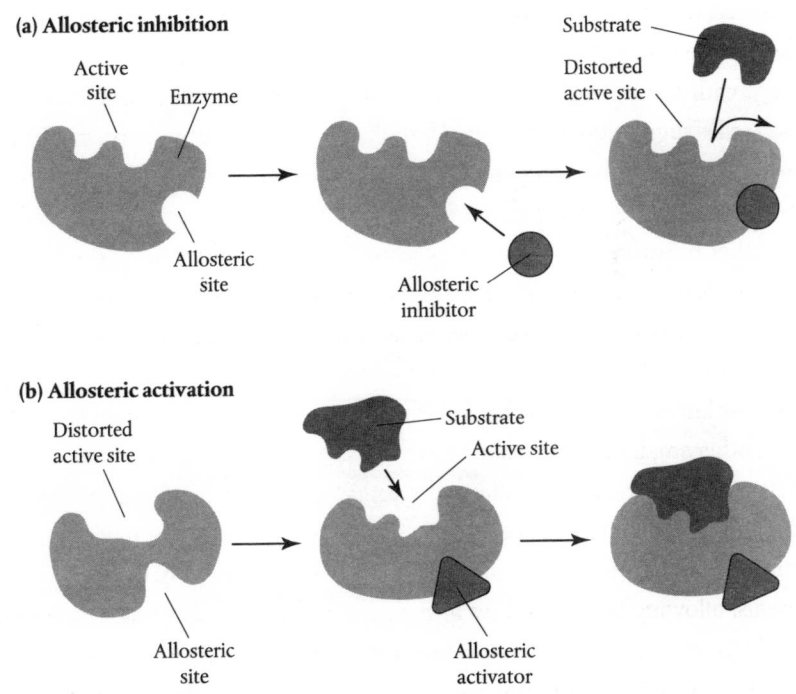

Figure 9. Allosteric control of enzyme activity

multicellular organisms, including our own species, albeit with some interesting twists. So cAMP also positively regulates gene expression in human cells; indeed, the connection between cAMP and the lac operon was merely further evidence of the importance of a signalling molecule originally discovered through a completely separate route, in mammalian liver.

We have already mentioned Earl Sutherland in passing, but his main contribution to science was the discovery of what have become known as 'second messengers', cAMP being just the first of these. Based at Western Reserve University in Cleveland, Ohio, Sutherland identified cAMP as the culmination of his quest to understand how the hormone adrenaline liberates glucose in the liver by stimulating the breakdown of glycogen, a polymerized form of this sugar molecule.[157] The importance of this carbohydrate store for everyday life is demonstrated by genetic diseases called glycogen storage disorders.[158] That sufferers will die unless fed a continual supply of glucose day and night shows how much we rely on our glycogen stores for normal existence. But until Sutherland's discovery, how signals outside the liver cell triggered changes inside it remained a mystery. He showed that cAMP was produced when adrenaline binds to proteins on the surface of the cell. Sutherland described the molecule as a second messenger by analogy with the hormone's role as the first messenger to the cell.[157] Initially, Sutherland's suggestion that a single molecule led to the numerous effects of adrenaline was met by disbelief. However, not only was he correct about the central role of cAMP in adrenaline's action, but subsequent studies showed that many other hormones stimulate its production. In addition, the idea of a second messenger turned out to have general relevance as other substances were shown to play similar roles in the cell. Sutherland was awarded a Nobel Prize for his discovery in 1971.[157]

We now know that many other substances can act as second messengers. These include other small molecules like cGMP, but also a charged atom or ion, calcium, and even a gas, nitric oxide. Indeed, the drug Viagra®, which became one of the best-selling drugs of all time because of its usefulness in treating impotence, works by stimulating the production of nitric oxide, which relaxes the blood vessels of the penis, allowing blood to flow into this organ, and thereby causing an erection.[159] Viagra® was originally developed as a treatment for angina—chest pains caused by restrictions in blood supply to the heart—but during initial clinical trials on healthy volunteers its ability to cause erections was noted, no doubt

accompanied by reactions ranging from alarm to delight in those being tested. At first, there was scepticism about the potency of the drug among clinicians, which was famously overcome by Dr Giles Brindley at the American Urological Society meeting in Las Vegas in 1983, when he injected some of the drug just before he was due to give his talk, and 'over the course of his lecture demonstrated to his audience visible evidence that such an injection could induce an erection'.[160] Subsequently, Viagra® was developed in a form to be taken orally, greatly aiding its appeal as a drug not only for treating impotence but also for more recreational use. Ironically, there are now concerns that inappropriate overuse of the drug could itself lead to permanent impotence.

Second messengers act as a relay system passing on signals from the cell surface to target proteins inside the cell. A particularly important set of target proteins activated by second messengers are called kinases; these enzymes add a phosphate group to other proteins and thereby alter their properties.[161] Protein kinase A, or PKA, is activated by cAMP. We've already seen how, in bacteria, cAMP directly binds to the CAP protein to positively switch on the lac operon. A similar positive role is played in human cells by the cAMP regulatory element binding protein, or CREB.[162] However, rather than being directly activated by cAMP, CREB is instead phosphorylated by PKA after the latter has been activated by the second messenger (see Figure 10). This indirect method of control of gene expression has the advantage of being more finely tuneable than in bacteria. This extra level of complexity almost certainly reflects the more complex nature of the signals controlling cellular processes in multicellular organisms like ourselves, where the cell not only responds to signals from the external environment but also from other cells within the body.

Just how complex a role gene regulatory proteins, also known as 'transcription factors', can play in multicellular organisms, was shown by recent studies that investigated the role of blood chemicals in the ageing process by the gruesome method of surgically attaching two mice together, one old, the other much younger, so they shared the same blood circulation system.[163] This approach was used in parallel with the more conventional method of giving blood transfusions from young to old mice. In both cases, the blood reversed age-related declines in memory and learning. After the treatment mice that were 18 months old, the equivalent of 70 years in a human, had acquired the enhanced learning abilities of a mouse that was only a few months old.[163] Saul Villeda of the

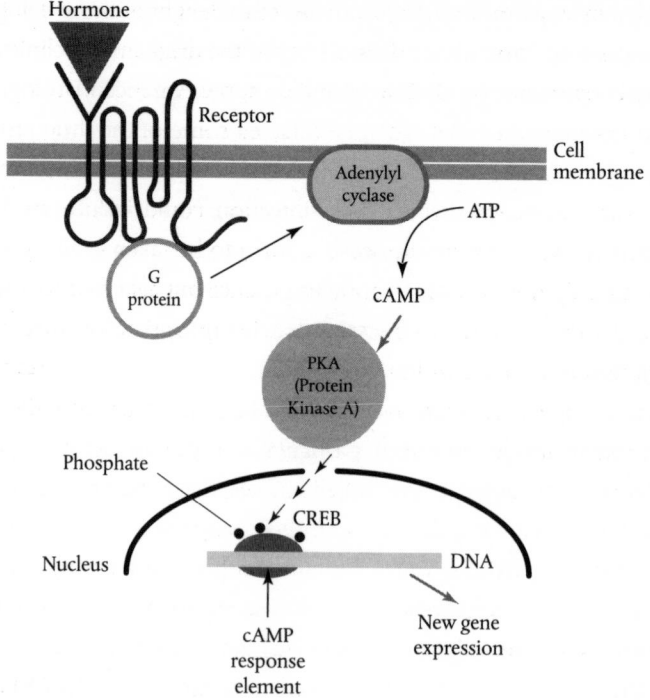

Figure 10. The cAMP signalling pathway leading to gene expression

University of California, who led the study, believes this shows 'there's something about young blood that can literally reverse the impairments you see in the older brain'.[164] Remarkably, these changes are primarily due to reactivation of CREB in a brain region called the hippocampus, that plays a central role in learning and memory, with the reactivated CREB turning on genes that regulate connections between nerve cells. This effect of young blood was traced to a protein called GDF11.[163] Before we get too excited about the possibilities for ageing humans, and whether Count Dracula was on to something after all (though presumably he would have needed to inject his victims' blood rather than drink it), it remains to be seen whether this kind of approach could be used in our own species. As Villeda said, 'I wish our manuscript could come with a big caption that says "Do not try this at home". We need a clinical trial to see if this applies to humans, and to see if there are effects that we don't want.'[164] In fact, GDF11 is currently being tested in clinical trials in aged humans. Whatever the outcome as an anti-ageing

treatment, here is a clear example of a transcription factor involved in a complex bodily process being influenced by signals from the rest of the body. But this raises another important question—how exactly do proteins like CAP and CREB exert their effects upon genes?

Remarkably, pioneers like Jacob and Monod worked out the basic roles of such proteins as the lac repressor and CAP without any knowledge of how these proteins physically interact with genes.[140] But as the 1960s drew to a close and flower power and the Beatles' psychedelic phase were succeeded by protests against the war in Vietnam and the violent assassinations of Malcolm X, Martin Luther King, and Bobby Kennedy, a new generation of scientists had decided the way forward lay in finding ways to directly isolate such transcription factors and characterize them. In fact, the struggles on the street and in the lab were not always so distant, as shown when Jonathan Beckwith, already mentioned as the co-discoverer of the CAP protein, in 1969 found a way to cut out the DNA composing the lac operon, and thus became the first person to physically isolate a gene.[165] For this breakthrough Beckwith was awarded the Eli Lilly Award in Microbiology, but in the spirit of the time he gave the $1,000 prize money to the radical Black Panther Party.[166] He also voiced publicly his concerns that such 'genetic engineering' might have a more sinister side, either in the creation of new, deadly pathogens, or as a tool of a repressive state. However, while there were many similar arguments in the first years of the molecular biology revolution, they did nothing to stop the growth of what was becoming a technological juggernaut. For new techniques were making it possible to do things Watson and Crick could only have dreamed about in 1953.

Two young scientists who decided to isolate and characterize a transcription factor for the first time were Walter Gilbert and Mark Ptashne, both junior members of the same department at Harvard University, where Watson had taken up a professorship after the discovery of the double helix. Watson once said one recipe for successful science was to 'take young researchers, put them together in virtual seclusion, give them an unprecedented degree of freedom and turn up the pressure by fostering competitiveness'.[167] This was precisely the situation that developed in his own department when Gilbert and Ptashne decided to independently isolate a transcription factor. While nominally working towards quite separate goals—Gilbert focused on the lac repressor, while Ptashne tackled the repressor in phage—the situation rapidly turned into a race to see who could

get to his goal first. At the time, Ptashne was heavily involved in the movement against the Vietnam War and even took part in a lecture tour of North Vietnam, in which he talked both about his scientific work and political activities even while the bombs were falling on the country. Horace Judson, who interviewed him at this time, noted his 'aviator-style spectacles, T-shirt, sawed-off blue-denim shorts, and sandals—more exposed skin than appeared prudent in a laboratory'.[168] But it was Ptashne's comment that 'people who claimed to be trying to isolate the repressor...weren't really willing to take the kind of risks that were necessary... *psychic* risks', that best gives a flavour of the highly-charged atmosphere in many molecular biology labs at this time. Meanwhile, for Gilbert, the repressor had become 'a holy grail...like isolating the neutrino...those of us who were involved in the isolation, of course, believed in its existence in a way other people did not'.[169]

Perhaps it was not so surprising that sheer force of will and an almost mystical faith in the likelihood of success were seen as necessary attributes for isolating a transcription factor, given that Monod's own calculations had indicated there were probably only seven or eight molecules of the lac repressor in a bacterial cell, or less than two thousandths of 1 per cent of the cell's protein.[169] Over the next few years, both Ptashne and Gilbert tried different biochemical strategies, use of radioactive labelling, and comparison of the properties of normal versus mutant bacteria, that led frustratingly close to their goals but then saw it vanish in a puff of smoke. And in the testosterone-fuelled environment of the Harvard department, both individuals knew that one's success would be viewed as the other's failure. Thankfully, both Ptashne and Gilbert finally achieved their goals of isolating their respective repressor proteins in publications that appeared almost simultaneously.[170] Success had come to both researchers without a resulting nervous breakdown, although the experience led Watson, qualifying his earlier remark about competiveness, to reflect that 'it is better that one's competitors be in a different city, if not country. Having them in the same building is a small model of hell.'[171] Most importantly, isolation of these transcription factors opened the way to that of other gene regulatory proteins, and made it possible to properly investigate the specific ways in which these proteins influence gene activity. In particular, such studies showed that transcription factors have a specific affinity for particular DNA sequences at the start of the gene they control, and illuminated the way they influence gene expression.

As we've seen, a key aspect of understanding how DNA functions as the hereditary molecule was the realization that its four different bases act as letters in a linear code. According to this view, the different sizes and shapes of the four bases are irrelevant. But when it comes to transcription factors, these differences become very important, since, as complex 3D structures themselves, proteins can only interact with other molecules through such properties of size and shape. To do so, transcription factors bind in the grooves of the DNA double helix where they can recognize a specific sequence by the differences in the shapes of the bases. Indeed, recent advances in X-ray diffraction have made it possible to identify the precise molecular interactions between transcription factors and their DNA target at a detailed level of structure.[172] But how does the binding of such factors determine whether a gene is turned on or off?

We've seen how mRNA is produced by RNA polymerase. However, on its own the polymerase is inactive and needs contact with proteins like CAP or CREB to activate it. By binding to DNA sequences at the start of a gene, such proteins are brought into close proximity to RNA polymerase, and this contact is sufficient to activate the polymerase. That transcription factors are themselves regulated by intracellular signals explains how information from the environment can influence gene action. This is one reason why, despite different cell types containing the same genomes, the proteins produced in such cells are very different. So heart cells typically contain proteins that regulate their contraction, while liver cells contain those involved in the metabolism of foodstuffs. The proteins produced in such different cell types differ partly because the cells contain different transcription factors, but also because of different incoming signals relayed by second messengers.

We can see now why such an enormous change took place when a differentiated cell nucleus was transplanted in an egg with its own nucleus removed, as happened during cloning of Gurdon's frogs, or Dolly the sheep. While an udder cell only contains the transcription factors needed to switch on genes involved in breast cell functions, like those involved in producing milk, in the egg a transplanted nucleus is exposed to quite different factors, those geared towards allowing the combined sperm and egg genomes to produce all the proteins required to make a whole new organism.[173] This is not all that needs to change in the transplanted nucleus, however, for another important difference between bacteria and multicellular organisms is that our DNA also comes wrapped in proteins that regulate accessibility of genes to transcription factors.

As we've seen in Chapter 2, in the late nineteenth century Friedrich Miescher and Walther Flemming showed that DNA in chromosomes is associated with proteins. Flemming gave the name chromatin to this combination of chromo-somal DNA and proteins.[174] In 1884 Albrecht Kossel, who had studied alongside Miescher, showed that the main protein component of chromatin was a single type of protein, which he called histone.[174] Kossel also showed that histone was a positively charged, basic protein, explaining its affinity for negatively charged, acidic DNA. We've seen that one reason it took so long for DNA to be accepted as the molecule of inheritance was its supposedly boring structure, which was revealed when Kossel identified the four nucleotide bases in DNA and RNA.[174] Instead, it seemed more likely that histone would somehow specify the genetic information; however, with the recognition of the importance of DNA in the 1950s, interest in histones slipped away. Ironically, it was the protein in chroma-tin, not the DNA, that was now seen as boring.

Such a view did not really change until the 1970s, when scientists began to scrutinize chromatin structure in much greater detail. In 1974, Donald and Ada Olins of the University of Tennessee studied chromatin under the electron microscope (the only microscope with sufficient resolution to visualize DNA directly because electrons have a much shorter wavelength than visible light) and made an exciting discovery.[175] We've seen how one view of genes is that they are analogous to beads on a string. But now the Olins saw that chromatin really did look like a string of beads; albeit with each bead covering a far smaller portion of DNA than a gene. Further studies by Roger Kornberg showed that the 'beads' were in fact an octamer of four pairs of different histone subtypes—H2A, H2B, H3, and H4—around which a segment of DNA coils to form what Kornberg called a 'nucleosome' (see Figure 11). Kornberg was the eldest son of Arthur Kornberg—the discoverer of DNA polymerase—and he made his own important discovery while working as a young postdoctoral scientist with Aaron Klug and his colleagues at the Laboratory of Molecular Biology in Cambridge. Klug had carried out his PhD with Rosalind Franklin at Birkbeck College, London, using X-ray diffraction to study the structure of viruses, a topic which Franklin had turned to following her work on DNA.[176] The expertise Klug gained at this time allowed him and his team to analyse the structure of the nucleosome in fine detail. These studies revealed that DNA is coiled just over two times around the histone octamer, while another histone, H1, remains outside this core and is only found in

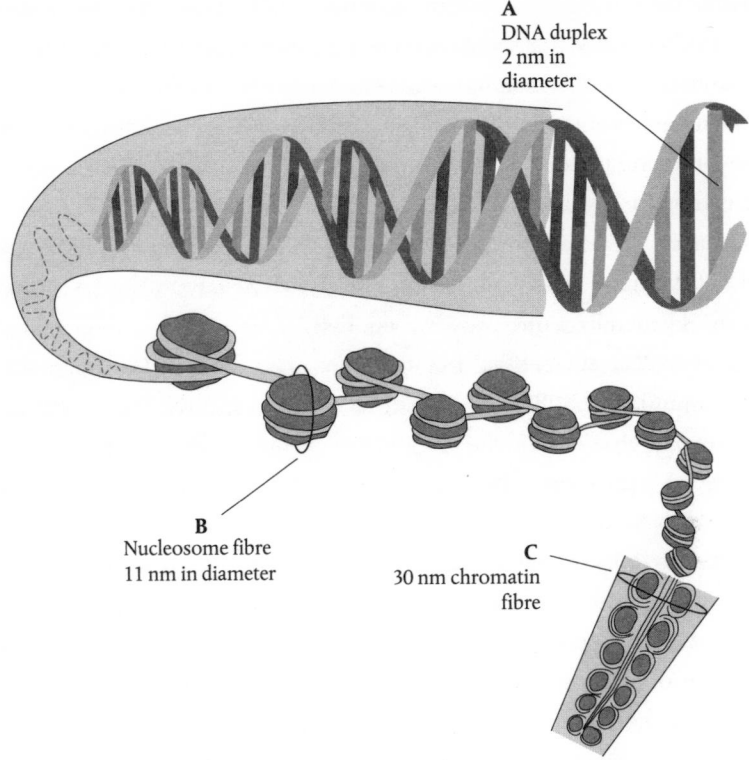

A
DNA duplex
2 nm in
diameter

B
Nucleosome fibre
11 nm in diameter

C
30 nm chromatin
fibre

Figure 11. Basic nucleosome structure of chromatin

particularly tightly packed DNA.[177] Klug's estimation of his work was that it was 'not necessarily glamorous, nor does it often produce immediate results, but it seeks to increase our basic understanding of living processes'.[178] Certainly, its significance was viewed as sufficiently important by the Nobel Prize committee, who awarded the prize to Klug in 1982. Kornberg would receive his own Nobel Prize in 2006 for working out the fine detail of the process of transcription in eukaryotes—species whose cells have a nucleus, which includes complex multi-cellular organisms like ourselves, but also the unicellular yeast.

Initially, histones were thought only important for packaging DNA into a manageable form in the nucleus. However, in the 1990s, Michael Grunstein at the University of California and David Allis at the Rockefeller University, New York, showed that addition of an acetyl group (chemical structure -COCH$_3$) to histones by the cellular machinery radically alters their interaction with DNA.[179]

Addition of the acetyl group loosens the histone–DNA association, while removal tightens it. Chemically, this makes sense, since the acetyl group removes a positive charge from the histone, making it less attractive to negatively charged DNA. And the enzymes—histone acetylases and deacetylases—that mediate these changes activate or repress gene expression respectively, by making DNA regulatory elements more or less accessible to transcription factors.[179]

Importantly, this discovery explained why the process of differentiation whereby 'totipotent' cells change into specialized cell types in a multicellular organism, is generally a one-way process. Only in exceptional circumstances, as during cloning, can such changes be reversed.[173] So the egg reprogrammes gene expression not only by providing a new set of transcription factors but also by making DNA control elements accessible to such factors. Despite these differences between gene expression in bacteria and multicellular organisms, one could still argue that they share much in common. So in both cases genes are switched on or off in response to incoming signals mediated by transcription factors that bind at the start of the genes they control. It was this that led Monod to claim 'what is true for E. coli is also true for the elephant'.[180] But as studies of gene regulation in multicellular organisms began to gather pace in the 1970s, other surprises were waiting on the horizon.

4

THE SPACIOUS GENOME

'It is a remarkable fact that the greater part (95 percent in the case of humans) of the genome might as well not be there, for all the difference it makes.'

Richard Dawkins

'Trying to read our DNA is like trying to understand software code—only with 90% of the code riddled with errors. It's very difficult in that case to understand and predict what that software code is going to do.' *Elon Musk*

The term 'survival of the fittest' generally conjures up images of lean, mean fighting machines, with lions, tigers, and great white sharks springing to mind. But really the only true measure of evolutionary success is an organism's ability to pass its genes on to the next generation. In this respect the humble bacterium is a clear winner. For bacteria have mastered the art of thriving in practically any environment on Earth, whether that be boiling hot springs in Yellowstone National Park, a dark and freezing lake deep under the Antarctic ice, or the confines of a human intestine.[181] Whether measured by cell number or sheer biomass, bacteria outperform every other life form on our planet. And a recent study that identified bacteria living happily a kilometre and a half below the Earth's crust shows the reach of these tiny organisms is even greater than suspected.[182] Such bacteria rely not on sunlight but on chemicals released by the rocks themselves. Bacteria have thrived over the three and a half billion years they have existed upon the planet, partly because of their small size and relative simplicity, which allows rapid reproduction and evolution, but also due to an ability to focus on one or a few sources of energy and exploit them as ruthlessly as possible.[181]

Bacterial genomes are admirably suited to this goal. The study of the lac operon showed that its genes are not only switched on simultaneously but transcribed

into a single mRNA molecule.[183] Subsequent studies showed that other bacterial genes with a similar function are linked in this way. An initial assumption was that a similar situation would exist in multicellular organisms, including humans. But as such genes were further investigated it became clear that they were transcribed into RNA as single, not multiple, entities. In addition, these genes were not adjacent; indeed, they were often located on completely different chromosomes. In other respects, though, gene regulation in bacteria and multicellular organisms seemed initially very similar. Jacob and Monod gave the name 'promoter' to the region where RNA polymerase but also transcription factors like CAP bind, and as researchers began studying gene regulation in multicellular organisms they found a similar arrangement of transcription factor binding sites at the start of genes. However, it soon became clear that such short-range influences were only part of the story. In particular, gene regulatory regions named 'enhancers', due to their potency in boosting gene expression, seemed unlike anything identified in bacteria.

Enhancers were first identified independently by Pierre Chambon at Strasbourg University and George Khoury at the US National Cancer Institute. Both scientists were studying animal viruses in the 1970s, because a popular idea at the time was that viruses were a primary cause of cancer. Remarkably, the link between viruses and cancer was identified over a hundred years ago, in 1911, by Peyton Rous, a pathologist at the Rockefeller University, New York.[184] Investigating the cause of tumours in farm poultry, Rous discovered that a cell-free tumour extract could cause cancer in chickens into which it was injected.[184] However, few people believed his claim that this showed cancer could be caused by an organism even smaller than a cell, namely a virus, and it was only after others confirmed his findings in the 1950s that Rous was finally awarded a Nobel Prize in 1966.

In fact, viruses only cause cancer in a minority of cases, such as certain types of human cervical cancer linked to infection by papillomaviruses. The discovery of this link by Harald zur Hausen of Heidelberg University has led to vaccination of teenage girls in some countries as a preventative measure, and to zur Hausen being awarded a Nobel Prize in 2008.[185] However, the focus on animal viruses in the 1970s also resulted in major insights into gene regulation in multicellular organisms, since such viruses reproduce by hijacking their host's own gene expression machinery. As such, because of their relative simplicity, studies of viruses offered an indirect way to investigate gene expression in multicellular organisms.

Enhancers were discovered by Chambon and Khoury while independently investigating which regions of viral genomes are most important for their regulation. Surprisingly, they found that some viral DNA sequences retained their potency even when thousands of base pairs away from the genes they regulated, and seemed equally capable of affecting a gene's activity whether located before or after it.[186] At first, enhancers were thought to be just a quirk of viruses, but then other studies showed that regulatory sequences acting many kilobases distant from the genes they controlled were also key features of human genes.[187] All this was most perplexing, for it completely contradicted the idea of genes, and their regulatory regions, as being compact units as established in bacteria.

If Jacob and Monod's findings had suggested that genes were like workshops, each producing its own specific product, on an incredibly long road—the chromosome—it now seemed that, in multicellular organisms, the on/off switch for each workshop could be miles down the road, with no obvious physical connection to the object it controlled. So how was such activity at a distance possible given that transcription factors were thought to directly interact with the RNA polymerase? One initial idea was that proteins binding to enhancers triggered a change in the DNA helix that was transmitted to the start of the gene. But how this might work remained unclear; instead, subsequent studies suggested that transcription factors bound to enhancers activate the RNA polymerase directly, by looping around the intervening DNA separating them (see Figure 12).[187] While enhancers activate genes, other DNA regions acting at a distance have the opposite effect, earning them the name of silencers.

One important feature of enhancers is their flexibility. Recently, Robert Tjian of the University of California has suggested that this flexibility may have been key to the development of complex multicellular life forms. An amazing aspect of multicellular life, whether a human or a fruitfly, is how a single cell—the fertilized egg—subsequently becomes an exquisitely structured organism with multiple types of cells, tissues, and organs, all working together in harmony. However, this creates a huge challenge, for not only must the individual cells of a developing multicellular organism respond to changes in their immediate environment, as a bacterium does in utilizing available nutrients, but regulatory mechanisms during embryogenesis must also be structured so that gene expression is tightly coordinated across the body.

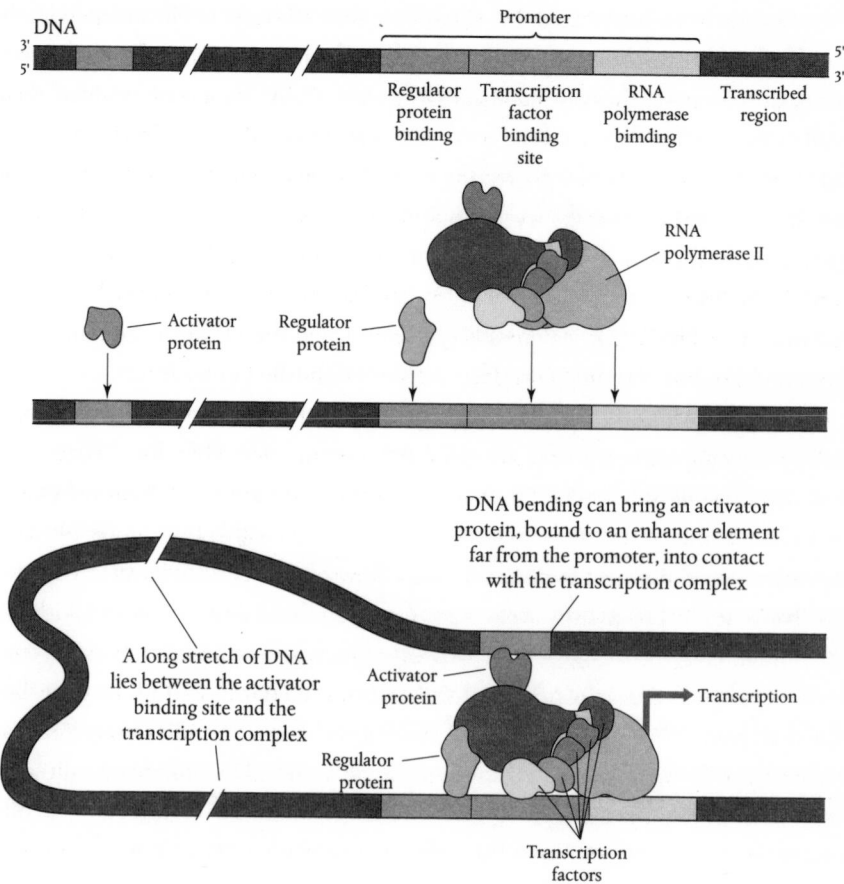

Figure 12. Enhancers and their relationship to the gene they control

One basic way in which an organism is structured is along its body axes.[188] Like other vertebrates we humans have a top and bottom, a back and front, plus a left and right side. Vertically, we have a head containing a brain at the top of our bodies, a torso with two arms at the upper end and two legs at the lower end, while in the other direction we have a back with a spine and shoulder blades and a front with chest and midriff. Finally, our internal organs are positioned according to a left–right asymmetry.[189] Most people's hearts are on their left side, although exceptions to this rule exist, and not just fictional characters like James Bond's adversary Dr No, who survived an assassination attempt because his heart was on his right.[190] So singer Donny Osmond, whose picture adorned the bedroom walls

of teenage girls across the world in the 1970s, also has his internal organs reversed in this way. He only found this out following a bad case of appendicitis that was initially misdiagnosed because his appendix was on the left instead of its normal right-hand position.[191] At a finer level of structuring, humans typically have five digits on their hands and feet, although people can be born with an abnormal number: the world record holder for the most digits being Akshat Saxena, an Indian boy born in 2010 with seven digits on each hand and ten on each foot.[192]

There has been scientific interest in the genes underpinning body axes for many years, partly reflecting a desire to understand the basic mechanisms of embryo development, but also because some abnormalities in human body 'patterning' pose serious threats to well-being and survival. A major step forward in our understanding of the genetics of body patterning came with the discovery of mutants affecting the body plan in fruitflies. The first such mutant was identified by Calvin Bridges in Thomas Morgan's laboratory in 1915, but it was Ed Lewis who first studied such mutants in detail. Lewis did his PhD with Alfred Sturtevant, the creator of the first genetic map, at the California Institute of Technology, where Lewis himself later established his own laboratory. It was here he discovered various mutants whose body symmetry was out of sync, such as flies with legs on their heads, or four instead of two wings.[193] Subsequent studies by Christiane Nusslein-Volhard at Tübingen University identified the genes linked to such bizarre mutants, a discovery that led to the award of a Nobel Prize to her and Lewis in 1995. These 'homeotic' genes, from the Greek for assimilation, code for transcription factors that switch on other genes, establishing a hierarchy of gene regulation, with genes involved in gross body patterning controlling those regulating a finer level of detail.[193] Remarkably, much the same genes that define different structures along the length of a fly are responsible for patterning our own human bodies.

One such set involved in body patterning are known as the pair-rule genes. These genes are expressed as seven stripes along the length of the fly embryo, which define where the different structures of the adult organism will later appear.[194] This complex pattern of expression is regulated by multiple enhancers, each specific for a different stripe, since if one is disabled by genetic engineering, this causes the loss of the stripe of expression it controls.[194] This provides a potential mechanism for the evolution of complex multicellular life forms, for by increasing the enhancers controlling a gene, each enhancer controlling the gene's expression in a different part of the embryo, evolution could first generate a

simple segmented structure, as in worms, and, subsequently, more complex structures, like limbs, wings, and so on.[195] This required, however, a dramatic loosening of the connection between a gene and its regulatory elements, in contrast to the tight link in bacteria.

But it isn't just the regulation of gene activity that is radically different in multicellular organisms, but the very structure of the genome itself. The first indication of this came from comparisons of genomes from different multicellular species. Such analysis identified huge discrepancies in the sizes of certain genomes compared to the apparent complexity of the species they came from.[196] The fact that some organisms had far more DNA than humans posed a potential threat to the view of ourselves as a superior species, if a greater amount of DNA was assumed to represent a more complex organism. Another possibility, though, was that the genomes of multicellular organisms contained an excess of non-functional 'junk' DNA, which varied between species. This possibility was bolstered by the first studies to examine the actual sequences of DNA in our genomes. In the 1960s, in the absence of any method for directly 'reading' the sequence of bases in DNA, Roy Britten and David Kohne at the Carnegie Institution in Washington, developed an ingenious way to do this indirectly.

If DNA is heated, eventually it acquires sufficient energy that the two strands of the double helix come apart. If the DNA is then cooled, because of the attraction of bases on the two strands for each other, eventually the double helix reassociates. Because it takes time for any piece of DNA to find its complementary sequence, Britten and Kohne assumed that the mouse genome would take much longer to reassociate than that of bacteria, given the latter's 100 times smaller size. Instead, they found that the reassociation occurred in waves: a quarter doing so rapidly, a further third more slowly, and only the remainder combining at the slow speed one would expect. The two researchers concluded that the more rapidly reassociating portions of the mouse genome must be highly repetitive, since such sequences are so similar they need not find their exact partners. To relate such genomic regions to a role in coding for proteins, Britten and Kohne next incorporated radioactivity into mouse mRNA and included this in the experiment. This showed that the mRNA only matched the slowest reassociating portion of the genome. It therefore seemed that over half the genome was made up of repetitive sequences, these being also 'non-coding' regions. This discovery would play an important part in the rise of the belief that protein-coding genes are

islands in a sea of 'junk' DNA, although Britten and Kohne themselves found this idea 'repugnant', preferring to believe that the function of repetitive DNA simply hadn't been identified.[197]

Further surprises were in store once scientists began to look more closely within genes themselves. As we've seen, while DNA acts as the ultimate repository of hereditary information, mRNA is the actual template for the assembly of an amino acid chain. As such, it seemed fair to assume that mRNA would be a direct replica of the DNA in order to fulfil this role. In bacteria this was found to be the case, with a one-to-one correspondence between the DNA and RNA molecules. But when scientists began similar comparisons in eukaryotes in the late 1970s, what they found was totally unexpected. The key discovery was made in 1977 by Phillip Sharp at the Massachusetts Institute of Technology and Richard Roberts at Cold Spring Harbor Laboratories.[198] While studying the reproductive cycle of adeno-viruses—which cause human illnesses ranging from the common cold to bronchitis and pneumonia—both were intrigued to find that adenoviral RNAs in the nucleus of the infected cell were much bigger than those in the cyto-plasm. Although at this time it was impossible to sequence DNA and RNA routinely, a comparison could be made by allowing them to bind to each other by the same 'base-pairing' that occurs in a DNA double helix. Studying such DNA–RNA hybrids under the electron microscope, a curious sight was observed: at regular intervals along the hybrid, large loops were seen. Further analysis identified these as DNA, indicating that only a small proportion of the DNA sequence in the gene was present in the mRNA. Curiously though, RNA from the nucleus was much longer and it perfectly matched the DNA of the gene. This suggested that, initially, an RNA spanning the length of the gene was produced but then it was substantially trimmed to size. This phenomenon was named splicing, by analogy with the way footage for a film is shot, with sections being cut out to create the final product (see Figure 13).[198] Rather confusingly, the discarded regions were named introns, for intragenic regions, and those that remained in the final mRNA were called exons, since these were expressed as protein. Any idea that splicing was some quirk of viral gene expression was soon quashed by further studies that showed it was also a feature of various human genes, such as the immunoglobulin genes and the globin genes that code for antibodies and haemoglobin respectively.[199]

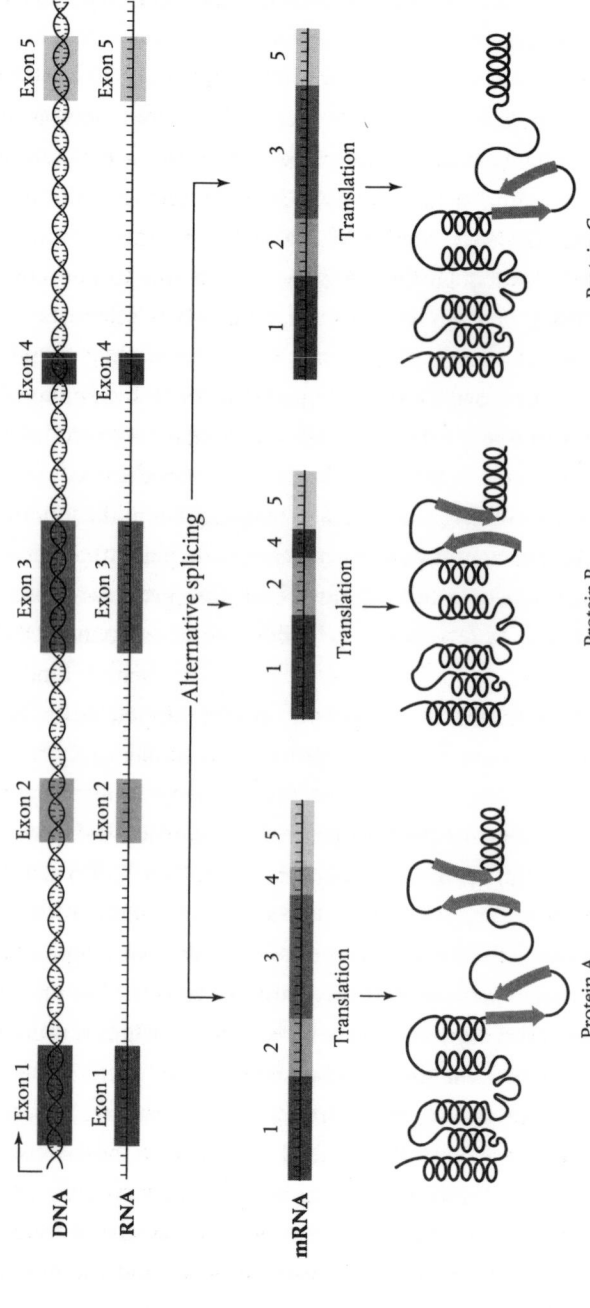

Figure 13. RNA splicing and alternative splicing

In fact, studies have shown that, in multicellular organisms, genes without introns are very much the exception, as well as highlighting the huge discrepancy in size between introns and exons.[199] So while the normal length of exons is less than 200 bases, introns can be anywhere from 2,000 to 11,000 bases long.[200] This disproportion in size is such that if the genome were a book, with the genes as different chapters, such chapters would contain chunks of only a paragraph or so of meaningful text, interspersed by pages of gibberish. So why has evolution allowed the creation of such long RNAs, if so much is subsequently thrown away? One reason may be the extra flexibility to the organism that can result. In different cell types of the body, or at specific stages of embryo development, different exons can be selected to be included in the final mRNA. This 'alternative splicing' means a single gene can code for many different proteins (as seen in Figure 13).[201] While there is still a flow of information from DNA to RNA to protein, this ensures that such information can go in different directions depending on the cellular environment. Alternative splicing can alter a protein's mode of action, regulation by cellular signals, or interaction with other proteins, to highlight just some ways in which a protein's function can be altered by this process. Its importance in humans is shown by the fact that over 90 per cent of our genes are alternatively spliced.[201]

Alternative splicing plays a particularly important role in the formation of antibodies by the immune system. It generates antibodies against a seemingly unlimited range of different foreign molecules, or antigens. Initially, there seemed two possible explanations for this, one being that when the body comes into contact with a foreign antigen it generates a specifically tailored antibody to match, an alternative being that it generates an almost infinite variety of different antibody molecules.[202] Using an analogy of buying a suit, these alternatives are like having one made-to-measure from a bespoke tailor, or buying a ready-made item from a high street clothing chain. Initially, the former model seemed most plausible, for how could the body generate such a huge variety of different forms of a protein? Yet this is indeed what happens, with alternative splicing being one mechanism whereby a single antibody gene can code for many different protein forms.[203]

Another reason why splicing might have been favoured in multicellular organisms is its potential benefits for evolutionary change. A crucial aspect of Darwin's theory of natural selection as a mechanism of evolution is its reliance on blind

chance. It is this aspect of Darwinism that can seem most threatening to those who look for some kind of guiding influence to life. In Darwin's own lifetime his theory was derided as 'the law of the higgledy-piggledy' by astronomer and philosopher John Herschel. This was ironic, given that Herschel himself probably stimulated Darwin to start thinking about evolution when they met at the former's home in Cape Town during the voyage of the *Beagle*.[204] For Herschel was sympathetic to the idea that new species could come into existence, which he called the 'mystery of mysteries', and indeed Darwin directly referred to this phrase and to Herschel in the *Origin of Species*. However, what the latter had in mind was a 'directed' evolution administered by God. Herschel also influenced Darwin in his general approach to science, through his statement that scientific discoveries are made when the mind 'leaps forward…by forming at once a bold hypothesis'. Unfortunately, Darwin's great idea was rather too bold for Herschel in the fact it went beyond conventional accepted notions.[204]

Others have argued that the chance of complex organisms such as human beings evolving is as likely as a tornado blowing through a junkyard, reassembling the dismembered remains of a Boeing 747 back into a fully functioning Jumbo Jet. This analogy, first used by the astronomer Fred Hoyle,[205] is based on a deep misunderstanding of natural selection: the variants available may arise by chance, but the actual selection, and therefore development of adaptations, is not arbitrary at all but moulded by the environmental conditions. However, it also neglects another feature about evolution, namely its conservatism, never creating anything purely from scratch but always borrowing from what is already there. And, in this respect, the division of eukaryotic genes into intron and exon regions seems to have played a very important role. So studies of proteins have shown these are composed of 'domains', each with their own discrete 3D structure separate from the rest of the protein.[206] Moreover, these structural domains often have a discrete function within a protein. Intriguingly, the same domains may crop up in proteins of quite different overall functions. It seems that, during evolution, new proteins have formed by mixing and matching existing domains. That protein domains often map onto specific exons, and are therefore already separated by introns at the DNA level, has been a key factor in allowing this process to occur: what is known as 'exon shuffling' (see Figure 14).[206]

Not that splicing doesn't have its disadvantages. In particular, serious genetic disorders can result from errors in the process.[207] One such disorder is Tay–Sachs

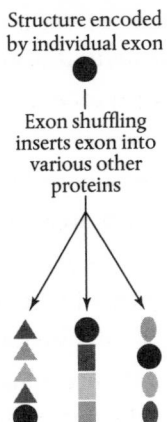

Figure 14. Exon shuffling as a central mechanism of protein evolution

disease, named after clinicians Waren Tay and Bernard Sachs, who, in the late nineteenth century, first noticed its occurrence among children of Ashkenazi Jewish immigrants in the US.[208] Symptoms begin as early as 6 months of age, when a previously normal child's development begins to slow, followed by rapid weakening of the muscles, loss of vision and hearing, and eventually full-scale dementia. Tragically, those with the condition die by the age of 3 to 5 years old. We now know this devastating disease is caused by a defect in the enzyme HexA, which normally breaks down a fatty substance called GM2 ganglioside.[209] In HexA's absence this substance builds up in cells of the nerves and brain, causing them to stop working normally and eventually destroying them. Tay–Sachs is a Mendelian recessive disorder, and, as such, is passed on by two carriers who do not themselves suffer from the disease. In one common form of Tay–Sachs, a mutation in an intron–exon junction means that the intron fails to be excised and so remains in the final mRNA where it disrupts the protein code, leading to a dysfunctional enzyme. Unfortunately, despite our detailed knowledge of the genetic basis of Tay–Sachs, this devastating disease remains incurable. However, there have been important steps forward in its prevention. This is mainly due to one man, Rabbi Josef Ekstein, who, having lost four of his children to the disease, set up a premarital testing service for potential couples in the Ashkenazi Jewish commu-nity, in which arranged marriages still play an important role.[210] If both individuals test positive they are told that the marriage cannot go ahead. This service has drawn some criticism on ethical grounds but its success at disease prevention

cannot be doubted, since the incidence of Tay–Sachs among Ashkenazi Jews is now less than in the general population.[208]

Such a link between splicing and disease was still some way in the future when splicing was first discovered. At that time, its main significance was providing more evidence of how different our own genomes are compared with those of bacteria, and how even genes themselves seem full of non-coding junk. But the full extent of non-coding DNA became most evident once the human genome itself was sequenced. The sequencing technique used was developed in 1977 by Fred Sanger, who as we saw in Chapter 2, two decades earlier, had obtained the first protein sequence. Sanger has referred to his career after successfully sequencing insulin as his 'lean years';[211] however, as his efforts resulted in him developing ways to sequence first RNA, then DNA, and the award of a second Nobel Prize, in this case leanness is a relative concept! Having tried numerous unsuccessful approaches in his bid to sequence DNA, he finally succeeded with one involving DNA polymerase, the enzyme that replicates DNA. Sanger realized that synthesis of a DNA strand from a template DNA could be used to 'read' the sequence of that template, if some way were found to interrupt DNA elongation in a manner specific to each base. He did this by generating modified nucleotides that were incapable of being linked to a subsequent nucleotide, so acting as a 'chain breaker'.[211] By having four tubes, each with a modified nucleotide corresponding to one of the four bases, a mixture of different lengths of DNA were obtained, each ending at either A,C, G, or T, depending upon the tube. By also radioactively tagging the DNA and separating it with a technique called gel electrophoresis, it was possible for the first time to 'read' the DNA sequence (see Figure 15). Sanger received a Nobel Prize for this discovery in 1980, making him one of the few people to have received the award twice.

Crucially, a refined version of Sanger's method, in which the four modified nucleotides each impart a different colour to the DNA and allow the process to be carried out in a single tube, made it possible to automate DNA sequencing. This was the approach used for the genome project.[212] The findings of this vast sequencing project were surprising in a number of different ways. The first surprise was the number of protein-coding genes in our genomes. A common estimate of the number of human genes prior to the genome project was 100,000. But the real figure is far lower, with a recent study quoting it as just over 22,000. This is more than a fruitfly, with 15,000 genes, or a chicken, with 17,000, but less

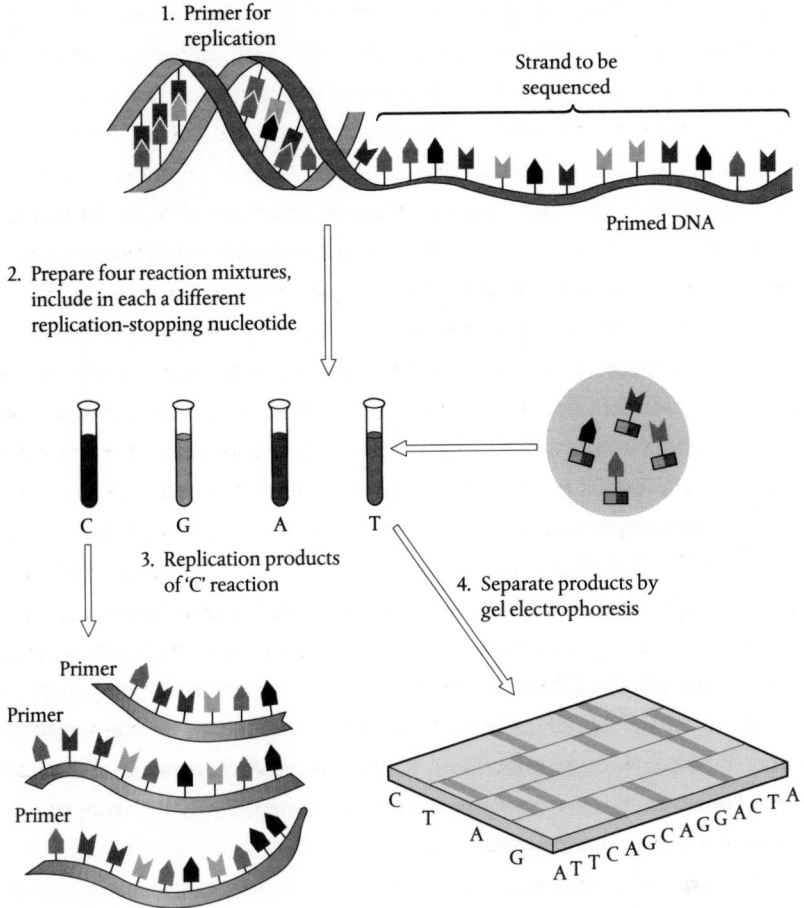

1. Primer for replication

Strand to be sequenced

Primed DNA

2. Prepare four reaction mixtures, include in each a different replication-stopping nucleotide

C   G   A   T

3. Replication products of 'C' reaction

4. Separate products by gel electrophoresis

Primer

Primer

Primer

C

T

A

G

ATTCAGCAGGACTA

Figure 15. Sanger's DNA sequencing method

than a grape, with over 30,000 genes (see Figure 16). So much for the genetic superiority of our species, at least as assessed by gene number alone. But the other big surprise was how little of our genomes are devoted to protein-coding sequence. So when the DNA present in our introns and between genes is compared to that coding for proteins, a seemingly insignificant 2 per cent is devoted to the latter. This finding greatly strengthened a claim made decades earlier by Susumu Ohno of City of Hope Medical Center in California, when he said, in 1972, that most of the human genome was what he called 'junk' DNA.[213] In this

Figure 16. Comparison of gene number between different species

first use of the phrase, Ohno was referring to 'pseudogenes', namely genes that originally resulted from the duplication of a functional gene, but which have become disabled through mutation, so they no longer produce a functional protein. However, this term soon became a popular way of referring to all the non-coding DNA in the genome.

At first glance, the existence of junk DNA seems to pose another problem for Crick's central dogma. If information flows in a one-way direction from DNA to RNA to protein, then there would be appear to be no function for such non-coding DNA. But if 'junk DNA' really is useless, then isn't it incredibly wasteful to carry it around in our genomes? After all, the reproduction of the genome that takes place during each cell division uses valuable cellular energy. And there is also the issue of packaging the approximately 3 billion base pairs of the human genome into the tiny cell nucleus. So surely natural selection would favour a situation where both genomic energy requirements and packaging needs are reduced fiftyfold? An influential explanation for how the majority of a genome could become junk rather than being eliminated by natural selection was put forward by Richard Dawkins of Oxford University in 1976 in his book *The Selfish Gene*. In this, he noted that 'if the "purpose" of DNA is to supervise the building of

bodies, it is surprising to find a large quantity of DNA which does no such thing. Biologists are racking their brains trying to think what useful task this apparently surplus DNA is doing...The simplest way to explain the surplus DNA is to suppose that it is a parasite, or at best a harmless but useless passenger.'[214] Francis Crick and Leslie Orgel later put this idea on a more formal scientific footing in 1980, in an article in which they presented evidence that such junk represented parasitical DNA, with an ability to reproduce itself but whose accumulation did not have enough of a detrimental effect on an organism's physiology or behaviour to allow it to be eliminated by natural selection.[215]

The existence of junk DNA has been proposed as further evidence that humans evolved by natural selection rather than being created by some supernatural being. In 1802, the theologian William Paley used the existence of an exquisitely complex biological structure like the human eye as evidence for God, saying 'Is it possible to believe that the eye was formed without any regard to vision?... Design must have had a designer.' [216] Darwin saw the human eye as a particular challenge for his theory, since its many sophisticated features seem interdependent, posing problems for his stress upon the power of gradual step-by-step change to transform life. His answer was to point to organisms with eyes ranging from simple to complex, and to suggest that evolution of the human eye involved similar organs as intermediates.[217]

But what if design is not always so perfect? Harvard palaeontologist Stephen Jay Gould believed that nature's oddities such as the panda's thumb—actually an enlarged wristbone, and which Gould saw as a rather clumsy solution to a design problem—serve as better proof of evolution's existence than more 'ideal' adaptations.[218] In this sense, what more perfect demonstration is there that nature is 'an excellent tinkerer, not a divine artificer', than the fact that 98 per cent of our own genome is useless? Certainly, this is an argument Dawkins has employed as evidence against a religious interpretation of life's origins, saying that there is no 'convincing reason why an intelligent designer should have created a pseudo-gene—a gene that does absolutely nothing and gives every appearance of being a superannuated version of a gene that used to do something—unless he was deliberately setting out to fool us'.[219] Similarly, Kenneth Miller of Brown University has observed that the genome resembles 'a hodgepodge of borrowed, copied, mutated, and discarded sequences and commands that has been cobbled together by millions of years of trial and error against the relentless test of survival.

It works, and it works brilliantly; not because of intelligent design, but because of the great blind power of natural selection.'[220]

This is a powerful argument, and one that I have much sympathy with, guided as I am by the principle that both life and the universe can be explained by purely materialist principles. However, using the uselessness of so much of the genome for such a purpose is also risky, for what if the so-called junk turns out to have an important function, but one that hasn't yet been identified? Whether such important functions exist within non-coding DNA has been one of the most hotly debated topics in genetics over the last few years. And one way in which this question first began to arise was through a reconsideration of the role of DNA's chemical cousin, RNA.

5

RNA OUT OF THE SHADOWS

'Because all of biology is connected, one can often make a breakthrough with an organism that exaggerates a particular phenomenon, and later explore the generality.'
                                                                            Thomas Cech

'As is a frequent occurrence in science, a general hypothesis was constructed from a few specific instances of a phenomenon.'
                                                                            Sidney Altman

Trying to conjure up the past is never easy, especially when that past is 3.7 billion years old. In his *Origin of Species*, Darwin was noticeably cagey about the precise way in which he believed life first arose on Earth, stating only that 'probably all the organic beings which have ever lived on this earth have descended from some primordial form, into which life was first breathed'.[221] However, writing in private to his friend the botanist Joseph Hooker, he was prepared to be more speculative. 'But if (and oh! what a big if!),' he wrote, 'we could conceive in some warm little pond, with all sorts of ammonia and phosphoric salts, lights, heat, electricity etc. present that a protein compound was chemically formed ready to undergo still more complex changes.'[222] This showed a recognition that the conditions that first gave rise to life might be very different to those in our current world. Meanwhile, the focus on proteins as central to life's origins reflected the idea, even at this time, that these molecules were key mediators of bodily processes. However, a more precise suggestion for the type of chemical environment likely to have existed on primeval Earth came in the 1920s from Russian biochemist Alexander Oparin, and J. B. S. Haldane.[223] Both independently proposed that our planet's early atmosphere was likely to have consisted of methane, ammonia, carbon dioxide, and water; with energy supplied by volcanic eruptions or lightning, this ought to have been sufficient to generate amino acids and other building blocks of life.

In 1953 Stanley Miller and Harold Urey at Chicago University first explored, experimentally, the possibility that such a mixture of simple chemicals could give rise to more complex molecular structures.[222] By exposing a mixture of water, methane, ammonia, and hydrogen in a sealed flask to an electric spark—to mimic lightning—and heat—to stimulate continual evaporation and condensation—they found that, within two weeks, amino acids had formed.[224] With the discovery that DNA acted as a linear code for the production of proteins, emphasis shifted to showing that its building blocks too could have been generated in a primeval soup, and, indeed, subsequent experiments with a slightly different starting mixture showed this was the case.[222] However, there was now a major conundrum to be solved in explaining how a DNA template coding for protein production could have come into existence. On the one hand, such a template is the repository of the information in the cell, but it is also relatively inert. Indeed, it is this inertness that makes DNA ideally suited to its role as genetic material, and the reason why it has recently proven possible to extract information from the DNA of Egyptian mummies, Neanderthal fossils, and woolly mammoth tissues revealed by melting glaciers.[225]

Proteins, on the other hand, are highly active, and easily degraded. However, as we saw in Chapter 3, without them the information in DNA would mean little, for its code can only be 'read' by proteins like RNA polymerase, that transcribe the DNA code into its RNA intermediary, and other regulatory proteins, that activate the polymerase. Yet this presents a 'chicken and egg' situation, for if DNA can only be replicated with the help of catalytic proteins, but such proteins can only be propagated through a DNA code, then how could either arise on its own?[226] An important clue to solving this conundrum emerged in 1981, from studies of the process whereby mRNA is generated by splicing, and is subsequently used as a template to produce a protein, so-called 'translation'. Ribosomes—the subcellular machines that take a particular mRNA and use it to produce a protein corresponding to the genetic code contained in the mRNA—are composed of ribosomal proteins but also of rRNA.[227] In fact, the ribosome is highly complex, containing almost a hundred different proteins and a variety of different RNAs. Studies of the spliceosome showed that it too was a complex structure composed of proteins and RNAs.[227]

When scientists first began studying the mechanism of action of ribosomes and spliceosomes it was assumed that the proteins would be responsible for catalysis,

with the RNAs performing an essentially structural role. This was an understandable assumption given that all the activities in life were believed to be carried out by special kinds of proteins called enzymes. These were first identified in 1879 by Eduard Buchner, who showed that yeast extracts lacking any living cells could still carry out the process of fermentation.[228] Then, almost fifty years later, in 1926, James Sumner crystallized an enzyme, urease, and showed it was a protein. We now know that enzymes are catalysts that allow the body's chemical reactions to take place in a fraction of the time they would require if left uncatalysed. Enzymes have a diversity of roles, digesting foods in the gut but transporting the digested products into the cell, transforming these into energy, and regulation of the genes coding for these processes.

However, when Thomas Cech of Colorado University began studying the molecular mechanisms underlying splicing in the early 1980s, he made a surprising discovery. Seeking to isolate and characterize the enzyme responsible for removal of the introns in rRNA in a single-celled eukaryotic organism called Tetrahymena, Cech found that the catalytic activity of the spliceosome was associated not with a protein, but a spliceosomal RNA.[229] Sidney Altman, at Yale University, was working on a different problem at this time—the generation of tRNAs in bacteria. His studies showed that such mature tRNAs are produced by a processing step, and, assuming this would be catalysed by an enzyme, he set out to isolate and characterize such an enzyme. But, like Cech, he found that the catalytic activity was due to an RNA.[230] Cech and Altman named such catalytic RNAs ribozymes, to stress the similarity with enzymes. Their suggestion was viewed with incredulity at first (you may be noting a pattern about great scientific discoveries by now), with some claiming that catalysis by RNAs was just a peculiar quirk of these systems. However, studies of the structure and mechanism of action of ribosomes—the protein production 'factories'—established the centrality of ribozyme action in the cell by showing that here too it was the rRNAs, not the ribosomal proteins, that constituted the ribosome's catalytic core.[231] The importance of Cech and Altman's discovery was acknowledged by the award of a Nobel Prize to them both in 1989. Altman later drew attention to two aspects of science, namely that 'hard work in stable surroundings could yield rewards, even if only in infinitesimally small increments', but also the emotional highs that could result from such work.[232] So, he recalled having 'resolved a problem that I had been working on for a year or more... The feeling of great satisfaction at having

solved my problem as well as having illuminated others kept me floating on air for weeks.'[233]

That RNA can function as a catalyst was initially puzzling, given that enzymes were thought to be the only molecules capable of forming complex 3D structures that provide specific catalytic pockets for the molecules they act upon. However, subsequent studies showed that RNA can form complex structures too.[234] We saw in Chapter 2 how DNA is a very uniform, some might say boring, molecule compared to proteins, with a chromosome's double helix structure the same from its start to its end. However, despite only having four types of bases like DNA, compared to the 20 amino acids in proteins, RNA can form complex 3D structures through the same base pairing that holds the DNA double helix together, but in a much more diverse manner than the latter. The discovery of ribozymes forced a reconsideration of RNA's role in the cell. Whether as a messenger or a component of the protein synthesis machinery, RNA had been relegated to a largely passive role in cellular function. But, with the discovery of its catalytic properties, speculation began as to what this meant for the molecule's function.[234] Was it possible, for instance, that RNA's flexibility of action reflected a past in which the molecule had played a much more central role in the replication of life than it now did? In fact, this possibility, named the 'RNA world hypothesis', was suggested as early as 1962 by Alexander Rich at the Massachusetts Institute of Technology, but his proposal had languished in the absence of evidence to support it.[226]

Now, with the discovery of ribozymes, the idea that on primeval Earth RNA had been both the molecule of inheritance and also the active motor of the cell, gained a new plausibility. According to this view, over time the more stable DNA usurped the role of RNA as the repository of life, while proteins increasingly took over the role of catalysis (see Figure 17).[226] Further support for the idea that RNA originally acted as the molecule of inheritance has emerged with the demonstration, in 2011, by Philipp Holliger at the Laboratory of Molecular Biology in Cambridge, that it is possible to artificially create a 'self-replicating' RNA molecule. This molecule not only replicates itself but can also generate another type of ribozyme, suggesting that once the first self-replicating RNA appeared, it might have generated a range of accessory molecular partners, kick-starting the evolution of more complex life forms. Another important clue as to RNA's past role comes from the fact that the second messengers cAMP and cGMP, and also the 'energy currency' of the cell ATP—whose chemical breakdown powers most catalytic

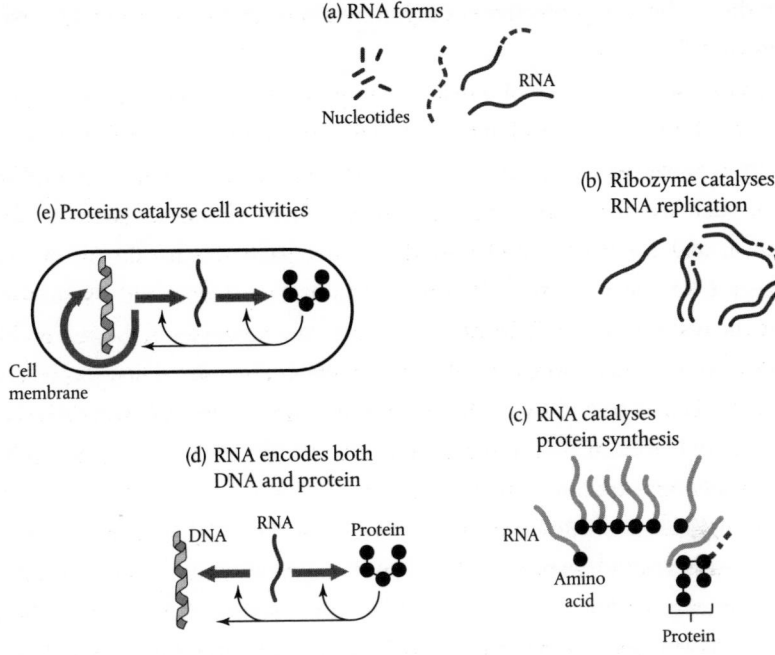

Figure 17. RNA world hypothesis

reactions—are all ribonucleotides or derived from these molecules, in line with a generalized role for RNA and its subsidiaries in the formation of early life.[226]

One important unresolved issue is how the origin of the first replication molecule relates to that of the first cell. We saw in Chapter 3 how the one-way flow of information from DNA to protein in Crick's central dogma ignores the fact that changes in the cellular environment, working through proteins that regulate gene expression, represent an important flow of information in the reverse direction. Similarly, discussion of life's origins has tended to assume the replicator arose first and then somehow acquired a cellular membrane. However, Jack Szostak at the Massachusetts General Hospital, who is 'interested in the related challenges of understanding the origin of life on the early earth and constructing synthetic cellular life in the laboratory', believes it more likely that a primitive cell formed first and then acquired replicator molecules, since it's hard to imagine how a replicating system could survive without a membrane to keep it from dispersing.[235] In line with this, recent studies suggest that primitive membranes could have been sufficiently permeable to allow important molecules

within their orbit, but protective enough to retain them so as to allow the first life to develop.[236]

Of course, in the absence of a machine to go back 3.7 billion years in time it's impossible to really be sure what happened in our evolutionary past. And perhaps the only way we will ever know is if life is discovered elsewhere in our solar system, such as on Jupiter's moon Europa where chemicals such as water, ammonia, and methane—similar to those that gave rise to life on our own planet—are known to exist.[226] Returning to our own planet and its life forms, despite the realization that RNA catalysed some key processes in the cell, and had probably been a much more central player in life as a whole, at first this role was very much seen as past glory, with RNA representing, in Jim Watson's words, an 'evolutionary heirloom'.[237] But more surprises were on the way, and they initially came through an experiment that went wrong.

A popular idea about scientific discovery is that it is a highly logical process, in which scientists put forward hypotheses and then, by demonstrating their validity by experiment, gradually move towards a truer picture of the natural world. Although patient deduction of the sort beloved by Sherlock Holmes is an important aspect of science, overly focusing on this underestimates the importance of luck in scientific discovery. In particular, experiments that don't give the desired result, but nevertheless reveal a view of the natural world not glimpsed previously, play a tremendously important role in science. One experiment that went wrong but led to a major insight was led by Richard Jorgensen, a plant scientist at the University of Arizona interested in the genetics of colour. He and his team tried to make a more intensely purple petunia by adding an additional pigment-producing gene to plants that were normally purple. However, instead of enhancing the colour, this genetic modification had completely the opposite effect, with the resulting flowers turning totally white, or becoming irregularly coloured.[238] As the normal and foreign genes seemed to cancel out each other's properties, Jorgensen and his colleagues called this phenomenon 'co-suppression'. Initially, the phenomenon was thought to be peculiar to petunias, but then other scientists started noticing similar results in other plant species. Subsequently, researchers studying the fungus Neurospora found that introducing additional copies of genes normally present in this organism silenced the effect of the normal genes.[239] But it still wasn't clear what caused the weird silencing effect, nor whether the phenomenon was confined to plants and fungi.

How silencing worked eventually emerged from studies focusing on the nematode worm *Caenorhabditis elegans*. This species was pioneered by Sydney Brenner, following his major contribution to cracking the genetic code, as a model organism for the study of embryo development.[240] By randomly mutating different genes with irradiation or mutagenic chemicals and then seeing whether such mutants had defects in embryogenesis, Brenner, and a growing army of 'worm specialists', began to identify many important genes involved in this process. One mechanism of development studied in detail was apoptosis, or 'programmed cell death'.[241] Although cell growth and division is a key aspect of embryogenesis, controlled cell death is also very important. Just as Michelangelo carved the statue of David from a single block of marble by hewing 'away the rough walls that imprison the lovely apparition to reveal it to the other eyes as mine see it',[242] so the embryo gains its detailed shape and form through trimming via cell death. Apoptosis also plays important roles during human development and in adult humans, for instance, in the destruction of cells that have become a health risk because their DNA is damaged.[240] Indeed, one way tumours develop is by ignoring the normal signals that trigger cell death. Sydney Brenner, who had never received a Nobel Prize for his work on the genetic code, finally did so in 2002, for discovering the mechanisms underlying apoptosis, which was made possible by the identification of worm mutants in which the process was defective.[240]

However, creating mutant nematodes is a laborious process, and some scientists wanted to find more direct ways of interfering with gene function. One such method was 'anti-sense' technology. This involved injecting a single strand of RNA complementary in its base sequence to a portion of a particular mRNA, the idea being that base pairing between the two would interfere with the mRNA's translation into protein. Andrew Fire and Craig Mello, at the University of Massachusetts Medical School, tried this technology in nematodes. They found that the anti-sense RNA did cause modest silencing of the gene, but, curiously, in another example of an experiment that went wrong, so did a control sense RNA, despite the fact it should not recognize the target mRNA by base pairing.[243,244] Even more surprising, when both anti-sense and sense RNA were added, this caused silencing that was a hundred times greater than with either component on its own. Because of this greatly enhanced effect, Fire and Mello realized the silencing agent must be double-stranded RNA, and the potency of the response

suggested that the process was a catalytic one, since tiny amounts of such RNA caused silencing.[243] Mello has discussed how developing a new technology can be 'exceedingly frustrating because you may never know how close you were to success, and failures quite often teach you nothing. Partly because of this, those working on technology development often tend to band together and share ideas more than would otherwise be common among scientists. This was certainly the case for Andrew Fire and me.'[244]

The search for the catalytic agent led to the discovery of a multi-subunit protein complex, called the RNA-induced silencing complex, or RISC for short (see Figure 18).[245] This complex has two components, the first being a protein named DICER, because it chops double-stranded RNA into much smaller fragments called short interfering RNAs, or siRNAs for short. The second component is the Argonaute proteins, which attach themselves to the siRNAs and transport them to their matching sequence target in the mRNA, which is then inactivated. It now became clear that the previous observations of silencing had accidentally

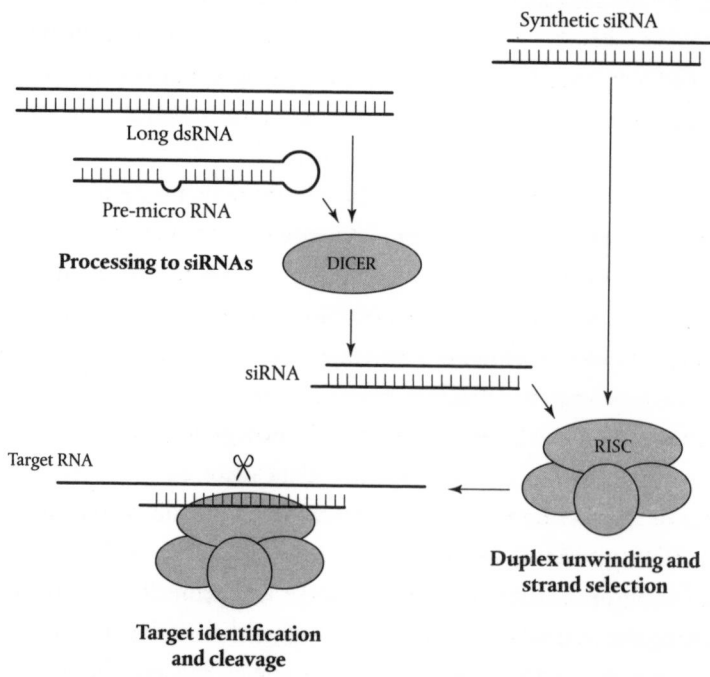

Figure 18. How RNA interference switches off gene expression

produced double-stranded RNA corresponding to a particular gene, which then activated RISC. According to Fire, 'we came into a field where a lot was already known. It was a complex jigsaw puzzle, and we were able to contribute one piece. Fortunately for us it was a very nice piece.'[246] He and Mello called the process 'RNA interference'. As a research tool, RNA interference provided, for the first time, a way to disable gene function in a rapid and flexible way.[246] No more would worm researchers have to painstakingly isolate mutants—now they could easily target specific genes by feeding worms bacteria expressing siRNAs, or just soak the worm in a solution containing such siRNAs.[241]

However, the real reason why RNA interference became such a big discovery, and would lead to the award of a Nobel Prize to Fire and Mello in 2006, was that it can be applied to many other species, including mammals.[245] In particular, the discovery that RNA interference can be applied to human cultured cells opened up exciting new possibilities for medical research, as it meant that, for the first time, human genes could be disabled in a very precise fashion. As such, it is now possible for scientists to study how 'knocking down' particular proteins affects processes in the human cell. One important use of RNA interference is in 'genome-wide screens'.[247] These use genome sequence information to create a 'library' of siRNAs covering all the genes in the genome. Cells in thousands of tiny culture dishes are then each exposed to a different siRNA, and whether this inhibits a specific cellular process has been used to identify genes involved in disorders ranging from Parkinson's disease to severe combined immune disorder, where patients lack a functioning immune system.

As well as providing new ways to diagnose human disease at the molecular level, there is much interest in using RNA interference in gene therapy. Standard gene therapy seeks to introduce a functional gene into cells where the normal gene is missing or unable to function. However, in some diseases such as cancer or types of dementia like Huntington's, it is the mutant protein that prevents the cell working normally. In such cases, selective elimination of this protein could be used to treat the disease.[248] RNA interference is so exquisitely sensitive to the sequence of the mRNA it targets, that if even a single base is different, as with the cancerous form of the RAS oncogene, then the mutant mRNA can be destroyed while leaving the normal form untouched. Unfortunately, the therapeutic potential of RNA interference has been slow to be realized.[248] While the process works extremely efficiently in human cells in culture, delivering sufficient quantities of

siRNAs to the right location in a living person has proven far from easy. However, progress has been made recently in finding ways to get around this problem.[249] For instance, one approach encapsulates siRNAs in 'nanoparticles' made of a mixture of fat and protein molecules, mimicking the way in which dietary cholesterol is absorbed into cells. Using such approaches, clinical trials are currently testing the potential of RNA interference as treatments for conditions ranging from high cholesterol in the blood, to hepatitis C infection, to various types of cancer.[249]

Therapeutic usefulness aside, the discovery of RNA interference raised an important question: given the presence of RISC in cells from plants to humans, what is the normal function of this protein complex? Through addressing this question it has become clear that RNA plays a far more multi-varied, and important, role in the cell than ever suspected. The first role suggested for the RNA interference process was that it protects the cell from infection by viruses. This certainly seems to be the case in plants.[250] Viruses that infect animal cells can have genomes made of DNA like our own, as in the case of the herpes virus, or of RNA, like the influenza virus. However, most plant viruses have an RNA genome, and, maybe because of this, RNA interference is one of the primary ways in which plants combat viral infection. In invertebrate species such as worms and flies, it also plays a central role in combating infection by viruses. Interestingly, viruses have found ways to fight back against such attempts to limit them.[250] For instance, some viruses make a protein that suppresses the RNA interference machinery. Others mutate their genomes so that the siRNAs the host organism uses against them are no longer effective. However, organisms have themselves evolved ways to override these tricks, in a kind of arms race between virus and host. In mammals, however, RNA interference does not seem to play a major role in combating viral infection. This may be because we have superseded such a need with our elaborate defence system, based on the antibody proteins of our immune system.

The discovery that both plants and animals employed siRNAs as a defence against pathogens demonstrated a new importance and flexibility of roles for RNA. But an even bigger surprise was still to come, as scientists began to realize that there are many other types of non-coding RNAs that exist normally in our cells. Currently, there are four known classes of non-coding RNAs, although each class almost certainly include many subclasses. First, there are the siRNAs, which,

as we've just discussed, regulate gene expression by destroying their target mRNAs. The second class are known as microRNAs, or miRNAs for short.[251] Their main mechanism of action is to prevent their target mRNA being used to make proteins by inhibiting its interaction with the ribosome. However, recent studies have shown that some miRNAs can also play stimulatory roles. So, in some circumstances, binding of a miRNA to its target mRNA enhances the latter's capacity to produce protein, while other miRNAs activate transcription of mRNAs themselves. Third, there are the piRNAs, which were first thought to be only present in the testicles and ovaries, where they act to safeguard the genomes of the eggs and sperm, an essential role given how important these are for forming the next generation.[252] However, more recently these have also been shown to play important roles in the brain. Their main action is to supress inappropriate 'mobility' of DNA elements in the genome, in ways we'll soon be exploring. The fourth class are the long non-coding RNAs, or lcRNAs.[253] These are defined mainly by length, all being over two hundred bases long, in contrast to the other three classes which are typically much smaller, at around twenty bases. These RNAs have various ways of regulating gene expression, but one particularly important role is to bring different parts of the genome together to form a complex 3D network of functionality, in ways we'll look at shortly. Between them, these different classes of non-coding RNAs act to regulate normal gene expression at practically every stage of this process. Since we are going to encounter non-coding RNAs throughout the remainder of this book, for now I just want to focus on one class—the miRNAs—in order to demonstrate the diversity of physiological processes that even one class of non-coding RNAs is involved in regulating.

It now seems that as many as half of all human genes are regulated by miRNAs.[254] Such miRNAs are related in sequence to the mRNAs of the genes they regulate, but typically can regulate multiple mRNA targets. Although miRNAs regulate a range of processes from embryo development through to adulthood, they have particularly pronounced roles in certain areas.[251] One such role is in stem cells: these cells are found throughout the body, but are particularly active in tissues that need continual replenishment like skin, blood, the gut lining, and the male gonads. Stem cells can divide indefinitely, but also generate all the cell types of the organ or tissue in which they are found. Some miRNAs are expressed in particular types of stem cells. By manipulating the mouse genome to prevent

the expression of these miRNAs, it has been possible to understand what functions they play in these cell types. Such manipulation of the genome makes use of another type of stem cells, so-called 'embryonic' stem cells, which have the potential to turn into any cell in the body. By modifying the genomes of such cells and then using them to create a mouse embryo, it is possible to generate a whole mouse with the gene modification.[255] While this approach has been mainly used to 'knock out' protein-coding genes in the mouse, in order to study their role in health and disease in a living mammal, it can be applied to any functional genomic element.

This approach has shown that miRNAs play key roles in many processes mediated by stem cells. One dramatic effect of blocking miRNA action is on the developing sperm.[251,256] A typical man produces about a thousand or so sperm in the time taken for one breath. What fuels this prodigious production process are the testicular stem cells. But when a specific miRNA only found in the testicles was knocked out, sperm production ground to an abrupt halt. Since some men are infertile because they fail to produce any sperm, there is now interest in whether this may sometimes be due to an miRNA defect. Conversely, a male contraceptive drug could be designed to specifically target the testicular miRNA; it would have to be very specific in its action though, for miRNAs have been shown to play other vital roles in the body and there could be severe consequences if these were blocked.

For instance, miRNAs play important roles in formation of blood cells. The complex nature of such regulation was shown by the fact that knocking out different miRNAs in mice upset the balance of the different types of blood cells in very specific ways.[251] So, while knocking out one miRNA led to the loss of certain white blood cells and a serious loss of immunity as a consequence, knocking out another depleted the red blood cells that carry oxygen in the blood, with resulting anaemia. In line with such a role, recent studies have shown that abnormal expression of miRNAs in humans is associated with some types of leukaemia—cancers of the blood.[257] Skin, hair, and the gut lining are all rapidly dividing tissues that rely on continual renewal by stem cells, so maybe it is not surprising that these too are badly affected when the miRNAs in such tissues are disabled.[251] Another important site of action for miRNAs is in the nervous system and brain.[251] So, inhibition of miRNA action in astroglial cells, which act as a support network for nerve cells, resulted in brain dysfunction and seizures. Curiously

though, inhibition of miRNAs in the forebrain resulted in an initial enhancement of learning and memory until, eventually, nerve degeneration set in. This provocative finding raises the question whether interfering with miRNAs in humans could promote learning in some circumstances. Interestingly, an important effect of brain miRNAs is on transcription factor CREB, which, as we saw in Chapter 3, plays a key role in learning and memory.[251] Other miRNAs regulate the heart and circulation.

So, starting from a failed attempt to turn a petunia purple, the discovery of RNA interference has revealed a whole new network of gene regulation mediated by RNAs and operating in parallel to the more established one of protein regulatory factors. However, another surprising discovery has emerged from the study of miRNAs: their point of origin. Studies have revealed that a surprising 60 per cent of miRNAs turn out to be recycled introns, with the remainder being generated from the regions between genes.[258] Yet these were the parts of the genome formerly viewed as junk. Does this mean we need a reconsideration of this question? This is an issue we will discuss in Chapter 6, in particular with regard to the ENCODE project, with its controversial findings that pose a challenge to the current consensus about how genes work, provoking both excitement but also deep disagreement.

6

IT'S A JUNGLE IN THERE!

'It's likely that 80 percent will go to 100 percent. We don't really have any large chunks of redundant DNA. This metaphor of junk isn't that useful.'

Ewan Birney

'Just because a piece of DNA has biological activity does not mean it has an important function in a cell. Most of the human genome is devoid of function and these people are wrong to say otherwise.'   *Dan Graur*

Metaphors have been central to biology as far back as Aristotle. In the seventeenth century, French scientist René Descartes compared animals to machines, and his English contemporary William Harvey described the heart as a pump. In the early twentieth century, the biochemist's view of the cell as a factory dominated, with structural proteins its bricks and mortar, and enzymes the machines that carry out the manufacturing process. As awareness grew of the commanding role of genes in cellular life, so did descriptions of the nucleus as the manager's office controlling activities on the factory floor of the cytoplasm. And, as we saw in Chapter 2, following the discovery of the DNA double helix the idea of life as a digital code became dominant. With the four nucleotide bases acting as the letters for this code, perhaps it was not surprising that the genome has become known as the book of life, although this description was clearly too old-fashioned for Walter Gilbert. He developed his own version of DNA sequencing alongside Sanger in the 1970s, sharing a Nobel Prize with the latter in 1980, and, from the late 1980s, became a central proponent of the human genome project. As part of his fundraising efforts at the time, he ended his seminars by holding up a glittering CD to the audience and declaring that 'soon I will be able to say "here is a human being; it's me"'.[259] Soon molecular biologists across the world were using this high-tech image to sell the

idea of a digitalized approach to biomedical science. However, at the completion of the project over a decade later in 2003, digital downloads were already making the CD metaphor look almost as dated as that of the book it replaced. A more fundamental problem with the metaphor had arisen though, for an e-book, like its paper form, is generally still expected to have a clear structure, with an introduction, conclusion, and a narrative sandwiched in the middle.

Yet an unexpected message of the human genome project was that the number of genes was much less than expected, and the proportion of non-coding DNA substantially greater than imagined. If the genome were a book, it seemed hard to escape the fact that the vast majority of it was complete gibberish. Not only that but the genes themselves were far from transparent, revealing little by DNA code alone about the cellular processes they mediated, the cell types and tissues they were expressed within, and the signalling pathways that regulated them, apart from what was already known from previous studies. Reflecting such concerns, the same year as the genome project was completed, a major new initiative was launched. Named ENCODE, for ENCylopedia of DNA Elements, its stated aim was to characterize all the 'functional' elements in the genome.[260] This seemed an acknowledgement that one book of life wasn't enough, and that while the human genome project might be compared to a dictionary, albeit a minimal one that merely listed the different words in a language, so an encyclopaedia was needed to provide detailed information about each gene and its relationship to the other genes in the genome. This was because, as Sydney Brenner noted about the genome project, 'getting the sequence will be the easy part as only technical issues are involved. The hard part will be finding out what it means, because this poses intellectual problems of how to understand the participation of the genes in the functions of living cells.'[261]

Importantly, ENCODE's scope was not to be limited to the protein-coding genes but would instead extend across the whole genome.[260] In part this reflected a growing recognition, stimulated by some of the discoveries we discussed in Chapters 4 and 5, that maybe some of the 'junk' in the genome was not as useless as had been supposed. In recognition of this fact, and showing that biologists are happy to borrow metaphors from whatever source they can, a new phrase increasingly used to describe the non-coding DNA, was that it represented the genome's 'dark matter'.[262] This term is more commonly used by cosmologists to refer to the 85 per cent of the universe that is invisible to the naked eye, and indeed

to any telescope, but is, nevertheless, presumed to exist to account for discrepancies between the universe's observed gravitational behaviour and its mass, implying that there must be much more mass than we can observe.[263] Given the difficulties in directly confirming the existence of this cosmological dark matter, or indeed telling us anything about its properties (although a recent study may have detected it in the Sun[264]), this might not seem a very helpful metaphor. But at least it conveyed the feeling that non-coding DNA could have an important function and was therefore worth investigating seriously.

ENCODE's initial focus was relatively cautious—a pilot project beginning in 2003 that surveyed only 1 per cent of the human genome. Its findings, published in 2007, were tantalizing, since they suggested that non-coding DNA was far more active than supposed.[265] This conclusion was sufficient to secure further major funding to survey the remaining 99 per cent of the genome. Involving 442 scientists from 32 institutions, and costing \$288 million, the ENCODE project was clearly an example of 'big science'.[260] An important issue was how genome function would be assessed. Unlike the original genome project—a straightforward, if daunting, matter of reading the 3 billion bases in our genome using a single method—diverse approaches would be required to study the genome as a living, functioning entity rather than just a series of letters (see Figure 19). One method involves identifying all the places in the genome where transcription factors bind to the DNA. As we saw in Chapter 3, such factors come in different shapes and sizes and relay information to the genes they control from diverse cellular signals. Historically, these factors had been studied one by one, with no sense of how their activity looked at a global level. However, one consequence of the genome project was the development of techniques that made it possible to do this. One such approach uses antibodies generated against transcription factors to purify such factors while they are still attached to their DNA target.[260] The latter can then be sequenced, creating a map showing where each regulatory factor binds in the genome.

Another approach measures differences in accessibility of different parts of the genome to identify regions of activity. Because control elements of active genes are less tightly bound to histones, which, as we saw in Chapter 3, wrap around the DNA but, when acetylated, do so much less tightly, they are both more accessible to transcription factors and also to enzymes called DNAases that cut unprotected DNA into fragments. By identifying parts of the genome that are susceptible to

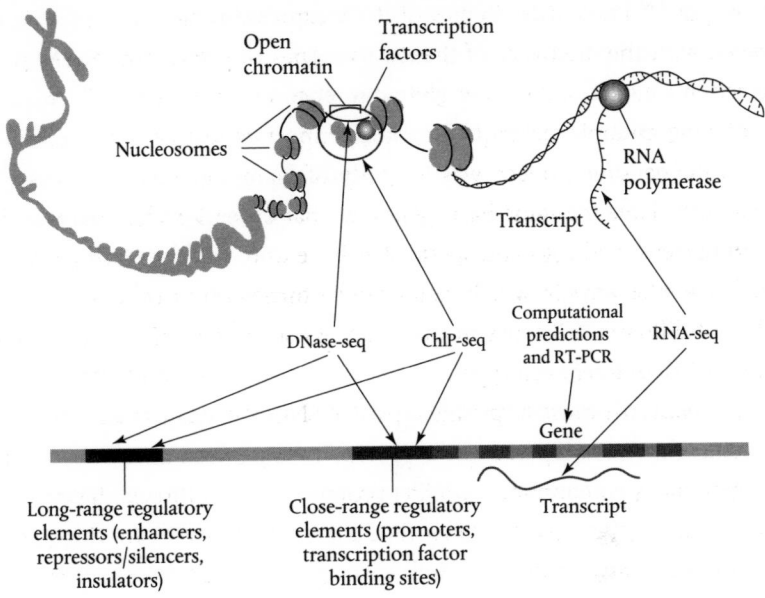

Figure 19. The different approaches used by ENCODE

being cut by such DNAases, a map can be constructed of those regions that are most accessible to transcription factors.[260] In fact, recent studies have shown that acetylation is merely one of a bewildering variety of chemical changes that affect histones, others being methylation and phosphorylation. The sheer number of these changes, each differently affecting gene expression, and the fact that such changes are highly responsive to incoming cellular signals, has given rise to the idea of a 'histone code' that operates parallel to the DNA code.[266] Importantly, whereas initially changes to histones were only thought to affect their association with DNA, more recent studies show that these can also act as a signal to recruit other proteins that regulate gene expression. Another important approach used by ENCODE involved cataloguing these histone modifications in the genome.

A third approach ENCODE used to investigate genome activity was surveying chemical changes in the DNA.[260] Studies in the 1980s first showed that addition of methyl (chemical structure $-CH_3$) groups to C nucleotides within genes and their regulatory regions profoundly affects their expression. As such, identification of methylated C nucleotides across the genome is another indicator of gene activity.[266] Finally, ENCODE studied activity in the genome by cataloguing its

RNA output.[260] Previously, studies of RNA expression had focused on mRNA. However, with the discovery of the diverse types of non-coding RNAs that we discussed in Chapter 5, the focus shifted to encompass these too.[267] In addition to employing multiple techniques, another important feature of ENCODE, compared to the genome project, was its study of many different cell types.[260] For while all cells have the same basic genome—bar exceptions like red blood cells with no nucleus, and eggs and sperm that have only half the DNA content of a normal cell—the ways in which genes can be turned on or off is as great as the number of different cell types in the body. As such, ENCODE studied genome activity in 147 different cell types.

Undoubtedly, the most surprising aspect of ENCODE was its discovery that, far from being inactive compared to the protein-coding genes, the other 98 per cent of the genome was humming with life, prompting Ewan Birney, the charismatic spokesperson for the project based at the Sanger Centre near Cambridge, England, to say 'it's like a jungle in there. It's full of things doing stuff.'[268] Initial claims from ENCODE leaders were that as much as 80 per cent of the human genome had a biochemical function. In fact, Birney went beyond even this, saying, 'it's likely that 80 percent will go to 100 percent'.[268] Echoing this, Thomas Gingeras of Cold Spring Harbor Laboratory, based at Long Island in the USA, said 'almost every nucleotide is associated with a function of some sort or another, and we now know where they are, what binds to them, what their associations are, and more'.[268] This conclusion was so radically different from the idea that most of the genome was 'junk', that John Stamatoyannopoulos of the University of Washington, predicted that the findings would 'change the way a lot of concepts are written about and presented in textbooks'.[269]

Based on studies that localized binding sites for regulatory proteins across the genome to 3.9 million different regions, Birney estimated that over 4 million 'switches' were scattered around the genome, devoted to controlling the activity of the genes—a startling imbalance given there are only just over 22,000 of the latter.[268] But it wasn't only gene switches that were detected in abundance. The study also found that 80 per cent of the genome was generating RNA transcripts.[260] In line with these transcripts having functional importance, many were found only in specific cellular compartments, indicating that they have fixed addresses where they operate. Surely there could hardly be a greater divergence from Crick's central dogma than this demonstration that RNAs were

produced in far greater numbers across the genome than could be expected if they were simply intermediaries between DNA and protein. Indeed, some ENCODE researchers argued that the basic unit of inheritance should now be considered as the transcript. So Stamatoyannopoulos claimed that 'the project has played an important role in changing our concept of the gene'.[270]

Another exciting development was ENCODE's claim to have provided an explanation for a problem that had confounded researchers ever since attempts began to identify the links between common diseases and specific parts of the genome. Such 'genome-wide association studies' work on the principle that, by taking a sufficient number of people—say half a million individuals who, being human, will suffer from various common diseases—and surveying common DNA sequence variants across the human genome, it should be possible to show which variants are associated with a particular disorder.[271] This, then, should identify the important genes, which, when defective, lead to someone succumbing to such a disorder. Since the completion of the genome project, many such studies have been carried out for issues ranging from cardiovascular disease, diabetes, and stroke, through to problems of the mind like schizophrenia and bipolar disorder.[272]

Some important DNA sequence variants have been linked to human disorders by this strategy. But a major problem in interpreting the significance of such findings was that 90 per cent of the DNA variants uncovered in this way were nowhere near any protein-coding genes.[271] However, many of these previous links with disease overlapped with regions of genomic activity identified by ENCODE. Importantly, regions previously implicated in a particular disease were active in precisely the cell type in which this disease occurs.[273] For instance, Birney pointed to the example of Crohn's disease, 'a pretty awful gut disease where the body attacks its own cells. There are a hundred places in the genome where we know a genetic change increases the risk of getting Crohn's. Many of those overlap with a switch identified by ENCODE.'[274] Particularly relevant, given that the body's immune system turns upon itself in Crohn's disease, was the fact that such genomic regions were active in T lymphocytes, which play a central role in mediating immunity. Such insights came from ENCODE surveying many different cell types. This analysis showed that although 4 million gene switches exist in total, which ones are active depends on cell type. This discovery emphasized the importance of cellular environment for gene expression, on a much greater scale than had been realized.[273]

Another surprise of the ENCODE project was how little conservation of genetic switches it detected between humans and other mammals. The project had been specifically carried out in parallel with a similar survey of the mouse genome to study this question. Although the similarity between mice and humans at the protein level is 97.5 per cent, ENCODE's comparison of regulatory regions in the human genome compared to that of the mouse showed a similarity of only 50 per cent.[275] Could this mean that while the proteins of the two species were largely alike, the factors controlling them were widely different? To investigate whether regions of the human genome unique to our species have important functional roles, comparisons of different human individuals were carried out by ENCODE researchers as part of the so-called '1000 Genomes Project'. This indicated that as much as 4 per cent of our genome that is not shared with other mammals is preserved amongst different people, suggesting it is newly under the influence of natural selection and, therefore, important.[275]

The ENCODE findings were widely reported both in glowing editorials in top science journals like *Nature* and *Science* but also across the media. Overall, the feeling was that here was a major new advance in our understanding of how the genome worked, with implications both for our understanding of our biology, and for the diagnosis and treatment of disease. Yet not everyone was so enamoured. Some months after the findings were published, an article, headed by Dan Graur of Houston University, appeared in the journal *Genome Biology and Evolution*,[276] attacking the findings in a vitriolic tone not normally associated with scientific debate, or at least not in the pages of an academic journal. According to the article, the claims of ENCODE were 'absurd', its statistics 'horrible', and it was 'the work of people who know nothing about evolutionary biology'. And, in response to claims by John Stamatoyannopoulos that the findings would necessitate a 're-writing of the textbooks', the article countered by saying that 'the textbooks dealing with marketing, mass-media hype, and public relations may well have to be rewritten'.[277] In a subsequent interview, Graur reiterated these points and added more caustic ones, claiming that 'this is not the work of scientists. This is the work of a group of badly trained technicians.'[278] And just in case his disdain for the project hadn't been fully appreciated, Graur also began showing a slide at the end of his presentations on the topic of a photograph of dollar bills taped together in the shape of a toilet paper roll—his view of what ENCODE had achieved with the $288 million spent on the project.[279]

So what was the motivation for such attacks? One claim made by Graur and his co-authors was that ENCODE researchers had confused biochemical activity with function. So just because huge areas of the genome are peppered with binding sites for regulatory proteins, modified histones, and evidence of large-scale RNA production outside of the protein-coding genes, this does not necessarily mean all are functional.[276] Rather, such activity may merely be genomic 'noise'. After all, if much of the genome can be junk, is it not possible that it may also generate junk activity? A central criticism raised by Graur and his co-authors was that a huge discrepancy existed between the large proportion of the human genome ENCODE leaders claimed was functional, compared to that predicted to be under the pressure of natural selection. As we saw in Chapter 1, variation within a species is believed to be ultimately due to changes in the genome caused by mutation, while the continued presence of such variants is linked to whether they have the characteristics necessary for survival in a particular environment, or are neutral enough in their effects that there is no pressure to eliminate them. But how can the influences of natural selection be gauged across the genome as a whole? Traditionally, the approach used is to compare the complete sequences of the genomes of different species, nucleotide by nucleotide. When used to compare the protein-coding portion of the genome, humans are seen to be 99 per cent similar to a chimpanzee,[280] 85 per cent similar to a mouse,[281] and, confirming the link between all life forms on the planet, even 50 per cent similar to a banana.[282]

But if the whole human genome is compared to that of the mouse, the similarity is far less, only around 5 per cent. And although a recent study comparing the genomes of different human individuals indicates a further amount of similarity that we all share, this only appears to be a further 4 per cent.[283] But, according to Graur and his co-authors, this made a mockery of the ENCODE claim that 80 per cent of our genomes are functional.[276] In particular, they accused ENCODE leaders of ignoring the role of 'purifying selection'. This is the process whereby natural selection prevents changes to DNA sequences in the genome because of their usefulness to the organism in which they occur. Without this selective pressure, there is nothing to stop mutations occurring and changing a particular sequence. But if only 9 per cent of the genome is 'conserved' in this way, then by definition only it can be functional, otherwise the conservation of sequence would be much greater. And, according to Graur and his co-authors, that means that the ENCODE claims of 80 per cent of the genome being

functional are 'absurd', because they 'assume that no deleterious mutations can ever occur in the regions they have deemed to be functional'. Indeed, such claims are akin to believing that 'a television set left on and unattended will still be in working condition after a million years because no natural events, such as rust, erosion, static electricity, and earthquakes can affect it'.[284]

Although the concerns raised by Graur and his co-authors were primarily directed at the underlying science of the ENCODE project, a more veiled concern of the article was the implications of the project's claims for the debate between creationists and evolutionists. We saw in Chapter 4 how the discovery of what appeared to be useless junk in the genome was used as evidence against the idea that a supernatural being designed life, including our own species. But if 80 or even 100 per cent actually turns out to be important, this might be seen to undermine the case for natural selection and let 'intelligent design' in through the back door. Or at least that seemed to be a concern of Graur and his co-authors, given that the title of their article was 'Function in the human genome according to the evolution-free gospel of ENCODE', and elsewhere they said that 'the only people that should be afraid of junk DNA are those claiming that natural processes are insufficient to explain life and that evolutionary theory should be supplemented or supplanted by an intelligent designer'.[285]

Finally, Graur and his co-authors used the opportunity to take a swipe at 'big science'. One consequence of the global recession is that obtaining the government grants that fund most university professors' research is becoming increasingly difficult. As such, there is increasing disquiet amongst some researchers that 'big science' projects like ENCODE are taking the bulk of available money. No matter that a single military fighter jet, at $350 million, can cost more than the combined ENCODE funding,[286] the accusation that the project was not just expensive but incompetent has achieved some resonance with researchers conducting the sort of 'small science' that has been the traditional norm, but who are now faced with a decreasing central pot of money.[284] Indeed, Graur reiterated this point about ENCODE in a recent interview, saying that 'when the average grant size in the biomedical sciences has been halved compared to 10 years ago, this is a scandal. If you pour $288 million into one project, you do not fund 500 other projects. You kill the careers of young scientists. They are reduced to becoming technicians.'[287]

Faced with such a strongly worded attack, the response from ENCODE researchers might have been expected to be similarly robust, or at least to address the key points raised by Graur and his colleagues. However, in an interview with *The Guardian* newspaper following the *Genome Biology and Evolution* paper, Ewan Birney would only say that 'the nature of the attacks against us is quite unfair and uncalled-for'. Birney also took part in an interview at the BBC with Chris Ponting of Oxford University, who had also criticized the ENCODE claims, albeit in more measured tones than Graur and his colleagues. Questioned by Ponting as to how much of the genome was 'vital for life', with the suggestion that this might be between 10 and 20 per cent, Birney seemed to agree with this suggestion, which left the basis for the previously claimed much higher figure of functionality unclear. Finally, asked by the BBC interviewer whether the ENCODE leaders had 'let the story get a bit away' from them, Birney's response was only that 'hindsight being such a cruel thing, [this] makes me think about what I could have done to minimize this kind of rather heated debate'.[288]

All of this was rather disappointing for anyone hoping to see a more vigorous defence of the original ENCODE claims, or an answer to the charge that such claims had been misplaced, either through incompetence or a desire to make a big splash with the media. However, others were prepared to be more vigorous in their defence. In particular, John Mattick and Marcel Dinger, of the Garvan Institute of Medical Research in Sydney, wrote an article for the *HUGO Journal*, official journal of the Human Genome Organisation, entitled 'The extent of functionality in the human genome'.[289] In this they responded in detail to the article by Graur and his co-authors. In response to the accusation that the apparent lack of sequence conservation of 90 per cent of the genome means that it has no function, Mattick and Dinger argued that regulatory elements and non-coding RNAs are much more relaxed in their link between structure and function, and therefore much harder to detect by standard measures of conservation. This could mean that 'conservation is relative', depending on the type of genomic structure being analysed.[289] Secondly, against the idea that the huge numbers of RNA transcripts produced by the genome are mainly random noise, Mattick and Dinger pointed to the fact that ENCODE had confirmed many preceding studies demonstrating that transcripts were produced in 'cell-type specific patterns' and showed 'dynamic regulation in embryo development, tissue differentiation, and disease', suggesting they play an important role in such processes.[289] The third point tackled was the

insinuation that claiming a large degree of function across the genome necessarily plays into the hands of those who want to reject the idea of biological evolution driven by natural selection. In answer to this, Mattick and Dinger argued that a high degree of functionality in the genome was 'entirely consistent with the tenets of evolution by natural selection', albeit along different lines to those who held to a view of the genome that was primarily focused on protein-coding genes.[290]

That Mattick was prepared to make such bold claims was no surprise to those familiar with his previous views on this topic. In fact, well before the ENCODE findings were published in 2012, he had been making the case that the genomes of multicellular organisms were far more complex in their mechanism of operation than had been imagined. So, in an article published in 2007 following the results of the initial ENCODE pilot project, Mattick said 'it is also now clear that the majority of the mammalian genome is expressed and that many mammalian genes are accompanied by extensive regulatory regions'.[291] In arguing for such a viewpoint, Mattick has suggested that the original concept of the genome as a digital code did not go far enough.[292] According to him, when Watson and Crick came up with their revolutionary proposal in the 1950s, one problem was that their views were coloured by the society of the time, this being a world of analogue devices like vinyl records and slide rules. As such, they conceived of the gene primarily as a recipe—albeit using a digital code—for analogue devices, the proteins. This led to the idea of a simple one-way transfer of information from DNA to proteins, which led to Crick's central dogma.

Yet now that we live in the digital age, we recognize that digital information can be highly multi-layered. And, according to Mattick, biologists are only just beginning to recognize that such multi-layered information is characteristic of our own genomes, with different forms of non-coding RNAs playing multiple roles in the different layers. In line with this idea, in a recent article in *Nature Reviews in Genetics*, entitled 'The rise of regulatory RNA', Mattick has claimed that 'RNA is the computational engine of cell biology, developmental biology, brain function and perhaps even evolution itself. The complexity and interconnectedness of these systems should not be cause for concern but rather the motivation for exploring the vast unknown universe of RNA regulation, without which we will not understand biology.'[293] A proponent of a similar viewpoint is Evelyn Fox Keller of the Massachusetts Institute of Technology, who believes recent 'genomic science has changed the very meaning of the term, turning the genome into an

entity far richer, more complex, and more powerful—simultaneously both more and less—than the pre-genomic genome, in ways that require us to rework our understanding of the relation between genes, genomes and genetics'.[294]

So who is right? Has ENCODE opened a new chapter in our understanding of the genome and how it works, or are the conclusions of the project's leaders flawed and misleading? To address this issue, it's time we began to dig deeper into those proposed multiple layers of the genome, like miners trying to find the richest seams, in order to gain further insights into what these layers are, and their relationship to each other. In doing so, we will not only look further at the role of the various types of non-coding RNAs, but also at the histone proteins that wrap around DNA. In addition, we will examine the chemical modifications that alter these proteins and the DNA itself. We will also study how such modifications are affected by changes in the environment of the cell and organism, and whether the genome as an entity is as stable as we have been led to believe. But before we do any of that, it's time to consider whether the original idea of the genome as a primarily linear object stretched out along a chromosome still holds, or whether, also like a mine, it is better understood in 3D. So if you are ready, let's get digging!

7

THE GENOME IN 3D

'Natural DNA is a tractless coil, like an unwound and tangled audiotape on the floor of the car in the dark.'
Kary Mullis

'The genome is like a panel of light switches in a room full of lights. These switches can be located far from the genes they regulate in the one-dimensional genome sequence but in three dimensions, the chromosome is folded so that they physically touch.'
Job Dekker

It's time to give the genome some physicality and some shape. A common view of chromosomes is of linear strands of DNA upon which the genes are dotted like beads on a string. In a very obvious sense chromosomes are linear entities, since each is an unbroken chain of bases, ranging from a quarter of a billion for the largest human chromosome 1, to 50 million for the smallest, chromosome 22.[295] Proteins are also linear molecules, albeit magnitudes smaller than even the smallest chromosome, but it has long been recognized that it is the 3D ordering of the amino acid chain that gives each specific protein its characteristic and unique properties. Now, however, there is a growing recognition that chromosomes too are complex 3D entities, so much so that ENCODE researcher Job Dekker of the University of Massachusetts Medical School recently said 'nothing in the genome makes sense, except in 3D',[296] paraphrasing a previous comment from renowned evolutionary biologist Theodosius Dobzhansky, who once said 'nothing in biology makes sense except in the light of evolution'.[297] So how did Dekker come to this conclusion and how exactly does a 3D genome function?

One factor that helped shape our image of chromosomes as solely linear entities was the genetic maps that scientists from Morgan and Sturtevant onwards began to construct, which reinforced the notion of such linearity. And while it is

ethically impossible to subject humans to massive doses of X-rays in order to stimulate mutations, or carry out mating experiments to study their transmission across generations, enough information has accumulated from investigations of families in which certain characteristics or diseases can be followed, to allow construction of such maps for our own species. So even before the genome project, detailed maps already existed of the relative positions of many human genes on each chromosome.[298]

The idea of chromosomes as linear entities was also reinforced by the shape chromosomes assume during the phase of cell division known as mitosis, when they become the tiny threads that Walther Flemming first observed, as we saw in Chapter 1. Chromosomes assume such a condensed linear form to ensure the two chromosome pairs segregate to each daughter cell in a tangle-free fashion.[299] Yet apart from this brief period in a cell's life, chromosomes normally assume a much looser form, with their DNA chains distributed across the 3D space of the cell nucleus. Not that this distribution is random; instead, it's been known for some years that DNA is densely packed. Indeed, it would be hard to imagine how the immensely long genome could be accommodated within the small nuclear space otherwise.[300] If all the DNA in a human cell were laid end to end, it would stretch for two metres. Yet the nucleus is only ten microns—less than one hundred thousandth this size—so how is this packaging problem solved?

The discovery of histones went a long way to providing an answer. By coiling the DNA into nucleosomes, the interaction with histones provides the first level of genomic packaging, but also makes possible a series of further levels of organization counterposed on top of each other like a set of Russian dolls.[301] Another important contributor to genomic packaging is the nuclear lamina, a fibrous network concentrated near the periphery of the nucleus that helps to organize the nuclear pores, holes in the nuclear membrane that allow molecules to travel between the nucleus and the rest of the cell. Recent studies have shown that the genomic regions associated with the nuclear lamina are those with low activity, which explains why early studies of stained cells first showed that the most condensed chromatin—the complex mixture of DNA, histones, and other proteins that genomes are composed of—is particularly concentrated around the periphery of the nucleus.[302]

The one type of human cell in which DNA is not primarily associated with histones is the sperm. We saw in Chapter 2 how Friedrich Miescher first isolated and characterized DNA from white blood cells in the pus from surgical bandages

while a young scientist working in Tübingen, Germany. Later, now based in his home city of Basel, Switzerland, he found another, slightly more salubrious source of DNA in salmon sperm, which he obtained in large quantities from the river Rhine near his laboratory. However, although his colleague Albrecht Kossel had shown that normally DNA is associated with histones, Miescher found that this is not true of the sperm: instead, its DNA is associated with another protein which he called protamine.[303] Histones and DNA are attracted to each other because of their respective basic and acidic chemical properties. Protamines are even more basic than histones and consequently have a greater affinity for DNA. Because of this, the sperm genome is packaged in an almost crystalline fashion. This allows the DNA to fit into the highly streamlined sperm head, an essential feature for a cell that must swim a great relative distance before it gets to its target, the egg. And just as Olympic swimmers shave or squeeze into high-tech supersuits to further streamline themselves, a recent study by scientists at the European Molecular Biology Laboratory in Grenoble showed that sperm streamlining is boosted by a protein called BRDT.[304]

The study showed that BRDT drives the replacement of histones by protamines by adding acetyl tags to the former. According to Saadi Khochbin, who led the study, 'in sperm, just before the DNA starts to hypercompact, these tags are added throughout the chromatin in a huge wave. If BRDT is absent, the extra compaction doesn't take place, and the sperm head would be less streamlined.'[305] Demonstrating the importance of this process for normal sperm function, male mice lacking BRDT are infertile. As well as aiding streamlining, such tight packaging helps to protect the sperm DNA from the potentially harmful bodily chemicals to which it is exposed during its journey through the female reproductive passage. However, recent studies have shown that a significant proportion of human sperm DNA—up to 15 per cent as opposed to only 1 per cent in mouse sperm—is associated with histones, with the genes first activated during embryo development being packaged in this way, in line with the idea that this looser association allows more rapid access of this part of the genome to transcription factors.[306] That the packaging of any particular region of the genome might affect its activity was first suggested many years ago by microscopy studies of cells exposed to different kinds of chemical stains, which revealed that chromatin exists in two main forms—a dark-staining tightly packed version called heterochromatin and a lighter-staining, looser form called euchromatin.[307] In addition, recent

studies indicate that, far from being a static structure, the 3D genome in the living cell is also highly dynamic, with structural changes in the chromatin being intimately linked to gene activity. Such recognition has come from experimental approaches that visualize the position of specific genes within the nucleus.

One such approach is called fluorescence *in situ* hybridization, or FISH for short. The fluorescently labelled DNA probes used in FISH are complementary to specific sequences in the genome and can be used to specifically identify the presence of a gene within a chromosome. 2D FISH has become an important clinical tool in the diagnosis of genetic abnormalities, particularly those associated with cancer.[308] In this approach, the probe is used to identify whether specific oncogenes are amplified in the genome. Normally, a gene is recognized as two spots of fluorescence, since there are two gene copies in a typical cell. However, in cancer, the cellular machinery that duplicates the genome at each cell division often breaks down, with some parts of the DNA being replicated more than once. And it's not a coincidence that the genome regions that tend to become amplified are those containing genes involved in cell growth and other processes that are subverted in cancer. Darwin and Wallace's theory of natural selection as the driving force of evolution views individual organisms in a species as subject to the 'survival of the fittest'. However, this principle is also central to cancer, as cells that overcome the normal limits governing cell growth and other forces limiting tumours, are selected for their superior qualities in this regard.[309] Through amplification of genomic regions with a high concentration of oncogenes, a cancerous cell can gain an advantage compared to other cells in the tumour. RAS is a particularly important oncogene because of the central role its non-mutated form plays in normal cell growth; it is amplified in up to 30 per cent of human cancers. 2D FISH can be used diagnostically to see whether this gene has become amplified in a cancer cell, since if this is the case, instead of two fluorescent spots, many more will be observed.

A further modification of 2D FISH is called chromosome painting.[310] In this approach the fluorescent probe targets DNA sequences across a whole chromosome. By using a different colour fluorescence for each chromosome, this technique makes it possible to easily identify all the different chromosomes in a cell. Previously, this meant laboriously comparing their different sizes and staining patterns with chemical dyes—such dyes give a pattern of bands unique to each chromosome but which can only be distinguished by someone trained to

recognize the subtle differences. Chromosome painting is used to identify people with genetic diseases involving chromosome 'translocations', where parts of one chromosome break off and become incorporated into a different chromosome during cell division.[310] By disrupting normal gene expression, such translocations can lead to disease, including cancer.

However, as well as being used to study condensed chromosomes, FISH has recently been used to study the location of genes in the uncondensed DNA that fills the 3D space of the nucleus in the so-called 'interphase' period between cell divisions.[311] Visualizing fluorescence in this 3D space is carried out using so-called 'confocal' microscopy. Typically, this uses a laser beam to scan across a 3D section and pick out a spot of fluorescence in high resolution. Combining this technique with FISH has made it possible to identify the precise position of a gene within the nucleus.[312] Such studies have shown that there are 'active' and 'inactive' regions of the nucleus, with genes that are switched on in the former, and genes that are switched off in the latter. Remarkably, when a gene's activity changes because of a cellular stimulus, its position in the nucleus also changes. Such changes occur, for instance, during stem cell differentiation: the process by which an unspecialized, rapidly dividing cell gives rise to a specialized cell type. 3D FISH showed that genes that keep the stem cell in its unspecialized state move into an inactive region upon differentiation, whereas genes that give the differentiated cell its specialized character move into an active region.[301] This shows that the nuclear space is a far more dynamic entity than previously thought.

Also revealed by recent studies is the complexity of the interactions between different genomic regions that occur within the 3D nuclear space. We saw in Chapter 4 how the discovery of enhancers was initially baffling since they can operate at a great distance from the genes they regulate. However, subsequent studies showed that enhancers, and the transcription factors bound to them, loop around to the gene promoter, and in this way can influence its expression. As important as these studies were, they were very much focused on the individual gene. However, over the last decade, new approaches that allow scientists to 'capture' interactions between different parts of the genome are revolutionizing our understanding of how these parts fit together. Such approaches use chemicals to cross-link the proteins that bind DNA, and then advanced sequencing technology to identify the DNA sequences to which such proteins are attached.[313] Importantly, this analysis is done on a 'global' scale so that all the interactions

occurring in the genome can be studied at once. By carrying out such analysis on a variety of cell types following physiological stimulation, it is becoming possible to build up a picture of how such interactions change during different cellular events.

Although the approaches discussed so far have greatly enhanced our understanding of how the genome operates in the 3D nuclear space, one significant limitation is that none involve study of the living cell. So 3D FISH is carried out on cells fixed with formaldehyde and then incubated with a fluorescent RNA probe. Similarly, methods that capture interactions between different genomic regions use cross-linking chemicals that kill the cell but freeze the molecular interactions within, and then fragment the DNA and associated protein. Although comparisons can be made between cells at different stages of differentiation or physiological stimulation, this is still a static picture. However, recently it has become possible to study genome interactions in a living cell in real time, through the use of fluorescent proteins first discovered in jellyfish, but which have since revolutionized the study of cellular processes by making it possible to fluorescently 'tag' molecules and follow their movement and activity.[314]

When Japanese biologist Osamu Shimomura, working at the Woods Hole Marine Biological Laboratory near Cape Cod, began studying why certain jellyfish were a striking green fluorescent colour, his main incentive was pure curiosity. But his discovery that a single protein—green fluorescent protein or GFP for short—was responsible for this property and the subsequent isolation of the gene coding for this protein, raised the possibility that GFP could be used to make the protein products of other genes 'visible' by genetically fusing the GFP gene to them.[314, 315] In fact, it was another scientist at Woods Hole, Douglas Prasher, who first cloned the GFP gene and suggested that it could be used as a fluorescent tag. However, Prasher was unable to obtain research funding to push his idea forward and instead two other scientists, Martin Chalfie and Roger Tsien, developed GFP in this way. Tsien had already found fame creating small molecules that fluoresce when they come into contact with cellular messengers, such as the calcium ions and cAMP that we discussed in Chapter 3.[316] This made it possible, for the first time, to 'visualize' changes in the concentrations of such messengers in the cell. Now, by mutating GFP in various ways, Tsien created a range of differently coloured fluorescent proteins, which, showing a characteristic humorous streak, he named after fruits.[314] So, in research papers it is now common to read about proteins tagged with banana, plum, tomato, grape, and so on. Quirky names aside,

the generation of differently coloured proteins that fluoresce at different wavelengths of light has made it possible to study the localization of two or more proteins in the cell at the same time, by giving them differently coloured tags.[317]

The importance of GFP was recognized by the award of a Nobel Prize to Shimomura, Chalfie, and Tsien in 2008. In his acceptance speech, Tsien drew attention to the fact that 'aspects of our work were fragile results of lucky circumstances' and how 'funding was difficult at times to obtain for basic research on obscure organisms like the jellyfish that was the source of GFP', adding that he hoped the award of the prize would reinforce 'recognition of the importance of basic science as the foundation for practical benefits to our health and economies'.[318] As a poignant illustration of this issue, during the Nobel announcements it emerged that Doug Prasher, who had originally cloned GFP, had left science, having failed to obtain funding for his research, and was working as a courtesy shuttle driver.[319] Subsequently, Tsien, who had always championed Prasher's input, not only paid for Prasher to attend the Nobel celebrations in Stockholm, but also offered him a job as a senior scientist in his laboratory. In his speech Tsien also noted the potential effects of environmental destruction, saying how 'over the last ten years, observed numbers of jellyfish in their Pacific Northwest habitat have declined by over a thousandfold...what other potential scientific breakthroughs may never happen because of man-made pollution and global warming?'[318]

Use of fluorescent tags such as GFP, coupled with very high resolution microscopy, is now making it possible to track the movements of individual transcription factors relative to the DNA elements to which they bind.[320] Such approaches will be vital in allowing scientists to study how changes in the cellular environment affect the expression of particular genes. The combination of these types of analysis has led to some major new insights. One is that even when chromosomes are in their uncondensed state, they generally occupy a defined region within the nucleus. But it has also become clear that, within such a chromosome 'territory', there are further levels of organization that divide the chromosome up into specifically defined structural and functional regions. In particular, recent studies have revealed an important sub-level of structure and function within the chromosome, so-called 'topologically associating domains' or TADs for short.[313] These are regions of the chromosome that can vary in size from a few hundred kilobases to several megabases. Within these regions there is a high level

of local contacts, while their boundaries act as a barrier to contacts with other regions. This finding goes some way to addressing a conundrum that has puzzled biologists ever since enhancers were first discovered, namely how gene regulatory elements that act over such long distances do not activate any random gene in the genome. In fact, it seems that TAD boundaries act as 'insulators' that prevent the influence of an enhancer spreading beyond the TAD in which it is contained.[321] Such insulating effects are mediated by proteins like cohesin, previously shown to be essential for chromosome segregation in dividing cells.[322] This shows that although there has been a tendency in the past to separate the replication of the genome from its expression, some key factors clearly regulate both processes.

One issue still to be fully resolved in understanding how the genome functions as a 3D entity is determining what drives enhancer looping. Initially, it was assumed that simple random movement brought enhancers into contact with the genes they control. Yet this makes it hard to explain a surprising finding of ENCODE, which is that only in a small minority of cases—less than 10 per cent— do enhancers interact with the nearest gene in their vicinity as assessed in a purely linear fashion along the chromosome.[313] Instead, the growing consensus is that enhancer looping is an active process. One possibility is that 'bridging' proteins fill the gap between an enhancer and the gene it controls, and, indeed, a protein called 'mediator' seems to play such a role.[323] However, the recent surprising finding that enhancers are transcribed into RNA, and abolishing production of such RNAs inhibits expression of the genes they control, suggests that such RNAs may also be involved.[324] A key question to address now is whether enhancer RNAs are involved in forming DNA loops, possibly by guiding the enhancer to its target gene. Recent studies suggest this may be the case, but enhancer RNAs may also act in other, as yet unidentified ways, upon gene expression.[325]

The 3D structure of the genome also seems to play an important role in the process of splicing. Although this might seem counterintuitive, given that splicing occurs at the RNA level, it is becoming increasingly obvious that transcription of genes and splicing of the resulting RNAs are tightly coordinated, so that chromatin structure can have a major impact on splicing. Recently, John Mattick and his colleague, Tim Mercer, at the Garvan Institute, have shown, in a collaborative project with John Stamatoyannopoulos, that the portions of a gene coding for exons are far more accessible in the 3D genome than those that code for introns.[326] Moreover, exons destined to be selected for alternative splicing in

particular cell types are also more accessible at the DNA level. Mercer believes this shows the genome is like 'a long and immensely convoluted grape vine, its twisted branches presenting some grapes to be plucked easily, while concealing others beyond reach. At the same time, imagine a lazy fruit picker only picking the grapes within easy reach. The same principle applies in the genome. Specific genes and even specific exons, are placed within easy reach by folding.'[327]

Although chromosome territories and TADs act to constrain gene expression in certain defined regions, there is also evidence that interactions between different regions of the genome can also sometimes occur over much greater distances, even between genes on different chromosomes. In particular, active genes from different chromosomes seem to congregate at sites called 'transcription factories' where substantial numbers of RNA polymerases and other enzymes involved in transcription are clustered. The idea of transcription factories was first proposed by Peter Cook and colleagues at Oxford University in the early 1990s.[328] They were using a labelled form of the nucleotide containing uracil, or U, found in RNA but not DNA, to visualize synthesis of RNA in the nucleus of a cell. In line with the idea that each individual gene is transcribed by its own RNA polymerase molecule, Cook and colleagues fully expected to see a homogenous distribution of labelling throughout the nucleus. Instead, they saw around three to five hundred concentrated clusters of transcriptional activity, and subsequent investigation with antibodies that recognized RNA polymerase proteins confirmed that these clusters contained such proteins. These findings led to the proposal that, rather than genes remaining stationary while the transcriptional machinery assembles around them, the situation is the other way around, with 'factories' composed of hundreds of RNA polymerases and associated enzymes being fixed at certain points in the nucleus while the genes to be transcribed come to them.[328]

The idea of transcription factories has been controversial since its first proposal, partly due to the difficulties of isolating such factories biochemically, and because there seems to be much variation between these entities in different cell types. However, the ability to capture interactions between different genomic regions has given a new lease of life to this idea by showing that genes from completely different parts of the genome that come together in the 3D nuclear space are associated with 'hot-spots' of transcriptional activity.[328] Tim Mercer believes this shows we need 'a new way of looking at things, one where the genome is folded around transcription machinery, rather than the other way around. Those genes

that come in contact with the transcription machinery get transcribed, while those parts which loop away are ignored.'[327] Formation of hot-spots of activity is likely to involve a combination of biochemical compatibility between different regulatory proteins, effects of insulators, the chromatin environment, and the 3D architecture of the nucleus, all acting together.

As well as changing our understanding of the basic mechanisms of gene expression such findings also have clinical implications. In particular, a recent study of the genes that generate haemoglobin has confirmed both the importance of contacts between genes on completely separate chromosomes and the existence of transcription factories, as well as their significance in diseases where globin expression is abnormal.[329] Haemoglobin is, of course, crucial to our existence, carrying, as it does, oxygen to our cells and carbon dioxide away from them. The protein also has a distinguished role in the history of molecular biology since Max Perutz solved its 3D structure, making this the first such protein structure to be so determined. For his efforts Perutz received a Nobel Prize in 1962, the same year as Watson, Crick, and Wilkins received theirs. However, it's not only in advancing our knowledge of protein structure that haemoglobin has played a central role, but also our understanding of how genes are regulated. We've seen how, although enhancers were first identified in adenovirus, one of the first to be identified in our own genome was in the beta-globin gene.[330] In fact, this gene is just one of a cluster that includes the epsilon-, gamma-, and delta-globin genes, which code for embryonic and foetal forms of haemoglobin. Remarkably, the order of expression of these genes during development mirrors the order in which they occur on the chromosome, while studies have shown that a complex regulatory element—the locus of control region or LCR—controls the expression of all the genes in the cluster.[330]

Studying the expression of the beta-globin gene is important clinically because a number of serious genetic diseases affect haemoglobin. One such disorder is sickle cell anaemia, where a mutation in a single DNA nucleotide changes an amino acid on the surface of the protein to one of a different character. This alters the 3D structure of the protein, so that instead of forming a soluble protein, aggregates are formed that both compromise the oxygen-carrying capacity of the protein and also cause the sickle-shaped red blood cells characteristic of this disorder.[331] Another group of genetic diseases affecting haemoglobin are the thalassaemias.[332] These come in multiple forms but all involve abnormalities in expression of either

the alpha- or beta-globin genes, which code for the alpha- and beta-globin proteins that make up haemoglobin in adult humans. Symptoms range from mild anaemia to fatal lack of properly functioning haemoglobin. Because mutations that cause thalassaemias can affect not only the protein-coding portions of the globin genes but also the regulatory regions that control them, studies of such mutations have led to important general insights about mechanisms of gene expression.[333] One unsolved issue is the question of how alpha- and beta-globin proteins are produced in evenly matched amounts, despite the genes coding for them being on completely different chromosomes. This is an important issue not only from a scientific point of view, but also for treatment of thalassaemias, because imbalances in the relative proportions of the alpha- and beta-globin protein chains can have toxic effects upon the cell.[332]

Studies investigating the interaction between different parts of the genome using cross-linking methods like those discussed, have shown that not only do the alpha- and beta-globin gene regulatory regions come into close contact, but they seem to be associated with the same transcription factory.[329] Understanding how this joint expression is regulated spatially in the genome could further our understanding of thalassaemias and lead to new ways to treat such disorders. In fact, this is just one case where understanding the 3D structure of the genome may aid diagnosis and treatment of disease. For instance, a breakdown in this 3D structure can occur during tumour formation. Cancer can be caused by activation of 'proto-oncogenes' or loss of function of 'tumour suppressor' genes.[334] Both classes of genes play important roles in regulating normal cell growth and division—it's only when they become mutated that they cause disease. We've seen how cancer can arise when a DNA region on one chromosome breaks and fuses with DNA from a different chromosome, such fusions being known as 'translocations'.[335] A cancer of the blood called Burkitt's lymphoma is triggered by a translocation in which the proto-oncogene MYC on chromosome 8, which plays a central role in cell growth, is brought into contact with the regulatory region for the immunoglobulin gene coding for antibodies on chromosome 14. Since antibodies are normally strongly expressed in B-lymphocytes of the immune system, this causes such cells to rapidly proliferate in a malignant fashion. Another translocation, known as the Philadelphia chromosome because of the city in which it was first identified, brings together two proto-oncogenes, BCR on chromosome 22 and ABL on chromosome 9, to form a fused protein BCR-ABL. This powerful stimulant to cell growth in white blood cells leads to a type of leukaemia.

Something that has puzzled cancer researchers for years is why certain gene combinations crop up so frequently in translocations. Now recent studies have shown that regions of the genome that fuse during translocations normally make close contact in the nucleus, and in the case of the MYC and antibody genes, are expressed by the same transcription factory.[336] So while breakage of chromosomes is a pathological process, its consequences will be partially determined by which genes are normally close to each other in the 3D nucleus. This has led Peter Cook and colleagues to suggest that characterization of the regulatory proteins involved in transcription factories, and how these change as a tumour develops, might lead to identification of new anti-cancer treatments.[337]

A breakdown of the 3D structure of the genome may also be one feature of the ageing process. So aged cells lack several key architectural proteins, and also have less condensed heterochromatin, than young cells. Further evidence of a link between ageing and genomic organization in the nucleus has come from studies of the premature human ageing disorder Hutchinson–Gilford Progeria syndrome.[338] Individuals with this disorder develop a wizened appearance and hair loss even as children, and generally die prematurely of a heart disorder or stroke. This disorder is caused by a mutation in the gene coding for lamin A, a protein involved in forming the nuclear lamina, and sufferers' cells show both a disorganized nuclear structure and also an absence of heterochromatin. How might a disorganized nucleus contribute to ageing? One possibility is that this exposes the genome to increased levels of DNA damage. Other premature ageing disorders in humans are due to defects in genes coding for 'DNA repair' enzymes that correct errors caused by UV radiation, environmental toxins, or simply mistakes made by DNA polymerase as it replicates the genome at each cell division. DNA that is less tightly organized in the nucleus may be more vulnerable to environmental insult, explaining why premature ageing is a feature of Hutchinson–Gilford Progeria syndrome.

Perhaps the most intriguing aspect of recent studies is the link identified between non-coding RNAs and long-range 3D interactions of the genome.[325] So although many non-coding RNAs have been shown to act locally to control expression of genes that they are located close to in the genome, there is also increasing evidence that some may act upon multiple targets that are much more distant. For instance, HOTAIR, a long non-coding RNA transcribed close to the HOX genes, members of the homeotic gene family, which, as we saw in Chapter 4,

control body patterning, binds to 800 locations in the genome across multiple chromosomes.[325] Recent evidence suggests that this pattern of binding may be intimately linked to the 3D structure, but also that long non-coding RNAs in particular may play a central role as a kind of 'scaffolding' that ties different regions of the genome together both structurally and also in terms of function. That such RNAs, by virtue of their sequence but also 3D shape, can bind DNA, RNA, and proteins, makes them ideal candidates for such a role. Importantly, the scaffolds that they form seem highly dynamic, and this may be a key factor in the regulation of gene activity in a global fashion across the genome.

Such findings demonstrate the importance of genome structure in both the normal and pathological state. Importantly, they show that the view of genes as isolated entities strung out like beads on a string along linear chromosomes is a poor misrepresentation of the complex reality of the 3D genome. Nevertheless, such findings can still be reconciled with the idea of the genome as an essentially stable repository of information which is passed down through the generations with both its primary structure, and the information it conveys, being constant through those generations. But are genomes really that stable? It is time to take a closer look.

8

THE JUMPING GENES

'If you know you are on the right track, if you have this inner knowledge, then nobody can turn you off... no matter what they say.'   *Barbara McClintock*

'Jumping genes are fundamental because they're agents of change. Everybody knows that organisms evolve. What makes them evolve is that their genes are dynamic and in motion.'   *Nina Fedoroff*

Imagine a map on which the key features moved about. This could make route-finding very difficult. If it were a map of England, one minute you might be heading south towards London, the next minute the capital city could have shifted north, next to York. Just as we expect the cities on road maps to maintain a constant position, so the scientists who first began to map the position of genes upon each chromosome did so with the justifiable assumption that, once located on the genetic map, those genes would stay in their allocated positions. This assumption may go some way to explaining the response when the geneticist Barbara McClintock announced in 1951, some two years before the discovery of the molecular structure of DNA, that portions of the genome could move about in the space of a few generations.[339] Unfortunately, despite the fact that McClintock had already made a name for herself establishing some key principles in genetics, such was the novelty of her findings that it took over three decades for them to be accepted by the scientific community. Even today, there is an ongoing debate about the functional significance of mobile elements, with the initial view that they are primarily parasitical entities only recently being challenged by evidence that they can play vital roles in gene regulation.

As a woman, McClintock faced many challenges in pursuing a career as a scientist in the early years of the twentieth century, not least from her own mother,

who, when McClintock's father was away at the front during World War I, initially tried to prevent her daughter from going to college because of a fear that this would make her 'umarriageable'.[340] Luckily, McClintock's father interceded on his return from the war just before college enrolment began, and Barbara began the academic career that would result in several major discoveries in genetics and finally a Nobel Prize. McClintock never did marry or meet anyone she wanted to share her life with, but her work has transformed our view of the genome in ways that resonate to this day.

McClintock's first important scientific finding was the demonstration that the crossing over that takes place in meiosis during formation of eggs and sperm involves a physical exchange between each chromosome pair. As we saw in Chapter 1, Thomas Morgan surmised that this must be the case based on Frans Janssens' observations but he had never directly shown it to be true. But when, working with corn, McClintock identified a mutant that had a chromosome with an unusually shaped end, she realized that here was a way to directly test the idea. By crossing the mutant with a normal plant and then observing the inheritance pattern of characteristics associated with the odd-shaped part of the chromosome, in what has been called 'one of the truly great experiments of modern biology' McClintock showed that inheritance of such characteristics was always accompanied by a physical exchange of this part of the chromosome.[341]

McClintock continued studying genetics in corn for the rest of her career. Another major discovery she made using the plant was the identification of two key structural elements of chromosomes—'telomeres' and 'centromeres'—from the Greek for 'end' and 'centre', this being their respective locations on the chromosome. The discovery of telomeres was made when, inspired by Hermann Muller's success in using radiation to induce mutations, McClintock tried this approach in corn. One mutation with a very obvious physical form that she identified was so-called 'ring' chromosomes, which formed when the ends of a chromosome fused together. McClintock surmised from this that there must be a structure at the ends of chromosomes that normally stabilized them, and that this had been compromised by mutation.[342] These telomeres are like the plastic tips on the ends of shoelaces and prevent the chromosome from fraying just as such tips protect the lace. But telomeres also have a tendency to shorten every time a cell divides. This tendency is offset in young cells by an enzyme called

telomerase, but as cells age this capacity diminishes, and this is one reason why cells in culture can only undergo a limited number of cell divisions before they die.[342] This limit can, however, be overcome in cancer cells which express telomerase at high levels. Telomerase is also active in eggs and sperm, so each new generation starts off life with re-lengthened telomeres.

In a recent study, mice were engineered to lack the telomerase enzyme and, as a consequence, suffered from advanced ageing.[343] However, when genetic engineering was used to reactivate telomerase in the mice for one month, surprisingly, not only did this stop the ageing, but it actually reversed the effects, so that the mice began to look significantly younger. As if they had drunk from Merlin's fountain of eternal youth, which, legend has it, still lies hidden in the Forest of Paimpont in Brittany, France,[344] shrivelled testes grew back to normal and the mice regained their fertility, the spleen, liver, and intestines recuperated from their degenerated state, and, in the brain, neural progenitor cells, which produce neurons and their supporting cells, were reactivated. Ronald DePinho of Harvard Medical School, who led the study, believes the findings show 'there's a point of return for age-associated disorders', while his colleague, David Sinclair, thinks that if a similar strategy could be used safely in humans, 'it could lead to breakthroughs in restoring organ function in the elderly and treating a variety of diseases of aging'.[345] However, David Harrison, who studies ageing at the Jackson Laboratory in Bar Harbor, Maine, believes 'telomere rejuvenation is potentially very dangerous unless you make sure that it does not stimulate cancer'. Harrison also questions whether mice lacking telomerase are a good model for human ageing, saying 'they are not studying normal ageing, but ageing in mice made grossly abnormal'.[345]

In contrast to telomeres, centromeres were identified by McClintock as bulges at the centre of each chromosome.[346] She noticed that these structures were always the first to line up at the centre of a cell before it began to divide, and it was the centromeres that seemed to guide each chromosome pair to an opposite pole of the cell. Such observations suggested that centromeres played a leading role in chromosome segregation. But the definitive evidence came yet again from the study of oddly shaped chromosomes that were the result of excessive irradiation with X-rays. After such treatment, some chromosomes had fused together so that they contained two centromeres. In this case, rather than being pulled towards one pole of the cell, the mutant chromosome was clearly being tugged in

two opposing directions, providing the first direct evidence of the central role played by centromeres in the segregation process.

Normally, centromeres guide this process in a very precise fashion during the cell divisions of mitosis that occur during embryo development. If this were not the case, multicellular organisms like ourselves could never develop with the correct number of chromosomes in each of the several trillion cells that make up our bodies. However, mistakes do sometimes occur during the formation of eggs and sperm during meiosis. This can result in an organism with only one, or an extra copy, of a particular chromosome, in contrast to the normal situation in which each cell has two. In humans, these conditions are not generally compatible with life, but there are exceptions, particularly with the sex chromosomes.[347] So women with Turner's syndrome have only one X chromosome; such women have short stature, a broad chest, low hairline, and low-set ears, plus dysfunctional ovaries that normally result in sterility, as well as specific mental differences. In contrast, men with Klinefelter's syndrome inherit not one but two X chromosomes to go with their Y chromosome. These men have less muscular bodies, less facial and body hair, and broader hips; with such subtle differences, this condition often goes unrecognized. Genetically engineered mice with abnormal numbers of sex chromosomes are being studied to further understand the effect of such changes upon the body and help devise treatments for the associated symptoms.[347]

The most well-known disorder associated with more than two copies of a non-sex chromosome is Down's syndrome, caused by three copies of chromosome 21.[348] People with this condition have characteristic facial features and learning difficulties, as well as heart defects in later life and a shortened life span. One of the main risk factors for Down's syndrome is the age of the mother. This suggests that the machinery that drives each chromosome 21 to opposite poles of the cell becomes defective as women age. Current studies are focusing on the interaction between centromeres and this machinery, and how this changes with maternal age, in order to understand why the segregation becomes faulty.[348] Ultimately, such studies could result in treatments that prevent such events occurring.

Given such pioneering initial discoveries in McClintock's career, one might assume that the importance of her subsequent findings would be accepted as readily. Unfortunately, this was not to be the case, because the nature of her next discovery challenged the very basis of genetics as it was perceived at the time.

McClintock discovered mobile genomic elements while studying the genetics of colour in corn. As consumers, we generally buy corn that is uniformly yellow; however, many supermarkets now also sell fancy varieties in which the different kernels are multicoloured, and it was the genetics of these varieties that McClintock studied. However, as she studied the pattern of inheritance of colour across successive generations, McClintock came to a surprising conclusion—the chromosomal position of the genes associated with the different colours appeared not to be fixed, but instead seemed highly mobile.[339]

McClintock named this process 'transposition' and the mobile elements 'transposons'. She proposed that transposons were not the genes for colour themselves but rather their controlling elements, and she suggested that this could explain why complex multicellular organisms composed of cells with identical sets of genes can have cells with very different functions.[349] As we've seen, the distinction between structural genes and the regulatory elements that control them is generally associated with Jacob and Monod. Yet McClintock made this distinction in a paper published in 1953, seven years before the French scientists drew attention to it in their report on the lac operon in 1960.[350] So why was her pioneering suggestion essentially ignored at the time?

One problem was that McClintock's linking of this insight to the idea that such regulatory elements can move about the genome was just too implausible for most scientists at the time to accept. As she herself put it, after presenting her new proposal at a scientific conference, her findings were received with 'puzzlement, even hostility'. One characteristic response was that of Joshua Lederberg, who, after a visit to McClintock's lab, remarked 'by God, that woman is either crazy or a genius'.[351] There was perhaps some justification for this response. The picture of each chromosome as a linear map with genes aligned along it resonated with the common sense view of a map as a static entity upon which the main features—seas, rivers, mountains, valleys, towns, and cities—do not move. Of course, if we studied successive maps of the same area over time, we would see gradual change, both in natural features, and in the cities, roads, and other features constructed by our species. In the same way, our own genomes were recognized as subject to change, but in a painfully slow incremental fashion, as different genes within the genome were affected by mutation. Yet here was McClintock arguing that genomic elements could move about in a rapid fashion, in the space of a few generations. Such was the incomprehension and indeed hostility that McClintock

encountered that, despite making other interesting new findings about the mobile elements—for instance that other 'suppressor' genes could inhibit their activity—she decided to stop publishing her work in this area. Instead, she diverted her studies into the origins of corn as a species, which she carried out during a series of trips to Central and South America where the plant originated.

But then, in the late 1960s and early 1970s, reports began to gradually filter in from other biologists of evidence for mobile elements in bacteria and yeast. Importantly, with new techniques for studying DNA at the molecular level discovered around this time, it finally became possible to show how transposition could occur. We now know there are two main types of transposons, both of which occur in the human genome (see Figure 20).[349] The first type replicate and then, just as text on a computer word file can be cut and pasted, they insert themselves elsewhere in the genome.[352] Although transposons of this type are no longer mobile in the human genome, they were active during the evolution of our

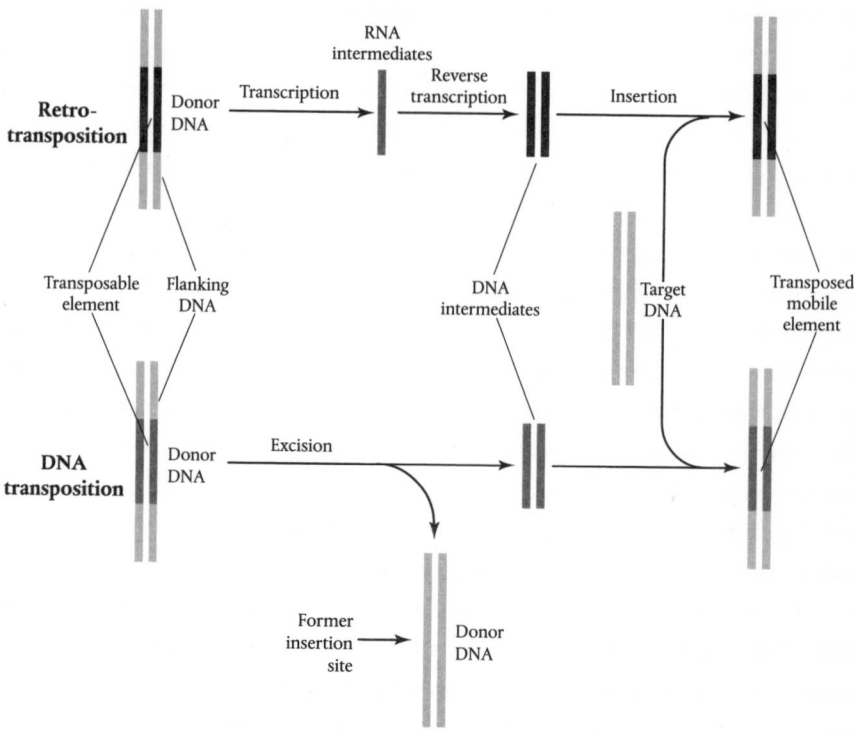

Figure 20. Transposons—how they move about

primate ancestors, about 37 million years ago.[353] The second type, which is still active in the human genome,[353] move via an RNA intermediate, which then turns back into DNA before it reinserts itself into the genome.[352] The recognition that RNA can code for DNA was one of the first challenges to Crick's central dogma that the information in DNA can only flow in one direction, via RNA to proteins. We saw in Chapter 3 how, since proteins are required to replicate and transcribe DNA, it could be equally valid to see information flowing back to DNA from proteins. Nevertheless, this is information flow in an indirect sense. In contrast, turning an RNA sequence into DNA is a very literal challenge to the central dogma, and this reversal of information requires a specific enzyme—reverse transcriptase.

In fact, reverse transcriptase was first discovered in quite a different context as a component of retroviruses, the most famous of which is HIV, the cause of AIDS.[354] Howard Temin of the University of Wisconsin, and David Baltimore of the Massachusetts Institute of Technology, made the discovery while studying RNA tumour viruses, this being another example, like the discovery of enhancers, where research into the link between viruses and cancer led to insights of great general relevance. An important clue as to how RNA tumour viruses work was the fact that, despite having an RNA genome, they have a permanent effect— tumour formation—on the tissues they infect. This led Temin to propose that since 'RNA is a transient molecule, so it must imprint itself on DNA'.[355] However, for years this notion was resisted because of the strength of the central dogma. Only when Temin and Baltimore independently isolated reverse transcriptase, the enzyme that carries out such imprinting by reversing the normal information flow, was the idea finally accepted. For the discovery Temin and Baltimore received a Nobel Prize in 1975. An important feature of RNA tumour viruses is that once conversion of the viral genome into DNA has taken place, it can now insert itself into the genome of the infected cell.[354] This ability to hide itself away in the genome of its host is one reason why HIV can be present in an infected individual for years before any overt symptoms are detected.

The discovery that retrotransposons also work via an RNA intermediate turned into DNA by reverse transcriptase came as a major surprise, for up till then this protein had been seen as something specific to retroviruses.[352] Such similarity has led to the suggestion that retrotransposons originally started life as retroviruses.[354] But it is also possible that retroviruses originated from retrotransposons. Deciding

which version of events is correct is difficult without access to a time machine to replay evolution. However, recent studies indicate reverse transcriptase may have a very ancient origin, raising the possibility that this enzyme may date back to a time when the RNA world that we discussed in Chapter 5, was being replaced with one centred on DNA.[356] So, far from being a quirk of nature, reverse transcriptase may have been a key architect in the biological world that we now inhabit.

The discovery of the mechanism of transposition meant that McClintock's pioneering ideas were finally vindicated, and would result in her being awarded the Nobel Prize for Physiology or Medicine in 1983, the first woman to win that prize unshared, at the age of 81. But as welcome as this belated recognition of her achievements was, for McClintock it was still only a partial victory. For, in contrast to her proposal that transposons played central roles in gene regulation, an idea that now became dominant was that these were parasitical elements with no purpose other than to propagate themselves. Justification for such an interpretation came from surprising findings that were beginning to emerge from other studies of the genome. So, not only were transposons now identified in multicellular animals as well as in plants, they appeared to be a major component of the genome in both cases. The reason why transposition was first detected in corn became clear when it emerged that this plant has a staggering 85 per cent of its genome devoted to these transposons.[349] But many other organisms also have significant proportions of these elements in their genomes. Even before the sequencing of the human genome it was clear that our species had vast numbers of these elements and the genome project confirmed the proportion to be 45 per cent.[350,357]

Such abundance, as well as an apparently simple repeating structure, meant that the idea of these elements as useless parasites quickly spread. Indeed, it was this discovery that played a significant part in the notion that the genome was largely junk, with Orgel and Crick arguing in 1980 that 'the spread of selfish DNA sequences within the genome can be compared to the spread of a not-too-harmful parasite within its host'.[358] However, the idea of harmlessness was challenged by the suggestion that, since transposons could move about, this was potentially very dangerous junk. For what was to stop one of these elements inserting itself within, or close to, an important gene, thereby disabling the gene or activating it in a non-regulated fashion? Evidence that this can happen in humans has come from a study of the disease haemophilia, caused by a defect in the gene for clotting

factor VIII.[349] The study showed that, in one patient, this gene had been disrupted by an insertion of a transposon. Other studies have shown that some cases of cancer have been triggered by a transposition event disrupting tumour suppressor genes or activating oncogenes.[359]

In general, though, our bodies seem to be very good at suppressing unwelcome transposon activity. So the suppressors that McClintock identified in corn have their equivalents in other species, including our own.[349] In particular, DNA methylation, which plays an important role generally in regulation of our genes as we saw in Chapter 6, is also important in keeping transposon activity in check. In addition, a recent study has shown that transposons themselves have evolved a mechanism for self-limiting their activity.[360] Transposition is driven by the enzyme transposase, and the study showed that once a certain number of copies of a transposon are created, transposase concentration rises to such a level that it begins to saturate its own binding sites. Ronald Chalmers at Nottingham University, who led the study, believes that this is in line with the idea that 'a successful parasite is not fatal to its host but lives in harmony with it'.[361] The effectiveness of such inhibitory mechanisms is such that one transposon isolated from fish genomes because of its potential usefulness for gene therapy was nicknamed 'Sleeping Beauty', because it had been 'reawakened' only by artificial means after a 'sleep' of 20 million years.[362]

One particular part of the body where transposon activity needs to be tightly regulated is in the genomes of sperm and eggs, for a transposon moving there to a new position could lead to sterility, the ultimate disaster from a Darwinian point of view. For this reason, the class of non-coding RNAs called piRNAs play a particularly important role in the gonads as suppressors of transposon activity. First discovered in fruitfly testicles by Alexei Aravin and colleagues at Moscow State University in 2001, they were subsequently shown to be present in the testicles and ovaries of all animal species, including humans.[363] piRNAs work by combining with piwi proteins, close relatives of the Argonaute proteins that are involved in RNA interference. The DNA sequences that code for piRNAs are bunched together in the genome in clusters. What was particularly surprising for researchers first investigating these clusters was the huge number of different piRNA sequences, there being at least 50,000 different varieties in mammals like ourselves, and maybe as many as 800,000, according to one recent study, in mice.[363] This diversity allows piRNAs to act like a mini immune system that

tracks down and disables different transposons, just as antibodies do in the body as a whole.

New evidence suggests, though, that in some circumstances the mechanisms that protect our DNA from transposons are undermined. In particular, certain human brain disorders can be caused by inappropriate transposon activity. Amyotrophic lateral sclerosis (ALS), also known as motor neurone disease or, in the USA, Lou Gehrig disease, after the famous baseball player that it affected, is caused by a degeneration of the nerve cells of the brain.[364] This disease leads to increasing inability to move, speak, swallow, and breathe, and usually results in death within ten years from respiratory failure, although another famous sufferer, physicist Stephen Hawking, has lived with the condition for more than fifty years.

Studies have shown that this disorder, as well as other neurodegenerative conditions such as Alzheimer's, are associated with defects in a protein called TDP-43.[364] A recent study, led by Josh Dubnau at Cold Spring Harbor Laboratory, has shown that TDP-43 normally binds to transposons and keeps them inactive.[365] The study also suggested that neurodegeneration can be triggered by an 'awakening' of the dormant transposons to which TDP-43 normally binds. Dubnau believes this indicates that 'TDP-43 normally functions to silence or repress the expression of potentially harmful transposons. When TDP-43 function is compromised, these mobile elements become overexpressed.'[366]

Studies like these confirm the idea of transposons as potentially dangerous parasites whose activity must be kept in check so as not to disrupt normal cellular and bodily function. Recently, however, evidence has been accumulating that transposons may have more beneficial roles. One such role is in the evolution of mammalian pregnancy.[367] A study has identified an unusually high proportion of transposon-derived regulatory elements near to genes involved in the development of the placenta, the tissue that nurtures the developing embryo and foetus in mammalian species like our own, and which distinguishes us from egg-laying mammals like the duck-billed platypus.[367] The placenta is a unique structure that acts as a bridge between the mother and her developing offspring, with the connecting role facilitated by a protein called syncytin. When expressed in cell lines syncytin causes neighbouring cells to fuse, and in the placenta this property is central for the fusion of the cells of the mother and her child. Yet syncytin originally started life as a retroviral gene that became incorporated into the genome as a mobile element. Indeed, its mechanism of action reflects this origin,

for in its original viral form the protein was located on the surface of the virus and helped the latter fuse with the cells it infected. These findings have led scientists studying this process to suggest that 'capture of a founding syncytin-like gene could have been instrumental in the dramatic transition from egg-laying to placental mammals'.[367]

A gene that began life as a transposon also plays a vital role in our immune system. As we've seen, a crucial way in which the body fights infection is through its ability to generate antibodies against a seemingly unlimited number of foreign molecules, or antigens. Although some of this diversity comes from alternative splicing, a far greater role is played by a rearrangement of the DNA in the immunoglobulin genes coding for such antibodies. Immunoglobulins are composed of four protein chains, two heavy chains and two light chains. Together they form a 'Y' shape, and the tips of the Y constitute the highly variable region that is subtly different in each different antibody.[368] A large part of this variability arises through a mixing and matching of a huge number of different sub-regions of the immunoglobulin genes. The protein mediating this rearrangement is an enzyme called RAG, which not only started life as a protein that regulates cutting and pasting of DNA transposons, but still plays this role today as it scrambles the different immunoglobulin gene sub-regions, in different permutations each time.[369]

Such examples might be viewed as important but still only isolated instances of the usefulness of transposition. However, a more controversial possibility now being debated is whether transposons have a far more central role in the process of gene regulation, just as McClintock originally proposed. This reappraisal of the role of transposons has emerged from global surveys of the regulatory elements in the genome conducted by projects like ENCODE. This has suggested that a surprising number of gene promoters originated as transposons.[349] So, at least 20 per cent of regulatory elements seem to have been derived from transposons, but the real figure may be significantly higher since the original character of these elements can often be hidden by mutation. Transposons have an obvious advantage in their potential to be co-opted into regulatory roles, since they already come equipped with sequences involved in gene expression. This is because these elements power their own movement in the genome and express genes that allow them to do this. Moreover, as transposons can also contain DNA sequences that respond to various hormones, this offers an intriguing possibility: that transposition might be strongly influenced by environmental pressures which lead to

changes in the hormonal state of the organism. Such a possibility would be in line with McClintock's suggestion, first made in 1950, that environmental changes that stressed the organism, such as heat shock and starvation, can trigger an increase in transposon activity.

Indeed, an increasing number of recent studies in plants have confirmed this ability of stress to activate transposons. Moreover, there is increasing evidence that stress can lead to such transposition-led changes in the genomes of mammalian species.[370] For instance, one study showed that changes in transposon activity in the mammalian brain can be triggered by stress. Post-traumatic stress disorder is a condition whereby people exposed to traumatic events can become stressed or frightened even when no longer in danger. In order to gain insights into this condition, studies have been conducted on rats subjected to repeated stress. The rats subsequently show a disproportionate reaction, such as a tendency to freeze, even when placed in a non-stressful situation. When gene expression in such rats was analysed, greatly increased transposon activity was detected in a brain region called the amygdala that is known to play an important role in emotional responses and decision-making.[370]

Clearly, this is another example in which activation of mobile elements has a negative impact upon the body. But there is also evidence that transposon activity might have a more creative role. In particular, recent studies have suggested that the genomes of different cells in human individuals may be far more different than previously suspected.[371] It has long been an assumption in biology that the different cells of human beings, like other multicellular organisms, have the same genome, bar exceptions like red blood cells, eggs and sperm, and antibody-producing cells, which respectively have no DNA, only half the amount of this substance, and a scrambling of the immunoglobulin genes. However, there is increasing evidence, based on the ability to sequence the whole genomes of individual cells, that the DNA in different cells in the body may be far more divergent than thought.[371]

To some extent, such diversity is due to mistakes made by the replication machinery during the DNA copying process that occurs every time a cell divides, or by mutations that can occur when a cell is exposed to radiation or toxic chemicals from the environment.[371] This is a significant cause of cancer, as oncogenes are activated or tumour suppressor genes disabled, whether by too much exposure to the sun, triggering melanomas, or smoking giving rise to lung

cancer. However, some of this diversity appears to be due to transposon activity and, intriguingly, this may play an important role in normal physiology. So, recent studies of the human brain have shown that active transposition is much more widespread than thought, suggesting that this might contribute to the plasticity which is such a characteristic feature of this organ.[370] And just as the immune system creates many genetically different antibody-producing cells to respond to foreign antigens, genome diversity in the nerve cells of the brain may allow it to respond to all the challenges that life throws at us.[371] It has even been proposed that such genetic diversity in the brain could be a significant cause of human individuality and explain why even identical twins can have quite different personalities and ways of dealing with situations.[370]

Such studies demonstrate that transposon activity may be important in the individual organism. However, what about another suggestion of McClintock's: that transposons play a central role in evolution? It is this that has proven to be the most controversial aspect of her work. McClintock argued that an increase in transposition might have benefits for the host organism facing environmental stresses, by initiating a rise in mutations that could provide an increase in variants for natural selection to act upon. Initially, this was thought unlikely since it was assumed that it could only occur in a fairly crude fashion, by disruption of gene function or non-specific activation of genes. However, McClintock always maintained there was a more creative side to transposition, and discoveries about the importance of transposons in forming new gene regulatory elements suggest she may have been right.

In addition, increasing evidence suggests that elevated transposon activity may accompany the origin of new species. For instance, a recent study has found that the timing of bat species' expansion coincided with an increase in transposon activity around 30 million years ago.[372] Moreover, this expansion also seems to have been linked to the creation of new miRNAs, which could have contributed to gene expression and therefore evolutionary novelty. David Ray of Mississippi State University, who led the study, believes this shows that 'transposable elements have the potential to shift evolution into overdrive by rapidly introducing large numbers of small RNAs. Those small RNAs don't change the proteins that genes code for but instead impact how and when the genes are expressed, thereby allowing for rapid changes in the way organisms interact with their environment.'[373] Other studies have suggested that increased transposon activity

accompanied the origins of other vertebrate groups.[374] Perhaps most provocatively, Roy Britten has proposed that the high level of recent transposition events in human evolution, and the dramatic changes in that evolution, such as the rapid growth of the brain, are intimately connected.[375] This is a subject to which we will return later when we consider the role of the genome in the evolution of human consciousness.

As we've seen, one of McClintock's central beliefs was that transposition drove evolution by sensing changes in the environment, for instance, those that led to stress. But this led to the criticism that there was no obvious mechanism whereby environmental changes could be communicated to the genome. This was something McClintock herself never explained adequately. Aware of this, in her Nobel Prize acceptance speech in 1983 she challenged biologists 'to determine the extent of knowledge the cell has of itself, and how it utilizes this knowledge in a "thoughtful" manner when challenged'.[376] On another occasion she spoke about 'smart cells', meaning that the genome as a whole must have some way of sensing, evaluating, and responding to changes in the environment. Unfortunately, this type of language seemed, to many critics, to verge on mysticism, and prompted one to ask 'does the organism...have foresight, conjuring up just the kind of restructuring that the occasion demands?'[376]

The problem was that, in the mid-1980s, there was still no conception of how signals from the environment might affect the genome's activity in such a 'thoughtful' manner, and, indeed, such an idea was anathema to many biologists, for whom it conjured up a long disregarded figure from the past, someone whose ideas had supposedly been discredited many years previously by Darwin. This scientist—Jean-Baptiste Lamarck—has, since that time, been spoken of generally as a figure of fun, but developments over recent decades have begun to challenge that view.

9

THE MARKS OF LAMARCK

'It is not the...character and form of the animal's bodily parts, that have given rise to its habits and particular structures. It is the habits and manner of life and the conditions in which its ancestors lived that have in the course of time fashioned its bodily form, organs and qualities.' *Jean-Baptiste Lamarck*

'We can't any longer have the conventional understanding of genetics which everybody peddles because it is increasingly obvious that epigenetics—actually things which influence the genome's function—are much more important than we realised.' *Robert Winston*

Paris at the end of the eighteenth century was not a safe place for aristocrats, or indeed anyone with a link to the old order. The French Revolution was in full swing and heads were rolling. As such, Jean-Baptiste Pierre Antoine de Monet, Knight of Lamarck, and keeper of the herbarium at the former Jardin de Roi, the king's garden, had significant reasons to be worried for his life. True, Lamarck was a respected scientist, being one of the foremost biologists of his era; indeed, it was he who introduced the words 'biology' and 'invertebrate' into our vocabulary.[377] However, Antoine Lavoisier, discoverer of oxygen, had also been a highly respected scientist, yet that had not prevented him being guillotined for being one of the king's tax collectors. Lamarck, though, was a disciple of Jean-Jacques Rousseau, now dead but still a leading intellectual influence on the revolution, and he could see exciting possibilities for the future despite the dangers. Sitting by the fire one night with his wife Marie, Lamarck recalled an occasion five years earlier when they had gathered at a spot not far from where the Eiffel Tower now stands, to watch inventor Jean-Pierre Blanchard embark upon one of the first manned hot-air balloon flights. Now turning to Marie, Lamarck said, 'If I can endure, I will ignite something new. If one idea can ascend like the balloon then I will be remembered. That is enough.'[378]

Lamarck did have an idea that would make him remembered, but, unfortunately, for most of the next 200 years, it would be as an object of scorn and ridicule. This great idea was his proposal, 50 years before Charles Darwin, that life arose through a process of biological evolution. In fact, he was not the only person coming to such a conclusion; most notably, so was Darwin's own grandfather, Erasmus Darwin. Nevertheless, it was Lamarck who became most associated with this idea, so that Charles Darwin himself would later acknowledge that 'Lamarck was the first man whose conclusions on the subject excited much attention...he first did the eminent service of arousing attention to the probability of all changes in the organic, as well as in the inorganic world, being the result of law, and not of miraculous interposition.'[379] At a time when the established view was that God created the world and all its life forms in seven days, with human beings at the pinnacle, Lamarck's bold idea was as revolutionary as the period in which it originated. For it suggested that material forces alone, and not some supernatural creator, could explain the origins of humankind, as well as showing that we were not as different from other species as we thought. Perhaps this was why Lamarck's ideas drew such venom in the years following the revolution, as Napoléon came to power and steered French society in a less radical direction. In particular, the naturalist Georges Cuvier mounted a bitter opposition to Lamarck's evolutionary ideas, both in the latter's lifetime and also after his death. Indeed, in one of the most backhanded 'eulogies' ever delivered at a funeral, Cuvier used this opportunity to mock and criticize Lamarck's theory of evolution even as his opponent lay fresh in his coffin, accusing him of being someone who 'constructed vast edifices on imaginary foundations'.[380]

Cuvier was, however, helped by some obvious potential flaws in Lamarck's proposed driving forces of evolution.[381] One was a tendency for organisms to become more complex, moving 'up' a ladder of progress. However, it was Lamarck's suggestion that the environment directly influences the hereditary material that was singled out for attack. An example often used to illustrate this suggestion is a giraffe stretching its neck to reach the highest leaves on a tree, and thereby somehow giving rise to descendants with slightly longer necks, as if sheer force of will were capable of modifying the biology of subsequent generations. But, as critics pointed out, if evolution really did work in this way, then why are blacksmiths' children not born with muscular forearms or young giraffes with much longer necks than their parents?

Lamarck's response was that such changes would be too slow to reveal themselves in a single generation, instead taking 'many thousands of years'.[382] Unfortunately, such a timescale was hard to grasp for eighteenth-century citizens, who would have surmised from reading the Bible that the Earth itself was only 8,000 years old. And it would be over a century before it was conclusively shown that our planet is far more ancient, at four and a half billion years old, leaving plenty of time for evolutionary changes to take place.[383] But there was another problem with Lamarckism, namely the lack of an obvious material basis for Lamarck's two proposed evolutionary drives. Not only was it unclear why organisms should tend towards greater complexity but, in the absence of any understanding of the material nature of the hereditary substance, it was not easy to imagine how this could be affected by the environment. These problems, together with the challenge that Lamarckism represented towards religious orthodoxy, was one of the reasons why it was only popular in the early nineteenth century with radical groups, such as the Chartists in Britain.[384] This association with radicalism may be one reason why Darwin held back for so many years from publishing his own theory of evolution by natural selection, and why the socialist Wallace was less inhibited in putting forward his version of that theory.[385]

The theory of natural selection, in contrast to Lamarckism, provided a clear mechanism for evolution in proposing that the different capacity of variants in a population to survive explained why some species have evolved and others have become extinct. Yet, as we've seen, this theory suffered from its own mechanistic flaw as long as inheritance was assumed to involve a blending of factors originating from each parents' blood, which would cancel out the very variation that was supposed to drive natural selection. And although the way out of this impasse had already been identified by Mendel in Darwin's own lifetime, unaware of this, the latter became increasingly unsure of the primacy of natural selection, ironically appealing to Lamarckian mechanisms as additional factors in the last years of his life.

However, when the importance of Darwin's ideas was resurrected by the rediscovery of Mendel's work, and then by the 'new synthesis' of Mendelism and Darwinism, Lamarckism was once again marginalized. With the discovery that DNA was the hereditary material that acted like a linear code, the new orthodoxy was that the environment could only influence inheritance through the random generation of mutations in the DNA sequence, the variants produced by such

mutations then becoming the raw material for natural selection to act upon. However, this is necessarily an indirect effect, in contrast to Lamarck's model, in which the act of a giraffe stretching for the highest leaves directly leads to an increase in neck lengths of subsequent generations. It also requires a far longer timescale than that envisaged by Lamarck. Recently, however, evidence has been emerging that Lamarck's proposal for a direct effect of the environment on the hereditary material may have not been so far off the mark at all, with one leading biologist, Eugene Koonin of the US National Institutes of Health, stating that 'Lamarck is back and perhaps with a vengeance'.[386] In particular, there has been a new recognition that gene activity may be altered in many ways that do not involve changes in the DNA sequence. What remains controversial, though, about such 'epigenetic' changes is whether their effects are only important over the lifetime of an organism or a few generations after, or instead have a significant influence on a longer timescale.

Although epigenetics has particularly flourished over the last decade, its origins go back much further. Indeed, the term was first proposed by British scientist Conrad Waddington in 1942; he created it by combining two terms, 'genetics' and 'epigenesis', the latter meaning the processes and events that bring the mature organism into existence.[387] In the 1930s Waddington travelled to the USA to work in Morgan's fly lab, where he began studying mutants as a way of understanding the mechanisms underlying embryo development. One mutant identified by Waddington had part of an antenna transformed into a segment of leg. He interpreted this as showing development is a series of branching decisions, regulated by the genes. In fact, we now know such changes are due to mutations in the homeotic genes, which, as we've seen, specify different bodily regions from head to foot and, remarkably, are lined up in the same order along the chromosome as the characteristics they impart to the embryo. In the absence of such molecular information, Waddington nevertheless came up with some interesting proposals. One was that developmental decision-making normally follows defined channels, with this 'canalization' meaning that a certain amount of genetic variation can be tolerated without obvious effects upon development, until a threshold is reached, at which point development can flip over into an alternative channel.[387]

According to Waddington, the development of the organism was not simply an outcome of the additive effects of all the individual genes, but rather their

interaction with each other in a dynamic system, meaning that changes in expression of any one gene must be considered in terms of their effect on that system. This resistance of the body to genetic variation may explain an interesting phenomenon noticed by scientists studying 'knockout' mice engineered to lack expression of a particular gene. As we mentioned in the Introduction, surprisingly many knockouts have far less effect on bodily form or function than might be expected.[388] One explanation for this phenomenon is that many genes occur as members of families. If one gene is knocked out, another family member may take its place by a process of 'remodelling'.[389] In addition, many important cellular processes are regulated by multiple signalling pathways acting in parallel, so loss of one of these might be compensated for by a greater activity of a parallel pathway. What remains unclear is why some knockouts have very pronounced effects while others have little. In this respect, Waddington's canalization may operate to varying degrees for different processes depending on the extent to which compensation can take place. Importantly, as we'll see in Chapter 11, this concept may help us understand genetic diseases in humans.

At a time when the molecular basis of the genome was still being worked out, Waddington's theories represented an important insight into the complexity of the relationship between genes and the bodily characteristics they influenced. But Waddington's research was heading in an even more surprising direction. Investigating whether changes in the embryo's environment could affect its development, he discovered that exposing fly embryos to high temperatures during their development led, in a few cases, to the disappearance of a vein in the fruitfly wing.[387] Clearly, this aspect of development was susceptible to perturbation by such treatment. What was surprising, though, was that when flies with the missing vein were bred with each other, and the temperature shock and selection were repeated for a few generations, it was possible to create a population in which all flies lacked the vein.

Waddington identified other examples of this phenomenon. For instance, he found that treating fly embryos with ether could induce the formation of flies with four wings rather than two, and combining ether treatment of embryos and selection across generations eventually gave rise to only four-winged flies.[387] Such examples raised a number of important questions. Clearly, here was a very artificial situation in which Waddington himself was selecting offspring with particular characteristics. Yet the fact that an environmentally induced change

could become heritable over a few generations suggested that something was happening to the hereditary material on a far shorter timescale than could be explained by spontaneous mutation.

Such a rapid influence of the environment seemed more in line with Lamarckism than with the new synthesis of Darwinism and Mendelism. But just as Lamarck's theory of evolution had foundered due to a lack of an obvious mechanism, so, in the 1940s, the lack of a clear idea about the material basis of the gene made it very difficult to even conceive how the environment could be acting in such a manner. If anything, the identification of DNA as the 'molecule of life' made Waddington's findings even harder to explain.[387] For if DNA operates as a digital code, and the only way this code can be altered is by mutations gradually changing the DNA sequence, then the speed of change in the examples discussed makes little sense.

As such, while the molecular biology revolution of the 1960s and '70s gathered pace, Waddington's findings were relegated, for many years, to the status of unexplained curiosities.[387] However, other evidence was emerging that suggested a far more direct influence of the environment on the hereditary material than would have been suspected, according to the standard orthodoxy of genetics, and some of it was in humans. Undoubtedly the most famous case of epigenetics affecting human health is the famine that affected Holland in the winter of 1944–45 at the end of World War II.[390] Because of a Nazi blockade on supplies entering the country, Dutch citizens suffered from an extreme lack of food. Such was the extent of the famine that starving people resorted to eating tulip bulbs and sugar beet to stay alive.[391] As it was, around 22,000 people died. However, the Dutch famine has become well known in scientific circles because of the surprising effects it had on women who were pregnant at this time, and their offspring. Strikingly, these fell into two categories. So women who were starved at the end of their pregnancy gave birth to children of a smaller birth weight. This was not so surprising; however, when girls born at this time grew up and themselves had children, these were also of reduced birth weight, despite their mothers having grown up in an affluent post-war society.[390] A different pattern was seen with women starved at the beginning of their pregnancy. While their subsequent access to food meant that they had offspring of normal birth weight, these children had a tendency to obesity, as if lack of food early in life had led to an urge to overindulge later in life by way of compensation. And in this case too, this tendency was passed on to their children.

Another historical example showing that food availability for one generation can affect not just children, but even grandchildren, of affected individuals, comes from Norrbotten, the northernmost county of Sweden, where the vagaries of the weather meant that, in the past, inhabitants could be subjected to famine, but also to periods of surplus.[392] Researchers studying whether such differences affected future generations found that grandchildren of men who had suffered famine lived longer than normal, while those of men who had lived through a time of surplus had a shorter lifespan. Such differences were linked to problems in cardiovascular health. So, in this case, a surplus of food was associated with detrimental effects on later generations. And since the effects were transmitted through men, this suggested that such effects were due to changes in the genome, not the womb.[392]

Such studies raised the question of how the environment might transmit such effects through the genome, given that they seem too rapid to involve a change in DNA sequence. In the end, a potential answer came from two discoveries that we discussed in Chapter 6, namely that DNA can be modified by methyl groups, and that the histones that wrap around DNA can also be modified chemically, for instance, by the addition of an acetyl group.[393] While acetylation of histones directly affects the tightness with which histones bind the DNA, thereby making the DNA more accessible to gene regulatory proteins, other histone modifications serve as a recognition signal for proteins, which then act to influence gene expression.[394] The proteins involved in epigenetic signalling have become known as 'writers' and 'readers': the former deposit epigenetic marks, while the latter interpret those marks and carry out the associated regulatory function. Other proteins act as 'erasers', by removing epigenetic marks. This reversibility of epigenetic changes is one crucial way in which they differ from genetic ones, since once a mutation occurs in DNA, this becomes a permanent feature. Why such proteins target one region of the genome over another has been unclear; however, recent studies suggest non-coding RNAs are central to this process.[395] This is part of an emerging dual aspect of such RNAs which can both recognize DNA elements due to sequence similarity, as well as co-opt proteins that modify DNA and its accompanying histones, thus directing epigenetic enzymes to specific gene targets.[395]

That epigenetic changes play key roles in our cells, there is now no doubt. We've already discussed the conundrum whereby a single cell, the fertilized egg,

can develop into an organism of thousands of different cell types, each with a different function, yet, in general, such different cell types contain the same genome. The discovery of transcription factors went some way to explaining this conundrum because it showed that different types of such factors in a cell would affect which genes were turned on or off. However, increasing evidence also implicates an important role for epigenetic changes.[396] Initially, epigenetic changes were thought to define cell specificity in a purely negative fashion, by preventing access of transcription factors to a gene; however, epigenetic features such as histone modifications are increasingly viewed as acting in a more positive, dynamic fashion.[397] In addition, epigenetic changes may affect the position of genes and their regulatory regions within the 3D nucleus, which, as we've seen, can greatly affect whether genes are turned on or off.

One curious feature of epigenetic changes during embryo development specific to mammals is a phenomenon called imprinting.[398] This involves certain genes being switched on or off, depending on whether they come from an individual's mother or father. The consequences of imprinting have been known since ancient times, when it was realized that animal hybrids generate different types of offspring depending on which species is the mother, and which is the father. So mating a male horse and a female donkey produces a hinny, while the opposite combination generates the more common mule. This suggested that there must be something different about the male and female genomes, for otherwise it is difficult to see why the two combinations should generate different types of animal.

The first experimental demonstration of this difference was made by Azim Surani at Cambridge University. In the 1980s Surani decided to investigate whether the genomes of two sperm, or two eggs, could develop normally when transplanted into an egg that had its own genome removed. If the two genomes were essentially the same, this ought to have resulted in the development of a normal embryo. Instead, Surani found that both combinations led to highly abnormal development.[398] He proposed that the male and female genomes must be modified, such that balanced development was only possible if both were present. Confirmation that this was the case came with the discovery that certain genes had a different pattern of methylation depending on whether they came from the father's or the mother's genome, which also affected whether they were turned on or off.

Why does such a phenomenon occur in mammals? One theory builds upon the fact that mammalian females bear their young internally, as opposed to laying eggs.[398] Because male mammals only have to invest a sperm in producing a new embryo, there is an evolutionary incentive for the paternal genome to boost growth of the embryo. However, female mammals must nurture the developing embryo inside their bodies at considerable cost to themselves; indeed, this could even become life-threatening should the new life form demand too many resources. The theory therefore predicts that genes switched on in the father's genome should boost embryo growth, while those in the mother suppress it. And, indeed, in general this seems to be the case. However, an opposing theory, for which there is also some evidence, has proposed that imprinted genes act cooperatively to optimize foetal development and the well-being of the mother. Given that at least 150 imprinted genes have been identified, with quite different characters, it is probable that elements of both theories may be correct.

Imprinting has been linked to a number of human diseases. In particular, genetic defects in imprinted genes can cause completely different symptoms depending on whether the disorder is inherited through the mother or father.[399] So Prader–Willi syndrome is associated with various symptoms, but the most prominent is an insatiable appetite, leading to life-threatening obesity. In contrast, individuals with Angelman syndrome have severe learning disabilities, jerky movements like hand-flapping, and engage in frequent laughter and smiling. Yet, despite their completely different characters, both syndromes are due to a loss of the same region of chromosome 15. However, while Angelman syndrome is caused by loss of expression of an imprinted gene that is normally only on in the maternal genome, Prader–Willi symptoms are due to an absence of expression of a neighbouring gene that is generally only on in the paternal genome. As well as playing a role in these severe disorders, there is increasing evidence that subtle differences in expression of imprinted genes can contribute to more common disorders like obesity, diabetes, psychiatric illness, and cancer.[398]

The role of epigenetic changes in embryo development explains why cloning remains a very inefficient process. For not only must the newly introduced genome come into contact with a whole new set of transcription factors, for these to influence its expression it must also undergo a fundamental change in its chromatin state. That such 'remodelling' can happen on a vast scale is remarkable in itself, but the fact that cloning is only successful in a small minority of attempts

shows that it is a far from assured event.[400] The examples just given also show the importance of epigenetic changes for normal development. But what relevance do such changes have to Lamarck's proposal that the environment can shape the hereditary material? In fact, a growing number of studies have shown that the epigenetic state of the genome is more responsive to environmental influences than previously suspected. One important influence on the epigenome is diet.[401] Substances ranging from green tea, garlic, carrots, broccoli, and cumin, can all affect the methylation state of different genes. The influence of diet on the epigenome is an active area of study, since it might point to ways to improve our health through the manipulation of diet, but also show whether consumption of cheap food full of fat and sugar—so-called 'junk food'—affects more than our waistlines.

Epigenetic changes also seem to be an important part of the body's response to stress. This response is mediated by a rise in 'stress hormones' like cortisol. Such hormones are released from the adrenal glands, these being stimulated by a region of the brain called the hypothalamus acting via the pituitary, the three together forming the HPA axis.[402] Stress hormones are members of the 'steroid hormone' family because of their chemical structure. Steroid hormones mediate their effects in the body by switching on certain target genes: to do this, the steroid hormone enters the cell across the cell membrane, and binds to a receptor inside the cell's cytoplasm. The combined hormone and receptor then effectively becomes a transcription factor that enters the nucleus and activates its target genes.

The effects of stress hormones on gene expression will persist as long as levels of these hormones in the blood remain high, but it was always assumed that, once they fell, so would the changes in gene expression. However, recent studies suggest that stress can cause more long-lasting epigenetic changes in the genome.[402] So, baby rats raised by mothers with a defect in their ability to look after their young grew up to have higher levels of methylation of the regulatory region, and so lower activity of the gene coding for the cortisol receptor. This effect was environmental, being also seen with rats born to biological mothers who did care for their young, but which were then fostered by uncaring mothers. A higher level of DNA methylation was also seen in the cortisol receptor gene in human suicide victims who had been abused as children.[402] In both rats and humans, therefore, stress early in life seems to desensitize the response to stress hormones, and this is mediated by epigenetic changes.

Recently, the effects of stress on the human genome have been shown to be more dramatic than had been imagined. We saw in Chapter 8 how the ends of chromosomes are protected by DNA sequences called telomeres that shorten each time a cell divides, and whose gradual loss in a person's lifetime are one cause of ageing. However, a recent study has shown that telomeres can shorten much more rapidly in children exposed to extremely stressful situations. The study examined two sets of 9-year-old boys, one being children who had grown up in a poor and unstable environment, the other being boys from more privileged backgrounds.[403] The first set typically lived with a single mother who had multiple partners, and had been exposed to domestic violence and other types of stress. An examination of telomere length in cells isolated from the two groups revealed that some of the boys in the stressful home environment had telomeres that were a staggering 40 per cent shorter than normal. However, this was only true of some of the boys, and further analysis revealed that affected individuals had differences in the genes coding for dopamine and serotonin, two brain neurotransmitters. Although these chemicals play vital roles in mediating human characteristics like love, happiness, self-confidence, and motivation, imbalances in the levels of these two substances in the brain are associated with depression, bipolar disorder, and schizophrenia. Given that shortening of telomeres has been linked to ageing and susceptibility to disease, these are worrying findings. But they also suggest that the link between stress and the epigenome is a complicated one, and may explain why, although stressful environments may trigger mental disorders, biological differences may also decide which individuals are most at risk and therefore in need of rapid intervention.

Findings such as these suggest that our genomes can be influenced by the environment in much more direct and dramatic ways than suspected, which is a vital necessary element if there is to be any truth in Lamarck's version of evolutionary change. However, a more controversial issue that remains to be properly addressed is the question of whether such epigenetic changes can be passed down to future generations, as Lamarckism requires, and to what extent this shapes evolution in the long term. In this respect, examples such as the Dutch famine offer tantalizing suggestions that the environment can influence future generations, but what is the evidence that this is linked to epigenetic changes? Studying such questions in humans is necessarily difficult, both in terms of obtaining tissue samples to analyse and of tracking individuals across generations,

which pose practical and ethical problems. However, studies of laboratory animals are helping our understanding of this issue. Such studies have shown that pregnant mice exposed to different diets or environmental toxins can pass on epigenetic changes, not just to sons and daughters, but also to grandchildren and great-grandchildren.[399]

Undoubtedly the biggest challenge for the idea that epigenetic changes can be transmitted across generations in mammals, including humans, is the existence of mechanisms that erase previous epigenetic marks in the egg and sperm and impose new ones. Because of this, from a genomic point of view at least, each new generation was, until recently, thought to start out as a blank slate. However, the notion that this process is an absolute one is now being challenged. So, previously it was thought that all the histones in the sperm genome were replaced by protamines; however, as we saw in Chapter 7, it now appears that as much as 15 per cent of human sperm DNA is associated with histones. Moreover, a recent study has shown that paternal diet affects the chemical modifications of such histones, which may therefore such carry such epigenetic marks into the next generation.[404] There is now also evidence that protamines themselves not only act to protect the sperm DNA during its journey to the egg, but may also carry epigenetic information into the embryo. In addition, there is increasing evidence that far more genomic regions than thought may escape the erasure of DNA methylation that occurs in epigenetic 'reprogramming' during sperm development.[405]

Perhaps most remarkable are recent studies indicating that some non-coding RNAs can be transmitted to the next generation via the sperm, and that these may guide the placement of epigenetic marks. One such study found that male mice subjected to stress as babies, produced offspring that showed depressive behaviour and a tendency to underestimate risk. Analysis of the sperm of the stressed mice showed that they contained an abnormally high expression of five miRNAs,[406] one of which, miR-375, had previously been linked to the stress response.[402] Remarkably, not only were the immediate offspring affected, but also the grandchildren of the stressed mice. Both offspring and grandchildren had abnormal levels of the five miRNAs in their blood and in the hippocampus, the latter being involved in both memory formation and the mediation of stress responses. To discount the possibility that the effects of stress were transmitted socially, the researchers isolated RNA from the sperm of the stressed mice and injected this into fertilized eggs from

unstressed parents—this also led to offspring with depressive behaviour and abnormal metabolism, characteristics that were passed on to subsequent generations.[406] This suggests that the effects of stress on future generations can be directly transmitted by sperm miRNAs.

How could stress lead to changes in miRNA levels in the sperm? One possibility is that stress hormones circulating in the blood make their way to the testicles, and trigger expression of miRNAs via stimulation of surface receptors on the sperm. However, an even more direct potential route has been recently identified, since miRNAs contained within 'exosomes'—membrane bound particles—have been observed entering sperm in the epididymis, the structure in which sperm are stored after they leave the testicles, prior to ejaculation.[407] It is possible, therefore, that miRNAs produced elsewhere in the body, for instance, the brain, could subsequently end up in the sperm and in the fertilized egg and embryo, providing a direct connection between the brains of one generation and the characteristics of future ones.

A major unresolved question is what relevance the propagation of epigenetic marks has for longer-term evolution. One interesting possibility is that such marks may facilitate more permanent genetic change. Such a possibility is based upon the discovery that methylated nucleotides are more prone to mutation than normal ones. Thinking along such lines, Eugene Koonin has recently argued that evolution may follow a 'two-phase process, with the first phase being the Lamarckian epigenetics and the second phase Darwinian selection of mutations'.[408] His proposal is that this would be akin to 'probing the waters...with epigenetic adaptation followed by the long-term genetic inheritance of the same adaptation should the challenge prove to be long-lasting'. If true, Koonin believes that this 'defies the common belief that evolution has no forecast'.[409]

Another possibility is that epigenetic changes make the genome more liable to transposition. As we've seen, stress may enhance transposition and, intriguingly, this seems to be linked to changes in the chromatin state of the genome, which permits repressed transposons to become active. It would therefore be very interesting if such a mechanism constituted a way for the environment to make a lasting, genetic mark. This would be in line with recent suggestions that an important mechanism of evolution is via 'genome resetting'—the periodic reorganization of the genome by newly amplified mobile DNA elements, which establishes new genetic programmes in embryo development. New evidence

suggests such a mechanism may be a key route whereby new species arise, and may have played an important role in the evolution of humans from apes.[410] This is very different from the traditional view of evolution as being driven by the gradual accumulation of mutations. Instead, it suggests that the genome is built 'Lego-like out of codons specifying protein domains', and evolutionary change is 'largely a matter of nonrandom codon reorganization by natural genetic engineering mechanisms like retrotransposition'.[411] Such a viewpoint would be in line with the Danish embryologist Søren Løvtrup's belief that 'evolution is not a question of making new materials, but rather of using old materials for new purposes'.[412] Such issues remain to be resolved. But our new understanding of the genome and epigenome are challenging our view of both disease and what it means to be human, and it is to these matters that we will shortly turn. However, first it is time to step back and address once more the question of how much functionality there is in the genome in light of the new information that we have gathered about the different levels of genomic activity. For, as well as being a continuing topic of controversy, this issue has a significant bearing on what will follow in the rest of this book.

10

CODE, NON-CODE, GARBAGE, AND JUNK

'Inspect every piece of pseudoscience and you will find a security blanket, a thumb to suck, a skirt to hold. What does the scientist have to offer in exchange? Uncertainty! Insecurity!'   *Isaac Asimov*

'I think people get it upside down when they say the unambiguous is the reality and the ambiguous merely uncertainty about what is really unambiguous. Let's turn it around the other way: the ambiguous is the reality and unambiguous is merely a special case of it, where we finally manage to pin down some very special aspect.'   *David Bohm*

In one of his more philosophical moments, which, being a Frenchman in the existential 1960s, was quite often, Jacques Monod said that 'in science, self-satisfaction is death...it is restlessness, anxiety, dissatisfaction, agony of mind that nourish science'.[413] This is an interesting reflection, given that a common conception about science is that it is primarily about assured facts. This viewpoint is not surprising when we consider how science is generally taught in school, and even to an extent at university, using textbooks or course notes in which scientific facts are displayed as things to be learned, not as objects to debate or dispute. Now, in a sense, there is a good reason why certain scientific claims are taught as facts, namely that, having been around for a substantial period of time and having been subject to ample efforts to disprove them, it is assumed that they correspond to real truths about the world. It is because of this that Euclid's principles of geometry, Newtonian mechanics, and Darwin's theory of natural selection are all accepted as central cornerstones of modern scientific thought.

It would be a mistake, though, to assume that such certainties characterize science at its most cutting edge, since, by definition, any true foray into the unknown must be highly uncertain. In discussing the ENCODE findings, we saw that a key question that polarized opinion about the significance of the findings was the question of how much of the genome could be considered 'functional' and how much was 'junk'. Having now looked in detail at novel features of the genome emerging from recent studies, namely its 3D character, the mobility of genetic elements, and links between genes and the environment mediated by epigenetic mechanisms, it is time to reassess this issue of genomic functionality. Here, however, we face a problem, which is that the approach used to assess such functionality has a substantial influence on the outcome of this assessment.[414] And since the choice of approach is itself influenced by whether one subscribes to a traditional picture of the genome, or a more radical one, this is an issue likely to be characterized by uncertainty for some time in the future.

As we discussed in Chapter 6, a traditional way of assessing functionality in the genome is to assume that important functional elements are those that show sequence conservation between different species. The idea is that such regions of the genome have survived 'purifying selection', the tendency of natural selection to weed out portions of the genome that have a non-functional role. So, a typical approach would be to compare the human genome with those of different mammalian species and identify how many nucleotide bases are retained between these two genomes. Chris Ponting and colleagues, who recently made such a comparison, have likened it to training 'a time-lapse camera on a single nucleotide position in your genome and, by winding back time, watch[ing] how it changed by chance mutations as it was passed back through the generations (and along the germline) over hundreds of millions of years'.[415] If a nucleotide is functional, then it should change only rarely. This is because change is mainly detrimental to survival and therefore less likely to have been propagated to subsequent generations.[416] However, if the nucleotide is not functional 'changes would not have been selected against and thus would have occurred more frequently'.[417]

Such a comparison between mice and humans reveals that while there is extensive sequence conservation in the protein-coding genes, around 85 per cent, conservation outside these regions is far less. Within these non-coding regions of the genome, however, certain elements stand out as being conserved, in particular regions linked to genes that are binding sites for transcription factors

and sequences that produce miRNAs, in line with the important roles identified for both these types of molecules as regulators of gene expression.[416,418] However, the remainder of the non-protein-coding genome showed far less conservation between mice and humans, such that only 3 per cent of the genome seems to be functional when assessed by these criteria.[418] This could imply lack of a functional role, although one problem with comparisons between the mouse and human genomes is that this might not detect genomic regions that are specific to our species, but might nevertheless have an important functional role. To address this issue, Ponting and colleagues also compared more closely related species, such as chimps and other primates, as well as looking at differences between different human individuals. When assessed by such criteria, this suggested that around 9 per cent of the human genome is functional.[418]

In contrast, another way of assessing functionality in the genome involves measuring its biochemical activity. This was the approach taken by the ENCODE researchers and, as we've seen, this has meant assuming that detection of transcription factor binding, DNA methylation and histone tags, and generation of non-coding RNAs, are all evidence of function. It was by this approach that ENCODE researchers came up with their high figure of 80 or more per cent functionality. Clearly though, this leaves us with a conundrum. So, while the estimate of 9 per cent functionality by Ponting and colleagues is a lot greater than the 2 per cent of the genome previously thought to be functional, it is clearly a lot less than 80 or more per cent. Is there any way of reconciling these two quite different figures? It is here that the debate becomes most heated. Those who believe the lower figure is the correct one argue that assuming biochemical activity equals function ignores the possibility that such activity might be just 'noise' and is impossible to reconcile with the apparent much lower levels of conservation. In contrast, those proposing a much higher figure believe that conservation is an imperfect measure of function for a number of reasons. One is that since many non-coding RNAs act as 3D structures, and because regulatory DNA elements are quite flexible in their sequence constraints, their easy detection by sequence conservation measurements will be much more difficult than for protein-coding regions. Using such criteria, John Mattick and colleagues have come up with much higher figures for the amount of functionality in the genome.[419] In addition, many epigenetic mechanisms that may be central for genome function will not be detectable through a DNA sequence comparison,

since they are mediated by chemical modifications of the DNA and its associated proteins that do not involve changes in DNA sequence. Finally, if genomes operate as 3D entities, then this may not be easily detectable in terms of sequence conservation.

Another potential problem in the way that sequence conservation has been used as a measure of functionality in the genome is the fact that such conservation needs to be measured against a reference point, which, in this case, is the repetitive DNA sequences that have accumulated in the genome through transposition. These sequences are assumed to be useless, and therefore their rate of mutation is taken to represent a 'neutral' reference; however, as John Mattick and his colleague Marcel Dinger, of the Garvan Institute, have pointed out, a flaw in such reasoning is 'the questionable proposition that transposable elements, which provide the major source of evolutionary plasticity and novelty, are largely non-functional'.[420] In fact, as we saw in Chapter 8, there is increasing evidence that while transposons may start off as molecular parasites, they can also play a central role in the creation of new regulatory elements, non-coding RNAs, and other such important functional components of the genome.[421] It is this that has led John Stamatoyannopoulos to conclude that 'far from being an evolutionary dustbin, transposable elements appear to be active and lively members of the genomic regulatory community, deserving of the same level of scrutiny applied to other genic or regulatory features'.[422] In fact, the emerging role for transposition in creating new regulatory mechanisms in the genome challenges the very idea that we can divide the genome into 'useful' and 'junk' components. A point that Sydney Brenner once made in reference to junk DNA was to distinguish between 'the rubbish we keep, which is junk, and the rubbish we throw away, which is garbage … everyone knows that you throw away garbage. But junk we keep in the attic until there may be some need for it.'[423] That previously useless items may take on new and important uses is important to bear in mind, against the idea that the functions of different genomic regions are fixed and unchanging.

The potential pitfalls of writing off elements in the genome as useless or parasitical has been demonstrated by a recent reconsideration of the role of pseudogenes. As we discussed in Chapter 4, these mutated, dysfunctional versions of protein-coding genes have traditionally been held up as a prime example of genomic garbage; indeed, it was in reference to pseudogenes that Ohno first coined the phrase 'junk' DNA.[424] Yet recent studies are forcing a reappraisal of

the functional role of these genetic 'duds'.[425] One particular type of pseudogene is the 'pseudoenzyme'. We mentioned in Chapter 1 that enzymes are the class of proteins that catalyse chemical reactions in the cell, and perform jobs that include transport of foodstuffs into the cell, transformation of these into energy, and regulation of the genes coding for all these processes, as well as a diversity of other cellular functions. Central to how enzymes work is their 'active site': the specific region in the enzyme in which catalysis take place. These active sites are characterized by a very precise amino acid sequence, which forms a similarly precise 3D structure in which catalysis takes place. Indeed, this precision is the key to how different enzymes are able to specifically catalyse their own unique chemical reaction amidst the hundreds of thousands of other reactions, all taking place simultaneously in the cell and organism.

Given the importance of enzymes in the body, it was not surprising that one of the first tasks of geneticists, following the completion of the Human Genome Project in 2003, was to catalogue all the genes that code for enzymes in the genome. Yet what was surprising was how many of those identified seemed to be catalytically inactive, as defined by the presence of debilitating mutations in their active sites.[425] So, of the 518 human kinases, enzymes which, as we saw in Chapter 3, activate other proteins by adding a phosphate group to them, around 10 per cent lacked at least one of three key amino acids necessary for catalysing the phosphate transfer. In another class of enzymes that modify proteins by adding a sulfate group, more than half the members of this class seemed to be catalytically inactive.[425] All of this confirmed the idea that the genome was littered with the remnants of 'dead' proteins. And although knowledge about the existence of pseudogenes was nothing new, the surprising number of pseudoenzymes came as somewhat of a shock to genome researchers, so much so that one of them, Gerard Manning at Genentech, a biotechnology company in California, recalls that 'we thought we must have got it wrong'.[426] Recently, though, as in a zombie horror movie, the dead are showing surprising signs of life.

In particular, recent studies have shown that just because pseudoenzymes are catalytically inactive, this doesn't prevent them playing important roles in the cell. In general, this involves the regulation of a 'living' cellular partner.[425] Why pseudogenes often have such an active partner relates to how they come into being in the first place. So, a typical way in which pseudogenes form is through the duplication of a functional gene. Mutation of one member of the pair can

disable it, while leaving its partner catalytically active. Initially, this was thought to be the end of the matter, but then biologists studying the evolution of pseudoenzymes became intrigued by the fact that the DNA sequences coding for some of them had changed little over millions of years of evolution. This suggested that these proteins had some function, for, as Patrick Eyers of Sheffield University, England, who was studying this question, puts it, 'biological systems don't bother keeping these proteins unless they are doing something important'.[426] In fact, subsequent studies have shown that pseudoenzymes have resisted change precisely because they have a variety of important roles assisting their catalytically active partner.[425] Such roles can include helping their partner to catalyse its specific reaction by forcing it into the correct shape, or acting as a bodyguard to transport it safely to its required location in the cell. The ability to play such specific roles is directly linked to the similarity between pseudoenzymes and their active partners since this allows the two to associate; yet, at the same time, the fact that pseudoenzymes are no longer required for catalysis has opened up a space for them to evolve in a variety of different ways that enhance their possibilities as regulatory agents.

The study of pseudoenzymes is not only driven by scientific curiosity: there is also now interest in this class of proteins as targets for new therapeutic drugs.[425] Pseudokinases in particular are being investigated as potential drug targets. This is because many kinases themselves are highly important targets for anti-cancer drugs, reflecting the role of this class of enzymes in normal cell growth but also in tumour formation. Such kinase inhibitors have been very successful, accounting for nearly $11 billion in sales in the USA alone. However, one drawback of such drugs is that because they target the enzyme's active site, and since this is fairly similar in different kinases, an inhibitor that targets one kinase can affect the activity of a different type, leading to unwelcome side-effects. So, although one of the most successful anti-kinase drugs, Gleevec®, has been effective in combating one form of leukaemia, it also causes abdominal pain, nausea, and fatigue. In contrast, because pseudokinases work through regions other than the active site, there is a hope that it might be possible to interfere with their activity, and therefore that of their catalytic partners, in a way that does not affect other types of kinases.[425]

Such new findings about the role of genomic elements previously presumed to be junk provide an important caution to the idea that we can simply write off such

elements. However, while this suggests a qualitative shift may be required in our understanding of genome function, it does not directly address the quantitative issue of whether claims of 80 or more per cent of the genome are warranted. In this respect, one issue that has puzzled scientists for many years is the so-called 'C-value paradox'. This was the term coined by C. A. Thomas of Harvard Medical School in 1971, to refer to the emerging evidence at that time that studies of the amount of DNA in the cells of different species seemed to bear no relationship to their complexity as organisms.[427] So, as Ford Doolittle of Dalhousie University, Canada, has noted, 'humans have a thousand times as much DNA as simple bacteria, but lungfish have at least 30 times more than humans, as do many flowering plants'.[428] At the other extreme is the *Fugu* pufferfish—a species prized as a delicacy in Japanese restaurants but so toxic that, if prepared incorrectly, it can rapidly result in death.[429] But *Fugu* is also of great interest to biologists because its genome is unusually compact—clocking in at a mere 400 million bases, compared to our own 3 billion bases. Yet, despite having a genome only one eighth the size of ours, *Fugu* possess a similar number of genes. This disparity raises questions about the wisdom of assigning functionality to the vast majority of the human genome, since, by the same token, this could imply that lungfish are far more complex than us from a genomic perspective, while the smaller amount of non-protein-coding DNA in the *Fugu* genome suggests that loss of such DNA is perfectly compatible with life in a multicellular organism.[428]

Not everyone is convinced about the value of these examples though. John Mattick, for instance, believes that organisms with a much greater amount of DNA than humans can be dismissed as exceptions because they are 'polyploid', that is, their cells have far more than the normal two copies of each gene, or their genomes contain an unusually high proportion of inactive transposons.[430] Mattick is also not convinced that *Fugu* provides a good example of a complex organism with no non-coding DNA. Instead, he points out that 89 per cent of this pufferfish's DNA is still non-protein coding, so the often-made claim that it is an example of a multicellular organism without such DNA is misleading.[431]

Perhaps one of the strongest arguments against the relatively small degree of sequence conservation in the genome being an accurate reflection of the true extent of functionality, is the fact that ENCODE and similar projects have shown that 'the vast majority of the mammalian genome is differentially transcribed in precise cell-specific patterns'.[430] Indeed, it was this cell-type specificity that led

Ewan Birney to predict that 80 per cent functionality might be an underestimate, because of the expectation that, as greater numbers of cell types were studied than in the ENCODE findings published in 2012, then more regions of the genome were likely to show activity in these new cell types. It's important at this point, though, to mention a criticism that has been raised about some of the cells that ENCODE analysed. The project studied a large variety of different human cell types; the idea being to survey genome activity across the whole human body. But this meant working with many so-called 'immortalized cell lines'—cells that have acquired the ability to divide indefinitely, like a cancer. Such cells have played an important role in medical research ever since the first such cell line was isolated from a woman called Henrietta Lacks in 1951.[432] Lacks was a poor black woman from Maryland in the US who was admitted to Johns Hopkins Hospital after feeling a 'knot' inside her; in fact, it was a highly malignant type of cervical cancer. Johns Hopkins had a progressive policy of treating poor people for free. There was another less benevolent side to the institution though, for during Lacks' treatment, and without her knowledge or consent, a sample of her tumour was removed by Howard Jones, the doctor treating her, and given to George Otto Gey, a clinician who was experimenting with ways to grow human cells in culture.

Previous attempts to culture normal human cells had all failed. We now know this is because such cells can only divide a finite number of times, typically about fifty, before they die. This 'Hayflick limit', named after Leonard Hayflick, the scientist who discovered it in 1962, is thought to be one reason why we all have finite lives, although ageing involves many other factors as well. However, unlike all previous attempts, Henrietta Lacks' cells not only multiplied at a phenomenal rate in the culture dish, but kept on dividing.[432] Tragically, Lacks succumbed to her cancer soon after being admitted to hospital. Her cells, though, had found immortality, and continue to be propagated in laboratories across the world to this day, having been used to develop a polio vaccine, played an important role in research into cancer and AIDS, and been used to assess the effects of radiation and toxic substances on human cells. Gey called Lacks' cells HeLa cells in a clumsy attempt to protect her anonymity, and for many years they were believed to have come from someone called Helen Lane. Lacks' family only found out by accident how important the cells had become in 1973, when they were asked for a blood sample by a scientist studying the genetics of HeLa. And only in August 2013, after

a long campaign for justice, did the family finally receive some acknowledgement for the unethical way they and Henrietta herself had been treated.[433]

In addition to showing that culture of cells outside the body was possible, the development of HeLa cells opened the way for the creation of many other immortalized human cell lines. While initially these were derived from cancers, just as HeLa cells had been, the development of ways to 'immortalize' cells in culture by exposing them to mutagenic chemicals, radiation, or adding oncogenes from viruses, made it possible to create a range of cell lines that retained properties of the organs or tissues from which they had originated. It was such cell lines that ENCODE used for some of its analyses, as well as stem cell lines that also have the capacity to divide indefinitely. Yet such types of cells are known to be transcriptionally 'permissive', making it possible that some of the high levels of transcriptional activity detected by ENCODE reflect this peculiarity, rather than being a general characteristic of all cells in the body.

The use of immortalized cell lines by ENCODE is one reason why we should treat some of its findings with caution. However, it's also important to note, as Stamatoyannopoulos does, that in contrast to the 'perception that ENCODE is largely a cell line centered endeavor ... overall ENCODE has sampled a vast range of primary cell types—indeed, these outnumber immortalized cell lines nearly three-to-one'.[434] Such 'primary' cells have been taken straight from the normal body, not immortalized. In addition, other studies have indicated that many functional elements identified by ENCODE, such as non-coding RNAs, show precise patterns of expression during embryo development and differentiation of stem cells into specialized cell types, as well as distinctive expression patterns across a complex structure like the brain.[435] Nevertheless, it remains possible that biochemical 'noise' might also have a precise expression pattern, which is why the ultimate way to test whether different elements in the genome are functional is to interfere with such elements in an experimental organism like a mouse, and assess the effect on the cell or organism.

The only problem with such a test is that, as we've seen, a surprising conclusion from mouse 'knockouts' of protein-coding genes is that elimination of the activity of a gene that has been identified as important by other criteria often has little effect on the whole organism, or very different effects to what was expected, presumably because of 'compensation' by other genes.[436] And if this is true of protein-coding genes, it's likely to be at least as much an issue for non-coding

regions of the genome. As such, if knocking out such a region does not have a significant negative effect on the organism, this will not necessarily mean that it does not have an important function. Another problem in trying to test the function of non-coding regions of the genome is the sheer number of such elements. Using traditional methods of gene knockout this would have made it difficult to test elements on such a scale. However, recently new methods of 'gene editing' are dramatically reducing the cost and also rapidly speeding up the process of making knockout animals.[437] As such, it is becoming possible to test the function of non-protein-coding elements across the breadth of the genome in ways that would have been undreamt of only a decade ago.

Chris Ponting and his colleague, Andrew Bassett at Oxford University, have recently demonstrated that such gene editing can be used to rapidly test the function of non-coding RNAs on a large scale in model organisms like the mouse, but also the zebrafish; the latter being particularly important for studying vertebrate development because its embryos grow outside the mother and are transparent, making them very amenable for studying embryogenesis.[438] However, these scientists have also drawn attention to the potential pitfalls of such an approach, namely that assessment of the effects of such intervention requires a clear idea of which cell types and tissues are likely to be affected, based on analysis of the expression pattern of such non-coding RNAs. In addition, interventions in the genome need to be carefully designed so that there are no unintended effects upon protein-coding genes.[439] Such considerations are already an issue for studies of knockouts of protein-coding genes, since, in a number of cases, effects upon the whole organism have been misinterpreted because attempts to knock out one gene ended up affecting a neighbouring gene because of unintended disruption of DNA elements that regulated the latter.[440] Indeed, as we become increasingly aware of the complexity of gene expression, and the densely packed nature of functional elements in the genome, some of which may be superimposed upon each other, so care will be needed when interfering with such elements and interpreting the results of such interventions.

A different problem in assessing the functional significance of different regions of the human genome is the fact that ENCODE showed that a significant proportion of the biochemical activity detected in the genome was only found in humans, and not in the mice which were being used as a point of comparison. This finding is one reason why some critics of ENCODE are sceptical about the

conclusions drawn by its researchers, since, if these regions really are functionally important, the findings would suggest that humans are far more different to mice than had been concluded by comparison of protein-coding sequences alone. To test whether this is the case, we, however, also face a practical problem, since if mouse knockouts are incapable of testing the functional significance of these genomic activities because they are only active in humans, not in mice, what alternative approaches will be available?

One possible route, if such regions of genomic activity are also found in other primates, would be to develop knockout versions of such species. Here the new gene editing technology is potentially of great importance, since one of the problems with traditional knockout technology was that it was effective in mice, but not other mammalian species. In contrast, the new technology can be applied to many species, with the result that the first knockout monkeys were recently created using such technology.[441] If regions of biochemical activity are identified that are only found in humans and other primates, but not in mice, for the first time it will now be possible to test the functional importance of such regions in a monkey model. However, if such regions are only found in our closest relatives, chimpanzees and other great apes, such an approach could pose ethical issues, given the opposition of some people to experimentation on such species, or indeed on any primate species.[441]

Of course, we face an even bigger problem in assessing the functional significance of biochemical activities in the genome that are restricted to humans alone. For, although such regions, if truly functional, might hold keys to the unique features that distinguish human beings from other species, how can we assess the significance of such regions given the impossibility, for ethical reasons, of creating genetically engineered knockout humans? One possible route would be to focus on human cells in culture. And, indeed, the new gene editing methods can easily be applied to human cells.[442] This means that it is now becoming almost routine to delete different regions of the human genome in cultured cells and then assess the effect on cell physiology. However, although this may allow characterization of the role of such regions in defined cellular processes, the approach has limited value for identifying important functions within a complex organ like the brain, or the body as a whole.

Critics of animal experimentation often argue that animal or human cells in culture could easily serve as a substitute for use of live animals in research. In fact,

such studies of cells in culture already form a central part of a typical research project. To take my own studies of the roles of chemical signals in important physiological processes as an example, at least half our recent research has used cultured cells. However, while we can learn a lot about basic cellular processes by studying cells in a culture dish, to understand the role of chemical signals and the genomic processes that they control in their full complexity, it is necessary to study the whole organism. This is not only because complex organs, such as the brain or the heart, are impossible to grow in culture, but also because different organs communicate with each other via hormones and other signalling molecules in a way that is only possible to study in a whole, living animal.

Faced with the impossibility of genetically engineering human beings as part of experimental science, there is, however, a different route to identifying functional roles for the non-coding parts of our genomes by looking for links between these regions and human disease. As we saw in Chapter 6, one surprising conclusion of studies of the link between the genome and disease that have been taking place since the completion of the Human Genome Project is that at least 90 per cent of such links are not in protein-coding genes but in the rest of the genome. This finding is, in itself, an important piece of evidence in support of the idea that such non-coding regions of the genome are important, but it also provides a way to begin to assess the effect of naturally occurring mutations in the non-coding genome. In effect, the individuals identified in this way constitute natural 'knock-outs', or other types of mutants in which the function of a particular gene is not knocked out but altered in some way. Because of this, studying these individuals may, on the one hand, reveal insights about the underlying molecular mechanisms of their disease, but also provide important information about the role of the non-coding genome in normal bodily function. There is a catch, however: the genetic basis of human disease is itself turning out to be far more complicated than many people had predicted, as we'll now explore in Chapter 11.

11

GENES AND DISEASE

'The success of the Human Genome Project will also soon let us see the essences of mental disease. Only after we understand them at the genetic level can we rationally seek out appropriate therapies for such illnesses as schizophrenia and bipolar disease.'   *Jim Watson*

'We have, in truth, learned nothing from the genome other than probabilities. How does a one or three percent increased risk for something translate into the clinic? It is useless information.'   *Craig Venter*

Genes and disease have been inextricably linked ever since the birth of human genetics. Maybe this reflects a general tendency of people to particularly notice abnormal or curious characteristics rather than more commonplace ones in fellow humans. Indeed, as we saw in Chapter 1, the first human condition to be linked to a genetic mechanism at the turn of the twentieth century was alkaptonuria, a disease that drew the attention of Archibald Garrod because of its association with urine that turns black on contact with air.[443] Garrod's insights eventually opened the door to recognition of a succession of other human diseases that followed Mendel's laws (see Figure 21). So, conditions like Huntington's chorea and cystic fibrosis are dominant and recessive diseases, respectively. In addition, there are sex-linked disorders, caused by defects in the X and Y chromosomes.[444,445] Because the Y chromosome is so small and contains few genes, Y-linked disorders are rare and few in number.[444] X-linked recessive disorders generally only affect men, since women have two X chromosomes (although there are exceptions, such as women with a condition called Turner's syndrome, who have only one X chromosome).[445] However, women can pass on these disorders to their sons. Haemophilia, where sufferers can bleed to death from a minor injury because of a defect in the blood-clotting response, is an X-linked disorder. The condition has

Condition	Gene (Chr. Location)	Inheritance Pattern
Congenital Deafness (nonsyndromic)	Connexin 26 (13q11)	Recessive
Tay–Sachs	hexosaminidase A (15q23)	Recessive
Familial hypercholesterolemia	LDL receptor (19p13)	Dominant
Sickle cell anemia	Beta-globin (11p15)	Recessive
Duchenne muscular dystrophy	Dystrophin (Xq21)	X-linked Recessive
Cystic Fibrosis	CFTR (7q31)	Recessive
Hemochromatosis	HFE (6p21)	Recessive
Huntington disease	Huntington (4p16)	Dominant

Figure 21. The different classes of single-gene disorders in humans

been known since the 2nd century AD, and ancient Jewish laws recognized that if a woman had two sons that died from circumcision her third son would not be required to be circumcised, showing some awareness of women as carriers.[446] Famously, Queen Victoria passed on the condition to many European royal males.[447] Indeed, the fact that the Russian Tsar and Tsarina's son had the disorder, and subsequently enlisted the monk and supposed faith healer Rasputin to treat the child, has been proposed as one of the destabilizing influences on the royal court that helped trigger the Russian Revolution. The discovery in 1991 of the remains of the Russian royal family, executed in 1918 at the height of the civil war that swept the country after the revolution, led to the demonstration that the haemophilia was due to a mutation in the intron–exon boundary of exon 4 of the clotting factor IX gene, showing this was a splicing disorder.[447]

The recognition that some human disorders followed the same inheritance patterns as Mendel's pea plants was a major step forward in human genetics. However, even the discovery that genes are made of DNA did not initially make it any easier to identify the specific gene defects responsible for such disorders, with the exception of conditions that affect the haemoglobin protein, like sickle cell anaemia and the thalassaemias. Here the link was obvious, given that these disorders were clearly connected with failure of the blood to transport oxygen in the normal manner. While both are recessive disorders, sickle cell is caused by a single amino acid change in the haemoglobin protein,[448] while thalassaemias are generally caused by a failure to properly produce the protein in normal amounts.[449] In 1949, Linus Pauling, who would receive a Nobel Prize in 1954

for his pioneering studies of protein structure, showed that the haemoglobin in sickle cell had an altered mobility upon separation using a technique called gel electrophoresis. This was the first demonstration of a link between an altered gene product and a disease, and Pauling predicted that 'medicine is just now entering into a new era [in which] scientists will have discovered the molecular basis of diseases, and will have discovered why molecules of certain drugs are effective in treatment, and others are not'.[450] However, these blood disorders are very much exceptions, and in general it has only been possible to identify the molecular defect responsible for single-gene disorders by a laborious search through the genome. This only became realizable in the 1970s when it became possible to cut and paste genes and sequence the DNA code itself. Armed with such tools, from the mid-1980s onwards, the molecular secrets of a series of single-gene disorders were finally revealed. So we now know the gene defects associated with recessive disorders like cystic fibrosis, dominant ones like Huntington's, and X-linked diseases like Duchenne's muscular dystrophy.

Huntington's has been recognized as a disorder since medieval times, but was only properly defined in 1872 when George Huntington described its successive symptoms of jerky movements, psychosis, and eventually full-scale dementia.[451] Identified as a dominant Mendelian disorder, the search for the affected gene was led by Nancy Wexler, who devoted her life to this quest after her own mother died of the disease.[452] A major breakthrough came with the discovery of an isolated community in Venezuela where a staggering half of the population were sufferers. Such concentrations of a specific genetic disease in a population are due to the 'founder effect', whereby a whole region is populated by descendants of an original carrier of a gene defect. This particular case provided an extended family of thousands of people who could be compared in genetic linkage studies, leading to the discovery of the huntingtin gene in 1993. This gene has a series of 'trinucleotide repeats', that is, the sequence CAG repeated over and over, at the start of its protein-coding region, resulting in a corresponding repeat of the amino acid glutamine.[451] Everyone has such repeats in their huntingtin protein; however, if an individual has more than thirty-five repeats, they will succumb to the disease, with the age at which they do so being related to how many extra repeats they have.

Huntington's disease has spread through the population in the past because most sufferers generally only show signs of the disorder between the ages of

35 and 44 years old. So people with the disease have often had children before realizing they themselves were sufferers, and, being a dominant disorder, the chance of these children succumbing is 50 per cent. One obstacle to treating the disorder is our continuing lack of understanding of the normal function of the huntingtin protein. Why the mutant protein causes the symptoms it does also remains unclear, although recent studies suggest that presence of the abnormal protein leads to enhanced cell death.[451] So, more than twenty years after the discovery of the huntingtin gene, the only really tangible outcome for sufferers is that a test is now available that shows how many CAG repeats an individual has in this gene, and therefore whether they will eventually succumb to the disease. A recent article in *The Guardian* newspaper by journalist Charlotte Raven, who took the test and now knows that she will eventually succumb to the disease, provides a moving account of what it feels like to live with this terrible knowledge.[453]

Much more is known about the proteins that are defective in cystic fibrosis and muscular dystrophy, recessive conditions associated not with the abnormal actions of a dominant mutant protein, but with the absence of a properly functioning normal protein. Cystic fibrosis has been known about at least since the eighteenth century, when literature warned 'woe to the child who tastes salty from a kiss on the brow, for he is cursed and soon must die', referring to the extra salt in the sweat of sufferers of this condition.[454] The disorder was only properly characterized in 1938, when Dorothy Andersen described patients with severe malfunction of the pancreas, the organ that produces our digestive enzymes as well as hormones like insulin, and linked such patients with those suffering from a lung disorder that left them highly vulnerable to asphyxiation and lung infections. In 1989, a team led by Francis Collins, who would later head the Human Genome Project, finally identified the defective gene, after a search which he compared to 'trying to find a burned-out light bulb in a house located somewhere between the East and West coasts without knowing the state, much less the town or street the house is on'.[455] The gene codes for the cystic fibrosis transporter protein, or CFTR, which regulates movement of chloride ions in and out of the 'epithelial' cells that form the inner boundaries of the lungs, pancreas, and some other tissues.[454] Lack of a functional CFTR protein leads to a build-up of salt in the sweat, and thick, sticky mucus accumulation in the lungs and pancreas, interfering with both digestion and breathing.

The most severe form of muscular dystrophy was first defined clinically in the mid-nineteenth century by Guillaume Duchenne, who gave his name to the disorder that he noted in boys who became progressively weaker, lost the ability to walk, and generally died in their teens.[456] Recently, a parent of a boy diagnosed with the disorder has described how what began as a routine check-up to find out why his son was slow in reaching certain pre-school 'milestones' turned into the realization that he would 'never play rugby, never make love, never make it to university, never realize his full potential'.[457] Duchenne's muscular dystrophy generally occurs in males and is carried by females, showing that it is an X-linked recessive disorder. In 1986, Louis Kunkel of Harvard Medical School identified the dystrophin gene, aided by the fact that some sufferers had obvious chunks missing from the X chromosome region where the gene was located.[456] In normal muscles the dystrophin protein links the surface membrane of the cell and its cytoskeleton, the protein structure that gives it shape and form. Lack of dystrophin destabilizes this interaction, leading to death of cells and muscle decay.[456]

When the CFTR gene was identified in 1989, the front cover of the journal *Science* featured a 4-year-old boy with cystic fibrosis sitting cross-legged framed by a rainbow of chromosomes.[458] Inside, editor Daniel Koshland confidently predicted that 'one in two thousand children born each year with a fatal defect now has a greater chance for a happy future'.[458] Geneticist Peter Goodfellow, who, a year later, would identify the SRY gene that single-handedly triggers the development of maleness in humans and other mammals, said 'the implications of this research are profound: there will be large spin offs in basic biology, especially in cell physiology, but the largest impact will be medical'.[458] However, we still lack a cure for these disorders despite having a much more detailed understanding of how the normal proteins work, and how defects in them lead to disease, so that Jack Riordan, co-discoverer of the CFTR gene, recently said that 'the disease has contributed much more to science than science has contributed to the disease'.[458]

One reason for this gap between understanding and ability to generate practical therapies is the difficulty in reconstituting a functional version of the proteins defective in these diseases, in the cells of a living person. Such 'gene therapy' is hampered both by the difficulties in getting artificial gene expression constructs into cells and expressing the missing protein without affecting expression of other genes. With Huntington's the goal is not to replace a missing functional gene, but to block expression of a dominant mutant version. As we've discussed, RNA

interference may hold some promise for this type of disorder, since siRNAs can precisely target a specific RNA sequence and thus block the expression of a mutant protein, but not the normal version. Here also though, a primary obstacle is effective delivery of siRNAs to a cell. Maybe this is why, despite the existence of a genetic test for Huntington's, many people at risk through a known family connection choose not to take the test; ironically, this includes Nancy Wexler, who helped develop it. Wexler believes it has taken so long to find a cure because 'every time you look under a rock for what the Huntington gene's doing, you find something fascinating and interesting, maybe relevant and maybe not. And so even figuring out what's relevant is tricky.'[452]

Not that the clinical scenario for single-gene disorders is totally bleak. Phenylketonuria, or PKU, is a recessive disorder affecting the enzyme that catalyses the transformation of the amino acid phenylalanine into tyrosine.[459] Because of this, phenylalanine entering the body as a component of many types of foodstuffs cannot be broken down, and instead accumulates to dangerous levels, leading to severe mental retardation, hyperactivity, and seizures during early childhood. Understanding the molecular nature of PKU has made a major difference to its treatment, by the simple practice of restricting phenylalanine in the diet.[460] Since excess phenylalanine only affects the developing brain, a more normal diet can be eaten after the teenage years. However, women with the disorder who become pregnant face a problem, since, although their children are unlikely to have the disorder because it is recessive, during the foetal stage they are highly vulnerable to their mother's blood. That is why pregnant women with PKU are advised to revert to an extremely strict diet, or not have children at all. PKU stands out as a success story partly because of the simplicity of the treatment. Unfortunately, many other metabolic disorders have proven less amenable to treatment simply by a change of diet.

As such, there is great interest still in the potential of gene therapy. The most promising situations are those in which the affected cells are most accessible, and indeed there has been partial success with a disease affecting a particularly accessible set of cells—those that make up the blood. One genetic disorder affecting white blood cells is an X-linked disorder, severe combined immunodeficiency, or SCID.[461] As we've seen, a key aspect of successful immunity is the production of antibodies by lymphocytes. This interaction is mediated by hormone-like substances called cytokines, and one type of SCID is caused by defects

in genes coding for these cytokines.[461] Such individuals effectively have no immune system and are extremely vulnerable to infectious diseases. Because lymphocytes are produced in the bone marrow, SCID has been a popular target for gene therapy, since affected cells can be removed, treated, and put back into the body.[461] However, a major issue to be properly resolved is how to safely introduce a gene expression construct into bone marrow cells.

One strategy is to use retroviruses. As we saw in Chapter 8, retroviral RNA genomes are transformed into DNA by the enzyme reverse transcriptase and then insert themselves into the genome of the host cell. This is one reason why HIV can go unnoticed in a person's body for so many years; it also means that retroviruses offer a way to transport gene constructs into the genome of a target cell therapeutically. A clinical trial carried out in France in the late 1990s used retroviruses engineered to carry a cytokine gene into the bone marrow cells of boys suffering from SCID.[461] In one respect the trial was a great success, with 17 out of 20 boys regaining a functional immune system. However, a serious problem with this approach became evident when five of the boys developed leukaemia. It became clear that insertion of the retroviral DNA into the host cell genome had activated an oncogene, those genes that normally play important roles in cell growth but which can cause cancer if overstimulated. The high proportion of those affected suggested that the insertion next to an oncogene wasn't accidental, although why remains unclear. While the leukaemia was subsequently treated, the problems it highlighted led to the suspension of the trial. Despite this setback there is still great interest in developing safe forms of gene therapy. One hope is that retroviruses can be engineered to target the genome without disrupting expression of other genes, although, given the number of regulatory elements identified by ENCODE, this may be far from easy.[461] Alternatively, adenoviruses can deliver proteins to cells without disrupting the genome.

Despite these problems, there is no doubt that the identification of genes defective in diseases with a Mendelian pattern of inheritance has greatly advanced our understanding of the molecular basis of these diseases, and hopefully, therefore, the possibility of developing effective ways to treat them. However, even for single-gene disorders much remains unclear about their manifestation across a population. So, while some cystic fibrosis sufferers die in their teens from lung failure, others only realize they have two faulty CFTR genes when they present at the infertility clinic—the male reproductive system also being affected by this

disorder—having no other obvious symptoms of the disease.[462] This variability is called the 'penetrance' of a disease. To some extent, it is due to different mutations in a gene having differing effects on the resulting protein; however, it also reflects the effects of other gene variants in an individual, and the unique environmental influences that individuals are subjected to during their lives, which can either counteract, or enhance, the effects of the gene variant in question.[463] So, sometimes the exact same gene mutation leads to severe symptoms in one person, but has no effect in another.[464]

If this is an issue for single-gene disorders, how about more common conditions such as heart disease, diabetes, cancer, and disorders of the mind like schizophrenia, bipolar disorder, and depression? A major selling point of the Human Genome Project was the claim that it would lead to greater understanding of such disorders. So, upon completion of the project in 2003, British science minister Lord Sainsbury said 'we now have the possibility of achieving all we ever hoped for from medicine'.[465] Daniel Koshland, editor of Science, promised that the basis for 'illnesses such as manic depression, Alzheimer's, schizophrenia and heart disease' would all be unravelled, with new drug treatments for these conditions sure to follow.[466] These pronouncements were echoed by Craig Venter, leader of the privately funded rival to the official genome project, who said, 'it is my belief that the basic knowledge that we're providing to the world will have a profound impact on the human condition and the treatments for disease and our view of our place on the biological continuum'.[467]

An important complement to the genome project was the creation of 'bio-banks' of DNA samples and medical information.[468] For instance, the UK Biobank aims to collect such samples from half a million individuals. The idea is then to identify gene variants associated with specific diseases in these individuals. In contrast to previous approaches that tested the role in disease of pre-selected 'candidate' genes, this approach is presumed to be unbiased, covering, as it does, the whole genome. This is possible because of the existence of maps of genetic 'markers' that occur at points along each of the 23 human chromosomes. One class of markers are called 'single nucleotide polymorphisms' or SNPs, alterations in specific nucleotide bases that vary between different human individuals.[469] Although SNPs may themselves cause a disease, importantly, this need not be the case. Rather, SNPs can associate with the real genetic cause of a disease because they are close enough on the chromosome to be 'linked' together, during the crossing over that takes place during meiosis.

Genome-wide association studies, or GWAS, have been a major focus of biomedical research in the decade since the completion of the genome project.[470] Such studies have examined over 200 diseases and human conditions, with over 4,000 SNP associations made. One estimate is that at least $250 million has been spent on such studies. So how successful has this approach been both in terms of helping us understand the molecular basis of diseases, and, as importantly, identifying new ways to diagnose and treat them? On the positive side, GWAS have highlighted some important novel links between genes and some common diseases, for instance, diabetes.[470,471] This condition, as commonly known, is associated with a high level of glucose in the blood; however, there are many other adverse effects, because insulin plays such a central role in the body. Insulin, which is secreted by the pancreas, is often known as the hormone of plenty because it regulates the accumulation of carbohydrate and fat stores and the growth of muscle following food intake. It exerts its effects by binding to a protein receptor on the surface of the cells it targets. This leads both to the transport of glucose into cells, but also regulation of a range of enzymes and other proteins involved in cell and tissue growth.

Type 1 diabetes occurs early in life and generally results in a total inability of the pancreas to produce insulin.[472] In contrast, type 2 diabetes occurs later in life and obesity is a major risk factor.[471] There is currently much talk about a diabetes 'epidemic', since the incidence of the disease has dramatically risen with rising levels of obesity. Since type 2 diabetes usually begins with an inability of tissues to respond to insulin, it was generally expected that defects would be concentrated in genes coding for the insulin receptor itself or other proteins that transmit its influence within the cell. Yet, GWAS have overwhelmingly identified a role in this disorder for genes involved in the formation and function of pancreatic beta cells.[470,471] This suggests that, although obesity is a trigger, individuals who succumb to type 2 diabetes are primarily those whose beta cells are less able to cope with the requirement for increased insulin production that occurs following the hormone's inability to manifest its effects in the body. In contrast, type 1 diabetes is mainly due to problems of auto-immunity.[472] Normally, the immune system distinguishes a person's own cells from bacteria, viruses, and other pathogens invading the body. However, this ability to distinguish self from non-self sometimes breaks down, resulting in auto-immunity. Type 1 diabetes is generally caused by auto-immune mechanisms destroying the pancreatic beta cells that

secrete insulin, although, in rare cases, the defect is in a regulatory region of the insulin gene.[472]

Despite these insights, there have been growing concerns in recent years about the practical value of GWAS. Surprisingly, it's not that this approach has failed to find links between the specific region of the genome and disease, but rather that it has identified a bewildering number of such links—but their effects are predicted to be tiny. Recently, Sir Alec Jeffreys of Leicester University, discoverer of the genetic fingerprinting technique, has argued that 'one of the great hopes for GWAS was that, in the same way that huge numbers of Mendelian disorders were pinned down at the DNA level and the gene and mutations involved identified, it would be possible to simply extrapolate from single gene disorders to complex multigenic disorders. That really hasn't happened.'[473] Or, as Jon McClellan and Mary-Claire King of Washington University have noted, 'to date, genome-wide association studies (GWAS) have published hundreds of common variants whose...frequencies are statistically correlated with various illnesses and traits. However, the vast majority of such variants have no established biological relevance to disease or clinical utility for prognosis or treatment.'[474] Perhaps most damning for the argument that GWAS simply need to improve their methods or the number of people being analysed, McClellan and King conclude that 'the general failure to confirm common risk variants is not due to a failure to carry out GWAS properly. The problem is underlying biology, not the operationalization of study design.'[475] These various points are worth considering in detail. We mentioned in Chapter 6 how 90 per cent of links between common diseases and the genome are in the non-protein-coding regions we've been discussing in this book. Yet media reports of such findings still tend to have headlines such as one that appeared recently on the BBC website entitled 'Eighty new genes linked to schizophrenia',[476] despite the fact that the links identified are overwhelmingly not to genes as traditionally defined, but to these non-coding regions. Indeed, an important aspect of the ENCODE project was its demonstration that many GWAS links that were disregarded because they were not in protein-coding genes, map closely to areas of the genome associated with important gene 'switches', or obvious biochemical activity.[477]

This at least helps to address previous concerns that most GWAS 'hits' are meaningless in terms of their link with gene function. However, a more fundamental problem is revealed by the study highlighted by the BBC, in which more than 100 genetic regions were linked to schizophrenia, 83 of which had never

been pinpointed before.[478] The leader of the study, Michael O'Donovan of Cardiff University, has concluded that 'finding a whole new bunch of genetic associations opens a window for well-informed experiments to unlock the biology of this condition and we hope ultimately new treatments'.[476] However, the fact that each of these one hundred or so differences is only predicted to have a tiny impact in terms of susceptibility to the disorder has led some critics to doubt how relevant such findings are for diagnosis and treatment.

The debate about the extent to which genetics determines susceptibility to mental disorders as compared to the influence of the environment is a long-standing one. The idea that mental illness is primarily a product of the environment reached its height in the work of psychiatrist R. D. Laing.[479] In his books *The Divided Self* and *Sanity, Madness and the Family*, Laing emphasized the pressures of modern life, particularly those within the nuclear family, as crucial triggers for schizophrenia; more controversially, he saw the disorder as a rational response to the 'madness' of modern society. Indeed, Laing once claimed that a schizophrenic teenager he encountered in a mental hospital who 'was terrified because the atom bomb was inside her', was less estranged from reality 'than the statesmen of the world who boast and threaten that they have Doomsday weapons'.[480] Influential during the 1960s, when mental illness could be viewed as part of a spectrum of rebelliousness personified by the phrase 'turn on, tune in, drop out', one problem with this viewpoint was that it ran the risk of glamorizing, and therefore potentially ignoring, the very real psychological pain and debilitating nature of schizophrenia for those who suffer from it.

In contrast, Jim Watson believes that schizophrenia is a straightforward genetic condition. Watson, whose own son Rufus has the condition, believes he has 'seen the failure of the environmental approach in a very personal way' since, 'for too long, my wife and I hoped that what Rufus needed was an appropriate challenge on which to focus. But as he passed into adolescence, I feared the origin of his diminished life lay in his genes. It was this realisation that led me to help to bring the human genome project into existence.'[481] However, the view that schizophrenia is purely a genetic disorder has trouble explaining some important facts. A recent study showed that black people of Caribbean origin living in Britain are nine times as likely to be diagnosed as schizophrenic as white Britons.[482] One explanation for this finding from a purely genetic point of view would be that this particular population is biologically more susceptible to schizophrenia; however,

this fails to explain why incidence levels amongst black people in the Caribbean itself are similar to those of British whites. The study concluded that racism was probably a key factor, both in terms of being diagnosed schizophrenic and as a trigger of the condition, but also that other factors specific to particular immigrant communities, such as differences in family structure, may explain why Afro-Caribbeans are so vulnerable in this respect. But, whatever the exact reasons, the study suggests that that 'biological or genetic susceptibility do not appear to explain high rates of schizophrenia in black Caribbeans'.[483]

Another problem with the idea that schizophrenia is a specific 'disease' with a common biological origin is the sheer diversity of symptoms used to classify it. These range from 'delusions, hallucinations, loosening of associations, disorganized speech and behaviour, illogical thinking, social isolation and cognitive deficit'.[484] Confusingly, one individual can be classified as schizophrenic by having one set of symptoms while another has a completely different set. This suggests that, rather than being a single 'disease', schizophrenia may encompass multiple related disorders. This ambiguity is also true of other mental conditions such as bipolar disorder, depression, and autism. Indeed, recent studies have suggested that these different disorders share elements in common and may even have common causes; moreover, there is a considerable overlap between such conditions and many behaviours that are considered 'normal'.[485] Coupled with this lack of precision in terms of diagnosis is a lack of understanding about the biological basis of mental disorders. So, while some scientists view schizophrenia as a problem of brain development, others believe it is due to degeneration of nerve cells. A sensible viewpoint would, therefore, seem to be that social factors play an important role in the development of mental disorders, but susceptibility to conditions such as schizophrenia, which probably encompasses a range of different disorders, is affected by real biological differences between individuals.[485] However, if these differences are due to many genetic variables, each with a tiny effect, it is perhaps understandable that some have concluded, like Craig Venter, that this is 'useless information' for identification of new diagnoses and treatments, not just for schizophrenia but other common conditions where GWAS have revealed a large number of weakly contributing factors.[486]

Recently, however, this scenario has been challenged by another possibility, which is that, far from common diseases being a product of many genetic differences all having a small, but cumulative effect on the body, instead, they

may be due to much rarer differences with a very powerful effect, but only in a few individuals.[487] The reason why this second scenario might be true is because of a potential flaw in GWAS, namely the assumption that common diseases are caused by common genetic differences that occur in at least 5 per cent of the population. This assumption has been partly a matter of necessity, since the databases that have been available do not include rarer genetic markers. However, it is possible that the links identified by GWAS actually reflect linkage with much rarer genetic differences that occur in a much smaller percentage of the population, these being the real causal agents of the disease.[487,488] A problem in testing such a possibility has been the prohibitive cost of sequencing whole genomes of many individuals in order to identify such rare differences. However, 'next-generation' approaches that generate DNA sequence for a fraction of the time and price of the Sanger method are now making it possible to address this issue directly.[489] And, tantalizingly, a recent study that focused on areas of the genome identified as linked to schizophrenia by GWAS, and carried out detailed sequence analysis in different individuals, did indeed identify rare differences that may have a considerable effect on specific genomic regions in certain individuals.[490]

A similar assessment as to which of the two scenarios just mentioned is correct is taking place in genetic studies of other common diseases.[471,488] In fact, as a recent review pointed out, 'it is likely that in a heterogeneous, complex genetic disorder such as schizophrenia, a subset of cases may be attributable to rare mutations with large effects while another subset may develop the disorder as a result of an interaction of multiple common variants of small effect'.[491] The exact situation will be important to resolve in terms of the future diagnosis and treatment of disease, for if a large number of common genetic differences contribute only a small amount to common diseases, this could make it very difficult to use such information to predict the chance of someone succumbing to a particular disease. Given that a number of commercial companies currently offer a disease prediction package based on known links between common SNPs and different diseases, this is an important concern.[492] The predictions made by such companies are advertised as giving individuals valuable information about their health and lifestyle choices. But they might also lead some people to worry unnecessarily about their health.

An original hope of GWAS was that the genes identified would be important new targets for drug design. While large numbers of potential targets have been

identified, some critics have questioned whether a drug targeting a gene product that only accounts for a small part of a disease's genetic effect will be particularly effective therapeutically. If, however, only one or a few rare genetic differences are strongly linked to the disease, but differently in each individual, this could imply a much stronger causative role for genetics in common conditions.[492] Such a conclusion poses its own problems for diagnosis and treatment though, for it would suggest that there is no common genetic mechanism for susceptibility to common diseases. As such, it could provide hope for the idea of a personalized medicine for each individual, but would also pose practical problems for drug companies seeking drug targets that would translate into pharmaceuticals that could be used to treat the population as a whole.[492]

Although detailed analysis of the genomes of large numbers of individuals is now being carried out, economic considerations mean that this effort is still largely focused on the coding exons of genes, the so-called 'exome'.[487,488] However, as we've seen, 90 per cent of current genetic links with disease are outside the protein-coding regions,[493] so this approach may fail to identify the great majority of such links. Further new developments in sequencing will, therefore, be necessary if detailed analysis of the whole of the genome in many individuals is to become possible, thus establishing which of the two scenarios discussed is true. Whatever the outcome of this analysis, it's clear that the idea that a few genes in most individuals would determine susceptibility to common diseases now looks false. Another unresolved issue is why the combined influence of all the genetic variants identified as contributing to a particular disease by GWAS seems to be much less than that estimated from studies of disease incidence in families, especially comparisons between identical and non-identical twins.[494] There are a number of possible explanations for such 'missing heritability'. One is that many more genetic variants still remain to be identified. However, another possibility is that the influence of such variants and the environment upon a particular disease do not combine in the simple additive fashion that has been supposed, reflecting the fact that the interactions between different gene products in the cell, whether proteins or non-coding RNAs, is a highly complex affair.[494] But if this is true of genetic variants and disease, then what does it tell us about the link between the genome and human characteristics generally? It's time to investigate what features of our genomes might make us specifically human, and, at the same time, distinguish us from other individuals. But first we need to define what it means to be human at all.

12

WHAT MAKES US HUMAN?

'Man is descended from a hairy, tailed quadruped, probably arboreal in its
habits.'   *Charles Darwin*

'The tool's function is to serve as the conductor of human influence on the
object of activity; it is externally oriented . . . The sign, on the other hand . . . is
aimed at mastering oneself.'   *Lev Vygotsky*

Skeleton of a crocodile. Nipple of a cat. Nose of a pig. Hair of a poodle. Thumb of
a monkey. Eyes of a baboon. Brain of a chimpanzee. If this sounds like a list of
ingredients for a witches' cauldron, think again, for it is merely a reminder of how
many general characteristics we share with other animals. In *The Origin of Species*
in 1859, Darwin was careful not to directly tackle the issue of human beings'
relationship to other organisms on the planet, saying only, cryptically, that 'light
will be thrown on the origin of man and his history'.[495] In fact, it was only in
1871, with *The Descent of Man*, that he applied his theory of natural selection
directly to our own species. The book's major theme was that human beings
share similarities in basic anatomy, physiology, and embryo development with
other mammalian species. In *The Expression of the Emotions in Man and Animals*,
published the following year, Darwin showed he wasn't afraid to include human
behaviour and society in this comparison. In contrast, as we've seen, Alfred
Wallace, co-discoverer of natural selection, found it unacceptable that this
mechanism could produce such an amazing entity as the human mind. Instead,
he argued that while natural selection could explain the workings of the human
body, our consciousness must have some more supernatural origin. It was this
that led Darwin to retort 'I hope you have not murdered too completely your
own and my child.'[496]

In fact, Darwin's fears were groundless, for it is the materialist view that has triumphed. It is now a starting point in neuroscience and psychology that any understanding of human consciousness must be based on molecular and cellular mechanisms shared with other species.[497] This viewpoint was greatly strengthened by the discovery of the DNA code, since comparing protein-coding sequences between humans and other mammalian species indicates that we share a huge amount in common with such species. So, as we saw in Chapter 6, humans and chimps share 99 per cent DNA similarity in protein-coding genes,[498] and even the tiny mouse is 85 per cent similar in this respect.[499] These similarities not only confirm Darwin's view of a continuum between ourselves and other organisms, but also justify the use of animals as surrogates for humans in studies of the mechanisms underlying our biology.[500] In terms of basic bodily functions there is much that is attractive about this approach. The way the heart, lungs, or kidneys of a mouse work is very similar to how these organs operate in our own bodies.[500] Within the cell, the same chemical messengers, like cAMP, control key physiological processes, while in the blood and extracellular fluid, the same hormones, cytokines, and neurochemicals, regulate similar functions in all mammals. So, although falling in or out of love, savouring a fine meal or rueing a bad one, appreciating a great piece of music or regretting a poor one, may seem particularly human activities, the chemicals shaping these responses are essentially the same as those producing pleasure and pain in our pet cat or the mouse that it's pursuing.[501]

Yet the fact remains that what is most remarkable about human beings is not what we have in common with other animals, but what distinguishes us as a species. One obvious difference is the technologies that are such familiar elements of modern human life. So, to write these words, I am using a desktop computer, whose speed and memory would have been undreamt of only decades ago. From time to time I will use the Internet to research a point, check my e-mail, or engage in any of the distractions that comes with continual access to the World Wide Web. This is all done in a building made of bricks and mortar, fully supplied with water, gas, and electricity. Outside, I can hear cars or the occasional plane. Being surrounded by such technology it is easy for those in the developed world to forget just how remarkable is our current existence. But while millions around the world live in far more primitive conditions, they still employ a staggering variety of different technologies, whether an Amazon tribesperson with their bow and arrow, or an Inuit building an igloo from snow blocks in the Arctic.

Of course, human beings are not the only species to use tools to transform the natural world. Although tool use was initially thought to occur only in primates, studies have shown that some birds also use sticks as tools.[502] What distinguishes humans, though, is that our tool use continues to evolve. In contrast, there is little sign that the life of a chimpanzee in the jungle is particularly different in comparison to when our two species diverged 7 to 8 million years ago. Yet, in the last 50,000 years, humans have gone from living in caves to sending spaceships to Mars. Therefore, there is clearly something unique about the way we humans have made tool use a systematic part of our lives, and our capacity to invent new tools with each new generation.

Another unique attribute of our species that underlies these abilities is our capacity for language. Compared to the sounds that animals make, human language is unique in being a conceptual framework of symbols that allow us to describe things in the world, their properties and current location, but also what happened to them in the past and might happen in the future.[503] Humans seem to almost effortlessly learn this complex symbolic system if exposed to it at a sufficiently early age. Evidence for the importance of such a 'critical period' comes from cases of unfortunate individuals who, through abuse, have been deprived of human contact in their early years, and who can subsequently learn words but seem incapable of fitting them into a conceptual framework of the type just mentioned.[504]

Our understanding of the biological basis of this critical period, and the unique language-learning capabilities of human children, has been greatly boosted by new ways to safely and non-invasively image brain activity in babies and toddlers newly exposed to language. Commenting on these approaches, neuroscientist and linguist Patricia Kuhl of Washington University said recently that 'this decade may represent the dawn of a golden age with regard to the developmental neuroscience of language in humans'.[505] Such techniques, referred to by acronyms like EEG, MEG, NIRS, and fMRI, either measure electrical properties of the brain or its metabolism, and can reveal changes occurring as rapidly as milliseconds, as well as their position in the brain. Such studies have shown that the critical period is not a single 'window' but rather successive ones attuned to different aspects of language—sounds, syntax, vocabulary—and are helping to define areas of the brain involved in language learning.

If our ability to transform the world using tools and our language capabilities are central to being human, how did they arise in the first place? To address this issue, we need to delve deeper into what is known about human evolution. When Darwin wrote the *Descent of Man*, the fossil evidence for human evolution was so sparse that he had to guess the likely sequence of events that led to modern human beings.[506] In so doing, he was influenced by the mainstream religious and philosophical thinking of his time, which saw rational thought as the key motor of cultural change. Accordingly, while acknowledging the importance of bipedalism, Darwin proposed that the key difference between apes and the first proto-humans was the latter's possession of a large brain.[506] To explain why a large brain would have evolved, he suggested that it had been stimulated by the growth of language, initially as a warning system. Finally, using their large brains, our ancestors developed tools.

We now know that such a sequence of events is wrong. Surprisingly, the person who guessed the correct order was not a biologist, but Friedrich Engels, better known for his political writings and partnership with Karl Marx.[506] Engels was familiar with Darwin's account of human evolution in the *Descent of Man*, but became unconvinced by the order of events proposed there. Instead, in an essay written in 1876, called 'The Part Played by Labour in the Transition from Ape to Man', he argued that the evolution of the human brain was a consequence, not a cause of tool use.[507] Engels proposed that our ape-like ancestors began to stand upright, this then 'freed the hands' for using tools, which led to socialized labour and the new opportunities and demands this imposed on human society.[507] Finally, this led to the growth of the brain and, at the same time, language, for human beings 'now had something to say to each other'. Importantly, the growth of the brain and of language and culture then further stimulated the growth of the brain. Engels believed his conception was a novel one, asking Marx to keep quiet about the idea, 'so that no lousy Englishman may steal it'.[508] However, he never published the essay in his lifetime, and instead it only appeared in print in 1896 in *Die Neue Zeit*, a German socialist newspaper, a year after Engels' death. There, it was ignored by the scientific world, which was to have unfortunate consequences for our understanding of human evolution.[506]

So when a crude hoax consisting of a human cranium joined to an orangutan's jawbone was planted in an archaeological dig in Piltdown, England, in 1912, it was taken seriously for fifty years because it fitted Darwin's proposed sequence of

human evolution. Meanwhile, Raymond Dart's discovery in South Africa in 1924 of the genuine partial remains of a creature with an ape-sized brain, but which was fully bipedal, was not taken seriously because it did not fit this sequence. In fact, it was only in the 1970s, when Donald Johanson found the famous 'Lucy', a complete 3.5 million-year-old skeleton of a small-brained bipedal ape, and Louis and Mary Leakey identified tool-using proto-humans with small brains, that the idea of bipedalism and tool use preceding the dramatic growth of the brain became accepted fact.[506]

While the development by proto-humans of different tools and their brain growth is now well established thanks to diverse fossil remains, the role that language played in our evolution remains much more uncertain.[509] This is because language leaves no trace in the fossil record, apart from indirectly in the structure of the mouths and throats of our ancestors. Difficulties in reaching a consensus about language evolution led the Linguistic Society of Paris in 1866 to ban debate on the topic because speculation was so far removed from any real evidence, a prohibition that influenced linguistics until the 1970s.[510] Since then, however, there have been more concerted attempts to study this question. To supplement the limited fossil evidence, studies have compared vocalization between ourselves and other species, investigated differences between existing human languages, and looked to indirect evidence for the existence of language in prehistoric societies such as signs of art, culture, and religion, which are presumed to require a complex language structure to sustain them.[511]

One suggestion put forward by Thomas Suddendorf of Queensland University, Australia, is that human language must have evolved in a society with significant levels of mutual trust.[512] The very separation of words as purely abstract symbols from the objects they relate to makes them ideal tools for deceit. However, while it is certainly possible to tell a bare-faced lie without batting an eyelid, it's precisely because our language ability is so conducive to lying that some believe it could only have arisen in a society operating on mutual trust.[512] This raises the question of why such a situation would arise in the first place. One possibility is that if human tool use evolved as a specifically social activity this would require a degree of trustworthiness for people to be able to work together. More positively, such shared labour would have led to the need to plan and organize such activities. The requirement for such planning could, in turn, have stimulated the development of a communication system that provided a sense of past, present, and future.

Another theory about human language, proposed by Robin Dunbar of Oxford University, sees it as having evolved to bind emerging human societies together.[513] In ape societies grooming helps to create social bonds and defuse tensions, and the 'gossip' theory of language origins sees it as a form of verbal grooming. However, it is important to recognize that human language is far more than a method of communication. Instead, it is tightly associated with a conceptual framework of symbols that makes our relationship to the world completely different to any other species, and any theory of its origins needs to explain this difference.[514]

So how did such a symbolic mind arise? A key challenge in answering this question is to explain how human consciousness, on the one hand, springs from the molecular and cellular mechanisms of an individual brain, and, on the other, is integrally linked to all the other 7 billion human brains on the planet by our location as individuals within wider human culture. One person who particularly sought to bridge this gap was the Russian psychologist Lev Vygotsky. He developed his theories about the mind over a decade, stretching from the early 1920s to his early death from tuberculosis in 1934, in a burst of creativity that led to some labelling him the 'Mozart of psychology' when his writings were rediscovered in the 1960s, having been banned by Stalin for their 'subversive' content.[515] Challenging the common view that human consciousness is primarily an individual affair, Vygotsky saw consciousness as a social construct, not in the crude sense of something written on a 'blank slate', but rather involving a complicated process of interaction between society and the inner psyche.[515] He drew a parallel between the way tools as external objects are 'aimed at mastering, and triumphing over, nature', with language based on words as inner objects, being 'a means of internal activity aimed at mastering oneself'.[516]

Vygotsky's studies of young children talking to themselves as they play showed that such 'egocentric speech' not only guides the child's activity but later becomes internalized as 'inner speech' and helps to create the thought processes of the individual. These studies also indicated that acquisition of speech restructures the brain so that thought is transformed from simple association to a process guided by a hierarchically ordered conceptual framework. This is an active process on the child's part, whereby the child seeks out the words and concepts that make sense of their everyday practical and social experience. Clearly, this ability must be based on real biological differences between humans and other species, but it also

requires a social environment and interaction with other human individuals. Vygotsky also believed that mental disorders like schizophrenia are characterized by a partial or complete breakdown of conceptual thinking and a regression to the level of thinking by association.[517]

Having now sketched a picture of some essential features of what it means to be human, it is time to see how we might link such attributes to the human genome. Ultimately, our human uniqueness must be based on genetic differences between ourselves and other species. However, while there is much discussion about the link between genes and human behaviour and society in many popular accounts, how well does this relate to what we have been learning about the genome? In the Introduction to this book, I mentioned how claims are often made about 'genes' coding for complex human characteristics like nationalism, intelligence, personality, sexual persuasion, and even men's supposed unwillingness to do the ironing. I criticized such claims because, in general, no attempt was made to identify these proposed genes, or if such an attempt was made, as with the so-called 'gay gene', it ended in failure. In addition, posing the issue this way often reveals a naïve understanding of the complexities of human behaviour and society, and their historical nature. Further confirmation of the potential difficulties faced by those seeking an easy answer to the question of what role genetics plays in determining complex human characteristics was demonstrated by a recent study that sought to identify genetic differences linked to intelligence. Previous attempts to link IQ to specific variations in genomic DNA sequence 'have led to a slew of irreproducible results', according to a recent commentary in *Nature*.[518] In response, the biggest study yet to investigate the genetics of intelligence recently focused on more than 100,000 people, its aim being 'to bring more rigour to studies of how genes contribute to behaviour'. Yet this study identified only three variants associated with intelligence, and, according to the *Nature* commentary, 'their effects are maddeningly small', while, overall, the findings were 'inconclusive', meaning that 'scientists looking for the genes underlying intelligence are in for a slog'.[518]

So can we expect to find any intelligible genetic basis for the different facets of human behaviour and society? I believe that we can, but only by engaging with the new insights emerging about our genomes at the molecular level, coupled with a more sophisticated awareness of the complexity of the human body, and its interactions with the environment and with other human beings and the culture that we have created. A surprising aspect of many popular accounts is how their

view of the gene seems anchored in the era of Mendel, when the gene was viewed as an abstract entity of no precise material form. Yet, as we've seen, not only do our genes' protein products exist in a cellular environment shared by thousands of other proteins, but the view of the genome as a linear entity upon which protein-coding genes are dotted like beads on a string, is being seriously challenged by new evidence that the genome is a complex 3D structure. In addition, the discovery that our genomes can respond to changes in both the cellular and the bodily environment through various epigenetic mechanisms means that the old division between nature and nurture appears far more fluid than previously suspected. At least in the lifetime of an individual, both the nutrients and also toxins our bodies encounter, as well as psychological stresses but also more positive experiences, may affect our genomes in a significant manner. What remains more uncertain and controversial is to what extent such epigenetic changes can be passed down to future generations. With these points in mind, it's time we looked more closely at what studies of our extinct ancestors, but also comparisons between humans and our closest animal relatives, can reveal about us both as humans and individuals.

A common but inaccurate view of evolution is as a ladder of progress in which species are like the rungs, with one species transforming into another in an orderly fashion. In contrast, Darwin himself saw evolution as more like a branch-ing tree, with different species as offshoots.[519] Current theories of human evolu-tion generally agree that *Homo sapiens* is merely the last existing member of a series of increasingly human-like species that diverged from our ape cousins about 6 million years ago. Studies of such past species have confirmed this progression, with ape-like creatures first beginning to walk upright (*Australopithecus afarensis*), use tools (*Homo habilis*), show signs of a rapidly growing brain (the unfortunately named *Homo erectus*), develop technology and perhaps even practise art in a more sophisticated manner (*Homo neanderthalensis*), eventually culminating in modern human beings (*Homo sapiens*) with all our unique attributes.[520] However, far from a ladder-like progression linking these species, there was considerable overlap in the period that they existed on the Earth, and this time was shared also with many other proto-human species (see Figure 22).

Fossil evidence has given us a sense of the physical forms of our proto-human ancestors: whether they walked upright and their height, the shape of their hands, the size and shape of their skulls, and, by extrapolation, their brains. Studies of

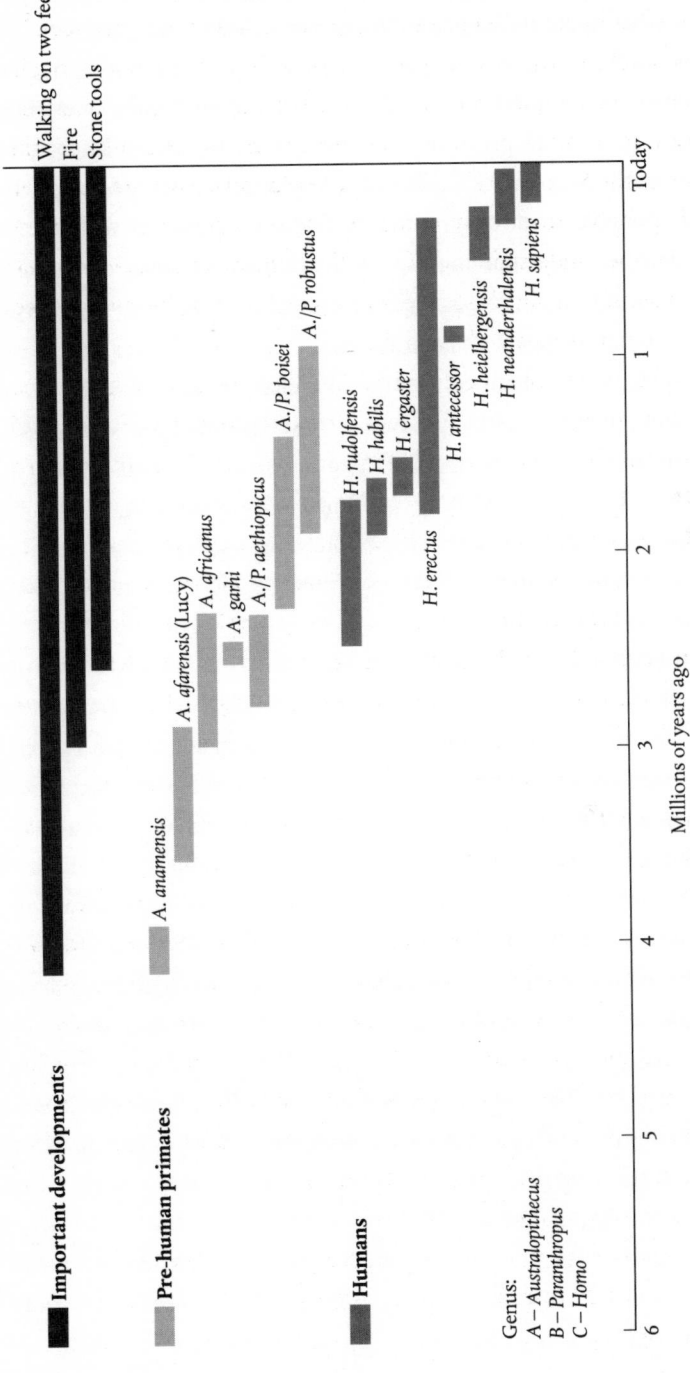

Figure 22. Human evolution timeline

tools and other artificial objects, works of art, and living spaces can all provide information about what might have gone on inside the heads of our ancestors.[521] But what of the genomes of these past species? Not so long ago it was thought impossible to address such a question directly. Recently, however, the Neanderthal genome and those of other proto-humans have been sequenced by Svante Pääbo and his team at the Max Planck Institute for Evolutionary Anthropology in Leipzig, making it possible to directly compare our own genomes with these extinct species.[522] Further understanding of how the human genome evolved has come from comparisons with our closest existing animal cousin, the chimpanzee, and by comparing human beings with each other.

In this latter respect, study of mitochondrial DNA has been very important. Mitochondria are the powerhouses of our cells, breaking down fats, sugars, and proteins, and transferring their energy to ATP, the cellular 'energy currency', in a process that requires oxygen.[523] The importance of this process for human life is shown by blocking it with cyanide, death following almost instantaneously. Yet mitochondria started off as free-living bacteria that became incorporated into our single-celled ancestors about 1.5 billion years ago, in a symbiotic relationship.[524] In line with this, mitochondria still retain some of their own genes, which have many similarities to those of bacteria. Mutations in mitochondrial genes cause defects in eyes, brain, heart, and muscle, these being high-energy-requiring tissues.[523,525] Such conditions are inherited from the mother, but affect both sexes; this pattern of transmission is due to the fact that, while egg and sperm both contain mitochondria, those of the sperm are destroyed once they enter the egg.[526]

Analysis of the mitochondrial genome in different human individuals has helped uncover the pattern of our evolution, since by estimating the mutation rate of the mitochondrial genome it is possible to treat the latter as a 'molecular clock'.[527] Two features of mitochondrial DNA—its maternal pattern of inheritance and the fact that, unlike chromosomal DNA, it's not reorganized by crossing over at each new generation—make it particularly amenable to studying the timescale of human origins, and the migration patterns of our ancestors. Insights have also come from studying the Y chromosome, since this is only inherited by males.[528] Such analysis suggests that *Homo sapiens* originated in East Africa about 150,000 years ago, from which point we eventually spread out across the world, first to the Middle East 60,000 years ago, and then to the rest of the world, reaching Europe 40,000 years ago.

Earlier groups of proto-humans, like *Homo erectus* and, later, *Homo neandertha-lensis*, also seem to have originated in Africa and then spread across the world. While *Homo erectus* appeared on the planet just under 2 million years ago and became extinct 150,000 years ago, Neanderthals appeared about a quarter of a million years ago and only became extinct 40,000 years ago. A question debated for many years is whether the emergence of our species led to the demise of the Neanderthals, and, if so, whether this was a direct or indirect effect. So, in William Golding's novel *The Inheritors*, written in 1955, we see prehistoric life from the perspective of a gentle, peaceful group of proto-humans, who meet a violent end at the hands of other proto-humans.[529] It is only at the end of the novel that we realize with a shock that the first, peaceful group are the Neanderthals, while their murderers are our own ancestors.

The idea of *Homo sapiens* wiping out other proto-human groups is certainly reconcilable with the fact that we have destroyed many other species, and continue to do so at alarming rates, since our advent on Earth.[530] However, the evidence for such a scenario is both sparse and contradictory, and it's just as likely that Neanderthals became extinct by simple out-competition for resources, or even because of changes in the climate and food resources that had nothing to do with modern humans.[531] Certainly, recent findings that indicate modern humans and Neanderthals coexisted in Europe for anything between 2,600 and 5,400 years, suggest that the process whereby Neanderthals disappeared once we met, was a gradual one.[532]

In addition, the picture has become complicated by the recent discovery that many people have a little bit of Neanderthal within them. Comparison of the Neanderthal genome with those of living human beings from across the world, shows that, on average, Europeans, but also people much further east in China and other parts of Asia, have around 1 to 3 per cent DNA of Neanderthal origin.[533] However, different people share different regions of their genomes with Neanderthals, so across the human population as a whole, humanity shares about 20 per cent of our genome with this species. In addition, another group of proto-humans, the Denisovans, ancient cousins of the Neanderthals whose remains were discovered in Siberia, share up to 8 per cent of their genome with modern Melanesian people who live in places such as Papua New Guinea and Fiji.[534] In contrast, people of sub-Saharan African descent have no Neanderthal or Denisovan DNA in their genomes, but may have residues of DNA from other proto-human groups that remained in Africa.[535]

Two recent detailed comparisons of Neanderthal and modern human genomes, one led by David Reich at Harvard Medical School, and the other by Joshua Akey at Washington University, showed that specific regions of the Neanderthal genome are represented but not others, suggesting that this selective retention has a functional basis.[536,537] Regions of the Neanderthal genome that are particularly prevalent in modern humans include genes active in keratinocytes, the cells that make skin, hair, and nails.[538] It is possible that acquiring these regions helped some humans to adapt to living in cold regions, since Neanderthals—who occupied a territory stretching from Western Europe to Siberia—were already adapted to a cold climate when they began to interbreed with modern humans newly arrived from the much hotter African subcontinent. A very specific adaptation of certain modern people living on the high altitude Tibetan plateau, the ability to thrive in a low oxygen environment, was recently shown to be due to a variant of a gene called EPAS1 that originated in Denisovans.[539]

We are also uncovering important clues about our own evolution from regions of the Neanderthal genome that are absent in modern humans. So, according to Akey, 'we find these gigantic holes in the human genomes where there are no surviving Neanderthal lineages. Most of these variations were removed in a couple of dozen generations.'[540] This suggests that such parts of the genome were harmful to human–Neanderthal hybrids and their descendants, and were purged rapidly as a consequence. That different living human individuals share different regions of their genomes with proto-humans, raises the question of whether different groups of people in the world, and individuals within those groups, have characteristics linked to these genomic regions. However, against such a possibility providing a biological basis to the view—typically used to assert white superiority—that humanity is strictly divided into different 'races', humans are far more similar genetically to each other than chimps, despite there being 7 billion of us compared with a few hundred thousand of them.[541]

An important reason for comparing the human genome with that of Neanderthals or other proto-humans is that this might allow us to identify genetic differences that underlie our unique attributes as a species. However, findings so far indicate that such differences are likely to be subtle. This is not surprising. Labelling someone a 'Neanderthal' usually signifies that a person is crude and uncultured; however, recent studies have challenged the view that our proto-human cousins were simple-minded brutes. There is evidence that Neanderthals

consciously buried their dead,[542] and were aware of the beneficial properties of herbs—with one study suggesting they may even have been partial to a soothing brew of camomile tea.[543] They also made a kind of glue for securing spear points by heating birch sap while protecting it from air by a method so sophisticated that archaeologists have had trouble replicating it. Such findings have led João Zilhão, an archaeologist at Barcelona University, to argue that Neanderthals were capable of abstract thinking, just like modern humans, on the basis that 'burying your dead is symbolic behaviour. Making sophisticated chemical compounds in order to haft your stone tools implies a capacity to think in abstract ways, a capacity to plan ahead, that's fundamentally similar to ours.'[544] A hotly debated question is whether Neanderthals practised art. Many excavations of places where they lived have unearthed lumps of pigment—red ochre and black manganese—that were sometimes worn down as if they had served as prehistoric crayons.[544] In another site three cockleshells were found with holes near one edge, and traces of pigment, implying they might have been worn as ornaments. Zilhão believes this shows Neanderthals decorated themselves both with body paint and jewellery. Most controversial of all is the discovery of cave paintings in Spain that may substantially predate the arrival of modern humans in Europe. One problem here is the uncertainty about the precise age of these paintings, with different methods for determining their age giving different results. So, while one estimate is of around 40,000 years old, the period in which modern humans are thought to have reached this region, the paintings may be substantially older. Much hangs on the precise age, for the later date could either mean that the pictures were painted by modern humans, or that Neanderthals merely copied them.[544]

Such disagreements matter because they impact on the sort of differences we might expect to see in a comparison between our genomes and those of Neanderthals. Of the few obvious genetic differences so far detected between ourselves and our Neanderthal cousins besides differences in skin cells, one noticeable change is in genes linked to autism and schizophrenia. Autism is the name for a range of conditions associated with difficulties in socializing and communicating with other people, and a tendency towards stereotyped or repetitive behaviours. As we've seen, recent genome-wide association studies have undermined the idea that one or a few gene defects determine mental disorders. Nevertheless, some genetic links appear stronger than others, such as the autism susceptibility candidate 2, or AUTS2, gene.[545] First identified in identical twins that were both

autistic, and subsequently in 36 unrelated individuals with autism and associated learning disabilities, many changes that affect this gene are in non-coding regions linked to its regulation. Recent studies in zebrafish and mice indicate that this gene codes for a transcription factor controlling the expression of genes involved in brain development. It is therefore interesting that AUTS2 and its associated regulatory regions were identified in a genome comparison between modern humans and Neanderthals as the most notable area of difference between the two species.[545] Other genomic regions that differ between ourselves and Neanderthals have also been linked to disorders of social interaction and learning.[546]

Further confirmation of a link between a tendency towards mental disorder and being human have come from a fascinating recent study that looked at epigenetic marks in Neanderthal and Denisovan genomes compared to those in modern humans.[547] As we saw in Chapter 6, chemical changes, like methylation in regulatory regions of genomic DNA, have a big impact upon whether a particular gene is turned on or off. It might seem an impossible task to identify such marks in proto-human genomes, given their extreme age and state of degradation, but researchers led by Liran Carmel at the University of Jerusalem, working with Pääbo's group in Leipzig, developed an ingenious way to do so by virtue of the fact that methylated nucleotides degrade to a different product than unmethylated ones do, during a process called deamination. This allowed the scientists to indirectly create a methylation map of such ancient genomes for the first time.[547] Since only two individuals—a Neanderthal and a Denisovan, both female—were analysed, the findings need to be treated as very preliminary, especially since the epigenomes of different individuals may vary considerably; however, Chris Stringer of London's Natural History Museum believes the study shows 'how we can begin to unlock epigenetic aspects of ancient genomes which have been hidden from us up to now'.[548] As well as finding differences in the activity profile of genes involved in skeletal development, which could account for the Neanderthal's shorter, stockier form and barrel chest, the study found that methylation differences between modern humans and Neanderthals were particularly prominent in genes linked to some mental disorders, with the suggestion that such genes were expressed at a much lower level in Neanderthals.[549]

These findings suggest that the very genetic changes that underlie modern humans' unique mental capabilities may also predispose us to such disorders. This further confirms the idea that attempts to find a gene 'for' schizophrenia or

autism may be misplaced, not only because of the large number of different genomic regions now linked to these disorders, but because such regions may normally play integral roles in the distinctive mental processes that define us as humans, such as creativity, abstract thought, and capacity for complex language. This possibility would be in line with suggestions that disorders like autism and schizophrenia are part of a broad spectrum of states of mind that overlap with those of the normal population.[550] It would also fit with the idea that there is a thin line between genius and insanity, and explain why many gifted mathematicians and abstract thinkers have shown autistic characteristics. Indeed, Fredrik Ullén, of the Karolinska Institute in Stockholm, has recently found that both highly creative people and those suffering from schizophrenia have a lower density of D2 receptors that bind to the neurotransmitter dopamine in the thalamus area of the brain.[551] Noting that 'fewer D2 receptors in the thalamus probably means a lower degree of signal filtering, and thus a higher flow of information from the thalamus', Ullén believes that such a barrage of uncensored information may help fan the creative spark.[552] However, while allowing creative individuals to make unusual connections in problem-solving situations that other people might miss, distortions in this ability in schizophrenics could lead to disturbing and destabilizing thoughts.

Despite these steps forward in studying ancient genomes both in terms of their DNA sequence and even their methylation state, we've seen in previous chapters how a complete picture of genomic activity needs to encompass many more factors, such as the mRNA transcripts generated, the gene regulatory proteins that regulate transcription, the multiple types of histone modifications, and the noncoding RNAs that we now know regulate gene expression at a variety of different levels.[553] Such factors need to be studied in different cell types, and, as importantly, during the development and growth of the body. As such, and given the absence of any living proto-human species to conduct such studies on, an alternative way of investigating how these different factors all come together to make us human is to study them in different cell types and stages of development, in both humans and our closest living relatives, chimpanzees. And, in particular, such analysis has focused upon one particular organ—the brain.

13

THE GENOME THAT BECAME CONSCIOUS

'An important stage of human thought will have been reached when the...
psychological, the objective and the subjective, are actually united, when the
tormenting conflicts or contradictions between my consciousness and my
body will have been factually resolved or discarded.'   *Ivan Pavlov*

'Science's biggest mystery is the nature of consciousness. It is not that we
possess bad or imperfect theories of human awareness; we simply have no
such theories at all.'   *Nick Herbert*

The human brain is the most complex structure in the known universe. Comparisons of the brain to a computer, or references to it as our 'wetware', analogous
to computer software, barely do justice to the true complexity of this organ. So
not only do our brains contain around 100 billion nerve cells, but each of these
can be connected to as many as 10,000 others, giving a total of some 100 trillion
nerve connections. As such, using our brains to try and understand how human
self-conscious awareness arose within this organ, why it is lacking in the brains
of our closest biological cousins, and relating this to the differences between
the human and chimp genomes, is undoubtedly the biggest challenge in biology
today. One of the most noticeable differences between humans and chimps is the
much greater brain/body ratio in our species. If it were down to differences in
body size alone, our brains should be 50 per cent bigger than those chimps; in
fact, they are 200 per cent larger.[554] We should be wary, though, of seeing size
alone as the defining feature of the human brain, since Neanderthals had an even
bigger brain/body ratio than ourselves.[555] Equally important is the fact that some
regions of the human brain are differently proportioned compared to chimps.

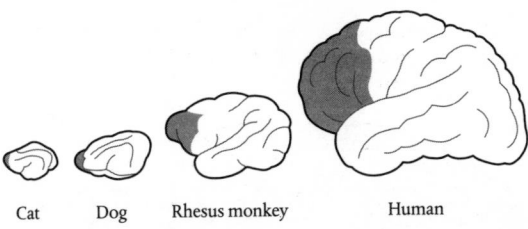

Cat   Dog   Rhesus monkey   Human

Figure 23. Prefrontal cortex in humans compared to other mammalian species

One region, called the prefrontal cortex, which has been implicated in complex thought, expression of personality, decision-making, and social interaction, is particularly pronounced in humans (see Figure 23).[554] Another region, the arcuate fasciculus, which connects parts of the brain implicated in language, is also visibly different in humans.

To gain insights into functional differences between our brains and that of chimps, recent studies have used a variety of different approaches. So Daniel Geschwind and his team at the University of California have been studying different patterns of expression of mRNA transcripts in human and chimp brains.[556] Because the brain is such a complex organ, such analysis has been carried out on numerous different brain regions (Figure 24). This revealed that there are major differences in the levels of thousands of RNA transcripts between the two species. Surprisingly, few of these differences appear to be specific to a particular brain region. There are two possible explanations for this. One is that the unique attributes of the human brain evolved without large-scale changes in the gross functional and structural composition of these regions. If true, this would tend to go against the idea that human brains are compartmentalized into modules, each responsible for a different behaviour. This view of the brain, vividly captured by Harvard University linguist Steven Pinker's analogy with a Swiss army knife with its multiple gadgets, is in line with the fact that injuries to the brain can often result in some apparently quite specific defects, for instance in language ability.[557] The idea of a 'modular' brain was subsequently linked to the proposal that different human characteristics are coded by specific genes that are only expressed within these modules.

This view of the human brain and the behaviour that results from it was challenged by the discovery that our genomes contain just over 20,000 genes, not much more than a worm or a fruitfly. These findings make it difficult to see

182

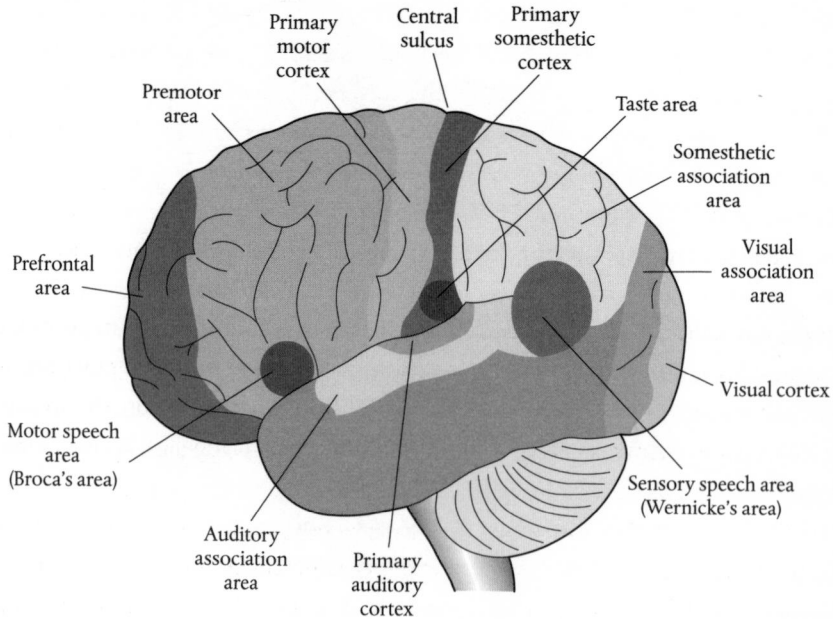

Figure 24. The human brain

how such a small number of genes could carry out the bewildering array of different human behaviours. As we saw in Chapters 4 and 5, though, genes have multiple ways to express themselves through alternative splicing, cell-type specific enhancers, and non-coding RNAs, so there is a danger of overemphasizing this point. The lack of differences in mRNA expression in different brain regions also argues against modularity, although it is possible that the regions analysed were too big to reveal differences in a few cell types. Finer-scale analysis will be required to address this issue. Fortunately, this is becoming increasingly feasible as new techniques make possible the study of the 'transcriptome' of single cells.

However, there are other reasons for doubting that particular human behaviours can be confined to specific regions of the brain in such a localized fashion. For instance, a recent study of electrical activity in the brains of monkeys engaged in problem-solving show that synchronization of brainwaves to form new communication circuits occurs across the prefrontal cortex and the striatum, two completely different brain regions.[558] Earl Miller of the Massachusetts Institute of Technology, who led the study, believes this shows 'there is some unknown

mechanism that allows these resonance patterns to form, and these circuits start humming together'.[559] Miller thinks the findings demonstrate a division of labour between the two brain regions, so that 'the striatum learns the pieces of the puzzle, and then the prefrontal cortex puts the pieces of the puzzle together', and have relevance for understanding how the human mind can absorb and analyse new information.[559] Learning and long-term memory formation are known to be associated with changes in the brain's synapses, or connections between nerve cells. But Miller thinks this process of 'synaptic plasticity' is too slow to account for the flexibility of the human mind. As he points out, 'if you can change your thoughts from moment to moment, you can't be doing it by constantly making new connections and breaking them apart in your brain. Plasticity doesn't happen on that kind of time scale.' Instead, he believes that the synchronized 'humming' he has identified 'foster[s] subsequent long-term plasticity changes in the brain, so real anatomical circuits can form. But the first thing that happens is they start humming together.'[559] What remains to be shown is how such global waves of electricity in the brain are subsequently translated into the changes in gene expression that underlie synaptic plasticity. The most likely mechanism for connecting these two phenomena is via 'second messengers'—small molecules such as cAMP, nitric oxide, or even the humble calcium ion—which, as we saw in Chapter 3, play a central role in switching genes on or off. Being small, second messengers not only operate inside cells, but they can also traverse the whole brain because of pores called 'gap junctions' that connect the different cells of this organ together. So studies using chemical probes that fluoresce when they come into contact with calcium ions, such as those designed by Roger Tsien,[560] show that learning is accompanied by calcium 'signals' that are distributed across different regions of the brain, and show complex properties in both time and space.[561] Such signals can have an immediate effect by acting upon calcium-sensitive enzymes, but they can also trigger changes in gene expression by activating transcription factors via addition of phosphate groups by calcium-regulated kinases such as CaMKII. In fact, recent studies have identified CaMKII as a key player in learning and memory, while defects in the activity of this protein seem to be one cause of psychiatric disorders such as schizophrenia, depression, and epilepsy.[562] An important question for future studies will be to study how the spread of electrical and chemical signals across the brain differs in humans compared to other species, how this relates to differences in gene expression in

different brain regions, and whether changes in these dynamic features of the human brain provide insights into some brain disorders.[561]

While insights can be gained by studying the differences between adult human and chimp brains, another important source of human uniqueness may lie in differences in brain development. As such, recent studies have investigated differences in mRNA levels in different regions of the brain at different developmental stages, both before and after birth.[554] One conclusion of such studies is that there are major differences in the times at which different genes are expressed during development in humans, compared to chimps, with some genes expressed substantially later in humans, others much earlier. Such differences are especially prominent in the prefrontal cortex compared to other brain regions. Genevieve Konopka, who studied this issue with Daniel Geschwind at the University of California, believes this shows that 'the intricate signalling pathways and enhanced cellular function that arose within the frontal lobe created a bridge to human evolution'.[563] Of particular interest is that genes involved in the formation of new synapses peak in expression several months after birth in chimp prefrontal cortex but only after 5 years of age in this region in humans (see Figure 25).[554] Moreover, electron microscope analysis of the synapses themselves shows that these are still being formed as late as 10 years old in humans.

According to Konopka, 'the biggest differences occurred in the expression of human genes involved in plasticity—the ability of the brain to process information and adapt'.[563] This would fit with the fact that human children have a much

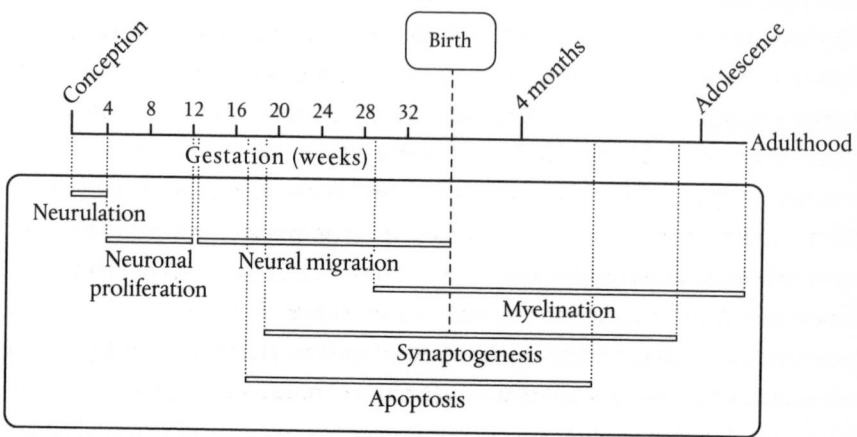

Figure 25. Timeline of human brain development

more extended period of learning than apes, and indicate that our brains are being restructured in response to such learning for a far longer period. Another important difference between humans and apes is the time at which 'myelination' of brain nerve cells takes place. The myelin sheath is a fatty, insulating layer that protects nerve cells and enhances the speed at which they transmit electrical impulses.[564] However, this comes at the expense of a capacity to form new connections and undergo changes in structure. Studies have shown that, while myelination is complete by the onset of puberty in chimps, in humans it still occurs up to the fourth decade of life.[554] Findings like these provide important new evidence for the idea that 'neoteny'—the retention of juvenile features in the adults of a species—has played an important role in human evolution. Evolutionary biologist Stephen Jay Gould, of Harvard University, in particular stressed the importance of this process on the basis that human adults have many physical features—a flatter and broader face, hairless body, large head to body ratio—in common with young, but not older, apes.[565] Such slowing of development was thought to allow a greater capacity for learning, but only now has its importance for brain evolution been confirmed at the molecular level.[554] Intriguingly, while we share many physical features in common with Neanderthals, their teeth seem to have matured much more rapidly than human teeth, akin to those of an ape, suggesting that, at least in some respects, the extent of neoteny in this species was less advanced than in modern humans.[566]

What would be interesting to explore is whether the restructuring of thought that Vygotsky believed took place in children via the 'tool' of language, and which we discussed in Chapter 12, can be linked to such dynamic changes in brain activity and subsequent changes in gene expression and plasticity. In this respect, an interesting finding of recent imaging studies is that there seem to be important overlaps between the human brain regions that mediate tool use and those governing language; however, these overlaps were not seen in other primates.[567] Another difference between humans and other primates is that human brains seem uniquely attuned to learning new tool use and language skills. This ability seems to be particularly associated with specific types of nerve cells called 'mirror' neurons, which can become activated both when a person is carrying out an action and when they are observing that action. This may explain one particular unique feature of infant humans, which is that they seem particularly capable of mimicking new actions and words; this could be one explanation why humans

seem uniquely capable of both learning from past ways of working, as well as inventing new ones.

The thousands of differences identified in the patterns of gene expression in the human brain compared to the chimp suggest that the 1 per cent difference between ourselves and apes at the level of protein-coding genes may mask much greater differences in terms of functional gene expression. But this also complicates the process of trying to identify the key differences that led to the unique attributes of consciousness and self-awareness that characterize our species. As such, there is increasing interest in identifying whether these large-scale changes in gene expression are due to a much smaller number of 'master-controller' genes. And, indeed, by comparing the regulatory elements adjacent to the genes whose expression is different in humans, it has been possible to identify certain transcription factors that activate gene expression on a global scale. One such factor, called MEF2A, has generated interest not only because it is a master regulator of synapse formation, but also because one of the enhancers that controls its expression is mutated in humans but not in Neanderthals, suggesting this may have contributed to a delay in synapse formation in humans, but not in our extinct cousins.[568] Another transcription factor that controls the expression of many genes in the brain and is altered in humans compared to chimps is coded by the CLOCK gene. This is one of a class of genes that regulates the body's circadian rhythm, or body clock, which governs our sleep/wake cycle. However, according to Daniel Geschwind, recent findings suggest 'that it orchestrates another function essential to the human brain', most likely one linked to brain plasticity.[563] Disruptions in the action of this gene have been implicated in mania-like behaviour in humans, providing further evidence that genetic attributes that make us uniquely human may also make us susceptible to mental disorders.[569]

However, it is not only transcription factors that control gene expression; there is growing evidence of key roles for miRNAs. Recent studies have increasingly focused on identifying miRNAs with important functions in the human brain. One such miRNA, miR-184, which is abundant in the prefrontal cortex of human brains but not those of chimps, has previously been shown to be an important regulator of nerve stem cell proliferation.[570] This is interesting since neurogenesis—the growth of new neurons from such stem cells—is important not just during brain development in the embryo, but is also increasingly being recognized

as a key process in the adult human brain.[571] Reflecting on this new-found role for non-coding RNAs in brain function, John Mattick and his colleague, Guy Barry of the University of Queensland in Australia, have recently argued that, while 'proteins form the core of basic cellular functioning...the increased sophistication, complexity, and plasticity of the regulatory RNA superstructure...has been at the heart of human cognitive advance'.[572] As evidence for this claim, Mattick and Barry point to studies showing that genomic regions that generate non-coding RNAs have been one of the main targets for mutation since humans diverged from chimps. They believe that emerging roles for numerous different classes of non-coding RNAs in the human brain suggest that they are 'temporally and spatially regulated to control both feedback ("hard-wired") processes during development and feed-forward ("soft-wired") processes during post-developmental cellular function'; this suggests that non-coding RNAs mediate processes like learning and memory through their link to multiple layers of further epigenetic processes.[572] One such process is RNA editing, in which RNA sequences are changed by conversion of nucleotide bases into modified forms. Interestingly, 'most of the edited sites occur in noncoding regions, implying that editing is not only modifying the structure-function properties of neuronal proteins, but also RNA-based regulatory circuits'.[573] That RNA editing in the brain is enhanced 35-fold in humans compared to mice, and has increased further during the transition from apes to humans, is seen by Mattick and Barry as further evidence of its important role in our evolution.

One important difference between the regulation of gene expression by non-coding RNAs compared to transcription factors, is that while the latter only control production of mRNAs, non-coding RNAs can affect the process at multiple levels. This has particular implications in nerve cells because of the highly differentiated structure of this cell type (see Figure 26). A typical nerve cell receives inputs of information from other nerve cells via structures called dendrites, of which it may have as many as 100,000. Its output to other nerve cells is concentrated on to a single axon; however, this usually has many branches, meaning that it can send signals to thousands of other nerve cells, but also to muscles and glands. The differing spatial reaches of nerve cells are shown by the fact that axons can be as short as a millimetre, or as long as a metre in the case of those that span the length of the spinal cord. When gene expression was thought to be regulated only at the level of mRNA production, it was assumed that all the

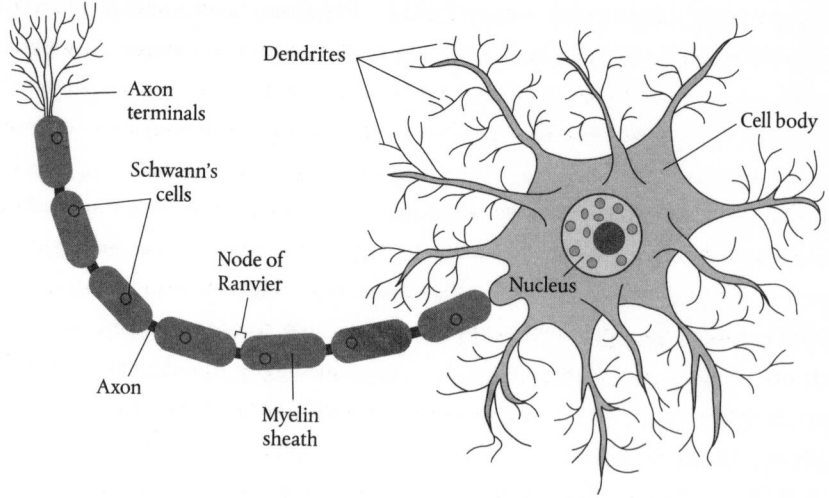

Figure 26. Structure of nerve cells

different parts of the nerve cell would contain similar types of proteins. However, it is now becoming clear that different regions of the nerve cell contain different populations of non-coding RNAs.[574] Given the capacity of non-coding RNAs to regulate translation of mRNAs into proteins, this suggests that specific dendrites or axon branches may have a unique protein profile, with important implications given the role of such structures in learning and memory. Moreover, the fact that one of the proteins whose translation is regulated by non-coding RNAs is the transcription factor CREB, whose role in learning and memory we discussed in Chapter 3, shows the potential complexity of the feedback processes involved.[575]

Such a focus on non-coding RNAs is important, given their rapidly emerging roles, but we should not forget the potential importance of other epigenetic mechanisms for human brain function, for instance, those involving chemical modifications to the DNA or the proteins that associate with it as part of the complex nature of chromatin. We've already discussed how epigenetic changes to the genome constitute a key way in which the cells of a developing embryo 'differentiate' into the myriad different cell types of the body, despite having identical genomes at the level of DNA sequence alone.[576] Such changes underlie the very different functional properties of such cells, for instance, the beat of a heart cell, the ability to conduct electrical impulses of a nerve cell, or the capacity of a liver cell to metabolize food and toxins. This differentiation of cells during

development is triggered by changes in the extracellular environment, primarily by growth factors and 'morphogens'—chemicals that induce changes in cell form and function—but also by contacts between different cells, that trigger changes within the embryonic cell via receptors on its surface.[577] Such a change in the internal state of a cell in response to environmental signals also occurs during learning and memory in the brain. A surprising revelation in recent years has been the discovery of how similar differentiation and development are to memory and learning at the molecular level. So, a remarkable number of the same genes and signalling pathways that regulate differentiation and development are employed in forming the synapses that mediate learning and memory. In addition, there is increasing evidence of great similarity in the epigenetic mechanisms underlying these two different processes.

In Chapter 6 we discussed the concept of a histone 'code'.[578] Far from being a simple on/off switch, the incredible variety of different ways of modifying histones means that this type of regulation can be specific to one or a few genes, as well as being finely graded like a dimmer switch, and it even has a built-in timing mechanism due to the fact that different modifications can be reversed at very different rates. In addition, it appears that DNA methylation may also form a similarly sophisticated code.[578] All this makes this type of gene regulation potentially ideally suited to forming one of the molecular bases of the complex processes of learning and memory. Indeed, the far-sighted Francis Crick proposed something along these lines as early as 1984, when he suggested that 'memory might be coded in alternations to particular stretches of chromosomal DNA'.[579] What he lacked was a mechanism for such changes; however, a number of recent studies have shown that interfering with histone modifications and DNA methylation has profound effects on memory and learning processes in animal models.[580,581] What still remains to be shown is whether distinct changes in modified histones or the methyl state of particular nucleotides within specific genes are responsible for particular memories. Hopefully, such is the sophistication with which it is becoming possible to identify such changes in specific genes, this idea may soon be tested in an animal model of learning. In addition, increasingly refined genetic engineering techniques are making it feasible to interfere with specific epigenetic changes in mice, with a view to seeing how they regulate learning and memory.

Finally, as we saw in Chapter 8, an exciting development of recent years has been the suggestion that transposition events may play a role in the development of individual human personalities. In particular, the hippocampus, the brain region associated with memory formation but also with forming new nerve cells through 'neurogenesis', seems to be particularly prone to transposon activity.[582] This activity seems to be very sensitive to changes in the environment, being boosted, for instance, in mice undergoing exercise regimes compared to those which remained sedentary. This finding has led to the proposal that, in humans, increased transposition activity could either change behaviour, allowing the individual to become more adaptable to a new environment, or, alternatively, increase the risk of mental disorders, depending on the particular environmental pressure. Findings such as these challenge the long-held idea that, at the cellular and genomic level, all cells in an individual's brain are essentially equivalent, as well as the notion that all humans are broadly similar in their cellular and genomic properties.[582] Instead, an individual's life experience may profoundly affect the way their brain works, so that even identical twins, traditionally assumed to be genetically identical, may differ considerably in their brain operation, depending on their particular experiences in life.

Combining what we've learned from recent studies of the differences in gene expression in humans compared to chimps and proto-humans like Neanderthals, with new findings from the fossil record, there would appear to be two distinct phases in the evolution of the human brain.[554] The first phase saw a long and gradual increase in brain size, accompanied by important changes in certain brain regions, and was shared to a varying degree by other proto-humans. This was followed by a second phase about 150,000 years ago, which saw more subtle developmental remodelling of the brain, leading to the unique characteristics of human consciousness that define our particular species. It is this that presumably underlies the explosion around 50,000 years ago of new technologies, art, and culture in human society that is still ongoing, taking our species to every corner of the Earth and even into outer space.[583]

One recurring feature of many genes and their regulators that seem to play important roles in human consciousness is their link with mental disorders.[554] So why have such differences arisen if they leave our species vulnerable to such disorders? One suggestion is that the very speed of the changes that accompanied the evolution of human consciousness allowed insufficient time to fine-tune these

new brain processes and render them robust enough to withstand environmental and natural genetic perturbations. Linking this possibility to their claims regarding the importance of non-coding RNAs in human brain function, Mattick and Barry have suggested that 'although the increase in mammalian cognitive ability has provided unique mechanisms to evolve exceptional skills, such as reasoning and awareness, it would also seem likely that a relatively new and increasingly complex regulatory system would have weaknesses and be vulnerable to stressors'.[584]

Another issue that remains to be properly addressed is how human evolution was able to occur so rapidly in the first place. As we saw in Chapter 1, the standard model of evolution is that change occurs through the natural selection of particular variants in a population, by virtue of their ability to survive, and, most importantly, reproduce, in a specific environment. That such different variants exist was discussed in Chapter 2 as being due to changes in the DNA sequence of the genome that occur because of the effects of radiation, chemicals, or other environmental insults. Such a mechanism is generally used to explain how our species arose, with initial mutations occurring that led to variants of apes that could walk upright, while subsequent mutations affecting the ability to use tools, growth of the brain, and so on. However, a potential problem with this model of human evolution is whether it is rapid enough to account for the astounding speed in which our species developed from brute animals to self-conscious beings. This is particularly an issue for the most recent phase of human evolution, since, while it took several million years for proto-humans to evolve from apes, development of sophisticated technologies, art, and culture, which are assumed to have required a new kind of self-conscious awareness, only seem to have taken off as recently as 50,000 years ago, this event itself only occurring 100,000 years after the appearance of modern humans on the planet.[583]

It is with this in mind, but also because of increasing awareness of the importance of epigenetic mechanisms of gene regulation, which might allow more rapid forms of evolution, that questions are now being asked as to whether such mechanisms might also have played a role in recent human evolution, particularly of the brain. Such a possibility requires two things to be true: firstly, that epigenetic changes can occur in the genomes of nerve cells in the brain, and, secondly, that such changes can be passed down to future generations. However, while epigenetic changes and transposition events in the brain are becoming increasingly implicated as mediators of our behavioural responses to life's stresses,

challenges, and opportunities, what evidence is there that such processes have had any long-term impact upon the evolution of our species?

As we mentioned in Chapter 2, a long-standing dogma, first put forward by August Weismann, is that whatever happens throughout our lifetimes to the non-sex cells in our bodies—the so-called 'somatic cells'—has no influence on future generations since it is only the sex cells, the eggs, and sperm, that pass on their genomes to our offspring.[585] What we also saw though, in Chapter 9, is that this dogma may finally be starting to be challenged. So, not only is there evidence from both animal experiments and observations of human populations that epigenetic changes may be passed down through several generations, but the mechanisms underlying such inheritance are now being identified. In particular, the finding that effects of stress in mice can be passed on to offspring by a route involving miRNAs in the sperm, and the detection of these miRNAs in the blood raises the possibility that the connection between the sex cells and the rest of the body, particularly the brain, may be more fluid than previously thought.[586]

Because of its capacity for radically restructuring the genome in a short space of time, transposition has been proposed as an important factor in human evolution. We saw in Chapter 8 how transposon activity can lead to disease by disrupting vital protein-coding genes. The potential threat to the continuation of a species, were such activity to occur freely in the eggs and sperm, has led to evolution of protective mechanisms, such as tight regulation of transposition by piRNAs. Yet we've also discussed a more creative aspect to transposon activity in the creation of new DNA regulatory elements. One puzzling aspect of transposition is that although increasing evidence suggests that this may have important functional roles in our brain cells, and therefore could conceivably increase our survival and reproduction prospects, this raises the question of what benefits the transposons themselves gain from their activity. More generally, could epigenetic events in the brain impact upon what is transmitted to future generations? In an interesting parallel, piRNAs, which were initially thought to be only expressed in the gonads, have now been shown to be also present in brain cells, and it has been suggested that they may play important roles in regulating specific patterns of transposition in individual nerve cells.[575] Could there be a more direct connection between the two organs than previously suspected? And, if so, could transposon activity in the brain affect the propagation of transposition effects to future offspring through the sperm, and therefore a transfer of the transposons themselves to the next

generation? As yet, no mechanism has been identified for such a connection but, analogous to how stress can be passed on to subsequent generations via miRNAs, it seems likely that these non-coding RNAs would play a role in such a process.

In considering what sort of information might be passed down across the generations through epigenetic means, the main focus has been upon the transmission of adverse effects such as stress. But there are also tantalizing hints that more positive life events might not only have a beneficial effect upon the brain through an epigenetic route in a person's lifetime, but that such effects might also influence further generations.[587] Quite how significant such effects are remains a matter of some controversy, and it is important at this point to introduce a note of caution, for, as Edith Heard of the Curie Institute and Robert Martienssen of the École Normale Supérieure in Paris, have warned, 'although the inheritance of epigenetic characters can certainly occur—particularly in plants—how much is due to the environment and the extent to which it happens in humans remain unclear'.[588] Heard and Martienssen point out that, while there does seem to be a basis for epigenetic influences extending across one or two generations in humans, as just outlined, evidence for more than this limited extent remains to be established. In addition, amidst the current interest in epigenetic mechanisms there is a danger in ignoring a far more obvious way in humans in which the experience of one generation affects those of the future. This is the fact, pointed out by Stephen Jay Gould, that 'human cultural evolution, in strong opposition to our biological history, is Lamarckian in character. What we learn in one generation, we transmit directly by teaching and writing.'[589] Of course, it's possible that both epigenetic mechanisms and social evolution might interact. If so, it seems likely that some of the 98 per cent of the genome previously assumed to be junk will play an important role in this process. Finally, if we have learned anything from recent discoveries about genomic and epigenetic mechanisms, it is that it's wise to keep an open mind. Or, as epigenetic researcher Brian Dias of Emory University, Atlanta, puts it, 'if science has taught me anything, it is to not discount the myriad ways of becoming and being'.[590] All of which means that, for those interested in the complex nexus of biological and social influence, even more exciting findings than those described in this book undoubtedly lie ahead.

CONCLUSION

The Case for Complexity

'The ultimate aim of the modern movement in biology is to explain all biology in terms of physics and chemistry.'   *Francis Crick*

'If we want to attain a living understanding of nature, we must become as flexible and mobile as nature herself.'   *Johann Wolfgang von Goethe*

From its inception, biology in the modern age has been characterized by a tension between two opposite poles. On the one hand, is the view expressed by seventeenth-century philosopher Francis Bacon that 'the nature of everything is best seen in its smallest portions',[591] a statement echoed by Francis Crick's claim that 'the ultimate aim of the modern movement in biology is to explain all biology in terms of physics and chemistry'.[592] On the other hand, there is the belief that biological systems have their own complex properties that must be explained in their own terms. First associated with the Romantic movement of the early nineteenth century, particularly through the utterances of poets like Coleridge and Wordsworth, this viewpoint was also held by some notable biologists at this time, such as Alexander von Humboldt and Lamarck, the latter expressing it through his belief that 'living beings have specific characteristics which cannot be reduced to those possessed by physical bodies'.[593] Indeed, these two activities could be combined in a single individual: so while Goethe is now primarily known as a literary figure, he also studied optics and the morphology of plants.

Goethe and his contemporaries faced a central problem, however, which was that the methods available to study the complexity that they recognized in nature were far too simple to do justice to it. So Lamarck sensed the potentially complex

nature of the relationship between organism, environment, and inheritance, but was unable to explain in material terms what might mediate this relationship. And although Goethe himself believed that future generations would remember him for his scientific investigations rather than his literary works, the opposite has been true. In contrast, it is the very reductionist approach that the Romantic poets and scientists abhorred that has been the dominant trend for the last two centuries.

A particularly powerful aspect of reductionism in modern biology has been its capacity to focus on one or a few elements that are isolated and studied separately as a way to illuminate the whole. In this book we've seen this process at work from Darwin onwards, whose theory of natural selection seemed so simple and straightforward to Thomas Huxley that he famously remarked 'How extremely stupid not to have thought of that!'[594] In choosing to focus on competition for scarce resources as the primary element in the evolutionary process, Darwin and Wallace gave less emphasis to the importance of cooperation in nature. Yet it could be argued that this has played an equal role in the origin of our species, whether through symbiosis, as when our single-celled ancestors fused with a bacterium, the latter becoming an energy-providing mitochondrion in return for a sheltering environment, or the way that cooperation in tool-using apes set them on the path to language and human consciousness. Darwin himself was far from ignorant of such considerations, for instance, once stating that 'in the long history of humankind (and animal kind, too) those who learned to collaborate and improvise most effectively have prevailed'.[595] Instead, it was individuals like Herbert Spencer, who first coined the phrase 'survival of the fittest', who were more responsible for the emphasis on crude competition in popularizations of Darwinism.[596] Nevertheless, Darwin's primary focus on competition helped ensure the success of natural selection as a principle, but has also been a factor in the distorted presentation, in some popular accounts, of how evolution works.

In genetics we've seen a similar demonstration of the power, but also the potentially distorting effects, of simplifying a complex process. The genius of Mendel was to recognize simple mathematical patterns in complex chains of inheritance. This focus on mathematics may be one reason why the importance of his work went unrecognized in his own lifetime, since biologists at that time were unused to thinking in such quantitative terms. However, another reason was that when Mendel tried to convince Carl von Nägeli, one of the world's most distinguished botanists at the time, of the importance of his findings, he failed

to do so partly because he couldn't demonstrate the same simple patterns of inheritance in the hawkweed plants that Nägeli sent him to test.[597] In fact, Mendel knew that even in peas some characteristics did not show the same straightforward rules of inheritance as the ones he used to illustrate his theory. Morgan also identified characteristics in fruitflies that failed to show a simple Mendelian pattern of inheritance but chose to ignore them.[598] Such simplification of genetics helped its success as an explanatory principle, and provided an important tool for understanding diseases like cystic fibrosis or Huntington's disease; however, it has also led to naïve expectations about the link between the genome and more common disorders that are only now being challenged by the reality of GWAS findings.

Another central principle in modern genetics is Weismann's proposal of a rigid division in multicellular organisms between the sex cells—the eggs and sperm—and the rest of the body, and his view that whatever happens in life to the body as a whole has no impact upon the only immortal part of the organism, the genetic material passed on to its descendants.[599] To back up his proposal, Weismann chose the rather barbaric route of cutting off the tails of 68 mice and showing that this did not result in any offspring born without tails over the next five generations.[599] In so doing, he helped boost the evolutionary synthesis of Darwinism and Mendelism; at the same time, his proposal seemed to shut the door firmly on Lamarck's view that the life experience of an organism could affect future generations, something that, as we've seen, is now being challenged in a number of important ways.

One view of Francis Crick's 'central dogma' of molecular biology is to see it as a modern version of Weismann's proposal.[600] So, just as Weismann's germ plasm was supposed to be the one pure and unchanging element of life, so, according to Richard Lewontin of Harvard University, DNA conceived as the central repository of information has assumed the mystical, self-renewing powers of the Holy Grail.[601] In cutting through the complexity of life as viewed by the biochemists, such a viewpoint played an invaluable role in opening up the genome to full view. Yet, at the same time, the one-sidedness of the central dogma has been exposed by the discovery of the myriad number of different ways in which DNA's information capacity can be modified by epigenetic mechanisms, both within the lifetime of an organism in different cells and tissues, and, more controversially, across generations too.

In summarizing some of the crucial developments of modern genetics, we can see both the strengths of the reductionist approach but also its weaknesses.

Typically, this approach seeks to reduce the complexity of life by focusing on one or two elements and then following these along a 'path of least resistance', just as a traveller may follow a path through a wood. There is no doubt that following such a path has allowed phenomenal progress in our understanding of genetics. However, just as a traveller will reach a destination by following a straight path, but may consequently miss important things on either side of the path, this, to some extent, has also been the case with molecular biology. Thankfully, though, this is not the end of the matter, because science also has an inbuilt mechanism that forces researchers to consider new paths of investigation even if this is not their original intention. We have seen this countless times in this book, where preconceptions about our genome, for instance, that it is a compact entity like that of a bacterium, were challenged by the discovery of enhancers, splicing, and so on. But it has also been true of the biggest biology project of all—the Human Genome Project.

Compared to the overwhelmingly positive headlines that greeted the 'first draft' of the genome, announced at a White House press conference in June 2000, media commentary about the tenth anniversary of this event was more subdued, and more critical. So a typical example was the New York Times, which, on 13 June 2010, ran a front-page story entitled 'A Decade Later, Gene Map Yields Few New Cures'.[602] Other media outlets and blogs across the world took up the theme that the project which had cost so much and taken almost a decade to complete had been largely an exercise in hype, and a failure in medical terms. One scientist particularly upset by such coverage was Eric Lander, director of the Broad Institute, a biomedical research institute in Cambridge, Massachusetts, and one of the leaders of the genome project. So he has rejected claims that he ever unduly hyped the project, arguing that 'I'm on record saying this is going to take a long time, and that the next step is to find the basis of disease, and then you have to make drugs…Going from the germ theory of disease to antibiotics that saved people's lives took 60 years. We might beat that. But anybody who thought in the year 2000 that we'd see cures in 2010 was smoking something.'[602]

In fact a survey of the claims made by those involved in the genome project at its inception uncovers some that are realistic, others that now seem overly simplistic, such as Jim Watson's claim in 1989 that 'we used to think our fate was in the stars. Now we know, in large measure, our fate is in our genes.'[603] Of course, one reason for such flowery phrases may have been the need to raise the $3 billion required to sequence the genome, which, in the 1980s, was an

unprecedented amount of money for a science project. A vision was required to enthuse the government agencies that would be bankrolling the project, even if that vision now, in retrospect, looks unrealistic. But this and other pronouncements made at the time, for instance, about the links between genetics and disease that would be uncovered by the genome project, also seem to me to betray a genuine naïvety about the complexity of this link, rather than being simply an attempt to hoodwink politicians into handing over taxpayers' money. Yet against those who argue that the Human Genome Project was a waste of money, it is important to stress both the very real successes of the post-genomic age, and also the way in which the more unexpected aspects of the project's findings have subsequently led to a more sophisticated understanding of the genome's complexity, and how we might harness this understanding in practical ways.

Discussing progress in science, Sydney Brenner once said that this 'depends on new techniques, new discoveries and new ideas, probably in that order'.[604] In this book, we've discussed some remarkable technologies that have been brought to bear upon the question of how our genomes function, both to regulate intracellular processes but also act as a repository of information for the next generation. One distinctive feature of molecular biology is the fact that many of its tools are themselves derived from life, whether this be DNA or RNA probes, antibodies, fluorescent proteins, enzymes to cut and paste DNA, or the polymerase used in DNA sequencing. However, we should also not forget the X-ray diffraction devices that first revealed the structures of DNA and proteins, or the microscopes and fluorescence imaging instruments that allow us to peer inside a cell and even visualize the very DNA and protein molecules themselves. Perhaps the most important legacy of the Human Genome Project besides the genome sequence itself was the introduction of massive computing power into biology, as well as robotic devices that have led to 'high-throughput' approaches becoming a routine aspect of modern biology.[605] One important consequence is that DNA sequencing itself has been transformed: Sanger's original method now having been superseded by others based on massive numbers of reactions all proceeding in parallel.[606] It is this that lies behind the dramatic reduction in cost of sequencing an individual human genome over recent years, which, according to George Church of Harvard University, 'dropped by a factor of 10 every year for the last five to six years, so it's a truly amazing exponential decrease compared to the computer industry'.[602]

This reduction in costs has exciting implications for medicine. As we've seen, the original assumption that common disorders such as heart disease, diabetes, or disorders of the mind like schizophrenia or autism would turn out to be caused by defects in one or a few genes has been undermined by the findings of genome-wide association studies. Yet it would be equally mistaken to underestimate the increasing capacity of genomic studies to pinpoint the molecular causes of some diseases now that is becoming possible to sequence an individual genome both rapidly and cheaply. Take, for instance, a recent case in which a 2-month-old baby boy was admitted to Children's Mercy Hospital in Kansas City, USA, with a mysterious ailment that had already caused his liver to fail and left him hovering at death's door.[607] By sequencing the boy's genome, within three days geneticist Stephen Kingsmore and his team at the hospital had pinpointed the cause of the ailment to a mutation linked to a rare condition in which an overactive immune system damages the liver and spleen. Armed with this diagnosis, the boy's doctors immediately gave him drugs to lower his immune response, with the consequence that he is now at home and healthy. In fact, this baby is just one of 44 sick infants whose genomes Kingsmore's group has sequenced, using a process that can provide a diagnosis in as little as 24 hours. In 28 of these cases the researchers were able to diagnose the illness, and in half of these they could recommend a treatment. Over the next five years Kingsmore is planning to sequence the genomes of 500 sick babies at the hospital, and this is just one of a number of projects across the breadth of the USA that are waiting for approval to carry out a similar exercise. Of course, such projects raise a number of ethical issues. The babies in these cases have given no consent for their genomes to be sequenced. And while the focus in this analysis has been on identifying the molecular defects linked to specific, potentially life-threatening conditions, important questions will need to be asked about who will have access to the sequence data, and how far doctors should be allowed to proceed in extracting information that is unrelated to the immediate disease from which the children are suffering.[607]

Advances in DNA sequencing are just one example of the ways in which high-throughput methods are transforming biology. This now makes it possible to investigate the cell's activities on a truly global scale, whether the object of study is RNA transcripts, DNA methylation, histone marks, or 3D interactions. Indeed, this was how ENCODE mapped a diverse number of biochemical activities across the whole genome. And, as we've seen, the findings of such analyses are revealing

an undreamt of complexity in the genome. Importantly, far from our biology being focused solely around the 2 per cent of our genomes that code for proteins, it is becoming clear that this is only the tip of the iceberg once we start to consider the 3D structure of the genome, non-coding RNAs, and all the epigenetic mechanisms that we've discussed.

As we've discussed in this book, a major part of the debate about the ENCODE findings has focused upon the question of what proportion of the genome is functional. Given that the two sides in this debate use quite different criteria to assess functionality it is likely that it will be some time before we have a clearer idea about who is most correct in this debate. Yet, in framing the debate in this quantitative way, there is a danger that we might lose sight of an exciting qualitative shift that has been taking place in biology over the last decade or so. So a previous emphasis on a linear flow of information, from DNA to RNA to protein through a genetic code, is now giving way to a much more complex picture in which multiple codes are superimposed upon each other. Such a viewpoint sees the gene as more than just a protein-coding unit; instead it can equally be seen as an accumulation of chemical modifications in the DNA or its associated histones, a site for non-coding RNA synthesis, or a nexus in a 3D network. Moreover, since we now know that multiple sites in the genome outside the protein-coding regions can produce RNAs, and that even many pseudo-genes are turning out to be functional, the very question of what constitutes a gene is now being challenged. Or, as Ed Weiss at the University of Pennsylvania recently put it, 'the concept of a gene is shredding'.[608] Such is the nature of the shift that now we face the challenge of not just recognizing the true scale of this complexity, but explaining how it all comes together to make a living, functioning, human being.

It's here, though, that we face a dilemma, which is whether the conceptual tools available to us in modern biology are sufficient to make sense of all this complexity and relate it not just to human disease, but also the other characteristics that distinguish us as a species and as individuals. In particular, although it is quite clear that reductionist methods have proven incredibly successful at identifying the molecules that make up the living cell and organism at an exquisite level of detail, what is now being debated is whether reductionism as a philosophy is capable of showing how all these molecules work together within an interrelated whole. Importantly, while such concerns go back at least as far as Goethe and his

contemporaries, they are now starting to be raised within the heart of molecular biology itself.

Take, for instance, a recent article by Marc van Regenmortel of the École Normale Supérieure de Biotechnologie in Strasbourg, written for *EMBO Reports*, a journal of the European Molecular Biology Organization, in which he has argued that 'the reductionist method of dissecting biological systems into their constituent parts has been effective in explaining the chemical basis of numerous living processes. However, many biologists now realize that this approach has reached its limit.'[609] Van Regenmortel believes this is due to the fact that reductionism's assumption that 'the isolated molecules and their structure have sufficient explanatory power to provide an understanding of the whole system' does not take into account that 'biological systems are extremely complex and have emergent properties that cannot be explained, or even predicted, by studying their individual parts'.[609]

Of course, it is one thing to state this problem and quite another to find a way to make sense of such complexity. In this respect, some would argue that the global nature of the new technologies that have emerged following the genome project addresses this issue. So, as well as genomics, we now have approaches to catalogue all proteins (the proteome), RNA molecules (the transcriptome), metabolites (the metabolome), and interactions (the interactome).[602] But it is one thing to catalogue this complexity, another to understand its functional significance. In fact Sydney Brenner, who, as we saw in Chapter 2, played a key role in cracking the genetic code, amongst other major contributions to molecular biology, has recently argued that 'this "omic" science has corrupted us. It has created the idea that if you just collect a lot of data, it will all work out.'[602] Instead, Brenner believes that the way forward lies in the recognition that the organizing principle for thinking about the genome is the cell. So, in an article published in 2010, he outlined a project called CellMap, whose aim would be to catalogue every type of cell in the body and detail how different genetic regions behave in each cellular environment.[602] In fact, as we saw in Chapter 6, such an aim has been central to ENCODE, with its survey of genomic activity in 147 different cell types.

There is a potential problem, however, in exchanging a catalogue of molecules for one of cells, with regard to a structure as complicated as the human brain. For, as we've seen, far from the brain being a collection of isolated cells, we must consider the fact that each cell can have as many as 10,000 connections to others

in the brain. One problem with merely cataloguing all the different types of brain cells and their genomic activities, is that this takes no account of how connections with other nerves might be affecting these activities. In fact, there are plans to address this issue, most notably through the Human Connectome Project.[610] This will map every single one of the 100 trillion nerve connections in the human brain by using sophisticated imaging techniques to study living brains, and high-throughput electron microscopy to study sections of dead brains. Amongst the thousands of individuals to be studied, the project will collect information from identical twins and their non-twin siblings, as well as individuals who suffer from various mental disorders. By mapping brain connections in these different cases, the project hopes to uncover the normal variation in human connectomes and how they change as humans learn, mature, and age.[610] Such is the aim, but the scale of the project is a daunting one. The connectome of the nematode worm, with 300 nerve cells joined by 7,000 connections, took a decade to complete. More recently, Hongkui Zeng and colleagues at the Allen Institute for Brain Science published a preliminary map of the connectome of the mouse brain, which has 75 million neurons. In comparison, the human brain has 100 billion nerve cells, as many as there are stars in the Milky Way. And, as Sebastian Seung, a neuroscientist at the Massachusetts Institute of Technology has pointed out, 'your connectome [has] a million times more connections than your genome has letters. Genomes are child's play compared with connectomes.'[610]

Such are the technical challenges faced by the connectome project, but there is also the question of whether the project really has the potential to deliver 'nothing less than the nature of human individuality', as is being promised in some quarters.[610] In particular, there are two potential flaws in the idea that simply mapping all the connections in the brain will be enough to reveal the underlying basis of human consciousness. One is the idea that an individual nerve cell can be treated as a 'black box' into which information is fed, and from which it emerges, without reference to the structure of the cell. Yet as we saw in Chapter 13, we now know that each nerve cell is composed of many functional sub-domains, with protein production in each regulated differently, depending on which type of non-coding RNAs it contains.[611] A second potential flaw is the focus on one-to-one connections between nerve cells. While, in itself, mapping all such connections in the brain is likely to be highly illuminating, it does not take into account the rapid and much more global connectivity that we've already discussed in the form of

electrical impulses and changes in the levels of second messengers such as calcium ions, which can spread across the brain in seconds.[612] Since calcium signals can both regulate the activity of important enzymes, as well as gene expression, such global connectivity also needs to be taken into consideration. In fact, moves are already underway to address the second of these issues, with some neuroscientists calling for a further brain scanning project, the 'dynome', whose aim will be to go beyond mapping mere brain anatomy and instead connect this to an understanding of brain dynamics.[613] As for the issue of the many sub-domains within nerve cells, one hope is that, as the non-coding RNAs present within the domains of different types of nerve cells are studied, some kinds of generalized patterns will emerge, relating to the different sorts of such RNAs and their spatial distribution within different categories of nerve cells.

In addition, though, there is a much bigger issue to be addressed, which is how, having catalogued all the different genomic activities in different nerve cells, the multiple types of such cells in the brain and their connections to each other, combined with an awareness of how the different regions of the brain interact at a more global level, we can thereby translate this into an awareness of how this all comes together to produce a self-conscious, thinking human brain. It is here that we may still have much to learn from the Romantic approach to the natural world, particularly the belief that the whole is present in every part of a biological system and each part is connected to the whole. One person who particularly espoused this approach in the context of human consciousness was Lev Vygotsky, whose view of the mind we discussed in Chapter 12. Vygotsky believed that science would only be able to truly decipher the material basis of consciousness by identifying a 'unit of analysis' that would be capable of reflecting all the complex interfunctional relationships that unite to produce it, from the individual nerve cell to the brain as a whole. In Vygotsky's view, such a unit of analysis had been identified in biology as a whole in the principle of natural selection, with its effects evident all the way from the conservation of a single protein sequence, through to the evolution of a whole species. However, Vygotsky argued that, for psychology, such a unit of analysis remained to be identified, as shown by its many competing and mutually exclusive explanations for how the mind worked. Today, one might add that although enormous strides have been made in the experimental neurosciences, the gap between them and the psychology of the mind remains huge.

So what might constitute such a unit of analysis for human consciousness? Based on the two central attributes that he believed constituted human uniqueness, Vygotsky believed that it must encompass both our ability to transform the world through tools and our capacity for language. But how would these two attributes manifest themselves at the cellular and genomic level in the brain? Not so long ago such a question would have been seen as a strictly one-way affair, with our genomes encoding such uniquely human attributes in the DNA sequence and transmitting this through proteins to nerve cell function. However, now that we are learning that our life experiences may significantly impact on our genomic activity, it is clear that we also need to incorporate this insight into our understanding of how the brain works. And somehow, while identifying the features of our brains that are uniquely human, we will also need to relate this to the underlying molecular and cellular mechanisms that we share with other species.

That a movement towards a more holistic way of looking at the brain is already happening should be clear from some of the cutting-edge studies that we have discussed in this book. And it is not only in this area of biology that a reconsideration of past ideas is under way. Indeed, it is surely not a coincidence that the biggest shifts in viewpoint are taking place in areas where the object of study is proving so complex that the limitations of previous approaches are becoming particularly apparent. Take, for instance, the study of metabolism, and particularly the role of organs such as the stomach, pancreas, liver, and fat tissue in this central process. Previously, the view of these different organs was of passive players controlled by signals originating in 'higher' centres, such as the hypothalamus in the brain. However, there is now an increasing recognition that each organ is an active player, sending out their own chemical signals both to each other, and back to the brain. That such a reassessment is now taking place is important given the current obesity 'epidemic', to stem which will require a more sophisticated view of the biological basis of appetite and satiety, as well as tackling the obvious social reasons for this epidemic—the surfeit of cheap, energy-rich foods, the high costs of healthier foodstuffs, and the lack of exercise that is becoming characteristic of so many in the developed world.

However, while old ways of thinking in biology are being challenged in these different areas, it would be a mistake to believe that everyone is convinced of the need for a new approach. Instead, despite emerging evidence of the intricacy of the links between our genomes and complex human diseases and characteristics,

I still attend far too many research seminars where speakers uncritically present their studies of mouse knockout 'models' of schizophrenia or autism. Apart from the difficulties of modelling these disorders in animals, given their social as well as biological component, the possibility that such single-gene knockouts might only be a crude approximation of the true genetic complexity of the human disorders, is rarely remarked upon. One reason for this may be that a complex state of affairs with multiple components is much harder to understand than one with just one, or a few, simple strands. However, it's surely a necessary step if biomedical research is to realize the promises made at the completion of the genome project and provide us with new and better means of treating disease.

Another important issue, and this, to some extent, depends upon who is correct about the extent of functionality in the human genome, is the question of how valid animal models are for understanding the true complexity of the human condition. As we've seen, one of the most surprising aspects of the ENCODE findings was the discovery that a significant amount of the biochemical activity in the genome appeared to be specific to humans. If this activity does turn out to reflect real function and not just 'noise', it would suggest that the biological differences between ourselves and other species may be greater than supposed. In fact, at the level of basic physiology there is clearly a huge amount of similarity between ourselves and a mouse, and, as such, experimentation on animals will continue to play a central role as models of human health and disease, including those of the mind. However, if we are to gain insights into the complexities of human disorders, and, as importantly, the normal human state, we will need to consider how we can supplement such studies with investigations in animals that are closer to our own species, such as other primates, but also studies in human beings themselves. In the former respect, the fact that new gene editing technologies mean it is becoming possible, for the first time, to generate knockout and other genetically modified versions of primates, offers the prospect of being able to study the effect of changes in the genome in such species. However, such a route will be controversial for some people and it will require careful consideration of the benefits of such an investigation compared to any suffering that may result in the animals being studied. Ethical considerations will be even more central to studies of human beings, whether this involves molecular analysis of the brains of dead individuals, or imaging studies of this organ in living subjects. However, one of the exciting aspects of the new genomic technologies is how

much information can now be gathered about the biochemical activity in the genomes of single human cells, while safe, non-invasive imaging methods can record electrical and chemical changes across the living human brain. Particularly as we learn more about the complex interacting role of biology and environment in shaping our lives, such complements to animal studies will become increasingly important. But so will a better appreciation of the complexities of human behaviour and society, both in terms of our lives today, as well as the events that have shaped them in the past. For, ultimately, it is our self-conscious awareness and ability to shape the world around us that is the most distinctive aspect of our species.

A concern shared by many is that we seem to have lost our way with regard to this particular ability in recent years. So, while we can now sequence a human baby's genome in twenty hours or image its brain patterns as it learns to speak, at the same time other children are dying for lack of clean water or being blown up by smart missiles in some distant war. Meanwhile, despite our vast technological capacities our governments and political leaders seem incapable of doing anything to tackle the most urgent issue of our times—the warming of the planet. So perhaps it's not surprising that some people feel more threatened than empowered by the growing prospect of scientists soon being able to decode the genomes of every individual on the planet. Personally, I am excited by this prospect, but it will need to be coupled with a real and democratic debate about the ways we intend to use this information. As such, my conclusion to this book is the hope that it has stimulated a desire to know more about the workings of the genome and how it affects our lives, but also that it has reaffirmed the importance of what truly distinguishes our species—that is, our potential to not only shape the world, but to do so for the good of every human being on the planet and all the other organisms (who are, after all, our biological cousins) with whom we share this miraculous blue biosphere within the cosmos.

GLOSSARY

Chromatin Complex of DNA, histones, and non-histone proteins from which eukaryotic chromosomes are formed. Condensation during mitosis yields the visible chromosomes.

Enhancer A regulatory sequence in eukaryotic DNA that may be located far from the gene it controls. Binding of transcription factors activates transcription of the associated gene.

Enzyme A biological molecule that acts as a catalyst. Most enzymes are proteins, but certain RNAs, called ribozymes, also have catalytic activity.

Epigenetic The study of heritable changes not caused by changes in the DNA sequence; also stable alterations in the transcriptional potential of a cell that are not necessarily heritable.

Gene editing A type of genetic engineering in which DNA is inserted, replaced, or removed from a genome using artificially engineered nucleases, or 'molecular scissors'.

Gene expression Overall process by which the information encoded in a gene is converted into an observable phenotype (most commonly production of a protein).

Genome-wide association study (GWAS) Investigation of many common genetic variants in different individuals to see if any variant is associated with a characteristic.

Histones A family of small proteins found in the chromatin of all eukaryotic cells, which associate with DNA in the nucleosome.

Insulator A DNA sequence that prevents a gene regulatory protein, bound to DNA in the control region of one gene, from influencing the transcription of adjacent genes.

Meiosis In eukaryotes, a special type of cell division that occurs during maturation of the eggs and sperm.

miRNA A microRNA is a small non-coding RNA molecule found in plants, animals, and some viruses, which functions in RNA silencing and regulation of gene expression.

Mitosis In eukaryotic cells, the process whereby the nucleus is divided to produce two genetically equivalent daughter nuclei.

mRNA The messenger RNA molecule specifies the amino acid sequence of a protein. It is translated into protein in a process catalysed by ribosomes.

Mutation A permanent, heritable change in the DNA sequence of a chromosome, usually in a single gene; commonly leads to a change in or loss of the normal function of the gene product.

Nucleosome Beadlike structure in eukaryotic chromatin. Composed of a short length of DNA wrapped around a core of histones; the fundamental structural unit of chromatin.

piRNAs Non-coding RNAs linked to gene silencing of transposons in germ cells, particularly those involved in sperm formation. Recently, also identified in the brain.

Promoter DNA sequence that determines the site of transcription initiation for RNA polymerase.

Protein kinase Enzyme that transfers the phosphate group of ATP to a target protein.

Pseudogene Gene that has accumulated multiple mutations that has rendered it inactive and non-functional.

Repetitive DNA Sequences of DNA in the genome that are found to be repeated, sometimes thousands of times over.

RNA interference The phenomenon of gene silencing mediated by the interaction of a double-stranded RNA, with a corresponding target messenger RNA.

Second messenger An intracellular signalling molecule whose concentration increases (or decreases) in response to the binding of an extracellular signal to a cell-surface receptor.

Silencer A regulatory sequence in eukaryotic DNA that may be located far from the gene it controls. Binding of transcription factors inhibits transcription of the associated gene.

siRNA Small interfering RNA. Functions by causing mRNA to be inactivated after transcription, resulting in no translation.

Splicing The process by which introns are excised and exons are joined back together in the post-transcriptional modification of RNA.

Transcription Process whereby one strand of a DNA molecule is used as a template for synthesis of a complementary RNA by RNA polymerase.

Transcription factor General term for any protein, other than RNA polymerase, required to initiate or regulate transcription in eukaryotic cells.

Translation The ribosome-mediated production of a protein whose amino acid sequence is specified by the nucleotide sequence in an mRNA.

Transposition The movement of a mobile DNA element into or out of a chromosome.

ENDNOTES

Introduction: How the Genome Lost Its Junk

1. Chandrasekhar, I., Wardrop, M., and Trotman, A., Phone hacking: timeline of the scandal, *The Telegraph*, <http://www.telegraph.co.uk/news/uknews/phone-hacking/8634176/Phone-hacking-timeline-of-a-scandal.html#June12> (2012).
2. Media Fellowships, *British Science Association*, <http://www.britishscienceassociation.org/science-society/media-fellowships> (2014).
3. *Eureka Alert*, <http://www.eurekalert.org/> (2014).
4. McCrimmon, O., ENCODE data describes function of human genome, *National Human Genome Research Institute*, <http://www.genome.gov/27549810> (2012).
5. Yong, E., ENCODE: the rough guide to the human genome, *Discover Magazine*, <http://blogs.discovermagazine.com/notrocketscience/2012/09/05/encode-the-rough-guide-to-the-human-genome/#.VAS6QsVdXh4> (2012).
6. Pennisi, E., Genomics. ENCODE project writes eulogy for junk DNA. *Science* 337: 1159–61 (2012), p. 1159.
7. Whipple, T. and Parrington, J., Rummage through 'junk' DNA finds vital material, *The Times*, <http://www.thetimes.co.uk/tto/science/genetics/article3529618.ece> (2012).
8. Connor, S., Scientists debunk 'junk DNA' theory to reveal vast majority of human genes perform a vital function, *The Independent*, <http://www.independent.co.uk/news/science/scientists-debunk-junk-dna-theory-to-reveal-vast-majority-of-human-genes-perform-a-vital-function-8106777.html> (2012).
9. Hanlon, M., 'Junk DNA' and the mystery of mankind's missing genes, *The Telegraph*, <http://www.telegraph.co.uk/science/9534185/Junk-DNA-and-the-mystery-of-mankinds-missing-genes.html> (2012).
10. Jha, A., Breakthrough study overturns theory of 'junk DNA' in genome, *The Guardian*, <http://www.theguardian.com/science/2012/sep/05/genes-genome-junk-dna-encode> (2012).
11. Pennisi, E., Genomics. ENCODE project writes eulogy for junk DNA. *Science* 337: 1159–61 (2012), p. 1159.
12. John Parrington articles—media fellowships 2012, *British Science Association*, <http://www.britishscienceassociation.org/john-parrington-articles-media-fellowships-2012> (2012).
13. Graur, D., Zheng, Y., Price, N., et al., On the immortality of television sets: 'function' in the human genome according to the evolution-free gospel of ENCODE. *Genome Biology and Evolution* 5: 578–90 (2013).
14. McKie, R., Scientists attacked over claim that 'junk DNA' is vital to life, *The Guardian*, <http://www.theguardian.com/science/2013/feb/24/scientists-attacked-over-junk-dna-claim> (2013).

15. Maher, B., Fighting about ENCODE and junk, *Nature News*. <http://blogs.nature.com/news/2012/09/fighting-about-encode-and-junk.html> (2012).
16. Keller, E. F., From gene action to reactive genomes. *The Journal of Physiology* 592: 2423–9 (2014), p. 2425.
17. Morris, D., *The Naked Ape: A Zoologist's Study of the Human Animal* (Bantam Books, 1967).
18. Morris, D., *The Naked Ape: A Zoologist's Study of the Human Animal* (Bantam Books, 1967), p. 56.
19. 1967: The Naked Ape steps out, *BBC*, http://news.bbc.co.uk/onthisday/hi/dates/stories/october/12/newsid_3116000/3116329.stm (2014).
20. Pagel, M., *Wired for Culture* (Penguin, 2012), p. 81.
21. Pagel, M., *Wired for Culture* (Penguin, 2012), p. 82.
22. Barkham, P., Iraq war 10 years on: mass protest that defined a generation, *The Guardian*, <http://www.theguardian.com/world/2013/feb/15/iraq-war-mass-protest> (2013).
23. Hamer, D. H., Hu, S., Magnuson, V. L., et al., A linkage between DNA markers on the X chromosome and male sexual orientation, *Science* 261: 321–7 (1993).
24. Kitzinger, J., Constructing and deconstructing the 'gay gene': media reporting of genetics, sexual diversity and 'deviance', in *Diversity without Deviance: Human Biology, Science and Society*, ed. G. Goodman and A. Ellison, 100–17 (Taylor & Francis, 2005).
25. Mustanski, B. S., Chivers, M. L., and Bailey, J. M., A critical review of recent biological research on human sexual orientation, *Annual Review of Sex Research* 13: 89–140 (2002).
26. Radford, T., The Selfish Gene by Richard Dawkins—book review, *The Guardian*, <http://www.theguardian.com/science/2012/aug/31/the-selfish-gene-richard-dawkins-review> (2012).
27. What they said: genome in quotes, *BBC*, <http://news.bbc.co.uk/1/hi/sci/tech/807126.stm> (2000).
28. Visscher, P. M., Brown, M. A., McCarthy, M. I., and Yang, J., Five years of GWAS discovery. *American Journal of Human Genetics* 90: 7–24 (2012).
29. Li, C., Personalized medicine—the promised land: are we there yet? *Clinical Genetics* 79: 403–12 (2011).
30. Rose, H. and Rose, S., How genes failed: Hilary Rose and Steven Rose on the limitations of biological determinism, *Socialist Worker*, <http://socialistworker.co.uk/art/29639/How+genes+failed%3A+Hilary+Rose+and+Steven+Rose+on+the+limitations+of+biological+determinism> (2012).
31. Van Regenmortel, M. H. V., Reductionism and complexity in molecular biology. *EMBO Reports* 5: 1016–20 (2004), p. 1016.
32. Parrington, J. and Coward, K., The spark of life. *The Biologist* 50: 5–10 (2003).
33. Parrington, J., Davis, L. C., Galione, A., and Wessel, G., Flipping the switch: how a sperm activates the egg at fertilization. *Developmental Dynamics* 236: 2027–38 (2007).
34. Doyle, A., McGarry, M. P., Lee, N. A., and Lee, J. J., The construction of transgenic and gene knockout/knockin mouse models of human disease. *Transgenic Research* 21: 327–49 (2012).
35. Fryer, R. M., Randall, J., Yoshida, T., et al., Global analysis of gene expression: methods, interpretation, and pitfalls. *Experimental Nephrology* 10: 64–74 (2002).
36. Levine, M., Cattoglio, C., and Tjian, R., Looping back to leap forward: transcription enters a new era. *Cell* 157: 13–25 (2014).
37. Gibcus, J. H. and Dekker, J. The hierarchy of the 3D genome. *Molecular Cell* 49: 773–82 (2013).
38. Morris, K. V. and Mattick, J. S., The rise of regulatory RNA. *Nature Reviews Genetics* 15: 423–37 (2014).
39. Rivera, C. M. and Ren, B., Mapping human epigenomes. *Cell* 155: 39–55 (2013).

40. Slotkin, R. K. and Martienssen, R., Transposable elements and the epigenetic regulation of the genome. *Nature Reviews Genetics* 8: 272–85 (2007).

41. Lupski, J. R., Genetics: genome mosaicism—one human, multiple genomes. *Science* 341: 358–9 (2013).

42. Reilly, M. T., Faulkner, G. J., Dubnau, J., et al., The role of transposable elements in health and diseases of the central nervous system. *The Journal of Neuroscience* 33: 17577–86 (2013).

43. Stindl, R., The telomeric sync model of speciation: species-wide telomere erosion triggers cycles of transposon-mediated genomic rearrangements, which underlie the saltatory appearance of nonadaptive characters. *Die Naturwissenschaften* 101: 163–86 (2014).

44. Pääbo, S., *Neanderthal Man* (Basic Books, 2014).

45. Ahmed, M. and Liang, P., Study of modern human evolution via comparative analysis with the Neanderthal genome. *Genomics & Informatics* 11: 230–8 (2013).

46. Li, C., Personalized medicine—the promised land: are we there yet? *Clinical Genetics* 79: 403–12 (2011).

Chapter 1: The Inheritors

47. Comparable odds to winning a Lotto jackpot, *Lottery*, <http://lottery.typepad.com/lottery/2012/06/comparable-odds-to-winning-a-lotto-jackpot.html> (2012).

48. Spector, D., The odds of you being alive are incredibly small, *Business Insider*, <http://www.businessinsider.com/infographic-the-odds-of-being-alive-2012-6> (2012).

49. Darwin, C., *Origin of Species* (John Murray, 1859).

50. Darwin, C., *Origin of Species* (John Murray, 1859), p. 78.

51. Shermer, M., *In Darwin's Shadow* (Oxford University Press, 2002), p. 161.

52. Young, R. M., Malthus on man—in animals no moral restraint. *Clio Medica* 59: 73–91 (2000).

53. Desmond, A. and Moore, J. R., *Darwin* (Michael Joseph, 1991), p. 468.

54. Desmond, A. and Moore, J. R., *Darwin* (Michael Joseph, 1991), p. 470.

55. Desmond, A. and Moore, J. R., *Darwin* (Michael Joseph, 1991), p. 469.

56. Darwin, C., *The Descent of Man* (John Murray, 1871), p. 485.

57. Shermer, M., *In Darwin's Shadow* (Oxford University Press, 2002), p. 159.

58. Gould, S. J. and Berry, A., *Infinite Tropics: An Alfred Russel Wallace Anthology* (Verso, 2003), p. 208.

59. Shermer, M., *In Darwin's Shadow* (Oxford University Press, 2002), p. 161.

60. Lennox, J., Aristotle's Biology, *Stanford Encylopedia of Philosophy*, <http://plato.stanford.edu/entries/aristotle-biology/> (2014).

61. Gregor Johann Mendel, *Complete Dictionary of Scientific Biography*, <http://www.encyclopedia.com/topic/Gregor_Johann_Mendel.aspx> (2008).

62. Badano, J. L. and Katsanis, N., Beyond Mendel: an evolving view of human genetic disease transmission. *Nature Reviews Genetics* 3: 779–89 (2002).

63. Watson, J. D., *DNA* (Arrow Books, 2004), p. 10.

64. Lenay, C., Hugo de Vries: from the theory of intracelullar pangenesis to the rediscovery of Mendel. *Life Sciences* 323: 1053–60 (2000).

65. Wallace, A., *Letters and Reminiscences* (Cassell, 1916), p. 108.

66. Kohler, R. E., *Lords of the Fly: Drosophila Genetics and the Experimental Life* (University of Chicago Press, 1994), p. 41.

67. Bowler, P. J., Hugo De Vries and Thomas Hunt Morgan: the mutation theory and the spirit of Darwinism. *Annals of Science* 35: 55–73 (1978).

68. Genes, Chromosomes, and the Origins of Modern Biology, *Columbia University*, <http://www.columbia.edu/cu/alumni/Magazine/Legacies/Morgan/> (2014).

69. Watson, J. D., *DNA* (Arrow Books, 2004), p. 14.

70. Paweletz, N., Walther Flemming: pioneer of mitosis research. *Nature Reviews Molecular and Cellular Biology* 2: 72–5 (2001).

71. Laubichler, M. D. and Davidson, E. H., Boveri's long experiment: sea urchin merogones and the establishment of the role of nuclear chromosomes in development. *Developmental Biology* 314: 1–11 (2008).

72. Wessel, G., Y does it work this way? Nettie Maria Stevens (July 7, 1861–May 4, 1912). *Molecular Reproduction and Development* 78 (2011).

73. Schramm, W., The history of haemophilia—a short review. *Thrombosis Research* 134S1: S4-S9 (2014).

74. Benson, K. R., T. H. Morgan's resistance to the chromosome theory. *Nature Reviews Genetics* 2: 469–74 (2001).

75. Carlson, E. A., H. J. Muller's contributions to mutation research. *Mutation Research* 752: 1–5 (2013).

76. Portin, P., The birth and development of the DNA theory of inheritance: sixty years since the discovery of the structure of DNA. *Journal of Genetics* 93: 293–302 (2014).

77. Koszul, R., Meselson, M., Van Doninck, K., et al., The centenary of Janssens's chiasmatype theory. *Genetics* 191: 309–17 (2012).

78. Brush, S. G., How theories became knowledge: Morgan's chromosome theory of heredity in America and Britain. *Journal of the History of Biology* 35: 471–535 (2002).

79. Maas, W., *Gene Action: A Historical Account* (Oxford University Press, 2002), p. 16.

80. Scriver, C. R., Garrod's foresight; our hindsight. *Journal of Inherited Metabolic Disease* 24: 93–116 (2001).

81. Edwards, A. W., Mathematizing Darwin. *Behavioral Ecology and Sociobiology* 65: 421–30 (2011).

82. Rao, V. and Nanjundiah, V., J. B. S. Haldane, Ernst Mayr and the Beanbag genetics dispute. *Journal of the History of Biology* 44: 233–81 (2011).

83. Haldane, J. B., A defense of beanbag genetics. 1964. *International Journal of Epidemiology* 37: 435–42 (2008).

84. Singer, M. and Berg, P., George Beadle: from genes to proteins. *Nature Reviews in Genetics* 5: 949–54 (2004).

Chapter 2: Life as a Code

85. Kean, S., *The Violinist's Thumb* (Doubleday, 2012), p. 18.

86. Dahm, R., Friedrich Miescher and the discovery of DNA. *Developmental Biology* 278: 274–88 (2005), p. 279.

87. Judson, H. F., *The Eighth Day of Creation* (Simon & Schuster, 1979), p. 30.

88. Watson, J. D., *DNA* (Arrow Books, 2004), p. 38.

89. Judson, H. F., *The Eighth Day of Creation* (Simon & Schuster, 1979), p. 59.

90. The Martha Chase Effect: Part 1, *Sciopic*, <http://sciopic.wordpress.com/2013/05/16/the-martha-chase-effect-part-1/> (2013).

91. *The Literature Network*, <http://www.online-literature.com/swift/3515/> (2014).

92. Watson, J. D., *The Annotated and Illustrated Double Helix* (Simon & Schuster, 2012).

93. Watson, J. D., *Avoid Boring People and Other Lessons from a Life in Science* (Oxford University Press, 2007), p. 39.

94. *James Watson: The double helix and beyond*, <http://www.npr.org/2012/11/16/165278526/james-watson-the-double-helix-and-beyond> (2012).

95. Landau, E., Watson: 'DNA was my only gold rush', *CNN*, <http://edition.cnn.com/2013/06/28/health/james-watson-dna/> (2013).

96. Watson, J. D., *The Annotated and Illustrated Double Helix* (Simon & Schuster, 2012), p. 37.

97. Jenkin, J., A unique partnership: William and Lawrence Bragg and the 1915 Nobel Prize in Physics. *Minerva* 39: 373–92 (2001).

98. Maddox, B., *Rosalind Franklin: The Dark Lady of DNA* (Harper Collins, 2002), p. 125.

99. The Randall letters: the DNA story at King's revisited, *King's College London Archive*, <http://dnaandsocialresponsibility.blogspot.co.uk/2010/08/randall-letters-dna-story-at-kings.html> (2010).

100. Watson, J. D., *The Annotated and Illustrated Double Helix* (Simon & Schuster, 2012), p. 182.

101. Wilkins, M., *The Third Man of the Double Helix* (Oxford University Press, 2003).

102. Maddox, B., *Rosalind Franklin: The Dark Lady of DNA* (Harper Collins, 2002), p. 127.

103. Watson, J. D., *The Annotated and Illustrated Double Helix* (Simon & Schuster, 2012), p. 200.

104. Watson, J. D., *The Annotated and Illustrated Double Helix* (Simon & Schuster, 2012), p. 209.

105. Kemp, M., The Mona Lisa of modern science. *Nature* 421: 416–20 (2003), p. 416.

106. Portin, P., The birth and development of the DNA theory of inheritance: sixty years since the discovery of the structure of DNA. *Journal of Genetics* 93: 293–302 (2014).

107. Judson, H. F., *The Eighth Day of Creation* (Simon & Schuster, 1979), p. 142.

108. Rose, S., Practicing biochemistry without a licence? *EMBO Reports* 12: 381 (2011), p. 381.

109. Watson, J. D. and Crick, F. H. C., Molecular structure of nucleic acids: a structure for deoxyribose nucleic acid. *Nature* 171: 737–8 (1953), p. 737.

110. Watson, J. D. and Crick, F. H. C., Genetical implications of the structure of deoxyribonucleic acid. *Nature* 171: 964–7 (1953).

111. Linus Pauling and the race for DNA, *Oregon State University Libraries*, <http://scarc.library.oregonstate.edu/coll/pauling/dna/quotes/all.html> (2014).

112. Maddox, B., *Rosalind Franklin: The Dark Lady of DNA* (Harper Collins, 2002), p. 307.

113. Sydney Brenner—biographical, *Nobel Media*, <http://www.nobelprize.org/nobel_prizes/medicine/laureates/2002/brenner-bio.html> (2002).

114. Watson, J. D., *DNA* (Arrow Books, 2004), p. 56.

115. Davis, T. H., Meselson and Stahl: the art of DNA replication. *Proceedings of the National Academy of Sciences of the United States of America* 101: 17895–6 (2004).

116. Lehman, I. R., Historical perspective: Arthur Kornberg, a giant of twentieth-century biochemistry. *Trends in Biochemical Sciences* 33: 291–6 (2008).

117. Stretton, A. O. W., The first sequence: Fred Sanger and insulin. *Genetics* 162: 527–32 (2002).

118. Judson, H., *The Eighth Day of Creation* (Simon & Schuster, 1979), p. 213.

119. Segre, G., The Big Bang and the genetic code. *Nature* 404: 437 (2000).

120. Gamow, G., *The Creation of the Universe* (Courier Dover Publications, 2004), p. 139.

121. Watson, J. D., *DNA* (Arrow Books, 2004), p. 64.

122. Watson, J. D., *DNA* (Arrow Books, 2004), p. 66.

123. Kresge, N., Simoni, R. D., and Hill, R., The discovery and isolation of RNA polymerase by Jerard Hurwitz. *Journal of Biological Chemistry* 281: e12–e14 (2006).

124. Watson, J. D., *DNA* (Arrow Books, 2004), p. 67.

125. Judson, H. F., *The Eighth Day of Creation* (Simon & Schuster, 1979), p. 282.

126. Pederson, T., Obituary: Paul C. Zamecnik (1912–2009). *Nature* 462: 423 (2009).

127. Sydney Brenner—biographical, *Nobel Media*, <http://www.nobelprize.org/nobel_prizes/medicine/laureates/2002/brenner-bio.html> (2002).

128. Pieribone, V., *Aglow in the Dark: The Revolutionary Science of Biofluorescence* (Harvard University Press, 2006), p. 113.

129. Judson, H. F., *The Eighth Day of Creation* (Simon & Schuster, 1979), pp. 436–41.

130. Shaw, K., The role of ribosomes in protein synthesis. *Nature Education* 1: 201 (2008).

131. Yanofsky, C., Establishing the triplet nature of the genetic code. *Cell* 128: 815–18 (2007).

132. Nazarali, A. J., Marshall Nirenberg 1927–2010. *Cellular and Molecular Neurobiology* 31: 805–7 (2011).

133. Crick, F. H. C., *What Mad Pursuit* (Basic Books, 1990), p. 109.

134. Judson, H. F., *The Eighth Day of Creation* (Simon & Schuster, 1979), p. 41.

135. Lewontin, R. C., *The Triple Helix* (Harvard University Press, 2000), p. 10.

136. Collins, N., *Sir John Gurdon, Nobel Prize winner, was 'too stupid' for science at school*, The Telegraph, <http://www.telegraph.co.uk/science/science-news/9594351/Sir-John-Gurdon-Nobel-Prize-winner-was-too-stupid-for-science-at-school.html> (2012).

137. Gurdon, J., Nuclear reprogramming in eggs. *Nature Medicine* 15: 1141–4 (2009).

138. Stanford, P. K., August Weismann's theory of the germ-plasm and the problem of unconceived alternatives. *History and Philosophy of the Life Sciences* 27: 163 (2005).

139. Gurdon, J. B., Interview with Sir John B. Gurdon, *Nobel Media*, <http://www.nobelprize.org/nobel_prizes/medicine/laureates/2012/gurdon-telephone.html> (2012).

Chapter 3: Switches and Signals

140. Jayaraman, R., Jacques Monod and the advent of the age of operons. *Resonance* 15: 1084–96 (2010).

141. Judson, H. F., *The Eighth Day of Creation* (Simon & Schuster, 1979), p. 357.

142. Jayaraman, R., Jacques Monod and the advent of the age of operons. *Resonance* 15: 1084–96 (2010), p. 1085.

143. Carroll, S. B., *Brave Genius: A Scientist, a Philosopher, and their Daring Adventures from the French Resistance to the Nobel Prize* (Broadway Books, 2014).

144. Watson, J. D., *DNA* (Arrow Books, 2004), p. 77.

145. Ullmann, A., In memoriam: Jacques Monod (1910–1976). *Genome Biology and Evolution* 3: 1025–33 (2011).

146. François Jacob, *The Telegraph*, <http://www.telegraph.co.uk/news/obituaries/10076471/Francois-Jacob.html> (2013).

147. Judson, H. F., *The Eighth Day of Creation* (Simon & Schuster, 1979), p. 402.

148. Judson, H. F., *The Eighth Day of Creation* (Simon & Schuster, 1979), p. 416.

149. Kay, L. E., *Who Wrote the Book of Life? A History of the Genetic Code* (Stanford University Press, 2000), p. 215.

150. Judson, H. F., *The Eighth Day of Creation* (Simon & Schuster, 1979), p. 373.

151. Englesberg, E. and Wilcox, G., Regulation: positive control. *Annual Review of Genetics* 8: 219–42 (1974).

152. Bussell, K., Accentuate the positive. *Nature Milestones*, S7, <http://www.nature.com/milestones/geneexpression/milestones/articles/milegene04.html> (2005).

153. Carroll, S. B., The main characters, *Sean B. Carroll website*, <http://seanbcarroll.com/main-characters/> (2014).

154. Muller-Hill, B., *The Lac Operon: A Short History of a Genetic Paradigm* (De Gruyter 1996).

155. Judson, H. F., *The Eighth Day of Creation* (Simon & Schuster, 1979), p. 418.
156. Ullmann, A., In memoriam: Jacques Monod (1910–1976). *Genome Biology and Evolution* 3: 1025–33 (2011), p. 1029.
157. Kresge, N., Simoni, R. D., and Hill, R., Earl W. Sutherland's discovery of cyclic adenine monophosphate and the second messenger system. *Journal of Biological Chemistry* 280: e39–40 (2005).
158. Hicks, J., Wartchow, E., and Mierau, G., Glycogen storage diseases: a brief review and update on clinical features, genetic abnormalities, pathologic features, and treatment. *Ultrastructural Pathology* 35: 183–96 (2011).
159. Rajfer, J., Discovery of NO in the penis. *International Journal of Impotence Research* 20: 431–6 (2008).
160. Rajfer, J., Discovery of NO in the penis. *International Journal of Impotence Research* 20: 431–6 (2008), p. 432.
161. Newman, R. H., Zhang, J., and Zhu, H., Toward a systems-level view of dynamic phosphorylation networks. *Frontiers in Genetics* 5: 263 (2014).
162. Sands, W. A. and Palmer, T. M., Regulating gene transcription in response to cyclic AMP elevation. *Cellular Signalling* 20: 460–6 (2008).
163. Villeda, S. A., Plambeck, K. E., Middeldorp, J., et al., Young blood reverses age-related impairments in cognitive function and synaptic plasticity in mice. *Nature Medicine* 20: 659–63 (2014).
164. Sample, I., Infusions of young blood may reverse effects of ageing, studies suggest, *The Guardian*, <http://www.theguardian.com/science/2014/may/04/young-blood-reverse-ageing-mice-studies> (2014).
165. Beckwith, J., Fifty years fused to lac. *Annual Review of Microbiology* 67: 1–19 (2013).
166. Kevles, D., Biologist at the barricades, *American Scientist*, <http://www.americanscientist.org/bookshelf/pub/biologist-at-the-barricades> (2003).
167. How the past informs the future, *Bright Boys*, <http://www.brightboys.org/PDF/Innovation_on_the_Verge.pdf> (2014).
168. Judson, H. F., *The Eighth Day of Creation* (Simon & Schuster, 1979), p. 588.
169. Judson, H. F., *The Eighth Day of Creation* (Simon & Schuster, 1979), p. 585.
170. Judson, H. F., *The Eighth Day of Creation* (Simon & Schuster, 1979), p. 590.
171. Watson, J. D., *Avoid Boring People and Other Lessons from a Life in Science* (Oxford University Press, 2007), pp. 257–8.
172. Burley, S. K., X-ray crystallographic studies of eukaryotic transcription initiation factors. *Philosophical Transactions of the Royal Society of London. Series B, Biological Sciences* 351: 483–9 (1996).
173. Gurdon, J. B. and Melton, D. A., Nuclear reprogramming in cells. *Science* 322: 1811–15 (2008).
174. Dahm, R., Friedrich Miescher and the discovery of DNA. *Developmental Biology* 278: 274–88 (2005).
175. Olins, D. E. and Olins, A. L., Chromatin history: our view from the bridge. *Nature Reviews Molecular Cell Biology* 4: 809–14 (2003).
176. Maddox, B., *Rosalind Franklin: The Dark Lady of DNA* (Harper, 2003), p. 229.
177. Travers, A. A. and Klug, A., The bending of DNA in nucleosomes and its wider implications. *Philosophical Transactions of the Royal Society B: Biological Sciences* 317: 537–61 (1987).
178. Klug, A., Aaron Klug's speech at the Nobel banquet, December 10, 1982, *Nobel Media*, <http://www.nobelprize.org/nobel_prizes/chemistry/laureates/1982/klug-speech.html> (1982).

179. Shahbazian, M. D. and Grunstein, M., Functions of site-specific histone acetylation and deacetylation. *Annual Review of Biochemistry* 76: 75–100 (2007).

180. Zimmer, C., E. coli: why I am in love with a bacterium, *The Telegraph*, <http://www.telegraph.co.uk/science/science-news/3345320/E.-coli-why-I-am-in-love-with-a-bacterium.html> (2008).

Chapter 4: The Spacious Genome

181. Hibbing, M. E., Fuqua, C., Parsek, M. R., and Peterson, S. B., Bacterial competition: surviving and thriving in the microbial jungle. *Nature Reviews Microbiology* 8: 15–25 (2010).

182. Lever, M. A., Rouxel, O., Alt, J. C., et al., Evidence for microbial carbon and sulfur cycling in deeply buried ridge flank basalt. *Science* 339: 1305–8 (2013).

183. Jayaraman, R., Jacques Monod and the advent of the age of operons. *Resonance* 15: 1084–96 (2010).

184. Weiss, R. A. and Vogt, P. K., 100 years of Rous sarcoma virus. *The Journal of Experimental Medicine* 208: 2351–5 (2011).

185. Mammas, I. N., Sourvinos, G., and Spandidos, D. A., The paediatric story of human papillomavirus. *Oncology Letters* 8: 502–6 (2014).

186. Khoury, G. and Gruss, P., Enhancer elements. *Cell* 33: 313–14 (1983).

187. Shlyueva, D., Stampfel, G., and Stark, A., Transcriptional enhancers: from properties to genome-wide predictions. *Nature Reviews Genetics* 15: 272–86 (2014).

188. Nowotschin, S. and Hadjantonakis, A. K., Cellular dynamics in the early mouse embryo: from axis formation to gastrulation. *Current Opinion in Genetics & Development* 20: 420–7 (2010).

189. Blum, M., Feistel, K., Thumberger, T., and Schweickert, A., The evolution and conservation of left-right patterning mechanisms. *Development* 141: 1603–13 (2014).

190. Notable persons with situs inversus, *My Hallucination*, <http://srsekhar.blogspot.co.uk/2008/10/notable-persons-with-situs-inversus.html> (2008).

191. Unique anatomy: situs inversus and interrupted IVC, *Into Another World*, <http://susanleighnoble.wordpress.com/2013/05/20/unique-anatomy-situs-inversus-interrupted-ivc/> (2013).

192. One-year-old Indian boy breaks world record after being born with THIRTY FOUR fingers and toes, *The Daily Mail*, <http://www.dailymail.co.uk/news/article-2018470/Akshat-Saxena-Indian-boy-born-34-fingers-toes-breaks-world-record.html> (2011).

193. Mallo, M., Wellik, D. M., and Deschamps, J., Hox genes and regional patterning of the vertebrate body plan. *Developmental Biology* 344: 7–15 (2010).

194. Smith, E. and Shilatifard, A., Enhancer biology and enhanceropathies. *Nature Structural & Molecular Biology* 21: 210–19 (2014).

195. Levine, M., Cattoglio, C., and Tjian, R., Looping back to leap forward: transcription enters a new era. *Cell* 157: 13–25 (2014).

196. Gregory, T. R., Coincidence, coevolution, or causation? DNA content, cell size, and the C-value enigma. *Biological Reviews* 76: 65–101 (2001).

197. Zimmer, C., The Case for Junk DNA, *National Geographic*, <http://phenomena.nationalgeographic.com/2014/05/09/the-case-for-junk-dna/> (2014).

198. Sharp, P. A., The discovery of split genes and RNA splicing. *Trends in Biochemical Sciences* 30: 279–81 (2005).

199. Breathnach, R. and Chambon, P., Organization and expression of eukaryotic split genes coding for proteins. *Annual Review of Biochemistry* 50: 349–83 (1981).
200. Hertel, K. J., Combinatorial control of exon recognition. *The Journal of Biological Chemistry* 283: 1211–15 (2008).
201. Gamazon, E. R. and Stranger, B. E., Genomics of alternative splicing: evolution, development and pathophysiology. *Human Genetics* 133: 679–87 (2014).
202. Halaby, D. M., Poupon, A., and Mornon, J. P., The immunoglobulin fold family: sequence analysis and 3D structure comparisons. *Protein Engineering* 12: 563–71 (1999).
203. Peterson, M. L., Mechanisms controlling production of membrane and secreted immunoglobulin during B cell development. *Immunologic Research* 37: 33–46 (2007).
204. Warner, B., Charles Darwin and John Herschel. *South African Journal of Science* 105: 432–3 (2009).
205. Hoyle, F., *Intelligent Universe: A New View of Creation and Evolution* (Michael Joseph Ltd., 1983).
206. Liu, M. and Grigoriev, A., Protein domains correlate strongly with exons in multiple eukaryotic genomes—evidence of exon shuffling? *Trends in Genetics: TIG* 20: 399–403 (2004).
207. Lewandowska, M. A., The missing puzzle piece: splicing mutations. *International Journal of Clinical and Experimental Pathology* 6: 2675–82 (2013).
208. Kaplan, F., Tay–Sachs disease carrier screening: a model for prevention of genetic disease. *Genetic Testing* 2: 271–92 (1998).
209. Mahuran, D. J., Biochemical consequences of mutations causing the GM2 gangliosidoses. *Biochimica et Biophysica Acta* 1455: 105–38 (1999).
210. George, A., The rabbi's dilemma, *New Scientist*, <http://www.newscientist.com/article/mg18124345.400-the-rabbis-dilemma.html?full=true#.VAg-Jo10wuQ> (2004).
211. Sanger, F., Sequences, sequences, and sequences. *Annual Reviews in Biochemistry* 57: 1–28 (1988).
212. Sulston, J. and Ferry, G., *The Common Thread* (Corgi, 2009).
213. Ohno, S., So much 'junk' DNA in our genome. *Brookhaven Symposium on Biology* 23: 366–70 (1972).
214. Dawkins, R., *The Selfish Gene: 30th Anniversary Edition* (Oxford University Press, 2006), p. 45.
215. Orgel, L. E. and Crick, F. H., Selfish DNA: the ultimate parasite. *Nature* 284: 604–7 (1980).
216. Clark, K. R., *Religion and the Sciences of Origins* (Palgrave Macmillan, 2014), p. 65.
217. Lamb, T. D., Collin, S. P., and Pugh, E. N., Jr., Evolution of the vertebrate eye: opsins, photoreceptors, retina and eye cup. *Nature Reviews Neuroscience* 8: 960–76 (2007).
218. Gould, S. J., *The Panda's Thumb: More Reflections in Natural History* (Penguin, 1990).
219. Dawkins, R., *The Greatest Show on Earth: The Evidence for Evolution* (Black Swan, 2010), p. 332.
220. Miller, K. R., Life's grand design. *Technology Review*, <http://www.millerandlevine.com/km/evol/lgd/> (1994).

Chapter 5: RNA Out of the Shadows

221. Darwin, C., *Origin of Species* (John Murray, 1859), p. 484.
222. Follmann, H. and Brownson, C., Darwin's warm little pond revisited: from molecules to the origin of life. *Die Naturwissenschaften* 96: 1265–92 (2009), p. 1265.
223. Tirard, S., Origin of life and definition of life, from Buffon to Oparin. *Origins of Life and Evolution of the Biosphere: The Journal of the International Society for the Study of the Origin of Life* 40: 215–20 (2010).

224. Miller, S. L. and Urey, H. C., Origin of life. *Science* 130: 1622–4 (1959).
225. Pääbo, S., *Neanderthal Man* (Basic Books, 2014).
226. Neveu, M., Kim, H. J., and Benner, S. A., The 'strong' RNA world hypothesis: fifty years old. *Astrobiology* 13: 391–403 (2013).
227. Staley, J. P. and Woolford, J. L., Jr., Assembly of ribosomes and spliceosomes: complex ribonucleoprotein machines. *Current Opinion in Cell Biology* 21: 109–18 (2009).
228. An introduction to enzymes, *Broad Institute*, <http://www.broadinstitute.org/~rivas/www/Biochem/enz.pdf> (2014).
229. Cech, T. R., Nobel lecture. Self-splicing and enzymatic activity of an intervening sequence RNA from Tetrahymena. *Bioscience Reports* 10: 239–61 (1990).
230. Altman, S., Nobel lecture. Enzymatic cleavage of RNA by RNA. *Bioscience Reports* 10: 317–37 (1990).
231. Korostelev, A. and Noller, H. F., The ribosome in focus: new structures bring new insights. *Trends in Biochemical Sciences* 32: 434–41 (2007).
232. Sidney Altman—biographical, *Nobel Media*, <http://www.nobelprize.org/nobel_prizes/chemistry/laureates/1989/altman-bio.html> (1989).
233. Levin, R. C., *The Work of the University* (Yale University Press, 2008), p. 42.
234. Ellington, A. D., Chen, X., Robertson, M., and Syrett, A., Evolutionary origins and directed evolution of RNA. *The International Journal of Biochemistry & Cell Biology* 41: 254–65 (2009).
235. Faculty Member—Jack Szostak, *Harvard University*, <http://dms.hms.harvard.edu/bbs/fac/Szostak.php> (2014).
236. Deamer, D. W., Origins of life: how leaky were primitive cells? *Nature* 454: 37–8 (2008).
237. Watson, J. D., *DNA* (Arrow Books, 2004), p. 81.
238. Napoli, C., Lemieux, C., and Jorgensen, R., Introduction of a chimeric chalcone synthase gene into petunia results in reversible co-suppression of homologous genes in trans. *The Plant Cell* 2: 279–89 (1990).
239. Billmyre, R. B., Calo, S., Feretzaki, M., et al., RNAi function, diversity, and loss in the fungal kingdom. *Chromosome Research: An International Journal on the Molecular, Supramolecular and Evolutionary Aspects of Chromosome Biology* 21: 561–72 (2013).
240. Sommer, R. J. and Bumbarger, D. J., Nematode model systems in evolution and development. *Wiley Interdisciplinary Reviews. Developmental Biology* 1: 389–400 (2012).
241. Putcha, G. V. and Johnson, E. M., 'Men are but worms': neuronal cell death in C. elegans and vertebrates. *Cell Death and Differentiation* 11: 38–48 (2004).
242. Shaikh, S. and Leonard-Amodeo, J., The deviating eyes of Michelangelo's David. *Journal of the Royal Society of Medicine* 98: 75–6 (2005), p. 75.
243. Fire, A., Xu, S., Montgomery, M. K., et al., Potent and specific genetic interference by double-stranded RNA in Caenorhabditis elegans. *Nature* 391: 806–11 (1998).
244. Craig C. Mello—biographical, *Nobel Media*, <http://www.nobelprize.org/nobel_prizes/medicine/laureates/2006/mello-bio.html> (2006).
245. Kurreck, J., RNA interference: from basic research to therapeutic applications. *Angewandte Chemie* 48: 1378–98 (2009).
246. Conger, K., Andrew Fire wins 2006 Nobel Prize in Physiology or Medicine, *Stanford University News Service*, <http://news.stanford.edu/pr/2006/pr-nobel-100206.html> (2006).
247. Campeau, E. and Gobeil, S., RNA interference in mammals: behind the screen. *Briefings in Functional Genomics* 10: 215–26 (2011).

248. Espiritu, M. J., Collier, A. C., and Bingham, J. P., A twenty-first-century approach to age-old problems: the ascension of biologics in clinical therapeutics. *Drug Discovery Today* 19: 1109–13 (2014).

249. Zhou, Y., Zhang, C., and Liang, W., Development of RNAi technology for targeted therapy—a track of siRNA based agents to RNAi therapeutics. *Journal of Controlled Release: Official Journal of the Controlled Release Society* 193: 270–81 (2014).

250. Incarbone, M. and Dunoyer, P., RNA silencing and its suppression: novel insights from in planta analyses. *Trends in Plant Science* 18: 382–92 (2013).

251. Sun, K. and Lai, E. C., Adult-specific functions of animal microRNAs. *Nature Reviews Genetics* 14: 535–48 (2013).

252. Watanabe, T. and Lin, H., Posttranscriptional regulation of gene expression by piwi proteins and piRNAs. *Molecular Cell* 56: 18–27 (2014).

253. Kapusta, A. and Feschotte, C., Volatile evolution of long noncoding RNA repertoires: mechanisms and biological implications. *Trends in Genetics* 30: 439–52 (2014).

254. Arora, S., Rana, R., Chhabra, A., et al., miRNA-transcription factor interactions: a combinatorial regulation of gene expression. *Molecular Genetics and Genomics* 288: 77–87 (2013).

255. Gama Sosa, M. A., De Gasperi, R., and Elder, G. A., Animal transgenesis: an overview. *Brain Structure & Function* 214: 91–109 (2010).

256. Van den Driesche, S., Sharpe, R. M., Saunders, P. T., and Mitchell, R. T., Regulation of the germ stem cell niche as the foundation for adult spermatogenesis: a role for miRNAs? *Seminars in Cell & Developmental Biology* 29: 76–83 (2014).

257. Undi, R. B., Kandi, R., and Gutti, R. K., MicroRNAs as haematopoiesis regulators. *Advances in Hematology* 2013: 695754 (2013).

258. Hesselberth, J. R., Lives that introns lead after splicing. *Wiley Interdisciplinary Reviews in RNA* 4: 677–91 (2013).

Chapter 6: It's a Jungle in There!

259. Rose, H. and Rose, S., *Genes, Cells and Brains* (Verso, 2012), p. 25.

260. Consortium, T. E. P., An integrated encyclopedia of DNA elements in the human genome. *Nature* 489: 57–74 (2012).

261. Brenner, S. Loose ends. *Current Biology* 5: 332 (1995).

262. Johnson, J. M., Edwards, S., Shoemaker, D., and Schadt, E. E., Dark matter in the genome: evidence of widespread transcription detected by microarray tiling experiments. *Trends in Genetics* 21: 93–102 (2005).

263. Ostriker, J. P. and Steinhardt, P., New light on dark matter. *Science* 300: 1909–13 (2003).

264. Sample, I., Dark matter may have been detected—streaming from the sun's core, *The Guardian*, <http://www.theguardian.com/science/2014/oct/16/dark-matter-detected-sun-axions> (2014).

265. Thomas, D. J., Rosenbloom, K. R., Clawson, H., et al., The ENCODE Project at UC Santa Cruz. *Nucleic Acids Research* 35: D663–7 (2007).

266. Rothbart, S. B. and Strahl, B. D., Interpreting the language of histone and DNA modifications. *Biochimica et Biophysica Acta* 1839: 627–43 (2014).

267. Dogini, D. B., Pascoal, V. D. B., Avansini, S. H., et al., The new world of RNAs. *Genetics and Molecular Biology* 37: 285–93 (2014).

268. Yong, E., ENCODE: the rough guide to the human genome, *Discover Magazine*, <http://blogs.discovermagazine.com/notrocketscience/2012/09/05/encode-the-rough-guide-to-the-human-genome/#.VAS6QsVdXh4> (2012).

269. Pennisi, E., Genomics. ENCODE project writes eulogy for junk DNA, *Science* 337: 1159–61 (2012), p. 1159.

270. Pennisi, E., Genomics. ENCODE project writes eulogy for junk DNA, *Science* 337: 1159–61 (2012), p. 1161.

271. Visscher, P. M., Brown, M. A., McCarthy, M. I., and Yang, J., Five years of GWAS discovery. *American Journal of Human Genetics* 90: 7–24 (2012).

272. Van der Sijde, M. R., Ng, A., and Fu, J., Systems genetics: from GWAS to disease pathways. *Biochimica et Biophysica Acta* 1842: 1903–1909 (2014).

273. Stamatoyannopoulos, J. A., What does our genome encode? *Genome Research* 22: 1602–11 (2012).

274. Whipple, T. and Parrington, J., Rummage through 'junk' DNA finds vital material, *The Times*, <http://www.thetimes.co.uk/tto/science/genetics/article3529618.ece> (2012).

275. Ward, L. D. and Kellis, M., Evidence of abundant purifying selection in humans for recently acquired regulatory functions. *Science* 337: 1675–8 (2012).

276. Graur, D., Zheng, Y., Price, N., et al., On the immortality of television sets: 'function' in the human genome according to the evolution-free gospel of ENCODE, *Genome Biology and Evolution* 5: 578–90 (2013).

277. Graur, D., Zheng, Y., Price, N., et al., On the immortality of television sets: 'function' in the human genome according to the evolution-free gospel of ENCODE, *Genome Biology and Evolution* 5: 578–90 (2013), p. 578.

278. McKie, R., Scientists attacked over claim that 'junk DNA' is vital to life, *The Guardian*, <http://www.theguardian.com/science/2013/feb/24/scientists-attacked-over-junk-dna-claim> (2013).

279. Bhattacharjee, Y., The vigilante. *Science* 343: 1306–9 (2014).

280. Spencer, G., New Genome Comparison Finds Chimps, Humans Very Similar at the DNA Level, *National Human Genome Research Institute*, <http://www.genome.gov/15515096> (2005).

281. Why mouse matters, *National Human Genome Research Institute*, <http://www.genome.gov/10001345> (2010).

282. DNA, *Natural History Museum*, <http://www.nhm.ac.uk/nature-online/evolution/what-is-the-evidence/morphology/dna-molecules/> (2014).

283. Haerty, W. and Ponting, C. P., No gene in the genome makes sense except in the light of evolution. *Annual Review of Genomics and Human Genetics* 15: 71–92 (2014).

284. Graur, D., Zheng, Y., Price, N., et al., On the immortality of television sets: 'function' in the human genome according to the evolution-free gospel of ENCODE, *Genome Biology and Evolution* 5: 578–90 (2013), p. 579.

285. Graur, D., Zheng, Y., Price, N., et al., On the immortality of television sets: 'function' in the human genome according to the evolution-free gospel of ENCODE, *Genome Biology and Evolution* 5: 578–90 (2013), p. 587.

286. Top 10 most expensive military planes, *TIME*, <http://content.time.com/time/photogallery/0,29307,1912203_1913325,00.html> (2014).

287. Bhattacharjee, Y., The vigilante. *Science* 343: 1306–9 (2014), p. 1309.

288. Gregory, T. R., *BBC interview with Ewan Birney*, *Genomicron*, <http://www.genomicron.evolverzone.com/2013/04/bbc-interview-with-ewan-birney/> (2013).

289. Mattick, J. S. and Dinger, M. E., The extent of functionality in the human genome. *The HUGO Journal* 7: 1–4 (2013).

290. Mattick, J. S. and Dinger, M. E., The extent of functionality in the human genome. *The HUGO Journal* 7: 1–4 (2013), p. 3.

291. Pheasant, M. and Mattick, J. S., Raising the estimate of functional human sequences. *Genome Research* 17: 1245–53 (2007), p. 1250.

292. Lewis, D., What is our junk DNA for?, *Cosmos Magazine*, <https://cosmosmagazine.com/life-sciences/what-our-junk-dna> (2014).

293. Morris, K. V. and Mattick, J. S., The rise of regulatory RNA. *Nature Reviews Genetics* 15: 423–37 (2014), p. 432.

294. Keller, E. F., From gene action to reactive genomes, *The Journal of Physiology* 592: 2423–9 (2014), p. 2425.

Chapter 7: The Genome in 3D

295. How many chromosomes do people have?, *Genetics Home Reference*, <http://ghr.nlm.nih.gov/handbook/basics/howmanychromosomes> (2014).

296. Yong, E., Getting to Know the Genome, *The Scientist*, <http://www.the-scientist.com/?articles.view/articleNo/32583/title/Getting-to-Know-the-Genome/> (2012).

297. Ayala, F. J., 'Nothing in biology makes sense except in the light of evolution': Theodosius Dobzhansky: 1900–1975. *Journal of Heredity* 68: 3–10 (1977), p. 3.

298. Hall, E., Reading maps of the genes: interpreting the spatiality of genetic knowledge. *Health & Place* 9: 151–61 (2003).

299. Paweletz, N., Walther Flemming: pioneer of mitosis research. *Nature Reviews Molecular and Cellular Biology* 2: 72–5 (2001).

300. Lavelle, C., Pack, unpack, bend, twist, pull, push: the physical side of gene expression. *Current Opinion in Genetics & Development* 25: 74–84 (2014).

301. Cremer, T. and Cremer, M., Chromosome territories. *Cold Spring Harbor Perspectives in Biology* 2: a003889 (2010).

302. Rodriguez, A. and Bjerling, P., The links between chromatin spatial organization and biological function. *Biochemical Society Transactions* 41: 1634–9 (2013).

303. Dahm, R., Friedrich Miescher and the discovery of DNA. *Developmental Biology* 278: 274–88 (2005).

304. Morinière, J., Rousseaux, S., Steuerwald, U., et al. Cooperative binding of two acetylation marks on a histone tail by a single bromodomain. *Nature* 461: 664–8 (2009).

305. Putting the squeeze on sperm DNA: streamlined sperm offer new way to read histone code, *Science Daily*, <http://www.sciencedaily.com/releases/2009/09/090930132652.htm> (2009).

306. Hammoud, S. S., Nix, D. A., Zhang, H., et al., Distinctive chromatin in human sperm packages genes for embryo development. *Nature* 460: 473–8 (2009).

307. Gibcus, J. H. and Dekker, J. The hierarchy of the 3D genome. *Molecular Cell* 49: 773–82 (2013).

308. Bishop, R., Applications of fluorescence *in situ* hybridization (FISH) in detecting genetic aberrations of medical significance. *Bioscience Horizons* 3: 85–95 (2010).

309. Berardi, M. J. and Fantin, V. R., Survival of the fittest: metabolic adaptations in cancer. *Current Opinion in Genetics & Development* 21: 59–66 (2011).

310. Liehr, T., Starke, H., Weise, A., et al., Multicolor FISH probe sets and their applications. *Histology and Histopathology* 19: 229–37 (2004).

311. Klonisch, T., Wark, L., Hombach-Klonisch, S., and Mai, S., Nuclear imaging in three dimensions: a unique tool in cancer research. *Annals of Anatomy = Anatomischer Anzeiger: Official Organ of the Anatomische Gesellschaft* 192: 292–301 (2010).

312. Tchélidzé, P., Chatron-Colliet, A., Thiry, M., et al., Tomography of the cell nucleus using confocal microscopy and medium voltage electron microscopy. *Critical Reviews in Oncology/Hematology* 69: 127–43 (2009).

313. Gorkin, D. U., Leung, D., and Ren, B., The 3D genome in transcriptional regulation and pluripotency. *Cell Stem Cell* 14: 762–75 (2014).

314. Zimmer, M., *Glowing Genes: A Revolution in Biotechnology* (Prometheus Books, 2005).

315. Tsien, R. Y., The green fluorescent protein. *Annual Review of Biochemistry* 67: 509–44 (1998).

316. Tsien, R. Y., Intracellular signal transduction in four dimensions: from molecular design to physiology. *Bowditch Lecture*, C723–C728 (1992).

317. Giepmans, B. N., Adams, S. R., Ellisman, M. H., and Tsien, R. Y., The fluorescent toolbox for assessing protein location and function. *Science* 312: 217–24 (2006).

318. Roger Y. Tsien's speech at the Nobel banquet, *Nobel Media*, <http://www.nobelprize.org/nobel_prizes/chemistry/laureates/2008/tsien-speech_en.html?print=1#.U_0AqMVdXh5> (2008).

319. How bad luck and bad networking cost Douglas Prasher a Nobel Prize, *Discover Magazine*, <http://discovermagazine.com/2011/apr/30-how-bad-luck-networking-cost-prasher-nobel> (2011).

320. Annibale, P. and Gratton, E., Advanced fluorescence microscopy methods for the real-time study of transcription and chromatin dynamics. *Transcription* 5: e28425 (2014).

321. Hou, C. and Corces, V. G., Throwing transcription for a loop: expression of the genome in the 3D nucleus. *Chromosoma* 121: 107–16 (2012).

322. Smallwood, A. and Ren, B., Genome organization and long-range regulation of gene expression by enhancers. *Current Opinion in Cell Biology* 25: 387–94 (2013).

323. Levine, M., Cattoglio, C., and Tjian, R., Looping back to leap forward: transcription enters a new era. *Cell* 157: 13–25 (2014).

324. Lai, F. and Shiekhattar, R., Enhancer RNAs: the new molecules of transcription. *Current Opinion in Genetics & Development* 25: 38–42 (2014).

325. Vance, K. W. and Ponting, C. P., Transcriptional regulatory functions of nuclear long noncoding RNAs. *Trends in Genetics* 30: 348–55 (2014).

326. Mercer, T. R., Edwards, S. L., Clark, M. B., et al., DNase I-hypersensitive exons colocalize with promoters and distal regulatory elements. *Nature Genetics* 45: 852–9 (2013).

327. Heather, A. The genome's 3D structure shapes how genes are expressed, *Garvan Institute*, <http://www.garvan.org.au/news-events/news/the-genome2019s-3d-structure-shapes-how-genes-are-expressed> (2013).

328. Papantonis, A. and Cook, P. R., Transcription factories: genome organization and gene regulation. *Chemical Reviews* 113: 8683–705 (2013).

329. Schoenfelder, S., Sexton, T., Chakalova, L., et al., Preferential associations between co-regulated genes reveal a transcriptional interactome in erythroid cells. *Nature Genetics* 42: 53–61 (2010).

330. Dean, A., In the loop: long range chromatin interactions and gene regulation. *Briefings in Functional Genomics* 10: 3–10 (2011).

331. Strandberg, B., Dickerson, R. E., and Rossmann, M. G., 50 years of protein structure analysis. *Journal of Molecular Biology* 392: 2–32 (2009).

332. Higgs, D. R., Engel, J. D., and Stamatoyannopoulos, G., Thalassaemia. *The Lancet* 379: 373–83 (2012).

333. Ginder, G. D., Epigenetic regulation of fetal globin gene expression in adult erythroid cells. *Translational Research: the journal of laboratory and clinical medicine* (2014).

334. Blanpain, C., Tracing the cellular origin of cancer. *Nature Cell Biology* 15: 126–34 (2013).

335. Nambiar, M., Kari, V., and Raghavan, S. C., Chromosomal translocations in cancer. *Biochimica et Biophysica Acta* 1786: 139–52 (2008).

336. Schwartz, M. and Hakim, O., 3D view of chromosomes, DNA damage, and translocations. *Current Opinion in Genetics & Development* 25: 118–25 (2014).

337. Deng, B., Melnik, S., and Cook, P. R., Transcription factories, chromatin loops, and the dysregulation of gene expression in malignancy. *Seminars in Cancer Biology* 23: 65–71 (2013).

338. Worman, H. J., Ostlund, C., and Wang, Y., Diseases of the nuclear envelope. *Cold Spring Harbor Perspectives in Biology* 2: a000760 (2010).

Chapter 8: The Jumping Genes

339. Keller, E. F., *A Feeling for the Organism: The Life and Work of Barbara McClintock* (W.H. Freeman and Company, 1983), p. 125.

340. Keller, E. F., *A Feeling for the Organism: The Life and Work of Barbara McClintock* (W.H. Freeman and Company, 1983), p. 30.

341. Keller, E. F., *A Feeling for the Organism: The Life and Work of Barbara McClintock* (W.H. Freeman and Company, 1983), p. 55.

342. Zakian, V. A., Telomeres: the beginnings and ends of eukaryotic chromosomes. *Experimental Cell Research* 318: 1456–60 (2012).

343. Jaskelioff, M., Muller, F. L., Paik, J.-H., et al., Telomerase reactivation reverses tissue degeneration in aged telomerase-deficient mice. *Nature* 469: 102–6 (2011).

344. Forêt de Paimpont, *France for Visitors*, <http://france-for-visitors.com/brittany/foret-de-paimpont.html> (2014).

345. Callaway, E., Telomerase reverses ageing process, *Nature News*, <http://www.nature.com/news/2010/101128/full/news.2010.635.html> (2010).

346. Cullen, J. H., *Barbara McClintock* (Chelsea House, 2003), p. 66.

347. Cox, K. H., Bonthuis, P. J., and Rissman, E. F., Mouse model systems to study sex chromosome genes and behavior: relevance to humans. *Frontiers in Neuroendocrinology* 35: 405–19 (2014).

348. Jones, K. T., Meiosis in oocytes: predisposition to aneuploidy and its increased incidence with age. *Human Reproduction Update* 14: 143–58 (2008).

349. Rebollo, R., Romanish, M. T., and Mager, D. L., Transposable elements: an abundant and natural source of regulatory sequences for host genes. *Annual Review of Genetics* 46: 21–42 (2012).

350. Keller, E. F., *A Feeling for the Organism: The Life and Work of Barbara McClintock* (W.H. Freeman and Company, 1983), pp. 175–8.

351. Keller, E. F., *A Feeling for the Organism: The Life and Work of Barbara McClintock* (W.H. Freeman and Company, 1983), p. 142.

352. O'Donnell, K. A. and Burns, K. H., Mobilizing diversity: transposable element insertions in genetic variation and disease. *Mobile DNA* 1: 21 (2010).

353. Ayarpadikannan, S. and Kim, H. S., The impact of transposable elements in genome evolution and genetic instability and their implications in various diseases. *Genomics and Informatics* 12: 98–104 (2014).

354. Weiss, R. A., On the concept and elucidation of endogenous retroviruses. *Philosophical Transactions of the Royal Society of London. Series B, Biological Sciences* 368: 20120494 (2013).

355. Lippincott, S., *David Baltimore: interviewed by Sara Lippincott*, <http://oralhistories.library.caltech.edu/168/1/Baltimore,D._OHO.pdf> (2009).

356. Boeke, J. D., The unusual phylogenetic distribution of retrotransposons: a hypothesis. *Genome Research* 13: 1975–83 (2003).

357. Alzohairy, A. M., Gyulai, G., Jansen, R. K., and Bahieldin, A., Transposable elements domesticated and neofunctionalized by eukaryotic genomes. *Plasmid* 69: 1–15 (2013).

358. Orgel, L. E. and Crick, F. H., Selfish DNA: the ultimate parasite. *Nature* 284: 604–7 (1980), p. 605.

359. Huang, C. R., Burns, K. H., and Boeke, J. D., Active transposition in genomes. *Annual Review of Genetics* 46: 651–75 (2012).

360. Claeys Bouuaert, C., Lipkow, K., Andrews, S. S., et al., The autoregulation of a eukaryotic DNA transposon. *eLife* 2: e00668 (2013).

361. Thorne, E. Why our prehistoric, parasitic 'jumping' genes don't send us into meltdown, *University of Nottingham*, <http://www.nottingham.ac.uk/news/pressreleases/2013/june/why-our-prehistoric,-parasitic-jumping-genes-dont-send-us-into-meltdown.aspx> (2013).

362. Vence, T., 'Sleeping Beauty' named Molecule of the Year, *BioTechniques*, <http://www.biotechniques.com/news/Sleeping-Beauty-named-Molecule-of-theyear/biotechniques-187068.html> (2010).

363. Leslie, M., The immune system's compact genetic counterpart. *Science* 339: 25–7 (2013).

364. Iguchi, Y., Katsuno, M., Ikenaka, K., et al., Amyotrophic lateral sclerosis: an update on recent genetic insights. *Journal of Neurology* 260: 2917–27 (2013).

365. Li, W., Jin, Y., Prazak, L., et al., Transposable elements in TDP-43-mediated neurodegenerative disorders. *PLoS One* 7: e44099 (2012).

366. Storm of 'awakened' transposons may cause brain-cell pathologies in ALS, other illnesses, *Science Daily*, <http://www.sciencedaily.com/releases/2012/09/120906123238.htm> (2012).

367. Dupressoir, A., Lavialle, C., and Heidmann, T., From ancestral infectious retroviruses to bona fide cellular genes: role of the captured syncytins in placentation. *Placenta* 33: 663–71 (2012), p. 663.

368. Halaby, D. M., Poupon, A., and Mornon, J. P., The immunoglobulin fold family: sequence analysis and 3D structure comparisons. *Protein Engineering* 12: 563–71 (1999).

369. Fugmann, S. D., The origins of the Rag genes—from transposition to V(D)J recombination. *Seminars in Immunology* 22: 10–16 (2010).

370. Reilly, M. T., Faulkner, G. J., Dubnau, J., et al., The role of transposable elements in health and diseases of the central nervous system. *The Journal of Neuroscience* 33: 17577–86 (2013).

371. Lupski, J. R., Genetics: genome mosaicism—one human, multiple genomes. *Science* 341: 358–9 (2013).

372. Platt, R. N. 2nd, Vandewege, M. W., Kern, C., et al. Large numbers of novel miRNAs originate from DNA transposons and are coincident with a large species radiation in bats. *Molecular Biology and Evolution* 31: 1536–45 (2014).

373. *Science Daily*, <http://www.sciencedaily.com/releases/2014/04/140401173134.htm> (2014).

374. Stindl, R., The telomeric sync model of speciation: species-wide telomere erosion triggers cycles of transposon-mediated genomic rearrangements, which underlie the saltatory appearance of nonadaptive characters. *Die Naturwissenschaften* 101: 163–86 (2014).

375. Britten, R. J., Transposable element insertions have strongly affected human evolution. *Proceedings of the National Academy of Sciences of the United States of America* 107: 19945–8 (2010).

376. Jorgensen, R. A., Restructuring the genome in response to adaptive challenge: McClintock's bold conjecture revisited. *Cold Spring Harbor Symposia on Quantitative Biology* 69: 349–54 (2004), p. 349.

Chapter 9: The Marks of Lamarck

377. Bard, J. B., The next evolutionary synthesis: from Lamarck and Darwin to genomic variation and systems biology. *Cell Communication and Signaling: CCS* 9: 30 (2011).

378. Honeywill, R., *Lamarck's Evolution: Two Centuries of Genius and Jealousy* (Murdoch Books, 2008), p. 6.

379. Darwin, C., *Origin of Species* (John Murray, 1869). p. xv.

380. Cuvier, G., Elegy of Lamarck, *The Victorian Web*, <http://www.victorianweb.org/science/science_texts/cuvier/cuvier_on_lamarck.htm> (2014).

381. Handel, A. E. and Ramagopalan, S. V., Is Lamarckian evolution relevant to medicine? *BMC Medical Genetics* 11: 73 (2010).

382. Bowler, P. J., *Evolution: The History of an Idea* (University of California Press, 2003).

383. Cavalier-Smith, T., Cell evolution and Earth history: stasis and revolution. *Philosophical Transactions of the Royal Society of London. Series B, Biological Sciences* 361: 969–1006 (2006).

384. Desmond, A. and Moore, J. R., *Darwin* (Michael Joseph, 1991), p. 286.

385. Shermer, M., *In Darwin's Shadow* (Oxford University Press, 2002), p. 45.

386. Koonin, E. V., Calorie restriction a Lamarck. *Cell* 158: 237–8 (2014), p. 238.

387. Slack, J. M., Conrad Hal Waddington: the last Renaissance biologist? *Nature Reviews Genetics* 3: 889–95 (2002).

388. Badano, J. L. and Katsanis, N., Beyond Mendel: an evolving view of human genetic disease transmission. *Nature Reviews Genetics* 3: 779–89 (2002).

389. Berridge, M. J., Bootman, M. D., and Roderick, H. L., Calcium signalling: dynamics, homeostasis and remodelling. *Nature Reviews Molecular Cell Biology* 4: 517–29 (2003).

390. Roseboom, T. J., van der Meulen, J. H., Ravelli, A. C., et al., Effects of prenatal exposure to the Dutch famine on adult disease in later life: an overview. *Molecular and Cellular Endocrinology* 185: 93–8 (2001).

391. Carey, N., *Beyond DNA: epigenetics*, http://www.naturalhistorymag.com/features/142195/beyond-dna-epigenetics (2012).

392. Pembrey, M. E., Male-line transgenerational responses in humans. *Human Fertility* 13: 268–71 (2010).

393. Choudhuri, S., From Waddington's epigenetic landscape to small noncoding RNA: some important milestones in the history of epigenetics research. *Toxicology Mechanisms and Methods* 21: 252–74 (2011).

394. Rothbart, S. B. and Strahl, B. D., Interpreting the language of histone and DNA modifications. *Biochimica et Biophysica Acta* 1839: 627–43 (2014).

395. Nakagawa, S. and Kageyama, Y., Nuclear lncRNAs as epigenetic regulators—beyond skepticism. *Biochimica et Biophysica Acta* 1839: 215–22 (2014).

396. Boland, M. J., Nazor, K. L., and Loring, J. F., Epigenetic regulation of pluripotency and differentiation. *Circulation Research* 115: 311–24 (2014).

397. Rothbart, S. B. and Strahl, B. D., Interpreting the language of histone and DNA modifications. *Biochimica et Biophysica Acta* 1839: 627–43 (2014).

398. Peters, J., The role of genomic imprinting in biology and disease: an expanding view. *Nature Reviews Genetics* 15: 517–30 (2014).

399. Zucchi, F. C., Yao, Y., and Metz, G. A., The secret language of destiny: stress imprinting and transgenerational origins of disease. *Frontiers in Genetics* 3: 96 (2012).

400. Narbonne, P., Miyamoto, K., and Gurdon, J. B., Reprogramming and development in nuclear transfer embryos and in interspecific systems. *Current Opinion in Genetics & Development* 22: 450–8 (2012).

401. Tammen, S. A., Friso, S., and Choi, S. W., Epigenetics: the link between nature and nurture. *Molecular Aspects of Medicine* 34: 753–64 (2013).

402. Griffiths, B. B. and Hunter, R. G., Neuroepigenetics of stress. *Neuroscience* 275C: 420–35 (2014).

403. Mitchell, C., Hobcraft, J., McLanahan, S. S., et al., Social disadvantage, genetic sensitivity, and children's telomere length. *Proceedings of the National Academy of Sciences of the United States of America* 111: 5944–9 (2014).

404. Campos, E. I., Stafford, J. M., and Reinberg, D., Epigenetic inheritance: histone bookmarks across generations. *Trends in Cell Biology* 24: 664–74 (2014).

405. Hughes, V., The sins of the father. *Nature* 507: 22–4 (2014).

406. Gapp, K., Jawaid, A., Sarkies, P., et al., Implication of sperm RNAs in transgenerational inheritance of the effects of early trauma in mice. *Nature Neuroscience* 17: 667–9 (2014).

407. Smythies, J., Edelstein, L., and Ramachandran, V., Molecular mechanisms for the inheritance of acquired characteristics-exosomes, microRNA shuttling, fear and stress: Lamarck resurrected? *Frontiers in Genetics* 5: 133 (2014).

408. Koonin, E. V., Calorie restriction a Lamarck. *Cell* 158: 237–8 (2014), p. 238.

409. Koonin, E. V., Calorie restriction a Lamarck. *Cell* 158: 237–8 (2014), p. 237.

410. Stindl, R., The telomeric sync model of speciation: species-wide telomere erosion triggers cycles of transposon-mediated genomic rearrangements, which underlie the saltatory appearance of nonadaptive characters. *Die Naturwissenschaften* 101: 163–86 (2014).

411. Stindl, R., The telomeric sync model of speciation: species-wide telomere erosion triggers cycles of transposon-mediated genomic rearrangements, which underlie the saltatory appearance of nonadaptive characters. *Die Naturwissenschaften* 101: 163–86 (2014), p. 173.

412. Stindl, R., The telomeric sync model of speciation: species-wide telomere erosion triggers cycles of transposon-mediated genomic rearrangements, which underlie the saltatory appearance of nonadaptive characters. *Die Naturwissenschaften* 101: 163–86 (2014), p. 176.

Chapter 10: Code, Non-Code, Garbage, and Junk

413. Jayaraman, R., Jacques Monod and the advent of the age of operons. *Resonance* 15: 1084–96 (2010), p. 1084.

414. Kellis, M., Wold, B., Snyder, M. P., et al., Defining functional DNA elements in the human genome. *Proceedings of the National Academy of Sciences of the United States of America* 111: 6131–8 (2014).

415. Haerty, W. and Ponting, C. P., No gene in the genome makes sense except in the light of evolution. *Annual Review of Genomics and Human Genetics* 15: 71–92 (2014), p. 72.

416. Haerty, W. and Ponting, C. P., No gene in the genome makes sense except in the light of evolution. *Annual Review of Genomics and Human Genetics* 15: 71–92 (2014).

417. Haerty, W. and Ponting, C. P., No gene in the genome makes sense except in the light of evolution. *Annual Review of Genomics and Human Genetics* 15: 71–92 (2014), p. 73.

418. Rands, C. M., Meader, S., Ponting, C. P., and Lunter, G., 8.2% of the human genome is constrained: variation in rates of turnover across functional element classes in the human lineage. *PLoS Genetics* 10: e1004525 (2014).

419. Pheasant, M. and Mattick, J. S., Raising the estimate of functional human sequences. *Genome Research* 17: 1245–53 (2007).

420. Mattick, J. S. and Dinger, M. E., The extent of functionality in the human genome. *The HUGO Journal* 7: 2 (2013).

421. Roberts, J. T., Cardin, S. E., and Borchert, G. M., Burgeoning evidence indicates that microRNAs were initially formed from transposable element sequences. *Mobile Genetic Elements* 4: e29255 (2014).

422. Stamatoyannopoulos, J. A., What does our genome encode? *Genome Research* 22: 1602–11 (2012).

423. Palazzo, A., Junk DNA—origin of the term, *Science Blogs*, <http://scienceblogs.com/transcript/2007/02/12/junk-dna-origin-of-the-term-1/> (2007).

424. Ohno, S., So much 'junk' DNA in our genome. *Brookhaven Symposium on Biology* 23: 366–70 (1972).

425. Leslie, M., 'Dead' enzymes show signs of life. *Science* 340: 25–7 (2013).

426. Leslie, M., 'Dead' enzymes show signs of life. *Science* 340: 25–7 (2013), p. 25.

427. Thomas, C. A., The genetic organization of chromosomes. *Annual Review of Genetics* 5: 237–56 (1971).

428. Doolittle, W. F., Is junk DNA bunk? A critique of ENCODE. *Proceedings of the National Academy of Sciences of the United States of America* 110: 5294–300 (2013), p. 5295.

429. Buerk, R., Fugu: the fish more poisonous than cyanide, *BBC*, <http://www.bbc.co.uk/news/magazine-18065372> (2012).

430. Mattick, J. S. and Dinger, M. E., The extent of functionality in the human genome. *The HUGO Journal* 7: 2 (2013).

431. Lewis, D., What is our junk DNA for?, *Cosmos Magazine*, <https://cosmosmagazine.com/life-sciences/what-our-junk-dna> (2014).

432. Skloot, R., *The Immortal Life of Henrietta Lacks* (Macmillan, 2010).

433. Henrietta Lacks: family win recognition for immortal cells, BBC, <http://www.bbc.co.uk/news/world-us-canada-23611189> (2013).

434. Stamatoyannopoulos, J. A., What does our genome encode? *Genome Research* 22: 1602–11 (2012), p. 1609.

435. Mattick, J. S. and Dinger, M. E., The extent of functionality in the human genome. *The HUGO Journal* 7: 2 (2013).

436. Badano, J. L. and Katsanis, N., Beyond Mendel: an evolving view of human genetic disease transmission. *Nature Reviews Genetics* 3: 779–89 (2002).

437. Gupta, R. M. and Musunuru, K., Expanding the genetic editing tool kit: ZFNs, TALENs, and CRISPR-Cas9. *Journal of Clinical Investigation* 124: 4154–61 (2014).

438. Bassett, A. R., Azzam, G., Wheatley, L., et al., Understanding functional miRNA-target interactions in vivo by site-specific genome engineering. *Nature Communications* 5: 4640 (2014).

439. Bassett, A. R., Akhtar, A., Barlow, D. P., et al., Considerations when investigating lncRNA function in vivo. *eLife* 3: e03058 (2014).

440. Meier, I. D., Bernreuther, C., Tilling, T., et al., Short DNA sequences inserted for gene targeting can accidentally interfere with off-target gene expression. *FASEB Journal: Official Publication of the Federation of American Societies for Experimental Biology* 24: 1714–24 (2010).

441. Cathomen, T. and Ehl, S., Translating the genomic revolution—targeted genome editing in primates. *New England Journal of Medicine* 370: 2342–5 (2014).

442. Niu, J., Zhang, B., and Chen, H., Applications of TALENs and CRISPR/Cas9 in human cells and their potentials for gene therapy. *Molecular Biotechnology* 56: 681–8 (2014).

Chapter 11: Genes and Disease

443. Scriver, C. R., Garrod's foresight; our hindsight. *Journal of Inherited Metabolic Disease* 24: 93–116 (2001).

444. Cox, K. H., Bonthuis, P. J., and Rissman, E. F., Mouse model systems to study sex chromosome genes and behavior: relevance to humans. *Frontiers in Neuroendocrinology* 35: 405–19 (2014).

445. Deng, X., Berletch, J. B., Nguyen, D. K., and Disteche, C. M., X chromosome regulation: diverse patterns in development, tissues and disease. *Nature Reviews Genetics* 15: 367–78 (2014).

446. Schramm, W., The history of haemophilia—a short review. *Thrombosis Research* 134S1: S4-S9 (2014).

447. Lannoy, N. and Hermans, C., The 'royal disease'—haemophilia A or B? A haematological mystery is finally solved. *Haemophilia: The Official Journal of the World Federation of Hemophilia* 16: 843–7 (2010).

448. Reed, W. and Vichinsky, E. P., New considerations in the treatment of sickle cell disease. *Annual Review of Medicine* 49: 461–74 (1998).

449. Higgs, D. R., Engel, J. D., and Stamatoyannopoulos, G., Thalassaemia. *The Lancet* 379: 373–83 (2012).

450. It's in the Blood!, *Oregon State University*, <http://scarc.library.oregonstate.edu/coll/pauling/blood/quotes/linus_pauling.html> (2014).

451. Kim, S. D. and Fung, V. S., An update on Huntington's disease: from the gene to the clinic. *Current Opinion in Neurology* 27: 477–83 (2014).

452. Wild, E., Interview: Alice and Nancy Wexler, *HDBuzz*, <http://en.hdbuzz.net/101> (2012).

453. Charlotte Raven: should I take my own life?, *The Guardian*, <http://www.theguardian.com/society/2010/jan/16/charlotte-raven-should-i-take-my-own-life> (2010).

454. Quinton, P. M., Cystic fibrosis: lessons from the sweat gland. *Physiology* 22: 212–25 (2007), p. 212.

455. Elmer-Dewitt, P., The Genetic Revolution, *TIME*: 46–50 (1994), p. 48.

456. Rahimov, F. and Kunkel, L. M., The cell biology of disease: cellular and molecular mechanisms underlying muscular dystrophy. *The Journal of Cell Biology* 201: 499–510 (2013).

457. Taussig, N., Our beautiful sons could die before us, *The Guardian*, <http://www.theguardian.com/lifeandstyle/2014/aug/16/our-beautiful-sons-could-die-before-us> (2014).

458. Pearson, H., Human Genetics: One Gene, Twenty Years, *Nature News*, <http://www.nature.com/news/2009/090708/full/460164a.html> (2009), p.165.

459. Scriver, C. R., Garrod's foresight; our hindsight. *Journal of Inherited Metabolic Disease* 24: 93–116 (2001).

460. Phenylketonuria, *NHS*, <http://www.nhs.uk/conditions/phenylketonuria/Pages/Introduction.aspx> (2014).

461. Touzot, F., Hacein-Bey-Abina, S., Fischer, A., and Cavazzana, M., Gene therapy for inherited immunodeficiency. *Expert Opinion on Biological Therapy* 14: 789–98 (2014).

462. Chen, H., Ruan, Y. C., Xu, W. M., et al., Regulation of male fertility by CFTR and implications in male infertility. *Human Reproduction Update* 18: 703–13 (2012).

463. Gallati, S., Disease-modifying genes and monogenic disorders: experience in cystic fibrosis. *The Application of Clinical Genetics* 7: 133–46 (2014).

464. Waalen, J. and Beutler, E., Genetic screening for low-penetrance variants in protein-coding genes. *Annual Review of Genomics and Human Genetics* 10: 431–50 (2009).

465. What they said: genome in quotes, *BBC*, <http://news.bbc.co.uk/1/hi/sci/tech/807126.stm> (2000).

466. Rose, H. and Rose, S., *Genes, Cells and Brains* (Verso, 2012), p. 25.

467. Genome announcement a milestone, but only a beginning, *CNN*, <http://edition.cnn.com/2000/HEALTH/06/26/human.genome.05/> (2000).

468. Kang, B., Park, J., Cho, S., et al., Current status, challenges, policies, and bioethics of biobanks. *Genomics & Informatics* 11: 211–17 (2013).

469. Nakamura, Y., DNA variations in human and medical genetics: 25 years of my experience. *Journal of Human Genetics* 54: 1–8 (2009).

470. Visscher, P. M., Brown, M. A., McCarthy, M. I., and Yang, J., Five years of GWAS discovery. *American Journal of Human Genetics* 90: 7–24 (2012).

471. Grarup, N., Sandholt, C. H., Hansen, T., and Pedersen, O., Genetic susceptibility to type 2 diabetes and obesity: from genome-wide association studies to rare variants and beyond. *Diabetologia* 57: 1528–41 (2014).

472. Wallberg, M. and Cooke, A., Immune mechanisms in type 1 diabetes. *Trends in Immunology* 34: 583–91 (2013).

473. Visscher, P. M., Brown, M. A., McCarthy, M. I., and Yang, J., Five years of GWAS discovery. *American Journal of Human Genetics* 90: 7–24 (2012), p. 7.

474. McClellan, J. and King, M. C., Genetic heterogeneity in human disease. *Cell* 141: 210–17 (2010), p. 213.

475. McClellan, J. and King, M. C., Genetic heterogeneity in human disease. *Cell* 141: 210–17 (2010), p. 216.

476. Mundasad, S., 'Eighty new genes linked to schizophrenia', *BBC*, <http://www.bbc.co.uk/news/health-28401693> (2014).

477. Stamatoyannopoulos, J. A., What does our genome encode? *Genome Research* 22: 1602–11 (2012).

478. Schizophrenia Working Group of the Psychiatric Genomics Consortium, Biological insights from 108 schizophrenia-associated genetic loci. *Nature* 511: 421–7 (2014).

479. Clarke, L., Ten years on: the abiding presence of R. D. Laing. *Journal of Psychiatric and Mental Health Nursing* 6: 313–20 (1999).

480. Laing, R. D., *The Divided Self: An Existential Study in Sanity and Madness* (Penguin, 1969), p. 12.

481. Sherwell, P., DNA father James Watson's 'holy grail' request, *The Telegraph*, <http://www.telegraph.co.uk/news/worldnews/northamerica/usa/5300883/DNA-father-James-Watsons-holy-grail-request.html> (2009).

482. Pinto, R., Ashworth, M., and Jones, R., Schizophrenia in black Caribbeans living in the UK: an exploration of underlying causes of the high incidence rate. *The British Journal of General Practice: The Journal of the Royal College of General Practitioners* 58: 429–34 (2008).

483. Pinto, R., Ashworth, M., and Jones, R., Schizophrenia in black Caribbeans living in the UK: an exploration of underlying causes of the high incidence rate. *The British Journal of General Practice: The Journal of the Royal College of General Practitioners* 58: 429–34 (2008), p. 433.

484. Singh, S., Kumar, A., Agarwal, S., et al., Genetic insight of schizophrenia: past and future perspectives. *Gene* 535: 97–100 (2014), p. 97.

485. Uher, R., Gene-environment interactions in severe mental illness. *Frontiers in Psychiatry* 5: 48 (2014).

486. SPIEGEL interview with Craig Venter: 'We Have Learned Nothing from the Genome', *Der Spiegel*, <http://www.spiegel.de/international/world/spiegel-interview-with-craig-venter-we-have-learned-nothing-from-the-genome-a-709174-2.html> (2010).

487. Saint Pierre, A. and Genine, E., How important are rare variants in common disease? *Briefings in Functional Genomics* 13: 353-61 (2014).

488. Panoutsopoulou, K., Tachmazidou, I., and Zeggini, E., In search of low-frequency and rare variants affecting complex traits. *Human Molecular Genetics* 22: R16–21 (2013).

489. Schreiber, M., Dorschner, M., and Tsuang, D., Next-generation sequencing in schizophrenia and other neuropsychiatric disorders. *American Journal of Medical Genetics. Part B, Neuropsychiatric Genetics: The Official Publication of the International Society of Psychiatric Genetics* 162B: 671–8 (2013).

490. Purcell, S. M., Moran, J. L., Fromer, M., et al., A polygenic burden of rare disruptive mutations in schizophrenia. *Nature* 506: 185–90 (2014).

491. Schreiber, M., Dorschner, M., and Tsuang, D., Next-generation sequencing in schizophrenia and other neuropsychiatric disorders. *American Journal of Medical Genetics. Part B, Neuropsychiatric Genetics: The Official Publication of the International Society of Psychiatric Genetics* 162B: 671–8 (2013), p. 672.

492. Li, C., Personalized medicine—the promised land: are we there yet? *Clinical Genetics* 79: 403–12 (2011).

493. St Laurent, G., Vyatkin, Y., and Kapranov, P., Dark matter RNA illuminates the puzzle of genome-wide association studies. *BMC Medicine* 12: 97 (2014).

494. Sadee, W., Hartmann, K., Seweryn, M., Pietrzak, M., Handelman, S. K., and Rempala, G. A. Missing heritability of common diseases and treatments outside the protein-coding exome. *Human Genetics.* 133: 1199–215 (2014).

Chapter 12: What Makes Us Human?

495. Darwin, C., *Origin of Species* (John Murray, 1859), p. 488.

496. Shermer, M., *In Darwin's Shadow* (Oxford University Press, 2002), p. 161.

497. Suddendorf, T., *The Gap* (Basic Books, 2013), p. 8.

498. Spencer, G., New Genome Comparison Finds Chimps, Humans Very Similar at the DNA Level, *National Human Genome Research Institute*, <http://www.genome.gov/15515096> (2005).

499. Why mouse matters, *National Human Genome Research Institute*, <http://www.genome.gov/10001345> (2010).

500. Swanson, K. S., Mazur, M. J., Vashisht, K., et al., Genomics and clinical medicine: rationale for creating and effectively evaluating animal models. *Experimental Biology and Medicine* 229: 866–75 (2004).

501. Debiec, J., Peptides of love and fear: vasopressin and oxytocin modulate the integration of information in the amygdala. *BioEssays: News and Reviews in Molecular, Cellular and Developmental Biology* 27: 869–73 (2005).

502. McGrew, W. C., Is primate tool use special? Chimpanzee and New Caledonian crow compared. *Philosophical Transactions of the Royal Society of London. Series B, Biological Sciences* 368: 20120422 (2013).

503. Suddendorf, T., *The Gap* (Basic Books, 2013), p. 65.

504. Suddendorf, T., *The Gap* (Basic Books, 2013), p. 74.

505. Kuhl, P. K., Brain mechanisms in early language acquisition. *Neuron* 67: 713–27 (2010), p. 713.

506. Trigger, B., Comment on Tobias, Piltdown, the case against Keith. *Current Anthropology* 33: 275 (1992).

507. Engels, F., The part played by labour in the transition from ape to man, *Marxists.org*, <http://www.marxists.org/archive/marx/works/1876/part-played-labour/> (1876).

508. Sheehan, H., *Marxism and the Philosophy of Science: A Critical History* (Humanities Press International, 1993), p. 24.

509. Stringer, C., *The Origin of our Species* (Allen Lane, 2011), p. 213.

510. Corballis, M., Not the last word, *American Scientist*, <http://www.americanscientist.org/bookshelf/pub/not-the-last-word> (2007).

511. Stringer, C., *The Origin of our Species* (Allen Lane, 2011), p. 158.

512. Suddendorf, T., *The Gap* (Basic Books, 2013), p. 76.

513. Dunbar, R., *Grooming, Gossip and the Evolution of Language* (Faber and Faber, 2004).

514. Deacon, T. W., *The Symbolic Species: The Co-evolution of Language and the Brain* (W. W. Norton & Company, 1998).

515. Van der Veer, R. and Valsiner, J., *Understanding Vygotsky: A Quest for Synthesis* (Blackwell, 1991).

516. Vygotsky, L. S., *Mind in Society* (Harvard University Press, 1978), p. 55.

517. Kozulin, A., *Vygotsky's Psychology* (Harvester Wheatsheaf, 1990), p. 225.

518. Callaway, E., 'Smart genes' prove elusive, *Nature News*, <http://www.nature.com/news/smart-genes-prove-elusive-1.15858> (2014).

519. Darwin's Tree of Life, *Natural History Museum*, <http://www.nhm.ac.uk/nature-online/evolution/tree-of-life/darwin-tree/> (2014).

520. Stringer, C., *The Origin of our Species* (Allen Lane, 2011), p. 266.

521. Stringer, C., *The Origin of our Species* (Allen Lane, 2011), p. 124.

522. Pääbo, S., *Neanderthal Man* (Basic Books, 2014).

523. Russell, O. and Turnbull, D., Mitochondrial DNA disease-molecular insights and potential routes to a cure. *Experimental Cell Research* 325: 38–43 (2014).

524. Rose, S., Lynn Margulis obituary, *The Guardian*, <http://www.theguardian.com/science/2011/dec/11/lynn-margulis-obtiuary> (2011).

525. Wong, L. J., Pathogenic mitochondrial DNA mutations in protein-coding genes. *Muscle & Nerve* 36: 279–93 (2007).

526. Sato, M. and Sato, K., Maternal inheritance of mitochondrial DNA by diverse mechanisms to eliminate paternal mitochondrial DNA. *Biochimica et Biophysica Acta* 1833: 1979–84 (2013).

527. Stringer, C., *The Origin of our Species* (Allen Lane, 2011), p. 23.

528. Stringer, C., *The Origin of our Species* (Allen Lane, 2011), p. 171.

529. Golding, W., *The Inheritors* (Faber and Faber, 1955).

530. Kolbert, E., *The Sixth Extinction* (Henry Holt & Company, 2014).

531. Stringer, C., *The Origin of our Species* (Allen Lane, 2011), p. 52.

532. Higham, T., Douka, K., Wood, R., et al., The timing and spatiotemporal patterning of Neanderthal disappearance. *Nature* 512: 306–9 (2014).

533. Pääbo, S., *Neanderthal Man* (Basic Books, 2014), p. 200.

534. Pääbo, S., *Neanderthal Man* (Basic Books, 2014), p. 243.

535. Pääbo, S., *Neanderthal Man* (Basic Books, 2014), p. 176.

536. Vernot, B. and Akey, J. M., Resurrecting surviving Neandertal lineages from modern human genomes. *Science* 343: 1017–21 (2014).

537. Sankararaman, S., Mallick, S., Dannemann, M., et al., The genomic landscape of Neanderthal ancestry in present-day humans. *Nature* 507: 354–7 (2014).

538. Pääbo, S., *Neanderthal Man* (Basic Books, 2014), p. 188.

539. Huerta-Sánchez, E., Jin, X., Asan, et al., Altitude adaptation in Tibetans caused by introgression of Denisovan-like DNA. *Nature* 512: 194–7 (2014).

540. Callaway, E., Modern human genomes reveal our inner Neanderthal, *Nature News*, <http://www.nature.com/news/modern-human-genomes-reveal-our-inner-neanderthal-1.14615> (2014).

541. Bowden, R. MacFie, T. S., Myers, S., et al. Genomic tools for evolution and conservation in the chimpanzee: Pan troglodytes ellioti is a genetically distinct population. *PLoS Genetics* 8: e1002504 (2012).

542. Stringer, C., *The Origin of our Species* (Allen Lane, 2011), p. 126.

543. Kaplan, M., Neanderthals ate their greens, *Nature News*, <http://www.nature.com/news/neanderthals-ate-their-greens-1.11030> (2012).

544. Appenzeller, T., Neanderthal culture: old masters. *Nature* 497: 302–4 (2013), p. 303.

545. Oksenberg, N., Stevison, L., Wall, J. D., and Ahituv, N., Function and regulation of AUTS2, a gene implicated in autism and human evolution. *PLoS Genetics* 9: e1003221 (2013).

546. Ahmed, M. and Liang, P., Study of modern human evolution via comparative analysis with the Neanderthal genome. *Genomics & Informatics* 11: 230–8 (2013).

547. Gokhman, D., Lavi, E., Prüfer, K., et al., Reconstructing the DNA methylation maps of the Neandertal and the Denisovan. *Science* 344: 523–7 (2014).

548. Pennisi, E., Ancient DNA holds clues to gene activity in extinct humans. *Science* 344: 245–6 (2014), p. 246.

549. Barras, C., Why we get autism but our Neanderthal cousins didn't, *New Scientist*, <http://www.newscientist.com/article/dn25443-why-we-get-autism-but-our-neanderthal-cousins-didnt.html#.U_X2zI10wuQ> (2014).

550. Seldon, H. L., Extended neocortical maturation time encompasses speciation, fatty acid and lateralization theories of the evolution of schizophrenia and creativity. *Medical Hypotheses* 69: 1085–9 (2007).

551. De Manzano, O., Cervenka, S., Karabanov, A., et al., Thinking outside a less intact box: thalamic dopamine D2 receptor densities are negatively related to psychometric creativity in healthy individuals. *PLoS One* 5: e10670 (2010).

552. Roberts, M., Creative minds 'mimic schizophrenia', *BBC*, <http://www.bbc.co.uk/news/10154775> (2010).

553. Kavanagh, D. H., Dwyer, S., O'Donovan, M. C., and Owen, M. J., The ENCODE project: implications for psychiatric genetics. *Molecular Psychiatry* 18: 540–2 (2013).

Chapter 13: The Genome That Became Conscious

554. Somel, M., Liu, X., and Khaitovich, P., Human brain evolution: transcripts, metabolites and their regulators. *Nature Reviews Neuroscience* 14: 112–27 (2013).

555. Ahmed, M. and Liang, P., Study of modern human evolution via comparative analysis with the Neanderthal genome. *Genomics & Informatics* 11: 230–8 (2013).

556. Konopka, G., Friedrich, T., Davis-Turak, J., et al., Human-specific transcriptional networks in the brain. *Neuron* 75: 601–17 (2012).

557. Pinker, S., *How the Mind Works* (Allen Lane, 1997), p. 27.

558. Antzoulatos, E. G. and Miller, E. K., Increases in functional connectivity between prefrontal cortex and striatum during category learning. *Neuron* 83: 216–25 (2014).

559. Synchronized brain waves enable rapid learning, *Science Daily*, <http://www.sciencedaily.com/releases/2014/06/140612121354.htm> (2012).

560. Tsien, R. Y., Intracellular signal transduction in four dimensions: from molecular design to physiology. *Bowditch Lecture*, C723–C728 (1992).

561. Leybaert, L. and Sanderson, M. J., Intercellular Ca(2+) waves: mechanisms and function. *Physiological Reviews* 92: 1359–92 (2012).

562. Robison, A. J., Emerging role of CaMKII in neuropsychiatric disease. *Trends in Neurosciences* 37: 653–62 (2014).

563. Schmidt, E., *More sophisticated wiring, not just a bigger brain, helped humans evolve beyond chimps*, <http://newsroom.ucla.edu/releases/more-sophisticated-wiring-not-237689> (2012).

564. Toga, A. W., Thompson, P. M., and Sowell, E. R., Mapping brain maturation. *Trends in Neurosciences* 29: 148–59 (2006).

565. Pievani, T., Many ways of being human, the Stephen J. Gould's legacy to palaeoanthropology (2002–2012). *Journal of Anthropological Sciences = Rivista di antropologia: JASS/Istituto italiano di antropologia* 90: 133–49 (2012).

566. Kelley, J., Neanderthal teeth lined up. *Nature* 428: 904–5 (2004).

567. Orban, G. A. and Caruana, F., The neural basis of human tool use. *Frontiers in Psychology* 5: 310 (2014).

568. Liu, X., Somel, M., Tang, L., et al., Extension of cortical synaptic development distinguishes humans from chimpanzees and macaques. *Genome Research* 22: 611–22 (2012).

569. Menet, J. S. and Rosbash, M., When brain clocks lose track of time: cause or consequence of neuropsychiatric disorders. *Current Opinion in Neurobiology* 21: 849–57 (2011).

570. Liu, C., Teng, Z.-Q., Santistevan, N. J., et al., Epigenetic regulation of miR-184 by MBD1 governs neural stem cell proliferation and differentiation. *Cell Stem Cell* 6: 433–44 (2010).

571. Braun, S. M. and Jessberger, S., Adult neurogenesis: mechanisms and functional significance. *Development* 141: 1983–6 (2014).

572. Barry, G. and Mattick, J. S., The role of regulatory RNA in cognitive evolution. *Trends in Cognitive Sciences* 16: 497–503 (2012), p. 499.

573. Barry, G. and Mattick, J. S., The role of regulatory RNA in cognitive evolution. *Trends in Cognitive Sciences* 16: 497–503 (2012), p. 500.

574. Smalheiser, N. R., The RNA-centred view of the synapse: non-coding RNAs and synaptic plasticity. *Philosophical Transactions of the Royal Society of London. Series B, Biological Sciences* 369: pii: 20130504 (2014).

575. Iyengar, B. R., Choudhary, A., Sarangdhar, M. A., et al., Non-coding RNA interact to regulate neuronal development and function. *Frontiers in Cellular Neuroscience* 8: 47 (2014).

576. Boland, M. J., Nazor, K. L., and Loring, J. F., Epigenetic regulation of pluripotency and differentiation. *Circulation Research* 115: 311–24 (2014).

577. Perrimon, N., Pitsouli, C., and Shilo, B. Z., Signaling mechanisms controlling cell fate and embryonic patterning. *Cold Spring Harbor Perspectives in Biology* 4: a005975 (2012).

578. Rothbart, S. B. and Strahl, B. D., Interpreting the language of histone and DNA modifications. *Biochimica et Biophysica Acta* 1839: 627–43 (2014).

579. Rudenko, A. and Tsai, L. H., Epigenetic regulation in memory and cognitive disorders. *Neuroscience* 264: 51–63 (2014), p. 51.

580. Rudenko, A. and Tsai, L. H., Epigenetic regulation in memory and cognitive disorders. *Neuroscience* 264: 51–63 (2014).

581. Guan, J. S., Xie, H., and Ding, X., The role of epigenetic regulation in learning and memory. *Experimental Neurology* pii: S0014-4886(14)00147-2 (2014).

582. Reilly, M. T., Faulkner, G. J., Dubnau, J., et al., The role of transposable elements in health and diseases of the central nervous system. *The Journal of Neuroscience* 33: 17577–86 (2013).

583. Stringer, C., *The Origin of our Species* (Allen Lane, 2011), p. 116.

584. Barry, G. and Mattick, J. S., The role of regulatory RNA in cognitive evolution. *Trends in Cognitive Sciences* 16: 497–503 (2012), p. 501.

585. Stanford, P. K., August Weismann's theory of the germ-plasm and the problem of unconceived alternatives. *History and Philosophy of the Life Sciences* 27: 163 (2005).

586. Gapp, K., Jawaid, A., Sarkies, P., et al., Implication of sperm RNAs in transgenerational inheritance of the effects of early trauma in mice. *Nature Neuroscience* 17: 667–9 (2014).

587. Hurley, D., Grandma's experiences leave a mark on your genes, *Discover Magazine*, <http://discovermagazine.com/2013/may/13-grandmas-experiences-leave-epigenetic-mark-on-your-genes> (2013).

588. Heard, E. and Martienssen, R. A., Transgenerational epigenetic inheritance: myths and mechanisms. *Cell* 157: 95–109 (2014), p. 95.

589. Heard, E. and Martienssen, R. A., Transgenerational epigenetic inheritance: myths and mechanisms. *Cell* 157: 95–109 (2014), p. 106.

590. Hughes, V., The sins of the father. *Nature* 507: 22–4 (2014), p. 24.

Conclusion: The Case for Complexity

591. Robertson, J. M., *The Philosophical Works of Francis Bacon* (Routledge, 2013), p. 429.

592. Van Regenmortel, M. H. V., Reductionism and complexity in molecular biology. *EMBO Reports* 5: 1016–20 (2004), p. 1016.

593. Boss, M. and Poggi, S., *Romanticism in Science: Science in Europe, 1790–1840* (Springer, 1993), p. 63.

594. Shanahan, T., *The Evolution of Darwinism: Selection, Adaptation and Progress in Evolutionary Biology* (Cambridge University Press, 2004), p. 2.

595. Anderson, A., A Time for Adaptation, *Huffington Post*, <http://www.huffingtonpost.com/anthony-anderson/a-time-for-adaptation_b_170948.html> (2011).
596. Herbert Spencer, *American Experience*, <http://www.pbs.org/wgbh/amex/carnegie/peopleevents/pande03.html> (2014).
597. Weiling, F., Historical study: Johann Gregor Mendel 1822–1884. *American Journal of Medical Genetics* 40: 1–25 (1991).
598. Hamilton, B. A. and Yu, B. D., Modifier Genes and the Plasticity of Genetic Networks in Mice. *PLoS Genetics* 8: e1002644 (2012).
599. Stanford, P. K., August Weismann's theory of the germ-plasm and the problem of unconceived alternatives. *History and Philosophy of the Life Sciences* 27: 163 (2005).
600. Keller, E. F., From gene action to reactive genomes, *The Journal of Physiology* 592: 2423–9 (2014).
601. Lewontin, R. C., *It Ain't Neccessarily So* (Granta, 2000), p. 138.
602. Cohen, J., The human genome, a decade later, *MIT Technology Review*, <http://m.technologyreview.com/featuredstory/422140/the-human-genome-a-decade-later/> (2011).
603. Malik, K., The gene genie, *New Statesman*, <http://www.newstatesman.com/node/138054> (2000).
604. Brenner, S., Life sentences: Detective Rummage investigates. *The Scientist* 16: 15 (2002).
605. Alterovitz, G., Liu, J., Chow, J., and Ramoni, M. F. Automation, parallelism, and robotics for proteomics. *Proteomics* 6: 4016–22 (2006).
606. Bahassi, E. M. and Stambrook, P. J., Next-generation sequencing technologies: breaking the sound barrier of human genetics. *Mutagenesis* 29: 303–10 (2014).
607. Reardon, S., Fast genetic sequencing saves newborn lives, *Nature News*, <http://www.nature.com/news/fast-genetic-sequencing-saves-newborn-lives-1.16027> (2014).
608. Finkel, E., The trouble with genes, *Cosmos Magazine*, <http://www.npc.org.au/assets/files/documents/journalismAwards/2011%20Awards/ElizabethFinkel_TheTroubleWithGenes.pdf> (2010).
609. Van Regenmortel, M. H. V., Reductionism and complexity in molecular biology. *EMBO Reports* 5: 1016–20 (2004), p. 1016.
610. Perkel, J. M., This is your brain: mapping the connectome, *Science*, <http://www.sciencemag.org/site/products/lst_20130118.xhtml> (2013).
611. Smalheiser, N. R., The RNA-centred view of the synapse: non-coding RNAs and synaptic plasticity. *Philosophical Transactions of the Royal Society of London. Series B, Biological Sciences* 369: pii: 20130504 (2014).
612. Leybaert, L. and Sanderson, M. J., Intercellular Ca(2+) waves: mechanisms and function. *Physiological Reviews* 92: 1359–92 (2012).
613. Kopell, N. J., Gritton, H. J., Whittington, M. A., and Kramer, M. A., Beyond the connectome: the dynome. *Neuron* 83: 1319–28 (2014).

INDEX OF NAMES

Bold type is used to indicate reference to figures.

INDEX OF SUBJECTS

Bold type is used to indicate reference to figures.

ANCESTORS IN OUR GENOME

The New Science of Human Evolution

Eugene E. Harris

978-0-19-997803-8 | Hardback | £18.99

'Simply indispensable for any reader wishing to learn about the latest research on human origins.'
Library Journal

'In the 'Age of Genomics,' this book is an absolute must-have for anyone interested in human evolution. In the most accessible manner, Eugene E. Harris enlightens how and why genomes represent such powerful evidence to understand our past.'
Jean-Jacques Hublin, Max Planck Institute for Evolutionary Anthropology

Geneticist Eugene Harris presents us with the complete and up-to-date account of the evolution of the human genome. Written from the perspective of population genetics, *Ancestors in Our Genome* traces human origins back to their earliest source among our human ancestors, and explains some of the challenging questions that scientists are currently attempting to answer. Harris draws upon extensive experience researching primate evolution in order to deliver a lively and thorough history of human evolution.

BIOCODE

The New Age of Genomics

Dawn Field and Neil Davies

978-0-19-968775-6 | Hardback | £16.99

'This lovely, reaching, important book shows us the front edge of a scientific movement that is transforming, simultaneously, science and our understanding of the world. If you want to understand the biological future, read this book.'

Rob Dunn

The living world runs on genomic software—what Dawn Field and Neil Davies call the 'biocode'—the sum of all DNA on Earth. Since the whole human genome was mapped in 2003, the new field of genomics has mushroomed and is now operating on an affordable, industrial scale. We can check our paternity, find out where our ancestors came from, and whether we are at risk of some diseases.

The ability to read DNA has changed how we view ourselves and understand our place in nature, and has opened up unprecedented possibilities. Already the first efforts at 'barcoding' entire ecological communities and creating 'genomic observatories' have begun. The future, the authors argue, will involve biocoding the entire planet.

Sign up to our quarterly e-newsletter **http://academic-preferences.oup.com/**

FREAKS OF NATURE

And what they tell us about evolution and development

Mark S. Blumberg

978-0-19-921306-1 | Paperback | £8.99

'This book offers a unique perspective, challenging our view of science, evolution, and social archetypes by examining the nature of malformations. It would be a worthwhile addition to the library of students and scholars alike.'

Kerby C. Oberg, MD, PhD, Loma Linda University

Two-legged goats, conjoined twins, 'Cyclops' infants with a single eye in the middle of their forehead, double-headed snakes, and Laloo, a man with a partially formed twin attached to his chest...In *Freaks of Nature*, Mark S. Blumberg turns a scientist's eye on these unusual examples of humans and other animals, showing how a subject once relegated to the sideshow can help explain some of the deepest complexities of biology.

Sign up to our quarterly e-newsletter **http://academic-preferences.oup.com/**

LIFE UNFOLDING

How the human body creates itself

Jamie A. Davies

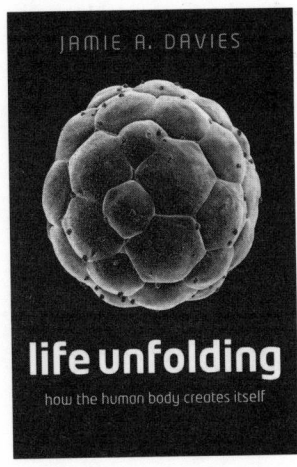

978-0-19-967353-7 | Hardback | £20.00

'A demanding but wonder-filled account of the simple interactions that create complex structures.'

New Scientist

Where did I come from? Why do I have two arms but just one head? How is my left leg the same size as my right one? Why are the fingerprints of identical twins not identical? How did my brain learn to learn? Why must I die?

Life Unfolding tells the story of human development from egg to adult, showing how our whole understanding of how we come to be has been transformed in recent years. Highlighting how embryological knowledge is being used to understand why bodies age and fail, Jamie A. Davies explores the profound and fascinating impacts of our newfound knowledge.

Sign up to our quarterly e-newsletter **http://academic-preferences.oup.com/**

MISMATCH

The Timebomb of Lifestyle Disease

Peter Gluckman and Mark Hanson

978-0-19-922838-6 | Paperback | £16.99

'Thought-provoking...this book conveys admirably, for a non-specialist reader, the implications of an important idea.'

Michael Sargent, Nature

'A fascinating and important journey through the development and evolution of human health.'

Lewis Wolpert

We have built a world that no longer fits our bodies. Our genes—selected through our evolution—and the many processes by which our development is tuned within the womb, limit our capacity to adapt to the modern urban lifestyle. There is a mismatch. We are seeing the impact of this mismatch in the explosion of diabetes, heart disease, and obesity. Bringing together the latest scientific research in evolutionary biology, development, medicine, anthropology, and ecology, Gluckman and Hanson argue that many of our problems as modern-day humans can be understood in terms of this fundamental and growing mismatch. It is an insight that we ignore at our peril.

Sign up to our quarterly e-newsletter **http://academic-preferences.oup.com/**

MISSING LINKS

In search of human origins

John Reader

978-0-19-927685-1 | Hardback | £25.00

This is the story of the search for human origins—from the Middle Ages, when questions of the earth's antiquity first began to arise, through to the latest genetic discoveries that show the interrelatedness of all living creatures. John Reader's passion for this quest, and the field of palaeoanthropology, began in the 1960s when he reported for *Life Magazine* on Richard Leakey's first fossil-hunting expedition to the badlands of East Turkana, in Kenya. Drawing on both historic and recent research, he tells the fascinating story of the science as it has developed from the activities of a few dedicated individuals, into the rigorous multidisciplinary work of today.

NATURE'S ORACLE

The life and work of W. D. Hamilton

Ullica Segerstrale

978-0-19-860728-1 | Paperback | £16.99

'As geniuses often are, he was a complex character and an exceptional challenge for any biographer. Ullica Segerstrale is ideally qualified to rise to that challenge. She achieves a genuinely affectionate yet warts-and-all portrait of her subject, combined with a good understanding of the deep subtleties of his thinking. Those who loved him, as I did, and those who wish to know more of the astonishing originality and versatility of his contributions to science, will treasure this book.'

Richard Dawkins

W. D. Hamilton was responsible for a revolution in thinking about evolutionary biology—a revolution that changed our understanding of life itself. In this illuminating and moving biography Ullica Segerstrale documents Hamilton's extraordinary life and work, revealing a man of immense intellectual curiosity, an uncompromising truth-seeker, a naturalist and jungle explorer, a risk-taker, an unconventional scientist with a poet's soul and a deep concern for life on earth and mankind's future.

Sign up to our quarterly e-newsletter **http://academic-preferences.oup.com/**

WHAT IS LIFE?

How Chemistry Becomes Biology

Addy Pross

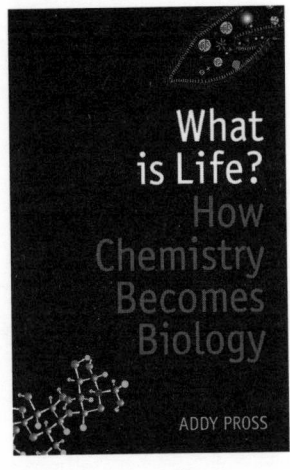

978-0-19-968777-0 | Paperback | £9.99

'I don't pretend to understand the chemistry—but by using analogies about boulders rolling down hills, and cars driving up them, Pross does a good job of explaining the principle.'

Brandon Robshaw, *Independent on Sunday*

Living things are hugely complex and have unique properties, such as self-maintenance and apparently purposeful behaviour which we do not see in inert matter. So how does chemistry give rise to biology? What could have led the first replicating molecules up such a path? Now, developments in the emerging field of 'systems chemistry' are unlocking the problem. The gulf between biology and the physical sciences is finally becoming bridged.

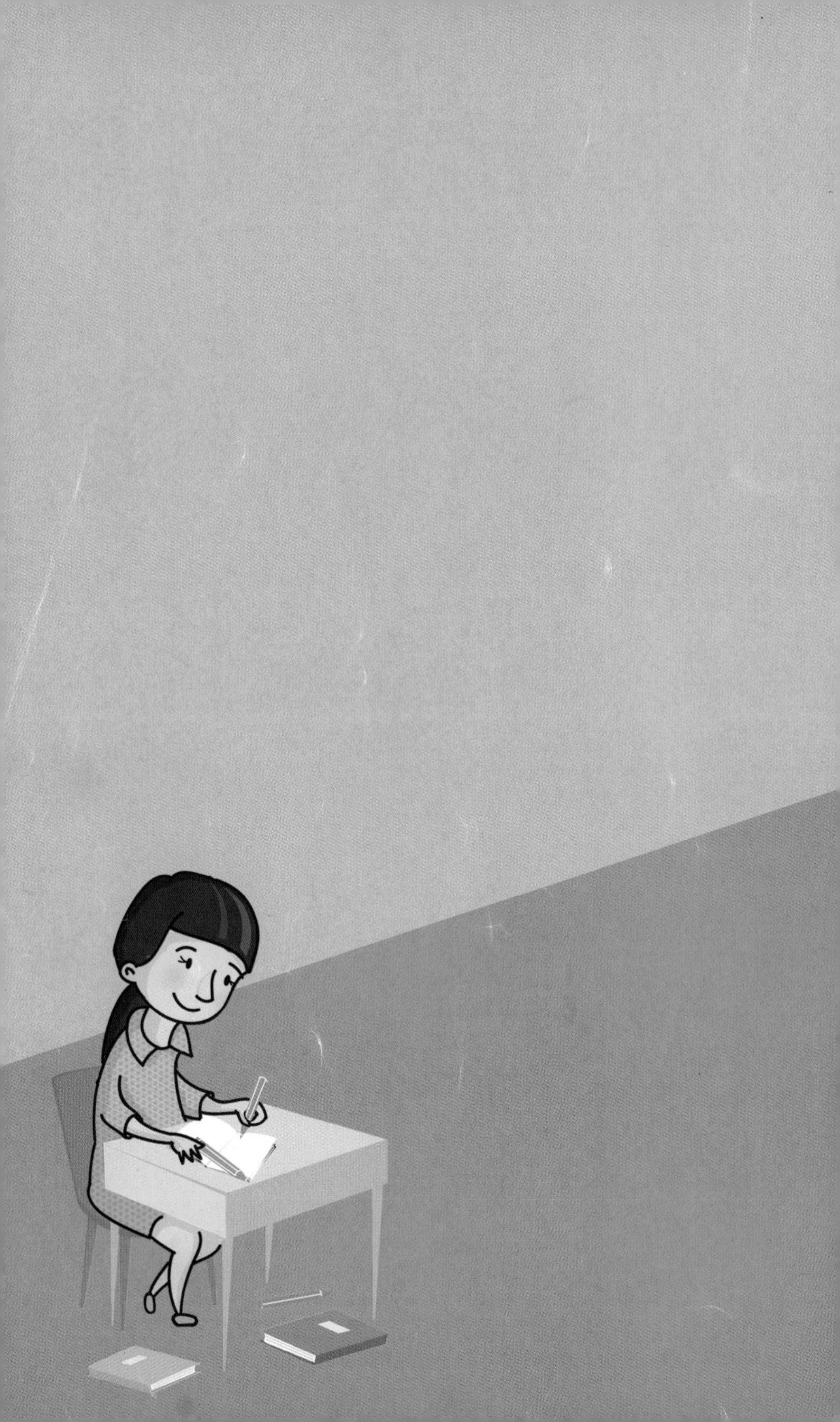

MANNERS MATTER
IN THE
CLASSROOM

BY **LORI MORTENSEN**

ILLUSTRATED BY
Lisa Hunt

CAPSTONE PRESS
a capstone imprint

First Graphics are published by Capstone Press,
151 Good Counsel Drive, P.O. Box 669, Mankato, Minnesota 56002.
www.capstonepub.com

Books published by Capstone Press are manufactured with paper
containing at least 10 percent post-consumer waste.

Library of Congress Cataloging-in-Publication Data
Mortensen, Lori, 1955–
Manners matter in the classroom / by Lori Mortensen ; Illustrated by Lisa Hunt.
    p. cm. — (First graphics)
  Includes bibliographical references and index.
ISBN 978-1-4296-5333-6 (library binding)
ISBN 978-1-4296-6223-9 (paperback)
  1. Etiquette for children and teenagers—Juvenile literature. 2. Elementary schools. 3.
Graphic novels. I. Hunt, Lisa (Lisa Jane), 1973– , ill. II. Title. III. Series.

BJ1857.C5M67 2011
395.5—dc22

                                        2010026607

Editor: **Shelly Lyons**
Designer: **Juliette Peters**
Art Director: **Nathan Gassman**
Production Specialist: **Eric Manske**

Printed in the United States of America in Stevens Point, Wisconsin.
072011   006285R

TABLE OF CONTENTS

MIND YOUR MANNERS

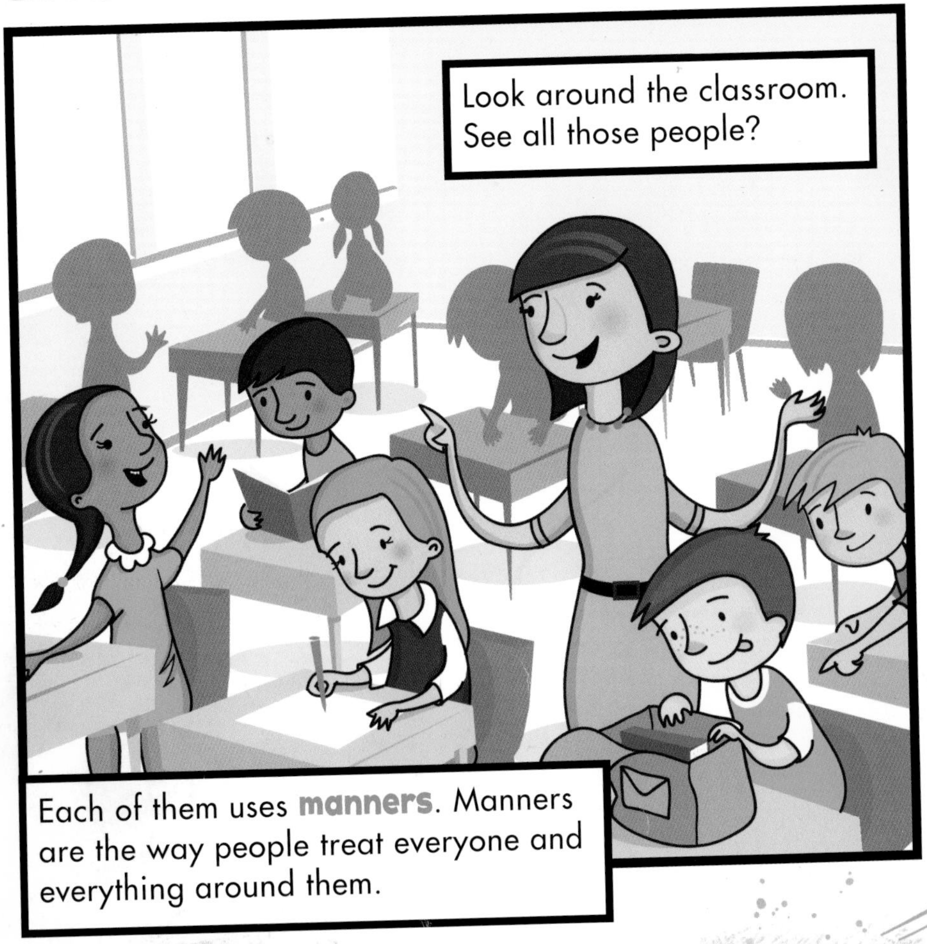
Look around the classroom. See all those people?
Each of them uses **manners**. Manners are the way people treat everyone and everything around them.

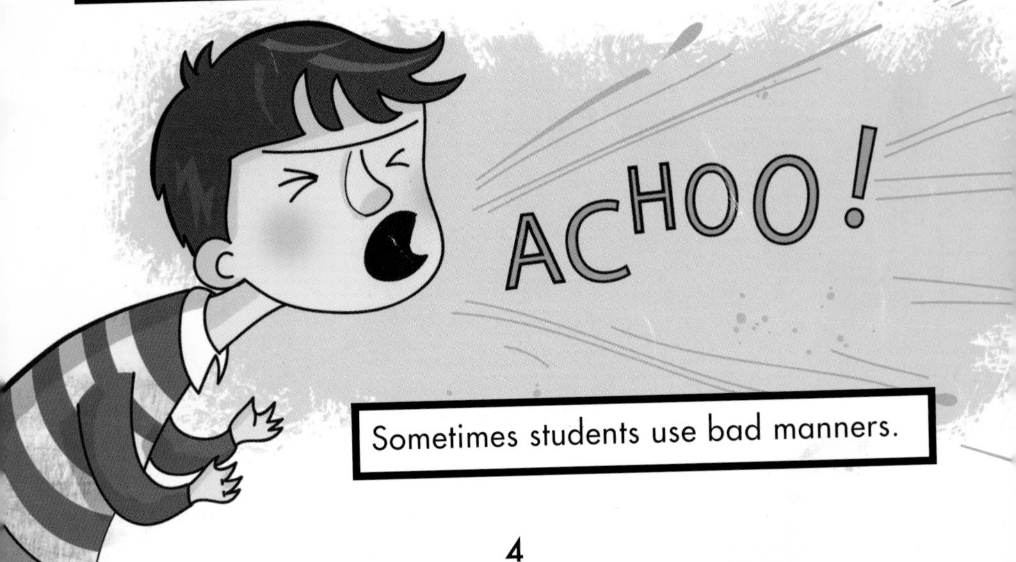
ACHOO!
Sometimes students use bad manners.

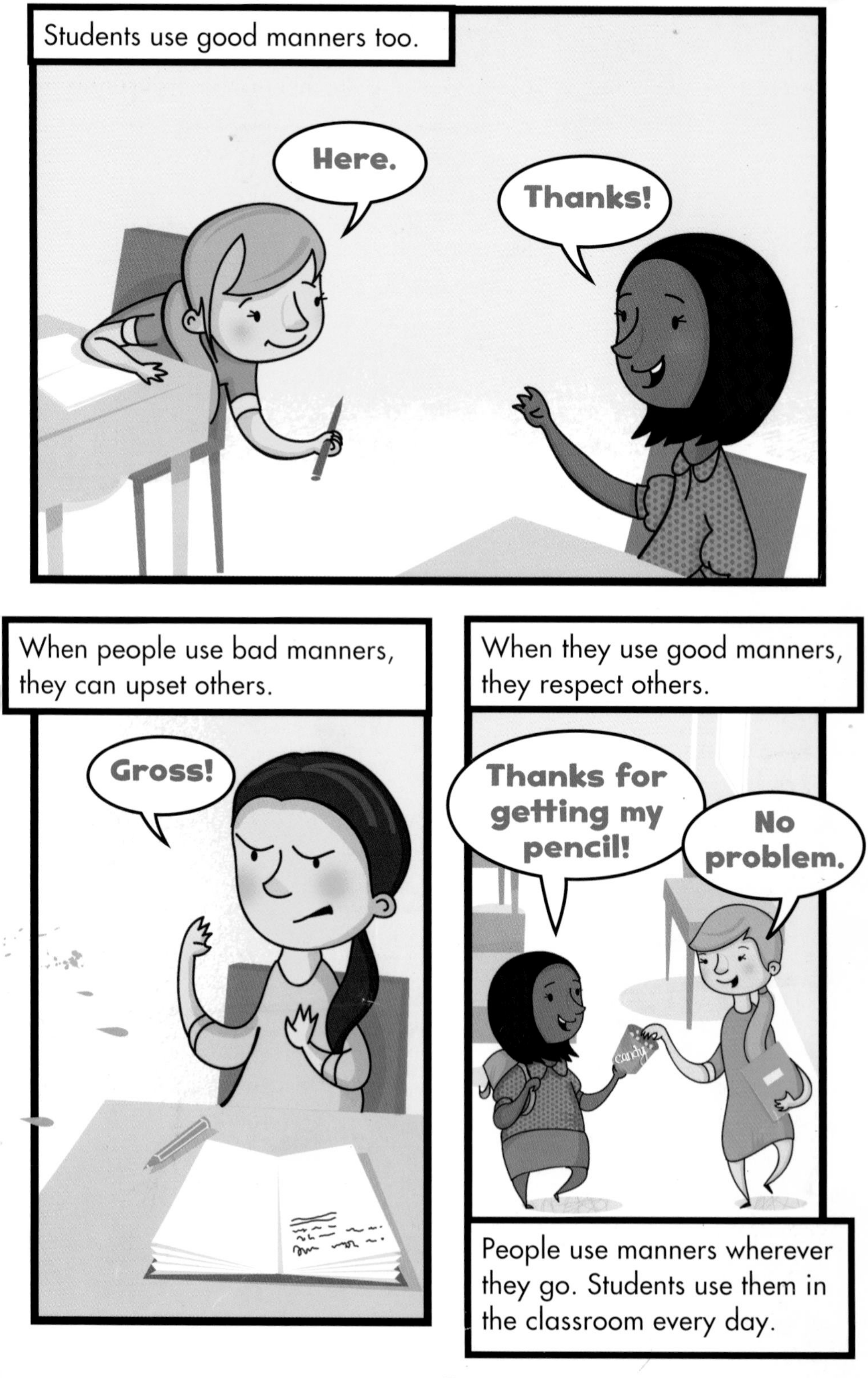
Students use good manners too.
Here.
Thanks!
When people use bad manners, they can upset others.
Gross!
When they use good manners, they respect others.
Thanks for getting my pencil!
No problem.
People use manners wherever they go. Students use them in the classroom every day.

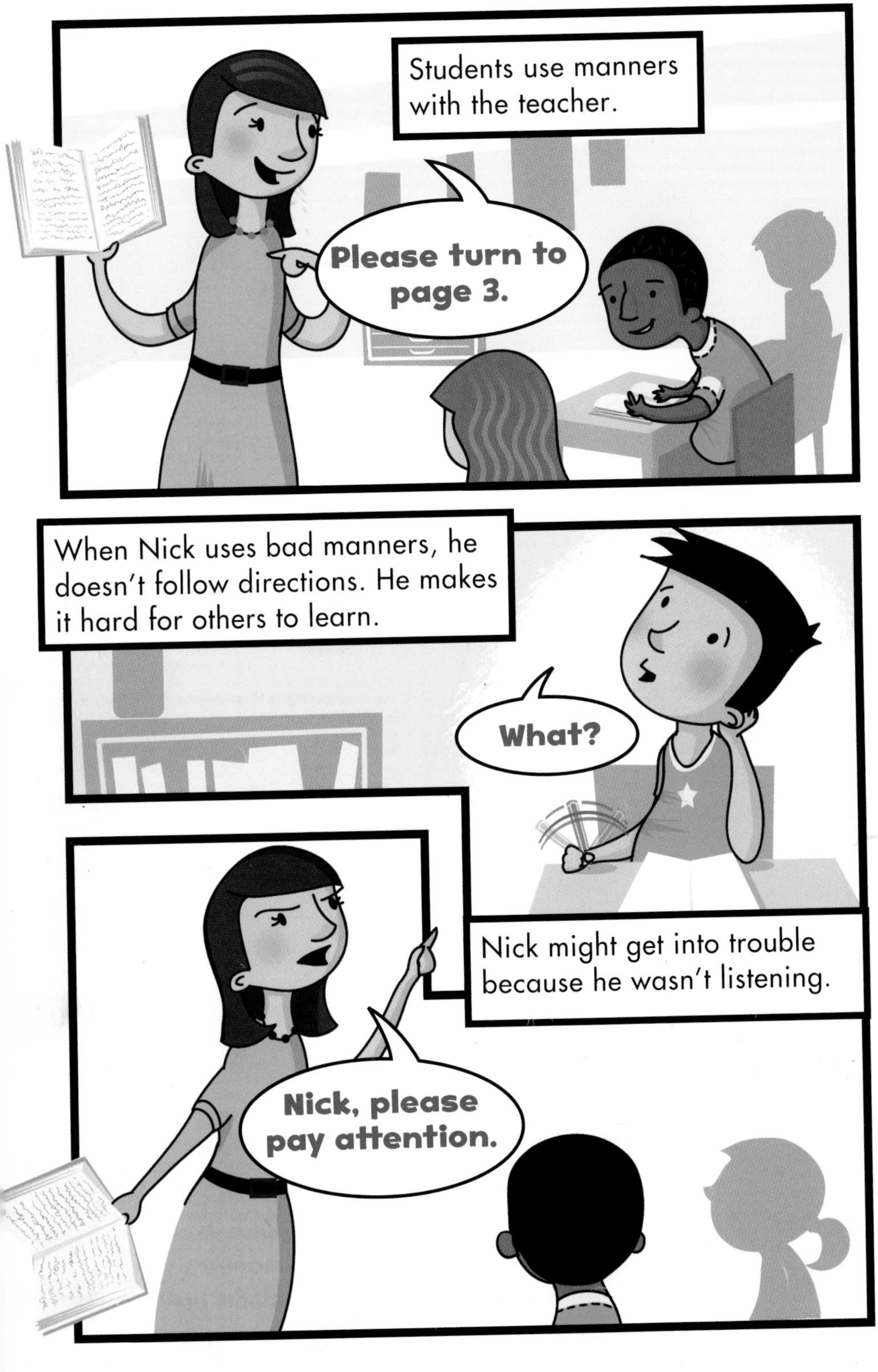
Students use manners with the teacher.
Please turn to page 3.
When Nick uses bad manners, he doesn't follow directions. He makes it hard for others to learn.
What?
Nick might get into trouble because he wasn't listening.
Nick, please pay attention.

7

Students use manners with classmates too. Kayla uses bad manners when she says mean things to a friend.

Nobody likes to be left out.

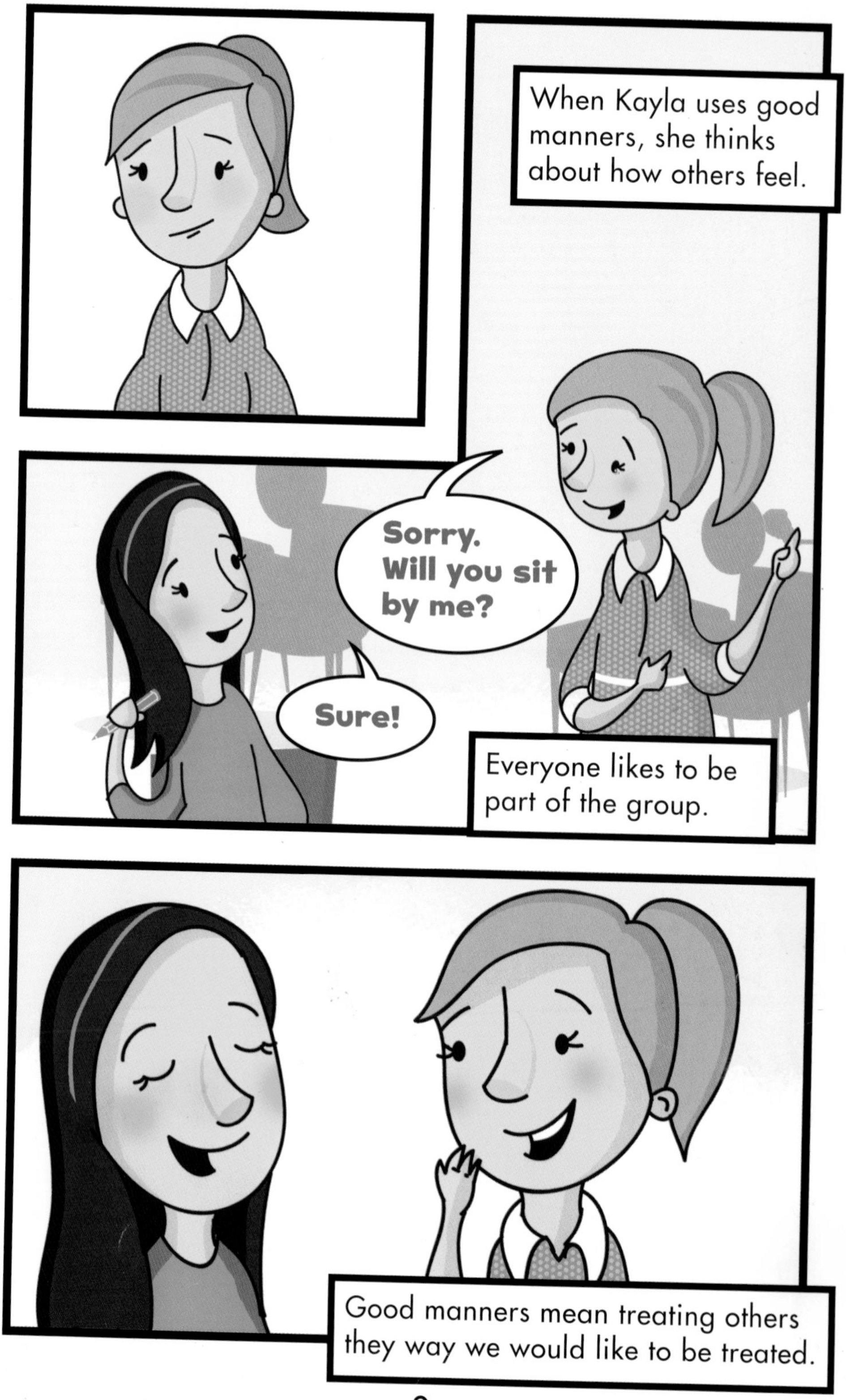
When Kayla uses good manners, she thinks about how others feel.
Sorry. Will you sit by me?
Sure!
Everyone likes to be part of the group.
Good manners mean treating others they way we would like to be treated.

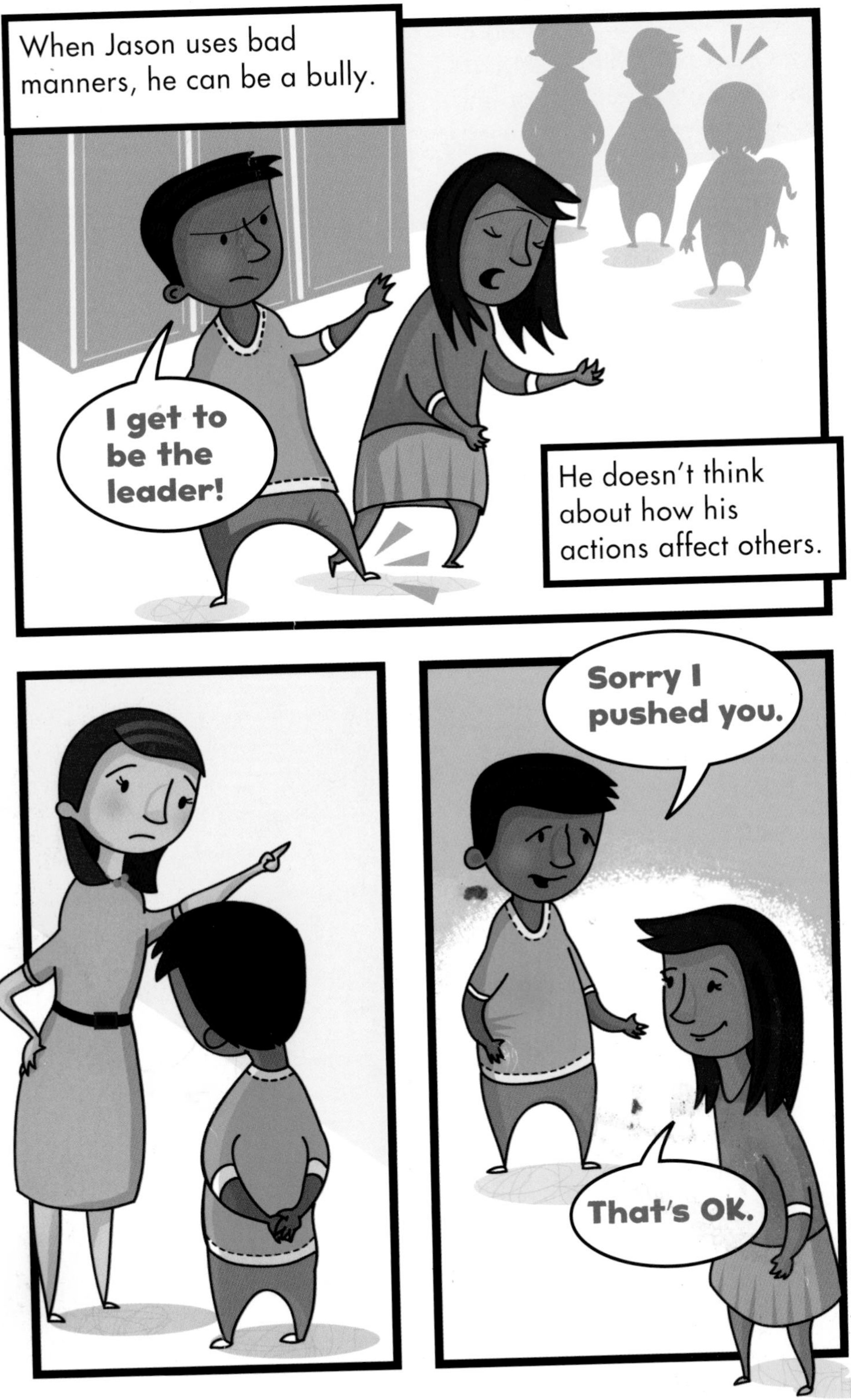
When Jason uses bad manners, he can be a bully.
I get to be the leader!
He doesn't think about how his actions affect others.
Sorry I pushed you.
That's OK.

When Jada uses good manners, she respects others. She asks nicely before getting in line.

Do you mind if my friend gets in line by me?

No problem!

When students use good manners, they all get along.

MANNERS AND STUFF

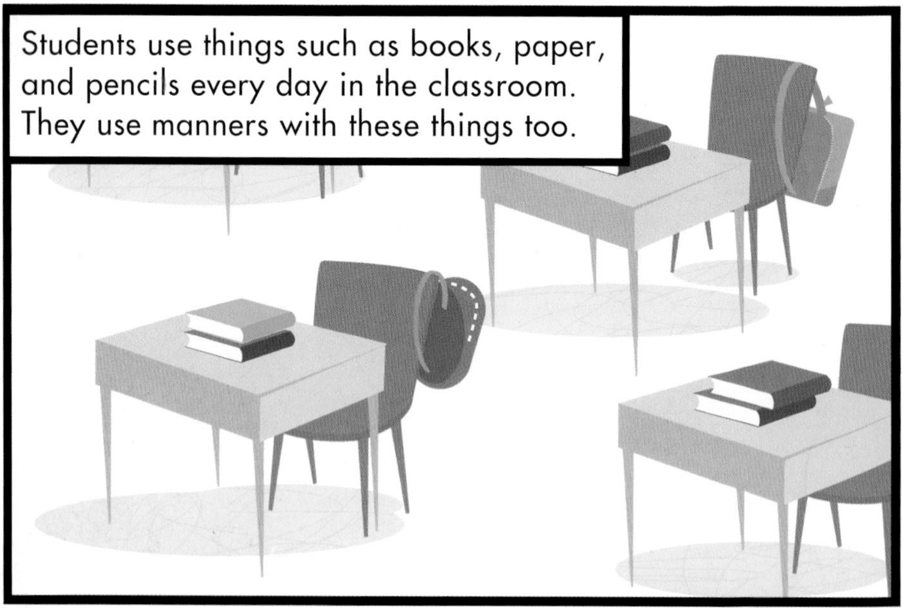
Students use things such as books, paper, and pencils every day in the classroom. They use manners with these things too.

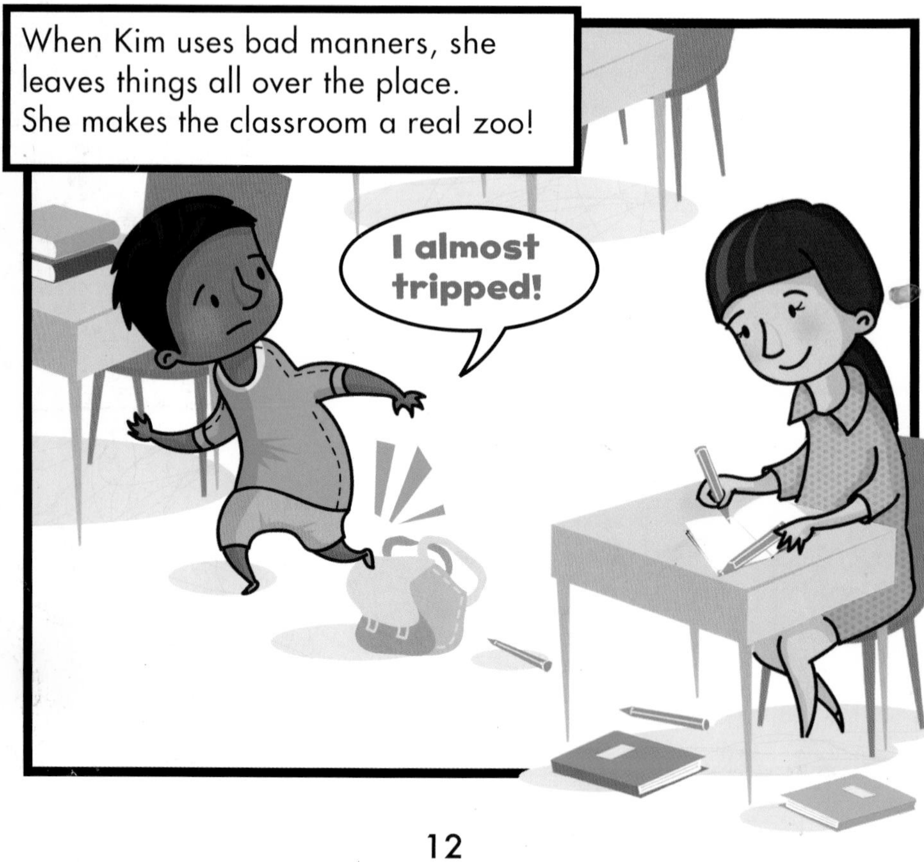
When Kim uses bad manners, she leaves things all over the place. She makes the classroom a real zoo!
I almost tripped!

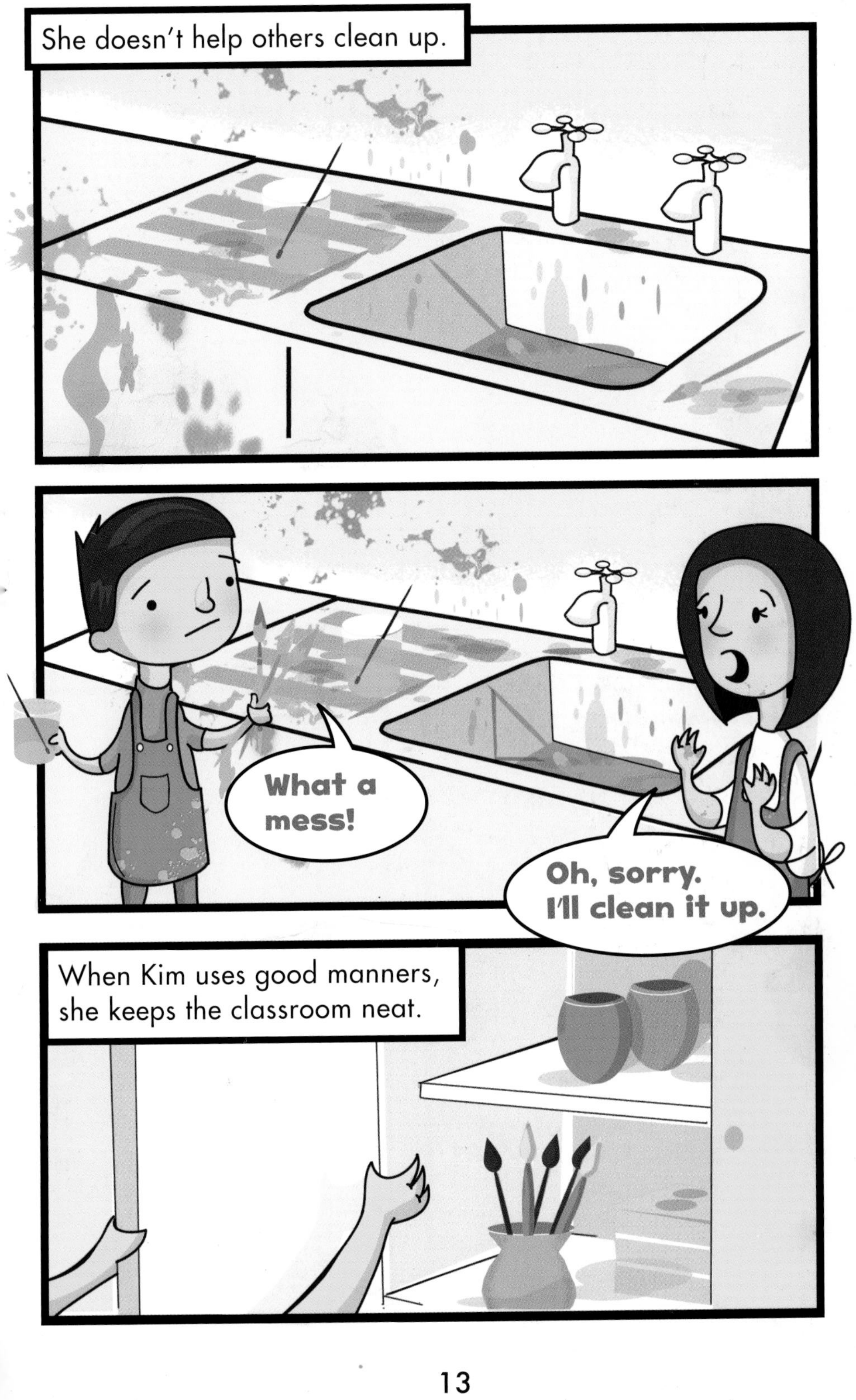
She doesn't help others clean up.
What a mess!
Oh, sorry. I'll clean it up.
When Kim uses good manners, she keeps the classroom neat.

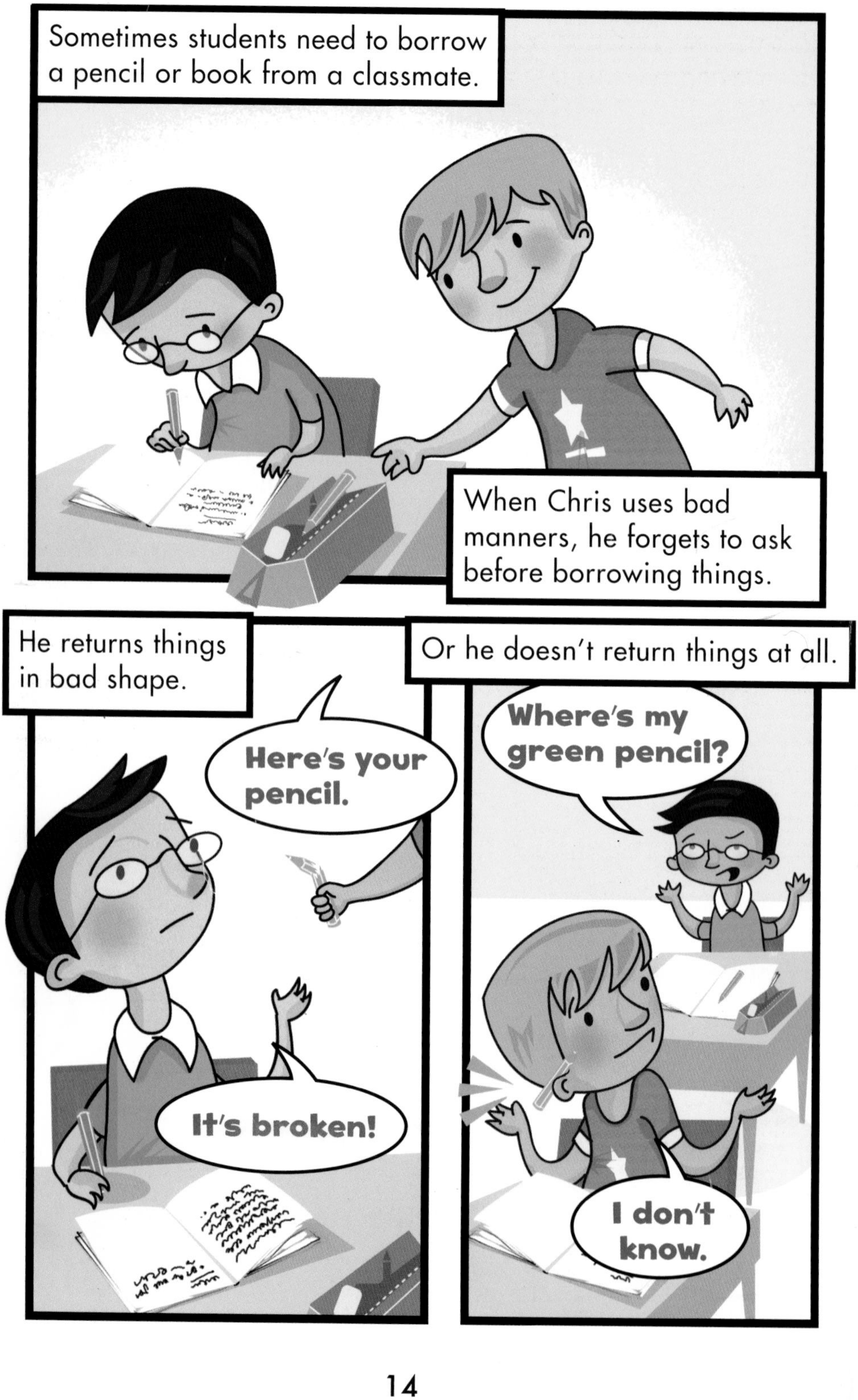
Sometimes students need to borrow a pencil or book from a classmate.
When Chris uses bad manners, he forgets to ask before borrowing things.
He returns things in bad shape.
Here's your pencil.
It's broken!
Or he doesn't return things at all.
Where's my green pencil?
I don't know.

15

QUIET, PLEASE

The classroom can be as noisy as lunchtime in the cafeteria.

Students use bad manners when they make lots of noise. Then no one can hear the teacher.

15

QUIET, PLEASE

The classroom can be as noisy as lunchtime in the cafeteria.

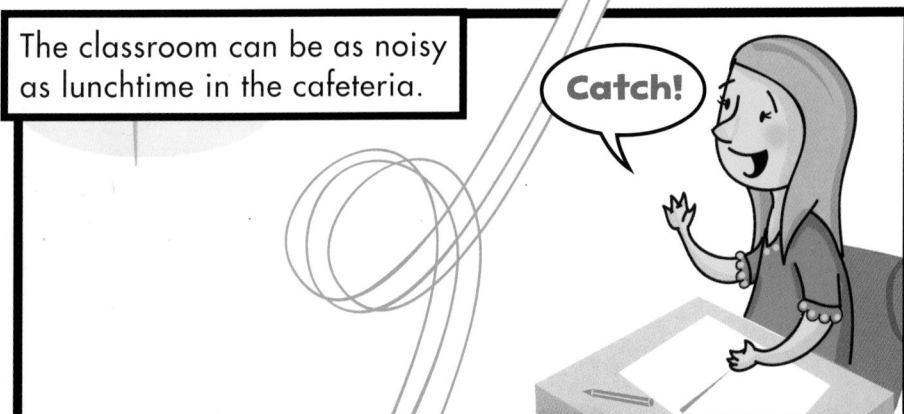

Students use bad manners when they make lots of noise. Then no one can hear the teacher.

17

When Zoe talks instead of works, she uses bad manners.

I'm bored! What's going on after school?

Some students use bad manners without talking at all.

Tap! Tap!

DRUM! DRUM! DRUM!

Hummm! Hummm! Hummm!

When Zoe uses good manners, she does her work quietly.

She doesn't bother others. And she gets a lot done!

Sometimes students make mistakes. That's normal. When Lilly uses bad manners, she seems uncaring.

bump!

Lilly uses good manners when she apologizes for mistakes.

Sorry. I tripped.

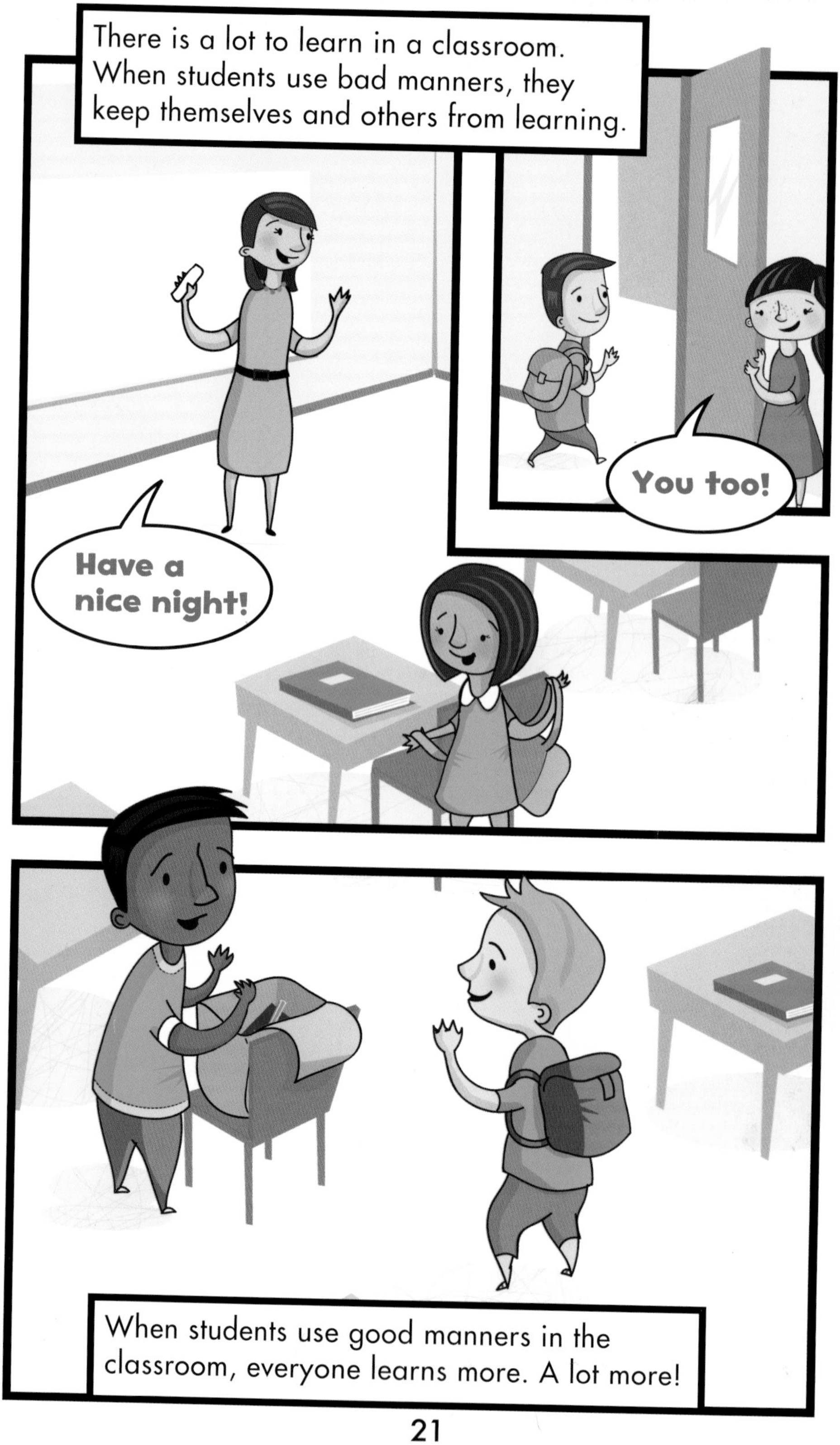
There is a lot to learn in a classroom. When students use bad manners, they keep themselves and others from learning.
Have a nice night!
You too!
When students use good manners in the classroom, everyone learns more. A lot more!

GLOSSARY

borrow—to use something for a certain amount of time before returning it

bully—someone who uses strength to harm those who are weaker

cafeteria—a place in a school where students eat

classmate—someone who is in the same class

respect—to show you care; respect means to treat others the way you would like to be treated

READ MORE

Goldberg, Whoopi. *Whoopi's Big Book of Manners.* New York: Hyperion Books for Children, 2006.

Keller, Laurie, *Do Unto Otters: A Book About Manners.* New York: Henry Holt, 2007.

Tourville, Amanda Doering. *Manners in the Lunchroom.* Way to Be! Minneapolis: Picture Window Books, 2009.

INTERNET SITES

FactHound offers a safe, fun way to find Internet sites related to this book. All of the sites on FactHound have been researched by our staff.

Here's all you do:

Visit *www.facthound.com*

Type in this code: 9781429653336

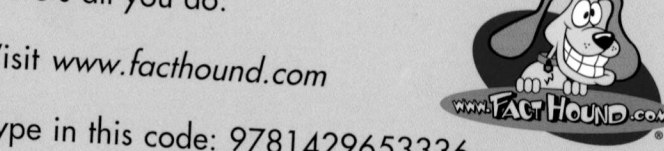

Super-cool stuff!

Check out projects, games and lots more at
www.capstonekids.com

INDEX

24